Contemporary Moral Issues in a Diverse Society

JULIE M. McDONALD

Saint Joseph's University

Wadsworth Publishing Company

I⟨T⟩P® An International Thomson Publishing Company

Belmont, CA · Albany, NY · Bonn · Boston · Cincinnati · Detroit · London · Madrid
Melbourne · Mexico City · New York · Paris · Singapore
Tokyo · Toronto · Washington

Philosophy Editor: Peter Adams
Assistant Editor: Kerri Abdinoor
Editorial Assistant: Kelly Bush
Marketing Manager: Dave Garrison
Print Buyer: Stacey Weinberger
Permissions Editor: Robert Kauser
Interior Designer: Lois Stanfield
Copy Editor: Jane Townsend
Cover Design: Adriane Bosworth
Cover Painting: National Gallery of Art
Compositor: Impact Publications
Printer: Malloy Lithographing

ON THE COVER

Lyonel Feininger (American, 1871–1956), *Zirchow VII*

Lyonel Feininger was born in New York but spent much of his life in Germany.[1] Writing about this painting, his son Lux tells us the following: "The date of the painting, 1918, marks a period in Lyonel Feininger's life almost completely overshadowed by his horror of the world war. . . . In this particular painting, a depth of structural unity, of interpenetration of light and substance, presented in deeply glowing color, is achieved. . . . [My father] . . . considered this to be one of his very major works. It was painted in Zehlendorf, that small suburb of Berlin, in those years an almost rural village, in which he was, as an 'enemy alien' severely restricted in his movements. . . . Travel was forbidden. Hunger was severely felt by everyone at this stage. . . ."[2] Lyonel Feininger painted this work during a period of uncertainty, violence, and powerful social upheaval; its vision nonetheless is one of "unity and reconciliation."

---

1. John Walker, *National Gallery of Art* (New York: Harry N. Abrahms, Inc., 1975: 602–603). 2. Walker, p. 602.

Library of Congress Cataloging-in-Publication Data
Contemporary moral issues in a diverse society / [collected by]
  Julie McDonald.
    p.   cm.
  ISBN 0-534-51321-2
  1. Ethics. 2. Social problems.   I. McDonald, Julie.
BJ1012.C659   1998
170--dc21
                              97-36695
                               CIP

For more information, contact Wadsworth Publishing Company, 10 Davis Drive, Belmont, CA 94002, or electronically at http://www.thomson.com/wadsworth.html

International Thomson Publishing Europe
Berkshire House 168-173
High Holborn
London, WC1V 7AA, England

Thomas Nelson Australia
102 Dodds Street
South Melbourne 3205
Victoria, Australia

Nelson Canada
1120 Birchmount Road
Scarborough, Ontario
Canada M1K 5G4

International Thomson Publishing GmbH
Königswinterer Strasse 418
53227 Bonn, Germany

International Thomson Editores
Campos Eliseos 385, Piso 7
Col. Polanco
11560 México D.F. México

International Thomson Publishing Asia
221 Henderson Road
#05-10 Henderson Building
Singapore 0315

International Thomson Publishing Japan
Hirakawacho Kyowa Building, 3F
2-2-1 Hirakawacho
Chiyoda-ku, Tokyo 102, Japan

International Thomson Publishing Southern Africa
Building 18, Constantia Park
240 Old Pretoria Road
Halfway House, 1685 South Africa

Brief Contents

Contents

Preface

MORAL ISSUES IN
OUR DIVERSE SOCIETY

In recent decades, undergraduate teaching in ethics has taken on a more and more applied orientation; courses in business ethics, medical ethics, philosophy of law, and the like have proliferated. Yet despite the increased emphasis on more concrete topics, philosophers have tended to isolate the "real" moral issues by abstracting them as far as possible from the supposedly irrelevant and thus dispensable details of the social matrix out of which they emerge. The methodological assumption governing this approach is that this type of abstraction is necessary to get at the "core" elements that constitute the particular moral problem, for example, conflicting rights or liberty claims.

This abstraction approach, as one may call it, has been challenged of late from many philosophical quarters. It too easily leads to the presumption that moral problems arise, as it were, in a social vacuum, and that the background details are irrelevant to the work of moral assessment. This, however, need not be the case, and to assume it as a methodological premise can seriously distort the resulting moral analysis. Recent work in philosophy has claimed that these abstract analyses are not neutral in the way that philosophers suggest or intend them to be. To reduce a particular moral problem to a conflict between one person's right to liberty and another's right to privacy might appear to be neutral and unbiased with respect to gender, race, or class, but this has been shown on occasion not to be the case. A number of philosophers recently have argued that to assume that the social dynamics of gender, race, ethnicity, social class, and sexual orientation are philosophically irrelevant is to give privilege to the perspective of those in society least disadvantaged by racial, ethnic, social class, and gender identities. Thus it is claimed that careful and responsible study of moral problems must take into account contextual factors such as these precisely in order to avoid an incomplete and potentially biased analysis.

Contemporary Moral Issues in a Diverse Society has been constructed in order to take this challenge into account. The essays collected here represent a wide variety of points of view—a wider variety than one would find in more traditional collections. A central organizing principle behind the anthology is that moral problems cannot, in general, be adequately analyzed apart from the social contexts in which they arise. Animated by this conviction in selecting articles and organizing chapters, I have focused on contexts where issues of gender, race, social class, sexual orientation, and health status are directly involved. Some of the classic articles in applied ethics—which embody what has felicitously been called "the view from nowhere"—are included. They are juxtaposed with less well-known pieces that take seriously the influence of gender, race, health status, and class on our understanding of contemporary moral controversies. This collection of readings encourages the student to acknowledge the diversity in structuring moral problems that may occur within his or her own community and perhaps within the very classroom in which these moral problems are being discussed. *Contemporary Moral Issues in a Diverse Society* deliberately sets out to broaden the scope of moral discussion by giving voice to those who believe that the social setting in which moral choice is faced is relevant to moral assessment.

The first chapter of this anthology, titled "Recognizing Difference and Entering Imaginatively into Others' Perspectives," opens with an essay by Martha Nussbaum, "Imagination and the Perspectives of Others." In it, she argues that one part of a careful and thorough moral analysis is the study of narratives that invite us in an imaginative way to enter into others' perspectives. Following Nussbaum's essay are numerous short pieces, which are by and large first person narratives of various experiences of exclusion and discrimination on the basis of race, gender, social class, health status, or sexual orientation. These narratives also show the complexities of the interplay among these aspects of social identity. This chapter includes Peggy McIntosh's much-admired piece on recognizing racial and sexual privileges; Marilyn Frye's brief analysis of oppression, illuminated by her metaphor of the birdcage; and Donna Langston's complementary essay on social class privilege. Chapter 1 thus encourages readers to try to imaginatively consider others' experiences and perspectives.

Each of the eight chapters that follow focuses on a particular moral issue: abortion; euthanasia and physician-assisted suicide; the death penalty; affirmative action; college speech codes; same-sex marriage; sexual violence; and new reproductive technologies.

The epilogue of the book, "Diverse Moral Perspectives and Moral Relativism," was written specifically for this anthology. I argue there that acknowledging a variety of perspectives in an analysis of moral problems does *not* force one to adopt a position of moral relativism or subjectivism. I assert that we ought to examine various perspectives, as each represents partial truth; only by drawing on many of these perspectives can we hope to aim at moral impartiality.

Moral Issues in a Diverse Society is supported by a web site. Students and faculty are invited to visit the web site at <http://www.sju.edu/MORAL>. The web site provides links to other relevant web sites and presents suggested reading materials and non-print resources.

ACKNOWLEDGMENTS

My greatest debt, of course, is to the authors who have graciously allowed me to reprint their works in this anthology. Catharine MacKinnon, Rosemarie Tong, Edward Iwata, Barbara Cox, Carol Gill and Diane Coleman were particularly helpful and generous with their support.

I am grateful to Peter Adams, Philosophy Editor at Wadsworth Publishing, who offered helpful advice. I also received constant encouragement from Clay Glad, Assistant Philosophy Editor. Bob Kauser and Jerry Holloway, from Wadsworth's Permissions and Production Departments respectively, answered countless questions with great patience. George Calmenson of The Book Company offered calm and wise support in the book's final stages and graciously tolerated last minute revisions. The book was greatly improved by the thoughtful suggestions of reviewers for Wadsworth: Allison Bailey, Illinois State University; Jeffrey R. DiLeo, Indiana University; Cynthia Freeland, University of Houston; and Joyce Hendricks, Central Michigan University.

My colleagues at Saint Joseph's University provided much needed support and assistance, particularly, John McCall, Joseph Godfrey, Elizabeth Linehan, John Kearney, Joanne Devlin, Judith Chapman, Marybeth Ayella, Lisa Baglione, F. Graham Lee, Claire Renzetti, and Sally Milliken. My students, especially Erin Hartshorn and Mary Malone offered valuable ideas on the selection of readings. And I am very grateful to those who stood for what must have seemed countless hours in front of photocopiers: Brian McAndrews, Mike McMahon, Erin McKenna, Megan Longshore, and Maryanne Crawford. Finally, special thanks to Ann, Ellen and Heather, Tim and Susan Corcoran, Moira and Kevin Whitelaw, Ethan Heppner, Steve McGovern, Barbara Wall, Carol Anthony, Lynette Goodstine, Robert Thornton, Richard Boyd, James Sterba, and M.A.N. & T.J.M.

1

Recognizing Difference and Entering Imaginatively into Others' Perspectives

Introduction

1.

Martha Nussbaum, "Imagination and the Perspectives of Others"

Patricia Williams, "The Death of the Profane"

Maureen T. Reddy, "Crossing the Color Line"

Richard Rodriguez, "Complexion"

Edward Iwata, "Race Without Face"

Nancy Mairs, "Carnal Acts: Disability"

Natasha Tarpley, "Testimony"

Amy Wang, "The Same Difference"

Andrew Sullivan, "Virtually Normal"

Dorothy Allison, "A Question of Class"

Paula Gunn Allen, "Where I Come from Is Like This"

2.

Peggy McIntosh, "White Privilege and Male Privilege: A Personal Account of Coming to See Correspondences Through Work in Women's Studies"

3.

Marilyn Frye, "Oppression: The Birdcage Metaphor"

4.

Donna Langston, "Tired of Playing Monopoly?"

5.

Kwame Anthony Appiah, "Racisms"

6.

Karen Fiser, "Philosophy and Disability"

*Being morally responsible means that we are accountable
for how we participate in constructing moral situations and
how we address others' vulnerability. We ourselves become
vulnerable by entertaining another point of view and thus
calling into question the 'given' status of our values, beliefs,
attachments, privileges, habits and other assumptions. To
the extent that we appreciate another viewpoint, it has
potentially transformative implications for our own.*

Audrey Thompson

In examining human persons and the moral controversies they face, philosophers have traditionally sought clarity by considering those topics apart from the contingent and thus seemingly irrelevant features of social life, such as a person's gender, race, and social class status. Philosophers assumed that a high level of abstraction would cause persons to be viewed as somehow fundamentally alike, and thus presumably equal. These philosophers sought to attend exclusively to the qualities that all human persons are thought to have in common, disregarding those that distinguish and differentiate us. Consequently, philosophers often depict human persons as interchangeable "agents" whose lives need be sketched out only in the broadest terms possible. Working with highly abstract accounts of persons, moral philosophers present and examine arguments about topics such as abortion, euthanasia, and the death penalty. For example, in studying the moral permissibility of the death penalty and of euthanasia, philosophers seek to talk about generic human agents in a way that strips them of their socially contingent features, such as their race and gender.

Lately, some philosophers have objected to this abstract manner of depicting persons and the moral conflicts they face; these philosophers encourage working with richer, more detailed understandings of persons, their relationships, and their communities. For them, doing good work in moral philosophy requires that one should be acquainted with human psychology and should also acquire a good deal of knowledge about the particulars that shape others' lives as well as one's own. Thus a complete analysis of moral problems requires that we attend to the ways in which the contingencies of social class, racial identity, physical disabilities, and gender affect our lives and hence the very structure of certain sorts of moral problems. When philosophers abstract from certain contingent aspects of social identity in their work, they may in fact distort some moral conflicts.

In seeking to think about the contours and structures of others' lives, one must be very cautious in assuming that others' lives are similar to his or her own; one should hesitate before extrapolating from one's own experiences to that of others. Having heard so frequently the injunction to put oneself in another person's shoes or position, most of us assume it's a simple task—it isn't.

Some scholars (including Martha Nussbaum, whose article opens this chapter) have suggested that moral philosophers should rely on various literary and other non-philosophical sources in order to learn about the significant details and particulars of others' lives. Certain novels, short stories, plays, and even autobiographies might serve us well as "moral texts." Narratives such as these offer up the nuances and complexities that often are overlooked in more traditional philosophic practices and that lead moral philosophers to describe humans as "agents X, Y, and Z." Philosopher Mark Johnson asks:

> Why do we learn more from narratives than from academic moral philosophy about what it is to be human, about the contingencies of life. . . ? The key to the answer is that our lives ultimately have a narrative structure. It is in sustained narratives, therefore, that we come closest to observing and participating in the reality of life as it is actually experienced and lived. We learn from, and are changed by, such narratives to the extent that we become imaginatively engaged in making fine discriminations of character and in determining what is morally salient in particular situations. We actually enter into the lives of the characters, and we perform acts of perception, decision, and criticism.[1]

It is important to note that these philosophers are not encouraging us to read narratives *in lieu of* studying abstract moral theories and critically examining arguments; rather, they suggest that we use narratives to supplement the more traditional philosophic texts. Martha Nussbaum's essay, "Imagination and the Perspectives of Others," explains more fully why philosophers ought to study narratives in order to understand better others' perspectives and lives.

The argument of this anthology is that features of our social identity—most notably, gender, race, social class, and sexual orientation—play an important role in structuring moral problems; thus the philosophic study of moral controversies requires some acquaintance with these aspects of our social identities. The readings that immediately follow Nussbaum's article are narrative, autobiographical accounts in which a number of women and men write about how their gender, social class, health status, race, ethnic background, and sexual preference have affected their lives. These readings serve as preparatory introductions for the more traditional philosophic readings in the following chapters. They are of necessity fairly brief. Ideally, students would read extended narratives, both fictional and autobiographical. The readings selected here are meant only to encourage students to read further along these lines.

As philosophers have sought to study the role the contingent features of social life might have in their moral analyses, they have realized that they also need to examine directly the ways in which race, ethnicity, and gender distinguish individuals as different from one another. Similarly, philosophers have sought to study and analyze the nature of discrimination, privilege, and oppression. Following the lead of social scientists, they have also questioned why it might be difficult to recognize in oneself discriminatory stances and attitudes. The readings at the end of this chapter offer a glimpse at the efforts philosophers and other theorists are making to study these morally significant features of persons and of our attitudes toward them.

---

1. Mark Johnson, *Moral Imagination: Implications of Cognitive Science for Ethics* (Chicago: University of Chicago Press, 1993) 196.

1.

Imagination and the Perspectives of Others

Martha Nussbaum

Martha Nussbaum is professor of law and ethics at the University of Chicago. Her most recent books include *The Therapy of Desire: Theory and Practice in Hellenistic Ethics; Poetic Justice; The Literary Imagination and Public Life; Love's Knowledge: Essays on Philosophy and Literature;* and *The Fragility of Goodness.* In this opening essay, Nussbaum argues that one virtue of good moral reasoning is the capacity to enter imaginatively into the lives of others, even quite distant others. She adds that this capacity is in part affective; imagining the lives of others requires emotional engagement. Given that emotional understanding of others' lives is an important part of moral reasoning, Nussbaum suggests that moral philosophers might enlargen and deepen their capacity for understanding by studying literature and other narrative accounts of particular lives, imagined or actual. Following Nussbaum's essay are a number of short autobiographical narratives that are intended to offer an opportunity to follow her suggestion. These stories were written by a number of women and men who testify to the painfulness and confusion of recognizing themselves as somehow "other" in this society. In many of these pieces, the writers speak to their experiences of feeling marginalized in some way as a result of one or another aspect of their given identities.

. . . Very often in today's political life we lack the capacity to see one another as fully human, as more than "dreams or dots." Often, too, those refusals of sympathy are aided and abetted by an excessive reliance on technical ways of modeling human behavior, especially those that derive from economic utilitarianism. These models can be very valuable in their place, but they frequently prove incomplete as a guide to political relations among citizens. Without the participation of the literary imagination, said [the poet Walt] Whitman, "things are grotesque, eccentric, fail of their full returns." We see much political argument today that is grotesque and eccentric in this way. The purpose of this book is to describe the ingredient of public discourse that Whitman found missing from his America and to show some roles it still might play in our own. It grows out of the conviction, which I share with Whitman, that storytelling and literary imagining are not opposed to rational argument, but can provide essential ingredients in a rational argument.

During the lifetimes of William James and John Dewey, it was taken for granted that academic philosophy, including philosophical discussion of literature and art, was part of public discourse. But during much of the present century, academic philosophy in the United States has had relatively few links with practical choice and public life. Recently, however, philosophers have once again become involved in public debate, not only about the basic issues of ethical and political theory, but also about more concrete issues in medicine, business, and law. During the past five years I, like numerous philosophical colleagues, have spent more and more time in professional schools—law schools in my case—giving visiting lectures and talking about issues with professional theorists and practitioners. In the spring of 1994, I taught law students for the first time, as a visiting professor in the law school at the University of Chicago. . . .

    The subject of my legal teaching was, in fact, storytelling, for the course I was asked to teach was Law and Literature. The law students and I read Sophocles, and Plato, and Seneca, and Dickens. In connection with the literary works, we discussed compassion and mercy, the role of the emotions in public judgment, what is involved in imagining the situation of someone different from oneself. We talked about ways in which texts of different types present human beings—seeing them, in some cases, as ends in themselves, endowed with dignity and individuality, in others as abstract undistinguishable units or as mere means to the ends of others. . . .

We talked, as well, about more concrete social issues, including gender, homosexuality, and race. In a lecture hall less than fifty yards away from the black metal fence in the law school parking lot that marks the "line" between the world of the university and the world of the inner-city Chicago slums, in a class with only one African-American member in seventy, we read Richard Wright's *Native Son*. Every Chicago place name marked a location we knew—though with respect to some of those locations almost all of us were in the position of Wright's Mary Dalton, when she says to Bigger Thomas that she has no idea how people live ten blocks away from her. "He knew as he stood there," says Wright of Bigger, "that he could never tell why he had killed. It was not that he did not really want to tell, but the telling of it would have involved an explanation of his entire life." We talked about the relevance of that passage to disputes about discretion and mercy in criminal sentencing—about a Supreme Court decision that instructs courts to treat defendants not "as members of a faceless, undifferentiated mass" but "as uniquely individual human beings."[1] What might the role of a novel such as Wright's be, in conveying to future judges and lawyers an understanding of that requirement? I did not invent the course Law and Literature; in fact, it had been for some years a regular part of the law school's curriculum. The legal profession's interest in the relationship between philosophy and literature had at first surprised me. Gradually I had come to see that what was being sought from such teaching was the investigation and principled defense of a humanistic and multivalued conception of public rationality that is powerfully exemplified in the common-

law tradition. This conception needs defending, since it has for some time been under attack from the more "scientific" conceptions offered by the law-and-economics movement. I had for some time been working on related philosophical ideas and had already begun to connect them to issues in the law. But the Chicago course marked the first time that I had tried to work out some of these ideas in the classroom, interacting with students who would shortly be lawyers and clerks for judges. Although I remain a legal amateur, and although I make this suggestion from the outside, still in considerable ignorance of the more technical and formal side of the law, which I am not proposing to demote and for which I have great respect, I believe more strongly than ever that thinking about narrative literature does have the potential to make a contribution to the law in particular, to public reasoning generally. . . .

The literary imagination is a part of public rationality, and not the whole. I believe that it would be extremely dangerous to suggest substituting empathetic imagining for rule-governed moral reasoning, and I am not making that suggestion. In fact, I defend the literary imagination precisely because it seems to me an essential ingredient of an ethical stance that asks us to concern ourselves with the good of other people whose lives are distant from our own. Such an ethical stance will have a large place for rules and formal decision procedures, including procedures inspired by economics. . . .

On the other hand, an ethics of impartial respect for human dignity will fail to engage real human beings unless they are made capable of entering imaginatively into the lives of distant others and to have emotions related to that participation. The emotions of the reader or spectator have been defended as essential to good ethical judgment by quite a few ethical theorists deeply concerned about impartiality—perhaps most notably by Adam Smith, whose *Theory of Moral Sentiments* is a central inspiration for the project of this book. Although these emotions have limitations and dangers, as I shall argue, and although their function in ethical reasoning must be carefully circumscribed, they also contain a powerful, if partial, vision of social justice and provide powerful motives for just conduct. . . .

My central subject is the ability to imagine what it is like to live the life of another person who might, given changes in circumstance, be oneself or one of one's loved ones. . . . Literature focuses on the possible, inviting its readers to wonder about themselves. . . . Unlike most historical works, literary works typically invite their readers to put themselves in the place of people of many different kinds and to take on their experiences. In their very mode of address to their imagined reader, they convey the sense that there are links of possibility, at least on a very general level, between the characters and the reader. The reader's emotions and imagination are highly active as a result, and it is the nature of this activity, and its relevance for public thinking, that interests me.

Historical and biographical works do provide us with empirical information that is essential to good choice. They may in fact also arouse the relevant forms of imaginative activity, if they are written in an inviting narrative style. But to the extent that they promote identification and sympathy in the reader, they resemble literary works. This is especially so if they show the effect of circumstances on the emotions and the inner world—a salient part of the contribution of the literary, as I shall argue.

Another way of putting this point is that good literature is disturbing in a way that history and social science writing frequently are not. Because it summons powerful emotions, it disconcerts and puzzles. It inspires distrust of conventional pieties and exacts a frequently painful confrontation with one's own thoughts and intentions. One may be told many things about people in one's own society and yet keep that knowledge at a distance. Literary works that promote identification and emotional reaction cut through those self-protective stratagems, requiring us to see and to respond to many things that may be difficult to confront—and they make this process palatable by giving us pleasure in the very act of confrontation. . . .

In its engagement with a general notion of the human being, [Dickens's *Hard Times*] (like many novels) is, I think, while particularistic, not relativistic. That is, it recognizes human needs that transcend boundaries of time, place, class, religion, and ethnicity, and it makes the focus of its moral deliberation the question of their adequate fulfillment. Its criticism of concrete political and social situations relies on a notion of what it is for a human being to flourish, and this notion itself, while extremely general and in need of further specification, is neither local nor sectarian. On the other hand, part of the idea of flourishing is a deep respect for qualitative difference—so the norm enjoins that governments, wherever they are, should attend to citizens in all their concreteness and variety, responding in a sensitive way to historical and personal contingencies. But that is itself a universal injunction and part of a universal picture of humanness. And it is by relying on this universal ideal that the novel, so different from a guidebook or even an anthropological field report, makes readers participants in the lives of people very different from themselves and also critics of the class distinctions that give people similarly constructed an unequal access to flourishing. Once again, these insights need corroboration from theoretical arguments; they are not complete in themselves. . . .

The literary judge . . . is committed to neutrality, properly understood. That is, she will not tailor her principles to the demands of political or religious pressure groups and will give no group or individual special indulgence or favor on account of their relation to her or her affiliations. She is a judicious spectator and does not gush with irrelevant or ungrounded sentiment. On the other hand, as I have argued here, her neutrality does not require a lofty distance from the social realities of the cases before her; indeed, she is enjoined to examine those realities searchingly, with imaginative concreteness and the emotional responses that are proper to the judicious spectator—or to his surrogate, the novel-reader. . . .

. . . [The] literary judge would look in particular for evidence that certain groups have suffered unequal disadvantages and therefore need more attention if they are to be shown a truly equal concern.

This concern for the disadvantaged is built into the structure of the literary experience, which was, as we saw, Adam Smith's model for the experience of the judicious spectator. The reader participates vicariously in numerous different lives, some more advantaged and some less. In realist social novels, which are my focus, these lives are self-consciously drawn from different social strata, and the extent to which these varied circumstances allow for flourishing is made part of the reader's experience. The reader enters each of these lives not knowing, so to speak, which one of them is hers—she identifies first with [one] and then with [another], living each of those lives in turn and becoming aware that her actual place is in many respects an accident of fortune. She has empathetic emotions appropriate to the living of the life and, more important, spectatorial emotions in which she evaluates the way fortune has made this life conducive or not conducive to flourishing. This means that she will notice especially vividly the disadvantages faced by the least well off. . . . Why should the literary imagination be any more connected with equality than with inequality, or with democratic rather than aristocratic ideals? Why is the sunlight of judicial vision specially concerned with the "helpless things"?

When we read *Hard Times* as sympathetic participants, our attention has a special focus. Since the sufferings and anxieties of the characters are among the central bonds between reader and work, our attention is drawn in particular to those characters who suffer and fear. Characters who are not facing any adversity simply do not hook us in as readers; there is no drama in a life in which things are going smoothly. This tragic sensibility leads the reader to investigate

with a particularly keen combination of identification and sympathy lives in which circumstance has played an impeding role. Sometimes, of course, the baneful circumstances are necessary and inevitable. Loved ones die; natural disasters destroy property and cities. Frequently, however, the tragedy that moves us is not necessary. Not all wars are inevitable; hunger and poverty and miserably unequal conditions of labor are not inevitable. Since we read a novel like *Hard Times* with the thought that we ourselves might be in a character's position—since our emotion is based in part on this sort of empathetic identification—we will naturally be most concerned with the lot of those whose position is worst, and we will begin to think of ways in which that position might have been other than it is, might be made better than it is.

One way in which the situation of the poor or oppressed is especially bad is that it might have been otherwise. We see this especially clearly when we see their situation side by side with the situation of the rich and prosperous. In this way our thought will naturally turn in the direction of making the lot of the worst off more similar to the lot of the rich and powerful: since we ourselves might be, or become, either of those two people, we want to raise the floor. This may not get all the way to complete equality (whether of resources or of welfare or of capability to function), but it does at least lead political thought in the direction of ameliorating persistent inequalities and providing all with a decent minimum. One might of course have these thoughts without being a "poet." But . . . the ability to imagine vividly, and then to assess judicially, another person's pain, to participate in it and then to ask about its significance, is a powerful way of learning what the human facts are and of acquiring a motivation to alter them. . . .

Literary understanding, I would therefore argue, promotes habits of mind that lead toward social equality in that they contribute to the dismantling of the stereotypes that support group hatred. For this purpose, in principle any literary work that has the characteristics I have discussed . . . would be valuable: in reading . . . we learn habits of "fancying" that we can then apply to other groups that come before us, whether or not those groups are depicted in the novels we have read. But it is also very valuable to extend this literary understanding by seeking out literary experiences in which we do identify sympathetically with individual members of marginalized or oppressed groups within our own society, learning both to see the world, for a time, through their eyes and then reflecting as spectators on the meaning of what we have seen. If one of the significant contributions of the novel to public rationality is its depiction of the interaction between shared human aspirations and concrete social circumstances, it seems reasonable that we should seek novels that depict the special circumstances of groups with whom we live and whom we want to understand, cultivating the habit of seeing the fulfillment or frustration of their aspirations and desires within a social world that may be characterized by institutional inequalities. . . .

NOTE

1. *Woodson v. North Carolina*, 428 U.S. 280, 304 (1976).

The Death of the Profane

Patricia Williams

Patricia Williams has written extensively about issues of race, civil rights, and constitutional law in leading law reviews and in books. She is professor of law, Columbia University. She is the author of *The Alchemy of Race and Rights* (Harvard) and *The Rooster's Egg: On the Persistence of Prejudice* (Harvard).

Buzzers are big in New York City. Favored particularly by smaller stores and boutiques, merchants throughout the city have installed them as screening devices to reduce the incidence of robbery: if the face at the door looks desirable, the buzzer is pressed and the door is unlocked. If the face is that of an undesirable, the door stays locked. Predictably, the issue of undesirability has revealed itself to be a racial determination. While controversial enough at first, even civil-rights organizations backed down eventually in the face of arguments that the buzzer system is a "necessary evil," that it is a "mere inconvenience" in comparison to the risks of being murdered, that suffering discrimination is not as bad as being assaulted, and that in any event it is not all blacks who are barred, just "17-year-old black males wearing running shoes and hooded sweatshirts."[1]

The installation of these buzzers happened swiftly in New York; stores that had always had their doors wide open suddenly became exclusive or received people by appointment only. I discovered them and their meaning one Saturday in 1986. I was shopping in Soho and saw in a store window a sweater that I wanted to buy for my mother. I pressed my round brown face to the window and my finger to the buzzer, seeking admittance. A narrow-eyed, white teenager wearing running shoes and feasting on bubble gum glared out, evaluating me for signs that would pit me against the limits of his social understanding. After about five seconds, he mouthed "We're closed," and blew pink rubber at me. It was two Saturdays before Christmas, at one o'clock in the afternoon; there were several white people in the store who appeared to be shopping for things for *their* mothers.

I was enraged. At that moment I literally wanted to break all the windows of the store and *take* lots of sweaters for my mother. In the flicker of his judgmental gray eyes, that saleschild had transformed my brightly sentimental, joy-to-the-world, pre-Christmas spree to a shambles. He snuffed my sense of humanitarian catholicity, and there was nothing I could do to snuff his, without making a spectacle of myself.

I am still struck by the structure of power that drove me into such a blizzard of rage. There was almost nothing I could do, short of physically intruding upon him, that would humiliate him the way he humiliated me. No words, no gestures, no prejudices of my own would make a bit of difference to him; his refusal to let me into the store—it was Benetton's, whose colorfully punnish ad campaign is premised on wrapping every one of the world's peoples in its cottons and woolens—was an outward manifestation of his never having let someone like me into the realm of his reality. He had no compassion, no remorse, no reference to me; and no desire to acknowledge me even at the estranged level of arm's-length transactor. He saw me only as one who would take his money and therefore could not conceive that I was there to give him money.

In this weird ontological imbalance, I realized that buying something in that store was like bestowing a gift, the gift of my commerce, the lucre of my patronage. In the wake of my outrage, I wanted to take back the gift of appreciation that my peering in the window must have appeared to be. I wanted to take it back in the form of unappreciation, disrespect, defilement. I wanted to work so hard at wishing he could feel what I felt that he would never again mistake my hatred for some sort of plaintive wish to be included. I was quite willing to disenfranchise myself, in the heat of my need to revoke the flattery of my purchasing power. I was willing to boycott Benetton's, random white-owned businesses, and anyone who ever blew bubble gum in my face again.

My rage was admittedly diffuse, even self-destructive, but it was symmetrical. The perhaps loose-ended but utter propriety of that rage is no doubt lost not just to the young man who actually barred me, but to those who would appreciate my being barred only as an abstract precaution, who approve of those who would bar even as they deny that they would bar *me*.

The violence of my desire to burst into Benetton's is probably quite apparent. I often wonder if the violence, the exclusionary hatred, is equally

apparent in the repeated public urgings that blacks understand the buzzer system by putting themselves in the shoes of white storeowners—that, in effect, blacks look into the mirror of frightened white faces for the reality of their undesirability; and that then blacks would "just as surely conclude that [they] would not let [themselves] in under similar circumstances."[2] (That some blacks might agree merely shows that some of us have learned too well the lessons of privatized intimacies of self-hatred and rationalized away the fullness of our public, participatory selves.)

On the same day I was barred from Benetton's, I went home and wrote the above impassioned account in my journal. On the day after that, I found I was still brooding, so I turned to a form of catharsis I have always found healing. I typed up as much of the story as I have just told, made a big poster of it, put a nice colorful border around it, and, after Benetton's was truly closed, stuck it to their big sweater-filled window. I exercised my first-amendment right to place my business with them right out in the street.

So that was the first telling of this story. The second telling came a few months later, for a symposium on Excluded Voices sponsored by a law review. I wrote an essay summing up my feelings about being excluded from Benetton's and analyzing "how the rhetoric of increased privatization, in response to racial issues, functions as the rationalizing agent of public unaccountability and, ultimately, irresponsibility." Weeks later, I received the first edit. From the first page to the last, my fury had been carefully cut out. My rushing, run-on-rage had been reduced to simple declarative sentences. The active personal had been inverted in favor of the passive impersonal. My words were different; they spoke to me upsidedown. I was afraid to read too much of it at a time—meanings rose up at me oddly, stolen and strange.

A week and a half later, I received the second edit. All reference to Benetton's had been deleted because, according to the editors and the faculty adviser, it was defamatory; they feared harassment and liability; they said printing it would be irresponsible. I called them and offered to supply a footnote attesting to this as my personal experience at one particular location and of a buzzer system not limited to Benetton's; the editors told me that they were not in the habit of publishing things that were unverifiable. I could not but wonder, in this refusal even to let me file an affidavit, what it would take to make my experience verifiable. The testimony of an independent white bystander? (a requirement in fact imposed in U.S. Supreme Court holdings through the first part of the century[3]).

Two days *after* the piece was sent to press, I received copies of the final page proofs. All reference to my race had been eliminated because it was against "editorial policy" to permit descriptions of physiognomy. "I realize," wrote one editor, "that this was a very personal experience, but any reader will know what you must have looked like when standing at that window." In a telephone conversation to them, I ranted wildly about the significance of such an omission. "It's irrelevant," another editor explained in a voice gummy with soothing and patience; "It's nice and poetic," but it doesn't "advance the discussion of any principle . . . This is a law review, after all." Frustrated, I accused him of censorship; calmly he assured me it was not. "This is just a matter of style," he said with firmness and finality.

Ultimately I did convince the editors that mention of my race was central to the whole sense of the subsequent text; that my story became one of extreme paranoia without the information that I am black; or that it became one in which the reader had to fill in the gap by assumption, presumption, prejudgment, or prejudice. What was most interesting to me in this experience was how the blind application of principles of neutrality, through the device of omission, acted either to make me look crazy or to make the reader participate in old habits of cultural bias.

That was the second telling of my story. The third telling came last April, when I was invited to participate in a law-school conference on Equality and Difference. I retold my sad tale of exclusion from Soho's most glitzy boutique, focusing in this version on the law-review editing process as a consequence of an ideology of style rooted in a social text of neutrality. I opined:

> Law and legal writing aspire to formalized, color-blind, liberal ideals. Neutrality is the standard for assuring these ideals; yet the adherence to it is often determined by reference

to an aesthetic of uniformity, in which difference is simply omitted. For example, when segregation was eradicated from the American lexicon, its omission led many to actually believe that racism therefore no longer existed. Race-neutrality in law has become the presumed antidote for race bias in real life. With the entrenchment of the notion of race-neutrality came attacks on the concept of affirmative action and the rise of reverse discrimination suits. Blacks, for so many generations deprived of jobs based on the color of our skin, are now told that we ought to find it demeaning to be hired, based on the color of our skin. Such is the silliness of simplistic either-or inversions as remedies to complex problems.

What is truly demeaning in this era of double-speak-no-evil is going to interviews and not getting hired because someone doesn't think we'll be comfortable. It is demeaning not to get promoted because we're judged "too weak," then putting in a lot of energy the next time and getting fired because we're "too strong." It is demeaning to be told what we find demeaning. It is very demeaning to stand on street corners unemployed and begging. It is downright demeaning to have to explain why we haven't been employed for months and then watch the job go to someone who is "more experienced." It is outrageously demeaning that none of this can be called racism, even if it happens only to, or to large numbers of, black people; as long as it's done with a smile, a handshake and a shrug; as long as the phantom-word "race" is never used.

The image of race as a phantom-word came to me after I moved into my late godmother's home. In an attempt to make it my own, I cleared the bedroom for painting. The following morning the room asserted itself, came rushing and raging at me through the emptiness, exactly as it had been for twenty-five years. One day filled with profuse and overwhelming complexity, the next day filled with persistently recurring memories. The shape of the past came to haunt me, the shape of the emptiness confronted me each time I was about to enter the room. The force of its spirit still drifts like an odor throughout the house.

The power of that room, I have thought since, is very like the power of racism as status quo: it is deep, angry, eradicated from view, but strong enough to make everyone who enters the room walk around the bed that isn't there, avoiding the phantom as they did the substance, for fear of bodily harm. They do not even know they are avoiding; they defer to the unseen shapes of things with subtle responsiveness, guided by an impulsive awareness of nothingness, and the deep knowledge and denial of witchcraft at work.

The phantom room is to me symbolic of the emptiness of formal equal opportunity, particularly as propounded by President Reagan, the Reagan Civil Rights Commission and the Reagan Supreme Court. Blindly formalized constructions of equal opportunity are the creation of a space that is filled in by a meandering stream of unguided hopes, dreams, fantasies, fears, recollections. They are the presence of the past in imaginary, imagistic form—the phantom-roomed exile of our longing.

It is thus that I strongly believe in the efficacy of programs and paradigms like affirmative action. Blacks are the objects of a constitutional omission which has been incorporated into a theory of neutrality. It is thus that omission is really a form of expression, as oxymoronic as that sounds: racial omission is a literal part of original intent; it is the fixed, reiterated prophecy of the Founding Fathers. It is thus that affirmative action is an affirmation; the affirmative act of hiring—or hearing—blacks is a recognition of individuality that re-places blacks as a social statistic, that is profoundly interconnective to the fate of blacks and whites either as sub-groups or as one group. In this sense, affirmative action is as mystical and beyond-the-self as an initiation ceremony. It is an act of verification and of vision. It is an act of social as well as professional responsibility.

The following morning I opened the local newspaper, to find that the event of my speech had commanded two columns on the front page of the Metro section. I quote only the opening lines: "Affirmative action promotes prejudice by denying the status of women and blacks, instead of affirming them as its name suggests. So said New York City attorney Patricia Williams to an audience Wednesday."[4]

I clipped out the article and put it in my journal. In the margin there is a note to myself: eventually, it says, I should try to pull all these threads together into yet another law-review article. The problem, of course, will be that in the hierarchy of law-review citation, the article in the newspaper will have more authoritative weight about me, as a so-called "primary resource," than I will have; it will take precedence over my own citation of the unverifiable testimony of my speech.

I have used the Benetton's story a lot, in speaking engagements at various schools. I tell it whenever I am too tired to whip up an original speech from scratch. Here are some of the questions I have been asked in the wake of its telling:

Am I not privileging a racial perspective, by considering only the black point of view? Don't I have an obligation to include the "salesman's side" of the story?

Am I not putting the salesman on trial and finding him guilty of racism without giving him a chance to respond to or cross-examine me?

Am I not using the store window as a "metaphorical fence" against the potential of his explanation in order to represent my side as "authentic"?

How can I be sure I'm right?

What makes my experience the real black one anyway?

Isn't it possible that another black person would disagree with my experience? If so, doesn't that render my story too unempirical and subjective to pay any attention to?

Always a major objection is to my having put the poster on Benetton's window. As one law professor put it: "It's one thing to publish this in a law review, where no one can take it personally, but it's another thing altogether to put your own interpretation right out there, just like that, uncontested, I mean, with nothing to counter it."[5]

Notes

1. "When 'By Appointment' Means Keep Out," *New York Times,* December 17, 1986, p. B1. Letter to the Editor from Michael Levin and Marguerita Levin, *New York Times,* January 11, 1987, p. E32.

2. *New York Times,* January 11, 1987, p. E32.

3. See generally *Blyew v. U.S.,* 80 U.S. 581 (1871), upholding a state's right to forbid blacks to testify against whites.

4. "Attorney Says Affirmative Action Denies Racism, Sexism," *Dominion Post* (Morgantown, West Virginia), April 8, 1988, p. B1.

5. These questions put me on trial—an imaginary trial where it is I who have the burden of proof—and proof being nothing less than the testimony of the salesman actually confessing yes yes I am a racist. These questions question my own ability to know, to assess, to be objective. And of course, since anything that happens to me is inherently subjective, they take away my power to know what happens to me in the world. Others, by this standard, will always know better than I. And my insistence on recounting stories from my own perspective will be treated as presumption, slander, paranoid hallucination, or just plain lies.

Recently I got an urgent call from Thomas Grey of Stanford Law School. He had used this piece in his jurisprudence class, and a rumor got started that the Benetton's story wasn't true, that I had made it up, that it was a fantasy, a lie that was probably the product of a diseased mind trying to make all white people feel guilty. At this point I realized it almost didn't make any difference whether I was telling the truth or not—that the greater issue I had to face was the overwhelming weight of a disbelief that goes beyond mere disinclination to believe and becomes active suppression of anything I might have to say. The greater problem is a powerfully oppressive mechanism for denial of black self-knowledge and expression. And this denial cannot be separated from the simultaneously pathological willingness to believe certain things about blacks—not to believe them, but things about them.

When students in Grey's class believed and then claimed that I had made it all up, they put me in a position like that of Tawana Brawley. I mean that specifically: the social consequence of concluding that we are liars operates as a kind of public absolution of racism—the conclusion is not merely that we are troubled or that I am eccentric, but that we, as liars, are the norm. Therefore, the nonbelievers can believe, things of this sort really don't happen (even in the face of statistics to the contrary). Racism or rape is all a big fantasy concocted by troublesome minorities and women. It is interesting to recall the outcry in every national medium, from the *New York Post* to the *Times* to the major networks, in the wake of the Brawley case: who will ever again believe a black woman who cries rape by a white man? . . . Now shift the frame a bit, and imagine a white male facing a consensus that he lied. Would there be a difference? Consider Charles Stuart, for example, the white Bostonian who accused a black man of murdering his pregnant wife and whose brother later alleged that in fact the brothers had conspired to murder her. Most people and the media not only did not claim but actively resisted believing that Stuart represented any kind of "white male" norm. Instead he was written off as a troubled weirdo, a deviant—again even in the face of spousal-abuse statistics to the contrary. There was not a story I could find that carried on about "who will ever believe" the next white man who cries murder.

Crossing the Color Line
Maureen T. Reddy

Maureen Reddy is an associate professor of English and director of the Women's Studies Program at Rhode Island College. Her previous books include *Sisters in Crime: Feminism and the Crime Novel; Narrating Mothers: Theorizing Maternal Subjectivities* (with Brenda Daly); *Crossing the Color Line: Race, Parenting, and Culture;* and *Mother Journeys: Feminists Write About Mothering* (coedited with Martha Roth and Amy Sheldon). She recently edited a collection of essays, *Everyday Acts Against Racism: Raising Children in a Multiracial World.*

Imagine:

Your nine-year-old son likes to play hide-and-seek games around the neighborhood with other children. One afternoon, you look out the kitchen window and see him crouching behind a neighbor's hedge, with his dark jacket pulled up over the back of his head for camouflage. Suddenly realizing that your child is now tall enough to be mistaken for a teenager, you call him into the house, away from the game. He thinks his greatest danger is being found by the child who is "It," but you know that he is at risk of being shot by someone who sees not a child playing, but the urban predator of television-fueled nightmares, ready to spring from the bushes.

You know that you have waited too long to warn him about this danger, and about others that are real and present now that he resembles an adolescent. He has to be told to keep his hands out of his pockets when he is in stores, for instance, lest he be seen as a shoplifter. He also must learn how to talk to the police who will surely stop him

From Maureen T. Reddy, *Crossing the Color Line: Race, Parenting, and Culture.* Copyright (c) 1994 by Maureen T. Reddy. Reprinted by permission of Rutgers University Press.

when he is out riding his bike some day soon. You ask your son to feed his pets and to make his bed, hoping the chores will give you enough time to figure out how to explain these facts of life to him without destroying his innocent sense of fun. You never faced such dangers as a child, and so you have no model to follow.

Unless you are white and your family is black, you probably will never confront exactly the dilemma I did early in 1992.[1] If everyone in your family is white, you would not have to teach your child to protect himself from these particular dangers. If you are black, you would have familial and personal experience to draw upon in teaching your children how to negotiate the world safely, with their self-esteem and sense of possibility protected. A white person in a black family starts from scratch.

Many Americans of all races want to believe that raising children is basically the same project, regardless of the children's and parents' races, arguing that child-rearing issues lack racial inflections.[2] And some aspects of parenting are indeed race-blind: toilet training, for example, or treating common childhood illnesses. However, I have learned as a white mother of black children that the race-blind issues tend to be the easier issues, and that far more of the hard questions I have about raising my children center on race. This should not be a surprise in a society as racialized as the one in which we live. Pick up a newspaper in any urban area in the United States on any day, and it is virtually certain that you will find at least one major story on race, with none of the news good: charges of racial discrimination in hiring practices, debates about affirmative action, high unemployment among so-called minority groups, racial violence, racial tensions—all these are front-page staples. The grim statistics on black life chances are familiar, at least in outline. Whereas blacks make up 12.1 percent of the U.S. population, they earn only 7.2 percent of the aggregate family income, and receive only 5.7 percent of all bachelor's degrees and 3.5 percent of doctorates awarded by U.S. colleges and universities.[3] Blacks are overrepresented in prisons (45.3 percent of inmates), as victims of crime (50.8 percent of murder victims, 33.2 percent of rape victims, and 30.8 percent of robbery victims were black in 1989–90), and in ill-paid occupations (25 percent

of hotel maids are black, for example, but only 0.9 percent of architects are).[4] In 1990, blacks were nearly three times as likely to be unemployed as were whites and nearly four times as likely to live in poverty, earning only approximately $580 for each $1,000 earned by white families.[5] Blacks have a far higher infant mortality rate than do whites, and if they live past infancy they are more likely to die young of hypertension, diabetes, or AIDS than are whites. The terrible facts that young black men are more than twice as likely to be homicide victims than they are to attend college and that murder is the leading cause of death for young black men are old news.

For the most part, even well-intentioned whites have no clear idea of the daily lives of their black fellow citizens, of what it feels like to live with racism every day. Worse yet, what it feels like to look at one's beloved children and to realize that the limited life chances limned by statistics are *their* life chances. Every so often, American whites are forced by some especially troubling public event to consider what such statistics might really mean to blacks, to confront at least briefly the flesh-and-blood reality of racism in America. The 1992 Los Angeles uprising might seem such an event, as it briefly focused attention on the "underclass," which was depicted as black by the media. In fact, though, the participants in the uprising were *not* all black; the media's persistence in portraying it as a black riot missed the point and misrepresented the case while reinforcing stereotypes about race. To my mind, one of the most powerful recent statements on the insidious extent of racism in our time came from Arthur Ashe in 1992. Frail, dying of AIDS, but as calm as ever, Ashe told an interviewer that having AIDS was not the most difficult thing he had ever had to deal with—being black was. Ashe's money and fame did not protect him from racism, as indeed nothing could.

And yet, the story on race is not all grim. Racism affects all black people, but racism is not the sum of black people's lives. Further, racism is subject to change, can even be eradicated through the collective efforts of blacks and whites working together. First, however, we as a nation need a serious, sustained, meaningful dialogue about race. . . .

When I met Doug, I was twenty-one, newly graduated from college, and I did not yet fully know that I was white; Doug, in contrast, knew for a certainty that he was black. Knowing that, he also knew that I was white. To paraphrase Thurgood Marshall, outside of his own house, Doug never had to look in a mirror to see that he was black. I, on the other hand, had been looking in mirrors for twenty-one years without recognizing my whiteness. And yet I was far from blind to racism, had read widely in black literature and history, and was deeply committed to the ideal of black liberation. If this is a paradox—awareness of racial inequality and commitment to its end alongside almost total lack of awareness of meanings of whiteness—and it is, it is one that many whites live with every day, with no discomfort.

It was only when I stopped being white, in some sense, that I began to understand what whiteness means in America. Under South African apartheid, the white partner of a black person was reclassified as "colored": legally, in other words, there was no such thing as a white/black marriage. Although we do not live under apartheid, a de facto reclassification happens here, too, I think: the white partner, in learning what being black in America entails, learns what whiteness means and loses or abandons at least some of that whiteness. Being white—unless you are an out-and-out racist—usually does not include any consciousness of whiteness as a social signifier, as a state with meanings of its own. Because whiteness is treated as the norm, identical to humanity, whiteness does not get marked as a category in most white people's lives. We do not think of white writers, for example, as a subcategory of the general category of "writer," although we do mark black writers this way: writer = white, much as mother = female . . . it simply goes without saying. To say someone's cultural background is white is to say nothing at all. As Richard Dyer points out in his essay on representations of whiteness in film, "White," this (false) sense of whiteness as a natural norm is an important component of white power, which "secures its dominance by seeming not to be anything in particular," by pretending to be invisible.[6] Making whiteness visible, becoming aware of whiteness as a social construction, moves one out of the mainstream of whiteness.

I *look* white, but that white skin conceals my inner life. This feeling of being costumed in one's own skin, of "masquerading" as white in public, may be the one thing white partners of black people, and especially white parents of black children, share regardless of other differences among us. Hettie Jones, the former wife of Amiri Baraka, says that she felt "misrepresented, minus a crucial dimension" when she went to work in a white office, without her husband and children. Jones quotes a white friend with black children who calls this feeling being "disguised in your own skin."[7] Similarly, out in public without her family, Jane Lazarre's protagonist Julia in her novel *Worlds Beyond My Control* feels "masked, colorless."[8] A white woman married to a black man, Julia walks alone through Manhattan feeling "like a woman disguised, one of those Halloween creatures with skin of some otherworldly green. Blacks treat her with short-fused hostility that has become ordinary on city streets, on buses, in banks. Whites murmur confessions of racial prejudice, thinking she is one of them."[9] Out without my family, I also feel disguised. In all-white groups, I feel like a secret spy, like Ralph Ellison's character who says "our [blacks'] life is a war" and claims he has been "a spy in the enemy's country ever since I give up my gun back in the Reconstruction."[10]

The process does not work the other way, however. The black partner does not become white, does not acquire white privilege, does not describe that feeling of masquerade, has *always* been a spy in the enemy's country. The color line is permeable in one direction only.

To explain how I became a racial bridge for my children, I need to explain how I came to marry a black man. The truest (and least satisfying, I realize) explanation is: I did not marry "a black man," I married Doug. Doug and I were friends before we became lovers, and therefore we knew a lot not only about each other, but also about each other's family and friends, well before we violated the great social taboo against interracial romance. Neither of us planned to fall in love with the other—who can plan such alchemy?—and we only talked about what crossing the color line might mean for us after it happened.

Much as I would like to believe that race played no meaningful role in Doug's and my initial attraction to each other, much as I want to say that love knows no color, of course race *must* have been important in some way. But in what way? And how to separate race's role from everything else that contributed to our finding each other? Nearly two decades later, excavating the layers of our relationship, especially those first heady months, seems impossible. Both of us were young and naive, and each of us separately accounted for the other's race in a purely negative way, as in "I don't care about race, my lover's race doesn't matter." But our races helped to make us what we were—and are—and so in that sense it *was* race that brought us together.

My daughter, nearing her second birthday, asks "why" about everything and sometimes says to me, "You love me, Mommy. Why?" Why indeed? "Because you are you," I tell her truthfully, which usually satisfies her. I want to make a parallel move here, saying I love Doug because he is Doug, and yet I know that is an inadequate explanation. Looking back, I recall that I was first attracted to Doug's calmness and gentleness, his intelligence, his dry humor, his physical self-confidence, his whole way of being in the world, and of course his race was part of all that. Having always felt like an outsider of sorts in the white lower-middle-class and working-class community in which I was raised, and later feeling appalled by the heedless attitude of entitlement I sensed in my wealthier college classmates, especially the white men, I found in Doug a kindred spirit. . . .

Through my experiences with Doug, I learned about the other side of racism, white skin privilege, which within a few years appeared to me like a vast underground network, whose surface I initially had mistaken for the whole. In myriad ways, white people's skin color smooths our paths, making our lives easier than the lives of people of color. We can expect to find housing in any neighborhood we can afford, for example, or (if we are men) to have our qualifications for job openings taken seriously. We can blend into most crowds— in restaurants, classrooms, corporations—if we wish, or if we prefer *not* to blend in, can assert our individuality in whatever manner we choose. We can see people like us in most films, television programs, advertisements, and public life, read about such people in newspapers, magazines, and our culture's "classic" works. We seldom are asked to speak for others of our race, although we may be asked to speak for others of our group if we are Catholics, Jews, or Mormons out of our contexts. African-American people are treated as being out of their contexts in most areas of this society.

The concept of white skin privilege is even harder than the concept of racism for many white Americans to comprehend fully, because very little in our society encourages us to examine the benefits that accrue to us strictly because of skin color. On the contrary, the dominant ideology of capitalist individualism works to obscure such knowledge, because recognition of white skin privilege undermines that ideology. If we get ahead through hard work *and* through racial privilege, then the notion of the United States as a place with freedom of opportunity obviously rests on beliefs that are demonstrably false and have *never* been true.[11]

In *Two Nations*, white sociologist Andrew Hacker tries to explain white skin privilege to his (white) readers through an imaginative exercise in which he asks us to fantasize about ourselves being forced to live as black people in America. What changes, material and psychological, would that alteration in race require? Hacker devotes a chapter to an overview of possible changes, discussing what it might be like to be black in this country. Well-intentioned as this exercise is, it does not begin to excavate the overlapping layers of privilege and lack of privilege, but touches on the surface. Derrick Bell points out that supposedly neutral government rules, encouraged by Supreme Court rulings, always disadvantage blacks. In effect, the Court "creates a property right in whiteness": every white person's first asset is this property.[12] Learning what this inequitable distribution of property means on a daily basis has been a process, an ongoing project for me.

Perhaps the greatest privilege of white skin is lack of consciousness about race: most white people are free to spend entire weeks, months, even years without thinking about race at all, or thinking of it in terms of others only. In contrast, I doubt that there are many black people above the age of six in the United States who can forget about race for even a single day.

This racial awareness, this constant consciousness, has been the biggest change in my life and the foundation of all other changes. Although I retain my white skin and many of its attendant privileges—when I'm out without my family, anyhow—I have lost the dangerous privilege of ignorance. From the mundane to the powerfully serious, race is always *there*, in my head and in the world. It is in this sense that everything is racial. Race, I believe, operates in some (often hidden) way in every aspect of life. The very hiddenness of race's workings creates massive problems unknown before the outlawing of certain discriminatory practice. Derrick Bell calls white American attitudes "racial schizophrenia": the very same whites who welcome blacks into their lives in some roles carefully discriminate against blacks in others. Whites' racial schizophrenia exacerbates the effects of racism on blacks. As Bell puts it, "Because bias is masked in unofficial practices and 'neutral' standards, we [blacks] must wrestle with the question whether race or some individual failing has cost us the job, denied us the promotion, or prompted our being rejected as tenants for an apartment. Either conclusion breeds frustration and alienation—and a rage we dare not show to others or admit to ourselves. . . ."[13]

When we decided to get married, we agreed to discuss the possibility of children later; neither of us was ready to have children, but we were both sure that our potential children's race was neither a barrier nor an incentive. Doug and I both knew people in interracial relationships who had decided never to have children because the burden of biracialism seemed to them too much to put on a child. We knew others who wanted biracial children because they believed such children were somehow more beautiful than either black or white children and they saw these children as advancing racial understanding. Both positions seemed to us not only racialist but also suffused with racism, as well as utterly wrongheaded in all kinds of ways. We had no qualms about bringing biracial children into the world, nor did we feel a missionary zeal to do so. We wanted to choose children as we had chosen each other: for themselves, whatever and whomever they might be, when the time was right. At the same time, we knew that our decision would have *some* racial dimension, even if we chose to ignore it, as in fact we did. . . .

When Sean was born, everything changed for me. I've heard mothers speak about what they did not know about motherhood before they became mothers themselves: the sleeplessness, the ways in which children impinge always on your consciousness, the simultaneous fragility and *permanence* of motherhood, the intensity of the experience, and the alteration of social status. I felt all this, and more, with the "more" mostly racial. Mothering Sean and now Ailis is not all of my life, but it has made the greatest difference in my life. As their mother, I feel implicated in issues of race in ways I did not before their births. . . .

With Sean's birth, I felt a more intensely personal stake in racial issues. It was my own child's life that was on the line when racial equality, affirmative action, and human rights were threatened, which is every day, everywhere, in this country. I began to think of myself as part of a community of mothers, and especially of mothers of black children. From the very beginning, mothering Sean shifted my position in the world, giving me a new standpoint and a new angle of vision.

When Sean was born in November of 1983, Doug and I had been married for four years and living in Minneapolis for almost all of that time, half a continent away from our families. My younger brother, Tom, had recently moved out to live with us, but everyone else awaited from a distance the birth of this first member of the next generation of our families.

The couples in our childbirth class and the women who were in my prenatal exercise class all had their babies before us, and every one had a boy. Both Doug and I assumed we would have a girl, based on some vague, mathematically insupportable idea about odds and just a feeling we both had. We were proved wrong when Sean appeared. When we made our calls an hour or so after Sean was born, everyone was effusively delighted, demanded photos by overnight mail, and announced various plans to fly out to us. The only odd comment came from my mother-in-law, who said, "A boy! That's *wonderful*—Daddy will be so happy! I'm relieved!" Relieved? "Oh, I probably shouldn't tell you this, but it's okay now that Sean's here and he's a boy," Marguerite said, "but Daddy said that if it wasn't a boy, he didn't care what it was." I spluttered a bit, and my mother-in-law said, "Don't take it personally, Maureen; that's what Daddy said to me, too, every time I was pregnant."

Well, *of course*, I took it personally: I am a woman, and a feminist, and objected to this valuing of boys over girls. I also was troubled by this vivid, early reminder that Doug and I would have to struggle with inequitable gender roles for our child, and to help him resist a racist, sexist system that, on one of its axes, favored him because of his maleness. Or more accurately, *seemed* to favor him: although maleness carries certain privileges, most of those privileges are in fact reserved for white males. Stereotypes of black masculinity—rapacious sexuality, violence, danger, threat—shorten black men's lives and mock the very notion of male privilege.

I also knew that simply resisting stifling race/gender definitions would not be enough: we would have to provide alternatives to fill the space resistance creates. In a world that offers few positive public images of black maleness, we would have to seek them out while also countering the vast number of soul-destroying stereotypes. As Ishmael Reed has remarked, the most familiar image of black men in the popular media is naked from the waist up, handcuffed, and thrown across a police car.[14] We did not want Sean to see black men in general or himself in particular through the racist lens, but I was not at all certain how Doug and I could help him to see himself through his own eyes, unclouded by racism or sexism. In addition to the obvious counter to racism unconditional love and real self-esteem provide, we both wanted to foster in Sean a sense of wide possibility through carefully choosing books and toys for him, and through encouraging lots of fantasy play.

One of the simpler pleasures of parenting, we thought, would be giving Sean toys and playing with him—wrong, wrong, wrong, as we learned on our first excursion to a toy store when Sean was just a few weeks old. Because Doug and I were among the first of our friends to have children, we had not been toy shopping since we were little more than children ourselves, and we therefore had no clear idea about what toys were available. Before our baby's birth, we had decided to buy toys on a gender-neutral basis—blocks, trucks, stuffed animals, and dolls, regardless of our child's sex— and to ban war toys and Barbie, for obvious rea-

sons. We had guessed that black dolls would be hard to find, but otherwise we had given little thought to race as a factor in toy shopping. After all, what could race have to do with blocks? Plenty, we discovered.

That first trip to a big toy store was enlightening: we found aisle upon aisle of toys of all varieties in packages that depicted only white children playing with them. At most, one-fifth of the toys we saw incorporated no exclusionary race or gender codes on their packages. Even fancy yuppie toys, carefully aimed at both sexes—European crib mobiles and the like—came in packages adorned with pictures of white babies. In the doll aisle, blond, blue-eyed dolls outnumbered black dolls fifty to one, and the only black male dolls were Cabbage Patch Kids, which were new to the market the year Sean was born and almost impossible to get. In an effort to support progressive manufacturers, we tried to buy toys that showed some sensitivity to racial diversity in their packaging, but we also ended up buying a lot of things that had to be removed from their boxes before we gave them to Sean. Obviously, though, we could not control everything in Sean's life as easily as we discarded troubling toy wrappings, and we knew that he would be bombarded by images and messages quite contrary to the vision of self we hoped to foster. What effect would these images have on him? And how powerful would our parental influence be? We waited and hoped.

At about two and a half or three, Sean began to say things that suggested he understood both race and sex as categories—as interrelated categories, in fact—and that he was trying to figure out the principles that govern those categories. Like most preschoolers, Sean had a passion for categorization and a sometimes overwhelming desire to organize the elements of his world into a system that made sense to him. He was single-mindedly dedicated to grasping the abstract principles to be extrapolated from specific observations. Sean was a tiny scientist, Doug and I were his reference library, and the world was his laboratory.

One evening, Sean asked me if he would get a vagina when he grew up. After explaining that he would always have a penis but no vagina, I remarked that I had been born with a vagina and still have one, and that his father was born with a penis and still has that. "Your sex doesn't change when you grow up," I concluded. A series of questions from Sean followed, focusing on people we know and whether they have vaginas or penises. That was the end of that, I thought. Months later, Sean once again brought up the penis/vagina issue, but phrased it this way: "Why do white people have vaginas, Mom?" He evidently thought genitalia determined race, not sex: generalizing from me and his father, Sean assumed all black people have penises, and all white people have vaginas. I had to return to our list of friends, reiterate who had penises and who vaginas, and remind him of each person's race before Sean would believe that a penis meant you were male, whether black or white, and a vagina meant you were female, independent of race.

Racial differences were apparently more noticeable to Sean than were sex differences, and I suppose this could have been predicted. After all, we were making major efforts to raise Sean in a gender-free way, emphasizing that the only real differences between boys and girls were biological. We were supported by friends and by the enlightened day-care center Sean attended, where both staff and parents identified themselves as feminists. Perhaps most important, when he was a toddler Sean never saw commercial television. At three, he did not choose playmates or toys on a gender-appropriate basis, nor did he seem to think much about differences between boys and girls, especially in comparison to several other children we knew, who made a big deal about gender roles from an early age. Sean could see skin-color differences between Doug and me, and knew that I have a vagina and Doug has a penis. He never saw other people naked, so he had no opportunity to notice black females with vaginas and white males with penises. It makes perfect sense, then, that he would jumble everything up and figure that skin color and genitalia were linked.

After figuring out the vagina/penis issue, Sean decided that other physical characteristics were sex-linked as well, once telling us that girls have blue eyes and boys have brown eyes. This statement emerged at a very unlikely time—quite late at night when he had awakened to go to the bathroom—which made me realize just how deeply

such issues concerned him. I explained that girls can have brown eyes and boys blue, and that many other possibilities exist, which Sean seemed to accept after recalling his brown-eyed aunt and blue-eyed uncle. He moved on to a different topic ("Why do I have to wash my hands if I don't touch the toilet?") and that seemed to be the end of it. As I tucked him back into bed, he said sleepily, "But boys have curly hair and girls don't," stuck his thumb in his mouth, and closed his eyes to signal the end of our discussion.

Sean's comments about race and his confusion about racial and sexual characteristics mirror social confusion. Race, unlike sex, has little to do with biology, popular mythology notwithstanding. As Henry Louis Gates trenchantly remarks, "Race is the ultimate trope of difference because it is so very arbitrary in its application. The biological criteria used to determine 'difference' in sex simply do not hold when applied to 'race.' Yet we carelessly use language in such a way as to *will* this sense of *natural* difference into our formulations."[15] Sex—but not gender—is an objective term of classification and therefore is comparatively easy to explain to a small child. Race and gender are subjective categories, social constructions, whose parameters constantly shift, change shape, mutate. Further, although both race and gender are socially constructed categories of analysis, they are *differently* constructed; consequently, understanding these constructions and resisting them requires quite different strategies.[16]

From about age three, Sean began to realize that racial differences were meaningful in some way beyond mere skin color, but he wasn't clear on what these meanings might be. For instance, he announced to me that people get darker as they get older and that dark people are older than light people. This makes sense as a general statement about the origins of humankind, but that wasn't his point. "No," I explained, "skin color isn't age-related. People come in all different colors and pretty much stay that way. Daddy was dark brown when he was little, and he's still dark brown. I was sort of pink when I was a baby and I'm still pink. You were light brown as a baby and you're still light brown." This seemed to make sense to Sean, and he moved on to another question ("Why is Big Bird yellow?").

A few weeks later, though, Sean once again said darker people are older than lighter people. I offered some examples of younger dark people (his friend Maggie, age two) and older light people (his grandfather, mid-sixties), and we laid that issue to rest, after agreeing that it's nice to have so many different shades of skin and hair and eyes in the world. Months passed with no further age/race commentary, but then one night while Doug was giving Sean a bath, Sean made a remark about "when you get old." It was the end of a long and exhausting day, and Doug jokingly replied, "I already *am* old!" Sean responded angrily, touching Doug's arm, "*That's* not old, Daddy! *That* [pointing to my skin] is old!" If dark skin doesn't signify age, then it must signify youth; Sean still wasn't willing to accept that skin color is independent of age and sex, all evidence of that independence carrying no weight on him.

As I look back now, Sean's early determination to figure out race's meaning strikes me as a nascent rage for order that rebelled against the intimations of chaos coming to him from the outside world. He was beginning to sense the social significance attached to race, and went looking for clues to explain that significance. The arbitrariness not only of racial distinctions themselves but also of race's social significance—when we think about it, using race as *the* crucial category depends on arbitrary historical choices that could just as easily have fastened on height or hair color or anything else for that matter—must have been apparent to him, and therefore Sean went looking for reassurances that the world was indeed an orderly place, with rules he could grasp. I think Sean felt that race *meant* something, and believed that meaning must attach to real, measurable, understandable differences, else the world might be terrifyingly unfathomable. . . .

Notes

1. Throughout this book I focus on blacks and whites, although I am well aware that many of the points I make about black people's lives in the United States could be made also about the lives of members of other "minority" groups. However, the particular stereotypes that could be applied to my son are not stereotypes of males in other groups.

2. Child development expert Bettye M. Caldwell, for instance, expressed this view in response to James P. Comer and Alvin F. Poussaint's *Raising Black Children* (New York: Plume, 1992). She told the *New York Times* that she has always worked against analyzing the differences between children in terms of race. See Carol Lawson, "Nurturing Black Children in an Unfriendly World," *New York Times*, 10 June 1993, C6.

3. Population figures come from the 1990 U.S. Census; family income from Andrew Hacker, *Two Nations* (New York: Scribners, 1992), 233; degree information from Hacker, *Two Nations*, 236.

4. The prison statistics come from Hacker, *Two Nations*, 197. The danger of arrest is so great for blacks, particularly young black males, that Comer and Poussaint devote a section of *Raising Black Children* to explaining what parents should do if their child is jailed (388–392). This material would never appear in a "color-blind"—that is, white-oriented—parenting manual. Victim and employment statistics from Hacker, *Two Nations*, 183 and 111 respectively.

5. Statistics from Hacker, *Two Nations*; unemployment, 103; poverty, 100; family earnings differential, 94.

6. Richard Dyer, "White," *Screen* 29, no. 4 (Autumn 1988): 44.

7. Hettie Jones, *How I Became Hettie Jones* (New York: Dutton, 1990), 202.

8. Jane Lazarre, *Worlds Beyond My Control* (New York: Dutton, 1991), xiv.

9. *Ibid.*, xiii–xiv.

10. Ralph Ellison, *Invisible Man* (1952; reprint, New York: Random House, 1972), 16.

11. Peggy McIntosh's "White Privilege and Male Privilege: A Personal Account of Coming to See Correspondences Through Work in Women's Studies," further details the privileges that attend whiteness in this society. In Margaret L. Andersen and Patricia Hill Collins, eds., *Race, Class, and Gender: An Anthology* (Belmont, Calif.: Wadsworth, 1992). I want to thank Martha Roth for pointing out the ways in which members of other "minority" groups are asked to speak for the entire group.

12. Derrick Bell, *Faces at the Bottom of the Well: The Permanence of Racism* (New York: Basic Books), 172.

13. *Ibid.*, 6.

14. Reed's remarks are quoted by bell hooks in *Yearning: race, gender, and cultural politics* (Boston: South End Press, 1990), 74.

15. Henry Louis Gates, Jr. "Writing 'Race' and the Difference It Makes," *Critical Inquiry* 12 (Autumn 1985): 5.

16. Patricia Hill Collins, *Black Feminist Thought: Knowledge, Consciousness, and the Politics of Empowerment* (New York: Routledge), 27.

Complexion

Richard Rodriguez

Richard Rodriguez's works include *Hunger of Memory, Days of Obligation,* and *Mexico's Children.* He is an editor at the *Pacific News Service* in San Francisco, a contributing editor for *Harper's* and the Sunday "Opinion" section of the *Los Angeles Times,* and occasionally appears as an essayist on the PBS television program "The NewsHour with Jim Lehrer."

Visiting the East Coast or the gray capitals of Europe during the long months of winter, I often meet people at deluxe hotels who comment on my complexion. (In such hotels it appears nowadays a mark of leisure and wealth to have a complexion like mine.) Have I been skiing? In the Swiss Alps? Have I just returned from a Caribbean vacation? No. I say no softly but in a firm voice that intends to explain: My complexion is dark. (My skin is brown. More exactly, terra-cotta in sunlight, tawny in shade. I do not redden in sunlight. Instead, my skin becomes progressively dark; the sun singes the flesh.)

When I was a boy the white summer sun of Sacramento would darken me so, my T-shirt would seem bleached against my slender dark arms. My mother would see me come up the front steps. She'd wait for the screen door to slam at my back. "You look like a *negrito,*" she'd say, angry, sorry to be angry, frustrated almost to laughing, scorn. "You know how important looks are in this country. With *los gringos* looks are all that they judge on. But you! Look at you! You're so careless!" Then she'd start in all over again. "You won't be satisfied till you end up looking like *los pobres* who work in the fields, *los braceros.*"

(*Los braceros*: Those men who work with their *brazos,* their arms; Mexican nationals who were licensed to work for American farmers in the 1950s. They worked very hard for very little money, my father would tell me. And what money they earned they sent back to Mexico to support their families, my mother would add. *Los pobres*— the poor, the pitiful, the powerless ones. But paradoxically also powerful men. They were the men with brown-muscled arms I stared at in awe on Saturday mornings when they showed up downtown like gypsies to shop at Woolworth's or Penney's. On Monday nights they would gather hours early on the steps of the Memorial Auditorium for the wrestling matches. Passing by on my bicycle in summer, I would spy them there, clustered in small groups, talking—frightening and fascinating men—some wearing Texas *sombreros* and T-shirts which shone fluorescent in the twilight. I would sit forward in the back seat of our family's '48 Chevy to see them, working alongside Valley highways: dark men on an even horizon, loading a truck amid rows of straight green. Powerful, powerless men. Their fascinating darkness—like mine—to be feared.)

"You'll end up looking just like them."

I

Regarding my family, I see faces that do not closely resemble my own. Like some other Mexican families, my family suggests Mexico's confused colonial past. Gathered around a table, we appear to be from separate continents. My father's face recalls faces I have seen in France. His complexion is white—he does not tan; he does not burn. Over the years, his dark wavy hair has grayed handsomely. But with time his face has sagged to a perpetual sigh. My mother, whose surname is inexplicably Irish—Moran—has an olive complexion. People have frequently wondered if, perhaps, she is Italian or Portuguese. And, in fact, she looks as though she could be from southern Europe. My mother's face has not aged as quickly as the rest of her body; it remains smooth and glowing—a cool tan—which her gray hair cleanly accentuates. My older brother has inherited her good looks. When he was a boy people would tell him that he looked like Mario Lanza, and hearing it he would smile with dimpled assurance. He would come home from high school with girl friends who seemed to me glamorous (because they were) blonds. And during those years I envied him his skin that burned red and peeled like the skin of the *gringos*. His complexion never darkened like mine. My youngest sister is exotically pale, almost ashen. She is delicately featured, Near Eastern, people have said. Only my older sister has a complexion as dark as mine, though her facial features are much less harshly defined than my own. To many people meeting her, she seems (they say) Polynesian. I am the only one in the family whose face is severely cut to the line of ancient Indian ancestors. My face is mournfully long, in the classical Indian manner; my profile suggests one of those beak-nosed Mayan sculptures—the eaglelike face upturned, open-mouthed, against the deserted, primitive sky.

"We are Mexicans," my mother and father would say, and taught their four children to say whenever we (often) were asked about our ancestry. My mother and father scorned those "white" Mexican-Americans who tried to pass themselves off as Spanish. My parents would never have thought of denying their ancestry. I never denied it: My ancestry is Mexican, I told strangers mechanically. But I never forgot that only my older sister's complexion was as dark as mine.

My older sister never spoke to me about her complexion when she was a girl. But I guessed that she found her dark skin a burden. I knew that she suffered for being a "nigger." As she came home from grammar school, little boys came up behind her and pushed her down to the sidewalk. In high school, she struggled in the adolescent competition for boyfriends in a world of football games and proms, a world where her looks were plainly uncommon. In college, she was afraid and scornful when dark-skinned foreign students from countries like Turkey and India found her attractive. She revealed her fear of dark skin to me only in adulthood when, regarding her own three children, she quietly admitted relief that they were all light.

That is the kind of remark women in my family have often made before. As a boy, I'd stay in the kitchen (never seeming to attract any notice), listening while my aunts spoke of their pleasure at having light children. (The men, some of whom were dark-skinned from years of working out of doors, would be in another part of the house.) It was the woman's spoken concern: the fear of having a dark-skinned son or daughter. Remedies were exchanged. One aunt prescribed to her sisters the elixir of large doses of castor oil during the last weeks of pregnancy. (The remedy risked an abortion.) Children born dark grew up to have their faces treated regularly with a mixture of egg white and lemon juice concentrate. (In my case, the solution never would take.) One Mexican-American friend of my mother's, who regarded it a special blessing that she had a measure of English blood, spoke disparagingly of her husband, a construction worker, for being so dark. "He doesn't take care of himself," she complained. But the remark, I noticed, annoyed my mother, who sat tracing an invisible design with her finger on the tablecloth.

There was affection too and a kind of humor about these matters. With daring tenderness, one of my uncles would refer to his wife as *mi negra*. An aunt regularly called her dark child *mi feito* (my little ugly one), her smile only partially hidden as she bent down to dig her mouth under his ticklish chin. And at times relatives spoke scornfully of pale, white skin. A *gringo's* skin resembled *masa*—baker's dough—someone remarked. Everyone laughed. Voices chuckled over the fact that the *gringos* spent so many hours in summer sunning themselves. ("They need to get sun because they look like *los muertos*.")

I heard the laughing but remembered what the women had said, with unsmiling voices, concerning dark skin. Nothing I heard outside the house, regarding my skin, was so impressive to me.

In public I occasionally heard racial slurs. Complete strangers would yell out at me. A teenager drove past, shouting, "Hey, Greaser! Hey, Pancho!" Over his shoulder I saw the giggling face of his girl friend. A boy pedaled by and announced matter-of-factly, "I pee on dirty Mexicans." Such remarks would be said so casually that I wouldn't quickly realize that they were being addressed to me. When I did, I would be paralyzed with embarrassment, unable to return the insult. (Those times I happened to be with white grammar school friends, *they* shouted back. Imbued with the mysterious kindness of children, my friends would never ask later why I hadn't yelled out in my own defense.)

In all, there could not have been more than a dozen incidents of name-calling. That there were so few suggests that I was not a primary victim of racial abuse. But that, even today, I can clearly remember particular incidents is proof of their impact. Because of such incidents, I listened when my parents remarked that Mexicans were often mistreated in California border towns. And in Texas. I listened carefully when I heard that two of my cousins had been refused admittance to an "all-white" swimming pool. And that an uncle had been told by some man to go back to Africa. I followed the progress of the southern black civil rights movement, which was gaining prominent notice in Sacramento's afternoon newspaper. But what most intrigued me was the connection between dark skin and poverty. Because I heard my mother speak so often about the relegation of dark people to menial labor, I considered the great victims of racism to be those who were poor and forced to do menial work. People like the farmworkers whose skin was dark from the sun.

After meeting a black grammar school friend of my sister's, I remember thinking that she wasn't really "black." What interested me was the fact that she wasn't poor. (Her well-dressed parents would come by after work to pick her up in a shiny green Oldsmobile.) By contrast, the garbage men who appeared every Friday morning seemed to me unmistakably black. (I didn't bother to ask my parents why Sacramento garbage men always were black. I thought I knew.) One morning I was in the backyard when a man opened the gate. He was an ugly, square-faced black man with popping red eyes, a pail slung over his shoulder. As he approached, I stood up. And in a voice that seemed to me very weak, I piped, "Hi." But the man paid me no heed. He strode past to the can by the garage. In a single broad movement, he overturned its contents into his larger pail. Our can came crashing down as he turned and left me watching, in awe.

"*Pobres negros,*" my mother remarked when she'd notice a headline in the paper about a civil rights demonstration in the South. "How the *gringos* mistreat them." In the same tone of voice she'd tell me about the mistreatment her brother endured years before. (After my grandfather's death, my grandmother had come to America with her son and five daughters.) "My sisters, we were still all just teenagers. And since *mi papá* was dead, my brother had to be the head of the family. He had to support us, to find work. But what skills did he have! Twenty years old. *Pobre.* He was tall, like

your grandfather. And strong. He did construction work. 'Construction!' The *gringos* kept him digging all day, doing the dirtiest jobs. And they would pay him next to nothing. Sometimes they promised him one salary and paid him less when he finished. But what could he do? Report them? We weren't citizens then. He didn't even know English. And he was dark. What chances could he have? As soon as we sisters got older, he went right back to Mexico. He hated this country. He looked so tired when he left. Already with a hunchback. Still in his twenties. But old-looking. No life for him here. *Pobre.*"

Dark skin was for my mother the most important symbol of a life of oppressive labor and poverty. But both my parents recognized other symbols as well.

My father noticed the feel of every hand he shook. (He'd smile sometimes—marvel more than scorn—remembering a man he'd met who had soft, uncalloused hands.)

My mother would grab a towel in the kitchen and rub my oily face sore when I came in from playing outside. "Clean the *graza* off of your face!" (*Greaser!*)

Symbols: When my older sister, then in high school, asked my mother if she could do light housework in the afternoons for a rich lady we knew, my mother was frightened by the idea. For several weeks she troubled over it before granting conditional permission: "Just remember, you're not a maid. I don't want you wearing a uniform." My father echoed the same warning. Walking with him past a hotel, I watched as he stared at a doorman dressed like a Beefeater. "How can anyone let himself be dressed up like that? Like a clown. Don't you ever get a job where you have to put on a uniform." In summertime neighbors would ask me if I wanted to earn extra money by mowing their lawns. Again and again my mother worried: "Why did they ask *you?* Can't you find anything better?" Inevitably, she'd relent. She knew I needed the money. But I was instructed to work after dinner. ("When the sun's not so hot.") Even then, I'd have to wear a hat. *Un sombrero de* baseball.

(*Sombrero.* Watching gray cowboy movies, I'd brood over the meaning of the broad-rimmed hat— that troubling symbol—which comically distinguished a Mexican cowboy from real cowboys.). . .

Race Without Face

Edward Iwata

Edward Iwata writes about business and financial issues for the *San Francisco Examiner*.
He and his wife, Virginia Mak, were educators at Stanford University's Okada House,
a residence hall and community center for students interested in Asian-American and
Asian issues.

I would soon discover I was different from white people. A cosmetic surgeon was about to cut into my face that gray winter morning. Hot lights glared as I lay on the operating table. Surgical tools clattered in containers, sharp metal against metal. I felt like a lamb awaiting a shearing of its wool. Shivering from the air-conditioned chill, I wondered if I'd made a mistake. Had my hatred of Oriental facial features, fanned by my desire to do well in a white world, blinded me so easily? An instant before the anesthetic numbed my brain cells, I felt the urge to cry out. I imagined ripping off my gown and sprinting to freedom. But at that point, even wetting my cracked lips was hard to do. "I trust you implicitly," I said, as a supplicant might beseech a priest.

Oddly, I imagined seeing, as if peering through a bloody gauze, the contours of two faces rushing toward me. One face was twisted into sadness. The other glowed with a look akin to pride. One white, one yellow; one white, one yellow. I did not know which was which.

A month earlier in her Beverly Hills medical office, the surgeon said she planned to taper the thick, round tip of my nose. She also wanted to build up my flat bridge with strips of cartilage.

"Oriental noses have no definition," she said, waving a clipboard like an inspector on an auto assembly line.

While she was at it, she suggested, why not work on the eyes, also? They looked dark and tired, even though I was twenty years old then. A simple slash along my eyelids would remove the fat cells that kept my eyes from springing into full, double-lidded glory.

Why not? I had thought. Didn't I want to distance myself from the faceless, Asian masses? I hated the pale image in the mirror. I hated the

slurs hurled at me that I couldn't shut out. I hated being a gook, a Nip.

It's a taboo subject, but true: Many people of color have, at some point in their youths, imagined themselves as Caucasian, the Nordic or Western European ideal. Hop Sing meets Rock Hudson. Michael Jackson magically transformed into Robert Redford.

For myself, an eye and nose job—or *blepharoplasty* and *rhinoplasty* in surgeons' tongue—would bring me the gift of acceptance. The flick of a scalpel would buy me respect.

To make the decision easier, a close friend loaned me $1500. I didn't tell my parents or anyone else about it.

The surgery was quick and painless. My friend drove me at dawn to the medical clinic. At 7 a.m. sharp, the surgeon, a brusque Hispanic woman, swept into the office and rushed passed us.

The next time I saw her, she was peering down at me and penciling lines on my face to guide her scalpel. A surgeon's mask and cap hid her own face; I saw only a large pair of eyes plotting the attack on my epidermis and cartilage. While I shivered, a nurse and an anesthesiologist laughed and gossiped.

"You have beautiful eyelashes, Edward," the surgeon said. It seemed like an odd thing to notice at that moment.

I tumbled into darkness. My last memory was a deep desire to yell or strike out, to stab the surgeon and her conspirators with their knives.

The surgeon went for my eyes first. Gently, she cut and scooped out the fat cells that lined my upper eyelid. That created a small furrow, which popped open my eyes a bit and created double-lids, every Asian model's dream.

Ignoring the blood, she then slit the upper inside of my nostril. Like a short-order cook trimming a steak, she carved the cartilage and snipped off bits of bone and tissue. Soon she was done.

After a coffee break or lunch, she would move on to the next patient.

Later that day, I was wheeled out of a bright recovery room. My head and limbs felt dull and heavy, as if buried in mud. A draft swept up my surgical gown and chilled my legs. Although my face was bound in bandages, I felt naked. Without warning, a sharp sense of loss engulfed me, a child away from home who is not sure why he aches so.

"Eddie, what did you do?" asked my mother when I next saw her. Then, her voice shaking, "Why did you do this? Were you ashamed of yourself?" As if struck by a lance, my legs weakened, my body cleaved. I was lost, flailing away in shadows, but I shrugged off her question and said something lame. I didn't sense at the time that whatever had compelled me to scar my face could also drive me further from home.

One week passed before I was brave enough to take my first look in the mirror. I stood in the bathroom, staring at my reflection until my feet got sore.

Stitch marks scarred my face like tracks on a drug addict's arm. My haggard eyes were rounder; my nose smaller and puggy. In the glare of the bathroom light, my skin seemed pale and washed out, a claylike shade of light brown. I looked like a medical illustration from a century ago, when doctors would have measured my facial angle and cranium size for racial intelligence.

I wanted to claw my new face.

The image I pictured in the mirror was an idealized Anglo man, an abstraction. I didn't realize at the time that my flaws were imagined, not real. I felt compelled to measure up to a cultural ideal in a culture that had never asked me what my ideal was.

Indeed, to many Anglos, the males of our culture are a mystery. Most whites know us only through the neutered images: Japanese salarymen. Sumo wrestlers. Sushi chefs. We're judged by our slant of eye and color of skin. We're seen only as eunuchs, as timid dentists and engineers. Books and movies portray us as ugly and demonic. We're truly a race of Invisible Men.

Clearly, Asian-American men have been psychologically castrated in this country. Our history is one of emasculation and accommodation. Japanese-Americans, for the most part, filed quietly into the internment camps. Proud Cantonese immigrants were trapped in their Chinatown ghettoes and bachelor societies by poverty and discrimination.

In the corporate arena, Asian-American men find their cultural values and strengths overshadowed by ego-driven, back-slapping, hyper-competitive whites. And, while socially we may be more "acceptable" than blacks and Hispanics, we are not acceptable enough to run legislatures, schools, corporations. Our women may be marriage material for whites, but our men are still seen as gooks. On the street, we're cursed or spat upon—even killed—because of our looks.

It cannot be denied, either, that we're regarded as kowtowing wimps not only by whites, but by a lot of Asian-American women—even those with racial and ethnic pride. Privately, they confess they see a lack of strong Asian-American men who fit an ideal of manhood: virile and sensitive, intelligent and intuitive, articulate and confident.

Of course, we must share part of the blame. Many of us grow up swallowing the stereotypes, accepting the role white society imposes on us. And aside from a handful of us in politics, law, the media, education, and the arts, the rest of us are too reserved and opinionless in the white world.

Simone de Beauvoir wrote that a woman "insinuates herself into a world that has doomed her to passivity." The same could have been said of too many Asian-American men, including myself.

I recall an episode four years ago when a former boss and I lunched at a Thai restaurant. I thought I deserved a promotion—new status, new duties, a bigger paycheck—real fast. He disagreed. Between bites of curry chicken, I was startled to hear this executive label me in words used for "docile" Asian men and "uppity" blacks.

"You're a quiet, reserved kind of guy," he said, waving his hands in the air. A few bites later, he veered the other way and portrayed me as a "cocky, arrogant young reporter . . . with a chip on your shoulder."

I was confused. Was I an obedient employee, or a hard-charging militant? And how could I be both? I ate my rice and said little. My face flushed with anger. Later that day, I left work early, fantasizing about a bloody, *ninja*-style revenge.

Why didn't I fight back? Instead of sitting silently, why didn't I challenge his superficial view of me?

Part of it was cultural. Our Eastern values are living, breathing elements in our lives, not topics we study in Zen Buddhism class. Regardless of how assimilated we may be, these values rise to claim our attention at unpredictable moments. So while I fancied myself a strong-minded journalist, I still felt shackled by cultural bonds, afraid of arguing back. It was the whole *deference* thing, this Asian habit of respecting authority to a fault.

I yearned for my boss' acceptance. I was blinded by my desire to fit in as a man, a journalist, a corporate player. In Japan, this could be called *ittaikan*, a longing for oneness with a person or a group. Readers of the Japanese psychiatrist Takeo Doi might think of it as *amae*, a passive dependency on another's love or kindness.

And so, by others and by ourselves, we're rendered impotent. I wasn't a limp lover. But outside my home or bedroom, I often felt powerless—desexed like a baby chick. It was as if I didn't exist. Employers didn't acknowledge my work. Professors in college rebuffed my remarks in the classroom. *Maître d*'s ignored my presence in restaurants. I felt voiceless, faceless.

A friend of mine, a San Francisco lawyer in her thirties, was thrilled to meet a liberal Japanese man from Tokyo after years of dating Asian-Americans. Several of her boyfriends had been bright and sensitive, but they lacked what she called "male energy"—a strength of purpose and destiny, a vision of one's goals in life.

"It's almost a *samurai* spirit that Asian-American men somehow lost in white society, as if they'd been neutered," she said. "Even though I'm a career woman, sometimes I want a man to take the lead, while I play the mothering role. . . . Reconnecting with a strong, decisive Asian male has been an eye-opener."

My friend's opinion is not unusual. Unfortunately some Asian-American men, scared of the nerd label, charge blindly in the opposite direction, aping Western notions of kick-ass masculinity: Rambo. Mike Tyson. Michael Milken. They become obsessed with the art of war, obsessed with competition. It's yet another stereotype, and equally damaging.

One example, a hot item in our community, is an all-male calendar, featuring pin-ups of Asian-American hunks. While the men photographed are all respected, the beefcake images they project are caricatures of the white physical ideal: the well-oiled, muscular body, the chiseled face, the hint of male power and violence. They're like minorities in beauty pageants who look more like the blond Miss American prototype than their own race.

"How warped that sense of manhood and beauty is," observes King-Kok Cheung, a literary scholar at UCLA. "In some ways, our internal oppression as Asians is greater than white oppression. We need to understand that anyone who is comfortable with himself is attractive."

Probably the biggest blow to my young psyche occurred at my predominantly white high school. My advanced English class boasted students who were versed in Petrarchan sonnets before I had learned to read baseball box scores. Even so, as a teenager I saw myself as a maverick writer in the manner of Jack Kerouac or Jack London. Mrs. Worthy, our strict teacher, showed me otherwise.

"Mr. Iwata, I'd like you to work on 'A Book is Like a Frigate' by Emily Dickinson," she said, assigning homework. "That shouldn't be too difficult to handle, even for you."

I still get chills when I recall my classmates shifting in their seats, their blue and green eyes staring at me. To Mrs. Worthy, I was the slow, quiet Asian boy who sat by the window, waiting for the school bus to dump me back in the inner-city.

Outside the classroom, media images confused me even more. Nowhere—from racist childrens' books to great literature to movies with evil Jap soldiers—did I see my true reflection in the larger world. Unlike students today, I had no Asian or Asian-American heroes, no cultural icons, to lead the way.

In sociological jargon, I was an Assimilationist, a Marginal Man, a Stranger. Like many Asian-Americans, I craved admiration and acceptance, mostly from whites. I worshipped Anglo models of success, the middle-class ethos carried to extremes.

But contrary to our shining image as model minorities, I learned I had *not* arrived. All the hard work and schooling and cosmetic surgery in the world couldn't change the way I looked, or the way I was perceived. I could not erase my skin color, no matter how hard I tried. My status in the white professional world was illusory; it did not transcend the harsh realities of race and class.

In my search for acceptance, I modeled myself after whites, especially in college—in speech and diction, style and dress, body language and eye contact. I thought I was a failure when no white coeds danced with me at a frat party. At beer busts, I avoided Asian-American women because they looked like the girls in my old neighborhood, with their moon faces and *daikon* (white radish) legs.

Before that, I used to hang with Hispanic buddies from East L.A. I was a *vato*, an *esé*, a buddha brother. And before that, I played basketball and dodged gangs in Crenshaw, a black and Asian neighborhood in Los Angeles. I wasn't cool, but I could fake it. When black classmates called me "nigger" or "homes" (short for "homeboy"), I smiled inside. Another mask.

At the same time, I fought the tug of family and culture. Seeking a place beyond my ken, I left Crenshaw to live on campus as a college freshman. I saw my new world as a stage ripe for rebellion.

My courses—journalism, literature, history— disappointed my parents. They hoped I would study medicine or business, like all good Japanese-American kids.

I was studying, all right: The science of interviewing accident victims for newspaper stories. Themes of Dionysian abandon, from Blake to Lord Byron. My literary hero was James Joyce, whose modernist art promised to transport me to Arabys unknown. I had not yet begun to study myself.

My bid for a cultural identity, a sense of manhood, quickened as my mother and father retired, and as Dad's health worsened. Clearly, a strong impulse pushed me to step up and fill their vacuum, to carry on a family legacy in some way.

My parents, Phillip and Midori, and sixteen relatives spent the years during World War II at Manzanar, the internment camp eight miles from the town of Independence in the Mojave Desert. When I was a kid, Mom never talked about Manzanar. Instead, she wove harmless tales for my brother, my sister, and me. The stories protected us from the truth.

Dad, a strong silent type, claimed he never cared about the political quest for redress—the twenty thousand dollars due each Japanese-American interned during the war. Interviewing him for the first story I did on Manzanar was not easy. "You don't have to write about this, do you?" he asked. Speaking to him the next time was even harder. "I told you I'm not a good person to interview," he snapped. "Talk to Mom again."

His reticence was understandable. Conservative Japanese-Americans hide their private faces in public. *Nomen no yo*, their ancestors said. *The face is like a Noh mask.* My mother and father calmly accepted their fates.

Like many Japanese-Americans, my parents veiled the past and white-washed their memories. They believed the government line that Uncle Sam sent them to the concentration camps for their own good, for their safety. The camps also gave them post-war opportunities by spreading them across the great land, they were told.

In truth, the internment was a horror for families, a civil rights disaster, the death of the old Japanese-American culture. For the men, the sense of powerlessness must have been devastating.

In my parents' desire to hide the past, I sensed a reflection of my own self-hate. Like most *sansei* (third generation), I ignored or never sought out the tragic facts of that era. As a student, I never read about the camps. As a young journalist, I picked up shards of history, but never the whole dark tale.

But after much cajoling, I persuaded my folks to join me on a pilgrimage to Manzanar in 1988. Only tumbleweeds, stone ruins, and barbed wire remained at the windy, desolate site. Nonetheless, the pilgrimage was a glimpse into a forgotten world, a gateway to the past. The ghosts were powerful. But I found no neat, easy answers.

There was no stopping now. The next spring, we flew to Japan. While trade wars dominated the news in Tokyo, my parents and I journeyed into the rural heart of our ancestral homeland.

For the first time, we met the Iwata and Kunitomi clans, who still live on the rice farms in Wakayama and Okayama that our families have owned since the eighteenth century. Among other revelations, I learned that the head of the Iwata family, my father's cousin, shared my Japanese name, Masao ("righteous boy").

Seated on a *tatami* floor at the Iwata homestead, we enjoyed *sukiyaki* and country-style vegetables we hadn't eaten since my grandmothers died several years ago. The *gohan* (steamed rice) was the lightest and sweetest we had ever tasted. Masao smiled broadly as he served the hot food, its steam rising toward the small family altar in the corner of the dining room.

At one point, I noticed Masao staring at Dad. His steady gaze was rude by Japanese standards. But apparently struck by the family resemblance, Masao couldn't avert his eyes from Dad's face. With their wavy hair and thick eyebrows, their dark skin and rakish grins, they could have been brothers.

I'm not a misty-eyed romantic longing for an ancestral past. Peering for gods in mountain shrines and temple ruins is not my idea of good journalism. Still, this was my flesh and blood seated in an old farmhouse on that warm spring night. I thought of a line from *No-No Boy*, a novel of WWII by John Okada: "If he was to find his way back to that point of wholeness and belonging, he must do so in the place where he had begun to lose it." Here was my point of origin, where my family began. As we scooped bowlfuls of rice into our hungry selves, a light rain wet the furrows of black soil in the field outside.

For me, Japan brought to the surface cultural conflicts and competing values. Even though I was as American as teriyaki chicken, the old Buddhist and Confucian values reached me in Southern California. *Giri* (obligation). *Omoiyari* (empathy). *Oyakoko* (filial piety). The Japanese, in fact, have a phrase unique to them: "*Jibun ga nai*," or "to have no self." They rarely use the first-person pronoun when they speak. Loyal *samurai* who followed their feudal barons to the grave had little over some Japanese-American kids.

Those values gave me strength—and also confused the hell out of me. The issue of personal independence and family ties was the most painful. How was I to pursue my goals, forge an identity, yet honor my parents without question? And if I chose filial piety, how was I to keep the bond strong without sacrificing my hard-won, American-style autonomy?

A Zen *koan* asks, "What was your face like before you were born?" I cannot know for sure how deeply the culture of my ancestors touches me, but I know I will never again see myself as a scarred, hollow man lost in the shadows, beating back death.

Japan freed my spirit and gave rise to an atavistic pride I had never known. The past, I realized, could be cradled like an heirloom found in an old trunk in the attic. I was a player in a family history that spanned the reigns of emperors, from feudal Japan to the modern Heisei Era, Year One—the year of my first visit to Japan. And my story would add a few scenes to that unfolding narrative.

After Manzanar and Japan, I began to see my surgery in a new slant of light. Like the victims of internment, I started coming to terms with my real and emotional scars.

Obviously, the surgery had been a rebellion against my "Japaneseness" and the traditional values of my parents. It was psychic surgery, an act of mutilation, a symbolic suicide. It was my self-hatred finding a stage.

Like many Asian Americans, I'm searching for a new cultural character and destiny.

Certainly, we need to change many of our past goals. While much is known of our drive toward the American dream, little is written of our worship of materialism, our narcissism, our obsession with showing that we've *arrived*. We're brilliant students of what historian Richard Hofstadter called "status politics," the effort to enhance one's social standing.

Somewhere between Asia and an "A+" in Achievement, we lost our way. The trappings of style and success—a fancy degree, a prestigious job, a Mercedes in every garage—have become more important than the accomplishments. Instead, the images we impress upon white society and other Asian-Americans are paramount. We have become the "racial bourgeoisie," a term coined by legal scholar Mari Matsuda. The hard work may bring "success," but this kind of success will not set us free.

The numbers reflect the reality. They tell a sad story, especially in education, supposedly our stronghold. Asian-Americans held 3.1 percent of administrative and management jobs in California colleges and universities, according to an analysis of 1980 census data by Amado Cabezas and Gary Kawaguchi of UC Berkeley's Ethnic Studies Department. Even more startling were the income figures. Asian-American faculty and staff were paid salaries *40 to 70 percent* of the mean annual income of white men. And this is only in one field.

A century ago, sugar plantation owners in Hawaii counted Asian laborers as part of their business supplies. Today, we're still regarded similarly: as bodies to fill affirmative-action goals, as background in movies. Even worse, we gladly accept what society imposes on us, so anxious are we to measure up to its standards of "success."

There is so much cultural brainwashing to undo, and so much to learn about our place in this country.

Many of us will not tolerate the status quo anymore. The *Miss Saigon* controversy reflects our rising anger. It's *our* March on Washington, *our* Stonewall gay riot, *our* Jackson, Mississippi. In other recent shows of strength, we've rallied around the racial killings of Asian-Americans. Our congressional and community leaders won redress payments for the internment of Japanese-Americans. And more Asian-Americans are filling seats in public office.

But where do we go next? And how do we define our community, if at all?

Clearly, we need new visions, new models. Elaine Kim, a UC Berkeley dean and ethnic studies scholar, says our community defies easy branding. The boundaries of Asian America are changing, fusing, changing again. "We're much more than white versus nonwhite, suburbanites versus urban people of color, East versus West, tradition versus modernity," she argues. "We're creating our culture every day."

Slowly and surely, a strong Asian-American culture is coming of age. It's a bold culture, unashamed and true to itself. It's a culture with a common destiny, *a community of the mind and soul*. And it's taking many forms—in plays and films, in literature and journalism, in history and the social sciences, in professional groups and political caucuses. We can certainly start by realizing we don't need to parrot anyone else's notions

of success and beauty. "We're not slaves to culture, but agents of culture, agents of change," says King-Kok Cheung. Instead of conforming to prefabricated images and stereotypes, we must define our own successes, our own personalities, our own images.

We must not vanish completely into the suburbs, nor must we isolate ourselves in our close-knit but ethnocentric Asian communities. Instead, we must find a new common ethos, a new aesthetic, a new psychology.

This new Asian America must transcend, yet embrace, our differences. It must value collective ethnic pride, yet respect individualism. It must honor equality of race and gender, and bury our hypocritical racism, sexism, and homophobia. And it must not hide behind moral self-righteousness or ideological rigidity, which poisons the radical left and fundamentalist right.

Our artists and scholars and educators, for the most part, create positive images, but we need many more; we cannot wait for Hollywood. Role models in all fields are important. Parents must teach their kids inner strength, not outer conformity. We must build more bridges with whites and others in a meaningful sense, not merely for show.

And as for Asian-American manhood? For Buddha's sake, let's use our imagination. The Lone Ranger and Bruce Lee are dead. We don't need to out-gun or measure up to anyone. We can return to the original meaning of compete, which comes from the Latin word *competere*, "to come together." Manhood now is a destructive, stereotyped, behavioral trap. Asian-Americans must recast our concept of masculinity, sculpting it into a larger definition of humanity.

For our role models, we can look to the past. The Japanese *bushido* ethic, the *samurai* spiritual and martial philosophy, is one. The scholarly Sage-King and Superior Man of Confucian thought is another, as is the Greek concept of *areté*—virtue in thought and action. All prized a male beauty and an ethos of strength and serenity, action and calmness, *yin* and *yang*.

To be sure, more Asian-American men are refusing to lock themselves into narrow roles and models. Rick Yuen, for example, a dean at Stanford, often finds himself caring for his two children and deferring to his wife, SF Community College board member Mabel Teng, on many family and career decisions. "I start with the basic assumption that we're men and women of equal standing," he says simply.

In the literary arts, playwrights David Henry Hwang and Philip Gotanda and poet David Mura explore themes of ethnic manhood and sexuality. In the social arena, gay Asians are starting to emerge, attacking the layer upon layer of racism and homophobia they face in the straight and gay worlds.

On a recent trip to Los Angeles, I stumbled across an irresistible metaphor for our culture. A journalist friend, Brenda Sunoo of the *Korea Times*, had invited me to join her family at a concert of young Asian-American musicians, all amateurs.

The concert was a romp in culture-bending and blending. There were Korean rappers. A Japanese folksinger. A Filipino multimedia artist. When the rap dancers blew a tricky move and fell to the ground, drawing laughs, they hid their faces in their hands in embarrassment. Another singer, his set delayed by technical problems, repeatedly thanked the audience for its patience.

The performers seemed much like Asian America: Shy but daring; apologetic but confident; imitative yet novel. "There's no blueprint for us,"

said Brenda. "Our history is being written now. Our individual choices will make us unique."

We've barely started to explore the beauty of our culture. With a little luck, the new Asian America will be a choral celebration, not an aria sung to an elite few. This will keep us from fading into white society as admired but bleached Americans.

We're trying to change the cultural paradigm, image by image. We have to. For it is how we see each other that will ultimately transform the world. How we see each other, and how we see ourselves.

So where does this all lead me? Do I feel more whole in my newfound identity? Have I tossed the masks slapped on me by society, my family, myself? Do I know why I cut off my nose to spite my race?

Yes, to all of the above. Now I see my image and others in a less harsh light. I know one's slant of eye and color of skin are bogus issues. For beyond acculturation, beyond racial identity, is the larger question of *kokoro*—Japanese for heart and soul. Make no mistake: I've learned I *am* different from white people. Not better, not worse, but distinct. The faces rushing toward me in my pre-surgical daze were neither white nor yellow. They were mine.

Carnal Acts: Disability

Nancy Mairs

Nancy Mairs is the author of several books of prose, including *Carnal Acts, Remembering the Bone House, Ordinary Time*, and *Voice Lessons*. She has also published poetry. The mother of three grown children, Nancy Mairs lives in Tucson, Arizona, with her husband, George.

For months now I've been consciously searching for representations of myself in the media, especially television. I know I'd recognize this self because of certain distinctive, though not unique, features: I am a forty-three-year-old woman crippled by multiple sclerosis; although I can still tot-

ter a short distance with the aid of a brace and a cane, more and more of the time I ride in a wheelchair. Because of these appliances and my peculiar gait, I'm easy to spot even in a crowd. So when I tell you I haven't noticed any woman like me on television, you can believe me.

Actually, last summer I did see a woman with multiple sclerosis portrayed on one of those medical dramas that offer an illness-of-the-week like the daily special at your local diner. In fact, that was the whole point of the show: that this poor young woman had MS. She was terribly upset (understandably, I assure you) by the diagnosis, and her response was to plan a trip to Kenya while she was still physically capable of making it, against the advice of the young, fit, handsome doctor who had fallen in love with her. And she almost did make it. At least, she got as far as a taxi to the airport, hotly pursued by the doctor. But at the last moment she succumbed to his blandishments and fled the taxi into his manly protective embrace. No escape to Kenya for this cripple.

Capitulation into the arms of a man who uses his medical powers to strip one of even the urge toward independence is hardly the sort of representation I had in mind. But even if the situation had been sensitively handled, according the woman her right to her own adventures, it wouldn't have been what I'm looking for. Such a television show, as well as films like *Duet for One* and *Children of a Lesser God,* in taking disability as its major premise, excludes the complexities that round out a character and make her whole. It's not about a woman who happens to be physically disabled; it's about physical disability as the determining factor of a woman's existence.

Take it from me, physical disability looms pretty large in one's life. But it doesn't devour one wholly. I'm not, for example, Ms. MS, a walking, talking embodiment of a chronic incurable degenerative disease. In most ways I'm just like every other woman of my age, nationality, and socioeconomic background. I menstruate, so I have to buy tampons. I worry about smoker's breath, so I buy mouthwash. I smear my wrinkling skin with lotions. I put bleach in the washer so my family's undies won't be dingy. I drive a car, talk on the telephone, get runs in my pantyhose, eat pizza. In most ways, that is, I'm the advertisers' dream: Ms. Great American Consumer. And yet the advertisers, who determine nowadays who will get represented publicly and who will not, deny the existence of me and my kind absolutely.

I once asked a local advertiser why he didn't include disabled people in his spots. His response seemed direct enough. "We don't want to give people the idea that our product is just for the handicapped," he said. But tell me truly now: If you saw me pouring out puppy biscuits, would

you think these kibbles were only for the puppies of cripples? If you saw my blind niece ordering a Coke, would you switch to Pepsi lest you be struck sightless? No, I think the advertiser's excuse masked a deeper and more anxious rationale: To depict disabled people in the ordinary activities of daily life is to admit that there is something ordinary about disability itself, that it might enter anybody's life. If it is effaced completely, or at least isolated as a separate "problem," so that it remains at a safe distance from other human issues, then the viewer won't feel threatened by her or his own physical vulnerability.

This kind of effacement or isolation has painful, even dangerous consequences, however. For the disabled person, these include self-degradation and a subtle kind of self-alienation not unlike that experienced by other minorities. Socialized human beings love to conform, to study others and then to mold themselves to the contours of those whose images, for good reasons or bad, they come to love. Imagine a life in which feasible others—others you can hope to be like—don't exist. At the least you might conclude that there is something queer about you, something ugly or foolish or shameful. In the extreme, you might feel as though you don't exist, in any meaningful social sense, at all. Everyone else is "there," sucking breath mints and splashing on cologne and swigging wine coolers. You're "not there." And if not there, nowhere.

But this denial of disability imperils even you who are able-bodied, and not just by shrinking your insight into the physically and emotionally complex world you live in. Some disabled people call you TAPs, or Temporarily Abled Persons. The fact is that ours is the only minority you can join involuntarily, without warning, at any time. And if you live long enough, as you're increasingly likely to do, you might well join it. The transition will probably be difficult from a physical point of view no matter what. But it will be a good bit easier psychologically if you are accustomed to seeing disability as a normal characteristic, one that complicates but does not ruin human existence. Achieving this integration, for disabled and able-bodied people alike, requires that we insert disability daily into our field of vision: quietly, naturally, in the small and common scenes of our ordinary lives.

Testimony

Natasha Tarpley

Natasha Tarpley is a 1993 graduate of Harvard University with a degree in African-American studies. Her work has appeared in *Essence, Callaloo, Obsidian II, African American Review*, and in the anthologies *In Search of Color Everywhere, Fast Talk, Full Volume*, and *City River of Voices*. In recent years, she has received poetry fellowships from the National Endowment for the Arts and the Massachusetts Cultural Council.

In the spring of my sophomore year at Harvard University, I was almost arrested in my own dormitory for attempting to take my computer to my nearby home. My younger brother had come in with me to help me carry it, and on our way out the door, the security guard stopped us. He told us not to move, that we weren't going anywhere. My brother was able to motion for my mother and younger sister, who were waiting in the car, to come in. My mother tried to talk to the guard, but to no avail. He called for back-up. At least four squad cars arrived on the scene immediately. At that point, it didn't matter that we were a family, that I was a Harvard student, that my mother—herself a Harvard graduate—was a parent dressed in a sophisticated business suit, that my sister was only in seventh grade or that my brother was a sophomore in high school. None of this made a difference. All that mattered was that we were Black.

I relay this incident because I learned from it a painful lesson, one that many Black students on campuses across the country are also learning: that my education, my family, my person, my life even, do not carry weight or have the same value as other students', white students', on this campus. That day, I lost part of myself; the part that had held some faint hope—albeit naive—that the words of acceptance and belonging, spoken behind toothy grins during freshmen orientation or student group meetings, were true; that I, as a student of this "grand and prestigious" institution, could move about as I chose and could claim the same rights and privileges as seemed to be bestowed upon others of my classmates.

At some point, the guard began stopping people who were walking in and out of the lobby, asking them if they could identify me, to prove that I actually lived in the building. I thought about those Black folks who had come before me, whose lives had had to be accounted for by others; whose destinies had been placed in the hands of strangers. It infuriated me that all of our protests and reasoning, and all of our identification "papers" laid out on the table, did not hold the same weight as the slight nod of a white person's head; an X marked by a white hand; a word spoken from a white mouth. That day, tears flowed where words had escaped me. But in many ways, this marked not only the breakdown of my old vocabulary, but also signified the beginning of new words and sounds, to describe and encompass both where I had been and the new direction in which I was heading.

Certainly the incident I have recounted is one that is not unfamiliar to many of us—Black students, parents, and families alike. This type of thing occurs daily on college campuses, neighborhood and city streets. James Baldwin writes, "while the tale of how we suffer and how we are delighted, and how we may triumph is never new, it must always be heard." Thus, while the stories we tell are important, it is the act of telling and of hearing them told that sets us free. And it is at this most vulnerable moment, at the meeting place of pain, joy, desire, and renewed hope, where we gather up the pieces of the stories that have been waiting to be told, and where our voices—although changing—are clear and strong enough for the telling that this . . . begins. Indeed this . . . is about the processes that we, young Black students and writers, go through in order to reach the point where we are able to open ourselves and release that which we held inside. And further, how this process of "coming into self" is connected to that of learning about, accepting, and loving one's Blackness.

Hence the title, *Testimony*, from the verb to testify; to bear witness, to bring forth, to claim and proclaim oneself as an intrinsic part of the world. The act of testifying or giving testimony has deep roots in African American history, reaching back to slavery (and before), to the places our ancestors created—behind somebody's wood cabin doubling as a makeshift church or meetinghouse, or in a nearby clearing—where they opened themselves up to one another, showed their scars, spoke of their day-to-day life, their hopes and dreams, prayed to their God, and tried to remember everything they had lost.

Testifying, although it has strong religious connotations, has also performed the important secular function of providing a means by which the salve could make herself visible, in a society which had rendered her invisible; by which he could explore the sound of his own voice when he had been rendered silent. Henry Louis Gates writes in his introduction to *Bearing Witness*, an anthology of Black autobiography: "If the individual black self could not exist before the law, it could and would be forged in language, as a testimony at once to the supposed integrity of the black self and against the social and political evils that delimited individual and group equality for all African Americans."

In this sense, testifying is not only a way to commune with one's Creator, but is also a way to define and redefine one's humanity; to ground oneself in community; to revel in the touch of hands and bodies familiar with the testifier's pain or joy, in voices that know how to reach her when she is far away and bring her back, making a bridge from this world to the next. And it is these simple gestures—touching and being touched, raising up one's voice—that helped to fill in the frame of the body, that gave it weight enough to anchor itself to the earth, instead of floating, a thin and airy shadow, above it.

Black people still live in a society in which we are often rendered invisible. The sun rises and sets to the deep gurgle, like a moan caught somewhere between the head and the feet, of a river of Black blood filling and overflowing. Black bodies, Black lives still hold little value, even to ourselves. This is evidenced by such national outrages as the Rodney King incident, as well as by those daily offenses to our personhood which somehow don't make national or local headlines: the subtle and blatant humiliation and discrimination that Black people experience on the job, at school, in their neighborhoods; Black children dying and killing one another, crimes punished only by the taking of another Black life.

In the classroom, Black students often find themselves fighting battles similar to those being waged against Black people on the streets. The same forces that work to silence and render invisible Black people outside of the classroom are also present in our educational systems. In interviews that I conducted with Black students on various college and university campuses, many students, particularly those at predominantly white institutions, spoke of discrepancies in grading and in the way they were treated. They talked as well about the pressure they felt to "speak for the race," as they were often one of a few or the only Black student in a class, their individual opinions and ideas pushed aside. But regardless of who they were supposedly speaking for, many Black students felt that their contributions were not valued or sufficiently recognized by the professor or other students.

James Baldwin writes that "to become educated . . . is to become inaccessibly independent, it is to acquire a dangerous way of assessing danger, and it is to hold in one's hands a means of changing reality." For many Black students, . . . the process of defining and redefining ourselves begins and ends with education. As a generation, we are among the first to taste the fruits of our parents' and grandparents' labors during the antisegregation and Civil Rights movements of the 1950s and 1960s, and are, as a result, able to make choices in terms of education and careers unimaginable forty or thirty, even twenty, years ago.

Although education takes many forms, oftentimes this journey to self begins with the choice to go to college. Armed with our parents' hopes, our own desires and interests, and perhaps, to some extent, expectations of achieving the mythical "American dream," we step foot on our respective campuses, reveling in our new found independence and the thrill of possibility spread out before us. And it is here that the real work begins; where we start to question ourselves, explore various options, and make choices about our identities.

One's arsenal of knowledge and one's education strongly influence how one sees oneself in relation to the rest of the world. We live our lives according to a cultural narrative, a story woven from the tales and lessons from the past which we perpetuate. For the most part, this narrative is Eurocentric, meaning that it has at its core a celebration and promulgation of European, or more accurately, white American value systems, achievements, and history. We understand that this framework could not and would not exist without Black people, for in addition to having helped create it, Black people also function as the "other" to which this "system" or narrative is diabolically opposed.

Thus, I envision the process of "becoming educated" much like that of climbing a staircase with missing steps. As Black students, we enter (and in many cases leave) institutions of "higher" learning with incomplete foundations. This is by no means meant to imply that Black students are not—at least—as smart, as capable, or as productive as students of other races. But it is meant to point out that most of us, for most of our lives, have been subject to educational systems—both public and private— which negate Blackness and Black contributions or achievements. Although American educational systems are becoming increasingly "multicultural," this is still problematic. Multiculturalism, insofar as I have seen, has not addressed the crucial issues of inclusion which it claims or, to be fair, sets out to achieve. Its rhetoric has not been accounted for in our lived and practical experiences.

In our climb up this incomplete staircase, we learn to skip over and avoid the wide and empty spaces of unknown Blackness. It is this rhetoric that we have bought into, which we use as a rope to pull us over these chasms, to get us from one step to the next. And if we have not bought the rhetoric, we have at least made the assumption that we have a right to express ourselves as individuals without being intruded upon, and to be treated with a certain degree of humanity. However, many of us reach a point where our expectations do not match our experience. The space between stairs becomes too wide to cross over, our rope will not reach, we lose our footing, or perhaps the entire foundation caves in.

But it is at this moment of destruction that we can begin to pick up the pieces and, with our own hands, put them in a new order, construct or reconstruct a new foundation. We begin the process of educating ourselves, "unlearning" and resynthesizing what we have learned in the past. . . .

We are among the first to take advantage of the advances made during the 1950s and 1960s; to live in a racially integrated society in which most of us have never confronted the legal and social segregation that our parents experienced and fought against. But we are also left to answer questions like, what does it mean to live in an integrated society? Is it—or was it ever—an appropriate solution, and what are its implications for the future? These remain questions for us, for they are issues with which our parents are still grappling. Although we are aware that racism exists, we make the dangerous assumption that we will be accorded, at the least, some common courtesy and respect. However, we learn our lessons the hard way and are thoroughly unprepared for the attacks which attempt to strip us of even these most basic elements of humanity. . . .

[M]any of us begin to wake from the dream of integration and confront its realities during our college careers. Although these are crude characterizations, there are several common responses to this. At one extreme, there are Black students who continue to try and fit into mainstream society at any cost, ignoring or tolerating racism, averting their eyes from other Black students, seeking friendship and partnership from those who are unlike themselves.

At the other extreme, some Black students, in response to the alienation and discrimination of which they have become increasingly aware, embrace essentialist notions of what it means to be Black. This can be equally as painful as the complete rejection of one's Blackness, for it imposes limitations, causing us to curb those interests which may not be perceived as "black enough" and to reject those who do not readily fit into this model or construct.

Others try to walk a tenuous middle ground between the two extremes, which often turns into a minefield, threatening to explode with every step. In most cases, these responses lead to further alienation and fragmentation; to hurtful and exclusive actions and situations which defeat the purpose of our newfound consciousness, and which serve to isolate a generation of people who have the potential to change the world.

In addition to confronting the issues raised by integration and the legacy left to us by our parents and ancestors, we are also grappling with our youth, the vast possibilities placed in our hands, and the responsibility of shaping those possibilities, of making something of ourselves. In many ways, this is our own struggle against invisibility and obsolescence. Perhaps, more than in any other area, the refusal to be rendered invisible is expressed most vividly in our art. Especially in the collage of Hip Hop, which, out of borrowed notes and fragments, creates a rhythm that matches the beating of our own hearts; and in rap, which refuses to allow the lives of Black youth to be confined and compressed into small urban spaces.

Increasingly, we are using our education to design structures for the future as well. Our poetry and other writings reflect the urgent need for change, to "MOVE," as Jennifer Smith writes. More and more Black students are choosing African and African-American or related studies as majors during college. . . .

In all genres and mediums, in all ways, this generation is involved in finding its voice, creating new traditions, laying a new foundation. At times we get distracted and confused. But part of the reason for this is that we are trying to define who and what we are in a society that requires its members to make binary choices, to choose sides—Black or white—with neither choice being more definitive or logical than the other. If we are to ask what it means to be integrated, for example, then we must also ask what it truly means to be Black, a question too big for one generation, and one which, perhaps, does not or should not have an answer. . . .

The Same Difference

Amy Wang

Amy Wang has recently won two awards from the Asian American Journalists Association.

It was on my way home that the moment of truth swept by—again.

There we were, a friend and I, heading north on the Pennsylvania Turnpike to central New York to visit my parents. Somehow our conversation had parted the curtains before my childhood memories, and before I knew it, I was telling him about an incident I have never quite forgotten.

As I spoke, it was almost as if my adult self were back in Pittsburgh, watching; strange how in my memory the sun is always glinting through a bright haze on that day. The trees are bare, or nearly so, with dark branches that reach out to splinter the sun's rays. I am walking alone, down a white concrete sidewalk littered with leaves, twigs, buckeyes. School is out for the day, and everyone is going home.

From behind come shouts, and I turn to see a group of children from school. A moment passes,

and I realize they are shouting at me. I listen for several seconds before the words whip into clarity:

Chink! Hey, chink! Chinky chinky chink!

They are running. I am frozen, my heart the only part of me moving, and it is pounding. Then one of them stoops, picks up a twig and hurls it at me. It lands short, a foot away on the sidewalk. Then I turn, still blocks from home, and run. The twigs keep coming, clattering close behind as the others shout and follow. As I run, I think of the steep steps to the front door and despair.

But when I reach the steps and turn around, only silence follows. And when my mother answers the doorbell's ring, she sees only her daughter, cheeks a little flushed, waiting to be let in. Almost instinctively, I know I must not tell her. It would only hurt her, and there is nothing she can do. Besides, it is nothing I want to discuss.

"Wow," he said. "And you were in sixth grade when this happened?"

"Six," I said. "I was 6 when this happened. I was in first grade."

Amy Wang, "The Same Difference," *The Philadelphia Inquirer Magazine* 12 December 1993: 9, 31. Reprinted with permission from *The Philadelphia Inquirer.*

He was clearly appalled, his eyes in far focus as he tried to understand how such a thing could happen to a small child. I was concentrating on the road, but even a sidelong glance showed he did not, could not, quite understand. And it was then that I felt the familiar stab of disappointment: the realization that no matter how long we traveled together, we would always be on parallel roads, moving on either side of a great divide. I would never know his assurance as he made his way through a world where his skin color was an assumption, and he would never know my anxiety as I made my way through a world where my skin color was an anguish.

We were silent, and after a while he fell asleep. "Wake me up when we get to Allentown," he had said as he drifted off, and we both smiled, remembering a classmate who had once padded an expense account for profit by driving from New York to Allentown and back twice in two days.

The thought of the old mill town triggered memories of another old mill town, where I had gotten my first job out of college. It was at the local newspaper, working nights on the copy desk. Our shifts ended at 1 a.m., and I often drove home through deserted streets, the hush broken only by the whir of an occasional street-cleaning machine or the clanking of a distant garbage truck. The other drivers on the streets at that hour seemed just as weary, just as intent on getting to bed.

In such an atmosphere I often dream, and so to this day a shadowy, slowed-down quality suffuses the memory of turning my head and looking out the side window one night just in time to see an old red Dodge draw up in the next lane at a traffic light. Inside, four young white crewcut men dressed in denim and flannel strain toward me, their faces distorted with hate, their mouths twisted with invective. Our windows are closed, so I am spared their actual words, but their frenzied pantomime leaves little to be imagined.

When the light turns green I pull away hastily, but they cruise alongside for the next few blocks. By the time they tire of me and swing into a left turn, I am seething with fear and rage. I wait until they are committed to the turn, then raise my middle finger. One of them looks back for a final insult, sees my gesture, and gapes—but only for a moment. He turns, and I know he is screaming at the driver to turn back. I gun it.

They never come after me, and I make it home alive. Numb, I crawl into bed. It is only after I lie down that I realize how they might have hurt me, the four of them with their huge Dodge against my tiny Nissan, and I begin to shake. As my mind tumbles, the phone rings. For a moment I think it is them, and then logic returns. I answer, and it is my boyfriend calling from Boston. I tell him what happened, melting into tears. He is sympathetic, but then he asks: "How do you know they weren't yelling at you because you were a woman?"

I don't, of course, but that is not the point. His whiteness rushes through the line with the very question. "It doesn't matter," I tell him, and suddenly I can't stand to hear his voice. I tell him I don't want to discuss it anymore, and hang up.

Somewhere along Route 79 in New York he said, "This is beautiful." I smiled, remembering the years I spent in Finger Lakes country: middle school, high school, college. Here were trees I had climbed, hills I had sledded down, malls I knew by heart; here were roads that led to memories and people who knew my history.

And it was because I had to come back here that another He was able to betray me. It was during the first summer I spent away from home, working at a magazine in New York. Picture now a pavilion on the grounds of a quiet country club where the staff is enjoying the annual company picnic, and there I am by the jukebox, hovering over the glassed-in 45s as a light mist dampens the grass. As The Contours wail "Do You Love Me," I sway to the beat, attracting a stranger's eyes. In a moment he is introducing himself; in an hour he is sitting by me in the bus taking us back to the city; in a week he is asking me out to dinner.

I am no longer thinking clearly. On my last day at the magazine, he watches as I clean out my desk, then asks me, in a low but urgent tone, not to forget him. He tells me he wants my address, and a sudden foreboding chill nearly stuns me with its iciness, sending shivers through my hand as I write out the address and phone number. Then I ask for his address and phone number. I do not think to ask him not to forget me.

Weeks go by without a word, and then one night, I know. The chill comes back. For days I hate white men, all of them, they all bear the blame for his misdeed. But I have known too many good ones for my fury to last, and finally I am forced to admit that I have been a fool, and that this time, at least, it had nothing to do with race.

"It could have happened to anyone," a (white male) friend tells me. "It happens to everyone."

I am not immediately consoled. But time goes on, and finally, so do I.

By the time we pulled into my parents' driveway, it was nearly dinnertime. I sprang out, glad to stretch, and bounded into the house, but he was slow to follow, and I had discarded my shoulder bag and greeted everyone by the time he finally appeared in the doorway. I went to introduce him, wondering why he was hanging back. Then he raised his eyes to mine as he came up the stairs, and I realized he was nervous. He was in my world now, and he was finally getting an inkling of what I went through every day.

Payback time. At last.

Then my mother was there, smiling and shaking his hand, and my father was right behind her, also smiling.

"Welcome," he said.

For a moment, I could see the horizon, where parallel lines sometimes seem to meet.

Virtually Normal

Andrew Sullivan

Andrew Sullivan was editor-in-chief of *The New Republic* from 1991 to 1996. He holds a B.A. in modern history and modern languages from Oxford University and a Ph.D. in political science from Harvard University. He is the author of *Virtually Normal: An Argument About Homosexuality* and numerous essays on political and cultural topics.

I remember the first time it dawned on me that I might be a homosexual. I was around the age of ten and had succeeded in avoiding the weekly soccer practice in my elementary school. I don't remember exactly how—maybe I had feigned a cold, or an injury, and claimed that because it was raining (it always seemed to be raining), I should be given the afternoon inside. I loathed soccer, partly because I wasn't very good at it and partly because I felt I didn't quite belong in the communal milieu in which it unfolded. The way it's played in English junior schools puts all the emphasis on team playing, and even back then this didn't appeal much to my nascent sense of *amour-propre*. But that lucky afternoon, I found myself sequestered with the girls, who habitually spent that time period doing sewing, knitting, and other appropriately feminine things. None of this, I remember, interested me much either; and I was happily engaged reading. Then a girl sitting next to me looked at me with a mixture of curiosity and disgust. "Why aren't you out with the boys playing football?" she asked. "Because I hate it," I replied. "Are you sure you're not really a girl under there?" she asked, with the suspicion of a sneer. "Yeah, of course," I replied, stung, and somewhat shaken.

It was the first time the fundamental homosexual dilemma had been put to me so starkly. It resonated so much with my own internal fears that I remember it vividly two decades later. Before then, most of what I now see as homosexual emotions had not been forced into one or the other gender category. I didn't feel as a boy or a girl; I felt as me. I remember vividly—perhaps I was five or six— being seated in the back of a car with my second cousin, a tousle-headed, wide-grinned kid a few years older, and being suddenly, unwittingly entranced by him. It was a feeling I had never felt before, the first inkling of a yearning that was only to grow stronger as the years went by. I remember too that around the age of eight, I joined a gang of four boys—modeled perhaps on the ubiquitous, vaguely homoerotic male pop groups common at the time—and developed a crush on one of them. He was handsome and effortlessly athletic, and in my difficult attempt to cement both a companionship and a premature love affair, I felt the first strains of the homosexual hurt that is the accompaniment of most homosexual lives. It was not so much the rejection; it was the combination of acceptance and rejection. It was feeling that that part of the male-male bond that worked—the part that works with most heterosexual male-male friendships—was also the part that destroyed the possibility of another, as yet opaque but far more complete longing that for me, but not for him, was inextricable from the relationship. It was a sense that longing was based on a structural lack of reciprocity; that love was about being accepted on the condition that you suppressed what you really felt.

Looking back, this inchoate ache was all that I knew of the homosexual experience. But I knew also, because of the absence of any mention of the subject, because of the lack of any tangible visible reflections of it in the world around me, that there was something wrong with it. So when that afternoon, I was abruptly asked whether I was actually a girl, I blanched and stammered. Had my friend seen something I thought was hidden? She had, of course, merely accused me of being a sissy—something all young geeks, whatever their fledgling sexual orientation, were well used to. But I wondered whether she hadn't detected something else, something deeper. How had she known? And what, anyway, was it? By the age of ten, the only answer I had been given was that I was simply the wrong gender, something that any brief perusal of my body would discount.

Maybe I should be clearer here. The longing was not sexual. I was too young to feel any explicit sexual desire. I had no idea what an expression of sexual love might be. So far as I can remember it, it was a desire to unite with another: not to possess, but to join in some way; not to lose myself, but to be given dimension. At the time, I also had fantasies of being part of some boys' gang, or a rock group—some institution that could legitimately incorporate the half-understood, half-felt emotions that were filtering through my system. Nowhere else in the world did I see relationships that incorporated this desire. There were many that intimated it—the soccer team, my father and his friends, the male atmosphere of the local pub or the rugby club—but all these, I divined even then, were somehow premised on a denial of the acknowledged intimacy

I had begun to crave. They were a simulacrum of acceptance. Because of their proximity to the very things I felt I wanted, they had developed a visceral hostility to the very thing that I was. So I had to be careful, in case they found out.

The secret, then, began when I was young. I hardly dared mention it to anyone; and the complete absence of any note of the subject in my family or in school, in television, newspapers, or even such books as I could get ahold of, made the secret that much more mystifying. I wondered whether there was any physical manifestation of this unmentionable fact. I was circumcised, unlike many other English boys: had that done it? I remember looking up physical descriptions of men and women in the local library to see if my own body corresponded to the shape of the male (I was, I determined, not broad-shouldered enough). When I was a little late going through puberty, I wondered whether that might be related, and half imagined that my voice might not break, and reveal my difference. Eventually, I succumbed to panic and mentioned it before God. I was in the communion line at my local parish church, Our Lady and Saint Peter's, the church that was linked to my elementary school. Please, I remember asking of the Almighty almost offhandedly as I walked up the aisle to receive communion from the mild-mannered Father Simmons for the umpteenth time, please, help me with *that*.

When people ask me whether homosexuality is a choice or not, I can only refer them to these experiences. They're the only thing I know for sure. Dozens of surveys have been written, countless questionnaires filled out, endless theories elaborated upon; but in most of these purportedly objective studies, opaque and troubling emotions are being reduced to statistics in front of strangers. I distrust them. But I don't fully distrust my own experience, or the experience of so many homosexuals I have met over the years. This experience is filtered, as all experience is, through the prism of reflection and self-reflection: it is not some raw datum in the empirical, verifiable world which I am presenting for review. But it is as honest a sketch as I can provide of the experience of finding oneself a homosexual.

Not that this was yet a truly sexual condition. In some sense, physical contact had, in a somewhat comic way, implanted itself in my mind. But it was still intensely abstract. I remember when I was around seven or eight seeing a bare-chested man on television one night and feeling such an intense longing for him that I determined to become a doctor. That way, I figured, I could render the man unconscious and lie on top of him when no one else was in the room. But then, I quickly realized, I would be found out and get into trouble. I spent most of the night awake, working out this scenario, and ending up as confused and as overcome by desire as when I began. But already I had divined that the expression of any kind of longing would have to take devious and subterranean forms. I would have to be an outlaw in order to be complete. I also remember making a joke in a debate competition at the age of twelve, at the time of a homosexual scandal involving the leader of the British Liberal Party. I joked that life was better under the Conservatives—or behind the Liberals, for that matter. It achieved a raucous response, but I had no idea what the analogy meant. Perhaps my schoolboy audience hadn't, either. We had learned the social levers of hostility to homosexuality before we had even the foggiest clue what they referred to.

My attraction to the same sex was not a desire as natural as sneezing, or eating, or sleeping, as some people claim. It was a secondary part of my psychological and emotional makeup; it operated in that confused and confusing part of my mind that was a fusion of involuntary desire and conscious aspiration. My first explicit sexual fondlings were with girls; but they were play, and carried no threat of emotional intimacy. Looking back, I realize I had no deep emotional ties to girls at all; they were friends, sometimes companions, sometimes soul mates. At elementary school, where I was academically ahead of my class, my closest colleagues were precocious girls. Their intellect I respected. But I had no longing to unite with them, and, looking back, didn't even want to talk with them much. I preferred hanging out with boys, traipsing through the neighboring woods with them, forming secret clubs, cycling around nearby lanes, playing childhood chase games (and in much of this, I guess I was indistinguishable from any other boy). But looking back, I also remember a nascent sense of a deeper, more intuitive, more emotional long-

ing. I have always enjoyed the company of women, sustained many deep, strong friendships, had countless, endless conversations; but I have never longed for a woman in the way that I have longed for a man, never yearned for her physical embrace or her emotional solidarity.

I was, in other words, virtually normal. Like many homosexuals, I have spent some time looking back and trying to decipher what might have caused my apparent aberration. One explanation does make some sort of sense. I had a very close relationship with my mother and a somewhat distant one with my father. My father provided very basic physical and practical support—when I had asthmatic attacks as a child, it was my father who picked me up in the middle of the night and calmed me down to help me breathe. He made my birthday cakes, picked me up from school, and provided a solid, if undemonstrative, base of emotional support. But it was my mother who filled my head with the possibilities of the world, who conversed with me as an adult, who helped me believe in my ability to do things in the wider world. It was her values that shaped and encouraged me; and my father who sought to ground me in reality, and to keep my inflated ego in some sort of check. In my adolescence I warred with my father and sided with my mother in the family fights that took place. And in all of this, I suppose, I follow a typical pattern of homosexual development.

But then so do many heterosexuals. Both my brother and sister grew up in the same atmosphere, and neither of them turned out to be homosexual. Many heterosexual boys have intense bonds with their mothers, and seek to recreate them in the women they eventually love. Many heterosexual boys fight with their fathers and loathe organized sports. And some homosexual boys may sense in their fathers—especially those who cast an extremely heterosexual image—a rejection that they then intensify and internalize. Because the son feels he cannot be what his father wants, he seeks refuge in the understanding of a perhaps more sympathetic mother, who can temporarily shield her gay son from the disappointment and latent suspicions of his father. In other words, homosexuality may actually cause a young boy to be distant from his father and close to his mother, rather than be caused by it.

But whatever its origins, by puberty, my nascent homosexual emotional makeup interacted with my burgeoning hormones to create the beginnings of a sexual implosion. Something like this, of course, happens to gay and straight kids alike; but gay children have a particularly weird time of it. It was then that the scope of my entire situation began to click into place in my head. My longings became so intense that I found myself drawing sketches of the men I desired; I cut out male models from glossy magazines and made catalogues of them; I moved from crushes to sexual obsessions. I could no longer hide from this explicit desire: there it was on paper, in my brain, before my eyes—an undeniable and powerful attraction to other boys and men. And of course, with all of this came an exquisite and inextricable sense of exhilaration as well as disgust. It was like getting on a plane for the first time, being exhilarated by its ascent, gazing with wonder out of the window, seeing the clouds bob beneath you, but then suddenly realizing that you are on the wrong flight, going to a destination which terrifies you, surrounded by people who inwardly appall you. And you cannot get off. You are filled with a lurching panic. You are one of them.

It is probably true that many teenagers experience something of this panic. Although there is an understandable desire to divide the world starkly into heterosexual desire and its opposite, most of us, I'd guess, have confronted the possibility at some time in our lives of the possibility of our own homosexuality. There is something of both attractions in all of us, to begin with. For the majority, it is resolved quite early; our society forces such a resolution. Except for a few who seem to retain throughout their lives a capacity for attraction to both sexes, for most of us the issue is largely resolved before the teenage years set in. On this, both experience and empirical study agree. It is not always—perhaps never—easy, for either the homosexual or the heterosexual. Sometimes, the strength of the other attraction requires such a forceful suppression that it resonates much later in life. How else to explain the sometimes violent fear and hostility to homosexuals that a few heterosexual males feel? And how else to account for the sense of distance and betrayal that haunts some homosexuals? In this early, panicked resolution—

one way or another—are the roots of many subsequent pathologies, pathologies that are not always pervious to reason.

But before the teenage years, panic is intermixed with pre-adult ambiguity. Many pubescent children play at sex with members of the same gender, before graduating on to the real thing. Many homosexuals do the exact opposite. For my part, my feelings were too strong and too terrifying to do anything but submerge them completely. There were, of course, moments when they took you unawares. Gay adolescents are offered what every heterosexual teenager longs for: to be invisible in the girls' locker room. But you are invisible in the boys' locker room, your desire as unavoidable as its object. In that moment, you learn the first homosexual lesson: that your survival depends upon self-concealment. I remember specifically coming back to high school after a long summer when I was fifteen and getting changed in the locker room for the first time again with a guy I had long had a crush on. But since the vacation, he had developed enormously: suddenly he had hair on his chest, his body had grown and strengthened, he was—clearly—no longer a boy. In front of me, he took off his shirt, and unknowingly, slowly, erotically stripped. I became literally breathless, overcome by the proximity of my desire. The gay teenager learns in that kind of event a form of control and sublimation, of deception and self-contempt, that never leaves his consciousness. He learns that that which would most give him meaning is most likely to destroy him in the eyes of other; that the condition of his friendships is the subjugation of himself.

In the development of any human being, these are powerful emotions. They form a person. The homosexual learns to make distinctions between his sexual desire and his emotional longings—not because he is particularly prone to objectification of the flesh, but because he needs to survive as a social and sexual being. The society separates these two entities, and for a long time the homosexual has no option but to keep them separate. He learns certain rules; and, as a with a child learning grammar, they are hard, later on in life, to unlearn.

It's possible, I think, that whatever society teaches or doesn't teach about homosexuality, this fact will always be the case. No homosexual child, surrounded overwhelmingly by heterosexuals, will feel at home in his sexual and emotional world, even in the most tolerant of cultures. And every homosexual child will learn the rituals of deceit, impersonation, and appearance. Anyone who believes political, social, or even cultural revolution will change this fundamentally is denying reality. This isolation will always hold. It is definitional of homosexual development. And children are particularly cruel. At the age of eleven, no one wants to be the odd one out; and in the arena of dating and hormones, the exclusion is inevitably a traumatic one.

It's also likely to be forlorn. Most people are liable to meet emotional rejection by sheer force of circumstance; but for a homosexual, the odds are simply far, far higher. My own experience suggests that somewhere between two and five percent of the population have involuntarily strong emotional and sexual attraction to the same sex. Which means that the pool of possible partners *starts* at one in twenty to one in fifty. It's no wonder, perhaps, that male homosexual culture has developed an ethic more of anonymous or promiscuous sex than of committed relationships. It's as if the hard lessons of adolescence lower permanently—by the sheer dint of the odds—the aspiration for anything more.

Did I know what I was? Somewhere, maybe. But it was much easier to know what I wasn't. I wasn't going to be able to enter into the world of dating girls; I wasn't going to be able to feel fully comfortable among the heterosexual climate of the male teenager. So I decided, consciously or subconsciously, to construct a trajectory of my life that would remove me from their company; give me an excuse, provide a dignified way out. In Anglo-Saxon culture, the wonk has such an option: he's too nerdy or intellectual to be absorbed by girls. And there is something masculine and respected in the discipline of the arts and especially the sciences. You can gain respect and still be different.

So I threw myself into my schoolwork, into (more dubiously) plays, into creative writing, into science fiction. Other homosexuals I have subsequently met pursued other strategies: some paradoxically threw themselves into sports, outjocking the jocks, gaining ever greater proximity, seeking respect, while knowing all the time that they were doomed to rejection. Others withdrew into isola-

tion and despair. Others still, sensing their difference, flaunted it. At my high school, an older boy insisted on wearing full makeup to class; and he was accepted in a patronizing kind of way, his brazen otherness putting others at ease. They knew where they were with him; and he felt at least comfortable with their stable contempt. The rest of us who lived in a netherworld of sexual insecurity were not so lucky.

Most by then had a far more acute sense of appearances than those who did not need to hide anything; and our sense of irony, and of aesthetics, assumed a precociously arch form, and drew us subtly together. Looking back, I realize that many of my best friends in my teen years were probably homosexual; and that somewhere in our coded, embarrassed dialogue we admitted it. Many of us also embraced those ideologies that seemed most alien to what we feared we might be: of the sports jock, of the altar boy, of the young conservative. They were the ultimate disguises. And our recognition of ourselves in the other only confirmed our desire to keep it quiet.

I should add that many young lesbians and homosexuals seem to have had a much easier time of it. For many, the question of sexual identity was not a critical factor in their life choices or vocation, or even a factor at all. Perhaps because of a less repressive upbringing or because of some natural ease in the world, they affected a simple comfort with their fate, and a desire to embrace it. These people alarmed me: their very ease was the sternest rebuke to my own anxiety, because it rendered it irrelevant. But later in life, I came to marvel at the naturalness of their self-confidence, in the face of such concerted communal pressure, and to envy it. I had the more common self-dramatizing urge of the tortured homosexual, trapped between feeling wicked and feeling ridiculous. It's shameful to admit it, but I was more traumatized by the latter than by the former; my pride was more formidable a force than my guilt.

When people ask the simple question What is a homosexual? I can only answer with stories like these. I could go on, but too many stories have already been told. Ask any lesbian or homosexual, and they will often provide a similar account. I was once asked at a conservative think tank what evidence I had that homosexuality was far more of an orientation than a choice, and I was forced to reply quite simply: my life. It's true that I have met a handful of lesbians and gay men over the years who have honestly told me that they genuinely had a choice in the matter (and a few heterosexuals who claim they too chose their orientation). I believe them; but they are the exception and not the rule. As homosexual lives go, my own was somewhat banal and typical.

This is not, of course, the end of the matter. Human experience begins with such facts, it doesn't end with them. There's a lamentable tendency to try to find some definitive solution to permanent human predicaments—in a string of DNA, in a conclusive psychological survey, in an analysis of hypothalami, in a verse of the Bible—in order to cut the argument short. Or to insist on the emotional veracity of a certain experience and expect it to trump any other argument on the table. But none of these things can replace the political and moral arguments about how a society should deal with the presence of homosexuals in its midst. I relate my experience here not to impress or to shock or to gain sympathy, but merely to convey what the homosexual experience is actually like. You cannot discuss something until you know roughly what it is.

It is also true, I think, that the lesbian experience is somewhat different than the homosexual male experience. Many lesbians argue that homosexuality is more often a choice for women than for men; that it involves a communal longing as much as an individual one; that it is far more rooted in moral and political choice than in ineradicable emotional or sexual orientation. Nevertheless, many lesbians also relate similar experiences to the one I have just related. Because girls and women can be less defensive about emotions and sexuality than boys and men, the sense of beleaguerment may be less profound than it is for boys, and the sense of self-contradiction less intense. But the coming to terms with something one already is, the slow unfolding of a self-realization around a basic emotional reality, is the same. In many, and probably most, cases, they cannot help it either.

The homosexual experience may be deemed an illness, a disorder, a privilege, or a curse; it may be deemed worthy of a "cure," rectified, embraced, or endured. *But it exists.* And it exists in something like the form I have just described. It occurs independently of the forms of its expression; it is bound up in that mysterious and unstable area where sexual desire and emotional longing meet; it reaches into the core of what makes a human being who he or she is. The origins of homosexuality are remarkably mysterious, and probably are due to a mixture of some genetic factors and very early childhood development (before the ages of five or six). But these arguments are largely irrelevant for the discussion that follows. The truth is that, for the overwhelming majority of adults, the condition of homosexuality is as involuntary as heterosexuality is for heterosexuals. Such an orientation is evident from the very beginning of the formation of a person's emotional identity. . . .

Given a choice, many homosexuals along the way would have preferred this were not so, which is about as good a piece of evidence that it is. Men married happily for years eventually crack and reveal the truth about themselves; people dedicated to extirpating homosexuality from the face of the earth have succumbed to the realization that they too are homosexual; individuals intent on ridding it from their systems have ended in defeat and sometimes despair; countless thousands have killed themselves in order not to face up to it, or often because they *have* finally faced up to it. They were not fleeing a chimera or chasing a deception; they were experiencing something real, whatever it was. . . .

By "homosexual," I mean simply someone who can tell a similar story to my own; someone who has found in his or her life that he or she is drawn emotionally and sexually to the same gender, someone who, practically speaking, has had no fundamental choice in the matter. Every society in human history has devised some way to account for this phenomenon, and to accommodate it. As I write, Western society is in the middle of a tense and often fevered attempt to find its own way on the matter. Amid a cacophony of passion and reason, propaganda and statistics, self-disclosures and bouts of hysteria, the subject is being ineluctably discussed. This . . . is an attempt to think through the arguments on all sides as carefully and honestly as possible; to take the unalterable experience of all of us, heterosexual and homosexual, and try to make some social and political sense of it.

A Question of Class

Dorothy Allison

Dorothy Allison's recent books include *Two or Three Things I Know for Sure, Bastard out of Carolina,* which was a National Book Award finalist in fiction, and *Trash.*

The first time I heard, "They're different than us, don't value human life the way we do," I was in high school in Central Florida. The man speaking was an army recruiter talking to a bunch of boys, telling them what the army was really like, what they could expect overseas. A cold angry feeling swept over me. I had heard the word *they* pronounced in that same callous tone before. *They,* those people over there, those people who are not us, they die so easily, kill each other so casually. They are different. *We,* I thought. *Me.*

When I was six or eight back in Greenville, South Carolina, I had heard that same matter-of-fact tone of dismissal applied to me. "Don't you play with her. I don't want you talking to them." Me and my family, we had always been *they.* Who am I? I wondered, listening to that recruiter. Who are my people? We die so easily, disappear so completely— we/they, the poor and the queer. I pressed my bony white trash fists to my stubborn lesbian mouth. The rage was a good feeling, stronger and purer than the shame that followed it, the fear and the sudden urge to run and hide, to deny, to pretend I did not know who I was and what the world would do to me.

My people were not remarkable. We were ordinary, but even so we were mythical. We were the *they* everyone talks about—the ungrateful poor. I grew up trying to run away from the fate that destroyed so many of the people I loved, and having learned the habit of hiding, I found I had also learned to hide from myself. I did not know who I was, only that I did not want to be *they,* the ones who are destroyed or dismissed to make the "real" people, the important people, feel safer. By the time I understood that I was queer, that habit of hiding was deeply set in me, so deeply that it was not a choice but an instinct. Hide, hide to survive, I thought, knowing that if I told the truth about

my life, my family, my sexual desire, my history, I would move over into that unknown territory, the land of they, would never have the chance to name my own life, to understand it or claim it.

Why are you so afraid? my lovers and friends have asked me the many times I have suddenly seemed a stranger, someone who would not speak to them, would not do the things they believed I should do, simple things like applying for a job, or a grant, or some award they were sure I could acquire easily. Entitlement, I have told them, is a matter of feeling like we rather than they. You think you have a right to things, a place in the world, and it is so intrinsically a part of you that you cannot imagine people like me, people who seem to live in your world, who don't have it. I have explained what I know over and over, in every way I can, but I have never been able to make clear the degree of my fear, the extent to which I feel myself denied: not only that I am queer in a world that hates queers, but that I was born poor into a world that despises the poor. The need to make my world believable to people who have never experienced it is part of why I write fiction. I know that some things must be felt to be understood, that despair, for example, can never be adequately analyzed; it must be lived. But if I can write a story that so draws the reader in that she imagines herself like my characters, feels their sense of fear and uncertainty, their hopes and terrors, then I have come closer to knowing myself as real, important as the very people I have always watched with awe.

I have known I was a lesbian since I was a teenager, and I have spent a good twenty years making peace with the effects of incest and physical abuse. But what may be the central fact of my life is that I was born in 1949 in Greenville, South Carolina, the bastard daughter of a white woman from a desperately poor family, a girl who had left the seventh grade the year before, worked as a waitress, and was just a month past fifteen when she had me. That fact, the inescapable impact of being born in a condition of poverty that this society finds shameful, contemptible, and somehow deserved, has had dominion over me to such an extent that I have spent my life trying to overcome or deny it. I have learned with great difficulty that the vast majority of people believe that poverty is a voluntary condition.

I have loved my family so stubbornly that every impulse to hold them in contempt has sparked in me a countersurge of pride—complicated and undercut by an urge to fit us into the acceptable myths and theories of both mainstream society and a lesbian-feminist reinterpretation. The choice becomes Steven Spielberg movies or Erskine Caldwell novels, the one valorizing and the other caricaturing, or the patriarchy as villain, trivializing the choices the men and women of my family have made. I have had to fight broad generalizations from every theoretical viewpoint.

Traditional feminist theory has had a limited understanding of class differences and of how sexuality and self are shaped by both desire and denial. The ideology implies that we are all sisters who should only turn our anger and suspicion on the world outside the lesbian community. It is easy to say that the patriarchy did it, that poverty and social contempt are products of the world of the fathers, and often I felt a need to collapse my sexual history into what I was willing to share of my class background, to pretend that my life both as a lesbian and as a working-class escapee was constructed by the patriarchy. Or conversely, to ignore how much my life was shaped by growing up poor and talk only about what incest did to my identity as a woman and as a lesbian. The difficulty is that I can't ascribe everything that has been problematic about my life simply and easily to the patriarchy, or to incest, or even to the invisible and much-denied class structure of our society.

In my lesbian-feminist collective we had long conversations about the mind/body split, the way we compartmentalize our lives to survive. For years I thought that that concept referred to the way I had separated my activist life from the passionate secret life in which I acted on my sexual desires. I was convinced that the fracture was fairly simple, that it would be healed when there was time and clarity to do so—at about the same point when I might begin

to understand sex. I never imagined that it was not a split but a splintering, and I passed whole portions of my life—days, months, years—in pure directed progress, getting up every morning and setting to work, working so hard and so continually that I avoided examining in any way what I knew about my life. Busywork became a trance state. I ignored who I really was and how I became that person, continued in that daily progress, became an automaton who was what she did.

I tried to become one with the lesbian-feminist community so as to feel real and valuable. I did not know that I was hiding, blending in for safety just as I had done in high school, in college. I did not recognize the impulse to forget. I believed that all those things I did not talk about, or even let myself think too much about, were not important, that none of them defined me. I had constructed a life, an identity in which I took pride, an alternative lesbian family in which I felt safe, and I did not realize that the fundamental me had almost disappeared.

It is surprising how easy it was to live that life. Everyone and everything cooperated with the process. Everything in our culture—books, television, movies, school, fashion—is presented as if it is being seen by one pair of eyes, shaped by one set of hands, heard by one pair of ears. Even if you know you are not part of that imaginary creature—if you like country music not symphonies, read books cynically, listen to the news unbelievingly, are lesbian not heterosexual, and surround yourself with your own small deviant community—you are still shaped by that hegemony, or your resistance to it. The only way I found to resist that homogenized view of the world was to make myself part of something larger than myself. As a feminist and a radical lesbian organizer, and later as a sex radical (which eventually became the term, along with pro-sex feminist, for those who were not anti-pornography but anti-censorship, those of us arguing for sexual diversity), the need to belong, to feel safe, was just as important for me as for any heterosexual, nonpolitical citizen, and sometimes even more important because the rest of my life was so embattled.

The first time I read the Jewish lesbian Irena Klepfisz's poems,[1] I experienced a frisson of recognition. It was not that my people had been "burned off the map" or murdered as hers had. No, we had been encouraged to destroy ourselves, made invisible because we did not fit the myths of the noble poor generated by the middle class. Even now, past forty and stubbornly proud of my family, I feel the draw of that mythology, that romanticized, edited version of the poor. I find myself looking back and wondering what was real, what was true. Within my family, so much was lied about, joked about, denied, or told with deliberate indirection, an undercurrent of humiliation or a brief pursed grimace that belied everything that had been said. What was real? The poverty depicted in books and movies was romantic, a backdrop for the story of how it was escaped.

The poverty portrayed by left-wing intellectuals was just as romantic, a platform for assailing the upper and middle classes, and from their perspective, the working-class hero was invariably male, righteously indignant, and inhumanly noble. The reality of self-hatred and violence was either absent or caricatured. The poverty I knew was dreary, deadening, shameful, the women powerful in ways not generally seen as heroic by the world outside the family.

My family's lives were not on television, not in books, not even comic books. There was a myth of the poor in this country, but it did not include us, no matter how hard I tried to squeeze us in. There was an idea of the good poor—hard-working, ragged but clean, and intrinsically honorable. I understood that we were the bad poor: men who drank and couldn't keep a job; women, invariably pregnant before marriage, who quickly became worn, fat, and old from working too many hours and bearing too many children; and children with runny noses, watery eyes, and the wrong attitudes. My cousins quit school, stole cars, used drugs, and took dead-end jobs pumping gas or waiting tables. We were not noble, not grateful, not even hopeful. We knew ourselves despised. My family was ashamed of being poor, of feeling hopeless. What was there to work for, to save money for, to fight for or struggle against? We had generations before us to teach us that nothing ever changed, and that those who did try to escape failed.

My mama had eleven brothers and sisters, of whom I can name only six. No one is left alive to tell me the names of the others. It was my grandmother who told me about my real daddy, a shiftless pretty man who was supposed to have married, had six children, and sold cut-rate life insurance to poor Black people. My mama married when I was a year old, but her husband died just after my little sister was born a year later.

When I was five, Mama married the man she lived with until she died. Within the first year of their marriage Mama miscarried, and while we waited out in the hospital parking lot, my stepfather molested me for the first time, something he continued to do until I was past thirteen. When I was eight or so, Mama took us away to a motel after my stepfather beat me so badly it caused a family scandal, but we returned after two weeks. Mama told me that she really had no choice; she could not support us alone. When I was eleven I told one of my cousins that my stepfather was molesting me. Mama packed up my sisters and me and took us away for a few days, but again, my stepfather swore he would stop, and again we went back after a few weeks. I stopped talking for a while, and I have only vague memories of the next two years.

My stepfather worked as a route salesman, my mama as a waitress, laundry worker, cook, or fruit packer. I could never understand, since they both worked so hard and such long hours, how we never had enough money, but it was also true of my mama's brothers and sisters who worked hard in the mills or the furnace industry. In fact, my parents did better than anyone else in the family. But eventually my stepfather was fired and we hit bottom—nightmarish months of marshals at the door, repossessed furniture, and rubber checks. My parents worked out a scheme so that it appeared my stepfather had abandoned us, but instead he went down to Florida, got a new job, and rented us a house. He returned with a U-Haul trailer in the dead of night, packed us up, and moved us south.

The night we left South Carolina for Florida, my mama leaned over the backseat of her old Pontiac and promised us girls, "It'll be better there." I don't know if we believed her, but I remember crossing Georgia in the early morning, watching the red clay hills and swaying grey blankets of moss recede through the back window. I kept looking at the trailer behind us, ridiculously small to contain everything we owned. Mama had packed nothing that wasn't fully paid off, which meant she had only two things of worth: her washing and sewing machines, both of them tied securely to the trailer walls. Throughout the trip I fantasized an accident that would burst that trailer, scattering old clothes and cracked dishes on the tarmac.

I was only thirteen. I wanted us to start over completely, to begin again as new people with nothing of the past left over. I wanted to run away from who we had been seen to be, who we had been. That desire is one I have seen in other members of my family. It is the first thing I think of when trouble comes—the geographic solution. Change your name, leave town, disappear, make yourself over. What hides behind that impulse is the conviction that the life you have lived, the person you are, is valueless, better off abandoned, that running away is easier than trying to change things, that change itself is not possible. Sometimes I think it is this conviction—more seductive than alcohol or violence, more subtle than sexual hatred or gender injustice—that has dominated my life and made real change so painful and difficult.

Moving to Central Florida did not fix our lives. It did not stop my stepfather's violence, heal my shame, or make my mother happy. Once there, our lives became controlled by my mother's illness and medical bills. She had a hysterectomy when I was about eight and endured a series of hospitalizations for ulcers and a chronic back problem. Through most of my adolescence she superstitiously refused to allow anyone to mention the word *cancer*. When she was not sick, Mama and my stepfather went on working, struggling to pay off what seemed an insurmountable load of debts.

By the time I was fourteen, my sisters and I had found ways to discourage most of our stepfather's sexual advances. We were not close, but we united against him. Our efforts were helped along when he was referred to a psychotherapist after he lost his temper at work, and was prescribed drugs that made him sullen but less violent. We were growing up quickly, my sisters moving toward dropping out of school while I got good grades and took every scholarship exam I could find. I was the first person in my family to graduate from high school, and the fact that I went on to college was nothing short of astonishing.

We all imagine our lives are normal, and I did not know my life was not everyone's. It was in Central Florida that I began to realize just how different we were. The people we met there had not been shaped by the rigid class structure that dominated the South Carolina Piedmont. The first time I looked around my junior high classroom and realized I did not know who those people were—not only as individuals but as categories, who their people were and how they saw themselves—I also realized that they did not know me. In Greenville, everyone knew my family, knew we were trash, and that meant we were supposed to be poor, supposed to have grim low-paid jobs, have babies in our teens, and never finish school. But Central Florida in the 1960s was full of runaways and immigrants, and our mostly white working-class suburban school sorted us out not by income and family background but by intelligence and aptitude tests. Suddenly I was boosted into the college-bound track, and while there was plenty of contempt for my inept social skills, pitiful wardrobe, and slow drawling accent, there was also something I had never experienced before: a protective anonymity, and a kind of grudging respect and curiosity about who I might become. Because they did not see poverty and hopelessness as a foregone conclusion for my life, I could begin to imagine other futures for myself.

In that new country, we were unknown. The myth of the poor settled over us and glamorized us. I saw it in the eyes of my teachers, the Lion's Club representative who paid for my new glasses, and the lady from the Junior League who told me about the scholarship I had won. Better, far better, to be one of the mythical poor than to be part of the *they* I had known before. I also experienced a new level of fear, a fear of losing what had never before been imaginable. Don't let me lose this chance, I prayed, and lived in terror that I might suddenly be seen again as what I knew myself to be. . . .

I am trying to understand how we internalize the myths of our society even as we resist them. I have felt a powerful temptation to write about my family as a kind of morality tale, with us as the heroes and middle and upper classes as the villains. It would be within the romantic myth, for example, to pretend that we were the kind of noble

Southern whites portrayed in the movies, mill workers for generations until driven out by alcoholism and a family propensity for rebellion and union talk. But that would be a lie. The truth is that no one in my family ever joined a union. . . .

Taken to its limits, the myth of the poor would make my family over into union organizers or people broken by the failure of the unions. As far as my family was concerned union organizers, like preachers, were of a different class, suspect and hated however much they might be admired for what they were supposed to be trying to achieve. Nominally Southern Baptist, no one in my family actually paid much attention to preachers, and only little children went to Sunday school. Serious belief in anything—any political ideology, any religious system, or any theory of life's meaning and purpose—was seen as unrealistic. It was an attitude that bothered me a lot when I started reading the socially conscious novels I found in the paperback racks when I was eleven or so. I particularly loved Sinclair Lewis's novels and wanted to imagine my own family as part of the working man's struggle.

"We were not joiners," my aunt Dot told me with a grin when I asked her about the union. My cousin Butch laughed at that, told me the union charged dues, and said, "Hell, we can't even be persuaded to toss money in the collection plate. An't gonna give it to no union man." It shamed me that the only thing my family wholeheartedly believed in was luck and the waywardness of fate. They held the dogged conviction that the admirable and wise thing to do was keep a sense of humor, never whine or cower, and trust that luck might someday turn as good as it had been bad—and with just as much reason. Becoming a political activist with an almost religious fervor was the thing I did that most outraged my family and the Southern working-class community they were part of.

Similarly, it was not my sexuality, my lesbianism, that my family saw as most rebellious; for most of my life, no one but my mama took my sexual preference very seriously. It was the way I thought about work, ambition, and self-respect. They were waitresses, laundry workers, counter girls. I was the one who went to work as a maid, something I never told any of them. They would have been angry if they had known. Work was just

work for them, necessary. You did what you had to do to survive. They did not so much believe in taking pride in doing your job as in stubbornly enduring hard work and hard times. At the same time, they held that there were some forms of work, including maid's work, that were only for Black people, not white, and while I did not share that belief, I knew how intrinsic it was to the way my family saw the world. Sometimes I felt as if I straddled cultures and belonged on neither side. I would grind my teeth at what I knew was my family's unquestioning racism while continuing to respect their pragmatic endurance. But more and more as I grew older, what I felt was a deep estrangement from their view of the world, and gradually a sense of shame that would have been completely incomprehensible to them.

"Long as there's lunch counters, you can always find work," I was told by my mother and my aunts. Then they'd add, "I can get me a little extra with a smile." It was obvious there was supposed to be nothing shameful about it, that needy smile across a lunch counter, that rueful grin when you didn't have rent, or the half-provocative, half-pleading way my mama could cajole the man at the store to give her a little credit. But I hated it, hated the need for it and the shame that would follow every time I did it myself. It was begging, as far as I was concerned, a quasi-prostitution that I despised even while I continued to rely on it. After all, I needed the money.

"Just use that smile," my girl cousins used to joke, and I hated what I knew they meant. After college, when I began to support myself and study feminist theory, I became more contemptuous rather than more understanding of the women in my family. I told myself that prostitution is a skilled profession and my cousins were never more than amateurs. There was a certain truth in this, though like all cruel judgments rendered from the outside, it ignored the conditions that made it true. The women in my family, my mother included, had sugar daddies, not johns, men who slipped them money because they needed it so badly. From their point of view they were nice to those men because the men were nice to them, and it was never so direct or crass an arrangement that they would set a price on their favors. Nor would they have described what they did as prostitution. Nothing made them angrier than the suggestion that the men who helped them out did it just for their favors. They worked for a living, they swore, but this was different. . . .

It is only as the child of my class and my unique family background that I have been able to put together what is for me a meaningful politics, to regain a sense of why I believe in activism, why self-revelation is so important for lesbians. There is no all-purpose feminist analysis that explains the complicated ways our sexuality and core identity are shaped, the way we see ourselves as parts of both our birth families and the extended family of friends and lovers we invariably create within the lesbian community. For me, the bottom line has simply become the need to resist that omnipresent fear, that urge to hide and disappear, to disguise my life, my desires, and the truth about how little any of us understand—even as we try to make the world a more just and human place. Most of all, I have tried to understand the politics of *they*, why human beings fear and stigmatize the different while secretly dreading that they might be one of the different themselves. Class, race, sexuality, gender—and all the other categories by which we categorize and dismiss each other—need to be excavated from the inside.

The horror of class stratification, racism, and prejudice is that some people begin to believe that the security of their families and communities depends on the oppression of others, that for some to have good lives there must be others whose lives are truncated and brutal. It is a belief that dominates this culture. It is what makes the poor whites of the South so determinedly racist and the middle class so contemptuous of the poor. It is a myth that allows some to imagine that they build their lives on the ruin of others, a secret core of shame for the middle class, a goad and a spur to the marginal working class, and cause enough for the homeless and poor to feel no constraints on hatred or violence. The power of the myth is made even more apparent when we examine how, within the lesbian and feminist communities where we have addressed considerable attention to the politics of marginalization, there is still so much exclusion and fear, so many of us who do not feel safe.

I grew up poor, hated, the victim of physical, emotional, and sexual violence, and I know that suffering does not ennoble. It destroys. To resist destruction, self-hatred, or lifelong hopelessness, we have to throw off the conditioning of being despised, the fear of becoming the *they* that is talked about so dismissively, to refuse lying myths and easy moralities, to see ourselves as human, flawed, and extraordinary. All of us—extraordinary.

Note

1. *A Few Words in the Mother Tongue: Poems, Selected and New* (Eighth Mountain Press: Portland, Oregon, 1990).

Where I Come from Is Like This
Paula Gunn Allen

Paula Gunn Allen is professor of English at UCLA. She is an accomplished poet, writer, and scholar who is of Laguna Pueblo and Sioux heritage. Her books include *Grandmothers of the Light: A Medicine Woman's Sourcebook* and *The Sacred Hoop: Recovering the Feminine in American Indian Traditions*.

I

Modern American Indian women, like their non-Indian sisters, are deeply engaged in the struggle to redefine themselves. In their struggle they must

reconcile traditional tribal definitions of women with industrial and postindustrial non-Indian definitions. Yet while these definitions seem to be more or less mutually exclusive, Indian women must somehow harmonize and integrate both in their own lives.

An American Indian woman is primarily defined by her tribal identity. In her eyes, her destiny is necessarily that of her people, and her sense of herself as a woman is first and foremost prescribed by her tribe. The definitions of woman's roles are as diverse as tribal cultures in the Americas. In some she is devalued, in others she wields considerable power. In some she is a familial/clan adjunct, in some she is as close to autonomous as her economic circumstances and psychological traits permit. But in no tribal definitions is she perceived in the same way as are women in western industrial and postindustrial cultures.

In the west, few images of women form part of the cultural mythos, and these are largely sexually charged. Among Christians, the madonna is the female prototype, and she is portrayed as essentially passive: her contribution is simply that of birthing. Little else is attributed to her and she certainly possesses few of the characteristics that are attributed to mythic figures among Indian tribes. This image is countered (rather than balanced) by the witch-goddess/whore characteristics designed to reinforce cultural beliefs about women, as well as western adversarial and dualistic perceptions of reality.

The tribes see women variously, but they do not question the power of femininity. Sometimes they see women as fearful, sometimes peaceful, sometimes omnipotent and omniscient, but they never portray women as mindless, helpless, simple, or oppressed. And while the women in a given tribe, clan, or band may be all these things, the individual woman is provided with a variety of images of women from the interconnected supernatural, natural, and social worlds she lives in.

As a half-breed American Indian woman, I cast about in my mind for negative images of Indian women, and I find none that are directed to Indian women alone. The negative images I do have are of Indians in general and in fact are more often of males than of females. All these images come to me from non-Indian sources, and they are always balanced by a positive image. My ideas of womanhood, passed on largely by my mother and grandmothers, Laguna Pueblo women, are about practicality, strength, reasonableness, intelligence, wit, and competence. I also remember vividly the women who came to my father's store, the women who held me and sang to me, the women at Feast Day, at Grab Days, the women in the kitchen of my Cubero home, the women I grew up with; none

of them appeared weak or helpless, none of them presented herself tentatively. I remember a certain reserve on those lovely brown faces; I remember the direct gaze of eyes framed by bright-colored shawls draped over their heads and cascading down their backs. I remember the clean cotton dresses and carefully pressed hand-embroidered aprons they always wore; I remember laughter and good food, especially the sweet bread and the oven bread they gave us. Nowhere in my mind is there a foolish woman, a dumb woman, a vain woman, or a plastic woman, though the Indian women I have known have shown a wide range of personal style and demeanor.

My memory includes the Navajo woman who was badly beaten by her Sioux husband; but I also remember that my grandmother abandoned her Sioux husband long ago. I recall the stories about the Laguna woman beaten regularly by her husband in the presence of her children so that the children would not believe in the strength and power of femininity. And I remember the women who drank, who got into fights with other women and with the men, and who often won those battles. I have memories of tired women, partying women, stubborn women, sullen women, amicable women, selfish women, shy women, and aggressive women. Most of all I remember the women who laugh and scold and sit uncomplaining in the long sun on feast days and who cook wonderful food on wood stoves, in beehive mud ovens, and over open fires outdoors.

Among the images of women that come to me from various tribes as well as my own are White Buffalo Woman, who came to the Lakota long ago and brought them the religion of the Sacred Pipe which they still practice; Tinotzin the goddess who came to Juan Diego to remind him that she still walked the hills of her people and sent him with her message, her demand and her proof to the Catholic bishop in the city nearby. And from Laguna I take the images of Yellow Woman, Coyote Woman, Grandmother Spider (Spider Old Woman), who brought the light, who gave us weaving and medicine, who gave us life. Among the Keres she is known as Thought Woman who created us all and who keeps us in creation even now. I remember Iyatiku, Earth Woman, Corn Woman, who guides and counsels the people to peace and who welcomes us home when we cast off this coil of flesh as huskers cast off the leaves that wrap the corn. I remember Iyatiku's sister, Sun Woman, who held metals and cattle, pigs and sheep, highways and engines and so many things in her bundle, who went away to the east saying that one day she would return.

II

Since the coming of the Anglo-Europeans beginning in the fifteenth century, the fragile web of identity that long held tribal people secure has gradually been weakened and torn. But the oral tradition has prevented the complete destruction of the web, the ultimate disruption of tribal ways. The oral tradition is vital; it heals itself and the tribal web by adapting to the flow of the present while never relinquishing its connection to the past. Its adaptability has always been required, as many generations have experienced. Certainly the modern American Indian woman bears slight resemblance to her forebears—at least on superficial examination—but she is still a tribal woman in her deepest being. Her tribal sense of relationship to all that is continues to flourish. And though she is at times beset by her knowledge of the enormous gap between the life she lives and the life she was raised to live, and while she adapts her mind and being to the circumstances of her present life, she does so in tribal ways, mending the tears in the web of being from which she takes her existence as she goes.

My mother told me stories all the time, though I often did not recognize them as that. My mother told me stories about cooking and childbearing; she told me stories about menstruation and pregnancy; she told me stories about gods and heroes, about fairies and elves, about goddesses and spirits; she told me stories about the land and the sky, about cats and dogs, about snakes and spiders; she told me stories about climbing trees and exploring the mesas; she told me stories about going to dances and getting married; she told me stories about dressing and undressing, about sleeping and waking; she told me stories about herself, about her mother, about her grandmother. She told me stories about grieving and laughing, about thinking and doing; she told me stories about school and about people; about darning and mending; she told me stories about turquoise and about gold;

she told me European stories and Laguna stories; she told me Catholic stories and Presbyterian stories; she told me city stories and country stories; she told me political stories and religious stories. She told me stories about living and stories about dying. And in all of those stories she told me who I was, who I was supposed to be, whom I came from, and who would follow me. In this way she taught me the meaning of the words she said, that all life is a circle and everything has a place within it. That's what she said and what she showed me in the things she did and the way she lives.

Of course, through my formal, white, Christian education, I discovered that other people had stories of their own—about women, about Indians, about fact, about reality—and I was amazed by a number of startling suppositions that others made about tribal customs and beliefs. According to the un-Indian, non-Indian view, for instance, Indians barred menstruating women from ceremonies and indeed segregated them from the rest of the people, consigning them to some space specially designed for them. This showed that Indians considered menstruating women unclean and not fit to enjoy the company of decent (nonmenstruating) people, that is, men. I was surprised and confused to hear this because my mother had taught me that white people had strange attitudes toward menstruation: they thought something was bad about it, that it meant you were sick, cursed, sinful, and weak and that you had to be very careful during that time. She taught me that menstruation was a normal occurrence, that I could go swimming or hiking or whatever else I wanted to do during my period. She actively scorned women who took to their beds, who were incapacitated by cramps, who "got the blues."

As I struggled to reconcile these very contradictory interpretations of American Indians' traditional beliefs concerning menstruation, I realized that the menstrual taboos were about power, not about sin or filth. My conclusion was later borne out by some tribes' own explanations, which, as you may well imagine, came as quite a relief to me.

The truth of the matter as many Indians see it is that women who are at the peak of their fecundity are believed to possess power that throws male power totally out of kilter. They emit such force that, in their presence, any male-owned or -dominated ritual or sacred object cannot do its usual task. For instance, the Lakota say that a menstruating woman anywhere near a yuwipi man, who is a special sort of psychic, spirit-empowered healer, for a day or so before he is to do his ceremony will effectively disempower him. Conversely, among many if not most tribes, important ceremonies cannot be held without the presence of women. Sometimes the ritual woman who empowers the ceremony must be unmarried and virginal so that the power she channels is unalloyed, unweakened by sexual arousal and penetration by a male. Other ceremonies require tumescent women, others the presence of mature women who have borne children, and still others depend for empowerment on postmenopausal women. Women may be segregated from the company of the whole band or village on certain occasions, but on certain occasions men are also segregated. In short, each ritual depends on a certain balance of power, and the positions of women within the phases of womanhood are used by tribal people to empower certain rites. This does not derive from a male-dominant view; it is not a ritual observance imposed on women by men. It derives from a tribal view of reality that distinguishes tribal people from feudal and industrial people.

Among the tribes, the occult power of women, inextricably bound to our hormonal life, is thought to be very great; many hold that we possess innately the blood-given power to kill—with a glance, with a step, or with a judicious mixing of menstrual blood into somebody's soup. Medicine women among the Pomo of California cannot practice until they are sufficiently mature; when they are immature, their power is diffuse and is likely to interfere with their practice until time and experience have it under control. So women of the tribes are not especially inclined to see themselves as poor helpless victims of male domination. Even in those tribes where something akin to male domination was present, women are perceived as powerful, socially, physically, and metaphysically. In times past, as in times present, women carried enormous burdens with aplomb. We were far indeed from the "weaker sex," the designation that white aristocratic sisters unhappily earned for us all.

I remember my mother moving furniture all over the house when she wanted it changed. She didn't wait for my father to come home and help—she just went ahead and moved the piano, a huge upright from the old days, the couch, the refrigerator. Nobody had told her she was too weak to do such things. In imitation of her, I would delight in loading trucks at my father's store with cases of pop or fifty-pound sacks of flour. Even when I was quite small I could do it, and it gave me a belief in my own physical strength that advancing middle age can't quite erase. My mother used to tell me about the Acoma Pueblo women she had seen as a child carrying hugh ollas (water pots) on their heads as they wound their way up the tortuous stairwell carved into the face of the "Sky City" mesa, a feat I tried to imitate with books and tin buckets. ("Sky City" is the term used by the Chamber of Commerce for the mother village of Acoma, which is situated atop a high sandstone table mountain.) I was never very successful, but even the attempt reminded me that I was supposed to be strong and balanced to be a proper girl.

Of course, my mother's Laguna people are Keres Indian, reputed to be the last extreme mother-right people on earth. So it is no wonder that I got notably nonwhite notions about the natural strength and prowess of women. Indeed, it is only when I am trying to get non-Indian approval, recognition, or acknowledgment that my "weak sister" emotional and intellectual ploys get the better of my tribal woman's good sense. At such times I forget that I just moved the piano or just wrote a competent paper or just completed a financial transaction satisfactorily or have supported myself and my children for most of my adult life.

Nor is my contradictory behavior atypical. Most Indian women I know are in the same bicultural bind: we vacillate between being dependent and strong, self-reliant and powerless, strongly motivated and hopelessly insecure. We resolve the dilemma in various ways: some of us party all of the time; some of us drink to excess; some of us travel and move around a lot; some of us land good jobs and then quit them; some of us engage in violent exchanges; some of us blow our brains out. We act in these destructive ways because we suffer from the societal conflicts caused by having to identify with two hopelessly opposed cultural definitions of women. Through this destructive dissonance we are unhappy prey to the self-disparagement common to, indeed demanded of, Indians living in the United States today. Our situation is caused by the exigencies of a history of invasion, conquest, and colonization whose searing marks are probably ineradicable. A popular bumper sticker on many Indian cars proclaims: "If You're Indian You're In," to which I always find myself adding under my breath, "Trouble."

III

No Indian can grow to any age without being informed that her people were "savages" who interfered with the march of progress pursued by respectable, loving, civilized white people. We are the villains of the scenario when we are mentioned at all. We are absent from much of white history except when we are calmly, rationally, succinctly, and systematically dehumanized. On the few occasions we are noticed in any way other than as howling, bloodthirsty beings, we are acclaimed for our noble quaintness. In this definition, we are exotic curios. Our ancient arts and customs are used to draw tourist money to state coffers, into the pocketbooks and bank accounts of scholars, and into support of the American-in-Disneyland promoters' dream.

As a Roman Catholic child I was treated to bloody tales of how the savage Indians martyred the hapless priests and missionaries who went among them in an attempt to lead them to the one true path. By the time I was through high school I had the idea that Indians were people who had benefited mightily from the advanced knowledge and superior morality of the Anglo-Europeans. At least I had, perforce, that idea to lay beside the other one that derived from my daily experience of Indian life, an idea less dehumanizing and more accurate because it came from my mother and the other Indian people who raised me. That idea was that Indians are a people who don't tell lies, who care for their children and their old people. You never see an Indian orphan, they said. You always know when you're old that someone will take care of you—one of your children will. Then they'd list the old folks who were being taken care of by this child or that. No child is ever considered illegitimate among the Indians, they said. If a girl gets pregnant, the baby is still part of the family, and the mother is too. That's what they said, and they showed me real people who lived according to those principles.

Of course the ravages of colonization have taken their toll; there are orphans in Indian country now, and abandoned, brutalized old folks; there are even illegitimate children, though the very concept still strikes me as absurd. There are battered children and neglected children, and there are battered wives and women who have been raped by Indian men. Proximity to the "civilizing" effects of white Christians has not improved the moral quality of life in Indian country, though each group, Indian and white, explains the situation differently. Nor is there much yet in the oral tradition that can enable us to adapt to these inhuman changes. But a force is growing in that direction, and it is helping Indian women reclaim their lives. Their power, their sense of direction and of self will soon be visible. It is the force of the women who speak and work and write, and it is formidable.

Through all the centuries of war and death and cultural and psychic destruction have endured the women who raise the children and tend the fires, who pass along the tales and the traditions, who weep and bury the dead, who are the dead, and who never forget. There are always the women, who make pots and weave baskets, who fashion clothes and cheer their children on at powwow, who make fry bread and piki bread, and corn soup and chili stew, who dance and sing and remember and hold within their hearts the dream of their ancient peoples—that one day the woman who thinks will speak to us again, and everywhere there will be peace. Meanwhile we tell the stories and write the books and trade tales of anger and woe and stories of fun and scandal and laugh over all manner of things that happen every day. We watch and we wait.

My great-grandmother told my mother: Never forget you are Indian. And my mother told me the same thing. This, then, is how I have gone about remembering, so that my children will remember too.

2.

White Privilege and Male Privilege:

A Personal Account of Coming to See Correspondences Through Work in Women's Studies

Peggy McIntosh

Peggy McIntosh is associate director of the Wellesley College Center for Research on Women. She is founder and co-director of the National SEED Project on Inclusive Curriculum. She has written many articles on women's studies, curriculum change, and systems of unearned privilege. In this famous essay, McIntosh argues that white men and white women are advantaged by numerous unacknowledged "white-skin" privileges. She explains that "white privilege is like an invisible weightless knapsack of special provisions, assurances, tools, maps, guides, codebooks, passports, visas, clothes, compass, emergency gear, and blank checks." McIntosh presents a partial list of her own white-skin privileges after reflecting upon her own experiences and observations.

Through work to bring materials and perspectives from Women's Studies into the rest of the curriculum, I have often noticed men's unwillingness to grant that they are overprivileged in the curriculum, even though they may grant that women are disadvantaged. Denials that amount to taboos surround the subject of advantages that men gain from women's disadvantages. These denials protect male privilege from being fully recognized, acknowledged, lessened, or ended.

Thinking through unacknowledged male privilege as a phenomenon with a life of its own, I realized that since hierarchies in our society are interlocking, there was most likely a phenomenon of white privilege that was similarly denied and protected, but alive and real in its effects. As a white person, I realized I had been taught about racism as something that puts others at a disadvantage, but had been taught not to see one of its corollary aspects, white privilege, which puts me at an advantage.

I think whites are carefully taught not to recognize white privilege, as males are taught not to recognize male privilege. So I have begun in an untutored way to ask what it is like to have white privilege. This paper is a partial record of my personal observations and not a scholarly analysis. It is based on my daily experiences within my particular circumstances.

I have come to see white privilege as an invisible package of unearned assets that I can count on cashing in each day, but about which I was "meant" to remain oblivious. White privilege is like an invisible weightless knapsack of special provisions, assurances, tools, maps, guides, codebooks, passports, visas, clothes, compass, emergency gear, and blank checks.

Since I have had trouble facing white privilege, and describing its results in my life, I saw parallels here with men's reluctance to acknowledge male privilege. Only rarely will a man go beyond acknowledging that women are disadvantaged to acknowledging that men have unearned advantage, or that unearned privilege has not been good for men's development as human beings, or for society's development, or that privilege systems might ever be challenged and *changed*.

I will review here several types or layers of denial that I see at work protecting, and preventing awareness about, entrenched male privilege. Then I will draw parallels, from my own experience, with the denials that veil the facts of white privilege. Finally, I will list forty-six ordinary and daily ways in which I experience having white privilege, by contrast with my African American colleagues in the same building. This list is not intended to be generalizable. Others can make their own lists from within their own life circumstances.

Writing this paper has been difficult, despite warm receptions for the talks on which it is based.[1] For describing white privilege makes one newly accountable. As we in Women's Studies work to reveal male privilege and ask men to give up some of their power, so one who writes about having white privilege must ask, "Having described it, what will I do to lessen or end it?"

The denial of men's overprivileged state takes many forms in discussions of curriculum change work. Some claim that men must be central in the curriculum because they have done most of what is important or distinctive in life or in civilization. Some recognize sexism in the curriculum but deny that it makes male students seem unduly important in life. Others agree that certain *individual* thinkers are male oriented but deny that there is any *systemic* tendency in disciplinary frameworks or epistemology to overempower men as a group. Those men who do grant that male privilege takes institutionalized and embedded forms are still likely to deny that male hegemony has opened doors for them personally. Virtually all men deny that male overreward alone can explain men's centrality in all the inner sanctums of our most powerful institutions. Moreover, those few who will acknowledge that male privilege systems have overempowered them usually end up doubting that we could dismantle these privilege systems. They may say they will work to improve women's status, in the society or in the university, but they can't or won't support the idea of lessening men's. In curricular terms, this is the point at which they say that they regret they cannot use any of the interesting new scholarship on women because the syllabus is full. When the talk turns to giving men less cultural room, even the most thoughtful and fair-minded of the men I know will tend to reflect, or fall back on, con-

servative assumptions about the inevitability of present gender relations and distributions of power, calling on precedent or sociobiology and psychobiology to demonstrate that male domination is natural and follows inevitably from evolutionary pressures. Others resort to arguments from "experience" or religion or social responsibility or wishing and dreaming.

After I realized, through faculty development work in Women's Studies, the extent to which men work from a base of unacknowledged privilege, I understood that much of their oppressiveness was unconscious. Then I remembered the frequent charges from women of color that white women whom they encounter are oppressive. I began to understand why we are justly seen as oppressive, even when we don't see ourselves that way. At the very least, obliviousness of one's privileged state can make a person or group irritating to be with. I began to count the ways in which I enjoy unearned skin privilege and have been conditioned into oblivion about its existence, unable to see that it put me "ahead" in any way, or put my people ahead, overrewarding us and yet also paradoxically damaging us, or that it could or should be changed.

My schooling gave me no training in seeing myself as an oppressor, as an unfairly advantaged person, or as a participant in a damaged culture. I was taught to see myself as an individual whose moral state depended on her individual moral will. At school, we were not taught about slavery in any depth; we were not taught to see slaveholders as damaged people. Slaves were seen as the only group at risk of being dehumanized. My schooling followed the pattern which Elizabeth Minnich has pointed out: whites are taught to think of their lives as morally neutral, normative, and average, and also ideal, so that when we work to benefit others, this is seen as work that will allow "them" to be more like "us." I think many of us know how obnoxious this attitude can be in men.

After frustration with men who would not recognize male privilege, I decided to try to work on myself at least by identifying some of the daily effects of white privilege in my life. It is crude work, at this stage, but I will give here a list of special circumstances and conditions I experience that I did not earn but that I have been made to feel are mine by birth, by citizenship, and by virtue of being a conscientious law-abiding "normal" person of goodwill. I have chosen those conditions that I think in my case *attach somewhat more to skin-color privilege* than to class, religion, ethnic status, or geographical location, though these other privileging factors are intricately intertwined. As far as I can see, my Afro-American co-workers, friends, and acquaintances with whom I come into daily or frequent contact in this particular time, place, and line of work cannot count on most of these conditions.

1. I can, if I wish, arrange to be in the company of people of my race most of the time.

2. I can avoid spending time with people whom I was trained to mistrust and who have learned to mistrust my kind or me.

3. If I should need to move, I can be pretty sure of renting or purchasing housing in an area which I can afford and in which I would want to live.

4. I can be reasonably sure that my neighbors in such a location will be neutral or pleasant to me.

5. I can go shopping alone most of the time, fairly well assured that I will not be followed or harassed by store detectives.

6. I can turn on the television or open to the front page of the paper and see people of my race widely and positively represented.

7. When I am told about our national heritage or about "civilization," I am shown that people of my color made it what it is.

8. I can be sure that my children will be given curricular materials that testify to the existence of their race.

9. If I want to, I can be pretty sure of finding a publisher for this piece on white privilege.

10. I can be fairly sure of having my voice heard in a group in which I am the only member of my race.

11. I can be casual about whether or not to listen to another woman's voice in a group in which she is the only member of her race.

12. I can go into a book shop and count on finding the writing of my race represented, into a supermarket and find the staple foods that fit with my cultural traditions, into a hairdresser's shop and find someone who can deal with my hair.

13. Whether I use checks, credit cards, or cash, I can count on my skin color not to work against the appearance that I am financially reliable.

14. I could arrange to protect our young children most of the time from people who might not like them.

15. I did not have to educate our children to be aware of systemic racism for their own daily physical protection.

16. I can be pretty sure that my children's teachers and employers will tolerate them if they fit school and workplace norms; my chief worries about them do not concern others' attitudes toward their race.

17. I can talk with my mouth full and not have people put this down to my color.

18. I can swear, or dress in secondhand clothes, or not answer letters, without having people attribute these choices to the bad morals, the poverty, or the illiteracy of my race.

19. I can speak in public to a powerful male group without putting my race on trial.

20. I can do well in a challenging situation without being called a credit to my race.

21. I am never asked to speak for all the people of my racial group.

22. I can remain oblivious to the language and customs of persons of color who constitute the world's majority without feeling in my culture any penalty for such oblivion.

23. I can criticize our government and talk about how much I fear its policies and behavior without being seen as a cultural outsider.

24. I can be reasonably sure that if I ask to talk to "the person in charge," I will be facing a person of my race.

25. If a traffic cop pulls me over or if the IRS audits my tax return, I can be sure I haven't been singled out because of my race.

26. I can easily buy posters, postcards, picture books, greeting cards, dolls, toys, and children's magazines featuring people of my race.

27. I can go home from most meetings of organizations I belong to feeling somewhat tied in, rather than isolated, out of place, outnumbered, unheard, held at a distance, or feared.

28. I can be pretty sure that an argument with a colleague of another race is more likely to jeopardize her chances for advancement than to jeopardize mine.

29. I can be fairly sure that if I argue for the promotion of a person of another race, or a program centering on race, this is not likely to cost me heavily within my present setting, even if my colleagues disagree with me.

30. If I declare there is a racial issue at hand, or there isn't a racial issue at hand, my race will lend me more credibility for either position than a person of color will have.

31. I can choose to ignore developments in minority writing and minority activist programs, or disparage them, or learn from them, but in any case, I can find ways to be more or less protected from negative consequences of any of these choices.

32. My culture gives me little fear about ignoring the perspectives and powers of people of other races.

33. I am not made acutely aware that my shape, bearing, or body odor will be taken as a reflection on my race.

34. I can worry about racism without being seen as self-interested or self-seeking.

35. I can take a job with an affirmative action employer without having my co-workers on the job suspect that I got it because of my race.

36. If my day, week, or year is going badly, I need not ask of each negative episode or situation whether it has racial overtones.

37. I can be pretty sure of finding people who would be willing to talk with me and advise me about my next steps, professionally.

38. I can think over many options, social, political, imaginative, or professional, without asking whether a person of my race would be accepted or allowed to do what I want to do.

39. I can be late to a meeting without having the lateness reflect on my race.

40. I can choose public accommodation without fearing that people of my race cannot get in or will be mistreated in the places I have chosen.

41. I can be sure that if I need legal or medical help, my race will not work against me.

42. I can arrange my activities so that I will never have to experience feelings of rejection owing to my race.

43. If I have low credibility as a leader, I can be sure that my race is not the problem.

44. I can easily find academic courses and institutions that give attention only to people of my race.

45. I can expect figurative language and imagery in all of the arts to testify to experiences of my race.

46. I can choose blemish cover or bandages in "flesh" color and have them more or less match my skin.

I repeatedly forgot each of the realizations on this list until I wrote it down. For me, white privilege has turned out to be an elusive and fugitive subject. The pressure to avoid it is great, for in facing it I must give up the myth of meritocracy. If these things are true, this is not such a free country; one's life is not what one makes of it; many doors open for certain people through no virtues of their own. These perceptions mean also that my moral condition is not what I had been led to believe. The appearance of being a good citizen rather than a troublemaker comes in large part from having all sorts of doors open automatically because of my color.

A further paralysis of nerve comes from literary silence protecting privilege. My clearest memories of finding such analysis are in Lillian Smith's unparalleled *Killers of the Dream* and Margaret Andersen's review of Karen and Mamie Fields' *Lemon Swamp*. Smith, for example, wrote about walking toward black children on the street and knowing they would step into the gutter; Andersen contrasted the pleasure that she, as a white child, took on summer driving trips to the south with Karen Fields' memories of driving in a closed car stocked with all necessities lest, in stopping, her black family should suffer "insult, or worse." Adrienne Rich also recognizes and writes about daily experiences of privilege, but in my observation, white women's writing in this area is far more often on systemic racism than on our daily lives as light-skinned women.[2]

In unpacking this invisible knapsack of white privilege, I have listed conditions of daily experience that I once took for granted, as neutral, normal, and universally available to everybody, just as I once thought of a male-focused curriculum as the neutral or accurate account that can speak for all. Nor did I think of any of these perquisites as bad for the holder. I now think that we need a more finely differentiated taxonomy of privilege, for some of these varieties are only what one would want for everyone in a just society, and others give license to be ignorant, oblivious, arrogant, and destructive.

Before proposing some more finely tuned categorization, I will make some observations about the general effects of these conditions on my life and expectations.

In this potpourri of examples, some privileges make me feel at home in the world. Others allow me to escape penalties or dangers that others suffer. Through some, I escape fear, anxiety, insult, injury, or a sense of not being welcome, not being real. Some keep me from having to hide, to be in disguise, to feel sick or crazy, to negotiate each transaction from the position of being an outsider or, within my group, a person who is suspected of having too close links with a dominant culture. Most keep me from having to be angry.

I see a pattern running through the matrix of white privilege, a pattern of assumptions that were passed on to me as a white person. There was one main piece of cultural turf; it was my own turf, and I was among those who could control the turf. I could measure up to the cultural standards and take advantage of the many options I saw around me to make what the culture would call a success of my life. *My skin color was an asset for any move I was educated to want to make.* I could think of myself as "belonging" in major ways and of making social systems work for me. I could freely disparage, fear, neglect, or be oblivious to anything outside of the dominant cultural forms. Being of the main culture, I could also criticize it fairly freely. My life was reflected back to me frequently enough so that I felt, with regard to my race, if not to my sex, like one of the real people.

Whether through the curriculum or in the newspaper, the television, the economic system, or the general look of people in the streets, I received daily signals and indications that my people counted and that others *either didn't exist or must be trying, not very successfully, to be like people of my race.* I was given cultural permission not to hear voices of people of other races or a tepid cultural tolerance for hearing or acting on such voices. I was also raised not to suffer seriously from anything that darker-skinned people might say about my group, "protected," though perhaps I should more accurately say *prohibited*, through the habits of my economic class and social group, from living in racially mixed groups or being reflective about interactions between people of differing races.

In proportion as my racial group was being made confident, comfortable, and oblivious, other groups were likely being made unconfident, uncomfortable, and alienated. Whiteness protected me from many kinds of hostility, distress, and violence, which I was being subtly trained to visit in turn upon people of color.

For this reason, the word "privilege" now seems to me misleading. Its connotations are too positive to fit the conditions and behaviors which "privilege systems" produce. We usually think of privilege as being a favored state, whether earned, or conferred by birth or luck. School graduates are reminded they are privileged and urged to use their (enviable) assets well. The word "privilege" carries the connotation of being something everyone must want. Yet some of the conditions I have described here work to systemically overempower certain groups. Such privilege simply *confers dominance*, gives permission to control, because of one's race or sex. The kind of privilege that gives license to some people to be, at best, thoughtless and, at worst, murderous should not continue to be referred to as a desirable attribute. Such "privilege" may be widely desired without being in any way beneficial to the whole society.

Moreover, though "privilege" may confer power, it does not confer moral strength. Those who do not depend on conferred dominance have traits and qualities that may never develop in those who do. Just as Women's Studies courses indicate that women survive their political circumstances to lead lives that hold the human race together, so "underprivileged" people of color who are the world's majority have survived their oppression and lived survivors' lives from which the white global minority can and must learn. In some groups, those dominated have actually become strong through *not* having all of these unearned advantages, and this gives them a great deal to teach the others. Members of so-called privileged groups can seem foolish, ridiculous, infantile, or dangerous by contrast.

I want, then, to distinguish between earned strength and unearned power conferred systemically. Power from unearned privilege can look like strength when it is, in fact, permission to escape or to dominate. But not all of the privileges on my list are inevitably damaging. Some, like the expectation that neighbors will be decent to you, or that your race will not count against you in court, should be the norm in a just society and should be considered as the entitlement of everyone. Others, like the privilege not to listen to less powerful people, distort the humanity of the holders as well as the ignored groups. Still others, like finding one's staple foods everywhere, may be a function of being a member of a numerical majority in the population. Others have to do with not having to labor under pervasive negative stereotyping and mythology.

We might at least start by distinguishing between positive advantages that we can work to spread, to the point where they are not advantages at all but simply part of the normal civic and social fabric, and negative types of advantage that unless rejected will always reinforce our present hierarchies. For example, the positive "privilege" of belonging, the feeling that one belongs within the human circle, as Native Americans say, fosters development and should not be seen as privilege for a few. It is, let us say, an entitlement that none of us should have to earn; ideally it is an *unearned entitlement*. At present, since only a few have it, it is an *unearned advantage* for them. The negative "privilege" that gave me cultural permission not to take darker-skinned Others seriously can be seen as arbitrarily conferred dominance and should not be desirable for anyone. This paper results from a process of coming to see that some of the power that I originally saw as attendant on being a human being in the United States consisted in *unearned advantage* and *conferred dominance*, as well as other kinds of special circumstance not universally taken for granted.

In writing this paper I have also realized that white identity and status (as well as class identity and status) give me considerable power to choose whether to broach this subject and its trouble. I can pretty well decide whether to disappear and avoid and not listen and escape the dislike I may engender in other people through this essay, or interrupt, answer, interpret, preach, correct, criticize, and control to some extent what goes on in reaction to it. Being white, I am given considerable power to escape many kinds of danger or penalty as well as to choose which risks I want to take.

There is an analogy here, once again, with Women's Studies. Our male colleagues do not have a great deal to lose in supporting Women's Studies, but they do not have a great deal to lose if they oppose it either. They simply have the power to decide whether to commit themselves to more equitable distributions of power. They will probably feel few penalties whatever choice they make; they do not seem, in any obvious short-term sense, the ones at risk, though they and we are all at risk because of the behaviors that have been rewarded in them.

Through Women's Studies work I have met very few men who are truly distressed about systemic, unearned male advantage and conferred dominance. And so one question for me and others like me is whether we will be like them, or whether we will get truly distressed, even outraged, about unearned race advantage and conferred dominance and if so, what we will do to lessen them. In any case, we need to do more work in identifying how they actually affect our daily lives. We need more down-to-earth writing by people about these taboo subjects. We need more understanding of the ways in which white "privilege" damages white people, for these are not the same ways in which it damages the victimized. Skewed white psyches are an inseparable part of the picture, though I do not want to confuse the kinds of damage done to the holders

of special assets and to those who suffer the deficits. Many, perhaps most, of our white students in the United States think that racism doesn't affect them because they are not people of color; they do not see "whiteness" as a racial identity. Many men likewise think that Women's Studies does not bear on their own existences because they are not female; they do not see themselves as having gendered identities. Insisting on the universal "effects" or "privilege" systems, then, becomes one of our chief tasks, and being more explicit about the *particular* effects in particular contexts is another. Men need to join us in this work.

In addition, since race and sex are not the only advantaging systems at work, we need to similarly examine the daily experience of having age advantage, or ethnic advantage, or physical ability, or advantage related to nationality, religion, or sexual orientation. Professor Marnie Evans suggested to me that in many ways the list I made also applies directly to heterosexual privilege. This is a still more taboo subject than race privilege: the daily ways in which heterosexual privilege makes some persons comfortable or powerful, providing supports, assets, approvals, and rewards to those who live or expect to live in heterosexual pairs. Unpacking that content is still more difficult, owing to the deeper imbeddedness of heterosexual advantage and dominance and stricter taboos surrounding these.

But to start such an analysis I would put this observation from my own experience: The fact that I live under the same roof with a man triggers all kinds of societal assumptions about my worth, politics, life, and values and triggers a host of unearned advantages and powers. After recasting many elements from the original list I would add further observations like these:

1. My children do not have to answer questions about why I live with my partner (my husband).

2. I have no difficulty finding neighborhoods where people approve of our household.

3. Our children are given texts and classes that implicitly support our kind of family unit and do not turn them against my choice of domestic partnership.

4. I can travel alone or with my husband without expecting embarrassment or hostility in those who deal with us.

5. Most people I meet will see my marital arrangements as an asset to my life or as a favorable comment on my likability, my competence, or my mental health.

6. I can talk about the social events of a weekend without fearing most listeners' reactions.

7. I will feel welcomed and "normal" in the usual walks of public life, institutional and social.

8. In many contexts, I am seen as "all right" in daily work on women because I do not live chiefly with women.

Difficulties and dangers surrounding the task of finding parallels are many. Since racism, sexism, and heterosexism are not the same, the advantages associated with them should not be seen as the same. In addition, it is hard to isolate aspects of unearned advantage that derive chiefly from social class, economic class, race, religion, region, sex, or ethnic identity. The oppressions are both distinct and interlocking, as the Combahee River Collective statement of 1977 continues to remind us eloquently.[3]

One factor seems clear about all of the interlocking oppressions. They take both active forms that we can see and embedded forms that members of the dominant group are taught not to see. In my class and place, I did not see myself as racist because I was taught to recognize racism only in individual acts of meanness by members of my group, never in invisible systems conferring racial dominance on my group from birth. Likewise, we are taught to think that sexism or heterosexism is carried on only through intentional, individual acts of discrimination, meanness, or cruelty, rather than in invisible systems conferring unsought dominance on certain groups. Disapproving of the systems won't be enough to change them. I was taught to think that racism could end if white individuals changed their attitudes; many men think sexism can be ended by individual changes in daily behavior toward women. But a man's sex provides advantage for him whether or not he approves of the way in which dominance has been conferred on his group. A "white" skin in the United States opens many doors for whites whether or not we approve of the way dominance has been conferred on us. Individual acts can palliate, but cannot end, these problems. To redesign social systems, we need first to acknowledge their colossal unseen dimensions. The silences and denials surrounding privilege are the key political tool here. They keep the thinking about equality or equity incomplete, protecting unearned advantage and conferred dominance by making these taboo subjects. Most talk by whites about equal opportunity seems to me now to be about equal opportunity to try to get into a position of dominance while denying that *systems* of dominance exist.

Obliviousness about white advantage, like obliviousness about male advantage, is kept strongly inculturated in the United States so as to maintain the myth of meritocracy, the myth that democratic choice is equally available to all. Keeping most people unaware that freedom of confident action is there for just a small number of people props up those in power and serves to keep power in the hands of the same groups that have most of it already. Though systemic change takes many decades, there are pressing questions for me and I imagine for some others like me if we raise our daily consciousness on the perquisites of being light-skinned. What will we do with such knowledge? As we know from watching men, it is an open question whether we will choose to use unearned advantage to weaken invisible privilege systems and whether we will use any of our arbitrarily awarded power to try to reconstruct power systems on a broader base.

NOTES

1. This paper was presented at the Virginia Women's Studies Association conference in Richmond in April, 1986, and the American Education Research Association conference in Boston in October, 1986, and discussed with two groups of participants in the Dodge seminars for Secondary School Teachers in New York and Boston in the spring of 1987.

2. Andersen, Margaret, "Race and the Social Science Curriculum: A Teaching and Learning Discussion." *Radical Teacher,* November, 1984, pp. 17–20. Smith, Lillian, *Killers of the Dream,* New York: W. W. Norton, 1949.

3. "A Black Feminist Statement," The Combahee River Collective, pp. 13–22 in G. Hull, P. Scott, B. Smith, Eds., *All the Women Are White, All the Blacks Are Men, But Some of Us Are Brave: Black Women's Studies,* Old Westbury, NY: The Feminist Press, 1982.

3.

Oppression: The Birdcage Metaphor

Marilyn Frye

Marilyn Frye teaches philosophy at Michigan State University. She is the author of *The Politics of Reality: Essays in Feminist Theory* and *Willful Virgin.* In this essay, Marilyn Frye acknowledges that it is difficult to recognize the power and the extent of institutionalized forms of oppression. In trying to help explain why it is difficult to see and understand such oppression, she draws on the metaphor of a wire birdcage: Each slender wire, by itself, does not enclose or imprison the bird; rather, the whole interwoven complex of slender wires creates the cage. When you focus visually on just one wire, you cannot see the other wires and the power they have when systematically organized into a cage. Frye suggests that this image makes it easier to "grasp one of the reasons why oppression can be hard to see and recognize: one can study the elements of an oppressive structure with great care and some good will without seeing the structure as a whole, and hence without seeing or being able to understand that one is looking at a cage."

. . . The word 'oppression' is a strong word. It repels and attracts. It is dangerous and dangerously fashionable and endangered. It is much misused, and sometimes not innocently.

The statement that women are oppressed is frequently met with the claim that men are oppressed too. We hear that oppressing is oppressive to those who oppress as well as to those they oppress. Some men cite as evidence of their oppression their much-advertised inability to cry. It is tough, we are told, to be masculine. When the stresses and frustrations of being a man are cited as evidence that oppressors are

oppressed by their oppressing, the word 'oppression' is being stretched to meaninglessness; it is treated as though its scope includes any and all human experience of limitation or suffering, no matter the cause, degree, or consequence. Once such usage has been put over on us, then if ever we deny that any person or group is oppressed, we seem to imply that we think they never suffer and have no feelings. We are accused of insensitivity; even of bigotry. For women, such accusation is particularly intimidating, since sensitivity is one of the few virtues that has been assigned to us. If we are found insensitive, we may fear we have no redeeming traits at all and perhaps are not real women. Thus are we silenced before we begin: the name of our situation drained of meaning and our guilt mechanisms tripped.

But this is nonsense. Human beings can be miserable without being oppressed, and it is perfectly consistent to deny that a person or group is oppressed without denying that they have feelings or that they suffer.

We need to think clearly about oppression, and there is much that mitigates against this. I do not want to undertake to prove that women are oppressed (or that men are not), but I want to make clear what is being said when we say it. We need this word, this concept, and we need it to be sharp and sure.

The root of the word 'oppression' is the element 'press'. *The press of the crowd; pressed into military service; to press a pair of pants; printing press; press the button.* Presses are used to mold things or flatten them or reduce them in bulk, sometimes to reduce them by squeezing out the gasses or liquids in them. Something pressed is something caught between or among forces and barriers which are so related to each other that jointly they restrain, restrict or prevent the thing's motion or mobility. Mold. Immobilize. Reduce.

The mundane experience of the oppressed provides another clue. One of the most characteristic and ubiquitous features of the world as experienced by oppressed people is the double bind—situations in which options are reduced to a very few and all of them expose one to penalty, censure or deprivation. For example, it is often a requirement upon oppressed people that we smile and be cheerful. If we comply, we signal our docility and our acquiescence in our situation. We need not, then, be taken note of. We acquiesce in being made invisible, in our occupying no space. We participate in our own erasure. On the other hand, anything but the sunniest countenance exposes us to being perceived as mean, bitter, angry or dangerous. This means, at the least, that we may be found "difficult" or unpleasant to work with, which is enough to cost one one's livelihood; at worst, being seen as mean, bitter, angry or dangerous has been known to result in rape, arrest, beating and murder. One can only choose to risk one's preferred form and rate of annihilation.

Another example: It is common in the United States that women, especially younger women, are in a bind where neither sexual activity nor sexual inactivity is all right. If she is heterosexually active, a woman is open to censure and punishment for being loose, unprincipled or a whore. The "punishment" comes in the form of criticism, snide and embarrassing remarks, being treated as an easy lay by men, scorn from her more restrained female friends. She may have to lie and hide her behavior from her parents. She must juggle the risks of unwanted pregnancy and dangerous contraceptives. On the other hand, if she refrains from heterosexual activity, she is fairly constantly harassed by men who try to persuade her into it and pressure her to "relax" and "let her hair down"; she is threatened with labels like "frigid," "uptight," "manhater," "bitch" and "cocktease." The same parents who would be disapproving of her sexual activity may be worried by her inactivity because it suggests she is not or will not be popular, or is not sexually normal. She may be charged with lesbianism. If a woman is raped, then if she has been heterosexually active she is subject to the presumption that she liked it (since her activity is presumed to show that she likes sex), and if she has not been heterosexually active, she is subject to the presumption that she liked it (since she is supposedly "repressed and frustrated"). Both heterosexual activity and heterosexual nonactivity are likely to be taken as proof that you wanted to be raped, and hence, of course, weren't *really* raped at all. You can't win. You are caught in a bind, caught between systematically related pressures.

Women are caught like this, too, by networks of forces and barriers that expose one to penalty, loss or contempt whether one works outside the home or not, is on welfare or not, bears children or not, raises children or not, marries or not, stays married or not, is heterosexual, lesbian, both or neither. Economic necessity; confinement to racial and/or sexual job ghettos; sexual harassment; sex discrimination; pressures of competing expectations and judgments about *women, wives* and *mothers* (in the society at large, in racial and ethnic subcultures and in one's own mind); dependence (full or partial) on husbands, parents or the state; commitment to political ideas; loyalties to racial or ethnic or other "minority" groups; the demands of self-respect and responsibilities to others. Each of these factors exists in complex tension with every other, penalizing or prohibiting all of the apparently available options. And nipping at one's heels, always, is the endless pack of little things. If one dresses one way, one is subject to the assumption that one is advertising one's sexual availability; if one dresses another way, one appears to "not care about oneself" or to be "unfeminine." If one uses "strong language," one invites categorization as a whore or slut; if one does not, one invites categorization as a "lady"—one too delicately constituted to cope with robust speech or the realities to which it presumably refers.

The experience of oppressed people is that the living of one's life is confined and shaped by forces and barriers which are not accidental or occasional and hence avoidable, but are systematically related to each other in such a way as to catch one between and among them and restrict or penalize motion in any direction. It is the experience of being caged in: all avenues, in every direction, are blocked or booby trapped.

Cages. Consider a birdcage. If you look very closely at just one wire in the cage, you cannot see the other wires. If your conception of what is before you is determined by this myopic focus, you could look at that one wire, up and down the length of it, and be unable to see why a bird would not just fly around the wire any time it wanted to go somewhere. Furthermore, even if, one day at a time, you myopically inspected each wire, you still could not see why a bird would have trouble going past the wires to get anywhere. There is no physical property of any one wire, *nothing* that the closest scrutiny could discover, that will reveal how a bird could be inhibited or harmed by it except in the most accidental way. It is only when you step back, stop looking at the wires one by one, microscopically, and take a macroscopic view of the whole cage, that you can see why the bird does not go anywhere; and then you will see it in a moment. It will require no great subtlety of mental powers. It is perfectly *obvious* that the bird is surrounded by a network of systematically related barriers, no one of which would be the least hindrance to its flight, but which, by their relations to each other, are as confining as the solid walls of a dungeon.

It is now possible to grasp one of the reasons why oppression can be hard to see and recognize: one can study the elements of an oppressive structure with great care and some good will without seeing the structure as a whole, and hence without seeing or being able to understand that one is looking at a cage and that there are people there who are caged, whose motion and mobility are restricted, whose lives are shaped and reduced. . . .

As the cageness of the birdcage is a macroscopic phenomenon, the oppressiveness of the situations in which women live our various and different lives is a macroscopic phenomenon. Neither can be *seen* from a microscopic perspective. But when you look macroscopically you can see it—a network of forces and barriers which are systematically related and which conspire to the immobilization, reduction and molding of women and the lives we live. . . .

4.
Tired of Playing Monopoly?

Donna Langston

Donna Langston, associate professor of women's studies at Mankato State University, reports that she has worked in a variety of positions, including that of secretary, waitress, factory worker, and crew member at an oil refinery. She is a Jewish lesbian who was raised and spent the majority of her adult life in an urban, working class/poor background. She is co-editor of *Changing Our Power.* In this essay, Langston challenges the American myth that we live in a "classless society" in which "ambition and intelligence alone are responsible for success." Langston suggests that the public denial of class structures makes these social divisions all the more powerful.

I. Magnin, Nordstrom, The Bon, Sears, Penneys, K mart, Goodwill, Salvation Army. If the order of this list of stores makes any sense to you, then we've begun to deal with the first question which inevitably arises in any discussion of class here in the U.S.—huh? Unlike our European allies, we in the U.S. are reluctant to recognize class differences. This denial of class divisions functions to reinforce ruling class control and domination. America is, after all, the supposed land of equal opportunity where, if you just work hard enough, you can get ahead, pull yourself up by your bootstraps. What the old bootstraps theory overlooks is that some were born with silver shoe horns. Female-headed households, communities of color, the elderly, disabled and children find themselves, disproportionately, living in poverty. If hard work were the sole determinant of your ability to support yourself and your family, surely we'd have a different outcome for many in our society. We also, however, believe in luck and, on closer examination, it certainly is quite a coincidence that the "unlucky" come from certain race, gender and class backgrounds. In order to perpetuate racist, sexist and classist outcomes, we also have to believe that the current economic distribution is unchangeable, has always existed, and probably exists in this form throughout the known universe, i.e., it's "natural." Some people explain or try to account for poverty or class position by focusing on the personal and moral merits of an individual. If people are poor, then it's something they did or didn't do; they were lazy, unlucky, didn't try hard enough, etc. This has the familiar ring of blaming the victims. Alternative explanations focus on the ways in which poverty and class position are due to structural, systematic, institutionalized economic and political power relations. These power relations are based firmly on dynamics such as race, gender, and class.

In the myth of the classless society, ambition and intelligence alone are responsible for success. The myth conceals the existence of a class society, which serves many functions. One of the main ways it keeps the working-class and poor locked into a class-based system in a position of servitude is by cruelly creating false hope. It perpetuates the false hope among the working-class and poor that they can have different opportunities in life. The hope that they can escape the fate that awaits them due to the class position they were born into. Another way the rags-to-riches myth is perpetuated is by creating enough visible tokens so that oppressed persons believe they, too, can get ahead. The creation of hope through tokenism keeps a hierarchical structure in place and lays the blame for not succeeding on those who don't. This keeps us from resisting and changing the class-based system. Instead, we accept it as inevitable, something we just have to live with. If oppressed people believe in equality of opportunity, then they won't develop class consciousness and will internalize the blame for their economic position. If the working-class and poor do not recognize the way false hope is used to control them, they won't get a chance to control their lives by acknowledging their class position, by claiming that identity and taking action as a group.

The myth also keeps the middle class and upper class entrenched in the privileges awarded in a class-based system. It reinforces middle- and upper-class beliefs in their own superiority. If we believe that anyone in society really can get ahead, then middle- and upper-class status and privileges must be deserved, due to personal merits, and enjoyed—and defended at all costs. According to this viewpoint, poverty is regrettable but acceptable, just the outcome of a fair game: "There have always been poor people, and there always will be."

Class is more than just the amount of money you have: it's also the presence of economic security. For the working class and poor, working and eating are matters of survival, not taste. However, while one's class status can be defined in important ways in terms of monetary income, class is also a whole lot more—specifically, class is also culture. As a result of the class you are born into and raised in, class is your understanding of the world and where you fit in; it's composed of ideas, behavior, attitudes, values, and language; class is how you think, feel, act, look, dress, talk, move, walk; class is what stores you shop at, restaurants you eat in; class is the schools you attend, the education you attain; class is the very jobs you will work at throughout your adult life. Class even determines when we marry and become mothers. Working-class women become mothers long before middle-class women receive their bachelor's degrees. We experience class at every level of our lives; class is who our friends are, where we live and work and even what kind of car we drive, if we own one, and what kind of health care we receive, if

any. Have I left anything out? In other words, class is socially constructed and all-encompassing. When we experience classism, it will be because of our lack of money (i.e., choices and power in this society) and because of the way we talk, think, act, move—because of our culture.

Class affects what we perceive as and what we have available to us as choices. Upon graduation from high school, I was awarded a scholarship to attend any college, private or public, in the state of California. Yet it never occurred to me or my family that it made any difference which college you went to. I ended up just going to a small college in my town. It never would have occurred to me to move away from my family for school, because no one ever had and no one would. I was the first person in my family to go to college. I had to figure out from reading college catalogs how to apply—no one in my family could have sat down and said, "Well, you take this test and then you really should think about . . ." Although tests and high school performance had shown I had the ability to pick up white middle-class lingo, I still had quite an adjustment to make—it was lonely and isolating in college. I lost my friends from high school—they were at the community college, vo-tech school, working, or married. I lasted a year and a half in this foreign environment before I quit college, married a factory worker, had a baby and resumed living in a community I knew. One middle-class friend in college had asked if I'd like to travel to Europe with her. Her father was a college professor and people in her family had actually travelled there. My family had seldom been able to take a vacation at all. A couple of times my parents were able—by saving all year—to take the family over to the coast on their annual two-week vacation. I'd seen the time and energy my parents invested in trying to take a family vacation to some place a few hours away; the idea of how anybody ever got to Europe was beyond me.

If class is more than simple economic status but one's cultural background, as well, what happens if you're born and raised middle-class, but spend some of your adult life with earnings below a middle-class income bracket—are you then working-class? Probably not. If your economic position changes, you still have the language, behavior, educational background, etc., of the middle class, which you can bank on. You will always have choices. Men who consciously try to refuse male privilege are still male; whites who want to challenge white privilege are still white. I think those who come from middle-class backgrounds need to recognize that their class privilege does not float out with the rinse water. Middle-class people can exert incredible power just by being nice and polite. The middle-class way of doing things is the standard—they're always right, just by being themselves. Beware of middle-class people who deny their privilege. Many people have times when they struggle to get shoes for the kids, when budgets are tight, etc. This isn't the same as long-term economic conditions without choices. Being working-class is also generational. Examine your family's history of education, work, and standard of living. It may not be a coincidence that you share the same class status as your parents and grandparents. If your grandparents were professionals, or your parents were professionals, it's much more likely you'll be able to grow up to become a yuppie, if your heart so desires, or even if you don't think about it.

How about if you're born and raised poor or working-class, yet through struggle, usually through education, you manage to achieve a different economic level: do you become middle class? Can you pass? I think some working class people may successfully assimilate into the middle class by learning to dress, talk, and act middle-class—to accept and adopt the middle-class way of doing things. It all depends on how far they're able to go. To succeed in the middle-class world means facing great pressures to abandon working-class friends and ways.

Contrary to our stereotype of the working class—white guys in overalls—the working class is not homogeneous in terms of race or gender. If you are a person of color, if you live in a female-headed household, you are much more likely to be working-class or poor. The experience of Black, Latino, American Indian or Asian American working classes will differ significantly from the white working classes, which have traditionally been able to rely on white privilege to provide a more elite position within the working class. Working-class people are often grouped together and stereotyped, but distinctions can be made among the working-class, working-poor and poor. Many working-class families are supported by unionized workers who possess marketable skills. Most working-poor families are supported by non-unionized, unskilled men and women. Many poor families are dependent on welfare for their income.

Attacks on the welfare system and those who live on welfare are a good example of classism in action. We have a "dual welfare" system in this country whereby welfare for the rich in the form of tax-free capital gain, guaranteed loans, oil depletion allowances, etc., is not recognized as welfare. Almost everyone in America is on some type of welfare; but, if you're rich, it's in the form of tax deductions for "business" meals and entertainment, and if you're poor, it's in the form of food stamps. The difference is the stigma and humiliation connected to welfare for the poor, as compared to welfare for the rich, which is called "incentives." Ninety-three percent of AFDC (Aid to Families with Dependent Children, our traditional concept of welfare) recipients are women and children. Eighty percent of food stamp recipients are single mothers, children, the elderly and disabled. Average AFDC payments are $93 per person, per month. Payments are so low nationwide that in only three states do AFDC benefits plus food stamps bring a household *up to* the poverty level. Food stamp benefits average $10 per person, per week (Sar Levitan, *Programs in Aid of the Poor for the 1980s*). A common focal point for complaints about "welfare" is the belief that most welfare recipients are cheaters—goodness knows there are no middle-class income tax cheaters out there. Imagine focusing the same anger and energy on the way corporations and big business cheat on their tax revenues. Now, there would be some dollars worth quibbling about. The "dual welfare" system also assigns a different degree of stigma to programs that benefit women and children, such as AFDC, and programs whose recipients are primarily male, such as veterans' benefits. The implicit assumption is that mothers who raise children do not work and therefore are not deserving of their daily bread crumbs.

Anti-union attitudes are another prime example of classism in action. At best, unions have been a very progressive force for workers, women and people of color. At worst, unions have reflected the same regressive attitudes which are out there in other social structures: classism, racism, and sexism. Classism exists within the working class. The aristocracy of the working class—unionized, skilled workers—have mainly been white and male and have viewed themselves as being better than unskilled workers, the unemployed and poor, who are mostly women and people of color. The white working class must commit itself to a cultural and ideological transformation of racist attitudes. The history of working people, and the ways we've resisted many types of oppression, are not something we're taught in school. Missing from our education is information about workers and their resistance.

Working-class women's critiques have focused on the following issues:

Education: White middle-class professionals have used academic jargon to rationalize and justify classism. The whole structure of education is a classist system. Schools in every town reflect class divisions: like the store list at the beginning of this article, you can list schools in your town by what classes of kids attend, and in most cities you can also list by race. The classist system is perpetuated in schools with the tracking system, whereby the "dumbs" are tracked into homemaking, shop courses and vocational school futures, while the "smarts" end up in advanced math, science, literature, and college-prep courses. If we examine these groups carefully, the coincidence of poor and working-class backgrounds with "dumbs" is rather alarming. The standard measurement of supposed intelligence is white middle-class English. If you're other than white middle-class, you have to become bilingual to succeed in the educational system. If you're white middle-class, you only need the language and writing skills you were raised with, since they're the standard. To do well in society presupposes middle-class background, experiences and learning for everyone. The tracking system separates those from the working class who can potentially assimilate to the middle class from all our friends, and labels us "college bound."

After high school, you go on to vocational school, community college, or college—public or private—according to your class position. Apart from the few who break into middle-class schools, the classist stereotyping of the working class as being dumb and inarticulate tracks most into vocational and low-skilled jobs. A few of us are allowed to slip through to reinforce the idea that equal opportunity exists. But for most, class position is destiny—determining our educational attainment and employment. Since we must overall abide by middle-class rules to succeed, the assumption is that we go to college in order to "better ourselves"—i.e., become more like them. I suppose it's assumed we have "yuppie envy" and desire nothing more than to be upwardly mobile individuals. It's assumed that we want to fit into their world. But many of us remain connected to our communities and families. Becoming college-educated doesn't mean we have to, or want to, erase our first and natural language and value system. It's important for many of us to remain in and return to our communities to work, live, and stay sane.

Jobs: Middle-class people have the privilege of choosing careers. They can decide which jobs they want to work, according to their moral or political commitments, needs for challenge or creativity. This is a privilege denied the working-class and poor, whose work is a means of survival, not choice. . . . Working-class women have seldom had the luxury of choosing between work in the home or market. We've generally done both, with little ability to purchase services to help with this double burden. Middle- and upper-class women can often hire other women to clean their houses, take care of their children, and cook their meals. Guess what class and race those "other" women are? Working a double or triple day is common for working-class women. Only middle-class women have an array of choices such as: parents put you through school, then you choose a career, then you choose when and if to have babies, then you choose a support system of working-class women to take care of your kids and house if you choose to resume your career. After the birth of my second child, I was working two part-time jobs—one loading trucks at night—and going to school during the days. While I was quite privileged because I could take my colicky infant with me to classes and the daytime job, I was in a state of continuous semi-consciousness. I had to work to support my family; the only choice I had was between school or sleep: Sleep became a privilege. A white middle-class feminist instructor at the university suggested to me, all sympathetically, that I ought to hire someone to clean my house and watch the baby. Her suggestion was totally out of my reality, both economically and socially. I'd worked for years cleaning other peoples' houses. Hiring a working-class woman to do the shit work is a middle-class woman's solution to any dilemma which her privileges, such as a career, may present her.

Mothering: The feminist critique of families and the oppressive role of mothering has focused on white middle-class nuclear families. This may not be an appropriate model for communities of class and color. Mothering and families may hold a different importance for working class women. Within this context, the issue of coming out can be a very painful process for working-class lesbians. Due to the homophobia of working-class communities, to be a lesbian is most often to be excommunicated from your family, neighborhood, friends and the people you work with. If you're working-class, you don't have such clearly demarcated concepts of yourself as an individual, but instead see yourself as part of a family and community that forms your survival structure. It is not easy to be faced with the risk of giving up ties which are so central to your identity and survival.

Individualism: Preoccupation with one's self—one's body, looks, relationships—is a luxury working-class women can't afford. Making an occupation out of taking care of yourself through therapy, aerobics, jogging, dressing for success, gourmet meals and proper nutrition, etc., may be responses that are directly rooted in privilege. The middle-class have the leisure time to be preoccupied with their own problems, such as their waistlines, planning their vacations, coordinating their wardrobes, or dealing with what their mother said to them when they were five—my!

The white middle-class women's movement has been patronizing to working-class women. Its supporters think we don't understand sexism. What we don't understand is white middle-class feminism. They act as though they invented the truth, the light, and the way, which they merely need to pass along to us lower-class drudges. What they invented is a distorted form of what working-class women already know—if you're female, life sucks. Only at least we were smart enough to know that it's not just being female, but also being a person of color or class, which makes life a quicksand trap. The class system weakens all women. It censors and eliminates images of female strength. The idea of women as passive, weak creatures totally discounts the strength, self-dependence and inter-dependence necessary to survive as working-class and poor women. My mother and her friends always had a less-than-passive, less-than-enamored attitude toward their spouses, male bosses, and men in general. I know from listening to their conversations, jokes and what they passed on to us, their daughters, as folklore. When I was five years old, my mother told me about how Aunt Betty had hit Uncle Ernie over the head with a skillet and knocked him out because he was raising his hand to hit her, and how he's never even thought about doing it since. This story was told to me with a good amount of glee and laughter. All the men in the neighborhood were told of the event as an example of what was a very acceptable response in the women's community for that type of male behavior. We kids in the neighborhood grew up with these stories of women giving husbands, bosses, the welfare system, schools, unions and men in general—hell, whenever they deserved it. For me there were many role models of women taking action, control and resisting what was supposed to be their lot. Yet many white middle-class feminists continue to view feminism like math homework, where there's only supposed to be one answer. Never occurs to them that they might be talking algebra while working-class women might be talking metaphysics.

Women with backgrounds other than white middle-class experience compounded, simultaneous oppression. We can't so easily separate our experiences by categories of gender, or race, or class, i.e., "I remember it well: on Saturday, June 3, I was experiencing class oppression, but by Tuesday, June 6, I was caught up in race oppression, then all day Friday, June 9, I was in the middle of gender oppression. What a week!" Sometimes, for example, gender and class reinforce each other. When I returned to college as a single parent after a few years of having kids and working crummy jobs—I went in for vocational testing. Even before I was tested, the white middle-class male vocational counselor looked at me, a welfare mother in my best selection from the Salvation Army racks, and suggested I quit college, go to vo-tech school and become a grocery clerk. This was probably the highest paying female working-class occupation he could think of. The vocational test results suggested I become an attorney. I did end up quitting college

once again, not because of his suggestion, but because I was tired of supporting my children in ungenteel poverty. I entered vo-tech school for training as an electrician and, as one of the first women in a non-traditional field, was able to earn a living wage at a job which had traditionally been reserved for white working-class males. But this is a story for another day. Let's return to our little vocational counselor example. Was he suggesting the occupational choice of grocery clerk to me because of my gender or my class? Probably both. Let's imagine for a moment what this same vocational counselor might have advised, on sight only, to the following people:

1. A white middle-class male: doctor, lawyer, engineer, business executive.

2. A white middle-class female: close to the same suggestion as #1 if the counselor was not sexist, or, if sexist, then: librarian, teacher, nurse, social worker.

3. A middle-class man of color: close to the same suggestions as #1 if the counselor was not racist, or, if racist, then: school principal, sales, management, technician.

4. A middle-class woman of color: close to the same suggestions as #3 if counselor was not sexist; #2 if not racist; if not racist or sexist, then potentially #1.

5. A white working-class male: carpenter, electrician, plumber, welder.

6. A white working-class female—well, we already know what he told me, although he could have also suggested secretary, waitress, and dental hygienist (except I'd already told him I hated those jobs).

7. A working-class man of color: garbage collector, janitor, fieldhand.

8. A working-class woman of color: maid, laundress, garment worker.

Notice anything about this list? As you move down it, a narrowing of choices, status, pay, working conditions, benefits and chances for promotions occurs. To be connected to any one factor, such as gender or class or race, can make life difficult. To be connected to multiple factors can guarantee limited economic status and poverty.

WAYS TO AVOID FACING CLASSISM

Deny Deny Deny: Deny your class position and privileges connected to it. Deny the existence or experience of the working-class and poor. You can even set yourself up (in your own mind) as judge and jury in deciding who qualifies as working-class by your white middle-class standards. So if someone went to college, or seems intelligent to you, not at all like your stereotypes, they must be middle-class.

Guilt Guilt Guilt: "I feel so bad, I just didn't realize!" is not helpful, but is a way to avoid changing attitudes and behaviors. Passivity— "Well, what can I do about it anyway?"—and anger—"Well, what do they want!"—aren't too helpful either. Again, with these responses, the focus is on you and absolving the white middle class from responsibility. A more helpful remedy is to take action. Donate your time and money to local foodbanks. Don't cross picket lines. Better yet, go join a picket line.

HOW TO CHALLENGE CLASSISM

If you're middle-class you can begin to challenge classism with the following:

1. Confront classist behavior in yourself, others and society. Use and share the privileges, like time or money, which you do have.

2. Make demands on working-class and poor communities' issues—anti-racism, poverty, unions, public housing, public transportation, literacy and day care.

3. Learn from the skills and strength of working people—study working and poor people's history; take some Labor Studies, Ethnic Studies, Women Studies classes.

Challenge elitism. There are many different types of intelligence: white middle-class, academic, professional intellectualism being one of them (reportedly). Finally, educate yourself, take responsibility and take action.

If you're working-class, just some general suggestions (it's cheaper than therapy—free, less time-consuming and I won't ask you about what your mother said to you when you were five):

1. Face your racism! Educate yourself and others, your family, community, any organizations you belong to; take responsibility and take action. Face your classism, sexism, heterosexism, ageism, able-bodiness, adultism. . . .

2. Claim your identity. Learn all you can about your history and the history and experience of all working and poor peoples. Raise your children to be anti-racist, anti-sexist and anti-classist. Teach them the language and culture of working peoples. Learn to survive with a fair amount of anger and lots of humor, which can be tough when this stuff isn't even funny.

3. Work on issues which will benefit your community. Consider remaining in or returning to your communities. If you live and work in white middle-class environments, look for working-class allies to help you survive with your humor and wits intact. How do working-class people spot each other? We have antenna.

We need not deny or erase the differences of working class cultures but can embrace their richness, their variety, their moral and intellectual heritage. We're not at the point yet where we can celebrate differences—not having money for a prescription for your child is nothing to celebrate. It's not time yet to party with the white middle class, because we'd be the entertainment ("Aren't they quaint? Just love their workboots and uniforms and the way they cuss!"). We need to overcome divisions among working people, not by ignoring the multiple oppressions many of us encounter, or by oppressing each other, but by becoming committed allies on all issues which affect working people: racism, sexism, classism, etc. An injury to one is an injury to all. Don't play by ruling class rules, hoping that maybe you can live on Connecticut Avenue instead of Baltic, or that you as an individual can make it to Park Place and Boardwalk. Tired of Monopoly? Always ending up on Mediterranean Avenue? How about changing the game?

5.

Racisms

Kwame Anthony Appiah

Kwame Anthony Appiah is professor of Afro-American studies and philosophy at Harvard University. He is the author of *In My Father's House: Africa in the Philosophy of Culture* and *Necessary Questions: An Introduction to Philosophy*, among other scholarly books. He has also published three novels. In this essay, Appiah challenges us to think about the very category of race and the corollary term *racism*. He distinguishes the concept of "racialism" from "racism," and then identifies several types of racism. He helps us to think clearly and critically about the often unnoticed presuppositions that undergird our use of the terms *race* and *racism*.

If the people I talk to and the newspapers I read are representative and reliable, there is a good deal of racism about. People and policies in the United States, in Eastern and Western Europe, in Asia and Africa and Latin America are regularly described as "racist." Australia had, until recently, a racist immigration policy; Britain still has one; racism is on the rise in France; many Israelis support Meir Kahane, an anti-Arab racist; many Arabs, according to a leading authority, are anti-Semitic racists;[1] and the movement to establish English as the "official language" of the United States is motivated by racism. Or, at least, so many of the people I talk to and many of the journalists with the newspapers I read believe.

But visitors from Mars—or from Malawi—unfamiliar with the Western concept of racism could be excused if they had some difficulty in identifying what exactly racism was. We see it everywhere, but rarely does anyone stop to say what it is, or to explain what is wrong with it. Our visitors from Mars would soon grasp that it had become at least conventional in recent years to express abhorrence for racism. They might even notice that those most often accused of it—members of the South African Nationalist party, for example—may officially abhor it also. But if they sought in the popular media of our day—in newspapers and magazines, on television or radio, in novels or films—for an explicit definition of this thing "we" all abhor, they would very likely be disappointed.

Now, of course, this would be true of many of our most familiar concepts. *Sister, chair, tomato*—none of these gets defined in the course of our daily business. But the concept of racism is in worse shape than these. For much of what we say about it is, on the face of it, inconsistent.

It is, for example, held by many to be racist to refuse entry to a university to an otherwise qualified "Negro" candidate, but not to be so to refuse entry to an equally qualified "Caucasian" one. But "Negro" and "Caucasian" are both alleged to be names of races, and invidious discrimination on the basis of race is usually held to be a paradigm case of racism. Or, to take another example, it is widely believed to be evidence of an unacceptable racism to exclude people from clubs on the basis of race; yet most people, even those who think of "Jewish" as a racial term, seem to think that there is nothing wrong with Jewish clubs, whose members do not share any particular religious beliefs, or Afro-American societies, whose members share the juridical characteristic of American citizenship and the "racial" characteristic of being black.

I say that these are inconsistencies "on the face of it," because, for example, affirmative action in university admissions is importantly different from the earlier refusal to admit blacks or Jews (or other "Others") that it is meant, in part, to correct. Deep enough analysis may reveal it to be quite consistent with the abhorrence of racism; even a shallow analysis suggests that it is intended to be so. Similarly, justifications can be offered for "racial" associations in a plural society that are not available for the racial exclusivism of the country club. But if we take racism seriously we ought to be concerned about the adequacy of these justifications.

In this essay, then, I propose to take our ordinary ways of thinking about race and racism and point up some of their presuppositions. And since popular concepts are, of course, usually fairly fuzzily and untheoretically conceived, much of what I have to say will seem to be both more theoretically and more precisely committed than the talk of racism and racists in our newspapers and on television. My claim is that these theoretical claims are required to make sense of racism as the practice of reasoning human beings. If anyone were to suggest that much, perhaps most, of what goes under the name "racism" in our world cannot be given such a rationalized foundation, I should not disagree: but to the extent that a practice cannot be rationally reconstructed it ought, surely, to be given up by reasonable people. The right tactic with racism, if you really want to oppose it, is to object to it rationally in the form in which it stands the best chance of meeting objections. The doctrines I want to discuss can be rationally articulated: and they are worth articulating rationally in order that we can rationally say what we object to in them.

RACIST PROPOSITIONS

There are at least three distinct doctrines that might be held to express the theoretical content of what we call "racism." One is the view—which I shall call *racialism*[2]—that there are heritable characteristics, possessed by members of our species, that allow us to divide them into a small set of races, in such a way that all the members of these races share certain traits and tendencies with each other that they do not share with members of any other race. These traits and tendencies characteristic of a race constitute, on the racialist view, a sort of racial essence; and it is part of the content of racialism that the essential heritable characteristics of what the nineteenth century called the "Races of Man" account for more than the visible morphological characteristics—skin color, hair type, facial features—on the basis of which we make our informal classifications. Racialism is at the heart of nineteenth-century Western attempts to develop a science of racial difference; but it appears to have been believed by others—for example, Hegel, before then, and many in other parts of the non-Western world since—who have had no interest in developing scientific theories.

Racialism is not, in itself, a doctrine that must be dangerous, even if the racial essence is thought to entail moral and intellectual dispositions. Provided positive moral qualities are distributed across the races, each can be respected, can have its "separate but equal" place. Unlike most Western-educated people, I believe—and I have argued elsewhere[3]—that racialism is false;

but by itself, it seems to be a cognitive rather than a moral problem. The issue is how the world is, not how we would want it to be.

Racialism is, however, a presupposition of other doctrines that have been called "racism," and these other doctrines have been, in the last few centuries, the basis of a great deal of human suffering and the source of a great deal of moral error.

One such doctrine we might call "extrinsic racism": extrinsic racists make moral distinctions between members of different races because they believe that the racial essence entails certain morally relevant qualities. The basis for the extrinsic racists' discrimination between people is their belief that members of different races differ in respects that *warrant* the differential treatment, respects—such as honesty or courage or intelligence—that are uncontroversially held (at least in most contemporary cultures) to be acceptable as a basis for treating people differently. Evidence that there are no such differences in morally relevant characteristics—that Negroes do not necessarily lack intellectual capacities, that Jews are not especially avaricious—should thus lead people out of their racism if it is purely extrinsic. As we know, such evidence often fails to change an extrinsic racist's attitudes substantially, for some of the extrinsic racist's best friends have always been Jewish. But at this point—if the racist is sincere—what we have is no longer a false doctrine but a cognitive incapacity, one whose significance I shall discuss later in this essay.

I say that the *sincere* extrinsic racist may suffer from a cognitive incapacity. But some who espouse extrinsic racist doctrines are simply insincere intrinsic racists. For *intrinsic racists*, on my definition, are people who differentiate morally between members of different races because they believe that each race has a different moral status, quite independent of the moral characteristics entailed by its racial essence. Just as, for example, many people assume that the fact that they are biologically related to another person—a brother, an aunt, a cousin—gives

them a moral interest in that person,[4] so an intrinsic racist holds that the bare fact of being of the same race is a reason for preferring one person to another. (I shall return to this parallel later as well.)

For an intrinsic racist, no amount of evidence that a member of another race is capable of great moral, intellectual, or cultural achievements, or has characteristics that, in members of one's own race, would make them admirable or attractive, offers any ground for treating that person as he or she would treat similarly endowed members of his or her own race. Just so, some sexists are "intrinsic sexists," holding that the bare fact that someone is a woman (or man) is a reason for treating her (or him) in certain ways.

There are interesting possibilities for complicating these distinctions: some racists, for example, claim, as the Mormons once did, that they discriminate between people because they believe that God requires them to do so. Is this an extrinsic racism, predicated on the combination of God's being an intrinsic racist and the belief that it is right to do what God wills? Or is it intrinsic racism because it is based on the belief that God requires these discriminations because they are right? (Is an act pious because the gods love it, or do they love it because it is pious?) Nevertheless, the distinctions between racialism and racism and between two potentially overlapping kinds of racism provide us with the skeleton of an anatomy of the propositional contents of racial attitudes.

RACIST DISPOSITIONS

Most people will want to object already that this discussion of the propositional content of racist moral and factual beliefs misses something absolutely crucial to the character of the psychological and sociological reality of racism, something I touched on when I mentioned that extrinsic racist utterances are often made by people who suffer from what I called a "cognitive incapacity." Part of the standard force of accusations of racism is that their objects are in some way *irrational*. The objection to Professor Shockley's claims about the intelligence of blacks is not just that they are false; it is rather that Professor Shockley seems, like many people we call "racist," to be unable to see that the evidence does not support his factual claims and that the connection between his factual claims and his policy prescriptions involves a series of non sequiturs.

What makes these cognitive incapacities especially troubling—something we should respond to with more than a recommendation that the individual, Professor Shockley, be offered psychotherapy—is that they conform to a certain pattern: namely, that it is especially where beliefs and policies that are to the disadvantage of nonwhite people that he shows the sorts of disturbing failure that have made his views both notorious and notoriously unreliable. Indeed, Professor Shockley's reasoning works extremely well in some other areas: that he is a Nobel Laureate in physics is part of what makes him so interesting an example.

This cognitive incapacity is not, of course, a rare one. Many of us are unable to give up beliefs that play a part in justifying the special advantages we gain (or hope to gain) from our positions in the social order—in particular, beliefs about the positive characters of the class of people who share that position. Many people who express extrinsic racist beliefs—many white South Africans, for example—are beneficiaries of social orders that deliver advantages to them by virtue of their "race," so that their disinclination to accept evidence that would deprive them of a justification for those advantages is just an instance of this general phenomenon.

So too, evidence that access to higher education is as largely determined by the quality of our earlier educations as by our own innate talents, does not, on the whole, undermine the confidence of college entrants from private schools in England or the United States or Ghana. Many of them continue to believe in the face of this evidence that their acceptance at

"good" universities shows them to be intellectually better endowed (and not just better prepared) than those who are rejected. It is facts such as these that give sense to the notion of false consciousness, the idea that an ideology can prevent us from acknowledging facts that would threaten our position.

The most interesting cases of this sort of ideological resistance to the truth are not, perhaps, the ones I have just mentioned. On the whole, it is less surprising, once we accept the admittedly problematic notion of self-deception, that people who think that certain attitudes or beliefs advantage them or those they care about should be able, as we say, to "persuade" themselves to ignore evidence that undermines those beliefs or attitudes. What is more interesting is the existence of people who resist the truth of a proposition while thinking that its wider acceptance would in no way disadvantage them or those individuals about whom they care—this might be thought to describe Professor Shockley; or who resist the truth when they recognize that its acceptance would actually advantage them—this might be the case with some black people who have internalized negative racist stereotypes; or who fail, by virtue of their ideological attachments, to recognize what is in their own best interests at all.

My business here is not with the psychological or social processes by which these forms of ideological resistance operate, but it is important, I think, to see the refusal on the part of some extrinsic racists to accept evidence against the beliefs as an instance of a widespread phenomenon in human affairs. It is a plain fact, to which theories of ideology must address themselves, that our species is prone both morally and intellectually to such distortions of judgment, in particular to distortions of judgment that reflect partiality. An inability to change your mind in the face of appropriate[5] evidence is a cognitive incapacity; but it is one that all of us surely suffer from in some areas of belief; especially in areas where our own interests or self-images are (or seem to be) at stake.

It is not, however, as some have held, a tendency that we are powerless to resist. No one, no doubt, can be impartial about everything—even about everything to which the notion of partiality applies; but there is no subject matter about which most sane people cannot, in the end, be persuaded to avoid partiality in judgment. And it may help to shake the convictions of those whose incapacity derives from this sort of ideological defense if we show them how their reaction fits into this general pattern. It is, indeed, because it generally *does* fit this pattern that we call such views "racism"—the suffix "-ism" indicating that what we have in mind is not simply a theory but an ideology. It would be odd to call someone brought up in a remote corner of the world with false and demeaning views about white people a "racist" if that person gave up those beliefs quite easily in the face of appropriate evidence.

Real live racists, then, exhibit a systematically distorted rationality, the kind of systematically distorted rationality that we are likely to call "ideological." And it is a distortion that is especially striking in the cognitive domain: extrinsic racists, as I said earlier, however intelligent or otherwise well informed, often fail to treat evidence against the theoretical propositions of extrinsic racism dispassionately. Like extrinsic racism, intrinsic racism can also often be seen as ideological; but since scientific evidence is not going to settle the issue, a failure to see that it is wrong represents a cognitive incapacity only on controversially realist views about morality. What makes intrinsic racism similarly ideological is not so much the failure of inductive or deductive rationality that is so striking in someone like Professor Shockley but rather the connection that it, like extrinsic racism, has with the interests—real or perceived—of the dominant group.[6] Shockley's racism is in a certain sense directed *against* nonwhite people: many believe that his views would, if accepted, operate against their objective interests, and he certainly presents the black "race" in a less than flattering light.

I propose to use the old-fashioned term "racial prejudice" in the rest of this essay to refer to the deformation of rationality in judgment that characterizes those whose racism is more than a theoretical attachment to certain propositions about race.

RACIAL PREJUDICE

It is hardly necessary to raise objections to what I am calling "racial prejudice"; someone who exhibits such deformations of rationality is plainly in trouble. But it is important to remember that propositional racists in a racist culture have false moral beliefs but may not suffer from racial prejudice. Once we show them how society has enforced extrinsic racist stereotypes, once we ask them whether they really believe that race in itself, independently of those extrinsic racist beliefs, justifies differential treatment, many will come to give up racist propositions, although we must remember how powerful a weight of authority our arguments have to overcome. Reasonable people may insist on substantial evidence if they are to give up beliefs that are central to their cultures.

Still, in the end, many will resist such reasoning; and to the extent that their prejudices are really not subject to any kind of rational control, we may wonder whether it is right to treat such people as morally responsible for the acts their racial prejudice motivates, or morally reprehensible for holding the views to which their prejudice leads them. It is a bad thing that such people exist; they are, in a certain sense, bad people. But it is not clear to me that they are responsible for the fact that they are bad. Racial prejudice, like prejudice generally, may threaten an agent's autonomy, making it appropriate to treat or train rather than to reason with them.

But once someone has been offered evidence both (1) that their reasoning in a certain domain is distorted by prejudice, and (2) that the distortions conform to a pattern that suggests a lack of impartiality, they ought to take special care in articulating views and proposing policies in that domain. They ought to do so because, as I have already said, the phenomenon of partiality in judgment is well attested in human affairs. Even if you are not immediately persuaded that you are yourself a victim of such a distorted rationality in a certain domain, you should keep in mind always that this is the usual position of those who suffer from such prejudices. To the extent that this line of thought is not one that itself falls within the domain in question, one can be held responsible for not subjecting judgments that *are* within that domain to an especially extended scrutiny; and this is a fortiori true if the policies one is recommending are plainly of enormous consequence.

If it is clear that racial prejudice is regrettable, it is also clear in the nature of the case that providing even a superabundance of reasons and evidence will often not be a successful way of removing it. Nevertheless, the racist's prejudice will be articulated through the sorts of theoretical propositions I dubbed extrinsic and intrinsic racism. And we should certainly be able to say something reasonable about why these theoretical propositions should be rejected.

Part of the reason that this is worth doing is precisely the fact that many of those who assent to the propositional content of racism do not suffer from racial prejudice. In a country like the United States, where racist propositions were once part of the national ideology, there will be many who assent to racist propositions simply because they were raised to do so. Rational objection to racist propositions has a fair chance of changing such people's beliefs.

EXTRINSIC AND INTRINSIC RACISM

It is not always clear whether someone's theoretical racism is intrinsic or extrinsic, and there is certainly no reason why we should expect to be able to settle the question. Since the issue probably never occurs to most people in these terms, we cannot suppose that they must have an answer. In fact, given the definition of the terms I offered, there is nothing barring someone from being both an intrinsic and an extrinsic racist, holding both that the bare fact of race provides a basis for treating members of his or her own race differently from others and that there are morally relevant characteristics that are differentially distributed among the races. Indeed, for reasons I shall discuss in a moment, *most* intrinsic racists are likely to express extrinsic racist beliefs, so that we should not be surprised that many people seem, in fact, to be committed to both forms of racism.

The Holocaust made unreservedly clear the threat that racism poses to human decency. But it also blurred our thinking because in focusing our attention on the racist character of the Nazi atrocities, it obscured their character as atrocities. What is appalling about Nazi racism is not just that it presupposes, as all racism does, false (racialist) beliefs—not simply that it involves a moral incapacity (the inability to extend our moral sentiments to all our fellow creatures) and a moral failing (the making of moral distinctions without moral differences)—but that it leads, first, to oppression and then to mass slaughter. In recent years, South African racism has had a similar distorting effect. For although South African racism has not led to killings on the scale of the Holocaust—even if it has both left South Africa judicially executing more (mostly black) people per head of population than most other countries and led to massive differences between the life chances of white and nonwhite South Africans—it *has* led to the systematic oppression and economic exploitation of people who are not classified as "white," and to the infliction of suffering on citizens of all racial classifications, not least by the police state that is required to maintain that exploitation and oppression.

Part of our resistance, therefore, to calling the racial ideas of those, such as the Black Nationalists of the 1960s, who advocate racial solidarity, by the same term that we use to describe the attitudes of Nazis or of members of the South African Nationalist party, surely resides in the fact that they largely did not contemplate using race as a basis for inflicting harm. Indeed, it seems to me that there is a significant pattern in the modern rhetoric of race, such that the discourse of racial solidarity is usually expressed through the language of *intrinsic* racism, while those who have used race as the basis for oppression and hatred have appealed to *extrinsic* racist ideas. This point is important for understanding the character of contemporary racial attitudes.

The two major uses of race as a basis for moral solidarity that are most familiar in the West are varieties of Pan-Africanism and Zionism. In each case it is presupposed that a "people," Negroes or Jews, has the basis for shared political life in the fact of being of the same race. There are varieties of each form of "nationalism" that make the basis lie in shared traditions; but however plausible this may be in the case of Zionism, which has in Judaism, the religion, a realistic candidate for a common and nonracial focus for nationality, the peoples of Africa have a good deal less in common culturally than is usually assumed. I discuss this issue at length in *In My Father's House: Essays in the Philosophy of African Culture,* but let me say here that I believe the central fact is this: what blacks in the West, like secularized Jews, have mostly in common is that they are perceived—both by themselves and by others—as belonging to the same race, and that this common race is used by others as the basis for discriminating against them. "If you ever forget you're a Jew, a goy will remind you." The Black Nationalists, like some Zionists, responded to their experience of racial discrimination by accepting the racialism it presupposed.[7]

Although race is indeed at the heart of Black Nationalism, however, it seems that it is the fact of a shared race, not the fact of a shared racial character, that provides the basis for solidarity. Where racism is implicated in the basis for national solidarity, it is intrinsic, not (or not only) extrinsic. It is this that makes the idea of fraternity one that is naturally applied in na-

tionalist discourse. For, as I have already observed, the moral status of close family members is not normally thought of in most cultures as depending on qualities of character; we are supposed to love our brothers and sisters in spite of their faults and not because of their virtues. Alexander Crummell, one of the founding fathers of Black Nationalism, literalizes the metaphor of family in these startling words:

> Races, like families, are the organisms and ordinances of God; and race feeling, like family feeling, is of divine origin. The extinction of race feeling is just as possible as the extinction of family feeling. Indeed, a race *is* a family.[8]

It is the assimilation of "race feeling" to "family feeling" that makes intrinsic racism seem so much less objectionable than extrinsic racism. For this metaphorical identification reflects the fact that, in the modern world (unlike the nineteenth century), intrinsic racism is acknowledged almost exclusively as the basis of feelings of community. We can surely, then, share a sense of what Crummell's friend and co-worker Edward Blyden called "the poetry of politics," that is, "the feeling of race," the feeling of "people with whom we are connected."[9] The racism here is the basis of acts of supererogation, the treatment of others better than we otherwise might, better than moral duty demands of us.

This is a contingent fact. There is no logical impossibility in the idea of racialists whose moral beliefs lead them to feelings of hatred for other races while leaving no room for love of members of their own. Nevertheless most racial hatred is in fact expressed through extrinsic racism: most people who have used race as the basis for causing harm to others have felt the need to see the other as independently morally flawed. It is one thing to espouse fraternity without claiming that your brothers and sisters have any special qualities that deserve recognition, and another to espouse hatred of others who have done nothing to deserve it.[10]

Many Afrikaners—like many in the American South until recently—have a long list of extrinsic racist answers to the question why blacks should not have full civil rights. Extrinsic racism has usually been the basis for treating people worse than we otherwise might, for giving them less than their humanity entitles them to. But this too is a contingent fact. Indeed, Crummell's guarded respect for white people derived from a belief in the superior moral qualities of the Anglo-Saxon race.

Intrinsic racism is, in my view, a moral error. Even if racialism were correct, the bare fact that someone was of another race would be no reason to treat them worse—or better—than someone of my race. In our public lives, people are owed treatment independently of their biological characters: if they are to be differently treated there must be some morally relevant difference between them. In our private lives, we are morally free to have aesthetic preferences between people, but once our treatment of people raises moral issues, we may not make arbitrary distinctions. Using race in itself as a morally relevant distinction strikes most of us as obviously arbitrary. Without associated moral characteristics, why should race provide a better basis than hair color or height or timbre of voice? And if two people share all the properties morally relevant to some action we ought to do, it will be an error—a failure to apply the Kantian injunction to universalize our moral judgments—to use the bare facts of race as the basis for treating them differently. No one should deny that a common ancestry might, in particular cases, account for similarities in moral character. But then it would be the moral similarities that justified the different treatment.

It is presumably because most people—outside the South African Nationalist party and the Ku Klux Klan—share the sense that intrinsic racism requires arbitrary distinctions that they are largely unwilling to express in situations that invite moral criticism. But I do not know how I would argue with someone who was willing to announce an intrinsic racism as a basic moral idea; the best one can do, perhaps, is to provide objections to possible lines of defense of it.

DE GUSTIBUS

It might be thought that intrinsic racism should be regarded not so much as an adherence to a (moral) proposition as the expression of a taste, analogous, say, to the food prejudice that makes most English people unwilling to eat horse meat, and most Westerners unwilling to eat the insect grubs that the !Kung people find so appetizing. The analogy does at least this much for us, namely, to provide a model of the way that *extrinsic* racist propositions can be a reflection of an underlying prejudice. For, of course, in most cultures food prejudices are rationalized: we say insects are unhygienic and cats taste horrible. Yet a cooked insect is no more health-threatening than a cooked carrot, and the unpleasant taste of cat meat, far from justifying our prejudice against it, probably derives from that prejudice.

But there the usefulness of the analogy ends. For intrinsic racism, as I have defined it, is not simply a taste for the company of one's "own kind," but a moral doctrine, one that is supposed to underlie differences in the treatment of people in contexts where moral evaluation is appropriate. And for moral distinctions we cannot accept that "de gustibus non est disputandum." We do not need the full apparatus of Kantian ethics to require that public morality be constrained by reason.

A proper analogy would be with someone who thought that we could continue to kill cattle for beef, even if cattle exercised all the complex cultural skills of human beings. I think it is obvious that creatures that shared our capacity for understanding as well as our capacity for pain should not be treated the way we actually treat cattle—that "intrinsic specieism" would be as wrong as racism. And the fact that most people think it is worse to be cruel to chimpanzees than to frogs suggests that they may agree with me. The distinction in attitudes surely reflects a belief in the greater richness of the mental life of chimps. Still, I do not know how I would *argue* against someone who could not see this; someone who continued to act on the contrary belief might, in the end, simply have to be locked up.

THE FAMILY MODEL

I have suggested that intrinsic racism is, at least sometimes, a metaphorical extension of the moral priority of one's family; it might, therefore, be suggested that a defense of intrinsic racism could proceed along the same lines as a defense of the family as a center of moral interest. The possibility of a defense of family relations as morally relevant—or, more precisely, of the claim that one may be morally entitled (or even obliged) to make distinctions between two otherwise morally indistinguishable people because one is related to one and not to the other—is theoretically important for the prospects of a philosophical defense of intrinsic racism. This is because such a defense of the family involves—like intrinsic racism—a denial of the basic claim, expressed so clearly by Kant, that from the perspective of morality, it is as rational agents *simpliciter* that we are to assess and be assessed. For anyone who follows Kant in this, what matters, as we might say, is not who you are but how you try to live. Intrinsic racism denies this fundamental claim also. And, in so doing, as I have argued elsewhere, it runs against the mainstream of the history of Western moral theory.[11]

The importance of drawing attention to the similarities between the defense of the family and the defense of the race, then, is not merely that the metaphor of family is often invoked by racism; it is that each of them offers the same general challenge to the Kantian stream of our moral thought. And the parallel with the defense of the family should be especially appealing to an intrinsic racist, since many of us who

have little time for racism would hope that the family is susceptible to some such defense.

The problem in generalizing the defense of the family, however, is that such defenses standardly begin at a point that makes the argument for intrinsic racism immediately implausible: namely, with the family as the unit through which we live what is most intimate, as the center of private life. If we distinguish, with Bernard Williams, between ethical thought, which takes seriously "the demands, needs, claims, desires, and generally, the lives of other people,"[12] and morality, which focuses more narrowly on obligation, it may well be that private life matters to us precisely because it is altogether unsuited to the universalizing tendencies of morality.

The functioning family unit has contracted substantially with industrialization, the disappearance of the family as the unit of production, and the increasing mobility of labor, but there remains that irreducible minimum: the parent or parents with the child or children. In this "nuclear" family, there is, of course, a substantial body of shared experience, shared attitudes, shared knowledge and beliefs; and the mutual psychological investment that exists within this group is, for most of us, one of the things that gives meaning to our lives. It is a natural enough confusion—which we find again and again in discussions of adoption in the popular media—that identifies the relevant group with the biological unit of *genitor, genetrix,* and *offspring* rather than with the social unit of those who share a common domestic life.

The relations of parents and their biological children are of moral importance, of course, in part because children are standardly the product of behavior voluntarily undertaken by their biological parents. But the moral relations between biological siblings and half-siblings cannot, as I have already pointed out, be accounted for in such terms. A rational defense of the family ought to appeal to the causal responsibility of the biological parent and the common life of the domestic unit, and not to the brute fact of biological relatedness, even if the former pair of considerations defines groups that are often coextensive with the groups generated by the latter. For brute biological relatedness bears no necessary connection to the sorts of human purposes that seem likely to be relevant at the most basic level of ethical thought.

An argument that such a central group is bound to be crucially important in the lives of most human beings in societies like ours is not, of course, an argument for any specific mode of organization of the "family": feminism and the gay liberation movement have offered candidate groups that could (and sometimes do) occupy the same sort of role in the lives of those whose sexualities or whose dispositions otherwise make the nuclear family uncongenial; and these candidates have been offered specifically in the course of defenses of a move toward societies that are agreeably beyond patriarchy and homophobia. The central thought of these feminist and gay critiques of the nuclear family is that we cannot continue to view any one organization of private life as "natural," once we have seen even the broadest outlines of the archaeology of the family concept.

If that is right, then the argument for the family must be an argument for a mode of organization of life and feeling that subserves certain positive functions; and however the details of such an argument would proceed it is highly unlikely that the same functions could be served by groups on the scale of races, simply because, as I say, the family is attractive in part exactly for reasons of its personal scale.

I need hardly say that rational defenses of intrinsic racism along the lines I have been considering are not easily found. In the absence of detailed defenses to consider, I can only offer these general reasons for doubting that they can succeed: the generally Kantian tenor of much of our moral thought threatens the project from the start; and the essentially unintimate nature of relations within "races" suggests that there is little prospect that the defense of the family—which seems an attractive and plausible project that extends ethical life beyond the narrow range of a universalizing morality—can be applied to a defense of races.

CONCLUSIONS

I have suggested that what we call "racism" involves both propositions and dispositions.

The propositions were, first, that there are races (this was *racialism*) and, second, that these races are morally significant either (a) because they are contingently correlated with morally relevant properties (this was *extrinsic racism*) or (b) because they are intrinsically morally significant (this was *intrinsic racism*).

The disposition was a tendency to assent to false propositions, both moral and theoretical, about races—propositions that support policies or beliefs that are to the disadvantage of some race (or races) as opposed to others, and to do so even in the face of evidence and argument that should appropriately lead to giving those propositions up. This disposition I called "racial prejudice."

I suggested that intrinsic racism had tended in our own time to be the natural expression of feelings of community, and this is, of course, one of the reasons why we are not inclined to call it racist. For, to the extent that a theoretical position is not associated with irrationally held beliefs that tend to the *disadvantage* of some group, it fails to display the *directedness* of the distortions of rationality characteristic of racial prejudice. Intrinsic racism may be as irrationally held as any other view, but it does not *have* to be directed *against* anyone.

So far as theory is concerned I believe racialism to be false: since theoretical racism of both kinds presupposes racialism, I could not logically support racism of either variety. But even if racialism were true, both forms of theoretical racism would be incorrect. Extrinsic racism is false because the genes that account for the gross morphological differences that underlie our standard racial categories are not linked to those genes that determine, to whatever degree such matters are determined genetically, our moral and intellectual characters. Intrinsic racism is mistaken because it breaches the Kantian imperative to make moral distinctions only on morally relevant grounds—granted that there is no reason to believe that race, *in se*, is morally relevant, and also no reason to suppose that races are like families in providing a sphere of ethical life that legitimately escapes the demands of a universalizing morality.

NOTES

1. Bernard Lewis, *Semites and Anti-Semites* (New York: Norton, 1986).

2. I shall be using the words "racism" and "racialism" with the meanings I stipulate; in some dialects of English they are synonyms, and in most dialects their definition is less than precise. For discussion of recent biological evidence see M. Nei and A. K. Roychoudhury, "Genetic Relationship and Evolution of Human Races," *Evolutionary Biology*, vol. 14 (New York: Plenum, 1983), pp. 1–59; for useful background see also M. Nei and A. K. Roychoudhury, "Gene Differences between Caucasian, Negro, and Japanese Populations," *Science*, 177 (August 1972), pp. 434–35.

3. See my "The Uncompleted Argument: Du Bois and the Illusion of Race," *Critical Inquiry*, 12 (Autumn 1985); reprinted in Henry Louis Gates (ed.), *"Race," Writing, and Difference* (Chicago: University of Chicago Press, 1986), pp. 21–37.

4. This fact shows up most obviously in the assumption that adopted children intelligibly make claims against their natural siblings: natural parents are, of course, causally responsible for their child's existence and that could be the basis of moral claims, without any sense that biological relatedness entailed rights or responsibilities. But no such basis exists for an interest in natural *siblings*; my sisters are not causally responsible for my existence. . . .

5. Obviously what evidence should *appropriately* change your beliefs is not independent of your social or historical situation. In mid-nineteenth-century America, in New England quite as much as in the heart of Dixie, the pervasiveness of the institutional support for the prevailing system of racist belief—the fact that it was reinforced by religion and state, and defended by people in the universities and colleges, who had the greatest cognitive authority—meant that it would have been appropriate to insist on a substantial body of evidence and argument before giving up assent to racist propositions. In California in the 1980s, of course, matters stand rather differently. To acknowledge this is not to admit to a cognitive relativism; rather, it is to hold that, at least in some domains, the fact that a belief is widely held—and especially by people in positions of cognitive authority—may be a good prima facie reason for believing it.

6. Ideologies, as most theorists of ideology have admitted, standardly outlive the period in which they conform to the objective interests of the dominant group in a society; so even someone who thinks that the dominant group in our society no longer needs racism to buttress its position can see racism as the persisting ideology of an earlier phase of society. (I say "group" to keep the claim appropriately general; it seems to me a substantial further claim that the dominant group whose interests an ideology serves is always a class.) I have argued, however, in "The Conservation of 'Race'" that racism continues to serve the interests of the ruling classes in the West; in *Black American Literature Forum*, 23 (Spring 1989), pp. 37–60.

7. As I argued in "The Uncompleted Argument: Du Bois and the Illusion of Race." The reactive (or dialectical) character of this move explains why Sartre calls its manifestations in Négritude an "antiracist racism"; see "Orphée Noir," his preface to Senghor's *Anthologie de la nouvelle poésie nègre et malagache de langue française* (Paris: PUF, 1948). Sartre believed, of course, that the synthesis of this dialectic would be the transcendence of racism; and it was his view of it as a stage—the antithesis—in that process that allowed him to see it as a positive advance over the original "thesis" of European racism. I suspect that the reactive character of antiracist racism accounts for the tolerance that is regularly extended to it in liberal circles; but this tolerance is surely hard to justify unless one shares Sartre's optimistic interpretation of it as a stage in a process that leads to the end of all racisms. (And unless your view of this dialectic is deterministic you should in any case want to play an argumentative role in moving to this next stage.)

For a similar Zionist response see Horace Kallen's "The Ethics of Zionism," *Maccabaean*, August 1906.

8. "The Race Problem in America," in Brotz's *Negro Social and Political Thought* (New York: Basic Books, 1966), p. 184.

9. *Christianity, Islam and the Negro Race* (1887; reprinted Edinburgh: Edinburgh University Press, 1967), p. 197.

10. This is in part a reflection of an important asymmetry: loathing, unlike love, needs justifying; and this, I would argue, is because loathing usually leads to acts that are *in se* undesirable, whereas love leads to acts that are large *in se* desirable—indeed, supererogatorily so.

11. See my "Racism and Moral Pollution," *Philosophical Forum*, 18 (Winter–Spring 1986–87), pp. 185–202.

12. *Ethics and the Limits of Philosophy* (Cambridge, Mass.: Harvard University Press, 1985), p. 12. I do not, as is obvious, share Williams's skepticism about morality.

6.
Philosophy and Disability

Karen Fiser

Karen Fiser is a philosopher and poet; she teachers poetry at Stanford University. Her philosophical essays examine issues of privacy and pain. Her poems have appeared in a number of magazines and journals. In this essay, Fiser challenges the ways in which philosophers have typically addressed physical disabilities. She seeks to explain why the disabled are in general the "invisible minority," and why philosophers are particularly prone to fail to acknowledge the existence of disability and chronic pain.

A few years after I became disabled, I began to notice how seldom philosophers acknowledge the existence of disability and chronic pain. It is probably important that, because I had been trained as a philosopher, it took me years to notice, though I myself had a disability. As human beings, we inevitably undergo physical limitation and loss, disease, disability, and chronic pain. If we do not suffer now, we will later. If we do not suffer ourselves, we love someone who does. By one recent estimate, there are close to 44 million disabled people in the United States (Congressional Research Service, 1984). In 1983 it was estimated that 60 million Americans were either partially or totally disabled by chronic pain (Morris, 1991, p. 19). Yet there is an absence in philosophy of meaningful discussion of these familiar facts of our human condition, even in contexts where one might expect to find it.

Philosophical discussions of personal identity, for example, commonly feature brains in vats, rational Martians, and person-stages. I have never seen a deep or careful discussion by a philosopher of the terrifying crises of personal identity familiar to people who become disabled as adults. Similarly, philosophical discussions of pain, though they abound, seem oddly triv-

ial and jejune next to any real experience of pain, especially chronic pain. One could simply never tell from reading philosophy that disabled people contribute to society or that their experience might enrich our understanding of what it is to live a human life.

Disabled people do sometimes appear in the philosophical literature. But, as Susan Wendell has noted, almost always the same two questions are being discussed: (1) How severely disabled does a person have to be before we are justified in withholding medical treatment and letting that person die? and (2) How disabled does a fetus need to be before it is permissible to prevent its being born? . . . Imagine yourself disabled, and see how this linkage of disability and death might strike you. It is as if there is no question of a *life* with disability, at all. It is simply assumed that disability in itself can be an appropriate basis for ending a human life, and the only morally troubling question is, *When?*

Involved in such a point of view is a cluster of attitudes and assumptions philosophers ought to question but apparently don't: we, the subjects here, can decide when persons whose disability places *them* at the margins (relative to *us*) may be allowed to live. There is a presumption that *we* have the right to ask this question, and that *we* have the capacity to answer it for ourselves on moral or conceptual or medical grounds, in the absence of any detailed knowledge of the lives of persons with disabilities or any real conversation with them on these issues. Related to this assumption is the fact that

Karen Fiser, "Philosophy, Disability, and Essentialism" in *Defending Diversity: Contemporary Philosophical Perspectives on Pluralism and Multiculturalism,* edited by Lawrence Foster and Patricia Herzog (Amherst: The University of Massachusetts Press, 1994): 83–101. Copyright (c) 1994 by the University of Massachusetts Press. Reprinted with permission.

the philosophers prescribing life or death for persons with disabilities are themselves able-bodied; if they weren't, they would not write as they do. There is no sense that disabled people are fully human subjects who can speak for themselves. Why does this seem plausible? We can see what is wrong with it by substituting any other minority group for persons with disabilities; what we have then is obviously, shockingly wrong. What does it mean that we don't notice this?

Even when philosophers do (rarely) attempt to discuss examples from the point of view of a person with a disability, their discussions are often marred by the same ignorant and contemptuous attitudes. Consider this passage from *Real People* by Kathleen V. Wilkes, in which she is comparing mental with physical disabilities:

> It is of course true that physical deficiency too may prevent him from engaging in such activities, but physical problems would at least leave open the possibility that he could pursue his interests indirectly—the physically handicapped can, for example, tell his friends and children, or write books, about how to care for begonias, what are the best routes up mountains, which philosophy books he would reread if only he were not blind, what he would say or do to support unilateralism or multilateralism if only he had the physical capacity. (Wilkes, 1988, pp. 94–95).

I suspect that most readers would read right past the offensive attitudes expressed in this passage without noticing them. A "physically handicapped" person could tell people how to care for begonias or write a book about it—*as opposed to* gardening? But, of course, disabled people do garden, and they also write books about topics more important than begonias. Stephen Hawking, a physicist with profound disabilities who wrote *A Brief History of Time*, did his important scientific work only *after* he became disabled. . . . Mark Wellman, a paraplegic, climbs mountains, he doesn't just write about it. Blind

people do read philosophy, and they write it as well. What "physical capacity" is required to support a political position or even to be active in politics? Franklin Roosevelt had an orthopedic disability, as we know, as have [Senator Kerrey and former Senator Bob Dole]. The clear implication of this paragraph is that disabled people usually don't do these things or can do them only "indirectly" or vicariously, simply because of their physical disabilities. But this is just not true.

Why would a philosopher make claims so at odds with facts we know very well when reminded of them? What accounts for the absence from our theories of real persons with real disabilities? Why can't we hear ourselves when we say offensive things about disabled people? I would like to suggest that we cannot end discrimination against persons with disabilities until we fundamentally change the way we think about and describe disability. We must reject the assumption (made by Wilkes in the paragraph quoted) that it even makes sense to say that if we know a person has a disability (belongs to a class of persons, for instance, persons with Down's syndrome or wheelchair users) we know what that person can do. We must stop making assumptions about what groups of people can do, and let them tell us.

DISABLING ASSUMPTIONS

I once gave my introductory ethics class an article to read, one of these Sunday supplement "super-crip" stories about people who triumph over their so-called handicaps. The story involved a man who refused to be beaten by his muscular dystrophy. It recounted how he insisted on driving and forcing himself to walk using crutches; the whole point of the article was to praise him for pushing himself always to do more. He and his wife went to a movie. He drove around until he finally found a parking place, and then they walked several blocks to the theater. But this had made them late, so he got angry at himself and insisted that they go home.

I asked my (all able-bodied) class to list the assumptions made by the author of the story. They didn't see any. Here are several: (1) It is better to use crutches than to use a wheelchair, even when using crutches is slower and makes you late for the movie; (2) using crutches to walk rather than a chair is courageous; (3) it is better for the disabled man to drive, even if it means he has to walk farther, than for his wife to drive and let him off in front of the theater; and (4) anger at himself for taking longer to get to the movie is an appropriate, healthy response (which *also* means he's courageous).

The members of my class did not notice these as assumptions because they shared them all. But most people with orthopedic disabilities do not hold these views; or, rather, if they do at first, they must (sometimes painfully) learn to discard them as disabling assumptions. The fact is, the dominant society is wheelchairphobic. People seem to feel a lot of emotion about wheelchairs, and they sometimes react oddly and unpredictably. I have had perfect strangers shout at me to *get out of that chair*. Once a woman congratulated the person standing next to me for having the courage it takes to walk! Sometimes people seem to feel called upon to *do* something, so they start pushing your chair vigorously without asking or speaking to you first.

Most people seem to assume you must be worse off if you're using a chair than you would be if you were standing. Many assume that if you use a chair, you're "confined" to it and can't walk. This is social prejudice born of ignorance. As one rehabilitation professional put it, "There are even times when the person who is walking is more disabled—because it takes twice as much energy to walk as it does if he would just sit down and wheel his chair" (Hooper, 1986, p. 21).

Many wheelchair users are in their chairs only half the day, or only when they are walking long distances. When I am walking, I am in pain with every step; when I am in my chair, I am in less pain, so I can do more. The chair empowers me. Pity is therefore not an appropriate response to someone using a wheelchair to walk. But if pity is inappropriate, so is the view that it takes more courage to walk with crutches. If you spent one day in a chair, you would know better. (By the way, doctors are not immune to these prejudices. Knowledge of the disease process does not equate to understanding the lives of people with disabilities.)

I myself went through a learning process. Like many others with my disability, I fought as hard as I could against using a wheelchair. I was especially afraid to teach in one. I endured many months of standing in front of my classes with excruciating, burning pain in my back and knees. Finally someone pointed out to me that it was actually *disabling* me to stand up, first because my obvious pain was distracting my class, and second because on days after I had stood I could not get out of bed. The price I was paying to keep standing on my own two feet was much too high.

As to assumption 3, that it's better for the man to drive than for his wife to drop him off, we overvalue personal autonomy in this culture, especially in men. But insisting on doing everything for oneself can be unrealistic and wrong, damaging to oneself and to others, when the circumstances have changed. Many disabled people go through a humbling transformation, learning to depend on others and to ask for help while not becoming overly dependent. The man in this story is going to have trouble if he keeps making his wife miss the movie because he insists on driving.

Finally, about assumption 4: people with any serious disability know that part of having a disability is constantly thinking out new ways to get something done and calculating how long it will take. Simple tasks become complex, requiring imagination and negotiation with others. Even one's relation to time has to change. In his memoir on becoming blind, John Hull tells of the profound changes in the sense of time and space occasioned by the onset of disability, describing a friend with multiple sclerosis who takes forty-five minutes to get his shoes tied. . . . Everything takes longer. You have to become more patient, not only with yourself, but with those for whom you must wait to receive help. Getting angry at oneself is the worst thing one could do. In this man's case, it seems a symptom of serious denial.

I have gone into such detail to make a point. People with disabilities are full, not diminished, human beings: they have real nonvicarious human lives to lead. You would not know that from reading philosophy.[1] There are many things to know about living a good life with a disability; most people begin to learn them only after they become disabled or someone close to them does. The accumulated wisdom and experience of disabled people is disregarded, as if it concerned only themselves. Its human importance is overlooked and discounted. For a long time in this country we have lived with what amounts to social and cultural segregation of people with disabilities. We seem content to remain ignorant about their lives and circumstances, and this ignorance often results in mistreatment and misunderstanding. But why should this be? Why do we think that ignorance and prejudice about people with disabilities is acceptable? Why do we think there is nothing important to learn from them about life?

If Kathleen Wilkes knew any disabled people well, I do not believe she would write philosophy as she does. Ethical theorists who knew about the lives of persons with Down's syndrome would not presume to generalize about their "diminished quality of life" or to give this as a reason for withholding medical treatment a "normal" child would receive.[2] When people refuse to look at the circumstances of a disabled person's life, they make abusive assumptions that disable the person. For example, in the case of Phillip Becker, a child with Down's syndrome who was institutionalized by his parents at birth, it was the refusal of the parents to see what he actually was like and was capable of that disabled him.

Because they saw him as someone who could not live a worthwhile life, they withheld their consent for Phillip to have his heart defect surgically repaired. The Heaths, a volunteer couple who had grown to love Phillip and saw him as a lively, likeable child who could learn and could enjoy his life, fought for him to have the same quality medical care he would have received without question if he had not been disabled.

There are many less dramatic examples of how the ignorant assumptions of the able-bodied actually create a handicap where the physical limitation involved need not do so. John Hull describes how sighted people do not understand that when a blind person is lost, he needs to be told precisely where he is; giving directions as one would to a sighted person (turn left at the corner, and then right) does not help. Similarly, when a blind person walks along with a friend, he must put a finger under the friend's elbow to stay with him. He therefore can't use his stick or attend in the same way to the route. This creates a dependency that the sighted person may assume is normal, when it is only a consequence of being with someone sighted.

Many persons previously thought to be "retarded" all their lives are now able to speak as a result of new techniques of facilitated communication on a computer keyboard. Men and women had been described and treated as if they were completely unable to learn, when in fact we were unable to communicate with them to find out what they knew. Many have lived whole lives waiting for us to find the key to unlock the prison of silence. Clearly, part of what was disabling them was other people's assumptions in the absence of real knowledge about what they could do.

Here is another, more everyday, kind of case. When I became disabled, I was constantly shamed by the fact that I would make plans and then have to change them. I would plan to attend a meeting and not be able to go. I would bend all my efforts to meet a certain professional goal and fail miserably because of unforeseen circumstances. When your pain level and energy are unpredictable, you feel as if you are at the mercy of factors you cannot control. That's because you are. You have to learn to take what a day bestows, even if it's not what you planned, and so do your friends, colleagues, and family. Before I understood this, I blamed myself and let others blame me. This shame was disabling.

Finally a wise friend whose husband had MS told me that this inability to predict even one's own future goes with the territory. You buy an adapted van so you can drive, only to find that your worsening condition makes further driving impossible. You fight for six months to have your employer accept the idea that a changed work schedule would enable you to function in your workplace, only to find that the new schedule is too much for you, and you have to start all over again.

Sometimes relationships cannot withstand the strain. Friends get hurt and angry that you don't do what you said you would do. Employers take it as your personal failing that you can't control your own life. All disabled persons can tell stories about problems at work, even jobs lost, because employers could not understand their behavior, and about friends and lovers who could not accept the realities of their situation and chose to disappear.

The important point here is that a person with a disability cannot be understood as the same person, with one added property—a disability. Or, to put this point differently: one cannot understand a person with a disability without coming to understand the nature of that particular disability and the demands it places on the person involved. For instance, if you don't understand that a person with multiple sclerosis suffering exacerbations of her condition can't predict what she will be able to do, you might wrongly conclude, from her failure to do, that she's unreliable or irresponsible.

THE INVISIBLE MINORITY

Often disabled people seem to be the invisible minority. Able-bodied people, even those who mean well, sometimes seem to overlook them or to view their problems as merely personal ones. Many people do not understand that discrimi-

nation against persons with disabilities is a serious problem that will not be solved easily. I heard a woman speak whose daughter had recently been a high school student who used a wheelchair. Her senior prom had been scheduled by the school in an inaccessible place. When the daughter protested that she wanted to attend and could not, many people got angry at her for causing so much trouble—after all, she was the only one affected.

When I heard this story, my thought was that if one student were excluded from a prom because the dance was held in a racially segregated country club, people would see that exclusion as clearly wrong and speak up for her. But when I tried that analogy out on able-bodied friends, they didn't think it was a good one. First of all, why would a wheelchair user need to go to a dance? If the school changed the dance to an accessible place, they thought, it would be a good thing to do, but they could not see that the student had a legal right to an accessible prom. This reaction troubled me. I began to fear that my able-bodied friends unconsciously saw people with disabilities as "less than," as if the disability *in itself* diminished their humanity, removing their right to choose for themselves. First of all, they tended to identify (somewhat defensively, it seemed to me) with the school authorities, seeing the problem in terms of expense and trouble to the school to benefit one person, and not of the student's civil rights. But, even more damaging, they seemed to take for granted that it was permissible for others to define the interests and abilities of a disabled person: she was disabled, so she could not dance and could have no interest in dancing. They did not perceive the obvious lack of respect inherent in this point of view.

Sometimes this lack of respect comes out in sadistic and abusive behavior. In *The Illness Narratives*, Arthur Kleinman tells the story of Paul Sensabaugh, a man who suffered brain injury and coma with severe injuries to the frontal and temporal lobes. . . . As a result, he underwent personality changes. His behavior became childish and impulsive. He was left with limited cognition. For him it became a struggle to do the simplest things. The biggest event of his day was going out to buy a paper. His daily routine became crucial to his sense of self-respect; it was important to be independent, to look "just the same as the others." Though his life had become severely circumscribed after his accident, he remained extremely conscious of other people's reactions and anxious to avoid shame. Dr. Kleinman remarks:

> I came to realize just how often he was shamed: by children in the hospital who gawked at him and mimicked his behavior; by patients or families who avoided sitting near him; by the hospital security personnel, who had a habit of making faces when he walked by; by the woman at the cash register who would say, "Come on, get goin', we can't wait all day while you count your change"; and worst of all, by the janitorial staff who called him "dummy."

One day the doctor was in a hurry and was brusque with Paul, impatiently cutting off his slow, painstaking attempts to talk. Paul responded:

> That's OK, Dr. Kleinman. I'm accustomed to it. I'm just a small person. I'm hardly a grownup anymore. I know the truth [beginning to cry]. I'm not altogether up here. I'm a half-wit like they said, aren't I? The world is too fast for me, isn't it? The people are too big. And when they get angry they can hurt you, can't they? It really is too dangerous a place for me. Maybe I should live in a home, you know what I mean, a home for people like me.

To me, the humanity and dignity of Paul's response provide the best answer to those who think that his disability, severe as it is, makes him less human or in any way renders his life less than a wholly human life. The point is, how do we as a society provide what he needs to live

the best life possible *for him*? Yet many people, meeting Paul on the street, would react to him with distaste, fear, condescension, or impatience, utterly failing to see that their own behavior is now creating the pain in his life and needs to change.

In fact, people with disabilities are often easy targets for verbal and physical abuse. Shocking as it is, many are victimized in their own homes. On the street, it is not unusual for wheelchair users to be taunted, beaten, and robbed.[3] Even when disabled people are not overtly abused, their dignity and personhood are continually assaulted. They are ignored, infantilized, treated as if they weren't there, spoken about in the third person: "Will you look after him? Will his chair fit in the elevator?" Taxi drivers pass wheelchair users by, because they think it's not worth their time to deal with the chair.

Able-bodied people often have great difficulty seeing how they contribute to the problems disabled people face. I once had a politically progressive colleague who loved Vietnamese peasants and every single member of the working class. Yet he kept scheduling meetings of a group to which we both belonged up a steep flight of stairs, which made it impossible for me to attend. He never could grasp that this was a political issue, much less a moral one. I could not get him to see the point. I wanted to call him a racist, because that's what it felt like: he refused to see what his privilege allowed him not to see, and I never had any power to make him act differently. (And that experience taught me a valuable lesson: never assume that someone who understands one form of oppression will necessarily notice or understand the oppression of disabled people. On the contrary, sometimes progressives are the worst, because they assume they're on your side, that they aren't among those who need to change, and that their behavior is beyond criticism. In other words, they do not think they need to learn anything from a disabled person because they already have the correct position.)

In an academic context, I have had colleagues tell me that disabled people aren't members of a minority group and therefore don't deserve any special attention in academic admissions or hiring. Yet these same colleagues will admit, if pressed, that there are no deaf or blind students in their classes, and that there are only a few wheelchair users on the campus. And they will admit, if you ask them, that they have no deaf or blind colleagues, and that there is maybe one faculty member with a visible disability, in another department. Do they think people with disabilities choose not to go to college or to teach in universities? The unfortunate fact is, they don't usually notice, one way or the other, because they are accustomed to the social, cultural, and economic segregation of disabled people.

I was talking recently with a colleague about how Stanford is heavily recruiting minority graduate students, flying them in for campus visits. I asked how many students with disabilities were among them, and there was a stunned silence. The committee had not even noticed that there weren't any.

Under heavy pressure from a strong and well-organized group of women of color, the president of a West Coast women's college pledged that, within five years, 10 percent of the faculty would be persons of color. The disabled students were in great pain about this decision. On the one hand, they did not wish to (and did not) oppose measures aimed at undoing the legacy of racism at the college. On the other hand, they knew that this measure would make it next to impossible to add any faculty with disabilities—there were none, and *no one had even noticed*. Once again, people with disabilities were invisible.

We should never assume that, by addressing the concerns of minority faculty and students, we have addressed the needs of faculty and students with disabilities. We do not know what those needs are without asking faculty and students with disabilities, and we cannot do that if there weren't any. Once we see this clearly, we can make it a priority to recruit minority students with disabilities, who are almost never mentioned. It is offensive to assume that faculty and students of color necessarily understand the issues of people with disabilities, or vice versa, just because one regards them both as minorities.

In fact, one cannot even safely assume that those with one disability automatically understand people with another. Though the dominant culture may lump together in one group called the disabled those whom they regard as physically defective or damaged, the fact is that, for example, people with orthopedic disabilities do not automatically understand the problems of blind people, and the community of deaf and hearing-impaired persons does not naturally identify with the problems of persons with cerebral palsy or developmental disabilities. They only so identify if they are politically aware enough to make such alliances.

Sometimes it is assumed that racial and ethnic discrimination is somehow more basic or more problematic and must be addressed first. This assumption often seems to rest on people's belief that attitudinal changes alone will do away with discrimination against the disabled. Or that, plus building a few ramps. This attitude was perfectly expressed by a college president who said that she preferred to regard all people as alike, just "differently abled." (This is akin to a racist who thinks she's non-racist saying that we're all alike under the skin.) Given the long history of active discrimination against disabled people, remaining neutral about this history, behaving as if we're all now magically somehow the same, makes the disabled person as an individual bear all the consequences of discrimination. The college president's view seemed to be that a change in attitude is already doing away with discrimination against persons with disabilities, but that racism is more serious and pervasive. . . .

We have all inherited a history of segregation, unexamined prejudice, privilege (relative to some other), and failure to see through our own ideological assumptions. No standpoint is immune to these shortcomings, however careful and responsible we try to be.

What does seem certain is that the only way we have to transcend these limits and to learn about the other, as Martha Minow has noted, is to talk with that person. . . . As a disabled person, I would like to see philosophers, including feminist theorists, stop merely consulting their intuitions about disability and start listening to disabled people talk about their own experiences. I would like to see them stop repeating biased and offensive language and assumptions about disability. And, finally, I would hope to see them working to correct not only the appalling silence about the lives of real human beings with real disabilities, but also the conditions underneath the silence.

NOTES

1. On the ethical significance of "having a human life to lead," see Diamond, 1991.

2. On this topic, see Asch and Fine, 1988, p. 299: "People who decide that Down's Syndrome or spina bifida automatically renders children or adults 'vegetables' or 'better off dead' simply know nothing about the lives of such people today—much less what those lives could be in a more inclusive, person-oriented society."

3. Personal communication from Bob Alexander, then chair of the Cambridge Commission on Handicapped Persons, in 1986.

WORKS CITED

Asch, Adrienne, and Michelle Fine. 1988. *Women with Disabilities*. Philadelphia: Temple University Press.

Blackwell-Stratton, Marian, et al. 1988. "Smashing Icons: Disabled Women and the Disability of Women's Movements," in Asch and Fine.

Bowe, Frank. 1984. *Disabled Women in America*. Washington, D.C.: President's Committee on Employment of the Handicapped.

Chang, Sucheng. 1990. "You're Short, Besides!" In *Making Face, Making Soul*, ed. Gloria Anzaldua. San Francisco: Aunt Lute Foundation.

Charmaz, Kathy. 1991. *Good Days, Bad Days*. New Brunswick, N.J.: Rutgers University Press.

Congressional Research Service. 1984. *Digest of Data on Persons with Disabilities*. Library of Congress, Report #84–115 EPW, principal investigator John L. Czajka.

Diamond, Cora. 1991. "The Importance of Being Human." In *Human Beings*, ed. David Cockburn. Cambridge: Cambridge University Press.

Dubus, Andre. 1991. *Broken Vessels*. Boston: Godine.

Easton, Carol. 1990. *Jacqueline du Pre*. New York: Summit.

Fiser, Karen. 1986. "Privacy and Pain." *Philosophical Investigations* 9, no. 1 (January), pp. 1–17.

Hooper, Ed. 1986. "More than a Long Walk." *Disability Rag*, January–February.

Hull, John M. 1990. *Touching the Rock: An Experience of Blindness*. New York: Pantheon.

Kent, Debra. 1987. "In Search of Liberation." In Saxton and Howe.

Kleinman, Arthur. 1988. *The Illness Narratives: Suffering, Healing, and the Human Condition*. New York: Basic Books.

Lugones, María C. 1991. "On the Logic of Pluralist Feminism." In *Feminist Ethics*, ed. Claudia Card. Lawrence: University Press of Kansas.

Lugones, María C., and Elizabeth V. Spelman. 1990. "Have We Got a Theory for You! Feminist Theory, Cultural Imperialism, and the Demand for 'The Woman's Voice.'" In *Hypatia Reborn: Essays in Feminist Philosophy*, ed. Azizah Y. Al-Hibri and Margaret A. Simons. Bloomington: Indiana University Press.

Mairs, Nancy. 1987. "On Being a Cripple." In Saxton and Howe.

Minow, Martha. 1990. *Making All the Difference: Inclusion, Exclusion, and American Law*. Ithaca, N.Y.: Cornell University Press.

Morris, David B. 1991. *The Culture of Pain*. Berkeley and Los Angeles: University of California Press.

Saxton, Marsha, and Florence Howe, eds. 1987. *With Wings*. New York: Feminist Press.

Scarry, Elaine. 1987. *The Body in Pain: The Making and Unmaking of the World*. New York: Oxford University Press.

Spelman, Elizabeth V. 1988. *Inessential Woman: Problems of Exclusion in Feminist Thought*. Boston: Beacon.

Stone, Deborah A. 1984. *The Disabled State*. Philadelphia: Temple University Press.

Wendell, Susan. 1989. "Toward a Feminist Theory of Disability." *Hypatia* 4, no. 2(Summer), pp. 104–24.

White, Michael, and John Gribben. 1992. *Stephen Hawking: A Life in Science*. New York: Dutton.

Wilkes, Kathleen. 1988. *Real People*. Oxford: Clarendon.

2

Abortion

Introduction

THE MORAL AND LEGAL CONTROVERSIES SURROUNDING ABORTION

Abortion remains a controversial issue in our country, even twenty-five years after the Supreme Court's ruling in *Roe v. Wade* (1973). Far from settling the matter or providing closure to this debate, this decision has generated intense disagreement over the legal and moral status of abortion.

The emphasis of this chapter is on the *moral* permissibility of abortion; the legal and constitutional issues are not directly addressed. Philosophers generally believe that the moral debate is prior to, and more fundamental than, the legal analysis. The moral analysis of abortion has, of course, obvious and important consequences for the legal and public policy debates.

FRAMING THE ABORTION DEBATE: THE STATUS OF THE FETUS

Philosophers writing about abortion have typically given prominence in their analyses to determining the status of the fetus. They have thought that moral judgments about the status of abortion would follow in a straightforward manner once the personhood status of the developing fetus was established. When philosophers use the term *person* in this sense, they do not employ it as a biological term indicating membership in a particular species. Rather, they use it as a moral and thus normative term. It typically is used to designate those who are members of our *moral* community, and who in light of their membership merit protection from other members of the community. Alternatively, membership in this community might be marked out by rights-based claims: *Persons* are those who have certain basic rights that must be honored and protected. If fetuses at a certain stage in their development were judged to be outside the class of persons, then abortion at that point would not be impermissible. On the other hand, if fetuses were deemed to be persons from the time of conception, fertilization, and/or implantation, then abortion would be impermissible except in a few cases, such as when the life of the pregnant woman is threatened by the continued development of the fetus. This theoretical framework is in Don Marquis's article in this chapter. Marquis asserts that "whether or not abortion is morally permissible stands or falls on whether or not a fetus is the sort of being whose life it is seriously wrong to end."[1]

RETHINKING THE MORAL FRAMEWORK FEMINIST ANALYSES

Other philosophers have suggested that we ought not focus on or limit the abortion debate to the questions surrounding the status of the fetus as a person. They have argued that our moral attention ought be directed to the *relationship* between the pregnant woman and the developing fetus. Others have argued that we must expand the scope of the debate to take into consideration the broader social context of child-bearing women and girls: Are safe and reliable contraceptives available for both women and men? What more can be done to ensure that

---

1. Don Marquis, "Why Abortion Is Immoral," p. 103.

girls and women are not coerced into sexual activity that might result in pregnancy? What role ought society take in providing health care and support to infants and young children and their parents? Whose responsibility is it to provide care for pre-school-age children? In short, these philosophers suggest that we cannot address the moral problems of abortion without also addressing the moral complexities of the oppression women and girls experience in our society.

7.

Abortion and the Concept of a Person

Jane English

Jane English taught philosophy at the University of North Carolina before her untimely death while mountain-climbing. In this essay, she argues that the abortion issue cannot be decided simply by examining the personhood status of the fetus; she contends that our concept of a person is not sharp enough to bear the weight of the entire moral debate over abortion. Even if the personhood status of the fetus were clear at each stage of development, conclusions about the moral permissibility of abortion cannot easily be drawn: In some cases, killing persons may be morally justified, and in certain instances, killing non-persons may not be morally permissible.

The abortion debate rages on. Yet the two most popular positions seem to be clearly mistaken. Conservatives maintain that a human life begins at conception and that therefore abortion must be wrong because it is murder. But not all killings of humans are murders. Most notably, self-defense may justify even the killing of an innocent person.

Liberals, on the other hand, are just as mistaken in their argument that since a fetus does not become a person until birth, a woman may do whatever she pleases in and to her own body. First, you cannot do as you please with your own body if it affects other people adversely.[1] Second, if a fetus is not a person, that does not imply that you can do to it anything you wish. Animals, for example, are not persons, yet to kill or torture them for no reason at all is wrong.

Jane English, "Abortion and the Concept of a Person," *Canadian Journal of Philosophy* 5 (October 1974): 233–243. Reprinted with permission of the *Canadian Journal of Philosophy*, The University of Calgary Press, and the Jane English Memorial Fund at the University of North Carolina.

At the center of the storm has been the issue of just when it is between ovulation and adulthood that a person appears on the scene. Conservatives draw the line at conception, liberals at birth. In this paper I first examine our concept of a person and conclude that no single criterion can capture the concept of a person and no sharp line can be drawn. Next I argue that if a fetus is a person, abortion is still justifiable in many cases; and if a fetus is not a person, killing it is still wrong in many cases. To a large extent, these two solutions are in agreement. I conclude that our concept of a person cannot and need not bear the weight that the abortion controversy has thrust upon it.

I

The several factions in the abortion argument have drawn battle lines around various proposed criteria for determining what is and what is not a person. For example, Mary Anne Warren[2] lists five features (capacities for reasoning, self-awareness, complex communications, etc.)

as her criteria for personhood and argues for the permissibility of abortion because a fetus falls outside this concept. Baruch Brody[3] uses brain waves. Michael Tooley[4] picks having-a-concept-of-self as his criterion and concludes that infanticide and abortion are justifiable, while the killing of adult animals is not. On the other side, Paul Ramsey[5] claims a certain gene structure is the defining characteristic. John Noonan[6] prefers conceived-of-humans and presents counterexamples to various other candidate criteria. For instance, he argues against viability as the criterion because the newborn and infirm would then be non-persons, since they cannot live without the aid of others. He rejects any criterion that calls upon the sorts of sentiments a being can evoke in adults on the grounds that this would allow us to exclude other races as non-persons if we could just view them sufficiently unsentimentally.

These approaches are typical: foes of abortion propose sufficient conditions for personhood which fetuses satisfy, while friends of abortion counter with necessary conditions for personhood which fetuses lack. But these both presuppose that the concept of a person can be captured in a straightjacket of necessary and/or sufficient conditions.[7] Rather, "person" is a cluster of features, of which rationality, having a self-concept and being conceived of humans are only a part.

What is typical of persons? Within our concept of a person we include, first, certain biological factors: descended from humans, having a certain genetic make-up, having a head, hands, arms, eyes, capable of locomotion, breathing, eating, sleeping. There are psychological factors: sentience, perception, having a concept of self and of one's own interests and desires, and the ability to use tools, the ability to use language or symbol systems, the ability to joke, to be angry, to doubt. There are rationality factors: the ability to reason and draw conclusions, the ability to generalize and to learn from past experience, the ability to sacrifice present interests for greater gains in the future.

There are social factors: the ability to work in groups and respond to peer pressures, the ability to recognize and consider as valuable the interests of others, seeing oneself as among "other minds," the ability to sympathize, encourage, love, the ability to evoke from others the responses of sympathy, encouragement, love, the ability to work with others for mutual advantage. Then there are legal factors: being subject to the law and protected by it, having the ability to sue and enter contracts, being counted in the census, having a name and citizenship, the ability to own property, inherit, and so forth.

Now the point is not that this list is incomplete, or that you can find counterinstances to each of its points. People typically exhibit rationality, for instance, but someone who was irrational would not thereby fail to qualify as a person. On the other hand, something could exhibit the majority of these features and still fail to be a person, as an advanced robot might. There is no single core of necessary and sufficient features which we can draw upon with the assurance that they constitute what really makes a person; there are only features that are more or less typical.

This is not to say that no necessary or sufficient conditions can be given. Being alive is a necessary condition for being a person, and being a U.S. Senator is sufficient. But rather than falling inside a sufficient condition or outside a necessary one, a fetus lies in the penumbra region where our concept of a person is not so simple. For this reason I think a conclusive answer to the question whether a fetus is a person is unattainable.

Here we might note a family of simple fallacies that proceed by stating a necessary condition for personhood and showing that a fetus has that characteristic. This is a form of the fallacy of affirming the consequent. For example, some have mistakenly reasoned from the premise that a fetus is human (after all, it is a human fetus rather than, say, a canine fetus), to the conclusion that it is a human. Adding an equivocation on 'being', we get the fallacious argument that since a fetus is something both living and human, it is a human being.

Nonetheless, it does seem clear that a fetus has very few of the above family of characteristics, whereas a newborn baby exhibits a much larger proportion of them—and a two-year-old has even more. Note that one traditional anti-abortion argument has centered on pointing out the many ways in which a fetus resembles a baby. They emphasize its development ("It already has ten fingers . . . ") without mentioning its dissimilarities to adults (it still has gills and a tail). They also try to evoke the sort of sympathy on our part that we only feel toward other persons ("Never to laugh . . . or feel the sunshine?"). This all seems to be a relevant way to argue, since its purpose is to persuade us that a fetus satisfies so many of the important features on the list that it ought to be treated as a person. Also note that a fetus near the time of birth satisfies many more of these factors than a fetus in the early months of development. This could provide reason for making distinctions among the different stages of pregnancy, as the U.S. Supreme Court has done.[8]

Historically, the time at which a person had been said to come into existence has varied widely. Muslims date personhood from fourteen days after conception. Some medievals followed Aristotle in placing ensoulment at forty days after conception for a male fetus and eighty days for a female fetus.[9] In European common law since the seventeenth century, abortion was considered the killing of a person only after quickening, the time when a pregnant woman first feels the fetus move on its own. Nor is this variety of opinions surprising. Biologically, a human being develops gradually. We shouldn't expect there to be any specific time or sharp dividing point when a person appears on the scene.

For these reasons I believe our concept of a person is not sharp or decisive enough to bear the weight of a solution to the abortion controversy. To use it to solve that problem is to clarify *obscurum per obscurius.*

II

Next let us consider what follows if a fetus is a person after all. Judith Jarvis Thomson's landmark article, "A Defense of Abortion,"[10] correctly points out that some additional argumentation is needed at this point in the conservative argument to bridge the gap between the premise that a fetus is an innocent person and the conclusion that killing it is always wrong. To arrive at this conclusion, we would need the additional premise that killing an innocent person is always wrong. But killing an innocent person is sometimes permissible, most notably in self-defense. Some examples may help draw out our intuitions or ordinary judgments about self-defense.

Suppose a mad scientist, for instance, hypnotized innocent people to jump out of the bushes and attack innocent passers-by with knives. If you are so attacked, we agree you have a right to kill the attacker in self-defense, if killing him is the only way to protect your life or to save yourself from serious injury. It does not seem to matter here that the attacker is not malicious but himself an innocent pawn, for your killing of him is not done in a spirit of retribution but only in self-defense.

How severe an injury may you inflict in self-defense? In part this depends upon the severity of the injury to be avoided: you may not shoot someone merely to avoid having your clothes torn. This might lead one to the mistaken conclusion that the defense may only equal the threatened injury in severity; that to avoid death you may kill, but to avoid a black eye you may only inflict a black eye or the equivalent. Rather, our laws and customs seem to say that you may create an injury somewhat, but not enormously, greater than the injury to be avoided. To fend off an attack whose outcome would be as serious as rape, a severe beating or the loss of a finger, you may shoot; to avoid having your clothes torn, you may blacken an eye.

Aside from this, the injury you may inflict should only be the minimum necessary to deter or incapacitate the attacker. Even if you know he intends to kill you, you are not justified in shooting him if you could equally well save yourself by the simple expedient of running away. Self-defense is for the purpose of avoiding harms rather than equalizing harms.

Some cases of pregnancy present a parallel situation. Though the fetus is itself innocent, it may pose a threat to the pregnant woman's well-being, life prospects or health, mental or physical. If the pregnancy presents a slight threat to her interests, it seems self-defense cannot justify abortion. But if the threat is on a par with a serious beating or the loss of a finger, she may kill the fetus that poses such a threat, even if it is an innocent person. If a lesser harm to the fetus could have the same defensive effect, killing it would not be justified. It is unfortunate that the only way to free the woman from the pregnancy entails the death of the fetus (except in very late stages of pregnancy). Thus a self-defense model supports Thomson's point that the woman has a right only to be freed from the fetus, not a right to demand its death.[11]

The self-defense model is most helpful when we take the pregnant woman's point of view. In the pre-Thomson literature, abortion is often framed as a question for a third party: do you, a doctor, have a right to choose between the life of the woman and that of the fetus? Some have claimed that if you were a passer-by who witnessed a struggle between the innocent hypnotized attacker and his equally innocent hypnotized victim, you would have no reason to kill either in defense of the other. They have concluded that the self-defense model implies that a woman may attempt to abort herself, but that a doctor should not assist her. I think the position of the third party is somewhat more complex. We do feel some inclination to intervene on behalf of the victim rather than the attacker, other things equal. But if both parties are innocent, other factors come into consideration. You would rush to the aid of your husband whether he was attacker or attackee. If a hypnotized famous violinist were attacking a skid row bum, we would try to save the individual who is of more value to society. These considerations would tend to support abortion in some cases.

But suppose you are a frail senior citizen who wishes to avoid being knifed by one of these innocent hypnotics, so you have hired a bodyguard to accompany you. If you are attacked, it is clear we believe that the bodyguard, acting as your agent, has a right to kill the attacker to save you from a serious beating. Your rights of self-defense are transferred to your agent. I suggest that we should similarly view the doctor as the pregnant woman's agent in carrying out a defense she is physically incapable of accomplishing herself.

Thanks to modern technology, the cases are rare in which a pregnancy poses as clear a threat to a woman's bodily health as an attacker brandishing a switchblade. How does self-defense fare when more subtle, complex, and long-range harms are involved?

To consider a somewhat fanciful example, suppose you are a highly trained surgeon when you are kidnapped by the hypnotic attacker. He says he does not intend to harm you but to take you back to the mad scientist who, it turns out, plans to hypnotize you to have a permanent mental block against all your knowledge of medicine. This would automatically destroy your career which would in turn have a serious adverse impact on your family, your personal relationships and your happiness. It seems to me that if the only way you can avoid this outcome is to shoot the innocent attacker, you are justified in so doing. You are defending yourself from a drastic injury to your life prospects. I think it is no exaggeration to claim that unwanted pregnancies (most obviously among teenagers) often have such adverse life-long consequences as the surgeon's loss of livelihood.

Several parallels arise between various views on abortion and the self-defense model. Let's suppose further that these hypnotized attackers only operate at night, so that it is well known that they can be avoided completely by the considerable inconvenience of never leaving your house after dark. One view is that since you could stay home at night, therefore if you go out and are selected by one of these hypnotized people, you have no right to defend yourself. This parallels the view that abstinence is the only acceptable way to avoid pregnancy. Others might hold that you ought to take along some defense such as Mace which will deter the hypnotized person without killing him, but that if this defense fails, you are obliged to submit to the resulting injury, no matter how severe it is. This parallels the view that contraception is all right but abortion is always wrong, even in cases of contraceptive failure.

A third view is that you may kill the hypnotized person only if he will actually kill you, but not if he will only injure you. This is like the position that abortion is permissible only if it is required to save a woman's life. Finally we have the view that it is all right to kill the attacker, even if only to avoid a very slight inconvenience to yourself and even if you knowingly walked down the very street where all these incidents have been taking place without taking along any Mace or protective escort. If we assume that a fetus is a person, this is the analogue of the view that abortion is always justifiable, "on demand."

The self-defense model allows us to see an important difference that exists between abortion and infanticide, even if a fetus is a person from conception. Many have argued that the only way to justify abortion without justifying infanticide would be to find some characteristic of personhood that is acquired at birth. Michael Tooley, for one, claims infanticide is justifiable because the really significant characteristics of a person are acquired some time after birth. But all such approaches look to characteristics of the developing human and ignore the relation between the fetus and the woman. What if, after birth, the presence of an infant or the need to support it posed a grave threat to the woman's sanity or life prospects? She could escape this threat by the simple expedient of running away. So a solution that does not entail the death of the infant is available. Before birth, such solutions are not available because of the biological dependence of the fetus on the woman. Birth is the crucial point not because of any characteristics the fetus gains, but because after birth the woman can defend herself by a means less drastic than killing the infant. Hence self-defense can be used to justify abortion without necessarily thereby justifying infanticide.

III

On the other hand, supposing a fetus is not after all a person, would abortion always be morally permissible? Some opponents of abortion seem worried that if a fetus is not a full-fledged person, then we are justified in treating it in any way at all. However, this does not follow. Nonpersons do get some consideration in our moral code, though of course they do not have the same rights as persons have (and in general they do not have moral responsibilities), and though their interests may be overridden by the interests of persons. Still, we cannot just treat them in any way at all.

Treatment of animals is a case in point. It is wrong to torture dogs for fun or to kill wild birds for no reason at all. It is wrong Period, even though dogs and birds do not have the same rights persons do. However, few people think it is wrong to use dogs as experimental animals, causing them considerable suffering in some cases, provided that the resulting research will probably bring discoveries of great benefit to people. And most of us think it is all right to kill birds for food or to protect our crops. People's rights are different from the consideration we give to animals, then, for it is wrong to experiment on people, even if others might later benefit a great deal as a result of their suffering. You might volunteer to be a subject, but this would be supererogatory; you certainly have a right to refuse to be a medical guinea pig.

But how do we decide what you may or may not do to non-persons? This is a difficult problem, one for which I believe no adequate account exists. You do not want to say, for instance, that torturing dogs is all right whenever the sum of its effects on people is good—when it doesn't warp the sensibilities of the torturer so much that he mistreats people. If that were the case, it would be all right to torture dogs if you did it in private, or if the torturer lived on a desert island or died soon afterward, so that his actions had no effect on people. This is an inadequate account, because whatever moral consideration animals get, it has to be indefeasible, too. It will have to be a general proscription of certain actions, not merely a weighing of the impact on people on a case-by-case basis.

Rather, we need to distinguish two levels on which consequences of actions can be taken into account in moral reasoning. The traditional objections to Utilitarianism focus on the fact that it operates solely on the first level, taking all the consequences into account in particular cases only. Thus Utilitarianism is open to "desert island" and "lifeboat" counterexamples because these cases are rigged to make the consequences of actions severely limited.

Rawls's theory could be described as a teleological sort of theory, but with teleology operating on a higher level.[12] In choosing the principles to regulate society from the original position, his hypothetical choosers make their decision on the basis of the total consequences of various systems. Furthermore, they are constrained to choose a general set of rules which people can readily learn and apply. An ethical theory must operate by generating a set of sympathies and attitudes toward others which reinforce the functioning of that set of moral principles. Our prohibition against killing people operates by means of certain moral sentiments including sympathy, compassion, and guilt. But if these attitudes are to form a coherent set, they carry us further: we tend to perform supererogatory actions, and we tend to feel similar compassion toward person-like non-persons.

It is crucial that psychological facts play a role here. Our psychological constitution makes it the case that for our ethical theory to work, it

must prohibit certain treatment of non-persons which are significantly person-like. If our moral rules allowed people to treat some personlike non-persons in ways we do not want people to be treated, this would undermine the system of sympathies and attitudes that makes the ethical system work. For this reason, we would choose in the original position to make mistreatment of some sorts of animals wrong in general (not just wrong in the cases with public impact), even though animals are not themselves parties in the original position. Thus it makes sense that it is those animals whose appearance and behavior are most like those of people that get the most consideration in our moral scheme.

It is because of "coherence of attitudes," I think, that the similarity of a fetus to a baby is very significant. A fetus one week before birth is so much like a newborn baby in our psychological space that we cannot allow any cavalier treatment of the former while expecting full sympathy and nurturative support for the latter. Thus, I think that anti-abortion forces are indeed giving their strongest arguments when they point to the similarities between a fetus and a baby, and when they try to evoke our emotional attachment to and sympathy for the fetus. An early horror story from New York about nurses who were expected to alternate between caring for six-week premature infants and disposing of viable 24-week aborted fetuses is just that—a horror story. These beings are so much alike that no one can be asked to draw a distinction and treat them so very differently.

Remember, however, that in the early weeks after conception, a fetus is very much unlike a person. It is hard to develop these feelings for a set of genes which doesn't yet have a head, hands, beating heart, response to touch or the ability to move by itself. Thus it seems to me that the alleged "slippery slope" between conception and birth is not so very slippery. In the early stages of pregnancy, abortion can hardly be compared to murder for psychological reasons, but in the latest stages it is psychologically akin to murder.

Another source of similarity is the bodily continuity between fetus and adult. Bodies play a surprisingly central role in our attitudes toward persons. One has only to think of the philosophical literature on how far physical identity suffices for personal identity or Wittgenstein's remark that the best picture of the human soul is the human body. Even after death, when all agree the body is no longer a person, we still observe elaborate customs of respect for the human body; like people who torture dogs, necrophiliacs are not to be trusted with people.[13] So it is appropriate that we show respect to a fetus as the body continuous with the body of a person. This is a degree of resemblance to persons that animals cannot rival.

Michael Tooley also utilizes a parallel with animals. He claims that it is always permissible to drown newborn kittens and draws conclusions about infanticide.[14] But it is only permissible to drown kittens when their survival would cause some hardship. Perhaps it would be a burden to feed and house six more cats or to find other homes for them. The alternative of letting them starve produces even more suffering than the drowning. Since the kittens get their rights secondhand, so to speak, *via* the need for coherence in our attitudes, their interests are often overridden by the interests of full-fledged persons. But if their survival would be no inconvenience to people at all, then it is wrong to drown them, *contra* Tooley.

Tooley's conclusions about abortion are wrong for the same reason. Even if a fetus is not a person, abortion is not always permissible, because of the resemblance of a fetus to a person. I agree with Thomson that it would be wrong for a woman who is seven months pregnant to have an abortion just to avoid having to postpone a trip to Europe. In the early months of pregnancy when the fetus hardly resembles a baby at all, then, abortion is permissible whenever it is in the interests of the pregnant woman or her family. The reasons would only need to outweigh the pain and inconvenience of the abortion itself. In the middle months, when the fetus comes to resemble a person, abortion would be justifiable only when the continuation of the pregnancy or the birth of the child would cause harms—physical, psychological, economic or social—to the woman. In the late months of pregnancy, even on our current assumption that a fetus is not a person, abortion seems to be wrong except to save a woman from significant injury or death.

The Supreme Court has recognized similar gradations in the alleged slippery slope stretching between conception and birth. To this point, the present paper has been a discussion of the moral status of abortion only, not its legal status. In view of the great physical, financial and sometimes psychological costs of abortion, perhaps the legal arrangement most compatible with the proposed moral solution would be the absence of restrictions, that is, so-called abortion "on demand."

So I conclude, first, that application of our concept of a person will not suffice to settle the abortion issue. After all, the biological development of a human being is gradual. Second, whether a fetus is a person or not, abortion is justifiable early in pregnancy to avoid modest harms and seldom justifiable late in pregnancy except to avoid significant injury or death.

NOTES

1. We also have paternalistic laws which keep us from harming our own bodies even when no one else is affected. Ironically, anti-abortion laws were originally designed to protect pregnant women from a dangerous but tempting procedure.

2. Mary Anne Warren, "On the Moral and Legal Status of Abortion," *Monist* 5 (1973), p. 55.

3. Baruch Brody, "Fetal Humanity and the Theory of Essentialism," in Robert Baker and Frederick Elliston (eds.), *Philosophy and Sex* (Buffalo, N.Y., 1975).

4. Michael Tooley, "Abortion and Infanticide," *Philosophy and Public Affairs* 1 (1971).

5. Paul Ramsey, "The Morality of Abortion," in James Rachels, ed., *Moral Problems* (New York, 1971).

6. John Noonan, "Abortion and the Catholic Church: A Summary History," *Natural Law Forum* 12 (1967):125–131.

7. Wittgenstein has argued against the possibility of so capturing the concept of a game, *Philosophical Investigations* (New York, 1958), §66–71.

8. Not because the fetus is partly a person and so has some of the rights of persons but rather because of the rights of personlike non-persons. . . .

9. Aristotle himself was concerned, however, with the different question of when the soul takes form. For historical data, see Jimmye Kimmey, "How the Abortion Laws Happened," *Ms.* 1 (April, 1973):48ff and John Noonan, *loc. cit.*

10. J. J. Thomson, "A Defense of Abortion," *Philosophy and Public Affairs* 1 (1971).

11. Ibid.

12. John Rawls, *A Theory of Justice* (Cambridge, Mass., 1971), §3–4.

13. On the other hand, if they can be trusted with people, then our moral customs are mistaken. It all depends on the facts of psychology.

14. Tooley, *op. cit.*

Choosing Disability

Laura Hershey

In 1983, when I was in college, local antiabortion protesters commemorated the tenth anniversary of *Roe* v. *Wade* with a rally. Our student feminist organization held a small counterdemonstration. Frantic in their zeal, anti-choice protesters assailed us with epithets like "slut" and "bitch." But the most hostile remark was directed at me. I was confronted by an angry nun whose "Abortion Is Murder" sign hung tiredly at her side. She stopped in front of me and aimed a pugnacious finger. "You see?" she announced. "God even let you be born!"

I'm not sure the sister realized that I had been part of the pro-choice demonstration. All she saw in me was a poster child for her holy crusade. I must have seemed to her an obvious mistake of nature: a severely disabled person, who, through a combination of divine intervention and legal restrictions, had been born anyway.

That was my first inkling of how attitudes about disability function in the volatile debate over reproductive rights. I understood that the nun and her co-crusaders were no friends of mine. To her, I was a former fetus who had escaped the abortionists. No room in that view for my identity as an adult woman; no room for the choices I might make. Now, more than a decade later, antiabortion groups are courting the disability community. The approach has become less clumsy, emphasizing respect for the lives of people with disabilities, and some activists have accepted the anti-choice message because they find it consistent with the goals of the disability rights movement. As a femi-

nist, however, I recoil at the "pro-life" movement's disregard for the lives and freedom of women.

But I cannot overlook the fact that when a prenatal test reveals the possibility of a "major defect," as the medical profession puts it, the pregnancy almost always ends in "therapeutic abortion." The prospect of bearing a child with disabilities causes such anxiety that abortion has become the accepted outcome—even among people who oppose abortion rights in general.

Indeed, fear of disability played a key role in the legalization of abortion in the United States in the 1960s. When thousands of pregnant women who had taken thalidomide (a drug used in tranquilizers) or had contracted rubella (German measles) gave birth to children with "defects," doctors called for easing abortion laws.

Today, despite three decades of activism by the disability community, and substantial disability rights legislation, avoiding disability is an important factor in the use and regulation of abortion. In a 1992 Time/CNN survey, for example, 70 percent of respondents favored abortion if a fetus was likely to be born deformed.

This is the quandary we face: the choices we all seek to defend—choices individual woman make about childbirth—can conflict with efforts to promote acceptance, equality, and respect for people with disabilities. I am inseparably committed to the empowerment of both people with disabilities and women. Therefore, my pro-choice stance must lie somewhere in the common ground between feminism and disability rights. I want to analyze social and scientific trends, and to vocalize my troubled feelings about where all of this may lead.

Reprinted by permission of *Ms. Magazine* (c) 1994.

I want to defy patriarchy's attempts to control women, and also to challenge an age-old bias against people with disabilities. I want to discuss the ethics of choice—without advocating restrictions on choice. To draw a parallel, feminists have no problem attacking sex-selective abortion used to guarantee giving birth to a child of the "right" sex (most often male), but we try to educate against the practice, rather than seek legislation.

In an effort to clarify my own thinking about these complex, interlocking issues, I have been reading and listening to the words of other disabled women. Diane Coleman, a Nashville-based disability rights organizer, is deeply concerned about the number of abortions based on fetal disability. Coleman sees this as a way that society expresses its complete rejection of people with disabilities, and the conviction that it would be better if we were dead. I find myself sharing her indignation.

Julie Reiskin, a social worker in Denver who is active in both disability rights and abortion rights, tells me, "I live with a disability, and I have a hard time saying, 'This is great.' I think that the goal should be to eliminate disabilities." It jars me to hear this, but Reiskin makes a further point that I find helpful. "Most abortions are not because there's something wrong with the fetus," she says. "Most abortions are because we don't have decent birth control." In other words, we should never have to use fetal disability as a reason to keep abortion legal: "It should be because women have the right to do what we want with our bodies, period," says Reiskin.

We are a diverse community, and it's no surprise to find divergent opinions on as difficult an issue as abortion. Our personal histories and hopes, viewed through the lens of current circumstances, shape our values and politics. Like all the women I interviewed, I must be guided by my own experiences of living with disability. At two year old, I still could not walk. Once I was diagnosed—I have a rare neuromuscular condition—doctors told my parents that I would live only another year or two. Don't bother about school, they advised; just buy her a few toys and make her comfortable until the end.

My parents ignored the doctors' advice. Instead of giving up on me, they taught me to read. They made sure I had a child-size wheelchair and a tricycle. My father built a sled for me, and when the neighborhood kids went to the park to fly downhill in fresh snow, he pulled me along. My mother performed much of my physical care, but was determined not to do all of it; college students helped out in exchange for housing. She knew that her own wholeness and my future depended on being able to utilize resources outside our home.

Now my life is my own. I have a house, a career, a partner, and a community of friends with and without disabilities. I rely on a motorized wheelchair for mobility, a voice-activated computer for my writing, and the assistance of Medicaid-funded attendants for daily needs—dressing, bathing, eating, going to the bathroom. I manage it all according to my own goals and needs.

My life contradicts society's stereotypes about how people with disabilities live. Across the country, thousands of other severely disabled people are surviving, working, loving, and agitating for change. I don't mean to paint a simplistic picture. Most of us work very hard to attain independence, against real physical and/or financial obstacles. Too many people are denied the kind of daily in-home assistance that makes my life possible. Guaranteeing such services has become a top priority for the disability rights movement.

Changes like these, amounting to a small revolution, are slow to reach the public consciousness. Science, on the other hand, puts progress into practice relatively quickly. Prenatal screening seems to give pregnant women more power—but is it actually asking women to ratify social prejudices through their reproductive "choices"? I cannot help thinking that in most cases, when a woman terminates a previously wanted pregnancy expressly to avoid giving birth to a disabled child, she is buying into obsolete assumptions about that child's future. And she is making a statement about the desirability or the relative worth of such a child. Abortion based on disability results from, and in turn strengthens, certain beliefs: children with disabilities (and by implication adults with disabilities) are a burden to family and society; life with a disability is scarcely worth living; preventing the birth is an act of kindness; women who bear disabled children have failed.

Language reinforces the negativity. Terms like "fetal deformity" and "defective fetus" are deeply stigmatizing, carrying connotations of inadequacy and shame. Many of us have been called "abnormal" by medical personnel, who view us primarily as "patients," subject to the definitions and control of the medical profession. "Medical professionals often have countless incorrect assumptions about our lives," says Diane Coleman. "Maybe they see us as failures on their part." As a result, doctors who diagnose fetuses with disabilities often recommend either abortion or institutionalization. "I really haven't heard very many say, 'It's O.K. to have a disability, your family's going to be fine,'" Coleman says.

The independent living movement, which is the disability community's civil rights movement, challenges this medical model. Instead of locating our difficulties within ourselves, we identify our oppression within a society that refuses to accommodate our disabilities. The real solution is to change society—to ensure full accessibility, equal opportunity, and a range of community support services—not to attempt to eliminate disabilities.

The idea that disability might someday be permanently eradicated—whether through prenatal screening and abortion or through medical research leading to "cures"—has strong appeal for a society wary of spending resources on human needs. Maybe there lurks, in the back of society's mind, the belief—the hope—that one day there will be no people with disabilities. That attitude works against the goals of civil rights and independent living. We struggle for integration, access, and support services, yet our existence remains an unresolved question. Under the circumstances, we cannot expect society to guarantee and fund our full citizenship.

My life of disability has not been easy or carefree. But in measuring the quality of my life, other factors—education, friends, and meaningful work, for example—have been decisive. If I were asked for an opinion on whether to bring a child into the world, knowing she would have the same limitations and opportunities I have had, I would not hesitate to say, "Yes."

I know that many women do not have the resources my parents had. Many lack education, are poor, or are without the support of friends and family. The problems created by these circumstances are intensified with a child who is disabled. No woman should have a child she can't handle or doesn't want. Having said that, I must also say that all kinds of women raise healthy, self-respecting children with disabilities, without unduly compromising their own lives. Raising a child with disabilities is difficult, but raising any child is difficult; just as you expect any other child to enrich your life, you can expect the same from a child with disabilities. But the media often portray raising a child with disabilities as a personal martyrdom. Disabled children, disabled *people*, are viewed as misfortunes.

I believe the choice to abort a disabled fetus represents a rejection of children who have disabilities. Human beings have a deep-seated fear of confronting the physical vulnerability that is part of being human. This terror has been dubbed "disabiliphobia" by some activists. I confront disabiliphobia every day: the usher who gripes that I take up too much room in a theater lobby; the store owner who insists that a ramp is expensive and unnecessary because people in wheelchairs never come in; the talk-show host who resents the money spent to educate students with disabilities. These are the voices of an age-old belief that disability compromises our humanity and requires us to be kept apart and ignored.

Disabiliphobia affects health care reform too. In the proposed Clinton health plan only people disabled through injury or illness—not those of us with congenital disabilities—will be covered. Is this exclusion premised on the assumption that those of us born with disabilities have lesser value and that our needs are too costly?

People with severe disabilities do sometimes require additional resources for medical and support services. But disabiliphobia runs deeper than a cost-benefit analysis. Witness the ordeal of Bree Walker, a Los Angeles newscaster with a mild physical disability affecting her hands and feet. In 1990, when Walker became pregnant with her second child, she knew the fetus might inherit her condition, as had the first. She chose to continue the pregnancy, which led talk-show hosts and listeners to feel they had the right to spend hours debating whether Walker should have the child (most said no). Walker received numerous hostile letters. The callers and letter writers seemed to be questioning her right to exist, as well as her child's.

Walker's experience also pointed out how easily disabiliphobia slips from decisions about fetuses with disabilities to decisions about people with disabilities. That's why abortion is an area where we fear that the devaluation of our lives could become enshrined in public policy. Prochoice groups must work to ensure that they do not support legislation that sets different standards based on disability.

A case in point is Utah's restrictive 1991 antiabortion law (which has since been declared unconstitutional). The law allowed abortions only in cases of rape, incest, endangerment of the woman's life, a profound health risk to the woman—or "fetal defect." According to Susanne Millsaps, director of Utah's NARAL affiliate, some disability rights activists wanted NARAL and other prochoice groups to join in opposing the "fetal defect" exemption. The groups did not specifically take a stand on the exemption; instead they opposed the entire law. I would agree that the whole statute had to be opposed on constitutional and feminist grounds. But I would also agree that there should have been a stronger response to the fetal disability exemption.

To group "fetal defect" together with rape, incest, and life-endangering complications is to reveal deep fears about disability. As Barbara Faye Waxman, an expert on the reproductive rights of women with disabilities, says: "In this culture, disability, in and of itself, is perceived as a threat to the welfare of the mother. I find that to be troublesome and offensive."

There is more at stake here than my feelings, or anyone else's, about a woman's decision. Rapidly changing reproductive technologies, combined with socially constructed prejudices, weigh heavily on any decision affecting a fetus with possible disabilities. While some women lack basic prenatal and infant care, huge amounts of money are poured into prenatal screening and genetic research. Approximately 450 disorders can now be predicted before birth. In most cases the tests reveal only the propensity for a condition, not the condition itself. The Human Genome Project aims to complete the DNA map, and to locate hundreds more physical and developmental attributes. There is little public debate about the worth or ultimate uses of this federally funded multibillion-dollar program. But there are issues with regard to abortion that we can no longer afford to ignore:

- Does prenatal screening provide more data for women's informed choices, or does it promote the idea that no woman should risk having a disabled child?
- Who decides whether a woman should undergo prenatal screening, and what she should do with the results?
- Are expensive, government-funded genetic research projects initiated primarily for the benefit of a society unwilling to support disability-related needs?
- Is society attempting to eradicate certain disabilities? Should this ever be a goal? If so, should all women be expected to cooperate in it?

The January/February 1994 issue of *Disability Rag & Resource*, a publication of the disability rights movement, devoted several articles to genetic screening. In one, feminist lawyer Lisa Blumberg argues that women are being coerced into accepting prenatal tests, and then pressured to terminate their pregnancies when disabling conditions appear likely. "Prenatal testing has largely become the decision of the doctor," Blumberg writes, and "the social purpose of these tests is to reduce the incidence of live births of people with disabilities."

A woman faced with this choice usually feels pressure from many directions. Family, friends, doctors, and the media predict all kinds of negative results should her child be disabled. At the same time, she is unlikely to be given information about community resources; nor is she encouraged to meet individuals who have the condition her child might be born with. This lack of exposure to real-life, nonmedical facts about living with a disability should make us wonder whether women are really making "informed" choices about bearing children with disabilities.

Few outside the disability community have dealt with these issues in any depth. "We are all aware of the potential for abuses in reproductive technology and in genetic testing," says Marcy Wilder, legal director for NARAL's national office in Washington, D.C. "I don't see that there have been widespread abuses—but we're certainly concerned." That concern has not led to any coalition-building with disability rights groups, however.

Many feminist disability rights activists report chilly responses when they attempt to network with pro-choice groups. Too often, when we object to positions that implicitly doubt the humanity of children born disabled, we are accused of being anti-choice. One activist I know recently told me about her experience speaking at a meeting of a National Organization of Women chapter. She mentioned feeling discomfort about the widespread abortion of disabled fetuses—and was startled by the members' reactions. "They said, 'How could you claim to be a feminist and pro-choice and even begin to think that there should be any limitations?' I tried to tell them I don't think there should be limitations, but that our issues need to be included."

On both sides, the fears are genuine, rational, and terrifying—if not always articulated. For the pro-choice movement, the fear is that questioning the motives and assumptions behind any reproductive decision could give ammunition to antiabortionists. Defenders of disability rights fear that the widespread use of prenatal testing and abortion for the purpose of eliminating disability could inaugurate a new eugenics movement. If we cannot unite and find ways to address issues of reproductive screening and manipulation, we all face the prospect that what is supposed to be a private decision—the termination of a pregnancy—might become the first step in a campaign to eliminate people with disabilities.

I am accusing the pro-choice movement not of spurring these trends, but of failing to address them. Most pro-choice organizations do not favor the use of abortion to eliminate disabilities, but their silence leaves a vacuum in which fear of disability flourishes.

Disabiliphobia and the "genetics enterprise," as activist Adrienne Asch calls it, have also had legal implications for the reproductive rights of all women. The tendency to blame social problems such as poverty and discrimination on individuals with disabilities and their mothers has made women vulnerable to the charge that they are undermining progress toward human "perfectability"—because they insist on a genuine choice. Some legal and medical experts have developed a concept called "fetal rights," in which mothers can be held responsible for the condition of their unborn or newborn children. According to Lisa Blumberg, "fetal rights" could more accurately be called "fetal quality control." For women with hereditary

disabilities who decide to have children this concept is nothing new. Society and medical professionals have often tried to prevent us from bearing and raising children. Disabled women know, as well as anyone, what it means to be deprived of reproductive choice. More broadly, decisions involving our health care, sexuality, and parenting have been made by others based on assumptions about our inabilities and/or our asexuality.

The right to control one's body begins with good gynecological care. Low income, and dependence on disability "systems," restrict access to that care. Like many women of disability, my health care choices are limited by the accessibility of medical facilities, and by providers' attitudes toward disability and their willingness to accept the low reimbursement of Medicaid. And Medicaid will not cover most abortions, a policy that discriminates against poor women and many women with disabilities.

Paradoxically, policy is often undermined by practice. Although public funding rarely pays for abortions, many women with disabilities are encouraged to have them—even when they would prefer to have a child. Doctors try to convince us an abortion would be best for "health reasons"—in which case, Medicaid will pay for it after all. "Abortions are easier for disabled women to get," says Nancy Moulton, a health care advocate in Atlanta, "because the medical establishment sees us as not being fit parents." Most women grow up amid strong if subtle pressures to become mothers. For those of us with disabilities, there is an equal or greater pressure to forgo motherhood. This pressure has taken the form of forced sterilization, lost custody battles, and forced abortion.

Consequently, for women with disabilities, reproductive freedom means more than being able to get an abortion. It is hard for many of us to relate to those in the reproductive rights movement whose primary concern is keeping abortions legal and available. But I believe our different perspectives on reproductive freedom are fundamentally compatible, like variations on a single theme.

Whatever the reason, feminist organizations seem inclined to overlook disability concerns. Feminist speakers might add "ableism" to their standard list of offensive "isms," but they do little to challenge it. Now more than ever, women with disabilities need the feminist movement's vigorous support. We need you to defend our rights as if they were your own—which they are. Here are a few suggestions:

- Recognize women with disabilities' equal stake in the pro-choice movement's goals. That means accepting us as women, not dismissing us as "other," or infirm, or genderless. Recognize us as a community of diverse individuals whose health needs, lifestyles, and choices vary.

- Defend all our reproductive rights: the right to appropriate education about sexuality and reproduction; to gynecological care, family planning services, and birth control; the right to be sexually active; to have children and to keep and raise those children, with assistance if necessary; and the right to abortion in accessible facilities, with practitioners who are sensitive to our needs.

- Remove the barriers that restrict the access of women with disabilities to services. Help to improve physical accessibility, arrange disability awareness training for staff and volunteers, and conduct outreach activities to reach women with disabilities.

- Continue struggling to build coalitions around reproductive rights and disability issues. There is plenty of common ground, although we may have to tiptoe through dangerous, mine-filled territory to get to it.

- Question the assumptions that seem to make bearing children with disabilities unacceptable.

Despite our rhetoric, abortion is not strictly a private decision. Individual choices are made in a context of social values; I want us to unearth, sort out, and appraise those values. I wouldn't deny any woman the right to choose abortion. But I would issue a challenge to all women making a decision whether to give birth to a child who may have disabilities.

The challenge is this: consider all relevant information, not just the medical facts. More important than a particular diagnosis are the conditions awaiting a child—community acceptance, access to buildings and transportation, civil rights protection, and opportunities for education and employment. Where these things are lacking or inadequate, consider joining the movement to change them. In many communities, adults with disabilities and parents of disabled children have developed powerful advocacy coalitions. I recognize that, having weighed all the factors, some women will decide they cannot give birth to a child with disabilities. It pains me, but I acknowledge their right and their choice.

Meanwhile, there is much work still to be done.

8.

Why Abortion Is Immoral

Don Marquis

Don Marquis is professor of philosophy at the University of Kansas, Lawrence. In this essay, he argues that with few exceptions abortions are immoral. He defends his view by arguing that fetuses have the same moral status or moral standing as do adult persons. Thus, the same reason that makes killing an adult immoral, namely, that it would deprive that person of a future, supports the conclusion that there is a strong presumption that any abortion is morally impermissible.

The view that abortion is, with rare exceptions, seriously immoral has received little support in the recent philosophical literature. No doubt

Reprinted by permission of the author and publisher from *The Journal of Philosophy,* Vol. 86, No. 4 (April 1989). Copyright (c) 1989 by The Journal of Philosophy, Inc.

most philosophers affiliated with secular institutions of higher education believe that the antiabortion position is either a symptom of irrational religious dogma or a conclusion generated by seriously confused philosophical argument. The purpose of this essay is to undermine this general belief. This essay sets out an argument that purports to show, as well as any argument in ethics can show, that abortion is, except possibly in rare cases, seriously immoral, that it is in the same moral category as killing an innocent adult human being.

The argument is based on a major assumption. Many of the most insightful and careful writers on the ethics of abortion—such as Joel Feinberg, Michael Tooley, Mary Anne Warren, H. Tristram Engelhardt, Jr., L. W. Sumner, John T. Noonan, Jr., and Philip Devine[1]—believe that whether or not abortion is morally permissible stands or falls on whether or not a fetus is the sort of being whose life it is seriously wrong to end. The argument of this essay will assume, but not argue, that they are correct.

Also, this essay will neglect issues of great importance to a complete ethics of abortion. Some anti-abortionists will allow that certain abortions, such as abortion before implantation or abortion when the life of a woman is threatened by a pregnancy or abortion after rape, may be morally permissible. This essay will not explore the casuistry of these hard cases. The purpose of this essay is to develop a general argument for the claim that the overwhelming majority of deliberate abortions are seriously immoral.

I

A sketch of standard anti-abortion and pro-choice arguments exhibits how those arguments possess certain symmetries that explain why partisans of those positions are so convinced of the correctness of their own positions, why they are not successful in convincing their opponents, and why, to others, this issue seems to be unresolvable. An analysis of the nature of this standoff suggests a strategy for surmounting it.

Consider the way a typical anti-abortionist argues. She will argue or assert that life is present from the moment of conception or that fetuses look like babies or that fetuses possess a characteristic such as a genetic code that is both necessary and sufficient for being human. Anti-abortionists seem to believe that (1) the truth

of all of these claims is quite obvious, and (2) establishing any of these claims is sufficient to show that abortion is morally akin to murder.

A standard pro-choice strategy exhibits similarities. The pro-choicer will argue or assert that fetuses are not persons or that fetuses are not rational agents or that fetuses are not social beings. Pro-choicers seem to believe that (1) the truth of any of these claims is quite obvious, and (2) establishing any of these claims is sufficient to show that an abortion is not a wrongful killing.

In fact, both the pro-choice and the anti-abortion claims do seem to be true, although the "it looks like a baby" claim is more difficult to establish the earlier the pregnancy. We seem to have a standoff. How can it be resolved?

As everyone who has taken a bit of logic knows, if any of these arguments concerning abortion is a good argument, it requires not only some claim characterizing fetuses, but also some general moral principle that ties a characteristic of fetuses to having or not having the right to life or to some other moral characteristic that will generate the obligation or the lack of obligation not to end the life of a fetus. Accordingly, the arguments of the anti-abortionist and the pro-choicer need a bit of filling in to be regarded as adequate.

Note what each partisan will say. The anti-abortionist will claim that her position is supported by such generally accepted moral principles as "It is always prima facie seriously wrong to take a human life" or "It is always prima facie seriously wrong to end the life of a baby." Since these are generally accepted moral principles, her position is certainly not obviously wrong. The pro-choicer will claim that her position is supported by such plausible moral principles as "Being a person is what gives an individual intrinsic moral worth" or "It is only seriously prima facie wrong to take the life of a member of the human community." Since these are generally accepted moral principles, the pro-choice position is certainly not obviously wrong. Unfortunately, we have again arrived at a standoff.

Now, how might one deal with this standoff? The standard approach is to try to show how the moral principles of one's opponent lose their plausibility under analysis. It is easy to see how this is possible. On the one hand, the anti-abortionist will defend a moral principle concerning the wrongness of killing which tends to be broad in scope in order that even fetuses at an early stage of pregnancy will fall under it. The problem with broad principles is that they often embrace too much. In this particular instance, the principle "It is always prima facie wrong to take a human life" seems to entail that it is wrong to end the existence of a living human cancer-cell culture, on the grounds that the culture is both living and human. Therefore, it seems that the anti-abortionist's favored principle is too broad.

On the other hand, the pro-choicer wants to find a moral principle concerning the wrongness of killing which tends to be narrow in scope in order that fetuses will *not* fall under it. The problem with narrow principles is that they often do not embrace enough. Hence, the needed principles such as "It is prima facie seriously wrong to kill only persons" or "It is prima facie wrong to kill only rational agents" do not explain why it is wrong to kill infants or young children or the severely retarded or even perhaps the severely mentally ill. Therefore, we seem again to have a standoff. The anti-abortionist charges, not unreasonably, that pro-choice principles concerning killing are too narrow to be acceptable; the pro-choicer charges, not unreasonably, that anti-abortionist principles concerning killing are too broad to be acceptable.

Attempts by both sides to patch up the difficulties in their positions run into further difficulties. The anti-abortionist will try to remove the problem of her position by reformulating her principle concerning killing in terms of human beings. Now we end up with: "It is always prima facie seriously wrong to end the life of a human being." This principle has the advantage of avoiding the problem of the human cancer-cell culture counterexample. But this advantage is purchased at a high price. For although it is clear that a fetus is both human and alive, it is not at all clear that a fetus is a human *being*. There is at least something to be said for the view that something becomes a human being only after a process of development, and that therefore first trimester fetuses and perhaps all fetuses are not yet human beings. Hence, the anti-abortionist, by this move, has merely exchanged one problem for another.[2]

The pro-choicer fares no better. She may attempt to find reasons why killing infants, young children, and the severely retarded is wrong which are independent of her major principle that is supposed to explain the wrongness of taking human life, but which will not also make abortion immoral. This is no easy task. Appeals to social utility will seem satisfactory only to those who resolve not to think of the enormous difficulties with a utilitarian account of the wrongness of killing and the significant social costs of preserving the lives of the unproductive.[3] A pro-choice strategy that extends the definition of 'person' to infants or even to young children seems just as arbitrary as an anti-abortion strategy that extends the definition of 'human being' to fetuses. Again, we find symmetries in the two positions and we arrive at a standoff.

There are even further problems that reflect symmetries in the two positions. In addition to counterexample problems, or the arbitrary application problems that can be exchanged for them, the standard anti-abortionist principle "It is prima facie seriously wrong to kill a human being," or one of its variants, can be objected to on the grounds of ambiguity. If 'human being' is taken to be a *biological* category, then the anti-abortionist is left with the problem of explaining why a merely biological category should make a moral difference. Why, it is asked, is it any more reasonable to base a moral conclusion on the number of chromosomes in one's cells than on the color of one's skin?[4] If 'human being', on the other hand, is taken to be a *moral* category, then the claim that a fetus is a human being cannot be taken to be a premise in the anti-abortion argument, for it is precisely what needs to be established. Hence, either the anti-abortionist's main category is a morally irrelevant, merely biological category, or it is of no use to the anti-abortionist in establishing (noncircularly, of course) that abortion is wrong.

Although this problem with the anti-abortionist position is often noticed, it is less often noticed that the pro-choice position suffers from an analogous problem. The principle "Only persons have the right to life" also suffers from an ambiguity. The term 'person' is typically defined in terms of psychological characteristics, although there will certainly be disagreement concerning which characteristics are most important. Supposing that this matter can be settled, the pro-choicer is left with the problem of explaining why *psychological* characteristics should make a *moral* difference. If the pro-choicer should attempt to deal with this problem by claiming that an explanation is not necessary, that in fact we do treat such a cluster of psychological properties as having moral significance, the sharp-witted anti-abortionist should have a ready response. We do treat being both living and human as having moral significance. If it is legitimate for the pro-choicer to demand that the anti-abortionist provide an explanation of the connection between the biological character of being a human being and the wrongness of being killed (even though people accept this connection), then it is legitimate for the anti-abortionist to demand that the pro-choicer provide an explanation of the connection between psychological criteria for being a person and the wrongness of being killed (even though that connection is accepted).[5]

Feinberg has attempted to meet this objection (he calls psychological personhood "commonsense personhood"):

The characteristics that confer commonsense personhood are not arbitrary bases for rights and duties, such as race, sex or species membership; rather they are traits that make sense out of rights and duties and without which those moral attributes would have no point or function. It is because people are conscious; have a sense of their personal identities; have plans, goals, and projects; experience emotions; are liable to pains, anxieties, and frustrations; can reason and bargain, and so on—it is because of these attributes that people have values and interests, desires and expectations of their own, including a stake in their own futures, and a personal well-being of a sort we cannot ascribe to unconscious or nonrational beings. Because of their developed capacities they can assume duties and responsibilities and can have and make claims on one another. Only because of their sense of self, their life plans, their value hierarchies, and their stakes in their own futures can they be ascribed fundamental rights. There is nothing arbitrary around these linkages (*op. cit.*, p. 270).

The plausible aspects of this attempt should not be taken to obscure its implausible features. There is a great deal to be said for the view that being a psychological person under some description is a necessary condition for having duties. One cannot have a duty unless one is capable of behaving morally, and a being's capability of behaving morally will require having a certain psychology. It is far from obvious, however, that having rights entails consciousness or rationality, as Feinberg suggests. We speak of the rights of the severely retarded or the severely mentally ill, yet some of these persons are not rational. We speak of the rights of the temporarily unconscious. The New Jersey Supreme Court based their decision in the Quinlan case on Karen Ann Quinlan's right to privacy, and she was known to be permanently unconscious at that time. Hence, Feinberg's claim that having rights entails being conscious is, on its face, obviously false.

Of course, it might not make sense to attribute rights to a being that would never in its natural history have certain psychological traits. This modest connection between psychological personhood and moral personhood will create a place for Karen Ann Quinlan and the temporarily unconscious. But then it makes a place for fetuses also. Hence, it does not serve Feinberg's pro-choice purposes. Accordingly, it seems that the pro-choicer will have as much difficulty bridging the gap between psychological personhood and personhood in the moral sense as the anti-abortionist has bridging the gap between being a biological human being and being a human being in the moral sense.

Furthermore, the pro-choicer cannot any more escape her problem by making person a purely moral category than the anti-abortionist could escape by the analogous move. For if person is a moral category, then the pro-choicer is left without the resources for establishing (noncircularly, of course) the claim that a fetus is not a person, which is an essential premise in her argument. Again, we have both a symmetry and a standoff between pro-choice and anti-abortion views.

Passions in the abortion debate run high. There are both plausibilities and difficulties with the standard positions. Accordingly, it is hardly surprising that partisans of either side embrace with fervor the moral generalizations that support the conclusions they preanalytically favor, and reject with disdain the moral generalizations of their opponents as being subject to inescapable difficulties. It is easy to believe that the counterexamples to one's own moral principles are merely temporary difficulties that will dissolve in the wake of further philosophical research, and that the counterexamples to the principles of one's opponents are as straightforward as the contradiction between *A* and *O* propositions in traditional logic. This might suggest to an impartial observer (if there are any) that the abortion issue is unresolvable.

There is a way out of this apparent dialectical quandary. The moral generalizations of both sides are not quite correct. The generalizations hold for the most part, for the usual cases. This suggests that they are all *accidental* generalizations, that the moral claims made by those on both sides of the dispute do not touch on the *essence* of the matter.

This use of the distinction between essence and accident is not meant to invoke obscure metaphysical categories. Rather, it is intended to reflect the rather atheoretical nature of the abortion discussion. If the generalization a partisan in the abortion dispute adopts were derived from the reason why ending the life of a human being is wrong, then there could not be exceptions to that generalization unless some special case obtains in which there are even more powerful countervailing reasons. Such generalizations would not be merely accidental generalizations; they would point to, or be based upon, the essence of the wrongness of killing, what it is that makes killing wrong. All this suggests that a necessary condition for resolving the abortion controversy is a more theoretical account of the wrongness of killing. After all, if we merely believe, but do not understand, why killing adult human beings such as ourselves is wrong, how could we conceivably show that abortion is either immoral or permissible?

II

In order to develop such an account, we can start from the following unproblematic assumption concerning our own case: it is wrong to kill *us*. Why is it wrong? Some answers can be easily eliminated. It might be said that what makes killing us wrong is that a killing brutalizes the one who kills. But the brutalization consists of being inured to the performance of an act that is hideously immoral; hence, the brutalization does not explain the immorality. It might be said that what makes killing us wrong is the great loss others would experience due to our absence. Although such hubris is understandable, such an explanation does not account for the wrongness of killing hermits, or those whose lives are relatively independent and whose friends find it easy to make new friends.

A more obvious answer is better. What primarily makes killing wrong is neither its effect on the murderer nor its effect on the victim's friends and relative, but its effect on the victim. The loss of one's life is one of the greatest losses one can suffer. The loss of one's life deprives one of all the experiences, activities, projects, and enjoyments that would otherwise have constituted one's future. Therefore, killing someone is wrong, primarily because the killing inflicts (one of) the greatest possible losses on the victim. To describe this as the loss of life can be misleading, however. The change in my biological state does not by itself make killing me wrong. The effect of the loss of my biological life is the loss to me of all those activities, projects, experiences, and enjoyments which would otherwise have constituted my future personal life. These activities, projects, experiences, and enjoyments are either valuable for their own sakes or are means to something else that is valuable for its own sake. Some parts of my future are not valued by me now, but will come to be valued by me as I grow older and as my values and capacities change. When I am killed, I am deprived both of what I now value which would have been part of my future personal life, but also what I would come to value. Therefore, when I die, I am deprived of all of the value of my future. Inflicting this loss on me is ultimately what makes killing me wrong. This being the case, it would seem that what makes killing *any* adult human being prima facie seriously wrong is the loss of his or her future.[6]

How should this rudimentary theory of the wrongness of killing be evaluated? It cannot be faulted for deriving an 'ought' from an 'is', for it does not. The analysis assumes that killing me (or you, reader) is prima facie seriously wrong. The point of the analysis is to establish which natural property ultimately explains the wrongness of the killing, given that it is wrong. A natural property will ultimately explain the

wrongness of killing, only if (1) the explanation fits with our intuitions about the matter and (2) there is no other natural property that provides the basis for a better explanation of the wrongness of killing. This analysis rests on the intuition that what makes killing a particular human or animal wrong is what it does to that particular human or animal. What makes killing wrong is some natural effect or other of the killing. Some would deny this. For instance, a divine-command theorist in ethics would deny it. Surely this denial is, however, one of those features of divine–command theory which renders it so implausible.

The claim that what makes killing wrong is the loss of the victim's future is directly supported by two considerations. In the first place, this theory explains why we regard killing as one of the worst of crimes. Killing is especially wrong, because it deprives the victim of more than perhaps any other crime. In the second place, people with AIDS or cancer who know they are dying believe, of course, that dying is a very bad thing for them. They believe that the loss of a future to them that they would otherwise have experienced is what makes their premature death a very bad thing for them. A better theory of the wrongness of killing would require a different natural property associated with killing which better fits with the attitudes of the dying. What could it be?

The view that what makes killing wrong is the loss to the victim of the value of the victim's future gains additional support when some of its implications are examined. In the first place, it is incompatible with the view that it is wrong to kill only beings who are biologically human. It is possible that there exists a different species from another planet whose members have a future like ours. Since having a future like that is what makes killing someone wrong, this theory entails that it would be wrong to kill members of such a species. Hence, this theory is opposed to the claim that only life that is biologically human has great moral worth, a claim which many anti-abortionists have seemed to adopt. This opposition, which this theory has in common with personhood theories, seems to be a merit of the theory.

In the second place, the claim that the loss of one's future is the wrong-making feature of one's being killed entails the possibility that the futures of some actual nonhuman mammals on our own planet are sufficiently like ours that it is seriously wrong to kill them also. Whether some animals do have the same right to life as human beings depends on adding to the account of the wrongness of killing some additional account of just what it is about my future or the futures of other adult human beings which makes it wrong to kill us. No such additional account will be offered in this essay. Undoubtedly, the provision of such an account would be a very difficult matter. Undoubtedly, any such account would be quite controversial. Hence, it surely should not reflect badly on this sketch of an elementary theory of the wrongness of killing that it is indeterminate with respect to some very difficult issues regarding animal rights.

In the third place, the claim that the loss of one's future is the wrong-making feature of one's being killed does not entail, as sanctity of human life theories do, that active euthanasia is wrong. Persons who are severely and incurably ill, who face a future of pain and despair, and who wish to die will not have suffered a loss if they are killed. It is, strictly speaking, the value of a human's future which makes killing wrong in this theory. This being so, killing does not necessarily wrong some persons who are sick and dying. Of course, there may be other reasons for a prohibition of active euthanasia, but that is another matter. Sanctity-of-human-life theories seem to hold that active euthanasia is seriously wrong even in an individual case where there seems to be good reason for it independently of public policy considerations. This consequence is most implausible, and it is a plus for the claim that the loss of a future of

value is what makes killing wrong that it does not share this consequence.

In the fourth place, the account of the wrongness of killing defended in this essay does straightforwardly entail that it is prima facie seriously wrong to kill children and infants, for we do presume that they have futures of value. Since we do believe that it is wrong to kill defenseless little babies, it is important that a theory of the wrongness of killing easily account for this. Personhood theories of the wrongness of killing, on the other hand, cannot straightforwardly account for the wrongness of killing infants and young children.[7] Hence, such theories must add special ad hoc accounts of the wrongness of killing the young. The plausibility of such ad hoc theories seems to be a function of how desperately one wants such theories to work. The claim that the primary wrong-making feature of a killing is the loss to the victim of the value of its future accounts for the wrongness of killing young children and infants directly; it makes the wrongness of such acts as obvious as we actually think it is. This is a further merit of this theory. Accordingly, it seems that this value of a future-like-ours theory of the wrongness of killing shares strengths of both sanctity-of-life and personhood accounts while avoiding weaknesses of both. In addition, it meshes with a central intuition concerning what makes killing wrong.

The claim that the primary wrong-making feature of a killing is the loss to the victim of the value of its future has obvious consequences for the ethics of abortion. The future of a standard fetus includes a set of experiences, projects, activities, and such which are identical with the futures of adult human beings and are identical with the futures of young children. Since the reason that is sufficient to explain why it is wrong to kill human beings after the time of birth is a reason that also applies to fetuses, it follows that abortion is prima facie seriously morally wrong.

This argument does not rely on the invalid inference that, since it is wrong to kill persons, it is wrong to kill potential persons also. The category that is morally central to this analysis is the category of having a valuable future like ours; it is not the category of personhood. The argument to the conclusion that abortion is prima facie seriously morally wrong proceeded independently of the notion of person or potential person or any equivalent. Someone may wish to start with this analysis in terms of the value of a human future, conclude that abortion is, except perhaps in rare circumstances, seriously morally wrong, infer that fetuses have the right to life, and then call fetuses "persons" as a result of their having the right to life. Clearly, in this case, the category of person is being used to state the *conclusion* of the analysis rather than to generate the *argument* of the analysis.

The structure of this anti-abortion argument can be both illuminated and defended by comparing it to what appears to be the best argument for the wrongness of the wanton infliction of pain on animals. This latter argument is based on the assumption that it is prima facie wrong to inflict pain on me (or you, reader). What is the natural property associated with the infliction of pain which makes such infliction wrong? The obvious answer seems to be that the infliction of pain causes suffering and that suffering is a misfortune. The suffering caused by the infliction of pain is what makes the wanton infliction of pain on me wrong. The wanton infliction of pain on other adult humans causes suffering. The wanton infliction of pain on animals causes suffering. Since causing suffering is what makes the wanton infliction of pain wrong and since the wanton infliction of pain on animals causes suffering, it follows that the wanton infliction of pain on animals is wrong.

This argument for the wrongness of the wanton infliction of pain on animals shares a number of structural features with the argument for the serious prima facie wrongness of abortion. Both arguments start with an obvious assumption concerning what it is wrong to do to

me (or you, reader). Both then look for the characteristic or the consequence of the wrong action which makes the action wrong. Both recognize that the wrong–making feature of these immoral actions is a property of actions sometimes directed at individuals other than postnatal human beings. If the structure of the argument for the wrongness of the wanton infliction of pain on animals is sound, then the structure of the argument for the prima facie serious wrongness of abortion is also sound, for the structure of the two arguments is the same. The structure common to both is the key to the explanation of how the wrongness of abortion can be demonstrated without recourse to the category of person. In neither argument is that category crucial.

This defense of an argument for the wrongness of abortion in terms of a structurally similar argument for the wrongness of the wanton infliction of pain on animals succeeds only if the account regarding animals is the correct account. Is it? In the first place, it seems plausible. In the second place, its major competition is Kant's account. Kant believed that we do not have direct duties to animals at all, because they are not persons. Hence, Kant had to explain and justify the wrongness of inflicting pain on animals on the grounds that "he who is hard in his dealings with animals becomes hard also in his dealing with men."[8] The problem with Kant's account is that there seems to be no reason for accepting this latter claim unless Kant's account is rejected. If the alternative to Kant's account is accepted, then it is easy to understand why someone who is indifferent to inflicting pain on animals is also indifferent to inflicting pain on humans, for one is indifferent to what makes inflicting pain wrong in both cases. But, if Kant's account is accepted, there is no intelligible reason why one who is hard in his dealings with animals (or crabgrass or stones) should also be hard in his dealings with men. After all, men are persons: animals are no more persons than crabgrass or stones. Persons are Kant's crucial moral category. Why, in short, should a Kantian accept the basic claim in Kant's argument?

Hence, Kant's argument for the wrongness of inflicting pain on animals rests on the claim that, in a world of Kantian moral agents, is demonstrably false. Therefore, the alternative analysis, being more plausible anyway, should be accepted. Since this alternative analysis has the same structure as the anti-abortion argument being defended here, we have further support for the argument for the immorality of abortion being defended in this essay.

Of course, this value of a future-like-ours argument, if sound, shows only that abortion is prima facie wrong, not that it is wrong in any or all circumstances. Since the loss of the future to a standard fetus, if killed, is, however, at least as great a loss as the loss of the future to a standard adult human being who is killed, abortion, like ordinary killing, could be justified only by the most compelling reasons. The loss of one's life is almost the greatest misfortune that can happen to one. Presumably abortion could be justified in some circumstances, only if the loss consequent on failing to abort would be at least as great. Accordingly, morally permissible abortions will be rare indeed unless, perhaps, they occur so early in pregnancy that a fetus is not yet definitely an individual. Hence, this argument should be taken as showing that abortion is presumptively very seriously wrong, where the presumption is very strong—as strong as the presumption that killing another adult human being is wrong.

III

How complete an account of the wrongness of killing does the value of a future-like-ours account have to be in order that the wrongness of abortion is a consequence? This account does not have to be an account of the necessary conditions for the wrongness of killing. Some persons in nursing homes may lack valuable human futures, yet it may be wrong to kill them

for other reasons. Furthermore, this account does not obviously have to be the sole reason killing is wrong where the victim did have a valuable future. This analysis claims only that, for any killing where the victim did have a valuable future like ours, having that future by itself is sufficient to create the strong presumption that the killing is seriously wrong.

One way to overturn the value of a future-like-ours argument would be to find some account of the wrongness of killing which is at least as intelligible and which has different implications for the ethics of abortion. Two rival accounts possess at least some degree of plausibility. One account is based on the obvious fact that people value the experience of living and wish for that valuable experience to continue. Therefore, it might be said, what makes killing wrong is the discontinuation of that experience for the victim. Let us call this the *discontinuation account*.[9] Another rival account is based upon the obvious fact that people strongly desire to continue to live. This suggests that what makes killing us so wrong is that it interferes with the fulfillment of a strong and fundamental desire, the fulfillment of which is necessary for the fulfillment of any other desires we might have. Let us call this the *desire account*.[10]

Consider first the desire account as a rival account of the ethics of killing which would provide the basis for rejecting the anti-abortion position. Such an account will have to be stronger than the value of a future-like-ours account of the wrongness of abortion if it is to do the job expected of it. To entail the wrongness of abortion, the value of a future-like-ours account has only to provide a sufficient, but not a necessary, condition for the wrongness of killing. The desire account, on the other hand, must provide us also with a necessary condition for the wrongness of killing in order to generate a pro-choice conclusion on abortion. The reason for this is that presumably the argument from the desire account moves from the claim that what makes killing wrong is interference with a very strong desire to the claim that abortion is not wrong because the fetus lacks a strong desire to live. Obviously, this inference fails if someone's having the desire to live is not a necessary condition of its being wrong to kill that individual.

One problem with the desire account is that we do regard it as seriously wrong to kill persons who have little desire to live or who have no desire to live or, indeed, have a desire not to live. We believe it is seriously wrong to kill the unconscious, the sleeping, those who are tired of life, and those who are suicidal. The value-of-a-human-future account renders standard morality intelligible in these cases; these cases appear to be incompatible with the desire account.

The desire account is subject to a deeper difficulty. We desire life, because we value the goods of this life. The goodness of life is not secondary to our desire for it. If this were not so, the pain of one's own premature death could be done away with merely by an appropriate alteration in the configuration of one's desires. This is absurd. Hence, it would seem that it is the loss of the goods of one's future, not the interference with the fulfillment of a strong desire to live, which accounts ultimately for the wrongness of killing.

It is worth noting that, if the desire account is modified so that it does not provide a necessary, but only a sufficient, condition for the wrongness of killing, the desire account is compatible with the value of a future-like-ours account. The combined accounts will yield an anti-abortion ethic. This suggests that one can retain what is intuitively plausible about the desire account without a challenge to the basic argument of this paper.

It is also worth noting that, if future desires have moral force in a modified desire account of the wrongness of killing, one can find support for an anti-abortion ethic even in the absence of a value of a future-like-ours account. If one decides that a morally relevant property, the possession of which is sufficient to make it

wrong to kill some individual, is the desire at some future time to live—one might decide to justify one's refusal to kill suicidal teenagers on these grounds, for example—then, since typical fetuses will have the desire in the future to live, it is wrong to kill typical fetuses. Accordingly, it does not seem that a desire account of the wrongness of killing can provide a justification of a pro-choice ethic of abortion which is nearly as adequate as the value of a human-future justification of an anti-abortion ethic.

The discontinuation account looks more promising as an account of the wrongness of killing. It seems just as intelligible as the value of a future-like-ours account, but it does not justify an anti-abortion position. Obviously, if it is the continuation of one's activities, experiences, and projects, the loss of which makes killing wrong, then it is not wrong to kill fetuses for that reason, for fetuses do not have experiences, activities, and projects to be continued or discontinued. Accordingly, the discontinuation account does not have the anti-abortion consequences that the value of a future-like-ours account has. Yet, it seems as intelligible as the value of a future-like-ours account, for when we think of what would be wrong with our being killed, it does seem as if it is the discontinuation of what makes our lives worthwhile which makes killing us wrong.

Is the discontinuation account just as good an account as the value of a future-like-ours account? The discontinuation account will not be adequate at all, if it does not refer to the *value* of the experience that may be discontinued. One does not want the discontinuation account to make it wrong to kill a patient who begs for death and who is in severe pain that cannot be relieved short of killing. (I leave open the question of whether it is wrong for other reasons.) Accordingly, the discontinuation account must be more than a bare discontinuation account. It must make some reference to the positive value of the patient's experiences. But, by the same token, the value of a future-like-ours account cannot be a bare future account either. Just having a future surely does not itself rule out killing the above patient. This account must make some reference to the value of the patient's future experiences and projects also. Hence, both accounts involve the value of experiences, projects, and activities. So far we still have symmetry between the accounts.

The symmetry fades, however, when we focus on the time period of the value of the experiences, etc., which has moral consequences. Although both accounts leave open the possibility that the patient in our example may be killed, this possibility is left open only in virtue of the utterly bleak future for the patient. It makes no difference whether the patient's immediate past contains intolerable pain, or consists in being in a coma (which we can imagine is a situation of indifference), or consists in a life of value. If the patient's future is a future of value, we want our account to make it wrong to kill the patient. If the patient's future is intolerable, whatever his or her immediate past, we want our account to allow killing the patient. Obviously, then, it is the value of that patient's future which is doing the work in rendering the morality of killing the patient intelligible.

This being the case, it seems clear that whether one has immediate past experiences or not does no work in the explanation of what makes killing wrong. The addition the discontinuation account makes to the value of a human future account is otiose. Its addition to the value-of-a-future account plays no role at all in rendering intelligible the wrongness of killing. Therefore, it can be discarded with the discontinuation account of which it is a part.

IV

The analysis of the previous section suggests that alternative general accounts of the wrongness of killing are either inadequate or unsuccessful in getting around the anti-abortion consequences of the value of a future-like-ours

argument. A different strategy for avoiding these anti-abortion consequences involves limiting the scope of the value of a future argument. More precisely, the strategy involves arguing that fetuses lack a property that is essential for the value-of-a-future argument (or for any anti-abortion argument) to apply to them.

One move of this sort is based upon the claim that a necessary condition of one's future being valuable is that one values it. Value implies a valuer. Given this one might argue that, since fetuses cannot value their futures, their futures are not valuable to them. Hence, it does not seriously wrong them deliberately to end their lives.

This move fails, however, because of some ambiguities. Let us assume that something cannot be of value unless it is valued by someone. This does not entail that my life is of no value unless it is valued by me. I may think, in a period of despair, that my future is of no worth whatsoever, but I may be wrong because others rightly see value—even great value—in it. Furthermore, my future can be valuable to me even if I do not value it. This is the case when a young person attempts suicide, but is rescued and goes on to significant human achievements. Such young people's futures are ultimately valuable to them, even though such futures do not seem to be valuable to them at the moment of attempted suicide. A fetus's future can be valuable to it in the same way. Accordingly, this attempt to limit the anti-abortion argument fails.

Another similar attempt to reject the anti-abortion position is based on Tooley's claim that an entity cannot possess the right to life unless it has the capacity to desire its continued existence. It follows that, since fetuses lack the conceptual capacity to desire to continue to live, they lack the right to life. Accordingly, Tooley concludes that abortion cannot be seriously prima facie wrong (*op. cit.*, pp. 46/7).

What could be the evidence for Tooley's basic claim? Tooley once argued that individuals have a prima facie right to what they desire and that the lack of the capacity to desire something undercuts the basis of one's right to it (*op. cit.*, pp. 44/5). This argument plainly will not succeed in the context of the analysis of this essay, however, since the point here is to establish the fetus's right to life on other grounds. Tooley's argument assumes that the right to life cannot be established in general on some basis other than the desire to life. This position was considered and rejected in the preceding section of this paper.

One might attempt to defend Tooley's basic claim on the grounds that, because a fetus cannot apprehend continued life as a benefit, its continued life cannot be a benefit or cannot be something it has a right to or cannot be something that is in its interest. This might be defended in terms of the general proposition that, if an individual is literally incapable of caring about or taking an interest in some *X*, then one does not have a right to *X* or *X* is not a benefit or *X* is not something that is in one's interest.[11]

Each member of this family of claims seems to be open to objections. As John C. Stevens[12] has pointed out, one may have a right to be treated with a certain medical procedure (because of a health insurance policy one has purchased), even though one cannot conceive of the nature of the procedure. And, as Tooley himself has pointed out, persons who have been indoctrinated, or drugged, or rendered temporarily unconscious may be literally incapable of caring about or taking an interest in something that is in their interest or is something to which they have a right, or is something that benefits them. Hence, the Tooley claim that would restrict the scope of the value of a future-like-ours argument is undermined by counterexamples.[13]

Finally, Paul Bassen[14] has argued that, even though the prospects of an embryo might seem to be a basis for the wrongness of abortion, an embryo cannot be a victim and therefore cannot be wronged. An embryo cannot be a victim, he says, because it lacks sentience. His central

argument for this seems to be that, even though plants and the permanently unconscious are alive, they clearly cannot be victims. What is the explanation of this? Bassen claims that the explanation is that their lives consist of mere metabolism and mere metabolism is not enough to ground victimizability. Mentation is required.

The problem with this attempt to establish the absence of victimizability is that both plants and the permanently unconscious clearly lack what Bassen calls "prospects" or what I have called "a future life like ours." Hence, it is surely open to one to argue that the real reason we believe plants and the permanently unconscious cannot be victims is that killing them cannot deprive them of a future life like ours; the real reason is not their absence of present mentation.

Bassen recognizes that his view is subject to this difficulty, and he recognizes that the case of children seems to support this difficulty, for "much of what we do for children is based on prospects." He argues, however, that in the case of children and in other such cases, "potentiality comes into play only where victimizability has been secured on other grounds" (*ibid.*, p. 333).

Bassen's defense of his view is patently question-begging, since what is adequate to secure victimizability is actually what is at issue. His examples do not support his own view against the thesis of this essay. Of course, embryos can be victims: when their lives are deliberately terminated, they are deprived of their futures of value, their prospects. This makes them victims, for it directly wrongs them.

The seeming plausibility of Bassen's view stems from the fact that paradigmatic cases of imagining someone as a victim involve empathy, and empathy requires mentation of the victim. The victims of flood, famine, rape, or child abuse are all persons with whom we can empathize. That empathy seems to be part of seeing them as victims.[15]

In spite of the strength of these examples, the attractive intuition that a situation in which there is victimization requires the possibility of empathy is subject to counterexamples. Consider a case that Bassen himself offers: "Posthumous obliteration of an author's work constitutes a misfortune for him only if he had wished his work to endure" (*op. cit.*, p. 318). The conditions Bassen wishes to impose upon the possibility of being victimized here seem far too strong. Perhaps this author, due to his unrealistic standards of excellence and his low self-esteem, regarded his work as unworthy of survival, even though it possessed genuine literary merit. Destruction of such work would surely victimize its author. In such a case, empathy with the victim concerning the loss is clearly impossible.

Of course, Bassen does not make the possibility of empathy a necessary condition for victimizability; he requires only mentation. Hence, on Bassen's actual view, this author, as I have described him, can be a victim. The problem is that the basic intuition that renders Bassen's view plausible is missing in the author's case. In order to attempt to avoid counterexamples, Bassen has made his thesis too weak to be supported by the intuitions that suggested it.

Even so, the mentation requirement on victimizability is still subject to counterexamples. Suppose a severe accident renders me totally unconscious for a month, after which I recover. Surely killing me while I am unconscious victimizes me, even though I am incapable of mentation during that time. It follows that Bassen's thesis fails. Apparently, attempts to restrict the value of a future-like-ours argument so that fetuses do not fall within its scope do not succeed.

V

In this essay, it has been argued that the correct ethic of the wrongness of killing can be extended to fetal life and used to show that there is a strong presumption that any abortion is morally impermissible. If the ethic of killing adopted here entails, however, that contraception is also seriously immoral, then there

would appear to be a difficulty with the analysis of this essay.

But this analysis does not entail that contraception is wrong. Of course, contraception prevents the actualization of a possible future of value. Hence, it follows from the claim that futures of value should be maximized that contraception is prima facie immoral. This obligation to maximize does not exist, however; furthermore, nothing in the ethics of killing in this paper entails that it does. The ethics of killing in this essay would entail that contraception is wrong only if something were denied a human future of value by contraception. Nothing at all is denied such a future by contraception, however.

Candidates for a subject of harm by contraception fall into four categories: (1) some sperm or other, (2) some ovum or other, (3) a sperm and an ovum separately, and (4) a sperm and an ovum together. Assigning the harm to some sperm is utterly arbitrary, for no reason can be given for making a sperm the subject of harm rather than the ovum. Assigning the harm to some ovum is utterly arbitrary, for no reason can be given for making an ovum the subject of harm rather than a sperm. One might attempt to avoid these problems by insisting that contraception deprives both the sperm and the ovum separately of a valuable future like ours. On this alternative, too many futures are lost. Contraception was supposed to be wrong, because it deprived us of one future of value, not two. One might attempt to avoid this problem by holding that contraception deprives the combination of sperm and ovum of a valuable future like ours. But here the definite article misleads. At the time of contraception, there are hundreds of millions of sperm, one (released) ovum and millions of possible combinations of all of these. There is no actual combination at all. Is the subject of the loss to be a merely possible combination? Which one? This alternative does not yield an actual subject of harm either. Accordingly, the immorality of contraception is not entailed by the loss of a future-like-ours argument simply because there is no nonarbitrarily identifiable subject of the loss in the case of contraception.

VI

The purpose of this essay has been to set out an argument for the serious presumptive wrongness of abortion subject to the assumption that the moral permissibility of abortion stands or falls on the moral status of the fetus. Since a fetus possesses a property, the possession of which in adult human beings is sufficient to make killing an adult human being wrong, abortion is wrong. This way of dealing with the problem of abortion seems superior to other approaches to the ethics of abortion, because it rests on an ethics of killing which is close to self-evident, because the crucial morally relevant property clearly applies to fetuses, and because the argument avoids the usual equivocations on 'human life', 'human being', or 'person'. The argument rests neither on religious claims nor on Papal dogma. It is not subject to the objection of 'speciesism.' Its soundness is compatible with the moral permissibility of euthanasia and contraception. It deals with our intuitions concerning young children.

Finally, this analysis can be viewed as resolving a standard problem—indeed, *the* standard problem—concerning the ethics of abortion. Clearly, it is wrong to kill adult human beings. Clearly, it is not wrong to end the life of some arbitrarily chosen single human cell. Fetuses seem to be like arbitrarily chosen human cells in some respects and like adult humans in other respects. The problem of the ethics of abortion is the problem of determining the fetal property that settles this moral controversy. The thesis of this essay is that the problem of the ethics of abortion, so understood, is solvable.

NOTES

1. Feinberg, "Abortion," in *Matters of Life and Death: New Introductory Essays in Moral Philosophy*, Tom Regan, ed. (New York: Random House, 1986), pp. 256–293; Tooley, "Abortion and Infanticide," *Philosophy and Public Affairs*, II, 1 (1972):37–65; Tooley, *Abortion and Infanticide* (New York: Oxford, 1984); Warren, "On the Moral and Legal Status of Abortion," *The Monist*, LVII, 1 (1973):43–61; Engelhardt, "The Ontology of Abortion," *Ethics*, LXXXIV, 3 (1974): 217–234; Sumner, *Abortion and Moral Theory* (Princeton: University Press, 1981); Noonan, "An Almost Absolute Value in History," in *The Morality of Abortion: Legal and Historical Perspectives*, Noonan, ed. (Cambridge: Harvard, 1970); and Devine, *The Ethics of Homicide* (Ithaca: Cornell, 1978).

2. For interesting discussions of this issue, see Warren Quinn, "Abortion: Identity and Loss," *Philosophy and Public Affairs*, XIII, 1 (1984:)24–54; and Lawrence C. Becker, "Human Being: The Boundaries of the Concept," *Philosophy and Public Affairs*, IV, 4 (1975):344–359.

3. For example, see my "Ethics and The Elderly: Some Problems," in Stuart Spicker, Kathleen Woodward, and David Van Tassel, eds., *Aging and the Elderly: Humanistic Perspectives in Gerontology* (Atlantic Highlands, NJ: Humanities, 1978), pp. 341–355.

4. See Warren, *op. cit.*, and Tooley, "Abortion and Infanticide."

5. This seems to be the fatal flaw in Warren's treatment of this issue.

6. I have been most influenced on this matter by Jonathan Glover, *Causing Death and Saving Lives* (New York: Penguin, 1977), ch. 3; and Robert Young, "What Is So Wrong with Killing People?" *Philosophy*, LIV, 210 (1979):515–528.

7. Feinberg, Tooley, Warren, and Engelhardt have all dealt with this problem.

8. "Duties to Animals and Spirits," in *Lectures on Ethics*, Louis Infeld, trans. (New York: Harper, 1963), p. 239.

9. I am indebted to Jack Bricke for raising this objection.

10. Presumably a preference utilitarian would press such an objection. Tooley once suggested that his account has such a theoretical underpinning. See his "Abortion and Infanticide," pp. 44/5.

11. Donald VanDeVeer seems to think this is self-evident. See his "Whither Baby Doe?" in *Matters of Life and Death*, p. 233.

12. "Must the Bearer of a Right Have the Concept of That to Which He Has a Right?" *Ethics*, XCV, 1 (1984):68–74.

13. See Tooley again in "Abortion and Infanticide," pp. 47–49.

14. "Present Sakes and Future Prospects: The Status of Early Abortion," *Philosophy and Public Affairs*, XI, 4 (1982): 322–326.

15. Note carefully the reasons he gives on the bottom of p. 316.

9.
Feminism and Abortion
Sally Markowitz

Professor Sally Markowitz teaches philosophy at Willamette University in Salem, Oregon. She presents one type of feminist perspective on the abortion issue. She argues that abortion is morally permissible if women find themselves facing unwanted pregnancies in a society in which they suffer discrimination and experience marked inequality.

In the past few decades, the issue of abortion, long of concern to women, has gained a prominent place in the platforms of politicians and a respectable, if marginal, one in the writings of moral philosophers. It is natural to speculate that the rise of and reactions to the women's liberation movement explain the feverish pitch of the recent debate, and no doubt there is much to this speculation. And yet, philosophical analyses of abortion have had surprisingly little to say directly about either women or feminism. Instead, their primary concern has been to decide whether or not the fetus is a person, with a right to life like yours or mine. That this question deserves philosophical attention becomes especially clear when we consider the frightening (if fanciful) ways it is asked and answered by those in power. Nevertheless, as many feminists and some philosophers have recognized, the way we respond to the problem of personhood will not necessarily settle the dispute over abortion once and for all. On some views, a full account must deal with the rights of pregnant women as well.

In fact, one popular defense of abortion is based on the woman's right to autonomy and avoids the personhood issue altogether. The central claim of the autonomy defense is that anti-abortion policies simply interfere in an impermissible way with the pregnant woman's autonomy. In what has become the classic philo-

sophical statement of this view, Judith Jarvis Thomson ingeniously argues that even if the fetus has a right to life, it need not also have the right to use its mother's body to stay alive. The woman's body is her own property, to dispose of as she wishes.[1] But autonomy theorists need not rest their case on the vaguely disturbing notion of the pregnant woman's property rights to her own body. For example, Jane English, in another version of the view, argues that a woman is justified in aborting if pregnancy and childbearing will prevent her from pursuing the life she wants to live, the expression of her own autonomy.[2]

Philosophers have come to call this strategy the "feminist" or "woman's liberation" approach, and indeed some version of it seems to be favored by many feminists.[3] This is no surprise since such a view may seem to be quite an improvement over accounts that regard personhood as the only essential issue. At least it recognizes women as bearers of rights as well as of babies. In what follows, however, I shall suggest that this defense may fall short of the feminist mark. Then I shall offer another defense, one derived not from the right to autonomy, but from an awareness of women's oppression and a commitment to a more egalitarian society.

I will assume throughout that the fetus has a serious right to life. I do so not because I believe this to be true, but rather because a feminist defense of abortion rights should be independent of the status of the fetus. For if, as many feminists believe, the move towards a sexually egalitarian society requires women's control of their reproductive lives, and if the

Sally Markowitz, "Abortion and Feminism," *Social Theory and Practice* 16 (Spring 1990):1–17. Reprinted with the permission of the author and *Social Theory and Practice*. Copyright (c) 1990.

permissibility of this control depends ultimately upon the status of the fetus, then the future of feminism rests upon how we resolve the personhood issue. This is not acceptable to most feminists. No doubt many feminists are comforted by arguments against the fetus's personhood. But regardless of the fetus's status, more must be said.

1.

What, then, from a feminist point of view, is wrong with an autonomy defense? Feminists should be wary on three counts. First, most feminists believe not only that women in our society are oppressed, but also that our failure to face the scope and depth of this oppression does much to maintain it. This makes feminists suspicious of perspectives, often called humanist or liberal ones, that focus only on the individual and de-emphasize the issue of gender by either refusing to acknowledge that women have less power than men or denying that this inequity is worth much attention. While liberals and humanists may try to discuss social issues, including abortion, with as little mention as possible of gender, feminists tend to search for the hidden, unexpected, and perhaps unwelcome ways in which gender is relevant. From this perspective, defenses of abortion which focus only on the personhood of the fetus are not essentially or even especially feminist ones since they completely avoid any mention of gender. Autonomy arguments, though, are not much of an improvement. They may take into account the well-being of individual women, but they manage to skirt the issue of women's status, as a group, in a sexist society.

Secondly, the autonomy defense incorporates a (supposedly) gender-neutral right, one that belongs to every citizen; there's nothing special about being a woman—except, of course, for the inescapable fact that only women find themselves pregnant against their wills. Some feminists have become disillusioned with this gender-neutral approach. They reject it both

on principle, because it shifts attention away from gender inequality, and for practical reasons, because it often works against women in the courts.[4] Instead, feminists have come to realize that sometimes gender should be relevant in claiming rights. Some of these rights, like adequate gynecological care, may be based on women's special physiology; others may stem from the special needs experienced by female casualties of a sexist society: the impoverished, divorced, or unwed mother, the rape victim, the anorexic teen, the coed who has been convinced that she lacks (or had better lack) mathematical aptitude. A thoroughly feminist analysis, then, will not hesitate, when appropriate, to claim a right on the basis of gender, rather than in spite of it.[5] And to do otherwise in the case of abortion may be not only to deny the obvious, but also to obscure the relation of reproductive practices to women's oppression.

The third problem feminists might have with an autonomy defense involves the content of the human ideal on which the right to autonomy rests. Some feminists, influenced by Marxist and socialist traditions, may reject an ideal that seems to be so intimately connected with the individualistic ideology of capitalism. Others may suspect that this ideology is not just capitalist but male-biased. And if feminists hesitate to justify abortion by appeal to a gender-neutral right derived from a gender-neutral ideal, they are even more suspicious of an ideal that seems to be gender neutral when really it's not. Increasingly, feminists reject the ideals of older feminists, like Simone de Beauvoir, who, in promoting for women what appeared to be an androgynous human ideal, unwittingly adopted one that was androcentric, or male-centered. Instead, feminists seek to free themselves from the misogynist perspective that sees women as incomplete men and ignores, devalues, or denies the existence of particularly female psychologies, values and experiences. On this view, to fashion a feminist human ideal we must look to women's values and experiences—or, at least, we must not look only to men's.[6]

This reevaluation has important implications for the abortion issue, since many feminists consider an overriding right to autonomy to be a characteristically male ideal, while nurturance and responsibility for other (the paradigmatic case of which, of course, is motherhood) to be characteristically female ones. Indeed, in the name of such women's values, some women who call themselves feminists have actually joined the anti-abortionist camp.[7] Most feminists, of course, don't go this far. But, paradoxically, many seem to find the ideal of autonomy less acceptable than the right to abortion it is supposed to justify. Clearly, something is awry. (I shall have more to say in section 4 about how autonomy is important to feminists.)

Feminists, therefore, need another argument. Instead of resting on an ideal many feminists reject, a feminist defense of abortion should somehow reflect an awareness of women's oppression and a commitment to ending it.

2.

Of all the philosophers, feminist and otherwise, who have discussed abortion, Alison Jaggar seems to be the only one to address the problem from this perspective. Jaggar argues that in societies where mothers bear the responsibility for pregnancy, birth and child-rearing, women should control abortion decisions. Women who live in other, more cooperative social communities (wherever they are), where members of both sexes share such responsibilities, cannot claim a right of the same force. The strength of a woman's say about whether or not to abort, then, should be relative to the amount of support (financial, emotional, physical, medical, and otherwise) she can expect from those around her.[8]

It is disheartening that the philosophical community has not paid Jaggar's paper the attention it merits in the decade and a half since its publication, but this lapse is hardly surprising. The notion of the individual's right to autonomy is so firmly entrenched that we have difficulty even entertaining other approaches. We find ourselves invoking such rights perhaps without realizing it even when we neither want nor need to. And, indeed, Jaggar is no exception; despite the promising intuition with which she starts, Jaggar finally offers us another, albeit more sophisticated, version of the autonomy argument. Quite simply, her argument implies that if abortion ought to be permissible in some societies but not in others, this is only because pregnancy and motherhood create obstacles to personal autonomy in some societies but not in others.

Jaggar bases her argument for abortion rights in our society on two principles. The first, or Right to Life principle, holds that

> the right to life, when it is claimed for a human being, means the right to a full human life and to whatever means are necessary to achieve this.... To be born, then, is only one of the necessary conditions for a full human life. The others presumably include nutritious food, breathable air, warm human companionship, and so on. If anyone has a right to life, she or he must be entitled to all of these.[9]

According to the second, or Personal Control Principle, "Decisions should be made by those, and only by those, who are importantly affected by them."[10] In our society, then, the state cannot legitimately set itself up as the protector of the fetus's right to life (as Jaggar has characterized it) because the mother and not the state will be expected to provide for this right, both during pregnancy and afterwards. But since, by the Personal Control Principle, only those whose lives will be importantly affected have the right to make a decision, in our society the pregnant woman should determine whether to continue her pregnancy.

Jaggar's argument incorporates both liberal and feminist perspectives, and there is a tension between them. Her argument is feminist rather than merely liberal because it does not rest exclusively on a universal right to autonomy.

Instead, it takes seriously the contingent and socially variable features of reproduction and parenting, their relationship to women's position in a society, and the effect of anti-abortion policy on this position. But her argument is also a liberal one. Consider, for example, the Personal Control Principle. While Jaggar doesn't explicitly spell out its motivation, she does state that the principle "provides the fundamental justification for democracy and is accepted by most shades of political opinion."[11] Surely this wide acceptance has something to do with the belief, equally widely held, that citizens should be able to decide for themselves what courses their lives should take, especially when some courses involve sacrifices or burdens. This becomes clear when Jaggar explains that an individual or organization has no moral claim as a protector of the right to life "that would justify its insistence on just one of the many conditions necessary to a full human life, in circumstances where this would place the burden of fulfilling all the other conditions squarely on the shoulders of some other individual or organization."[12] Once again we have an appeal to a universal right to personal autonomy, indeed a right based on an ideal which not only might be unacceptable to many feminists, but may cast the net too widely even for some liberals. For example, one might claim that taxation policies designed to finance social programs interfere with personal choices about how to spend earnings, a matter that will have important consequences for one's life. Such a view also permits a range of private actions which some liberals may believe are immoral: for example, an adult grandchild may decide to stop caring for a burdensome and senile grandparent if such care places a heavy burden on the grandchild.

I shall not attempt to pass judgment here on the desirability of either redistributing income through taxation or passing laws requiring us to be Good Samaritans in our private lives. Nor do I want to beg the question, which I shall discuss later, of whether reproductive autonomy is, in all circumstances, overridingly important in a

way other sorts of autonomy may not be. I can leave these matters open because a feminist defense of abortion need not depend on how we settle them. For there is a significant difference between the sacrifices required by restrictive abortion policies and those required by enforcing other sorts of Good Samaritanism: taxes and laws against letting the aged or handicapped starve to death apply to everyone; those prohibiting abortion apply only to women. While anyone might end up with a helpless, cantankerous grandparent and most of us end up paying taxes, only women end up pregnant. So anti-abortion laws require sacrifice not of everyone, but only of women.

3.

This brings us to what I regard as the crucial question: When, if ever, can people be required to sacrifice for the sake of others? And how can feminists answer this question in a way that rests not on the individual right to personal autonomy, but on a view of social reality that takes seriously power relations between genders? I suggest the following principle, which I shall call the Impermissible Sacrifice Principle: *When one social group in a society is systematically oppressed by another, it is impermissible to require the oppressed group to make sacrifices that will exacerbate or perpetuate this oppression.* (Note that this principle does not exempt the members of oppressed groups from *all* sorts of sacrifices just because they are oppressed; they may be as morally responsible as anyone for rendering aid in some circumstances. Only sacrifices that will clearly perpetuate their oppression are ruled out.)

The Impermissible Sacrifice Principle focuses on power relationships between groups rather than on the rights of individuals. This approach will suit not only feminists but all who recognize and deplore other sorts of systematic social oppression as well. Indeed, if we take our opposition to oppression seriously, this approach may be necessary. Otherwise, when policy decisions are made, competing goals and commitments may distract us from the conditions we claim to deplore and encourage decisions that allow such conditions to remain. Even worse, these other goals and commitments can be used as excuses for perpetuating oppression. Testing policies against the Impermissible Sacrifice Principle keeps this from happening.

Feminists should welcome the applicability of the Impermissible Sacrifice Principle to groups other than women. Radical feminists are sometimes accused of being blind to any sort of oppression but their own. The Impermissible Sacrifice Principle, however, enables feminists to demonstrate solidarity with other oppressed groups by resting the case for abortion on the same principle that might, for example, block a policy requiring the poor rather than the rich to bear the tax burden, or workers rather than management to take a pay cut. On the other hand, feminists may worry that the Impermissible Sacrifice Principle, taken by itself, may not yield the verdict on abortion feminists seek. For if some radical feminists err by recognizing only women's oppression, some men err by not recognizing it at all. So the Impermissible Sacrifice Principle must be supplemented by what I shall call the Feminist Proviso: *Women are, as a group, sexually oppressed by men; and this oppression can neither be completely understood in terms of, nor otherwise reduced to, oppressions of other sorts.*

Feminists often understand this oppression to involve men's treating women as breeding machines, sexual or aesthetic objects, nurturers who need no nurturance. Women become alienated from their bodies, their sexuality, their work, their intellect, their emotions, their moral agency. Of course, feminists disagree about exactly how to formulate this analysis, especially since women experience oppression differently depending on their class, race, and ethnicity. But however we decide to understand women's oppression, we can be sure an anti-abortion policy will make it worse.

Adding the Feminist Proviso, then, keeps (or makes) sexism visible, ensuring that women are one of the oppressed groups to which the Principle applies. This should hardly need saying. Yet by focusing on other sorts of oppression the Principle might cover, men often trivialize or ignore feminists' demands and women's pain. For example, someone (perhaps a white male) who is more sympathetic to the claims of racial minorities or workers than to those of women might try to trivialize or deny the sexual oppression of a white, affluent woman (perhaps his wife) by reminding her that she's richer than an unemployed black male and so should not complain. The Feminist Proviso also prevents an affluent white women who rejects the unwelcome sexual advances of a minority or working class male from being dismissed (or dismissing herself) as a racist or classist. She may well be both. But she also lives in a world where, all things being equal, she is fair sexual game, in one way or another, for any male.[12] Finally, the Impermissible Sacrifice Principle in conjunction with the Feminist Proviso might be used to block the view that a black or Third World woman's first obligation is to bear children to swell the ranks of the revolution, regardless of the consequences of maternity within her culture. Having children for this reason may be a legitimate choice; but she also may have independent grounds to refuse.

I have added the Feminist Proviso so that the Impermissible Sacrifice Principle cannot be used to frustrate a feminist analysis. But I must also emphasize that the point is not to pit one oppressed group against another, but to make sure that the men in otherwise progressive social movements do not ignore women's oppression or, worse, find "politically correct" justifications for it. Women refuse to wait until "after the revolution" not just because they are impatient, but also because they have learned that not all revolutions are feminist ones.

The Impermissible Sacrifice Principle and the Feminist Proviso together, then, justify abortion on demand for women *because they live in a sexist society.* This approach not only gives a more explicitly feminist justification of abortion than the autonomy defense; it also gives a stronger one. For autonomy defenses are open to objections and qualifications that a feminist one avoids. Consider the ways the feminist approach handles these four challenges to the autonomy defense.

First, some philosophers have dismissed autonomy defenses by suggesting blithely that we simply compensate the pregnant woman.[13] Of what, though, will such compensation consist? Maternity leave? Tax breaks? Prenatal health care? Twenty points added to her civil-service exam score? Such benefits lighten one's load, no doubt. But what women suffer by being forced to continue unwanted pregnancies is not merely a matter of finances or missed opportunities; in a sexist society, there is reason to expect that an anti-abortion policy will reinforce a specifically *sexual* oppression, whatever sorts of compensation are offered. Indeed, even talk of compensation may be misguided, since it implies a prior state when things were as they should be; compensation seeks to restore the balance after a temporary upset. But in a sexist society, there is no original balance; women's oppression is the status quo. Even if individual women are compensated by money, services, or opportunities, sexual oppression may remain.

Second, an autonomy defense may seem appropriate only in cases where a woman engages in "responsible" sex: it is one thing to be a victim of rape or even contraceptive failure, one might argue; it is quite another voluntarily to have unprotected intercourse. A feminist defense suggests another approach. First, we might question the double standard that requires that women pay for "irresponsible" sex while men don't have to, even though women are oppressed by men. More importantly, if we focus on the *way* women are oppressed, we may understand many unwanted pregnancies to result from fear and paralysis rather than irresponsibility. For in a sexist society, many women simply do not believe they can control the conditions under which they have sex. And, sad to say, often they may be right.[14]

Third, what about poor women's access to abortion? The sort of right the autonomy theorists invoke, after all, seems to be a right to noninterference by the state. But this negative right seems to be in tension with a demand for state-funded abortions, especially since not everyone supports abortion. At any rate, we will need another argument to justify the funding of abortion for poor women. The defense I suggest, however, is clearly committed to providing all women with access to abortion, since to allow abortions only for those who can afford them forces poor women, who are doubly oppressed, to make special sacrifices. An egalitarian society must liberate all women, not just the rich ones.

Finally, autonomy defenses allow, indeed invite, the charge that the choice to abort is selfish. Even Thomson finds abortion, while not unjust, often to be "selfish" or "indecent." Although she has deprived nothing of its rights, the woman who aborts has chosen self-interested autonomy over altruism in the same way one might choose to watch while a child starves. Of course, one is tempted to point out that the (largely male) world of commerce and politics thrives on such "morally indecent" but legal actions. But then feminists are reduced to claiming a right to be as selfish as men are. Moreover, once the specter of selfishness is raised, this defense does not allow feminists to make enough of male anti-abortionists' motives. On an autonomy defense, these motives are simply not relevant, let alone damning, and feminists who dwell on them seem to be resorting to *ad hominems*. From a feminist perspective, however, abortion is a political issue, one which essentially concerns the interests of and power relations between men and women. Thus, what women and men can expect to gain or lose from an abortion policy becomes the point rather than the subject of *ad hominem* arguments.[15]

The approach I propose does well on each of these important counts. But its real test comes when we weigh the demands of the Impermissible Sacrifice Principle against fetal rights; for we have required that a feminist analysis be independent of the status of the fetus. Indeed, we may even be tempted to regard fetuses as constituting just the sort of oppressed group to whom the principle applies, and surely a fetus about to be aborted is in worse shape than the woman who carries it.

However, it may not make sense to count fetuses as an oppressed group. A disadvantaged one, perhaps. But the Impermissible Sacrifice Principle does not prescribe that more disadvantaged groups have a right to aid from less disadvantaged ones; it focuses only on the particular disadvantage of social oppression. That the fetus has a serious right to life does not imply that it's the sort of being that can be oppressed, if it cannot yet enter into the sorts of social relationships that constitute oppression. I cannot argue for this here; in any case, I suspect my best argument will not convince everyone. But feminists have another, more pointed response.

Whether or not we can weigh the disadvantage of fetuses against the oppression of women, we must realize what insisting on such a comparison does to the debate. It narrows our focus, turning it back to the conflict between the rights of fetuses and of women (even if now this conflict is between the rights of groups rather than of individuals). This is certainly not to deny that fetal rights should be relevant to an abortion policy. But feminists must insist that the oppression of women should be relevant too. And it is also relevant that unless our society changes in deep and global ways, anti-abortion policies, intentionally or not, will perpetuate women's oppression by men. This, then, is where feminists must stand firm.

Does this mean that instead of overriding the fetus's right to life by women's right to autonomy, I am proposing that feminists override the fetus's right by the right of women to live in a sexually egalitarian society? This is a difficult position for feminists but not an impossible one, especially for feminists with utilitarian leanings. Many feminists, for example, see sexism as responsible for a culture of death: war, violence, child abuse, ecological disaster. Eradicate sexism, it might be argued, and we will save more lives than we will lose. Some feminists might even claim that an oppressed woman's fate can be worse than that of an aborted fetus. Although I will not argue for such claims, they may be less implausible than they seem. But feminists need not rest their case on them. Instead, they may simply insist that society must change so that women are no longer oppressed. Such changes, of course, may require of men sacrifices unwelcome beyond their wildest dreams. But that, according to a feminist analysis, is the point.

So we should not see the choice as between liberating women and saving fetuses, but between two ways of respecting the fetus's right to life. The first requires women to sacrifice while men benefit. The second requires deep social changes that will ensure that men no longer gain and women lose through our practices of sexuality, reproduction, and parenthood. To point out how men gain from women's compulsory pregnancy is to steal the misplaced moral thunder from those male authorities—fathers, husbands, judges, congressmen, priests, philosophers—who, exhorting women to do their duty, present themselves as the benevolent, disinterested protectors of fetuses against women's selfishness. Let feminists insist that the condition for refraining from having abortions is a sexually egalitarian society. If men do not respond, and quickly, they will have indicated that fetal life isn't so important to them after all, or at least not important enough to give up the privileges of being male in a sexist society. If this makes feminists look bad, it makes men look worse still.

4.

My defense maintains what seems to me to be Jaggar's most important insight: the strength of a right to abortion depends on women's condition in a particular society. But where Jaggar's argument seems motivated by the goal of securing personal autonomy for women, mine is not. Instead I tie the permissibility of abortion directly to the goal of ending sexism. As I have suggested, this is a strength from the feminist point of view, since many feminists are not completely sure about their attitudes towards the liberal ideal of autonomy. But it remains to be asked, then, why feminists so often invoke an autonomy right. Are most feminists really liberal individualists at heart? Not necessarily. For it is easy to conflate two motivations for insisting upon a right to autonomy. One is the liberal conviction that personal autonomy is overridingly and intrinsically valuable; the other is the feminist conviction that in our society such autonomy for women frustrates and represents freedom from male domination. This is especially true of reproductive autonomy, for obvious reasons. Feminists see men making decisions about women's reproductive lives and then benefitting by the resulting gaps in power. This exploitation must be stopped if we are to achieve sexual equality, and the easiest way to stop it in a society like ours is to wrest this control from men and give it to individual women. So it's not necessarily that women work towards a sexually egalitarian society simply to secure for themselves the degree of personal autonomy now reserved for men. Instead, by frustrating male dominance, women's autonomy will promote a more sexually egalitarian society.

These considerations allow us more fully to understand why some feminists resist a human ideal based on nurturance rather than autonomy. Such resistance does not merely reflect an attachment to an individualistic and, some would claim, androcentric human ideal. Nor are these feminist critics, for the most part, claiming they simply don't want to be nurturers. Their skepticism seems to have a more pragmatic and political basis: nurturing is fine, but not if only women do it. As Simone de Beauvoir put it in 1982, motherhood, despite its new feminist glorification, "is still the most skillful way there is of turning women into slaves."[16] On top of the demands of motherhood, moreover, women are expected to nurture men as well, rather than be nurtured by them. This makes for a hard and often an unrewarding day's work. The ultimate goal for feminists, then, is not to cease to nurture, nor even to nurture less, but to resist or transform relationships where nurturance becomes an expression of powerlessness.

But if nurturance isn't something women should avoid, neither is the liberal ideal of autonomy necessarily something women should embrace, except, again, insofar as it frustrates exploitation by men. Indeed, in a truly egalitarian society, women might not even think in terms of this ideal.

Some feminists might concede this point for autonomy in general but insist that sexual and reproductive autonomy are another matter: surely any sexually egalitarian society must include the right to abortion. This objection might take various forms. One might claim, for example, that pregnancy involves a woman's relation to her own body, over which she needs control for her emotional health and sense of identity. Or one might emphasize the special vulnerability to male oppression, physical and psychological, an anti-abortion policy might be expected to encourage, whatever the society. Both objections, though, are inconclusive for the same reason: Neither takes seriously enough how deeply our natures are shaped by gender; and gender, according to most feminists, is socially constructed. For example, one's relationship to one's body, according to feminist psychologist Nancy Chodorow, depends on one's socially constructed gender identity. "We cannot know," claims Chodorow, "what children would make of their bodies in a nonsexually organized social world."[17] The same, it would seem, goes for adult women. Similarly, the claim that any sexually egalitarian society requires that individual women have complete control over abortion decisions seems to reflect a biological determinism many feminists would reject. Need women's potential vulnerability in pregnancy inevitably be exploited by men? In a society like ours, no doubt it will be. But what do we know about the behavior of men in a truly sexually egalitarian society? True, such a society is difficult to imagine. But this suggests only that we avoid dogmatism in our view of what such a society requires, especially when our certainty rests on intuitions about a human nature that may be almost wholly shaped by the very social organization we wish to change.

Of course, a sexually egalitarian society may turn out to require abortion rights; human (or, at least, male) nature may be, sad to say, only so malleable. Feminists, though, should not be troubled by this possibility: we need not show that abortion rights are necessary in all societies to argue that they are necessary in ours. In any case, since the verdict is not in, it is a good thing that a feminist defense need not rely on it.

Finally, since my discussion unequivocally assumes a feminist perspective, the approach I suggest may seem far removed from the standard ones popular in legal and philosophical circles. This should come as no surprise, since most philosophers and judges are not feminists. While feminists might regret this, they forget it at their own risk. The standard defenses of abortion—those that focus on autonomy rights or the status of the fetus—simply do not reflect or even acknowledge feminist concerns, and so such defenses are bound to frustrate the feminists who rely on them. This is not to say that feminists cannot in good faith use standard autonomy and non-personhood defenses when it is pragmatic to do so, but only that such defenses do not tell the whole (or even the right) story.

In any case, I hope my discussion has brought to light for everyone a dimension of the abortion issue too often ignored by philosophers: the relationship between reproductive practices and the liberation (or oppression) of women. After all, many philosophers, feminist and otherwise, reject utilitarianism because it seems to allow, indeed to require, sacrifices from arbitrarily chosen individuals for the sake of the general good. If such a consequence strikes us as undesirable, how much more so is a policy that requires significant sacrifices not merely from random individuals, but from members of an oppressed group, a group whose oppression, in fact, arises from and will be made worse by these very sacrifices? At least until we have a sexually egalitarian society, it is impermissible to forbid women to have abortions. If we sincerely believe (as I see no reason to) that abortion is at least *prima facie* wrong because it violates an overriding right of the fetus, our view should provide all the more incentive to change society so that women are no longer oppressed. As long as anti-abortionists reject or ignore the necessity of such change, the burden of moral proof, if not the blame, surely rests on them.

NOTES

1. Judith Jarvis Thomson, "A Defense of Abortion," *Philosophy and Public Affairs* 1 (1971): 47–66.

2. Jane English, "Abortion and the Concept of a Person," in *Today's Moral Problems*, ed. by Richard A. Wasserstrom, (New York: Macmillan, 1985), pp. 448–57.

3. Peter Singer, *Practical Ethics* (Cambridge: Cambridge University Press, 1979), p. 113.

4. Catharine A. MacKinnon, *Feminism Unmodified: Discourses on Life and Law* (Cambridge: Harvard University Press, 1987), pp. 35–36.

5. See, for example, Alison Jaggar, *Feminism, Politics and Human Nature* (Totowa, New Jersey: Rowman and Allanheld, 1983), especially Parts One and Two; and Catharine A. MacKinnon, *Feminism Unmodified: Discourses on Life and Law*.

6. See Sara Ruddick, "Maternal Thinking," *Feminist Studies* 6 (1980):345–46; Nancy Chodorow, *The Reproduction of Mothering: Psychoanalysis and the Sociology of Gender* (Berkeley and Los Angeles: University of California Press, 1978); Carol Gilligan, *In a Different Voice: Psychological Theory and Women's Development* (Cambridge: Harvard University Press, 1982).

7. Sidney Callahan, "A Pro-Life Feminist Makes Her Case," *Commonweal* (April 25, 1986), quoted in the *Utne Reader* 20 (1987):104–108.

8. Alison Jaggar, "Abortion and a Woman's Right to Decide," in *Philosophy and Sex*, ed. Robert Baker and Frank Elliston (Buffalo: Prometheus Press, 1975), pp. 324–37.

9. "Abortion and a Woman's Right to Decide," p. 328.

10. "Abortion and a Woman's Right to Decide," p. 328.

11. "Abortion and a Woman's Right to Decide," p. 329.

12. For classic discussions of sexism in the civil rights movement, see Susan Brownmiller, *Against Our Will: Men,*

Women, and Rape (New York: Simon and Schuster, 1975), especially pp. 210–55; and Michelle Wallace, *Black Macho and the Myth of the Superwoman* (New York: Dial Press, 1978).

13. Michael Tooley, "Abortion and Infanticide," in Joel Feinberg, ed., *The Problem of Abortion* (Belmont, California: Wadsworth, 1983).

14. MacKinnon, *Feminism Unmodified*, p. 95.

15. This approach also allows us to understand the deep divisions between women on this issue. For many women in

traditional roles fear the immediate effects on their lives of women's liberation generally and a permissive abortion policy in particular. On this, see Kristen Luker, *Abortion and the Politics of Motherhood* (Berkeley: University of California Press, 1984), especially pp. 158–215.

16. Alice Schwarzer, *After the Second Sex: Conversations with Simone de Beauvoir* (New York: Pantheon, 1984), p. 114.

17. Nancy Chodorow, "Feminism and Difference," *Socialist Review* 46 (1979): 66.

10.
Feminist Analyses of Women and Abortion
Susan Sherwin

Susan Sherwin is professor of philosophy and women's studies at Dalhousie University in Halifax, Canada. In this essay, an excerpt from her book *No Longer Patient: Feminist Ethics and Health Care,* she directly examines the differences between feminist and non-feminist analyses of the moral permissibility of abortion.

Although abortion has long been an important issue in bioethics, the distinctive analysis of feminist ethics is generally overlooked in the discussion. Authors and readers commonly presume a familiarity with the feminist position and equate it with other liberal defenses of women's right to choose abortion; but feminist ethics yields a different analysis of the moral questions surrounding abortion from that usually offered by liberal abortion arguments.[1] Although feminists agree with some of the conclusions of nonfeminist arguments on abortion, they often disagree with the way the issues are formulated and with the reasoning that is offered in the mainstream literature.

Feminist reasoning in support of women's right to choose abortion is significantly different from the reasoning used by nonfeminist supporters of similar positions. For instance, most feminist accounts evaluate abortion policy within a broader framework, according to its place among the social institutions that support

the subordination of women. In contrast, most nonfeminist discussions of abortion consider the moral or legal permissibility of abortion in isolation; they ignore (and thereby obscure) relevant connections with other social practices, including the ongoing power struggle within sexist societies over the control of women and their reproduction. Feminist arguments take into account the actual concerns that particular women attend to in their decision-making on abortion, such as the nature of a woman's feelings about her fetus, her relationships with her partner, other children she may have, and her various obligations to herself and others. In contrast, most nonfeminist discussions evaluate abortion decisions in their most abstract form (for example, questioning what sort of being a fetus is); from this perspective, specific questions of context are deemed irrelevant. In addition, nonfeminist arguments in support of choice about abortion are generally grounded in masculinist conceptions of freedom (such as privacy, individual choice, and individuals' property rights with respect to their own bodies), which do not meet the needs, interests, and intuitions of many of the women concerned.

Feminists also differ from nonfeminists in their conception of what is morally at issue with abortion. Nonfeminists focus exclusively on the morality and legality of performing abortions, whereas feminists insist that other issues, including the accessibility and delivery of abortion services, must also be addressed. Disputes about abortion arise even at the stage of defining the issue and setting the moral parameters for discussion. Although many nonfeminist bioethicists agree with feminists about which abortion policies should be supported, they tend to accept the proposals of the antifeminists as to what is morally at issue in developing that policy.

Thus although feminists welcome the support of nonfeminists in pursuing policies that grant women control over abortion decisions, they generally envision policies for this purpose that are very different from those considered by their nonfeminist sympathizers. Feminist ethicists promote a model for addressing the provision of abortion services different from the one conceived in traditional bioethical arguments. For example, Kathleen McDonnell urges feminists to develop an implicitly "'feminist morality' of abortion. . . . At its root it would be characterized by the deep appreciations of the complexities of life, the refusal to polarize and adopt simplistic formulas" (McDonnell 1984, 52). Here I propose one conception of the shape such an analysis should take.

WOMEN AND ABORTION

The most obvious difference between feminist and nonfeminist approaches to abortion lies in the relative attention each gives in its analysis to the interests and experiences of women. Feminist analysis regards the effects of unwanted pregnancies on the lives of women individually and collectively as the central element in the moral examination of abortion; it is considered self-evident that the pregnant woman is the subject of principal concern in abortion decisions. In many nonfeminist accounts, however, not only is the pregnant woman not perceived as

central, she is often rendered virtually invisible. Nonfeminist theorists, whether they support or oppose women's right to choose abortion, generally focus almost all their attention on the moral status of the fetus.[2]

In pursuing a distinctively feminist ethics, it is appropriate to begin with a look at the role of abortion in women's lives. The need for abortion can be very intense; no matter how appalling and dangerous the conditions, women from widely diverse cultures and historical periods have pursued abortions. No one denies that if abortion is not made legal, safe, and accessible in our society, women will seek out illegal and life-threatening abortions to terminate pregnancies they cannot accept. Antiabortion activists seem willing to accept this cost, although liberals definitely are not; feminists, who explicitly value women, judge the inevitable loss of women's lives that results from restrictive abortion policies to be a matter of fundamental concern.

Antiabortion campaigners imagine that women often make frivolous and irresponsible decisions about abortion, but feminists recognize that women have abortions for a wide variety of compelling reasons. Some women, for instance, find themselves seriously ill and incapacitated throughout pregnancy; they cannot continue in their jobs and may face insurmountable difficulties in fulfilling their responsibilities at home. Many employers and schools will not tolerate pregnancy in their employees or students, and not every woman is able to put her job, career, or studies on hold. Women of limited means may be unable to take adequate care of children they have already borne, and they may know that another mouth to feed will reduce their ability to provide for their existing children. Women who suffer from chronic disease, who believe themselves too young or too old to have children, or who are unable to maintain lasting relationships may recognize that they will not be able to care properly for a child when they face the decision. Some who are homeless, addicted to drugs, or diagnosed as carrying the AIDS virus may be unwilling to allow a child to enter the world with the handicaps that would result from the mother's condition. If the fetus is a result of rape or incest, then the psychological pain of carrying it may be unbearable, and the woman may recognize that her attitude to the child after birth will be tinged with bitterness. Some women learn that the fetuses that they carry have serious chromosomal anomalies and consider it best to prevent them from being born with a condition that is bound to cause them to suffer. Others, knowing the fathers to be brutal and violent, may be unwilling to subject a child to the beatings or incestuous attacks they anticipate; some may have no other realistic way to remove the child (or themselves) from the relationship.[3]

Finally, a woman may simply believe that bearing a child is incompatible with her life plans at the time. Continuing a pregnancy may have devastating repercussions throughout a woman's life. If the woman is young, then a pregnancy will likely reduce her chances of pursuing an education and hence limit her career and life opportunities: "The earlier a woman has a baby, it seems, the more likely she is to drop out of school; the less education she gets, the more likely she is to remain poorly paid, peripheral to the labor market, or unemployed, and the more children she will have" (Petchesky 1985, 150). In many circumstances, having a child will exacerbate the social and economic forces already stacked against a woman by virtue of her sex (and her race, class, age, sexual orientation, disabilities, and so forth). Access to abortion is necessary for many women if they are to escape the oppressive conditions of poverty.[4]

Whatever the specific reasons are for abortion, most feminists believe that the women concerned are in the best position to judge whether abortion is the appropriate response to a pregnancy. Because usually only the woman choosing abortion is properly situated to weigh all the relevant factors, most feminists resist attempts to offer general, abstract rules for determining when abortion is morally justified.[5]

Women's personal deliberations about abortion involve contextually defined considerations that reflect their commitments to the needs and interests of everyone concerned, including themselves, the fetuses they carry, other members of their household, and so forth. Because no single formula is available for balancing these complex factors through all possible cases, it is vital that feminists insist on protecting each woman's right to come to her own conclusions and resist the attempts of other philosophers and moralists to set the agenda for these considerations. Feminists stress that women must be acknowledged as full moral agents, responsible for making moral decisions about their own pregnancies. Women may sometimes make mistakes in their moral judgments, but no one else can be assumed to have the authority to evaluate and overrule their judgments.[6]

Even without patriarchy, bearing a child would be a very important event in a woman's life, because it involves significant physical, emotional, social, and (usually) economic changes for her. The ability to exert control over the incidence, timing, and frequency of childbearing is often tied to a woman's ability to control most other things she values. Because we live in a patriarchal society, it is especially important to ensure that women have the authority to control their own reproduction.[7] Despite the diversity of opinion found among feminists on most other matters, most feminists agree that women must gain full control over their own reproductive lives if they are to free themselves from male dominance.[8]

Moreover, women's freedom to choose abortion is linked to their ability to control their own sexuality. Women's subordinate status often prevents them from refusing men sexual access to their bodies. If women cannot end the unwanted pregnancies that result from male sexual dominance, then their sexual vulnerability to particular men may increase, because caring for an(other) infant involves greater financial needs and reduced economic opportunities for women.[9] As a result, pregnancy often forces women to become dependent on particular men. Because a woman's dependence on a man is assumed to entail her continued sexual loyalty to him, restriction of abortion serves to commit women to remaining sexually accessible to particular men and thus helps to perpetuate the cycle of oppression.

In contrast to most nonfeminist accounts, feminist analyses of abortion direct attention to how women get pregnant. Those who reject abortion seem to believe that women can avoid unwanted pregnancies "simply" by avoiding sexual intercourse. These views show little appreciation for the power of sexual politics in a culture that oppresses women. Existing patterns of sexual dominance mean that women often have little control over their sexual lives. They may be subject to rape by their husbands, boyfriends, colleagues, employers, customers, fathers, brothers, uncles, and dates, as well as by strangers. Often the sexual coercion is not even recognized as such by the participants but is the price of continued "good will"—popularity, economic survival, peace, or simply acceptance. Many women have found themselves in circumstances where they do not feel free to refuse a man's demands for intercourse, either because he is holding a gun to her head or because he threatens to be emotionally hurt if she refuses (or both). Women are socialized to be compliant and accommodating, sensitive to the feelings of others, and frightened of physical power; men are socialized to take advantage of every opportunity to engage in sexual intercourse and to use sex to express dominance and power. Under such circumstances, it is difficult to argue that women could simply "choose" to avoid heterosexual activity if they wish to avoid pregnancy. Catharine MacKinnon neatly sums it up: "The logic by which women are supposed to consent to sex [is]: preclude the alternatives, then call the remaining option 'her choice'" (MacKinnon 1989, 192).

Furthermore, women cannot rely on birth control to avoid pregnancy. No form of contraception that is fully safe and reliable is avail-able, other than sterilization; because women may wish only to avoid pregnancy temporarily, not permanently, sterilization is not always an acceptable choice. The pill and the IUD are the most effective contraceptive means offered, but both involve significant health hazards to women and are quite dangerous for some.[10] No woman should spend the thirty to forty years of her reproductive life on either form of birth control. Further, both have been associated with subsequent problems of involuntary infertility, so they are far from optimal for women who seek to control the timing of their pregnancies.

The safest form of birth control involves the use of barrier methods (condoms or diaphragms) in combination with spermicidal foams or jelly. But these methods also pose difficulties for women. They are sometimes socially awkward to use. Young women are discouraged from preparing for sexual activity that might never happen and are offered instead romantic models of spontaneous passion; few films or novels interrupt scenes of seduction for a partner to fetch contraceptives. Many women find their male partners unwilling to use barrier methods of contraception, and they often find themselves in no position to insist. Further, cost is a limiting factor for many women. Condoms and spermicides are expensive and are not covered under most health care plans.[11] Only one contraceptive option offers women safe and fully effective birth control: barrier methods with the backup option of abortion.[12]

From a feminist perspective, the central moral feature of pregnancy is that it takes place in women's bodies and has profound effects on women's lives. Gender-neutral accounts of pregnancy are not available; pregnancy is explicitly a condition associated with the female body.[13] Because only women experience a need for abortion, policies about abortion affect women uniquely. Therefore, it is important to consider how proposed policies on abortion fit into general patterns of oppression for women. Unlike nonfeminist accounts, feminist ethics demands that the effects of abortion policies on the oppression of women be of principal consideration in our ethical evaluations.

THE FETUS

In contrast to feminist ethics, most nonfeminist analysts believe that the moral acceptability of abortion turns entirely on the question of the moral status of the fetus. Even those who support women's right to choose abortion tend to accept the premise of the antiabortion proponents that abortion can be tolerated only if we can first prove that the fetus lacks full personhood.[14] Opponents of abortion on demand that we define the status of the fetus either as a being that is valued in the same way as other humans and hence is entitled not to be killed or as a being that lacks in all value. Rather than challenging the logic of this formulation, many defenders of abortion have concentrated on showing that the fetus is indeed without significant value (Tooley 1972, Warren 1973); others, such as L. W. Sumner (1981), offer a more subtle account that reflects the gradual development of fetuses and distinguishes between early fetal stages, where the relevant criterion for personhood is absent, and later stages, where it is present. Thus the debate often rages between abortion opponents, who describe the fetus as an "innocent," vulnerable, morally important, separate being whose life is threatened and who must be protected at all costs, and abortion supporters, who try to establish that fetuses are deficient in some critical respect and hence are outside the scope of the moral community. In both cases, however, the nature of the fetus as an independent being is said to determine the moral status of abortion.

The woman on whom the fetus depends for survival is considered as secondary (if she is considered at all) in these debates. The actual experiences and responsibilities of real women are not perceived as morally relevant to the debate, unless these women too, can be proved innocent by establishing that their pregnancies are a result of rape or incest.[15] In some contexts,

women's role in gestation is literally reduced to that of "fetal containers"; the individual women disappear or are perceived simply as mechanical life-support systems.[16]

The current rhetoric against abortion stresses that the genetic makeup of the fetus is determined at conception and the genetic code is incontestably human. Lest there be any doubt about the humanity of the fetus, we are assailed with photographs of fetuses at various stages of development that demonstrate the early appearance of recognizably human characteristics, such as eyes, fingers, and toes. Modern ultrasound technology is used to obtain "baby's first picture" and stimulate bonding between pregnant women and their fetuses (Petchesky 1987). That the fetus in its early stages is microscopic, virtually indistinguishable to the untrained eye from fetuses of other species, and lacking in the capacities that make human life meaningful and valuable is not deemed relevant by the self-appointed defenders of the fetus. The antiabortion campaign is directed at evoking sympathetic attitudes toward a tiny, helpless being whose life is threatened by its own mother; the fetus is characterized as a being entangled in an adversarial relationship with the (presumably irresponsible) woman who carries it (Overall 1987). People are encouraged to identify with the "unborn child," not with the woman whose life is also at issue.

In the nonfeminist literature, both defenders and opponents of women's right to choose abortion agree that the difference between a late-term fetus and a newborn infant is "merely geographical" and cannot be considered morally significant. Daniel Callahan (1986), for instance, maintains a pro-choice stand but professes increasing uneasiness about this position in light of new medical and scientific developments that increase our knowledge of embryology and hasten the date of potential viability for fetuses; he insists that defenders of women's right to choose must come to terms with the question of the fetus and the effects of science on the fetus's prospects apart from the woman who carries it.

Arguments that focus on the similarities between infants and fetuses, however, generally fail to acknowledge that a fetus inhabits a woman's body and is wholly dependent on her unique contribution to its maintenance, whereas a newborn is physically independent, although still in need of a lot of care.[17] One can only view the distinction between being in or out of a woman's womb as morally irrelevant if one discounts the perspective of the pregnant woman; feminists seem to be alone in recognizing the woman's perspective as morally important to the distinction.[18]

In antiabortion arguments, fetuses are identified as individuals; in our culture, which views the (abstract) individual as sacred, fetuses qua individuals are to be honored and preserved. Extraordinary claims are made to establish the individuality and moral agency of fetuses. At the same time, the women who carry these fetal individuals are viewed as passive hosts whose only significant role is to refrain from aborting or harming their fetuses. Because it is widely believed that a woman does not actually have to do anything to protect the life of her fetus, pregnancy is often considered (abstractly) to be a tolerable burden to protect the life of an individual so like us.[19]

Medicine has played its part in supporting these attitudes. Fetal medicine is a rapidly expanding specialty, and it is commonplace in professional medical journals to find references to pregnant women as "the maternal environment." Fetal surgeons now have at their disposal a repertoire of sophisticated technology that can save the lives of dangerously ill fetuses; in light of the excitement of such heroic successes, it is perhaps understandable that women have disappeared from their view. These specialists see the fetuses as their patients, not the women who nurture the fetuses. As the "active" agents in saving fetal lives (unlike the pregnant women, whose role is seen as purely passive), doctors perceive themselves as developing independent relationships with the fetuses they treat. Barbara Katz Rothman observes: "The medical

model of pregnancy, as an essentially parasitic and vaguely pathological relationship, encourages the physician to view the fetus and mother as two separate patients, and to see pregnancy as inherently a conflict of interest between the two" (Rothman 1986, 25).

Perhaps even more distressing than the tendency to ignore the woman's agency altogether and view her as a passive participant in the medically controlled events of pregnancy and childbirth is the growing practice of viewing women as genuine threats to the well-being of the fetus. Increasingly, women are described as irresponsible or hostile toward their fetuses, and the relationship between them is characterized as adversarial. Concern for the well-being of the fetus is taken as license for doctors to intervene to ensure that women comply with medical "advice." Courts are called upon to enforce the doctors' orders when moral pressure alone proves inadequate, and women are being coerced into undergoing unwanted cesarean deliveries and technologically monitored hospital births (Annas 1982; Rodgers 1989; Nelson and Milliken 1990). Some states have begun to imprison women for endangering their fetuses through drug abuse and other socially unacceptable behaviors (Annas 1986). Mary Anne Warren reports that a bill was recently introduced in an Australian state that makes women liable to criminal prosecution "if they are found to have smoked during pregnancy, eaten unhealthful foods, or taken any other action which can be shown to have adversely affected the development of the fetus" (Warren 1989, 60).

In other words, some physicians have joined antiabortion campaigners in fostering a cultural acceptance of the view that fetuses are distinct individuals who are physically, ontologically, and socially separate from the women whose bodies they inhabit and that they have their own distinct interests. In this picture, pregnant women are either ignored altogether or are viewed as deficient in some crucial respect, and hence they can be subject to coercion for the sake of their fetuses. In the former case, the interests of the women concerned are assumed to be identical with those of the fetus; in the latter, the women's interests are irrelevant, because they are perceived as immoral, unimportant, or unnatural. Focus on the fetus as an independent entity has led to presumptions that deny pregnant women their roles as active, independent, moral agents with a primary interest in what becomes of the fetuses they carry. The moral question of the fetus's status is quickly translated into a license to interfere with women's reproductive freedom.

A FEMINIST VIEW OF THE FETUS

Because the public debate has been set up as a competition between the rights of women and those of fetuses, feminists have often felt pushed to reject claims of fetal value, in order to protect women's needs. As Kathryn Adelson (1987) has argued, however, viewing abortion in this way "rips it out of the context of women's lives." Other accounts of fetal value are more plausible and less oppressive to women.

On a feminist account fetal development is examined in the context in which it occurs, within women's bodies, rather than in the isolation of imagined abstraction. Fetuses develop in specific pregnancies that occur in the lives of particular women. They are not individuals housed in generic female wombs or full persons at risk only because they are small and subject to the whims of women. Their very existence is relationally defined, reflecting their development within particular women's bodies; that relationship gives those women reason to be concerned about them. Many feminists argue against a perspective that regards the fetus as an independent being and suggest that a more accurate and valuable understanding of pregnancy would involve regarding the pregnant woman "as a biological and social unit" (Rothman 1986, 25).

On this view, fetuses are morally significant, but their status is relational rather than absolute. Unlike other human beings, fetuses do not have any independent existence; their existence is uniquely tied to the support of a specific other. Most nonfeminist accounts have ignored the relational dimension of fetal development and have presumed that the moral status of fetuses could be resolved solely in terms of abstract, metaphysical criteria of personhood as applied to the fetus alone (Tooley 1972; Warren 1973). Throughout much of the nonfeminist literature, commentators argue that some set of properties (such as genetic heritage, moral agency, self-consciousness, language use, or self-determination) will entitle all who possess it to be granted the moral status of persons. They seek some feature by which we can neatly divide the world into moral persons (who are to be valued and protected) and others (who are not entitled to the same group privileges).

This vision, however, misinterprets what is involved in personhood and what is especially valued about persons. Personhood is a social category, not an isolated state. Persons are members of a community, and they should be valued in their concrete, discrete, and different states as specific individuals, not merely as conceptually undifferentiated entities. To be a morally significant category, personhood must involve personality as well as biological integrity.[20] It is not sufficient to consider persons simply as Kantian atoms of rationality, because persons are embodied, conscious beings with particular social histories. Annette Baier has developed a concept of persons as "second persons," which helps explain the sort of social dimension that seems fundamental to any moral notion of personhood:

> A person, perhaps, is best seen as one who was long enough dependent upon other persons to acquire the essential arts of personhood. Persons essentially are *second* persons, who grow up with other persons. . . . The fact that a person has a life *history*, and that a people collectively have a history depends upon the humbler fact that each person has a childhood in which a cultural heritage is

transmitted, ready for adolescent rejection and adult discriminating selection and contribution. Persons come after and before other persons (Baier 1985: 84–5).

Persons, in other words, are members of a social community that shapes and values them, and personhood is a relational concept that must be defined in terms of interactions and relationships with others.[21]

Because humans are fundamentally relational beings, it is important to remember that fetuses are characteristically limited in the "relationships" in which they can "participate"; within those relationships, they can make only the most restricted "contributions."[22] After birth human beings are capable of a much wider range of roles in relationships with a broad variety of partners; that very diversity of possibility and experience leads us to focus on the abstraction of the individual as a constant through all these different relationships. Until birth, however, no such variety is possible, so the fetus must be understood as part of a complex entity that includes the woman who currently sustains the fetus and who will, most likely, be principally responsible for it for many years to come.

A fetus is a unique sort of human entity, then, for it cannot form relationships freely with others, and others cannot readily form relationships with it. A fetus has a primary and particularly intimate sort of "relationship" with the woman in whose womb it develops; connections with any other persons are necessarily indirect and must be mediated through the pregnant woman. The relationship that exists between a woman and her fetus is clearly asymmetrical, because she is the only party to it who is capable of even considering whether the interaction should continue; further, the fetus is wholly dependent on the woman who sustains it, whereas she is quite capable of surviving without it.

Most feminist views of what is valuable about persons reflect the social nature of indi-

vidual existence. No human, especially no fetus, can exist apart from relationships; efforts to speak of the fetus itself, as if it were not inseparable from the woman in whom it develops, are distorting and dishonest. Fetuses have a unique physical status—within and dependent on particular women. That gives them also a unique social status. However much some might prefer it to be otherwise, no one other than the pregnant woman in question can do anything to support or harm a fetus without doing something to the woman who nurtures it. Because of this inexorable biological reality, the responsibility and privilege of determining a fetus's specific social status and value must rest with the woman carrying it.

Many pregnancies occur to women who place a very high value on the lives of the particular fetuses they carry and choose to see their pregnancies through to term, despite the possible risks and costs involved; it would be wrong of anyone to force such a woman to terminate her pregnancy. Other women, or some of these same women at other times, value other things more highly (for example, their freedom, their health, or previous responsibilities that conflict with those generated by the pregnancies), and so they choose not to continue their pregnancies. The value that women ascribe to individual fetuses varies dramatically from case to case and may well change over the course of any particular pregnancy. The fact that fetal lives can neither be sustained nor destroyed without affecting the women who support them implies that whatever values others may attach to fetuses generally or to specific fetuses individually should not be allowed to outweigh the ranking that is assigned to them by the pregnant women themselves.

No absolute value attaches to fetuses apart from their relational status, which is determined in the context of their particular development. This is not the same, however, as saying that they have no value at all or that they have merely instrumental value, as some liberal suggest. The value that women place on their own fetuses is the sort of value that attaches to an emerging human relationship.

Nevertheless, fetuses are not persons, because they have not developed sufficiently in their capacity for social relationships to be persons in any morally significant sense (that is, they are not yet second persons). In this way they differ from newborns, who immediately begin to develop into persons by virtue of their place as subjects in human relationships; newborns are capable of some forms of communication and response. The moral status of fetuses is determined by the nature of their primary relationship and the value that is created there. Therefore, feminist accounts of abortion emphasize the importance of protecting women's rights to continue or to terminate pregnancies as each sees fit.

THE POLITICS OF ABORTION

Feminist accounts explore the connections between particular social policies and the general patterns of power relationships in our society. With respect to abortion in this framework, Mary Daly observes that "one hundred percent of the bishops who oppose the repeal of antiabortion laws are men and one hundred percent of the people who have abortions are women. . . . To be comprehended accurately, they [arguments against abortion] must be seen within the context of sexually hierarchical society" (Daly 1973, 106).

Antiabortion activists appeal to arguments about the unconditional value of human life. When we examine their rhetoric more closely, however, we find other ways of interpreting their agenda. In addition to their campaign to criminalize abortion, most abortion opponents condemn all forms of sexual relations outside of heterosexual marriage, and they tend to support patriarchal patterns of dominance within such marriages. Many are distressed that liberal abortion policies support permissive sexuality by allowing women to "get away with" sex outside of marriage. They perceive that ready access

to abortion supports women's independence from men.[23]

Although nonfeminist participants in the abortion debates often discount the significance of its broader political dimensions, both feminists and antifeminists consider them crucial. The intensity of the antiabortion movement correlates closely with the increasing strength of feminism in achieving greater equality for women. The original American campaign against abortion can be traced to the middle of the nineteenth century, that is, to the time of the first significant feminist movement in the United States (Luker 1984). Today abortion is widely perceived as supportive of increased freedom and power for women. The campaign against abortion intensified in the 1970s, which was a period of renewed interest in feminism. As Rosalind Petchesky observes, the campaign rested on some powerful symbols: "To feminists and antifeminists alike, it came to represent the image of the 'emancipated woman' in her contemporary identity, focused on her education and work more than on marriage or childbearing; sexually active outside marriage and outside the disciplinary boundaries of the parental family; independently supporting herself and her children; and consciously espousing feminist ideas" (Petchesky 1984, 241). Clearly, much more than the lives of fetuses is at stake in the power struggle over abortion.

When we place abortion in the larger political context, we see that most of the groups active in the struggle to prohibit abortion also support other conservative measures to maintain the forms of dominance that characterize patriarchy (and often class and racial oppression as well). The movement against abortion is led by the Catholic church and other conservative religious institutions, which explicitly endorse not only fetal rights but also male dominance in the home and the church. Most opponents of abortion also oppose virtually all forms of birth control and all forms of sexuality other than monogamous, reproductive sex; usually, they also resist having women assume positions of authority in the dominant public institutions (Luker 1984). Typically, antiabortion activists support conservative economic measures that protect the interests of the privileged classes of society and ignore the needs of the oppressed and disadvantaged (Petchesky 1985). Although they stress their commitment to preserving life, many systematically work to dismantle key social programs that provide life necessities to the underclass. Moreover, some current campaigns against abortion retain elements of the racism that dominated the North American abortion literature in the early years of the twentieth century, wherein abortion was opposed on the grounds that it amounted to racial suicide on the part of whites.[24]

In the eyes of its principal opponents, then, abortion is not an isolated practice; their opposition to abortion is central to a set of social values that runs counter to feminism's objectives. Hence antiabortion activists generally do not offer alternatives to abortion that support feminist interests in overturning the patterns of oppression that confront women. Most deny that there are any legitimate grounds for abortion, short of the need to save a woman's life—and some are not even persuaded by this criterion (Nicholson 1977). They believe that any pregnancy can and should be endured. If the mother is unable or unwilling to care for the child after birth, then they assume that adoption can be easily arranged.

It is doubtful, however, that adoptions are possible for every child whose mother cannot care for it. The world abounds with homeless orphans; even in the industrialized West, where there is a waiting list for adoption of healthy (white) babies, suitable homes cannot always be found for troubled adolescents; inner-city, AIDS babies, or many of the multiply handicapped children whose parents may have tried to care for them but whose marriages broke under the strain.

Furthermore, even if an infant were born healthy and could be readily adopted, we must recognize that surrendering one's child for adoption is an extremely difficult act for most women. The bond that commonly forms between women and their fetuses over the full term of pregnancy is intimate and often intense; many women find that it is not easily broken after birth. Psychologically, for many women adoption is a far more difficult response to unwanted pregnancies than abortion. Therefore, it is misleading to describe pregnancy as merely a nine-month commitment; for most women, seeing a pregnancy through to term involves a lifetime of responsibility and involvement with the resulting child and, in the overwhelming majority of cases, disproportionate burden on the woman through the child-rearing years. An ethics that cares about women would recognize that abortion is often the only acceptable recourse for them.

EXPANDING THE AGENDA

The injunction of feminist ethics to consider abortion in the context of other issues of power and oppression means that we need to look beyond the standard questions of its moral and legal acceptability. This implies, for instance, that we need to explore the moral imperatives of ensuring that abortion services are actually available to all women who seek them. Although medically approved abortions are technically recognized as legal (at least for the moment) in both Canada and the United States, many women who need abortions cannot obtain them; accessibility is still associated with wealth and privilege in many regions.[25] In Canada vast geographical areas offer no abortion services at all, so unless the women of those regions can afford to travel to urban clinics, they have no meaningful right to abortion. In the United States, where there is no universal health insurance, federal legislation (under the Hyde amendment) explicitly denies the use of public money for abortions. Full ethical discussion of abortion reveals the necessity of removing the economic, age, and racial barriers that currently restrict access to medically acceptable abortion services.[26]

The moral issues extend yet further. Feminism demands respect for women's choices; even if the legal and financial barriers could be surpassed, this condition may remain unmet. The focus of many political campaigns for abortion rights has been to make abortion a matter of medical, not personal, choice, suggesting that doctors (but not necessarily women) can be trusted to choose responsibly. Feminists must insist on respect for women's moral agency. Therefore, feminism requires that abortion services be provided in an atmosphere that is supportive of the choices that women make. This could be achieved by offering abortions in centers that deal with all matters of reproductive health in an open, patient-centered manner, where respectful counseling on all aspects of reproductive health is available.[27]

Furthermore, the moral issues surrounding abortion include questions of how women are treated when they seek abortions. All too frequently hospital-based abortions are provided by practitioners who are uneasy about their role and treat the women involved with hostility and resentment.[28] Health care workers involved in providing abortions must recognize that abortion is a legitimate option that should be carried out with respect and concern for the physical, psychological, and emotional well-being of the patient. In addition, we need to turn our moral attention to the effects of antiabortion protests on women. Increasingly, many antiabortion activists have personalized their attacks and focused their energies on harassing the women who enter and leave abortion clinics, thereby requiring them to pass a gauntlet of hostile protesters to obtain abortions. Such arrangements are not conducive to positive health care, so these protests, too, must be subject to moral criticism within the ethics of health care.

Feminist ethics promotes the value of reproductive freedom, which is defined as the condition under which women are able to make truly voluntary choices about their reproductive lives. Women must have control over their reproduction if patriarchal dominance over women is to be brought to an end. In addition to reliable and caring abortion services, then, women also need access to safe and effective birth control, which would provide them with other means of avoiding pregnancy.[29]

Moreover, we must raise questions about politics of sexual domination in this context. Many men support women's right to abortion because they perceive that if women believe that they can engage in intercourse without having to accept an unwanted pregnancy, they will become more sexually available. Some of the women who oppose abortion resist it for this very reason; they do not want to support a practice that increases women's sexual vulnerability. Feminists need to develop an analysis of reproductive freedom that includes sexual freedom as it is defined by women, not men. Such an analysis would, for example, include women's right to refuse sex. Because this right can only be assured if women have power equal to men's and are not subject to domination because of their sex, women's freedom from oppression is itself an element of reproductive freedom.

Finally, it is important to stress that feminist accounts do not deny that fetuses have value. They ask that fetuses be recognized as existing within women's pregnancies and not as separate, isolated entities. Feminists positively value fetuses that are wanted by the women who carry them; they vigorously oppose practices that force women to have abortions they do not want. No women should be subjected to coerced abortion or sterilization. Women must be assured of adequate financial and support services for the care of their children, so that they are not forced to abort fetuses that they would otherwise choose to carry. Further, voluntarily pregnant women should have access to suitable pre- and postnatal care and nutrition, lest wanted fetuses be unnecessarily harmed or lost.

Feminists perceive that far more could be done to protect and care for fetuses if the state directed its resources toward supporting women who choose to continue their pregnancies, rather than draining those resources to police the women who try to terminate undesired pregnancies. Unlike their conservative counterparts, feminists recognize that caring for the women who maintain the lives of fetuses is not only a more legitimate policy than is regulating them but also probably more effective at ensuring the health and well-being of more fetuses and, ultimately, of more infants.

In sum, then, feminist ethics demands that moral discussions of abortion reflect a broader agenda than is usually found in the arguments put forth by bioethicists. Only by reflecting on the meaning of ethical pronouncements on actual women's lives and the connections that exist between judgments on abortion and the conditions of domination and subordination can we come to an adequate understanding of the moral status of abortion in a particular society.

NOTES

1. Much of the philosophic literature on abortion characterizes the possible moral positions on the issue as falling within three slots along a continuum: conservative (no abortions are morally acceptable, except, perhaps, when the woman's life is at stake), moderate (abortions are permissible under certain circumstances), or liberal (abortion should be available "on demand"). See, e.g., Wertheimer (1971) or Sumner (1981).

2. Technically, the term "fetus" does not cover the entire period of development. Medical practitioners prefer to distinguish between differing stages of development with such terms as "conceptus," "embryo" (and, recently, "pre-embryo"), and "fetus." Because these distinctions are not relevant to the discussion here, I follow the course common to discussions in bioethics and feminism and use the term "fetus" to cover the entire period of development from conception to the end of pregnancy through either birth or abortion.

3. Bearing a child can keep a woman within a man's sphere of influence against her will. The Canadian news media were dominated in the summer of 1989 by the story of Chantel Daigle, a Quebec woman who faced injunctions granted to her former boyfriend by two lower courts against her choice of abortion before she was finally given permission for abortion by the Supreme Court of Canada. Daigle's explanation to the media of her determination to abort stressed her recogni-

tion that if she was forced to bear this child, she would never be free from the violent father's involvement in her life.

4. Feminists believe that it is wrong of society to make childbearing a significant cause of poverty in women, but the reality of our social and economic structures in North America is that it does. In addition to their campaigns for greater reproductive freedom for women, feminists also struggle to ensure that women receive greater support in child-rearing; in efforts to provide financial stability and support services to those who provide care for children, feminists would welcome the support of those in the antiabortion movement who sincerely want to reduce the numbers of abortions.

5. Among the exceptions here, see Overall (1987), who seems willing to specify some conditions under which abortion is immoral (78–79).

6. Critics continue to base the debate on the possibility that women might make frivolous abortion decisions; hence they want feminists to agree to setting boundaries on acceptable grounds for choosing abortion. Feminists, however, should resist this injunction. There is no practical way of drawing a line fairly in the abstract; cases that may appear "frivolous" at a distance often turn out to be substantive when the details are revealed. There is no evidence to suggest that women actually make the sorts of choices worried critics hypothesize about: for example, the decision of a woman eight-months pregnant to abort because she wants to take a trip or gets in "a tiff" with her partner. These sorts of fantasies, on which demands to distinguish between legitimate and illegitimate personal reasons for choosing abortion rest, reflect an offensive conception of women as irresponsible. They ought not to be perpetuated. Women seeking moral guidance in their own deliberations about choosing abortion do not find such hypothetical discussions of much use.

7. In her monumental historical analysis of the early roots of Western patriarchy, Lerner (1986) determined that patriarchy began in the period from 3100 to 600 B.C., when men appropriated women's sexual and reproductive capacity; the earliest states entrenched patriarchy by institutionalizing the sexual and procreative subordination of women to men.

8. Some women claim to be feminist yet oppose abortion; some even claim to offer a feminist argument against abortion (see Callahan 1987). For reasons that I develop in this chapter, I do not believe a thorough feminist analysis can sustain a restrictive abortion policy, although I do acknowledge that feminists need to be wary of some of the arguments proposed in support of liberal policies on abortion.

9. The state could do a lot to ameliorate this condition. If it provided women with adequate financial support, removed the inequities in the labor market, and provided affordable and reliable child care, pregnancy need not so often lead to a woman's dependence on a particular man. That it

does not do so is evidence of the state's complicity in maintaining women's subordinate position with respect to men.

10. The IUD has proven so hazardous and prone to lawsuits, it has been largely removed from the market in the United States (Pappert 1986). It is also disappearing from other Western countries but is still being purchased by population-control agencies for use in the developing world (LaCheen 1986).

11. For a more detailed discussion of the limitations of current contraceptive options, see Colodny (1989); for the problems of cost, see esp. 34–35.

12. See Petchesky (1985), esp. chap. 5, where she documents the risks and discomforts associated with pill use and IUDs and the increasing rate at which women are choosing the option of diaphragm or condom, with the option of early, legal abortions as backup.

13. Eisenstein (1988) has developed an interesting account of sexual politics, which identifies the pregnant body as the central element in the cultural subordination of women. She argues that pregnancy (either actual or potential) is considered the defining characteristic of all women, and because it is not experienced by men, it is classified as deviance and considered grounds for different treatment.

14. Thomson (1971) is a notable exception to this trend.

15. Because she was obviously involved in sexual activity, it is often concluded that the noncoerced woman is not innocent but guilty. As such, she is judged far less worthy than the innocent being she carries within her. Some who oppose abortion believe that an unwanted pregnancy is a suitable punishment for "irresponsible" sex.

16. This seems reminiscent of Aristotle's view of women as flowerpots where men implant the seed with all the important genetic information and the movement necessary for development and the women's job is that of passive gestation, like the flowerpot. See Whitbeck (1973) and Lange (1983).

17. Some are so preoccupied with the problem of fetuses being "stuck" in women's bodies that they seek to avoid this geographical complication altogether, completely severing the ties between woman and fetus. For example, Bernard Nathanson, an antiabortion activist with the zeal of a new convert, eagerly anticipates the prospect of artificial wombs as alternative means for preserving the lives of fetuses and "dismisses the traditional reverence for birth as mere 'mythology' and the act of birth itself as an 'insignificant event'" (cited in McDonnell 1984, 113).

18. Cf. Warren (1989) and Tooley (1972).

19. The definition of pregnancy as a purely passive activity reaches its ghoulish conclusion in the increasing acceptability of sustaining brain-dead women on life-support systems to continue their functions as incubators until the fetus can be safely delivered. For a discussion of this trend, see Murphy (1989).

20. This apt phrasing is taken from Petchesky (1985), 342.

21. E.g., Held (1987b) argues that personhood is a social status, created by the work of mothering persons.

22. Fetuses are almost wholly individuated by the women who bear them. The fetal "contributions" to the relationship are defined by the projections and interpretations of the pregnant woman in the latter stages of pregnancy, if she chooses to perceive fetal movements in purposeful ways (e.g., "it likes classical music, spicy food, exercise").

23. See Luker (1984), esp. chaps. 6 and 7, and Petchesky (1985), esp. chaps. 7 and 8, for documentation of these associations in the U.S. antiabortion movement and Collins (1985), esp. chap. 4, and McLaren and McLaren (1986) for evidence of similar trends in the Canadian struggle.

24. See McLaren and McLaren (1986) and Petchesky (1985).

25. When abortion was illegal, many women nonetheless managed to obtain abortions, but only the relatively privileged women with money were able to arrange safe, hygienic abortions; poor women were often constrained to rely on dangerous, unacceptable services. In the United States court rulings have ensured that rich and middle-class women have, for the moment, relatively easy access to well-run clinics and hospitals, but because public hospitals are mostly unwilling to offer abortion services and federal law prohibits the use of Medicaid funding for abortion, many poor women still find legal, safe abortions out of reach (Petchesky 1985). In Canada, too, abortion services are most readily available to middle-class, urban, mature women. This suggests that financial circumstances may be a more significant factor in determining women's access to abortion than abortion's legal status.

26. Some feminists suggest we seek recognition of the legitimacy of nonmedical abortion services. This would reduce costs and increase access dramatically, with no apparent increase in risk as long as services were provided by trained, responsible practitioners who were concerned with the well-being of their clients. It would also allow the possibility of increasing women's control over abortion. See, e.g., McDonnell (1984).

27. For a useful model of such a center, see Van Wagner and Lee (1989).

28. A poignant collection of some women's unfortunate experiences with hospital abortions is offered in *Telling Our Secrets,* produced by CARAL (1990).

29. Therefore, the Soviet model, in which abortions have been relatively accessible, is also unacceptable, because there the unavailability of birth control forces women to rely on multiple abortions to control their fertility.

The Ambivalence of Abortion: One Woman's Experience

Linda Bird Francke (Originally published under the pseudonym "Jane Doe.")

"Jane Doe," thirty-eight, had an abortion in New York City in 1973. The mother of three children, then three, five, and eleven, Jane had just started a full-time job in publishing. She and her husband, an investment banker, decided together that another baby would add an almost unbearable strain to their lives, which were already overfull. What Jane had not anticipated was the guilt and sadness that followed the abortion. She wrote about the experience shortly thereafter and filed the story away. Three years later she reread it and decided it might be helpful to other women who experience the ambivalence of abortion. The *New York Times* ran it on their Op-Ed page in May 1976. This is what she wrote:

> We were sitting in a bar on Lexington Avenue when I told my husband I was pregnant. It is not a memory I like to dwell on. Instead of the champagne and hope which had heralded the impending births of the first, second, and third child, the news of this one was greeted with shocked silence and Scotch. "Jesus," my husband kept saying to himself, stirring the ice cubes around and around. "Oh, Jesus."
>
> Oh, how we tried to rationalize it that night as the starting time for the movie came and went. My husband talked about his plans for a career change in the next year, to stem the staleness that fourteen years with the same investment-banking firm had brought him. A new baby would preclude that option.
>
> The timing wasn't right for me either. Having juggled pregnancies and child care with what freelance jobs I could fit in between feedings, I had just taken on a full-time job. A new baby would put me right back in the nursery just when our youngest child was finally school age. It was time for *us*, we tried to rationalize. There just wasn't room in our lives now for another baby. We both agreed. And agreed. And agreed.

How very considerate they are at the Women's Services, known formally as the Center for Reproductive and Sexual Health. Yes, indeed, I could have an abortion that very Saturday morning and be out in time to drive to the country that afternoon. Bring a first morning urine specimen, a sanitary belt and napkins, a money order or $125 cash—and a friend.

My friend turned out to be my husband, standing awkwardly and ill at ease as men always do in places that are exclusively for women, as I checked in at nine A.M. Other men hovered around just as anxiously, knowing they had to be there, wishing they weren't. No one spoke to each other. When I would be cycled out of there four hours later, the same men would be slumped in their same seats, locked downcast in their cells of embarrassment.

The Saturday morning women's group was more dispirited than the men in the waiting room. There were around fifteen of us, a mixture of races, ages and backgrounds. Three didn't speak English at all and a fourth, a pregnant Puerto Rican girl around eighteen, translated for them.

There were six black women and a hodgepodge of whites, among them a T-shirted teenager who kept leaving the room to throw up and a puzzled middle-aged woman from Queens with three grown children.

"What form of birth control were you using?" the volunteer asked each one of us. The answer was inevitably "none." She then went on to describe the various forms of birth control available at the clinic, and offered them to each of us.

The youngest Puerto Rican girl was asked through the interpreter which she'd like to use: the loop, diaphragm, or pill. She shook her head "no" three times. "You don't want to come back here again, do you?" the volunteer pressed. The girl's head was so low her chin rested on her breastbone. "*Si*," she whispered.

We had been there two hours by that time, filling out endless forms, giving blood and urine, receiving lectures. But unlike any other group of women I've been in, we didn't talk.

Our common denominator, the one which usually floods language and economic barriers into familiarity, today was one of shame. We were losing life that day, not giving it.

The group kept getting cut back to smaller, more workable units, and finally I was put in a small waiting room with just two other women. We changed into paper bathrobes and paper slippers, and we rustled whenever we moved. One of the women in my room was shivering and an aide brought her a blanket.

"What's the matter?" the aide asked her. "I'm scared," the woman said. "How much will it hurt?" The aide smiled. "Oh, nothing worse than a couple of bad cramps," she said. "This afternoon you'll be dancing a jig."

I began to panic. Suddenly the rhetoric, the abortion marches I'd walked in, the telegrams sent to Albany to counteract the Friends of the Fetus, the Zero Population Growth buttons I'd worn, peeled away, and I was all alone with my microscopic baby. There were just the two of us there, and soon, because it was more convenient for me and my husband, there would be one again.

How could it be that I, who am so neurotic about life that I step over bugs rather than on them, who spend hours planting flowers and vegetables in the spring even though we rent out the house and never see them, who make sure the children are vaccinated and inoculated and filled with vitamin C, could so arbitrarily decide that this life shouldn't be?

"It's not a life," my husband had argued, more to convince himself than me. "It's a bunch of cells smaller than my fingernail."

But any woman who has had children knows that certain feeling in her taut, swollen breasts, and the slight but constant ache in her uterus that signals the arrival of life. Though I would march myself into blisters for a woman's right to exercise the option of motherhood, I discovered there in the waiting room that I was not the modern woman I thought I was.

When my name was called, my body felt so heavy the nurse had to help me into the examining room. I waited for my husband to burst through the door and yell "stop," but of course he didn't. I concentrated on three black spots in the acoustic ceiling until they grew in size to the shape of saucers, while the doctor swabbed my insides with antiseptic.

"You're going to feel a burning sensation now," he said, injecting the Novocaine into the neck of the womb. The pain was swift and severe, and I twisted to get away from him. He was hurting my baby, I reasoned, and the black saucers quivered in the air. "Stop," I cried. "Please stop." He shook his head, busy with his equipment. "It's too late to stop now," he said. "It'll just take a few more seconds."

What good sports we women are. And how obedient. Physically the pain passed even before the hum of the machine signaled that the vacuuming of my uterus was completed, my baby sucked up like ashes after a cocktail party. Ten minutes start to finish. And I was back on the arm of the nurse.

There were twelve beds in the recovery room. Each one had a gaily flowered draw sheet and a soft green or blue thermal blanket. It was all very feminine. Lying on these beds for an hour or more were the shocked victims of their sex, their full wombs now stripped clean, their futures less encumbered.

It was very quiet in that room. The only voice was that of the nurse, locating the new women who had just come in so she could monitor their blood pressure, and checking out the recovered women who were free to leave.

Juice was being passed about, and I found myself sipping a Dixie cup of Hawaiian Punch. An older woman with tightly curled bleached hair was just getting up from the next bed. "That was no goddamn snap," she said, resting before putting on her miniskirt and high white boots. Other women came and went, some walking out as dazed as they had entered, others with a bounce that signaled they were going right back to Bloomingdale's.

Finally then, it was time for me to leave. I checked out, making an appointment to return in two weeks for an IUD insertion. My husband was slumped in the waiting room, clutching a single yellow rose wrapped in a wet paper towel and stuffed into a baggie.

We didn't talk the whole way home, but just held hands very tightly. At home there were more yellow roses and a tray in bed for me and the children's curiosity to divert.

It had certainly been a successful operation. I didn't bleed at all for two days just as they had predicted, and then I bled only moderately for another four days. Within a week my breasts had subsided and the tenderness vanished, and my body felt mine again instead of the eggshell it becomes when it's protecting someone else.

My husband and I are back to planning our summer vacation and his career switch.

And it certainly does make more sense not to be having a baby right now—we say that to each other all the time. But I have this ghost now. A very little ghost that only appears when I'm seeing something beautiful, like the full moon on the ocean last weekend. And the baby waves at me. And I wave at the baby. "Of course, we have room," I cry to the ghost. "Of course, we do."

I am "Jane Doe." Using a pseudonym was not the act of cowardice some have said it was, but rather an act of sympathy for the feelings of my family. My daughters were too young then to understand what an abortion was, and my twelve-year-old son (my husband's stepson) reacted angrily when I even broached the subject of abortion to him. Andrew was deeply moralistic, as many children are at that age, and still young enough to feel threatened by the actions of adults; his replies to my "suppose I had an abortion" queries were devastating. "I think abortion is okay if the boy and girl aren't married, and they just made a mistake," he said. "But if you had an abortion, that would be different. You're married, and there is no reason for you not to have another baby. How could you just kill something—no matter how little it is—that's going to grow and have legs and wiggle its fingers?"

"I would be furious with you if you had an abortion. I'd lose all respect for you for being so selfish. I'd make you suffer and remind you of it all the time. I would think of ways to be mean. Maybe I'd give you the silent treatment or something.

"If God had meant women to have abortions, He would have put buttons on their stomachs."

I decided to wait until he was older before we discussed it again.

There were other considerations as well. My husband and I had chosen not to tell our parents about the abortion. My mother was very ill at the time and not up to a barrage of phone calls from her friends about "what Linda had written in the newspaper." And there were my parents-in-law,

who had always hoped for a male grandchild to carry on the family name. So I avoided the confessional and simply wrote what I thought would be a helpful piece for other women who might have shared my experience.

The result was almost great enough to be recorded on a seismograph. Interpreting the piece as anti-abortion grist, the Right-to-Lifers reproduced it by the thousands and sent it to everyone on their mailing lists. In one Catholic mailing, two sentences were deleted from the article: one that said I was planning to return to the clinic for an IUD insertion, and the other the quote from a middle-aged woman, "That was no goddamn snap." Papers around the country and in Canada ran it, culminating in its appearance in the Canadian edition of the *Reader's Digest,* whose staff took it upon their editorial selves to delete the last paragraph about the "little ghost" because they considered it "mawkish." They also changed the title from "There Just Wasn't Room in Our Lives for Another Baby" to "A Successful Operation" in the hopes that it would change their magazine's pro-abortion image.

Hundreds of letters poured into the *New York Times*, some from Right-to-Lifers, who predictably called me a "murderer," and others from pro-choice zealots who had decided the article was a "plant" and might even have been written by a man. Women wrote about their own abortions, some of which had been positive experiences and some disastrous. One woman even wrote that she wished her own mother had had an abortion instead of subjecting her to a childhood that was "brutal and crushing." Many of the respondents criticized me, quite rightly, for not using birth control in the first place. I was stunned, and so was the *New York Times*. A few weeks later they ran a sampling of the letters and my reply, which follows:

> The varied reactions to my abortion article do not surprise me at all. They are all right. And they are all wrong. There is no issue so fundamental as the giving of life, or the cessation of it. These decisions are the most personal one can ever make and each person facing them reacts in her own way. It is not black-and-white as the laws governing abortion are forced to be. Rather it is the gray area whose core touches our definition of ourselves that produces "little

ghosts" in some, and a sense of relief in others.

I admire the woman who chose not to bear her fourth child because she and her husband could not afford to give that child the future they felt necessary. I admire the women who were outraged that I had failed to use any form of contraception. And I ache for the woman whose mother had given birth to her even though she was not wanted, and thus spent an empty, lonely childhood. It takes courage to take the life of someone else in your own hands, and even more courage to assume responsibility for your own.

I had my abortion over two years ago. And I wrote about it shortly thereafter. It was only recently, however, that I decided to publish it. I felt it was important to share how one person's abortion had affected her, rather than just sit by while the pro and con groups haggled over legislation.

The effect has indeed been profound. Though my husband was very supportive of me, and I, I think, of him, our relationship slowly faltered. As our children are girls, my husband anguished at the possibility that I had been carrying a son. Just a case of male macho, many would argue. But still, that's the way he feels, and it is important. I hope we can get back on a loving track again.

Needless to say, I have an IUD now, instead of the diaphragm that is too easily forgotten. I do not begrudge my husband his lack of contraception. Condoms are awkward. Neither do I feel he should have a vasectomy. It is profoundly difficult for him to face the possibility that he might never have that son. Nor do I regret having the abortion. I am just as much an avid supporter of children by choice as I ever was.

My only regret is the sheer irresponsibility on my part to become pregnant in the first place. I pray to God that it will never happen again. But if it does, I will be equally thankful that the law provides women the dignity to choose whether to bring a new life into the world or not.

I had obviously and unintentionally touched a national nerve. With abortion becoming an everyday occurrence since the Supreme Court ruling in 1973, which overturned the right of individual states to intervene in a woman's decision to abort in the first trimester (twelve weeks) of pregnancy and to intervene in the second trimester (twenty-four weeks) only to ensure medical practices "reasonably related to maternal health," American women of all ages, races, and backgrounds were facing the same sort of dilemma I had. . . .

. . . So much has happened in the short time since abortion was legalized that only now is there an opportunity to draw breath and begin to evaluate what the 1973 Supreme Court decision has wrought, and what repercussions the 1977 Supreme Court decision upholding states' rights to withhold abortion funding for the poor will have. Abortion is not new by any means. But confronting the fact of it without furtiveness and danger is. The quantum leap from women's age-old need and desire to control their reproductive lives to their sanctioned ability finally to do so has raised questions of ethics and morality that have yet to be answered. Perhaps they never will be.

Another Woman's Experience: I'm 38, and Running Out of Time

Paulette Mason (a pseudonym)

I need some advice. I'm pregnant—15 weeks pregnant. And I'm not married. Please don't think that I don't believe in family values. I do. I'm not promiscuous; it's just that I was lonely and I liked this man a lot. We used birth control but it failed. I

didn't know I was pregnant because I didn't have the usual symptoms. Everything that a woman expects to have happen on a monthly basis continued to happen. I never learned that this was possible in high school hygiene; we didn't have sex education, just the seven food groups.

The man I got pregnant by doesn't want to have anything to do with me or the child. I want to have the baby; I'm 38 and I'm running out of time. I've been thinking about how and when and whether I could have a child for a couple of years now. I agree with Marilyn Quayle; for a woman like me, it's an essential part of my nature to make a home with a man and raise a child.

The father of my baby also believes in family values. That's why he wants me to get an abortion. He feels children should be raised in a two-parent home, and since he has no intention of being that other parent, it would be unfair to the child to raise it alone. He's an active Democrat, but he doesn't think Murphy Brown is a good role model.

"You're not Murphy Brown," he said to me. "You're not a rich independent yuppie who can afford to scoff at convention and go it alone. You've been reading too many women's magazines loaded with feminist junk. You barely make a living. How can you support and nurture a child? You don't even have a steady job." (I work freelance.) "I bet you don't even have health insurance," he said. As a matter of fact, I don't have health insurance.

After I got off the phone, I looked into getting insurance. It turned out that no one would insure me; my pregnancy was considered a previous condition. Then I looked into Medicaid and city health clinics. The social worker I talked to said I made too much money to qualify. I called a hospital and found out that if I required a C-section it would cost about $12,000. I didn't have that much in the bank. If the baby were born prematurely, it would cost about $1,000 a day to keep her alive in the hospital nursery. If something was wrong with the baby, I'd be in debt to the hospital for the rest of my life. But I didn't want to let money be the critical factor in this decision.

Finally, I was able to find one insurance company that was willing to insure me and the baby for possible complications. "Boy, am I glad I found you guys," I told the insurance agent. He agreed I was lucky; his company was the only one he knew of that would insure pregnant women.

I thought maybe I could go on welfare so that I could stay at home during those all-important first two years. But when I looked into welfare, it turned out that even with food stamps I wouldn't be able to live on it. The social worker I spoke to said that most women on welfare have some income off the books and live with family members.

My parents live on Social Security and small pensions. My brother is unemployed. He says that since the recession, it's been hard to find work.

I made up a budget. After I factored in health insurance for me and the baby ($4,000) and child care help ($300 a week for full-time baby-sitting), I was many thousands of dollars short.

I looked into child support. The man I got pregnant by lives out of state. The lawyers and court officials I spoke to said that it could easily take two years for me to get a court order. I was at wit's end. Then I got a brainstorm. I called the Catholic church. I figured it was against abortions and so was I. I asked the woman who answered the phone, Can you help me keep my baby? She told me that her agency primarily helped girls from the South Bronx and what they offered them was infant foster care. That was the very day the newspapers in New York were filled with stories about a foster family that had starved a child to death. I mentioned this to the social worker. She said: "We're very careful. All our families are fingerprinted and their records checked."

Things seemed so hopeless by then. I went to a doctor who did second-trimester abortions, which are a good deal more complicated than first-trimester abortions. In the second trimester, the fetus is sufficiently large so that it has to be dismembered to be removed. When I heard the doctor use the word dismember, I started to cry—for myself and my baby and what might have been my future.

If a surgeon isn't skillful, the uterus can be perforated, leading to infection, sterility, even hysterectomy. The procedure takes two days. On the first day, the woman's cervix is dilated. I asked the doctor, "Will it hurt?" The doctor said that sometimes it doesn't hurt but other times it hurts a lot, and women leave sobbing and doubled over in pain. "It's very traumatic to many women," he said, "because they know that they've started a process that will end in termination and there's nothing that can be done to stop it once it starts."

On the second day, the actual procedure is carried out. The woman undresses, puts on a paper gown, is wheeled into an operating room, her legs are put into stirrups and an anesthesiologist puts her under. When she wakes up in the recovery room, her baby is gone. When the doctor explained all this to me, I started to cry again. "I don't know what to do," I told the doctor. The doctor said it was my choice. He said: "Nobody likes to get an abortion, especially a late abortion. I've performed thousands of operations and I've never met a woman who was happy about it. Do you think you can take good care of a child? That's really the question."

This has been agonizing for me. I think about the way I want to have a baby, and about paying someone to act like a mother to my child, and about what I'll say when my child asks why her father didn't want her, and about what I'll feel like during the 24 hours my cervix is dilating and I'm waiting for the end. When I think about adoption, I think about spending the rest of my life wondering where my baby, the baby I wanted, is, and if she's happy and how she turned out. And I think, What would Dan Quayle want me to do?

The Death of Guadalupe Negron

Lynette Holloway

Section (i) The Family of Guadalupe Negron Mourn Her Death

After a blink of his long black lashes and a thoughtful pause, the 5-year-old son of Guadalupe Negron and Jose Callejas drove his father to cry with a short phrase in Spanish.

"I miss my mother," said the child, Byron, his eyes glistening with tears as he sat next to his father.

"I miss her, too," Mr. Callejas said last week in his lawyer's office. The child, realizing his father's anguish, moved to comfort him. And they held each other for a moment.

Mrs. Negron, 33, died two years ago after a botched abortion by Dr. David Benjamin, a Queens obstetrician convicted of second-degree murder on Tuesday for her death.

Dr. Benjamin became the first doctor in the state convicted of murder in connection with a medical procedure performed on a patient. He is to be sentenced on September 12 [1995] by Justice Robert J. Hanophy in State Supreme Court in Jamaica, Queens, and faces the possibility of 25 years to life in prison.

Mr. Callejas, 39, a Honduran immigrant who has three children with Mrs. Negron, praised the jury's decision, speaking through an interpreter. But he also spoke of a family torn apart by the loss of its core.

The divided family lives in the High Bridge section of the Bronx: Byron with his father in a studio; his brothers, Alexander, 11, and Dennis, 8, in a cramped apartment with Mrs. Negron's niece, Elena DeMonzon. Mrs. Negron's fourth son, Carlos, 14, from a previous relationship, also lives with Ms. DeMonzon, who is 22.

"There is a void in my life now that can never be filled," Mr. Callejas said. Along with Mr. Callejas, Mrs. Negron, a recent immigrant to the United States, sold ices from carts, but she wanted to become a home attendant, and had applied for a job.

Mrs. Negron was married to Herminio Negron, yet had been living with Mr. Callejas, her longtime sweetheart, since her three-year marriage started to dissolve. When she realized she was pregnant with her fifth child, she and Mr. Callejas discussed abortion, he said.

"I didn't know for sure if she was going to have it done," he said, "but I wanted her to go to a hospital where I knew it would be safe."

But Mrs. Negron wanted privacy. She found an ad in a Spanish-language newspaper that promised just that. The place was Dr. Benjamin's Metro Women's Center on Roosevelt Avenue in Corona, Queens. She was five months pregnant.

"I kissed her goodbye," Mr. Callejas said, remembering the morning she went to the clinic, on July 9, 1993, and adding that he wished he had held her a little longer. "I didn't know she was going to have the abortion. We really had not finished discussing it."

Section (ii): A Physician on Trial for the Death of Guadalupe Negron's Death

Fearing that he could lose his medical license, a Queens doctor intentionally misled paramedics who arrived at his office two years ago to treat a 33-year-old woman who bled to death after an abortion, prosecutors said yesterday as they began their murder case against the doctor.

Barry A. Schwartz, the chief assistant district attorney of Queens, said in his opening statement to the jury that Dr. David Benjamin told paramedics that the woman, Guadalupe Negron, had suffered a heart attack when in fact she had bled to death while the doctor was in a separate room performing another abortion.

Dr. Benjamin, 58, who faces charges of second-degree murder and evidence tampering, is believed by the Queens District Attorney's office to be the first doctor in New York State charged with murder involving the death of a patient during a medical procedure.

Defense lawyers tried to knock down the prosecutor's theory, arguing that the woman had suffered a heart attack by the time paramedics arrived, saying it took them 25 minutes to reach Dr. Benjamin's storefront office in Corona. There was no attempt at coverup, they said. But there was a problem.

Michael Doyle, one of Dr. Benjamin's lawyers, admitted that his client had mistakenly thought the woman was 13 weeks pregnant, instead of 18 to 20 weeks, but he said the doctor took every possible step to save her when complications arose.

"It was a mistake," Mr. Doyle told the jury. "It was a bad mistake. But he did not knowingly take on a procedure he did not have the skills to perform properly."

Dr. Benjamin showed no emotion throughout the first day of the trial, which is expected to last about two weeks.

As armed court officers escorted him into the wood-paneled courtroom yesterday morning and past a phalanx of reporters and cameras, he proclaimed, "I'm innocent."

Inside the courtroom, there appeared to be no family members for either Dr. Benjamin or Mrs. Negron.

Dr. Benjamin's license was revoked in June 1993, after 25 years of practice, for "gross incompetence and negligence" in five previous cases. In these, women he treated suffered life-threatening perforations to their uteruses—the same injury that led to Mrs. Negron's death, officials said. But Dr. Benjamin was allowed by law to continue practice three weeks longer, or until the State Administrative Board of Review upheld the revocation of his license on July 30.

None of this was known to Mrs. Negron on July 8 of that year, when she left her home in the Bronx with $750 and persuaded her niece to drive her to Dr. Benjamin's office, at the Metro Women's Clinic at 102–21 Roosevelt Avenue. Afraid to tell her husband that she was pregnant with a fifth child, and worried about losing her job as a nurse's aide, she had decided to get an abortion.

Defense lawyers said yesterday that Dr. Benjamin performed a successful abortion even after discovering Mrs. Negron's pregnancy was further along than he initially realized, but that he put her back on the operating table a second time after she complained of pain and bleeding. When Dr. Benjamin informed her that she should go to a hospital, defense attorneys said, she became agitated, ripping out her intravenous tubes and sitting up while the doctor was working inside her uterus, causing a three-inch perforation.

But Mr. Schwartz, the prosecutor, contended that the doctor caused the rip when he performed the abortion, allowing her to bleed in the recovery room furnished with bloody couches without offering the slightest bit of help and went on to perform another abortion.

He charged that Dr. Benjamin performed an abortion that should have taken several hours and quite possibly a day in about two hours.

"She died because she bled to death," Mr. Schwartz argued. "The doctor tore her insides, trying to pull big things through a small hole."

The final blow came, Mr. Schwartz said, when Dr. Benjamin called 911 "all too late" and then tried to cover up his missteps, telling paramedics she had suffered a heart attack and suppressing Mrs. Negron's medical records.

Mr. Schwartz said Dr. Benjamin wrote a note for paramedics describing Mrs. Negron's condition. He told jurors, "You won't see a word about the laceration. You won't see a word about the heavy bleeding. Cover-up." The prosecutor said that Dr. Benjamin had shown "depraved indifference" to his patient's life, adding, "What he did and what he didn't do constitute murder."

Two search warrants, executed at his office and home, failed to turn up Mrs. Negron's medical records, prosecutors said. But defense lawyers handed prosecutors the records on Wednesday, saying they were never subpoenaed.

Outside the courtroom, one defense lawyer, Brad Leventhal, blamed a slow response by an Emergency Medical Service ambulance for the woman's death. "EMS responded so poorly to this call," he said. "They waited 25 minutes before the ambulance arrived." Mr. Doyle contended there was no initial evidence that the woman's uterus had been perforated, which is why his client told paramedics about the heart attack. "When she sat up on the table, she effectively cut off her life support," Mr. Doyle said. But Dr. Benjamin worked hard to save her, Mr. Doyle said. "The doctor took measures to save her life and continued emergency proceedings while waiting for EMS," Mr. Doyle said. Prosecutors, however, charged that an emergency worker discovered that Dr. Benjamin had mistakenly inserted into Mrs. Negron's stomach a breathing tube that was supposed to be inserted in her trachea. By that time, she had no pulse or respiration, the indictment said.

Abortion: A Matter of Choice

Judy D. Simmons

Abortion is a great equalizer of women. Whatever their age, class or race, women tend to walk the same way after ending a pregnancy. They sort of hunch their shoulders, fold their arms rather protectively across their upper bodies, and take small steps. Of course, they're pretty woozy when they come out; most stay in the recovery room only long enough to get conscious and unsteadily upright. Nobody wants to spend a lot of time sipping tea and eating cookies in the clinic, any more than she hangs around the dentist's office after oral surgery or looks forward to a chummy tête-a-tête following an audit by the Internal Revenue Service.

Aborting a pregnancy isn't the high point of a woman's day. Nor, however, is it the melodramatic tragedy, social cancer, mortal sin, legislative crisis or genocidal master plan that various segments of the American public represent it to be. Women have been preventing and aborting pregnancies as long as they've been women. African queen and pharaoh Hatshepsut, who reigned in Egypt between 1500 and 1479 B.C., invented a method of birth control.

Numerous African women enslaved in the United States aborted pregnancies rather than bear children into slavery or give birth to the products of slave masters' rapes, notes Paula Giddings in her book, *When and Where I Enter.* A sixty-seven-year-old woman I know who has lived in a number of places in this country told me that every town she was ever in had its abortionist, and everyone knew where to find him or her. Abortion has been either legal or not a matter of public-policy intervention in many nations for ages. Like so many things one deals with in life, abortion is an uncomfortable but not uncommon experience. In the case of a girl we'll call Renee—a fifteen-year-old with a troubled home life, some emotional deficits and little practical awareness—abortion is a necessity, a mercy and a chance to build a better life.

These were my thoughts a few years back as I sat in a Westchester County, New York, women's clinic waiting for Renee to emerge from the inner sanctum where the abortions are done. These thoughts are a good deal more reasonable and coherent than the ones I had when I ended my first pregnancy in 1963. At that time, abortions were illegal in the United States. I traveled to Tijuana, Mexico, from Sacramento, California, where I lived and went to college. I can remember having one clear idea: If the place looked and felt like a butcher shop, I'd come home and let the pregnancy come to term. I had heard about the coathanger and knitting-needle abortions that were the standard methods for poor and nonwhite women before the 1973 *Roe v. Wade* Supreme Court decision that legalized abortion; and I had read about women being rendered sterile or dying as the aftermath of "back-alley" abortions. My thoughts at that time were sheer, simple fear and an awful sadness. A phase of my life was ending—an innocence, if you'll allow me that. Deciding to *have an abortion* went against every dream I'd had since I was seven or eight and found out how interestingly babies are made.

I was always a dreamy girl. As a preschooler I dreamed that I flew around heaven with a blue-eyed, blond-haired Jesus. I dreamed—until I actually did it at seventeen—that I'd be reunited with my father, who had divorced me and my mother when I was five. From the time I went from Rhode Island to segregated Alabama when I was seven, I dreamed I'd escape the red-clay dust, the gnats, the slop pails and the prejudiced white folks and get back up North to be Somebody.

Naturally, the deepest dream was that I would marry an intelligent, handsome, God-fearing man, be his divine helpmeet, have six children (to compensate for my only-child loneliness, I guess) and live happily ever after. To me, love, sex, marriage, children, goodness and happiness were all wrapped up in one romantic religious package that automatically came in the mail when you were old enough. Finding out that this wasn't so, in a scant three months of 1963, emotionally devastated me.

As I waited for Renee I pondered the similarities and differences in our abortion situations. In the twenty-odd years gone by between the two experiences, abortion has been legalized in the United States—that is an obvious difference. What's not so obvious, perhaps, is the psychological difference that makes. Renee didn't have to contact what amounted to an underground network and have a password (a previous patient's code name) to make her appointment. She didn't have to fly far away from home, family and friends and cross a national border feeling as if she had a flashing neon sign on her forehead saying ABORTION. She didn't have to fear being arrested when

she went for a post-abortion checkup if the doctor decided to help some lout of a prosecutor polish his reputation by meddling in a personal matter that should never be part of the legal system.

Renee wasn't totally ignorant about the procedure and what to expect following it. I thought I'd have terrible cramps and bleed to the point of hemorrhage. Imagine my surprise when I returned to the hotel, fell asleep and woke up feeling wonderful, with only the discomfort of being famished from not having eaten all day. I then proceeded to eat the most delicious fried chicken ever sold by a restaurant. Relief is a great flavor-enhancer. If there's one cause I might take up the gun for, it's that girls and women should always be able to get safe, legal, caring, "sunshine" abortions. No one should be subjected to the terror of clandestine activity in addition to the other stresses that usually surround a decision to abort.

The similarities between Renee's experience and mine are an old story. Renee was impregnated by a man ten years her senior who said he was going to marry her. My "fiance" was thirteen years older than I. Renee's seducer was in an authority position—a security guard at her junior high school. Mine was my thirty-one-year-old languages professor (white and, it later turned out, gay). Renee was hungry for love and protection to make her feel wanted and worthwhile. So was I. Like most young girls—indeed, like many people in the United States—Renee imposed fantasy on reality, acting on the assumption that what she felt and wanted to happen was really what was happening. So did I. But it ain't easy, especially when you're a teenager whose awakening glands can make you think mud looks like fudge and smells like perfume.

The similarity between Renee and me that makes me angry is that adult women never talked to us *realistically* about being a woman, lover and mother. When I spoke with Renee the day before she went for the abortion, she showed no awareness of why her mother might stay married to Renee's tyrant of a stepfather, who was making advances toward Renee and terrorizing the family with physical violence, meanness about money and refusal to allow them visitors and telephone calls.

The kid wasn't anywhere near ready for parental responsibility, as far as I could tell. When I told her that the pretty cribs she saw on television cost upwards of four hundred bucks, her eyes got big. She told me that if she gave birth she'd have to go live with an aunt whose daughter, also a teenager, had recently had a baby. When I asked her why her aunt would want another teen with a child in the house, and where the money would come from to support them all, Renee just looked overwhelmed. Then I asked Renee why a twenty-four-year-old man who already had small children and lived with a grown woman would seduce a scrawny, underdeveloped child like Renee and not even protect her.

Renee's answers to these questions revealed that she'd been acting her age, playing the appropriate early teen games of get a boy to lie to you, compete with the other girl, send messages through friends, play hide and seek with parents. But Renee was the only teenager in that game, a vulnerable kid who feels she's unloved and unwanted by both her parents. *Where are the people who are supposed to supervise and protect this young girl?* I wondered. Renee's mother and aunts clearly didn't have any greater hopes for her than that she follow in their stunted footsteps of early motherhood, broken relationships, undeveloped skills and enforced dependence on men who may exact a high price for their support.

I know a woman who had her first child out of wedlock at thirteen, another at seventeen, then got married and had two more kids before her husband left her. The woman was very nearly crazy with bills and parental responsibilities. When she suspected that her sixteen-year-old daughter might be messing around, she responded to my query about a heart-to-heart mother-daughter discussion of responsible sex and birth control with a haughty, "I'm not going to talk to her about those things. She'll think I'm condoning sex." Condoning sex! Did this woman's mother "condone" her having sex and a baby at thirteen? "My mother? Hell, no." Did that stop her from doing both? "I don't care. If my daughter's going to mess around, she'll just have to take the consequences." I ran screaming into the night.

Why, why, generation after generation, do we send young girls out ignorant? Sure, I remember comments from women such as "You better take care of yourself" and "You lie down with dogs, you get up with fleas," or "Girl, it's hard to be a woman." These are vague warnings indeed when the lust tide of puberty rises; when the guys are so sleek, sweet, masterful and full of smiles; when the experimental necking and petting sets the heated sap to running; when the first real manly hand touches your breast, and you feel a strange, silky saliva slide down your throat and discover a new reason for panties to get wet. Don't grown women remember what it's like to be fresh meat and jail-bait? You have to beat dudes off with a stick. Sometime, somewhere, somebody's gonna get ya.

In theory, it's fine to say that men have an equal responsibility to protect against pregnancy and disease. In fact, God bless the child who's got her own, and God helps her who helps herself. Giving young girls a chance to develop their intellectual and spiritual possibilities, protecting them with supervision, information and devices as necessary, schooling them in the realities of sex, mating and motherhood counter the pervasive fantasies and compelling hungers of body and soul—all this is women's work, women's responsibility, women's mission. 'Cause we're the ones who get jammed up.

I don't know why so many women are reluctant to give their daughters of the flesh or spirit a shot at a better life. In my meaner moods I think it's because the adult women are deeply jealous of the younger girls' freshness, their very possibilities. Misery loves company. And, I suppose, some women think that women must sacrifice themselves on the biological altar—it's our punishment for tempting Adam in the Garden.

A conversation with my close friend Gigi gave me another thought: Maybe good, loving mothers are afraid that if they talk to their children about the down sides of motherhood and mating, their children will feel that Mother doesn't love or want them *really* and fall into a Freudian soup of neuroses. Or, said another friend, maybe mothers are embarrassed to discuss "intimate" things with youngsters since some inference may be drawn about Momma's own experience.

There may be another, sadder reason that some women don't prepare girls for the worst as well as the best. For many mothers and wives, filling those roles is the only identity they have, the only status they hold. If they start thinking about what they could have done in addition to or instead of tying themselves down so early and completely, they might feel very wasted. Few people volunteer to think that they've sold themselves short in life.

It's been said ad nauseam that we human beings use very little of our potential. One of my basic values is that more aware, skilled people participate in world affairs to rescue us human beings from the thieves and thugs who run everything for their own private or class interests. We shouldn't volunteer for slavery and exploitation, but that's just what we do when we place sexual and emotional gratification ahead of education and economic viability. We cannot teach our children what we ourselves don't know, and we cannot protect them if we have no personal and social power.

Obviously, I'm not as concerned about an embryo's right to life as I am about a child's quality of life, and the things that destroy it. What about war—nuclear and otherwise—social injustice and the irrevocable death penalty? What about the bombing of children in Libya, the slaughter in the Middle East and South Africa, or the United States government's devoting a hundred million dollars to sustain and heighten violence in Nicaragua? What about classism and racism, which condemn children to falling down elevator shafts and out of windows in slum houses, or poor nutrition, lousy medical care, police brutality and unemployed, crazed or simply juvenile parents? What about the feminization of poverty that results from too many girls and women having children before developing intellectual coping skills and economic positioning, whether or not there are husbands present?

Perhaps we can moderate the notion that becoming a mother means one has done something intrinsically special and sacred. Every species of animal and plant I've heard of reproduces itself. It doesn't take a creative genius or intellectual giant to have sex and reproduce other human animals, although it may take both to rear the human animal into a decent human being in this complex perilous time. It's the rearing that separates the women from the girls, not the birthing.

Had I been clear about these things when I aborted my pregnancy, I wouldn't have substituted the role of "tragic abortee" for the rejected role of "mother," nor punished myself for going against the prevailing notion that becoming a mother should be the crowning fulfillment of every woman's life. Biologically speaking, what I aborted at eight weeks wasn't a cute, cuddly baby. Between eight weeks and nine months anything could happen: spontaneous abortion, a car accident, the world blowing up, a thalidomide distortion—you name it. There's no guarantee that pregnancy means getting a perfect reflection of oneself in a lovely little package. Of course, chances are that I would have had a healthy baby, but my point is that it was foolish and unnecessary to torture myself with guilt over an *assumption,* a hope, a fantasy, that the embryonic cells might have become another Dr. Martin Luther King, Jr. They might also have become Charles Manson, or have never become a fully developed human being at all.

My decision to abort was quite practical as well. At the time, I was living with three roommates in Sacramento, financed by student loans and part-time jobs. The jobs I'd had—waitress, telephone magazine sales, nannying and civil-service clerkships—were dead-end enough to convince me I'd never make it into financial comfort and an advantaged lifestyle if I didn't get a degree, and certainly not if I were supporting and rearing a child. Plus, it had been understood from the day I was born that I would get a bachelor's degree at least, if not a master's. It would disgrace the whole family if I came home with a big belly, no degree and no husband. Out-of-wedlock wasn't fashionable or respectable in 1963. Having a child and releasing her or him for adoption was out as far as I was concerned. No kid of mine was going to wander the planet without my knowing its circumstances.

Furthermore, I was a child of divorce who had longed to have my father around, or to have my mother replace him with a stepfather. I thought—probably still think—that being wanted and loved by both a woman and a man is advantageous for a child's balanced development. (Maybe this idea is just my last romantic notion—certainly other parenting arrangements have worked well for many.) Although conventional wisdom emphasizes that boys need fathers, I think girls also need the consistent, nonsexual attention of a loving, committed man to help them understand male culture and to develop other aspects of their being than women tend to evoke. I did not and do not want the sole responsibility of rearing children. For me, it's just too much.

I think it's very important for girls and women to give themselves the chance to develop more than their biological and emotional abilities. This doesn't mean not being mothers and wives, but rather being other things as well. The world is profoundly in need of the "feminine" characteristics— empathy, cooperation and conciliation, nurturing and sharing.

Women cannot affect human affairs beyond the personal and familial by being only mothers and marginal survival workers. The hand that rocks the cradle does not, in fact, rule the world— it just rocks the cradle. Harriet Tubman, Sojourner Truth and Mary McLeod Bethune didn't educate and free enslaved Africans by just rocking cradles. Women didn't get the vote, found Planned Parent-hood or get abortion legalized in this country by only rocking cradles. Dorothy Height (National Council of Negro Women), Jewell Jackson McCabe (National Coalition of 100 Black Women), Faye Wattleton (Planned Parenthood), Marian Wright Edelman (Children's Defense Fund) and Barbara C. Jordan (professor and former Texas congress-woman) have not contributed to the improvement of hundreds of thousands of lives by rocking cra-dles. They rock the boat.

To be all that we can be—even if we join the Army—we must control the timing and circum-stances of motherhood. Since telling people to ab-stain from something as necessary, basic and pleasurable as sex doesn't seem to work, that means using contraception in the first place and abortion as a last resort. I'm not saying that every young mother lives a blighted life. I just want to maximize the odds in favor of girls, women and children. That's the name of this tune.

11.
A Critical Review of Feminist Analyses of Abortion
Ronald Dworkin

Ronald Dworkin is professor of jurisprudence at Oxford University and professor of law and of philosophy at New York University. He is the author of *Life's Dominion: An Argument about Abortion, Euthanasia, and Individual Freedom*. In this essay, he questions some femi-nist approaches to the abortion debate that emphasize the unique relationship between the pregnant woman and the fetus, a relationship deemed unlike all other moral relationships in human society. Dworkin asserts that abortion is not a unique type of moral problem, and it should not be viewed as cut from a different cloth. He finds in the abortion debate the same type of choices (albeit magnified) that we must make throughout our lives about the value of life and the meaning of death.

Women who regard themselves as feminists, or as part of the "women's movement," do not nec-essarily all have the same set of convictions, and it is a crude mistake to treat them as if they did. There are serious divisions of opinion within feminism over the strategies for improving the political, economic, and social position of women—for example, over the ethics and the wisdom of censoring literature which some fem-inists find demeaning to women. Feminists also disagree about deeper questions: about the char-acter and roots of sexual and gender discrimina-tion, about whether women are genetically different from men in moral sensibility or per-ception, and whether the goal of feminism

Ronald Dworkin, "Feminism and Abortion," *The New York Review of Books* (June 10, 1993). Reprinted with permission from *The New York Review of Books*. Copyright (c) 1993 Nyrev, Inc.

should be simply to erase formal and informal discrimination or to aim instead at a thoroughly genderless world in which roughly as many fathers as mothers are in primary charge of children, and roughly as many women as men hold top military positions. Feminists even disagree over whether abortion should be permitted: there *are* "pro-life" feminists. The feminist views I shall discuss here are only those concerned with the special connection between a pregnant woman and the fetus she carries.

In the United States, during the decades before *Roe* v. *Wade*, feminists were leaders in the campaigns to repeal anti-abortion laws in various states: they argued, with an urgency and power unmatched by any other group, for the rights that *Roe* finally recognized. They have since expressed deep disgust with Supreme Court decisions that have allowed states to restrict those rights in various ways, and they have demonstrated in support of their position, risking, in some cases, violent injury at the hands of anti-abortion protesters. Nevertheless, some feminists are among the most savage critics of the arguments Justice Blackmun used in his opinion justifying the *Roe* decision; they insist that the Court reached the right result but for very much the wrong reason. Some of them suggest that the decision may in the end have worked to the detriment rather than the benefit of women.

Blackmun's opinion argued that women have a general constitutional right to privacy and that it follows from that general right that they have the right to an abortion before the end of the second trimester of their pregnancy. Some feminists object that the so-called right to privacy is a dangerous illusion and that a woman's freedom of choice about abortion in contemporary societies, dominated by men, should be defended not by an appeal to privacy but instead as an essential aspect of any genuine attempt to improve sexual equality. It is not surprising that feminists should want to defend abortion rights in as many ways as possible, and certainly not

surprising that some should call attention to sexual inequality as part of the reason why women need such rights. But why should they be eager not only to claim an additional argument from equality but actually to reject the right to privacy argument on which the Court had relied? Why shouldn't they urge both arguments, and as many others as seem pertinent?

Many of the various reasons feminist writers offer to explain their rejection of the right to privacy are unconvincing, but it is important to see why, not only because some of the mistaken claims on which they rest have been influential but in order to see why we must look for more convincing explanations. Professor Catharine MacKinnon, for example, a prominent feminist lawyer, argues that the right-to-privacy argument presupposes what she regards as a fallacious distinction between matters that are in principle private, like the sexual acts and decisions of couples, which government should not attempt to regulate or supervise, and those that are in principle public, like public health, foreign affairs, and economic policy, about which government must of course legislate. That distinction, she believes, is mistaken, and dangerous for women in several ways. It supposes that women really are free to make decisions for themselves within the private space they occupy, though in fact, she insists, women are often very unfree in the so-called private realm; men often force sexual compliance upon them in private, and this private sexual domination both reflects and helps to sustain the political and economic subordination of women in the public community.

Appealing to a right to privacy is dangerous, MacKinnon suggests, in two ways. First, insisting that sex is a private matter implies that the government has no legitimate concern with what happens to women behind the bedroom door, where they may be raped or mauled. Second, the claim that abortion is a private matter seems to imply that government has no responsibility to help finance abortion for poor pregnant women as it helps finance childbirth for them. (Other feminists expand on this point. Basing the right to an abortion on a right to privacy seems to suggest, they say, that government does all it needs to do for sexual equality by allowing women this free choice, which ignores the larger truth that any substantial advance toward equality will require considerable public expenditure on welfare and other programs directed to women.) MacKinnon argues that the Supreme Court's 1980 decision in *Harris* v. *McRae*, which reversed Judge John Dooling's decision that the Hyde Amendment prohibiting the use of federal funds to finance abortion was unconstitutional, was a direct result of the Court's rhetoric about privacy in *Roe* v. *Wade*.

Is this persuasive? It is certainly true that many women are sexually intimidated and that a presumption of much criminal and civil law—that women who have sexual intercourse have either been raped or have freely and willingly consented—is much too crude, and the American law of sexual harassment has begun slowly to change (in part thanks to Professor MacKinnon's work) to reflect that realization. But there is no evident connection between these facts and MacKinnon's claims about the rhetoric of privacy. The right to privacy that the Court recognized in *Roe* v. *Wade* in no way assumes that all or even some women are genuinely free agents in sexual decisions. On the contrary, that women are often dominated by men makes it more rather than less important to insist that women should have a constitutionally protected right to control the use of their own bodies.

MacKinnon, it is true, disparages the motives of men who favor women's right to abortion. Liberal abortion rules, she says, allow men to use women sexually with no fear of any consequences of paternity; allow them, she says, quoting a feminist colleague, to fill women up, vacuum them out, and fill them up again. But her suspicion of men who are her allies, even if it

were well founded, would offer no ground for her taking a more critical view of the right-to-privacy argument than of any other argument for liberal abortion rules that men might support.

Nor is the second reason she gives against the right to privacy argument—that recognizing privacy in sex means that the law will not protect women from marital rape or help to finance abortions—any more persuasive, for she conflates different senses of "privacy." Sometimes privacy is territorial: people have a right to privacy in the territorial sense when they are entitled to do as they wish in a certain specified space: inside their own homes, for example. Sometimes privacy is a matter of confidentiality: we say that people may keep their political convictions private, meaning that they need not disclose how they have voted.

Sometimes, however, privacy means something different from either of these senses: It means sovereignty over personal decisions. The Supreme Court long ago held, for example, that the constitutional right of privacy includes the right of parents of German descent to send their children to a private school in which German is taught. That is a matter of sovereignty over a particular parental decision that the Court believed should be protected; it is not a matter of either territorial privacy or secrecy. (It is true that in *Griswold* v. *Connecticut* one justice said that the law must not forbid contraceptives because if it did, policemen would have to search bedrooms. But he alone urged that rationale, and the Court explicitly rejected it in a decision soon after when it held that the right to privacy meant that teen-agers were free to buy contraceptives in drugstores.)

The right to privacy that the Court endorsed in *Roe* v. *Wade* is plainly privacy in the sense of sovereignty over particular, specified decisions, and it does not follow from the government's protection of a woman's sovereignty over the use of her own body for procreation that it is indifferent to how her partner treats her—or how she treats him—inside her home. On the contrary, a right not to be raped or sexually violated is another example of a right to control how one's body is used. Nor does it follow that the government has no responsibility to assure the economic conditions that make the exercise of the right possible and its possession valuable. Recognizing that women have a constitutional right to determine how their own bodies are to be used is a prerequisite, not a barrier, to the further claim that the government must ensure that this right is not illusory.

The explanations that MacKinnon and some other feminists give for their opposition to the language of privacy do not go to the heart of the matter. But other passages in their work suggest a far stronger explanation: claiming that a right to *privacy* protects a woman's decision whether to abort a fetus assimilates pregnancy to other situations that are very unlike it; the effect of that assimilation is to obscure the special meaning of pregnancy for women and to denigrate its unique character by overlooking it. The claim of privacy, according to these feminists, treats pregnancy as if a woman and her fetus were morally and genetically separate entities. It treats pregnancy, MacKinnon says, as if it were just another case in which two separate entities have either deliberately or accidentally become connected in some way, and one party plainly has a "sovereign right" to sever the connection if it wishes.

MacKinnon offers examples of other such cases: the relationship between an employee and her employer, or between a tenant on short lease and his landlord, or (in a reference to a well-known article about abortion by the philosopher Judith Jarvis Thomson that many feminists dislike[1]) between a sick violinist and a woman who wakes to find that the violinist has been connected by tubes to her body, an attachment that must be maintained for nine months if the violinist is to remain alive. MacKinnon insists that pregnancy is not like those relation-

ships; in a striking passage, she describes what pregnancy is like from the perspective of a woman.

> In my opinion and in the experience of many pregnant women, the fetus is a human form of life. It is alive. . . . More than a body part but less than a person, where it is, is largely what it is. From the standpoint of the pregnant woman, it is both me and not me. It "is" the pregnant woman in the sense that it is in her and of her and is hers more than anyone's. It "is not" her in the sense that she is not all that is there.

MacKinnon also cites the poet Adrienne Rich's comment, "The child that I carry for nine months can be defined *neither* as me nor as not-me."

By ignoring the unique character of the relationship between a pregnant woman and her fetus, by neglecting the mother's perspective and assimilating her situation to that of a landlord or a woman strapped to a violinist, the privacy claim obscures, in particular, the special *creative* role of a woman in pregnancy. Her fetus, MacKinnon argues, is not merely "in her" as an inanimate object might be, or something alive but alien that has been transplanted into her body. It is "of her and is hers more than anyone's" because it is, more than anyone else's, her creation and her responsibility; it is alive because *she* has made it come alive; she already has an intense physical and emotional investment in it unlike that which any other person, even its father, has. Because of these physical and emotional connections it is as wrong to say that the fetus is separate from her as to say that it is not.

All these aspects of a pregnant woman's experience—everything special, complex, ironic, and tragic about pregnancy and abortion—are neglected in the liberal explanation that women have a right to abortion because they are entitled to sovereignty over personal decisions, an explanation that would apply with equal force to a woman's right to choose her own clothing.

The most characteristic and fundamental feminist claim is that women's sexual subordination must be made a central feature of the abortion debate. MacKinnon puts the point in a particularly striking way: If women were truly equal with men, she says, the political status of a fetus would be different from what it is now. That seems paradoxical: How can the inequality of women, however unjustified, doom fetuses— half of whom are female—to a lower status, and a lesser right to live, than they would otherwise have? This objection to MacKinnon's argument, like so much else in the public and philosophical debate about abortion, presupposes that the pivotal issue is whether a fetus is a person with interests and rights of its own. The objection would be sound if that were the central issue— if the debate were about a fetus's status in that sense. But MacKinnon's point becomes not only sensible but powerful if we take her to be discussing a fetus's status in the sense I have just discussed—as a creative achievement and responsibility. Then the crucial question is whether and when abortion is an unjustifiable waste of something of intrinsic creative importance, and MacKinnon's point is the arresting one that the intrinsic importance of a new human life may well depend on the meaning and freedom of the act that created it.

If women were free and equal to men in their sexual relationships, feminists say—if they had a more genuinely equal role in forming the moral, cultural, and economic environment in which children are conceived and raised—then the status of a fetus would be different because it would be more genuinely and unambiguously the woman's own intended and wanted creation rather than something imposed upon her. Abortion would then more plainly be, as many women now think it is, a kind of self-destruction, a woman destroying something into which

she had mixed herself. Women cannot take that view of abortion now, some feminists argue, because too often sexual intercourse is, to some degree, rape, and pregnancy is too often the result not of creative achievement but of uncreative subordination, and also because the costs of an unwanted pregnancy are so unfairly distributed, falling so heavily and disproportionately on them.

This argument, at least put in the way I have put it here, may be overstated. It takes no notice of the creative function of the father, for example, and though it shows what is objectionable in relying wholly on the concept of privacy to defend a woman's right to an abortion, it does not prove that the Supreme Court was misguided in relying on that concept in deciding the constitutional issue in *Roe* v. *Wade*. After all, appealing to privacy does not deny the ways in which pregnancy is a unique relationship or the ambivalent and complex character of many pregnant women's attitudes toward the fetuses they carry. In fact, the best argument for applying the constitutional right of privacy to abortion emphasizes the special psychic as well as physical costs of unwanted pregnancies. I do not believe, finally, that even a great and general improvement in equality between men and women in the United States would either undercut the argument that women have a constitutional right to abortion or obviate the need for such a right.

In spite of these important reservations, the feminist arguments of MacKinnon and others have added a very important dimension to the abortion debate. It is true that many women's attitudes toward abortion are affected by a contradictory sense of both identification with and oppression by their pregnancies, and that the sexual, economic, and social subordination of women contributes to that undermining sense of oppression. In a better society, in which child rearing was supported as enthusiastically as abortion was discouraged, the status of a fetus probably would change, because women's sense of pregnancy and motherhood as creative activities would be more genuine and less compromised, and the inherent value of their own lives less threatened. The feminist arguments reveal another way, then, in which our understanding is cramped and our experience distorted by the one-dimensional idea that the abortion controversy turns only on whether a fetus is a person from the moment of conception. Most feminists do not hold that a fetus is a person with moral rights of its own, but they do insist that it is a creature of moral consequence. They emphasize not the woman's right suggested by the rhetoric of privacy, but a woman's responsibility to make a complex decision that she is best placed to make.

That is explicitly the message of another prominent feminist lawyer, Professor Robin West, who argues that if the Supreme Court one day overrules *Roe* v. *Wade*, and the battle over abortion shifts from courtrooms to legislatures, women will not succeed in defending abortion rights if they emphasize privacy, which suggests selfish, willful decisions taken behind a veil of immunity from public censure. Instead, she says, women should emphasize responsibility, and she offers what she calls a responsibility-based argument to supplement the right-based claims of *Roe*.

> Women need the freedom to make reproductive decisions not merely to vindicate a right to be left alone, but often to strengthen their ties to others: to plan responsibly and have a family for which they can provide, to pursue professional or work commitments made to the outside world, or to continue supporting their families or communities. At other times the decision to abort is necessitated, not by a murderous urge to end life, but by the harsh reality of a financially irresponsible partner, a society indifferent to the care of children, and a workplace incapable of accommodating or supporting the needs

of working parents. . . . Whatever the reason, the decision to abort is almost invariably made within a web of interlocking, competing, and often irreconcilable responsibilities and commitments.[2]

West is obviously assuming that the audience to which this argument is addressed has firmly rejected the view that a fetus is a person. If her claims were interpreted as proposing that a woman may murder another *person* in order to "strengthen her ties to others," or because her husband is financially irresponsible, or because society does not mandate maternity leave, these claims would be politically suicidal for the feminist cause. West assumes what I have been arguing, that most people recognize, even when their rhetoric does not, that the real argument against abortion is that it is irresponsible to waste human life without a justification of appropriate importance.

West and other feminists often refer to the research of the sociologist Professor Carol Gilligan of Harvard University. In a much-cited study, Gilligan argued that, at least in American society, women characteristically think about moral issues in ways different from men.[3] Women who are faced with difficult moral decisions, she said, pay less attention to abstract moral principles than men do, but feel a greater responsibility to care for and nurture others, and to prevent hurt or pain. She relied on, among other research studies, interviews with twenty-nine women contemplating abortion who had been referred to her research program by counseling services. These women were not typical of all women considering abortion; although twenty-one of them did have abortions following the discussions (of the others, four had their babies, two miscarried, and two could not be reached to learn of their decision), they were all at least willing to discuss their decisions with a stranger and to delay their abortions to do so.

One feature of the responses is particularly striking. Though many of the twenty-nine women in the study were in considerable doubt about what was the right decision to make, and agonized over it, none of them, apparently, traced that doubt to any uncertainty or perplexity over the question of whether a fetus is a person with a right to live. At least one—a twenty-nine-year-old Catholic nurse—said she believed in the principle that a fetus is a person and that abortion is murder, but it is doubtful that she really did believe that, since she also said that she had come to think that abortion might sometimes be justified because it fell into "a 'gray' area," just as she now thought, on the basis of her nursing experience, that euthanasia might sometimes be justified in spite of her church's teaching to the contrary. In any case, even she worried, like the others, not about the metaphysical status of the fetus but about a conflict of responsibilities she believed she owed to family, to others, and to herself.

The women in the study did not see this conflict as one between simple self-interest and their responsibilities to others but rather as a conflict between genuine responsibilities on both sides, of having to decide—as a twenty-five-year-old who had already had one abortion put it—how to act in a "decent, human kind of way, one that leaves maybe a slightly shaken but not totally destroyed person." Some of them said that the selfish choice would be to have their babies. One nineteen-year-old felt that "it is a choice of hurting myself [by an abortion] or hurting other people around me. What is more important?" Or, as a seventeen-year-old put it, "What I want to do is to have the baby, but what I feel I should do, which is what I need to do, is have an abortion right now, because sometimes what you want isn't right." When she wanted the child, she said, she wasn't thinking of the responsibilities that go with it, and that was selfish.

All of Gilligan's subjects talked and wondered about responsibility, and not about mur-

der. They sometimes talked of responsibility to the child, but they meant the future hypothetical child, not the existing embryo—they meant that it would be wrong to have a child one could not care for properly. They also worried about other people who would be affected by their decision. One, in her late twenties, said that a right decision depends on awareness of "what it will do to your relationship with the father or how it will affect him emotionally." They talked of responsibility to themselves, but they had in mind not their pleasure, or doing what they wanted now, but their responsibilities to make something of their own lives. One adolescent said, "Abortion, if you do it for the right reasons, is helping you to start over and do different things." A musician in her late twenties said that her choice for abortion was selfish because it was for her "survival," but she meant surviving in her work, which, she said, was "where I derive the meaning of what I am."

Gilligan says, in summary, "Here the conventional feminine voice emerges with great clarity, defining the self and proclaiming its worth on the basis of the ability to care for and protect others." But her subjects talked of another, more abstract, kind of responsibility as well: responsibility to what they called "the world." One said, "I don't need to pay off my imaginary debts to the world through this child, and I don't think that it is right to bring a child into the world and use it for that purpose." Another said that it would be selfish for her to decide to have an abortion because it denied "the survival of the child, another human being," but she did not mean that abortion was murder or that it violated any fetal rights. She put it in very different, more impersonal, and abstract terms: "Once a certain life has begun, it shouldn't be stopped artificially."

This is a brief but careful and accurate statement of what, beneath all the screaming rhetoric about rights and murder, most people think is the real moral defect in abortion. Abortion wastes the intrinsic value—the sanctity, the inviolability—of a human life and is therefore a grave moral wrong unless the intrinsic value of other human lives would be wasted in a decision *against* abortion. Each of Gilligan's subjects was exploring and reacting to that terrible conflict. Each was trying, above all, to take the measure of her responsibility for the intrinsic value of her *own* life, to locate the awful decision she had to make in that context, to see the decisions about whether to cut off new life, with its own intrinsic value, as part of a larger challenge to show respect for all life by living well and responsibly herself. Deciding about abortion is not a unique problem, disconnected from all other decisions, but rather a dramatic and intensely lit example of choices people must make throughout their lives, all of which express convictions about the value of life and the meaning of death.

NOTES

1. Judith Jarvis Thomson, "A Defense of Abortion," *Philosophy and Public Affairs* I, No. 1 (Fall 1971).

2. Robin West, "Taking Freedom Seriously," *Harvard Law Review*, Vol. 104, No. 1 (November 1990), pp. 84–85.

3. Carol Gilligan, *In a Different Voice* (Harvard University Press, 1982).

3

Euthanasia and Physician-Assisted Suicide

A GROWING DEBATE

In the early 1990s, the push to make voluntary active euthanasia or assisted suicide available in our society seemed restricted to West Coast ballot initiatives, such as those in Oregon, California, and Washington and to the isolated and controversial efforts of Dr. Jack Kevorkian and the activities and publications of relatively small organizations such as the Hemlock Society.[1] However by the mid-1990s, the demand to "legalize" euthanasia spread throughout the country, growing increasingly larger and more vocal. Demands for the government's affirmation of a "right to die" were further fueled by two Federal Appellate Court decisions in 1996, which prompted the United States Supreme Court to study physician-assisted suicide.

Although it is clear that the debate over euthanasia has increased sharply in the 1990s, it is often unclear what exactly is being debated; those staking out positions use many different terms to describe what it is they seek to defend or to decry, for example, *the right to die, mercy killing, assisted suicide, physician-assisted suicide, physician-assisted death, physician aid-in-dying, self-deliverance, pulling the plug,* and so on. These popular terms and slogans are vague and imprecise; they also bear strong ideological markings.[2] And so it is often difficult to determine what is at issue.

DEFINING VOLUNTARY ACTIVE EUTHANASIA AND PHYSICIAN-ASSISTED SUICIDE

Philosophers seek to avoid these slippery slogans in order to gain clarity and thus to examine arguments more carefully. In this chapter, we examine the debate over *voluntary active euthanasia* and *physician-assisted suicide*. We shall define *voluntary active euthanasia as the intentional and direct termination of a person's life when that person is terminally ill or when his or her death is imminent, and where that person is a competent adult who voluntarily, consistently, and repeatedly requests the termination of his or her life.*[3] We shall define a terminally ill person as one who has an incurable or irreversible condition that is highly likely to cause his or her death within a relatively short time (six months or less) with or without treatment.[4] Note that this definition of voluntary active euthanasia does not indicate *who* the actual or final agent of death is—the terminally ill person who self-administers the lethal dose, a friend or family member of this person, or a physician.

It is at this point that we need to address the relationship between voluntary active euthanasia and physician-assisted suicide. While some philosophers and policy-makers distinguish sharply between the two, many do not. Following Dan Brock, whose article opens this chapter, we shall view the two as very closely related, if distinguishable at all. Brock states that "a paradigm case of physician-assisted suicide is a patient's ending his or her life with a lethal dose of a medication requested of and provided by a physician for that purpose."[5] He then suggests that "a paradigm case of voluntary active euthanasia is a physician's administering the lethal dose, often because the patient is unable to do so."[6] What distinguishes the two, then, is who actually administers the lethal dose, in other words, "who acts last." Brock concludes that because in each case "the physician plays an active and necessary causal role" there is "no significant, intrinsic difference between the two."[7]

ARGUMENTS IN FAVOR OF VOLUNTARY ACTIVE EUTHANASIA

The central question of this chapter is whether any form of voluntary active euthanasia is *morally permissible*. Many defenders of euthanasia justify their positions by appealing to the values of liberty, autonomy, and self-determination: Rational, competent adults should have the right to make responsible decisions regarding their own lives, provided they respect others' right to self-determination. Respecting an individual's right to self-determination includes allowing him or her to commit euthanasia. Legal prohibitions on euthanasia thus constitute unwarranted government intervention in a fundamental exercise of autonomy. In a similar type of argument, supporters argue that making voluntary active euthanasia available to the terminally ill allows them a measure of dignity in the face of the final and ravaging stages of their illnesses. Other defenders appeal to the value of mercy to support the claim that euthanasia is morally acceptable and ought be made available in our society: Those committed to the value of mercy would in certain cases agree to assist terminally ill persons in their efforts to end their lives. To refuse to accede to the requests of a terminally ill person suffering unbearable pain would be cruel, callous, and heartless. Philosophers Dan Brock and Margaret Pabst Battin offer defenses of euthanasia in their articles in this chapter; both rely strongly on the value of self-determination in their respective defenses of euthanasia.

ARGUMENTS AGAINST VOLUNTARY ACTIVE EUTHANASIA

Some opponents of euthanasia find it morally objectionable because it involves someone forming and acting on a direct intention to bring about a human person's death. They argue that it is morally impermissible to directly intend to terminate the life of a human person no matter the circumstances; the sanctity of persons makes such an intention intrinsically evil.

Philosophers who support this line of reasoning argue that we can make a clear moral distinction between allowing someone to die by withholding or withdrawing life-saving medical resources, and directly *and* actively seeking to end a person's life by administering a lethal dose. Thus, these critics argue, although it is morally acceptable for competent, terminally ill persons to refuse any medical treatment other than palliative care or to consent to the withdrawal of life-sustaining medical treatments, it is morally wrong to directly and intentionally act to bring about the death of terminally ill persons.

Other critics stop short of arguing that each and every instance of voluntary active euthanasia is morally evil. Their concerns are instead based on fear of undesirable consequences that might ensue should society make euthanasia widely available. They worry that if society should sanction even very restricted forms of euthanasia or physician-assisted suicide, then inevitably abuses would occur—

abuses that would disproportionately affect the most vulnerable members of society. Variations on this consequentialist argument point to the possible negative consequences with respect to the health-care professions: If society were to permit physician-assisted suicide, what might be the effect on physicians and other health-care professionals? Might not this erode patients' trust in physicians and nurses? Consequentialist arguments of this sort are often called "slippery slope" arguments.

RACE, GENDER, CLASS, AND VOLUNTARY ACTIVE EUTHANASIA

Although there is an obvious connection between gender and abortion, and, as we shall see in the next chapter, a notable one between race and class and the death penalty, some might think that a moral analysis of voluntary active euthanasia is unlikely to be influenced by concerns about gender or race or social class, and so on. A terminal illness accompanied by intolerable pain can affect anyone, regardless of gender or race or sexual orientation or social class. Yet a number of philosophers and social scientists have recently argued that a thorough moral analysis of this issue must examine how gender, race, and economic status affect our health care decisions, our access to health care, and our relationships with health care professionals. Scholars who explicitly work out of feminist and African-American perspectives have of late made significant contributions to bioethics or medical ethics; indeed, many believe these fields have been transformed and reinvigorated by work attentive to race and gender.[8] The reading by Susan M. Wolf in this chapter gives some hint of these projects.

The role of gender in the euthanasia debate gained public attention briefly when it was noted that the first eight persons who received assistance from the infamous Dr. Jack Kevorkian in ending their lives were all female.[9] Feminist Susan Wolf offers more subtle reasons why we ought consider gender an important variable in our analysis. She writes, "established gender differences in health care (including the adequacy of pain relief), in health care insurance, in suicidal behavior, and in societal expectations about who should be self-sacrificing give reason to think that gender may play an important role."[10] Feminists have, of late, criticized the underpinnings of moral arguments whose conclusions turn by and large on a solitary individual's liberty-rights or claims to autonomy, for example, the primary argument offered by defenders of voluntary active euthanasia. Feminist scholars often recommend that more attention be paid to the socially situated self or the self-in-relation-to-others. In doing so, they argue, we discover that the reasons why some persons seek physician-assisted suicide or euthanasia have more to do with their fear of burdening their families than their desire to be in control of their lives. Medical ethicist Dr. Mark Siegler noted the following in a recent debate on this topic: [If voluntary active euthanasia is legalized] it's going to expand it widely for large numbers of people who may not want this so much, particularly, I'm deeply afraid [for] . . . the vulnerable populations, the poor, the uninsured, the disabled, the mentally and physically incapacitated, racial and cultural minorities. They're the people who will have most to fear from this policy, not the civil libertarians who [will] have one more right. . . . [T]he exit polls on the West Coast [when residents of California and Oregon, respectively, voted on measures to legalize physician-assisted suicide] demonstrate consistently that the people who are most against assisted suicide tend to be the elderly, African Americans, Asians, and women, interestingly enough. Those in favor tend to be young men, people in control of their lives, who are successful."[11] The congressional testimony of disabled-rights activists Carol Gill and Diane Coleman found in this chapter raises very directly the concern over the growing social acceptance of euthanasia and physician-assisted suicide that is felt by persons with disabilities.

NOTES

1. Peter Steinfels, "Beliefs: Why the liberal agenda might one day include the battle over euthanasia and assisted suicide," *The New York Times*, 15 July 1995: A28.

2. The overt political attempts to label the types of policies in question strike many philosophers as at best confused and at worst deliberately deceptive. Consider California's Proposition 161, which sought to legalize "physician-assisted death" or "aid in dying." "Aid in dying" was defined as "a medical procedure that will terminate the life of the qualified patient in a painless, humane and dignified manner whether administered by the physician at the patient's choice or direction or whether the physician provides means to the patient for self-administration." (Proposed Law, 161. Death with Dignity Act. Section 2525.2 [k].) The proposed law then asserts the following: "Requesting and receiving aid-in-dying by a qualified patient in accordance with this title shall not, for any purpose, constitute a suicide." (Section 2525.16) A few lines later, the text affirms "Nothing in this Act shall be construed to condone, authorize, or approve mercy killing." (2525.23).

3. See pages 163–164 of Dan W. Brock's article in this chapter, "Voluntary Active Euthanasia: An Overview and Defense."

4. Brock 163–164.

5. Brock 164.

6. Brock 164.

7. Brock 164.

8. As evidence of this transformation, see for example, Helen Bequaert Holmes and Laura Purdy, eds., *Feminist Perspectives in Medical Ethics* (Bloomington, IN: Indiana University Press, 1992); Susan Sherwin, *No Longer Patient: Feminist Ethics and Health Care* (Philadelphia: Temple University Press, 1992); Harley Flack and Edmund Pellegrino, eds., *African-American Perspectives on Biomedical Ethics* (Washington, D.C.: Georgetown University Press, 1992); Mary Briody Mahowald, *Women and Children in Health Care: An Unequal Majority* (New York: Oxford University Press, 1993); Annette Dula and Sara Goering, *It Just Ain't Fair: The Ethics of Health Care for African-Americans* (London: Praeger Publishers, 1994); Joan C. Callahan, ed., *Reproduction, Ethics and the Law: Feminist Perspectives* (Bloomington, IN: Indiana University Press, 1995); Susan M. Wolf, ed., *Feminism & Bioethics: Beyond Reproduction* (New York: Oxford University Press, 1996); and Laura Purdy, *Reproducing Persons: Issues in Feminist Bioethics* (Ithaca, NY: Cornell University Press, 1996).

9. See Katharine Seelye, "Dr. Kevorkian and the Women He's Helped," *The Philadelphia Inquirer*, 20 December 1992: C1, C3.

10. Susan M. Wolf, "Introduction," in *Feminism & Bioethics: Beyond Reproduction* (New York: Oxford, 1995): 31.

11. Dr. Mark Siegler, director of the Center for Clinical Medical Ethics at the University of Chicago, "A Debate with Professor Margaret Pabst Battin," *The NewsHour with Jim Lehrer*, April 8, 1996.

12.

Voluntary Active Euthanasia: An Overview and Defense

Dan W. Brock

Dan W. Brock, Ph.D., is a professor of philosophy and biomedical ethics at Brown University. He is also the director of the Center for Biomedical Ethics at Brown. In this essay, Brock surveys a wide range of arguments used by both opponents and proponents of voluntary active euthanasia. He critically evaluates these arguments, particularly those based on the potential consequences—good and bad—of making euthanasia available in our society. Brock concludes by admitting that he believes that on the whole the stronger arguments are on the side of the proponents. In particular, he favors arguments grounded in the values of individual self-determination and individual well-being.

Since the case of Karen Quinlan first seized public attention fifteen years ago, no issue in biomedical ethics has been more prominent than the debate about forgoing life-sustaining treatment. Controversy continues regarding some aspects of that debate, such as forgoing life-sustaining nutrition and hydration, and relevant law varies some from state to state. Nevertheless, I believe it is possible to identify an emerging consensus that competent patients, or the surrogates of incompetent patients, should be permitted to weigh the benefits and burdens of alternative treatments, including the alternative of no treatment, according to the patient's values, and either to refuse any treatment or to select from among available alternative treatments. This consensus is reflected in bioethics scholarship, in reports of prestigious bodies such as the President's Commission for the Study of Ethical Problems in Medicine, The Hastings Center, and the American Medical Association, in a large body of judicial decisions in courts around the country, and finally in the beliefs and practices of health care professionals who care for dying patients.[1]

More recently, significant public and professional attention has shifted from life-sustaining treatment to euthanasia—more specifically, vol-

untary active euthanasia—and to physician-assisted suicide. Several factors have contributed to the increased interest in euthanasia. In the Netherlands, it has been openly practiced by physicians for several years with the acceptance of the country's highest court.[2] In 1988 there was an unsuccessful attempt to get the question of whether it should be made legally permissible on the ballot in California. In November 1991 voters in the state of Washington defeated a widely publicized referendum proposal to legalize both voluntary active euthanasia and physician-assisted suicide. Finally, some cases of this kind, such as "It's Over, Debbie," described in the *Journal of the American Medical Association,* the "suicide machine" of Dr. Jack Kevorkian, and the cancer patient "Diane" of Dr. Timothy Quill, have captured wide public and professional attention.[3] Unfortunately, the first two of these cases were sufficiently problematic that even most supporters of euthanasia or assisted suicide did not defend the physicians' actions in them. As a result, the subsequent debate they spawned has often shed more heat than light. My aim is to increase the light, and perhaps as well to reduce the heat, on this important subject by formulating and evaluating the central ethical arguments for and against voluntary active euthanasia and physician-assisted suicide. My evaluation of the arguments leads me, with reservations to be noted, to support permitting both practices. My primary aim, however, is not to argue for euthanasia, but to identify

Dan W. Brock, "Voluntary Active Euthanasia," *Hastings Center Report* 22 (March/April 1992): 10–22. Used with the permission of the author and the *Hastings Center Report.* Copyright (c) 1992.

confusions in some common arguments, and problematic assumptions and claims that need more defense or data in others. The issues are considerably more complex than either supporters or opponents often make out; my hope is to advance the debate by focusing attention on what I believe the real issues under discussion should be.

In the recent bioethics literature some have endorsed physician-assisted suicide but not euthanasia.[4] Are they sufficiently different that the moral arguments for one often do not apply to the other? A paradigm case of physician-assisted suicide is a patient's ending his or her life with a lethal dose of medication requested of and provided by a physician for that purpose. A paradigm case of voluntary active euthanasia is a physician's administering the lethal dose, often because the patient is unable to do so. The only difference that need exist between the two is the person who actually administers the lethal dose—the physician or the patient. In each, the physician plays an active and necessary causal role.

In physician-assisted suicide the patient acts last (for example, Janet Adkins herself pushed the button after Dr. Kevorkian hooked her up to his suicide machine), whereas in euthanasia the physician acts last by performing the physical equivalent of pushing the button. In both cases, however, the choice rests fully with the patient. In both the patient acts last in the sense of retaining the right to change his or her mind until the point at which the lethal process becomes irreversible. How could there be a substantial moral difference between the two based only on this small difference in the part played by the physician in the causal process resulting in death? Of course, it might be held that the moral difference is clear and important—in euthanasia the physician kills the patient whereas in physician-assisted suicide the patient kills him- or herself. But this is misleading at best. In assisted suicide the physician and patient together kill the patient. To see this, suppose a physician

supplied a lethal dose to a patient with the knowledge and intent that the patient will wrongfully administer it to another. We would have no difficulty in morality or the law recognizing this as a case of joint action to kill for which both are responsible.

If there is no significant, intrinsic moral difference between the two, it is also difficult to see why public or legal policy should permit one but not the other; worries about abuse or about giving anyone dominion over the lives of others apply equally to either. As a result, I will take the arguments evaluated below to apply to both and will focus on euthanasia.

My concern here will be with *voluntary* euthanasia only—that is, with the case in which a clearly competent patient makes a fully voluntary and persistent request for aid in dying. Involuntary euthanasia, in which a competent patient explicitly refuses or opposes receiving euthanasia, and nonvoluntary euthanasia, in which a patient is incompetent and unable to express his or her wishes about euthanasia, will be considered here only as potential unwanted side-effects of permitting voluntary euthanasia. I emphasize as well that I am concerned with *active* euthanasia, not withholding or withdrawing life-sustaining treatment, which some commentators characterize as "passive euthanasia." Finally, I will be concerned with euthanasia where the motive of those who perform it is to respect the wishes of the patient and to provide the patient with a "good death," though one important issue is whether a change in legal policy could restrict the performance of euthanasia to only those cases.

A last introductory point is that I will be examining only secular arguments about euthanasia, though of course many people's attitudes to it are inextricable from their religious views. The policy issue is only whether euthanasia should be permissible, and no one who has religious objections to it should be required to take any part in it, though of course this would not fully satisfy some opponents.

THE CENTRAL ETHICAL ARGUMENT FOR VOLUNTARY ACTIVE EUTHANASIA

The central ethical argument for euthanasia is familiar. It is that the very same two fundamental ethical values supporting the consensus on patient's rights to decide about life-sustaining treatment also support the ethical permissibility of euthanasia. These values are individual self-determination or autonomy and individual well-being. By self-determination as it bears on euthanasia, I mean people's interest in making important decisions about their lives for themselves according to their own values or conceptions of a good life, and in being left free to act on those decisions. Self-determination is valuable because it permits people to form and live in accordance with their own conception of a good life, at least within the bounds of justice and consistent with others doing so as well. In exercising self-determination people take responsibility for their lives and for the kinds of persons they become. A central aspect of human dignity lies in people's capacity to direct their lives in this way. The value of exercising self-determination presupposes some minimum of decision-making capacities or competence, which thus limits the scope of euthanasia supported by self-determination; it cannot justifiably be administered, for example, in cases of serious dementia or treatable clinical depression.

Does the value of individual self-determination extend to the time and manner of one's death? Most people are very concerned about the nature of the last stage of their lives. This reflects not just a fear of experiencing substantial suffering when dying, but also a desire to retain dignity and control during this last period of life. Death is today increasingly preceded by a long period of significant physical and mental decline, due in part to the technological interventions of modern medicine. Many people adjust to these disabilities and find meaning and value in new activities and ways. Others find the impairments and burdens in the last stage of their lives at some point sufficiently great to make life no longer worth living. For many patients near death, maintaining the quality of one's life, avoiding great suffering, maintaining one's dignity, and insuring that others remember us as we wish them to become of paramount importance and outweigh merely extending one's life. But there is no single, objectively correct answer for everyone as to when, if at all, one's life becomes all things considered a burden and unwanted. If self-determination is a fundamental value, then the great variability among people on this question makes it especially important that individuals control the manner, circumstances, and timing of their dying and death.

The other main value that supports euthanasia is individual well-being. It might seem that individual well-being conflicts with a person's self-determination when the person requests euthanasia. Life itself is commonly taken to be a central good for persons, often valued for its own sake, as well as necessary for pursuit of all other goods within a life. But when a competent patient decides to forgo all further life-sustaining treatment then the patient, either explicitly or implicitly, commonly decides that the best life possible for him or her with treatment is of sufficiently poor quality that it is worse than no further life at all. Life is no longer considered a benefit by the patient, but has now become a burden. The same judgment underlies a request for euthanasia: continued life is seen by the patient as no longer a benefit, but now a burden. Especially in the often severely compromised and debilitated states of many critically ill or dying patients, there is no objective standard, but only the competent patient's judgment of whether continued life is no longer a benefit.

Of course, sometimes there are conditions, such as clinical depression, that call into question whether the patient has made a competent choice, either to forgo life-sustaining treatment or to seek euthanasia, and then the patient's choice need not be evidence that continued life is no longer a benefit for him or her. Just as with decisions about treatment, a determination of incompetence can warrant not honoring the patient's choice; in the case of treatment, we then transfer decisional authority to a surrogate, though in the case of voluntary active euthanasia a determination that the patient is incompetent means that choice is not possible.

The value or right of self-determination does not entitle patients to compel physicians to act contrary to their own moral or professional values. Physicians are moral and professional agents whose own self-determination or integrity should be respected as well. If performing euthanasia became legally permissible, but conflicted with a particular physician's reasonable understanding of his or her moral or professional responsibilities, the care of a patient who requested euthanasia should be transferred to another.

Most opponents do not deny that there are some cases in which the values of patient self-determination and well-being support euthanasia. Instead, they commonly offer two kinds of arguments against it that on their view outweigh or override this support. The first kind of argument is that in any individual case where considerations of the patient's self-determination and well-being do support euthanasia, it is nevertheless always ethically wrong or impermissible. The second kind of argument grants that in some individual cases euthanasia may *not* be ethically wrong, but maintains nonetheless that public or legal policy should never permit it. The first kind of argument focuses on features of any individual case of euthanasia, while the second kind focuses on social or legal policy. In the next section I consider the first kind of argument.

EUTHANASIA IS THE DELIBERATE KILLING OF AN INNOCENT PERSON

The claim that any individual instance of euthanasia is a case of deliberate killing of an innocent person is, with only minor qualifica-

tions, correct. Unlike forgoing life-sustaining treatment, commonly understood as allowing to die, euthanasia is clearly killing, defined as depriving of life or causing the death of a living being. While providing morphine for pain relief at doses where the risk of respiratory depression and an earlier death may be a foreseen but unintended side effect of treating the patient's pain, in a case of euthanasia the patient's death is deliberate or intended even if in both the physician's ultimate end may be respecting the patient's wishes. If the deliberate killing of an innocent person is wrong, euthanasia would be nearly always impermissible.

In the context of medicine, the ethical prohibition against deliberately killing the innocent derives some of its plausibility from the belief that nothing in the currently accepted practice of medicine is deliberate killing. Thus, in commenting on the "It's Over, Debbie" case, four prominent physicians and bioethicists could entitle their paper "Doctors Must Not Kill."[5] The belief that doctors do not in fact kill requires the corollary belief that forgoing life-sustaining treatment, whether by not starting or by stopping treatment, is allowing to die, not killing. Common though this view is, I shall argue that it is confused and mistaken.

Why is the common view mistaken? Consider the case of a patient terminally ill with ALS disease. She is completely respirator dependent with no hope of ever being weaned. She is unquestionably competent but finds her condition intolerable and persistently requests to be removed from the respirator and allowed to die. Most people and physicians would agree that the patient's physician should respect the patient's wishes and remove her from the respirator, though this will certainly cause the patient's death. The common understanding is that the physician thereby allows the patient to die. But is that correct?

Suppose the patient has a greedy and hostile son who mistakenly believes that his mother will never decide to stop her life-sustaining treatment and that even if she did her physician would not remove her from the respirator. Afraid that his inheritance will be dissipated by a long and expensive hospitalization, he enters his mother's room while she is sedated, extubates her, and she dies. Shortly thereafter the medical staff discovers what he has done and confronts the son. He replies, "I didn't kill her, I merely allowed her to die. It was her ALS disease that caused her death." I think this would rightly be dismissed as transparent sophistry—the son went into his mother's room and deliberately killed her. But, of course, the son performed just the same physical actions, did just the same thing, that the physician would have done. If that is so, then doesn't the physician also kill the patient when he extubates her?

I underline immediately that there are important ethical differences between what the physician and the greedy son do. First, the physician acts with the patient's consent whereas the son does not. Second, the physician acts with a good motive—to respect the patient's wishes and self-determination—whereas the son acts with a bad motive—to protect his own inheritance. Third, the physician acts in a social role through which he is legally authorized to carry out the patient's wishes regarding treatment whereas the son has no such authorization. These and perhaps other ethically important differences show that what the physician did was morally justified whereas what the son did was morally wrong. What they do *not* show, however, is that the son killed while the physician allowed to die. One can either kill or allow to die with or without consent, with a good or bad motive, within or outside of a social role that authorizes one to do so.

The difference between killing and allowing to die that I have been implicitly appealing to here is roughly that between acts and omissions resulting in death.[6] Both the physician and the greedy son act in a manner intended to cause death, do cause death, and so both kill. One reason this conclusion is resisted is that on a different understanding of the distinction between killing and allowing to die, what the physician

does is allow to die. In this account, the mother's ALS is a legal disease whose normal progression is being held back or blocked by the life-sustaining respiratory treatment. Removing this artificial intervention is then viewed as standing aside and allowing the patient to die of her underlying disease. I have argued elsewhere that this alternative account is deeply problematic, in part because it commits us to accepting that what the greedy son does is to allow to die, not kill.[7] Here, I want to note two other reasons why the conclusion that stopping life support is killing is resisted.

The first reason is that killing is often understood, especially within medicine, as unjustified causing of death; in medicine it is thought to be done only accidentally or negligently. It is also increasingly widely accepted that a physician is ethically justified in stopping life support in a case like that of the ALS patient. But if these two beliefs are correct, then what the physician does cannot be killing, and so must be allowing to die. Killing patients is not, to put it flippantly, understood to be part of physicians' job description. What is mistaken in this line of reasoning is the assumption that all killings are *unjustified* causings of death. Instead, some killings are ethically justified, including many instances of stopping life support.

Another reason for resisting the conclusion that stopping life support is often killing is that it is psychologically uncomfortable. Suppose the physician had stopped the ALS patient's respirator and had made the son's claim, "I didn't kill her, I merely allowed her to die. It was her ALS disease that caused her death." The clue to the psychological role here is how naturally the "merely" modifies "allowed her to die." The characterization as allowing to die is meant to shift felt responsibility away from the agent—the physician—and to the lethal disease process. Other language common in death and dying contexts plays a similar role; "letting nature takes its course" or "stopping prolonging the dying process" both seem to shift responsibility from the physician who stops life support to the fatal disease process. However psychologically helpful these conceptualizations may be in making the difficult responsibility of a physician's role in the patient's death bearable, they nevertheless are confusions. Both physicians and family members can instead be helped to understand that it is the patient's decision and consent to stopping treatment that limits their responsibility for the patient's death and that shifts the responsibility to the patient.

Many who accept the difference between killing and allowing to die as the distinction between acts and omissions resulting in death have gone on to argue that killing is not in itself morally different from allowing to die.[8] In this account, very roughly, one kills when one performs an action that causes the death of a person (we are in a boat, you cannot swim, I push you overboard, and you drown), and one allows to die when one has the ability and opportunity to prevent the death of another, knows this, and omits doing so, with the result that the person dies (we are in a boat, you cannot swim, you fall overboard, I don't throw you an available life ring, and you drown). Those who see no moral difference between killing and allowing to die typically employ the strategy of comparing cases that differ in these and no other potentially morally important respects. This will allow people to consider whether the mere difference that one is a case of killing and the other of allowing to die matters morally, or whether instead it is other features that make most cases of killing worse than most instances of allowing to die. Here is such a pair of cases:

Case 1. A very gravely ill patient is brought to a hospital emergency room and sent up to the ICU. The patient begins to develop respiratory failure that is likely to require intubation very soon. At that point the patient's family members and long-standing physician arrive at the ICU and inform the ICU staff that there had been extensive discussion about future care with the patient when he was unquestionably competent. Give his grave and terminal illness, as well as his

state of debilitation, the patient had firmly rejected being placed on a respirator under any circumstances, and the family and physician produce the patient's advance directive to that effect. The ICU staff do not intubate the patient, who dies of respiratory failure.

Case 2. The same as Case 1 except that the family and physician are slightly delayed in traffic and arrive shortly after the patient has been intubated and placed on the respirator. The ICU staff extubate the patient, who dies of respiratory failure.

In Case 1 the patient is allowed to die, in Case 2 he is killed, but it is hard to see why what is done in Case 2 is significantly different morally than what is done in Case 1. It must be other factors that make most killings worse than most allowings to die, and if so, euthanasia cannot be wrong simply because it is killing instead of allowing to die.

Suppose both my arguments are mistaken. Suppose that killing is worse than allowing to die and that withdrawing life support is not killing, although euthanasia is. Euthanasia still need not for that reason be morally wrong. To see this, we need to determine the basic principle for the moral evaluation of killing persons. What is it that makes paradigm cases of wrongful killing wrongful? One very plausible answer is that killing denies the victim something that he or she values greatly—continued life or a future. Moreover, since continued life is necessary for pursuing any of a person's plans and purposes, killing brings the frustration of all of these plans and desires as well. In a nutshell, wrongful killing deprives a person of a valued future, and of all the person wanted and planned to do in that future.

A natural expression of this account of the wrongness of killing is that people have a moral right not to be killed.[9] But in this account of the wrongness of killing, the right not to be killed, like other rights, should be waivable when the person makes a competent decision that continued life is no longer wanted or a good, but is instead worse than no further life at all. In this view, euthanasia is properly understood as a case of a person having waived his or her right not to be killed.

This rights view of the wrongness of killing is not, of course, universally shared. Many people's moral views about killing have their origins in religious views that human life comes from God and cannot be justifiably destroyed or taken away, either by the person whose life it is or by another. But in a pluralistic society like our own with a strong commitment to freedom of religion, public policy should not be grounded in religious beliefs which many in that society reject. I turn now to the general evaluation of public policy on euthanasia.

WOULD THE BAD CONSEQUENCES OF EUTHANASIA OUTWEIGH THE GOOD?

The argument against euthanasia at the policy level is stronger than at the level of individual cases, though even here I believe the case is ultimately unpersuasive, or at best indecisive. The policy level is the place where the main issues lie, however, and where moral considerations that might override arguments in favor of euthanasia will be found, if they are found anywhere. It is important to note two kinds of disagreement about the consequences for public policy of permitting euthanasia. First, there is empirical or factual disagreement about what the consequences would be. This disagreement is greatly exacerbated by the lack of firm data on the issue. Second, since on any reasonable assessment there would be both good and bad consequences, there are moral disagreements about the relative importance of different effects. In addition to these two sources of disagreement, there is also no single, well-specified policy proposal for legalizing euthanasia on which policy assessments can focus. But without such specification, and especially without explicit procedures for protecting against well-intentioned misuse and ill-intentioned abuse, the consequences for policy are largely speculative. Despite these difficulties, a preliminary account of the main likely good and bad consequences is possible. This should help clarify where better data or more moral analysis and argument are needed, as well as where policy safeguards must be developed.

Potential Good Consequences of Permitting Euthanasia

What are the likely good consequences? First, if euthanasia were permitted it would be possible to respect the self-determination of competent patients who want it, but now cannot get it because of its illegality. We simply do not know how many such patients and people there are. In the Netherlands, with a population of about 14.5 million (in 1987), estimates in a recent study were that about 1,900 cases of voluntary active euthanasia or physician-assisted suicide occur annually. No straightforward extrapolation to the United States is possible for many reasons, among them, that we do not know how many people here who want euthanasia now get it, despite its illegality. Even with better data on the number of persons who want euthanasia but cannot get it, significant moral disagreement would remain about how much weight should be given to any instance of failure to respect a person's self-determination in this way.

One important factor substantially affecting the number of persons who would seek euthanasia is the extent to which an alternative is available. The widespread acceptance in the law, social policy, and medical practice of the right of a competent patient to forgo life-sustaining treatment suggests that the number of competent persons in the United States who would want euthanasia if it were permitted is probably relatively small.

A second good consequence of making euthanasia legally permissible benefits a much larger group. Polls have shown that a majority of the American public believes that people should have a right to obtain euthanasia if they want it.[10] No doubt the vast majority of those who support this right to euthanasia will never in fact come to want euthanasia for themselves. Nevertheless, making it legally permissible would reassure many people that if they ever do want euthanasia they would be able to obtain it. This reassurance would supplement the broader control of the process of dying given by the right to decide about life-sustaining treatment. Having fire insurance on one's house benefits all who have it, not just those whose houses actually burn down, by reassuring them that in the unlikely event of their house burning down, they will receive the money needed to rebuild it. Likewise, the legalization of euthanasia can be thought of as a kind of insurance policy against being forced to endure a protracted dying process that one has come to find burdensome and unwanted, especially when there is no life-sustaining treatment to forgo. The strong concern about losing control of their care expressed by many people who face serious illness likely to end in death suggests that they give substantial importance to the legalization of euthanasia as a means of maintaining this control.

A third good consequence of the legalization of euthanasia concerns patients whose dying is filled with severe and unrelievable pain or suffering. When there is a life-sustaining treatment that, if foregone, will lead relatively quickly to death, then doing so can bring an end to these patients' suffering without recourse to euthanasia. For patients receiving no such treatment, however, euthanasia may be the only release from their otherwise prolonged suffering and agony. This argument from mercy has always been the strongest argument for euthanasia in those cases to which it applies.[11]

The importance of relieving pain and suffering is less controversial than is the frequency with which patients are forced to undergo untreatable agony that only euthanasia could relieve. If we focus first on suffering cased by physical pain, it is crucial to distinguish pain that *could* be adequately relieved with modern methods of pain control, though it in fact is not, from pain that is relievable only by death.[12] For

a variety of reasons, including some physicians' fear of hastening the patient's death, as well as the lack of a publicly accessible means for assessing the amount of the patient's pain, many patients suffer pain that could be, but is not, relieved.

Specialists in pain control, as for example the pain of terminally ill cancer patients, argue that there are very few patients whose pain could not be adequately controlled, though sometimes at the cost of so sedating them that they are effectively unable to interact with other people or their environment. Thus, the argument from mercy in cases of physical pain can probably be met in a large majority of cases by providing adequate measures of pain relief. This should be a high priority, whatever our legal policy on euthanasia—the relief of pain and suffering has long been, quite properly, one of the central goals of medicine. Those cases in which pain could be effectively relieved, but in fact is not, should only count significantly in favor of legalizing euthanasia if all reasonable efforts to change pain management techniques have been tried and have failed.

Dying patients often undergo substantial psychological suffering that is not fully or even principally the result of physical pain.[13] The knowledge about how to relieve this suffering is much more limited than in the case of relieving pain, and efforts to do so are probably more often unsuccessful. If the argument from mercy is extended to patients experiencing great and unrelievable psychological suffering, the numbers of patients to which it applies are much greater.

One last good consequence of legalizing euthanasia is that once death has been accepted, it is often more humane to end life quickly and peacefully, when that is what the patient wants. Such a death will often be seen as better than a more prolonged one. People who suffer a sudden and unexpected death, for example by dying quickly or in their sleep from a heart attack or stroke, are often considered lucky to have died in this way. We care about how we die in part because we care about how others remember us, and we hope they will remember us as we were in "good times" with them and not as we might be when disease has robbed us of our dignity as human beings. As with much in the treatment and care of the dying, people's concerns differ in this respect, but for at least some people, euthanasia will be a more humane death than what they have often experienced with other loved ones and might otherwise expect for themselves.

Some opponents of euthanasia challenge how much importance should be given to any of these good consequences of permitting it, or even whether some would be good consequences at all. But more frequently, opponents cite a number of bad consequences that permitting euthanasia would or could produce, and it is to their assessment that I now turn.

Potential Bad Consequences of Permitting Euthanasia

Some of the arguments against permitting euthanasia are aimed specifically against physicians, while others are aimed against anyone being permitted to perform it. I shall first consider one argument of the former sort. Permitting physicians to perform euthanasia, it is said, would be incompatible with their fundamental moral and professional commitment as healers to care for patients and to protect life. Moreover, if euthanasia by physicians became common, patients would come to fear that a medication was intended not to treat or care, but instead to kill, and would thus lose trust in their physicians. This position was forcefully stated in a paper by Willard Gaylin and his colleagues:

> The very soul of medicine is on trial. . . .
> This issue touches medicine at its moral center; if this moral center collapses, if physicians become killers or are even licensed to kill, the profession—and, therewith, each physician—will never again be worthy of trust and respect as healer and comforter and protector of life in all its frailty.

These authors go on to make clear that, while they oppose permitting anyone to perform euthanasia, their special concern is with physicians doing so:

> We call on fellow physicians to say that they will not deliberately kill. We must also say to each of our fellow physicians that we will not tolerate killing of patients and that we shall take disciplinary action against doctors who kill. And we must say to the broader community that if it insists on tolerating or legalizing active euthanasia, it will have to find nonphysicians to do its killing.[14]

If permitting physicians to kill would undermine the very "moral center" of medicine, then almost certainly physicians should not be permitted to perform euthanasia. But how persuasive is this claim? Patients should not fear, as a consequence of permitting *voluntary* active euthanasia, that their physicians will substitute a lethal injection for what patients want and believe is part of their care. If active euthanasia is restricted to cases in which it is truly voluntary, then no patient should fear getting it unless she or he has voluntarily requested it. (The fear that we might in time also come to accept nonvoluntary, or even involuntary, active euthanasia is a slippery slope worry I address below.) Patients' trust of their physicians could be increased, not eroded, by knowledge that physicians will provide aid in dying when patients seek it.

Might Gaylin and his colleagues nevertheless be correct in their claim that the moral center of medicine would collapse if physicians were to become killers? This question raises what at the deepest level should be the guiding aims of medicine, a question that obviously cannot be fully explored here. But I do want to say enough to indicate the direction that I believe an appropriate response to this challenge should take. In spelling out above what I called the positive argument for voluntary active euthanasia, I suggested that two principal values—respecting patients' self-determination and promoting their well-being—underlie the consensus that competent patients, or the surrogates of incompetent patients, are entitled to refuse any life-sustaining treatment and to choose from among available alternative treatments. It is the commitment to these two values in guiding physicians' actions as healers, comforters, and protectors of their patients' lives that should be at the "moral center" of medicine, and these two values support physicians' administering euthanasia when their patients make competent requests for it.

What should not be at that moral center is a commitment to preserving patients' lives as such, without regard to whether those patients want their lives preserved or judge their preservation a benefit to them. Vitalism has been rejected by most physicians, and despite some statements that suggest it, is almost certainly not what Gaylin and colleagues intended. One of them, Leon Kass, has elaborated elsewhere the view that medicine is a moral profession whose proper aim is "the naturally given end of health," understood as the wholeness and well-working of the human being; "for the physician, at least, human life in living bodies commands respect and reverence—*by its very nature.*" Kass continues, "the deepest ethical principle restraining the physician's power is not the autonomy or freedom of the patient; neither is it his own compassion or good intention. Rather, it is the dignity and mysterious power of human life itself."[15] I believe Kass is in the end mistaken about the proper account of the aims of medicine and the limits on physicians' power, but this difficult issue will certainly be one of the central themes in the continuing debate about euthanasia.

A second bad consequence that some foresee is that permitting euthanasia would weaken society's commitment to provide optimal care for dying patients. We live at a time in which the control of health care costs has become, and is likely to continue to be, the dominant focus of health care policy. If euthanasia is seen as a cheaper alternative to adequate care and treatment, then we might become less scrupulous about providing sometimes costly support and other services to dying patients. Particularly if our society comes to embrace deeper and more explicit rationing of health care, frail, elderly, and dying patients will need to be strong and effective advocates for their own health care and other needs, although they are hardly in a position to do this. We should do nothing to weaken their ability to obtain adequate care and services.

This second worry is difficult to assess because there is little firm evidence about the likelihood of the feared erosion in the care of dying patients. There are at least two reasons, however, for skepticism about this argument. The first is that the same worry could have been directed at recognizing patients' or surrogates' rights to forgo life-sustaining treatment, yet there is no persuasive evidence that recognizing the right to refuse treatment has caused a serious erosion in the quality of care of dying patients. The second reason for skepticism about this worry is that only a very small proportion of deaths would occur from euthanasia if it were permitted. In the Netherlands, where euthanasia under specified circumstances is permitted by the courts, though not authorized by statute, the best estimate of the proportion of overall deaths that result from it is about 2 percent.[16] Thus, the vast majority of critically ill and dying patients will not request it, and so will still have to be cared for by physicians, families, and others. Permitting euthanasia should not diminish people's commitment and concern to maintain and improve the care of these patients.

A third possible bad consequence of permitting euthanasia (or even a public discourse in which strong support for euthanasia is evident) is to threaten the progress made in securing the rights of patients or their surrogates to decide about and to refuse life-sustaining treatment.[17] This progress has been made against the backdrop of a clear and firm legal prohibition of euthanasia, which has provided a relatively bright line limiting the dominion of others over patients' lives. It has therefore been an important reassurance to concerns about how the authority to take steps ending life might be misused, abused, or wrongly extended.

Many supporters of the right of patients or their surrogates to refuse treatment strongly oppose euthanasia, and if forced to choose might well withdraw their support of the right to refuse treatment rather than accept euthanasia. Public policy in the last fifteen years has generally let life-sustaining treatment decisions be made in health care setting between physicians and patients or their surrogates, and without the involvement of the courts. However, if euthanasia is made legally permissible greater involvement of the courts is likely, which could in turn extend to a greater court involvement in life-sustaining treatment decisions. Most agree, however, that increased involvement of the courts in these decisions would be undesirable, as it would make sound decisionmaking more cumbersome and difficult without sufficient compensating benefits.

As with the second potential bad consequence of permitting euthanasia, this third consideration too is speculative and difficult to assess. The feared erosion of patients' or surrogates' rights to decide about life-sustaining treatment, together with greater court involvement in those decisions, are both possible. However, I believe there is reason to discount this general worry. The legal rights of competent patients and, to a lesser degree, surrogates of incompetent patients to decide about treatment are very firmly embedded in a long line of informed consent and life-sustaining treatment cases, and are not likely to be eroded by a debate over, or even acceptance of, euthanasia. It will not be accepted without safeguards that reassure the public about abuse, and if that debate shows the need for similar safeguards for some life-sustaining treatment decisions they should be adopted there as well. In neither case are the only possible safeguards greater court involvement, as the recent growth of institutional ethics committees shows.

The fourth potential bad consequence of permitting euthanasia has been developed by David Velleman and turns on the subtle point that making a new option or choice available to people can sometimes make them worse off, even if once they have the choice they go on to choose what is best for them.[18] Ordinarily, people's continued existence is viewed by them as a given, a fixed condition with which they must cope. Making euthanasia available to people as an option denies them the alternative of staying alive by default. If people are offered the option of euthanasia, their continued existence is now a choice for which they can be held responsible and which they can be asked by others to justify. We care, and are right to care, about being able to justify ourselves to others. To the extent that our society is unsympathetic to justifying a severely dependent or impaired existence, a heavy psychological burden of proof may be placed on patients who think their terminal illness or chronic infirmity is not a sufficient reason for dying. Even if they otherwise view their life as worth living, the opinion of others around them that it is not can threaten their reason for living and make euthanasia a rational choice. Thus the existence of the option becomes a subtle pressure to request it.

This argument correctly identifies the reason why offering some patients the option of euthanasia would not benefit them. Velleman takes it not as a reason for opposing all euthanasia, but for restricting it to circumstances where there are "unmistakable and overpowering reasons for persons to want the option of euthanasia," and for denying the option in all other cases. But there are at least three reasons why such restriction may not be warranted. First, polls and other evidence support that most Americans believe euthanasia should be permitted (though the recent defeat of the referendum to permit it in the state of Washington raises some doubt about this support). Thus, many more people seem to want the choice than would be made worse off by getting it. Second, if giving people the option of ending their life really makes them worse off, then we should not only prohibit euthanasia, but also take back from people the right they now have to decide about life-sustaining treatment. The feared harmful effect should already have occurred from securing people's right to refuse life-sustaining treatment, yet there is no evidence of any such widespread harm or any broad public desire to rescind that right. Third, since there is a wide range of conditions in which reasonable people can and do disagree about whether they would want continued life, it is not possible to restrict the permissibility of euthanasia as narrowly as Velleman suggests without thereby denying it to most persons who would want it; to permit it only in cases in which virtually everyone would want it would be to deny it to most who would want it.

A fifth potential bad consequence of making euthanasia legally permissible is that it might weaken the general legal prohibition of homicide. This prohibition is so fundamental to civilized society, it is argued, that we should do nothing that erodes it. If most cases of stopping life support are killing, as I have already argued, then the court cases permitting such killing have already in effect weakened this prohibition. However, neither the courts nor most people have seen these cases as killing and so as challenging the prohibition of homicide. The courts have usually grounded patients' or their surrogates' rights to refuse life-sustaining treatment in rights to privacy, liberty, self-determination, or bodily integrity, not in exceptions to homicide laws.

Legal permission for physicians or others to perform euthanasia could not be grounded in patients' rights to decide about medical treatment. Permitting euthanasia would require qualifying, at least in effect, the legal prohibition against homicide, a prohibition that in general does not allow the consent of the victim to justify or excuse the act. Nevertheless, the very same fundamental basis of the right to decide about life-sustaining treatment—respecting a person's self-determination—does support euthanasia as well. Individual self-determination

has long been a well-entrenched and fundamental value in the law, and so extending it to euthanasia would not require appeal to novel legal values or principles. That suicide or attempted suicide is no longer a criminal offense in all states indicates an acceptance of individual self-determination in the taking of one's own life analogous to that required for voluntary active euthanasia. The legal prohibition (in most states) of assisting in suicide and the refusal in the law to accept the consent of the victim as a possible justification of homicide are both arguably a result of difficulties in the legal process of establishing the consent of the victim after the fact. If procedures can be designed that clearly establish the voluntariness of the person's request for euthanasia, it would under those procedures represent a carefully circumscribed qualification on the legal prohibition of homicide. Nevertheless, some remaining worries about this weakening can be captured in the final potential bad consequence, to which I will now turn.

This final potential bad consequence is the central concern of many opponents of euthanasia and, I believe, is the most serious objection to a legal policy permitting it. According to this "slippery slope" worry, although active euthanasia may be morally permissible in cases in which it is unequivocally voluntary and the patient finds his or her condition unbearable, a legal policy permitting euthanasia would inevitably lead to active euthanasia being performed in many other cases in which it would be morally wrong. To prevent those other wrong cases of euthanasia we should not permit even morally justified performance of it.

Slippery slope arguments of this form are problematic and difficult to evaluate.[19] From one perspective, they are the last refuge of conservative defenders of the status quo. When all the opponent's objections to the wrongness of euthanasia itself have been met, the opponent then shifts ground and acknowledges both that it is not in itself wrong and that a legal policy which resulted only in its being performed would not be bad. Nevertheless, the opponent maintains, it should still not be permitted because doing so would result in its being performed in other cases in which it is not voluntary and would be wrong. In this argument's most extreme form, permitting euthanasia is the first and fateful step down the slippery slope to Nazism. Once on the slope we will be unable to get off.

Now it cannot be denied that it is *possible* that permitting euthanasia could have these fateful consequences, but that cannot be enough to warrant prohibiting it if it is otherwise justified. A similar *possible* slippery slope worry could have been raised to securing competent patients' rights to decide about life support, but recent history shows such a worry would have been unfounded. It must be relevant how likely it is that we will end with horrendous consequences and an unjustified practice of euthanasia. How *likely* and *widespread* would the abuses and unwarranted extensions of permitting it be? By abuses, I mean the performance of euthanasia that fails to satisfy the conditions required for voluntary active euthanasia, for example, if the patient has been subtly pressured to accept it. By unwarranted extensions of policy, I mean later changes in legal policy to permit not just voluntary euthanasia, but also euthanasia in cases in which, for example, it need not be fully voluntary. Opponents of voluntary euthanasia on slippery slope grounds have not provided the data or evidence necessary to turn their speculative concerns into well-grounded likelihoods.

It is at least clear, however, that both the character and likelihood of abuses of a legal policy permitting euthanasia depend in significant part on the procedures put in place to protect against them. I will not try to detail fully what such procedures might be, but will just give some examples of what they might include:

1. The patient should be provided with all relevant information about his or her medical condition, current prognosis,

available alternative treatments, and the prognosis of each.

2. Procedures should ensure that the patient's request for euthanasia is stable or enduring (a brief waiting period could be required) and fully voluntary (an advocate for the patient might be appointed to ensure this).

3. All reasonable alternatives must have been explored for improving the patient's quality of life and relieving any pain or suffering.

4. A psychiatric evaluation should ensure that the patient's request is not the result of a treatable psychological impairment such as depression.[20]

These examples of procedural safeguards are all designed to ensure that the patient's choice is fully informed, voluntary, and competent, and so a true exercise of self-determination. Other proposals for euthanasia would restrict its permissibility further—for example, to the terminally ill—a restriction that cannot be supported by self-determination. Such additional restrictions might, however, be justified by concern for limiting potential harms from abuse. At the same time, it is important not to impose procedural or substantive safeguards so restrictive as to make euthanasia impermissible or practically infeasible in a wide range of justified cases.

These examples of procedural safeguards make clear that it is possible to substantially reduce, though not to eliminate, the potential for abuse of a policy permitting voluntary active euthanasia. Any legalization of the practice should be accompanied by a well-considered set of procedural safeguards together with an ongoing evaluation of its use. Introducing euthanasia into only a few states could be a form of carefully limited and controlled social experiment that would give us evidence about the benefits and harms of the practice. Even then firm and uncontroversial data may remain elusive, as the continuing controversy over what has taken place in the Netherlands in recent years indicates.[21]

The Slip into Nonvoluntary Active Euthanasia

While I believe slippery slope worries can largely be limited by making necessary distinctions both in principle and in practice, one slippery slope concern is legitimate. There is reason to expect that legalization of voluntary active euthanasia might soon be followed by strong pressure to legalize some nonvoluntary euthanasia of incompetent patients unable to express their own wishes. Respecting a person's self-determination and recognizing that continued life is not always of value to a person can support not only voluntary active euthanasia, but some nonvoluntary euthanasia as well. These are the same values that ground competent patients' right to refuse life-sustaining treatment. Recent history here is instructive. In the medical ethics literature, in the courts since Quinlan, and in norms of medical practice, that right has been extended to incompetent patients and exercised by a surrogate who is to decide as the patient would have decided in the circumstances if competent.[22] It has been held unreasonable to continue life-sustaining treatment that the patient would not have wanted just because the patient now lacks the capacity to tell us that. Life-sustaining treatment for incompetent patients is today frequently forgone on the basis of a surrogate's decision, or less frequently on the basis of an advance directive executed by the patient while still competent. The very same logic that has extended the right to refuse life-sustaining treatment from a competent patient to the surrogate of an incompetent patient (acting with or without a formal advance directive from the patient) may well extend the scope of active euthanasia. The argument will be, Why continue to force unwanted life on patients just because they have now lost the capacity to request euthanasia from us?

A related phenomenon may reinforce this slippery slope concern. In the Netherlands, what the courts have sanctioned has been clearly restricted to voluntary euthanasia. In itself, this serves as some evidence that permitting it need *not* lead to permitting the nonvoluntary variety. There is some indication, however, that for many Dutch physicians euthanasia is no longer viewed as a special action, set apart from their usual practice and restricted only to competent persons. Instead, it is seen as one end of a spectrum of caring for dying patients. When viewed in this way it will be difficult to deny euthanasia to a patient for whom it is seen as the best or most appropriate form of care simply because that patient is now incompetent and cannot request it.

Even if voluntary active euthanasia should slip into nonvoluntary active euthanasia, with surrogates acting for incompetent patients, the ethical evaluation is more complex than many opponents of euthanasia allow. Just as in the case of surrogates' decision to forgo life-sustaining treatment for incompetent patients, so also surrogates' decisions to request euthanasia for incompetent persons would often accurately reflect what the incompetent person would have wanted and would deny the person nothing that he or she would have considered worth having. Making nonvoluntary active euthanasia legally permissible, however, would greatly enlarge the number of patients on whom it might be performed and substantially enlarge the potential for misuse and abuse. As noted above, frail and debilitated elderly people, often demented or otherwise incompetent and thereby unable to defend and assert their own interests, may be especially vulnerable to unwanted euthanasia.

For some people, this risk is more than sufficient reason to oppose the legalization of voluntary euthanasia. But while we should in general be cautious about inferring much from the experience in the Netherlands to what our own experience in the United States might be, there may be one important lesson that we can learn from them. One commentator has noted that in the Netherlands families of incompetent patients have less authority than do families in the United States to act as surrogates for incompetent patients in making decisions to forgo life-sustaining treatment.[24] From the Dutch perspective, it may be we in the United States who are *already* on the slippery slope in having given surrogates broad authority to forgo life-sustaining treatment for incompetent persons. In this view, the more important moral divide, and the more important with regard to potential for abuse, is not between forgoing life-sustaining treatment and euthanasia, but instead between voluntary and nonvoluntary performance of either. If this is correct, then the more important issue is ensuring the appropriate principles and procedural safeguards for the exercise of decisionmaking authority by surrogates for incompetent persons in *all* decisions at the end of life. This may be the correct response to slippery slope worries about euthanasia.

I have cited both good and bad consequences that have been thought likely from a policy change permitting voluntary active euthanasia, and have tried to evaluate their likelihood and relative importance. Nevertheless, as I noted earlier, reasonable disagreement remains both about the consequences of permitting euthanasia and about which of these consequences are more important. The depth and strength of public and professional debate about whether, all things considered, permitting euthanasia would be desirable or undesirable reflects these disagreements. While my own view is that the balance of considerations supports permitting the practice, my principal purpose here has been to clarify the main issues.

THE ROLE OF PHYSICIANS

If euthanasia is made legally permissible, should physicians take part in it? Should only physicians be permitted to perform it, as is the case in the Netherlands? In discussing whether euthanasia is incompatible with medicine's commitment to curing, caring for, and comforting patients, I argued that it is not at odds with a proper understanding of the aims of medicine, and so need not undermine patients' trust in their physicians. If that argument is correct, then physicians probably should not be prohibited, either by law or by professional norms, from taking part in a legally permissible practice of euthanasia (nor, of course, should they be compelled to do so if their personal or professional scruples forbid it). Most physicians in the Netherlands appear not to understand euthanasia to be incompatible with their professional commitments.

Sometimes patients who would be able to end their lives on their own nevertheless seek the assistance of physicians. Physician involvement in such cases may have important benefits to patients and others beyond simply assuring the use of effective means. Historically, in the United States suicide has carried a strong negative stigma that many today believe unwarranted. Seeking a physician's assistance, or what can almost seem a physician's blessing, may be a way of trying to remove that stigma and show others that the decision for suicide was made with due seriousness and was justified under the circumstances. The physician's involvement provides a kind of social approval, or more accurately helps counter what would otherwise be unwarranted social disapproval.

There are also at least two reasons for restricting the practice of euthanasia to physicians only. First, physicians would inevitably be involved in some of the important procedural safeguards necessary to a defensible practice, such as seeing to it that the patient is well-informed about his or her condition, prognosis, and possible treatments, and ensuring that all reasonable means have been taken to improve the quality of the patient's life. Second, and probably more important, one necessary protection against abuse of the practice is to limit the persons given authority to perform it, so that they can be held accountable for their exercise of that authority. Physicians, whose training and professional norms give some assurance that they would perform euthanasia responsibly, are an appropriate group of persons to whom the practice may be restricted.

ACKNOWLEDGMENTS

Earlier versions of this paper were presented at the American Philosophical Association Central Division meetings (at which David Velleman provided extremely helpful comments), Massachusetts General Hospital, Yale University School of Medicine, Princeton University, Brown University, and as the Brin Lecture at The Johns Hopkins School of Medicine. I am grateful to the audiences on each of these occasions, to several anonymous reviewers, and to Norman Daniels for helpful comments. The paper was completed while I was a Fellow in the Program in Ethics and the Professions at Harvard University.

NOTES

1. President's Commission for the Study of Ethical Problems in Medicine and Biomedical and Behavioral Research, *Deciding to Forego Life-Sustaining Treatment* (Washington, D.C.: U.S. Government Printing Office, 1983); The Hastings Center, *Guidelines on the Termination of Life-Sustaining Treatment and Care of the Dying* (Bloomington: Indiana University Press, 1987); *Current Opinions of the Council on Ethical and Judicial Affairs of the American Medical Association—1989: Withholding or Withdrawing Life-Prolonging Treatment* (Chicago: American Medical Association, 1989); George Annas and Leonard Glantz, "The Right of Elderly Patients to Refuse Life-Sustaining Treatment," *Millbank Memorial Quarterly* 64, suppl. 2 (1986): 95–162; Robert F. Weir, *Abating Treatment with Critically Ill Patients* (New York: Oxford University Press, 1989); Sidney J. Wanzer et al. "The Physician's Responsibility toward Hopelessly Ill Patients," *NEJM* 310 (1984): 955–59.

2. M.A.M. de Wachter, "Active Euthanasia in the Netherlands," *JAMA* 262, no. 23 (1989): 3315–19.

3. Anonymous, "It's Over, Debbie," *JAMA* 259 (1988): 272; Timothy E. Quill, "Death and Dignity," *NEJM* 322 (1990): 1881–83.

4. Wanzer et al., "The Physician's Responsibility toward Hopelessly Ill Patients: A Second Look," *NEJM* 320 (1989): 844–49.

5. Willard Gaylin, Leon R. Kass, Edmund D. Pellegrino, and Mark Siegler, "Doctors Must Not Kill," *JAMA* 259 (1988): 2139–40.

6. Bonnie Steinbock, ed., *Killing and Allowing to Die* (Englewood Cliffs, N.J.: Prentice Hall, 1980).

7. Dan W. Brock, "Forgoing Food and Water: Is It Killing?" in *By No Extraordinary Means: The Choice to Forgo Life-Sustaining Food and Water,* ed. Joanne Lynn (Bloomington: Indiana University Press, 1986), pp. 117–31.

8. James Rachels, "Active and Passive Euthanasia," *NEJM* 292 (1975): 78–80; Michael Tooley, *Abortion and Infanticide* (Oxford: Oxford University Press, 1983). In my paper, "Taking Human Life," *Ethics* 95 (1985): 851–65, I argue in more detail that killing in itself is not morally different from allowing to die and defend the strategy of argument employed in this and the succeeding two paragraphs in the text.

9. Dan W. Brock, "Moral Rights and Permissible Killing," in *Ethical Issues Relating to Life and Death,* ed. John Ladd (New York: Oxford University Press, 1979), pp. 94–117.

10. P. Painton and E. Taylor, "Love or Let Die," *Time,* 19 March 1990, pp. 62–71; *Boston Globe*/Harvard University Poll, *Boston Globe,* 3 November 1991.

11. James Rachels, *The End of Life* (Oxford: Oxford University Press, 1986).

12. Marcia Angell, "The Quality of Mercy," *NEJM* 306 (1982): 98–99; M. Donovan, P. Dillon, and L. Mcguire, "Incidence and Characteristics of Pain in a Sample of Medical-Surgical Inpatients," *Pain* 30 (1987): 69–78.

13. Eric Cassell, *The Nature of Suffering and the Goals of Medicine* (New York: Oxford University Press, 1991).

14. Gaylin et al., "Doctors Must Not Kill."

15. Leon R. Kass, "Neither for Love Nor Money: Why Doctors Must Not Kill," *The Public Interest* 94 (1989): 25–46; cf. also his *Toward a More Natural Science: Biology and Human Affairs* (New York: The Free Press, 1985), chs. 6–9.

16. Paul J. Van der Maas et al., "Euthanasia and Other Medical Decisions Concerning the End of Life," *Lancet* 338 (1991): 669–74.

17. Susan M. Wolf, "Holding the Line on Euthanasia," Special Supplement, *Hastings Center Report* 19, no. 1 (1989): 13–15.

18. My formulation of this argument derives from David Velleman's statement of it in his commentary on an earlier version of this paper delivered at the American Philosophical Association Central Division meetings; a similar point was made to me by Elisha Milgram in discussion on another oc-

casion. For more general development of the point see Thomas Schelling, *The Strategy of Conflict* (Cambridge, Mass.: Harvard University Press, 1960); and Gerald Dworkin, "Is More Choice Better Than Less?" in *The Theory and Practice of Autonomy* (Cambridge: Cambridge University Press, 1988).

19. Frederick Schauer, "Slipper Slopes," *Harvard Law Review* 99 (1985): 361–83; Wibren van der Burg, "The Slippery Slope Argument," *Ethics* 102 (October 1991): 42–65.

20. There is evidence that physicians commonly fail to diagnose depression. See Robert I. Misbin, "Physicians Aid in Dying," *NEJM* 325 (1991): 1304–7.

21. Richard Fenigsen, "A Case against Dutch Euthanasia," Special Supplement, *Hastings Center Report* 19, no. 1 (1989): 22–30.

22. Allen E. Buchanan and Dan W. Brock, *Deciding for Other: The Ethics of Surrogate Decisionmaking* (Cambridge: Cambridge University Press, 1989).

23. Van der Maas et al., "Euthanasia and Other Medical Decisions."

24. Margaret P. Battin, "Seven Caveats Concerning the Discussion of Euthanasia in Holland," *American Philosophical Association Newsletter on Philosophy and Medicine* 89, no. 2 (1990).

Oregon's Ballot Measure 16: The "Death with Dignity Act" (1994)

Editor's Note: On November 8, 1994, the "Death with Dignity Act" (Measure 16) was approved by Oregon voters by a 52 percent to 48 percent vote. It was to have gone into effect on December 8th of that year but was blocked by court action.

Summary

Allows terminally ill adult Oregon residents voluntary informed choice to obtain physician's prescription for drugs to end life. Removes criminal penalties for qualifying physician-assisted suicide. Applies when physicians predict patient's death within 6 months. Requires:

15-day waiting period;

2 oral, 1 written request;

second physician's opinion;

counseling if either physician believes patient has mental disorder, impaired judgment from depression.

Person has choice whether to notify next of kin. Health care providers immune from civil, criminal liability for good faith compliance.

Written Request for Medication to End One's Life in a Humane and Dignified Manner

2.01 *Who May Initiate a Written Request for Medication*

An adult who is capable, is a resident of Oregon, and has been determined by the attending physician and consulting physician to be suffering from a terminal disease, and who has voluntarily expressed his or her wish to die, may make a written request for medication for the purpose of ending his or her life in a humane and dignified manner in accordance with this Act.

2.02 *Form of the Written Request*

(1) A valid request for medication under this Act shall be in substantially the form described in Section 6 of this Act, signed and dated by the patient and witnessed by at least two individuals who, in the presence of the patient, attest that to the best of their knowledge and belief the patient is capable, acting voluntarily, and is not being coerced to sign the request.

(2) One of the witnesses shall be a person who is not:

(a) A relative of the patient by blood, marriage or adoption;

(b) A person who at the time the request is signed would be entitled to any portion of the estate of the qualified patient upon death under any will or by operation of law; or

(c) An owner, operator or employee of a health care facility where the qualified patient is receiving medical treatment or is a resident.

(3) The patient's attending physician at the time the request is signed shall not be a witness.

(4) If the patient is a patient in a long term care facility at the time the written request is made, one of the witnesses shall be an individual designated by the facility and having the qualifications specified by the Department of Human Resources by rule.

Safeguards

3.01 Attending Physician Responsibilities

The attending physician shall:

(1) Make the initial determination of whether a patient has a terminal disease, is capable, and has made the request voluntarily;

(2) Inform the patient of:
   (a) his or her medical diagnosis;
   (b) his or her prognosis;
   (c) the potential risks associated with taking the medication to be prescribed;
   (d) the probable result of taking the medication to be prescribed;
   (e) the feasible alternatives, including, but not limited to, comfort care, hospice care and pain control.

(3) Refer the patient to a consulting physician for medical confirmation of the diagnosis, and for determination that the patient is capable and acting voluntarily;

(4) Refer the patient for counseling if appropriate pursuant to Section 3.03;

(5) Request that the patient notify next of kin;

(6) Inform the patient that he or she has an opportunity to rescind the request at any time and in any manner, and offer the patient an opportunity to rescind at the end of the 15-day waiting period pursuant to Section 3.06;

(7) Verify, immediately prior to writing the prescription for medication under this Act, that the patient is making an informed decision;

(8) Fulfill the medical record documentation requirements of Section 3.09;

(9) Ensure that all appropriate steps are carried out in accordance with this Act prior to writing a prescription for medication to en-

able a qualified patient to end his or her life in a humane and dignified manner.

3.02 Consulting Physician Confirmation

Before a patient is qualified under this Act, a consulting physician shall examine the patient and his or her relevant medical records and confirm, in writing, the attending physician's diagnosis that the patient is suffering from a terminal disease, and verify that the patient is capable, is acting voluntarily, and has made an informed decision.

3.03 Counseling Referral

If in the opinion of the attending physician or the consulting physician a patient may be suffering from a psychiatric or psychological disorder, or depression causing impaired judgment, either physician shall refer the patient for counseling. No medication to end a patient's life in a humane and dignified manner shall be prescribed until the person performing the counseling determines that the person is not suffering from a psychiatric or psychological disorder, or depression causing impaired judgment.

3.04 Informed Decision

No person shall receive a prescription for medication to end his or her life in a humane and dignified manner unless he or she has made an informed decision as defined in Section 1.01(7). Immediately prior to writing a prescription for medication under this Act, the attending physician shall verify that the patient is making an informed decision.

3.05 Family Notification

The attending physician shall ask the patient to notify next of kin of his or her request for medication pursuant to this Act. A patient who declines or is unable to notify next of kin shall not have his or her request denied for that reason.

3.06 Written and Oral Requests

In order to receive a prescription for medication to end his or her life in a humane and dignified manner, a qualified patient shall have made an oral request and a written request, and reiterate the oral request to his or her attending physician no less than fifteen (15) days after making the initial oral request. At the time the qualified patient makes his or her second oral request, the attending physician shall offer the patient an opportunity to rescind the request.

3.07 Right to Rescind Request

A patient may rescind his or her request at any time and in any manner without regard to his or her mental state. No prescription for medication under this Act may be written without the attending physician offering the qualified patient an opportunity to rescind the request.

3.08 Waiting Periods

No less than fifteen (15) days shall elapse between the patient's initial and oral request and the writing of a prescription under this Act. No less than 48 hours shall elapse between the patient's written request and the writing of a prescription under this Act. . . .

3.10 Residency Requirements

Only requests made by Oregon residents, under this Act, shall be granted. . . .

4.01 Immunities

Except as provided in Section 4.02:

(1) No person shall be subject to civil or criminal liability or professional disciplinary action for participating in good faith compliance with this Act. This includes being present when a qualified patient takes the prescribed medication to end his or her life in a humane and dignified manner. . . .

(4) No health care provider shall be under any duty, whether by contract, by statute or by any other legal requirement to participate in the provision to a qualified patient of medication to end his or her life in a humane and dignified manner. If a health care provider is unable or unwilling to carry out a patient's request under this Act, and the patient transfers his or her care to a new health care provider, the prior health care provider shall transfer, upon request, a copy of the patient's relevant medical records to the new health care provider.

Form of the Request

6.01 Form of the request

A request for a medication as authorized by this Act shall be in substantially the following form:

REQUEST FOR MEDICATION TO END MY LIFE IN A HUMANE AND DIGNIFIED MANNER

I, _____, am an adult of sound mind.

I am suffering from _____, which my attending physician has determined is a terminal disease and which has been medically confirmed by a consulting physician.

I have been fully informed of my diagnosis, prognosis, the nature of medication to be prescribed and potential associated risks, the expected result, and the feasible alternatives, including comfort care, hospice care and pain control.

I request that my attending physician prescribe medication that will end my life in a humane and dignified manner.

INITIAL ONE:

_____ I have informed my family of my decision and taken their opinions into consideration.

_____ I have decided not to inform my family of my decision.

_____ I have no family to inform of my decision.

I understand that I have the right to rescind this request at any time.

I understand the full import of this request and I expect to die when I take the medication to be prescribed.

I make this request voluntarily and without reservation, and I accept full moral responsibility for my actions.

Signed: _____

Dated: _____

DECLARATION OF WITNESSES

We declare that the person signing this request:
(a) Is personally known to us or has provided proof of identity;
(b) Signed this request in our presence;

(c) Appears to be of sound mind and not under duress, fraud or undue influence;

(d) Is not a patient for whom either of us is attending physician.

_____
Date   Witness 1/
_____
Date   Witness 2/

Note: One witness shall not be a relative (by blood, marriage or adoption) of the person signing this request, shall not be entitled to any portion of the person's estate upon death and shall not own, operate or be employed at a health care facility where the person is a patient or resident. If the patient is an inpatient at a health care facility, one of the witnesses shall be an individual designated by the facility.

13.
The Case for Euthanasia: Mercy and Autonomy

Margaret Pabst Battin

Margaret Pabst Battin is professor of philosophy and adjunct professor of internal medicine, Division of Medical Ethics, University of Utah. She has written and edited numerous books, among them a study of philosophical issues in suicide, a collection on age-rationing of medical care, a text on professional ethics, and a study of ethical issues in organized religion. In this essay, she argues that the moral values of mercy and autonomy support arguments that establish the moral permissibility of euthanasia. Indeed, Battin argues that in certain circumstances the principle of medical mercy may impose an *obligation* on the physician to help his or her patient achieve a painless death.

INTRODUCTION

Because it arouses questions about the morality of killing, the effectiveness of consent, the duties of physicians, and equity in the distribution of resources, the problem of euthanasia is one of the most acute and uncomfortable contemporary problems in medical ethics. It is not a new problem; euthanasia has been discussed—and practiced—in both Eastern and Western cultures from the earliest historical times to the present. But because of medicine's new technological capacities to extend life, the problem is much more pressing than it has been in the past, and both the discussion and practice of euthanasia are more widespread. Despite this, much of contemporary Western culture remains strongly opposed to euthanasia: doctors ought not kill people, its public voices maintain, and ought not let them die if it is possible to save life.

I believe that this opposition to euthanasia is in serious moral error—on grounds of mercy, autonomy, and justice. I shall argue for the rightness of granting a person a humane, merciful death, if he or she wants it, even when this can be achieved only by a direct and deliberate killing. . . .

THE ARGUMENT FROM MERCY

The principle of mercy asserts that *where possible, one ought to relieve the pain or suffering of another person, when it does not contravene that person's wishes, where one can do so without undue costs to oneself, where one will not violate other moral obligations, where the pain or suffering itself is not necessary for the sufferer's attainment of some overriding good, and where the pain or suffering can be relieved without precluding the sufferer's attain-*

ment of some overriding good.[1] This principle might best be called the principle of medical mercy, to distinguish it from principles concerning mercy in judicial contexts.[2] Stated in this relatively weak form and limited by these provisos, the principle of (medical) mercy is not controversial, though the point I wish to argue here certainly is: contexts that require mercy sometimes require euthanasia as a way of granting mercy— both by direct killing and by letting die.

Although philosophers do not agree on whether moral agents have positive duties of beneficence, including duties to those in pain, members of the medical world are not reticent about asserting them. "Relief of pain is the least disputed and most universal of the moral obligations of the physician," writes one doctor. "Few things a doctor does are more important than relieving pain," says another.[3] These are not simply assertions that the physician ought "do no harm," as the Hippocratic oath is traditionally interpreted, but assertions of positive obligation. It might be argued that the physician's duty of mercy derives from a special contractual or fiduciary relationship with the patient, but I think that this is in error: rather, the duty of (medical) mercy is generally binding on all moral agents[4] and it is only by virtue of their more frequent exposure to pain and their specialized training in its treatment that this duty falls more heavily on physicians and nurses than on others. Hence, though we may call it the principle of "medical" mercy, it asserts an obligation that we all have.

This principle of mercy establishes two component duties:

1. the duty not to cause further pain or suffering; and
2. the duty to act to end pain or suffering already occurring.

Under the first of these, for a physician or other caregiver to extend mercy to a suffering patient may mean to refrain from procedures that cause further suffering—provided, of course, that the treatment offers the patient no

overriding benefits. So, for instance, the physician must refrain from ordering painful tests, therapies, or surgical procedures when they cannot alleviate suffering or contribute to a patient's improvement or cure. Perhaps the most familiar contemporary medical example is the treatment of burn victims when survival is unprecedented; if with the treatments or without them the patient's chance of survival is nil, mercy requires the physician not to impose the debridement treatments, which are excruciatingly painful, when they can provide the patient no benefit at all.

Although the demands of mercy in burn contexts have become fairly well recognized in recent years,[5] other practices that the principles of mercy would rule out remain common. For instance, repeated cardiac resuscitation is sometimes performed even though a patient's survival is highly unlikely; although patients in arrest are unconscious at the time of resuscitation, it can be a brutal procedure, and if the patient regains consciousness, its aftermath can involve considerable pain. (On the contrary, of course, attempts at resuscitation would indeed be permitted under the principle of mercy if there were some chance of survival with good recovery, as in hypothermia or electrocution.) Patients are sometimes subjected to continued unproductive, painful treatment to complete a research protocol, to train student physicians, to protect the physician or hospital from legal action, or to appease the emotional needs of family members; although in some specific cases such practices may be justified on other grounds, in general they are prohibited by the principle of mercy. Of course, whether a painful test or therapy will actually contribute to some overriding good for the patient is not always clear. Nevertheless, the principle of mercy directs that where such procedures can reasonably be expected to impose suffering on the patient without overriding benefits for him or her, they ought not be done.

In many such cases, the patient will die whether or not the treatments are performed.

In some cases, however, the principle of mercy, may also demand withholding treatment that could extend the patient's life if the treatment is itself painful or discomforting and there is very little or no possibility that it will provide life that is pain-free or offers the possibility of other important goods. For instance, to provide respiratory support for a patient in the final, irreversible stages of a deteriorative disease may extend his life but will mean permanent dependence and incapacitation; though some patients may take continuing existence to make possible other important goods, for some patients continued treatment means the pointless imposition of continuing pain. "Death," whispered Abe Perlmutter, the Florida ALS victim who pursued through the courts his wish to have the tracheotomy tube connecting him to a respirator removed, "can't be any worse than what I'm going through now."[6] In such cases, the principle of mercy demands that the "treatments" no longer be imposed, and that the patient be allowed to die.

But the principle of mercy may also demand "letting die" in a still stronger sense. Under its second component, the principle asserts a duty to act to end suffering that is already occurring. Medicine already honors this duty through its various techniques of pain management, including physiological means like narcotics, nerve blocks, acupuncture, and neurosurgery, and psychotherapeutic means like self-hypnosis, conditioning, and good old-fashioned comforting care. But there are some difficult cases in which pain or suffering is severe but cannot be effectively controlled, at least as long as the patient remains sentient at all. Classical examples include tumors of the throat (where agonizing discomfort is not just a matter of pain but of inability to swallow, "air hunger," or acute shortness of breath), tumors of the brain or bone, and so on. Severe nausea, vomiting, and exhaustion may increase the patient's misery. In these cases, continuing life—or at least continuing consciousness—may mean continuing pain. Consequently, mercy's demand for euthanasia takes

hold here: mercy demands that the pain, even if with it the life, be brought to an end.

Ending the pain, though with it the life, may be accomplished through what is usually called "passive euthanasia," withholding or withdrawing treatment that could prolong life. In the most indirect of these cases, the patient is simply not given treatment that might extend his or her life—say, radiation therapy in advanced cancer. In the more direct cases, life-saving treatments deliberately withheld in the face of an immediate, lethal threat—for instance, antibiotics are withheld from a cancer patient when an overwhelming infection develops, since though either the cancer or the infection will kill the patient, the infection does so sooner and in a much gentler way. In all of the passive euthanasia cases, properly so called, the patient's life could be extended; it is mercy that demands that he or she be "allowed to die."

But the second component of the principle of mercy may also demand the easing of pain by means more direct than mere allowing to die; it may require *killing*. This is usually called "active euthanasia," and despite borderline cases (for instance, the ancient Greek practice of infanticide by exposure), it can in general be conceptually distinguished from passive euthanasia. In passive euthanasia, treatment is withheld that could support failing bodily functions, either in warding off external threats or in performing its own processes; active euthanasia, in contrast, involves the direct interruption of ongoing bodily processes that otherwise would have been adequate to sustain life. However, although it may be possible to draw a conceptual distinction between passive and active euthanasia, this provides no warrant for the ubiquitous view that killing is morally worse than letting die.[7] Nor does it support the view that withdrawing treatment is worse than withholding it. If the patient's condition is so tragic that continuing life brings only pain, and there is no other way to relieve the pain than by death, then the more merciful act is not one that merely removes support for bodily processes and waits for eventual death to ensue; rather, it is one that brings the pain—and the patient's life—to an end *now*. If there are grounds on which it is merciful not to prolong life, then there are also grounds on which it is merciful to terminate it at once. The easy overdose, the lethal injection (successors to the hemlock used for this purpose by non-Hippocratic physicians in ancient Greece[8]), are what mercy demands when no other means will bring relief.

But, it may be objected, the cases we have mentioned to illustrate intolerable pain are classical ones; such cases are controllable now. Pain is a thing of the medical past, and euthanasia is no longer necessary, though it once may have been, to relieve pain. Given modern medical technology and recent remarkable advances in pain management, the sufferings of the mortally wounded and dying can be relieved by less dramatic means. For instance, many once-feared, painful diseases—tetanus, rabies, leprosy, tuberculosis—are now preventable or treatable. Improvements in battlefield first-aid and transport of the wounded have been so great that the military *coup de grâce* is now officially obsolete. We no longer speak of "mortal agony" and "death throes" as the probable last scenes of life. Particularly impressive are the huge advances under the hospice program in the amelioration of both the physical and emotional pain of terminal illness,[9] and our culturewide fears of pain in terminal cancer are no longer justified: cancer pain, when it occurs, can now be controlled in virtually all cases. We can now end the pain without also ending the life.

This is a powerful objection, and one very frequently heard in medical circles. Nevertheless, it does not succeed. It is flatly incorrect to say that all pain, including pain in terminal illness, is or can be controlled. Some people still die in unspeakable agony. With superlative care, many kinds of pain can indeed be reduced in many patients, and adequate control of pain in terminal illness is often quite easy to achieve. Nevertheless, complete, universal, fully reliable pain control is a myth. Pain is not yet a "thing

of the past," nor are many associated kinds of physical distress. Some kinds of conditions, such as difficulty in swallowing, are still difficult to relieve without introducing other discomforting limitations. Some kinds of pain are resistant to medication, as in elevated intracranial pressure or bone metastases and fractures. For some patients, narcotic drugs are dysphoric. Pain and distress may be increased by nausea, vomiting, itching, constipation, dry mouth, abscesses and decubitus ulcers that do not heal, weakness, breathing difficulties and offensive smells. Severe respiratory insufficiency may mean—as Joanne Lynn describes it—"a singularly terrifying and agonizing final few hours."[10] Even a patient receiving the most advanced and sympathetic medical attention may still experience episodes of pain, perhaps alternating with unconsciousness, as his or her condition deteriorates and the physician attempts to adjust schedules and dosages of pain medication. Many dying patients, including half of all terminal cancer patients, have little or no pain,[11] but there are still cases in which pain management is difficult and erratic. Finally, there are cases in which pain control is theoretically possible but for various extraneous reasons does not occur. Some deaths take place in remote locations where there are no pain-relieving resources. Some patients are unable to communicate the nature or extent of their pain. And some institutions and institutional personnel who have the capacity to control pain do not do so, whether from inattention, malevolence, fears of addiction, or divergent priorities in resources.

In all these cases, of course, the patient can be sedated into unconsciousness; this does indeed end the pain. But in respect of the patient's experience, this is tantamount to causing death: the patient has no further conscious experience and thus can achieve no goods, experience no significant communication, satisfy no goals. Furthermore, adequate sedation, by depressing respiratory function, may hasten death. Thus, though it is always technically possible to achieve relief from pain, at least when the appropriate resources are available, the price may be functionally and practically equivalent, at least from the patient's point of view, to death. And this, of course, is just what the issue of euthanasia is about.

Of course, to see what the issue is about is not yet to reach its resolution, or to explain why attitudes about this issue are so starkly divergent. Rather, we must examine the logic of the argument for euthanasia and observe in particular how the principle of mercy functions in the overall case. The canon "One ought to act to end suffering," the second of the abstract duties generated by the principle of mercy, can be traced to the more general principle of beneficence. But its application in a given case also involves a minor premise that is ostensive in character: it points to an alleged case of suffering. This person is suffering, the applied argument from mercy holds, in a way that lays claim on us for help in relieving that pain.

It may be difficult to appreciate the force of this argument if its character is not adequately recognized. By asserting the abstract duty of mercy and pointing to specific occasions of pain, the argument generates the conclusion that we ought not let these cases of pain occur: not only ought we prevent them from occurring if we can, but also we ought to bring them to an end if they do. In practice, most arguments for euthanasia on grounds of mercy are pursued by the graphic evocation of cases: the tortures suffered by victims of awful diseases.

But this argument strategy is problematic. The evocation of cases may be very powerful, but it is also subject to a certain unreliability. After all, pain is, in general, not well remembered by those not currently suffering it, and though bystanders may be capable of very great sympathy, no person can actually feel another's pain. Suffering that does not involve pain may be even harder for the bystander to assess. Conversely, however, bystanders sometimes seem to suffer more than the patient: pain, particularly in those for whom one has strong emotional attachments, is notoriously difficult to

watch. Furthermore, sensitivity on the part of others to pain and suffering is very much subject to individual differences in experience with pain, beliefs concerning the purpose of suffering and pain, fears about pain, and physical sensitivity to painful stimuli. Yet there is no objective way to establish how seriously the ostensive premise of the argument from mercy should be taken in any specific case, or how one should respond. Clearly, such a premise can be taken too seriously—so that concern for another's pain or suffering outweighs all other considerations—or one can be far too cavalier about the facts. To break a promise to a patient—say, not to intubate him—because you perceive that he is in pain may be to overreact to his suffering. However, it is morally repugnant to stand by and watch another person suffer when one could prevent it; and it is a moral failing too to be insensitive, when there is no overriding reason for doing so, to the fact that another person is in pain.

The principle of mercy holds that suffering ought to be relieved—unless, among other provisos, the suffering itself will give rise to some overriding benefit or unless the attainment of some benefit would be precluded by relieving the pain. But it might be argued that life itself is a benefit, always an overriding one. Certainly life is usually a benefit, one that we prize. But unless we accept certain metaphysical assumptions, such as "life is a gift from God," we must recognize that life is a benefit because of the experiences and interests associated with it. For the most part, we prize these, but when they are unrelievedly negative, life is not a benefit after all. Philippa Foot treats this as a conceptual point: "Ordinary human lives, even very hard lives, contain a minimum of basic goods, but when these are absent the idea of life is no longer linked to that of good."[12]

Such basic goods, she explains, include not being forced to work far beyond one's capacity; having the support of a family or community; being able to more or less satisfy one's hunger; having hopes for the future; and being able to lie down to rest at night. When these goods are missing, she asserts, the connection between *life* and *good* is broken, and we cannot count it as a benefit to the person whose life it is that his life is preserved.

These basic goods may all be severely compromised or entirely absent in the severely ill or dying patient. He or she may be isolated from family or community, perhaps by virtue of institutionalization or for various other reasons; he or she may be unable to eat, to have hopes for the future, or even to sleep undisturbed at night. Yet even for someone lacking all of what Foot considers to be basic goods, the experiences associated with life may not be unrelievedly negative. We must be very cautious in asserting of someone, even someone in the most abysmal-seeming conditions of the severely ill or dying, that life is no longer a benefit, since the way in which particular experiences, interests, and "basic goods" are valued may vary widely from one person to the next. Whether a given set of experiences constitutes a life that is a benefit to the person whose life it is is not a matter for *objective* determination, though there may be very good external clues to the way in which that person is in fact valuing them. It is, in the end, very much a function of subjective preference and choice. For some persons, life may be of value even in the grimmest conditions, for others, not. The crucial point is this: when a suffering person is conscious enough to have any experience at all, whether that experience counts as a benefit overriding the suffering or not is relative to that person and can be decided ultimately only by him or her.[13]

If this is so, then we can no longer assume that the cases in which euthanasia is indicated on grounds of mercy are infrequent or rare. It is true that contemporary pain management techniques do make possible the control of pain to a considerable degree. But unless pain and discomforting symptoms are eliminated altogether without loss of function, the underlying problem for the principle of mercy remains: how does *this* patient value life, how does he or she weigh death against pain? We are accustomed to assume that only patients suffering extreme, irremediable pain could be candidates for euthanasia at all and do not consider whether some patients might choose death in preference to comparatively moderate chronic pain, even when the condition is not a terminal one. Of course, a patient's perceptions of pain are extremely subject to stress, anxiety, fear, exhaustion, and other factors, but even though these perceptions may vary, the underlying weighing still demands respect. This is not just a matter of differing sensitivities to pain, but of differing values as well: for some patients, severe pain may be accepted with resignation or even pious joy, whereas for others mild or moderate discomfort is simply not worth enduring. Yet, without appeal to religious beliefs about the spiritual value of suffering, we have no objective way to determine how much pain a person *ought* to stand. Consequently, we cannot assume that euthanasia is justified, if at all, in only the most severe cases. Thus, the issue of euthanasia looms larger, rather than smaller, in the contemporary medical world.

That we cannot objectively determine whether life is a benefit to a person or whether pain outweighs its value might seem to undermine all possibility of appeal to the principle of mercy. But I think it does not. Rather, it shows simply that the issue is more complex, and that we must recognize that the principle of mercy itself demands recognition of a second fundamental principle relevant in euthanasia cases: the principle of autonomy. If the sufferer is the best judge of the relative values of that suffering and other benefits to himself, then his own choices in the matter of mercy ought to be respected. To impose "mercy" on someone who insists that despite his suffering life is still valuable to him would hardly be mercy; to withhold mercy from someone who pleads for it, on the basis that his life could still be worthwhile for him, is insensitive and cruel. Thus, the principle of mercy is conceptually tied to that of autonomy, at least insofar as what guarantees the best application of the principle—and hence, what guarantees the proper response to the ostensive premise in the argument from mercy—is respect for the patient's own wishes concerning the relief of his suffering or pain.

To this issue we now turn.

THE ARGUMENT FROM AUTONOMY

The second principle supporting euthanasia is that of (patient) autonomy: *one ought to respect a competent person's choices, where one can do so without undue costs to oneself, where doing so will not violate other moral obligations, and where these choices do not threaten harm to other persons or parties.* This principle of autonomy, though limited by these provisos, grounds a person's right to have his or her own choices respected in determining the course of medical treatment, including those relevant to euthanasia: whether the patient wishes treatment that will extend life, though perhaps also suffering, or whether he or she wants the suffering relieved, either by being killed or by being allowed to die. It would of course also require respect for the choices of the person whose condition is chronic but not terminal, the person who is disabled though not dying, and the person not yet suffering at all, but facing senility or old age. Indeed, the principle of autonomy would require respect for self-determination in the matter of life and death in any condition at all, provided that the choice is freely and rationally made and does not harm others or violate other moral rules. Thus, the principle of autonomy would protect a much wider range of life-and-death acts than those we call euthanasia, as well as those performed for reasons of mercy.

Support for patient autonomy in matters of life and death is partially reflected in U.S. law, in which a patient's right to passive voluntary euthanasia (though it is not called by this name) is established in a long series of cases. In 1914, in the case *Schloendorff v. New York Hospital*,[14] Justice Cardozo asserted that "every human being of adult years and sound mind has a right

to determine what shall be done with his own body" and held that the plaintiff, who had been treated against his will, had the right to refuse treatment; more recent cases, including *Yetter*,[15] *Perlmutter*,[16] and *Bartling*,[17] establish that the competent adult has the right to refuse medical treatment, on religious or personal grounds, even if it means he or she will die. (Exceptions include some persons with dependents and persons who suffer from communicable diseases that pose a risk to the public at large.) Furthermore, the patient has the right to refuse a component of a course of treatment, even though he or she consents to others; this is established in the Jehovah's Witnesses cases in which patients refused blood transfusions but accepted surgery and other care. In many states, the law also recognizes passive voluntary euthanasia of the no longer competent adult who has signed a refusal-of-treatment document while still competent; such documents, called "natural death directives" or "living wills," protect the physician from legal action for failure to treat if he or she follows the patient's antecedent request to be allowed to die. (By 1985, 35 states and the District of Columbia had enacted such laws.) Additionally, the "durable power of attorney" permits a person to designate a relative, friend, or other person to make treatment decisions on his or her behalf after he or she is no longer competent; these may include decisions to refuse life sustaining treatment. Many hospitals have adopted policies permitting the writing of orders not to resuscitate, or "no code" orders, which stipulate that no attempt is to be made to revive a patient following a cardiorespiratory arrest. These policies typically are stated to require that such orders be issued only with the concurrence of the patient, if competent, or the patient's family or legal guardian. In theory at least, living wills, no-code orders, durable powers of attorney, and similar devices are designed to protect the patient's voluntary choice to refuse life-prolonging treatment.

These legal mechanisms for refusal of treatment all protect individual autonomy in matters of euthanasia: the right to choose to live or to die. But it is crucial to see that they all protect only passive euthanasia, not any more active form. The Natural Death Act of California, like similar legislation in other states, expressly states that "nothing in this Act shall be construed to condone, authorize, or approve mercy killing."[18] Likewise, the living will directs only the withholding or cessation of treatment, in the absence of which the patient will die.[19] A durable power of attorney permits the same choices on behalf of the patient by a designated second party. These legal mechanisms are sometimes said to protect the "right to die," but it is important to see that this is only the right to be *allowed* to die, not to be helped to die or to have death actively brought about. However, we have already seen that allowing to die is sometimes less merciful than direct, humane killing: the principle of mercy demands the right to be killed, as well as to be allowed to die. Thus, the protections offered by the legal mechanisms now available may be seen as truncated conclusions from the principle of patient autonomy that supports them; this principle should protect not only the patient's choice of refusal of treatment but also a choice of a more active means of death.

It is often objected that autonomy in euthanasia choices should not be recognized in practice, whether or not it is accepted in principle, because such choices are often erroneously made. One version of this argument points to physician error. Physicians make mistakes, it holds, and since medicine in any case is not a rigorous science, predictions of oncoming, painful death with no possibility of cure are never wholly reliable. People diagnosed as dying rapidly of inexorable cancers have survived, cancer-free, for dozens of years; people in cardiac failure or long-term irreversible coma have revived and regained full health. Although some of this can be attributed simply to physician error, we must also guard against the more pernicious phenomenon of the "hanging of crepe," in which the physician (usually not

intentionally) delivers a prognosis dimmer than is actually warranted by the facts. If the patient succumbs, the physician cannot be blamed, since that is what was predicted; but if the patient survives, the physician is credited with the cure.[20] Other factors interfering with the accuracy of a diagnosis or prognosis include impatience on the part of a physician with a patient who is not doing well, difficulties in accurately estimating future complications, ignorance of a treatment or cure that is about to be discovered or is on the way, and a host of additional factors arising when the physician is emotionally involved, inexperienced, uninformed, or incompetent.[21]

A second argument pointing to the possibility of erroneous choice on the part of the patient asserts the very great likelihood of impairment of the patient's mental processes when seriously ill. Impairing factors include depression, anxiety, pain, fear, intimidation by authoritarian physicians or institutions, and drugs used in medical treatment that affect mental status. Perhaps a person in good health would be capable of calm, objective judgment even in such serious matters as euthanasia, so this view holds, but the person as patient is not. Depression, extremely common in terminal illness, is a particular culprit: it tends to narrow one's view of the possibilities still open; it may make recovery look impossible, it may screen off the possibilities, even without recovery, of significant human relationships and important human experience in the time that is left.[22] A choice of euthanasia in terminal illness, this view holds, probably reflects largely the gloominess of the depression, not the gravity of the underlying disease or any genuine intention to die.

If this is so, ought not the euthanasia request of a patient be ignored for his or her own sake? According to a limited paternalist view (sometimes called "soft" or "weak" paternalism), intervention in a person's choices for his or her own sake is justified if the person's thinking is impaired. Under this principle, not every euthanasia request should be honored;

such requests should be construed, rather, as pleas for more sensitive physical and emotional care.

It is no doubt true that many requests to die are pleas for better care or improved conditions of life. But this still does not establish that all euthanasia requests should be ignored, because the principle of paternalism licenses intervention in a person's choices just *for his or her own good.* Sometimes the choice of euthanasia, though made in an impaired, irrational way, may seem to serve the person's own good better than remaining alive. Thus, since the paternalist, in intervening, must act for the sake of the person in whose liberty he or she interferes, the paternalist must take into account not only the costs for the person of failing to interfere with a euthanasia decision when euthanasia was not warranted (the cost is death, when death was not in this person's interests) but also the costs for that person of interfering in a decision that was warranted (the cost is continuing life—and continuing suffering—when death would have been the better choice).[23] The likelihood of these two undesirable outcomes must then be weighed. To claim that "there's always hope" or to insist that "the diagnosis could be wrong" in a morally responsible way, one must weigh not only the cost of unnecessary death to the patient but also the costs to the patient of dying in agony if the diagnosis is right and the cure does not materialize. But cases in which the diagnosis is right and the cure does not materialize are, unfortunately, much more frequent than cases in which the cure arrives or the diagnosis is wrong. The "there's always hope" argument, used to dissuade a person from choosing euthanasia, is morally irresponsible unless there is some quite good reason to think there actually *is* hope. Of course, the "diagnosis could be wrong" argument against euthanasia is a good one in areas or specialties in which diagnoses are frequently inaccurate (the chief of one neurology service admitted that on initial diagnoses "we get it right about 50 percent of the time"), or where there is a systematic bias in favor of unduly grim prog-

noses—but it is not a good argument against euthanasia in general. Similarly, "a miracle cure may be developed tomorrow" is also almost always irresponsible. The paternalist who attempts to interfere with a patient's choice of euthanasia must weigh the enormous suffering of those to whom unrealistic hopes are held out against the benefits to those very few whose lives are saved in this way.

As limited paternalism, extended "strong" or "hard" paternalism—permitting intervention not merely to counteract impairment but also to avoid great harm—provides a special case when applied to euthanasia situations. The hard paternalist may be tempted to argue that because death is the greatest of harms, euthanasia choices must always be thwarted. But the initial premise of this argument is precisely what is at issue in the euthanasia dispute itself, as we've seen: is death the worst of harms that can befall a person, or is unrelieved, hopeless suffering a still worse harm? The principle of mercy obliges us to relieve suffering when it does not serve some overriding good; but the principle itself cannot tell us whether sheer existence—life—is an overriding good. In the absence of an objectively valid answer, we must appeal to the individual's own preferences and values. Which is the greater evil—death or pain? Some persons may adopt religious answers to this question, others may devise their own; but the answer always is tied to the person whose life it is, and cannot be supplied in any objective way. Hence, unless he or she can discover what the suffering person's preferences and values are, the hard paternalist cannot determine whether intervening to prolong life or to terminate it will count as acting for that person's sake.

Of course, there are limits to such a claim. When there is no evidence of suffering or pain, mental or physical, and no evidence of factors like depression, psychoactive drugs, or affect-altering disease that might impair cognitive functioning, an external observer usually can accurately determine whether life is a benefit: unless the person has an overriding commitment to a principle or cause that requires sacrifice of that life, life *is* a benefit to him or her. (But such a person, of course, is probably not a patient.) Conversely, when there is every evidence of pain and little or no evidence of factors that might outweigh the pain, such as cognitive capacities that might give rise to other valuable experience, then an external observer generally can also accurately determine the value of this person's life: it is a disbenefit, a burden, to him. (Given pain and complete cognitive incapacity, such a person is almost always a patient.) It is when both pain and cognitive capacities are found that the person-relative character of the value of life becomes most apparent, and most demanding of respect.

Thus, if we view the spectrum of persons from fully healthy through severely ill to decerebrate or brain-dead, we may assert that the principle of autonomy operates most strongly at the middle of this range. The more severe a person's pain and suffering, when his or her condition is not so diminished as to preclude cognitive capacities altogether, the stronger the respect we must accord his or her own view of whether life is a benefit or not. At both ends of the scale, however, paternalistic considerations come into play: if the person is healthy and without pain, we will interfere to keep him or her alive (preventing, for instance, suicide attempts); if his or her life means only pain, we act for the person's sake by causing him or her to die (as we should for certain severely defective neonates). But when the patient retains cognitive capacities, the greater is his or her suffering, and the more his or her choices concerning it deserve our respect. When the choice that is faced is death or pain, it is the patient who must choose which is worse.

We saw earlier that in euthanasia issues the principle of mercy is conceptually tied to the principle of autonomy, at least for its exercise; we now see that the principle of autonomy is dependent on the principle of mercy in certain sorts of cases. It is *not* dependent in this way, however, in those cases most likely to generate euthanasia requests. That someone voluntarily and knowingly requests release from what he or she experiences as misery is sufficient, other things being equal, for the request to be honored; although this request is rooted in the patient's desire for mercy, we cannot insist on independent, objective evidence that mercy would in fact be served, or that death is better than pain. We can demand such evidence to protect a perfectly healthy person, and we can summon it to end the sufferings of someone who can no longer choose; but we cannot demand it or use it for the seriously ill person in pain. To claim that an incessantly pain-racked but conscious person cannot make a rational choice in matters of life and death is to misconstrue the point: he or she, better than anyone else, can make such a choice, based on intimate acquaintance with pain and his or her own beliefs and fears about death. If the patient wishes to live, despite such suffering, he or she must be allowed to do so; or the patient must be granted help if he or she wishes to die.

But this introduces a further problem. The principle of autonomy, when there are no countervailing considerations on paternalistic grounds or on grounds of harm to others, supports the practice of voluntary euthanasia and, in fact, any form of rational, voluntary suicide. We already recognize a patient's right to refuse any or all medical treatment and hence correlative duties of noninterference on the part of the physician to refrain from treating the patient against his or her will. But does the patient's right of self-determination also give rise to any positive obligation on the part of the physician or other bystander to actively produce death? Pope John Paul II asserts that "no one may ask to be killed";[24] Peter Williams argues that a person does not have a right to be killed even though to kill him might be humane.[25] But I think that both the Pope and Williams are wrong. Although we usually recognize only that the principle of autonomy generates rights to noninterference, in some circumstances a right of self-determination does generate claims to assistance or to the provision of goods.

We typically acknowledge this in cases of handicap or disability. For instance, the right of a person to seek an education ordinarily generates on the part of others only an obligation not to interfere with his or her attendance at the university, provided the person meets its standards; but the same right on the part of a person with a severe physical handicap may generate an obligation on the part of others to provide transportation, assist in acquiring textbooks, or provide interpretive services. The infant, incapable of earning or acquiring its own nourishment, has a right to be fed. There is a good deal of philosophic dispute about such claims, and public policies vary from one administration and court to the next. But if, in a situation of handicap or disability, a right to self-determination can generate claim rights (rights to be aided) as well as noninterference rights, the consequences for euthanasia practices are far-reaching indeed. Some singularly sympathetic cases—like that of the completely paralyzed cerebral palsy victim Elizabeth Bouvier—have brought this issue to public attention. But notice that in euthanasia situations, most persons are handicapped with respect to producing for themselves an easy, "good," merciful death. The handicaps are occasionally physical, but most often involve lack of knowledge of how to bring this about and lack of access to means for so doing. If a patient chooses to refuse treatment and so die, he or she still may not know what components of the treatment to refuse in order to produce an easy rather than painful death; if the person chooses death by active means, he or she may not know what drugs or other methods would be appropriate, in what dosages, and in any case he or she may be unable to obtain them. Yet full autonomy is not achieved until one can both choose and act upon one's choices. It is here, in these cases of "handicap" that afflict many or most patients, that rights to self-determination may generate obligations on the part of physicians (provided, perhaps, that they do not have principled objections to participation in such activities themselves[26]). The physi-

cian's obligation is not only to respect the patient's choices but also to make it possible for the patient to act upon his or her choices. This means supplying the knowledge and equipment to enable the person to stay alive, if he or she so chooses; this is an obligation physicians now recognize. But it may also mean providing the knowledge, equipment, and help to enable the patient to die, if that is his or her choice; this is the other part of the physician's obligation, not yet recognized by the medical profession or the law in the United States.[27]

This is not to say that any doctor should be forced to kill any person who asks that: other contravening considerations—particularly that of ascertaining that the request is autonomous and not the product of coerced or irrational choice, and that of controlling abuses by unscrupulous physicians, relatives, or patients—would quickly override. Nor would the physician have an obligation to assist in "euthanasia" for someone not severely ill. But when the physician is sufficiently familiar with the patient to know the seriousness of the condition and the earnestness of the patient's request, when the patient is sufficiently helpless, and when there are no adequate objections on grounds of personal scruples or social welfare, then the principle of autonomy—like the principle of mercy—imposes on the physician the obligation to help the patient in achieving an easy, painless death. . . .

NOTES

I'd like to thank Arthur G. Lipman, Pharm. D., and Howard Wilcox, M.D., as well as my colleagues in philosophy, Bruce Landesman and Leslie Francis, for comments on earlier drafts of this chapter.

1. Perhaps the principle of (medical) mercy is stronger than this and asserts a duty to relieve the suffering of others even at some substantial cost to oneself, or in violation of others of these provisos. The quite weak form of the principle, as I have stated it here, requires, for instance, that one ought not stand idly by (all other things being equal) when one could easily help an injured person but does not require feats of physical or financial heroism or self-sacrifice. This is not to say that I think a stronger version of the duty to re-

lieve suffering (as defended, for instance, by Susan James, "The Duty to Relieve Suffering," *Ethics* [October 1982] 93:4–21), could not be supported, but that the stronger version is not necessary for the case I am making here: a prima facie duty to participate in both passive and active euthanasia, at least in a more permissive legal climate, is entailed even by the very weak form of the principle of mercy.

Incidentally, although much of the medical literature distinguishes between pain and suffering, I have not chosen to do so here: it would raise difficult mind/body problems, and in any case the two are clearly intertwined. I grant, however, that the principle of (medical) mercy would meet still broader assent if phrased to require the relieving of physical pain alone.

2. It is important not to confuse the principle of (medical) mercy with a principle permitting or requiring judicial mercy. In judicial and political contexts, such as pardons or amnesties, the individual on whom penalties have been or are about to be imposed may have no claim to benevolent treatment, and the issue concerns whether mercy may or should be granted. Many authors treat judicial mercy as a work of individual supererogation, not a requirement or duty, and some suggest that it is morally forbidden: one ought not excuse a person guilty of a crime. However, we are concerned here not with judicial mercy, but rather with mercy as it arises primarily in medical contexts: injuries, illnesses, disabilities, degenerative processes, and genetic defect or disease. Unlike pain or suffering inflicted in judicial contexts, in the medical context these are not warranted by the past actions of the suffering individual, but are usually of natural or accidental origin and in most cases are beyond the individual's control: pain and suffering are something that happen to him or her, not something the patient has earned. The principle of medical mercy is usually taken to apply even in cases in which a medical condition is caused or exacerbated by the individual's voluntary behavior, as in smokers' diseases or injuries from attempted suicide. It is consistent to hold that mercy is supererogatory (or perhaps morally forbidden) in judicial or political contexts, but also that it is required in medical ones.

3. Edmund D. Pellegrino, M.D., "The Clinical Ethics of Pain Management in the Terminally Ill," *Hospital Formulary* 17 (November 1982): 1495–96; and Marcia Angell, "The Quality of Mercy," *New England Journal of Medicine* 306 (January 1982): 98–99.

4. For instance, I take it to be a moral duty, and not merely a nice thing to do, to help a child remove a painful splinter from a finger when the child cannot do so alone and when this can be done without undue costs to oneself. (I assume that the splinter case satisfies the other provisos of the principle of medical mercy.) Similarly, I take it to be a moral duty to stop the bleeding of a person who has been wounded or to pull someone from a fire, though in very many of the cases in which such circumstance arise (wars, accidents) this duty is abrogated because we cannot do so without risks to

ourselves. The duty of medical mercy is not simply equivalent to either nonmaleficence or beneficence, though perhaps derived from them, since the former is understood as a duty to refrain from causing harm and the latter to do good in a positive sense; the duty of medical mercy requires one to counteract harms one did not cause, though it may not require conferring additional positive benefits.

5. See Sharon H. Imbus and Bruce E. Zawacki, "Autonomy for Burned Patients When Survival Is Unprecedented," *New England Journal of Medicine* 297 (August 11, 1977): 309–311.

6. See Mary Voboril, *Miami Herald,* Saturday, July 1, 1978; see also note 17.

7. An extensive discussion of the conceptual and moral distinctions between killing and letting die begins with Jonathan Bennett, "Whatever the Consequences," *Analysis* 26 (1966): 83–97, and, after the American Medical Association's stand prohibiting mercy killing but permitting cessation of treatment, continues in James Rachels's "Active and Passive Euthanasia," *New England Journal of Medicine* 292 (January 9, 1975): 78–80, and many subsequent papers.

8. See Ludwig Edelstein, "The Hippocratic Oath," in *Ancient Medicine: Selected Papers of Ludwig Edelstein*, ed. Owsei Temkin and C. Lilian Temkin (Baltimore: The Johns Hopkins University Press, 1967), esp. 9–15, on the Greek physician's role in euthanasia.

9. Hospice, founded and directed by Cicely Saunders, is a movement devoted to the development of institutions for providing palliative but medically nonaggressive care for terminal patients. In addition to its extraordinary contribution in developing methods of prophylactic pain control, according to which analgesics are administered on a scheduled basis in advance of experienced pain, Hospice has also emphasized attention to the emotional needs of the patient's family. An account of the theory and methodology of Hospice can be found in various publications by Saunders, including "Terminal Care of Medical Oncology," in *Medical Oncology*, ed. K. D. Bagshawe (Oxford: Blackwell, 1975), 563–576.

10. Joanne Lynn, M.D., "Supportive Care for Dying Patients: An Introduction for Health Care Professionals," Appendix B of the President's Commission for the Study of Ethical Problems in Medicine and Biomedical and Behavioral Research, *Deciding to Forgo Life-Sustaining Treatment* (Washington, D.C.: Government Printing Office, 1983), 295.

11. Robert G. Twycross, "Voluntary Euthanasia," in *Suicide and Euthanasia: The Rights of Personhood,* ed. Samuel E. Wallace and Albin Eser (Knoxville: The University of Tennessee Press, 1981), 89.

12. Philippa Foot, "Euthanasia," *Philosophy & Public Affairs* 6 (Winter 1977): 95.

13. To discover what one's own views are, try the following thought experiment. Imagine that you have been captured by a gang of ruthless and superlatively clever criminals, whom you know with certainty will never be caught or

change their minds. They plan either to execute you now, or to torture you unremittingly for the next twenty years and then put you to death. Which would be worse? Does your view change if the length of the torture period is reduced to twenty days or twenty minutes, and if so, why? How severe does the torture need to be?

14. 211 N.Y. 127, 129; 105 N.E. 92, 93 (1914).

15. *In re Yetter,* 62 Pa. D.&C. 2d 619 (1973).

16. *Satz v. Perlmutter,* 362 S. 2d 160 (Fla. App. 1978), affirmed by Florida Supreme Court 379 So. 2d 359 (1980).

17. *Bartling v. Superior Court,* 2 Civ. No. B007907 (Calif. App. 1984).

18. California Health & Safety Code, Sections 7195–7196.

19. The living will and durable power of attorney forms valid in different states are distributed by Choice in Dying, 200 Varig Street, New York, NY 10014. Copies are also available from hospitals and attorneys.

20. M. Siegler, "Pascal's Wager and the Hanging of Crepe," *The New England Journal of Medicine* 293 (1975): 853–857.

21. See also a study of other factors associated with differences in prognosis and treatment decisions: R. Pearlman, T. Inui, and W. Carter, "Variability in Physician Bioethical Decision-Making," *Annals of Internal Medicine* 97 (September 1982): 420–425.

22. The effects of depression on the choice concerning whether to live or die are described by Richard B. Brandt, "The Morality and Rationality of Suicide," in *A Handbook for the Study of Suicide,* ed. Seymour Perlin (New York: Oxford University Press, 1975), 61–76, and reprinted in part in M. Pabst Battin and David J. Mayo, eds., *Suicide: The Philosophical Issues* (New York: St. Martin's Press, 1980), 117–132.

23. I've considered elsewhere the symmetrical argument that if death is in some circumstances actually better than life, the paternalist should be prepared to override a patient's

choice of life. See M. Pabst Battin, *Ethical Issues in Suicide* (Englewood Cliffs, N.J.: Prentice-Hall, 1982), 160–175.

24. Vatican Congregation for the Doctrine of the Faith, "Declaration on Euthanasia," June 26, 1980; see Section II, "Euthanasia."

25. Peter C. Williams, "Rights and the Alleged Right of Innocents to Be Killed," *Ethics* 87 (1976–77): 383–394.

26. This proviso may appear to resemble similar provisos exempting physicians, nurses, and other caregivers who have principled objections to participating in abortions. But I am much less certain that weight should be given to the scruples of physicians in euthanasia cases, at least at the time of need. As I will suggest in the final section of this chapter, the patient has an obligation to make his or her wishes concerning euthanasia known in advance in a foreseeable decline; if the physician objects, it is his or her duty to excuse himself or herself from the case and from the care of the patient altogether *before* the patient's deteriorating condition prevents or makes it difficult to transfer to another physician; the doctor cannot simply voice his or her objections when the patient finally reaches the point of requesting help in dying. The physician should of course object if, for instance, he or she believes that the patient is acting on faulty information; but the physician ought not introduce a principled objection to participation in euthanasia in general at this late date.

27. To this end, the British and Scottish voluntary euthanasia societies have published booklets of explicit information concerning methods of suicide for distribution to their members; the Dutch voluntary euthanasia society has published a handbook intended specifically for physicians, and voluntary physician-assisted euthanasia is legally tolerated in Holland. In the United States, Hemlock, a society advocating legalization of voluntary euthanasia and assisted suicide, also makes available similar information.

AIDS Patients' Silent Companion Is Often Suicide, Experts Discover

Seth Mydans

Whenever Jim Lee opens his refrigerator, his two carefully hoarded bottles of Seconal are there, reminding him that he is soon to die, and that like large numbers of people with AIDS, he is preparing when the time is right to take his own life.

"I don't need these pills to remind me that I'm dying; whenever I look in the mirror and see my

Kaposi's I'm reminded," he said, referring to the cancerous blotches that are a common mark of AIDS. "Whenever I have a fever I'm reminded."

Doctors and social workers and AIDS patients say there are many people like Mr. Lee, facing the near certainty of an agonizing death, surrounded by friends and lovers dying in the same ugly way, who have made long-term preparations for suicide.

Far from everyone follows through with the preparations, but studies show that although it is largely hidden and hard to confirm, suicide is more common among people with AIDS than among people with other terminal illnesses.

Mr. Lee, a 53-year-old landscape gardener, says that his decision is a liberating one, that he draws from the sight of his Seconal bottles—as he does not from the sight of his Kaposi's sarcoma—a sense of dignity, strength and even life.

"It's incredible," he said. "Once you do this small preparation, you have such a sense of power. You've taken power away from the medical profession. You've taken power away from the disease. I'm in control now."

But as suicide has become acknowledged as a common option among infected people, a backlash has developed within the community of people with AIDS, a feeling that the real dignity lies in seeing the disease through to its end.

A Taboo Issue

Part of that reaction arises from an emerging perception of AIDS as potentially more manageable with the appearance of new drugs and improved techniques of treatment.

"If there is a strong trend amid the AIDS population toward suicide, I think there is an even stronger reaction against it," said Fred Clark, 40, a former restaurant employee who works with Mr. Lee for a private AIDS counseling group called Being Alive.

He said that there had been sharp debates on the issue in the group, and that the objections of some members had made suicide something of a taboo issue for open discussion.

"I have AIDS and I'm willing to face whatever comes," Mr. Clark said.

"You don't want to see people suffer, and I've seen a lot of people suffer," he said, "especially when it gets into dementia and people start having seizures and trembling and they can't swallow and their mom is sitting there holding their hands—it's just a pathetic scene."

1988 Suicide Study

The basic study of AIDS and suicide, published in 1988 by a group of researchers led by Dr. Peter Marzuk of Cornell University Medical College, found that AIDS patients were 36 times more likely to take their own lives than the entire population of men 20 to 59 years old.

This rate is higher than that of patients with other chronic and eventually fatal diseases, Dr. Marzuk said in an interview.

"What we're finding is that AIDS carries with it a high risk of suicide," said Dr. Marzuk, who has estimated that 1,000 AIDS patients will probably have taken their lives by 1991.

He said that his findings, based on medical examiners' reports, were confirmed in a later California study, but that both probably understated the true figures because suicide is often secret.

Suicides among AIDS patients have become fairly common, said Andrew Weisser, a spokesman for AIDS Project Los Angeles, a private center. Last December alone, he said, at least 5 of the 2,000 patients associated with his group, took their own lives.

Mr. Lee now draws inspiration from other men who chose what he calls self-deliverance. Some of their stories are told in the extensive obituary section of *Update*, a newspaper published for the gay community of Southern California.

A Farewell to Friends

In the pages of *Update*, Mr. Lee read of Kenneth Larry Hill, a 49-year-old actor, who scheduled and attended his own wake, said good-bye to his friends and family, and died that evening.

He also read of Thomas Gerard Wiswell, a 38-year old actor, artist and writer, who shot himself in the head, the newspaper reported, "taking the precaution to wear a hooded sweatshirt so he wouldn't make a mess."

Mr. Wiswell also left an envelope with extra money for a cleaning person, and labeled his possessions as bequests to his friends.

"As his final task," *Update* reported, "Tom Wiswell had gone the mile to the Mayfair Market and stocked his refrigerator with Italian sausage because it was a food his brother liked. It also had a label: 'This is for Don's lunch.'"

Mr. Lee's is a small refrigerator, in a kitchen whose window overlooks the garden where his helper is tending his plots of cactus. When his fever is high, he can get a soft drink, and it is just a few steps to his daybed, where he also plans one day to lie down to die.

"It's a bachelor's refrigerator," Mr. Lee said, slipping the two small brown bottles of pills back onto their shelf. "Just the normal things: Reddi-Whip, champagne, beer, lots of fruit, yogurt and preservative-free mayonnaise."

An Orderly Departure

Mr. Lee was found to have AIDS two and a half years ago, and as he has grown sicker and weaker, he has begun his own preparations for an orderly departure. He has visited a printer to prepare death notices and he is sending what he calls thank-you notes to friends, bidding them farewell.

Bare nails in his walls are evidence that he has begun giving away the artworks, antiques and books he has collected over the years.

"I'm a 53-year-old man and this is it: this is the end," Mr. Lee said.

Using a prescription from a sympathetic doctor, Mr. Lee has already accumulated more than a lethal dose of Seconal, a strong sleeping pill. When he reaches double the dose, he said, he can begin giving away surplus pills to his friends with AIDS.

14.

The Disability Rights Opposition to Physician-Assisted Suicide

Diane Coleman and Carol Gill

Diane Coleman, an attorney, and Carol Gill, a psychologist, are activists who work to secure rights for persons with disabilities. Coleman is one of the founders of the grassroots disabled-rights group called Not Dead Yet, which has been active in challenging efforts to make physician-assisted suicide legally available. She also represents American Disabled for Attendant Programs Today (ADAPT). Coleman notes that she has been disabled since birth due to spinal muscular atrophy and has used a wheelchair since the age of eleven. Dr. Gill is a clinical and research psychologist who specializes in health and disability. She identifies herself as "a woman with a disability" who uses a motorized wheelchair and a nighttime ventilator.

In their testimony, Coleman and Gill argue that the so-called "right-to-die," defended by proponents of physician-assisted suicide, may very well become the "duty to die" for many persons with disabilities. They fear that physician-assisted suicide may not be a genuine "choice" for persons with disabilities, who live in a society that routinely discriminates against them and frequently treats them as costly burdens to the rest of society.

Most proponents of physician-assisted suicide would say that a representative of the disability community does not really belong on this panel today. They would say that physician-assisted suicide pertains to people who are terminally ill, not disabled.

This testimony was presented by Diane Coleman and Carol Gill on April 29, 1996, before the Judiciary Committee of the U.S. House of Representatives. Reprinted with permission of Diane Coleman and Carol Gill. The appendix is part of the *amici curiae* brief filed by the organizations Not Dead Yet and American Disabled for Attendant Programs Today (ADAPT) in support of petitioners seeking to challenge the 2nd Circuit Court Ruling in *Quill* v. *Vacco* (1996). (The U.S. Supreme Court reversed this ruling in 1997. See *Vacco* v. *Quill*, pp. 239–243 below.)

The concerns of people with disabilities were similarly dismissed as irrelevant in the context of withdrawal of life-sustaining treatment or "passive euthanasia." Nevertheless, courts did not carefully protect non-terminal people with disabilities from a too hasty "final exit." Indeed, court after court declared that people with disabilities were essentially the same as people with terminal illnesses, stating that routine disability-related health care was artificially prolonging life, or that it did not matter how extended the individual's life-expectancy might be if their quality of life rendered their life "meaningless." This occurred in numerous appellate court cases involving people with quadriplegia, often locked away in nursing homes without hope of in-home support services, and it even occurred in a case involving a woman with cerebral palsy.

No court, or professional whose judgment the courts respected, examined the suicidal feelings of Elizabeth Bouvia, David Rivlin, Larry McAfee, Hector Rodas or Kenneth Bergstedt. All courts attributed the individual's desire to die to their physical disabilities per se rather than to events and circumstances in their lives, such as a miscarriage, loss of spouse and confinement to nursing homes. All courts superficially concluded that the individual's despair was not suicidal, not treatable or deserving of appropriate intervention. These individuals were granted a so-called "right to die" without being offered adequate supports for living. These highly publicized cases are the tip of an unexplored iceberg, one that proponents of physician-assisted suicide prefer to ignore. But the legal foundation for applying physician-assisted suicide to nonterminal people with disabilities is already firmly entrenched in our judicial system, and disabled people are beginning to feel that we are riding on the Titanic.

1. People with disabilities do not have adequate protection from either the courts or disability organizations. The courts have consistently excused parents who have murdered children with disabilities. A woman in Wisconsin escaped sentencing after admittedly starving her son with cerebral palsy to death. She said she was responding to family pressure and the message of a T.V. show on euthanasia. A west coast mother recently killed her brain injured non-verbal teenaged daughter. The judge said her actions were understandable, that other parents could be expected to react in the same way. He sentenced her to community service. Meanwhile, disability watchdog organizations are losing funding. There have never been enough of these to serve people with disabilities adequately; now many are forced to shut down.

2. People with disabilities and incurable chronic diseases have experienced a long history of persecution and genocide. At the turn of the century, Chicago's Ugly Law ordered people with visible disabilities to hide themselves from public view. In the 1930's, 200,000 people with disabilities were put to death by Nazi physicians who were inspired by the contemporary euthanasia movements of England and the U.S. Three years ago, a European judge ordered a hotel to refund money to a vacationing couple because they claimed their holiday was ruined by the presence of disabled people in the dining room. A physically disabled German man committed suicide after verbal and physical assaults by skinheads. There has been a rise in hate crimes against people with disabilities, internationally. A U.S. government report on child abuse recently found that children with disabilities are twice as likely to be abused as children who are nondisabled, simply because of their disabilities. Suffice it to say, contempt for life with disability is very much around us. In this context, we should be extended more protections of our lives, as a minority group at risk, instead of fewer protections.

3. Assisted suicide will not remain confined to the imminently dying. Individuals and groups who have spearheaded this push for assisted suicide have clearly intended people with disabilities to be targeted once laws are relaxed for terminally ill people. In *Final Exit*, Hemlock Society founder Derek Humphrey writes: "What can those of us who sympathize with a justified suicide by a handicapped person do to help? . . . When we have statutes on the books permitting lawful physician aid-in-dying for the terminally ill, I believe that along with this reform there will come a more tolerant attitude to the other exceptional cases." Kevorkian has openly admitted that he designed his suicide device as an answer for quadriplegics. He has said that he perceives physical disability as a cause of extreme human suffering that can be addressed by "medicide." He also argued, as did the Nazis, that society will benefit from the deaths of incurably disabled people. Chillingly, he wrote: ". . . the voluntary self-elimination of individual and mortally diseased or crippled lives taken collectively can only enhance the preservation of public health and welfare." The courts have not prevented this man from following through on his intention to "enhance" society by eliminating people with disabilities who despair in the face of society's crushing oppression. [Editor's note: See Appendix, pp. 202–203 below.]

4. Assisted suicide enthusiasts have reinforced public prejudice and fear regarding disability. They describe our physical status or our simple need for human assistance, tools and technology as "pitiful," "helpless," "hopeless," "miserable," and inherently "undignified." This is an insult to our lifestyles. For example, many people with disabilities routinely manage incontinence through a variety of methods advertised in numerous disability magazines. These negative labels also promote myths about disability and "quality of life." Experienced people with disabilities have learned that there's more to life than toileting independently. Research consistently indicates that "quality of life" is determined by social supports and meaningful involvement in one's environment, not degree of disability. Most people with disabilities say that public misconceptions about disability trouble them far more than their physical limitations. If promoters of assisted suicide genuinely cared about people with disabilities, they would stop contributing to these negative public attitudes. Instead, they exploit disability prejudice in their public statements and expensive political advertisements to frighten the public into endorsing assisted suicide.

5. As long as people with disabilities are disenfranchised and treated as unwelcome and costly burdens on society, assisted suicide is forced "choice." Assisted suicide is not a free choice as long as people with disabilities are denied adequate healthcare, affordable personal assistance in our own homes, assistive technology, equal education, nondiscriminatory employment, and free access to our communities' structures and transportation systems. Based on recent developments in both public and private managed care, it is already possible in some states for impoverished disabled, elderly and chronically ill people to get assistance to die, but impossible for them to get shoes, eyeglasses, and tooth repair. Indeed, the 9th Circuit Court decision in effect recognizes assisted

suicide as an acceptable solution to the economic burdens of healthcare. The so called "right to die" has become the "duty to die," with Court approval. [Editor's note: The U.S. Supreme Court reversed the 9th Circuit Court's ruling in 1997. See *Washington* v. *Glucksberg,* pp. 239–243 below.]

6. The great majority of problems that lead people with disabilities, chronic conditions, and even terminal illnesses to seek hastened deaths are remediable through other means, such as assisted independent living outside of nursing homes, sophisticated pain management, death counseling for individuals and families, augmentative communication technology, hospice support, etc. Unfortunately, our nation's health care system has not responded adequately or consistently to these important human needs. Most citizens, particularly poor citizens, must fight for access to health care every step of the way. Many physicians have limited knowledge or skills in pain management, and no knowledge of even the most simple and inexpensive disability-related technology and services. To legalize assisted suicide in a country that has been a pioneer in suicide prevention is a backward step into primitiveness.

7. Physicians must not be given the power to decide who lives and who is escorted to death. As disabled historian Hugh Gallagher warns, the Nazi experience demonstrates how easily compassionate and well-educated physicians can lose their moral compass. Furthermore, research shows that physicians learn very little about disabled people during medical training, they are poor at diagnosing treatable depression, they are often uninformed about options such as pain management and supported living for people with disabilities, and they have a high suicide rate, themselves. Moreover, research shows that physicians consistently and dramatically underestimate quality of life for people with disabilities compared to the assessments of people with disabilities themselves. In addition, most individuals with disabilities report longstanding problems with physicians, citing disability prejudice, ignorance about the disability lifestyle, and medical abuse as commonly issuing from physicians.

It is unlikely that doctors will become more careful and accountable for our lives when current permissive attitudes about physician-assisted suicide are given the status of law.

8. The 2nd Circuit Court decision [*Quill v. Vacco*] illustrates the logic that propels us down the slippery slope to endangerment. In numerous court cases since 1985 involving "passive euthanasia," "right to die" proponents have argued that passively withdrawing life supports was neither suicide nor mercy killing—it was just letting nature take its course. Now, the Court's decision articulates that there is no essential difference between assisted suicide and death from withdrawal of life supports. Will the next decision challenge the distinction between assisted suicide and mercy killing, or the distinction between voluntary requests to die and proxy requests or decisions made without consent at all? That is exactly what happened in the Netherlands—a country often cited by assisted suicide proponents as the model for the U.S. Specifically, according to a Dutch governmental report in 1990, 5,941 persons were given lethal injections without consent. Of those, 1,474 were fully competent, according to their physicians. In 8% of the cases, doctors admitted there were unexplored options. Regardless of options, they euthanized unconsenting patients because of such express reasons as "low quality of life," "no prospect of improvement," "the family could not take any more." (*Doctor Assisted Suicide and the Euthanasia Movement*, ed. by Gary E. McCuen.)

9. In fact, people with disabilities have already been endangered by relaxation of laws and policies protecting their lives. Medical rehabilitation specialists report that quadriplegics and other significantly disabled people are dying wrongfully in increasing numbers because emergency room physicians judge their quality of life as low and, therefore, withhold aggressive treatment. Disabled people who need ventilators are often not offered assisted breathing as an option. Those who already use ventilators report that they are increasingly asked by medical personnel to consider "do not resuscitate" orders and withdrawal of life support. Children with non-terminal disabilities who never asked to die are killed "gently" by the denial of routine treatment. People with relatively mild disabilities are routinely denied life saving organ transplants. Many people with disabilities are terrified that managed care will further abridge their already limited options for life-extending treatments. Oregon's attempt to ration healthcare based on "quality of life" judgments (judgments made by nondisabled people) demonstrated how quickly the deck can be stacked against the lives of people with costly conditions. In the Netherlands, where disabled children, and adults with multiple sclerosis, quadriplegia, and depression are commonly assisted to die, disabled citizens express fear. Some carry wallet cards asking not to be euthanized. Dutch physicians follow a practice not to offer assisted ventilation to quadriplegics. Those who visit the U.S. have expressed surprise to see quadriplegics actively engaged in life with the use of costly portable ventilators and mouth-controlled power wheelchairs. Not surprisingly, the hospice movement is virtually non-existent in the Netherlands. When assisted death is a ready solution, there is little incentive to develop life-enhancing supportive services for "incurables."

10. Many proponents of physician-assisted suicide have expressed the belief that adequate safeguards can be adopted to protect vulnerable people from various forms of pressure and abuse if the practice is legalized in conformance with the 2nd and 9th Circuit Court opinions. This view is at best naive and at worst deliberately misleading. Similar statements were made during the last decade in the context of the withdrawal of life-sustaining treatment, but no meaningful safeguards have been established. In particular, people with disabilities are notably absent from hospital medical ethics committees. If, in fact, proponents of physician-assisted suicide believe that adequate safeguards against treatable suicidal feelings can be established, then they should be willing to allow physician-assisted [suicide] for any citizen, regardless of their health status, after those safeguards have been observed. However, no one has proposed that physician-assisted suicide be made available to all citizens on a non-discriminatory basis. Indeed, science fiction movies have been made depicting the atrocities of such a practice in futuristic society. But it appears that such practices are acceptable today if "only" applied to a loosely defined group of seriously ill or impaired individuals. The fact is that proponents of physician-assisted suicide are willing to risk the lives of hundreds of thousands of severely disabled people who are not terminally ill in order to secure a right to active euthanasia that would effectively shield them from legal scrutiny of their conduct. People with disabilities protest this cavalier devaluation of our lives.

11. Assisted suicide is discriminatory. As a policy, it singles out ill and disabled people as fitting subjects for dying. Meanwhile, neither the public nor health professionals endorse this so-called "autonomous" decision for young, healthy Americans. If there is a constitutional right to control one's death through assistance, it should apply to all citizens, not just those judged (or misjudged) to have a deficient life.

12. Assisted suicide is classist. Those who are used to privilege, and the control over one's life that privilege affords, will benefit from having one more choice—the choice to die by their own schedule. Such individuals expect to control all aspects of their lives. Either they cannot truly fathom the experience of disenfranchised groups, or they are willing to risk the safety of many (society's poor and oppressed) to ensure their personal access to more options. On the other hand, those who lack privilege, who are socially devalued and feared, those who are denied meaningful options to live, will be endangered by legalization of assisted suicide. The historical reality of disabled people's experience is that society does not adequately support our lives unless pressured by strong legal sanctions. The Congress of the United States acknowledged that disabled people are a discrete and insular minority in its passage of the Americans with Disabilities Act in 1990. We are entitled to the equal protection of the laws under the 14th Amendment of the U.S. Constitution. The laws that protect our lives have

often been the only buffer between us and annihilation. Now, under the guise of a 14th Amendment protection of an alleged liberty interest in assisted suicide, a certain class of people will be denied the 14th Amendment's equal protection of laws providing for suicide prevention when one poses a danger to oneself.

13. There is virtually no research on suicide and suicidal wishes in people with disabilities. This is a direct reflection of how little our lives are valued. Physicians, such as Timothy Quill, who propose guidelines for "safe" assisted death admit that the social consequences of assisted suicide are unknown. Yet they argue that legalizing physician assisted suicide will open up this area for investigation. At what cost to whom? It is hard to imagine a physician defending this kind of research design for any other group of people. Why are ill and disabled persons dispensable?

14. People with disabilities and incurable illnesses deserve the same social supports and commitment to suicide intervention as any other citizen. Although proponents of assisted suicide often emphasize its rationality, suicidologists tell us there is always a powerful emotional force and the pain of unmet needs underlying the desire to die. Most death requests, even in terminally ill people, are propelled by despair and treatable depression. As two such experts stated recently (Herbert Hendin and Gerald Klermand in *Amer. J. of Psychiatry* Jan. 1993):

> Advocates of physician-assisted suicide try to convey the impression that in terminally ill patients the wish to die is totally different from suicidal intent in those without terminal illness. However, like other suicidal individuals, patients who desire an early death during a terminal illness are usually suffering from a treatable mental illness, most commonly a depressive condition. Strikingly, the overwhelming majority of the terminally ill fight for life to the end. Some may voice suicidal thoughts in response to transient depression or severe pain, but these patients usually respond well to treatment

for depressive illness and pain medication and are grateful to be alive.

In fact, periods of depression are common in people adjusting to new or progressive disabilities. Such depression and concomitant suicidal feelings can persist for months or even years if not addressed with support and treatment from those experienced in working with people with disabilities.

15. Women with disabilities will be particularly endangered by the legalization of assisted suicide. Research indicates that women with disabilities are even more socially devalued than disabled men. We are also more likely to bear the stresses of poverty and social isolation. As women, we are twice as likely as men to suffer from depression. A study by DisAbled Women's network (DAWN) in Canada indicates that rates of depression and suicide may be even higher for women with disabilities than other women due to our multiple stresses, our high incidence of abuse, and our internalization of society's message that we are useless and inferior as women. If anyone doubts that women will be exploited and endangered by assisted suicide, that doubter should study Kevorkian's "clients." The first eight were all middle aged or elderly women with chronic illnesses and disabilities. Many said they feared being a burden on others. An autopsy on one of them revealed no evidence of any physical illness. Women with disabilities are going to be the first to feel a "duty to die."

16. People with disabilities in our country are increasingly caught in a perilous bind. On one side, recent assaults on the Americans with Disabilities Act and the Individuals with Disabilities Education Act threaten our hope of equal opportunity, and managed care threatens our access to basic healthcare and long-term services. On the other side, sanctioned assisted suicide allows our healthcare professionals to offer the final solution.

CONCLUSION

People have always been afraid to face the practical difficulties and losses associated with aging, illness and disability. In today's society, with cutbacks in health care and the human service "safety net," and with growing isolation from the supports our families could once more easily provide, people's fears are understandably growing. As a culture, we must address these very real human needs and fears.

But, particularly in the absence of a constitutional right to physician care, a right to physician-assisted suicide is not the answer. While a few may have all the options that money can buy and choose the final solution with complete understanding and freedom, the majority who are offered this option are people that society is all too ready to abandon as too costly and unproductive—people who can only depend on the protection of the law. The depth and breadth of this abandonment is only understood by those who live it everyday.

We ask all who care about social injustice to believe us when we state that disability-based discrimination in this culture is deep-seated, virtually unconscious, pervasive and overwhelming. This discrimination against millions of Americans must be understood and reversed, in ways that few can even envision, long before we discuss expanding the ways in which society's unwanted can be killed.

But if, in the prevailing confusion and despair of our culture, physician-assisted suicide will become a constitutional right for some, then it must be a constitutional right for all, nondisabled as well as disabled. The same safeguards, or lack of safeguards, that apply to some must apply to all. Those who have asserted the 14th Amendment's right to liberty as the legal foundation for a steady expansion of the right to die in the last decade cannot be allowed to continue to ignore the 14th Amendment's Equal Protection clause.

The assertion that people with disabilities are not threatened by physician-assisted suicide is false, based on virtually every court precedent to date, as well as actual practice in our culture today. The fact that its proponents continue to dismiss and marginalize the input of the disability community on this topic leads us to believe that they may actually feel that our untimely deaths are ultimately acceptable in the interest of the "greater good."

Then we can only call upon this Congress and the good people of our nation to resist our being singled out, to resist this form of discrimination. We are the proverbial "canaries in the coal-mine," the barometers of our value system. If we are declared expendable, who will be next?

APPENDIX

. . . The following people were Kevorkian's "patients" through September 7, 1996:

Name, Age, Date Died, Status and Condition at Time of Death

JANET ADKINS, 54, 6/4/90. Not terminal. Had Alzheimer's disease.

SHERRY MILLER, 43, 10/23/91. Not terminal. Had multiple sclerosis with disorganization of motor control in legs and arms.

MARJORIE WANTZ, 58, 10/23/91. Not terminal. Had severe pelvic pain.

SUSAN WILLIAMS, 52, 5/15/92. Not terminal. Had multiple sclerosis and was blind.

LOIS HAWES, 52, 9/26/92. Terminal stages of lung cancer.

CATHERINE ANDREYEV, 46, 11/23/92. Terminal stages of breast cancer.

MARCELLA LAWRENCE, 67, 12/15/92. Not terminal. Had heart disease, emphysema and arthritis.

MARGUERITE TATE, 70, 12/15/92. Terminal stages of Lou Gehrig's disease.

JACK MILLER, 53, 1/20/93. Terminal stages of bone cancer. Also had emphysema.

STANLEY BALL, 82, 2/4/93. Not terminal. Had pancreatic cancer.

MARY BIERNAT, 73, 2/4/93. Had breast and chest cancer. Unclear whether terminal.

ELAINE GOLDBAUM, 47, 2/8/93. Not terminal. Had multiple sclerosis, was blind and used a wheelchair.

HUGH GALE, 70, 2/15/93. Unclear whether terminal. Had emphysema and congestive heart disease.

JONATHAN GRENZ, 44, 2/18/93. Terminal. Had throat cancer.

MARTHA RUWART, 41, 2/18/93. Terminal. Had duodenal and ovarian cancer.

RON MANSUR, 54, 5/16/93. Unclear whether terminal. Had lung and bone cancer.

THOMAS HYDE, 30, 8/4/93. Terminal. Had Lou Gehrig's disease.

DONALD O'KEEFE, 73, 9/9/93. Terminal. Had bone cancer.

MERIAN FREDERICK, 72, 10/22/93. Not terminal stage of Lou Gehrig's disease.

ALI KHALILI, 61, 11/22/93. Not terminal. Had progressive bone disease and multiple myeloma.

MARGARET GARRISH, 72, 11/26/94. Not terminal. Had double amputation from chronic degenerative joint disease.

JOHN EVANS, 77, 5/8/95. Not terminal. Had chronic lung disease.

NICHOLAS LOVING, 27, 5/12/95. Not terminal stage of Lou Gehrig's disease.

ERIKA GARCELLANO, 60, 6/26/95. Not terminal stage of Lou Gehrig's disease.

ESTHER COHAN, 46, 8/25/95. Not terminal. Had multiple sclerosis.

PATRICIA CASHMAN, 58, 11/8/95. Not terminal. Had breast cancer.

LINDA HENSLEE, 48, 1/29/96. Not terminal. Had multiple sclerosis.

AUSTIN BASTABLE, 53, 5/6/96. Not terminal. Had multiple sclerosis.

RUTH NEUMAN, 69, 6/10/96. Not terminal. Was overweight and had diabetes.

LONA JONES, 58, 6/18/96. Not terminal. Had a brain tumor.

BETTE LOU HAMILTON, 67, 6/20/96. Not terminal. Had a degenerative neurological disease.

SHIRLEY CLINE, 63, 7/4/96. Not terminal. Had colon cancer.

REBECCA BADGER, 39, 7/9/96. Not terminal. Had multiple sclerosis.

ELIZABETH MERCZ, 59, 8/6/96. Not terminal. Had Lou Gehrig's disease.

JUDITH CURREN, 42, 8/15/96. Not terminal. Had chronic fatigue syndrome and muscle disorder.

DORTHA SIEBENS, 76, 8/20/96. Not terminal. Had Lou Gehrig's disease.
PATRICIA SMITH, 40, 8/22/96. Not terminal. Had multiple sclerosis.
PAT DIGANGL, 66, 8/22/96. Not terminal. Had debilitating muscle illness.

JACK LEATHERMAN, 73, 9/2/96. Terminal. Had pancreatic cancer.
ISABEL CORREA, 60, 9/7/96. Not terminal. Had severe pain from a spinal cord condition.

Hospice and End-of-Life Care

Joanne Lynn et al.

While the hospice has medieval roots as a service to pilgrims and other travelers, the modern hospice movement began during the late 1960s as a response to the complex needs of persons who were terminally ill and close to death. The first contemporary hospices were founded in England, including the well-known St. Christopher's Hospice in London, which was established in 1966 by Cicely Saunders, M.D. (Stoddard, 1990).

The success of the hospice movement in England and the publication of Elisabeth Kübler-Ross's findings about the dying person's experience (Kübler-Ross, 1969) gave rise to the hospice movement in the United States. The Connecticut Hospice, established in 1974, was the first hospice program in the United States. The number of persons using hospice programs has increased every year since. The 1,935 programs in the United States provided services to over 246,000 persons in 1992 (National Hospice Organization [NHO] *Newsline*, 1993). In the United States, cancer patients account for 78 percent of hospice admissions; AIDS patients, 4 percent; those with cardiac diseases, 10 percent; those with Alzheimer's-type dementia, 1 percent; those with renal disease, 1 percent; and patients with all other diagnoses, 6 percent (National Hospice Organization, 1993). Eighty-nine percent of hospices in the United States are non-profit organizations (NHO, 1993).

In the United States, the hospice has gained wide-spread acceptance, both as a program of health services and as a change agent in the dominant health-care system. The health-care systems of most European countries have integrated hospice care as an option, and hospices are slowly emerging in Latin American, African, and Asian countries.

The Philosophy of Hospice Care

Hospice care is ordinarily perceived as an alternative to hospital-based, conventional health care. Hospice is not defined by the locus of care, however. The goal of hospice care is to ensure that dying persons live as fully and comfortably as possible, a goal that can be achieved in a variety of settings, including the patient's place of residence and in-patient hospice units.

Hospice is a concept that embraces a philosophy of caring, combined with the best medical knowledge and clinical skills to provide care that is both compassionate and competent. In selecting hospice care, a dying person chooses health care that focuses on comfort and function rather than on cure or prolongation of life. Hospice care does not aim to shorten life nor to prolong dying. Its providers realistically deal with grief and death, but with a focus on quality living. Hospice care seeks to advance the patient's goals and to provide support and assistance for family and friends during the patient's dying and the bereavement period thereafter.

Since the outcomes to be valued or avoided vary greatly among dying patients, hospice providers must be as familiar with the patient's values and priorities as they are with clinical medicine. The success of hospice care depends on the ongoing commitment to provide the kind of comfort and caring that is supportive of the patient's goals and values. An array of services is necessary to meet the physiological, emotional, social, and spiritual needs of the dying, including medical care, nursing, social services, pastoral care, volunteers, therapists, nursing assistants, homemakers, and bereavement counselors. Effectiveness of the hospice team requires collaboration and substantial cross-disciplinary expertise.

Hospices originally depended entirely upon the efforts of volunteers, but that has changed. Although most of the care and support is now provided by paid professionals, volunteers still offer an important element of community commitment and solidarity, as well as an array of concrete services.

Hospice programs in the United States have had to work within a complex and often uncertain reimbursement system. Although the number of insurance companies and managed-care systems that offer payment for hospice services has increased, many do not have a specific hospice benefit and all vary greatly. A great deal of time and effort is required to estimate likely payments for prospective hospice patients. Dying patients often discover that their hospice coverage is too thin or uncertain to provide the services they will need.

Following several years of an experimental program at twenty-six hospices, Medicare was restructured in 1986 to provide a hospice benefit alternative for most U.S. citizens over sixty-five years of age. Patients choosing the Medicare hospice option are obligated to forfeit most benefits for hospitalization and other aggressive therapies that might require hospitalization. Approximately 35 percent of all hospices in the United States are authorized Medicare providers. The Medicare hospice program pays the hospice provider on a per diem capitated basis, with four rates of pay that depend upon service intensity (though almost all payments have been at the lowest rate). This effectively makes the hospice program the "at risk" insurer, since costly patients must be balanced by inexpensive ones. This financial structure has substantial conflicts of interest for providers and serious barriers to enrollment for potential patients.

Perversely, the advent of a Medicare hospice program and ensuing acceptance of some hospice benefits in most private insurance and managed-care programs in the United States has diminished the availability of philanthropic funds and volunteers to provide charitable care. Along with the popularity of hospice services and the constraints imposed on access, a major problem for hospice staffs and administrators has been to find creative and equitable responses to the mandate to limit access even in the face of obvious patient need.

Symptom Management

Hospice has made its best known contributions in the area of effective symptom management. The judicious use of pharmacological agents for pain and effective treatment for the other discomforts associated with terminal disease allow the patient to die with comfort and dignity. Because of the complex nature of symptoms, especially pain, symptom management includes technologically intensive nonpharmaceutical approaches, such as radiation and nerve blocks, as well as more interactive methods, such as relaxation techniques, imagery, acupuncture, and therapeutic touch. A combination of therapies can result in comfort for nearly all patients. Most estimates hold that fewer than 5 percent of dying patients must be substantially sedated in order to be comfortable.

These treatment strategies have given rise to serious ethical concerns (Gibson, 1984). Specific practices aimed at relieving suffering may also shorten life. For example, the use of substantial amounts of narcotics to relieve the physical pain of advanced cancer might hasten debilitation; morphine administered to those dying from respiratory insufficiency effectively sedates those struggling to breathe but also predictably hastens death. The careful evaluation of all alternatives by a trained clinical team, together with a well-informed patient or surrogate who understands the implications of treatment, usually makes it possible to negotiate such difficult decisions. However, efforts must continue to clarify and define acceptable standards of practice. There is a real risk of inattentive overmedication. Patient comfort and control, not physiological imbalances or habitual responses to abnormalities, must be the guide to service delivery.

Ethical Issues in Patient Care

Although hospice care is preferable to conventional care for many who are dying, changes in the health-care system—indeed, in hospice care itself—have created some difficult ethical issues. Advances in medical science continue to generate new and expanded technologies to prolong life, seeming to call into question the wisdom of forgoing treatment. Proponents of the right to life and of assisted suicide engage in heated debates, with each agreeing only that hospice offers too limited a set of treatment options. Society has become increasingly focused on inexpensive care, rather than quality care, for the dying.

The complexity of information that must now be given to the patient regarding services available and financial implications, at a time when he or she is experiencing the impact of death coming close, often makes it unrealistic to expect a patient to make an informed decision about hospice. When a patient does not have decision-making capacity, hospice regulations and state laws in the United States are often unclear about what would constitute appropriate surrogate decision making.

A hallmark of hospice care has been its focus on the patient and family as the "unit of care." Although the patient's interests are of primary concern, the life of a patient necessarily affects the lives of those closest to him or her. Most patients will consider family interests when making decisions. Family-focused care works well as long as there is agreement, but difficulty arises when family preferences conflict with patient choices. What happens when a family wants artificial feeding started, but the patient has clearly refused such intervention? If a patient has asked to go home to die, and the family is physically and emotionally unable to comply, how should the care proceed? Patient autonomy cannot supersede all other considerations, but the balance is, as yet, not clear.

Killing Versus Letting Die

One of the more controversial ethical issues involved in hospice care focuses on the distinction between active euthanasia and allowing death to occur as a result of the disease process, without intervention. In the context of hospice care, a well-informed patient (or surrogate, acting in the patient's best interest) can refuse treatment and accept a plan of care that is focused on comfort rather than life extension. Some people thereby may die sooner then they would otherwise. The deliberate act of inducing death in order to terminate hopeless suffering or a meaningless existence has been distinguished, in medical ethics, from allowing a terminally ill patient to die with peace of mind and his or her symptoms relieved (Crowley, 1988; U.S. President's Commission, 1993, Hastings Center, 1987). Nevertheless, in practice the delineation of wrongful killings from acceptable practice is challenged by cases requiring exceedingly high doses of narcotics to ease pain, or by forgoing a treatment that might well grant many more months of life.

Hospice supports the patient's right to choose to end his or her life naturally, and perhaps earlier than necessary, by forgoing life-prolonging medical intervention. If a patient is strongly pressured to accept hospice care (e.g., if it is the only course of care paid for by his or her health insurance), he or she may not be exercising a truly free choice for an earlier, "natural" death; for such a person, who may have preferred medical care in a more aggressive setting, the pressure to accept hospice care may well convey a weakness in the societal commitment to sustain life. On the other hand, the refusal of hospice providers to offer assistance in deliberate suicide also acts as a constraint on self-determination, one whose justification is currently involved in controversy.

Artificial Nutrition and Hydration

Providing food and water to those who are unable to feed themselves is ordinarily seen as a fundamental societal obligation. Failure to treat the malnutrition and dehydration that often accompanies the dying process creates an apparent ethical conundrum for the hospice care provider, especially since tube feeding and intravenous hydration seem so simple. Clearly, some patients are harmed by the artificial provision of food and water, since such interventions can cause suffering by inducing fluid overload, requiring restraints, and occasioning other complications. Patients often die more comfortably without artificial hydration and nutrition, and those who are able to communicate rarely want artificial feeding. Patients and their surrogates must be aware of alternatives regarding the provision of nutrition and hydration and the likely effects of choices to use or to forgo artificial support (Lynn, 1986).

Access to Hospice Care

The decision to enter a hospice program usually follows the patient's choice to forgo life-sustaining treatment, or the recognition that there is no treatment offering life extension. What sorts of life-extending treatment should remain available in hospice care has been quite controversial. The decision to use hospice requires the patient (or surrogate) to understand the services that will be provided, and hospice has traditionally required a substantial standard of consent. The patients must usually acknowledge that the illness is in its final stage, life expectancy is limited, and death will occur within approximately six months. Life expectancy is difficult to predict. Prognosticating life span for terminal illness relies upon woefully inadequate data, is quite imprecise in most circumstances even if substantial data is collected, and is an uncomfortable challenge to physicians' usual professional experience and practice. Patients are often denied access to hospice because their physicians are too uncertain about prognosis. Only with cancer is there regularly a discernible terminal phase of a month or less, so uncertainty with prognosis acts to deny access to those dying of most organ system failures or dementia.

Another limitation upon access has been the requirement under most U.S. financing strategies to provide most services in the home. While this comports with the dominant image of hospice, it also is insensitive to the presence of large numbers of persons in need who do not have homes, or do not have adequate homes, or do not have available unpaid family caregivers to serve them at home.

Conclusion

Hospice care as an organized and recognized part of the health-care delivery system is a relatively recent phenomenon that has become institutionalized in Great Britain and the United States and is growing in most other parts of the world.

The commitment to comprehensiveness in care plans, patient preferences as arbiters of the course of care, and effective symptom management have made hospice care a desirable alternative choice for care at the end of life for many patients, though hospice programs have focused upon those dying of cancer.

Hospice care regularly encounters the problems of decision making about the treatment of dying persons, and thus regularly confronts conventional issues of medical ethics such as the distinction between killing and letting die, the uncertain obligation to provide nutrition and hydration, and the problem of informed consent. Resolution of these problems is complicated by a commitment to serve the family as well as the patients.

Finally, hospice as a program of health services in the United States has had troubling problems induced by having administrative reasons to exclude many persons who would benefit greatly from hospice care and by having to provide services more efficiently than conventional health care. Access to hospice has been arbitrarily limited by policies aiming to constrain costs, but utilization of hospice has also been unjustifiably encouraged by the same considerations.

Reference

Crowley, Margaret A. 1988. "The Hospice Movement: A Renewed View of the Death Process." *Journal of Contemporary Health Law and Policy* 4, no. 4: 295–320.

Gibson, Donald E. 1984. "Hospice: Morality and Economics." *Gerontologist* 24, no. 1: 4–8.

Hastings Center. 1987. *Guidelines on the Termination of Life-Sustaining Treatment and the Care of the Dying.* Bloomington: Indiana University Press.

Kübler-Ross, Elisabeth. 1969. *On Death and Dying.* New York: Macmillan.

Lynn, Joanne, ed. 1986. *By No Extraordinary Means: The Choice to Forgo Life-Sustaining Food and Water.* Bloomington: University of Indiana Press.

National Hospice Organization. *1993. Newsline.*

Stoddard, Sandol. 1990. "Hospice: Approaching the 21st Century." *American Journal of Hospice and Palliative Care* 7, no. 2: 27–30.

U.S. President's Commission For the Study of Ethical Problems in Medicine and Biomedical and Behavioral Research. 1983. *Deciding to Forgo Life-Sustaining Treatment: A Report on the Ethical, Medical and Legal Issues in Treatment Decisions.* Washington, D.C.

15.
A Feminist Critique of Physician-Assisted Suicide
Susan M. Wolf

Susan M. Wolf is associate professor of law and medicine at the University of Minnesota Law School, and a faculty associate at the university's Center for Biomedical Ethics. She begins her essay by pointing out that most of the debate over euthanasia and physician-assisted suicide is about a patient who does not exist, namely, "a patient with no gender, race or insurance status." Wolf argues that we must attend to the role that gender, among other factors, might have in shaping this cluster of moral dilemmas. She asks if women, who have traditionally been socialized into attaching great value to self-sacrifice, might not be more vulnerable to subtle pressures should euthanasia and physician-assisted suicide become widely available in our society.

The debate in the United States over whether to legitimate physician-assisted suicide and active euthanasia has reached new levels of intensity. Oregon has become the first state to legalize physician-assisted suicide, and there have been campaigns, ballot measures, bills, and litigation in other states in attempts to legalize one or both practices.[1] Scholars and others increasingly urge either outright legalization or some other form of legitimation, through recognition of an affirmative defense of "mercy killing" to a homicide prosecution or other means.[2]

Yet the debate over whether to legitimate physician-assisted suicide and euthanasia (by which I mean active euthanasia, as opposed to the termination of life-sustaining treatment)[3] is most often about a patient who does not exist— a patient with no gender, race, or insurance status. This is the same generic patient featured in most bioethics debates. Little discussion has focused on how differences between patients might alter the equation.

Even though the debate has largely ignored this question, there is ample reason to suspect that gender, among other factors, deserves analysis. The cases prominent in the American debate mostly feature women patients. This occurs against a backdrop of a long history of cultural images revering women's sacrifice and self-sacrifice. Moreover, dimensions of health status and health care that may affect a patient's vulnerability to considering physician-assisted suicide and euthanasia—including depression, poor pain relief, and difficulty obtaining good health care—differentially plague women. And suicide patterns themselves show a strong gender effect: women less often complete suicide, but more often attempt it.[4] These and other factors raise the question of whether the dynamics surrounding physician-assisted suicide and euthanasia may vary by gender.

Indeed, it would be surprising if gender had no influence. Women in America still live in a society marred by sexism, a society that particularly disvalues women with illness, disability, or merely advanced age. It would be hard to explain if health care, suicide, and fundamental dimensions of American society showed marked differences by gender, but gender suddenly dropped out of the equation when people became desperate enough to seek a physician's help in ending their lives.

What sort of gender effects might we expect? There are four different possibilities. First, we might anticipate a higher incidence of women than men dying by physician-assisted suicide and euthanasia in this country. This is an empirical claim that we cannot yet test; we currently

Susan M. Wolf, "Gender, Feminism, and Death: Physician-Assisted Suicide and Euthanasia," in *Feminism & Bioethics: Beyond Reproduction*, ed. Susan M. wolf (New York: Oxford University Press, 1996): 282–317. Copyright (c) 1996 The Hastings Center. Reprinted by permission of The Hastings Center.

lack good data in the face of the illegality of the practices in most states[5] and the condemnation of the organized medical profession.[6] The best data we do have are from the Netherlands and are inconclusive. As I discuss below, the Dutch data show that women predominate among patients dying through euthanasia or administration of drugs for pain relief, but not by much. In the smaller categories of physician-assisted suicide and "life-terminating events without . . . request," however, men predominate. And men predominate too in making requests rejected by physicians. It is hard to say what this means for the United States. The Netherlands differs in a number of relevant respects, with universal health care and a more homogeneous society. But the Dutch data suggest that gender differences in the United States will not necessarily translate into higher numbers of women dying. At least one author speculates that there may in fact be a sexist tendency to discount and refuse women's requests.[7]

There may, however, be a second gender effect. Gender differences may translate into women seeking physician-assisted suicide and euthanasia for somewhat different reasons than men. Problems we know to be correlated with gender—difficulty getting good medical care generally, poor pain relief, a higher incidence of depression, and a higher rate of poverty—may figure more prominently in women's motivation. Society's persisting sexism may figure as well. And the long history of valorizing women's self-sacrifice may be expressed in women's requesting assisted suicide or euthanasia.

The well-recognized gender differences in suicide statistics also suggest that women's requests for physician-assisted suicide and euthanasia may more often than men's requests be an effort to change an oppressive situation rather than a literal request for death. Thus some suicidologists interpret men's predominance among suicide "completers" and women's among suicide "attempters" to mean that women more often engage in suicidal behavior with a goal other than "completion."[8] The rela-

tionship between suicide and the practices of physician-assisted suicide and euthanasia itself deserves further study; not all suicides are even motivated by terminal disease or other factors relevant to the latter practices. But the marked gender differences in suicidal behavior are suggestive.

Third, gender differences may also come to the fore in physicians' decisions about whether to grant or refuse requests for assisted suicide or euthanasia. The same historical valorization of women's self-sacrifice and the same background sexism that may affect women's readiness to request may also affect physicians' responses. Physicians may be susceptible to affirming women's negative self-judgments. This might or might not result in physicians agreeing to assist; other gender-related judgments (such as that women are too emotionally labile, or that their choices should not be taken seriously) may intervene.[9] But the point is that gender may affect not just patient but physician.

Finally, gender may affect the broad public debate. The prominent U.S. cases so far and related historical imagery suggest that in debating physician-assisted suicide and euthanasia, many in our culture may envision a woman patient. Although the AIDS epidemic has called attention to physician-assisted suicide and euthanasia in men, the cases that have dominated the news accounts and scholarly journals in the recent renewal of debate have featured women patients. Thus we have reason to be concerned that at least some advocacy for these practices may build on the sense that these stories of women's deaths are somehow "right." If there is a felt correctness to these accounts, that may be playing a hidden and undesirable part in catalyzing support for the practices' legitimation.

Thus we have cause to worry whether the debate about and practice of physician-assisted suicide and euthanasia in this country are gendered in a number of respects. Serious attention to gender therefore seems essential. Before we license physicians to kill their patients or to assist patients in killing themselves, we had better understand the dynamic at work in that encounter, why the practice seems so alluring that we should court its dangers, and what dangers are likely to manifest. After all, the consequences of permitting killing or assistance in private encounters are serious, indeed fatal. We had better understand what distinguishes this from other forms of private violence, and other relationships of asymmetrical power that result in the deaths of women. And we had better determine whether tacit assumptions about gender are influencing the enthusiasm for legalization.

Yet even that is not enough. Beyond analyzing the way gender figures into our cases, cultural imagery, and practice, we must analyze the substantive arguments. For attention to gender, in the last two decades particularly, has yielded a wealth of feminist critiques and theoretical tools that can fruitfully be brought to bear. After all, the debate over physician-assisted suicide and euthanasia revolves around precisely the kind of issues on which feminist work has focused: what it means to talk about rights of self-determination and autonomy; the reconciliation of those rights with physicians' duties of beneficence and caring; and how to place all of this in a context including the strengths and failures of families, professionals, and communities, as well as real differentials of power and resources.

The debate over physician-assisted suicide and euthanasia so starkly raises questions of rights, caring, and context that at this point it would take determination *not* to bring to bear a literature that has been devoted to understanding those notions. Indeed, the work of Lawrence Kohlberg bears witness to what an obvious candidate this debate is for such analysis.[10] It was Kohlberg's work on moral development, of course, that provoked Carol Gilligan's *In A Different Voice*, criticizing Kohlberg's vision of progressive stages in moral maturation as one that was partial and gendered.[11] Gilligan proposed that there were really two different approaches to moral problems, one that emphasized generalized rights and universal principles, and the other that instead emphasized contextualized

caring and the maintenance of particular human relationships. She suggested that although women and men could use both approaches, women tended to use the latter and men the former. Both approaches, however, were important to moral maturity. Though Gilligan's and others' work on the ethics of care has been much debated and criticized, a number of bioethicists and health care professionals have found a particular pertinence to questions of physician caregiving.[12]

Embedded in Kohlberg's work, one finds proof that the euthanasia debate in particular calls for analysis in the very terms that he employs, and that Gilligan then critiques, enlarges, and reformulates. For one of the nine moral dilemmas Kohlberg used to gauge subjects' stage of moral development was a euthanasia problem. "Dilemma IV" features "a woman" with "very bad cancer" and "in terrible pain." Her physician, Dr. Jefferson, knows she has "only about six months to live." Between periods in which she is "delirious and almost crazy with pain," she asks the doctor to kill her with morphine. The question is what he should do.[13]

The euthanasia debate thus demands analysis along the care, rights, and context axes that the Kohlberg–Gilligan debate has identified.[14] Kohlberg himself used this problem to reveal how well respondents were doing in elevating general principles over the idiosyncrasies of relationship and context. It is no stretch, then, to apply the fruits of more than a decade of feminist critique. The problem has a genuine pedigree.

The purpose of this chapter thus is twofold. First, I explore gender's significance for analyzing physician-assisted suicide and euthanasia. Thus I examine the prominent cases and cultural images, against the background of cautions recommended by what little data we have from the Netherlands. Finding indications that gender may well be significant, I investigate what that implies for the debate over physician-assisted suicide and euthanasia. Clearly more research is required. But in the meantime, patients' vulnerability to requesting these fatal interventions because of failures in health care and other background conditions, or because of a desire not to die but to alter circumstances, introduces reasons why we should be reluctant to endorse these practices. Indeed, we should be worried about the role of the physician in these cases, and consider the lessons we have learned from analyzing other relationships that result in women's deaths. What we glean from looking at gender should lead us to look at other characteristics historically associated with disadvantage, and thus should prompt a general caution applicable to all patients.

My second purpose is to go beyond analysis of gender itself, to analysis of the arguments offered on whether to condone and legitimate these practices. Here is where I bring to bear the feminist literature on caring, rights, and context. I criticize the usual argument that patients' rights of self-determination dictate legitimation of physician-assisted suicide and euthanasia, on the grounds that this misconstrues the utility of rights talk for resolving this debate, and ignores essential features of the context. I then turn to arguments based on beneficence and caring. It is no accident that the word "mercy" has figured so large in our language about these problems; they do involve questions of compassion and caring. However, a shallow understanding of caring will lead us astray, and I go on to elaborate what a deep and contextualized understanding demands. I argue that physicians should be guided by a notion of "principled caring." Finally, I step back to suggest what a proper integration of rights and caring would look like in this context, how it can be coupled with attention to the fate of women and other historically disadvantaged groups, and what practical steps all of this counsels.

This chapter takes a position. As I have before, I oppose the legitimation of physician-assisted suicide and euthanasia.[15] Yet the most important part of what I do here is urge the necessity of feminist analysis of this issue. Physician-assisted suicide and euthanasia are difficult problems on which people may disagree. But I hope to persuade that attending to gender and feminist concerns in analyzing these problems is no longer optional.

GENDER IN CASES, IMAGES, AND PRACTICE

The tremendous upsurge in American debate over whether to legitimate physician-assisted suicide and euthanasia in recent year has been fueled by a series of cases featuring women. The case that seems to have begun this series is that of Debbie, published in 1988 by the *Journal of the American Medical Association (JAMA)*.[16] JAMA published this now infamous, first-person, and anonymous account by a resident in obstetrics and gynecology of performing euthanasia. Some subsequently queried whether the account was fiction. Yet it successfully catalyzed an enormous response.

The narrator of the piece tells us that Debbie is a young woman suffering from ovarian cancer. The resident has no prior relationship with her, but is called to her bedside late one night while on call and exhausted. Entering Debbie's room, the resident finds an older woman with her, but never pauses to find out who that second woman is and what relational context Debbie acts within. Instead, the resident responds to the patient's clear discomfort and to her words. Debbie says only one sentence, "Let's get this over with." It is unclear whether she thinks the resident is there to draw blood and wants that over with, or means something else. But on the strength of that one sentence, the resident retreats to the nursing station, prepares a lethal injection, returns to the room, and administers it. The story relates this as an act of mercy under the title, "It's Over, Debbie," as if in caring response to the patient's words.

The lack of relationship to the patient; the failure to attend to her own history, relationships, and resources; the failure to explore beyond the patient's presented words and engage her in conversation; the sense that the cancer diagnosis plus the patient's words demand death; and the construal of that response as an act of mercy are all themes that recur in the later cases. The equally infamous Dr. Jack Kevorkian has provided a slew of them.

They begin with Janet Adkins, a 54-year-old Oregon woman diagnosed with Alzheimer's disease.[17] Again, on the basis of almost no relationship with Ms. Adkins, on the basis of a diagnosis by exclusion that Kevorkian could not verify, prompted by a professed desire to die that is a predictable stage in response to a number of dire diagnoses, Kevorkian rigs her up to his "Mercitron" machine in a parking lot outside Detroit in what he presents as an act of mercy.

Then there is Marjorie Wantz, a 58-year-old woman without even a diagnosis.[18] Instead, she has pelvic pain whose source remains undetermined. By the time Kevorkian reaches Ms. Wantz, he is making little pretense of focusing on her needs in the context of a therapeutic relationship. Instead, he tells the press that he is determined to create a new medical specialty of "obitiatry." Ms. Wantz is among the first six potential patients with whom he is conferring. When Kevorkian presides over her death there is another woman who dies as well, Sherry Miller. Miller, 43, has multiple sclerosis. Thus neither woman is terminal.

The subsequent cases reiterate the basic themes.[19] And it is not until the ninth "patient" that Kevorkian finally presides over the death of a man.[20] By this time, published criticism of the predominance of women had begun to appear.[21]

Kevorkian's actions might be dismissed as the bizarre behavior of one man. But the public and press response has been enormous, attesting to the power of these accounts. Many people have treated these cases as important to the debate over physician-assisted suicide and euthanasia. Nor are Kevorkian's cases so aberrant—they pick up all the themes that emerge in "Debbie."

But we cannot proceed without analysis of Diane. This is the respectable version of what Kevorkian makes strange. I refer to the story [Editor's note: see "The Story of Diane," pp. 231–234 below] published by Dr. Timothy Quill in the *New England Journal of Medicine*, recounting his assisting the suicide of his patient Diane.[22] She is a woman in her forties diagnosed with leukemia, who seeks and obtains from Dr. Quill a prescription for drugs to take her life. Dr. Quill cures some of the problems with the prior cases. He does have a real relationship with her, he knows her history, and he obtains a psychiatric consult on her mental state. He is a caring, empathetic person. Yet once again we are left wondering about the broader context of Diane's life—why even the history of other problems that Quill describes has so drastically depleted her resources to deal with this one, and whether there were any alternatives. And we are once again left wondering about the physician's role— why he responded to her as he did, what self-scrutiny he brought to bear on his own urge to comply, and how he reconciled this with the arguments that physicians who are moved to so respond should nonetheless resist.[23]

These cases will undoubtedly be joined by others, including cases featuring men, as the debate progresses. Indeed, they already have been. Yet the initial group of cases involving women has somehow played a pivotal role in catalyzing reexamination of two of the most fundamental and long-standing prohibitions in medicine. These are prohibitions that have been deemed by some constitutive of the physician's role: above all, do no harm; and give no deadly drug, even if asked. The power of this core of cases seems somehow evident.

This collection of early cases involving women cries out for analysis. It cannot be taken as significant evidence predicting that more women may die through physician-assisted suicide and euthanasia; these individual cases are no substitute for systematic data. But to understand what they suggest about the role of gender, we need to place them in context.

The images in these cases have a cultural lineage. We could trace a long history of portrayals of women as victims of sacrifice and self-sacrifice. In Greek tragedy, that ancient source of still reverberating images, "suicide . . . [is] a woman's solution."[24] Almost no men die in this way. Specifically, suicide is a wife's solution; it is one of the few acts of autonomy open to her. Wives use suicide in these tragedies often to join their husbands in death. The other form of death specific to women is the sacrifice of young women who are virgins. The person putting such a woman to death must be male.[25] Thus "[i]t is by men that women meet their death, and it is for men, usually, that they kill themselves."[26] Men, in contrast, die by the sword or spear in battle.[27]

The connection between societal gender roles and modes of death persists through history. Howard Kushner writes that "Nineteenth-century European and American fiction is littered with the corpses of . . . women. . . . [T]he cause was always . . . rejection after an illicit love affair. . . . If women's death by suicide could not be attributed to dishonor, it was invariably tied to women's adopting roles . . . assigned to men."[28] By the mid-nineteenth century characterizations of women's suicides meshed with the ideology described by Barbara Welter as that of 'True Womanhood. . . .' Adherence to the virtues of 'piety, purity, submissiveness and domesticity' translated into the belief that 'a "fallen woman" was a "fallen angel."'. . .[29] Even after statistics emerged showing that women completed suicide less often than men, the explanations offered centered on women's supposedly greater willingness to suffer misfortune, their lack of courage, and less arduous social role.[30]

Thus, prevailing values have imbued women's deaths with specific meaning. Indeed, Carol Gilligan builds on images of women's suicides and sacrifice in novels and drama, as well as on her on own data, in finding a psychology and even an ethic of self-sacrifice among women. Gilligan finds one of the "conventions of femininity" to be "the moral equation of goodness with self-sacrifice."[31] "[V]irtue for women lies in self-sacrifice. . . ."[32]

Given this history of images and the valorization of women's self-sacrifice, it should come as no surprise that the early cases dominating the debate about self-sacrifice through physician-assisted suicide and euthanasia have been cases of women. In Greek tragedy only women were candidates for sacrifice and self-sacrifice,[33] and to this day self-sacrifice is usually regarded as a feminine not masculine virtue.

This lineage has implications. It means that even while we debate physician-assisted suicide and euthanasia rationally, we may be animated by unacknowledged images that give the practices a certain gendered logic and felt correctness. In some deep way it makes sense to us to see these women dying, it seems right. It fits an old piece into a familiar, ancient puzzle. Moreover, these acts seem good; they are born of virtue. We may not recognize that the virtues in question—female sacrifice and self-sacrifice—are ones now widely questioned and deliberately rejected. Instead, our subconscious may harken back to older forms, reembracing those ancient virtues, and thus lauding these women's deaths.

Analyzing the early cases against the background of this history also suggests hidden gender dynamics to be discovered by attending to the facts found in the accounts of these cases, or more properly the facts not found. What is most important in these accounts is what is left out, how truncated they are. We see a failure to attend to the patient's context, a readiness on the part of these physicians to facilitate death, a seeming lack of concern over why these women turn to these doctors for deliverance. A clue about why we should be concerned about each of these omissions is telegraphed by data from exit polls on the day Californians defeated a referendum measure to legalize active euthanasia. Those polls showed support for the measure lowest among women, older people, Asians, and African Americans, and highest among younger men with postgraduate education and incomes over $75,000 per year.[34] The *New York Times* analysis was that people from more vulnerable groups were more worried about allowing physicians actively to take life. This may suggest concern not only that physicians may be too ready to take their lies, but also that these patients may be markedly vulnerable to seeking such relief. Why would women, in particular, feel this?

Women are at greater risk for inadequate pain relief.[35] Indeed, fear of pain is one of the reasons most frequently cited by Americans for supporting legislation to legalize euthanasia.[36] Women are also at greater risk for depression.[37] And depression appears to underlie numerous requests for physician-assisted suicide and euthanasia.[38] These factors suggest that women may be differentially driven to consider requesting both practices.

That possibility is further supported by data showing systematic problems for women in relationship to physicians. As an American Medical Association report on gender disparities recounts, women receive more care even for the same illness, but the care is generally worse. Women are less likely to receive dialysis, kidney transplants, cardiac catheterization, and diagnostic testing for lung cancer. The report urges physicians to uproot "social or cultural biases that could affect medical care" and "presumptions about the relative worth of certain social roles."[39]

This all occurs against the background of a deeply flawed health care system that ties health insurance to employment. Men are differentially represented in the ranks of those with private health insurance, women in the ranks of the others—those either on government entitlement programs or uninsured.[40] In the U.S. two-tier health care system, men dominate in the higher-quality tier, women in the lower.

Moreover, women are differentially represented among the ranks of the poor. Many may feel they lack the resources to cope with disability and disease. To cope with Alzheimer's, breast cancer, multiple sclerosis, ALS, and a host of other diseases takes resources. It takes not only the financial resource of health insurance, but

also access to stable working relationships with clinicians expert in these conditions, in the psychological issues involved, and in palliative care and pain relief. It may take access to home care, eventually residential care, and rehabilitation services. These are services often hard to get even for those with adequate resources, and almost impossible for those without. And who are those without in this country? Disproportionately they are women, people of color, the elderly, and children.[41]

Women may also be driven to consider physician-assisted suicide or euthanasia out of fear of otherwise burdening their families.[42] The dynamic at work in a family in which an ill member chooses suicide or active euthanasia is worrisome. This worry should increase when it is a woman who seeks to "avoid being a burden," or otherwise solve the problem she feels she poses, by opting for her own sacrifice. The history and persistence of family patterns in this country in which women are expected to adopt self-sacrificing behavior for the sake of the family may pave the way too for the patient's request for death. Women requesting death may also be sometimes seeking something other than death. The dominance of women among those attempting but not completing suicide in this country suggests that women may differentially engage in death-seeking behavior with a goal other than death. Instead, they may be seeking to change their relationships or circumstances.[43] A psychiatrist at Harvard has speculated about why those women among Kevorkian's "patients" who were still capable of killing themselves instead sought Kevorkian's help. After all, suicide has been decriminalized in this country, and step-by-step instructions are readily available. The psychiatrist was apparently prompted to speculate by interviewing about twenty physicians who assisted patients' deaths and discovering that two-thirds to three-quarters of the patients had been women. The psychiatrist wondered whether turning to Kevorkian was a way to seek a relationship.[44] The women also found a supposed "expert" to rely upon, someone to whom they could yield control. But then we must wonder what circumstances, what relational context, led them to this point.

What I am suggesting is that there are issues relating to gender left out of the accounts of the early prominent cases of physician-assisted suicide and euthanasia or left unexplored that may well be driving or limiting the choices of these women. I am not suggesting that we should denigrate these choices or regard them as irrational. Rather, it is the opposite—that we should assume these decisions to be rational and grounded in a context. That forces us to attend to the background failures in that context.

Important analogies are offered by domestic violence. Such violence has been increasingly recognized as a widespread problem. It presents some structural similarities to physician-assisted suicide and especially active euthanasia. All three can be fatal. All three are typically acts performed behind closed doors. In the United States, all three are illegal in most jurisdictions, though the record of law enforcement on each is extremely inconsistent. Though men may be the victims and women the perpetrators of all three, in the case of domestic violence there are some conceptions of traditional values and virtues that endorse the notion that a husband may beat his wife. As I have suggested above, there are similarly traditional conceptions of feminine self-sacrifice that might bless a physician's assisting a woman's suicide or performing euthanasia.

Clearly, there are limits to the analogy. But my point is that questions of choice and consent have been raised in the analysis of domestic violence against women, much as they have in the case of physician-assisted suicide and active euthanasia. If a woman chooses to remain in a battering relationship, do we regard that as a choice to be respected and reason not to intervene? While choosing to remain is not consent to battery, what if a woman says that she "deserves" to be beaten—do we take that as reason to condone the battering? The answers that have been developed to these questions are instructive, be-

cause they combine respect for the rationality of women's choices with a refusal to go the further step of excusing the batterer. We appreciate now that a woman hesitating to leave a battering relationship may have ample and rational reasons: well-grounded fear for her safety and that of her children, a justified expectation of economic distress, and warranted concern that the legal system will not effectively come to her aid. We further see mental health professionals now uncovering some of the deeper reasons why some women might say at some point they "deserve" violence. Taking all of these insights seriously has led to development of a host of new legal, psychotherapeutic, and other interventions meant to address the actual experiences and concerns that might lead women to "choose" to stay in a violent relationship or "choose" violence against them. Yet none of this condones the choice of the partner to batter or, worse yet, kill the woman. Indeed, the victim's consent, we should recall, is no legal defense to murder.

All of this should suggest that in analyzing why women may request physician-assisted suicide and euthanasia, and why indeed the California polls indicate that women may feel more vulnerable to and wary of making that request, we have insights to bring to bear from other realms. Those insights render suspect an analysis that merely asserts women are choosing physician-assisted suicide and active euthanasia, without asking why they make that choice. The analogy to other forms of violence against women behind closed doors demands that we ask why the woman is there, what features of her context brought her there, and why she may feel there is no better place to be. Finally, the analogy counsels us that the patient's consent does not resolve the question of whether the physician acts properly in deliberately taking her life through physician-assisted suicide or active euthanasia. The two people are separate moral and legal agents.[45]

This leads us from consideration of why women patients may feel vulnerable to these practices, to the question of whether physicians may be vulnerable to regarding women's requests for physician-assisted suicide and euthanasia somewhat differently from men's. There may indeed be gender-linked reasons for physicians in this country to say "yes" to women seeking assistance in suicide or active euthanasia. In assessing whether the patient's life has become "meaningless," or a "burden," or otherwise what some might regard as suitable for extinguishing at her request, it would be remarkable if the physician's background views did not come into play on what makes a woman's life meaningful or how much of a burden on her family is too much.[46]

Second, there is a dynamic many have written about operating between the powerful expert physician and the woman surrendering to his care.[47] It is no accident that bioethics has focused on the problem of physician paternalism. Instead of an egalitarianism or what Susan Sherwin calls "amicalism,"[48] we see a vertically hierarchical arrangement built on domination and subordination. When the patient is female and the doctor male, as is true in most medical encounters, the problem is likely to be exacerbated by the background realities and history of male dominance and female subjugation in the broader society. Then a set of psychological dynamics are likely to make the male physician vulnerable to acceding to the woman patient's request for active assistance in dying. These may be a complex combination of rescue fantasies[49] and the desire to annihilate. Robert Burt talks about the pervasiveness of this ambivalence, quite apart from gender: "Rules governing doctor-patient relations must rest on the premise that anyone's wish to help a desperately pained, apparently helpless person is intertwined with a wish to hurt that person, to obliterate him from sight."[50] When the physician is from a dominant social group and the patient from a subordinate one, we should expect the ambivalence to be heightened. When the "help" requested *is* obliteration, the temptation to enact both parts of the ambivalence in a single act may be great.

This brief examination of the vulnerability of women patients and their physicians to collaboration on actively ending the woman's life in a way reflecting gender roles suggests the need to examine the woman's context and where her request for death comes from, the physician's context and where his accession comes from, and the relationship between the two. We need to do that in a way that uses rather than ignores all we know about the issues plaguing the relations between women and men, especially suffering women and powerful expert men. The California exit polls may well signal both the attraction and the fear of enacting the familiar dynamics in a future in which it is legitimate to pursue that dynamic to the death. It would be implausible to maintain that medicine is somehow exempt from broader social dynamics. The question, then, is whether we want to bless deaths driven by those dynamics.

All of this suggests that physician-assisted suicide and euthanasia, as well as the debate about them, may be gendered. I have shown ways in which this may be true even if women do not die in greater numbers. But exploring gender would be incomplete without examining what data we have on its relationship to incidence. As noted above, those data, which are from the Netherlands, neither support the proposition that more women will die from these practices, nor provide good reason yet to dismiss the concern. We simply do not know how these practices may play out by gender in the United States. There is no good U.S. data, undoubtedly because these practices remain generally illegal.[51] And the Dutch data come from another culture, with a more homogeneous population, a different health care system providing universal coverage, and perhaps different gender dynamics.[52]

The status of physician-assisted suicide and euthanasia in the Netherlands is complex. Both practices remain criminal, but both are tolerated under a series of court decisions, guidelines from the Dutch medical association, and a more recent statute that carve out a domain in which the practices are accepted. If the patient is competent and contemporaneously requests assisted suicide or euthanasia, the patient's suffering cannot be relieved in any other way acceptable to the patient, a second physician concurs that acceding to the request is appropriate, and the physician performing the act reports it to permit monitoring and investigation, then the practices are allowed.

Dutch researchers have been reporting rigorous empirical research on the practices only in the past several years.[53] The team led by Dr. Paul van der Maas and working at governmental request published the first results of their nationwide study in 1991.[54] They found that "medical decisions concerning the end of life (MDEL)" were made in 38 percent of all deaths in the Netherlands, and thus were common. They differentiated five different types of MDEL's: non-treatment decisions (which are neither physician-assisted suicide nor active euthanasia) caused 17.5 percent of deaths; administration of opiod drugs for pain and symptomatic relief (which would be considered active euthanasia in the United States if the physician's intent were to end life, rather than simply to relieve pain or symptoms with the foreseeable risk of hastening death) accounted for another 17.5 percent; active euthanasia at the patient's request (excluding the previous category) accounted for 1.8 percent; physician-assisted suicide (in which the patient, not physician, administers the drugs) covered 0.3 percent. Finally, there was a category of "life-terminating events without explicit and persistent request" accounting for 0.8 percent. In more than half of these cases, the patient had expressed a desire for euthanasia previously, but was no longer able to communicate by the time a decision had to be made and effectuated.

Women predominated in all of these categories except for the two rarest, but not by a great deal.[55] Thus, the ratio of females to males is 52:48 for euthanasia,[56] the same for death from drugs for pain and symptomatic relief, and 55:45 for non-treatment decisions.[57] This is

against a background ratio of 48:52 for all deaths in the Netherlands.[58] However, in the much smaller categories of physician-assisted suicide and "life-terminating events without explicit and persistent request," men predominated by 68:32 and 65:35 respectively.[59] Why would men predominate in these two categories? In the case of physician-assisted suicide, the researchers suggest that we are talking about younger, urbanized males who have adopted a more demanding style as patients[60] and may be seeking control.[61] Perhaps women, in contrast, are more often surrendering to their fate and relinquishing control to the physicians whom they ask to take their lives. Unfortunately, the researchers do not venture an explanation of why males predominate in the category of people who die from "life-terminating events without explicit and persistent request." This is numerically the smallest category, and one that should not occur at all under the Dutch guidelines because these are not contemporaneously competent patients articulating a request. Thus the numbers may be particularly unreliable here, if there is reluctance to report this illicit activity. Finally, the researchers report that more males than females made requests for physician-assisted suicide and euthanasia that physicians refused (55:45).[62]

What can we learn from the Dutch data that is relevant to the United States? There are causes for caution in making the cross-cultural comparison. There may be fewer reasons to expect a gender difference in the Dutch practices of euthanasia and physician-assisted suicide (as we would define these terms, that is, including the administration of drugs for pain relief and palliation, when the physician's purpose is to end life). First, the Netherlands provides universal health care coverage, while the United States's failure to provide universal coverage and tolerance for a two-tier health care system differentially disadvantages women (and other historically oppressed groups), leaving them with fewer means to cope with serious illness and more reason to consider seeking death. Second, the Netherlands presents greater homogeneity in race and ethnicity.[63] Again, this means that the United States presents more opportunities for and history of oppression based on difference. Third, we have to wonder whether elderly women in the United States face more difficulties and thus more reason to consider physician-assisted suicide and euthanasia than those in the Netherlands. A significant number in the United States confront lack of financial resources and difficulties associated with the absence of universal health coverage. Older women in the United States may also find themselves disvalued. "[T]here is evidence that the decision to kill oneself is viewed as most 'understandable' when it is made by an older woman."[64] Finally, it is worth speculating whether gender dynamics differ in the Netherlands.

Apart from that speculation, the differences in Dutch demographics and health care would be reasons to expect no gender differential in the Netherlands in the practices we are examining. The fact that we nonetheless see something of a gender difference in the case of most deaths intentionally caused by a physician at the patient's request should heighten our concern about gender differences in the United States. Given the general illegality of euthanasia and physician-assisted suicide currently in this country, decent data would be difficult to gather. Yet there seems to be reason to attend to gender in what studies we can do, and in our analysis of these problems. Studies planned for Oregon, the one American jurisdiction to legalize physician-assisted suicide so far, should surely investigate gender.

Attending to gender in the data available from the Netherlands, in the images animating the American debate, and in the cases yielding those images thus suggests that our customarily gender-neutral arguments about the merits of physician-assisted suicide and euthanasia miss much of the point. Though one can certainly conceive of a gender-neutral practice, that may be far from what we have, at least in the United States, with our history of inequalities.

Equally troubling, our failure thus far to attend to gender in debating these practices may represent more than mere oversight. It may be a product of the same deep-rooted sexism that makes the self-destruction of women in Greek tragedy seem somehow natural and right. Indeed, there is something systematic in our current submerging of gender. The details left out of the usual account of a case of assisted suicide or euthanasia—what failures of relationship, context, and resources have brought the woman to this point; precisely why death seems to her the best remaining option; what elements of self-sacrifice motivate her choice—are exactly the kind of details that might make the workings of gender visible.

They are also the kind of details that might make the workings of race, ethnicity, and insurance status visible as well. The sort of gender analysis that I have pursued here should also provoke us to other analyses of the role played by these other factors. To focus here on just the first of these, there is a long history of racism in medicine in this country, as vividly demonstrated by the horrors of the Tuskegee Syphilis Study.[65] We now are seeing new studies showing a correlation between race and access to cardiac procedures, for instance.[66] Although analysis of the meaning of these correlations is in progress, we have ample reason to be concerned, to examine the dynamic at work between patients of color and their physicians, and to be wary of expanding the physician's arsenal so that he or she may directly take the patient's life.

This sort of analysis will have to be detailed and specific, whether exploring gender, race, or another historic basis for subordination. The cultural meaning, history, and medical profession's use of each of those categories is specific, even though we can expect commonalities. The analysis will also have to pay close attention to the interaction, when a patient presents multiple characteristics that have historically occasioned discrimination and disadvantage.[67] How all of these categories function in the context of physician-assisted suicide and euthanasia will bear careful examination.

Probably the category of gender is the one we actually know most about in that context. At least we have the most obvious clues about that category, thanks to the gendered nature of the imagery. We would be foolish not to pursue those clues. Indeed, given grounds for concern that physician-assisted suicide and euthanasia may work in different and troubling ways when the patient is a woman, we are compelled to investigate gender.

FEMINISM AND THE ARGUMENTS

Shifting from the images and stories that animate debate and the dynamics operating in practice to analysis of the arguments over physician-assisted suicide and euthanasia takes us further into the concerns of feminist theory. Arguments in favor of these practices have often depended on rights claims. More recently, some authors have grounded their arguments instead on ethical concepts of caring. Yet both argumentative strategies have been flawed in ways that feminist work can illuminate. What is missing is an analysis that integrates notions of physician caring with principled boundaries to physician action, while also attending to the patient's broader context and the community's wider concerns. Such an analysis would pay careful attention to the dangers posed by these practices to the historically most vulnerable populations, including women.

Advocacy of physician-assisted suicide and euthanasia has hinged to a great extent on rights claims. The argument is that the patient has a right of self-determination or autonomy that entitles her to assistance in suicide or euthanasia. The strategy is to extend the argument that self-determination entitles the patient to refuse unwanted life-sustaining treatment by maintaining that the same rationale supports patient entitlement to more active physician assistance in death. Indeed, it is sometimes argued that there is no principled difference between termination

of life-sustaining treatment and the more active practices.

The narrowness and mechanical quality of this rights thinking, however, is shown by its application to the stories recounted above. That application suggests that the physicians in these stories are dealing with a simple equation: given an eligible rights bearer and her assertion of the right, the correct result is death. What makes a person an eligible rights bearer? Kevorkian seems to require neither a terminal disease nor thorough evaluation of whether the patient has non-fatal alternatives. Indeed, the Wantz case shows he does not even require a diagnosis. Nor does the Oregon physician-assisted suicide statute require evaluation or exhaustion of non-fatal alternatives; a patient could be driven by untreated pain, and still receive physician-assisted suicide. And what counts as an assertion of the right? For Debbie's doctor, merely "Let's get this over with." Disease plus demand requires death.

Such a rights approach raises a number of problems that feminist theory has illuminated. I should note that overlapping critiques of rights have been offered by Critical Legal Studies,[68] Critical Race Theory,[69] and some communitarian theory.[70] Thus some of these points would be echoed by those critiques.[71] Yet as will be seen, feminist theory offers ways to ground evaluation of rights and rights talk[72] in the experiences of women.

In particular, feminist critiques suggest three different sorts of problems with the rights equation offered to justify physician-assisted suicide and euthanasia. First, it ignores context, both the patient's present context and her history. The prior and surrounding failures in her intimate relationships, in her resources to cope with illness and pain, and even in the adequacy of care being offered by the very same physician fade into invisibility next to the bright light of a rights bearer and her demand. In fact, her choices may be severely constrained. Some of those constraints may even be alterable or removable. Yet attention to those dimensions of decision is discouraged by the absolutism of the equation: either she is an eligible rights bearer or not; either she has asserted her right or not. There is no room for conceding her competence and request, yet querying whether under all the circumstances her choices are so constrained and alternatives so unexplored that acceding to the request may not be the proper course. Stark examples are provided by cases in which pain or symptomatic discomfort drives a person to request assisted suicide or euthanasia, yet the pain or discomfort are treatable. A number of Kevorkian's cases raise the problem as well: Did Janet Adkins ever receive psychological support for the predictable despair and desire to die that follow dire diagnoses such as Alzheimer's? Would the cause of Marjorie Wantz's undiagnosed pelvic pain been ascertainable and even ameliorable at a better health center? In circumstances in which women and others who have traditionally lacked resources and experience oppression are likely to have fewer options and a tougher time getting good care, mechanical application of the rights equation will authorize their deaths even when less drastic alternatives are or should be available. It will wrongly assume that all face serious illness and disability with the resources of the idealized rights bearer—a person of means untroubled by oppression. The realities of women and others whose circumstances are far from that abstraction's will be ignored.

Second, in ignoring context and relationship, the rights equation extols the vision of a rights bearer as an isolated monad and denigrates actual dependencies. Thus it may be seen as improper to ask what family, social, economic, and medical supports she is or is not getting; this insults her individual self-governance. Nor may it be seen as proper to investigate alternatives to acceding to her request for death; this too dilutes self-rule. Yet feminists have reminded us of the actual embeddedness of persons and the descriptive falseness of a vision of each as an isolated individual.[73] In addition, they have argued normatively that a society comprised of isolated

individuals, without the pervasive connections and dependencies that we see, would be undesirable.[74] Indeed, the very meaning of the patient's request for death is socially constructed; that is the point of the prior section's review of the images animating the debate. If we construe the patient's request as a rights bearer's assertion of a right and deem that sufficient grounds on which the physician may proceed, it is because we choose to regard background failures as irrelevant even if they are differentially motivating the requests of the most vulnerable. We thereby avoid real scrutiny of the social arrangements, governmental failures, and health coverage exclusions that may underlie these requests. We also ignore the fact that these patients may be seeking improved circumstances more than death. We elect a myopia that makes the patient's request and death seem proper. We construct a story that clothes the patient's terrible despair in the glorious mantle of "rights."

Formulaic application of the rights equation in this realm thus exalts an Enlightenment vision of autonomy as self-governance and the exclusion of interfering others. Yet as feminists such as Jennifer Nedelsky have argued, this is not the only vision of autonomy available.[75] She argues that a superior vision of autonomy is to be found by rejecting "the pathological conception of autonomy as boundaries against others," a conception that takes the exclusion of others from one's property as its central symbol. Instead, "If we ask ourselves what actually enables people to be autonomous, the answer is not isolation but relationships . . . that provide the support and guidance necessary for the development and experience of autonomy." Nedelsky thus proposes that the best "metaphor for autonomy is not property, but childrearing. There we have encapsulated the emergence of autonomy through a relationship with others."[76] Martha Minow, too, presents a vision of autonomy that resists the isolation of the self, and instead tries to support the relational context in which the rights bearer is embedded.[77] Neither author counsels abandonment of autonomy and rights. But they propose fundamental revisions that would rule out the mechanical application of a narrow rights equation that would regard disease or disability, coupled with demand, as adequate warrant for death.[78]

In fact, there are substantial problems with grounding advocacy for the specific practices of physician-assisted suicide and euthanasia in a rights analysis, even if one accepts the general importance of rights and self-determination. I have elsewhere argued repeatedly for an absolute or near-absolute moral and legal right to be free of unwanted life-sustaining treatment.[79] Yet the negative right to be free of unwanted bodily invasion does not imply an affirmative right to obtain bodily invasion (or assistance with bodily invasion) for the purpose of ending your own life.

Moreover, the former right is clearly grounded in fundamental entitlements to liberty, bodily privacy, and freedom from unconsented touching; in contrast there is no clear "right" to kill yourself or be killed. Suicide has been widely decriminalized, but decriminalizing an act does not mean that you have a positive right to do it and to command the help of others. Indeed, if a friend were to tell me that she wished to kill herself, I would not be lauded for giving her the tools. In fact, that act of assistance has *not* been decriminalized. That continued condemnation shows that whatever my friend's relation to the act of suicide (a "liberty," "right," or neither), it does not create a right in her sufficient to command or even permit my aid.

There are even less grounds for concluding that there is a right to be killed deliberately on request, that is, for euthanasia. There are reasons why a victim's consent has traditionally been no defense to an accusation of homicide. One reason is suggested by analogy to Mill's famous argument that one cannot consent to one's own enslavement: "The reason for not interfering . . . with a person's voluntary acts, is consideration for his liberty. . . . But by selling himself for a slave, he abdicates his liberty; he foregoes any future use of it. . . ."[80] Similarly, acceding

to a patient's request to be killed wipes out the possibility of her future exercise of her liberty. The capacity to command or permit another to take your life deliberately, then, would seem beyond the bounds of those things which you have a right grounded in notions of liberty. We lack the capacity to bless another's enslavement of us or direct killing of us. How is this compatible then with a right to refuse life-sustaining treatment? That right is not grounded in any so-called "right to die," however frequently the phrase appears in the general press.[81] Instead, it is grounded in rights to be free of unwanted bodily invasion, rights so fundamental that they prevail even when the foreseeable consequence is likely to be death.

Finally, the rights argument in favor of physician-assisted suicide and euthanasia confuses two separate questions: what the patient may do, and what the physician may do. After all, the real question in these debates is not what patients may request or even do. It is not at all infrequent for patients to talk about suicide and request assurance that the physician will help or actively bring on death when the patient wants;[82] that is an expected part of reaction to serious disease and discomfort. The real question is what the doctor may do in response to this predictable occurrence. That question is not answered by talk of what patients may ask; patients may and should be encouraged to reveal everything on their minds. Nor is it answered by the fact that decriminalization of suicide permits the patient to take her own life. The physician and patient are separate moral agents. Those who assert that what a patient may say or do determines the same for the physician, ignore the physician's separate moral and legal agency. They also ignore the fact that she is a professional, bound to act in keeping with a professional role and obligations. They thereby avoid a necessary argument over whether the historic obligations of the physician to "do no harm" and "give no deadly drug even if asked" should be abandoned.[83] Assertion of what the patient may do does not resolve that argument.

The inadequacy of rights arguments to legitimate physician-assisted suicide and euthanasia has led to a different approach, grounded on physicians' duties of beneficence. This might seem to be quite in keeping with feminists' development of an ethics of care.[84] Yet the beneficence argument in the euthanasia context is a strange one, because it asserts that the physician's obligation to relieve suffering permits or even commands her to annihilate the person who is experiencing the suffering. Indeed, at the end of this act of beneficence, no patient is left to experience its supposed benefits. Moreover, this argument ignores widespread agreement that fears of patient addiction in these cases should be discarded, physicians may sedate to unconsciousness, and the principle of double effect permits giving pain relief and palliative care in doses that risk inducing respiratory depression and thereby hastening death. Given all of that, it is far from clear what patients remain in the category of those whose pain or discomfort can only be relieved by killing them.

Thus this argument that a physician should provide so much "care" that she kills the patient is deeply flawed. A more sophisticated version, however, is offered by Howard Brody.[85] He acknowledges that both the usual rights arguments and traditional beneficence arguments have failed. Thus he claims to find a middle path. He advocates legitimation of physician-assisted suicide and euthanasia "as a compassionate response to one sort of medical failure," namely, medical failure to prolong life, restore function, or provide effective palliation. Even in such cases, he does not advocate the creation of a rule providing outright legalization. Instead, "compassionate and competent medical practice" should serve as a defense in a criminal proceeding.[86] Panels should review the practice case by case; a positive review should discourage prosecution.

There are elements of Brody's proposal that seem quite in keeping with much feminist work: his rejection of a binary either–or analysis, his skepticism that a broad rule will yield a proper resolution, his requirement instead of a case-by-case approach. Moreover, the centrality that he accords to "compassion" again echoes feminist work on an ethics of care. Yet ultimately he offers no real arguments for extending compassion to the point of killing a patient, for altering the traditional boundaries of medical practice, or for ignoring the fears that any legitimation of these practices will start us down a slippery slope leading to bad consequences. Brody's is more the proposal of a procedure—what he calls "not resolution but adjudication," following philosopher Hilary Putnam—than it is a true answer to the moral and legal quandaries.

What Brody's analysis does accomplish, however, is that it suggests that attention to method is a necessary, if not sufficient, part of solving the euthanasia problem. Thus we find that two of the most important current debates in bioethics are linked—the debate over euthanasia and the debate over the proper structure of bioethical analysis and method.[87] The inadequacies of rights arguments to establish patient entitlement to assisted suicide and euthanasia are linked to the inadequacies of a "top-down" or deductive bioethics driven by principles, abstract theories, or rules. They share certain flaws: both seem overly to ignore context and the nuances of cases; their simple abstractions overlook real power differentials in society and historic subordination; and they avoid the fact that these principles, rules, abstractions, and rights are themselves a product of historically oppressive social arrangements. Similarly, the inadequacies of beneficence and compassion arguments are linked to some of the problems with a "bottom-up" or inductive bioethics built on cases, ethnography, and detailed description. In both instances it is difficult to see where the normative boundaries lie, and where to get a normative keel for the finely described ship.

What does feminism have to offer these debates? Feminists too have struggled extensively with the question of method, with how to integrate detailed attention to individual cases with rights, justice, and principles. Thus in criticizing

Kohlberg and going beyond his vision of moral development, Carol Gilligan argued that human beings should be able to utilize both an ethics of justice and an ethics of care. "To understand how the tension between responsibilities and rights sustains the dialectic of human development is to see the integrity of two disparate modes of experience that are in the end connected. . . . In the representation of maturity, both perspectives converge. . . ."[88] What was less clear was precisely how the two should fit together. And unfortunately for our purposes, Gilligan never took up Kohlberg's mercy killing case to illuminate a care perspective or even more importantly, how the two perspectives might properly be interwoven in that case.

That finally, I should suggest, is the question. Here we must look to those feminist scholars who have struggled directly with how the two perspectives might fit. Lawrence Blum has distinguished eight different positions that one might take, and that scholars have taken, on "the relation between impartial morality and a morality of care:"[89] (1) acting on care is just acting on complicated moral principles; (2) care is not moral but personal; (3) care is moral but secondary to principle and generally adds mere refinements or supererogatory opportunities; (4) principle supplies a superior basis for moral action by ensuring consistency; (5) care morality concerns evaluation of persons while principles concern evaluation of acts; (6) principles set outer boundaries within which care can operate; (7) the preferability of a care perspective in some circumstances must be justified by reasoning from principles; and (8) care and justice must be integrated. Many others have struggled with the relationship between the two perspectives as well.

Despite this complexity, the core insight is forthrightly stated by Owen Flanagan and Kathryn Jackson: "[T]he most defensible specification of the moral domain will include issues of both right and good."[90] Martha Minow and Elizabeth Spelman go further. Exploring the axis of abstraction versus context, they argue against dichotomizing the two and in favor of recognizing their "constant interactions."[91] Indeed, they maintain that a dichotomy misdescribes the workings of context. "[C]ontextualists do not merely address each situation as a unique one with no relevance for the next one. . . . The basic norm of fairness—treat like cases alike—is fulfilled, not undermined, by attention to what particular traits make one case like, or unlike, another."[92] Similarly, "[w]hen a rule specifies a context, it does not undermine the commitment to universal application to the context specified; it merely identifies the situations to be covered by the rule."[93] If this kind of integration is available, then why do we hear such urgent pleas or attention to context? "[T]he call to context in the late twentieth century reflects a critical argument that prevailing legal and political norms have used the form of abstract, general, and universal prescriptions while neglecting the experiences and needs of women of all races and classes, people of color, and people without wealth."[94]

Here we find the beginning of an answer to our dilemma. It appears that we must attend to both context and abstraction, peering through the lenses of both care and justice. Yet our approach to each will be affected by its mate. Our apprehension and understanding of context or cases inevitably involves categories, while our categories and principles should be refined over time to apply to some contexts and not others.[95] Similarly, our understanding of what caring requires in a particular case will grow in part from our understanding of what sort of case this is and what limits principles set to our expressions of caring; while our principles should be scrutinized and amended according to their impact on real lives, especially the lives of those historically excluded from the process of generating principles.[96]

This last point is crucial and a distinctive feminist contribution to the debate over abstraction versus context, or in bioethics, principles versus cases. Various voices in the bioethics debate over method—be they advocating casuistry, specified principlism, principlism itself, or some other position—present various solutions to the question of how cases and principles or other higher-order abstractions should interconnect. Feminist writers too have substantive solutions to offer, as I have suggested. But feminists also urge something that the mainstream writers on bioethics method have overlooked altogether, namely, the need to use cases and context to reveal the systematic biases such as sexism and racism built into the principles or other abstractions themselves. Those biases will rarely be explicit in a principle. Instead, we will frequently have to look at how the principle operates in actual cases, what it presupposes (such as wealth or life options), and what it ignores (such as preexisting sexism or racism among the very health care professionals meant to apply it).[97]

What, then, does all this counsel in application to the debate over physician-assisted suicide and euthanasia? This debate cannot demand a choice between abstract rules or principles and physician caring. Although the debate has sometimes been framed that way, it is difficult to imagine a practice of medicine founded on one to the exclusion of the other. Few would deny that physician beneficence and caring for the individual patient are essential. Indeed, they are constitutive parts of the practice of medicine as it has come to us through the centuries and aims to function today. Yet that caring cannot be unbounded. A physician cannot be free to do whatever caring for or empathy with the patient seems to urge in the moment. Physicians practice a profession with standards and limits in the context of a democratic polity that itself imposes further limits.[98] These considerations have led the few who have begun to explore an ethics of care for physicians to argue that the notion of care in that context must be carefully delimited and distinct from the more general caring of a parent for a child (although there are limits, too, on what a caring parent may do).[99] Physicians must pursue what I will call "principled caring."

This notion of principled caring captures the need for limits and standards, whether techni-

cally stated as principles or some other form of generalization. Those principles or generalizations will articulate limits and obligations in a provisional way, subject to reconsideration and possible amendment in light of actual cases. Both individual cases and patterns of cases may specifically reveal that generalizations we have embraced are infected by sexism or other bias, either as those generalizations are formulated or as they function in the world. Indeed, given that both medicine and bioethics are cultural practices in a society riddled by such bias and that we have only begun to look carefully for such bias in our bioethical principles and practices, we should expect to find it.

Against this background, arguments for physician-assisted suicide and euthanasia—whether grounded on rights or beneficence—are automatically suspect when they fail to attend to the vulnerability of women and other groups. If our cases, cultural images, and perhaps practice differentially feature the deaths of women, we cannot ignore that. It is one thing to argue for these practices for the patient who is not so vulnerable, the wealthy white male living on Park Avenue in Manhattan who wants to add yet another means of control to his arsenal. It is quite another to suggest that the woman of color with no health care coverage or continuous physician relationship, who is given a dire diagnosis in the city hospital's emergency room, needs then to be offered direct killing.

To institute physician-assisted suicide and euthanasia at this point in this country—in which many millions are denied the resources to cope with serious illness, in which pain relief and palliative care are by all accounts woefully mishandled, and in which we have a long way to go to make proclaimed rights to refuse life-sustaining treatment and to use advance directives working realities in clinical settings—seems, at the very least, to be premature. Were we actually to fix those other problems, we have no idea what demand would remain for these more drastic practices and in what category of patients. We know, for example, that the remaining category is likely to include very few, if any, patients in pain, once inappropriate fears of addiction, reluctance to sedate to unconsciousness, and confusion over the principle of double effect are overcome.

Yet against those background conditions, legitimating the practices is more than just premature. It is a danger to women. Those background conditions pose special problems for them. Women in this country are differentially poorer, more likely to be either uninsured or on government entitlement programs, more likely to be alone in their old age, and more susceptible to depression. Those facts alone would spell danger. But when you combine them with the long (indeed, ancient) history of legitimating the sacrifice and self-sacrifice of women, the danger intensifies. That history suggests that a woman requesting assisted suicide or euthanasia is likely to be seen as doing the "right" thing. She will fit into unspoken cultural stereotypes.[100] She may even be valorized for appropriate feminine self-sacrificing behavior, such as sparing her family further burden or the sight of an unaesthetic deterioration. Thus she may be subtly encouraged to seek death. At the least, her physician may have a difficult time seeing past the legitimating stereotypes and valorization to explore what is really going on with this particular patient, why she is so desperate, and what can be done about it. If many more patients in the Netherlands ask about assisted suicide and euthanasia than go through with it,[101] and if such inquiry is a routine part of any patient's responding to a dire diagnosis or improperly managed symptoms and pain, then were the practices to be legitimated in the United States, we would expect to see a large group of patients inquiring. Yet given the differential impact of background conditions in the United States by gender and the legitimating stereotypes of women's deaths, we should also expect to see what has been urged as a neutral practice show marked gender effects.

Is it possible to erect a practice that avoids this? No one has yet explained how. A recent article advocating the legitimation of physician-assisted suicide, for example, acknowledges the need to protect the vulnerable (though it never lists women among them).[102] But none of the seven criteria it proposes to guide the practice involves deeply inquiring into the patient's life circumstances, whether she is alone, or whether she has health care coverage. Nor do the criteria require the physician to examine whether gender or other stereotypes are figuring in the physician's response to the patient's request. And the article fails to acknowledge the vast inequities and pervasive bias in social institutions that are the background for the whole problem. There is nothing in the piece that requires we remedy or even lessen those problems before these fatal practices begin.

The required interweaving of principles and caring, combined with attention to the heightened vulnerability of women and others, suggests that the right answer to the debate over legitimating these practices is at least "not yet" in this grossly imperfect society and perhaps a flat "no." Beneficence and caring indeed impose positive duties upon physicians, especially with patients who are suffering, despairing, or in pain. Physicians must work with these patients intensively; provide first-rate pain relief, palliative care, and symptomatic relief; and honor patients' exercise of their rights to refuse life-sustaining treatment and use advance directives. Never should the patient's illness, deterioration, or despair occasion physician abandonment. Whatever concerns the patient has should be heard and explored, including thoughts of suicide, or requests for aid or euthanasia.

Such requests should redouble the physician's efforts, prompt consultation with those more expert in pain relief or support care, suggest exploration of the details of the patient's circumstances, and a host of other efforts. What such requests should not do is prompt our collective legitimation of the physician's saying "yes" and actively taking the patient's life. The mandates of caring fail to bless killing the person for whom one cares. Any such practice in the United States will inevitably reflect enormous background inequities and persisting societal biases. And there are special reasons to expect gender bias to play a role.

The principles bounding medical practice are not written in stone. They are subject to reconsideration and societal renegotiation over time. Thus the ancient prohibitions against physicians assisting suicide and performing euthanasia do not magically defeat proposals for change. (Nor do mere assertions that "patients want it" mandate change, as I have argued above.)[103] But we ought to have compelling reasons for changing something as serious as the limits on physician killing, and to be rather confident that change will not mire physicians in a practice that is finally untenable.

By situating assisted suicide and euthanasia in a history of women's deaths, by suggesting the social meanings that over time have attached to and justified women's deaths, by revealing the background conditions that may motivate women's requests, and by stating the obvious—that medicine does not somehow sit outside society, exempt from all of this—I have argued that we cannot have that confidence. Moreover, in the real society in which we live, with its actual and for some groups fearful history, there are compelling reasons not to allow doctors to kill. We cannot ignore that such practice would allow what for now remains an elite and predominantly male profession to take the lives of the "other." We cannot explain how we will train the young physicians both to care for the patient through difficult straits and to kill. We cannot protect the most vulnerable.

CONCLUSION

Some will find it puzzling that elsewhere we seek to have women's voices heard and moral agency respected, yet here I am urging that physicians not accede to the request for assisted suicide and euthanasia. Indeed, as noted above, I have elsewhere maintained that physicians must honor patients' requests to be free of unwanted life-sustaining treatment. In fact, attention to gender and feminist argument would urge some caution in both realms. As Jay Katz has suggested, any patient request or decision of consequence merits conversation and exploration.[104] And analysis by Steven Miles and Alison August suggests that gender bias may be operating in the realm of the termination of life-sustaining treatment too.[105] Yet finally there is a difference between the two domains. As I have argued above, there is a strong right to be free of unwanted bodily invasion. Indeed, for women, a long history of being harmed specifically through unwanted bodily invasion such as rape presents particularly compelling reasons for honoring a woman's refusal of invasion and effort to maintain bodily intactness. When it comes to the question of whether women's suicides should be aided, however, or whether women should be actively killed, there is no right to command physician assistance, the dangers of permitting assistance are immense, and the history of women's subordination cuts the other way. Women have historically been seen as fit objects for bodily invasion, self-sacrifice, and death at the hands of others. The task before us is to challenge all three.[106]

Certainly some women, including some feminists, will see this problem differently. That may be especially true of women who feel in control of their lives, are less subject to subordination by age or race or wealth, and seek yet another option to add to their many. I am not arguing that women should lose control of their lives and selves. Instead, I am arguing that when women request to be put to death or ask help in taking their own lives, they become part of a broader social dynamic of which we have properly learned to be extremely wary. These are fatal practices. We can no longer ignore questions of gender or the insights of feminist argument.

NOTES

My thanks to Arthur Applbaum, Larry Blum, Alta Charo, Norman Daniels, Johannes J. M. van Delden, Rebecca Dresser, Jorge Garcia, Henk ten Have, Warren Kearney, Elizabeth Kiss, Steven Miles, Christine Mitchell, Remco Oostendorp, Lynn Peterson, Dennis Thompson, and Alan Wertheimer for help at various stages, to the *Texas Journal on Women and the Law* at the University of Texas Law School for the opportunity to elicit comments on an earlier version, and to participants in the University of Minnesota Law School Faculty Workshop for valuable suggestions. Kent Spies and Terrence Dwyer of the University of Minnesota Law School provided important research assistance. Work on this chapter was supported in part by a Fellowship in the Program in Ethics and the Professions at Harvard University.

1. See, for example, Pamela Carroll, "Proponents of Physician-Assisted Suicide Continuing Efforts," *ACP Observer*, February 1992, p. 29 (describing state initiatives in Washington, California, Michigan, New Hampshire, and Oregon). Subsequently, Oregon voters made that state the first to legalize physician-assisted suicide. See 1995 Oregon Laws, Ch. 3, I. M. No. 16. But see also *Lee v. Oregon,* 869 F. Supp. 1491 (D. Or. 1994), entering an injunction preventing the statute from going into effect. Further legal proceedings will decide the statute's fate. For attempts to legalize physician-assisted suicide through litigation, see *Compassion in Dying* v. *Washington,* 850 F. Supp. 1454 (W. D. Wash. 1994), *rev'd,* 49 F.3d 586 (9th Cir. 1995); *Quill v. Koppel,* 870 F. Supp. 78 (S.D.N.Y. 1994). See also *Hobbins v. Attorney General,* 527 N.W. 2d 714 (Mich. 1994).

2. See, for example, Howard Brody, "Assisted Death—A Compassionate Response to a Medical Failure," *New England Journal of Medicine* 327 (1992): 1384–88; Timothy E. Quill, Christine K. Cassel, and Diane E. Meier, "Care of the Hopelessly Ill: Proposed Clinical Criteria for Physician-Assisted Suicide," *New England Journal of Medicine* 327 (1992): 1380–84; Guy I. Benrubi, "Euthanasia—The Need for Procedural Safeguards," *New England Journal of Medicine,* 326 (1992): 197–99; Christine K. Cassel and Diane E. Meier, "Morals and Moralism in the Debate Over Euthanasia and Assisted Suicide," *New England Journal of Medicine* 323 (1990): 750–52; James Rachels, *The End of Life* (Oxford, England: Oxford University Press, 1986).

3. I restrict the term "euthanasia" to active euthanasia, excluding the termination of life-sustaining treatment, which has sometimes been called "passive euthanasia." Both law and ethics now treat the termination of treatment quite differently from the way they treat active euthanasia, so to use "euthanasia" to refer to both invites confusion. See generally "Report on the Council on Ethical and Judicial Affairs of the American Medical Association," *Issues in Law & Medicine* 10 (1994): 91–97, 92.

4. See Howard I. Kushner, "Women and Suicide in Historical Perspective," in Joyce McCarl Nielsen, ed., *Feminist Re-search Methods: Exemplary Readings in the Social Sciences* (Boulder, CO: Westview Press, 1990), 193–206, 198–200.

5. See Alan Meisel, *The Right to Die* (New York, NY: John Wiley & Sons, 1989), 62, & *1993 Cumulative Supplement No. 2,* 50–54.

6. See Council on Ethical and Judicial Affairs, *Code of Medical Ethics: Current Opinions with Annotations* (Chicago, IL: American Medical Association, 1994), 50–51; "Report of the Board of Trustees of the American Medical Association," *Issues in Law & Medicine* 10 (1994): 81–90; "Report of the Council on Ethical and Judicial Affairs;" *Report of the Council on Ethical and Judicial Affairs of the American Medical Association: Euthanasia* (Chicago, IL: American Medical Association, 1989). There are U.S. data on public opinion and physicians' self-reported practices. See, for example, "Report of the Board of Trustees." But the legal and ethical condemnation of physician-assisted suicide and euthanasia in the United States undoubtedly affect the self-reporting and render this a poor indicator of actual practices.

7. See Nancy S. Jecker, "Physician-Assisted Death in the Netherlands and the United States: Ethical and Cultural Aspects of Health Policy Development," *Journal of the American Geriatrics Society* 42 (1994): 672–78, 676.

8. See generally Howard I. Kushner, "Women and Suicidal Behavior: Epidemiology, Gender, and Lethality in Historical Perspective," in Silvia Sara Canetto and David Lester, eds., *Women and Suicidal Behavior* (New York, NY: Springer, 1995).

9. Compare Jecker, "Physician-Assisted Death," 676, on reasons physicians might differentially refuse women's requests.

10. See Lawrence Kohlberg, *The Philosophy of Moral Development: Moral Stages and the Idea of Justice,* vol. I (San Francisco, CA: Harper & Row, 1981); Lawrence Kohlberg, *The Psychology of Moral Development: The Nature and Validity of Moral Stages,* vol. II (San Francisco, CA: Harper & Row, 1984).

11. See Carol Gilligan, *In A Different Voice: Psychological Theory and Women's Development* (Cambridge, MA: Harvard University Press, 1982).

12. Gilligan's work has prompted a large literature, building upon as well as criticizing her insights and methodology. See, for example, the essays collected in Larrabee, ed., *An Ethic of Care.* On attention to the ethics of care in bioethics and on feminist criticism of the ethics of care, see my Introduction to [Wolf's book].

13. See Kohlberg, *The Psychology of Moral Development,* 644–47.

14. On the Kohlberg–Gilligan debate, see generally Lawrence A. Blum, "Gilligan and Kohlberg: Implications for Moral Theory," in Larrabee, ed., *An Ethic of Care,* 49–68; Owen Flanagan and Kathryn Jackson, "Justice, Care, and Gender: The Kohlberg–Gilligan Debate Revisited," in Larrabee, ed., *An Ethic of Care,* 69–84; Seyla Benhabib, "The Generalized and the Concrete Other: The Kohlberg–Gilligan

Controversy and Feminist Theory," in Seyla Benhabib and Drucilla Cornell, eds., *Feminism as Critique: On the Politics of Gender* (Minneapolis, MN: University of Minnesota Press, 1987), 77–95.

15. See, for example, Susan M. Wolf, "Holding the Line on Euthanasia," *Hastings Center Report* 19 (Jan./Feb. 1989): special supp. 13–15.

16. See "It's Over, Debbie," *Journal of the American Medical Association* 259 (1988): 272.

17. See Timothy Egan, "As Memory and Music Faded, Oregon Woman Chose Death," *New York Times*, June 7, 1990, p. A1; Lisa Belkin, "Doctor Tells of First Death Using His Suicide Device," *New York Times*, June 6, 1990, p. A1.

18. See "Doctor Assists in Two More Suicides in Michigan," *New York Times*, October 24, 1991, p. A1 (Wantz and Miller).

19. See "Death at Kevorkian's Side Is Ruled Homicide," *New York Times*, June 6, 1992, p. 10; "Doctor Assists in Another Suicide," *New York Times*, September 27, 1992, p. 32; "Doctor in Michigan Helps a 6th Person To Commit Suicide," *New York Times*, November 24, 1992, p. A10; "2 Commit Suicide, Aided by Michigan Doctor," *New York Times*, December 16, 1992, p. A21.

20. See "Why Dr. Kevorkian Was Called In," *New York Times*, January 25, 1993, p. A16.

21. See B. D. Colen, "Gender Question in Assisted Suicides," *Newsday*, November 25, 1992, p. 17; Ellen Goodman, "Act Now to Stop Dr. Death," *Atlanta Journal and Constitution*, May 27, 1992, p. A11.

22. See Timothy E. Quill, "Death and Dignity—A Case of Individualized Decision Making," *New England Journal of Medicine* 324 (1991): 691–94.

23. On Quill's motivations, see Timothy E. Quill, "The Ambiguity of Clinical Intentions," *New England Journal of Medicine* 329 (1993): 1039–40.

24. Nicole Loraux, *Tragic Ways of Killing a Woman*, Anthony Forster, trans. (Cambridge, MA: Harvard University Press, 1987), 8.

25. *Ibid.*, 12.

26. *Ibid.*, 23.

27. *Ibid.*, 11.

28. Kushner, "Women and Suicidal Behavior," 16–17 (citations omitted).

29. Kushner, "Women and Suicide in Historical Perspective," 195, citing Barbara Welter, "The Cult of True Womanhood: 1820–1860," *American Quarterly* 18 (1966): 151–55.

30. *Ibid.*, 13–19.

31. Gilligan, *In A Different voice*, 70.

32. *Ibid.*, 13–19.

33. Loraux in *Tragic Ways of Killing a Woman* notes the single exception of Ajax.

34. See Peter Steinfels, "Help for the Helping Hands in Death," *New York Times*, February 14, 1993, sec. 4, pp. 1, 6.

35. See Charles S. Cleeland et al., "Pain and Its Treatment in Outpatients with Metastatic Cancer," *New England Journal of Medicine* 330 (1994): 592–96.

36. See Robert J. Blendon, U. S. Szalay, and R. A. Knox, "Should Physicians Aid Their Patients in Dying?" *Journal of the American Medical Association* 267 (1992): 2658–62.

37. See William Coryell, Jean Endicott, and Martin B. Keller, "Major Depression in a Non-Clinical Sample: Demographic and Clinical Risk Factors for First Onset," *Archives of General Psychiatry* 49 (1992): 117–25.

38. See Susan D. Block and J. Andrew Billings, "Patient Requests to Hasten Death: Evaluation and Management in Terminal Care," *Archives of Internal Medicine* 154 (1994): 2039–47.

39. Council on Ethical and Judicial Affairs, American Medical Association, "Gender Disparities in Clinical Decision Making," *Journal of the American Medical Association* 266 (1991): 559–62, 561–62.

40. See Nancy S. Jecker, "Can an Employer-Based Health Insurance System Be Just?" *Journal of Health Politics, Policy & Law* 18 (1993): 657–73; Employee Benefit Research Institute (EBRI), *Sources of Health Insurance and Characteristics of the Uninsured: Analysis of the March 1992 Current Population Survey*, EBRI Issue Brief No. 133 (Jan. 1993).

41. The patterns of uninsurance and underinsurance are complex. See, for example, Employee Benefit Resources Institute, *Sources of Health Insurance*. Recall that the poorest and the elderly are covered by Medicaid and Medicare, though they are subject to the gaps and deficiencies in quality of care that plague those programs.

42. Lawrence Schneiderman et al. purport to show that patients already consider burdens to others in making termination of treatment decisions, and—more importantly... —that men do so more than women. See Lawrence J. Schneiderman et al., "Attitudes of Seriously Ill Patients toward Treatment that Involves High Cost and Burdens on Others," *Journal of Clinical Ethics* 5 (1994): 109–12. But Peter A. Ubel and Robert M. Arnold criticize the methodology and dispute both conclusions in "The Euthanasia Debate and Empirical Evidence: Separating Burdens to Others from One's Own Quality of Life," *Journal of Clinical Ethics* 5 (1994): 155–58.

43. See, for example, Kushner, "Women and Suicidal Behavior."

44. See Colen, "Gender Question in Assisted Suicides."

45. Another area in which we do not allow apparent patient consent or request to authorize physician acquiescence is sex between doctor and patient. Even if the patient requests sex, the physician is morally and legally bound to refuse. The considerable consensus that now exists on this,

however, has been the result of a difficult uphill battle. See generally Howard Brody, *The Healer's Power* (New Haven, CT: Yale University Press, 1992), 26–27; Nanette Gartrell, et al., "Psychiatrist-Patient Sexual Contact: Results of a National Survey. Part 1. Prevalence," *American Journal of Psychiatry* 143 (1986): 1126–31.

46. As noted above, though, Nancy Jecker speculates that a physician's tendency to discount women's choices may also come into play. See Jecker, "Physician-Assisted Death," 676. Compare Silvia Sara Canetto, "Elderly Women and Suicidal Behavior," in Canetto and Lester, eds., *Women and Suicidal Behavior*, 215–33, 228, asking whether physicians are more willing to accept women's suicides.

47. See, for example, Susan Sherwin, *No Longer Patient: Feminist Ethics and Health Care* (Philadelphia, PA: Temple University Press, 1992); Barbara Ehrenreich and Deirdre English, *For Her Own Good: 150 Years of the Experts' Advice to Women* (New York, NY: Doubleday, 1978).

48. Sherwin, *No Longer Patient*, 157.

49. Compare Brody, "The Rescue Fantasy," in *The Healer's Art*, ch. 9.

50. Robert A. Burt, *Taking Care of Strangers* (New York, NY: Free Press, 1979), vi. See also Steven H. Miles, "Physicians and Their Patients' Suicides," *Journal of the American Medical Association* 271 (1994); 1786–88. I discuss the significance of the ambivalence in euthanasia context in Wolf, "Holding the Line on Euthanasia."

51. In an article advocating the legitimation of physician-assisted suicide, the authors nonetheless note the lack of good data on U.S. practice: "From 3 to 37 percent of physicians responding to anonymous surveys reported secretly taking active steps to hasten a patient's death, but these survey data were flawed by low response rates and poor design." Quill, Cassel, and Meier, "Care of the Hopelessly Ill," 1381 (footnotes with citations omitted).

52. On relevant differences between the United States and the Netherlands, see Jecker, "Physician-Assisted Death;" "Report of the Board of Trustees;" Margaret Battin, "Voluntary Euthanasia and the Risks of Abuse: Can We Learn Anything from the Netherlands?" *Law, Medicine & Health Care* 20 (1992): 133–43.

53. There have been two major teams of researchers. The first, conducting research at governmental request, has produced publications including Loes Pijnenborg, Paul J. van der Maas, Johannes J. M. van Delden, and Caspar W. N. Looman, "Life-terminating acts without explicit request of patient," *Lancet* 341 (1993): 1196–99; Paul J. van der Maas, Johannes J. M. van Delden, and Loes Pijnenborg, "Euthanasia and other Medical Decisions Concerning the End of Life: An investigation performed upon request of the Commission of Inquiry into the Medical Practice concerning Euthanasia," *Health Policy* 22 (1992): 1– 262; and Paul J. van der Maas, Johannes J. M. van Delden, Loes Pijnenborg, and Caspar W. N. Looman, "Euthanasia and other medical decisions con-

cerning the end of life," *Lancet* 338 (1991): 669–74. The second team's publications include G. van der Wal, J. T. van Eijk, H. J. Leenen, and C. Speeuwenberg, "The use of drugs for euthanasia and assisted suicide in family practice" (Medline translation of Dutch title), *Nederlands Tijdschrift Voor Geneeskunde* 136 (1992): 1299–305; same authors, "Euthanasia and assisted suicide by physicians in the home situation. 2. Suffering of the patients" (Medline translation of Dutch title), same journal 135 (1991): 1599–603; and same authors, "Euthanasia and assisted suicide by physicians in the home situation. I. Diagnoses, age and sex of patients," same journal 135 (1991): 1593–98. More recently the latter group has published Gerrit van der Wal and Robert J. M. Dillmann, "Euthanasia in the Netherlands," *British Medical Journal* 308 (1994): 1346–49; M. T. Muller et al., "Voluntary Active Euthanasia and Physician-Assisted Suicide in Dutch Nursing Homes: Are the Requirements for Prudent Practice Properly Met?" *Journal of the American Geriatrics Society* 42 (1994): 624–29; G. van der Wal et al., "Voluntary Active Euthanasia and Physician-Assisted Suicide in Dutch Nursing Homes: Requests and Administrations," *Journal of the American Geriatrics Society* 42 (1994): 620–23.

54. van der Maas et al., "Euthanasia," *Lancet*.

55. Henk ten Have has pointed out to me that women have also predominated in the court cases on physician-assisted suicide and euthanasia in the Netherlands. Personal communication, April 1993. Ideally, those judicial opinions will be translated into English or be analyzed by someone bilingual, permitting comparison to the textual analysis of U.S. judicial opinions in Steven Miles and Alison August, "Courts, Gender, and 'the Right to die,'" *Law, Medicine & Health Care* 18 (1990): 85–95.

56. van der Maas, van Delden, and Pijnenborg, "Euthanasia," *Health Policy*, 50.

57. van der Maas et al., "Euthanasia," *Lancet*, 671.

58. Johannes J. M. van Delden, personal communication, April 2, 1993.

59. Pijnenborg et al., "Life-terminating acts without explicit request of patient;" van der Maas, van Delden, and Pijnenborg, "Euthanasia," *Health Policy*, 50; Johannes J. M. van Delden, personal communication, April, 1993. Note that the 1991 *Lancet* article combines euthanasia, physician-assisted suicide, and "life-terminating events without explicit and persistent request," labeling the combination "euthanasia and related MDEL," and reporting a combined gender ratio of 61:39, with males predominating. See van der Maas et al., "Euthanasia," *Lancet*, 670–71. However, as I indicate in text, when you separate the three subcategories, women predominate for euthanasia.

60. Note that in *Lancet*, the researchers addressed both euthanasia and physician-assisted suicide in stating that, "Euthanasia and assisted suicide were more often found in deaths in relatively young men and in the urbanised western Netherlands, and this may be an indication of a shift to-

wards a more demanding attitude of patients in matters concerning the end of life." van der Maas et al., "Euthanasia," *Lancet*, 673. See also Pijnenborg et al., "Life-terminating acts without explicit request of patient." However, in their subsequent *Health Policy* publication, they reported that euthanasia was *not* more often found in men, though physician-assisted suicide was. van der Maas, van Delden, and Pijnenborg, "Euthanasia," *Health Policy*, 50.

61. Johannes J. M. van Delden, personal communication, April 1993.

62. See van der Maas, van Delden, and Pijnenborg, "Euthanasia," *Health Policy*, 52.

63. Compare, for example, "Netherlands: Ethnic Minority Population to Reach One Million by 2000," *Financieele Dagblad*, March 3, 1994 (ethnic minority population will then be 6.6 percent) with U.S. Department of Commerce, Bureau of the Census, *Statistical Abstract of the United States 1993*, 113th ed., 18 (20 percent of the 1990 population was non-white).

64. Canetto, "Elderly Women and Suicidal Behavior," 225–26 (citation omitted). I am grateful to Alta Charo for suggesting I also consider the preponderance of women in American nursing homes. See *Census of the Population, 1990: General Population Characteristics of the United States* (Washington, DC: Government Printing Office, 1992), 48 (1,278,433 women in nursing homes versus 493,609 men). On suicidal behavior, both attempted and completed, in U.S. nursing homes see Nancy J. Osgood, Barbara A. Brant, and Aaron Lipman, *Suicide Among the Elderly in Long-Term Care Facilities* (New York, NY: Greenwood Press, 1991).

65. There is a substantial literature on the Tuskegee study. See, for example, Arthur L. Caplan, "When Evil Intrudes," Harold Edgar, "Outside the Community," Patricia A. King, "The Dangers of Difference," and James H. Jones, "The Tuskegee Legacy: AIDS and the Black Community," all in "Twenty Years After: The Legacy of the Tuskegee Syphilis Study," *Hastings Center Report* 22 (Nov.–Dec. 1992): 29–40; James H. Jones, *Bad Blood: The Tuskegee Syphilis Experiment* (New York, NY: Free Press, 1981); Allan M. Brandt, "Racism and Research: The Case of the Tuskegee Syphilis Study," *Hastings Center Report* 8 (Dec. 1978): 21–28.

66. See Mark B. Wenneker and Arnold M. Epstein, "Racial Inequalities in the Use of Procedures for Patients with Ischemic Heart Disease in Massachusetts," *Journal of the American Medical Association* 261 (1989): 233–57. See also Robert J. Blendon et al., "Access to Medical Care for Black and White Americans: A Matter of Continuing Concern," *Journal of the American Medical Association* 261 (1989): 278–81; Craig K. Svensson, "Representation of American Blacks in Clinical Trials of New Drugs," *Journal of the American Medical Association* 261 (1989): 263–65.

67. On the intersection of race and gender, for example, see Kimberlé Crenshaw, "Demarginalizing the Intersection of Race and Sex: A Black Feminist Critique of Antidiscrimination Doctrine, Feminist Theory and Antiracist Politics," *Chicago Legal Forum* 1989: 139–67. See also Patricia Hill Collins, *Black Feminist Thought: Knowledge, Consciousness, and the Politics of Empowerment* (New York, NY: Routledge, 1991). On the intersection of race and gender in health, see Evelyn C. White, ed. *The Black Women's Health Book: Speaking for Ourselves* (Seattle, WA: Seal Press, 1990).

68. See, for example, Morton J. Horowitz, "Rights," *Harvard Civil Rights-Civil Liberties Law Review* 23 (1988): 393–406; Mark Tushnet, "An Essay on Rights," *Texas Law Review* 62 (1984): 1363–403.

69. Though there is overlap in the rights critiques of Critical Legal Studies (CLS) and Critical Race Theory, "[t]he CLS critique of rights and rules is the most problematic aspect of the CLS program, and provides few answers for minority scholars and lawyers." Richard Delgado, "The Ethereal Scholar: Does Critical Legal Studies Have What Minorities Want?" *Harvard Civil Rights–Civil Liberties Law Review* 22 (1987): 301–22, 304 (footnote omitted). Patricia Williams, indeed, has argued the necessity of rights discourse: "[S]tatements . . . about the relative utility of needs over rights discourse overlook that blacks have been describing their needs for generations. . . . For blacks, describing needs has been a dismal failure. . . ." Patricia J. Williams, *The Alchemy of Race and Rights* (Cambridge, MA: Harvard University Press, 1991), 151.

70. See, for example, Mary Ann Glendon, *Rights Talk: The Impoverishment of Political Discourse* (New York, NY: Free Press, 1991).

71. Margaret Farley has helpfully traced commonalities as well as distinctions between feminist theory and other traditions, noting that it is wrong to demand of any one critical stream that it bear no relation to the others. See Margaret A. Farley, "Feminist Theology and Bioethics," in Earl E. Shelp, ed., *Theology and Bioethics: Exploring the Foundations and Frontiers* (Boston, MA: D. Reidel, 1985), 163–85.

72. I take the term "rights talk" from Glendon, *Rights Talk*.

73. See, for example, Jean Grimshaw, *Philosophy and Feminist Thinking* (Minneapolis, MN: University of Minnesota Press, 1986), 175.

74. See, for example, Naomi Scheman, "Individualism and the Objects of Psychology," in Sandra Harding and Merrill B. Hintikka, eds., *Discovering Reality: Feminist Perspectives on Epistemology, Metaphysics, Methodology, and the Philosophy of Science* (Boston, MA: D. Reidel, 1983), 225–40, 240.

75. See Jennifer Nedelsky, "Reconceiving Autonomy: Sources, Thoughts and Possibilities," *Yale Journal of Law and Feminism* 1 (1989): 7–36.

76. Ibid., 12–13.

77. See Martha Minow, *Making All the Difference: Inclusion, Exclusion, and American Law* (Ithaca, NY: Cornell University Press, 1990).

78. Another author offering a feminist revision of autonomy and rights is Diana T. Meyers in "The Socialized Individual

and Individual Autonomy: An Intersection between Philosophy and Psychology," in Eva Feder Kittay and Diana T. Meyers, eds., *Women and Moral Theory* (Savage, MD: Rowman & Littlefield, 1987), 139–53. See also Elizabeth M. Schneider, "The Dialectic of Rights and Politics: Perspectives from the Women's Movement," *New York University Law Review* 61 (1986): 589–652. There is a large feminist literature presenting a critique of rights, some of it rejecting the utility of such language. See, for example, Catharine MacKinnon, "Feminism, Marxism, Method and the State: Toward Feminist Jurisprudence," *Signs* 8 (1983): 635–58, 658 ("Abstract rights will authorize the male experience of the world.").

79. See, for example, Susan M. Wolf, "Nancy Beth Cruzan: In No Voice At All," *Hastings Center Report* 20 (Jan.–Feb. 1990): 38–41; *Guidelines on the Termination of Life-Sustaining Treatment and the Care of the Dying* (Bloomington, IN: Indiana University Press & The Hastings Center, 1987).

80. John Stuart Mill, "On Liberty," in Marshall Cohen, ed., *The Philosophy of John Stuart Mill: Ethical, Political and Religious* (New York, NY: Random House, 1961), 185–319, 304.

81. Leon R. Kass also argues against the existence of a "right to die" in "Is There a Right to Die?" *Hastings Center Report* 23 (Jan.–Feb. 1993): 34–43.

82. The Dutch studies show that even when patients know they can get assisted suicide and euthanasia, three times more patients ask for such assurance from their physicians than actually die that way. See van der Maas et al., "Euthanasia," *Lancet*, 673.

83. On these obligations and their derivation, see Leon R. Kass, "Neither for Love nor Money: Why Doctors Must Not Kill," *The Public Interest* 94 (Winter 1989): 25–46; Tom L. Beauchamp and James F. Childress, *Principles of Biomedical Ethics*, 4th ed. (New York, NY: Oxford University Press, 1994), 189, 226–27.

84. See Leslie Bender, "A Feminist Analysis of Physician-Assisted Dying and Voluntary Active Euthanasia," *Tennessee Law Review* 59 (1992): 519–46, making a "caring" argument in favor of "physician-assisted death."

85. Brody, "Assisted Death."

86. James Rachels offers a like proposal. See Rachels, *The End of Life*.

87. For a summary of the debate over the proper structure of bioethics, see David DeGrazia, "Moving Forward in Bioethical Theory: Theories, Cases, and Specified Principlism," *Journal of Medicine and Philosophy* 17 (1992): 511–40. There have been several different attacks on a bioethics driven by principles, which is usually taken to be exemplified by Beauchamp and Childress, *Principles of Biomedical Ethics*. Clouser and Gert argue for a bioethics that would be even more "top-down" or deductive, proceeding from theory instead of principles. See K. Danner Clouser and Bernard Gert, "A Critique of Principlism," *Journal of Medicine and Philosophy* 15 (1990): 219–36. A different at-

tack is presented by Ronald M. Green, "Method in Bioethics: A Troubled Assessment," *Journal of Medicine and Philosophy* 15 (1990): 179–97. Hoffmaster argues for an ethnography driven, "bottom-up" or inductive bioethics. Barry Hoffmaster, "The Theory and Practice of Applied Ethics," *Dialogue*, XXX (1991): 213–34. Jonsen and Toulmin have urged a revival of casuistry built on case-by-case analysis. Albert R. Jonsen and Stephen Toulmin, *The Abuse of Casuistry: A History of Moral Reasoning* (Berkeley, CA: University of California Press, 1988). Beauchamp and Childress discuss these challenges at length in the 4th edition of *Principles of Biomedical Ethics*.

88. See Gilligan, *In A Different Voice*, 174. Lawrence Blum points out that Kohlberg himself stated that "the final, most mature stage of moral reasoning involves an 'integration of justice and care that forms a single moral principle,'" but that Kohlberg, too, never spelled out what the integration would be. See Lawrence A. Blum, "Gilligan and Kohlberg: Implications for Moral Theory," *Ethics* 98 (1988): 472–91, 482–83 (footnote with citation omitted).

89. See Blum, "Gilligan and Kohlberg," 477.

90. Owen Flanagan and Kathryn Jackson, "Justice, Care, and Gender: The Kohlberg-Gilligan Debate Revisited," in Larrabee, ed., *An Ethic of Care*, 69–84, 71.

91. Martha Minow and Elizabeth V. Spelman, "In Context," *Southern California Law Review* 63 (1990): 1597–652, 1625.

92. *Ibid.*, 1629.

93. *Ibid.*, 1630–31.

94. *Ibid.*, 1632–33.

95. There are significant similarities here to Henry Richardson's proposal of "specified principlism." See DeGrazia, "Moving Forward in Bioethical Theory."

96. On the importance of paying attention to who is doing the theorizing and to what end, including in feminist theorizing, see María C. Lugones and Elizabeth V. Spelman, "Have We Got a Theory for You! Feminist Theory, Cultural Imperialism and the Demand for 'The Woman's Voice,'" *Women's Studies International Forum* 6 (1983): 573–81.

97. I have elsewhere argued that health care institutions should create processes to uncover and combat sexism and racism, among other problems. See Susan M. Wolf, "Toward a Theory of Process," *Law, Medicine & Health Care* 20 (1992): 278–90.

98. On the importance of viewing the medical profession in the context of the democratic polity, see Troyen Brennan, *Just Doctoring: Medical Ethics in the Liberal State* (Berkeley, CA: University of California Press, 1991).

99. See, for example, Howard J. Curzer, "Is Care A Virtue For Health Care Professionals?" *Journal of Medicine and Philosophy* 18 (1993): 51–69; Nancy S. Jecker and Donnie J. Self, "Separating Care And Cure: An Analysis Of Historical And Contemporary Images Of Nursing And Medicine," *Journal of Medicine and Philosophy* 16 (1991): 285–306.

100. Compare Canetto, "Elderly Women and Suicidal Behavior," finding evidence of this with respect to elderly women electing suicide.

101. See van der Maas, van Delden, and Pijnenborg, "Euthanasia," *Health Policy*, 51–55, 145–46; van der Wal et al., "Voluntary Active Euthanasia and Physician-Assisted Suicide in Dutch Nursing Homes."

102. See Quill, Cassel, and Meier, "Care of the Hopelessly Ill."

103. In these two sentences, I disagree both with Kass's suggestion that the core commitments of medicine are set for all time by the ancient formulation of the doctor's role and with Brock's assertion that the core commitment of medicine is to do whatever the patient wants. See Kass, "Neither for Love Nor Money;" Dan Brock, "Voluntary Active Euthanasia," *Hastings Center Report* 22 (Mar.–Apr. 1992): 10–22.

104. See Jay Katz, *The Silent World of Doctor and Patient* (New York, NY: Free Press, 1984), 121–22.

105. See Miles and August, "Gender, Courts, and the 'Right to Die.'"

106. While a large literature analyzes the relationship between terminating life-sustaining treatment and the practices of physician-assisted suicide and euthanasia, more recently attention has turned to the relationship between those latter practices and abortion. On the question of whether respect for women's choice of abortion requires legitimation of those practices, see, for example, Seth F. Kreimer, "Does Pro-choice Mean Pro-Kevorkian? An Essay on *Roe, Casey,* and the Right to Die," *American University Law Review* 44 (1995): 803–54. Full analysis of why respect for the choice of abortion does not require legitimation of physician-assisted suicide and euthanasia is beyond the scope of this chapter. However, the courts themselves are beginning to argue the distinction. See Compassion in Dying v. Washington, 49 F.3d 586 (9th Cir. 1995). On gender specifically, there are strong arguments that gender equity and concern for the fate of women demand respect for the abortion choice, whereas I am arguing that gender concerns cut the other way when it comes to physician-assisted suicide and euthanasia.

The Case of Diane

Timothy E. Quill, M.D.

Timothy E. Quill, M.D., is an internist and associate professor of medicine and psychiatry at the University of Rochester School of Medicine and Dentistry, New York. He was one of the plaintiffs in the case on physician-assisted suicide decided by the Second Circuit Court of Appeals, *Quill* v. *Vacco* (1996).

Diane was feeling tired and had a rash. A common scenario, though there was something subliminally worrisome that prompted me to check her blood count. Her hematocrit was 22, and the white-cell count was 4.3 with some metamyelocytes and unusual white cells. I wanted it to be viral, trying to deny what was staring me in the face. Perhaps in a repeated count it would disappear. I called Diane and told her it might be more serious than I had initially thought—that the test needed to be repeated and that if she felt worse, we might have to move quickly. When she pressed for the possibilities, I reluctantly opened the door to leukemia. Hearing the word seemed to make it exist. "Oh

shit!" she said. "Don't tell me that." Oh, shit! I thought, I wish I didn't have to.

Diane was no ordinary person (although no one I have ever come to know has been really ordinary). She was raised in an alcoholic family and had felt alone for much of her life. She had vaginal cancer as a young woman. Through much of her adult life, she had struggled with depression and her own alcoholism. I had come to know, respect, and admire her over the previous eight years as she confronted these problems and gradually overcame them. She was an incredibly clear, at times brutally honest, thinker and communicator. As she took control of her life, she developed a strong sense of independence and confidence. In the previous three-and-one-half years, her hard work had paid off. She was completely abstinent from alcohol, she had established much deeper connections with her husband, college-age son, and several friends, and her business and her

Timothy E. Quill, "Death and Dignity: A Case of Individualized Decision Making," *New England Journal of Medicine* 324, No. 10 (March 7, 1991): 691–694. Reprinted by permission of the *New England Journal of Medicine*. Copyright (c) 1991 by the Massachusetts Medical Society. All rights reserved.

artistic work were blossoming. She felt she was really living fully for the first time.

Not surprisingly, the repeated blood count was abnormal, and detailed examination of the peripheral blood smear showed myelocytes. I advised her to come into the hospital, explaining that we needed to do a bone marrow biopsy and make some decisions relatively rapidly. She came to the hospital knowing what we would find. She was terrified, angry, and sad. Although we knew the odds, we both clung to the thread of possibility that it might be something else.

The bone marrow confirmed the worst: acute myelomonocytic leukemia. In the face of this tragedy, we looked for signs of hope. This is an area of medicine in which technological intervention has been successful, with cures 25 percent of the time—long-term cures. As I probed the costs of these cures, I heard about induction chemotherapy (three weeks in the hospital, prolonged neutropenia, probable infectious complications, and hair loss; 75 percent of patients respond, 25 percent do not). For the survivors, this is followed by consolidation chemotherapy (with similar side effects; another 25 percent die, for a net survival of 50 percent). Those still alive, to have a reasonable chance of long-term survival, then need bone marrow transplantation (hospitalization for two months and whole-body irradiation, with complete-killing of the bone marrow, infectious complications, and the possibility for graft-versus-host disease—with a survival of approximately 50 percent, or 25 percent of the original group). Though hematologists may argue over the exact percentages, they don't argue about the outcome of no treatment—certain death in days, weeks, or at most a few months.

Believing that delay was dangerous, our oncologist broke the news to Diane and began making plans to insert a Hickman catheter and begin induction chemotherapy that afternoon. When I saw her shortly thereafter, she was enraged at his presumption that she would want treatment, and devastated by the finality of the diagnosis. All she wanted to do was go home and be with her family. She had no further questions about treatment and in fact had decided that she wanted none. Together we lamented her tragedy and the unfairness of life. Before she left, I felt the need to be sure

that she and her husband understood that there was some risk in delay, that the problem was not going to go away, and that we needed to keep considering the options over the next several days. We agreed to meet in two days.

She returned in two days with her husband and son. They had talked extensively about the problem and the options. She remained very clear about her wish not to undergo chemotherapy and to live whatever time she had left outside the hospital. As we explored her thinking further, it became clear that she was convinced she would die during the period of treatment and would suffer unspeakably in the process (from hospitalization, from lack of control over her body, from the side effects of chemotherapy, and from pain and anguish). Although I could offer support and my best effort to minimize her suffering if she chose treatment, there was no way I could say any of this would not occur. In fact, the last four patients with acute leukemia at our hospital had died very painful deaths in the hospital during various stages of treatment (a fact I did not share with her). Her family wished she would choose treatment but sadly accepted her decision. She articulated very clearly that it was she who would be experiencing all the side effects of treatment and that odds of 25 percent were not good enough for her to undergo so toxic a course of therapy, given her expectations of chemotherapy and hospitalization and the absence of a closely matched bone marrow donor. I had her repeat her understanding of the treatment, the odds, and what to expect if there were no treatment. I clarified a few misunderstandings, but she had a remarkable grasp of the options and implications.

I have been a longtime advocate of active, informed patient choice of treatment or nontreatment, and of a patient's right to die with as much control and dignity as possible. Yet there was something about her giving up a 25 percent change of long-term survival in favor of almost certain death that disturbed me. I had seen Diane fight and use her considerable inner resources to overcome alcoholism and depression, and I half expected her to change her mind over the next week. Since the window of time in which effective treatment can be initiated is rather narrow, we met several times that week. We obtained a second hematology consultation and talked at length about the meaning and implications of treatment and nontreatment. She talked to a psychologist she had seen in the past. I gradually understood the decision from her perspective and became convinced that it was the right decision for her. We arranged for home hospice care (although at that time Diane felt reasonably well, was active, and looked healthy), left the door open for her to change her mind, and tried to anticipate how to keep her comfortable in the time she had left.

Just as I was adjusting to her decision, she opened up another area that would stretch me profoundly. It was extraordinarily important to Diane to maintain control of herself and her own dignity during the time remaining to her. When this was no longer possible, she clearly wanted to die. As a former director of a hospice program, I know how to use pain medicines to keep patients comfortable and lessen suffering. I explained the philosophy of comfort care, which I strongly believe in. Although Diane understood and appreciated this, she had known of people lingering in what was called relative comfort, and she wanted no part of it. When the time came, she wanted to take her life in the least painful way possible. Knowing of her desire for independence and her decision to stay in control, I thought this request made perfect sense. I acknowledged and explored this wish but also thought that it was out of the realm of currently accepted medical practice and that it was more than I could offer or promise. In our discussion, it became clear that preoccupation with her fear of a lingering death would interfere with Diane's getting the most out of the time she had left until she found a safe way to ensure her death. I feared the effects of a violent death on her family, the consequences of an ineffective suicide that would leave her lingering in precisely the state she dreaded so much, and the possibility that a family member would be forced to assist her, with all the legal and personal repercussions that would follow. She discussed this at length with her family. They believed that they should respect her choice. With this in mind, I told Diane that information was available from the Hemlock Society that might be helpful to her.

A week later she phoned me with a request for barbiturates for sleep. Since I knew that this was an essential ingredient in a Hemlock Society suicide, I asked her to come to the office to talk things over. She was more than willing to protect me by participating in a superficial conversation about her insomnia, but it was important to me to know how she planned to use the drugs and to be sure that she was not in despair or overwhelmed in a way that might color her judgment. In our discussion, it was apparent that she was having trouble sleeping, but it was also evident that the security of having enough barbiturates available to commit suicide when and if the time came would leave her secure enough to live fully and concentrate on the present. It was clear that she was not despondent and that in fact she was making deep, personal connections with her family and close friends. I made sure that she knew how to use the barbiturates for sleep, and also that she knew the amount needed to commit suicide. We agreed to meet regularly, and she promised to meet with me before taking her life, to ensure that all other avenues had been exhausted. I wrote the prescription with an uneasy feeling about the boundaries I was exploring—spiritual, legal, professional, and personal. Yet I also felt strongly that I was setting her free to get the most out of the time she had left, and to maintain dignity and control on her own terms until her death.

The next several months were very intense and important for Diane. Her son stayed home from college, and they were able to be with one another and say much that had not been said earlier. Her husband did his work at home so that he and Diane could spend more time together. She spent time with her closest friends. I had her come into the hospital for a conference with our residents, at which she illustrated in a most profound and personal way the importance of informed decision making, the right to refuse treatment, and the extraordinarily personal effects of illness and interaction with the medical system. There were emotional and physical hardships as well. She had periods of intense sadness and anger. Several times she became very weak, but she received transfusions as an outpatient and responded with marked improvement of symptoms. She had two serious infections that responded surprisingly well to empirical courses of oral antibiotics. After three tumultuous months, there were two weeks of relative calm and well-being, and fantasies of a miracle began to surface.

Unfortunately, we had no miracle. Bone pain, weakness, fatigue, and fevers began to dominate her life. Although the hospice workers, family members, and I tried our best to minimize the suffering and promote comfort, it was clear that the end was approaching. Diane's immediate future held what she feared the most—increasing discomfort, dependence, and hard choices between pain and sedation. She called up her closest friends and asked them to come over to say good-bye, telling them that she would be leaving soon. As we had agreed, she let me know as well. When we met, it was clear that she knew what she was doing, that she was sad and frightened to be leaving, but that she would be even more terrified to stay and suffer. In our tearful goodbye, she promised a reunion in the future at her favorite spot on the edge of Lake Geneva, with dragons swimming in the sunset.

Two days later her husband called to say that Diane had died. She had said her final goodbyes to her husband and son that morning, and asked them to leave her alone for an hour. After an hour, which must have seemed an eternity, they found her on the couch, lying very still and covered by her favorite shawl. There was no sign of struggle. She seemed to be at peace. They called me for advice about how to proceed. When I arrived at their house, Diane indeed seemed peaceful. Her husband and son were quiet. We talked about what a remarkable person she had been. They seemed to have no doubts about the course she had chosen or about their cooperation, although the unfairness of her illness and the finality of her death were overwhelming to us all.

I called the medical examiner to inform him that a hospice patient had died. When asked about the cause of death, I said, "acute leukemia." He said that was fine and that we should call a funeral director. Although acute leukemia was the truth, it was not the whole story. Yet any mention of suicide would have given rise to a police investigation and probably brought the arrival of an ambulance crew for resuscitation. Diane would have become a "coroner's case," and the decision to perform an autopsy would have been made at the discretion of the medical examiner. The family or I

could have been subject to criminal prosecution, and I to professional review, for our roles in support of Diane's choices. Although I truly believe that the family and I gave her the best care possible, allowing her to define her limits and directions as much as possible, I am not sure the law, society, or the medical profession would agree. So I said "acute leukemia" to protect all of us, to protect Diane from an invasion into her past and her body, and to continue to shield society from the knowledge of the degree of suffering that people often undergo in the process of dying. Suffering can be lessened to some extent, but in no way eliminated or made benign, by the careful intervention of a competent, caring physician, given current social constraints.

Diane taught me about the range of help I can provide if I know people well and if I allow them to say what they really want. She taught me about life, death, and honesty and about taking charge and facing tragedy squarely when it strikes. She taught me that I can take small risks for people that I really know and care about. Although I did not assist in her suicide directly, I helped indirectly to make it possible, successful, and relatively painless. Although I know we have measures to help control pain and lessen suffering, to think that people do not suffer in the process of dying is an illusion. Prolonged dying can occasionally be peaceful, but more often the role of the physician and family is limited to lessening but not eliminating severe suffering.

I wonder how many families and physicians secretly help patients over the edge into death in the face of such severe suffering. I wonder how many severely ill or dying patients secretly take their lives, dying alone in despair. I wonder whether the image of Diane's final aloneness will persist in the minds of her family, or if they will remember more the intense, meaningful months they had together before she died. I wonder whether Diane struggled in that last hour, and whether the Hemlock Society's way of death by suicide is the most benign. I wonder why Diane, who gave so much to so many of us, had to be alone for the last hour of her life. I wonder whether I will see Diane again, on the shore of Lake Geneva at sunset, with dragons swimming on the horizon.

16.

Active and Passive Euthanasia

James Rachels

James Rachels is professor of philosophy at the University of Alabama at Birmingham. He is the author of numerous articles and three books, *The Elements of Moral Philosophy, The End of Life: Euthanasia and Morality,* and *Created from Animals: The Moral Implications of Darwinism.* In this well-known essay, Rachels challenges the traditional moral distinction between killing and letting die. The philosophical debate over this distinction has received fresh attention in recent legal battles over physician-assisted suicide.

The distinction between active and passive euthanasia is thought to be crucial for medical ethics. The idea is that it is permissible, at least in some cases, to withhold treatment and allow a patient to die, but it is never permissible to take any direct action designed to kill the patient. This doctrine seems to be accepted by most doctors, and it is endorsed in a statement adopted by the House of Delegates of the American Medical Association on December 4, 1973:

> The intentional termination of the life of one human being by another—mercy killing—is contrary to that for which the medical profession stands and is contrary to the policy of the American Medical Association.
>
> The cessation of the employment of extraordinary means to prolong the life of the body when there is irrefutable evidence that biological death is imminent is the decision of the patient and/or his immediate family. The advice and judgment of the physician should be freely available to the patient and/or his immediate family.

However, a strong case can be made against this doctrine. In what follows I will set out some of the relevant arguments, and urge doctors to reconsider their views on this matter.

To begin with a familiar type of situation, a patient who is dying of incurable cancer of the throat is in terrible pain, which can no longer be satisfactorily alleviated. He is certain to die within a few days, even if present treatment is continued, but he does not want to go on living for those days since the pain is unbearable. So he asks the doctor for an end to it, and his family joins in the request.

Suppose the doctor agrees to withhold treatment, as the conventional doctrine says he may. The justification for his doing so is that the patient is in terrible agony, and since he is going to die anyway, it would be wrong to prolong his suffering needlessly. But now notice this. If one simply withholds treatment, it may take the patient longer to die, and so he may suffer more than he would if more direct action were taken and a lethal injection given. This fact provides strong reason for thinking that, once the initial decision not to prolong his agony has been made, active euthanasia is actually preferable to passive euthanasia, rather than the reverse. To say otherwise is to endorse the option that leads to more suffering rather than less, and is contrary to the humanitarian impulse that prompts the decision not to prolong his life in the first place.

Part of my point is that the process of being "allowed to die" can be relatively slow and painful, whereas being given a lethal injection is relatively quick and painless. Let me give a different sort of example. In the United States about one in 600 babies is born with Down's syndrome. Most of those babies are otherwise healthy—that is, with only the usual pediatric care, they will proceed to an otherwise normal

James Rachels, "Active and Passive Euthanasia," *The New England Journal of Medicine*, Vol. 292 (1975): 78–80.
Reprinted by permission of *The New England Journal of Medicine*. Copyright (c) 1975 by the Massachusetts Medical Society. All rights reserved.

infancy. Some, however, are born with congenital defects such as intestinal obstructions that require operations if they are to live. Sometimes, the parents and the doctor will decide not to operate, and let the infant die. Anthony Shaw describes what happens then:

> . . . When surgery is denied [the doctor] must try to keep the infant from suffering while natural forces sap the baby's life away. As a surgeon whose natural inclination is to use the scalpel to fight off death, standing by and watching a salvageable baby die is the most emotionally exhausting experience I know. It is easy at a conference, in a theoretical discussion, to decide that such infants should be allowed to die. It is altogether different to stand by in the nursery and watch as dehydration and infection wither a tiny being over hours and days. This is a terrible ordeal for me and the hospital staff—much more so than for the parents who never set foot in the nursery.[1]

I can understand why some people are opposed to all euthanasia, and insist that such infants must be allowed to live. I think I can also understand why other people favor destroying these babies quickly and painlessly. But why should anyone favor letting "dehydration and infection wither a tiny being over hours and days"? The doctrine that says that a baby may be allowed to dehydrate and wither, but may not be given an injection that would end its life without suffering, seems so patently cruel as to require no further refutation. The strong language is not intended to offend, but only to put the point in the clearest possible way.

My second argument is that the conventional doctrine leads to decisions concerning life and death made on irrelevant grounds.

Consider again the case of the infants with Down's syndrome who need operations for congenital defects unrelated to the syndrome to live. Sometimes, there is no operation, and the baby dies, but when there is no such defect, the baby lives on. Now, an operation such as that to remove an intestinal obstruction is not prohibitively difficult. The reason why such operations are not performed in these cases is, clearly, that the child has Down's syndrome and the parents and doctor judge that because of that fact it is better for the child to die.

But notice that this situation is absurd, no matter what view one takes of the lives and potentials of such babies. If the life of such an infant is worth preserving, what does it matter if it needs a simple operation? Or, if one thinks it better that such a baby should not live on, what difference does it make that it happens to have an unobstructed intestinal tract? In either case, the matter of life and death is being decided on irrelevant grounds. It is the Down's syndrome, and not the intestines, that is the issue. The matter should be decided, if at all, on that basis, and not be allowed to depend on the essentially irrelevant question of whether the intestinal tract is blocked.

What makes this situation possible, of course, is the idea that when there is an intestinal blockage, one can "let the baby die," but when there is no such defect there is nothing that can be done, for one must not "kill" it. The fact that this idea leads to such results as deciding life or death on irrelevant grounds is another good reason why the doctrine should be rejected.

One reason why so many people think that there is an important moral difference between active and passive euthanasia is that they think killing someone is morally worse than letting someone die. But is it? Is killing, in itself, worse than letting die? To investigate this issue, two cases may be considered that are exactly alike except that one involves killing whereas the other involves letting someone die. Then, it can be asked whether this difference makes any difference to the moral assessments. It is important that the cases be exactly alike, except for this one difference, since otherwise one cannot be confident that it is this difference and not some other that accounts for any variation in the assessments of the two cases. So, let us consider this pair of cases:

In the first, Smith stands to gain a large inheritance if anything should happen to his six-year-old cousin. One evening while the child is taking his bath, Smith sneaks into the bathroom and drowns the child, and then arranges things so that it will look like an accident.

In the second, Jones also stands to gain if anything should happen to his six-year-old cousin. Like Smith, Jones sneaks in planning to drown the child in his bath. However, just as he enters the bathroom Jones sees the child slip and hit his head, and fall face down in the water. Jones is delighted; he stands by, ready to push the child's head back under if it is necessary, but it is not necessary. With only a little thrashing about, the child drowns all by himself, "accidentally," as Jones watches and does nothing.

Now Smith killed the child, whereas Jones "merely" let the child die. That is the only difference between them. Did either man behave better from a moral point of view? If the difference between killing and letting die were in itself a morally important matter, one should say that Jones' behavior was less reprehensible than Smith's. But does one really want to say that? I think not. In the first place, both men acted from the same motive, personal gain, and both had exactly the same end in view when they acted. It may be inferred from Smith's conduct that he is a bad man, although that judgment may be withdrawn or modified if certain further facts are learned about him—for example, that he is mentally deranged. But would not the very same thing be inferred about Jones from his conduct? And would not the same further considerations also be relevant to any modification of this judgment? Moreover, suppose Jones pleaded, in his own defense, "After all, I didn't do anything except just stand there and watch the child drown. I didn't kill him; I only let him die." Again, if letting die were in itself less bad than killing, this defense should have at least some weight. But it does not. Such a "defense" can only be regarded as a grotesque perversion of moral reasoning. Morally speaking, it is no defense at all.

Now, it may be pointed out, quite properly, that the cases of euthanasia with which doctors are concerned are not like this at all. They do not involve personal gain or the destruction of normal healthy children. Doctors are concerned only with cases in which the patient's life is of no further use to him, or in which the patient's life has become or will soon become a terrible burden. However, the point is the same in these cases: the bare difference between killing and letting die does not, in itself, make a moral difference. If a doctor lets a patient die for humane reasons, he is in the same moral position as if he had given the patient a lethal injection for humane reasons. If his decision was wrong—if, for example, the patient's illness was in fact curable—the decision would be equally regrettable no matter which method was used to carry it out. And if the doctor's decision was the right one, the method used is not in itself important.

The AMA policy statement isolates the crucial issue very well; the crucial issue is "the intentional termination of the life of one human being by another." But after identifying this issue, and forbidding "mercy killing," the statement goes on to deny that the cessation of treatment is the intentional termination of a life. This is where the mistake comes in, for what is the cessation of treatment, in these circumstances, if it is not "the intentional termination of the life of one human being by another"? Of course it is exactly that, and if it were not, there would be no point to it.

Many people will find this judgment hard to accept. One reason, I think, is that it is very easy to conflate the question of whether killing is, in itself, worse than letting die, with the very different question of whether most actual cases of killing are more reprehensible than most actual cases of letting die. Most actual cases of killing are clearly terrible (think, for example, of all the murders reported in the newspapers), and one hears of such cases every day. On the other hand, one hardly ever hears of a case of letting die, except for the actions of doctors who are motivated by humanitarian reasons. So one learns to think of killing in a much worse light than of letting die. But this does not mean that there is something about killing that makes it in itself worse than letting die, for it is not the bare difference between killing and letting die that makes the difference in these cases. Rather, the other factors—the murderer's motive of personal gain, for example, contrasted with the doctor's humanitarian motivation—account for different reactions to the different cases.

I have argued that killing is not in itself any worse than letting die; if my contention is right, it follows that active euthanasia is not any worse than passive euthanasia. What arguments can be given on the other side? The most common, I believe, is the following:

"The important difference between active and passive euthanasia is that, in passive euthanasia, the doctor does not do anything to bring about the patient's death. The doctor does nothing, and the patient dies of whatever ills already afflict him. In active euthanasia, however, the doctor does something to bring about the patient's death: he kills him. The doctor who gives the patient with cancer a lethal injection has himself caused his patient's death; whereas if he merely ceases treatment, the cancer is the cause of the death."

A number of points need to be made here. The first is that it is not exactly correct to say that in passive euthanasia the doctor does nothing, for he does do one thing that is very important: he lets the patient die. "Letting someone die" is certainly different, in some respects, from other types of action—mainly in that it is a kind of action that one may perform by way of not performing certain other actions. For example, one may let a patient die by way of not giving medication, just as one may insult someone by way of not shaking his hand. But for any purpose of moral assessment, it is a type of action nonetheless. The decision to let a patient die is subject to moral appraisal in the same way that a decision to kill him would be subject to moral appraisal: it may be assessed as wise or unwise, compassionate or sadistic, right or wrong. If a doctor deliberately let a patient die who was suffering from a routinely curable illness, the doctor would certainly be to blame for what he had done, just as he would be to blame if he had needlessly killed the patient. Charges against him would then be appropriate. If so, it would be no defense at all for him to insist that he didn't "do anything." He would have done something very serious indeed, for he let his patient die.

Fixing the cause of death may be very important from a legal point of view, for it may determine whether criminal charges are brought against the doctor. But I do not think that this notion can be used to show a moral difference between active and passive euthanasia. The reason why it is considered bad to be the cause of someone's death is that death is regarded as a great evil—and so it is. However, if it has been decided that euthanasia—even passive euthanasia—is desirable in a given case, it has also been decided that in this instance death is no greater an evil than the patient's continued existence. And if this is true, the usual reason for not wanting to be the cause of someone's death simply does not apply.

Finally, doctors may think that all of this is only of academic interest—the sort of thing that philosophers may worry about but that has no practical bearing on their own work. After all, doctors must be concerned about the legal consequences of what they do, and active euthanasia is clearly forbidden by the law. But even so, doctors should also be concerned with the fact that the law is forcing upon them a moral doctrine that may well be indefensible, and has a considerable effect on their practices. Of course, most doctors are not now in the position of being coerced in this matter; for they do not regard themselves as merely going along with what the law requires. Rather, in statements such as AMA policy statement that I have quoted, they are endorsing this doctrine as a central point of medical ethics. In that statement, active euthanasia is condemned not merely as illegal but as "contrary to that for which the medical profession stands," whereas passive euthanasia is approved. However, the preceding considerations suggest that there is really no moral difference between the two, considered in themselves (there may be important moral differences in some cases in their *consequences*, but, as I pointed out, these differences may make active euthanasia, and not passive euthanasia, the morally preferable option). So,

whereas doctors may have to discriminate between active and passive euthanasia to satisfy the law, they should not do any more than that. In particular, they should not give the distinction any added authority and weight by writing it into official statements of medical ethics.

NOTE

1. Shaw, A.: "Doctor, Do We Have a Choice?" *The New York Times Magazine*, January 30, 1972, p. 54.

Washington v. Glucksberg and Vacco v. Quill (1997)

United States Supreme Court

Editor's Note: In June, 1997, the U.S. Supreme Court ruled unanimously that terminally ill adults do not have a constitutionally protected "right to doctor-assisted suicide." The Court thus upheld state laws in Washington and New York which prohibit physician-assisted suicide; these state laws had been invalidated by lower courts in 1996. Chief Justice William Rehnquist wrote the two decisions, *Washington v. Glucksberg* (upholding the state law in Washington) and *Vacco v. Quill* (affirming the ban in New York State). In both cases, concurring opinions were offered by Justices Sandra Day O'Connor, Stephen Breyer and David Souter. The Justices make clear that these rulings do not preclude debate about assisted suicide in legislative spheres. Rehnquist states "our holding permits this debate to continue, as it should in a democratic society."

Part I. Washington v. Glucksberg

The question presented in this case is whether Washington's prohibition against "caus[ing]" or "aid[ing]" a suicide offends the 14th Amendment to the United States Constitution. We hold that it does not. . . .

The plaintiffs asserted "the existence of a liberty interest protected by the 14th Amendment which extends to a personal choice by a mentally competent, terminally ill adult to commit physician-assisted suicide." Relying primarily on *Planned Parenthood v. Casey* and *Cruzan v. Director, Missouri Dept. of Health,* the district court agreed, and concluded that Washington's assisted-suicide ban is unconstitutional because it "places an undue burden on the exercise of (that) constitutionally pro-

tected liberty interest." The district court also decided that the Washington statute violated the Equal Protection Clause's requirement that "'all persons similarly situated . . . be treated alike.'"

A panel of the Court of Appeals for the Ninth Circuit reversed, emphasizing that "[i]n the 205 years of our existence no constitutional right to aid in killing oneself has ever been asserted and upheld by a court of final jurisdiction." The Ninth Circuit reheard the case *en banc,* reversed the panel's decision, and affirmed the district court. . . .

In almost every state indeed, in almost every Western democracy it is a crime to assist a suicide. The states' assisted-suicide bans are not innovations. Rather, they are long-standing expressions of the states' commitment to the protection and preservation of all human life. Indeed, opposition to and condemnation of suicide and, therefore, of assisting suicide are consistent and enduring themes of our philosophical, legal, and cultural

United States Supreme Court, *Washington v. Glucksberg*, No. 96-110, and *Vacco v. Quill*, No 95-1858 (June 26, 1997).

heritages. More specifically, for over 700 years, the Anglo-American common-law tradition has punished or otherwise disapproved of both suicide and assisting suicide . . . .

The due process clause guarantees more than fair process, and the "liberty" it protects includes more than the absence of physical restraint. The clause also provides heightened protection against government interference with certain fundamental rights and liberty interests. In a long line of cases, we have held that, in addition to the specific freedoms protected by the Bill of Rights, the "liberty" specially protected by the due process clause includes the rights to marry, to have children, to direct the education and upbringing of one's children, to marital privacy, to use contraception, to bodily integrity, and to abortion. We have also assumed, and strongly suggested, that the due process clause protects the traditional right to refuse unwanted lifesaving medical treatment.

But we "ha[ve] always been reluctant to expand the concept of substantive due process because guideposts for responsible decision making in this uncharted area are scarce and open-ended." . . .

Our established method of substantive-due-process analysis has two primary features: First, we have regularly observed that the due process clause specially protects those fundamental rights and liberties which are, objectively, "deeply rooted in this nation's history and tradition," and "implicit in the concept of ordered liberty," such that "neither liberty nor justice would exist if they were sacrificed." Second, we have required in substantive-due-process cases a "careful description" of the asserted fundamental liberty interest. Our nation's history, legal traditions, and practices thus provide the crucial "guideposts for responsible decision making," that direct and restrain our exposition of the due process clause. . . .

Turning to the claim at issue here, the Court of Appeals stated that "[p]roperly analyzed, the first issue to be resolved is whether there is a liberty interest in determining the time and manner of one's death," or, in other words, "[i]s there a right to die?" Similarly, respondents assert a "liberty to choose how to die" and a right to "control of one's final days," and describe the asserted liberty as "the right to choose a humane, dignified death," and "the liberty to shape death." . . .

The Washington statute at issue in this case prohibits "aid[ing] another person to attempt suicide," Wash. Rev. Code s9A.36.060(1) (1994), and, thus, the question before us is whether the "liberty" specially protected by the due process clause includes a right to commit suicide which itself includes a right to assistance in doing so. We now inquire whether this asserted right has any place in our nation's traditions. Here, as discussed above, we are confronted with a consistent and almost universal tradition that has long rejected the asserted right, and continues explicitly to reject it today, even for terminally ill, mentally competent adults. To hold for respondents, we would have to reverse centuries of legal doctrine and practice and strike down the considered policy choice of almost every state.

The history of the law's treatment of assisted suicide in this country has been and continues to be one of the rejection of nearly all efforts to permit it. That being the case, our decisions lead us to conclude that the asserted "right" to assistance in committing suicide is not a fundamental liberty interest protected by the due process clause. The Constitution also requires, however, that Washington's assisted-suicide ban be rationally related to legitimate government interests. This requirement is unquestionably met here. As the court below recognized, Washington's assisted-suicide ban implicates a number of state interests.

First, Washington has an "unqualified interest in the preservation of human life." The state's prohibition on assisted suicide, like all homicide laws, both reflects and advances its commitment to this interest. . . .

Relatedly, all admit that suicide is a serious public health problem, especially among persons in otherwise vulnerable groups. The state has an interest in preventing suicide and in studying, identifying and treating its causes. Those who attempt suicide, terminally ill or not, often suffer from depression or other mental disorders. Research indicates, however, that many people who request physician-assisted suicide withdraw that request if their depression and pain are treated. The New York task force, however, expressed its concern that, because depression is difficult to diagnose, physicians and medical professionals often fail to respond adequately to seriously ill patients' needs. Thus, legal physician-assisted suicide could make it more difficult for the state to protect depressed or mentally ill persons, or those who are suffering from untreated pain, from suicidal impulses.

The state also has an interest in protecting the integrity and ethics of the medical profession. In contrast to the Court of Appeals' conclusion that "the integrity of the medical profession would [not] be threatened in any way by [physician-assisted suicide]," the American Medical Association, like many other medical and physicians' groups, has concluded that "[p]hysician-assisted suicide is fundamentally incompatible with the physician's role as healer." And physician-assisted suicide could, it is argued, undermine the trust that is essential to the doctor-patient relationship by blurring the time-honored line between healing and harming.

Next, the state has an interest in protecting vulnerable groups including the poor, the elderly, and disabled persons from abuse, neglect and mistakes. The Court of Appeals dismissed the state's concern that disadvantaged persons might be pressured into physician-assisted suicide as "ludicrous on its face." We have recognized, however, the real risk of subtle coercion and undue influence in end-of-life situations.

The state's interest here goes beyond protecting the vulnerable from coercion; it extends to protecting disabled and terminally ill people from prejudice, negative and inaccurate stereotypes and "societal indifference." The state's assisted-suicide ban reflects and reinforces its policy that the lives of terminally ill, disabled and elderly people must be no less valued than the lives of the young and healthy and that a seriously disabled person's suicidal impulses should be interpreted and treated the same way as anyone else's.

Finally, the state may fear that permitting assisted suicide will start it down the path to voluntary and perhaps even involuntary euthanasia. The Court of Appeals struck down Washington's assisted-suicide ban only "as applied to competent, terminally ill adults who wish to hasten their deaths by obtaining medication prescribed by their doctors."

[The State of] Washington insists, however, that the impact of the court's decision will not and cannot be so limited. If suicide is protected as a matter of constitutional right, it is argued, "every man and woman in the United States must enjoy it." The Court of Appeals' decision, and its expansive reasoning, provide ample support for the state's concerns. . . .

Throughout the nation, Americans are engaged in an earnest and profound debate about the morality, legality, and practicality of physician-assisted suicide. Our holding permits this debate to continue, as it should in a democratic society.

Justice David Souter, Concurring Opinion in Washington v. Glucksberg

Respondents base their claim on the traditional right to medical care and counsel, subject to the limiting conditions of informed, responsible choice when death is imminent, conditions that support a strong analogy to rights of care in other situations in which medical counsel and assistance have been available as a matter of course. There can be no stronger claim to a physician's assistance than at the time when death is imminent, a moral judgment implied by the state's own recognition of the legitimacy of medical procedures necessarily hastening the moment of impending death.

In my judgment, the importance of the individual interest here, as within that class of "certain interests" demanding careful scrutiny of the state's contrary claim, cannot be gainsaid. Whether that interest might in some circumstances, or at some time, be seen as "fundamental" to the degree entitled to prevail is not, however, a conclusion that I need to draw here, for I am satisfied that the state's interests described in the following section are sufficiently serious to defeat the present claim that its law is arbitrary or purposeless. . . .

One must bear in mind that the nature of the right claimed, if recognized as one constitutionally required, would differ in no essential way from other constitutional rights guaranteed by enumeration or derived from some more definite textual source than "due process." An unenumerated right should not therefore be recognized, with the effect of displacing the legislative ordering of things, without the assurance that its recognition would prove as durable as the recognition of those other rights differently derived.

To recognize a right of lesser promise would simply create a constitutional regime too uncertain to bring with it the expectation of finality that is one of this Court's central obligations in making constitutional decisions. Legislatures, however, are not so constrained. The experimentation that should be out of the question in constitutional adjudication displacing legislative judgments is entirely proper, as well as highly desirable, when the legislative power addresses an emerging issue like assisted suicide.

The Court should accordingly stay its hand to allow reasonable legislative consideration. While I do not decide for all time that respondents' claim should not be recognized, I acknowledge that legislative institutional competence as the better one to deal with that claim at this time.

Part II: *Vacco v. Quill*

In New York, as in most states, it is a crime to aid another to commit or attempt suicide, but patients may refuse even lifesaving medical treatment. The question presented by this case is whether New York's prohibition on assisting suicide therefore violates the equal protection clause of the 14th Amendment. We hold that it does not.

Petitioners are various New York public officials. Respondents Timothy E. Quill, Samuel C. Klagsbrun and Howard A. Grossman are physicians who practice in New York. They assert that although it would be "consistent with the standards of [their] medical practice[s]" to prescribe lethal medication for "mentally competent, terminally ill patients" who are suffering great pain and desire a doctor's help in taking their own lives, they are deterred from doing so by New York's ban on assisting suicide.

Respondents, and three gravely ill patients who have since died, sued the state's Attorney General [Dennis Vacco] in the United States District Court. They urged that because New York permits a competent person to refuse life-sustaining medical treatment, and because the re-

fusal of such treatment is "essentially the same thing" as physician-assisted suicide, New York's assisted-suicide ban violates the equal protection clause.

The district court disagreed. The court noted New York's "obvious legitimate interests in preserving life, and in protecting vulnerable persons," and concluded that "[u]nder the United States Constitution and the Federal system it establishes, the resolution of this issue is left to the normal democratic processes within the state." . . .

On their faces, neither New York's ban on assisting suicide nor its statutes permitting patients to refuse medical treatment treat anyone differently than anyone else or draw any distinctions between persons. *Everyone,* regardless of physical condition, is entitled, if competent, to refuse unwanted lifesaving medical treatment; *no one* is permitted to assist a suicide. Generally speaking, laws that apply evenhandedly to all "unquestionably comply" with the equal protection clause.

The court of appeals, however, concluded that some terminally ill people—those who are on life-support systems—are treated differently than those who are not, in that the former may "hasten death" by ending treatment but the latter may not "hasten death" through physician-assisted suicide. This conclusion depends on the submission that ending or refusing life-saving medical treatment "is nothing more nor less than assisted suicide." Unlike the court of appeals, we think the distinction between assisting suicide and withholding life-sustaining treatment, a distinction widely recognized and endorsed in the medical profession and in our legal tradition, is both important and logical; it is certainly rational. . . .

The state enacted its current assisted-suicide statutes in 1965. Since then, New York has acted several times to protect patients' common-law right to refuse treatment. In so doing, however, the state has neither endorsed a general right to "hasten death" nor approved physician-assisted suicide. Quite the opposite: The state has reaffirmed the line between "killing" and "letting die." . . .

For all these reasons, we disagree with respondents' claim that the distinction between refusing lifesaving medical treatment and assisted suicide is "arbitrary" and "irrational." Granted, in some cases, the line between the two may not be clear, but certainty is not required, even were it possible.

Justice Sandra Day O'Connor, Concurring Opinion in Vacco v. Quill

The Court frames the issue in this case as whether the due process clause of the Constitution protects a "right to commit suicide which itself includes a right to assistance in doing so" and concludes that our nation's history, legal traditions, and practices do not support the existence of such a right. I join the court's opinions because I agree that there is no generalized right to "commit suicide."

But respondents urge us to address the narrower question whether a mentally competent person who is experiencing great suffering has a constitutionally cognizable interest in controlling the circumstances of his or her imminent death. I see no need to reach that question in the context of the facial challenges to the New York and Washington laws at issue here.

The parties and *amici* agree that in these states a patient who is suffering from a terminal illness and who is experiencing great pain has no legal barriers to obtaining medication, from qualified physicians, to alleviate that suffering, even to the point of causing unconsciousness and hastening death. In this light, even assuming that we would recognize such an interest, I agree that the state's interest in protecting those who are not truly competent or facing imminent death, or those whose decisions to hasten death would not truly be voluntary, are sufficiently weighty to justify a prohibition against physician-assisted suicide.

Justice Stephen Breyer, Concurring Opinion in Vacco v. Quill

I agree with the Court in *Vacco* v. *Quill* that the articulated state interests justify the distinction drawn between physician-assisted suicide and withdrawal of life-support. I also agree with the Court that the critical question in both of the cases before us is whether "the 'liberty' specially protected by the due process clause includes a right" of the sort that the respondents assert. I do not agree, however, with the Court's formulation of that claimed "liberty" interest.

The Court describes it as a "right to commit suicide with another's assistance." But I would not reject the respondents' claim without considering a different formulation, for which our legal tradition may provide greater support. That formulation would use words roughly like a "right to die with dignity." But irrespective of the exact words used, at its core would lie personal control over the manner of death, professional medical assistance, and the avoidance of unnecessary and severe physical suffering combined. . . .

I do not believe, however, that this Court need or now should decide whether or not such a right is "fundamental."

4

Death Penalty

THE USE OF THE DEATH PENALTY

The use of the death penalty as a form of punishment has a long and complex history in this country. At times, state authorities have resorted to this penalty not infrequently, and have done so without great public outcry, as for example in the early part of the twentieth century. Its use then waned sharply in the late 1960s.[1] In a landmark ruling in 1972, *Furman* v. *Georgia*, the U.S.

Supreme Court struck down states' death penalty laws on procedural grounds; they found that states' patterns of use, at that time, violated the Eighth Amendment's prohibition of "cruel and unusual" punishment. Those states that used the death penalty were forced to put a halt to the practice until a decision four years later, *Gregg* v. *Georgia*, in which the Supreme Court judged that the death penalty need not in principle violate the Eighth Amendment.[2] Various states, most notably those in the South, resumed their use of the death penalty in the wake of this decision. By the mid-1990s, as one commentator observed, the death penalty seemed to be "enjoying an unbridled popularity boom."[3]

In this chapter, we are concerned with the question of the moral justification of the State's use of the death penalty: Is it ever morally permissible for the State deliberately and directly to kill an individual as punishment for his or her crimes? As indicated in earlier chapters, our focus is on the broad moral arguments on both sides of this debate. We are not directly concerned here with constitutional issues, although court decisions on this issue have often included thoughtful moral analyses.

PROPONENTS OF THE DEATH PENALTY

Defenders of the death penalty often justify it on grounds of its alleged ability to deter future criminals from committing capital offenses. Arguments of this type are often referred to as "forward-looking" defenses. In contrast, other proponents offer "backward-looking" justifications; they argue that regardless of its purported consequences with respect to the future behavior of potential criminals, the death penalty is simply the just desert of those who murder others. By committing the heinous crime of murder, the convicted murderer has forfeited his or her status as a member of our moral community.

OPPONENTS OF THE DEATH PENALTY

Critics of the death penalty argue that it can never be morally justified as it is inherently inhumane and cruel. They suggest that other forms of punishment are available that are not as brutal and as savage. Other opponents find it unjustifiable due to the likelihood of errors in the criminal justice system: The very possibility that the State might wrongly convict an innocent person should preclude it from ever instituting an irreversible form of punishment such as death.

In recent years, critics of the death penalty have looked more carefully at the details of the cases in which defendants have received the death penalty and in which it has actually been administered in our society. These scholars assert that we cannot debate the moral status of the death penalty in the abstract or with respect to an ideal world. Rather, we must examine it in its full social context, drawing on the empirical work of social scientists in order to study how, when, and to whom it is administered in our society. They argue that racism and sharp social class divisions stubbornly persist in our society—despite all the rhetoric of civics classes to the contrary—and that in a society with such unjust inequalities, we cannot expect that the death penalty could be fairly administered, and thus it ought be banned. Studies document that most death row prisoners are poor and thus are unlikely to be able to mount full-fledged legal defenses and investigations. Researchers have also determined that racial and ethnic minorities are disproportionately represented among death row populations.[4] Other research claims to show that racial prejudices distort how and when the death penalty is meted out in our courts: Controlling for other variables, researchers report that those convicted of killing white persons are more likely to be sentenced to death than those found guilty of murdering blacks.

Those who argue that our entrenched patterns of discrimination make it impossible for us to fairly administer such a severe form of punishment often point to the "conversion" of Supreme Court Justice Harry Blackmun in his final years on the bench. After years of accepting the constitutionality of the death penalty, Justice Blackmun suddenly declared that he had revised his position[5]; his dissenting opinion in a 1994 decision involving a Texas death penalty case, *Callins v. Collins*, gives sobering witness to the reasons for his change of mind:

> From this day forward, I no longer shall tinker with the machinery of death. For more than twenty years I have endeavored—indeed, I have struggled—along with a majority of this Court, to develop procedural and substantive rules that would lend more than the appearance of fairness to the death penalty endeavor. Rather than continue to coddle the Court's delusion that the desired level of fairness has been achieved and the need for regulation eviscerated, I feel morally and intellectually obligated simply to concede that the death penalty experiment has failed. It is virtually self-evident to me now that no combination of procedural rules or substantive regulations ever can save the death penalty from its inherent constitutional deficiencies. The basic question—does the system accurately and consistently determine which defendants 'deserve' to die?—cannot be answered in the affirmative.[6]

NOTES

1. American Civil Liberties Union, "The Death Penalty: Briefing Paper 8," p. 1.

2. ACLU, Briefing Paper 8, p. 1.

3. Linda Greenhouse, "A Capacity to Change as Well as to Challenge," *The New York Times*, 27 February 1994, Sec. 4, p. 4.

4. ACLU, "Briefing Paper 8," p. 1.

5. Linda Greenhouse, "A Capacity to Change as Well as to Challenge," *The New York Times*, 27 February, 1994, Sec. 4, p. 4.

6. Justice Harry Blackmun, Dissenting Opinion in *Callins v. Collins*, 1994.

17.

The Ultimate Punishment: A Defense

Ernest van den Haag

Ernest van den Haag retired as the John M. Olin Professor of Jurisprudence and Public Policy at Fordham University. His most recent books are *Punishing Criminals* and *The Death Penalty: A Debate* (with John P. Conrad). He is a well-known advocate of the death penalty. In this essay, he defends the death penalty on grounds of its deterrent effect, arguing as well that it is a fitting retribution for murder. He concludes, "Execution of those who have committed heinous murders may deter only one murder per year. If it does, it seems quite warranted. It is also the only fitting retribution for murder I can think of."

In an average year about 20,000 homicides occur in the United States. Fewer than 300 convicted murderers are sentenced to death. But because no more than thirty murderers have been executed in any recent year, most convicts sentenced to death are likely to die of old age. Nonetheless, the death penalty looms large in discussions: it raises important moral questions independent of the number of executions.

The death penalty is our harshest punishment. It is irrevocable: it ends the existence of those punished, instead of temporarily imprisoning them. Further, although not intended to cause physical pain, execution is the only corporal punishment still applied to adults. These singular characteristics contribute to the perennial, impassioned controversy about capital punishment.

I. DISTRIBUTION

Consideration of the justice, morality, or usefulness of capital punishment is often conflated with objections to its alleged discriminatory or capricious distribution among the guilty. Wrongly so. If capital punishment is immoral, no distribution among the guilty could make it moral. If capital punishment is moral, no distribution would make it immoral. Improper distribution cannot affect the quality of what is distributed, be it punishments or rewards. Discriminatory or capricious distribution thus could not justify abolition of the death penalty. Further, maldistribution inheres no more in capital punishment than in any other punishment.

Maldistribution between the guilty and the innocent is, by definition, unjust. But the injustice does not lie in the nature of the punishment. Because of the finality of the death penalty, the most grievous maldistribution occurs when it is imposed upon the innocent. However, the frequent allegations of discrimination and capriciousness refer to maldistribution among the guilty and not to the punishment of the innocent.

Maldistribution of any punishment among those who deserve it is irrelevant to its justice or morality. Even if poor or black convicts guilty of capital offenses suffer capital punishment, and other convicts equally guilty of the same crimes do not, a more equal distribution, however desirable, would merely be more equal. It would not be more just to the convicts under sentence of death.

Punishments are imposed on persons, not on racial or economic groups. Guilt is personal. The only relevant question is: does the person to be executed deserve the punishment? Whether or not others who deserved the same punishment, whatever their economic or racial group, have avoided execution is irrelevant. If they have, the guilt of the executed convicts would not be diminished, nor would their punishment be less deserved. To put the issue starkly, if the death penalty were imposed on guilty blacks, but not on guilty whites, or, if it were imposed by a lottery among the guilty, this irrationally discriminatory or capricious distribution would neither make the penalty unjust, nor cause anyone to be unjustly punished, despite the undue impunity bestowed on others.

Equality, in short, seems morally less important than justice. And justice is independent of distributional inequalities. The ideal of equal justice demands that justice be equally distributed, not that it be replaced by equality. Justice requires that as many of the guilty as possible be punished, regardless of whether others have avoided punishment. To let these others escape the deserved punishment does not do justice to them, or to society. But it is not unjust to those who could not escape.

These moral considerations are not meant to deny that irrational discrimination, or capriciousness, would be inconsistent with constitutional requirements. But I am satisfied that the Supreme Court has in fact provided for adherence to the constitutional requirement of equality as much as is possible. Some inequality is indeed unavoidable as a practical matter in any system. But, *ultra posse nemo obligatur*. (Nobody is bound beyond ability.)

Recent data reveal little direct racial discrimination in the sentencing of those arrested and convicted of murder. The abrogation of the death penalty for rape has eliminated a major source of racial discrimination. Concededly, some discrimination based on the race of murder victims may exist; yet, this discrimination affects criminal victimizers in an unexpected way. Murderers of whites are thought more likely to be executed than murderers of blacks. Black victims, then, are less fully vindicated than white ones. However, because most black murderers kill blacks, black murderers are spared the death penalty more often than are white murderers. They fare better than most white murderers. The motivation behind unequal distribution of the death penalty may well have been to discriminate against blacks, but the result has favored them. Maldistribution is thus a straw man for empirical as well as analytical reasons.

II. MISCARRIAGES OF JUSTICE

In a recent survey Professors Hugo Adam Bedau and Michael Radelet found that 7000 persons were executed in the United States between 1900 and 1985 and that 25 were innocent of capital crimes. Among the innocents they list Sacco and Vanzetti as well as Ethel and Julius Rosenberg. Although their data may be questionable, I do not doubt that, over a long enough period, miscarriages of justice will occur even in capital cases.

Despite precautions, nearly all human activities, such as trucking, lighting, or construction, cost the lives of some innocent bystanders. We do not give up these activities, because the advantages, moral or material, outweigh the unintended losses. Analogously, for those who think the death penalty just, miscarriages of justice are offset by the moral benefits and the usefulness of doing justice. For those who think the death penalty unjust even when it does not miscarry, miscarriages can hardly be decisive.

III. DETERRENCE

Despite much recent work, there has been no conclusive statistical demonstration that the death penalty is a better deterrent than are alternative punishments. However, deterrence is less than decisive for either side. Most abolitionists acknowledge that they would continue to favor abolition even if the death penalty were shown to deter more murders than alternatives could deter. Abolitionists appear to value the life of a convicted murderer or, at least, his nonexecution, more highly than they value the lives of the innocent victims who might be spared by deterring prospective murderers.

Deterrence is not altogether decisive for me either. I would favor retention of the death penalty as retribution even if it were shown that the threat of execution could not deter prospective murderers not already deterred by the threat of imprisonment. Still, I believe the death penalty, because of its finality, is more feared than imprisonment, and deters some prospective murderers not deterred by the threat of imprisonment. Sparing the lives of even a few prospective victims by deterring their murderers is more important than preserving the lives of convicted murderers because of the possibility, or even the probability, that executing them would not deter others. Whereas the lives of the victims who might be saved are valuable, that of the murderer has only negative value, because of his crime. Surely the criminal law is meant to protect the lives of potential victims in preference to those of actual murderers.

Murder rates are determined by many factors; neither the severity nor the probability of the threatened sanction is always decisive. However, for the long run, I share the view of Sir James Fitzjames Stephen: "Some men, probably, abstain from murder because they fear that if they committed murder they would be hanged. Hundreds of thousands abstain from it because they regard it with horror. One great reason why they regard it with horror is that murderers are hanged." Penal sanctions are useful in the long run for the formation of the internal restraints so necessary to control crime. The severity and finality of the death penalty is appropriate to the seriousness and the finality of murder.

IV. INCIDENTAL ISSUES: COST, RELATIVE SUFFERING, BRUTALIZATION

Many nondecisive issues are associated with capital punishment. Some believe that the monetary cost of appealing a capital sentence is excessive. Yet most comparisons of the cost of life imprisonment with the cost of execution, apart from their dubious relevance, are flawed at least by the implied assumption that life prisoners will generate no judicial costs during their imprisonment. At any rate, the actual monetary costs are trumped by the importance of doing justice.

Others insist that a person sentenced to death suffers more than his victim suffered, and that this (excess) suffering is undue according to the *lex talionis* (rule of retaliation). We cannot know whether the murderer on death row suffers more than his victim suffered; however, unlike the murderer, the victim deserved none of the suffering inflicted. Further, the limitations of the *lex talionis* were meant to restrain private vengeance, not the social retribution that has taken its place. Punishment—regardless of the motivation—is not intended to revenge, offset, or compensate for the victim's suffering, or to be measured by it. Punishment is to vindicate the law and the social order undermined by the crime. This is why a kidnapper's penal confinement is not limited to the period for which he imprisoned his victim; nor is a burglar's confinement meant merely to offset the suffering or the harm he caused his victim; nor is it meant only to offset the advantage he gained.

Another argument heard at least since Beccaria is that, by killing a murderer, we encourage, endorse, or legitimize unlawful killing. Yet, although all punishments are meant to be unpleasant, it is seldom argued that they legitimize the unlawful imposition of identical unpleasantness. Imprisonment is not thought to legitimize kidnapping; neither are fines thought to legitimize robbery. The difference between murder and execution, or between kidnapping and imprisonment, is that the first is unlawful and undeserved, the second a lawful and deserved punishment for an unlawful act. The physical similarities of the punishment to the crime are irrelevant. The relevant difference is not physical, but social.

V. JUSTICE, EXCESS, DEGRADATION

We threaten punishments in order to deter crime. We impose them not only to make the threats credible but also as retribution (justice) for the crimes that were not deterred. Threats and punishments are necessary to deter and deterrence is a sufficient practical justification for them. Retribution is an independent moral justification. Although penalties can be unwise, repulsive, or inappropriate, and those punished can be pitiable, in a sense the infliction of legal punishment on a guilty person cannot be unjust. By committing the crime, the criminal volunteered to assume the risk of receiving a legal punishment that he could have avoided by not committing the crime. The punishment he suffers is the punishment he voluntarily risked suffering and, therefore, it is no more unjust to him than any other event for which one knowingly volunteers to assume the risk. Thus, the death penalty cannot be unjust to the guilty criminal.

There remain, however, two moral objections. The penalty may be regarded as always excessive as retribution and always morally degrading. To regard the death penalty as always excessive, one must believe that no crime—no matter how heinous—could possibly justify capital punishment. Such a belief can be neither corroborated nor refuted; it is an article of faith.

Alternatively, or concurrently, one may believe that everybody, the murderer no less than the victim, has an imprescriptible (natural?) right to life. The law therefore should not deprive anyone of life. I share Jeremy Bentham's view that any such "natural and imprescriptible rights" are "nonsense upon stilts."

Justice Brennan has insisted that the death penalty is "uncivilized," "inhuman," inconsistent with "human dignity" and with "the sanctity of life," that it "treats members of the human race as nonhumans, as objects to be toyed with and discarded," that it is "uniquely degrading to human dignity" and "by its very nature, [involves] a denial of the executed person's humanity." Justice Brennan does not say why he thinks execution "uncivilized." Hitherto most civilizations have had the death penalty, although it has been discarded in Western Europe, where it is currently unfashionable probably because of its abuse by totalitarian regimes.

By "degrading," Justice Brennan seems to mean that execution degrades the executed convicts. Yet philosophers, such as Immanuel Kant and G.F.W. Hegel, have insisted that, when deserved, execution, far from degrading the executed convict, affirms his humanity by affirming his rationality and his responsibility for his actions. They thought that execution, when deserved, is required for the sake of the convict's dignity. (Does not life imprisonment violate human dignity more than execution, by keeping alive a prisoner deprived of all autonomy?)

Common sense indicates that it cannot be death—our common fate—that is inhuman. Therefore, Justice Brennan must mean that death degrades when it comes not as a natural or accidental event, but as a deliberate social imposition. The murderer learns through his punishment that his fellow men have found him unworthy of living; that because he has murdered, he is being expelled from the community of the living. This degradation is self-inflicted. By murdering, the murderer has so dehumanized himself that he cannot remain among the living. The social recognition of his self-degradation is the punitive essence of execution. To believe, as Justice Brennan appears to, that the degradation is inflicted by the execution reverses the direction of causality. Execution of those who have committed heinous murders may deter only one murder per year. If it does, it seems quite warranted. It is also the only fitting retribution for murder I can think of.

A Glimpse of Executions Might Change Some Minds

Claude Lewis

The irony and idiocy of the death penalty was underscored again last week in McAlester, Okla. Only hours before the scheduled execution of convicted murderer Robert Brecheen, he tried to kill himself with an overdose of drugs. So prison officials revived him so they could kill him in the prescribed manner with a lethal injection of other drugs.

Brecheen's experience may at first seem unusual, but the history of executions in the United States is replete with events that range from the bizarre to the barbarous.

The last official public execution was a hanging in Owensboro, Ky., in 1936. Back then, murders conducted by the state involved community and political participation.

It was not unusual for as many as 20,000 people to attend some killings. Executions were sometimes turned into near-festivals, with popcorn and soft drink venders hawking wares as if the crowd, anticipating a death, were watching a sporting event.

Follow, if you dare, the description provided by Clinton Duffy, warden of San Quentin from 1942 to 1954, who oversaw as many as 60 hangings:

"The man hit bottom, and I observed that he was fighting by pulling on the straps, wheezing, whistling, trying to get air. (I noticed) that blood was oozing through the black cap. I observed also that he urinated, defecated, and the droppings fell on the floor, and the stench was terrible. I also saw witnesses pass out and had to be removed from the witness room. Some of them threw up. When he was taken down and the cap removed, big hunks of flesh were torn off the sides of his face where the noose had been."

In 1896, a witness described the horror of an Illinois hanging when the rope was too short:

"We were forced to stand there in horrified fascination while the tortured creature danced crazily at the end of the rope, lunging like a gigged frog,

kicking and twirling in mad futility . . . . Five long minutes dragged by, 10, 15, 20, and still the suffering man struggled and fought with gruesome silence that chilled one to the marrow."

For some, electricity seemed more clinical and humane. Texas newsman Don Reid, who attended 189 executions in 22 years, disagreed. He wrote about the stench of burning flesh, the contortions, the voltage racing through the body, the arching of the back, the violence, the horror and the smell of burning sweat and steam and the smoke that fills the room.

Once, Reid recalled, a man failed to die on schedule. Writhing in pain, he was nearly thrown from the chair. The officials moved him to a cot where he finally died. More electricity was set up and the warden ordered the dead man strapped to the chair again. For 30 seconds, current coursed through his body. Then, the warden wiped his brow and declared: "Gentleman, justice has been done."

However it's done, executions say at least as much about the states—and the public—that permit them as they do about the loathsome misbehavior of the men, and occasionally women, who wind up on death row.

The death penalty is now a hot political issue with opponents labeling the practice "uncivilized," while proponents shout that legal injections are "humane." Nowadays, the terrible reality involved in orchestrated killings is largely unseen.

More often than we hear, innocent people are executed. Supporters of condemned journalist, Mumia Abu-Jamal, now seeking a new trial, say they wish to prevent such a miscarriage.[1]

Certainly, politics—and poverty—are factors in whether someone is sentenced to death. The greatest number of executions occur among those who have suffered abuse, those with poor legal representation and minorities. They make up the bulk of our spiritually, socially and morally impoverished citizens. Even the retarded are not always spared execution. Rarely are the wealthy put to death.

Claude Lewis, "A Glimpse of Executions Might Change Some Minds," *The Philadelphia Inquirer,* 14 August 1995: A9. Reprinted with permission from *The Philadelphia Inquirer.*

The desire for revenge is strong in a nation beside itself with rage concerning the rampant abuse visited upon innocent men, women and children around the country.

Still, it is folly to use death as a tool to punish people whose cruel behavior moves us to seek revenge rather than justice. Despite arguments to the contrary, the death penalty is not a deterrent to major crimes, including murder. Because of the appeal process, a death sentence is usually far [more] costly than a life sentence.

Pam Tucker, secretary of the Pennsylvania Coalition to Abolish the Death Penalty, said, "There's more than irony involved in bringing a person back to health, like the Brecheen case, and then killing them. Such practices underscore the absurdity of the death penalty. But the killing continues."

Note

1. *Editor's Note:* Mumia Abu-Jamal was convicted of, and sentenced to die for, the 1981 murder of Philadelphia police officer Daniel Faulkner. Supporters of Mumia Abu-Jamal—a journalist and former radio reporter—have sought a new trial for him on the grounds that his original defense attorney was not competent and information favorable to his defense was withheld from the jury.

18.

Justice, Civilization, and the Death Penalty

Jeffrey H. Reiman

Jeffrey Reiman is William Fraser McDowell Professor of Philosophy at The American University in Washington, D.C. His recent books include *The Rich Get Richer and the Poor Get Prison: Ideology, Class, and Criminal Justice* and *Justice and Modern Moral Philosophy.* Reiman argues that even though the death penalty may be a just punishment for a person convicted of murder, the abolition of the death penalty is one of the hallmarks of a civilized, modern state.

On the issue of capital punishment, there is as clear a clash of moral intuitions as we are likely to see. Some (now a majority of Americans) feel deeply that justice requires payment in kind and thus that murderers should die; and others (once, but no longer, nearly a majority of Americans) feel deeply that the state ought not be in the business of putting people to death.[1] Arguments for either side that do not do justice to the intuitions of the other are unlikely to persuade anyone not already convinced. And, since, as I shall suggest, there is truth on both sides, such arguments are easily refutable, leaving us with nothing but conflicting intuitions and no guidance from reason in distinguishing the better from the worse. In this context, I shall try to make an argument for the abolition of the death penalty that does justice to the intuitions on both sides. I shall sketch out a conception of retributive justice that accounts for the justice of executing murderers, and then I shall argue that *though the death penalty is a just punishment for murder*, abolition of the death penalty is a part of the civilizing mission of modern states. . . .

I. JUST DESERTS AND JUST PUNISHMENTS

In my view, the death penalty is a just punishment for murder because the *lex talionis*, an eye for an eye, and so on, is just, although, as I shall suggest at the end of this section, it can only be rightly applied when its implied preconditions are satisfied. The *lex talionis* is a version of retributivism. Retributivism—as the word itself suggests—is the doctrine that the offender should be *paid back* with suffering he deserves because of the evil he has done, and the *lex talionis* asserts that injury equivalent to that he imposed is what the offender deserves. But the *lex talionis* is not the only version of retributivism. Another, which I shall call "proportional retributivism," holds that what retribution requires is not equality of injury between crimes and punishments, but "fit" or proportionality, such that the worst crime is punished with the society's worst penalty, and so on, though the society's worst punishment need not duplicate the injury of the worst crime.[2] Later, I shall try to show how a form of proportional retributivism is compatible with acknowledging the justice of the *lex talionis*. Indeed, since I shall defend the justice of the *lex talionis*, I take such compatibility as a necessary condition of the validity of any form of retributivism.

There is nothing self-evident about the justice of the *lex talionis* nor, for that matter, of retributivism.[3] The standard problem confronting those who would justify retributivism is that of overcoming the suspicion that it does no more than sanctify the victim's desire to hurt the offender back. Since serving that desire amounts to hurting the offender simply for the satisfaction that the victim derives from seeing the offender suffer, and since deriving satisfaction from the suffering of others seems primitive, the policy of imposing suffering on the offender for no other purpose than giving satisfaction to his victim seems primitive as well. Consequently, defending retributivism requires showing that the suffering imposed on the wrongdoer has some worthy point beyond the satisfaction of victims. In what follows, I shall try to identify a proposition—which I call the *retributivist principle*—that I take to be the nerve of retributivism. I think this principle accounts for the justice of the *lex talionis* and indicates the point of the suffering demanded by retributivism. Not to do too much of the work of the death penalty

advocate, I shall make no extended argument for this principle beyond suggesting the considerations that make it plausible. I shall identify these considerations by drawing, with considerable license, on Hegel and Kant.

I think that we can see the justice of the *lex talionis* by focusing on the striking affinity between it and the *golden rule*. The *golden rule* mandates "Do unto others as you would have others do unto you," while the *lex talionis* counsels "Do unto others as they have done unto you." It would not be too far-fetched to say that the *lex talionis* is the law enforcement arm of the golden rule, at least in the sense that if people were actually treated as they treated others, then everyone would necessarily follow the golden rule because then people could only willingly act toward others as they were willing to have others act toward them. This is not to suggest that the *lex talionis* follows from the golden rule, but rather that the two share a common moral inspiration: the equality of persons. Treating others as you *would* have them treat you means treating others as equal to you, because adopting the golden rule as one's guiding principle implies that one counts the suffering of others to be as great a calamity as one's own suffering, that one counts one's right to impose suffering on others as no greater than their right to impose suffering on one, and so on. This leads to the *lex talionis* by two approaches that start from different points and converge.

I call the first approach "Hegelian" because Hegel held (roughly) that crime upsets the quality between persons and retributive punishment restores that equality by "annulling" the crime. As we have seen, acting according to the golden rule implies treating others as your equals. Conversely, violating the golden rule implies the reverse: Doing to another what you would *not* have that person do to you violates the equality of persons by asserting a right toward the other that the other does not possess toward you. Doing back to you what you did "annuls" your violation by reasserting that the other has the same right toward you that you assert toward him. Punishment according to the *lex talionis* cannot heal the injury that the other has suffered at your hands, rather it rectifies the indignity he has suffered, by restoring him to equality with you.

"Equality of persons" here does not mean equality of concern for their happiness, as it might for a utilitarian. On such a (roughly) utilitarian understanding of equality, imposing suffering on the wrongdoer equivalent to the suffering he has imposed would have little point. Rather, equality of concern for people's happiness would lead us to impose as little suffering on the wrongdoer as was compatible with maintaining the happiness of others. This is enough to show that retributivism (at least in this "Hegelian" form) reflects a conception of morality quite different from that envisioned by utilitarianism. Instead of seeing morality as administering doses of happiness to individual recipients, the retributivist envisions morality as maintaining the relations appropriate to equally sovereign individuals. A crime, rather than representing a unit of suffering added to the already considerable suffering in the world, is an assault on the sovereignty of an individual that temporarily places one person (the criminal) in a position of illegitimate sovereignty over another (the victim). The victim (or his representative, the state) then has the right to rectify this loss of standing relative to the criminal by meting out a punishment that reduces the criminal's sovereignty in the degree to which he vaunted it above his victim's. It might be thought that this is a duty, not just a right, but that is surely too much. The victim has the right to forgive the violator without punishment, which suggests that it is by virtue of having the right to punish the violator (rather than the duty) that the victim's quality with the violator is restored.

I call the second approach "Kantian" since Kant held (roughly) that, since reason (like justice) is no respecter of the sheer difference between individuals, when a rational being decides to act in a certain way toward his fellows, he implicitly authorizes similar action by

his fellows toward him. A version of the golden rule, then, is a requirement of reason: Acting rationally, one always acts as he would have others act toward him. Consequently, to act toward a person as he has acted toward others is to treat him as a rational being, that is, as if his act were the product of a rational decision. From this, it may be concluded that we have a duty to do to offenders what they have done, since this amounts to according them the respect due rational beings. Here too, however, the assertion of a duty to punish seems excessive, since, if this duty arises because doing to people what they have done to others is necessary to accord them the respect due rational beings, then we would have a duty to do to all rational persons *everything*—good, bad, or indifferent—that they do to others. The point rather is that, by his acts, a rational being *authorizes* others to do the same to him, he doesn't *compel* them to. Here too, then, the argument leads to a right, rather than a duty, to exact the *lex talionis*. And this is supported by the fact that we can conclude from Kant's argument that a rational being cannot validly complain of being treated in the way he has treated others, and where there is no valid complaint, there is no injustice, and where there is no injustice, others have acted within their rights. It should be clear that the Kantian argument also rests on the equality of persons, because a rational agent only implicitly authorizes having done to him action similar to what he has done to another, if he and the other are similar in the relevant ways.

The "Hegelian" and "Kantian" approaches arrive at the same destination from opposite sides. The "Hegelian" approach starts from the victim's equality with the criminal, and infers from it the victim's right to do to the criminal what the criminal has done to the victim. The "Kantian" approach starts from the criminal's rationality, and infers from it the criminal's authorization of the victim's right to do to the criminal what the criminal has done to the victim. Taken together, these approaches support the following proposition: The equality and rationality of persons implies that an offender deserves and his victim has the right to impose suffering on the offender equal to that which he imposed on the victim. This is the proposition I call the *retributivist principle*, and I shall assume henceforth that it is true. This principle provides that the *lex talionis* is the criminal's just desert and the victim's (or as his representative, the state's) right. Moreover, the principle also indicates the point of retributive punishment, namely, it affirms the equality and rationality of persons, victims and offenders alike.[4] And the point of this affirmation is, like any moral affirmation, to make a statement, to the criminal, to impress upon him his equality with his victim (which earns him a like fate) and his rationality (by which his actions are held to authorize his fate), and to the society, so that recognition of the equality and rationality of persons becomes a visible part of our shared moral environment that none can ignore in justifying their actions to one another. . . .

The truth of the retributivist principle establishes the justice of the *lex talionis*, but, since it establishes this as a right of the victim rather than a duty, it does not settle the question of whether or to what extent the victim or the state should exercise this right and exact the *lex talionis*. This is a separate moral question because strict adherence to the *lex talionis* amounts to allowing criminals, even the most barbaric of them, to dictate our punishing behavior. It seems certain that there are at least some crimes, such as rape or torture, that we ought not try to match. And this is not merely a matter of imposing an alternative punishment that produces an equivalent amount of suffering, as, say, some number of years in prison that might "add up" to the harm caused by a rapist or a torturer. Even if no amount of time in prison would add up to the harm caused by a torturer, it still seems that we ought not torture him even if this were the only way of making him suffer as much as he has made his victim suffer. Or, consider someone who has committed several murders in cold blood. On the *lex talionis*, it would seem

that such a criminal might justly be brought to within an inch of death and then revived (or to within a moment of execution and then reprieved) as many times as he has killed (minus one), and then finally executed. But surely this is a degree of cruelty that would be monstrous.[5] . . .

I suspect that it will be widely agreed that the state ought not administer punishments of the sort described above even if required by the letter of the *lex talionis*, and thus, even granting the justice of *lex talionis*, there are occasions on which it is morally appropriate to diverge from its requirements. . . .

This way of understanding just punishment enables us to formulate proportional retributivism so that it is compatible with acknowledging the justice of the *lex talionis*: If we take the *lex talionis* as spelling out the offender's just deserts, and if other moral considerations require us to refrain from matching the injury caused by the offender while still allowing us to punish justly, then surely we impose just punishment if we impose the closest morally acceptable approximation to the *lex talionis*. Proportional retributivism, then, in requiring that the worst crime be punished by the society's worst punishment and so on, could be understood as translating the offender's just desert into its nearest equivalent in the society's table of morally acceptable punishments. Then the two versions of retributivism (*lex talionis* and proportional) are related in that the first states what just punishment would be if nothing but the offender's just desert mattered, and the second locates just punishment at the meeting point of the offender's just deserts and the society's moral scruples. And since this second version only modifies the requirements of the *lex talionis* in light of other moral considerations, it is compatible with believing that the *lex talionis* spells out the offender's just deserts, much in the way that modifying the obligations of promisers in light of other moral considerations is compatible with believing in the binding nature of promises. . . .

II. CIVILIZATION, PAIN, AND JUSTICE

As I have already suggested, from the fact that something is justly deserved, it does not automatically follow that it should be done, since there may be other moral reasons for not doing it such that, all told, the weight of moral reasons swings the balance against proceeding. The same argument that I have given for the justice of the death penalty for murderers proves the justice of beating assaulters, raping rapists, and torturing torturers. Nonetheless, I believe, and suspect that most would agree, that it would not be right for us to beat assaulters, rape rapists, or torture torturers, *even though it were their just deserts*—and even if this were the only way to make them suffer as much as they had made their victims suffer. Calling for the abolition of the death penalty, though it be just, then, amounts to urging that as a society we place execution in the same category of sanction as beating, raping, and torturing, and treat it as something it would not be right for us to do to offenders, *even if it were their just deserts*. . . .

Progress in civilization is characterized by a lower tolerance for one's own pain and that suffered by others. And this is appropriate, since, via growth in knowledge, civilization brings increased power to prevent or reduce pain and, via growth in the ability to communicate and interact with more and more people, civilization extends the circle of people with whom we empathize.[6] If civilization is characterized by lower tolerance for our own pain and that of others, then publicly refusing to do horrible things to our fellows both signals the level of our civilization *and, by our example, continues the work of civilizing*. And this gesture is all the more powerful if we refuse to do horrible things to those who deserve them. I contend then that the more things we are able to include in this category, the more civilized we are and the more civilizing. Thus we gain from including torture in this category, and if execution is especially horrible, we gain still more by including it. . . .

What can be said of reducing the horrible things that we do to our fellows even when deserved? First of all, given our vulnerability to pain, it seems clearly a gain. Is it however an unmitigated gain? That is, would such a reduction ever amount to a loss? It seems to me that there are two conditions under which it would be a loss, namely, if the reduction made our lives more dangerous, or if not doing what is justly deserved were a loss in itself. Let us leave aside the former, since, as I have already suggested and as I will soon indicate in greater detail, I accept that if some horrible punishment is necessary to deter equally or more horrible acts, then we may have to impose the punishment. Thus my claim is that reduction in the horrible things we do to our fellows is an advance in civilization *as long as our lives are not thereby made more dangerous*, and that it is only then that we are called upon to extend that reduction as part of the work of civilization. Assuming then, for the moment, that we suffer no increased danger by refraining from doing horrible things to our fellows when they justly deserve them, does such refraining to do what is justly deserved amount to a loss?

It seems to me that the answer to this must be that refraining to do what is justly deserved is only a loss where it amounts to doing an injustice. But such refraining to do what is just is not doing what is unjust, unless what we do instead falls below the bottom end of the range of just punishments. Otherwise, it would be unjust to refrain from torturing torturers, raping rapists, or beating assaulters. In short, I take it that if there is no injustice in refraining from torturing torturers, then there is no injustice in refraining to do horrible things to our fellows generally, when they deserve them, as long as what we do instead is compatible with believing that they do deserve them. And thus that if such refraining does not make our lives more dangerous, then it is no loss, and given our vulnerability to pain, it is a gain. Consequently, reduction in the horrible things we do to our fellows, when not necessary to our protection, is an advance in civilization that we are called upon to continue once we consciously take upon ourselves the work of civilization.

To complete the argument, however, I must show that execution is horrible enough to warrant its inclusion alongside torture. Against this it will be said that execution is not especially horrible since it only hastens a fate that is inevitable for us.[7] I think that this view overlooks important differences in the manner in which people reach their inevitable ends. I contend that execution is especially horrible, and it is so in a way similar to (though not identical with) the way in which torture is especially horrible. I believe we view torture as especially awful because of two of its features, which also characterize execution: intense pain and the spectacle of one human being completely subject to the power of another. This latter is separate from the issue of pain since it is something that offends us about unpainful things, such as slavery (even voluntarily entered) and prostitution (even voluntarily chosen as an occupation).[8] Execution shares this separate feature, since killing a bound and defenseless human being enacts the total subjugation of that person to his fellows. I think, incidentally, that this accounts for the general uneasiness with which execution by lethal injection has been greeted. Rather than humanizing the event, it seems only to have purchased a possible reduction in physical pain at the price of increasing the spectacle of subjugation—with no net gain in the attractiveness of the death penalty. Indeed, its net effect may have been the reverse.

In addition to the spectacle of subjugation, execution, even by physically painless means, is also characterized by a special and intense psychological pain that distinguishes it from the loss of life that awaits us all. Interesting in this regard is the fact that although we are not terribly squeamish about the loss of life itself, allowing it in war, self-defense, as a necessary cost of progress, and so on, we are, as the extraordinary hesitance of our courts testifies, quite reluctant to execute. I think this is because execution involves the most psychologically painful features of deaths. We normally regard death from human causes as worse than death from natural causes, since a humanly caused shortening of life lacks the consolation of unavoidability. And we normally regard death whose coming is foreseen by its victim as worse than sudden death, because a foreseen death adds to the loss of life the terrible consciousness of that impending loss.[9] As a humanly caused death whose advent is foreseen by its victim, an execution combines the worst of both.

Thus far, by analogy with torture, I have argued that execution should be avoided because of how horrible it is to the one executed. But there are reasons of another sort that follow from the analogy with torture. Torture is to be avoided not only because of what it says about *what* we are willing to do to our fellows, but also because of what it says about *us* who are willing to do it. To torture someone is an awful spectacle not only because of the intensity of pain imposed, but because of what is required to be able to impose such pain on one's fellows. The tortured body cringes, using its full exertion to escape the pain imposed upon it—it literally begs for relief with its muscles as it does with its cries. To torture someone is to demonstrate a capacity to resist this begging, and that in turn demonstrates a kind of hardheartedness that a society ought not parade.

And this is true not only of torture, but of all severe corporal punishment. Indeed, I think this constitutes part of the answer to the puzzling question of why we refrain from punishments like whipping, even when the alternative (some months in jail versus some lashes) seems more costly to the offender. Imprisonment is painful to be sure, but it is a reflective pain, one that comes with comparing what is to what might have been, and that can be temporarily ignored by thinking about other things. But physical pain has an urgency that holds body and mind in a fierce grip. Of physical pain, as Orwell's Winston Smith recognized, "you could only wish one thing: that it should stop."[10]

Refraining from torture in particular and corporal punishment in general, we both refuse to put a fellow human being in this grip *and* refuse to show our ability to resist this wish. The death penalty is the last corporal punishment used officially in the modern world. And it is corporal not only because administered via the body, but because the pain of foreseen, humanly administered death strikes us with the urgency that characterizes intense physical pain, causing grown men to cry, faint, and lose control of their bodily functions. There is something to be gained by refusing to endorse the hardness of heart necessary to impose such a fate.

By placing execution alongside torture in the category of things we will not do to our fellow human beings even when they deserve them, we broadcast the message that totally subjugating a person to the power of others *and* confronting him with the advent of his own humanly administered demise is too horrible to be done by civilized human beings to their fellows even when they have earned it: too horrible to do, and too horrible to be capable of doing. And I contend that broadcasting this message loud and clear would in the long run contribute to the general detestation of murder and be, to the extent to which it worked itself into the hearts and minds of the populace, a deterrent. In short, refusing to execute murderers though they deserve it both reflects and continues the taming of the human species that we call civilization. Thus, I take it that the abolition of the death penalty, though it is just punishment for murder, is part of the civilizing mission of modern states.

III. CIVILIZATION, SAFETY, AND DETERRENCE

Earlier I said that judging a practice too horrible to do even to those who deserve it does not exclude the possibility that it could be justified if necessary to avoid even worse consequences. Thus, were the death penalty clearly proven a better deterrent to the murder of innocent peo-

ple than life in prison, we might have to admit that we had not yet reached a level of civilization at which we could protect ourselves without imposing this horrible fate on murderers, and thus we might have to grant the necessity of instituting the death penalty.[11] But this is far from proven. The available research by no means clearly indicates that the death penalty reduces the incidence of homicide more than life imprisonment does. Even the econometric studies of Isaac Ehrlich, which purport to show that each execution saves seven or eight potential murder victims, have not changed this fact, as is testified to by the controversy and objections from equally respected statisticians that Ehrlich's work has provoked.[12]

Conceding that it has not been proven that the death penalty deters more murders than life imprisonment, van den Haag has argued that neither has it been proven that the death penalty does *not* deter more murders,[13] and thus we must follow common sense which teaches that the higher the cost of something, the fewer people will choose it, and therefore at least some potential murderers who would not be deterred by life imprisonment will be deterred by the death penalty. Van den Haag writes:

> . . . our experience shows that the greater the threatened penalty, the more it deters.
>
> . . . Life in prison is still life, however unpleasant. In contrast, the death penalty does not just threaten to make life unpleasant—it threatens to take life altogether. This difference is perceived by those affected. We find that when they have the choice between life in prison and execution, 99% of all prisoners under sentence of death prefer life in prison. . . .
>
> From this unquestioned fact a reasonable conclusion can be drawn in favor of the superior deterrent effect of the death penalty. Those who have the choice in practice . . . fear death more than they fear life in prison. . . . If they do, it follows that the threat of the death penalty, all other things equal, is likely to deter more than the threat

of life in prison. One is most deterred by what one fears most. From which it follows that whatever statistics fail, or do not fail, to show, the death penalty is likely to be more deterrent than any other. [pp. 68–69]

Those of us who recognize how common-sensical it was, and still is, to believe that the sun moves around the earth, will be less willing than Professor van den Haag to follow common sense here, especially when it comes to doing something awful to our fellows. Moreover, there are good reasons for doubting common sense on this matter. Here are four:

1. From the fact that one penalty is more feared than another, it does not follow that the more feared penalty will deter more than the less feared, unless we know that the less feared penalty is not fearful enough to deter everyone who can be deterred—and this is just what we don't know with regard to the death penalty. Though I fear the death penalty more than life in prison, I can't think of any act that the death penalty would deter me from that an equal likelihood of spending my life in prison wouldn't deter me from as well. Since it seems to me that whoever would be deterred by a given likelihood of death would be deterred by an *equal* likelihood of life behind bars, I suspect that the common-sense argument only seems plausible because we evaluate it unconsciously assuming that potential criminals will face larger likelihoods of death sentences than of life sentences. If the likelihoods were equal, it seems to me that where life imprisonment was improbable enough to make it too distant a possibility to worry much about, a similar low probability of death would have the same effect. After all, we are undeterred by small likelihoods of death every time we walk the streets. And if life imprisonment were sufficiently probable to pose a real deterrent threat, it would pose as much of a deterrent threat as death. And this is just what most of the research we have on the comparative deterrent impact of execution versus life imprisonment suggests.

2. In light of the fact that roughly 500 to 700 suspected felons are killed by the police in the line of duty every year, and the fact that the number of privately owned guns in America is substantially larger than the number of households in America, it must be granted that anyone contemplating committing a crime *already* faces a substantial risk of ending up dead as a result.[14] It's hard to see why anyone *who is not already deterred by this* would be deterred by the addition of the more distant risk of death after apprehension, conviction, and appeal. Indeed, this suggests that people consider risks in a much crueler way than van den Haag's appeal to common sense suggests—which should be evident to anyone who contemplates how few people use seatbelts (14% of drivers, on some estimates), when it is widely known that wearing them can spell the difference between life (outside prison) and death.[15]

3. Van den Haag has maintained that deterrence doesn't work only by means of cost-benefit calculations made by potential criminals. It works also by the lesson about the wrongfulness of murder that is slowly learned in a society that subjects murderers to the ultimate punishment (p. 63). But if I am correct in claiming that the refusal to execute even those who deserve it has a civilizing effect, then the refusal to execute also teaches a lesson about the wrongfulness of murder. My claim here is admittedly speculative, but no more so than van den Haag's to the contrary. And my view has the added virtue of accounting for the failure of research to show an increased deterrent effect from executions *without having to deny the plausibility of van den Haag's common-sense argument that at least some additional potential murderers will be deterred by the prospect of the death penalty*. If there is a deterrent effect from *not executing*, then it is understandable that while executions will deter some murderers, this effect will be balanced out by the weakening of the deterrent effect of not executing, such that no net reduction in murders will result.[16] And this, by the way, also disposes of van den Haag's argument that, in the absence of knowledge one way or the other on the deterrent effect of executions, we should execute murderers rather than risk the lives of innocent people whose murders might have been deterred if we had. If there is a deterrent effect of not executing, it follows that we risk innocent lives either way. And if this is so, it seems that the only reasonable course of action is to refrain from imposing what we know is a horrible fate.[17]

4. Those who still think that van den Haag's common-sense argument for executing murderers is valid will find that the argument proves more than they bargained for. Van den Haag maintains that, in the absence of conclusive evidence on the relative deterrent impact of the death penalty versus life imprisonment, we must follow common sense and assume that if one punishment is more fearful than another, it will deter some potential criminals not deterred by the less fearful punishment. Since people sentenced to death will almost universally try to get their sentences changed to life in prison, it follows that death is more fearful than life imprisonment, and thus that it will deter some additional murderers. Consequently, we should institute the death penalty to save the lives these additional murderers would have taken. But, since people sentenced to be tortured to death would surely try to get their sentences changed to simple execution, the same argument proves that death-by-torture will deter still more potential murderers. Consequently, we should institute death-by-torture to save the lives these additional murderers would have taken. Anyone who accepts van den Haag's argument is then confronted with a dilemma: Until we have conclusive evidence that capital punishment is a greater deterrent to murder than life imprisonment, we must grant *either* that we should not follow common sense and not impose the death penalty; *or* we should follow common sense and torture murderers to death. In short, either we must abolish the electric chair or reinstitute the rack. Surely, this is the *reductio ad absurdum* of van den Haag's common-sense argument.

CONCLUSION

I believe that, taken together, these arguments prove that we should abolish the death penalty though it is a just punishment for murder.

NOTES

1. Asked, in a 1981 Gallup Poll, "Are you in favor of the death penalty for persons convicted of murder?" 66.25% were in favor, 25% were opposed, and 8.75% had no opinion. Asked the same question in 1966, 47.5% were opposed, 41.25% were in favor, and 11.25% had no opinion (Timothy J. Flanagan, David J. van Alstyne, and Michael R. Gottfredson, eds., *Sourcebook of Criminal Justice Statistics—1981*, U.S. Department of Justice, Bureau of Justice Statistics [Washington, D.C.: U.S. Government Printing Office, 1982], p. 209).

2. The most extreme form of retributivism is the law of retaliation: 'an eye for an eye' " (Stanley I. Benn, "Punishment," *The Encyclopedia of Philosophy* 7, ed. Paul Edwards [New York: Macmillan, 1967], p. 32). Hugo Bedau writes: "retributive justice need not be thought to consist of *lex talionis*. One may reject that principle as too crude and still embrace the retributive principle that the severity of punishments should be graded according to the gravity of the offense" (Hugo Bedau, "Capital Punishment," in *Matters of Life and Death*, ed. Tom Regan [New York: Random House, 1980], p. 177). See also, Andrew von Hirsch, "Doing Justice: The Principle of Commensurate Deserts," and Hyman Gross, "Proportional Punishment and Justifiable Sentences," in *Sentencing*, eds. H. Gross and A. von Hirsch (New York: Oxford University Press, 1981), pp. 243–56 and 272–83, respectively.

3. Stanley Benn writes: "to say 'it is fitting' or 'justice demands' that the guilty should suffer is only to affirm that punishment is right, not to give grounds for thinking so" (Benn, "Punishment," p. 30).

4. Herbert Morris defends retributivism on parallel grounds. See his "Persons and Punishment," *The Monist* 52, no. 4 (October 1968): 475–501. Isn't what Morris calls "the right to be treated as a person" essentially the right of a rational being to be treated only as he has authorized, implicitly or explicitly, by his own free choices?

5. Bedau writes: "Where criminals set the limits of just methods of punishment, as they will do if we attempt to give exact and literal implementation to *lex talionis*, society will find itself descending to the cruelties and savagery that criminals employ. But society would be deliberately authorizing such acts, in the cool light of reason, and not (as is often true of vicious criminals) impulsively or in hatred and anger or with an insane or unbalanced mind. Moral restraints, in

short, prohibit us from trying to make executions perfectly retributive" (Bedau, "Capital Punishment," p. 176).

6. Van den Haag writes that our ancestors "were not as repulsed by physical pain as we are. The change has to do not with our greater smartness or moral superiority but with a new outlook pioneered by the French and American revolutions [namely, that assertion of human equality and with it 'universal identification'], and by such mundane things as the invention of anesthetics, which make pain much less of an everyday experience" ([Ernest van den Haag and John P. Conrad, *The Death Penalty: A Debate* (New York: Plenum Press, 1983)], p. 215; cf. van den Haag's *Punishing Criminals* [New York: Basic Books, 1975], pp. 196–206).

7. Van den Haag seems to waffle on the question of the unique awfulness of execution. For instance, he takes it not to be revolting in the way that earcropping is, because "We all must die. But we must not have our ears cropped" (p. 190), and here he cites John Stuart Mill's parliamentary defense of the death penalty in which Mill maintains that execution only *hastens* death. Mill's point was to defend the claim that "There is not . . . any human infliction which makes an impression on the imagination so entirely out of proportion to its real severity as the punishment of death" (Mill, "Parliamentary Debate," p. 273). And van den Haag seems to agree since he maintains that, since "we cannot imagine our own nonexistence. . . , [t]he fear of the death penalty is in part the fear of the unknown. It . . . rests on a confusion" (pp. 258–59). On the other hand, he writes that "Execution sharpens our separation anxiety because death becomes clearly foreseen. . . . Further, and perhaps most important, when one is executed he does not just die, he is put to death, forcibly expelled from life. He is told that he is too depraved, unworthy of living with other humans" (p. 258). I think, incidentally, that it is an overstatement to say that we cannot imagine our own nonexistence. If we can imagine any counterfactual experience, for example, how we might feel if we didn't know something that we do in fact know, then it doesn't seem impossible to imagine what it would "feel like" not to live. I think I can arrive at a pretty good approximation of this by trying to imagine how things "felt" to me in the eighteenth century. And, in fact, the sense of the awful difference between being alive and not that enters my experience when I do this makes the fear of death—not as a state, but as the absence of life—seem hardly to rest on a confusion.

8. I am not here endorsing this view of voluntarily entered slavery or prostitution. I mean only to suggest that it is *the belief* that these relations involve the extreme subjugation of one person to the power of another that is at the basis of their offensiveness. What I am saying is quite compatible with finding that this belief is false with respect to voluntarily entered slavery or prostitution.

9. This is no doubt partly due to modern skepticism about an afterlife. Earlier peoples regarded a foreseen death as a blessing allowing time to make one's peace with God. Writing

of an early Middle Ages, Phillippe Aries says, "In this world that was so familiar with death, sudden death was a vile and ugly death; it was frightening; it seemed a strange and monstrous thing that nobody dared talk about" (Phillippe Aries, *The Hour of Our Death* [New York: Vintage, 1982], p. 11).

10. George Orwell, *1984* (New York: New American Library, 1983; originally published in 1949), p. 197.

11. I say "might" here to avoid the sticky question of just how effective a deterrent the death penalty would have to be to justify overcoming our scruples about executing. It is here that the other considerations often urged against capital punishment—discrimination, irrevocability, the possibility of mistake, and so on—would play a role. Omitting such qualifications, however, my position might crudely be stated as follows: *Just desert limits what a civilized society may do to deter crime, and deterrence limits what a civilized society may do to give criminals their just deserts.*

12. Isaac Ehrlich, "The Deterrent Effect of Capital Punishment: A Question of Life or Death," *American Economic Review* 65 (June 1975): 397–417. For reactions to Ehrlich's work, see Alfred Blumstein, Jacqueline Cohen, and Daniel Nagin, eds., *Deterrence and Incapacitation: Estimating the Effects of Criminal Sanctions on Crime Rates* (Washington, D.C.: National Academy of Sciences, 1978), esp. pp. 59–63 and 336–60; Brian E. Forst, "The Deterrent Effect on Capital Punishment: A Cross-State Analysis," *Minnesota Law Review* 61 (May 1977): 743–67, Deryck Beyleveld, "Ehrlich's Analysis of Deterrence," *British Journal of Criminology* 22 (April 1982): 101–23, and Isaac Ehrlich, "On Positive Methodology, Ethics and Polemics in Deterrence Research," *British Journal of Criminology* 22 (April 1982): 124–39. Much of the criticism of Ehrlich's work focuses on the fact that he found a deterrence impact of executions in the period from 1993–1969, which includes the period 1963–1969, a time when hardly any executions were carried out and crime rates rose for reasons that are arguably independent of the existence or nonexistence of capital punishment. When the 1963–1969 period is excluded, no significant deterrent effect shows. Prior to Ehrlich's work, research on the comparative deterrent impact of the death penalty versus life imprisonment indicated no increase in the incidence of homicide in states that abolished the death penalty and no greater incidence of homicide in states without the death penalty compared to similar states with the death penalty. See Thorsten Sellin, *The Death Penalty* (Philadelphia: American Law Institute, 1959).

13. Van den Haag writes: "Other studies published since Ehrlich's contend that his results are due to the techniques and periods he selected, and that different techniques and periods yield different results. Despite a great deal of research on all sides, one cannot say that the statistical evidence is conclusive. Nobody has claimed to have *disproved* that the death penalty may deter more than life imprisonment. But one cannot claim, either, that it has been proved statistically in a conclusive manner that the death penalty

does deter more than alternative penalties. This lack of proof does not amount to disproof" (p. 65).

14. On the number of people killed by the police, see Lawrence W. Sherman and Robert H. Langworthy, "Measuring Homicide by Police Officers," *Journal of Criminal Law and Criminology* 70, no. 4 (Winter 1979): 546–60; on the number of privately owned guns, see Franklin Zimring, *Firearms and Violence in American Life* (Washington, D.C.: U.S. Government Printing Office, 1968), pp. 6–7.

15. *AAA World* (Potomac ed.) 4, no. 3 (May–June 1984), pp. 18c and 18i.

16. A related claim has been made by those who defend the so-called brutalization hypothesis by presenting evidence to show that murders *increase* following an execution. See, for example, William J. Bowers and Glenn L. Pierce, "Deterrence or Brutalization: What Is the Effect of Executions?" *Crime & Delinquency* 26, no. 4 (October 1980): 453–84. They conclude that each execution gives rise to two additional homicides in the month following and that these are real additions, not just a change in timing of the homicides (ibid., p. 481). My claim, it should be noted, is not identical to this, since, as I indicate in the text, what I call "the deterrence effect of not executing" is not something whose impact is to be seen immediately following executions but over the long haul, and, further, my claim is compatible with finding no net increase in murders due to executions. Nonetheless, should the brutalization hypothesis be borne out by further

studies, it would certainly lend support to the notion that there is a deterrent effect of not executing.

17. Van den Haag writes: "If we were quite ignorant about the marginal deterrent effects of execution, we would have to choose—like it or not—between the certainty of the convicted murderer's death by execution and the likelihood of the survival of future victims of other murderers on the one hand, and on the other his certain survival and the likelihood of the death of new victims. I'd rather execute a man convicted of having murdered others than put the lives of innocents at risk. I find it hard to understand the opposite choice" (p. 69). Conway was able to counter this argument earlier by pointing out that the research on the marginal deterrent effects of execution was not *inconclusive* in the sense of *tending to point both ways*, but rather in the sense of *giving us no reason to believe that capital punishment saves more lives than life imprisonment.* He could then answer van den Haag by saying that the choice is not between risking the lives of murderers and risking the lives of innocents, but between killing a murderer with no reason to believe lives will be saved and sparing a murderer with no reason to believe lives will be lost (Conway, "Capital Punishment and Deterrence," [*Philosophy & Public Affairs* 3, no. 4], pp. 442–43). This, of course, makes the choice to spare the murderer more understandable than van den Haag allows. Events, however, have overtaken Conway's argument. The advent of Ehrlich's research, contested though it may be, leaves us in fact with research that tends to point both ways.

Death Penalty Statistics
Rick Halperin

Editor's Note: Rick Halperin, a member of the history department at Southern Methodist University (SMU), collects and publishes death penalty statistics on his web site. SMU is located in Texas, which puts far more prisoners to death than any other state.

U.S. Executions 1997 (as of mid–1997)

1997	Overall	Date	Name	State	Method
1	359	1/8	Earl Van Denton	AR	Lethal Injection
2	360	1/8	Paul Ruiz	AR	Lethal Injection
3	361	1/8	Kirt Wainwright	AR	Lethal Injection
4	362	1/10	Billy Wayne Waldrop	AL	Electrocution
5	363	1/23	Randy Greenawalt	AZ	Lethal Injection
6	364	1/29	Eric Schneider	MO	Lethal Injection
7	365	2/6	Michael George	VA	Lethal Injection
8	366	2/10	Richard Brimage, Jr.	TX	Lethal Injection
9	367	2/26	Coleman Wayne Gray	VA	Lethal Injection

Rick Halperin, "Death Penalty Statistics," http://www.smu.edu/~deathpen/ 9 May 1997. Reprinted with the permission of Rick Halperin.

1997	Overall	Date	Name	State	Method
10	368	3/12	John Kennedy Barefield	TX	Lethal Injection
11	369	3/25	Pedro Medina	FL	Electrocution
12	370	4/2	David Lee Herman	TX	Lethal Injection
13	371	4/3	David Spence	TX	Lethal Injection
14	372	4/14	Billy Joe Woods	TX	Lethal Injection
15	373	4/16	Kenneth Gentry	TX	Lethal Injection
16	374	4/21	Benjamin Herbert Boyle	TX	Lethal Injection
17	375	4/24	John Ashley Brown, Jr.	LA	Lethal Injection
18	376	4/29	Ernest Baldree	TX	Lethal Injection
19	377	5/2	Walter Hill	AL	Electrocution
20	378	5/6	Terry Washington	TX	Lethal Injection
21	379	5/8	Scott Carpenter	OK	Lethal Injection

Methods of execution and numbers executed by that method in the USA are: electrocution (129), firing squad (2), gas chamber (9), hanging (3), and lethal injection (236).

U.S. Executions 1996

1996	Overall	Date	Name	State	Method
1	314	1/4	Walter Correll Jr.	VA	Lethal Injection
2	315	1/23	Richard Townes Jr.	VA	Lethal Injection
3	316	1/25	Billy Bailey	DE	Hanging
4	317	1/26	John Taylor	UT	Firing Squad
5	318	1/30	William Flamer	DE	Lethal Injection
6	319	2/9	Leo Jenkins	TX	Lethal Injection
7	320	2/16	Edward Horsley	AL	Electrocution
8	321	2/21	Jeffrey Sloxan	MO	Lethal Injection
9	322	2/23	William Bonin	CA	Lethal Injection
10	323	2/27	Kenneth Granviel	TX	Lethal Injection
11	324	3/1	Antonio James	LA	Lethal Injection
12	325	3/30	Richard Moran	NV	Lethal Injection
13	326	4/10	Doyle Williams	MO	Lethal Injection
14	327	4/19	James Clark	DE	Lethal Injection
15	328	4/26	Benjamin Brewer	OK	Lethal Injection
16	329	5/3	Keith Williams	CA	Lethal Injection
17	330	5/31	Robert South	SC	Lethal Injection
18	331	6/19	Daren Bolton	AZ	Lethal Injection
19	332	7/17	John Joubert	NE	Electrocution
20	333	7/17	Joseph Savino	VA	Lethal Injection
21	334	7/18	Tommie Smith	IN	Lethal Injection
22	335	7/19	Fred Kornahrens	SC	Lethal Injection
23	336	7/31	Emmett Nave	MO	Lethal Injection
24	337	8/7	Thomas Battle	MO	Lethal Injection
25	338	8/8	William Frank Parker	AR	Lethal Injection
26	339	8/9	Steven Hatch	OK	Lethal Injection
27	340	8/21	Richard Oxford	MO	Lethal Injection
28	341	8/22	Luis Mata	AZ	Lethal Injection
29	342	9/6	Michael Torrence	SC	Lethal Injection
30	343	9/6	Douglas Wright	OR	Lethal Injection

1996	Overall	Date	Name	State	Method
31	344	9/18	Ray Lee Stewart	IL	Lethal Injection
32	345	9/18	Joe Gonzales	TX	Lethal Injection
33	346	10/4	Larry Gene Bell	SC	Electrocution
34	347	10/21	John Earl Bush	FL	Electrocution
35	348	11/14	Larry Lonchar	GA	Electrocution
36	349	11/15	Doyle Cecil Lucas	SC	Lethal Injection
37	350	11/15	Ellis Wayne Felker	GA	Electrocution
38	351	11/21	Ronald Bennett	VA	Lethal Injection
39	352	11/22	Frank Middleton	SC	Lethal Injection
40	353	12/3	Gregory Beaver	VA	Lethal Injection
41	354	12/6	John Mills, Jr.	FL	Electrocution
42	355	12/10	Larry Stout	VA	Lethal Injection
43	356	12/11	Richard Zeitvogel	MO	Lethal Injection
44	357	12/12	Lem Tuggle	VA	Lethal Injection
45	358	12/16	Ronald Hoke	VA	Lethal Injection

Executions by State (from January 1976 to May 1997)

Texas	116
Florida	39
Virginia	39
Louisiana	24
Missouri	24
Georgia	22
Alabama	15
Arkansas	15
South Carolina	11
Oklahoma	9
Delaware	8
Illinois	8
North Carolina	8
Arizona	7
Nevada	6
Utah	5
California	4
Indiana	4
Mississippi	4
Nebraska	2
Pennsylvania	2
Washington	2
Idaho	1
Maryland	1
Montana	1
Oregon	1
Wyoming	1

Total executions   379

U.S. Executions by Year, 1976–1996

1976	0
1977	1
1978	0
1979	2
1980	0
1981	1
1982	2
1983	5
1984	21
1985	18
1986	18
1987	25
1988	11
1989	16
1990	23
1991	14
1992	31
1993	38
1994	31
1995	56
1996	45

19.

Race and the Death Penalty

Anthony G. Amsterdam

Anthony G. Amsterdam is a law professor at the New York University School of Law, Clinical Law Center. In this essay, he criticizes the United States Supreme Court decision *McCleskey v. Georgia* (1987), which addressed race and the death penalty. Warren McCleskey, a black man, was sentenced by the state of Georgia to die for the murder of a white man, an on-duty police officer. The Supreme Court ruled that McCleskey could be constitutionally sentenced to die despite overwhelming statistical evidence that juries in Georgia imposed the death penalty in a pattern that reflected the race of the convicted murderers and of their victims. In the *McCleskey* case, the Supreme Court acknowledged research that showed that in Georgia, blacks who killed whites were twenty-two times more likely to be sentenced to death than were blacks who killed blacks, yet it upheld Warren McCleskey's sentence, arguing that he would have to prove that the jurors in his particular case were discriminatory. Amsterdam argues that it is against the fundamental values of our society for a public institution to treat people differently solely as a consequence of their race. He concludes that "toleration of racism cannot be justified by the . . . interest of the society in fighting crime."

There are times when even truths we hold self-evident require affirmation. For those who have invested our careers and our hopes in the criminal justice system, this is one of those times. Insofar as the basic principles that give value to our lives are in the keeping of the law and can be vindicated or betrayed by the decisions of any court, they have been sold down the river by a decision of the Supreme Court of the United States less than a year old [in 1988].

I do not choose by accident a metaphor of slavery. For the decision I am referring to is the criminal justice system's *Dred Scott* case. It is the case of Warren McCleskey, a black man sentenced to die for the murder of a white man in Georgia. The Supreme Court held that McCleskey can be constitutionally put to death despite overwhelming unrebutted and unexplained statistical evidence that the death penalty is being imposed by Georgia juries in a pattern which reflects the race of convicted murderers and their victims and cannot be accounted for by any factor other than race.

This is not just a case about capital punishment. The Supreme Court's decision, which amounts to an open license to discriminate against people of color in capital sentencing, was placed upon grounds that implicate the entire criminal justice system. Worse still, the Court's reasoning makes us all accomplices in its toleration of a racially discriminatory administration of criminal justice.

Let us look at the *McCleskey* case. His crime was an ugly one. He robbed a furniture store at gunpoint, and he or one of his accomplices killed a police officer who responded to the scene. McCleskey may have been the triggerman. Whether or not he was, he was guilty of murder under Georgia law.

But his case in the Supreme Court was not concerned with guilt. It was concerned with why McCleskey had been sentenced to death instead of life imprisonment for his crime. It was concerned with why, out of seventeen defendants charged with the killings of police officers in Fulton County, Georgia between 1973 and 1980, only Warren McCleskey—a black defendant charged with killing a white officer—

Anthony Amsterdam, "Race and the Death Penalty" (as appeared in *Criminal Justice Ethics* Vol. 7, No. 1 [Winter/Spring 1988] pp. 2, 84–86). Reprinted by permission of The Institute For Criminal Justice Ethics, 899 Tenth Avenue, New York, NY 10019. Reprinted also by permission of the author.

had been chosen for a death sentence. In the only other one of these seventeen cases in which the predominantly white prosecutor's office in Atlanta had pushed for the death penalty, a black defendant convicted of killing a black police officer had been sentenced to life instead.

It was facts of that sort that led the NAACP Legal Defense Fund to become involved in McCleskey's case. They were not unfamiliar facts to any of the lawyers who, like myself, had worked for the Legal Defense Fund for many years, defending Blacks charged with serious crimes throughout the South. We knew that in the United States black defendants convicted of murder or rape in cases involving white victims have always been sentenced to death and executed far out of proportion to their numbers, and under factual circumstances that would have produced a sentence of imprisonment—often a relatively light sentence of imprisonment—in identical cases with black victims or white defendants or both.

Back in the mid-sixties the Legal Defense Fund had presented to courts evidence of extensive statistical studies conducted by Dr. Marvin Wolfgang, one of the deans of American criminology, showing that the grossly disproportionate number of death sentences which were then being handed out to black defendants convicted of the rape of white victims could not be explained by any factor other than race. Prosecutors took the position then that these studies were insufficiently detailed to rule out the influence of every possible non-racial factor, and it was largely for that reason that the courts rejected our claims that our black death-sentenced clients had been denied the Equal Protection of the Laws. Fortunately, in 1972 we had won a Supreme Court decision that saved the lives of all those clients and outlawed virtually every death penalty statute in the United States on procedural grounds; and when the States enacted new death-penalty laws between 1973 and 1976, only three of them reinstated capital punishment for rape. Now that it no longer mattered much, the prosecutors could afford to take

another tack. When we argued against the new capital murder statutes on the ground that the Wolfgang studies had shown the susceptibility of capital sentencing laws to racially discriminatory application, the Government of the United States came into the Supreme Court against us saying, Oh, yes, Wolfgang was "a careful and comprehensive study, and we do not question its conclusion that during the twenty years between [1945 and 1965] . . . , in southern states, there was discrimination in rape cases." However, said the Government, this "research does not provide support for a conclusion that racial discrimination continues, . . . or that it applies to murder cases."

So we were well prepared for this sort of selective agnosticism when we went to court in the *McCleskey* case. The evidence that we presented in support of McCleskey's claim of racial discrimination left nothing out. Our centerpiece was a pair of studies conducted by Professor David Baldus, of the University of Iowa, and his colleagues, which examined 2,484 cases of murder and non-negligent manslaughter that occurred in Georgia between 1973, the date when its present capital murder statute was enacted, and 1979, the year after McCleskey's own death sentence was imposed. The Baldus team got its data on these cases principally from official state records, supplied by the Georgia Supreme Court and the Georgia Board of Pardons and Paroles.

Through a highly refined protocol, the team collected information regarding more than five hundred factors in each case—information relating to the demographic and individual characteristics of the defendant and the victim, the circumstances of the crime and the strength of the evidence of guilt, and the aggravating and mitigating features of each case: both the features specified by Georgia law to be considered in capital sentencing and every factor recognized in the legal and criminological literature as theoretically or actually likely to affect the choice of life or death. Using the most reliable and advanced techniques of social-science research, Baldus processed the data through a wide array of sophisticated statistical procedures, including multiple-regression analyses based upon alternative models that considered and controlled for as few as 10 or as many as 230 sentencing factors in each analysis. When our evidentiary case was presented in court, Baldus reanalyzed the data several more times to take account of every additional factor, combination of factors, or model for analysis of factors suggested by the State of Georgia's expert witnesses, its lawyers, and the federal trial judge. The Baldus study has since been uniformly praised by social scientists as the best study of any aspect of criminal sentencing ever conducted.

What did it show? That death sentences were being imposed in Georgia murder cases in a clear, consistent pattern that reflected the race of the victim and the race of the defendant and could not be explained by any non-racial factor. For example:

1. Although less than 40 percent of Georgia homicide cases involve white victims, in 87 percent of the cases in which a death sentence is imposed, the victim is white. White-victim cases are almost eleven times more likely to produce a death sentence than are black-victim cases.

2. When the race of the defendant is considered too, the following figures emerge: 22 percent of black defendants who kill white victims are sentenced to death; 8 percent of white defendants who kill white victims are sentenced to death; 1 percent of black defendants who kill black victims are sentenced to death; 3 percent of white defendants who kill black victims are sentenced to death. It should be noted that out of the roughly 2,500 Georgia homicide cases found, only 64 involved killings of black victims by white defendants, so the 3 percent death-sentencing rate in this category represents a total of two death sentences over a six-year period. Plainly, the reason why racial discrimination against black defendants does not appear even more glaringly evident is that most black murderers kill black victims; almost no identified white murderers kill black victims; and virtually

nobody is sentenced to death for killing a mere black victim.

3. No non-racial factor explains these racial patterns. Under multiple regression analysis, the model with the maximum explanatory power shows that after controlling for legitimate non-racial factors, murderers of white victims are still being sentenced to death 4.3 times more often than murderers of black victims. Multiple regression analysis also shows that the race of the victim is as good a basis for predicting whether or not a murderer will be sentenced to death as are the aggravating circumstances which the Georgia statute explicitly says should be considered in favor of a death sentence, such as whether the defendant has a prior murder conviction, or whether he is the primary actor in the present murder.

4. Across the whole universe of cases, approximately 5 percent of Georgia killings result in a death sentence. Yet when more than 230 non-racial variables are controlled for, the death-sentencing rate is 6 percentage points higher in white-victim cases than in black-victim cases. What this means is that in predicting whether any particular person will get the death penalty in Georgia, it is less important to know whether or not he committed a homicide in the first place than to know whether, if he did, he killed a white victim or a black one.

5. However, the effects of race are not uniform across the entire range of homicide cases. As might be expected, in the least aggravated sorts of cases, almost no one gets a death sentence; in the really gruesome cases, a high percentage of both black and white murderers get death sentences; so it is in the mid-range of cases— cases like McCleskey's—that race has its greatest impact. The Baldus study found that in these mid-range cases the death-sentencing rate for killers of white victims is 34 percent as compared to 14 percent for killers of black victims. In other words, out of every thirty-four murderers sentenced to death for killing a white victim, twenty of them would not have gotten death sentences if their victims had been black.

The bottom line is this: Georgia has executed eleven murderers since it passed its present statute in 1973. Nine of the eleven were black. Ten of the eleven had white victims. Can there be the slightest doubt that this revolting record is the product of some sort of racial bias rather than a pure fluke?

A narrow majority of the Supreme Court pretended to have such doubts and rejected McCleskey's Equal-Protection challenge to his death sentence. It did not question the quality or the validity of the Baldus study, or any of the findings that have been described here. It admitted that the manifest racial discrepancies in death sentencing were unexplained by any non-racial variable, and that Baldus's data pointed to a "likelihood" or a "risk" that race was at work in the capital sentencing process. It essentially conceded that if a similar statistical showing of racial bias had been made in an employment-discrimination case or in a jury-selection case, the courts would have been required to find a violation of the Equal Protection Clause of the Fourteenth Amendment. But, the Court said, racial discrimination in capital sentencing cannot be proved by a pattern of sentencing results: a death-sentenced defendant like McCleskey must present proof that the particular jury or the individual prosecutor, or some other decision-maker in his own case, was personally motivated by racial considerations to bring about his death. Since such proof is never possible to obtain, racial discrimination in capital sentencing is never possible to prove.

The Court gave four basic reasons for this result. First, since capital sentencing decisions are made by a host of different juries and prosecutors, and are supposed to be based upon "innumerable factors that vary according to the characteristics of the individual defendant and the facts of the particular capital offense," even sentencing patterns that are explicable by race and inexplicable except by race do not necessarily show that any single decision-maker in the system is acting out of a subjective purpose to discriminate. Second, capital punishment laws are important for the protection of society; the "[i]mplementation of these laws necessarily requires discretionary judgments"; and, "[b]ecause discretion is essential to the criminal justice process, we [sh]ould demand exceptionally clear proof before we . . . infer that the discretion has been abused." Third, this same respect for discretionary judgments makes it imprudent to require juries and prosecutors to explain their decisions, so it is better to ignore the inference of racial discrimination that flows logically from their behavior than to call upon them to justify such behavior upon non-racial grounds.

Fourth, more is involved than capital punishment. "McCleskey's claim . . . throws into serious question the principles that underlie our entire criminal justice system." This is so because "the Baldus study indicates a discrepancy that appears to correlate with race," and "[a]pparent disparities in sentencing are an inevitable part of our criminal justice system." "Thus," says the Court, "if we accepted McCleskey's claim that racial bias has impermissibly tainted the capital sentencing decision, we could soon be faced with similar claims as to other types of penalty. Moreover, the claim that . . . sentence rests on the irrelevant factor of race easily could be extended to apply to claims based on unexplained discrepancies that correlate to membership in other minority groups, and even to gender"—and even to claims based upon "the defendant's facial characteristics, or the physical attractiveness of the . . . victim." In other words, if we forbid racial discrimination in meting out sentences of life or death, we may have to face claims of discrimination against Blacks, or against women, or perhaps against ugly people, wherever the facts warrant such claims, in the length of prison sentences, in the length of jail sentences, in the giving of suspended sentences, in the making of pretrial release decisions, in the invocation of recidivist sentencing enhancements, in the prosecutor's decisions whether to file charges, and how heavily to load up the charges, against black defendants as compared with white defendants or against ugly defendants as compared with ravishingly beautiful defendants; and of course the whole criminal justice system will then fall down flat and leave us in a state of anarchy. In thirty years of reading purportedly serious judicial opinions, I have never seen one that came so close to Thomas De Quincy's famous justification for punishing the crime of murder: "If once a man indulges himself in murder, very soon he comes to think little of robbing; and from robbing he next comes to drinking and Sabbath-breaking, and from that to incivility and procrastination."

Notice that the Court's version of this slippery-slope argument merely makes explicit what is implied throughout its opinion in the *McCleskey* case. Its decision is not limited to capital sentencing but purports to rest on principles which apply to the whole criminal justice system. Every part of that system from arrest to sentencing and parole, in relation to every crime from murder to Sabbath-breaking, involves a multitude of separate decision-makers making individualized decisions based upon "innumerable [case-specific] factors." All of these decisions are important for the protection of society from crime. All are conceived as "necessarily requir[ing] discretionary judgments." In making these discretionary judgments, prosecutors and judges as well as jurors have traditionally been immunized from inquiry into their motives. If this kind of discretion implies the power to treat black people differently from white people and to escape the responsibility for explaining why one is making life-and-death decisions in an apparently discriminatory manner, it implies a tolerance for racial discrimination throughout the length and breadth of the administration of criminal justice. What the Supreme Court has held, plainly, is that the very nature of the criminal justice system requires that its workings be excluded from the ordinary rules of law and even logic that guarantee equal protection to racial minorities in our society.

And it is here, I suggest, that any self-respecting criminal justice professional is obliged to speak out against this Supreme Court's conception of the criminal justice system. We must reaffirm that there can be no justice in a system which treats people of color differently from white people, or treats crimes against people of color differently from crimes against white people.

We must reaffirm that racism is itself a crime, and that the toleration of racism cannot be justified by the supposed interest of society in fighting crime. We must pledge that when anyone—even a majority of the Supreme Court—tells us that a power to discriminate on grounds of race is necessary to protect society from crime, we will recognize that we are probably being sold another shipment of propaganda to justify repression. Let us therefore never fail to ask the question whether righteous rhetoric about protecting society from crime really refers to protecting only white people. And when the answer, as in the McCleskey case, is that protecting only white people is being described as "protecting society from crime," let us say that we are not so stupid as to buy this version of the Big Lie, nor so uncaring as to let it go unchallenged.

Let us reaffirm that neither the toleration of racism by the Supreme Court nor the pervasiveness of racism in the criminal justice system can make it right, and that these things only make it worse. Let us reaffirm that racism exists, and is against the fundamental law of this Nation, whenever people of different races are treated differently by any public agency or institution as a consequence of their race and with no legitimate non-racial reason for the different treatment. Let us dedicate ourselves to eradicating racism, and declaring it unlawful, not simply in the superficial, short-lived situation where we can point to one or another specific decision-maker and show that his decisions were the product of conscious bigotry, but also in the far more basic, more intractable, and more destructive situations where hundreds upon hundreds of different public decision-makers, acting like

Georgia's prosecutors and judges and juries—without collusion and in many cases without consciousness of their own racial biases—combine to produce a pattern that bespeaks the profound prejudice of an entire population.

Also, let us vow that we will never claim—or stand by unprotestingly while others claim for us—that, because our work is righteous and important, it should be above the law. Of course, controlling crime is vital work; that is why we give the agencies of criminal justice drastic and unique coercive powers, including the powers of imprisonment and death. And of course discretion in the execution of such powers is essential. But it is precisely because the powers that the system regulates are so awesome, and because the discretion of its actors is so broad, that it cannot be relieved of accountability for the exercise of that discretion. Nor can it be exempted from the scrutiny that courts of law are bound to give to documented charges of discrimination on the ground of race by any agency of government. Let us declare flatly that we neither seek nor will accept any such exemption,

and that we find it demeaning to be told by the Supreme Court that the system of justice to which we have devoted our professional lives cannot do its job without a special dispensation from the safeguards that assure to people of every race the equal protection of the law.

This is a stigma criminal justice practitioners do not deserve. Service in the criminal justice system should be a cause not for shame but for pride. Nowhere is it possible to dedicate one's labors to the welfare of one's fellow human beings with a greater sense that one is needed and that the quality of what one does can make a difference. But to feel this pride, and to deserve it, we must consecrate ourselves to the protection of all people, not a privileged few. We must be servants of humanity, not of caste. Whether or not the Supreme Court demands this of us, we must demand it of ourselves and of our coworkers in the system. For this is the faith to which we are sworn by our common calling: that doing justice is never simply someone else's job; correcting injustice is never simply someone else's responsibility.

Studies Find Death Penalty Tied to Race of the Victims

Erik Eckholm

About half of all the people who are murdered each year in the United States are black. Yet since 1977, when a firing squad in Utah initiated the modern era of capital punishment, the overwhelming majority of people who have been executed—85 percent—had killed a white person.

Only 11 percent had killed a black person.

Such a huge disparity seems to suggest that racial factors may be influencing how the death penalty is dispensed—but in different ways than some people had suspected.

While death penalty opponents had long feared that the race of the killer would play a pro-

nounced role in determining who would be executed and that blacks would be put to death far more frequently than whites, several studies suggest that the most significant distinction is the race of the victim.

Other things being equal, the studies show, killers of white people are more likely to receive death sentences than killers of blacks. This disparity, civil rights advocates say, shows that the judicial system places more value on the lives of whites than of blacks.

Whether similar racial disparities are likely to occur in New York and what, if anything, should be done to prevent it have been topics of dispute in Albany as legislators prepare to revive the death penalty.

But the experience of other states suggests to many experts that such patterns will be hard to eliminate. "Some people are being sentenced to death based on race, and I find that morally and legally objectionable," said Dr. David C. Baldus, professor of law at the University of Iowa and director of what is widely considered the most authoritative study of racial factors in capital punishment.

The question of race is among the mostly politically charged and highly studied issues in capital punishment. And it goes to the heart of a question that troubles many opponents: whether the imposition of the death penalty is inherently unfair.

Shortly before he retired from the United States Supreme Court last year, Justice Harry A. Blackmun cited intractable racial disparities as one of the reasons why he had turned against capital punishment altogether.

But bias, if it exists, is no reason to slow down executions, said Ernest van den Haag, former professor of jurisprudence at Fordham University in New York. "The fact that a murderer who gets the death penalty could point to a murderer who didn't," he said, "does not make him any less guilty."

Although the strength of some of the research findings is disputed, numerous studies around the country have reached these basic conclusions:

- Disparities in death sentencing are most often related to the race of the victim. When the victim is white, the death penalty is imposed more often whether the killer is black or white. In one study, the presence of a white victim did as much to increase the chances of a death sentence as the fact that the murder was committed during an armed robbery.

- Bias does not necessarily occur at the most visible point of the judicial process—when juries decide whether to recommend death. Often, disparities arise from earlier decisions by prosecutors, like whether to allow the defendant to plead guilty to a lesser charge or whether to ask for the death penalty at all.

- The disparities are concentrated among certain kinds of murder cases that account for perhaps one-fifth to one-fourth of the total. In a majority of murders—crimes of passion, killings in barroom brawls—death is rarely imposed. In a small number of especially grisly crimes like multiple murders, death sentences are frequent

regardless of race. But for murders that fall into a middle ground—the killing of a shopkeeper in a robbery, say, or a murder by a person with a serious felony record—prosecutors and juries are more likely to agonize over the propriety of a death sentence, and hidden biases are more likely to creep in, the studies suggest.

In a 1990 review of 28 studies on race and the death penalty, the General Accounting Office in Washington said, "In 82 percent of the studies, race of victim was found to influence the likelihood of being charged with capital murder or receiving the death penalty." The office described the trend as "remarkably consistent" through research of varied quality and scope, and pointed to crucial gaps in some reports that found no bias.

The same review described as "equivocal" the evidence that the race of the defendant mattered: several studies found signs that blacks convicted of murder were more likely to be executed, especially in rural areas, but others found white defendants at higher risk, especially in cities, and some studies found no differences.

Laws Once Gave Penalties by Race

To many people, the likelihood of bias seems greatest in interracial killings, with blacks who kill whites more likely to receive death sentences. The sheer numbers appear to bear that out: over the last 18 years, 88 black men have been executed for killing whites, while only two white men have been executed for killing blacks.

But most of the studies indicate that when the nature of the crimes is taken into account as well as the fact that black-on-white killings are more frequent than white-on-black killings, the evidence of extra bias disappears. Again, the true bias arises from the race of the victim, regardless of the killer's race.

Discrimination in murder penalties by the race of the victim has a long history, especially in the South. In the days of slavery, laws in many states openly specified different penalties, said George H. Kendall, associate counsel of the NAACP Legal Defense and Educational Fund, with death the automatic sanction when a black killed a white.

"Those laws were swept away after the Civil War, but the customs that grew up around them remained," Mr. Kendall said.

In a classic 1944 study of American race relations, "An American Dilemma," Gunnar Myrdal found that when blacks committed crimes against each other without involving whites, the legal consequences were lower than when whites were harmed. "The sentences for even major crimes are ordinarily reduced when the victim is another Negro," he wrote.

Because of its size and detail, the most persuasive evidence of bias comes from a study of Georgia in the 1970's led by Dr. Baldus. Looking at 1,050 murder cases, researchers tried to weed out the influence of 39 factors that might affect penalties, from the past record of the defendant to whether the killing was committed in the course of another crime like robbery or rape to the motives and means of the killing.

After those factors are eliminated, Mr. Baldus said in a recent interview, a clear racial effect remained: when the murder victim was white, the chance of a death penalty was roughly doubled in certain kinds of cases, the ones falling into that middle ground.

Just How Reliable Are the Studies?

Some statisticians question whether the Baldus study, let alone others of lesser sweep, really prove bias. Stephen P. Klein, a researcher at the Rand Corporation, said the available statistical methods were incapable of showing cause and effect.

He noted that the number of actual death sentences in question in such studies was small and that uncounted, often intangible factors, like the credibility of witnesses at trial, might well explain the apparent racial disparities.

Dr. Samuel R. Gross, a professor of law at the University of Michigan and an author of a study that found bias in eight states, said there was no reason to think that uncounted factors would wipe out the racial differences found in numerous studies around the country.

The focus on the race of victims, rather than defendants, has a paradoxical effect. Since most murders involve killers and victims of the same race, eliminating the disparity linked to the race of the victim would likely mean that the proportion, and perhaps the absolute number, of blacks on death row would rise.

If killers of black people were executed at the rate of killers of whites, many more blacks would receive death sentences. If, on the other hand, killers of whites were executed at the same rate as killers of blacks, many whites would be spared.

But a jump in death sentences for blacks would be unlikely, said Mr. Kendall of the legal defense fund, which opposes the death penalty on the ground that it is inherently unfair and unworkable.

"If everything were fair, I think we'd see a lot fewer capital cases over all," he said. Now, he said, the death penalty is used especially when a high-profile victim is murdered, usually a white person. Given the enormous public expense of capital cases, "we're not going to see a big increase in black victim cases," he said.

Efforts to Offset Racial Disparities

Whether racial disparities seen in other parts of the country will extend to New York when it institutes the death penalty cannot be known. Dr. Baldus and others caution against assuming that studies in one place and time apply to any other. But he added that his recent analysis of death sentencing in New Jersey in the 1980's produced preliminary evidence of similar bias, though the numbers are still small.

Mr. Kendall said that if anything, the country appeared to be moving backward in race relations and that prejudice was by no means limited to the South. "I don't see anything about New York that would make the process work any differently here than anywhere else," he said.

What might be done to purge the death penalty of bias is unclear. As one countermeasure, New York legislators apparently plan, in capital cases, to permit lawyers to question potential jurors in private about their racial attitudes.

New York may also call for research on racial aspects of death-sentencing over time to detect any disparities. But it apparently will not take the step that civil rights advocates want most: to write into the law that statistical evidence of disparities should be a powerful weapon in court for individual defendants facing death.

If prosecutors had no legitimate explanation for detected disparities, Mr. Kendall said, then death sentences in the affected subgroup of defendants should be overturned.

The Baldus study itself was the centerpiece of an appeal to the United States Supreme Court in 1987 by a black man in Georgia who had been sentenced to death for murdering a white police officer. In the case, *McCleskey v. Kemp,* the defendant argued that his penalty should be revoked, based on the evidence of systematic discrimination in cases like his.

The Supreme Court, by a 5-to-4 vote, rejected the appeal, arguing that he also had to prove actual discrimination in the handling of his own case.

But defense lawyers say that that standard has harmed their search for racial fairness.

"It's almost impossible to prove purposeful discrimination in a single case," said Dale Jones, an assistant public defender in Trenton.

For the last several years, civil rights groups have sought to write a "racial justice" provision into Federal criminal law, which would require quantitative studies of racial patterns in death sentencing and give powerful courtroom standing to any findings. But last year, Congress, as it adopted a new crime bill, rejected the proposal. Opponents belittled the evidence of bias and said such a law could be used in court to bog down any application of the death penalty.

Dr. van den Haag, the death penalty proponent, questioned the importance of research showing bias by the race of the victim. And even if discrimination exists, he said, the solution is not to abolish the death penalty but to end disparities— by increasing executions of the favored group.

Dr. Baldus said the issue was not whether blacks or whites get their share of death sentences but whether justice is tainted by inappropriate considerations. "The real concern isn't the number of black people on death row," he said. "It's the integrity of the system."

20.
Does It Matter If the Death Penalty Is Arbitrarily Administered?

Stephen Nathanson

Stephen Nathanson is professor of philosophy at Northeastern University. His books include *An Eye for an Eye: The Morality of Punishing by Death* and *Should We Consent to be Governed?* He argues that the state institution of the death penalty ought to be abolished because it has been and will continue to be arbitrarily imposed. He also anticipates, and responds to, some of Ernest van den Haag's objections to the argument from arbitrariness.

I

In this article, I will examine the argument that capital punishment ought to be abolished because it has been and will continue to be imposed in an arbitrary manner.

This argument has been central to discussions of capital punishment since the Supreme Court ruling in the 1972 case *Furman v. Georgia.* In a 5–4 decision, the Court ruled that capital punishment as then administered was unconstitutional. Although the Court issued several opinions, the problem of arbitrariness is widely seen as having played a central role in the Court's thinking. As Charles Black, Jr., has put it,

> . . . The decisive ground of the 1972 Furman case anti-capital punishment ruling—the ground persuasive to the marginal justices needed for a majority—was that, out of a large number of persons "eligible" in law for

Stephen Nathanson, "Does It Matter If the Death Penalty Is Arbitrarily Administered?" *Philosophy And Public Affairs* 14 (Spring 1985). Copyright (c) 1985 by Princeton University Press. Reprinted by permission of Princeton University Press.

the punishment of death, a few were selected as if at random, by no stated (or perhaps statable) criteria, while all the rest suffered the lesser penalty of imprisonment.[1]

Among those justices moved by the arbitrariness issue, some stressed the discriminatory aspects of capital punishment, the tendency of legally irrelevant factors like race and economic status to determine the severity of sentence, while others emphasized the "freakish" nature of the punishment, the fact that it is imposed on a minuscule percentage of murderers who are not obviously more deserving of death than others.

Although the Supreme Court approved new death penalty laws in *Gregg v. Georgia* (1976), the reasoning of *Furman* was not rejected. Rather, a majority of the Court determined that Georgia's new laws would make arbitrary imposition of the death penalty much less likely. By amending procedures and adding criteria which specify aggravating and mitigating circumstances, Georgia had succeeded in creating a system of "guided discretion," which the court accepted in the belief that it was not likely to yield arbitrary results.

The *Gregg* decision has prompted death penalty opponents to attempt to show that "guided discretion" is an illusion. This charge has been supported in various ways. Charles Black has supported it by analyzing both the legal process of decision making in capital cases and the legal criteria for determining who is to be executed. He has argued that, appearances to the contrary, there are no meaningful standards operating in the system. Attacking from an empirical angle, William Bowers and Glenn Pierce have tried to show that even after *Furman* and under new laws, factors like race and geographic location of the trial continue to play a large role and that the criteria which are supposed to guide judgment do not separate those sentenced into meaningfully distinct groups. Perhaps the most shocking conclusion of Bowers and Pierce concerns the large role played by the race of the killer and the victim, as the chances of execution are by far the greatest when blacks kill whites and least when whites kill blacks.[2]

The upshot of both these approaches is that "guided discretion" is not working and, perhaps, cannot work. If this is correct and if the argument for arbitrariness is accepted, then it would appear that a return from *Gregg* to *Furman* is required. That is, the Court should once again condemn capital punishment as unconstitutional.

I have posed these issues in terms of the Supreme Court's deliberations. Nonetheless, for opponents of the death penalty, the freakishness of its imposition and the large role played by race and other irrelevant factors are a moral as well as a legal outrage. For them, there is a fundamental moral injustice in the practice of capital punishment and not just a departure from the highest legal and constitutional standards.

II

The argument from arbitrariness has not, however, been universally accepted, either as a moral or a constitutional argument. Ernest van den Haag, an articulate and longtime defender of the death penalty, has claimed that the Supreme Court was wrong to accept this argument in the first place and thus that the evidence of arbitrariness presented by Black, Bowers and Pierce and others is beside the point. In his words:

> . . . the abolitionist argument from capriciousness, or discretion, or discrimination, would be more persuasive if it were alleged that those selectively executed are not guilty. But the argument merely maintains that some other guilty, but more favored persons, or groups, escape the death penalty. This is hardly sufficient for letting anyone else found guilty escape the penalty. On the contrary, that some guilty persons or groups elude it argues for extending the death penalty to them.[3]

Having attacked the appeal to arbitrariness, van den Haag goes on to spell out his own conception of the requirements of justice. He writes:

> Justice requires punishing the guilty—as many of the guilty as possible, even if only some can be punished—and sparing the innocent—as many of the innocent as possible, even if not all are spared. It would surely be wrong to treat everybody with equal injustice in preference to meting out justice at least to some. . . . [I]f the death penalty is morally just, *however discriminatorily applied to only some of the guilty*, it does remain just *in each case* in which it is applied. (emphasis added)[4]

Distinguishing sharply between the demands of justice and the demands of equality, van den Haag claims that the justice of individual punishments depends on individual guilt alone and not on whether punishments are equally distributed among the class of guilty persons.

Van den Haag's distinction between the demands of justice and the demands of equality parallels the distinction drawn by Joel Feinberg between "noncomparative" and "comparative" justice.[5] Using Feinberg's terminology, we can express van den Haag's view by saying that he believes that the justice of a particular punishment is a *noncomparative* matter. It depends solely on what a person deserves and not on how others are treated. For van den Haag, then, evidence of arbitrariness and discrimination is irrelevant, so long as those who are executed are indeed guilty and deserve their punishment.

There is no denying the plausibility of van den Haag's case. In many instances, we believe it is legitimate to punish or reward deserving individuals, even though we know that equally deserving persons are unpunished or unrewarded. Consider two cases:

A. A driver is caught speeding, ticketed, and required to pay a fine. We know that the percentage of speeders who are actually punished is extremely small, yet we would probably regard it as a joke if the driver protested that he was being treated unjustly or if someone argued that no one should be fined for speeding unless all speeders were fined.

B. A person performs a heroic act and receives a substantial reward, in addition to the respect and admiration of his fellow citizens. Because he deserves the reward, we think it just that he receive it, even though many equally heroic persons are not treated similarly. That most heroes are unsung is no reason to avoid rewarding this particular heroic individual.

Both of these instances appear to support van den Haag's claim that we should do justice whenever we can in individual cases and that failure to do justice in all cases is no reason to withhold punishment or reward from individuals.

III

Is the argument from arbitrariness completely unfounded then? Should we accept van den Haag's claim that "unequal justice is justice still"?

In response to these questions, I shall argue that van den Haag's case is not as strong as it looks and that the argument from arbitrariness can be vindicated.

As a first step in achieving this, I would like to point out that there are in fact several different arguments from arbitrariness. While some of these arguments appeal to the random and freakish nature of the death penalty, others highlight the discriminatory effects of legally irrelevant factors. Each of these kinds of arbitrariness raises different sorts of moral and legal issues.

For example, though we may acknowledge the impossibility of ticketing all speeding drivers and still favor ticketing some, we must not find every way of determining which speeders are ticketed equally just. Consider the policy of ticketing only those who travel at extremely high speeds, as opposed to that of ticketing every tenth car. Compare these with the policy of giving tickets only to speeders with beards and long hair or to speeders whose cars bear bumper stickers expressing unpopular political views. While I shall not pursue this point in detail, I take it to be obvious that these different selection policies are not all equally just or acceptable.

A second difference between versions of the argument from arbitrariness depends on whether or not it is granted that we can accurately distinguish those who deserve to die from those who do not. As van den Haag presents the argument, it assumes that we are able to make this distinction. Then, the claim is made that from this class of people who deserve to die, only some are selected for execution. The choice of those specific persons from the general class of persons who deserve to die is held to be arbitrary.

Van den Haag neglects a related argument which has been forcefully defended by Charles Black. Black's argument is that the determination of *who* deserves to die—the first step—is itself arbitrary. So his claim is not merely that arbitrary factors determine who among the deserving will be executed. His point is that the determination of who deserves to die is arbitrary. His main argument is that

> the official choices—by prosecutors, judges, juries, and governors—that divide those who are to die from those who are to live are on the whole not made, and cannot be made, under standards that are consistently meaningful and clear, but that they are often made, and in the foreseeable future will continue often to be made, under no standards at all or under pseudo-standards without discoverable meaning.[6]

According to Black, even the most conscientious officials could not make principled judgments about desert in these instances, because our laws do not contain clear principles for differentiating those who deserve to die from those who do not. While I shall not try to summarize Black's analysis of the failures of post-*Furman* capital punishment statutes, it is clear that if van den Haag were to meet this argument,

he would have to provide his own analysis of these laws in order to show that they do provide clear and meaningful standards. Or, he would have to examine the actual disposition of cases under these laws to show that the results have not been arbitrary. Van den Haag does not attempt to do either of these things. This seems to result from a failure to distinguish (a) the claim that judgments concerning *who deserves to die* are arbitrarily made, from (b) the claim that judgments concerning *who among the deserving shall be executed* are arbitrarily made.

Van den Haag may simply assume that the system does a decent job of distinguishing those who deserve to die from those who do not, and his assumption gains a surface plausibility because of his tendency to oversimplify the nature of the judgments which need to be made. In contrast to Black, who stresses the complexity of the legal process and the complexity of the judgments facing participants in that process, van den Haag is content to say simply that "justice requires punishing the guilty. . . and sparing the innocent." This maxim makes it look as if officials and jurors need only divide people into two neat categories, and if we think of guilt and innocence as *factual* categories, it makes it look as if the only judgment necessary is whether a person did or did not kill another human being.

In fact, the problems are much more complicated than this. Not every person who kills another human being is guilty of the same crime. Some may have committed no crime at all, if their act is judged to be justifiable homicide. Among others, they may have committed first-degree murder, second-degree murder, or some form of manslaughter. Furthermore, even if we limit our attention to those who are convicted of first-degree murder, juries must consider aggravating and mitigating circumstances in order to judge whether someone is guilty enough to deserve the death penalty. It is clear, then, that simply knowing that someone is factually guilty of killing another person is far from sufficient for determining that he deserves to die, and if prosecutors, juries, and judges do not have criteria which enable them to classify those who are guilty in a just and rational way, then their judgments about who deserves to die will necessarily be arbitrary and unprincipled.

Once we appreciate the difficulty and complexity of the judgments which must be made about guilt and desert, it is easier to see how they might be influenced by racial characteristics and other irrelevant factors. The statistics compiled by Bowers and Pierce show that blacks killing whites have the greatest chance of being executed, while whites killing blacks have the least chance of execution. What these findings strongly suggest is that officials and jurors think that the killing of a white by a black is a more serious crime than the killing of a black by a white. Hence, they judge that blacks killing whites *deserve* a more serious punishment than whites killing blacks. Given the bluntness of our ordinary judgments about desert and the complexity of the choices facing jurors and officials, it may not be surprising either that people find it difficult to make the fine discriminations required by law or that such judgments are influenced by deep-seated racial or social attitudes.

Both legal analysis and empirical studies should undermine our confidence that the legal system sorts out those who deserve to die from those who do not in a nonarbitrary manner. If we cannot be confident that those who are executed in fact deserve to die, then we ought not to allow executions to take place at all.

Because van den Haag does not distinguish this argument from other versions of the argument from arbitrariness, he simply neglects it. His omission is serious because this argument is an independent, substantial argument against the death penalty. It can stand even if other versions of the argument from arbitrariness fall.

IV

I would like now to turn to the form of the argument which van den Haag explicitly deals with and to consider whether it is vulnerable to his criticisms. Let us assume that there is a class of people whom we know to be deserving of death. Let us further assume that only some of these people are executed and that the executions are arbitrary in the sense that those executed have not committed worse crimes than those not executed. This is the situation which Justice Stewart described in *Furman*. He wrote:

> These death sentences are cruel and unusual in the same way that being struck by lightning is cruel and unusual. For of all the people convicted of rapes and murders in 1967 and 1968, *many just as reprehensible as these*, the petitioners are among *a capriciously selected random handful* upon whom the sentence of death has in fact been imposed. (emphasis added)[7]

What is crucial here (and different from the argument previously discussed) is the assumption that we can judge the reprehensibility of both the petitioners and others convicted of similar crimes. Stewart does not deny that the petitioners deserve to die, but because other equally deserving people escape the death penalty for no legally respectable reasons, the executions of the petitioners, Stewart thought, would violate the Eighth and Fourteenth Amendments.

This is precisely the argument van den Haag rejected. We can sum up his reasons in the following rhetorical questions: How can it possibly be unjust to punish someone if he deserves the punishment? Why should it matter whether or not others equally deserving are punished?

I have already acknowledged the plausibility of van den Haag's case and offered the examples of the ticketed speeder and the rewarded hero as instances which seem to confirm his view. Nonetheless, I think that van den Haag is profoundly mistaken in thinking that the justice of a reward or punishment depends solely on whether the recipient deserves it.

Consider the following two cases which are structurally similar to A and B (given above) but which elicit different reactions:

C. I tell my class that anyone who plagiarizes will fail the course. Three students plagiarize papers, but only one receives a failing grade. The other two, in describing their motivation, win my sympathy, and I give them passing grades.

D. At my child's birthday party, I offer a prize to the child who can solve a particular puzzle. Three children, including my own, solve the puzzle. I cannot reward them all, so I give the prize to my own child.

In both cases, as in van den Haag's, only some of those deserving a reward or punishment receive it. Unlike cases A and B, however, C and D do not appear to be just, in spite of the fact that the persons rewarded or punished deserve what they get. In these cases, the justice of giving them what they deserve appears to be affected by the treatment of others.

About these cases I am inclined to say the following. The people involved have not been treated justly. It was unjust to fail the single plagiarizer and unjust to reward my child. It would have been better—because more just—to have failed no one than to have failed the single student. It would have been better to have given a prize to no one than to give the prize to my child alone.

The unfairness in both cases appears to result from the fact that the reasons for picking out those rewarded or punished are irrelevant and hence that the choice is arbitrary. If I have a stated policy of failing students who plagiarize, then it is unjust for me to pass students with whom I sympathize. Whether I am sympathetic or not is irrelevant, and I am treating the student whom I do fail unjustly because I am not acting simply on the basis of desert. Rather, I am acting on the basis of desert plus degree of sympathy. Likewise, in the case of the prize, it appears that I am preferring my own child in giving out the reward, even though I announced that receipt of the award would depend only on success in solving the puzzle.

This may be made clearer by varying the plagiarism example. Suppose that in spite of my stated policy of failing anyone who plagiarizes, I

am regularly lenient toward students who seem sufficiently repentant. Suppose further that I am regularly more lenient with attractive female students than with others. Or suppose that it is only redheads or wealthy students whom I fail. If such patterns develop, we can see that whether a student fails or not does not depend simply on being caught plagiarizing. Rather, part of the explanation of a particular student's being punished is that he or she is (or is not) an attractive female, redheaded or wealthy. In these instances, I think the plagiarizers who are punished have grounds for complaint, even though they were, by the announced standards, clearly guilty and deserving of punishment.

If this conclusion is correct, then doing justice is more complicated than van den Haag realizes. He asserts that it would be "wrong to treat everybody with equal injustice in preference to meting out justice at least to some." If my assessment of cases C and D is correct, however, it is better that everyone in those instances be treated "unjustly" than that only some get what they deserve. Whether one is treated justly or not depends on how others are treated and not solely on what one deserves.[8]

In fact, van den Haag implicitly concedes this point in an interesting footnote to his essay. In considering the question of whether capital punishment is a superior deterrent, van den Haag mentions that one could test the deterrent power of the death penalty by allowing executions for murders committed on Monday, Wednesday, and Friday, while setting life imprisonment as the maximum penalty for murders committed on other days. In noting the obstacles facing such an experiment, he writes:

> . . . it is not acceptable to our sense of justice that *people guilty of the same crime would get different punishments* and that the difference would be made to depend deliberately on *a factor irrelevant to the nature of the crime* or of the criminal. (emphasis added)[9]

Given his earlier remarks about the argument from arbitrariness, this is a rather extraordinary comment, for van den Haag concedes that the justice of a punishment is not solely determined by what an individual deserves but is also a function of how equally deserving persons are treated in general.

In his case, what he finds offensive is that there is no difference between what the Monday, Wednesday, Friday murderers deserve and what the Tuesday, Thursday, Saturday, and Sunday murderers deserve. Yet the morally irrelevant factor of date is decisive in determining the severity of the punishment. Van den Haag (quite rightly) cannot swallow this.

Yet van den Haag's example is exactly parallel to the situation described by opponents of the death penalty. For, surely, the race of the criminal or victim, the economic or social status of the criminal or victim, the location of the crime or trial and other such factors are as irrelevant to the gravity of the crime and the appropriate severity of the punishment as is the day of the week on which the crime is committed. It would be as outrageous for the severity of the punishment to depend on these factors as it would be for it to depend on the day of the week on which the crime was committed.

In fact, it is more outrageous that death sentences depend on the former factors because a person can control the day of the week on which he murders in a way in which he cannot control his race or status. Moreover, we are committed to banishing the disabling effects of race and economic status from the law. Using the day of the week as a critical factor is at least not invidiously discriminatory, as it neither favors nor disfavors previously identifiable or disadvantaged groups.

In reply, one might contend that I have overlooked an important feature of van den Haag's example. He rejected the deterrence experiment not merely because the severity of punishment depended on irrelevant factors but also because the irrelevant factors were *deliberately* chosen as the basis of punishment. Perhaps it is the fact that irrelevant factors are deliberately chosen which makes van den Haag condemn the proposed experiment.

This is an important point. It certainly makes matters worse to decide deliberately to base life and death choices on irrelevant considerations. However, even if the decision is not deliberate, it remains a serious injustice if irrelevant considerations play this crucial role. Individuals might not even be aware of the influence of these factors. They might genuinely believe that their judgments are based entirely on relevant considerations. It might require painstaking research to discover the patterns underlying sentencing, but once they are known, citizens and policymakers must take them into consideration. Either the influence of irrelevant factors must be eradicated or, if we determine that this is impossible, we may have to alter our practices more radically.

This reasoning, of course, is just the reasoning identified with the *Furman* case. As Justice Douglas wrote:

> A law that stated that anyone making more than $50,000 would be exempt from the death penalty would plainly fall, as would a law that in terms said that blacks, those who never went beyond the fifth grade in school, those who make less than $3,000 a year, or those who were unpopular or unstable should be the only people executed. A law which in the overall view reaches the same result in practice has no more sanctity than a law which in terms provides the same.[10]

The problem, in Douglas's view, was that the system left life and death decisions to the "uncontrolled discretion of judges or juries," leading to the unintended but nonetheless real result that death sentences were based on factors which had nothing to do with the nature of the crime.

What I want to stress here is that the arbitrariness and discrimination need not be purposeful or deliberate. We might discover, as critics allege, that racial prejudice is so deeply rooted in our society that prosecutors, juries, and judges cannot free themselves from prejudice when determining how severe a punishment for a crime should be. Furthermore, we might conclude that these tendencies cannot be eradicated, especially when juries are called upon to make subtle and complex assessments of cases in the light of confusing, semi-technical criteria. Hence, although no one *decides* that race will be a factor, we may *predict* that it will be a factor, and this knowledge must be considered in evaluating policies and institutions.

If factors *as irrelevant as* the day of the crime determine whether people shall live or die and if the influence of these factors is ineradicable, then we must conclude that we cannot provide a just system of punishment and even those who are guilty and deserving of the most severe punishments (like the Monday killers in van den Haag's experiment) will have a legitimate complaint that they have been treated unjustly.

I conclude, then, that the treatment of *classes* of people is relevant to determining the justice of punishments for *individuals* and van den Haag is wrong to dismiss the second form of the argument from arbitrariness. That argument succeeds in showing that capital punishment is unjust and thus provides a powerful reason for abolishing it.

V

Supporters of the death penalty might concede that serious questions of justice are raised by the influence of arbitrary factors and still deny that this shows that capital punishment ought to be abolished. They could argue that some degree of arbitrariness is present throughout the system of legal punishment, that it is unreasonable to expect our institutions to be perfect, and that acceptance of the argument from arbitrariness would commit us to abolishing all punishment.

In fact, van den Haag makes just these points in his essay. He writes:

> The Constitution, though it enjoins us to minimize capriciousness, does not enjoin a standard of unattainable perfection or exclude penalties because that standard has not been attained. . . . I see no more merit in the attempt to persuade the courts to let all

capital-crime defendants go free of capital punishment because some have wrongly escaped it than I see in an attempt to persuade the courts to let all burglars go because some have wrongly escaped imprisonment.[11]

It is an important feature of this objection that it could be made even by one who conceded the injustice of arbitrarily administered death sentences. Rather than agreeing that capital punishment should be abolished, however, this objection moves from the premise that the flaws revealed in capital punishment are shared by *all* punishments to the conclusion that we must either (a) reject all punishments (because of the influence of arbitrary factors on them) or (b) reject the idea that arbitrariness provides a sufficient ground for abolishing the death penalty.

Is there a way out of this dilemma for death penalty opponents?

I believe that there is. Opponents of the death penalty may continue to support other punishments, even though their administration also involves arbitrariness. This is not to suggest, of course, that we should be content with arbitrariness or discrimination in the imposition of any punishment.[12] Rather the point is to emphasize that the argument from arbitrariness counts against the death penalty with special force. There are two reasons for this.

First, death is a much more severe punishment than imprisonment. This is universally acknowledged by advocates and opponents of the death penalty alike. It is recognized in the law by the existence of special procedures for capital cases. Death obliterates the person, depriving him or her of life and thereby, among other things, depriving him or her of any further rights of legal appeal, should new facts be discovered or new understandings of the law be reached. In this connection, it is worth recalling that many people were executed and are now dead because they were tried and sentenced under the pre-*Furman* laws which allowed the "uncontrolled discretion of judges and juries."

Second, though death is the most severe punishment in our legal system, it appears to be unnecessary for protecting citizens, while punishments generally are thought to promote our safety and well-being. The contrast between death and other punishments can be brought out by asking two questions. What would happen if we abolished all punishments? And, what would happen if we abolished the death penalty?

Most of us believe that if all punishments were abolished, there would be social chaos, a Hobbesian war of all against all. To do away with punishment entirely would be to do away with the criminal law and the system of constraints which it supports. Hence, even though the system is not a just one, we believe that we must live with it and strive to make it as fair as possible. On the other hand, if we abolish capital punishment, there is reason to believe that nothing will happen. There is simply no compelling evidence that capital punishment prevents murders better than long-term prison sentences. Indeed, some evidence even suggests that capital punishment increases the number of murders. While I cannot review the various empirical studies of these questions here, I think it can plausibly be asserted that the results of abolishing punishment generally would be disastrous, while the results of abolishing capital punishment are likely to be insignificant.[13]

I conclude then that the argument from arbitrariness has special force against the death penalty because of its extreme severity and its likely uselessness. The arbitrariness of other punishments may be outweighed by their necessity, but the same cannot be said for capital punishment.

VI

In closing, I would like to comment briefly on one other charge made by van den Haag, the charge that the argument from arbitrariness is a "sham" argument because it is not the real reason why people oppose the death penalty. Those who use this argument, van den Haag claims, would oppose capital punishment even if it were not arbitrarily imposed.

At one level, this charge is doubly fallacious. The suggestion of dishonesty introduced by the word "sham" makes the argument into an *ad hominem*. In addition, the charge suggests that there cannot be more than one reason in support of a view. There are many situations in which we offer arguments and yet would not change our view if the argument were refuted, not because the argument is a sham, but because we have additional grounds for what we believe.

Nonetheless, van den Haag's charge may indicate a special difficulty for the argument from arbitrariness, for the argument may well strike people as artificial and legalistic. Somehow, one may feel that it does not deal with the real issues—the wrongness of killing, deterrence, and whether murderers deserve to die.

Part of the problem, I think, is that our ordinary moral thinking involves specific forms of conduct or general rules of personal behavior. The argument from arbitrariness deals with a feature of an *institution*, and thinking about institutions seems to raise difficulties for many people. Believing that an individual murderer deserves to die for a terrible crime, they infer that there ought to be capital punishment, without attending to all of the implications for other individuals which will follow from setting up this practice.

The problem is similar to one that John Stuart Mill highlighted in *On Liberty*. For many people, the fact that an act is wrong is taken to be sufficient ground for its being made illegal. Mill argued against the institutionalization of all moral judgments, and his argument still strikes many people as odd. If the act is wrong, they ask, shouldn't we do everything in our power to stop it? What they fail to appreciate, however, are all of the implications of institutionalizing such judgments.

Likewise, people ask, If so and so deserves to die, shouldn't we empower the state to execute him? The problem, however—or one of many problems—is that institutionalizing this judgment about desert yields a system which makes neither moral nor legal sense. Moreover, it perpetuates and exacerbates the liabilities and disadvantages which unjustly befall many of our fellow citizens. These are genuine and serious problems, and those who have raised them in the context of the capital punishment debate have both exposed troubling facts about the actual workings of the criminal law and illuminated the difficulties of acting justly. Most importantly, they have produced a powerful argument against authorizing the state to use death as a punishment for crime.

NOTES

1. *Capital Punishment: The Inevitability of Caprice and Mistake*, 2d ed. (New York: W. W. Norton & Co., 1981), p. 20.

2. Ibid., *passim*; W. Bowers and G. Pierce, "Arbitrariness and Discrimination under Post-*Furman* Capital Statutes," *Crime & Delinquency* 26 (1980): 563–635. Reprinted in *The Death Penalty in America*, 3d ed. ed. Hugo Bedau (New York: Oxford University Press, 1982), pp. 206–24.

3. "The Collapse of the Case Against Capital Punishment," *National Review*, 31 March 1978: 397. A briefer version of this paper appeared in the *Criminal Law Bulletin* 14 (1978): 51–68 and is reprinted in Bedau, pp. 323–33.

4. Ibid.

5. "Noncomparative Justice," in *Rights, Justice, and the Bounds of Liberty: Essays in Social Philosophy* (Princeton, NJ: Princeton University Press, 1980); originally published in the *Philosophical Review* 83 (1974): 297–338.

6. Black, *Capital Punishment*, p. 29.

7. Reprinted in Bedau, pp. 263–64.

8. Using Feinberg's terminology, these can be described as cases in which the criteria of comparative and noncomparative justice conflict with one another. I am arguing that in these instances, the criteria of comparative justice take precedence. Although Feinberg does discuss such conflicts, it is unclear to me from his essay whether he would agree with this claim.

9. Van den Haag, "The Collapse of the Case Against Capital Punishment," p. 403, n. 12. (This important footnote does not appear in the shorter version of the paper.)

10. Reprinted in Bedau, pp. 255–56.

11. Van den Haag, "The Collapse of the Case Against Capital Punishment," p. 397.

12. For a discussion of the role of discrimination throughout the criminal justice system and recommendations for reform, see American Friends Service Committee, *Struggle for Justice* (New York: Hill and Wang, 1971).

13. In support of the superior deterrent power of the death penalty, van den Haag cites I. Ehrlich, "The Deterrent Effect of Capital Punishment: A Question of Life and Death," *American Economic Review* 65 (1975): 397–417. Two reviews of the evidence on deterrence, both of which criticize Ehrlich at length, are Hans Zeisel, "The Deterrent Effect of the Death Penalty: Facts v. Faith," and Lawrence Klein et al., "The Deterrent Effect of Capital Punishment: An Assessment of the Evidence." (Both of these articles appear in Bedau.) The thesis that executions increase the number of homicides is defended by W. Bowers and G. Pierce in "Deterrence or Brutalization: What is the Effect of Executions?," *Crime & Delinquency* 26 (1980): 453–84.

My thanks are due to Hugo Bedau, William Bowers, Richard Daynard, and Ernest van den Haag for reactions to my thinking about the death penalty. I would especially like to thank Ursula Bentele for helpful discussions and access to unpublished research, Nelson Lande for spirited comments (both philosophical and grammatical), and John Troyer, whose keen and persistent criticisms of my views forced me to write this article.

21.
Refuting Reiman and Nathanson
Ernest van den Haag

Ernest van den Haag responds here to Jeffrey Reiman and Stephen Nathanson's arguments. He asserts that Reiman fails to show that the death penalty is necessarily inconsistent with "advanced" "civilizations." He also questions Reiman's efforts to justify alternative punishments as appropriate to the crime of murder. He accuses Nathanson of preferring "equal injustice"(letting all get away with murder if some do) to "unequal justice" (punishing some deservedly guilty murderers, even if a few do escape their rightful punishment).

I shall consider Jeffrey Reiman's view of the punishment offenders deserve before turning to his moral scruples, alleged to justify lesser punishments, and to the discriminatory distribution of the death penalty which Stephen Nathanson stresses.

Reiman believes the death penalty is deserved by some murderers, but should never be imposed. Moral scruples should preclude it. If the punishment deserved according to the *lex talionis* is morally repugnant, we may impose less, provided the suffering imposed *in lieu* of what is deserved is proportional to the suffering inflicted on the crime victim. However, suffering exceeding that of his victim can never be deserved by the offender; to impose it would be "unjust for the same reasons that make punishment of the innocent unjust."[1]

MEASUREMENT

How do we know whether the punitive suffering to be imposed on the offender is less or "equal to that which he imposed on the victim" so as not to exceed what he deserves?[2] Cardinal and interpersonal measurement of suffering would be required to find out. Although ordinal measurement is possible in some cases, the cardinal and interpersonal measurement required by Reiman's scheme is not.[3] How many days must the kidnapper be confined, to suffer as much, but no more, than his victim? If he kept his victim three days, are three days of confinement correct? Or three hundred? Or one thousand? If he half-starved his victim, should we do as much to him, or, how do we commute starvation into additional time?

Punishment for kidnapping can be, within limits, of the same kind as the crime, although all we can actually do to conform to Reiman's pre-

Ernest van den Haag, "Refuting Reiman and Nathanson," *Philosophy And Public Affairs* 14 (Spring 1985). Copyright (c) 1985 by Princeton University Press. Reprinted by permission of Princeton University Press.

scription even here is to confine for a longer time the kidnapper who kept his victim for a longer time. We have no way of comparing the victim's suffering with the victimizer's, and to limit the latter accordingly. Execution too bears some similarity to the murderer's crime. But confinement? How do we make it commensurate with murder? What about the punishment for assault, burglary, or rape? How do we compare the pain suffered by the victims with the pain to be imposed on the offender by confinement, to make sure that the latter not exceed the former? There is no way of applying Reiman's criterion of desert. Fortunately, we don't need to.

ACTUAL DESERT

Even if, somehow, we knew that three days' confinement inflicts as much pain as his victim suffered on the kidnapper who kept his victim three days, we would feel that the kidnapper deserves much more punishment. That feeling would be appropriate. The offender imposed undeserved suffering on his victim. Why should society not impose undeserved (in Reiman's terminology) suffering on the offender? It would be undeserved only if one accepts Reiman's flawed view of retribution, for, in addition to whatever he deserves for what his victim suffered, the offender also deserves punishment for breaking the law, for imposing undeserved unlawful suffering on someone. Retributionism of any kind cannot authorize less, despite Reiman's view that suffering imposed on the criminal is unjust when it exceeds the suffering of his victim.

Although occasionally he indicates awareness of the social harm caused by crime and even of the social function of punishment, Reiman treats crimes as though involving but a relationship between victim and offender, implemented by judicial authorities.[4] From this faulty premise he infers that retribution should not exceed the harm done to the victim, an idea derived from the *lex talionis*. But that primitive rule was meant to limit the revenge private parties could exact for what was regarded as private harm. The function of the rule was to guard against social disruption by unlimited and indefinitely extended vengeance.

Crimes are no longer regarded merely as private harms. Retribution for the suffering of the individual victims, however much deserved, is not punishment any more than restitution is. Punishment must vindicate the disrupted public order, the violated law, must punish for the social harm done. If my neighbor is burglarized or robbed, he is harmed. But we all must take costly precautions, and we all feel and are threatened: crime harms society as it harms victims. Hence, punishment must, whenever possible, impose pain believed to exceed the pain suffered by the individual victim of crime. No less is deserved. Punishment must be determined by the total gravity of the crime, the social as well as the individual harm, and by the need to deter from the harmful crime. There are ordinal limits to deserved punishments, but cardinal upper limits are set only by harm, habit and sentiment—not by victim suffering.

Let me now turn to the moral scruples which should lead us to reduce punishment to less than what is deserved in some cases. I share some of Reiman's scruples: although he deserves it, I do not want to see the torturer tortured. Other scruples strike me as unjustified.

POVERTY AND CULPABILITY

Reiman believes "that the vast majority of murders in America are a predictable response to the frustrations and disabilities of impoverished social circumstances" which could be, but are not remedied because "others in America benefit," wherefore we have "no right to exact the full cost . . . from our murderers until we have done everything possible to rectify the conditions that produce their crimes."[5] Murder here seems to become the punishment for the sins of the wealthy. According to Reiman, "the vast majority" of current murderers are not fully culpable,

since part of the blame for their crimes must be placed on those who fail to "rectify the conditions that produce their crimes."

I grant that certain social conditions predictably produce crime more readily than others. Does it follow that those who commit crimes in criminogenic conditions are less responsible, or blameworthy, than they would be if they did not live in these conditions? Certainly not. Predictability does not reduce responsibility. Reiman remains responsible for his predictable argument. Culpability is reduced only when the criminal's ability to control his actions, or to realize that they are wrong, is abnormally impaired. If not, the social conditions in which the criminal lives have no bearing on his responsibility for his acts. Conditions, such as poverty, just or unjust, may increase the temptation to commit crimes. But poverty is neither a necessary nor a sufficient condition for crime, and thus certainly not a coercive one. If there is no compulsion, temptation is no excuse. The law is meant to restrain, and to hold responsible, those tempted to break it. It need not restrain those not tempted, and it cannot restrain those who are unable to control their actions.

Reiman's claim, that even "though criminals can control their actions, when crimes are predictable responses to unjust circumstances, then those who benefit from and do not remedy those conditions bear some responsibility for the crimes and thus the criminals cannot be held *wholly* responsible for them . . ." seems quite unjustified. Those responsible for unjust conditions must be blamed for them,[6] but not for crimes that are "predictable responses to unjust circumstances," if the respondents could have avoided these crimes, as most people living in unjust conditions do.

If crimes are political, that is, address not otherwise remediable "unjust circumstances," they may be held to be morally, if not legally, excusable, on some occasions.[7] But the criminal's moral, let alone legal, responsibility for a crime which he committed for personal gain and could have avoided, is not diminished merely because he lives in unjust circumstances, and his crime was a predictable response to them. Suppose the predictable response to unjust wealth were drunken driving, or rape. Would his wealth excuse the driver or the rapist? Why should poverty, if wealth would not?[8]

Crime is produced by many circumstances, "just" and "unjust." The most just society may have no less crime than the least just (unless "just" is defined circularly as the absence of crime). Tracing crime to causal circumstances is useful and may help us to control it. Suggesting that they *eo ipso* are excuses confuses causality with nonresponsibility. *Tout comprendre ce n'est pas tout pardonner*, Mme. de Staël's followers to the contrary notwithstanding. Excuses require specific circumstances that diminish the actor's control over his actions.

Since "unjust circumstances" do not reduce the responsibility of criminals for their acts, I shall refrain from discussing whether Reiman's circumstances really are unjust, or merely unequal, and whether they do exist because someone benefits from them and could be eliminated if the alleged beneficiaries wished to eliminate them. I am not sure that unjust circumstances always can be remedied, without causing worse injustices. Nor do I share Reiman's confidence that we know what social justice is, or how to produce it.

CIVILIZATION

Reiman thinks that the death penalty is not civilized, because it involves the total subjugation of one person to others, as does slavery, or prostitution.[9]

Whereas slavery usually is not voluntary, the murderer runs the risk of execution voluntarily: he could avoid it by not murdering. I find nothing uncivilized in imposing the risk of subjugation and death on those who decide to murder.

Nota bene: Persons who act with diminished capacity, during moments of passion, are usually convicted of manslaughter rather than murder. Even if convicted of murder, they are not sentenced to death; only if the court believes the murderer did have a choice, and intended to murder, can he receive the death sentence.

Reiman refers to research finding a brutalization effect, such that executions lead to more homicides. The data are unpersuasive. Some researchers find an increase, some a decrease, of homicides immediately after an execution.[10] Either effect seem[s] ephemeral, involving bunching, rather than changes in the annual homicide rate.

To argue more generally, as Reiman also does, that capital punishment is inconsistent with the advancement of civilization, is to rely on arbitrary definitions of "advancement" and "civilization" for a circular argument. If civilization actually had "advanced" in the direction Reiman, quoting Durkheim, thinks it has, why is that a reason for not preferring "advancement" in some other, perhaps opposite, direction? I cannot find the *moral* (normative) argument in Reiman's description.

DETERRENCE

The death penalty should be retained if abolition would endanger us, Reiman believes. But he does not believe that abolition would. He may be right. However, some of his arguments seem doubtful.

He thinks that whatever marginal deterrent effect capital punishment has, if it has any, is not needed, since life imprisonment provides all the deterrence needed. How can it be ascertained that punishment x deters "everyone who can be deterred" so that punishment x-plus would not deter additional persons? I can see no way to determine this, short of experiments we are unlikely to undertake. Reiman may fear life imprisonment as much, or more, than death. Couldn't someone else fear death more and be insufficiently deterred by life imprisonment?

I cannot prove conclusively that the death penalty deters more than life imprisonment, or that the added deterrence is needed. Reiman cannot prove conclusively that the added deterrence is not needed, or produced. I value the life of innocents more than the life of murderers. Indeed, I value the life of murderers negatively. Wherefore I prefer over- to underprotection. I grant this is a preference.

SELF-DEFENSE

Reiman also believes that murderers who are not deterred by the risk they run because their victims may defend themselves with guns will not be deterred by the risk of execution. This seems unrealistic. Murderers rarely run much risk from self-defense since they usually ambush unsuspecting victims.

TORTURE

On my reasoning, Reiman contends, torture should be used, since it may deter more than execution; or else, even if more deterrent than alternatives, the death penalty should be abolished as torture was: "either we must abolish the electric chair or reinstitute the rack," is his colorful phrase. But there is a difference. I do not oppose torture as undeserved or nondeterrent (although I doubt that the threat of the rack, or of anything adds deterrence to the threat of execution), but simply as repulsive. Death is not; nor is the death penalty. Perhaps repulsiveness is not enough to exclude the rack. If Reiman should convince me that the threat of the rack adds a great deal of deterrence to the threat of execution he might persuade me to overcome my revulsion and to favor the rack as well. It certainly can be deserved.

MORAL THEORY

In *The Death Penalty: A Debate*[11] I noted that only when punishments are based not on retribution alone, but also on deterrence, they rest on a theory, that is, on a correlation of recurrent facts to a prediction: punishment x will, *ceteris paribus*, reduce the rate of crime y by 10%, and x-plus will bring a reduction of 20%. Reiman censures me for using "theory" when I should have written "empirical theory." He is right. Further, deterrence does not morally justify any punishment, unless one has first accepted the moral desirability of reducing crime, and the tolerability of the costs. I should have pointed that out. Finally, I did not mean to deny that there are moral theories to justify retribution. They strike me as more dependent on feeling than empirical theories are. More to the point, unlike deterrence theory, justice theories are not meant to predict the effect of various punishments, and are not capable of determining, except ordinally, what these punishments should be, although they can help to justify the distribution of punishments.[12]

MODES OF EXECUTION

As Reiman stresses, the spectacle of execution is not pretty. Nor is surgery. Wherefore both should be attended only by the necessary personnel.[13] I do not find Reiman's aesthetic or moral scruples sufficient to preclude execution or surgery. However, I share his view that lethal injections are particularly unpleasant, not so much because of the subjugation which disturbs him, but because of the veterinary air. (We put animals "to sleep" when sick or inconvenient.) In contrast, shooting strikes me as dignified; it is painless too and probably the best way of doing what is necessary.

LIFE IMPRISONMENT

Reiman proposes life imprisonment without parole instead of execution. Although less feared, and therefore likely to be less deterrent, actual lifelong imprisonment strikes me as more cruel than execution even if perceived as less harsh. Its comparative cruelty was stressed already by Cesare Bonesana, Marchese di Beccaria, and by many others since.

Life imprisonment also becomes undeserved over time. A person who committed a murder when twenty years old and is executed within five years—far too long and cruel a delay in my opinion—is, when executed, still the person who committed the murder for which he is punished. His identity changes little in five years. However, a person who committed a murder when he was twenty years old and is kept in prison when sixty years old, is no longer the same person who committed the crime for which he is still being punished. The sexagenarian is unlikely to have much in common with the twenty-year-old for whose act he is being punished; his legal identity no longer reflects reality. Personality and actual identity are not that continuous. In effect, we punish an innocent sexagenarian who does not deserve punishment, instead of a guilty twenty-year-old who did. This spectacle should offend our moral sensibilities more than the deserved execution of the twenty-year-old. Those who deserve the death penalty should be executed while they deserve it, not kept in prison when they no longer deserve any punishment.

DISCRIMINATION

Disagreeing with the Supreme Court, Stephen Nathanson believes that the death penalty still is distributed in an excessively capricious and discriminatory manner. He thinks capital punishment is "unjust" because poor blacks are more likely to be sentenced to death than wealthy whites. Further, blacks who murdered whites are more likely to be executed than those who murdered blacks.[14] This last discrimination has been thrown into relief recently by authors who seem to be under the impression that they have revealed a new form of discrimination against black murderers. They have not. The practice invidiously discriminates against black victims of murder, who are not as fully, or as often, vindicated as white victims are. However, discrimination against a class of victims, although invidious enough, does not amount to discrim-

ination against their victimizers. The discrimination against black victims, the lesser punishment given their murderers, actually favors black murderers, since most black victims are killed by black murderers. Stephen Nathanson and Jeffrey Reiman appear to think that they have captured additional discrimination against black defendants. They are wrong.

Neither the argument from discrimination against black victims, nor the argument from discrimination against black murderers, has any bearing on the guilt of black murderers, or on the punishment they deserve.

Invidious discrimination is never defensible. Yet I do not see wherein it, in Reiman's words, "would constitute a separate and powerful argument for abolition," or does make the death penalty "unjust" for those discriminatorily selected to suffer it, as Stephen Nathanson believes.[15] If we grant that some (even all) murderers of blacks, or, some (even all) white and rich murderers, escape the death penalty, how does that reduce the guilt of murderers of whites, or of black and poor murderers, so that they should be spared execution too? Guilt is personal. No murderer becomes less guilty, or less deserving of punishment, because another murderer was punished leniently, or escaped punishment altogether. We should try our best to bring every murderer to justice. But if one got away with murder wherein is that a reason to let anyone else get away? A group of murderers does not become less deserving of punishment because another equally guilty group is not punished, or punished less. We can punish only a very small proportion of all criminals. Unavoidably they are selected accidentally. We should reduce this accidentality as much as possible but we cannot eliminate it.[16]

EQUAL INJUSTICE AND UNEQUAL JUSTICE

Reiman and Nathanson appear to prefer equal injustice—letting all get away with murder if some do—to unequal justice: punishing some guilty offenders according to desert, even if others get away. Equal justice is best, but unattainable. Unequal justice is our lot in this world. It is the only justice we can ever have, for not all murderers can be apprehended or convicted, or sentenced equally in different courts. We should constantly try to bring every offender to justice. But meanwhile unequal justice is the only justice we have, and certainly better than equal injustice—giving no murderer the punishment his crime deserves.

MORE DISCRIMINATION

Nathanson insists that some arbitrary selections among those equally guilty are not "just." He thinks that selecting only bearded speeders for ticketing, allowing the cleanshaven to escape, is unjust. Yet the punishment of the bearded speeders is not unjust. The escape of the clean-shaven ones is. I never maintained that a discriminatory distribution is just—only that it is irrelevant to the guilt and deserved punishment of those actually guilty.

Nathanson further suggests that it is not just to spare some student plagiarizers punishment for (I suppose) irrelevant reasons, while punishing others. Again the distribution is discriminatory, i.e., unjust. But the punishment of the plagiarizers selected is not. (The non-punishment of the others is.) Nathanson thinks that giving a prize only to one of three deserving children (his own) is unjust. Not to the deserving child. Only to the others, just as it was unjust not to punish the others who deserved it, but not unjust to punish the deserving plagiarizers who were irrelevantly selected.[17]

Nathanson taxes me with inconsistency because in a footnote I wrote that irrelevant discriminations are "not acceptable to our sense of justice." They are not. But I did not say that those who deserved the punishment received, or the reward, were unjustly treated, that is, did not deserve it and should not have received it. Rather those equally situated also should have received it, and the distribution was offensive because they did not. Whenever possible this inequality should be corrected, but certainly not by not distributing the punishment, or the reward at issue, or by not giving it to the deserving. Rather by giving it as well to those who because of discrimination did not get it. (I might have done better to write in my footnote that discriminatory distributions offend our sense of *equal* justice. But neither the Constitution nor I favor replacing justice with equality.)

Nathanson quotes the late Justice Douglas suggesting that a law which deliberately prescribes execution only for the guilty poor, or which has that effect, would be unconstitutional. Perhaps. But the vice would be in exempting the guilty rich; the guilty poor would remain guilty, and deserving of prescribed punishment even if the guilty rich escape legally or otherwise.[18]

Further on Nathanson points out that the inevitable capriciousness in the distribution of punishments (only a very small percentage of offenders are ever punished and the selection unavoidably is morally arbitrary) while no reason to abolish punishment in general, may still be an argument for abolishing capital punishment because of its unique severity, and because we could survive without. We can survive without many things, which is not reason for doing without, if one thinks, as I do, that we survive *better* with. As for the unique severity of the death penalty it is, of course, the reason for imposing it for uniquely heinous crimes. The guilt of those who committed them is not diminished, if they are selected by a lottery from among all those guilty of the crime.

Following Charles Black, Nathanson notes that those executed are not necessarily the worst murderers, since there is no way of selecting these. He is right. It seems quite sufficient, however, that those executed, though not the worst, are bad enough to deserve execution. That others who deserved it even more got away, does not make those executed insufficiently deserving.

Nathanson goes on to insist that "not every person who kills another is guilty of the same crime." True. Wherefore the law makes many distinctions, leaving only a small group of those guilty of homicide eligible for the death penalty. Further, capital punishment is not mandated. The court must decide in each case whether or not to impose it. To impose capital punishment, courts must find that the aggravating circumstances attending the murder outweigh the mitigating ones, both of which must be listed in the law. Nathanson is right in pointing out that the criteria listed in the law are not easy to apply. If they were, we would not need the judgment of the court. That judgment is not easy to make. It may seem too severe, or not severe enough, in some cases, as would mandated penalties. So what else is new?

NOTES

1. See Jeffrey H. Reiman, "Justice, Civilization, and the Death Penalty: Answering van den Haag," *Philosophy & Public Affairs* 14, no. 2: 128. Unless otherwise noted, all my quotations are taken from Reiman's article.

2. This question arises only when the literal *lex talionis* is abandoned—as Reiman proposes to do, for good reason—in favor of the proportional retribution he suggests. How, by the way, would we punish a skyjacker? Summing up the suffering of all the skyjacked passengers? What about the damage to air traffic?

3. The order of punishments is notoriously hard to coordinate with the order of crimes: even when punishments are homogeneous, crimes are not.

4. Perhaps Reiman's excessive reliance on the Hegelian justification of retribution (to vindicate the quality of victim and offender) or on the Kantian version (to vindicate the rationality of both) is to blame.

5. Reiman does not say here that murder deserves less than the death penalty, but only that "the vast majority of murderers" deserve less because impoverished. However, wealthy murderers can be fully culpable, so that we may "exact the full cost" from them.

6. Who are they? They are not necessarily the beneficiaries, as Reiman appears to believe. I benefit from rent control, which I think unjust to my landlord, but I'm not responsible for it. I may benefit from low prices for services or goods, without being responsible for them, or for pre-

dictable criminal responses to them. Criminals benefit from the unjust exclusionary rules of our courts. Are they to blame for these rules?

7. See my *Political Violence & Civil Disobedience, passim* (New York: Harper & Row, 1972) for a more detailed argument.

8. Suppose unjust wealth tends to corrupt, and unjust poverty does not. Would the wealthy be less to blame for their crimes?

9. Prostitution does not involve total subjugation and is voluntary. In an ambiguous footnote Reiman asserts that it is the perception of prostitution as subjugation that makes it offensive. But this perception, derived from pulp novels more than from reality, is not what makes the voluntary act offensive. Rather, it is the sale of sex as a fungible service, divorced from affection and depersonalized that is offensive. Anyway, when something is offensive because misperceived it is not the thing that is offensive.

10. David P. Philips, "The Deterrent Effect of Capital Punishment: New Evidence on an Old Controversy," *The American Journal of Sociology* (July 1980). For further discussion see loc. cit., July 1982. See also Lester, *Executions as a Deterrent to Homicides* 44 *Psychological Rep.* 562 (1979).

11. Ernest van den Haag and John P. Conrad (New York: Plenum Press, 1983).

12. See my *Punishing Criminals* (New York: Basic Books, 1975) which is superseded to some extent by the views expressed in my "Criminal Law as a Threat System 73, *Journal of Criminal Law and Criminology* 2 (1982).

13. Both spectacles when graphically shown may also give rise to undesirable imitations or inspirations.

14. Despite some doubts, I am here granting the truth of both hypotheses.

15. Stephen Nathanson, "Does It Matter If the Death Penalty Is Arbitrarily Administered?" *Philosophy & Public Affairs* 14, no. 2. Unless otherwise noted, all further quotations are taken from Nathanson's article.

16. Discrimination or capriciousness is (when thought to be avoidable and excessive) sometimes allowed by the courts as a defense. Apparently this legal device is meant to reduce discrimination and capriciousness. But those spared because selected discriminatorily for punishment do not become any less deserving of it as both Reiman and Nathanson think, although not punishing them is used as a means to foster the desired equality in the distributions of punishments.

17. There will be some difficulty in explaining to the children who did not get the reward, why they did not, but no difficulty in explaining why one deserving child got it—unless the children share Nathanson's difficulty in distinguishing between justice and equality.

18. See [note] 16.

A Declaration of Life

Editor's Note: This document is an "advance directive" that individuals opposed to the death penalty may sign. (It is similar to the advance directive one might sign in order to be considered as an organ donor.) The person who signs the "Declaration of Life" declares "that should I die as a result of a violent crime, I request that the person or persons found guilty for my killing not be subject to . . . the death penalty . . . no matter how heinous their crime or how much I have suffered." It has been circulated by religious organizations which seek to abolish the death penalty, particularly the Sisters of Mercy of the Americas and the Friends (Quaker) Committee to Abolish the Death Penalty.

I, the undersigned, being of sound and disposing mind and memory, do hereby in the presence of witnesses make this Declaration of Life,

I believe that the killing of one human being by another is morally wrong.

I believe it is morally wrong for any state or other governmental entity to take the life of a human being for any reason.

I believe that capital punishment is not a deterrent to crime and serves only the purpose of revenge.

THEREFORE, I hereby declare that should I die as a result of a violent crime, I request that the person or persons found guilty of homicide for my killing not be subject to or put in jeopardy of the death penalty under any circumstances, no matter how heinous their crime or how much I may have suffered. The death penalty would only increase my suffering.

I request that the Prosecutor or District Attorney having the jurisdiction of the person or persons alleged to have committed my homicide not file or prosecute an action for capital punishment as a result of my homicide.

I request that this Declaration be made admissible in any trial of any person charged with my homicide, and read and delivered to the jury. I also request the Court to allow this Declaration to be admissible as a statement of the victim at the sentencing of the person or persons charged and convicted of my homicide; and, to pass sentence in accordance with my wishes.

I request that the Governor or other executive officer(s) grant pardon, clemency or take whatever action is necessary to stay and prohibit the carrying out of the execution of any person or persons found guilty of my homicide.

This Declaration is not meant to be, and should not be taken as, a statement that the person or persons who have committed my homicide should go unpunished.

I request that my family and friends take whatever actions are necessary to carry out the intent and purpose of this Declaration; and, I further request them to take no action contrary to this Declaration.

I request that, should I die under the circumstances as set forth in the Declaration and the death penalty is requested, my family, friends and personal representative deliver copies of this Declaration as follows: to the Prosecutor or District Attorney having jurisdiction over the person or persons charged with my homicide; to the Attorney representing the person or persons charged with my homicide; to the judge presiding over the case involving my homicide; for recording, to the Recorder of the County in which my homicide took place and to the recorder of the County in which the person or persons charged with my homicide are to be tried; to all newspapers, radio and television stations of general circulation in the County in which my homicide took place and the County in which the person or persons charged with my homicide are to be tried; and, to any other person, persons or entities my family, friends or personal representative deem appropriate in order to carry out my wishes as set forth herein.

I affirm under the pains and penalties for perjury that the above Declaration of Life is true.

WITNESS

_____

_____
printed name

DECLARANT

_____

_____
printed name

_____
Social Security Number

STATE OF _____)

COUNTY OF _____)

Before me, a Notary Public in and for said county and state, personally appeared the Declarant and acknowledged the execution of the foregoing instrument this _____ day of _____ 19_____.

_____

WITNESS my hand and notarial seal.

_____

NOTARY PUBLIC
_____
Printed Name

My commission expires:

_____

County of Residence:

_____

Please send a copy of this notarized form to: Cherish Life Circle, Convent of Mercy, 273 Willoughby Ave., Brooklyn, NY 11205

5

Affirmative Action

WHAT IS AFFIRMATIVE ACTION?

Affirmative action policies continue to arouse passionate—and indeed often intemperate—debate in political, economic, and educational circles. In general, affirmative action programs aim to benefit particular classes of persons who are underrepresented in various institutions and professions due to past and current patterns of discrimination and blocked opportunities. As might be expected, the terms used to describe affirmative action initiatives are imprecise and often reflect strong ideological positions: *quota systems, reverse discrimination, preferential treatment, set asides, numerical goals, timetables, diversity mandates,* and so on.

Affirmative action policies can be used to guide decisions at different levels in a variety of social institutions. They help to determine who should be admitted to undergraduate and professional programs of study, and who should be favored with scholarships; who should be hired and promoted in the private sector in large corporations; who should be hired and promoted in the civil service, for example, in police and fire departments; who should be given special access to training programs in the civil service; and which companies should receive federal and state contracts for new construction, procurement of goods, and the maintenance of public facilities. Programs of this sort must in addition clearly specify their intended beneficiaries, something that often is no simple matter. Affirmative action programs of the past three decades have typically defined recipients in terms of racial or ethnic background as well as gender; an increasing body of work in the 1990s has, however, shown the complexities involved with establishing the needed racial and ethnic categories.[1] Some have suggested that we abandon race- and gender-based preferences in favor of "need-based" criteria.[2]

DIFFERENT TYPES OF AFFIRMATIVE ACTION PROGRAMS

Given its multiple forms and extensions and its many and contested labels, affirmative action is hard to define. Thus, debates over it are likely to be seriously flawed unless attention is given its many meanings. Because there is no standard definition of the term *affirmative action,* one cannot assume a consistent use of it in the articles in this chapter. In reading each article, one must be very careful to determine how the terms of the debate are being used. (One should be especially on guard when an author fails to explain how he or she defines *affirmative action* or *preferential treatment*; this may not be an unintentional omission on the author's part.) One way to gain some clarity about the multiple usages of this term is to enumerate several different types of programs that are described as affirmative action. Note that this is by no means a complete catalog of the many ways in which the term has come to be used; it attempts only to point out some important distinctions.

PROCEDURAL OR "WEAK"
AFFIRMATIVE ACTION

The most basic type of affirmative action initiative, often referred to as "proce-dural" or "weak" affirmative action, seeks to expand the pool of qualified appli-cants who will be considered for admission, hiring, training, promotion, or the awarding of contracts.[3] To be more specific, this type of program seeks to identify qualified members of minority groups who have traditionally been overlooked or excluded from consideration, specifically racial minorities and white women. Ini-tiatives of this sort require that employers publicly and fairly advertise job open-ings rather than rely exclusively on word of mouth among friends and associates to generate a pool of applicants. Such programs may take more active forms, as when an organization deliberately acts to reach out to minority candidates. For example, a large city newspaper that has very few members of a particular mi-nority group on its professional staff may recruit candidates at a national con-vention of journalists belonging to that group.[4] Or again, increasing the pool of qualified candidates might involve designing and implementing training pro-grams so as ensure that traditionally underrepresented minorities would be bet-ter prepared to meet the desired standards. An example of this would be a nonprofit group that offers pre-apprenticeship training programs to women typ-ically employed in low-wage "pink-collar" jobs. The training would prepare them to enter highly-paid skilled labor positions.[5]

The term *weak affirmative action* is somewhat misleading in that it might sug-gest that these programs are ineffective or of little consequence. This is not at all the case. Programs falling under this broad rubric have been quite effective in opening up schools, workplaces, and professions to white women and to African Americans and Hispanics. Students born in the last twenty or so years might very well take many of these successful programs for granted, not realizing how rev-olutionary they were even as late as the 1970s.

TIE-BREAKER AFFIRMATIVE ACTION

Another type of affirmative action program might be described as a "tie-breaker" plan: If there are two "equally qualified" applicants for one position, and if one belongs to a group that historically has been discriminated against and is un-derrepresented in the relevant institution, then the tie should be broken by giv-ing the position to the minority candidate. For example, if two promising undergraduates are being considered for the same graduate fellowship, and if they received the same score on the graduate entrance record examination and have basically identical college grades and class ranks in very similar programs of study, then the "tie" between the two would be broken by favoring the minor-ity student.

PREFERENTIAL TREATMENT
AFFIRMATIVE ACTION

A more controversial type of affirmative action program involves giving positive preference to a minority candidate. Such a program would, for example, involve white females or persons identified as members of racial or ethnic minority groups being permitted to count their minority status as part of their qualifications.

QUOTAS, SET-ASIDES, AND TIMETABLE
AFFIRMATIVE ACTION

More contentious still are programs in which quotas or timetables are used to advance target groups. Programs of this sort might require that a certain percentage of open positions or federal contracts or seats in a medical school class be set aside for minorities. These programs might demand, for example, that the minority representation in a business firm or university roughly reflect the representation of that minority group in the local community. A company might be required to fill future vacancies with minority workers until its proportion of minority employees is similar to that of the surrounding locale or labor market. It is well to bear in mind that this type of affirmative action is relatively rare in American business and is implemented only under very special circumstances. Generally it is used only as a last resort and is, because of its nature, understood to be a temporary measure.

ARGUMENTS FOR AND AGAINST
AFFIRMATIVE ACTION

In examining the arguments for and against affirmative action, one must be careful to stipulate exactly which type of program is being defended or criticized. It is not enough simply to state that one is opposed to, or in favor of, affirmative action—a specific type should be identified before its merits are debated. Few persons object to procedural or weak affirmative action. The other types of programs are the ones that usually draw the critical attention, especially preferential treatment programs and quota systems.

Some critics of affirmative action argue that almost all forms of affirmative action are unfair as they violate a basic right that citizens be treated equally and have equal opportunities to advance in society. In his essay in this chapter, Thomas Nagel writes, "The charge of unfairness arouses the deepest disagreements. To be passed over because of membership in a group one was born into, where this has nothing to do with one's individual qualifications for a position, can arouse strong feelings of resentment. It is a departure from the ideal . . . that people should be judged so far as possible on the basis of individual characteristics rather than involuntary group membership."[6]

Other critics point out the undesirable consequences and potentially self-defeating features of preferential treatment and quotas. One such argument concludes that any form of affirmative action in the business world that is used to give preference to a "less well-qualified" candidate over a "more qualified" one will ultimately lead to economic inefficiencies in the market system, and therefore should be banned. Others push the consequentialist argument in a different direction, claiming that strong affirmative action programs will only result in heightened racial and ethnic awareness and thus increased tension in our country. A similar argument expresses worry that strong affirmative action programs tend to undermine the self-esteem of the groups involved.

Proponents of strong affirmative action often point out that they do not find it desirable in and of itself. Some support such programs as a temporary (but not necessarily short-term) measure to redress past harms and to counteract *continuing* discrimination. Others justify these programs as less than desirable instruments that are nonetheless the most effective means of bringing about a more equitable society. Unless and until better tools are found to alleviate social injustice, these supporters find strong forms of affirmative action necessary.

NOTES

1. See, for example, the following anthologies: Naomi Zack, ed., *American Mixed Race: The Culture of Microdiversity* (Lanham, Maryland: Rowman and Littlefield Publishers, 1995); Richard Delgado, ed., *Critical Race Theory: The Cutting Edge* (Philadelphia: Temple University Press, 1995); Becky Thompson and Sangeeta Tyagi, eds. *Names We Call Home: Autobiography on Racial Identity* (New York: Routledge, 1996).

2. See Richard Kahlenberg's essay in this chapter, "Class, Not Race."

3. My debt to John McCall's work should be very obvious to those familiar with it. See John J. McCall and Joseph R. DesJardins, *Contemporary Issues in Business Ethics*, 3rd ed. (Belmont, California: Wadsworth, 1996).

4. Deirdre Carmody, "Magazines Try to Fill a Void in Minority Hiring," *The New York Times*, 18 July 1994: D6.

5. The term *pink-collar* refers to certain types of work in which women have traditionally been employed, for example, serving food in restaurants, typing, cleaning hotel rooms, providing childcare, or in-home health care. These jobs typically do not require much formal education, are low paying, and permit frequent entry, departure, and reentry into the labor force. According to a 1995 U.S. Bureau of Labor Statistics Current Population Survey, in 1994, 90 percent of child-care workers were women, as were 89 percent of nursing aides and attendants, 91 percent of hairdressers and cosmetologists, 95 percent of licensed practical nurses, 96 percent of private household workers, and 98 percent of secretaries, stenographers, and typists. In contrast, women made up only 2 percent of electricians, 1 percent of plumbers, pipe fitters and steamfitters, 1 percent of carpenters, 6 percent of painters, 17 percent of telephone installers and repairers, and 1 percent of bricklayers and stonemasons in 1994.

6. Thomas Nagel, "A Defense of Affirmative Action," pp. 318–322.

22.
The Moral Status of Affirmative Action

Louis P. Pojman

Louis P. Pojman teaches philosophy at West Point Academy. In this essay, he presents the distinction between weak and strong forms of affirmative action; he also details some of the history of the civil rights movement, which gave rise to government mandated affirmative action programs. Pojman then outlines and explains some of the standard arguments typically given by both opponents and proponents of affirmative action. He concludes that although affirmative action programs were well intentioned, they cannot and will not improve our society.

"A ruler who appoints any man to an office, when there is in his dominion another man better qualified for it, sins against God and against the State." (*The Koran*).

"[Affirmative action] is the meagerest recompense for centuries of unrelieved oppression." (Quoted by Shelby Steele as the justification for affirmative action.)

Hardly a week goes by but that the subject of affirmative action does not come up. Whether in the guise of reverse discrimination, preferential hiring, nontraditional casting, quotas, goals and timetables, minority scholarships, or race norming, the issue confronts us as a terribly perplexing problem. Last summer's Actor's Equity debacle over the casting of the British actor, Jonathan Pryce, as a Eurasian in Miss Saigon; Assistant Secretary of Education Michael Williams' judgment that Minority Scholarships are unconstitutional; the "Civil Rights Bill of 1991," reversing recent decisions of the Supreme Court which constrain preferential hiring practices; the demand that Harvard Law School hire a black female professor; grade stipends for black students at Pennsylvania State University and other schools; the revelations of race norming in state employment agencies; as well as debates over quotas, underutilization guidelines, and diversity in employment; all testify to the importance of this subject for contemporary society.

There is something salutary as well as terribly tragic inherent in this problem. The salutary aspect is the fact that our society has shown itself committed to eliminating unjust discrimination. Even in the heart of Dixie there is a recognition of the injustice of racial discrimination. Both sides of the affirmative action debate have good will and appeal to moral principles. Both sides are attempting to bring about a better society, one that is color-blind, but they differ profoundly on the morally proper means to accomplish that goal.

And this is just the tragedy of the situation: Good people on both sides of the issue are ready to tear each other to pieces over a problem that has no easy or obvious solution. And so the voices become shrill and the rhetoric hyperbolic. The same spirit which divides the pro-choice movement from the right to life movement on abortion divides liberal pro-affirmative action advocates from liberal anti-affirmative action advocates. This problem, more than any other, threatens to destroy the traditional liberal consensus in our society. I have seen family members and close friends who until recently fought on the same side of the barricades against racial injustice divide in enmity over this issue. The anti-affirmative liberals

Louis P. Pojman, "The Moral Status of Affirmative Action," *Public Affairs Quarterly*. Reprinted with permission of the *Public Affairs Quarterly* and the author.

("liberals who've been mugged") have tended towards a form of neoconservatism and the pro-affirmative liberals have tended to side with the radical left to form the "politically correct ideology" movement.

In this paper I will confine myself primarily to affirmative action policies with regard to race, but much of what I say can be applied to the areas of gender and ethnic minorities.

I. DEFINITIONS

First let me define my terms:

Discrimination is simply judging one thing to differ from another on the basis of some criterion. "Discrimination" is essentially a good quality, having reference to our ability to make distinctions. As rational and moral agents we need to make proper distinctions. To be rational is to discriminate between good and bad arguments, and to think morally is to discriminate between reasons based on valid principles and those based on invalid ones. What needs to be distinguished is the difference between rational and moral discrimination on the one hand, and irrational and immoral discrimination on the other hand.

Prejudice is a discrimination based on irrelevant grounds. It may simply be an attitude which never surfaces in action, or it may cause prejudicial actions. A prejudicial discrimination in action is immoral if it denies someone a fair deal. So discrimination on the basis of race or sex where these are not relevant for job performance is unfair. Likewise, one may act prejudicially in applying a relevant criterion on insufficient grounds, as in the case where I apply the criterion of being a hard worker but then assume, on insufficient evidence, that the black man who applies for the job is not a hard worker.

There is a difference between *prejudice* and *bias*. Bias signifies a tendency towards one thing rather than another where the evidence is incomplete or based on non-moral factors. For example, you may have a bias towards blondes

and I towards redheads. But prejudice is an attitude (or action) where unfairness is present—where one *should* know or do better, as in the case where I give people jobs simply because they are redheads. Bias implies ignorance or incomplete knowledge, whereas prejudice is deeper, involving a moral failure—usually a failure to pay attention to the evidence. But note that calling people racist or sexist without good evidence is also an act of prejudice. I call this form of prejudice "defamism," for it unfairly defames the victim. It is a contemporary version of McCarthyism.

Equal opportunity is offering everyone a fair chance at the best positions that society has at its disposal. Only native aptitude and effort should be decisive in the outcome, not factors of race, sex, or special favors.

Affirmative action is the effort to rectify the injustice of the past by special policies. Put this way, it is Janus-faced or ambiguous, having both a backward-looking and a forward-looking feature. The backward-looking feature is its attempt to correct and compensate for past injustice. This aspect of affirmative action is strictly deontological. The forward-looking feature is its implicit ideal of a society free from prejudice; this is both deontological and utilitarian.

When we look at a social problem from a backward-looking perspective we need to determine who has committed or benefited from a wrongful or prejudicial act and to determine who deserves compensation for that act.

When we look at a social problem from a forward-looking perspective we need to determine what a just society (one free from prejudice) would look like and how to obtain that kind of society. The forward-looking aspect of affirmative action is paradoxically race-conscious, since it uses race to bring about a society which is not race-conscious, which is color-blind (in the morally relevant sense of this term).

It is also useful to distinguish two versions of affirmative action. *Weak affirmative action* involves such measures as the elimination of segregation (namely the idea of "separate but equal"), widespread advertisement to groups not previously represented in certain privileged positions, special scholarships for the disadvantaged classes (e.g., all the poor), using underrepresentation or a history of past discrimination as a tie breaker when candidates are relatively equal, and the like.

Strong affirmative action involves more positive steps to eliminate past injustice, such as reverse discrimination, hiring candidates on the basis of race and gender in order to reach equal or near equal results, proportionate representation in each area of society.

II. A BRIEF HISTORY OF AFFIRMATIVE ACTION

1. After a long legacy of egregious racial discrimination the forces of civil justice came to a head during the decade of 1954–1964. In the 1954 U.S. Supreme Court decision, *Brown v. Board of Education*, racial segregation was declared inherently and unjustly discriminatory, a violation of the constitutional right to equal protection, and in 1964 Congress passed the Civil Rights Act which banned all forms of racial discrimination.

During this time the goal of the Civil Rights Movement was equal opportunity. The thinking was that if only we could remove the hindrances to progress, invidious segregation, discriminatory laws, and irrational prejudice against blacks, we could free our country from the evils of past injustice and usher in a just society in which the grandchildren of the slave could play together and compete with the grandchildren of the slave owner. We were after a color-blind society in which every child had an equal chance to attain the highest positions based not on his skin color but on the quality of his credentials. In the early 60s when the idea of reverse discrimination was mentioned in civil rights groups, it was usually rejected as a new racism. The Executive Director of the NAACP, Roy Wilkins, stated this posi-

tion unequivocally during congressional consideration of the 1964 civil rights law. "Our association has never been in favor of a quota system. We believe the quota system is unfair whether it is used for [blacks] or against [blacks] . . . [We] feel people ought to be hired because of their ability, irrespective of their color. . . . We want equality, equality of opportunity and employment on the basis of ability."[1]

So the Civil Rights Act of 1964 was passed outlawing discrimination on the basis of race or sex.

> Title VII, Section 703(a) Civil Rights Act of 1964: It shall be an unlawful practice for an employer (1) to fail or refuse to hire or to discharge any individual or otherwise to discriminate against any individual with respect to his compensation, terms, conditions, or privileges of employment, because of such individual's race, color, sex, or national origin; or
>
> (2) to limit, segregate, or classify his employees or applicants for employment in any way which would deprive or tend to deprive any individual of employment opportunities or otherwise adversely affect his status as an employee because of such individual's race, color, religion, sex, or national origin. [42 U.S.C.2000e–2(a)]
>
> . . . Nothing contained in this title shall be interpreted to require any employer to grant preferential treatment to any individual or to any group on account of an imbalance which may exist with respect to the total numbers or percentage of persons of any race . . . employed by any employer . . . in comparison with the total or percentage of persons of such race . . . in any community, State, section, or other areas, or in the available work force in any community, State, section, or other area. [42 U.S.C.2000e–2(j)]

The Civil Rights Act of 1964 espouses a meritocratic philosophy, calling for equal opportunity and prohibiting reverse discrimination as just another form of prejudice. The Voting Rights

Act (1965) was passed and Jim Crow laws throughout the South were overturned. Schools were integrated and public accommodations opened to all. Branch Rickey's promotion of Jackie Robinson from the minor leagues in 1947 to play for the Brooklyn Dodgers was seen as the paradigm case of this kind of equal opportunity—the successful recruiting of a deserving person.

2. But it was soon noticed that the elimination of discriminatory laws was not producing the fully integrated society that leaders of the civil rights movement had envisioned. Eager to improve the situation, in 1965 President Johnson went beyond equal opportunity to affirmative action. He issued the famous Executive Order 11246 in which the Department of Labor was enjoined to issue government contracts with construction companies on the basis of race. That is, it would engage in reverse discrimination in order to make up for the evils of the past. He explained the act in terms of the shackled runner analogy.

> Imagine a hundred yard dash in which one of the two runners has his legs shackled together. He has progressed ten yards, while the unshackled runner has gone fifty yards. How do they rectify the situation? Do they merely remove the shackles and allow the race to proceed? Then they could say that "equal opportunity" now prevailed. But one of the runners would still be forty yards ahead of the other. Would it not be the better part of justice to allow the previously shackled runner to make up the forty-yard gap; or to start the race all over again? That would be affirmative action towards equality. (President Lyndon Johnson, 1965, inaugurating the affirmative action policy of Executive Order 11246).

In 1967 President Johnson issued Executive Order 11375 extending affirmative action (henceforth "AA") to women. Note here that AA originates in the executive branch of government. Until the Kennedy-Hawkins Civil Rights Act of 1990, AA policy was never put to a vote or passed by Congress. Gradually, the benefits of AA were extended to Hispanics, native Americans, Asians, and handicapped people.[2]

The phrase "An Equal Opportunity/Affirmative Action Employer" ("AA/EO") began to appear as official public policy. But few noticed an ambiguity in the notion of "AA" which could lead to a contradiction in juxtaposing it with "EO," for there are two types of AA. At first AA was interpreted as, what I have called, "weak affirmative action," in line with equal opportunity, signifying wider advertisement of positions, announcements that applications from blacks would be welcomed, active recruitment and hiring blacks (and women) over *equally* qualified men. While few liberals objected to these measures, some expressed fears of an impending slippery slope towards reverse discrimination.

However, except in professional sports—including those sponsored by universities—weak affirmative action was not working, so in the late 60s and early 70s a stronger version of affirmative action was embarked upon—one aimed at equal results, quotas (or "goals"—a euphemism for "quotas"). In *Swann v. Charlotte-Mecklenburg* (1971), regarding the busing of children out of their neighborhood . . . to promote integration, the Court, led by Justice Brennan, held that affirmative action was implied in *Brown* and was consistent with the Civil Rights Act of 1964. The NAACP now began to support reverse discrimination.

Thus began the search for minimally qualified blacks in college recruitment, hiring, and the like. Competence and excellence began to recede into second place as the quest for racial, ethnic, and gender diversity became the dominant goals. The slogan "We have to become race conscious in order to eliminate race consciousness" became the paradoxical justification for reverse discrimination.

3. In 1968 the Department of Labor ordered employers to engage in utilization studies as part of its policy of eliminating discrimination in the workplace. The office of Federal Contract

Compliance of the U.S. Department of Labor (Executive Order 11246) stated that employers with a history of *underutilization* of minorities and women were required to institute programs that went beyond passive nondiscrimination through deliberate efforts to identify people of "affected classes" for the purpose of advancing their employment. Many employers found it wise to adopt policies of preferential hiring in order to preempt expensive government suits.

Employers were to engage in "utilization analysis" of their present work force in order to develop "specific and result-oriented procedures": to which the employer commits *every good-faith effort* in order to provide "relief for members of an '*affected class*', who by virtue of *past discrimination* continue to suffer the present effects of that discrimination." This self-analysis is supposed to discover areas in which such affected classes are underused, considering their availability and skills. "*Goals and timetables* are to be developed to guide efforts to correct deficiencies in the employment of affected classes of people in each level and segment of the work force." Affirmative action also calls for "rigorous examination" of standards and criteria for job performance, not so as to "dilute necessary standards" but in order to ensure that "arbitrary and discriminatory employment practices are eliminated" and to eliminate unnecessary criteria which "have had the effect of eliminating women and minorities" either from selection or promotion.[3]

4. In 1969 two important events occurred. (a) The Philadelphia Plan—The Department of Labor called for "goals and timetables" for recruiting minority workers. In Philadelphia area construction industries, where these companies were all-white, family-run businesses, the contractor's union took the case to court on the grounds that Title VII of the Civil Rights Act prohibits quotas. The Third Circuit Court of Appeals upheld the Labor Department, and the Supreme Court refused to hear it. This case became the basis of the EEOC's aggressive pursuit of "goals and timetables" in other business situations.

(b) In the Spring of 1969 James Forman disrupted the service of Riverside Church in New York City and issued the Black Manifesto to the American Churches, demanding that they pay blacks $500,000,000 in reparations. The argument of the Black Manifesto was that for three and a half centuries blacks in America have been "exploited and degraded, brutalized, killed and persecuted" by whites; that this was part of the persistent institutional patterns of first, legal slavery and then, legal discrimination and forced segregation; and that through slavery and discrimination whites had procured enormous wealth from black labor with little return to blacks. These facts were said to constitute grounds for reparations on a massive scale. The American churches were but the first institutions to be asked for reparations.[4]

5. The Department of Labor issued guidelines in 1970 calling for hiring representatives of *underutilized* groups. "*Nondiscrimination* requires the elimination of all existing discriminatory conditions, whether purposeful or inadvertent. . . . Affirmative action requires . . . the employer to make additional efforts to recruit, employ and promote qualified members of groups formerly excluded" (HEW Executive Order 22346, 1972). In December of 1971 Guidelines were issued to eliminate underutilization of minorities, aiming at realignment of the job force at every level of society.

6. In *Griggs v. Duke Power Company* (1971) the Supreme Court interpreted Title VII of the Civil Rights Act as forbidding use of aptitude tests and high school diplomas in hiring personnel. These tests were deemed presumptively discriminatory, employers having the burden of proving such tests relevant to performance. The notion of *sufficiency* replaced that of excellence or best qualified, as it was realized (though not explicitly stated) that the goal of racial diversity required compromising the standards of competence.

7. In 1977, the EEOC called for and *expected* proportional representation of minorities in every area of work (including universities).

8. In 1978 the Supreme Court addressed the Bakke case. Alan Bakke had been denied admission to the University of California at Davis Medical School even though his test scores were higher than the sixteen blacks who were admitted under the affirmative action quota program. He sued the University of California and the U.S. Supreme Court ruled (*University of California v. Bakke*, July 28, 1978) in a 5 to 4 vote that reverse discrimination and quotas are illegal except (as Justice Powell put it) when engaged in for purposes of promoting diversity (interpreted as a means to extend free speech under the First Amendment) and restoring a situation where an institution has had a history of prejudicial discrimination. The decision was greeted with applause from anti-AA quarters and dismay from pro-AA quarters. Ken Tollett lamented, "The affirmance of Bakke would mean the reversal of affirmative action; it would be an officially sanctioned signal to turn against blacks in this country. . . . Opposition to special minority admissions programs and affirmative action is anti-black."[5]

But Tollett was wrong. The Bakke case only shifted the rhetoric from "quota" language to "goals and timetables" and "diversity" language. In the '80s affirmative action was alive and well, with preferential hiring, minority scholarships, and race norming prevailing in all walks of life. No other white who has been excluded from admission to college because of his race has ever won his case. In fact only a year later, Justice Brennan was to write in *U.S. Steel v. Weber* that prohibition of racial discrimination against "any individual" in Title VII of the Civil Rights Act did not apply to discrimination against whites.[6]

9. Perhaps the last step in the drive towards equal results took place in the institutionalization of grading applicants by group-related standards, race norming. Race norming is widely practiced but most of the public is unaware of it, so let me explain it.

Imagine that four men come into a state employment office in order to apply for a job. One is black, one Hispanic, one Asian, and one white. They take the standard test (a version of the General Aptitude Test Battery or VG-GATB). All get a composite score of 300. None of them will ever see that score. Instead the numbers will be fed into a computer and the applicants' percentile ranking emerges. The scores are group-weighted. Blacks are measured against blacks, whites against whites, Hispanics against Hispanics. Since blacks characteristically do less well than other groups, the effect is to favor blacks. For example, a score of 300 as an accountant will give the black a percentile score of 87, a Hispanic a percentile score of 74 and a white or oriental a score of 47. The black will get the job as the accountant. (See the box entitled "Percentile Conversion Tables").

This is known as race norming. Until an anonymous governmental employee recently blew the whistle, this practice was kept a secret in several state employment services. Prof. Linda Gottfredson of the University of Delaware, one of the social scientists to expose this practice, has since had her funding cut off. In a recent letter to the *New York Times* she writes:

> One of America's best-kept secrets is that the Employment Service of the Department of Labor has unabashedly promulgated quotas. In 1981 the service recommended that state employment agencies adopt a race-conscious battery to avoid adverse impact when referring job applicants to employers.
> . . . The score adjustments are not trivial. An unadjusted score that places a job applicant at the 15th percentile among whites would, after race-norming, typically place a black near the white 50th percentile. Likewise, unadjusted scores at the white 50th percentile would, after race-norming, typically place a black near the 85th percentile for white job applicants. . . . [I]ts use by 40 states in the last decade belies the claim that *Griggs* did not lead to quotas.[7]

10. In the *Ward Cove, Richmond,* and *Martin* decisions of the mid-80s the Supreme Court

Percentile Conversion Tables

Jobs are grouped into five broad families: Family I includes, for example, machinists, cabinet makers, and tool makers; Family II includes helpers in many types of agriculture, manufacturing, and so on; Family III includes professional jobs such as accountant, chemical engineer, nurse, editor; Family IV includes bus drivers, bookkeepers, carpet layers; Family V includes exterminators, butchers, file clerks. A raw score of 300 would convert to the following percentile rankings:

	I	II	III	IV	V
Black	79	59	87	83	73
Hispanic	62	41	74	67	55
Other	39	42	47	45	42

SOURCES: Virginia Employment Commission: U.S. Department of Labor. Employment and Training Administration, Validity Generalization Manual (Section A: Job Family Scoring).

limited preferential hiring practices, placing a greater burden of proof on the plaintiff, now required to prove that employers have discriminated. The Kennedy-Hawkins Civil Rights Act of 1990, which was passed by Congress last year, sought to reverse these decisions by requiring employers to justify statistical imbalances not only in the employment of racial minorities but also that of ethnic and religious minorities. Wherever underrepresentation of an "identified" group exists, the employer bears the burden of proving he is innocent of prejudicial behavior. In other words, the bill would make it easier for minorities to sue employers. President Bush vetoed the bill, deeming it a subterfuge for quotas. A revised bill is now in Congressional committee.

Affirmative action in the guise of underutilized or "affected groups" now extends to American Indians and Hispanics (including Spanish nobles) but not Portuguese, Asians, the handicapped, and in some places Irish and Italians. Estimates are that 75 percent of Americans may obtain AA status as minorities: everyone except the white nonhandicapped male. It is a strange policy that affords special treatment to the children of Spanish nobles and illegal immigrants but not the children of the survivors of Russian pogroms or Nazi concentration camps.

Of course, there is nothing new about the notions of racial discrimination and preferential treatment. The first case of racial discrimination is the fall of man, as standardly interpreted, in which the whole race is held accountable and guilty of Adam's sin. The notion of collective responsibility also goes way back in our history. The first case of preferential treatment is God's choosing Abel's sacrifice of meat and rejecting Cain's vegetarian sacrifice—which should give all Jewish-Christian vegetarians something to think about! The first case of preferential treatment in Greek mythology is that of the Achaian horse race narrated in the 23rd book of the *Iliad*. Achilles had two prizes to give out. First prize went to the actual winner. Antilochus, son of Nestor, came in second, but Achilles decided to give second prize to Eumelius because he was of a nobler rank, even though he had come in last. Antilochus complained, saying in effect, "If it is preordained that some other criterion than merit is to count for the award, why should we have a race at all?" Achilles was moved by this logic and gave the prize to Antilochus, offering Eumelius a treasure of his own.

Neither is affirmative action primarily an American problem. Thomas Sowell has recently written a book on the international uses of preferential treatment, *Preferential Policies: An International Perspective,* in which he analyzes government-mandated preferential policies in India, Nigeria, Malaysia, Sri Lanka, and the United States.[8] We will consider Sowell's study towards the end of this paper.

III. ARGUMENTS FOR AFFIRMATIVE ACTION

Let us now survey the main arguments typically cited in the debate over affirmative action. I will briefly discuss seven arguments on each side of this issue.

1. Need for Role Models

This argument is straightforward. We all have need of role models, and it helps to know that others like us can be successful. We learn and are encouraged to strive for excellence by emulating our heroes and role models.

However, it is doubtful whether role models of one's own racial or sexual type are necessary for success. One of my heroes was Gandhi, an Indian Hindu, another was my grade school science teacher, one Miss DeVoe, and another was Martin Luther King. More important than having role models of one's own type is having genuinely good people, of whatever race or gender, to emulate. Furthermore, even if it is of some help to people with low self-esteem to gain encouragement from seeing others of their particular kind in leadership roles, it is doubtful whether this need is a sufficient condition to justify preferential hiring or reverse discrimination. What good is a role model who is inferior to other professors or business personnel? Excellence will rise to the top in a system of fair opportunity. Natural development of role models will come more slowly and more surely. Proponents of preferential policies simply lack the patience to let history take its own course.

2. The Need of Breaking the Stereotypes

Society may simply need to know that there are talented blacks and women, so that it does not automatically assign them lesser respect or status. We need to have unjustified stereotype beliefs replaced with more accurate ones about the talents of blacks and women. So we need to engage in preferential hiring of qualified minorities even when they are not the most qualified.

Again, the response is that hiring the less qualified is neither fair to those better qualified who are passed over nor an effective way of removing inaccurate stereotypes. If competence is accepted as the criterion for hiring, then it is unjust to override it for purposes of social engineering. Furthermore, if blacks or women are known to hold high positions simply because of reverse discrimination, then they will still lack the respect due to those of their rank. In New York City there is a saying among doctors, "Never go to a black physician under 40," referring to the fact that AA has affected the medical system during the past fifteen years. The police use "Quota Cops" and "Welfare Sergeants" to refer to those hired without passing the standardized tests. (In 1985 180 black and Hispanic policemen, who had failed a promotion test, were promoted anyway to the rank of sergeant.) The destruction of false stereotypes will come naturally as qualified blacks rise naturally in fair competition (or if it does not—then the stereotypes may be justified). Reverse discrimination sends the message home that the stereotypes are deserved—otherwise, why do these minorities need so much extra help?

3. Equal Results Argument

Some philosophers and social scientists hold that human nature is roughly identical, so that on a fair playing field the same proportion from every race and gender and ethnic group would attain to the highest positions in every area of endeavor. It would follow that any inequality of results itself is evidence for inequality of opportunity. John Arthur, in discussing an intelligence test, Test 21, puts the case this way.

History is important when considering governmental rules like Test 21 because low scores by blacks can be traced in large measure to the legacy of slavery and racism: Segregation, poor schooling, exclusion from trade unions, malnutrition, and poverty have all played their roles. Unless one assumes that blacks are naturally less able to pass the test, the conclusion must be that the results are themselves socially and legally constructed, not a mere given for which law and society can claim no responsibility.

The conclusion seems to be that genuine equality requires equal results. Obviously blacks have been treated unequally throughout U.S. history, and just as obviously the economic and psychological effects of that inequality linger to this day, showing up in lower income and poorer performance in school and on tests than whites achieve. Since we have no reason to believe that differences in performance can be explained by factors other than history, equal results are a good benchmark by which to measure progress made toward genuine equality.[9]

The result of a just society should be equal numbers in proportion to each group in the work force.

However, Arthur fails even to consider studies that suggest that there are innate differences between races, sexes, and groups. If there are genetic differences in intelligence and temperament within families, why should we not expect such differences between racial groups and the two genders? Why should the evidence for this be completely discounted?

Perhaps some race or one gender is more intelligent in one way than another. At present we have only limited knowledge about genetic differences, but what we do have suggests some difference besides the obvious physiological traits.[10] The proper use of this evidence is not to promote discriminatory policies but to be *open* to the possibility that innate differences may have led to an overrepresentation of certain groups in certain areas of endeavor. It seems that on average blacks have genetic endowments favoring them in the development of skills necessary for excellence in basketball.

Furthermore, on Arthur's logic, we should take aggressive AA against Asians and Jews since they are overrepresented in science, technology, and medicine. So that each group receives its fair share, we should ensure that 12 percent of U.S. philosophers are black, reduce the percentage of Jews from an estimated 15 percent to 2 percent—firing about 1,300 Jewish philosophers. The fact that Asians are producing 50 percent of Ph.D.'s in science and math and blacks less than 1 percent clearly shows, on this reasoning, that we are providing special secret advantages to Asians.

But why does society have to enter into this results game in the first place? Why do we have to decide whether all difference is environmental or genetic? Perhaps we should simply admit that we lack sufficient evidence to pronounce on these issues with any certainty—but if so, should we not be more modest in insisting on equal results? Here is a thought experiment. Take two families of different racial groups, Green and Blue. The Greens decide to have only two children, to spend all their resources on them, to give them the best education. The two Green kids respond well and end up with achievement test scores in the 99th percentile. The Blues fail to practice family planning. They have fifteen children. They can only afford two children, but lack of ability or whatever prevents them from keeping their family down. Now they need help for their large family. Why does society have to step in and help them? Society did not force them to have fifteen children. Suppose that the achievement scores of the fifteen children fall below the 25th percentile. They cannot compete with the Greens. But now enters AA. It says that it is society's fault that the Blue children are not as able as the Greens and that the Greens must pay extra taxes to enable the Blues to compete. No restraints are put on the Blues regarding family size. This seems unfair to the Greens. Should the Green children be made to bear responsibility for the consequences of the Blues' voluntary behavior?

My point is simply that Arthur needs to cast his net wider and recognize that demographics and child-bearing and -rearing practices are crucial factors in achievement. People have to take some responsibility for their actions. The equal results argument (or axiom) misses a greater part of the picture.

4. The Compensation Argument

The argument goes like this: Blacks have been wronged and severely harmed by whites. Therefore white society should compensate blacks for the injury caused them. Reverse discrimination in terms of preferential hiring, contracts, and scholarships is a fitting way to compensate for the past wrongs.

This argument actually involves a distorted notion of compensation. Normally, we think of compensation as owed by a specific person A to another person B whom A has wronged in a specific way C. For example, if I have stolen your car and used it for a period of time to make business profits that would have gone to you, it is not enough that I return you car. I must pay you an amount reflecting your loss and my ability to pay. If I have only made $5,000 and only have $10,000 in assets, it would not be possible for you to collect $20,000 in damages—even though that is the amount of loss you have incurred.

Sometimes compensation is extended to groups of people who have been unjustly harmed by the greater society. For example, the U.S. government has compensated Japanese-Americans who were interred during the Second World War, and the West German government has paid reparations to the survivors of Nazi concentration camps. But here a specific people have been identified who were wronged in an identifiable way by the government of the nation in question.

On the face of it the demand by blacks for compensation does not fit the usual pattern. Perhaps Southern states with Jim Crow laws could be accused of unjustly harming blacks, but it is hard to see that the U.S. government was involved in doing so. Furthermore, it is not clear that all blacks were harmed in the same way or whether some were *unjustly* harmed or harmed more than poor whites and others (e.g., short people). Finally, even if identifiable blacks were harmed by identifiable social practices, it is not clear that most forms of affirmative action are appropriate to restore the situation. The usual practice of a financial payment seems more appropriate than giving a high-level job to someone unqualified or only minimally qualified, who, speculatively, might have been better qualified had he not been subject to racial discrimination. If John is the star tailback of our college team with a promising professional future, and I accidentally (but culpably) drive my pick-up truck over his legs, and so cripple him, John may be due compensation, but he is not due the tailback spot on the football team.

Still, there may be something intuitively compelling about compensating members of an oppressed group who are minimally qualified. Suppose that the Hatfields and the McCoys are enemy clans and some youths from the Hatfields go over and steal diamonds and gold from the McCoys, distributing it within the Hatfield economy. Even though we do not know which Hatfield youths did the stealing, we would want to restore the wealth, as far as possible, to the McCoys. One way might be to tax the Hatfields, but another might be to give preferential treatment in terms of scholarships and training programs and hiring to the McCoys.[11]

This is perhaps the strongest argument for affirmative action, and it may well justify some weak versions of AA, but it is doubtful whether it is sufficient to justify strong versions with quotas and goals and timetables in skilled positions. There are at least two reasons for this. First, we have no way of knowing how many people of group G would have been at competence level L had the world been different. Secondly, the normal criterion of competence is a strong prima facie consideration when the most important positions are at stake. There are two reasons for this: (1) Society has given people expectations that if they attain certain levels of excellence they will be awarded appropriately and (2) filling the most important positions with the best qualified is the best way to insure efficiency in job-related areas and in society in general. These reasons are not absolutes. They can be overridden. But there is a strong presumption in their favor so that a burden of proof rests with those who would override them.

At this point we get into the problem of whether innocent non-blacks should have to pay a penalty in terms of preferential hiring of blacks. We turn to that argument.

5. Compensation from Those Who Innocently Benefited from Past Injustice

White males as innocent beneficiaries of unjust discrimination of blacks and women have no grounds for complaint when society seeks to rectify the tilted field. White males may be innocent of oppressing blacks and minorities (and women), but they have unjustly benefited from that oppression or discrimination. So it is perfectly proper that less qualified women and blacks be hired before them.

The operative principle is: He who knowingly and willingly benefits from a wrong must help pay for the wrong. Judith Jarvis Thomson puts it this way. "Many [white males] have been direct beneficiaries of policies which have downgraded blacks and women . . . and even those who did not directly benefit . . . had, at any rate, the advantage in the competition which comes of the confidence in one's full membership [in the community], and of one's right being recognized as a matter of course."[12] That is, white males obtain advantages in self-respect and self-confidence deriving from a racist system that denies these to blacks and women.

Objection. As I noted in the previous section, compensation is normally individual and specific. If *A* harms *B* regarding *x*, *B* has a right to compensation from *A* in regards to *x*. If *A* steals *B*'s car and wrecks it, *A* has an obligation to com-

pensate *B* for the stolen car, but *A*'s son has no obligation to compensate *B*. Furthermore, if *A* dies or disappears *B* has no moral right to claim that society compensate him for the stolen car—though if he has insurance, he can make such a claim to the insurance company. Sometimes a wrong cannot be compensated, and we just have to make the best of an imperfect world.

Suppose my parents, divining that I would grow up to have an unsurpassable desire to be a basketball player, bought an expensive growth hormone for me. Unfortunately, a neighbor stole it and gave it to little Lew Alcindor, who gained the extra 18 inches—my 18 inches—and shot up to an enviable 7 feet 2 inches. Alias Kareem Abdul Jabbar, he excelled in basketball, as I would have done had I had my proper dose.

Do I have a right to the millions of dollars that Jabbar made as a professional basketball player—the unjustly innocent beneficiary of my growth hormone? I have a right to something from the neighbor who stole the hormone, and it might be kind of Jabbar to give me free tickets to the Laker basketball games, and perhaps I should be remembered in his will. As far as I can see, however, he does not *owe* me anything, either legally or morally.

Suppose further that Lew Alcindor and I are in high school together and we are both qualified to play basketball, only he is far better than I. Do I deserve to start in his position because I would have been as good as he is had someone not cheated me as a child? Again, I think not. But if being the lucky beneficiary of wrongdoing does not entail that Alcindor (or the coach) owes me anything in regards to basketball, why should it be a reason to engage in preferential hiring in academic positions or highly coveted jobs? If minimal qualifications are not adequate to override excellence in basketball, even when the minimality is a consequence of wrongdoing, why should they be adequate in other areas?

6. The Diversity Argument

It is important that we learn to live in a pluralistic world, learning to get along with other races and cultures, so we should have fully integrated schools and employment situations. Diversity is an important symbol and educative device. Thus preferential treatment is warranted to perform this role in society.

But, again, while we can admit the value of diversity, it hardly seems adequate to override considerations of merit and efficiency. Diversity for diversity's sake is moral promiscuity, since it obfuscates rational distinctions, and unless those hired are highly qualified the diversity factor threatens to become a fetish. At least at the higher levels of business and the professions, competence far outweighs considerations of diversity. I do not care whether the group of surgeons operating on me reflect racial or gender balance, but I do care that they are highly qualified. And likewise with airplane pilots, military leaders, business executives, and, may I say it, teachers and professors. Moreover, there are other ways of learning about other cultures besides engaging in reverse discrimination.

7. Anti-Meritocratic (Desert) Argument to Justify Reverse Discrimination: "No One Deserves His Talents"

According to this argument, the competent do not deserve their intelligence, their superior character, their industriousness, or their discipline; thus they have no right to the best positions in society; therefore society is not unjust in giving these positions to less (but still minimally) qualified blacks and women. In one form this argument holds that since no one deserves anything, society may use any criteria it pleases to distribute goods. The criterion most often designated is social utility. Versions of this argument are found in the writings of John Arthur, John Rawls, Bernard Boxill, Michael Kinsley, Ronald Dworkin, and Richard Wasserstrom. Rawls writes, "No one deserves his place in the distribution of native endowments, any more than one deserves one's initial starting place in society. The assertion that a man deserves the superior character that enables him to make the

effort to cultivate his abilities is equally problematic; for his character depends in large part upon fortunate family and social circumstances for which he can claim no credit. The notion of desert seems not to apply to these cases."[13] Michael Kinsley is even more adamant:

> Opponents of affirmative action are hung up on a distinction that seems more profoundly irrelevant: treating individuals versus treating groups. What is the moral difference between dispensing favors to people on their "merits" as individuals and passing out society's benefits on the basis of group identification?
>
> Group identifications like race and sex are, of course, immutable. They have nothing to do with a person's moral worth. But the same is true of most of what comes under the label "merit." The tools you need for getting ahead in a meritocratic society—not all of them but most: talent, education, instilled cultural values such as ambition—are distributed just as arbitrarily as skin color. They are fate. The notion that people somehow "deserve" the advantages of these characteristics in a way they don't "deserve" the advantage of their race is powerful, but illogical.[14]

It will help to put the argument in outline form.

1. Society may award jobs and positions as it sees fit as long as individuals have no claim to these positions.

2. To have a claim to something means that one has earned it or deserves it.

3. But no one has earned or deserves his intelligence, talent, education or cultural values which produce superior qualifications.

4. If a person does not deserve what produces something, he does not deserve its products.

5. Therefore better qualified people do not deserve their qualifications.

6. Therefore, society may override their qualifications in awarding jobs and positions

as it sees fit (for social utility or to compensate for previous wrongs).

So it is permissible if a minimally qualified black or woman is admitted to law or medical school ahead of a white male with excellent credentials or if a less qualified person from an "underutilized" group gets a professorship ahead of a far better qualified white male. Sufficiency and underutilization together outweigh excellence.

Objection. Premise 4 is false. To see this, reflect that just because I do not deserve the money that I have been given as a gift (for instance) does not mean that I am not entitled to what I get with that money. If you and I both get a gift of $100 and I bury mine in the sand for five years while you invest yours wisely and double its value at the end of five years, I cannot complain that you should split the increase 50/50 since neither of us deserved the original gift. If we accept the notion of responsibility at all, we must hold that persons deserve the fruits of their labor and conscious choices. Of course, we might want to distinguish moral from legal desert and argue that, morally speaking, effort is more important than outcome, whereas, legally speaking, outcome may be more important. Nevertheless, there are good reasons in terms of efficiency, motivation, and rough justice for holding a strong prima facie principle of giving scarce high positions to those most competent.

The attack on moral desert is perhaps the most radical move that egalitarians like Rawls and company have made against meritocracy, but the ramifications of their attack are far-reaching. The following are some of its implications. Since I do not deserve my two good eyes or two good kidneys, the social engineers may take one of each from me to give to those needing an eye or a kidney—even if they have damaged their organs by their own voluntary actions. Since no one deserves anything, we do not deserve pay for our labors or praise for a job well done or first prize in the race we win.

The notion of moral responsibility vanishes in a system of leveling.

But there is not good reason to accept the argument against desert. We do act freely and, as such, we are responsible for our actions. We deserve the fruits of our labor, reward for our noble feats and punishment for our misbehavior.

We have considered seven arguments for affirmative action and have found no compelling case for strong AA and only one plausible argument (a version of the compensation argument) for weak AA. We must now turn to the arguments against affirmative action to see whether they fare any better.[15]

IV. ARGUMENTS AGAINST AFFIRMATIVE ACTION

1. Affirmative Action Requires Discrimination Against a Different Group

Weak affirmative action weakly discriminates against new minorities, mostly innocent young white males, and strong affirmative action strongly discriminates against these new minorities. . . . this discrimination is unwarranted, since, even if some compensation to blacks were indicated, it would be unfair to make innocent white males bear the whole brunt of the payments. In fact, it is poor white youth who become the new pariahs on the job market. The children of the wealthy have no trouble getting into the best private grammar schools and, on the basis of superior early education, into the best universities, graduate schools, managerial and professional positions. Affirmative action simply shifts injustice, setting blacks and women against young white males, especially ethnic and poor white males. It does little to rectify the goal of providing equal opportunity to all. If the goal is a society where everyone has a fair chance, then it would be better to concentrate on support for families and early education and decide the matter of university admissions and job hiring on the basis of traditional standards of competence.

2. Affirmative Action Perpetuates the Victimization Syndrome

Shelby Steele admits that affirmative action may seem "the meagerest recompense for centuries of unrelieved oppression" and that it helps promote diversity. At the same time, though, notes Steele, affirmative action reinforces the spirit of victimization by telling blacks that they can gain more by emphasizing their suffering, degradation, and helplessness than by discipline and work. This message holds the danger of blacks becoming permanently handicapped by a need for special treatment. It also sends to society at large the message that blacks cannot make it on their own.

Leon Wieseltier sums up the problem this way.

> The memory of oppression is a pillar and a strut of the identity of every people oppressed. It is no ordinary marker of difference. It is unusually stiffening. It instructs the individual and the group about what to expect of the world, imparts an isolating sense of aptness. . . . Don't be fooled, it teaches, there is only repetition. For that reason, the collective memory of an oppressed people is not only a treasure but a trap.
>
> In the memory of oppression, oppression outlives itself. The scar does the work for the wound. That is the real tragedy: that injustice obtains the power to distort long after it has ceased to be real. It is a posthumous victory for the oppressors, when pain becomes a tradition. And yet the atrocities of the past must never be forgotten. This is the unfairly difficult dilemma of the newly emancipated and the newly enfranchised: An honorable life is not possible if they remember too little and a normal life is not possible if they remember too much.[16]

With the eye of recollection, which does not "remember too much," Steele recommends a policy that offers "educational and economic development of disadvantaged people regardless of race

and the eradication from our society—through close monitoring and severe sanctions—of racial and gender discrimination."[17]

3. Affirmative Action Encourages Mediocrity and Incompetence

Last spring Jesse Jackson joined protesters at Harvard Law School in demanding that the Law School faculty hire black women. Jackson dismissed Dean of the Law School Robert C. Clark's standard of choosing the best qualified person for the job as "cultural anemia." "We cannot just define who is qualified in the most narrow vertical, academic terms," he said. "Most people in the world are yellow, brown, black, poor, non-Christian and don't speak English, and they can't wait for some white males with archaic rules to appraise them."[18] It might be noted that if Jackson is correct about the depth of cultural decadence at Harvard, blacks might be well advised to form and support their own more vital law schools and leave places like Harvard to their archaism.

At several universities, the administrations have forced departments to hire members of minorities even when far superior candidates were available. Shortly after obtaining my Ph.D in the late 70s I was mistakenly identified as a black philosopher (I had a civil rights record and was once a black studies major) and was flown to a major university, only to be rejected for a more qualified candidate when it [was] discovered that I was white.

Stories of the bad effects of affirmative action abound. The philosopher Sidney Hook writes that "At one Ivy League university, representatives of the Regional HEW demanded an explanation of why there were no women or minority students in the Graduate Department of Religious Studies. They were told that a reading knowledge of Hebrew and Greek was presupposed. Whereupon the representatives of HEW advised orally: 'Then end those old-fashioned programs that require irrelevant languages. And start up programs on relevant things which minority group students can study without learning languages.'"[19]

Nicholas Capaldi notes that the staff of HEW itself was one-half women, three-fifths members of minorities, and one-half black—a clear case of racial over-representation.

In 1972 officials at Stanford University discovered a proposal for the government to monitor curriculum in higher education: the "Summary Statement . . . Sex Discrimination Proposed HEW Regulation to Effectuate Title IX of the Education Amendment of 1972" to "establish and use internal procedure for reviewing curricula, designed both to ensure that they do not reflect discrimination on the basis of sex and to resolve complaints concerning allegations of such discrimination, pursuant to procedural standards to be prescribed by the Director of the office of Civil Rights." Fortunately, Secretary of HEW Caspar Weinberger, when alerted to the intrusion, assured Stanford University that he would never approve of it.[20]

Government programs of enforced preferential treatment tend to appeal to the lowest possible common denominator. Witness the 1974 HEW Revised Order No. 14 on Affirmative Action expectations for preferential hiring: "Neither minorities nor female employees should be required to possess higher qualifications than those of the lowest qualified incumbents."

Furthermore, no tests may be given to candidates unless it is *proved* to be relevant to the job.

> No standard or criteria which have, by intent or effect, worked to exclude women or minorities as a class can be utilized, unless the institution can demonstrate the necessity of such standard to the performance of the job in question.
>
> Whenever a validity study is called for . . . an investigation of suitable selection procedures and suitable alternative methods of using the selection procedure which have as little adverse impact as possible. . . . Whenever the user is shown an alternative selection

procedure with evidence of less adverse impact and substantial evidence of validity for the same job in similar circumstances, the user should investigate it to determine the appropriateness of using or validating it in accord with these guidelines.[21]

At the same time Americans are wondering why standards in our country are falling and the Japanese are getting ahead. Affirmative action with its twin idols, Sufficiency and Diversity, is the enemy of excellence. I will develop this thought below (IV.6.).

4. Affirmative Action Policies Unjustly Shift the Burden of Proof

Affirmative action legislation tends to place the burden of proof on the employer who does not have an "adequate" representation of "underutilized" groups in his work force. He is guilty until proven innocent. I have already recounted how in the mid-80s the Supreme Court shifted the burden of proof back onto the plaintiff, while Congress is now attempting to shift the burden back to the employer. Those in favor of deeming disproportional representation "guilty until proven innocent" argue that it is easy for employers to discriminate against minorities by various subterfuges, and I agree that steps should be taken to monitor against prejudicial treatment. But being prejudiced against employers is not the way to attain a just solution to discrimination. The principle: Innocent until proven guilty applies to employers as well as criminals. Indeed, it is clearly special pleading to reject this basic principle of Anglo-American law in this case of discrimination while adhering to it everywhere else.

5. An Argument from Merit

Traditionally, we have believed that the highest positions in society should be awarded to those who are best qualified—as the Koran states in the quotation at the beginning of this paper. Rewarding excellence both seems just to the individuals in the competition and makes for efficiency. Note that one of the most successful acts of integration, the recruitment of Jackie Robinson in the late 40s, was done in just this way, according to merit. If Robinson had been brought into the major league as a mediocre player or had batted .200 he would have been scorned and sent back to the minors where he belonged.

Merit is not an absolute value. There are times when it may be overridden for social goals, but there is a strong prima facie reason for awarding positions on its basis, and it should enjoy a weighty presumption in our social practices.

In a celebrated article Ronald Dworkin says that "Bakke had no case" because society did not owe Bakke anything. That may be, but then why does it owe anyone anything? Dworkin puts the matter in Utility terms, but if that is the case, society may owe Bakke a place at the University of California at Davis, for it seems a reasonable rule-utilitarian principle that achievement should be rewarded in society. We generally want the best to have the best positions, the best qualified candidate to win the political office, the most brilliant and competent scientist to be chosen for the most challenging research project, the best qualified pilots to become commercial pilots, only the best soldiers to become generals. Only when little is at stake do we weaken the standards and content ourselves with sufficiency (rather than excellence)—there are plenty of jobs where "sufficiency" rather than excellence is required. Perhaps we now feel that medicine or law or university professorships are so routine that they can be performed by minimally qualified people—in which case AA has a place.

But note, no one is calling for quotas or proportional representation of *underutilized* groups in the National Basketball Association where blacks make up 80 percent of the players. But if merit and merit alone reigns in sports, should it not be valued at least as much in education and industry?

6. The Slippery Slope

Even if strong AA or reverse discrimination could meet the other objections, it would face a tough question: Once you embark on this project, how do you limit it? Who should be excluded from reverse discrimination? Asians and Jews are over-represented, so if we give blacks positive quotas, should we place negative quotas on these other groups? Since white males, "WMs," are a minority which is suffering from reverse discrimination, will we need a new affirmative action policy in the twenty-first century to compensate for the discrimination against WMs in the late twentieth century?

Furthermore, affirmative action has stigmatized the *young* white male. Assuming that we accept reverse discrimination, the fair way to make sacrifices would be to retire *older* white males who are more likely to have benefited from a favored status. Probably the least guilty of any harm to minority groups is the young white male—usually a liberal who has been required to bear the brunt of ages of past injustice. Justice Brennan's announcement that the Civil Rights Act did not apply to discrimination against whites shows how the clearest language can be bent to serve the ideology of the moment.[22]

7. The Mounting Evidence Against the Success of Affirmative Action

Thomas Sowell of the Hoover Institute has shown in his book *Preferential Policies: An International Perspective* that preferential hiring almost never solves social problems. It generally builds in mediocrity or incompetence and causes deep resentment. It is a short-term solution which lacks serious grounding in social realities.

For instance, Sowell cites some disturbing statistics on education. Although twice as many blacks as Asian students took the nationwide Scholastic Aptitude Test in 1983, approximately fifteen times as many Asian students scored above 700 (out of a possible 800) on the mathematics half of the SAT. The percentage of Asians who scored above 700 in math was also more than six times higher than the percentage of American Indians and more than ten times higher than that of Mexican Americans—as well as more than double the percentage of whites. As Sowell points out, in all countries studied, "intergroup performance disparities are huge" (108).

> There are dozens of American colleges and universities where the median combined verbal SAT score and mathematics SAT score total 1200 or above. As of 1983 there were fewer than 600 black students in the entire U.S. with combined SAT scores of 1200. This meant that, despite widespread attempts to get a black student "representation" comparable to the black percentage of the population (about 11 percent), there were not enough black students in the entire country for the Ivy League alone to have such a "representation" without going beyond the pool—even if the entire pool went to the eight Ivy League colleges.[23]

Often it is claimed that a cultural bias is the cause of the poor performance of blacks on SATs (or IQ tests), but Sowell shows that these test scores are actually a better predictor of college performance for blacks than for Asians and whites. He also shows the harmfulness of the effect on blacks of preferential acceptance. At the University of California, Berkeley, where the freshman class closely reflects the actual ethnic distribution of California high school students, more than 70 percent of blacks fail to graduate. All 312 black students entering Berkeley in 1987 were admitted under "affirmative action" criteria rather than by meeting standard academic criteria. So were 480 out of 507 Hispanic students. In 1986 the median SAT score for blacks at Berkeley was 952, for Mexican Americans 1,014, for American Indians 1,082, and for Asian Americans 1,254. (The average SAT for all students was 1,181.)

The result of this mismatching is that blacks who might do well if they went to a second-tier or third-tier school where their test scores would

indicate they belong, actually are harmed by preferential treatment. They cannot compete in the institutions where high abilities are necessary.

Sowell also points out that affirmative action policies have mainly assisted middle-class blacks, those who have suffered least from discrimination. "Black couples in which both husband and wife are college educated overtook white couples of the same description back in the early 1970s and continued to at least hold their own in the 1980s" (115).

Sowell's conclusion is that similar patterns of results obtained from India to the United States wherever preferential policies exist. "In education, preferential admissions policies have led to high attrition rates and substandard performances for those preferred students . . . who survived to graduate." In all countries the preferred tended to concentrate in less difficult subjects which lead to less remunerative careers. "In the employment market, both blacks and untouchables at the higher levels have advanced substantially while those at the lower levels show no such advancement and even some signs of retrogression. These patterns are also broadly consistent with patterns found in countries in which majorities have created preferences for themselves . . . " (116).

The tendency has been to focus at the high-level end of education and employment rather than on the lower level of family structure and early education. But if we really want to help the worst off improve, we need to concentrate on the family and early education. It is foolish to expect equal results when we begin with grossly unequal starting points—and discriminating against young white males is no more just than discriminating against women, blacks or anyone else.

CONCLUSION

Let me sum up. The goal of the Civil Rights movement and of moral people everywhere has been equal opportunity. The question is: How best to get there? Civil Rights legislation removed the legal barriers to equal opportunity, but did not tackle the deeper causes that produced differential results. Weak affirmative action aims at encouraging minorities in striving for the highest positions without unduly jeopardizing the rights of majorities, but the problem of weak affirmative action is that it easily slides into strong affirmative action where quotas, "goals," and equal results are forced into groups, thus promoting mediocrity, inefficiency, and resentment. Furthermore, affirmative action aims at the higher levels of society—universities and skilled jobs—yet if we want to improve our society, the best way to do it is to concentrate on families, children, early education, and the like. Affirmative action is, on the one hand, too much, too soon and on the other hand, too little, too late.

Martin Luther said that humanity is like a man mounting a horse who always tends to fall off on the other side of the horse. This seems to be the case with affirmative action. Attempting to redress the discriminatory iniquities of our history, our well-intentioned social engineers engage in new forms of discriminatory iniquity and thereby think that they have successfully mounted the horse of racial harmony. They have only fallen off on the other side of the issue.[24]

NOTES

1. Quoted in William Bradford Reynolds, "Affirmative Action is Unjust" in D. Bender and B. Leone (eds.), *Social Justice* (St. Paul, MN, 1984), p. 23.

2. Some of the material in this section is based on Nicholas Capaldi's *Out of Order: Affirmative Action and the Crisis of Doctrinaire Liberalism* (Buffalo, NY, 1985), chapters 1 and 2. Capaldi, using the shackled runner analogy, divides the history into three stages: a *platitude stage* "in which it is reaffirmed that the race is to be fair, and a fair race is one in which no one has either special disadvantages or special advantages (equal opportunity)"; a *remedial stage* in which victims of past discrimination are to be given special help in overcoming their disadvantages; and a *realignment stage* "in which all runners will be reassigned to those positions on the course that they would have had if the race had been fair from the beginning" (p. 18f).

3. Wanda Warren Berry, "Affirmative Action is Just" in D. Bender, *op. cit.*, p. 18.

4. Robert Fullinwider, *The Reverse Discrimination Controversy* (Totowa, NJ, 1970), p 25.

5. Quoted in Fullinwider *op. cit.*, p. 4f.

6. See Lino A. Graglia, "'Affirmative Action,' the Constitution, and the 1964 Civil Rights Act," *Measure,* no. 92 (1991).

7. Linda Gottfredson, "Letters to the Editor," *New York Times,* Aug. 1, 1990 issue. Gender-norming is also a feature of the proponents of affirmative action. Michael Levin begins his book *Feminism and Freedom* (New Brunswick, 1987) with federal court case *Beckman v. NYFD* in which 88 women who failed the New York City Fire Department's entrance exam in 1977 filed a class-action sex discrimination suit. The court found that the physical strength component of the test was not job-related, and thus a violation of Title VII of the Civil Rights Act, and ordered the city to hire forty-nine of the women. It further ordered the fire department to devise a special, less-demanding physical strength exam for women. Following EEOC guidelines, if the passing rate for women is less than 80 percent that of the passing rate of men, the test is presumed invalid.

8. Thomas Sowell, *Preferential Policies: An International Perspective* (New York, 1990).

9. John Arthur, *The Unfinished Constitution* (Belmont, CA, 1990), p. 238.

10. See Phillip E. Vernon's excellent summary of the literature in *Intelligence: Heredity and Environment* (New York, 1979) and Yves Christen "Sex Differences in the Human Brain" in Nicholas Davidson (ed.), *Gender Sanity* (Lanham, 1989) and T. Bouchard et al., "Sources of Human Psychological Differences: The Minnesota Studies of Twins Reared Apart," *Science,* vol.250 (1990).

11. See Michael Levin, "Is Racial Discrimination Special?" *Policy Review,* Fall issue (1982).

12. Judith Jarvis Thomson, "Preferential Hiring" in Marshall Cohen, Thomas Nagel and Thomas Scanlon (eds.), *Equality and Preferential Treatment* (Princeton, 1977).

13. John Rawls, *A Theory of Justice* (Cambridge, 1971), p. 104; See Richard Wasserstrom "A Defense of Programs of Preferential Treatment," *National Forum* (Phi Kappa Phi Journal), vol. 58 (1978). See also Bernard Boxill, "The Morality of Preferential Hiring," *Philosophy and Public Affairs,* vol. 7 (1978).

14. Michael Kinsley, "Equal Lack of Opportunity," *Harper's,* June issue (1983).

15. There is one other argument which I have omitted. It is one from precedence and has been stated by Judith Jarvis Thomson in the article cited earlier:

"Suppose two candidates for a civil service job have equally good test scores, but only one job is available. We could decide between them by coin-tossing. But in fact we do allow for declaring for *A* straightaway, where *A* is a veteran, and *B* is not. It may be that *B* is a non-veteran through no fault of his own. . . . Yet the fact is that *B* is not a veteran and *A* is. On the assumption that the veteran has served his country, the country owes him something. And it is plain that giving him preference is not an unjust way in which part of that debt of gratitude can be paid" (p. 379f).

The two forms of preferential hiring are analogous. Veteran's preference is justified as a way of paying a debt of gratitude; preferential hiring is a way of paying a debt of compensation. In both cases innocent parties bear the burden of the community's debt, but it is justified.

My response to this argument is that veterans should not be hired in place of better qualified candidates, but that benefits like the GI scholarships are part of the contract with veterans who serve their country in the armed services. The notion of compensation only applies to individuals who have been injured by identifiable entities. So the analogy between veterans and minority groups seems weak.

16. Quoted in Jim Sleeper, *The Closest of Strangers* (New York, 1990), p. 209.

17. Shelby Steele, "A Negative Vote on Affirmative Action," *New York Times*, May 13, 1990 issue.

18. *New York Times*, May 10, 1990 issue

19. Nicholas Capaldi, *op.cit.,* p. 85.

20. Cited in Capaldi, *op.cit.,* p. 95.

21. *Ibid.*

22. The extreme form of this New Speak is incarnate in the Politically Correct Movement ("PC" ideology) where a new orthodoxy has emerged, condemning white, European culture and seeing African culture as the new savior of us all. Perhaps the clearest example of this is Paula Rothenberg's book *Racism and Sexism* (New York, 1987) which asserts that there is no such thing as black racism; only whites are capable of racism (p. 6). Ms. Rothenberg's book has been scheduled as required reading for all freshmen at the University of Texas. See Joseph Salemi, "Lone Star Academic Politics," no. 87 (1990).

23. Thomas Sowell, *op. cit.,* p. 108.

24. I am indebted to Jim Landesman, Michael Levin, and Abigail Rosenthal for comments on a previous draft of this paper. I am also indebted to Nicholas Capaldi's *Out of Order* for first making me aware of the extent of the problem of affirmative action.

State of California, Proposition 209: Prohibition Against Discrimination or Preferential Treatment by State and Other Public Entities

Editor's Note: On November 5, 1996, California voters approved Ballot Proposition 209 by a vote of 54 percent to 46 percent. Opponents of the measure immediately filed suit in federal court, claiming that Proposition 209 would violate the Equal Protection Clause of the U.S. Constitution.

Part One: Summary of Proposition 209

- Prohibits the state, local governments, districts, public universities, colleges, and schools, and other government instrumentalities from discriminating against or giving preferential treatment to any individual or group in public employment, public education, or public contracting on the basis of race, sex, color, ethnicity, or national origin.

- Does not prohibit reasonably necessary, bona fide qualifications based on sex and actions necessary for receipt of federal funds.

- Mandates enforcement to extent permitted by federal law.

- Requires uniform remedies for violations. Provides for severability of provisions if invalid.

Part Two: Text of Proposition 209

Prohibition Against Discrimination Or Preferential Treatment by State and Other Public Entities. Initiative Constitutional Amendment.

This initiative measure is submitted to the people in accordance with the provisions of Article II, Section 8 of the [California] Constitution. This initiative measure expressly amends the Constitution by adding a section thereto . . .

Proposed Amendment to Article I

Section 31 is added to Article I of the *California Constitution* as follows:

(a) The state shall not discriminate against, or grant preferential treatment to, any individual or group on the basis of race, sex, color, ethnicity, or national origin in the operation of

The Secretary of State of California. Text downloaded from the official California Secretary of State's website: California Ballot Pamphlet. General Election. November 5, 1996. http://www.ss.ca.gov/Vote96/html/BP/home.htm. November 9, 1996.

public employment, public education, or public contracting.

(b) This section shall apply only to action taken after the section's effective date.

(c) Nothing in this section shall be interpreted as prohibiting bona fide qualifications based on sex which are reasonably necessary to the normal operation of public employment, public education, or public contracting.

(d) Nothing in this section shall be interpreted as invalidating any court order or consent decree which is in force as of the effective date of this section.

(e) Nothing in this section shall be interpreted as prohibiting action which must be taken to establish or maintain eligibility for any federal program, where ineligibility would result in a loss of federal funds to the state.

(f) For the purposes of this section, "state" shall include, but not necessarily be limited to, the state itself, any city, county, city and county, public university system, including the University of California, community college district, school district, special district, or any other political subdivision or governmental instrumentality of or within the state.

(g) The remedies available for violations of this section shall be the same, regardless of the injured party's race, sex, color, ethnicity, or national origin, as are otherwise available for violations of then-existing California antidiscrimination law.

(h) This section shall be self-executing. If any part or parts of this section are found to be in conflict with federal law or the United States Constitution, the section shall be implemented to the maximum extent that federal law and the United States Constitution permit. Any provision held invalid shall be severable from the remaining portions of this section.

Part Three: Analysis of Proposition 209 by the Legislative Analyst

Background

The federal, state, and local governments run many programs intended to increase opportunities for various groups—including women and racial and ethnic minority groups. These programs are commonly called "affirmative action" programs. For example, state law identifies specific goals for the participation of women-owned and minority-owned companies on work involved with state contracts. State departments are expected, but not required, to meet these goals, which include that at least 15 percent of the value of contract work should be done by minority-owned companies and at least 5 percent should be done by women-owned companies. The law requires departments, however, to reject bids from companies that have not made sufficient "good faith efforts" to meet these goals.

Other examples of affirmative action programs include:

- Public college and university programs such as scholarship, tutoring, and outreach that are targeted toward minority or women students.
- Goals and timetables to encourage the hiring of members of "underrepresented" groups for state government jobs.
- State and local programs required by the federal government as a condition of receiving federal funds (such as requirements for minority-owned business participation in state highway construction projects funded in part with federal money).

Proposal

This measure would eliminate state and local government affirmative action programs in the areas of public employment, public education, and public contracting to the extent these programs involve "preferential treatment" based on race, sex, color, ethnicity, or national origin. The specific programs affected by the measure, however, would depend on such factors as (1) court rulings on what types of activities are considered "preferential treatment" and (2) whether federal law requires the continuation of certain programs.

The measure provides exceptions to the ban on preferential treatment when necessary for any of the following reasons:

- To keep the state or local governments eligible to receive money from the federal government.
- To comply with a court order in force as of the effective date of this measure (the day after the [November 5, 1996] election).

- To comply with federal law or the United States Constitution.
- To meet privacy and other considerations based on sex that are reasonably necessary to the normal operation of public employment, public education, or public contracting.

Fiscal Effect

If this measure is approved by the voters, it could affect a variety of state and local programs. These are discussed in more detail below.

Fiscal Effect—Public Employment and Contracting

The measure would eliminate affirmative action programs used to increase hiring and promotion opportunities for state or local government jobs, where sex, race, or ethnicity are preferential factors in hiring, promotion, training, or recruitment decisions. In addition, the measure would eliminate programs that give preference to women-owned or minority-owned companies on public contracts. Contracts affected by the measure would include contracts for construction projects, purchases of computer equipment, and the hiring of consultants. These prohibitions would not apply to those government agencies that receive money under federal programs that require such affirmative action.

The elimination of these programs would result in savings to the state and local governments. These savings would occur for two reasons. First, government agencies no longer would incur costs to administer the programs. Second, the prices paid on some government contracts would decrease. This would happen because bidders on contracts no longer would need to show "good faith efforts" to use minority-owned or women-owned subcontractors. Thus, state and local governments would save money to the extent they otherwise would have rejected a low bidder— because the bidder did not make a "good faith effort"—and awarded the contract to a higher bidder.

Based on available information, we estimate that the measure would result in savings in employment and contracting programs that could total tens of millions of dollars each year.

Fiscal Effect—Public Schools and Community Colleges

The measure also could affect funding for public schools (kindergarten through grade 12) and community college programs. For instance, the measure could eliminate, or cause fundamental changes to, voluntary desegregation programs run by school districts. (It would not, however, affect court-ordered desegregation programs.) Examples of desegregation spending that could be affected by the measure include the special funding given to (1) "magnet" schools (in those cases where race or ethnicity are preferential factors in the admission of students to the schools) and (2) designated "racially isolated minority schools" that are located in areas with high proportions of racial or ethnic minorities. We estimate that up to $60 million of state and local funds spent each year on voluntary desegregation programs may be affected by the measure.

In addition, the measure would affect a variety of public school and community college programs such as counseling, tutoring, outreach, student financial aid, and financial aid to selected school districts in those cases where the programs provide preferences to individuals or schools based on race, sex, ethnicity, or national origin. Funds spent on these programs total at least $15 million each year.

Thus, the measure could affect up to $75 million in state spending in public schools and community colleges.

The State Constitution requires the state to spend a certain amount each year on public schools and community colleges. As a result, under most situations, the Constitution would require that funds that cannot be spent on programs because of this measure instead would have to be spent for other public school and community college programs.

Fiscal Effect—University of California and California State University

The measure would affect admissions and other programs at the state's public universities. For example, the California State University (CSU) uses race and ethnicity as factors in some of its admissions decisions. If this initiative is passed by the voters, it could no longer do so. In 1995, the

Regents of the University of California (UC) changed the UC's admissions policies, effective for the 1997–98 academic year, to eliminate all consideration of race or ethnicity. Passage of this initiative by the voters might require the UC to implement its new admissions policies somewhat sooner.

Both university systems also run a variety of assistance programs for students, faculty, and staff that are targeted to individuals based on sex, race, or ethnicity. These include programs such as outreach, counseling, tutoring, and financial aid. The two systems spend over $50 million each year on programs that probably would be affected by passage of this measure.

Fiscal Effect—Summary

As described above, this measure could affect state and local programs that currently cost well in excess of $125 million annually. The actual amount of this spending that might be saved as a result of this measure could be considerably less, for various reasons:

- The amount of spending affected by this measure could be less depending on (1) court rulings on what types of activities are considered

"preferential treatment" and (2) whether federal law requires continuation of certain programs.

- In most cases, any funds that could not be spent for existing programs in public schools and community colleges would have to be spent on other programs in the schools and colleges.

- In addition, the amount affected as a result of this measure would be less if any existing affirmative action programs were declared unconstitutional under the United States Constitution. For example, five state affirmative action programs are currently the subject of a lawsuit. If any of these programs are found to be unlawful, then the state could no longer spend money on them—regardless of whether this measure is in effect.

- Finally, some programs we have identified as being affected might be changed to use factors other than those prohibited by the measure. For example, a high school outreach program operated by the UC or the CSU that currently uses a factor such as ethnicity to target spending could be changed to target instead high schools with low percentages of UC or CSU applications.

23.
A Defense of Affirmative Action

Thomas Nagel

Thomas Nagel is professor of philosophy and law at New York University. His recent books include *The View from Nowhere, Equality and Partiality,* and *Other Minds: Critical Essays 1969–1994.* In this essay, Nagel draws the standard distinction between weak and strong forms of affirmative action and defends certain types of strong affirmative action programs as legitimate and perhaps indispensable means of promoting a more just society. He argues for his position by showing that the standard anti-affirmative action arguments are clearly outweighed by society's need to take exceptional measures "to remove the stubborn residues of racial caste."

The term "affirmative action" has changed in meaning since it was first introduced. Originally it referred only to special efforts to ensure equal

Thomas Nagel, "A Defense of Affirmative Action." Testimony before the Subcommittee on the Constitution of the Senate Judiciary Committee, January 18, 1981. Used with the permission of the author.

opportunity for members of groups that had been subject to discrimination. These efforts included public advertisement of positions to be filled, active recruitment of qualified applicants from the formerly excluded groups, and special training programs to help them meet the standards for admission or appointment. There was also close attention to procedures of appointment, and sometimes to the results, with a view to detecting continued discrimination, conscious or unconscious.

More recently the term has come to refer also to some degree of definite preference for members of these groups in determining access to positions from which they were formerly excluded. Such preference might be allowed to influence decisions only between candidates who are otherwise equally qualified, but usually it involves the selection of women or minority members over other candidates who are better qualified for the position.

Let me call the first sort of policy "weak affirmative action" and the second "strong affirmative action." It is important to distinguish them, because the distinction is sometimes blurred in practice. It is strong affirmative action—the policy of preference—that arouses controversy. Most people would agree that weak or precautionary affirmative action is a good thing, and worth its cost in time and energy. But this does not imply that strong affirmative action is also justified.

I shall claim that in the present state of things it is justified, most clearly with respect to blacks. But I also believe that a defender of the practice must acknowledge that there are serious arguments against it, and that it is defensible only because the arguments for it have great weight. Moral opinion in this country is sharply divided over the issue because significant values are involved on both sides. My own view is that while strong affirmative action is intrinsically undesirable, it is a legitimate and perhaps indispensable method of pursuing a goal so important to the national welfare that it can be justified as a temporary, though not short-term, policy for both public and private institutions. In this respect it is like other policies that impose burdens on some for the public good.

THREE OBJECTIONS

I shall begin with the argument against. There are three objections to strong affirmative action:

that it is inefficient; that it is unfair; and that it damages self-esteem.

The degree of inefficiency depends on how strong a role racial or sexual preference plays in the process of selection. Among candidates meeting the basic qualifications for a position, those better qualified will on the average perform better, whether they are doctors, policemen, teachers, or electricians. There may be some cases, as in preferential college admissions, where the immediate usefulness of making educational resources available to an individual is thought to be greater because of the use to which the education will be put or because of the internal effects on the institution itself. But by and large, policies of strong affirmative action must reckon with the costs of some lowering in performance level: the stronger the preference, the larger the cost to be justified. Since both the costs and the value of the results will vary from case to case, this suggests that no one policy of affirmative action is likely to be correct in all cases, and that the cost in performance level should be taken into account in the design of a legitimate policy.

The charge of unfairness arouses the deepest disagreements. To be passed over because of membership in a group one was born into, where this has nothing to do with one's individual qualifications for a position, can arouse strong feelings of resentment. It is a departure from the ideal—one of the values finally recognized in our society—that people should be judged so far as possible on the basis of individual characteristics rather than involuntary group membership.

This does not mean that strong affirmative action is morally repugnant in the manner of racial or sexual discrimination. It is nothing like those practices, for though like them it employs race and sex as criteria of selection, it does so for entirely different reasons. Racial and sexual discrimination are based on contempt or even loathing for the excluded group, a feeling that certain contacts with them are degrading to members of the dominant group, that they are fit only for subordinate positions or menial work. Strong affirmative action involves none of this: it is simply a means of increasing the social and economic strength of formerly victimized groups, and does not stigmatize others.

There is an element of individual unfairness here, but it is more like the unfairness of conscription in wartime, or of property condemnation under the right of eminent domain. Those who benefit or lose out because of their race or sex cannot be said to deserve their good or bad fortune.

It might be said on the other side that the beneficiaries of affirmative action deserve it as compensation for past discrimination, and that compensation is rightly exacted from the group that has benefited from discrimination in the past. But this is a bad argument, because as the practice usually works, no effort is made to give preference to those who have suffered most from discrimination, or to prefer them especially to those who have benefited most from it, or been guilty of it. Only candidates who in other qualifications fall on one or other side of the margin of decision will directly benefit or lose from the policy, and these are not necessarily, or even probably, the ones who especially deserve it. Women or blacks who don't have the qualifications even to be considered are likely to have been handicapped more by the effects of discrimination than those who receive preference. And the marginal white male candidate who is turned down can evoke our sympathy if he asks, "Why me?" (A policy of explicitly *compensatory* preference, which took into account each individual's background of poverty and discrimination, would escape some of these objections, and it has its defenders, but it is not the policy I want to defend. Whatever its merits, it will not serve the same purpose as direct affirmative action.)

The third objection concerns self-esteem, and is particularly serious. While strong affirmative action is in effect, and generally known to be so, no one in an affirmative action category who gets a desirable job or is admitted to a selective university can be sure that he or she has not benefited from the policy. Even those who would have made it anyway fall under suspicion, from themselves and from others: it comes to be widely felt that success does not mean the same thing for women and minorities. This painful damage to esteem cannot be avoided. It should make any defender of strong affirmative action want the practice to end as soon as it has achieved its basic purpose.

JUSTIFYING AFFIRMATIVE ACTION

I have examined these three objections and tried to assess their weight, in order to decide how strong a countervailing reason is needed to justify such a policy. In my view, taken together they imply that strong affirmative action involving significant preference should be undertaken only if it will substantially further a social goal of the first importance. While this condition is not met by all programs of affirmative action now in effect, it is met by those which address the most deep-seated, stubborn, and radically unhealthy divisions in the society, divisions whose removal is a condition of basic justice and social cohesion.

The situation of black people in our country is unique in this respect. For almost a century after the abolition of slavery we had a rigid racial caste system of the ugliest kind, and it only began to break up twenty-five years ago. In the South it was enforced by law, and in the North, in a somewhat less severe form, by social convention. Whites were thought to be defiled by social or residential proximity to blacks, intermarriage was taboo, blacks were denied the same level of public goods—education and legal protection—as whites, were restricted to the most menial occupations, and were barred from any positions of authority over whites. The visceral feelings of black inferiority and untouchability that this system expressed were deeply ingrained in the members of both races, and they continue, not surprisingly, to have their effect. Blacks still form, to a considerable extent, a hereditary social and economic community characterized by widespread poverty, unemployment, and social alienation.

When this society finally got around to moving against the caste system, it might have done no more than to enforce straight equality of opportunity, perhaps with the help of weak affirmative action, and then wait a few hundred years while things gradually got better. Fortunately it decided instead to accelerate the process by both public and private institutional action, because there was wide recognition of the intractable character of the problem posed by this insular minority and its place in the nation's history and collective consciousness. This has not been going on very long, but the results are already impressive, especially in speeding the advancement of blacks into the middle class. Affirmative action has not done much to improve the position of poor and unskilled blacks. That is the most serious part of the problem, and it requires a more direct economic attack. But increased access to higher education and upper-level jobs is an essential part of what must be achieved to break the structure of drastic separation that was left largely undisturbed by the legal abolition of the caste system.

Changes of this kind require a generation or two. My guess is that strong affirmative action for blacks will continue to be justified into the early decades of the next century, but that by then it will have accomplished what it can and will no longer be worth the costs. One point deserves special emphasis. The goal to be pursued is the reduction of a great social injustice, not proportional representation of the races in all institutions and professions. Proportional racial representation is of no value in itself. It is not a legitimate social goal, and it should certainly not be the aim of strong affirmative action, whose drawbacks make it worth adopting only against a serious and intractable social evil.

This implies that the justification for strong affirmative action is much weaker in the case of other racial and ethnic groups, and in the case of women. At least, the practice will be justified in a narrower range of circumstances and for a shorter span of time than it is for blacks. No other group has been treated quite like this, and no other group is in a comparable status. Hispanic-Americans occupy an intermediate position, but it seems to me frankly absurd to include persons of oriental descent as beneficiaries of affirmative action, strong or weak. They are not a severely deprived and excluded minority, and their eligibility serves only to swell the numbers that can be included on affirmative action reports. It also suggests that there is a drift in the policy toward adopting the goal of racial proportional representation for its own sake. This is a foolish mistake, and should be resisted. The only legitimate goal of the policy is to reduce egregious racial stratification.

With respect to women, I believe that except over the short term, and in professions or institutions from which their absence is particularly marked, strong affirmative action is not warranted and weak affirmative action is enough. This is based simply on the expectation that the social and economic situation of women will improve quite rapidly under conditions of full equality of opportunity. Recent progress provides some evidence for this. Women do not form a separate hereditary community, characteristically poor and uneducated, and their position is not likely to be self-perpetuating in the same way as that of an outcast race. The process requires less artificial acceleration, and any need for strong affirmative action for women can be expected to end sooner than it ends for blacks.

I said at the outset that there was a tendency to blur the distinction between weak and strong affirmative action. This occurs especially in the use of numerical quotas, a topic on which I want to comment briefly.

A quota may be a method of either weak or strong affirmative action, depending on the circumstances. It amounts to weak affirmative action—a safeguard against discrimination—if, and only if, there is independent evidence that average qualifications for the positions being filled are no lower in the group to which a minimum quota is being assigned than in the applicant group as a whole. This can be presumed true of unskilled jobs that most people can do, but it becomes less likely, and harder to establish, the greater the skill and education required for the position. At these levels, a quota proportional to population, or even to representation of the group in the applicant pool, is almost certain to amount to strong affirmative action. Moreover it is strong affirmative action of a particularly crude and indiscriminate kind, because it permits no variation in the degree of preference on the basis of costs in efficiency, depending on the qualification gap. For this rea-

son I should defend quotas only were they serve the purpose of weak affirmative action. On the whole, strong affirmative action is better implemented by including group preference as one factor in appointment or admission decisions, and letting the results depend on its interaction with other factors.

I have tried to show that the arguments against strong affirmative action are clearly outweighed at present by the need for exceptional measures to remove the stubborn residues of racial caste. But advocates of the policy should acknowledge the reasons against it, which will ensure its termination when it is no longer necessary. Affirmative action is not an end in itself, but a means of dealing with a social situation that should be intolerable to us all.

The Ampersand Problem: Women & Minorities—The Erasure of Black Women

Elizabeth Spelman

[G]ender can be treated in a way that obscures the race and class identity of privileged women—for example, of contemporary white middle-class women.... —and simultaneously makes it hard to conceive of women who are not of that particular class and race as "women."[1] Precisely insofar as a discussion of gender and gender relations is really, even if obscurely, about a particular group of women and their relation to a particular group of men, it is unlikely to be applicable to any other group of women. At the same time, the particular race and class identity of those referred to simply as "women" becomes explicit when we see the inapplicability of statements about "women" to women who are not of that race or class.

[S]ome of these points are illustrated tellingly in an article in the *New York Times* about how

From *Inessential Woman: Problems of Exclusion in Feminist Thought* by Elizabeth V. Spelman. Copyright (c) 1988 by Elizabeth V. Spelman. Reprinted by permission of Beacon Press, Boston.

"women and Blacks" have fared in the U.S. military.[2] The author of the article does not discuss women who are Black or Blacks who are women. Indeed, it is clear that the "women" referred to are white, the "Blacks" referred to are male, even though, in a chart comparing the numbers and the placement of "women" and "Blacks," a small note appears telling the reader that Black women are included in the category "Blacks."[3] There are several things to note about the sexual and racial ontology of the article. The racial identity of those identified as "women" does not become explicit until reference is made to Black women, at which point it also becomes clear that the category "women" excludes Black women. In the contrast between "women" and "Blacks" the usual contrast between "men" and "women" is dropped, even though the distinction is in effect between a group of men and a group of women. But the men in question are not called men. They are called "Blacks."

It is not easy to think about gender, race, and class in ways that don't obscure or underplay their effects on one another. The crucial question is how the links between them are conceived. . . . [We often] find an additive analysis of the various elements of identity and of various forms of oppression: there's sex *and* race *and* class; there's sexism *and* racism *and* classism. . . . [A]ttempts to bring in elements of identity other than gender, to bring in kinds of oppression other than sexism, still have the effect of obscuring the racial and class identity of those described as "women," still make it hard to see how women not of a particular race and class can be included in the description. . . . Ironically, the categories and methods we may find most natural and straightforward to use as we explore the connections between sex and race, sexism and racism, confuse those connections rather than clarify them. . . .

In the process of comparing racism and sexism, Richard Wasserstrom describes the ways in which women and Blacks have been stereotypically conceived of as less fully developed than white men: In the United States, "men and women are taught to see men as independent, capable, and powerful; men and women are taught to see women as dependent, limited in abilities, and passive."[4] But who is taught to see Black men as "independent, capable, and powerful," and by whom are they taught? Are Black men taught that? Black women? White men? White women? Similarly, who is taught to see Black women as "dependent, limited in abilities, and passive"? If this stereotype is so prevalent, why then have Black women had to defend themselves against the images of matriarch and whore?

Wasserstrom continues:

As is true for race, it is also a significant social fact that to be a female is to be an entity or creature viewed as different from the standard, fully developed person who is male as well as white. But to be female, as opposed to being black, is not to be conceived of as simply a creature of less worth. That is one important thing that differentiates sexism from racism: the ideology of sex, as opposed to the ideology of race, is a good deal more complex and confusing. Women are both put on a pedestal and deemed not fully developed persons.[5]

He leaves no room for the Black woman. For a Black woman cannot be "female, as opposed to being Black"; she is female *and* Black. Since Wasserstrom's argument proceeds from the assumption that one is either female or Black, it cannot be an argument that applies to black women. Moreover, we cannot generate a composite image of the Black women from Wasserstrom's argument, since the description of women as being put on a pedestal, or being dependent, never generally applied to Black women in the United States and was never meant to apply to them.

Wasserstrom's argument about the priority of sexism over racism has an odd result, which stems from the erasure of Black women in his analysis. He wishes to claim that in this society sex is a more fundamental fact about people than race. Yet his description of women does not apply to the Black woman, which implies that being Black is a more fundamental fact about her than being a woman and hence that her sex is not a more fundamental fact about her than her race. I am not saying that Wasserstrom actually believes this is true, but that paradoxically the terms of his theory force him into that position. If the terms of one's theory require that a person is either female or Black, clearly there is no room to describe someone who is both.

Notes

1. This chapter is a slightly revised version of my "Theories of Race and Gender: The Erasure of Black Women," in *Quest: a feminist quarterly* 5, no. 4 (1982): 36–62.

2. Richard Halloran, "Women, Blacks, Spouses Transforming the Military," *New York Times*, 25 August 1986, A1 and A14.

3. See also Gloria T. Hull, Patricia Bell Scott, and Barbara Smith, eds., *All the Women Are White, All the Blacks Are Men, But Some of Us Are Brave: Black Women's Studies* (Old Westbury, N.Y.: Feminist Press, 1982).

4. Richard A. Wasserstrom, "Racism and Sexism," in *Philosophy and Women*, ed. Sharon Bishop and Marjorie Weinzweig (Belmont, Cal: Wadsworth, 1979), 8. Reprinted from "Racism, Sexism, and Preferential Treatment: An Approach to the Topics," *UCLA Law Review* (February 1977): 581–615.

5. *Ibid.*

24.

Why Do We Need Affirmative Action?

Laura M. Purdy

Laura M. Purdy is a professor of philosophy at Wells College. She has also taught at Hamilton College and Cornell University. She has written on a number of public policy issues, including the rights of children, new reproductive technologies, and affirmative action. In her essay, Purdy encourages us to examine the affirmative action debate in its full social context. She suggests that if the debate over affirmative action is to be adequately conducted, then we must begin with a more comprehensive understanding of social issues. In particular, she challenges us to rethink the notion of qualifications, for example, qualifications for university admission and employment. She believes that those who debate affirmative action are often too quick to assume that they know how to evaluate "qualifications" of competing candidates.

Why is affirmative action sometimes morally required? Three general strategies for defending affirmative action have been suggested. One is that it appropriately compensates members of disadvantaged groups for past discrimination, another is that it counteracts current and ongoing discrimination, and a third is that it helps to secure more equality in society.

Affirmative action has been the subject of a great deal of controversy and confusion. Part of it has arisen because of conflicting definitions of affirmative action, and of the related notions of preferential treatment and reverse discrimination. A second problem has been that the populations for which it has been pressed vary in significant ways among themselves. Thus, for example, points which might be relevant to the situation of white middle class women might not be so for members of certain ethnic minorities. Hence, remedies that make sense for the one will not necessarily do so for the other. Thirdly, even for the same group, some proposals address the particular problem better than others and so, even where some action is well warranted, not every remedy will be equally justifiable. Accordingly, steps that would seem morally reasonable or even mandatory for one

situation (admission to higher education, for instance) might be thoroughly inappropriate for another (such as tenuring a faculty member). These problems would create some obstacles to intelligent discussion, even if affirmative action were not such a deeply political issue. But it is such an issue, not only because it involves fundamental concepts in ethics and political philosophy (concepts that bear upon our most basic ways of looking at the world and about which there is substantial debate), but also because it appears to be a zero-sum game: any victory for members of one class appears to be a loss for another. That the debate is mostly conducted by those with something to lose, whether it be a job, or just the satisfaction of knowing they deserve their job, helps to keep tempers hot.

Whatever the reasons for controversy, many people seem to have reached the conclusion that little more can usefully be said about the issue: we shall simply have to agree to disagree, and attempt to find compromises—fighting it out in schools, workplaces, legislatures, and courts. Given the prevailing political winds, however, existing affirmative action programs are clearly in jeopardy. In any case, it is doubtful that anything worthwhile remains to be said about this issue; consequently, despite this pessimism about further reasoned debate here, I believe it is worth another look. This paper starts with

Laura M. Purdy, "Why Do We Need Affirmative Action?" *Journal of Social Philosophy* 25 (1994): 133–143. Reprinted by permission of the *Journal of Social Philosophy*.

definitions and moves on to questions about qualifications; compensation arguments raise additional issues about how this society allocates social resources and the values that drive such allocations.

WHAT IS AFFIRMATIVE ACTION?

Some people distinguish between the kind of procedural practices that increase the probability of finding qualified individuals in the relevant classes, and the substantive· ones that advantage members of such classes. I take it for granted that such procedural practices are morally necessary, as do most people: the rancor here is focused on substantive rules that benefit individuals who are members of certain groups like white women, African Americans, and the disabled.

Substantive affirmative action principles can take various forms. One ("weak" affirmative action), involves selecting members of disadvantaged groups (hereafter "Ds") whenever their qualifications are as good as those of their competitors; another ("strong"), involves selecting them even when they are somewhat less qualified. Both of these practices may be known as "preferential treatment." Preferential treatment is used both by proponents and by opponents of affirmative action to describe what it requires in practice. "Reverse discrimination," on the other hand, tends to be used by opponents of affirmative action, and seems generally intended to convey the idea that systematically preferring candidates in certain classes is as unjust as the kind of discrimination that spurred affirmative action policies in the first place.

These definitions raise some questions. First and foremost, how do we judge "qualifications"?

QUALIFICATIONS

Opponents of affirmative action programs often assume that we know what the right qualifications are for any given enterprise, and that judg-

ments about them are generally unproblematic. But there are good reasons for doubting whether these beliefs are as solid as they are taken to be: our conception of appropriate qualifications may be too high, too narrow, or just plain unwarranted.

There are surely enterprises for which we can be reasonably confident that we know what it takes to do a job well, since they require clearly definable and measurable skills. A good typist, for example, needs speed and accuracy and these abilities are easily and reliably measured by means of a typing test.

But requirements for many other ventures are a good deal less clear. In question may be both what it takes to achieve a given result, and what result is desirable. We like to think, for instance, that only the most literate students can think philosophically. Yet I have often been surprised at the acuity of otherwise quite savage students, as well as by untutored children. In fact, students at all levels are sometimes clearly capable of doing well in courses for which they lack prerequisites. This is not to say that having certain skills and knowledge is not desirable, but that we may sometimes overlook alternative ways to acquire them, judge them necessary when they are not, or mistakenly link them with others.

Another example of debatable standards of qualification comes from the heart of the affirmative action debate, admission to professional schools. One might reasonably infer from discussions of *Bakke*, for instance, that the standards for admission to medical school are valid and clear; at most, there seem to be a few questions about the relevance of social issues like the importance of role models for white women or the probability of practicing in underserved populations for minorities. Thus discussion centers on whether it is unjust to select traditionally less qualified students rather than more qualified ones in order to promote these nontraditional ends. But what about even the relatively prosaic decision-making difficulties that admissions committees face with several non-commensurable measures, like GPA, MCATs, recommendations, prestige of school, and so forth? And as I have argued elsewhere, it also fails to take account of bias embedded in those measures.[1]

But that is just the tip of the iceberg. Do the MCATs really measure what an individual knows? More to the point, do their scales validly portray the relationship between someone's score and success in medical studies? Worse yet, what do we know about the relationship between success in medical school and good doctoring? The inadequacies of the contemporary medical establishment are becoming increasingly evident, and the education of physicians plays no small role in the crisis. For this and other reasons, medical education clearly needs fundamental rethinking, a process pursued more or less actively at any given time by those involved. Some changes would make quite a difference in our conception of who is most qualified for medical school. What, for example, about a requirement that aspiring doctors first work as nurses, in order to test and reinforce their capacity for conscientious caring?[2] Until such issues are better settled, why confine the debate to the narrow questions now so often regarded as central? Medicine is not the only field where this point is relevant.

Examples of the widespread tendency to set unnecessary and hence overly restrictive standards for opportunities and performance can easily be found in legal cases. For example, in the 1971 *Griggs v. Duke Power Company*, the Supreme Court found that the company's employment standards (a high school diploma, and certain scores on an aptitude test) unreasonably excluded blacks from its better paying jobs, for those requirements hadn't been shown to be relevant to the jobs in question.[3] Height and weight rules have similarly operated to exclude white women and members of small ethnic groups from some occupations. They have been found unconstitutional under Title VII when potential employers could neither show why the requirement was relevant nor would let applicants attempt to prove that they could do the job anyway. Interestingly, as Judith Baer points out, in some situations "the relevance of these requirements could not be proved even in instances where common sense might suggest that they were sound: height requirements for police officers, for example. The assertion that taller officers are more impressive authority figures than their shorter counterparts may seem plausible, but there is no evidence to support this hypothesis."[4] Recourse to such notions as "authority figure" might also suggest unjustifiable assumptions about how to understand a given job, perhaps giving undue priority to specific ways of dealing with people.[5]

That in turn raises the more general point that what is considered important or desirable is often a contestable moral or political issue. Examples that will be familiar to academics are the relative valuation of different areas of specialization within a discipline, or the ranking of different approaches to certain problems. For example, as Sheila Ruth has pointed out, the discipline of philosophy has had—and still has to a considerable extent—a hierarchy by which such "central" areas as metaphysics, epistemology, philosophy of language, and logic are considered the most prestigious, as well as a hierarchy of abstractness valuing more theoretical work above the more applied.[6] These judgments create a network of effects, ranging from what gets published, to who and what wins the prestigious positions and prizes. Yet, it is hardly clear that the initial premises of this system are justified, and hence at least some judgments about who is better qualified will be seriously questionable.

This issue becomes especially pressing as we make decisions about the aims of enterprises for which individuals are being selected. Education, for example, is currently being torn by debate about whether it should be passing on "traditional wisdom" or helping to create a more just world. Yet that choice bears fundamentally on who is most qualified for many jobs. In particular, overtly "political" work, long anathema in academe, must now in some cases by taken seriously. Doing so is especially difficult for those who see the status quo as politically neutral since they are used to rejecting politically aware scholarship without having to distinguish good from bad.

The upshot of all this is that we should be much warier of the view that takes it for granted that we know how to evaluate qualifications. What follows is that there needs to be a great deal more to affirmative action decisions than whether it is ever defensible to prefer those with "worse" qualifications.

COMPENSATION

Arguments from compensation assume that although Ds have suffered discrimination in the past, it no longer keeps them from deserved positions. Hence, such arguments focus on whether Ds deserve special help because of that past discrimination. Whether they do so or not seems to me to depend on the present effects of that discrimination, and what kind of special help might be at issue.[7]

There is no space here to address the interesting and voluminous debate on this topic. However, there are a couple of general points about the issue worth noting. First, compensation arguments tend to assume that discrimination no longer occurs and that merit is now the basis of all competitive selection. That assumption changes our conception of the affirmative action debate and makes it seem less pressing and more theoretical than it really is. It is also, as I will argue shortly, unrealistic.

But second, even if such discrimination disappeared tomorrow, that would not compensate African-Americans, for instance, for the injustices done to them. Merit-based decision-making rewards achievement, but downplays factors that lead to lack of achievement even where they are compounded by further injustice. The more relevant issue here is not the old injustice of enslavement, but a second and ongoing injustice that magnifies it, namely inequality of social services. Especially significant here are those that, like health care and schooling, help prepare children for higher education and the job market. As long as parents' unequal resources play so large a role in children's access to such services, equality of opportunity will not exist.[8] Such inequality is bad enough when it rests on bad luck; it is surely even more intolerable when it is built on prior injustice. However, it is, unlike slavery, something that could be remedied. And if it were, it seems to me that compensation arguments based solely on past injustice, such as slavery, might, like its other legacies, wither away.

In short, many of the intriguing moral questions raised by affirmative action could well be rendered moot by a minimally just society that allocated resources more fairly than does ours to create true equality of opportunity.[9] Wouldn't it therefore be more sensible for philosophers and lawyers to wait to cross some moral bridges once the issue has been situated in its larger context? Without that context, papers rejecting this remedy or that remedy may be quite right, but nevertheless fall short of articulating just social policy.

This analytical approach is symptomatic of the more general fragmentation of our social thinking, such that if one remedy is rejected, perhaps appropriately, there is no guarantee that another better one will be promoted instead. Thus, for example, it may be true that some children's schooling has been so inadequate that they cannot benefit from university work. At present, institutions of higher education may admit them to make amends, knowing that they are likely to fail. It would be more sensible to provide comprehensive special programs to help them cope; in a time of scarcity, however, such programs may divert scarce resources from the central (and defensible) mission of the school. Yet failing to admit them, or refusing to provide programs—in themselves perhaps justifiable policies—could well mean that nothing at all will be done. That is a morally untenable consequence.

Also responsible in part for current situations that seem to call for affirmative action is the overall scarcity of resources devoted to human needs. Such scarcity means that competition for education, jobs, and basic well-being is far more ferocious than necessary. If the stakes were lower, affirmative action measures would not be seen as the winner-take-all, zero-sum game that now provokes such bitterness. More spending on education would help provide everybody with excellent educational opportunities, and getting into a prestige school would become less important. If there were enough jobs for all, and each guaranteed a living wage, access to the most attractive positions would not be such a desperate matter. So here, as elsewhere, questions about affirmative action deflect our attention from the larger picture, leading us to downplay or ignore altogether morally untenable social arrangements.[10]

ONGOING DISCRIMINATION

Opponents of affirmative action programs generally suppose that discrimination against Ds is now only a trivial factor in social choices. Thus to take race, sex, or any other non-merit based characteristic into account constitutes the same kind of discrimination—this time against members of the mainstream—that was originally rejected for Ds. Implicit in this argument is the assumption that in the absence of affirmative action programs, merit is the driving force behind competitive choices. Hence affirmative action constitutes objectionable reverse discrimination.

This argument collapses if the underlying premise about ongoing discrimination is false, however. Yet that premise seems dubious, at best, as there is much evidence of both continuing direct prejudice and institutional discrimination against members of certain ethnic minorities, women, gays, lesbians, and the disabled.

It is surely undeniable that many people are still very prejudiced, and that sexism, racism, and a variety of other isms are flourishing.[11] Although relatively few educated people would

now admit to such prejudice, that does not mean that they are free of it, and overt manifestations of it are still quite common. Consider, for instance, the kinds of harassment and insults women, ethnic minorities, and gay people still face in public places when they overstep the bounds sanctioned by tradition: even conservative opponents of speech codes cannot deny the existence of the hate speech that has triggered those policies. More subtle, but still powerful, opposition to the most basic tenets of equality for Ds is still widespread. For example, I recently gave a talk on women's and men's social roles at a nearby Rotary Club. Its members, mostly middle-aged white males, and prime movers in the town, so far from disputing my claims that women are not yet free to define their own nature, were clearly upset at that prospect. This talk was given, not in 1952, but in 1992.

Feminists have been documenting the inequalities between females and males for years, and while perhaps not every such inequality is a result of discrimination, many obviously do result from it. [12] A similar case could be made with respect to certain other groups.[13]

Ignoring the evidence here makes the lives of non-Ds more comfortable, as they can then enjoy their privilege in good conscience: if, after all, differences in well-being are merely a result of free choices, they are justifiable.

However, there is good reason for thinking that the status quo is often not the result of free and informed choices, and that, even if it were, some of the enormous discrepancies in well-being that now exist would be indefensible. Take, for instance, the handicaps women often suffer as a result of their responsibility for child-rearing. Suppose Josie opts for the "traditional" route in life, perhaps finishing high school or college, marrying Joe, and staying at home to care for their children. If she is lucky, she will be happy in her marriage, and her husband will provide for her and the children. But what if her marriage doesn't work out? The best-case scenario is that her ex-husband continues to take some responsibility for the children, as well as for her support. But how many ex-wives find themselves in that position? Far more frequently, Joe's child support does not even cover the children's needs, let alone her own. So, out to work she must go. But because she lacks job skills and experience, and must be on call for the children, her job will most likely be poorly paid, quite possibly without such benefits as health insurance. From these meager earnings she must also pay for daycare, if her children are young. Anybody who doubts the ubiquity of this scenario should consult the literature on the feminization of poverty.[14]

Are the choices that led to this outcome free and well informed? It is arguable that women's decision to choose this traditional path is both less free than it seems, and less free than it ought to be. Despite considerable progress toward the idea that women, like men, should be free to choose the nature of the life they will lead, many girls are still brought up to believe that they are to be nurturers of men and children. This message is reinforced by a variety of powerful vehicles like movies, books, magazines, and advertisements. They are also a conduit of the pronatalism that encourages girls and women to think that having and rearing children is natural, inevitable and fun: when was the last time you saw a dirty diaper in a Pampers ad? Or a sulky child in a plug for baby food?[15] Politicians and pundits who blame society's ills on working women are common enough these days, too; the evils of daycare is a perennial topic of debate.[16] Of course, even the apparently free and informed choices girls and women now make will become more obviously less free as abortion becomes ever more unavailable, especially if contraception follows in its footsteps.[17]

The power of these influences certainly shows up in many women students. Even if they are aware of divorce statistics, they resist the idea that their own marriage is as likely to collapse as succeed; the feminization of poverty might as well be happening in Timbuktu. Sadly, the social cover-up of these trends plus the "it-can't-happen to-me" syndrome prevents many

from building what protection they can for these contingencies into their planning. These are not informed choices.

But suppose they were? Opponents of progressivism, including certain forms of affirmative action, seem to believe that the social arrangements that make these choices so imprudent for women are natural and immutable. That is not the case. Tax policy and social programs are routinely used by governments to encourage people to behave in ways that are perceived as desirable. Instead of leaving women and children to suffer impoverishment, they could be used here to protect women who stay at home with their children. That they aren't suggests that society doesn't really value women's homemaking activities, or else that it cynically figures that women can be persuaded to do them at their own risk.

Keeping women in the home full or part-time under the present circumstances has many benefits for society taken as a whole, despite the drawbacks for women themselves. First, when women put husbands and children first, they do not compete for more desirable places in the work world. Secondly, men benefit from women's domestic work, for they will provide otherwise unobtainable or prohibitively expensive services. The military, corporations, and educational institutions have long assumed that when they hire a man, a woman's services are included. Thirdly, when women are in charge of children, society is spared the expense of making other arrangements for their care. Last, but not least, society benefits from a reasonable number of children. This last point is often reflected by those who claim that children are a personal luxury and that women ought therefore to take full responsibility for the ones they produce. The real agenda here is revealed, however, when women have fewer children than is thought necessary, whether for canon fodder, business interests, or "racial purity": women's choices are then described as selfish or sick.[18]

Given these perceived social benefits, it is surely wrong to penalize the women who have provided them. A just social policy would support women who choose to do this work so that they do not risk impoverishment. However, even were such a policy in place, affirmative action might be necessary to recognize the disvalued skills women have acquired, and to help ensure that their time at home does not hold them back for the rest of their lives. Comparable issues may well exist for people in other categories.

CONCLUSION

This paper has considered some rather general issues relevant to affirmative action. It suggests that coming up with a just affirmative action policy will require a more comprehensive understanding of social issues than is yet evident in much of the debate. Because the issues are broad, but also presuppose detailed knowledge of specific situations, compelling solutions to contemporary problems will not be forthcoming anytime soon. Nor, even where they are, can we expect immediately to right underlying injustices and therefore render moot affirmative action controversies now resting upon them.

Affirmative action decisions must therefore—like others—be made in unjust contexts. Unfortunately, debate about how to make the best of bad circumstances is still necessary; it is also valuable, so long as it does not obscure the need for larger analysis. Perhaps emphasizing the need for that larger analysis will help temper the tone of the debate, whether philosophical or legal, even if it does not give us instant answers.

NOTES

1. I have argued elsewhere that both past prejudice biases much evidence and that present prejudice can bias perception of the evidence. See "In Defense of Hiring Apparently Less Qualified Women," *Journal of Social Philosophy*, Vol. 15 (Summer 1984), 26–33.

2. That would also help democratize the profession.

3. Judith A. Baer, *Women in American Law* (New York: Holmes and Meier Publishers, Inc., 1991), pp. 88–89.

4. Baer, p. 89

5. The social reluctance to question such matters is demonstrated in at least two other cases. In *Boyd v. Ozark Airlines*, 568 F. 2d 50 (8th Circ. 1977), an appellate panel let stand a height requirement for pilots because of the cockpit design of aircraft—despite the fact that airplanes are, like cars, often redesigned (Baer, p. 89). And, in *Dothard v. Rawlinson*, whereas the Court held height and weight requirements to be unconstitutional for Alabama prison guards, it refused to strike down a same-sex rule adopted instead—even though other states successfully guard male inmates with females (Baer, p. 90).

6. Sheila Ruth, "Methodocracy, Misogyny and Bad Faith: The Response of Philosophy," *Men's Studies Unmodified: The Impact of Feminism on the Academic Disciplines*, ed. Dale Spender (London: Pergamon Press, 1980).

7. For a useful discussion, see Bernard Boxill, *Blacks and Social Justice* (Totowa, NJ: Rowman and Allenheld, 1984), especially chap.7.

8. Skeptics might start by skimming Jonathan Kozol's *Savage Inequalities*, with its hungry and ill children, housed in rotting buildings where classes are lucky to have teachers or books. They should pay special attention to the Appendix, which lays out the disparities in school funding among districts. To deny that Manhasset's $15,084 per capita buys a better education than New York City's $7,299 is less plausible. (Jonathan Kozol, *Savage Inequalities* (New York: Crown Publishers, Inc. 1991).

9. A related, but perhaps more utopian point, is that positions of at least modest security and comfort would be accessible to everybody. And, a better society would redistribute both positions and income in such a way that more enjoyable jobs would be available, so that the competition for them would be reduced. No doubt most of my readers will object that these ideals are hopelessly unrealistic, but that shouldn't stop us from doing what we can.

10. My comments here presuppose very different social possibilities from those currently taken for granted by many people in the United States. Obviously, this is not the place to argue in detail about those issues. However, the following points should provide some preliminary food for thought on the part of those who find my suggestions utopian. There is considerable literature on the economic feasibility of converting defense spending to civilian uses. The current resistance to cutting military spending ignores studies that show that only 17,000 jobs in missile production are created from $1,000,000,000 in industrial investment, whereas it creates respectively 25,000 jobs in petrochemicals, 48,000 jobs in the health-sector, 62,000 jobs in educational services, or 65,000 retail jobs. (Alan S. Miller, *Gaia Connections* [Savage, Maryland: Rowman & Littlefield, 1991], pp. 63–69.)

11. For disheartening examples of misogyny, see Fidelis Morgan, *A Misogynist's Sourcebook* (London: Jonathan Cape, 1989). To believe that such deeply embedded attitudes, and ones that are so openly expressed, no longer exert any influence on society, would be implausible. Considerable evidence about other Ds is easily available.

12. For useful summaries, see *The American Woman 1990–1991: A Status Report*, ed. Sara E. Rix for the Women's Research and Education Institute (NY: Norton and Norton, 1990) and *Sisterhood is Global*, ed. Robin Morgan (NY: Anchor Books, 1984).

The first notes in the Introduction that "in this country many women are double- or triple-working in families, jobs, and public roles, and they are often stretched to the limit. . . . Many women are alone—with children, but without jobs or adequate support. Many are ill-housed, undereducated, and underemployed. There are not only glass ceilings atop women who have risen part way in corporate life; plenty of steel caps still hold the lid on initial opportunities" (p.22). The rest of the book provides support for these claims.

Morgan's introduction to the second is still more shocking. She begins her lengthy description of the inferior position of women with a quotation from Kurt Waldheim's "Report to the UN Commission on the Status of Women": "While women represent half the global population and one-third of the labor force, they receive only one-tenth of the world income and own less than one percent of world property. The also are responsible for two-thirds of all working hours" (p. 1).

Since these are not states of affairs that would be chosen by anybody, they strongly suggest the failure of societies to safeguard women's interests equally with those of men. Against such a failure the objection that women's plight is just the result of their own choices rings hollow.

13. See for example, Gertrude Ezorsky, *Racism and Injustice* (Ithaca: Cornell University Press, 1991), chap. 1; also, Tom L. Beauchamp, "The Justification of Reverse Discrimination," *Social Justice and Preferential Treatment: Women and*

Racial Minorities in Education and Business, ed. William T. Blackstone and Robert D. Heslep (Athens, GA.: University of Georgia Press, 1977), especially part 2; and my "In Defense of Hiring Apparently Less Qualified Women," *Journal of Social Philosophy*, Vol. 15 (Summer 1984), 26–33. Prejudice against such Ds as the disabled and homosexuals could also be documented.

14. For more information see Hilda Scott, *Working Your Way to the Bottom: The Feminization of Poverty* (London: Pandora Press, 1984).

15. For a compelling argument about the nature and force of pronatalist messages, see *Pronatalism: The Myth of Mom and Apple Pie*, ed. Ellen Peck and Judith Senderowitz (New York: Thomas Y. Crowell, 1974).

16. See, for example, George Gilder, *Sexual Suicide* (NY: Bantam Books, 1973), Robert D. McCracken, *Fallacies of Women's Liberation* (Boulder: Shields Publishing, Inc., 1972), or Michael Levin, *Feminism and Freedom* (New Brunswick, NJ: Transaction Books, 1987).

17. Consider the interesting statistic that some 30 percent of first year college men and 20 percent of first year college women still think that women's place is the home! See "This Year's College Freshmen: Attitudes and Characteristics," *Chronicle of Higher Education*, 37, n. 20 (30 January 1991): A30–31.

18. A glance or two at history provides evidence for this claim. A good place to start is with the nineteenth-century debate about education for women: if women got too much education, their reproductive organs would shrivel and they wouldn't have enough children. (Edward H. Clarke, *Sex in Education: A Fair Chance for the Girls* (Boston: James R. Osgood and Co., 1873) This theme surfaces periodically, especially in the literature on eugenics. For an excellent overview of the nineteenth century, see Carroll Smith-Rosenberg and Charles Rosenberg, "The Female Animal: Medical and Biological Views of Woman and Her Role in Nineteenth-Century America," *Concepts of Health and Disease*, ed. Arthur L. Caplan, H. Tristram Engelhardt, Jr., and James L. McCartney (Reading, MA: Addison-Wesley Publishing Co., 1981).

Legally Sanctioned Special Advantages Are a Way of Life in the United States
Benjamin DeMott

During years of service on academic committees, I've read stacks of "autobiographical statements" composed by candidates for Rhodes scholarships and other prestigious fellowships. Almost by con-

Benjamin DeMott, "Legally Sanctioned Special Advantages Are a Way of Life in the United States," *The Chronicle of Higher Education* 27 February 1991: A40. Copyright (c) 1991 Benjamin DeMott. Reprinted by permission of the author.

vention these achievers cite evidence attesting to their readiness to "try everything" in the way of learning—including private lessons in skills ranging from dressage, bassoon playing, and wilderness-survival techniques to ballet, ice dancing, tennis, chess, and Russian.

The point the achievers seem determined to get across is that they are venturesome. As one candidate put it in a homily that I have encountered in several versions: "There was only one rule in my family. You had to try everything. You had to give it a fair try and afterward, if you didn't like it, okay: Quit. But you had to make the effort."

Such assertions convey an important self-concept—that of people independent, unafraid of embarrassment or failure, aware of the endless range of pleasures and satisfactions life offers to those eager to seize them, proud of the capacity for commitment. Usually students see that capacity—a shade self-deceivingly—as a purely personal trait; they habitually see expensive advantages and options as proof of individual merit.

This innocent self-deception comes to mind often as I follow the national debate on affirmative action. American rhetoric has long insisted that the rules for success are the same for everyone and that merit is the key to advancement. The rhetoric of merit figures prominently in the affirmative-action debate—fairness, level playing field, preferential treatment, competition, fear of competition, and so on. And one theme surfaces time and again, favored not only by representatives of the majority culture but also lately by some minority representatives, as well. The substance of the theme is that special advantages of any sort are alien to the American way.

In my view, this is a wrong-headed belief, disturbingly oblivious of the vast structure of legally sanctioned special advantages that undergirds many Americans' individual achievements and comforts. In numberless ways, public policy contravenes the rhetoric denigrating special advantages. The evidence is omnipresent. The weekly journal *Tax Notes* recently pointed out that the non-poor population of the United States will receive a government benefit worth $60-billion in 1991—a clear special advantage—thanks to the deductibility of mortgage interest and property taxes. As renters, most of the working poor are ineligible for this benefit.

Comparable provisions—special advantages for the non-poor partly paid for by the taxes of the working poor—abound throughout our tax code. In 1989, writing in the *Population Research and Policy Review*, sociologists Leonard Beeghley and Jeffrey Dwyer listed some 30 different forms of federal tax subsidies that are awarded to the non-

poor; these subsidies are worth hundreds of billions of dollars each year. People whose annual income is under $75,000 are ineligible for many of these subsidies. Only about one black family in 25 has an income that large.

To those who qualify for them, American tax shelters appear benign, color-blind, "democratic." But along this democratic byway some people clearly are more equal than others. Because most whites earn more than blacks, tax shelters favor whites; in many instances the degree of favoritism is staggering. When the cash benefits of a government policy are 25 times more likely to go to white families than to black families, and when that pattern has been in place for decades with barely a whisper of public protest, it's preposterous to speak—as many do in arguments over affirmative action—as though the idea of special advantages were un-American.

No less preposterous is the notion that student superstardom in colleges and universities is a function solely of native brilliance and individual true grit. Once hailed as democracy's front line, this country's schools long ago ceased functioning as equalizers. During the last three to four decades, educational researchers and historians have labored to explain why this happened, measuring the distance between a meritocratic school system and the system as it now functions.

The pioneering contribution to this inquiry was "Elmtown's Youth," August Hollingshead's 1949 study of how social and economic class affected the treatment of poor, middle-class, and upper-middle-class pupils by teachers and principals in one Midwestern high school. The most penetrating research was conducted for Congress by the Coleman Commission at the height of the civil-rights movement.

The Coleman Report, published in 1966, established that class influenced the achievement of students throughout their schooling because it shaped their attitudes toward teachers, their familiarity with the materials of learning, their study habits and the environment in which they studied, and their classroom participation. (In this context, it is clear that training in the skills and arts of commitment, like that provided by private lessons, is an immense advantage to any student.) The most recent confirmation and updating of the Coleman Commission's report appeared in William Julius Wilson's 1987 book, *The Truly Disadvantaged: The Inner City, the Underclass & Public Policy.*

Other research has documented that well-off students with weak academic records are far more likely to attend college than hard-up students with strong records; that "multi-track" or "open transfer" school systems create permanent enclaves of students of the same social class instead of fostering mobility; and that state financing arrangements provide low subsidies for the least-advantaged students attending two-year colleges and high subsidies for the most-advantaged attending flagship universities. Still other studies have shown that scholarship funds, advertised as democratizing influences at private colleges and universities, often are awarded to students with extremely large family incomes.

A body of inquiry has established, furthermore, that teachers' conceptions of "ideal" pupils typically equate class-connected characteristics such as accent, appearance, manner, and deportment with "natural or inborn intelligence." Similar skewing has been noted in standards adopted by testing agencies. For example, the verbal behavior of middle- and upper-middle-class children identified as "intelligent" has become the yardstick for evaluating all students, with predictable consequences for speakers of "Black English."

The point of citing all this isn't to deny that pure merit sometimes receives a fair shake in elementary and secondary schools. Everyone who teaches knows of occasions when worth has risen despite obstacles; faith that a caring teacher can help in this process sustains thousands of academicians. But it's one thing to acknowledge the possibility that students can overcome the odds and quite another to condone the excessively moralized assumptions—the fantasies of unconditioned individual accomplishment ("I did it my way")—that turn up in students' life stories and in adults' critiques of affirmative action.

The affirmative-action cause has failings, of course. Manipulative politicos easily exploit them to drive a wedge between working-class whites and blacks. The country would be better off if its politics focused less on race and more on the ways in which bad schools, bad jobs, bad housing, and frightening crime rates wreck life for blacks and whites. And it certainly would be harder to denigrate affirmative-action programs if they helped the working poor of all races as much as they help middle-class members of minority groups.

But righting ancient wrongs is complex work, beset with anomaly; succeeding at it requires exceptionally high levels of self-awareness and social realism. That is why it makes sense to challenge people who think sweetheart deals, insider trading, and special advantages for particular groups are alien to the American way of life. Let's face up to the awkward truth: Special advantages are and have been for generations as American as blueberry pie.

25.

Class, Not Race

Richard Kahlenberg

Richard Kahlenberg argues that public policies such as affirmative action programs might be more successful (or at least meet less resistance) if they shifted from race-based criteria to class-based criteria. If we seek to move toward a more just society, perhaps we ought to attend more to differences in social and economic class, and extend preferences to those who are economically disadvantaged. Shifting from color-consciousness to class-consciousness might offer clear advantages both in the administration of affirmative action programs and in garnering of public support for these programs.

In an act that reflected panic as much as cool reflection, Bill Clinton said recently that he is reviewing all federal affirmative action programs to see "whether there is some other way we can reach [our] objective without giving a preference by race or gender." As the country's mood swings violently against affirmative action, and as Republicans gear up to use the issue to bludgeon the Democratic coalition yet again in 1996, the whole project of legislating racial equality seems suddenly in doubt. The Democrats, terrified of the issue, are now hoping it will just go away. It won't. But at every political impasse, there is a political opportunity. Bill Clinton now has a chance, as no other Democrat has had since 1968, to turn a glaring liability for his party into an advantage—without betraying basic Democratic principles.

There is, as Clinton said, a way "we can work this out." But it isn't the *Bakke* straddle," which says yes to affirmative action (race as a factor) but no to quotas. It isn't William Julius Wilson's call to "emphasize" race-neutral social programs, while downplaying affirmative action. The days of downplaying are gone; we can count on the Republicans for that. The way out—an idea Clinton hinted at—is to introduce the principle of race neutrality and the goal of aiding the disadvantaged into affirmative action preference programs themselves: to base preferences, in education, entry-level employment and public contracting, on class, not race.

Were Clinton to propose this move, the media would charge him with lurching to the right. Jesse Jackson's presidential campaign would surely soon follow. But despite its association with conservatives such as Clarence Thomas, Antonin Scalia and Dinesh D'Souza, the idea of class-based affirmative action should in fact appeal to the left as well. After all, its message of addressing class unfairness and its

political potential for building cross-racial coalitions are traditional liberal staples.

For many years, the left argued not only that class was important, but also that it was more important than race. This argument was practical, ideological and politic. An emphasis on class inequality meant Robert Kennedy riding in a motorcade through cheering white and black sections of racially torn Gary, Indiana, in 1968, with black Mayor Richard Hatcher on one side, and white working-class boxing hero Tony Zale on the other.

Ideologically, it was clear that with the passage of the Civil Rights Act of 1964, class replaced caste as the central impediment to equal opportunity. Martin Luther King Jr. moved from the Montgomery Boycott to the Poor People's Campaign, which he described as "his last, greatest dream," and "something bigger than just a civil rights movement for Negroes." RFK told David Halberstam that "it was pointless to talk about the real problem in America being black and white, it was really rich and poor, which was a much more complex subject."

Finally, the left emphasized class because to confuse class and race was seen not only as wrong but as dangerous. This notion was at the heart of the protest over Daniel Patrick Moynihan's 1965 report, *The Negro Family: The Case for National Action,* in which Moynihan depicted the rising rates of illegitimacy among poor blacks. While Moynihan's critics were wrong to silence discussion of illegitimacy among blacks, they rightly noted that the title of the report, which implicated all blacks, was misleading, and that fairly high rates of illegitimacy also were present among poor whites—a point which Moynihan readily endorses today. (In the wake of the second set of L.A. riots in 1992, Moynihan rose on the Senate floor to reaffirm that family structure "is not an issue of race but of class. . . . It is class behavior.")

The irony is that affirmative action based on race violates these three liberal insights. It provides the ultimate wedge to destroy Robert Kennedy's coalition. It says that despite civil

Richard Kahlenberg, "Class, Not Race," *The New Republic*, 3 April 1995: 21, 24–26. Reprinted by permission of *The New Republic*, (c) 1995, The New Republic, Inc.

rights protections, the wealthiest African American is more deserving of preference than the poorest white. It relentlessly focuses all attention on race.

In contrast, Lyndon Johnson's June 1965 address to Howard University, in which the concept of affirmative action was first unveiled, did not ignore class. In a speech drafted by Moynihan, Johnson spoke of the bifurcation of the black community, and, in his celebrated metaphor, said we needed to aid those "hobbled" in life's race by past discrimination. This suggested special help for disadvantaged blacks, not all blacks; for the young Clarence Thomas, but not for Clarence Thomas's son. Johnson balked at implementing the thematic language of his speech. His Executive Order 11246, calling for "affirmative action" among federal contractors, initially meant greater outreach and required hiring without respect to race. In fact, LBJ rescinded his Labor Department's proposal to provide for racial quotas in the construction industry in Philadelphia. It fell to Richard Nixon to implement the "Philadelphia Plan," in what Nixon's aides say was a conscious effort to drive a wedge between blacks and labor. (Once he placed racial preferences on the table, Nixon adroitly extricated himself, and by 1972 was campaigning against racial quotas.)

The ironies were compounded by the Supreme Court. In the 1974 case, *DeFunis v. Odegaard,* in which a system of racial preferences in law school admissions was at issue, it was the Court's liberal giant, William O. Douglas, who argued that racial preferences were unconstitutional, and suggested instead that preferences be based on disadvantage. Four years later, in the *Bakke* case, the great proponent of affirmative action as a means to achieve "diversity" was Nixon, appointee Lewis F. Powell Jr. Somewhere along the line, the right wing embraced Douglas and Critical Race Theory embraced Powell.

Today, the left pushes racial preferences, even for the most advantaged minorities, in order to promote diversity and provide role models for disadvantaged blacks—an argument which, if it came from Ronald Reagan, the left would rightly dismiss as trickle-down social theory. Today, when William Julius Wilson argues the opposite of the Moynihan report—that the problems facing the black community are rooted more in class than race—it is Wilson who is excoriated by civil rights groups. The left can barely utter the word "class," instead resorting to euphemisms such as "income groups," "wage earners," and "people who play by the rules."

For all of this, the left has paid a tremendous price. On a political level, with a few notable exceptions, the history of the past twenty-five years is a history of white, working-class Robert Kennedy Democrats turning first into Wallace Democrats, then into Nixon and Reagan Democrats and ultimately into today's Angry White Males. Time and again, the white working class votes its race rather than its class, and Republicans win. The failure of the left to embrace class also helps turn poor blacks, for whom racial preferences are, in Stephen Carter's words, "stunningly irrelevant," toward Louis Farrakhan.

On the merits, the left has committed itself to a goal—equality of group results—which seems highly radical, when it is in fact rather unambitious. To the extent that affirmative action, at its ultimate moment of success, merely creates a self-perpetuating black elite along with a white one, its goal is modest—certainly more conservative than real equality of opportunity, which gives blacks and whites and other Americans of all economic strata a fair chance at success.

The priority given to race over class has inevitably exacerbated white racism. Today, both liberals and conservatives conflate race and class because it serves both of their purposes to do so. Every year, when SAT scores are released, the breakdown by race shows enormous gaps between blacks on the one hand and whites and Asians on the other. The NAACP cites these figures as evidence that we need to do more. Charles Murray cites the same statistics as evidence of intractable racial differences. We rarely see a breakdown of scores by class, which would show enormous gaps between rich and poor, gaps that would help explain the differences in scores by race.

On the legal front, it once made some strategic sense to emphasize race over class. But when states moved to the remedial phrase—and began trying to address past discrimination—the racial focus became a liability. The strict scrutiny that struck down Jim Crow is now used, to varying degrees, to curtail racial preferences. Class, on the other hand, is not one of the suspect categories under the Fourteenth Amendment, which leaves class-based remedies much less assailable.

If class-based affirmative action is a theory that liberals should take seriously, how would it work in practice? In this magazine, Michael Kinsley has asked, "Does Clarence Thomas, the sharecropper's kid, get more or fewer preference points than the unemployed miner's son from Appalachia?" Most conservative proponents of class-based affirmative action have failed to explain their idea with any degree of specificity. Either they're insincere—offering the alternative only for tactical reasons—or they're stumped.

The former is more likely. While the questions of implementation are serious and difficult, they are not impossible to answer. At the university level, admissions committees deal every day with precisely the type of apples-and-oranges question that Kinsley poses. Should a law school admit an applicant with a 3.2 GPA from Yale or a 3.3 from Georgetown? How do you compare those two if one applicant worked for the Peace Corps but the other had slightly higher LSATs?

In fact, a number of universities already give preferences for disadvantaged students in addition to racial minorities. Since 1989 Berkeley has granted special consideration to applicants "from socioeconomically disadvantaged backgrounds . . . regardless of race or ethnicity." Temple University Law School has, since the 1970s, given preference to "applicants who have over-

come exceptional and continuous economic deprivation." And at Hastings College of Law, 20 percent of the class is set aside for disadvantaged students through the Legal Equal Opportunity Program. Even the U.C.-Davis medical program challenged by Allan Bakke was limited to "disadvantaged" minorities, a system which Davis apparently did not find impossible to administer.

Similar class-based preference programs could be provided by public employers and federal contractors for high school graduates not pursuing college, on the theory that at that age their class-based handicaps hide their true potential and are not at all of their own making. In public contracting, government agencies could follow the model of New York's City's old class-based program, which provided preferences based not on the ethnicity or gender of the contractor, but to small firms located in New York City which did part of their business in depressed areas or employed economically disadvantaged workers.

The definition of class or disadvantage may vary according to context, but if, for example, the government chose to require class-based affirmative action from universities receiving federal funds, it is possible to devise an enforceable set of objective standards for deprivation. If the aim of class-based affirmative action is to provide a system of genuine equality of opportunity, a leg up to promising students who have done well despite the odds, we have a wealth of sociological data to devise an obstacles test. While some might balk at the very idea of reducing disadvantage to a number, we currently reduce intellectual promise to numbers—SATs and GPAs—and adding a number for disadvantage into the calculus just makes deciding who gets ahead and who does not a little fairer.

There are three basic ways to proceed: with a simple, moderate or complex definition. The simple method is to ask college applicants their family's income and measure disadvantage by that factor alone, on the theory that income is a good proxy for a whole host of economic disadvantages (such as bad schools or a difficult learning environment). This oversimplified approach is essentially the tack we've taken with respect to compensatory race-based affirmative action. For example, most affirmative action programs ask applicants to check a racial box and sweep all the ambiguities under the rug. Even though African Americans have, as Justice Thurgood Marshall said in *Bakke,* suffered a history "different in kind, not just degree, from that of other ethnic groups," universities don't calibrate preferences based on comparative group disadvantage (and, in the Davis system challenged by Bakke, two-thirds of the preferences went to Mexican-Americans and Asians, not blacks). We also ignore the question of when an individual's family immigrated in order to determine whether the family was even theoretically subject to the official discrimination in this country on which preferences are predicated.

"Diversity" was supposed to solve all this by saying we don't care about compensation, only viewpoint. But, again, if universities are genuinely seeking diversity of viewpoints, they should inquire whether a minority applicant really does have the "minority viewpoint" being sought. Derrick Bell's famous statement—"the ends of diversity are not served by people who look black and think white"—is at once repellent and a relevant critique of the assumption that all minority members think alike. In theory, we need some assurance from the applicant that he or she will in fact interact with students of different backgrounds, lest the cosmetic diversity of the freshman yearbook be lost to the reality of ethnic theme houses.

The second way to proceed, the moderately complicated calculus of class, would look at what sociologists believe to be the Big Three determinants of life chances: parental income, education and occupation. Parents' education, which is highly correlated with a child's academic achievement, can be measured in number of years. And while ranking occupations might seem hopelessly complex, various attempts to do so objectively have yielded remarkable consistent results—from the Barr Scale of the early 1920s to Alba Edwards' Census rankings of the 1940s to the Duncan Scores of the 1960s.

The third alternative, the complex calculus of disadvantage, would count all the factors mentioned, but might also look at net worth, the quality of secondary education, neighborhood influences and family structure. An applicant's family wealth is readily available from financial aid forms, and provides a long-term view of relative disadvantage, to supplement the "snapshot" picture that income provides. We also know that schooling opportunities are crucial to a student's life chances, even controlling for home environment. Some data suggest that a disadvantaged student at a middle-class school does better on average than a middle-class student at a school with high concentrations of poverty. Objective figures are available to measure secondary school quality—from per student expenditure, to the percentage of students receiving free or reduced-price lunches, to a school's median score on standardized achievement tests. Neighborhood influences, measured by the concentration of poverty within Census tracts or zip codes, could also be factored in, since numerous studies have found that living in a low-income community can adversely affect an individual's life chances above and beyond family income. Finally, everyone from Dan Quayle to Donna Shalala agrees that children growing up in single-parent homes have a tougher time. This factor could be taken into account as well.

The point is not that this list is the perfect one, but that it *is* possible to devise a series of fairly objective and verifiable factors that measure the degree to which a teenager's true potential has been hidden. (As it happens, the complex definition is the one that disproportionately benefits African Americans. Even among similar income groups, blacks are more likely than whites to live in concentrated poverty, go to bad schools and live in single-parent homes.) It's just not true that a system of class preferences is inherently harder to administer than a system based on race. Race only seems simpler because we have ignored the ambiguities. And racial preferences are just as easy to ridicule. To paraphrase Kinsley, does a new Indian immigrant get fewer or more points than a third-generation Latino whose mother is Anglo?

Who should benefit? Mickey Kaus, in "Class Is In," . . . argued that class preferences should be reserved for the underclass. But the injuries of class extend beyond the poorest. The offspring of the working poor and the working class lack advantages, too, and indeed SAT scores correlate lockstep with income at every increment. Unless you believe in genetic inferiority, these statistics suggest unfairness is not confined to the underclass. As a practical matter, a teenager who emerges from the underclass has little chance of surviving at an elite college. At Berkeley, administrators found that using a definition of disadvantaged, under which neither parent attended a four-year college and the family could not afford to pay $1,000 in education expenses, failed to bring in enough students who were likely to pass.

Still, there are several serious objections to class-based preferences that must be addressed.

1. *We're not ready to be color-blind because racial discrimination continues to afflict our society.* Ron Brown says affirmative action "continues to be needed not to redress grievances of the past, but the current discrimination that continues to exist." This is a relatively new theory, which conveniently elides the fact that preferences were supposed to be temporary. It also stands logic on its head. While racial discrimination undoubtedly still exists, the Civil Rights Act of 1964 was meant to address prospective discrimination. Affirmative action—discrimination in itself—makes sense only to the extent that there is a current-day legacy of *past* discrimination which new prospective laws cannot reach back and remedy.

In the contexts of education and employment, the Civil Rights Act already contains powerful tools to address intentional and unintentional discrimination. The Civil Rights Act of 1991 reaffirmed the need to address unintentional discrimination—by requiring employers to justify employment practices that are statistically more likely to hurt minorities—but it did so without crossing the line to required preferences. This principle also applies to Title VI of the Civil Rights Act, so that if, for example, it can be shown that the SAT produces an unjustified disparate impact, a university can be barred from using it. In addition, "soft" forms of affirmative action, which require employers and universities to broaden the net and interview people from all races are good ways of ensuring positions are not filled by word of mouth, through wealthy white networks.

We have weaker tools to deal with discrimination in other areas of life—say, taxi drivers who refuse to pick up black businessmen—but how does a preference in education or employment remedy that wrong? By contrast, there is nothing illegal about bad schools, bad housing and grossly stunted opportunities for the poor. A class preference is perfectly appropriate.

2. *Class preferences will be just as stigmatizing as racial preferences.* Kinsley argues that "any debilitating self-doubt that exists because of affirmative action is not going to be mitigated by being told you got into Harvard because of your 'socioeconomic disadvantage' rather than your race."

But class preferences are different from racial preferences in at least two important respects. First, stigma—in one's own eyes and the eyes of others—is bound up with the question of whether an admissions criterion is accepted as legitimate. Students with good grades aren't seen as getting in "just because they're smart." And there appears to be a societal consensus—from

Douglas to Scalia—that kids from poor backgrounds deserve a leg up. Such a consensus has never existed for class-blind racial preference.

Second, there is no myth of inferiority in this country about the abilities of poor people comparable to that about African Americans. Now, if racial preferences are purely a matter of compensatory justice, then the question of whether preferences exacerbate white racism is not relevant. But today racial preferences are often justified by social utility (bringing different racial groups together helps dispel stereotypes) in which case the social consequences are highly relevant. The general argument made by proponents of racial preferences—that policies need to be grounded in social reality, not ahistorical theory—cuts in favor of the class category. Why? Precisely because there is no stubborn myth for it to reinforce.

Kaus makes a related argument when he says that class preferences "will still reward those who play the victim." But if objective criteria are used to define the disadvantaged, there is no way to "play" the victim. Poor and working-class teenagers are the victims of class inequality not of their own making. Preferences, unlike, say, a welfare check, tell poor teenagers not that they are helpless victims, but that we think their long-run potential is great, and we're going to give them a chance—if they work their tails off—to prove themselves.

3. *Class preferences continue to treat people as members of groups as opposed to individuals.* Yes. But so do university admissions policies that summarily reject students below a certain SAT level. It's hard to know what treating people as individuals means. (Perhaps if university admissions committees interviewed the teachers of each applicant back to kindergarten to get a better picture of their academic potential, we'd be treating them more as individuals.) The question is not whether we treat people as members of groups—that's inevitable—but whether the group is a relevant one. And in measuring disadvantage (and hidden potential) class is surely a much better proxy than race.

4. *Class-based affirmative action will not yield a diverse student body in elite colleges.* Actually, there is reason to believe that class preferences will disproportionately benefit people of color in most contexts—since minorities are disproportionately poor. In the university context, however, class-based preferences were rejected during the 1970s in part because of fear that they would produce inadequate numbers of minority students. The problem is that when you control for income, African American students do worse that white and Asian students on the SAT—due in part to differences in culture and linguistic patterns, and in part to the way income alone as a measurement hides other class-based differences among ethnic groups.

The concern is a serious and complicated one. Briefly, there are four responses. First, even Murray and Richard Herrnstein agree that the residual racial gap in scores has declined significantly in the past two decades, so the concern, though real, is not as great as it once was. Second, if we use the sophisticated definition of class discussed earlier—which reflects the relative disadvantage of blacks vis-à-vis whites of the same income level—the racial gap should close further. Third, we can improve racial diversity by getting rid of unjustified preferences—for alumni kids or students from underrepresented geographic regions—which disproportionately hurt people of color. Finally, if the goal is to provide genuine equal opportunity, not equality of group result, and if we are satisfied that a meritocratic system which corrects for class inequality is the best possible approximation of that equality, then we have achieved our goal.

5. *Class-based affirmative action will cause as much resentment among those left out as race-based affirmative action.* Kinsley argues that the rejected applicant in the infamous Jesse Helms commercial from 1990 would feel just as angry for losing out on a class-based as a race-based preference, since both involve "making up for past injustice." The difference, of course, is that class preferences go to the actual victims of class injury, mooting the whole question of intergenerational justice. In the racial context, this was called "victim specificity." Even the Reagan administration was in favor of compensating actual victims of racial discrimination.

The larger point implicit in Kinsley's question is a more serious one: that any preference system, whether race- or class-based, is "still a form of zero-sum social engineering." Why should liberals push for class preferences at all? Why not just provide more funding for education, safer schools, better nutrition? The answer is that liberals should do these things; but we cannot hold our breath for it to happen. In 1993, when all the planets were aligned—a populist Democratic president, Democratic control of both Houses of Congress—they produced what *The New York Times* called "A BUDGET WORTHY OF MR. BUSH." Cheaper alternatives, such as preferences, must supplement more expensive strategies of social spending. Besides, to the extent that class preferences help change the focus of public discourse from race to class, they help reforge the coalition needed to sustain the social programs liberals want.

Class preferences could restore the successful formula on which the early civil rights movement rested: morally unassailable underpinnngs and a relatively inexpensive agenda. It's crucial to remember that Martin Luther King Jr. called for special consideration based on class, not race. After laying out a forceful argument for the special debt owed to blacks, King rejected the call for a Negro Bill of Rights in favor of a Bill of Rights for the Disadvantaged. It was King's insight that there were nonracial ways to remedy racial wrongs, and the injuries of class deserve attention along with the injuries of race.

None of this is to argue that King would have opposed affirmative action if the alternative were to do nothing. For Jesse Helms to invoke King's color-blind rhetoric now that it is in the interests of white people to do so is the worst kind of hypocrisy. Some form of compensation is necessary, and I think affirmative action, though deeply flawed, is better than nothing.

But the opportunity to save affirmative action of any kind may soon pass. If the Supreme Court continues to narrow the instances in which racial preferences are justified, if California voters put an end to affirmative action in their state and if Congress begins to roll back racial preferences in legislation which President Clinton finds hard to veto—or President Phil Gramm signs with gusto—conservatives will have less and less reason to bargain. Now is the time to call their bluff.

26.

Opinion in *University of California v. Bakke* (1978)

Justice Lewis F. Powell, Jr.

The 1978 United States Supreme Court decision *University of California v. Bakke* and the 1996 Fifth Circuit Appellate Court decision *Cheryl Hopwood et al. v. State of Texas* (the following article) are two extremely important federal rulings on the issue of race and affirmative action in higher education.

The Bakke case began in the mid-1970s when Allen Bakke, a white male, was denied admission to the medical school at the University of California at Davis. At that time, the medical school had an admission policy which reserved 16 of the 100 places in the first year class for minority students. Allen Bakke was precluded from being considered for these 16 slots because of his race; the students who were admitted to fill these 16 seats in the incoming class had lower undergraduate G.P.A.'s and lower M.C.A.T. scores than Bakke. He then filed suit against the University of California. The trial court ruled in his favor concluding that he had been the victim of *invidious* racial discrimination, a decision in turn supported by the California Supreme Court. The University of California then appealed to the United States Supreme Court.

The controlling opinion in the Supreme Court decision was written by Justice Powell and represented only a 5-4 plurality of the court. Powell's opinion in part affirmed and in part reversed the California court's decision: Bakke's 14th Amendment rights had been violated by the special admission policy at Davis as he had been "totally excluded" on the basis of his race from competing for those 16 slots set aside for minority students. Yet, Powell argued that the State of California nonetheless had a legitimate interest in devising admission policies where an applicant's race and ethnic origin would be considered along with other factors. Thus while the Supreme Court ruled that the particular UC-Davis Medical School admission policy in effect at that time was unconstitutional, it did *not* rule that race could *not* be considered in university admissions programs.

I

Over the past 30 years, this Court has embarked upon the crucial mission of interpreting the Equal Protection Clause with the view of assuring to all persons "the protection of equal laws," in a Nation confronting a legacy of slavery and racial discrimination. Because the landmark decisions in this area arose in response to the continued exclusion of Negroes from the mainstream of American society, they could be characterized as involving discrimination by the "majority" white race against the Negro minority. But they need not be read as depending upon that characterization for their results. It suffices to say that "[o]ver the years, this Court has consistently repudiated '[d]istinctions between citizens solely because of their ancestry' as being 'odious to a free people whose institutions are founded upon the doctrine of equality.'"

Petitioner [the University of California] urges us to adopt for the first time a more restrictive view of the Equal Protection Clause and hold that discrimination against members of the white "majority" cannot be suspect if its purpose can be characterized as "benign." The clock of our liberties, however, cannot be turned back to 1868. It is far too late to argue that the guarantee of equal protection to *all* persons permits the recognition of special wards entitled to a degree of protection greater than that accorded others. "The Fourteenth Amendment is not directed solely against discrimination due to a 'two-class theory'—that is, based upon differences between 'white' and Negro." . . .

II

We have held that in "order to justify the use of a suspect classification, a State must show that its purpose or interest is both constitutionally permissible and substantial and that its use of the classification is 'necessary. . . to the accomplishment' of its purpose or the safeguarding of its interest." The special admissions program purports to serve the purposes of: (i) "reducing the historic deficit of traditionally disfavored minorities in medical schools and in the medical profession"; (ii) countering the effects of societal discrimination; (iii) increasing the number of physicians who will practice in communities currently underserved; and (iv) obtaining the educational benefits that flow from an ethnically diverse student body. It is necessary to decide which, if any, of these purposes is substantial enough to support the use of a suspect classification.

A

If petitioner's purpose is to assure within its student body some specified percentage of a particular group merely because of its race or ethnic origin, such a preferential purpose must be rejected not as insubstantial but as facially invalid. Preferring members of any one group for no reason other than race or ethnic origin is discrimination for its own sake. This the Constitution forbids.

B

The State certainly has a legitimate and substantial interest in ameliorating, or eliminating where feasible, the disabling effects of identified discrimination. The line of school desegregation cases, commencing with *Brown v. Board of Education* (1954) attests to the importance of this state goal and the commitment of the judiciary to affirm all lawful means toward its attainment. In the school cases, the States were required by court order to redress the wrongs worked by specific instances of racial discrimination. That goal was far more focused than the remedying of the effects of "societal discrimination," an amorphous concept of injury that may be ageless in its reach into the past.

We have never approved a classification that aids persons perceived as members of relatively victimized groups at the expense of other innocent individuals in the absence of judicial, legislative, or administrative findings of constitutional or statutory violations. After such findings have been made, the governmental interest in preferring members of the injured groups at the expense of others is substantial, since the legal rights of the victims must be vindicated. In such a case, the extent of the injury and the consequent remedy will have been judicially, legislatively, or administratively defined. Also,

the remedial action usually remains subject to continuing oversight to assure that it will work the least harm possible to other innocent persons competing for the benefit. Without such findings of constitutional or statutory violations, it cannot be said that the government has any greater interest in helping one individual than in refraining from harming another. Thus, the government has no compelling justification for inflicting such harm.

Petitioner does not purport to have made, and is in no position to make, such findings. Its broad mission is education, not the formulation of any legislative policy or the adjudication of particular claims of illegality. . . . [I]solated segments of our vast governmental structures are not competent to make those decisions, at least in the absence of legislative mandates and legislatively determined criteria. Before relying upon these sorts of findings in establishing a racial classification, a governmental body must have the authority and capability to establish, in the record, that the classification is responsive to identified discrimination. Lacking this capability, petitioner has not carried its burden of justification on this issue.

Hence, the purpose of helping certain groups whom the faculty of the Davis Medical School perceived as victims of "societal discrimination" does not justify a classification that imposes disadvantages upon persons like respondent [Allen Bakke], who bear no responsibility for whatever harm the beneficiaries of the special admissions program are thought to have suffered. To hold otherwise would be to convert a remedy heretofore reserved for violations of legal rights into a privilege that all institutions throughout the Nation could grant at their pleasure to whatever groups are perceived as victims of societal discrimination. That is a step we have never approved.

C

Petitioner identifies, as another purpose of its program, improving the delivery of health-care services to communities currently underserved. It may be assumed that in some situations a State's interest in facilitating the health care of its citizens is sufficiently compelling to support the use of a suspect classification. But there is virtually no evidence in the record indicating that petitioner's special admissions program is either needed or geared to promote that goal. The court below addressed this failure of proof:

> "The University concedes it cannot assure that minority doctors who entered under the program, all of whom expressed an 'interest' in practicing in a disadvantaged community, will actually do so. It may be correct to assume that some of them will carry out this intention, and that it is more likely they will practice in minority communities than the average white doctor. Nevertheless, there are more precise and reliable ways to identify applicants who are genuinely interested in the medical problems of minorities than by race. An applicant of whatever race who has demonstrated his concern for disadvantaged minorities in the past and who declares that practice in such a community is his primary professional goal would be more likely to contribute to alleviation of the medical shortage than one who is chosen entirely on the basis of race and disadvantage. In short, there is no empirical data to demonstrate that any one race is more selflessly socially oriented or by contrast that another is more selfishly acquisitive."

Petitioner simply has not carried its burden of demonstrating that it must prefer members of particular ethnic groups over all other individuals in order to promote better health-care delivery to deprived citizens. Indeed, petitioner has not shown that its preferential classification is likely to have any significant effect on the problem.

D

The fourth goal asserted by petitioner is the attainment of a diverse student body. This clearly is a constitutionally permissible goal for an institution of higher education. Academic freedom, though not a specifically enumerated constitutional right, long has been viewed as a special concern of the First Amendment. The freedom of a university to make its own judgments as to education includes the selection of its student body.

Ethnic diversity, however, is only one element in a range of factors a university properly may consider in attaining the goal of a heterogeneous student body. Although a university must have wide discretion in making the sensitive judgments as to who should be admitted, constitutional limitations protecting individual rights may not be disregarded. Respondent urges—and the courts below have held—that petitioner's dual admissions program is a racial classification that impermissibly infringes his rights under the Fourteenth Amendment. As the interest of diversity is compelling in the context of a university's admissions program, the question remains whether the program's racial classification is necessary to promote this interest.

III

A

It may be assumed that the reservation of a specified number of seats in each class for individuals from the preferred ethnic groups would contribute to the attainment of considerable ethnic diversity in the student body. But petitioner's argument that this is the only effective means of serving the interest of diversity is seriously flawed. In a most fundamental sense the argument misconceives the nature of the state interest that would justify consideration of race or ethnic background. It is not an interest in simple ethnic diversity, in which a specified percentage of the student body is in effect guaranteed to be members of selected ethnic groups, with the remaining percentage an undifferentiated aggregation of students. The diversity that furthers a compelling state interest encompasses a far broader array of qualifications and characteristics of which racial or ethnic origin is but a single though important element. Petitioner's special admissions program, focused *solely* on ethnic diversity, would hinder rather than further attainment of genuine diversity.

Nor would the state interest in genuine diversity be served by expanding petitioner's two-track system into a multitrack program with a prescribed number of seats set aside for each identifiable category of applicants. Indeed, it is inconceivable that a university would thus pursue the logic of petitioner's two-track program to the illogical end of insulating each category of applicants with certain desired qualifications from competition with all other applicants.

The experience of other university admissions programs, which take race into account in achieving the educational diversity valued by the First Amendment, demonstrates that the assignment of a fixed number of places to a minority group is not a necessary means toward that end. An illuminating example is found in the Harvard College program:

> "In recent years Harvard College has expanded the concept of diversity to include students from disadvantaged economic, racial and ethnic groups. Harvard College now recruits not only Californians or Louisianans but also blacks and Chicanos and other minority students. . . .
>
> "In practice, this new definition of diversity has meant that race has been a factor in some admission decisions. When the Committee on Admissions reviews the large middle group of applicants who are 'admissible' and deemed capable of doing good work in their courses, the race of an applicant may tip the balance in his favor just as geographic origin or a life spent on a farm may tip the balance in other candidates' cases. A farm boy from Idaho can bring something to Harvard College that a Bostonian cannot offer. Similarly, a black student can usually bring something that a white person cannot offer. . . .

> "In Harvard College admissions the Committee has not set target-quotas for the number of blacks, or of musicians, football players, physicists or Californians to be admitted in a given year. . . . But that awareness [of the necessity of including more than a token number of black students] does not mean that the Committee sets a minimum number of blacks or of people from west of the Mississippi who are to be admitted. It means only that in choosing among thousands of applicants who are not only 'admissible' academically but have other strong qualities, the Committee, with a number of criteria in mind, pays some attention to distribution among many types and categories of students."

In such an admissions program, race or ethnic background may be deemed a "plus" in a particular applicant's file, yet it does not insulate the individual from comparison with all other candidates for the available seats. The file of a particular black applicant may be examined for his potential contribution to diversity without the factor of race being decisive when compared, for example, with that of an applicant identified as an Italian-American if the latter is thought to exhibit qualities more likely to promote beneficial educational pluralism. Such qualities could include exceptional personal talents, unique work or service experience, leadership potential, maturity, demonstrated compassion, a history of overcoming disadvantage, ability to communicate with the poor, or other qualifications deemed important. In short, an admissions program operated in this way is flexible enough to consider all pertinent elements of diversity in light of the particular qualifications of each applicant, and to place them on the same footing for consideration, although not necessarily according them the same weight. Indeed, the weight attributed to a particular quality may vary from year to year depending upon the "mix" both of the student body and the applicants for the incoming class.

This kind of program treats each applicant as an individual in the admissions process. The applicant who loses out on the last available seat to another candidate receiving a "plus" on the basis of ethnic background will not have been foreclosed from all consideration for that seat simply because he was not the right color or had the wrong surname. It would mean only that his combined qualifications, which may have included similar nonobjective factors, did not outweigh those of the other applicant. His qualifications would have been weighed fairly and competitively, and he would have no basis to complain of unequal treatment under the Fourteenth Amendment.

It has been suggested that an admissions program which considers race only as one factor is simply a subtle and more sophisticated—but no less effective—means of according racial preference than the Davis program. A facial intent to discriminate, however, is evident in petitioner's preference program and not denied in this case. No such facial infirmity exists in an admissions program where race or ethnic background is simply one element—to be weighed fairly against other elements—in the selection process. "A boundary line," as Mr. Justice Frankfurter remarked in another connection, "is none the worse for being narrow." And a court would not assume that a university, professing to employ a facially nondiscriminatory admissions policy, would operate it as a cover for the functional equivalent of a quota system. In short, good faith would be presumed in the absence of a showing to the contrary in the manner permitted by our cases.

B

In summary, it is evident that the Davis special admissions program involves the use of an explicit racial classification never before countenanced by this Court. It tells applicants who are not Negro, Asian, or Chicano that they are totally excluded from a specific percentage of the seats in an entering class. No matter how strong their qualifications, quantitative and extracurricular, including their own potential for contribution to educational diversity, they are never afforded the chance to compete with applicants from the preferred groups for the special admissions seats. At the same time, the preferred applicants have the opportunity to compete for every seat in the class.

The fatal flaw in petitioner's preferential program is its disregard of individual rights as guaranteed by the Fourteenth Amendment. Such rights are not absolute. But when a State's distribution of benefits or imposition of burdens hinges on ancestry or the color of a person's skin or ancestry, that individual is entitled to a demonstration that the challenged classification is necessary to promote a substantial state interest. Petitioner has failed to carry this burden. For this reason, that portion of the California court's judgment holding petitioner's special admissions program invalid under the Fourteenth Amendment must be affirmed.

C

In enjoining petitioner from ever considering the race of any applicant, however, the courts below failed to recognize that the State has a substantial interest that legitimately may be served by a properly devised admissions program involving the competitive consideration of race and ethnic origin. For this reason, so much of the California court's judgment as enjoins petitioner from any consideration of the race of any applicant must be reversed.

White Woman Accuses Law School of Bias

Richard Bernstein

From Cheryl J. Hopwood's point of view, if overcoming past hardship was counted as a plus when applying to the University of Texas Law School, she should have been among the more qualified candidates.

Ms. Hopwood's father died when she was a girl and she was reared under difficult circumstances by her mother. She worked all through high school and put herself through both community college and the California State University at Sacramento, where she graduated with a 3.8 grade point average. Then, having become a Texas resident, she did well enough on the law school admissions test to get into a category of law school applicant that is almost automatically admitted at Texas.

But Cheryl Hopwood was not admitted, and she believes the reason is that she is white. That has put her at the center of a lawsuit against the University of Texas that, if she wins, could make it far more difficult for universities nationwide to follow the affirmative action policies that have guided them for two decades. A decision in the matter is expected in the next few days, certainly weeks.

"The Texas approach to affirmative action is in the mainstream of the approach used by law schools and other schools throughout the country," said Harry Reasoner, a lawyer for the university. "That would be put at risk if this were formally condemned by the court and no alternatives are offered."

Race as a Factor

The suit brought by Ms. Hopwood and three other plaintiffs is being widely compared to a landmark case of 16 years ago, *Bakke v. Regents of the University of California*. The United States Supreme Court, in a 5-to-4 decision, required that Allan P.

Bakke be admitted to medical school, ruling that the school violated his rights when it rejected him on the ground that he was white.

The Court endorsed affirmative action in the Bakke case, saying that taking race and ethnicity into account in university admissions is permissible, but only if done in a flexible way and for the purpose of redressing the effects of past racial injustice. Race, in other words, can be a factor in selecting candidates for admission, but not the sole factor, the Court said.

Ms. Hopwood has argued that in setting up admissions targets for black and Mexican-American applicants, the university went far beyond what the Supreme Court permitted in Bakke, using race and ethnicity as the all-important criteria for admission and thus violating the plaintiffs' rights to equal treatment.

"Race should just not be a determining factor in admissions policy at the level of law school," she said in a recent telephone interview from her home in San Antonio. "At that level I'm competing with others who have B.A. degrees and they're not people who necessarily have more disadvantaged backgrounds than I have."

The case, argued last month before Judge Sam Sparks in Federal District Court in Austin, offered an unusually candid look at the admissions process used by a major law school, a process normally shrouded in secrecy. Called by the plaintiffs as hostile witnesses, university officials said that the institution set aside roughly 15 percent of its law school seats for blacks and Mexican-Americans, who are admitted under different criteria from all other students, including other minority students. Law school deans from Stanford University and the universities of Minnesota, Michigan and North Carolina testified that they used similar preferences for minority applicants.

The Texas system, portrayed as a discriminatory quota by the plaintiffs, was defended by the university on several grounds, among them that race is only one factor among many considered by the admissions panel and that since the Texas affirmative action program is "narrowly tailored" to remedy the effects of past bias, it is permitted by Bakke.

Most important, university officials said, in a state that is 40 percent black and Mexican-American, the law school's affirmative action program works. Although minority students are admitted at a lower standard than whites, they said, all can do the required work and almost all graduate and pass the bar exam.

"We see minority graduates of ours as elected officials, working in prominent law firms, as members of the Texas Legislature and the Federal bench," said Michael Charlot, the law school's acting dean. Federico F. Peña, the Secretary of Transportation, is among the school's minority graduates. "To the extent that there are minorities in important offices in Texas, they are often our graduates," Mr. Charlot said.

Almost Full Circle

There is a historic poignancy to the renewed legal conflict over affirmative action occurring at the University of Texas, the scene of one of the early landmark Supreme Court decisions leading to the dismantling of segregation in higher education.

In that case, Sweatt v. Painter, the Court decided in 1950 that the university's ban on black students in the law school—and Texas's creation of the Law School for Coloreds—was unconstitutional. Heman Sweatt, who brought the case, became the first black student at the university's law school, but he dropped out, citing its atmosphere of racism.

Judge Sparks must weigh the merits of a nearly inverse accusation: that the university discriminates so avidly in favor of blacks and Mexican-Americans that the rights of whites are being violated.

Witnesses testified during the trial, for example, that virtually every black and Mexican-American student admitted to the law school is given a scholarship, without regard for financial need. As a result, said Terral R. Smith, a lawyer for the plaintiffs: "The university is not helping poor black people with affirmative action. It is denying people like Hopwood and giving special privileges to upper-middle-class black people and Mexican-Americans."

While there are no data to support this assertion, the anecdotal evidence is compelling, Mr. Smith said in an interview. "When you talk to professors, they admit that the black students who can do the work are usually those whose parents have been successful," he said.

According to the law school, its affirmative action policy works like this: Every one of roughly 4,000 applicants is assigned a Texas Index number, a combination of undergraduate grade point average and law school admissions test score. The numbers range from about 145 to 220. Under examination by plaintiffs' lawyers, law school officials acknowledged that blacks and Mexican-Americans are given something close to automatic admission at index numbers substantially below those of many whites who are rejected, including all four plaintiffs in the case.

The head of the law school's admissions committee, Stanley Johanson, admitted under questioning that no black or Mexican-American applicants who were state residents and had a Texas Index of 185 or higher were denied admission. Ms. Hopwood's index was 199 and the three other plaintiffs, white men, had 198.

Mr. Johanson also said that had Ms. Hopwood been black or Mexican-American she would "in all probability" have been accepted.

"Hopwood is the epitome of who is harmed by affirmative action," said Mr. Smith, a former state legislator. "If she had been black, she would have been admitted. Every black applicant that had her credentials got a $7,000 scholarship and free tuition."

A law school memorandum entered into evidence by plaintiffs' lawyers showed that in 1992, the year Ms. Hopwood applied, the law school rejected 668 white candidates before it rejected a single black candidate. And admissions statistics indicated that among candidates with indexes between 189 and 192, 6 percent of the more than 500 white applicants were admitted while 89 percent of the 23 Mexican-American applicants and all 4 black applicants were admitted.

"Six percent versus 100 percent shows that you're giving quite a bit of weight to race," said Michael Rosman, a lawyer for the Center for Individual Rights in Washington, a public interest firm that represents clients in First Amendment and civil rights cases. The center devised much of the plaintiffs' legal strategy and drafted most of the briefs in the Hopwood case.

The university maintains that the national pool of minority candidates able to compete on an equal basis with whites is so small that, if affirmative action were abandoned, the law school would revert almost to the kind of all-white institution it was in the days of Jim Crow. And in the entering class of 1992, they noted, there were 41 blacks and 55 Mexican-Americans.

"Are there white applicants who were not admitted who would have gotten in if they had been black?" asked Samuel Issacharoff, a law professor at the school and member of the legal team that argued the case. "The answer is clearly yes. That's the nature of a racial preference."

But, he said, while affirmative action is not "cost free," it is an essential tool to enable minorities to overcome a legacy of past discrimination.

Minority students who testified in the university's behalf agreed that if there were no serious effort to recruit blacks and Mexican-Americans, they would probably have gone to law school elsewhere.

As for Ms. Hopwood, the university's lawyers said that her studies at a university with generally low academic standards counted against her and could have explained her rejection just as much as her race.

But in a trial involving few disputes over facts, Ms. Hopwood's educational credentials may be relatively unimportant. Indeed, the case seems to come down to a value judgment about what price it is fair and legal to ask whites to pay to provide opportunities previously denied nonwhites. "The law school has never denied that there are costs to affirmative action," said Barry D. Burgdorf, a lawyer for the university. "Hopwood is a cost. But the Supreme Court has said several times that you can have innocent victims to get the benefit."

My Equal Opportunity, Your Free Lunch
David K. Shipler

Tormented by their white classmates, Hispanic students at a leading law school needed reassurance. They were being told that they didn't deserve to be there because they had scored lower than whites on the Law School Admission Test. And they wanted this smear refuted.

"I tried to be very candid with them," the law school's dean later recalled. It was true, he told them: their scores on the L.S.A.T., the standard benchmark for admission, were somewhat lower. But if they worked extremely hard, he said, they could make up for "differences in past credentials."

An awful silence descended. "I just looked into their eyes as I was talking," the dean remembers, "and I thought, 'I can't bear this; it's too painful.' Their hopes and expectations about what would be said were defeated. There was just a feeling of betrayal."

The incident illustrates the discomfort and denial affirmative action arouses in a society that champions the boundless potential of individual merit. Neither benefactors nor beneficiaries like to reveal the compromises that sometimes are made to bring more minorities into universities and workplaces. But the defenders had better start talking plainly if they want to save the system, in one form or another, from the gathering storm of outrage that is about to be harnessed by conservative Republicans.

Some rough political choices lie ahead. Should affirmative action be retained? Should preference

Looking at Class-Based Results

One alternative to affirmative action would use selection criteria modified on the basis of income and parent's education rather than race.

There is a direct correlation between income levels and scores . . .
S.A.T. scores by parents' income level in 1994. All scores out of 800 possible.

	Verbal	Math
Less than $10,000	350 points	416
$10,000 to $20,000	377	435
$20,000 to $30,000	402	454
$30,000 to $40,000	416	469
$40,000 to $50,000	429	482
$50,000 to $60,000	437	492
$60,000 to $70,000	446	502
$70,000 or more	469	531

SOURCE: The College Board

be given to people on the basis of income rather than race? Should the system be—and can it be—scrapped altogether?

How It All Began

Three decades ago, the phrase affirmative action was coined as a catch-all for racial preference programs and goals—but not rigid quotas, which courts rarely permit. The efforts have produced a legacy of tangible successes and poisonous resentments, a revolution in recruiting and hiring alongside the deepening decay of poverty.

Affirmative action has never sat well with most white Americans. Last year, only 16 percent endorsed preferences for blacks in hiring and promotion, according to a survey by the National Opinion Research Center at the University of Chicago. To the majority, affirmative action has gone too far for too long. It is ideologically repulsive, because it vitiates the myth that this country's bounty is open to anyone who has brains and works hard. How much more satisfying it would be to decide that remedial measures are no longer needed.

That appeal has already emerged as the Republicans' approach during the build-up to the 1996 elections. What looms is likely to be a coarse campaign of sloganeering that could heighten tensions along the lines of class and race. Its outcome will shape a vital dimension of the country's future by maintaining, revising or eventually eliminating institutional preferences for minorities and women.

Since affirmative action programs are supposed to be temporary remedies, the question is how much longer the country will have to take this unpleasant medicine. To anyone who wants to see women and minorities participate fully in this society, the answer seems to be that more patience is required.

Habits of interaction between sexes and races die with difficulty. Patterns of discrimination and economic disadvantage can leave deep and lasting scars on a person's "credentials." These sometimes fade after a generation, and often they do not; it is still too early to see how well the children of those who were first helped less than a generation ago will do in adulthood.

That is why the most perceptive companies and colleges look past test scores for qualities missed by conventional measurements—a fact they often fudge to avoid labeling ethnic or racial groups in a way that would undermine self-esteem and reinforce the majority's resentments.

They have a point. But self-doubts among minorities, and prejudices against them, did not begin with affirmative action. Nor are they abated by euphemism and evasion.

Making Allowances

Every statistic that is ferreted out can be turned into a weapon. Universities, well aware of this, do not publicize their students' test scores by race. But some admissions officers acknowledge that they make allowances for lower scores among blacks and Hispanic students and, at some colleges, for low-income whites.

"It would be naive to have a single standard to apply to all groups if, on a national level, you know that the test operates differently," said Karl M. Furstenberg, Dean of Admissions at Dartmouth. "We make decisions on individuals, not on groups. But we know about these national patterns, so when you read individual applications you recalibrate the criteria."

The rationale of affirmative action lies in the recognition that even if discrimination is eliminated, the handicaps of poor schooling and impoverished family life remain severe obstacles; color-blindness in choosing applicants is not enough. So, in the words of one Federal regulation, the institution "must take affirmative action to overcome the effects of prior discrimination." This means seeking the best candidates from excluded groups even if their qualifications on paper don't always match those of white men.

White males have long benefited from unstated preferences as fraternity brothers, golfing buddies, children of alumni and the like—unconscious biases that go largely unrecognized until affirmative action forces recruiters to think about how they gravitate to people like themselves. Changing or eliminating those preferences breeds backlash. Polls show most Americans believe less qualified blacks get hired or promoted over whites, though few seem to know whites who are victims of reverse discrimination.

"Blacks are such a small fraction of the population that the lost opportunities to white men are really minuscule," said Barbara R. Bergmann, an economics professor at the American University in Washington.

One strategy that may gain ground would shift affirmative action to target class, or, more precisely, income.

The most critical gateway at which racial preferences can make a difference may be entry to college, where many blacks realize middle-class aspirations. Even while most low-income blacks have been left untouched by affirmative action, the small percentage who are attractive to good colleges are wooed and financed, and later sought by graduate schools and corporations.

For years, such elite colleges as Dartmouth, Harvard and the Massachusetts Institute of Technology have mixed race and class to give low-income white youngsters admission preferences similar to those for minorities. But with Federal scholarships cut, some other schools are taking the opposite tack, satisfying affirmative-action goals with middle-class blacks and selecting other students who can pay. Fewer than 10 percent of last fall's college freshmen came from families with incomes under $20,000.

If income replaced race entirely as a qualifier for preferences, whites would be the major beneficiaries, and racial integration would probably decline.

Of the 14.6 million poor Americans under the age of 18, fully 61 percent are white. And since whites tend to outscore blacks and Hispanic students on the standard admissions test even where their family incomes are the same, many middle-class black and Hispanic students would continue to need preferential treatment to make up the gap.

Within each racial and ethnic group, average Scholastic Aptitude Test[1] scores increase as income rises, from a mean total of 766 out of 1,600 for those from families earning under $10,000 a year, to a score of 1000 in the bracket over $70,000. Consequently, economic disadvantage becomes a factor in assessing scores. If two applicants have the same grades and scores, but one is wealthy and the other poor, "I would argue that they're not performing equally," said Mr. Furstenberg, the Dartmouth dean. The low-income student's scores may "represent a greater achievement," he said.

Marlyn McGrath Lewis, director of admissions for Harvard and Radcliffe, said: "We have particular interest in students from a modest background. Coupled with high achievement and a high ambition level and energy, a background that's modest can really be a help. We know that's the best investment we can make: a kid who's hungry."

Although College Board achievement and S.A.T. scores are good predictors of freshman grades, she said, they become less reliable later. Furthermore, a study of three classes of Harvard alumni over three decades found a high correlation between "success"—defined by income, community involvement and professional satisfaction—and two criteria that might not ordinarily be associated with Harvard freshmen: low S.A.T. scores and a blue-collar background.

Doing Without

Without affirmative action, many institutions would resegregate. A Federal judge in Texas ruled as much last August in upholding the University of Texas Law School's program. The mean L.S.A.T. score of all 500 students entering the school in 1992 was 162 (on a scale from 120 to 200), putting them at the 89th percentile; the mean for blacks was 158, at the 78th percentile.[2]

The law school argued that if only grades and test scores had been considered, the class would have had only 9 blacks instead of 41, and 18 Mexican-Americans instead of 55, which Judge Sam Sparks ruled would have been tokenism.

"Until society sufficiently overcomes the effects of pervasive racism," he wrote, "affirmative action is necessary."

The four rejected white applicants who brought the suit have appealed.

The structure of affirmative action has been built by decisions of all three branches of government. Therefore, not all preferences for minorities and women are susceptible to change by Presidential order or even by Congress. They are supported not only by intricate Federal laws and regulations, but also by court interpretations of the Fourteenth Amendment's equal protection clause and by institutional self-interest that has gone beyond original legal mandates.

In some quarters, affirmative action has been driven by pragmatism. Without a draft, for example, the military wants to tap the full reservoir of a work force in which the percentage of whites is declining. Colleges often want diverse student bodies not only to forestall discrimination lawsuits but also to enrich the educational experience.

"The curriculum has been forced to respond in a way that's more truthful and inclusive," said Mary M. Childers, Dartmouth's Director of Affirmative Action. "The social life of students is richer and more heterogeneous and conflict-ridden in a way that prepares them for the actual world out there."

The gap between mean S.A.T. scores for blacks and whites is narrowing, but it is still large. Last year, the mean totaled 938 for whites and 740 for blacks. This reinforces the determination of many admissions officers to avoid reducing people to test score results.

"Intellectual talent and other forms of human talent exist in all segments of the population," said Mr. Furstenberg of Dartmouth. "What we're trying to do is find the greatest talent."

Designing that search is also the nation's task.

Notes

1. *Editor's Note*: This article refers incorrectly to the standardized test given for college admissions. It is called the "Scholastic *Assessment* Test," not the "Scholastic *Achievement* Test."

2. *Editor's Note*: *The New York Times* later corrected the figures originally given for the range of scores on the standardized test for law school applicants. It is 120 to 180, not 120 to 200 as reported in the original article.

27.

Cheryl Hopwood et al. v. State of Texas (1996)

United States Court of Appeals, Fifth Circuit

Editor's Note: On March 18, 1996 the United States Court of Appeals for the Fifth Circuit (which covers Texas, Mississippi, and Louisiana) ruled in *Hopwood v. Texas* that the University of Texas Law School "may not use race as a factor in law school admissions." The State of Texas appealed to the Supreme Court which announced on July 1st of that year that it would *not* hear an appeal to the Hopwood decision.

OPINION: JERRY E. SMITH, CIRCUIT JUDGE:

With the best of intentions, in order to increase the enrollment of certain favored classes of minority students, the University of Texas School of Law... discriminates in favor of those applicants by giving substantial racial preferences ... [to] blacks and Mexican Americans, to the detriment of whites and non-preferred minorities. The question we decide today... is whether the Fourteenth Amendment permits the school to discriminate in this way.

We hold that it does not. The law school has presented no compelling justification, under the Fourteenth Amendment or Supreme Court precedent, that allows it to continue to elevate some races over others, even for the wholesome purpose of correcting perceived racial imbalance in the student body. "Racial preferences appear to 'even the score'... only if one embraces the proposition that our society is appropriately viewed as divided into races, making it right that an injustice rendered in the past to a black man should be compensated for by discriminating against a white." *City of Richmond v. J.A. Croson Co.*, (1989) (Scalia, J., concurring in the judgment).

*   *   *   *   *

The University of Texas School of Law is one of the nation's leading law schools, consistently ranking in the top twenty.... Accordingly, admission to the law school is fiercely competitive, with over 4,000 applicants a year competing to be among the approximately 900 offered admission to achieve an entering class of about 500 students....

Numbers are therefore paramount for admission. In the early 1990s, the law school largely based its initial admissions decisions upon an applicant's so-called Texas Index ("TI") number, a composite of undergraduate grade point average ("GPA") and Law School Aptitude Test ("LSAT") score. The law school used this number as a matter of administrative convenience in order to rank candidates and to predict, roughly, one's probability of success in law school....

Of course, the law school did not rely upon numbers alone. The admissions office necessarily exercised judgment in interpreting the individual scores of applicants, taking into consideration factors such as the strength of a student's undergraduate education, the difficulty of his major, and significant trends in his own grades and the undergraduate grades at his respective college (such as grade inflation)....

... For the class entering in 1992..., the law school placed the typical applicant in one of three categories according to his TI score: "presumptive admit," "presumptive deny," or a middle "discretionary zone." An applicant's TI category determined how extensive a review his application would receive.

Most, but not all, applicants in the presumptive admit category received offers of admission with little review.... [O]nly five to ten percent [were changed] to the discretionary zone because of weaknesses in their applications, generally a non-competitive major or a weak undergraduate education.

Applicants in the presumptive denial category also received little consideration....

Applications in the middle range were subjected to the most extensive scrutiny. . . .

Blacks and Mexican Americans were treated differently from other candidates, however. First, compared to whites and non-preferred minorities, the TI ranges that were used to place them into the three admissions categories were lowered to allow the law school to consider and admit more of them. . . . [T]he presumptive TI admission score for resident whites and non-preferred minorities was 199. Mexican American and blacks needed a TI of only 189 to be presumptively admitted. The difference in the presumptive-deny ranges is even more striking. The presumptive denial score for "non-minorities" was 192; the same score for blacks and Mexican Americans was 179.

. . . According to the law school, 1,992 resident white applicants had a mean GPA of 3.53 and an LSAT of 164. Mexican Americans scored 3.27 and 158; blacks scored 3.25 and 157. . . .

These disparate standards greatly affected a candidate's chance of admission. . . . Out of the pool of resident applicants who fell within this range (189–192 inclusive), 100% of blacks and 90% of Mexican Americans, but only 6% of whites, were offered admission.

The stated purpose of this lowering of standards was to meet an "aspiration" of admitting a class consisting of 10% Mexican Americans and 5% blacks, proportions roughly comparable to the percentages of those races graduating from Texas colleges. . . .

* * * * *

Cheryl Hopwood, Douglas Carvell, Kenneth Elliott, and David Rogers (the "plaintiffs") applied for admission to the 1992 entering law school class. All four were white residents of Texas and were rejected.

The plaintiffs were considered as discretionary zone candidates. Hopwood, worth a GPA of 3.8 and an LSAT of 39 (equivalent to a three-digit LSAT of 160), had a TI of 199, a score barely within the presumptive-admit category for resident whites, which was 199 and up. She was dropped into the discretionary zone

for resident whites (193 to 198), however, because . . . [it was] decided her educational background overstated the strength of her GPA. . . .

* * * * *

The central purpose of the Equal Protection Clause "is to prevent the States from purposefully discriminating between individuals on the basis of race." It seeks ultimately to render the issue of race irrelevant in governmental decision making. ("A core purpose of the Fourteenth Amendment was to do away with all governmentally imposed discrimination.") . . .

Accordingly, discrimination based upon race is highly suspect. "Distinctions between citizens solely because of their ancestry are by their very nature odious to a free people whose institutions are founded upon the doctrine of equality," and "racial discriminations are in most circumstances irrelevant and therefore prohibited. . . ." *Hirabayashi v. United States*, 320 U. S. 81, 100 (1943). Hence, "preferring members of any one group for no reason other than race or ethnic origin is discrimination for its own sake. This the Constitution forbids." *Regents of Univ. of Cal. v. Bakke*, 438 U.S. 265, 307 (1978) (opinion of Powell, J.); see also *Loving v. Virginia*, 388 U.S. 1, 11 (1967); *Brown v. Board of Educ.*, 347 U.S. 483, 493–94 (1954). These equal protection maxims apply to all races. *Adarand Constructors v. Pena*, 115 S. Ct. 2097, 2111 (1995).

In order to preserve these principles, the Supreme Court recently has required that any governmental action that expressly distinguishes between persons on the basis of race be held to the most exacting scrutiny. Furthermore, there is now absolutely no doubt that courts are to employ strict scrutiny when evaluating all racial classifications, including those characterized by their proponents as "benign" or "remedial."

Strict scrutiny is necessary because the mere labeling of a classification by the government as "benign" or "remedial" is meaningless. As Justice O'Connor indicated in *Croson*:

> Absent searching judicial inquiry into the justifications for such race-based measures, there is simply no way of determining what

classifications are "benign" or "remedial" and what classifications are in fact motivated by illegitimate notions of racial inferiority or simple racial politics. Indeed, the purpose of strict scrutiny is to "smoke out" illegitimate uses of race by assuring that the legislative body is pursuing a goal important enough to warrant use of a highly suspect tool. The test also ensures that the means chosen "fit" this compelling goal so closely that there is little or no possibility that the motive for the classification was illegitimate racial prejudice or stereotype. (plurality opinion).

* * * * *

. . . [W]hen evaluating the proffered governmental interest for the specific racial classification, to decide whether the program in question narrowly achieves that interest, we must recognize that "the rights created by . . . the Fourteenth Amendment are, by its terms, guaranteed to the individual. The rights established are personal rights." Thus, the Court consistently has rejected arguments conferring benefits on a person based solely upon his membership in a specific class of persons.

* * * * *

Justice Powell's separate opinion in *Bakke* provided the original impetus for recognizing diversity as a compelling state interest in higher education. In that case, Allan Bakke, a white male, was denied admission to the Medical School of the University of California at Davis, a state-run institution. . . .

Under the medical school's admissions system, the white applicants, who comprised the majority of the prospective students, applied through the general admissions program. A special admissions program was reserved for members of "minority groups" or groups designated as "economically and/or educationally disadvantaged." The university set aside sixteen of the one hundred positions in the entering class for candidates from the special program.

The California Supreme Court struck down the program on equal protection grounds. . . . The United States Supreme Court affirmed in part and reversed in part in an opinion announced by Justice Powell. 438 U.S. at 271–72 (opinion of Powell, J.). The Court reached no consensus on a justification for its result, however. Six Justices filed opinions, none of which garnered more that four votes (including the writer's). The two major opinions one four-Justice opinion by Justices Brennan, White, Marshall, and Blackmun and one by Justice Stevens in which Chief Justice Burger and Justices Stewart and Rehnquist joined reflected completely contrary views of the law.

While Justice Powell found the program unconstitutional under the Equal Protection Clause and affirmed Bakke's admission, Justice Stevens declined to reach the constitutional issue and upheld Bakke's admission under Title VI. Justice Powell also concluded that the California Supreme Court's proscription of the consideration of race in admissions could not be sustained. This became the judgment of the Court, as the four-Justice opinion by Justice Brennan opined that racial classifications designed to serve remedial purposes should receive only intermediate scrutiny. These Justices would have upheld the admissions program under this intermediate scrutiny, as it served the substantial and benign purpose of remedying past societal discrimination.

Hence, Justice Powell's opinion has appeared to represent the "swing vote," and though, in significant part, it was joined by no other Justice, it has played a prominent role in subsequent debates concerning the impact of *Bakke*. . . .

* * * * *

Here, the plaintiffs argue that diversity is not a compelling governmental interest under superseding Supreme Court precedent. Instead, they believe that the Court finally has recognized that only the remedial use [*i.e.*, when there is evidence of past discrimination] of race is compelling. . . .

We agree with the plaintiffs that any consideration of race or ethnicity by the law school for the purpose of achieving a diverse student body is not a compelling interest under the Fourteenth Amendment. Justice Powell's argument in *Bakke* garnered only his own vote and has never represented the view of a majority of the Court in Bakke or any other case. Moreover, subsequent Supreme Court decisions regarding education state that non-remedial state interests will never justify racial classifications. Finally, the classification of persons on the basis of race for the purpose of diversity frustrates, rather than facilitates, the goals of equal protection.

* * * * *

Justice O'Connor . . . , in her . . . dissent in *Metro Broadcasting*, joined by Justices Rehnquist, Scalia, and Kennedy, explained this position:

> [the Court] has recognized only one [compelling state] interest: remedying the effects of racial discrimination. The interest in increasing the diversity of broadcast viewpoints is clearly not a compelling interest. It is simply too amorphous, too insubstantial, and too unrelated to any legitimate basis for employing racial classifications.

* * * * *

In short, there has been no indication from the Supreme Court, other than Justice Powell's lonely opinion in *Bakke*, that the state's interest in diversity constitutes a compelling justification for governmental race-based discrimination. Subsequent Supreme Court case law strongly suggests, in fact, that it is not.

Within the general principles of the Fourteenth Amendment, the use of race in admissions for diversity in higher education, contradicts, rather than furthers, the aims of equal protection. Diversity fosters, rather than minimizes, the use of race. It treats minorities as a group, rather than as individuals. It may further remedial purposes but, just as likely, may promote improper racial stereotypes, thus fueling racial hostility.

* * * * *

While the use of race *per se* is proscribed, state-supported schools may reasonably consider a host of factors—some of which may have some correlation with race—in making admissions decisions. The federal courts have no warrant to intrude on those executive and legislative judgments unless the distinctions intrude on specific provisions of federal law or the Constitution. A university may properly favor one applicant over another because of his ability to play the cello, make a downfield tackle, or understand chaos theory. An admissions process may also consider an applicant's home state or relationship to school alumni. Law schools specifically may look at things such as unusual or substantial extracurricular activities in college, which may be atypical factors affecting undergraduate grades. Schools may even consider factors such as whether an applicant's parents attended college or the applicant's economic and social background.

* * * * *

We now turn to the district court's determination that "the remedial purpose of the law school's affirmative action program is a compelling government objective." The plaintiffs argue that the court erred by finding that the law school could employ racial criteria to remedy the present effects of past discrimination in Texas's primary and secondary schools. The plaintiffs contend that the proper unit for analysis is the law school, and the state has shown no recognizable present effects of the law school's past discrimination. The law school, in response, notes Texas's well-documented history of discrimination in education and argues that its effects continue today at the law school, both in the level of educational attainment of the average minority applicant and in the school's reputation.

In contrast to its approach to the diversity rationale, a majority of the Supreme Court has held that a state actor may racially classify where it has a "strong basis in the evidence for its conclusion that remedial action was necessary." *Croson*, 488 U.S. at 500. . . .

* * * * *

. . . [O]ne cannot conclude that the law school's past discrimination has created any current hostile environment for minorities. While the school once did practice *de jure* discrimination in denying admission to blacks, the Court in *Sweatt v. Painter*, 339 U.S. 629 (1950), struck down the law school's program. Any other discrimination by the law school ended in the 1960s. *Hopwood*, 861 F. Supp. at 555.

By the late 1960s, the school had implemented its first program designed to recruit minorities, and it now engages in an extensive minority recruiting program that includes a significant amount of scholarship money. The vast majority of the faculty, staff, and students at the law school had absolutely nothing to do with any discrimination that the law school practiced in the past.

In such a case, one cannot conclude that a hostile environment is the present effect of past discrimination. Any racial tension at the law school is most certainly the result of present societal discrimination and, if anything, is contributed to, rather than alleviated by, the overt and prevalent consideration of race in admissions.

*   *   *   *   *

In sum, the law school has failed to show a compelling state interest in remedying the present effects of past discrimination sufficient to maintain the use of race in its admissions system. Accordingly, it is unnecessary for us to examine the district's determination that the law school's admissions program was not narrowly tailored to meet the compelling interests that the district court erroneously perceived.

*   *   *   *   *

In summary, we hold that the University of Texas School of Law may not use race as a factor in deciding which applicants to admit in order to achieve a diverse student body, to combat the perceived effects of a hostile environment at the law school, to alleviate the law school's poor reputation in the minority community, or to eliminate any present effects of past discrimination by actors other than the law school. Because the law school has proffered these justifications for its use of race in admissions, the plaintiffs have satisfied their burden of showing that they were scrutinized under an unconstitutional admissions system. The plaintiffs are entitled to reapply under an admissions system that invokes none of these serious constitutional infirmities. . . .

WIENER, CIRCUIT JUDGE, SPECIALLY CONCURRING:

"We judge best when we judge least, particularly in controversial matters of high public interest." In this and every other appeal, we should decide only the case before us, and should do so on the narrowest possible basis. Mindful of this credo, I concur in part and, with respect, specially concur in part.

The sole substantive issue in this appeal is whether the admissions process employed by the law school for 1992 meets muster under the Equal Protection Clause of the Fourteenth Amendment. The law school offers alternative justifications for its race-based admissions process, each of which, it insists, is a compelling interest: (1) remedying the present effects of past discrimination (present effects) and (2) providing the educational benefits that can be obtained only when the student body is diverse (diversity). As to present effects, I concur in the panel opinion's analysis: Irrespective of whether the law school or the University of Texas system as a whole is deemed the relevant governmental unit to be tested, neither has established the existence of present effects of past discrimination sufficient to justify the use of a racial classification. As to diversity, however, I respectfully disagree with the panel opinion's conclusion that diversity can never be a compelling governmental interest in a public graduate school. Rather than attempt to decide that issue, I would take a considerably narrower path—and, I believe, a more appropriate one—to reach an equally narrow result: I would assume *arguendo* that diversity can be a compelling interest but conclude that the admissions process here under scrutiny was not narrowly tailored to achieve diversity.

*   *   *   *   *

In this light, the limited racial effects of the law school's preferential admissions process, targeting exclusively blacks and Mexican Americans, more closely resembles a set aside or quota system for those two disadvantaged minorities than it does an academic admissions program narrowly tailored to achieve true diversity. I concede that the law school's 1992 admissions process would increase the percentages of black

faces and brown faces in that year's entering class. But facial diversity is not true diversity, and a system thus conceived and implemented simply is not narrowly tailored to achieve diversity.

* * * * *

The [Hopwood] Decision Is Flatly, Unequivocally Wrong

Michael A. Olivas

It is 1978, and I am in my constitutional-law class at Georgetown University Law Center, where I am a night student, struggling to understand the mysteries of equal protection and the Fourteenth Amendment. The march through the syllabus comes to a screeching halt when my professor comes into class bearing a photocopy of a Supreme Court opinion, *Regents of the University of California v. Allan Bakke*. My professor says, in an awestruck voice, "Affirmative action as we know it is over. They admitted Bakke."

Now it is nearly 20 years later, and last week my phone explodes. Reporters are hounding me for a quick analysis of *Hopwood* v. *Texas*, a case just decided by the U.S. Court of Appeals for the Fifth Circuit. I am rushed, and my computer won't cooperate to pull up the case from its memory banks. Someone is sending me the full, 70-page version by overnight mail, but until I see it I can just listen, incredulously, as reporters read excerpts to me. One reporter—from Fort Worth, I believe—asks, "Professor, is it the end of affirmative action? Did they admit Hopwood?"

Well, no and no, but I'm still sick at heart. Who knew in 1978 that we were at the high point of affirmative action, that its wave had crested, that the *Bakke* decision is what we must fight to protect nearly 20 years later?

The decision by the three-judge panel in *Hopwood* v. *Texas*, a lawsuit filed by four white students who had been refused admission to the University

of Texas Law School in 1992, is both more and less than the decision in *Regents* v. *Bakke*. It is more harsh and unyielding in its analysis and result than was *Bakke*, which I teach each spring in my education-law course. But it is also less compelling and intuitive than Justice Lewis F. Powell's carefully crafted and nuanced plurality opinion, which struck down the use of quotas and set-asides for minority-group students but upheld the use of race as an acceptable criterion in admissions.

While some legal absolutists have lampooned Justice Powell's balancing act, it served a great purpose in reassuring universities that they still had discretion and latitude in choosing from among their many applicants. *Hopwood*, however, is far from nuanced: It is stark, almost Manichaean. To this panel, nearly all is black and white (literally, since the judges also seem to believe that Mexican Americans in Texas never faced any state action to discriminate against them). The judges see the choices as an admissions process based on race or on merit; admission of qualified students or preferential treatment. If not legally sure-footed, the court's world view is asserted with assurance.

In my reading of *Hopwood*, though, the judges do get it wrong, both in legal terms and in the practicalities of the admissions process. Remarkably, two of the three judges attempt to overturn *Bakke,* or to suggest that the Supreme Court has abandoned it. The judges say that the U.T. law school relied too much on Justice Sandra Day O'Connor's opinion in a teacher-layoff case "for the proposition that Justice Powell's *Bakke* formulation is still viable." Elsewhere, they characterize Justice Powell's decision as a "lonely" opinion. Whereas

Michael A. Olivas, "The Decision Is Flatly, Unequivocally Wrong," *The Chronicle of Higher Education* 29 March 1996: B3. Reprinted by permission of the author.

Justice Powell began his *Bakke* opinion by holding that diversity "clearly is a constitutionally permissible goal for an institution of higher education," this panel boldly states that "any consideration of race or ethnicity by the law school for the purpose of achieving a diverse student body is not a compelling interest under the Fourteenth Amendment."

That is flatly, unequivocally wrong. While it is true that in decisions on teacher layoffs and city and federal set-asides for minority businesses, the Supreme Court has trimmed back the reach of affirmative action—striking down federal set-asides unless they are very narrowly drawn and, in general, requiring very exacting tests to justify preference programs—*Bakke* remains the law of the land. For instance, Justice Sandra Day O'Connor wrote in the teacher-layoff case, *Wygant v. Jackson Board of Education*: "Although its precise contours are uncertain, a state interest in the promotion of racial diversity has been found to be sufficiently 'compelling,' at least in the context of higher education, to support the use of racial considerations in furthering that interest."

And in a decision just last June, on set-asides of federal highway funds for minority-owned companies (*Adarand Constructors v. Peña*), Justice O'Connor wrote: "When race-based action is necessary to further a compelling interest, such action is within the constitutional constraints if it satisfies the 'narrow tailoring' test this Court has set out in previous cases." That hardly sounds like the death knell for well-crafted admissions programs.

As this panel misreads *Bakke*, so it misreads the admissions process. Plaintiff Cheryl Hopwood was a single mother with a child born with cerebral palsy. The panel said her "unique background . . . would bring a different perspective to the law school." But when she applied, the law school did not have this information. Incredibly, she provided no letters of recommendation and no personal statement outlining her "unique background." Yet, she is certain she was displaced from her rightful seat in law school by less-qualified minorities. How could the committee have known of her special considerations? Another of the plaintiffs presented a letter of recommendation from a professor who described his academic performance at his

small college, where he graduated 98th in a class of 247, as "uneven, disappointing, and mediocre."

That such students could obtain high scores on an index utilizing only grade-point averages and scores on the Law School Admission Test is a clear indication of why law schools look to features other than mere scores. Any law school would be wary of incomplete applications or ones where letters of recommendation singled out a student for "mediocre" academic achievement.

The white beneficiaries of racial practices often assume that they have reached their station in life on their merits, and that members of minority groups have advanced only through bending of the rules. Critics of affirmative action, and many federal judges, have become convinced that higher scores on tests translate into more-meritorious applications, and that relying on "objective" measures constitutes a fair, race-neutral process. The evidence for this proposition is exceedingly thin; indeed, a substantial body of research and academic common practice refute it.

The heavy reliance on test scores and the near-magical properties accorded them inflate the narrow, modest use to which any standardized scores should be put. Accepted psychometric principles, testing-industry norms of good practice, and research on the efficacy of testing all suggest more modest claims for test scores, standing alone or combined with other measures. Test scores are, at best, imperfect measures that modestly predict first-year grades; first-year grades are only a small part of an aptitude for study of the law.

More important, the same score means different things for different populations. Careful studies of predictive validity consistently show that scores from standardized tests are less predictive of Hispanic students' first-year grade-point averages (both underpredicting and overpredicting) than the scores of Anglo students. If research consistently shows that test scores predict differently and less well for different populations, including men and women, this weakens substantially the claim by affirmative-action critics that the L.S.A.T. or other standardized tests should be given more weight in the admissions process.

The plaintiffs and the Fifth Circuit panel act as though a massive dislocation of deserving whites has occurred because many undeserving students of color have taken whites' rightful places. The data simply contradict this. The number of white law students today is at an all-time high: more than 120,000, or 85 per cent of the total enrollment in the 50 states and the District of Columbia. Blacks constitute just over 6 per cent, and members of other minority groups an even smaller percentage. For Mexican Americans and Puerto Ricans—among the fastest-growing ethnic-minority groups in the country—those enrollment figures represent an actual decline in numbers and in proportion since the early 1980s.

In 1990, white students took 79 percent of all the L.S.A.T. exams given, and 58 per cent of all the whites who applied to law schools were admitted; of all groups, only Asian Americans were admitted at a greater rate (61 per cent). There is no evidence of slippage here, no hint of unfairness. And no law school can afford to admit unqualified students; its spaces are too precious.

Moreover, it was not "lesser qualified" minorities who displaced the *Hopwood* plaintiffs. More whites were taken off the U.T. law school's waiting list in 1992 than the total number of minority-group students enrolled in the law school. Virtually all of the applicants in the pool, and certainly applicants with credentials such as those of the black and Mexican-American students admitted, can succeed at U.T.'s law school.

Admissions programs today at nearly all law schools are more thorough and better administered than at any point in the history of legal education. The sheer crush of applicants—Georgetown receives more than 10,000 applications a year for fewer than 1,000 places—means that admissions officers can choose among many exceptionally qualified people. This is a key point. When they choose among thousands of applicants, all of whom have the credentials to do the work, admissions committees are doing exactly what they are charged to do: They are assembling a qualified, diverse student body. *Bakke* sanctions this, common sense dictates it, and no anecdotal horror stories or isolated allegations can change this central fact.

I urge the U.T. law school to seek review of the *Hopwood* case by the entire Fifth Circuit, especially since the concurring opinion of one of the three judges reads much as my own dissent would read. Failing that, they should seek review by the Supreme Court. The law school will have to read more files in the future, to discover the Cheryl Hopwoods and the Ana Maria Garcias among future applicants. But the effort remains essential, just as it was when *Bakke* was decided in 1978.

Ruling Out Race: A Bold Step to Make Colleges Colorblind

Michael S. Greve

Editor's Note: Michael S. Greve is executive director of the Center for Individual Rights, which, along with Theodore B. Olson and Douglas Cox of Gibson, Dunn, and Crutcher, represented two of the plaintiffs in the *Hopwood* case.

The U.S. Court of Appeals for the Fifth Circuit has struck a powerful blow for a colorblind Constitution. The court held last week that the University of Texas Law School "may not use race as a factor in law school admissions."

In deciding the case known as *Hopwood* v. *State of Texas*, the court rejected the notion that achiev-

ing racial "diversity" in a student body can ever be a sufficiently compelling reason for racial discrimination, and it confined the remedial use of racial preferences to very narrow circumstances. Under the court's reasoning, virtually no state college or university may maintain race-based affirmative-action programs.

The Fifth Circuit's holding is a dramatic victory for the plaintiffs, four white applicants to the University of Texas Law School's 1992 entering class, who claimed that they had been denied admission because of their race. Beyond its immediate results,

---

Michael S. Greve, "Ruling Out Race: A Bold Step to Make Colleges Colorblind," *The Chronicle of Higher Education* 29 March 1996: B2. Copyright (c) 1996 by Michael S. Greve. Reprinted by permission of the author.

the *Hopwood* decision offers the hope that we may, at long last, get beyond divisive racial games.

In 1992, as in preceding and subsequent years, the law school admitted applicants largely (though not exclusively) on the basis of the "Texas Index" or T. I., a weighted combination of an applicant's score on the Law School Admission Test and grade-point average. However, to insure that each entering class had an enrollment that was roughly 5 per cent black and 10 per cent Mexican American, applicants from those two groups were admitted with substantially lower scores than those of other applicants. All of the plaintiffs had T. I. scores that would have guaranteed their admission had they been members of the preferred minority groups.

In August 1994, U.S. District Judge Sam Sparks held that the plaintiffs had been subjected to unconstitutional discrimination on the basis of race. Judge Sparks ruled that the law school's use of a separate subcommittee to screen applications from black and Mexican-American students violated the Constitution. And he suggested that cutoff scores differing by race—which the law school had used to classify applicants within each racial group as "presumptive admits," "presumptive denials," or "discretionary admits"—were also unconstitutional. However, he upheld the use of racial "goals" and preferences in the admission process, and he denied the plaintiffs meaningful relief.

The Fifth Circuit now has reversed Judge Sparks on both points: It has forbidden the use of race in student admissions and has held that the plaintiffs may be entitled to compensatory damages. And while the three-judge panel declined to issue an injunction ordering the law school to admit the plaintiffs, the judges made plain that they expected the law school to comply with the principles laid out in their opinion. Should the school fail to do so, the court remarked, an injunction and, possibly, punitive damages would be appropriate.

The *Hopwood* decision strikes not merely at the scope of race-based affirmative action or at the techniques used in the process, but, more broadly, at the two presumed state interests on which affirmative action has been based—remedying historical discrimination and "diversity."

Under long-established and unquestioned precedent, a law school or other government agency may use narrowly tailored, race-conscious remedies to redress the effects of its past discrimination. But the Fifth Circuit helpfully clarified that the law school could remedy only the effects of its own discrimination, not that of the university at large or, as the defendants had maintained, of the entire Texas education system. (Otherwise, any state agency could embark upon boundless, timeless preference schemes under the pretense of remedying discrimination elsewhere in the system.) Although unexceptional from a legal standpoint, this holding means that state colleges and universities—just about all of which ceased discriminating against minorities decades ago—no longer will be able to use past discrimination as a basis for racial preferences.

Of even greater practical importance is the Fifth Circuit's holding that consideration of race or ethnicity "for the purpose of achieving a diverse student body is not a compelling interest under the Fourteenth Amendment." That amendment guarantees all citizens equal protection of the laws. In the 1978 Supreme Court decision, *Regents of the University of California* v. *Allan Bakke*, Justice Lewis F. Powell said the interests of "diversity" justified the use of mild racial preferences or "plus" factors (though not quotas). But as the Fifth Circuit observed, this position was not adopted by any other Justice in deciding *Bakke* and has "never represented the view of a majority of the Court in *Bakke* or any other case."

This is hardly a novel or shocking insight. Several Supreme Court cases—from the 1989 decision in *City of Richmond* v. *J. A. Croson* (which restricted cities' ability to funnel a portion of their contracts to minority-owned companies) to last year's decision in *Adarand Constructors* v. *Pena* (which subjected federal set-aside programs to strict judicial scrutiny)—have either said or plainly implied that remedying past discrimination was the only constitutionally permissible rationale for racial preferences. The Fifth Circuit's *Hopwood* opinion simply explains this position, albeit in a particularly clear and lucid form.

The education establishment's jeremiads notwithstanding, *Hopwood* does not mean that universities must now admit students by test scores alone, or that they must ignore diversity, properly understood. The Fifth Circuit indicated that colleges may use qualitative admission criteria and even criteria that correlate with race—"such as whether an applicant's parents attended college or the applicant's economic and social background"—provided they do not do so because of race or in a racially discriminatory manner. And colleges may still select students with an eye toward insuring, for instance, a diversity of viewpoints on campus. It is only the use of race (per se or as a proxy for other characteristics) that is forbidden.

And the reason why it is forbidden, the Fifth Circuit explained, is that "the classification of persons on the basis of race for the purpose of diversity frustrates, rather than facilitates, the goals of equal protection," which is to get the government out of the business of classifying its citizens by race.

The significance of this holding lies in its realization that we cannot get beyond race by constantly taking it into account, and also in its long-overdue acknowledgment that there is no middle ground between the constitutional command of colorblindness on one hand and quota games on the other. Justice Powell's lone *Bakke* opinion—quotas, no, mild race preferences, yes—was an attempt to find such middle ground. But college officials across the country concluded from the opinion that quotas are okay, so long as you disguise them: They made race enough of a "plus" to reach predetermined racial percentages—even if the "plus" was so large as to swamp all other considerations in the admissions process.

At U. T.'s law school, the "presumptive admit" scores on the Texas Index for blacks and Mexican Americans were substantially lower than the "presumptive deny" scores for all other applicants. This meant that applicants with identical qualifications were automatically rejected or accepted depending on their race alone. The fact that the law school had ended the use of a separate minority-admissions committee and the use of racially separate cutoff scores at the time of the district court's ruling in *Hopwood* made no material difference.

Those changes merely meant that the law school was reaching its minority-enrollment "goals" without physically separating applicants' files. As long as race is allowed to enter into the admissions process in any form, there is practically no way to prevent institutions from playing a "diversity" shell game.

After *Hopwood*, the game is up—not simply at U. T.'s law school, but across the country. Technically, of course, the opinion binds only educational institutions in the Fifth Circuit (which covers Texas, Mississippi, and Louisiana), and the defendants may yet persuade the Supreme Court to hear the case. But the message of *Hopwood* is unequivocal, and its interpretation of the applicable Supreme Court decisions is highly persuasive.

No doubt, college and university administrators and "civil rights" advocates will sound dire warnings—as U. T.'s law school did throughout the *Hopwood* litigation—that the demise of de facto quotas for blacks and Mexican Americans means "resegregation" and "lily-white schools" (members of other minority groups, such as Asians and non-Mexican Hispanics, evidently count as "lily white"). But this inflammatory talk—a discredited establishment's last stand in defense of a morally bankrupt affirmative-action regime—is unlikely to resonate in the courts or among voters.

Hopwood is of one piece with the Supreme Court's *Adarand* decision and appellate cases such as *Podberesky* v. *Kirwan*, in which the Fourth Circuit declared the University of Maryland's race-based scholarships unconstitutional. And, come November, the voters of California are likely to approve the California Civil Rights Initiative, which will commit the state's government to colorblindness in contracting, employment, and education.

In short, the broad trend toward official colorblindness is unmistakable. To be sure, racial quotas and preferences are supported by powerful, entrenched interests; they and self-righteous college officials and lawyers may decide to meet *Hopwood* with massive resistance. But the Fifth Circuit's decision offers plaintiffs who believe that they have suffered reverse discrimination a clean shot at discriminatory admissions policies, as well as the prospect of meaningful remedies if they are found to have suffered discrimination. Many more plaintiffs such as those in *Hopwood* now will come forward.

In decency and fairness, universities should ask themselves what can be gained from forcing college applicants, who are young only once, to dismantle the invidious edifice of quotas—one lawsuit, one institution at a time.

Myths About Minorities

Mari J. Matsuda and Charles R. Lawrence III

The United States Court of Appeals for the Fifth Circuit recently ruled that the affirmative action program at the University of Texas Law School was unconstitutional. The court's decision drastically limits affirmative action at public universities within the Fifth Circuit's jurisdiction and if sustained could sound the death knell for affirmative action programs across the country.

This is how the Fifth Circuit panel opens its opinion: "In order to increase the enrollment of certain favored classes of minority students, the University of Texas School of Law discriminates in favor of those applicants by giving substantial racial preferences in its admissions program. The beneficiaries of this system are black and Mexican-Americans, to the detriment of whites and nonpreferred minorities."

There are several myths embedded in this statement. The first is that beneficiaries of affirmative action are a "favored class." In fact, schools like the University of Texas instituted affirmative action precisely because blacks and Mexican-Americans are disadvantaged. For instance, a series of Federal court cases has found long-standing discrimination against blacks and Mexican-Americans in elementary and secondary schools. The vast majority of public schools remain segregated, and about 40 percent of black and Hispanic children live in poverty compared with just 19 percent of white children. The term "favored minority" erases these grim statistics. It is as though the best thing to be, now, in Texas, is a member of one of these two groups.

The court also uses the word "discriminates," borrowing from the power that word attained in earlier civil rights cases. This is the myth of reverse discrimination. A university that seeks to admit a diverse student body is not discriminating in the same way that the universities did during Jim Crow days. But the court equates the two and buries the larger truth: Racial discrimination is prevalent in spite of our legal prohibitions. An at-tempt to remedy the effects of past and continuing discrimination against nonwhites is not equal to putting up "whites only" signs.

The next rhetorical myth the court invokes is "racial preference." When Americans are asked their opinion of "racial preferences," not surprisingly most say they are against preferences. But this term paints a false picture of affirmative action. Like all good law schools, the one at the University of Texas selected individuals from a large pool of qualified applicants. No law school relies on grades and test scores alone to do this, just as no smart consumer looking for a good lawyer would. For a number of reasons—including the need to redress past discrimination and the need for diversity—law schools look beyond the numbers.

The finest universities in the country are the most diverse. Contrary to the myth that diversity "softens" standards—another word used in the Fifth Circuit's opinion—institutions like the University of California at Berkeley found that their standards went up as they became more diverse.

The final and most damaging myth is in the court's phrase: "to the detriment of whites and other minorities." The belief is that affirmative action takes from one and gives to an unqualified other and that no white people benefit from diversity. Yet the talents and abilities that it takes to negotiate an increasingly complex world are not one-dimensional. Interaction with different cultures, belief systems and presumptions helps make us smarter. Creative intelligence challenges existing premises. This kind of critical thought is what we teach in universities. We teach it best when the classroom is rich with diversity, not impoverished by it as the Fifth Circuit presumes.

In a state with a long history of subjugating blacks and Mexicans, there is reason to be concerned that these groups have a fair chance at access to legal education. Whether the University of Texas chose the most effective means of attaining that goal is unclear, but the court's choice of language perpetuates the myth that there is nothing for "the rest of us" to gain by attempting to remedy the most egregious exclusions.

6

College Speech Codes

WORDS THAT WOUND

"Sticks and stones may break my bones, but names will never hurt me." Grade-school students have often been taught to recite this refrain when they suffer name-calling and other verbal insults on the playground or in school bathrooms and corridors. Many adults can recall childhood experiences involving cruel taunts, vicious barbs, and painful verbal jabs. Parents and school authorities urged us to ignore these verbal affronts, which, it was suggested, couldn't cause "real" harm, as could physical assaults. The simple refrain was offered over and over again as a self-evident truth. And yet I suspect that many of us harbored lingering doubts as to its truth, especially in light of the deep and lasting pain caused by other children's mean-spirited remarks, and the relative impermanence of bruises and broken bones long since healed.[1]

SPEECH CODES ON COLLEGE CAMPUSES

Although many associate disparaging and hurtful name-calling with elementary school, for some, the experience continues when they move on to college. As universities have sought to create more diverse communities than in past decades, they also have witnessed an increase in verbal and symbolic hostilities motivated by various forms of prejudice. In recent years, administrators and faculty at a number of major universities in the United States decided that statements such as the above refrain constituted an inadequate response to students' complaints of verbal harassment related to their racial, ethnic, sexual, or health status. Thus, in the late 1980s and early 1990s they implemented "speech codes" designed to restrict the use of hate speech, typically defined as "racist, sexist, homophobic, or ethnically demeaning speech. . . . "[2] Universities that instituted speech codes quickly found them to be extremely controversial. The proposed codes varied greatly in their definitions of "hate speech" as well as in the nature of the punishments meted out to violators.

Institutions that sought to put such codes into effect included the University of Michigan, the University of Wisconsin, the University of Pennsylvania, Brown, Stanford, Emory, and the University of Texas. The University of Pennsylvania, for example, adopted (and later rescinded) a policy that prohibited "any verbal or symbolic" behavior that "insults or demeans the person . . . on the basis of his or her race, color, ethnicity or national origin."[3] The University of Wisconsin adopted a speech code (subsequently struck down by a federal district judge) that barred "slurs or epithets that were based on a person's race, sex, religion, sexual orientation, disability, or ethnic origin."[4] The University threatened penalties if a student's use of such slurs and epithets created a "hostile learning environment" for another member of the university community.[5] A later version of the UW code (repealed by the university's Board of Regents) sought to punish a person who used "epithets directed specifically toward individuals with the purpose of creating a hostile educational environment on the basis of their race, gender, or sexual preference."[6] In the wake of legal challenges and internal campus pressures, some universities have abandoned their efforts to enact speech codes; others have sought to amend or rewrite their codes to avoid court challenges. Not all universities, however, have retreated in the face of these problems. In 1995, the University of Massachusetts at Amherst set forth what one commentator described as a "sweeping" new speech code. The associate chancellor, Susan Pearson, argued that "universities have a responsibility not to abandon the effort just because a few efforts were pronounced inadequate by the courts."[7]

ARGUMENTS IN FAVOR
OF COLLEGE SPEECH CODES

Defenders of speech codes argue that they are necessary to sustain learning environments in which minorities and other persons traditionally underrepresented on college campuses will have some measure of protection from verbal and symbolic harassment. In the absence of such safeguards, vulnerable student populations are less likely to have genuine equality of opportunity to pursue higher education, and thus are less likely to advance in society. As Charles Lawrence argues in his article in this chapter, "In recent years, university campuses have seen a resurgence of racial violence and a corresponding rise in the incidence of verbal and symbolic assault and harassment to which blacks and other traditionally subjugated groups are subjected.[8]

Unlike those who face harassment in public and open places, college students are in effect a "captive" audience. Measures that would allow a person to avoid harassment, such as averting the eyes or avoiding particular streets, will not suffice if the harassment is taking place in the classroom or dormitory or cafeteria. And as Lawrence argues, "regulation of otherwise protected speech has been permitted when . . . unwilling listeners cannot avoid the speech. Racist posters, flyers, and graffiti in dorms, classrooms, bathrooms, and other common living spaces would fall within the reasoning of these cases. Minority students should not be required to remain in their rooms to avoid racial assault. . . . I would argue that the university's responsibility for ensuring these students receive an equal educational opportunity provides a compelling justification for regulations that ensure them safe passage in all common areas."[9]

ARGUMENTS AGAINST
COLLEGE SPEECH CODES

Critics of college speech codes argue that these policies limit freedom of speech and thought, which are essential to the unfettered pursuit of truth within our universities. They assert that if there is any social institution within which freedom of speech must be protected, clearly it is the university. Speech codes, however well crafted, will ultimately have a chilling effect on the free exchange of ideas both within and without the classroom. Some critics suggest that university officials surely can find alternate ways of creating welcoming environments for minorities on their campuses, instead of supporting measures that threaten the very mission of the university. In response to the argument that college campuses are special types of communities within which students are not always free to walk away from hateful speech, opponents stress the continuity of college life and "real life": Minorities cannot, unfortunately, expect to be sheltered from verbal assaults once they leave the campus environment; shouldn't colleges help their students prepare for post-college experiences? Critics of a more pragmatic bent worry that it is nearly impossible to craft workable policies banning certain kinds of speech as well as certain symbolic gestures and images. They suggest that if university communities are really concerned with eliminating discrimination and bigotry from within their midst, then they ought develop curricular programs to educate students about problems of prejudice and racism.

NOTES

1. See Richard Delgado, "Words that Wound: A Tort Action for Racial Insults, Epithets, and Name Calling," 17 HARV. C.R.-C.L. REV. 133 (1982).

2. American Association of University Professors, "Statement on Freedom of Expression and Campus Speech Codes," p. 402.

3. "University of Pennsylvania May Drop Curbs on Speech," *Chicago Tribune*, February 2, 1994, p. 14.

4. Michele N-K. Collison, "Hate-Speech Code at U. of Wisconsin Voided by Court," *Chronicle of Higher Education*, October 23, 1991: A1.

5. Collison, A1.

6. "Regents Strike Down Wisconsin Speech Code," *The Chronicle of Higher Education*, 23 September, 1992: A5.

7. Christopher Shea, "Another College Proposes a Sweeping Speech Code," *The Chronicle of Higher Education*, 17 November, 1995: A37.

8. Charles R. Lawrence III, "If He Hollers Let Him Go: Regulating Racist Speech on Campus," p. 366.

9. Lawrence, p. 379.

28.

If He Hollers Let Him Go: Regulating Racist Speech on Campus

Charles R. Lawrence III

Charles R. Lawrence III is professor of law at Georgetown University. He coauthored *The Bakke Case: The Politics of Inequalities* and has written numerous articles in the areas of public education and race relations. In this essay, Lawrence defends narrowly tailored policies that are aimed at racist speech that causes direct, substantial injury to members of the campus community. He criticizes civil libertarians, who, in the name of free speech, automatically reject all campus efforts to respond to racist speech. Lawrence challenges the abstract framework of libertarians' arguments wherein they seem to presuppose an idealized society with genuine equality of opportunity, free of all culturally ingrained forms of racism. He encourages us to listen carefully to the victims of racist speech, and to acknowledge that deep-rooted and institutionalized forms of racism have prevented our colleges and universities from being the ideal, open marketplaces for the free and unfettered exchange of ideas.

Racist incidents occur at the University of Michigan, University of Massachusetts-Amherst, University of Wisconsin, University of New Mexico, Columbia University, Wellesley College, Duke University, and University of California-Los Angeles. (*Ms.* magazine, October, 1987)

The campus ought to be the last place to legislate tampering with the edges of first amendment protections.

University of Michigan:
"Greek Rites of Exclusion": Racist leaflets

Charles R. Lawrence III, "If He Hollers Let Him Go: Regulating Racist Speech on Campus," *Duke University Law Journal* (1990): 432. Reprinted by permission of *Duke University Law Journal* and the author.

The title of this chapter was inspired by the novel by Chester Himes, *If He Hollers Let Him Go* (1945).

distributed in dorms; white students paint themselves black and place rings in their noses at "jungle parties." (*The Nation*, July 1987)

Silencing a few creeps is no victory if the price is an abrogation of free speech. Remember censorship is an ugly word too.

Northwest Missouri State University: White Supremacists distribute flyers stating: "The Knights of the Ku Klux Klan are Watching You." (Klanwatch Intelligence Report No. 42, February 1988 [*Klanwatch*])

Kansas University: KKK members speak. (*Klanwatch*)

Temple University: White Student Union formed. (*Klanwatch*)

Stanford University: Aryan Resistance literature distributed. (*Klanwatch*)

Stockton State College (New Jersey): Invisible Empire literature distributed. (*Klanwatch*)

Memphis State University: Bomb threats at Jewish Student Union. (*Klanwatch*)

Arizona State University: Shot fired at Hillel Foundation building. (*Klanwatch*)

The harm that censors allege will result unless speech is forbidden rarely occurs.

Dartmouth College: Black professor called "a cross between a welfare queen and a bathroom attendant" and the *Dartmouth Review* purported to quote a Black student, "Dese boys be sayin' that we be comin' here to Dartmut an' not takin' the classics." (*The Nation*, February 27, 1989)

Yes, speech is sometimes painful. Sometimes it is abusive. That is one of the prices of a free society.

Purdue University: Counselor finds "Death Nigger" scratched on her door. (*The Nation*, February 27, 1989)

More speech, not less, is the proper cure for offensive speech.

Smith College: African student finds message slipped under her door that reads, "African Nigger do you want some bananas? Go back to the Jungle." (*New York Times*, October 19, 1988).

Speech cannot be banned simply because it is offensive.

University of Michigan: Campus radio station broadcasts a call from a student who "joked": "Who are the most famous black women in history? Aunt Jemima and Mother Fucker." (*The Nation*, February 27, 1989)

Those who don't like what they are hearing or seeing should try to change the atmosphere through education. That is what they will have to do in the real world after they graduate.

University of Michigan: A student walks into class and sees this written on the blackboard: "A mind is a terrible thing to waste—especially on a nigger." (*Chicago Tribune*, April 23, 1989)

People of color, women, and gays and lesbians owe their vibrant political movements in large measure to their freedom to communicate. If speech can be banned because it offends someone, how long will it be before the messages of these groups are themselves found offensive?

Stanford University: "President Donald Kennedy refused yesterday to consider amnesty for students who took over his office last week. . . . Kennedy insisted that the probe of violations of the Stanford behavior code go forward. The students [who were demanding more minority faculty and ethnic studies reforms] consider the prospect of disciplinary action unfair in view of Stanford's decision earlier this year not to punish two white students who defaced a poster of 19th century composer Ludwig von Beethoven to portray a stereotypical black face, then tacked it up in a predominantly black dormitory. The two incidents differ sharply, Kennedy said. The poster was admittedly racially offensive. But its defacement probably was protected by constitutional freedoms. However, the office takeover was clearly a violation of Stanford's policy against campus disruption." (*San Francisco Chronicle*, May 25, 1989)

Now it's the left that is trying to restrict free speech. Though the political labels have shifted, the rationale is the same: Our adversaries are dangerous and therefore should not be allowed to speak.

In recent years, university campuses have seen a resurgence of racial violence and a corresponding rise in the incidence of verbal and symbolic assault and harassment to which blacks and other traditionally subjugated groups are subjected. The events listed above were gathered from newspapers and magazine reports of racist incidents on campuses. The accompanying italicized statements criticizing proposals to regulate racism on campus were garnered from conversations, debates, and panel discussions at which I was present. Some were recorded verbatim and are exact quotes; others paraphrase the sentiment expressed. I have heard some version of each of these arguments many times over. These incidents are but a small sampling of the hate speech to which minorities are subjected on a daily basis on our nation's college campuses. There is a heated debate in the civil liberties community concerning the proper response to incidents of racist speech on campus. Strong disagreements have arisen between those individuals who believe that racist speech such as that described above should be regulated by the university or some public body and those individuals who believe that racist expression should be protected from all public regulation. At the center of the controversy is a tension between the constitutional values of free speech and equality. Like the debate over affirmative action in university admissions, this issue has divided old allies and revealed unrec-

ognized or unacknowledged differences in the experience, perceptions, and values of members of long-standing alliances. It also has caused considerable soul searching by individuals with longtime commitments to both the cause of political expression and the cause of racial equality.

I write this chapter from within the cauldron of this controversy. I make no pretense of dispassion or objectivity, but I do claim a deep commitment to the values that motivate both sides of the debate. I have spent the better part of my life as a dissenter. As a high school student I was threatened with suspension for my refusal to participate in a civil defense drill, and I have been a conspicuous consumer of my first amendment liberties ever since. I also have experienced the injury of the historical, ubiquitous, and continuous defamation of American racism. I grew up with Little Black Sambo and Amos and Andy, and I continue to receive racist tracts in the mail and shoved under my door. As I struggle with the tension between these constitutional values, I particularly appreciate the experience of both belonging and not belonging that gives to African Americans and other outsider groups a sense of duality. W.E.B. DuBois—scholar and founder of the National Association for the Advancement of Colored People (NAACP)—called the gift and burden inherent in the dual, conflicting heritage of all African Americans their "second-sight."[1]

The double consciousness of groups outside the ethnic mainstream is particularly apparent in the context of this controversy. Blacks know and value the protection the first amendment affords those of us who must rely upon our voices to petition both government and our neighbors for redress of grievances. Our political tradition has looked to "the word,"[2] to the moral power of ideas, to change the system when neither the power of the vote nor that of the gun were available. This part of us has known the experience of belonging and recognizes our common and inseparable interest in preserving the right of free speech for all. But we also know the experience of the outsider. The framers excluded us from the protection of the first amendment. The same Constitution that established rights for others endorsed a story that proclaimed our inferiority. It is a story that remains deeply ingrained in the American psyche. We see a different world than that seen by Americans who do not share this historical experience. We often hear racist speech when our white neighbors are not aware of its presence.

It is not my purpose to belittle or trivialize the importance of defending unpopular speech against the tyranny of the majority. There are very strong reasons for protecting even racist speech. Perhaps the most important reasons are that it reinforces our society's commitment to the value of tolerance, and that by shielding racist speech from government regulation, we are forced to combat it as a community. These reasons for protecting racist speech should not be set aside hastily, and I will not argue that we should be less vigilant in protecting the speech and associational rights of speakers with whom most of us would disagree.

But I am deeply concerned about the role that many civil libertarians have played, or the roles we have failed to play, in the continuing, real-life struggle through which we define the community in which we live. I fear that by framing the debate as we have—as one in which the liberty of free speech is in conflict with the elimination of racism—we have advanced the cause of racial oppression and placed the bigot on the moral high ground, fanning the rising flames of racism. Above all, I am troubled that we have not listened to the real victims, that we have shown so little empathy or understanding for their injury, and that we have abandoned those individuals whose race, gender, or sexual orientation provokes others to regard them as second-class citizens. These individuals' civil liberties are most directly at stake in the debate. In this chapter I focus on racism. Although I will not address violent pornography and homophobic hate speech directly, I will draw on the experience of women and gays as victims of hate speech where they operate as instructive analogues.

I have set two goals in constructing this chapter. The first goal is limited and perhaps overly modest, but it is nonetheless extremely important: I will demonstrate that much of the argument for protecting racist speech is based on the distinction that many civil libertarians draw between direct, face-to-face racial insults, which they think deserve first amendment protection, and all other fighting words, which they find unprotected by the first amendment. I argue that the distinction is false, that it advances none of the purposes of the first amendment, and that the time has come to put an end to the ringing rhetoric that condemns all efforts to regulate racist speech, even narrowly drafted provisions aimed at racist speech that results in direct, immediate, and substantial injury.

I also urge the regulation of racial epithets and vilification that do not involve face-to-face encounters—situations in which the victim is part of a captive audience and the injury is experienced by all members of a racial group who are forced to hear or see these words. In such cases, the insulting words are aimed at an entire group with the effect of causing significant harm to individual group members.

My second goal is more ambitious and more indeterminate. I propose several ways in which the traditional civil liberties position on free speech does not take into account important values expressed elsewhere in the Constitution. Further, I argue that even those values the first amendment itself is intended to promote are frustrated by an interpretation that is acontextual and idealized, by presupposing a world characterized by equal opportunity and the absence of societally created and culturally ingrained racism.

This chapter is divided into four parts: The first part explores whether our Constitution already commits us to some regulation of racist speech. I argue that it does; that this is the meaning of *Brown v. Board of Education*.[3] For the time being, I would ask only that the reader be open to considering this interpretation of *Brown*. This interpretation is useful even for those who believe the censorship of any expression cannot ultimately be condoned: *Brown* can help us better understand the injury of racist speech, an understanding that is vital to our discussion.

I also consider the implications of the state action doctrine in understanding *Brown* and argue that the public/private ideology promoted by that doctrine plays a critical role in advancing racism and clouding our vision of the appropriate role for the community in disestablishing systematic, societal group defamation.

The second part considers the debate over regulation of racial harassment on campus. I argue that carefully drafted regulations can and should be sustained without significant departures from existing first amendment doctrine. The regulation of racist fighting words should not be treated differently from the regulation of garden-variety fighting words, and captive audiences deserve no less protection when they are held captive by racist speakers. I also suggest that rules requiring civility and respect in academic discourse encourage rather than discourage the fullest exchange of ideas. Regulations that require minimal civility of discourse in certain designated forums are not incursions on intellectual and political debate.

The third part explores the nature of the injury inflicted by racist hate speech and examines the unstated assumptions that lie at the core of first amendment theory. In this part, I urge reconsideration of the history of racism in the United States; the ubiquity and continued vitality of culturally engendered conscious and unconscious beliefs about the inferiority of nonwhites, and the effect of inequities of power on the marketplace of ideas.

In the last part, I argue that civil libertarians must examine not just the substance of our position on racist speech but also the ways in which we enter the debate. The way the debate has been framed makes heroes out of bigots and fans the flames of racial violence. I also consider the reasons for some civil libertarians' resistance to even minimal and narrowly drafted regulations of racist harassment.

BROWN V. BOARD OF EDUCATION: A CASE ABOUT REGULATING RACIST SPEECH

The landmark case of *Brown v. Board of Education* is not one we normally think of as concerning speech. As read most narrowly, the case is about the rights of Black children to equal educational opportunity. But *Brown* can also be read more broadly to articulate a principle central to any substantive understanding of the equal protection clause, the foundation on which all antidiscrimination law rests. This is the principle of equal citizenship. Under that principle, "Every individual is presumptively entitled to be treated by the organized society as a respected, responsible, and participating member."[4] The principle further requires the affirmative disestablishment of society practices that treat people as members of an inferior or dependent caste, as unworthy to participate in the larger community. The holding in *Brown*—that racially segregated schools violate the equal protection clause—reflects the fact that segregation amounts to a demeaning, caste-creating practice. The prevention of stigma was at the core of the Supreme Court's unanimous decision in *Brown* that segregated public schools are inherently unequal. Observing that the segregation of Black pupils "generates a feeling of inferiority as to their status in the community,"[5] Chief Justice Earl Warren recognized what a majority of the Court had ignored almost sixty years earlier in *Plessy v. Ferguson*.[6] The social meaning of racial segregation in the United States is the designation of a superior and an inferior caste, and segregation proceeds "on the ground that colored citizens are . . . inferior and degraded."[7]

The key to this understanding of *Brown* is that the practice of segregation, the practice the Court held inherently unconstitutional, was *speech*. *Brown* held that segregation is unconstitutional not simply because the physical separation of Black and white children is bad or because resources were distributed unequally among Black and white schools. *Brown* held that segregated schools were unconstitutional primarily because of the *message* segregation conveys—the message that Black children are an untouchable caste, unfit to be educated with white children. Segregation serves its purpose by conveying an idea. It stamps a badge of inferiority upon Blacks, and this badge communicates a message to others in the community, as well as to Blacks wearing the badge, that is injurious to Blacks. Therefore, *Brown* may be read as regulating the content of racist speech. As a regulation of racist speech, the decision is an exception to the usual rule that regulation of speech content is presumed unconstitutional.

The Conduct/Speech Distinction

Some civil libertarians argue that my analysis of *Brown* conflates speech and conduct. They maintain that the segregation outlawed in *Brown* was discriminatory conduct, not speech, and the defamatory message conveyed by segregation simply was an incidental by-product of that conduct. This position is often stated as follows: "Of course segregation conveys a message, but this could be said of almost all conduct. To take an extreme example, a murderer conveys a message of hatred for his victim. But we would not argue that we cannot punish the murder—the primary conduct—merely because of this message, which is its secondary by-product."[8] The Court has been reluctant to concede that the first amendment has any relevance whatsoever in examples like this one, because the law would not be directed at anything resembling speech or at the views expressed. In such a case the regulation of speech is truly incidental to the regulation of the conduct.

These same civil libertarians assert that I suggest that all conduct with an expressive component should be treated alike—namely, as unprotected speech. This reading of my position clearly misperceives the central point of my argument. I do not contend that *all* conduct with an expressive component should be treated as unprotected speech. To the contrary, my suggestion that *racist* conduct amounts to speech is

premised upon a unique characteristic of racism—namely its reliance upon the defamatory message of white supremacy to achieve its injurious purpose. I have not ignored the distinction between the speech and conduct elements of segregation, although, as the constitutional scholar Lawrence Tribe explained, "Any particular course of conduct may be hung almost randomly on the 'speech' peg or the 'conduct' peg as one sees fit."[9] Rather, my analysis turns on that distinction; I ask the question of whether there is a purpose to outlawing segregation that is unrelated to its message and conclude that the answer is no.

If, for example, John W. Davis, counsel for the Board of Education of Topeka, Kansas, had been asked during oral argument in *Brown* to state the board's purpose in educating Black and white children in separate schools, he would have been hard pressed to answer in a way unrelated to the purpose of designating Black children as inferior. If segregation's primary goal is to convey the message of white supremacy, then *Brown's* declaration that segregation is unconstitutional amounts to a regulation of the message of white supremacy. Properly understood, *Brown* and its progeny require that the systematic group defamation of segregation be disestablished. Although the exclusion of Black children from white schools and the denial of educational resources and association that accompany exclusion can be characterized as conduct, these particular instances of conduct are concerned primarily with communicating the idea of white supremacy. The nonspeech elements are by-products of the main message rather than the message being simply a by-product of unlawful conduct.

The public accommodations provisions of the Civil Rights Act of 1964[10] illuminate why laws against discrimination also regulate racist speech. The legislative history and the Supreme Court's opinions upholding the act establish that Congress was concerned that Blacks have access to public accommodations to eliminate impediments to the free flow of interstate commerce, but this purpose could have been achieved through a regime of separate but equal accommodations.

Title II of the Civil Rights Act goes farther; it incorporates the principle of the inherent inequality of segregation and prohibits restaurant owners from providing separate places at the lunch counter for "whites" and "coloreds." Even if the same food and the same service are provided, separate but equal facilities are unlawful. If the signs indicating separate facilities remain in place, then the statute is violated despite proof that restaurant patrons are free to disregard the signs. Outlawing these signs graphically illustrates my point that antidiscrimination laws are primarily regulations of the content of racist speech.

In the summer of 1966, Robert Cover and I were working as summer interns with C. B. King in Albany, Georgia. One day we stopped for lunch at a take-out chicken joint. The establishment was housed in a long diner-like structure with an awning extending from each of two doors in the side of the building. A sign was painted at the end of each awning. One said White, the other Colored. Bob and I entered the "white" side together, knowing we were not welcome to do so. When the proprietor took my order, I asked if he knew that the signs on his awnings were illegal under Title II of the Civil Rights Act of 1964. He responded, "People can come in this place through any door they want to." What this story makes apparent is that the signs themselves violate the antidiscrimination principle even when the conduct of denial of access is not present.

Another way to understand the inseparability of racist speech and discriminatory conduct is to view individual racist acts as part of a totality. When viewed in this manner, white supremacists' conduct or speech is forbidden by the equal protection clause. The goal of white supremacy is not achieved by individual acts or even by the cumulative acts of a group, but rather it is achieved by the institutionalization of the ideas of white supremacy. The institutionalization of white supremacy within our culture has created conduct on the society level that is greater than the sum of individual racist acts. The racist acts of millions of individuals are mutually reinforcing and cumulative because the status quo of institutionalized white supremacy remains long after deliberate racist actions subside.

Professor Kendall Thomas describes the way in which racism is simultaneously speech (a socially constructed meaning or idea) and conduct by asking us to consider the concept of "race" not as a noun but as a verb. He notes that race is a social construction. The meaning of "Black" or "white" is derived through a history of acted-upon ideology. Moreover, the cultural meaning of race is promulgated through millions of ongoing contemporaneous speech/acts. Thus, he says, "We are raced." The social construction of race is an ongoing process.[11]

It is difficult to recognize the institutional significance of white supremacy or how it *acts* to harm, partially because of its ubiquity. We simply do not see most racist conduct because we experience a world in which whites are supreme as simply "the world." Much racist conduct is considered unrelated to race or regarded as neutral because racist conduct maintains the status quo, the status quo of the world as we have known it. Catharine MacKinnon has observed that "To the extent that pornography succeeds in constructing social reality, it becomes invisible as harm." Thus, pornography "is more act-like than thought-like."[12] This truth about gender discrimination is equally true of racism.

Just because one can express the idea or message embodied by a practice such as white supremacy does not necessarily equate that practice with the idea. Slavery was an idea as well as a practice, but the Supreme Court recognized the inseparability of idea and practice in the institution of slavery when it held the enabling clause of the thirteenth amendment clothed Congress with the power to pass "all laws necessary and proper for abolishing all badges and incidents of slavery in the United States."[13] This understanding also informs the regulation of speech/conduct in the public accommodations provisions of the Civil Rights Act of 1964 discussed above. When the racist restaurant or hotel owner puts a Whites Only sign in his window, his sign is more than speech. Putting up the sign is more than an act excluding Black patrons who see the sign. The sign is part of the larger practice of segregation and white supremacy that constructs and maintains a culture in which nonwhites are excluded from full citizenship. The inseparability of the idea and practice of racism is central to *Brown's* holding that segregation is inherently unconstitutional.

Racism is both 100 percent speech and 100 percent conduct. Discriminatory conduct is not racist unless it also conveys the message of white supremacy—unless it is interpreted within the culture to advance the structure and ideology of white supremacy. Likewise, all racist speech constructs the social reality that constrains the liberty of nonwhites because of their race. By limiting the life opportunities of others, this act of constructing meaning also makes racist speech conduct.

The Public/Private Distinction

There are critics who would contend that *Brown* is inapposite because the equal protection clause only restricts government behavior, whereas the first amendment protects the speech of private persons. They say, "Of course we want to prevent the state from defaming Blacks, but we must continue to be vigilant about protecting speech rights, even of racist individuals, from the government. In both cases our concern must be protecting the individual from the unjust power of the state."

At first blush, this position seems persuasive, but its persuasiveness relies upon the mystifying properties of constitutional ideology. In particular, I refer to the state action doctrine. Roughly stated,

> The [state action] doctrine holds that although someone may have suffered harmful treatment of a kind that one might ordinarily describe as a deprivation of liberty or a denial of equal protection of the laws, that occurrence excites no constitutional concern unless the proximate active perpetrators of the harm include persons exercising the special authority or power of the government of a state.[14]

By restricting the application of the fourteenth amendment to discrimination implicating the government, the state action rule immunizes private discriminators from constitutional scrutiny. In so doing, it leaves untouched the largest part of the vast system of segregation in the United States. The *Civil Rights Cases*[15] in which this doctrine was firmly established stands as a monument preserving American racial discrimination. Although the origin of state action is textual, countervailing values of privacy, freedom of association, and free speech all have been used to justify the rule's exculpation of private racism.

For example, it is argued that a white family's decision to send its children to private school or to move to a racially exclusive suburb should be accorded respect in spite of the fourteenth amendment's requirement of nondiscrimination because these decisions are part of the right to individual familial autonomy. In this way, the state action rule's rather arbitrary limit on the scope of the antidiscrimination principle is transformed into a right of privacy—which is presented as the constitutional embodiment of an affirmative, neutral, and universally shared value. A new and positive image emerges—an image that has been abstracted from its original context.

In the abstract, the right to make decisions about how we will educate our children or with whom we will associate is an important value in American society. But when we decontextualize by viewing this privacy value in the abstract, we ignore the way it operates in the real world. We do not ask ourselves, for example, whether it is a value to which all people have equal access. And we do not inquire about who has the resources to send their children to private school or move to an exclusive suburb. The privacy value, when presented as an ideal, seems an appropriate limitation on racial justice because we naively believe that everyone has an equal stake in this value.

I do not mean to suggest that privacy or autonomy has no normative value; there is some point at which the balance ought to be struck in its favor *after full consideration of the inequities that might accompany that choice*. What is objectionable about the privacy language that I am discussing here is that it ignores inequities and assumes we all share equally in the value being promoted.

The Supreme Court's treatment of the abortion controversy provides the most striking example of the fact that the right of autonomous choice is not shared by rich and poor alike. In *Roe v. Wade*, the Court declared in no uncertain terms that the right of privacy "is broad enough to encompass a woman's decision whether or not to terminate her pregnancy."[16] Yet, in *Harris v. McRae*, the Court with equal certainty asserted, "It simply does not follow that a woman's freedom of choice carries with it a constitutional entitlement to the financial resources to avail herself of the full range of protected choices."[17]

The argument that distinguishes private racist speech from the government speech outlawed by *Brown* suffers from the same decontextualizing ideology. If the government is involved in a joint venture with private contractors to engage in the business of defaming Blacks, should it be able to escape the constitutional mandate that makes that business illegal simply by handing over the copyright and the printing presses to its partners in crime? I think not. And yet this is the essence of the position that espouses first amendment protection for those partners.

In an insightful article considering the constitutional implications of government regulation of pornography, the legal scholar Frank Michelman observed that the idea of state action plays a crucial, if unspoken, role for judges and civil libertarians who favor an absolute rule against government regulation of private pornographic publications (or racist speech), even when that expression causes "effects fairly describable . . . as deprivations of liberty and denials of equal protection of the laws."[18] He noted that judges and civil libertarians would not balance the evils of private subversions of liberty and equal protec-

tion against the evils of government censorship because "the Constitution, through the state action doctrine, in effects tells them not to." Michelman suggests that the state action doctrine, by directing us to the text of the fourteenth amendment, diverts our attention from the underlying issue—whether we should balance the evils of private deprivations of liberty against the government deprivations of liberty that may arise out of state regulations designed to avert those private deprivations.

A person who responds to the argument that *Brown* mandates the abolition of racist speech by reciting the state action doctrine fails to consider that the alternative to regulating racist speech is infringement of the claims of Blacks to liberty and equal protection. The best way to constitutionally protect these competing interests is to balance them directly. To invoke the state action doctrine is to circumvent our value judgment as to how these competing interests should be balanced.

The deference usually given to the first amendment values in this balance is justified using the argument that racist speech is unpopular speech, that like the speech of civil rights activists, pacifists, and religious and political dissenters, it is in need of special protection from majoritarian censorship. But for over three hundred years, racist speech has been the liturgy of the leading established religion of the United States, the religion of racism. Racist speech remains a vital and regrettably popular characteristic of the U.S. vernacular. It must be noted that there has not yet been satisfactory retraction of the government-sponsored defamation in the slavery clauses,[19] the *Dred Scott* decision,[20] the Black codes, the segregation statutes, and countless other group libels. The injury to Blacks is hardly redressed by deciding the government must no longer injure our reputation if one then invokes the first amendment to ensure that racist speech continues to thrive in an unregulated private market.

Consider, for example, the case of *McLaurin v. Oklahoma State Regents*,[21] in which the University of Oklahoma graduate school, under order by a federal court to admit McLaurin, a Black student, designated a special seat, roped off from other seats, in each classroom, the library, and the cafeteria. The Supreme Court held that this arrangement was unconstitutional because McLaurin could not have had an equal opportunity to learn and participate if he was humiliated and symbolically stigmatized as an untouchable. Would it be any less injurious if all McLaurin's classmates had shown up at class wearing blackface? Should this symbolic speech be protected by the Constitution? Yet, according to a *Time* magazine report, in the fall of 1988 at the University of Wisconsin, "Members of the Zeta Beta Tau fraternity staged a mock slave auction, complete with some pledges in blackface."[22] More recently, at the same university, white male students trailed Black female students shouting, "I've never tried a nigger before."[23] These young women were no less severely injured than was McLaurin simply because the university did not directly sponsor their assault. If the university fails to protect them in their right to pursue their education free from this kind of degradation and humiliation, then surely there are constitutional values at stake.

It is a very sad irony that the first instinct of many civil libertarians is to express concern for possible infringement of the assailants' liberties while barely noticing the constitutional rights of the assailed. Shortly after *Brown*, many Southern communities tried to escape the mandate of desegregation by closing public schools and opening private (white) academies. These attempts to avoid the fourteenth amendment through the privatization of discrimination consistently were invalidated by the courts. In essence, the Supreme Court held that the defamatory message of segregation would not be insulated from constitutional proscription simply because the speaker was a nongovernment entity.

The Supreme Court also has indicated that Congress may enact legislation regulating private racist speech. In upholding the public accommodations provisions of Title II of the Civil Rights Act of 1964 in *Heart of Atlanta Motel v. United States*,[24] the Court implicitly rejected the argument that the absence of state action meant that private discriminators were protected by first amendment free speech and associational rights. Likewise in *Bob Jones University v. United States*,[25] the Court sustained the Internal Revenue Service decision to discontinue tax-exempt status for a college with a policy against interracial dating and marriage. The college framed its objection in terms of the free exercise of religion, arguing its policy was religiously motivated, but the Court found that the government had "a fundamental, overriding interest in eradicating racial discrimination in education" that "substantially outweighs whatever burden denial of tax benefits" placed on the college's exercise of its religious beliefs.[26] It is difficult to believe that the university would have fared any better under free speech analysis or if the policy had been merely a statement of principle rather than an enforceable disciplinary regulation. Regulation of private racist speech also has been held constitutional in the context of prohibition of race-designated advertisements for employees, home sales, and rentals.

Thus *Brown* and the antidiscrimination law it spawned provide precedent for my position that the content regulation of racist speech is not only permissible but may be required by the Constitution in certain circumstances. This precedent may not mean that we should advocate the government regulation of all racist speech, but it should give us pause in assuming absolutist positions about regulations aimed at the message or idea such speech conveys. If we understand *Brown*—the cornerstone of the civil rights movement and equal protection doctrine—correctly, and if we understand the necessity of disestablishing the system of signs and symbols that signal Blacks' inferiority, then we should not proclaim that all racist speech that stops short of physical violence must be defended.

RACIST SPEECH AS THE FUNCTIONAL EQUIVALENT OF FIGHTING WORDS

Much recent debate over the efficacy of regulating racist speech has focused on the efforts by colleges and universities to respond to the burgeoning incidents of racial harassment on their campuses. At Stanford, where I teach, there has been considerable controversy over whether racist and other discriminatory verbal harassment should be regulated and what form any regulation should take. Proponents of regulation have been sensitive to the danger of inhibiting expression, and the current regulation (which was drafted by my colleague Tom Grey) manifests that sensitivity. It is drafted somewhat more narrowly than I would have preferred, leaving unregulated hate speech that occurs in settings where there is a captive audience, but I largely agree with this regulation's substance and approach. I include it here as one example of a regulation of racist speech that I would argue violates neither first amendment precedent nor principle. The regulation reads as follows:

Fundamental Standard Interpretation: Free Expression and Discriminatory Harassment

1. Stanford is committed to the principles of free inquiry and free expression. Students have the right to hold and vigorously defend and promote their opinions, thus entering them into the life of the University, there to flourish or wither according to their merits. Respect for this right requires that students tolerate even expression of opinions which they find abhorrent. Intimidation of students by other students in their exercise of this right, by violence or threat of violence, is therefore considered to be a violation of the Fundamental Standard.

2. Stanford is also committed to principles of equal opportunity and nondiscrimination. Each student has the right to equal access to a Stanford education, without discrimination on the basis of sex, race, color, handicap, religion, sexual orientation, or national and ethnic origin. Harassment of students on the basis of any of these characteristics tends to create a hostile environment that makes access to education for those subjected to it less than equal. Such discriminatory harassment is therefore considered to be a violation of the Fundamental Standard.

3. This interpretation of the Fundamental Standard is intended to clarify the point at which protected free expression ends and prohibited discriminatory harassment begins. Prohibited harassment includes discriminatory intimidation by threats of violence, and also includes personal vilification of students on the basis of their sex, race, color, handicap, religion, sexual orientation, or national and ethnic origin.

4. Speech or other expression constitutes harassment by vilification if it:
   a) is intended to insult or stigmatize an individual or a small number of individuals on the basis of their sex, race, color, handicap, religion, sexual orientation, or national and ethnic origin; and
   b) is addressed directly to the individual or individuals whom it insults or stigmatizes; and
   c) makes use of "fighting" words or nonverbal symbols.
   In the context of discriminatory harassment, "fighting" words or nonverbal symbols are words, pictures or symbols that, by virtue of their form, are commonly understood to convey direct and visceral hatred or contempt for human beings on the basis of their sex, race, color, handicap, religion, sexual orientation, and national and ethnic origin.[27]

This regulation and others like it have been characterized in the press as the work of "thought police," but the rule does nothing more than prohibit intentional face-to-face insults, a form of speech that is unprotected by the first amendment. When racist speech takes the form of face-to-face insults, catcalls, or other assaultive speech aimed at an individual or a small group of persons, then it falls within the "fighting words" exception to first amendment protection. The Supreme Court has held that words that "by their very utterance inflict injury or tend to incite an immediate breach of the peace"[28] are not constitutionally protected.

Face-to-face racial insults, like fighting words, are undeserving of first amendment protection for two reasons. The first reason is the immediacy of the injurious impact of racial insults. The experience of being called "nigger," "spic," "Jap," or "kike" is like receiving a slap in the face. The injury is instantaneous. There is neither an opportunity for intermediary reflection on the idea conveyed nor an opportunity for responsive speech. The harm to be avoided is both clear and present. The second reason that racial insults should not fall under protected speech relates to the purpose underlying the first amendment. The purpose of the first amendment is to foster the greatest amount of speech. Racial insults disserve that purpose. Assaultive racist speech functions as a preemptive strike. The racial invective is experienced as a blow, not a proffered idea, and once the blow is struck, it is unlikely that dialogue will follow. Racial insults are undeserving of first amendment protection because the perpetrator's intention is not to discover truth or initiate dialogue, but to injure the victim.

The fighting words doctrine anticipates that the verbal slap in the face of insulting words will provoke a violent response, resulting in a breach of the peace. When racial insults are hurled at minorities, the response may be silence or flight rather than a fight, but the preemptive effect on further speech is the same. Women and minorities often report that they find themselves speechless in the face of discriminatory verbal attacks. This inability to respond is not the result of oversensitivity among these groups, as some individuals who oppose protective regulation have argued. Rather it is the product of

several factors, all of which evidence the non-speech character of the initial preemptive verbal assault. The first factor is that the visceral emotional response to personal attack precludes speech. Attack produces an instinctive, defensive psychological reaction. Fear, rage, shock, and flight all interfere with any reasoned response. Words like "nigger," "kike," and "faggot" produce physical symptoms that temporarily disable the victim, and the perpetrators often use these words with the intention of producing this effect. Many victims do not find words of response until well after the assault, when the cowardly assaulter has departed.

A second factor that distinguishes racial insults from protected speech is the preemptive nature of such insults—words of response to such verbal attacks may never be forthcoming because speech is usually an inadequate response. When one is personally attacked with words that denote one's subhuman status and untouchability, there is little, if anything, that can be said to redress either the emotional or reputational injury. This is particularly true when the message and meaning of the epithet resonates with beliefs widely held in society. This preservation of widespread beliefs is what makes the face-to-face racial attack more likely to preempt speech than other fighting words do. The racist name caller is accompanied by a cultural chorus of equally demeaning speech and symbols. Segregation and other forms of racist speech injure victims because of their dehumanizing and excluding message. Each individual message gains its power because of the cumulative and reinforcing effect of countless similar messages that are conveyed in a society where racism is ubiquitous.

The subordinated victims of fighting words also are silenced by their relatively powerless position in society. Because of the significance of power and position, the categorization of racial epithets as fighting words provides an inadequate paradigm; instead one must speak of their functional equivalent. The fighting words doctrine presupposes an encounter between two persons of relatively equal power who have been acculturated to respond to face-to-face insults with violence: The fighting words doctrine is a paradigm based on a white male point of view. It captures the "macho" quality of male discourse. It is accepted, justifiable, and even praiseworthy when "real men" respond to personal insult with violence. (Presidential candidate George Bush effectively emulated the most macho—and not coincidentally most violent—of movie stars, Clint Eastwood, when he repeatedly used the phrase, "Read my lips!" Any teenage boy will tell you the subtext of this message: "I've got nothing else to say about this and if you don't like what I'm saying we can step outside.") The fighting words doctrine's responsiveness to this male stance in the world and its blindness to the cultural experience of women is another example of how neutral principles of law reflect the values of those who are dominant.

Black men also are well aware of the double standard that our culture applies in responding to insult. Part of the culture of racial domination through violence—a culture of dominance manifested historically in thousands of lynchings in the South and more recently in the racial violence at Howard Beach and Bensonhurst—is the paradoxical expectation on the part of whites that Black males will accept insult from whites without protest, yet will become violent without provocation. These expectations combine two assumptions: First, that Blacks as a group—and especially Black men—are more violent; and second, that as inferior persons, Blacks have no right to feel insulted. One can imagine the response of universities if Black men started to respond to racist fighting words by beating up white students.

In most situations, minorities correctly perceive that a violent response to fighting words will result in a risk to their own life and limb. This risk forces targets to remain silent and submissive. This response is most obvious when women submit to sexually assaultive speech or when the racist name caller is in a more powerful position—the boss on the job or a member

of a violent racist group. Certainly, we do not expect the Black woman crossing the Wisconsin campus to turn on her tormentors and pummel them. Less obvious, but just as significant, is the effect of pervasive racial and sexual violence and coercion on individual members of subordinated groups, who must learn the survival techniques of suppressing and disguising rage and anger at an early age.

One of my students, a white, gay male, related an experience that is quite instructive in understanding the fighting words doctrine. In response to my request that students describe how they experienced the injury of racist speech, Michael told a story of being called "faggot" by a man on a subway. His description included all of the speech-inhibiting elements I have noted previously. He found himself in a state of semishock, nauseous, dizzy, unable to muster the witty, sarcastic, articulate rejoinder he was accustomed to making. He was instantly aware of the recent spate of gay bashing in San Francisco and that many of these incidents had escalated from verbal encounters. Even hours later when the shock subsided and his facility with words returned, he realized that any response was inadequate to counter the hundreds of years of societal defamation that one word— "faggot"—carried with it. Like the word "nigger" and unlike the word "liar," it is not sufficient to deny the truth of the word's application, to say, "I am not a faggot." One must deny the truth of the word's meaning, a meaning shouted from the rooftops by the rest of the world a million times a day. The complex response "Yes, I am a member of the group you despise and the degraded meaning of the word you use is one that I reject" is not effective in a subway encounter. Although there are many of us who constantly and in myriad ways seek to counter the lie spoken in the meaning of hateful words like "nigger" and "faggot," it is a nearly impossible burden to bear when one is ambushed by a sudden, face-to-face hate speech assault.

But there is another part of my discussion with Michael that is equally instructive. I asked if he could remember a situation when he had been verbally attacked with reference to his being a white male. Had he ever been called a "honkey," a "chauvinist pig," or "mick"? (Michael is from a working-class Irish family in Boston.) He said that he had been called some version of all three and that although he found the last one more offensive than the first two, he had not experienced—even in that subordinated role—the same disorienting powerlessness he had experienced when attacked for his membership in the gay community. The question of power, of the context of the power relationships within which speech takes place, and the connection to violence must be considered as we decide how best to foster the freest and fullest dialogue within our communities. Regulation of face-to-face verbal assault in the manner contemplated by the proposed Stanford provision will make room for more speech than it chills. The provision is clearly within the spirit, if not the letter, of existing first amendment doctrine.

The proposed Stanford regulation, and indeed regulations with considerably broader reach, can be justified as necessary to protect a captive audience from offensive or injurious speech. Courts have held that offensive speech may not be regulated in public forums such as streets and parks where listeners may avoid the speech by moving on or averting their eyes,[29] but the regulation of otherwise protected speech has been permitted when the speech invades the privacy of unwilling listeners' homes or when unwilling listeners cannot avoid the speech.[30] Racist posters, flyers, and graffiti in dorms, classrooms, bathrooms, and other common living spaces would fall within the reasoning of these cases. Minority students should not be required to remain in their rooms to avoid racial assault. Minimally, they should find a safe haven in their dorms and other common rooms that are a part of their daily routine. I would argue that the university's responsibility for ensuring these students receive an equal educational opportunity provides a compelling justification for

regulations that ensure them safe passage in all common areas. Black, Latino, Asian, or Native American students should not have to risk being the target of racially assaulting speech every time they choose to walk across campus. The regulation of vilifying speech that cannot be anticipated or avoided would not preclude announced speeches and rallies where minorities and their allies would have an opportunity to organize counterdemonstrations or avoid the speech altogether.

KNOWING THE INJURY AND STRIKING THE BALANCE: UNDERSTANDING WHAT IS AT STAKE IN RACIST SPEECH CASES

I argued in the last section that narrowly drafted regulations of racist speech that prohibit face-to-face vilification and protect captive audiences from verbal and written harassment can be defended within the confines of existing first amendment doctrine. Here I argue that many civil libertarians who urge that the first amendment prohibits any regulation of racist speech have given inadequate attention to the testimony of individuals who have experienced injury from such speech. These civil libertarians fail to comprehend both the nature and extent of the injury inflicted by racist speech. I further urge that understanding the injury requires reconsideration of the balance that must be struck between our concerns for racial equality and freedom of expression.

The arguments most commonly advanced against the regulation of racist speech go something like this: We recognize that minority groups suffer pain and injury as the result of racist speech, but we must allow this hate mongering for the benefit of society as a whole. Freedom of speech is the lifeblood of our democratic system. It is a freedom that enables us to persuade others to our point of view. Free speech is especially important for minorities because often it is their only vehicle for rallying support for redress of their grievances. Even though we do not wish anyone to be persuaded that racist lies are true, we cannot allow the public regulation of racist invective and vilification because any prohibition broad enough to prevent racist speech would catch in the same net forms of speech that are central to a democratic society.

Whenever we argue that racist epithets and vilification must be allowed, not because we would condone them ourselves but because of the potential danger the precedent of regulation would pose for the speech of all dissenters, we are balancing our concern for the free flow of ideas and the democratic process with our desire for equality. This kind of categorical balance is struck whenever we frame any rule—even an absolute rule. It is important to be conscious of the nature and extent of injury to both concerns when we engage in this kind of balancing. In this case, we must place on one side of the balance the nature and extent of the injury caused by racism. We must also consider whether the racist speech we propose to regulate is advancing or retarding the values of the first amendment.

Understanding the Injury Inflicted by Racist Speech

There can be no meaningful discussion about how to reconcile our commitment to equality and our commitment to free speech until we acknowledge that racist speech inflicts real harm and that this harm is far from trivial. I should state that more strongly: To engage in a debate about the first amendment and racist speech without a full understanding of the nature and extent of the harm of racist speech risks making the first amendment an instrument of domination rather than a vehicle of liberation. Not everyone has known the experience of being victimized by racist, misogynist, or homophobic speech, and we do not share equally the burden of the societal harm it inflicts. Often we are too quick to say we have heard the victims' cries when we have not; we are too eager to assure ourselves we have experienced the same injury and therefore can make the constitutional balance without danger of mismeasurement. For many of us who have fought for the rights of oppressed minorities, it is difficult to accept that by underestimating the injury from racist speech we too might be implicated in the vicious words we would never utter. Until we have eradicated racism and sexism and no longer share in the fruits of those forms of domination, we cannot legitimately strike the balance without hearing the protest of those who are dominated. My plea is simply that we listen to the victims.

Members of my own family were involved in a recent incident at a private school in Wilmington, Delaware, that taught me much about both the nature of the injury racist speech inflicts and the lack of understanding many whites have of that injury.

A good Quaker school dedicated to a deep commitment to and loving concern for all the members of its community, Wilmington Friends School also became a haven for white families fleeing the court-ordered desegregation of the Wilmington public schools. In recent years, the school strove to meet its commitment to human equality by enrolling a small (but significant) group of minority students and hiring an even smaller number of Black faculty and staff. My sister Paula, a gifted, passionate, and dedicated teacher, was the principal of the lower school. Her sons attended the high school. My brother-in-law, John, teaches geology at the University of Delaware. He is a strong, quiet, loving man, and he is white. My sister's family had moved to Wilmington, shouldering the extra burdens and anxieties borne by an interracial family moving to a town where, not long ago, the defamatory message of segregation graced the doors of bathrooms and restaurants. Within a year they had made a place as well-loved and respected members of the community, particularly the school community, where Paula was viewed as a godsend and my nephews made many good friends.

In May of their second year in Wilmington, an incident occurred that shook the entire school community, but was particularly painful to my sister's family and others who found themselves the objects of hateful speech. In a letter to the school community explaining a decision to expel four students, the school's headmistress described the incident as follows:

On Sunday evening, May 1, four students in the senior class met by prearrangement to paint the soccer kickboard, a flat rectangular structure, approximately 8 ft. by 25 ft., standing in the midst of the Wilmington Friends School playing fields. They worked for approximately one hour under bright moonlight and then went home.

What confronted students and staff the following morning, depicted on the kickboard, were racist and anti-Semitic slogans and, most disturbing of all, threats of violent assault against one clearly identified member of the senior class. The slogans written on the kickboard included "Save the land, join the Klan," and "Down with Jews"; among the drawings were at least twelve hooded Ku Klux Klansmen, Nazi swastikas, and a burning cross. The most frightening and disturbing depictions, however, were those that threatened violence against one of our senior Black students. He was drawn, in a cartoon figure, identified by his name, and his initials, and by the name of his mother. Directly to the right of his head was a bullet, and farther to the right was a gun with its barrel directed toward the head. Under the drawing of the student, three Ku Klux Klansmen were depicted, one of whom was saying that the student "dies." Next to the gun was a drawing of a burning cross under which was written "Kill the Tarbaby."[31]

When I visited my sister's family a few days after this incident, the injury they had suffered was evident. The wounds were fresh. My sister, a care giver by nature and vocation, was clearly in need of care. My nephews were quiet. Their faces betrayed the aftershock of a recently inflicted blow and a newly discovered vulnerability. I knew the pain and scars were no less enduring because the injury had not been physical. And when I talked to my sister, I realized

the greatest part of her pain came not from the incident itself, but rather from the reaction of white parents who had come to the school in unprecedented numbers to protest the offending students' expulsion. "It was only a prank." "No one was physically attacked." "How can you punish these kids for mere words, mere drawings." Paula's pain was compounded by the failure of these people with whom she lived and worked to recognize that she had been hurt, to understand in even the most limited way the reality of her pain and that of her family.

Many people called the incident "isolated." But Black folks know that no racial incident is "isolated" in the United States. That is what makes the incidents so horrible, so scary. It is the knowledge that they are *not* the isolated unpopular speech of a dissident few that makes them so frightening. These incidents are manifestations of an ubiquitous and deeply ingrained cultural belief system, an American way of life. Too often in recent months, as I have debated this issue with friends and colleagues, I have heard people speak of the need to protect "offensive" speech. The word offensive is used as if we were speaking of a difference in taste, as if I should learn to be less sensitive to words that "offend" me. I cannot help but believe that those people who speak of offense—those who argue that this speech must go unchecked—do not understand the great difference between offense and injury. They have not known the injury my sister experienced, have not known the fear, vulnerability, and shame experienced by the Wisconsin students described at the beginning of this chapter. There is a great difference between the offensiveness of words that you would rather not hear because they are labeled dirty, impolite, or personally demeaning and the *injury* inflicted by words that remind the world that you are fair game for physical attack, that evoke in you all of the millions of cultural lessons regarding your inferiority that you have so painstakingly repressed, and that imprint upon you a badge of servitude and subservience for all the world to see. It is instructive that the chief proponents of restricting people who inflict these injuries are women and people of color, and there are few among these groups who take the absolutist position that any regulation of this speech is too much.

Again, *Brown v. Board of Education* is a useful case for our analysis. *Brown* is helpful because it articulates the nature of the injury inflicted by the racist message of segregation. When one considers the injuries identified in the *Brown* decision, it is clear that racist speech causes tangible injury, and it is the kind of injury for which the law commonly provides, and even requires, redress.

Psychic injury is no less an injury than being struck in the face, and it often is far more severe. *Brown* speaks directly to the psychic injury inflicted by racist speech in noting that the symbolic message of segregation affected "the hearts and minds" of Negro children "in a way unlikely ever to be undone."[32] Racial epithets and harassment often cause deep emotional scarring and feelings of anxiety and fear that pervade every aspect of a victim's life. Many victims of hate propaganda have experienced physiological and emotional symptoms, such as rapid pulse rate and difficulty in breathing.

A second injury identified in *Brown*, and present in my example, is reputational injury. As Professor Tribe has noted, "Libelous speech was long regarded as a form of personal assault . . . that government could vindicate . . . without running afoul of the constitution."[33] Although *New York Times v. Sullivan* and its progeny have subjected much defamatory speech to constitutional scrutiny—on the reasoning that "debate on public issues should be uninhibited, robust, and wide-open"[34] and should not be "chilled" by the possibility of libel suits—these cases also demonstrate a concern for balancing the public's interest in being fully informed with the competing interest of defamed persons in vindicating their reputation.

The interest of defamed persons is even stronger in racial defamation cases than in the *Sullivan* line of cases. The *Sullivan* rule protects statements of fact that are later proven erroneous. But persons who defame a racial group with racial epithets and stereotyped caricatures are not concerned that they may have "guessed wrong" in attempting to ascertain the truth. The racial epithet is the expression of a widely held belief. It is invoked as an assault, not as a statement of fact that may be proven true or false. Moreover, if the *Sullivan* rule protects erroneous speech because of an ultimate concern for the discovery of truth, then the rule's application to racial epithets must be based on an acceptance of the possible "truth" of racism, a position that, happily, most first amendment absolutists are reluctant to embrace. Furthermore, the rationale of *Sullivan* and its progeny is that public issues should be vigorously debated and that, as the Supreme Court held in *Gertz v. Robert Welch, Inc.*, there is "no such thing as a false idea."[35] But are racial insults ideas? Do they encourage wide-open debate?

Brown is a case about group defamation. The message of segregation was stigmatizing to Black children. To be labeled unfit to attend school with white children injured the reputation of Black children, thereby foreclosing employment opportunities and the right to be regarded as respected members of the body politic. An extensive discussion on the constitutionality or efficacy of group libel laws is beyond the scope of this chapter, and it must suffice for me to note that although *Beauharnais v. Illinois*,[36] which upheld an Illinois group libel statute, has fallen into disfavor with some commentators, *Brown* remains an instructive case. By identifying the inseparability of discriminatory speech and action in the case of segregation, where the injury is inflicted by the meaning of the segregation, *Brown* limits the scope of *Sullivan*. *Brown* reflects the understanding that racism is a form of subordination that achieves its purposes through group defamation.

The third injury identified in *Brown* is the denial of equal educational opportunity. *Brown* recognized that even where segregated facilities are materially equal, Black children did not have an equal opportunity to learn and participate in the school community if they bore the additional burden of being subjected to the humiliation and psychic assault that accompanies the message of segregation. University students bear an analogous burden when they are forced to live and work in an environment where at any moment they may be subjected to denigrating verbal harassment and assault. The testimony of nonwhite students about the detrimental effect of racial harassment on their academic performance and social integration in the college community is overwhelming. A similar injury is recognized and addressed in the requirement of Title VII of the Civil Rights Act that employers maintain a nondiscriminatory, nonhostile work environment and in federal and state regulations prohibiting sexual harassment on campuses as well as in the workplace.

All three of these very tangible, continuing, and often irreparable forms of injury—psychic, reputational, and the denial of equal educational opportunity—must be recognized, accounted for, and balanced against the claim that a regulation aimed at the prevention of these injuries may lead to restrictions on important first amendment liberties.

The Other Side of the Balance: Does the Suppression of Racial Epithets Weigh for or Against Speech?

In striking a balance, we also must think about what we are weighing on the side of speech. Most Blacks—unlike many white civil libertarians—do not have faith in free speech as the most important vehicle for liberation. The first amendment coexisted with slavery, and we still are not sure it will protect us to the same extent that it protects whites. It often is argued that minorities have benefited greatly from first amendment protection and therefore should guard it jealously. We are aware that the struggle for racial equality has relied heavily on the persuasion of peaceful protest protected by the first amendment, but experience also teaches us that our petitions often go unanswered until protests

disrupt business as usual and require the self-interested attention of those persons in power.

Paradoxically, the disruption that renders protest speech effective usually causes it to be considered undeserving of first amendment protection. Note the cruel irony in the news story cited at the beginning of this chapter that describes the Stanford president's justification for prosecuting students engaged in a peaceful sit-in for violation of the university's Fundamental Standard: The protesting students were punished, but the racist behavior the students were protesting went unpunished. This lack of symmetry was justified on the grounds that punishment might violate the bigots' first amendment rights—a particularly ironic result given Professor Derrick Bell's observation that it was Black students' civil rights protests that underlay the precedents upon which white students relied to establish their first amendment rights in school and university settings. As in so many other areas, a policy that Blacks paid the price for is used against them and on behalf of whites. Once one begins to doubt the existence of a symmetry between official reactions to racism and official reactions to protests against racism, the absolutist position loses credence: It becomes difficult for us to believe that fighting to protect speech rights for racists will ensure our own speech rights. Our experience is that the American system of justice has never been symmetrical where race is concerned. No wonder we see equality as a precondition of free speech and place more weight on that side of the balance aimed at the removal of the badges and incidents of slavery that continue to flourish in our culture.

Blacks and other people of color are equally skeptical about the absolutist argument that even the most injurious speech must remain unregulated because in an unregulated marketplace of ideas the best ideas will rise to the top and gain acceptance. Our experience tells us the opposite. We have seen too many demagogues elected by appealing to U.S. racism. We have seen too many good, liberal politicians shy away from the issues that might brand them as too closely allied with us. The American marketplace of ideas was founded with the idea of the racial inferiority of nonwhites as one of its chief commodities, and ever since the market opened, racism has remained its most active item in trade.

But it is not just the prevalence and strength of the idea of racism that make the unregulated marketplace of ideas an untenable paradigm for those individuals who seek full and equal personhood for all. The real problem is that the idea of the racial inferiority of nonwhites infects, skews, and disables the operation of a market (like a computer virus, sick cattle, or diseased wheat). It trumps good ideas that contend with it in the market. It is an epidemic that distorts the marketplace of ideas and renders it dysfunctional.

Racism is irrational. Individuals do not embrace or reject racist beliefs as the result of reasoned deliberation. For the most part, we do not even recognize the myriad ways in which the racism that pervades our history and culture influences our beliefs. But racism is ubiquitous. We are all racists. Often we fail to see it because racism is so woven into our culture that it seems normal. In other words, most of our racism is unconscious. So it must have been with the middle-aged, white, male lawyer who thought he was complimenting a Mexican-American law student of mine who had applied for a job with his firm. "You speak very good English," he said. But she was a fourth-generation Californian, not the stereotypical poor immigrant he unconsciously imagined she must be.

The disruptive and disabling effect on the market of an idea that is ubiquitous and irrational, but seldom seen or acknowledged, should be apparent. If the community is considering competing ideas about providing food for children, shelter for the homeless, or abortions for pregnant women, and the choices made among the proposed solutions are influenced by the idea that some children, families, or women are less deserving of our sympathy because they are racially inferior, then the market is not func-

tioning as either John Stuart Mill or Oliver Wendell Holmes envisioned it. In the term used by constitutional theorist John Ely, there is a "process defect."[37]

Professor Ely coined the term *process defect* in the context of developing a theory to identify instances in which legislative action should be subjected to heightened judicial scrutiny under the equal protection clause. Ely argued that the courts should interfere with the normal majoritarian political process when the defect of prejudice bars groups subject to widespread vilification from participation in the political process and causes governmental decisionmakers to misapprehend the costs and benefits of their actions. This same process defect that excludes vilified groups and misdirects the government operates in the marketplace of ideas. Mill's vision of truth emerging through competition in the marketplace of ideas relies on the ability of members of the body politic to recognize "truth" as serving their interest and to act on that recognition.[38] As such, this vision depends upon the same process that James Madison referred to when he described his vision of a democracy in which the numerous minorities within our society would form coalitions to create majorities with overlapping interests through pluralist wheeling and dealing.[39] Just as the defect of prejudice blinds white voters to interests that overlap with those of vilified minorities, it also blinds them to the "truth" of an idea or the efficacy of solutions associated with that vilified group. And just as prejudice causes the governmental decisionmakers to misapprehend the costs and benefits of their actions, it also causes all of us to misapprehend the value of ideas in the market.

Prejudice that is unconscious or unacknowledged causes the most significant distortions in the market. When racism operates at a conscious level, opposing ideas may prevail in open competition for the rational or moral sensibilities of the market participant. But when individuals are unaware of their prejudice, neither reason nor moral persuasion will likely succeed.

Racist speech also distorts the marketplace of ideas by muting or devaluing the speech of Blacks and other despised minorities. Regardless of intrinsic value, their words and ideas become less salable in the marketplace of ideas. An idea that would be embraced by large numbers of individuals if it were offered by a white individual will be rejected or given less credence if its author belongs to a group demeaned and stigmatized by racist beliefs.

An obvious example of this type of devaluation is the Black political candidate whose ideas go unheard or are rejected by white voters, although voters would embrace the same ideas if they were championed by a white candidate. Once again, the experience of one of my gay students provides a paradigmatic example of how ideas are less acceptable when their authors are members of a group that has been victimized by hatred and vilification. Bob had not "come out" when he first came to law school. During his first year, when issues relating to heterosexism came up in class or in discussions with other students, he spoke to these issues as a sympathetic "straight" white male student. His arguments were listened to and taken seriously. In his second year, when he had come out and his classmates knew that he was gay, he found that he was not nearly as persuasive an advocate for his position as when he was identified as straight. He was the same person saying the same things, but his identity gave him less authority. Similarly, Catharine MacKinnon argues that pornography causes women to be taken less seriously as they enter the public arena.[40] Racial minorities have the same experiences on a daily basis as they endure the microaggression of having their words doubted, or misinterpreted, or assumed to be without evidentiary support, or when their insights are ignored and then appropriated by whites who are assumed to have been the original authority.

Finally, racist speech decreases the total amount of speech that reaches the market by coercively silencing members of those groups who are its targets. I noted earlier in this chapter the ways in which racist speech is inextricably linked with racist conduct. The primary purpose and effect of the speech/conduct that constitutes white supremacy is the exclusion of nonwhites from full participation in the body politic. Sometimes the speech/conduct of racism is direct and obvious. When the Klan burns a cross on the lawn of a Black person who joined the NAACP or exercised the right to move to a formerly all-white neighborhood, the effect of this speech does not result from the persuasive power of an idea operating freely in the market. It is a threat; a threat made in the context of a history of lynchings, beatings, and economic reprisals that made good on earlier threats; a threat that silences a potential speaker. Such a threat may be difficult to recognize because the tie between the speech and the threatened act is unstated. The tie does not need to be explicit because the promised violence is systemic. The threat is effective because racially motivated violence is a well-known historical and contemporary reality. The threat may be even more effective than a phone call that takes responsibility for a terrorist bomb attack and promises another, a situation in which we easily recognize the inextricable link between the speech and the threatened act. The Black student who is subjected to racial epithets, like the Black person on whose lawn the Klan has burned a cross, is threatened and silenced by a credible connection between racist hate speech and racist violence. Certainly the recipients of hate speech may be uncommonly brave or foolhardy and ignore the system of violence in which this abusive speech is only a bit player. But it is more likely that we, as a community, will be denied the benefit of many of their thoughts and ideas.

Again MacKinnon's analysis of how first amendment law misconstrues pornography is instructive. She notes that in concerning themselves only with government censorship, first amendment absolutists fail to recognize that whole segments of the population are systematically silenced by powerful private actors. "As a result, [they] cannot grasp that the speech of some silences the speech of others in a way that is not simply a matter of competition for airtime."[41]

Asking Victim Groups to Pay the Price

Whenever we decide that racist hate speech must be tolerated because of the importance of tolerating unpopular speech, we ask Blacks and other subordinated groups to bear a burden for the good of society—to pay the price for the societal benefit of creating more room for speech. And we assign this burden to them without seeking their advice or consent. This amounts to white domination, pure and simple. It is taxation without representation. We must be careful that the ease with which we strike the balance against the regulation of racist speech is in no way influenced by the fact the cost will be borne by others. We must be certain that the individuals who pay the price are fairly represented in our deliberation and that they are heard.

Even as our discussions concerning the efficacy of regulating racist speech on campuses continue, they evidence our lack of attention to the costs of constitutional injury borne by the victims. I have had scores of conversations about this topic over the past several months with students, colleagues, university administrators, ACLU board members, reporters, friends, relatives, and strangers. By now there is an experience of déjà vu each time I am asked to explain how a good civil libertarian like myself—a veteran of 1960s sit-ins and demonstrations, a progressive constitutional law professor, and a person who has made antiestablishment speech his vocation—could advocate censorship. I try to be patient, articulate, and good natured as I set forth the concerns and the arguments explored in this chapter. I try to listen carefully, to remain open to others' experiences and to my own strong instincts against governmental incursion on individual liberty.

Often when I am at my best, even the most steadfast defenders of the first amendment faith will concede that these are persuasive arguments. They say they agree with much of what I have said, they recognize I am proposing narrowly framed restrictions on only the most abusive, least substantive forms of racist speech, and they understand the importance of hearing the victims' stories. Then they say, "But I'm afraid I still come out differently from you in the end. I still don't see how we can allow even this limited regulation of racist speech without running some risk of endangering our first amendment liberties."

One of these encounters occurred at a recent dinner with colleagues in New York. My good friend and former colleague john powell—john is national legal director of the ACLU and he is Black—was in attendance. He told the following story:

> My family was having Thanksgiving dinner at the home of friends. We are vegetarians and my two kids were trying to figure out which of the two dressings on the table was the vegetarian dressing and which was the meat dressing. One of our hosts pointed to one of the dressings and said, "This is the regular dressing and the other is the vegetarian dressing." I corrected him saying, "There is no such thing as 'regular' dressing. There is meat dressing and there is vegetarian dressing, but neither one of them is regular dressing."

This incident reminded powell of the discussions he has had with his colleagues on the subject of regulating racist speech. "Somehow," he said,

> I always come away from these discussions feeling that my white colleagues think about the first amendment the way my friend thought about "regular" [meat] dressing, as an amendment for regular people or all people, and that they think of the equal protection clause of the fourteenth amendment the way my friend thought about vegetarian dressing, as a special amendment for a minority of different people.

Inevitably, in these conversations, those of us who are nonwhite bear the burden of justification, of justifying our concern for protection under our "special" amendment. It is not enough that we have demonstrated tangible and continuing injury committed against the victims of racist speech. There can be no public remedy for our special fourteenth amendment injury until we have satisfied our interlocutors that there is no possible risk of encroachment on their first amendment—the "regular" amendment.

If one asks why we always begin by asking whether we can afford to fight racism rather than asking whether we can afford not to, or if one asks why my colleagues who oppose all regulation of racist speech do not feel that the burden is theirs to justify a reading of the first amendment that requires sacrificing rights guaranteed under the equal protection clause, then one sees an example of how unconscious racism operates in the marketplace of ideas.

Well-meaning individuals who are committed to equality without regard to race and who have demonstrated that commitment in many arenas do not recognize where the burden of persuasion has been placed in this discussion. When they do, they do not understand why. Even as I experienced the frustration of always bearing the burden of persuasion, I did not see the source of my frustration or understand its significance until powell told his story about the Thanksgiving dressing. Unfortunately, our unconscious racism causes even those of us who are the direct victims of racism to view the first amendment as the "regular" amendment—an amendment that works for all people—and the equal protection clause and racial equality as a special-interest amendment important to groups that are less valued.

Derrick Bell has noted that often in our constitutional history the rights of Blacks have been sacrificed because sacrifice was believed necessary to preserve the greater interests of the whole.[42] It is not just the actual sacrifice that is racist but also the way the "whole with the greater interests" gets defined. Today in a world committed to the idea of equality, we rarely notice the sacrifice or how we have avoided noticing the sacrifice by defining the interests of whites as the whole, "the regular." When we think this way, when we see the potential danger of incursions on the first amendment but do not see existing incursions on the fourteenth amendment, our perceptions have been influenced by an entire belief system that makes us less sensitive to the injury experienced by nonwhites. Unaware, we have adopted a worldview that takes for granted Black sacrifice.

Richard Delgado has suggested there is another way in which those of us who abhor racist speech but insist that it cannot be regulated may be, perhaps unwittingly, benefiting from the presence of "a certain amount of low-grade racism" in the environment:

> I believe that racist speech benefits powerful white-dominated institutions. The highly educated, refined persons who operate the University of Wisconsin, other universities, major corporations, would never, ever themselves utter a racial slur. That is the last thing they would do.
>
> Yet, they benefit, and on a subconscious level they know they benefit, from a certain amount of low-grade racism in the environment. If an occasional bigot or redneck calls one of us a nigger or spick one night late as we're on our way home from the library, that is all to the good. Please understand that I am not talking about the very heavy stuff—violence, beatings, bones in the nose. That brings out the TV cameras and the press and gives the university a black eye. I mean the daily, low-grade largely invisible stuff, the hassling, cruel remarks, and other things that would be covered by rules. This kind of behavior keeps non-white people on edge, a little off balance. We get these occasional reminders that we are different, and not really wanted. It prevents us from digging in too strongly, starting to think we could really belong here. It makes us a little introspective, a

little unsure of ourselves; at the right low-grade level it prevents us from organizing on behalf of more important things. It assures that those of us of real spirit, real pride, just plain leave—all of which is quite a substantial benefit for the institution.[43]

"WHICH SIDE ARE (WE) ON?"

However one comes out on the question of whether racist hate speech should be artificially distinguished from other fighting words and given first amendment protection, it is important to examine and take responsibility for the effects of how one participates in the debate. It is important to consider how our voice is heard. We must ask ourselves whether in our well-placed passion for preserving our first amendment freedoms we have been forceful enough in our personal condemnation of ideas we abhor, whether we have neglected our alliances with victims of the oppressive manifestations of the continuing dominance of these racist ideas within our communities and within ourselves.

At the core of the argument that we should resist all government regulation of speech is the ideal that the best cure for bad speech is good speech and that ideas that affirm equality and the worth of all individuals ultimately will prevail over racism, sexism, homophobia, and anti-Semitism because they are better ideas. Despite an optimism regarding the human capacity for good that can only be explained by faith, I am skeptical of ideals that provide the vehicle for oppressive ideology. I do not believe that truth will prevail in a rigged game or in a contest where the referees are on the payroll of the proponents of falsity. The argument that good speech ultimately drives out bad speech rests on a false premise unless those of us who fight racism are vigilant and unequivocal in that fight.

There is much about the way many civil libertarians have participated in the debate over the regulation of racist speech that causes the victims of that speech to wonder which side the civil libertarians are on. Those who raise their voices in protest against public sanctions against racist speech have not organized private protests against the voices of racism. It has been people of color, women, and gays who have held vigils at offending fraternity houses, staged candlelight marches and counterdemonstrations, and distributed flyers calling upon their classmates and colleagues to express their outrage at pervasive racism, sexism, and homophobia in their midst and to show their solidarity with its victims.

Traditional civil libertarians have been conspicuous largely in their absence from these group expressions of condemnation. Their failure to participate in this marketplace response to speech with more speech is often justified, paradoxically, as concern for the principle of free speech. When racial minorities or other victims of hate speech hold counterdemonstrations or engage in picketing, leafleting, heckling, or booing of racist speakers, civil libertarians often accuse them of private censorship, of seeking to silence opposing points of view. When both public and private responses to racist speech are rejected as contrary to the principle of free speech, it is no wonder that the victims of racism do not consider first amendment absolutists allies.

Blacks and other racial minorities also are made skeptical by the resistance encountered when we approach traditional civil liberties groups like the ACLU with suggestions that they at least reconsider the ways in which they engage in this complex debate concerning speech and equality. Traditional civil liberties lawyers typically have elected to stand by as universities respond to the outbreak of hate speech by adopting regulations that often are drafted with considerable attention to appeasing various, widely diverging political constituencies with only passing concern for either free speech or equality. Not surprisingly, these regulations are vague and overbroad. I believe that there is an element of unconscious collusion in the failure of universities, some with top-notch legal staffs and fine law schools, to draft narrow, carefully crafted regulations. For example, it is difficult to believe that anyone at the University of Michigan Law School was consulted in drafting the regulation that was struck down at that university.[44] It is almost as if the university administrators purposefully wrote an unconstitutional regulation so that they could say to the Black students, "We tried to help you, but the courts just won't let us do it." Such sloppy regulations provide easy prey for the white-hatted defenders of the first amendment faith who dutifully march into court to have them declared unconstitutional. Nor do some civil liberties lawyers stop there. They go on to point to the regulations' inadequacies as evidence that any regulation against racist speech may chill expression that should be protected.

Minority delegates to the 1989 ACLU biennial convention proposed a different approach. Their approach was to have the ACLU offer its expertise to schools and universities at the beginning of the legislative process instead of waiting until the end to attack a predictably unacceptable regulation. In the view of minority delegates, hearings should be held on university campuses where the incidence and nature of the injury of racist speech could be carefully documented and responses that were least restrictive of protected speech could be recommended. Such an approach would serve two important purposes. It would give civil libertarians an opportunity to influence the process from the outset, ensuring that the regulation reflected their constitutional concerns. It also would signal to racial minorities and other hate speech victims that the civil liberties community is aware of and concerned about issues of equality as well as free speech. But this approach to racist speech incidents was rejected at the national convention and has faced strong opposition when proposed to regional ACLU boards.

There is also a propensity among some civil libertarians to minimize the injury to the victims of racist speech and distance themselves from it by characterizing individual acts of racial harassment as aberrations, as isolated incidents in a community that is otherwise free of racism.

When those persons who argue against the regulation of racist speech speak of "silencing a few creeps" or argue that "the harm that censors allege will result unless speech is forbidden rarely occurs," they demonstrate an unwillingness even to acknowledge the injury. Moreover, they disclaim any responsibility for its occurrence. A recent conversation with a colleague about an incident at Stanford exemplifies this phenomenon. Two white freshmen had defaced a poster bearing the likeness of Beethoven. They had colored the drawing of Beethoven brown, given it wild curly hair, big lips, and red eyes and posted it on the door of a black student's dorm room in Ujamaa, the Black theme house. An investigation of the incident revealed that the two white students involved had been in an argument with the same Black student the night before. The white students contested the Black student's assertion that Beethoven was of African descent. It appeared that the Sambo-like defacement of the portrait was the white students' final rebuttal to the Black student's claim of familial relationship with the great composer—that this caricature was meant to ridicule the idea that such a genius could be Black—could be "Sambo."

My colleague shared my outrage at these students' behavior but went on to say that he thought I had misinterpreted the import of the incident in viewing it as a manifestation of more widespread racism at Stanford. He was inclined to explain the students' behavior as that of two rather isolated, ignorant, misguided youths acting out against the dominant liberal culture. This hardly seemed an accurate description to me. The message conveyed by the defaced poster replicated, in a crude form, an argument that was being made by much of the Stanford faculty in the then-current debate over Stanford's course requirement in Western Civilization. The thrust of much of the argument for maintaining a Eurocentric curriculum that included no contributions of people of color was that there were no significant non-European contributions to be included. The students' defacement had added a graphic footnote to that argument. It seemed to me—contrary to my colleague's explanation of the students' behavior—that they were imitating their role models in the professorate, not rebelling against them.

In its most obvious manifestations, the recent outbreak of racism on our campuses provides an opportunity to examine the presence of less overt forms of racism within our educational institutions. But the debate that has followed these incidents has focused on the first amendment freedoms of the perpetrators rather than the university community's responsibility for creating an environment where such acts occur. The resurgence of flagrant racist acts has not occurred in a vacuum. It is evidence of more widespread resistance to change by those holding positions of dominance and privilege in institutions, which until recently were exclusively white. An atmosphere that engenders virulent racist speech is inseparable from practices that exclude minorities from university professorships and attitudes that devalue their contributions to the culture. Those who are marginalized in these institutions—by their token inclusion on faculties and administrations, by the exclusion of their cultures from core curricula, and by an ideology of diversity and multiculturalism that seems to require assimilation more than real change in the university—see their colleagues' attention to free speech as an avoidance of these larger issues of equality.

I believe that the speech/acts that "race" us must all be fought simultaneously, for they are mutually dependent parts of a whole. At Stanford I have responded to some of my colleagues who have urged that we turn our attention from the relatively trivial concern of racist speech to more important concerns like affirmative action by suggesting that we tie the two efforts together. Why not hold the university responsible for individual violations of a regulation against racial harassment, much as the employer is held responsible under Title VII of the Civil Rights Act for the harassing acts of its employees? Each time a violation of the regulation against racist speech occurs there would be a public intervention in the form of a hearing and a public announcement of the judicial body's findings of fact. Instead of the university punishing the individuals involved, an affirmative remedy or reparation would be made by the university to the injured class. The university might set aside a slot for a minority professor or fund an additional full scholarship for a minority student, or cancel classes for a day and hold a university-wide teach-in on racism. Such a proposal would directly address the institution's responsibility for maintaining a discrimination-free environment; it would have the symbolic value provided by a clear university position against certain forms of racist speech, and it would avoid first amendment problems by placing public sanctions on the institution rather than the individual speaker. If minority students knew that concrete institutional resources were being spent to change the atmosphere of racism on campus, they would be less concerned that individual racist speakers were escaping punishment. As things are, minority students hear the call for focus on racist attitudes and practices rather than on racist speech as "just a lot of cheap talk."

When the ACLU enters the debate by challenging the University of Michigan's efforts to provide a safe harbor for its Black, Latino, and Asian students (in a climate that a colleague of mine compared unfavorably with Mississippi in the 1960s), we should not be surprised that nonwhite students feel abandoned. When we respond to Stanford students' pleas for protection by accusing them of seeking to silence all who disagree with them, we paint the harassing bigot as a martyred defender of democracy. When we valorize bigotry, we must assume some responsibility for the assaultive acts of those emboldened by their newfound status as defenders of the faith. We must find ways to engage actively in speech and action that resists and counters the racist ideas the first amendment protects. If we fail in this duty, the victims of hate speech rightly assume we are aligned with their oppressors.

We must also begin to think creatively as lawyers. We must embark upon the development of a first amendment jurisprudence that is grounded in the reality of our history and contemporary experience, particularly the experiences of the victims of oppression. We must eschew abstractions of first amendment theory that proceed without attention to the dysfunction in the marketplace of ideas created by racism and unequal access to that market. We must think hard about how best to launch legal attacks against the most assaultive and indefensible forms of hate speech. Good lawyers can create exceptions and narrow interpretations limiting the harm of hate speech without opening the floodgates of censorship. We must weigh carefully and critically the competing constitutional values expressed in the first and fourteenth amendments.

A concrete step in this direction is the abandonment of overstated rhetorical and legal attacks on individuals who conscientiously seek to frame a public response to racism that preserves our first amendment liberties. I have ventured a second step in this chapter by suggesting that the regulation of certain face-to-face racial vilification on university campuses may be justified under current first amendment doctrine as an analogy to the protection of certain classes of captive audiences. Most important, we must continue this discussion. It must be a discussion in which the victims of racist speech are heard. We must be attentive to the achievement of the constitutional ideal of equality as we are to the ideal of untrammeled expression. There can be no true free speech where there are still masters and slaves.

EPILOGUE

"Eeny, meeny, miney, mo."

It is recess time at the South Main Street School. It is 1952, and I am nine. Eddie Becker, Muck Makowski, John Thomas, Terry Flynn, Howie Martin, and I are standing in a circle, each with our right foot thrust forward. The toes of our black, high-top Keds sneakers touch, forming a tight hub of white rubber at the center, our skinny, blue-jeaned legs extending like spokes from the hub. Heads bowed, we are intently watching Muck, who is hunkered down on one knee so that he can touch our toes as he calls out the rhyme. We are enthralled and entranced by the drama of this boyhood ritual, this customary pregame incantation. It is no less important than the game itself.

But my mind is not on the ritual. I have lost track of the count that will determine whose foot must be removed from the hub, who will no longer have a chance to be a captain in this game. I hardly feel Muck's index finger as it presses through the rubber to my toes. My mind is on the rhyme. I am the only Black boy in this circle of towheaded prepubescent males. Time stands still for me. My palms are sweaty and I feel a prickly heat at the back of my neck. I know that Muck will not say the word.

"Catch a tiger by the toe."

The heads stay down. No one looks at me. But I know that none of them is picturing the capture of a large striped animal. They are thinking of me, imagining my toe beneath the white rubber of my Kids sneaker—my toe attached to a large, dark, thick-lipped, burr-headed American fantasy/nightmare.

"If he hollers let him go."

Tigers don't holler. I wish I could right now.

My parents have told me to ignore this word that is ringing unuttered in my ears. "You must not allow those who speak it to make you feel small or ugly," they say. They are proud, Mississippi-bred Black professionals and longtime political activists. Oft-wounded veterans of the war against the racist speech/conduct of Jim Crow and his many relations, they have, on countless occasions, answered the bad speech/conduct of racism with the good speech/conduct of their lives—representing the race; being smarter, cleaner, and more morally upright than white folk to prove that Black folk are equal, are fully human—refuting the lies of the cultural myth that is American racism. "You must know that it is their smallness, their ugliness of which this word speaks," they say.

I am struggling to heed their words, to follow their example, but I feel powerless before this word and its minions. In a moment's time it has made me an other. In an instant it has rebuilt the wall between my friends' humanity and my own, the wall that I have so painstakingly disassembled.

I was good at games, not just a good athlete, but a strategist, a leader. I knew how to make my teammates feel good about themselves so that they played better. It just came naturally to me. I could choose up a team and make the members feel like family. When other folks felt good, I felt good too. Being good at games was the main tool I used to knock down the wall I'd found when I came to this white school in this white town. I looked forward to recess because that was when I could do the most damage to the wall. But now this rhyme, this word, had undone all my labors.

"Eeny, meeny, miney, mo."

I have no memory of who got to be captain that day or what game we played. I just wished Muck had used "One potato, two potato . . . " We always used that at home.

NOTES

1. W.E.B. DuBois, *The Souls of Black Folk* 16–17 (1953).

2. V. Harding, *There Is a River* 82 (1981).

3. 347 U.S. 483 (1954).

4. Karst, *Citizenship, Race and Marginality*, 30 Wm. & Mary L. Rev. 1, 1 (1988).

5. 347 U.S. at 494.

6. 163 U.S. 537 (1896).

7. *Id.* at 560 (J. Harlan, dissenting).

8. *See, e.g.,* Strossen, *Regulating Racist Speech on Campus: A Modest Proposal?* Duke L. J. 484 at 541–43 (1990).

9. L. Tribe, *American Constitutional Law* §12–7 at 827 (2d ed. 1988).

10. 42 U.S.C. §2000a (1982).

11. K. Thomas, Comments at Frontiers of Legal Thought Conference, Duke Law School (Jan. 26, 1990).

12. C. MacKinnon, *Toward a Feminist Theory of the State*, 204 (1989).

13. *Jones v. Alfred H. Mayer Co.*, 392 U.S. 409, 439 (1968) (upholding Congress's use of the "badge of servitude" idea to justify federal legislation prohibiting racially discriminatory practices by private persons).

14. Michelman, *Conceptions of Democracy in American Constitutional Argument: The Case of Pornography Regulation*, 56 Tenn. L. Rev. 291, 306 (1989).

15. 109 U.S. 3 (1883).

16. 410 U.S. 113 (1973).

17. 448 U.S. 297, 316 (1980).

18. *See* Michelman, *supra* note 14, at 306–07.

19. U.S. Const. art. I, §2, cl. 3 and §9, cl. 1; art. IV, §2, cl. 3.

20. *Dred Scott v. Sanford*, 60 U.S. (19 How.) 393 (1857).

21. 339 U.S. 637 (1950).

22. *A Step Toward Civility*, Time, May 1, 1989, at 43.

23. *Id.*

24. *Heart of Atlanta Motel, Inc. v. United States*, 379 U.S. 241, 258 (1964); *see also Roberts v. United States Jaycees*, 468 U.S. 609, 624 (1984)(Court upheld the public accommodations provision of the Minnesota Human Rights Act).

25. 461 U.S. 574, 595 (1983).

26. 461 U.S. at 604.

27. Interpretation of the Fundamental Standard defining when verbal or nonverbal abuse violates the student conduct code adopted by the Stanford University Student Conduct Legislative Council, March 14, 1990. *SCLC Offers Revised Reading of Standard*, Stanford Daily, Apr. 4, 1990, §1, col. 4.

It is important to recognize that this regulation is not content neutral. It prohibits "discriminatory harassment" rather than just plain harassment, and it regulates only discriminatory harassment based on "sex, race, color, handicap, religion, sexual orientation, and national and ethnic origin." It is arguably viewpoint neutral with respect to these categories, although its reference to "words . . . that, by virtue of their form, are commonly understood to convey direct and visceral hatred or contempt" probably means that there will be many more epithets that refer to subordinated groups than words that refer to superordinate groups covered by the regulation.

28. *Chaplinsky v. New Hampshire*, 315 U.S. 568, 572 (1942).

29. *See Cohen v. California*, 403 U.S. 15, 21 (1971) (holding that the state could not excise, as offensive conduct, particular epithets from public discourse); *Erznoznik v. City of Jacksonville*, 43 U.S. 205, 209 (1975) (overturning a city ordinance that deterred drive-in theaters from showing movies containing nudity).

30. *See Kovacks v. Cooper*, 336 U.S. 77, 86 (1949) (right to free speech not abridged by city ordinance outlawing use of sound trucks on city streets); *Federal Communication Comm'n v. Pacifica Found.*, 438 U.S. 726, 748 (1978) (limited first amendment protection of broadcasting that extends into privacy of home); Rowan v. United States Post Office Dep't,

397 U.S. 728, 736 (1970) (unwilling recipient of sexually arousing material had right to instruct Postmaster General to cease mailings to protect recipient from unwanted communication of "ideas").

31. Letter from Dulany O. Bennett to parents, alumni, and friends of the Wilmington Friends School (May 17, 1988).

32. 347 U.S. at 494.

33. L. Tribe, *supra* note 9, at 861.

34. 376 U.S. 254, 270.

35. 418 U.S. 323, 339 (1974).

36. 343 U.S. 250 (1952).

37. J. Ely, Democracy and Distrust, 103–04, 135–79 (1980).

38. J. S. Mill, On Liberty, ch. 2 (1859).

39. J. Madison, The Federalist No. 51, at 323–24 (C. Rossiter ed. 1961).

40. MacKinnon, *Not a Moral Issue*, 2 Yale L. & Pol'y Rev. 321, 325–26, 335 (1984).

41. C. MacKinnon, *supra* note 12, at 206.

42. D. Bell, Racism and American Law, 30 (2nd ed. 1980).

43. R. Delgado, Address to State Historical Society, Madison, Wis. (Apr. 24, 1989). Delgado drew an analogy to Susan Brownmiller's observation that rape is the crime of all men against all women. Men who would never commit rape and who abhor it nonetheless benefit from the climate of terror that the experience of rape helps create.

44. 721 F.Supp. 852 (1989).

Pomona College Assesses Limits of Its Free-Speech Wall

Twenty years ago, students at Pomona College, a small liberal arts institution east of Los Angeles, began scrawling and painting their passions on a gray cinder-block wall, turning what had been built as a flood barrier into a free-speech forum and public art display.

Over the past five years, expressions of bigotry and calls for violence against minorities have appeared on the wall in addition to less controversial messages like "Relax" and "Remember World AIDS Day." Now, after a scrawled "Kill O. J." appeared on the wall after the verdict in the O. J. Simpson trial, college officials are considering whether this symbol of free speech has become so hurtful that it should be torn down.

The college president, Peter W. Stanley, has appointed a committee of faculty members, students and college administrators to study the issue and recommend a solution. Its report is expected by Feb. 28.

"What we are trying to figure out is if the benefit is worth the pain of the disruption," said David Menefee-Libey, an associate professor of politics who is on the committee.

Pomona is not the first college faced with the task of fighting "hate speech" without infringing on freedom of expression and academic liberty.

Stanford University, for example, recently tried to institute a speech code, but the courts struck down the code as unconstitutional.

The first disturbing message appeared on Pomona's wall five years ago when an "Asian American Studies Now" sign was painted over to read "Asian Students Die." Since then, other messages, many directed against blacks and homosexuals, have caused outcries. But it was the "Kill O. J." message, which appeared with a drawing of a noose, that prompted college officials to re-assess the wall, said the college's associate dean of students, Toni Clark.

Faculty members on the evaluation committee say they are not trying to limit student speech or apply speech codes. "This isn't a question of free speech versus censorship," Mr. Menefee-Libey said. "What this is about is how do we engage each other and what do we do when individuals say antagonistic, stupid things."

But some students say that any effort to regulate what is permitted on the wall will be an unacceptable limit on speech.

"I'm not for censorship," said Nissa Perez, 21, a senior at Scripps College, which, with Pomona and three adjacent campuses, make up the Claremont Colleges.

Speaking of the wall, Ms. Perez said, "I basically don't walk around it if I don't like what's on it." The wall, 5 feet high and 200 feet long, stands between the college library and the student dormitories on the northern side of the campus.

"College Assesses Limits of Its Free-Speech Wall," *The New York Times*, 03 January 1996: B6. Copyright (c) 1996 The New York Times Company. Reprinted with permission.

For twenty years a flood wall on the Pomona College campus has served as an unofficial bulletin board, but the appearance of hateful messages and racist comments in recent years prompted administrators to consider whether the bounds of free speech had been crossed.

Luis Sinco/NYT Pictures, "The Walker Campus Wall, Pomona College," *The New York Times*, 03 January 1996. Copyright (c) 1996 by the New York Times Co. Reprinted with permission.

One change under consideration would require anyone putting something on the wall to affix his or her name as well. That, Ms. Clark said, would force students to "assume responsibility for their actions."

Opponents argue that requiring signatures [would] just be another form of censorship. "There is a certain chilling effect that would come from that," said Leo Flynn, a professor of politics at Pomona. "Anonymity is an important constitutional component."

Over the years, Pomona administrators never interfered with messages on the wall, Ms. Clark said, unless the message was "personally directed or obviously obscene." When one appeared, the college had it promptly painted over, and that never drew a protest.

Editor's Note: According to Pomona College officials, the wall still stands and continues to serve as an informal campus message center. No policies have been adopted to regulate students' use of the wall.

29.

In Defense of Prejudice: Why Incendiary Speech Must Be Protected

Jonathan Rauch

Jonathan Rauch is the author of *Kindly Inquisitors: The New Attacks on Free Thought* and is a writer for *The Economist*. An opponent of speech codes, Rauch argues that support for intellectual pluralism is inconsistent with the institution of speech codes. If we want a society in which we have genuine freedom of expression, intellectual freedom, and a tolerant pluralism, then we must accept the inevitable and regrettable costs—racism, sexism, and homophobia. Rauch concludes that "an enlightened and efficient intellectual regime lets a million prejudices bloom, including many that you or I may regard as hateful or grotesque. It avoids any attempt to stamp out prejudice, because stamping out prejudice really means forcing everyone to share the same prejudice, namely, that of whoever is in authority."

The war on prejudice is now, in all likelihood, the most uncontroversial social movement in America. Opposition to "hate speech," formerly identified with the liberal left, has become a bipartisan piety. In the past year, groups and factions that agree on nothing else have agreed that the public expression of any and all prejudices must be forbidden. On the left, protesters and editorialists have insisted that Francis L. Lawrence resign as president of Rutgers University for describing blacks as "a disadvantaged population that doesn't have that genetic, hereditary background to have a higher average." On the other side of the ideological divide, Ralph Reed, the executive director of the Christian Coalition, responded to criticism of the religious right by calling a press conference to denounce a supposed outbreak of "namecalling, scapegoating, and religious bigotry." Craig Rogers, an evangelical Christian student at California State University, recently filed a $2.5 million sexual-harassment suit against a lesbian professor of psychology, claiming that anti-male bias in one of her lectures violated campus rules and left him feeling "raped and trapped."

In universities and on Capitol Hill, in workplaces and newsrooms, authorities are declaring that there is no place for racism, sexism, homophobia, Christian-bashing, and other forms of prejudice in public debate or even in private thought. "Only when racism and other forms of prejudice are expunged," say the crusaders for sweetness and light, "can minorities be safe and society be fair." So sweet, this dream of a world without prejudice. But the very last thing society should do is seek to utterly eradicate racism and other forms of prejudice.

Jonathan Rauch, "In Defense of Prejudice: Why Incendiary Speech Must Be Protected," *Harper's Magazine* 290 (May 1995): 37–44. Copyright (c) 1995 by *Harper's Magazine*. All rights reserved. Reproduced from the May issue by special permission.

I suppose I should say, in the customary I-hope-I-don't-sound-too-defensive tone, that I am not a racist and that this is not an article favoring racism or any other particular prejudice. It is an article favoring intellectual pluralism, which permits the expression of various forms of bigotry and always will. Although we like to hope that a time will come when no one will believe that people come in types and that each type belongs with its own kind, I doubt such a day will ever arrive. By all indications, *Homo sapiens* is a tribal species for whom "us versus them" comes naturally and must be continually pushed back. Where there is genuine freedom of expression, there will be racist expression. There will also be people who believe that homosexuals are sick or threaten children or—especially among teenagers—are rightful targets of manly savagery. Homosexuality will always be incomprehensible to most people, and what is incomprehensible is feared. As for anti-Semitism, it appears to be a hardier virus than influenza. If you want pluralism, then you get racism and sexism and homophobia, and communism and fascism and xenophobia and tribalism, and that is just for a start. If you want to believe in intellectual freedom and the progress of knowledge and the advancement of science and all those other good things, then you must swallow hard and accept this: for as thickheaded and wayward an animal as us, the realistic question is how to make the best of prejudice, not how to eradicate it.

Indeed, "eradicating prejudice" is so vague a proposition as to be meaningless. Distinguishing prejudice reliably and nonpolitically from non-prejudice, or even defining it crisply, is quite hopeless. We all feel we know prejudice when we see it. But do we? At the University of Michigan, a student said in a classroom discussion that he considered homosexuality a disease treatable with therapy. He was summoned to a formal disciplinary hearing, for violating the school's policy against speech that "victimizes" people based on "sexual orientation." Now, the evidence is abundant that this particular hypothesis is wrong, and any American homosexual can attest to the harm that the student's hypothesis has inflicted on many real people. But was it a statement of prejudice or of misguided belief? Hate speech or hypothesis? Many Americans who do not regard themselves as bigots or haters believe that homosexuality is a treatable disease. They may be wrong, but are they all bigots? I am unwilling to say so, and if you are willing, beware. The line between a prejudiced belief and a merely controversial one is elusive, and the harder you look the more elusive it becomes. "God hates homosexuals" is a statement of fact, not of bias, to those who believe it; "American criminals are disproportionately black" is a statement of bias, not of fact, to those who disbelieve it.

Who is right? You may decide, and so may others, and there is no need to agree. That is the great innovation of intellectual pluralism (which is to say, of post-Enlightenment science, broadly defined). We cannot know in advance or for sure which belief is prejudice and which is truth, but to advance knowledge we don't need to know. The genius of intellectual pluralism lies not in doing away with prejudices and dogmas but in channeling them—making them socially productive by pitting prejudice against prejudice and dogma against dogma, exposing all to withering public criticism. What survives at the end of the day is our base of knowledge.

What they told us in high school about this process is very largely a lie. The Enlightenment tradition taught us that science is orderly, antiseptic, rational, the province of detached experimenters and high-minded logicians. In the popular view, science stands for reason against prejudice, open-mindedness against dogma, calm consideration against passionate attachment—all personified by pop-science icons like the magisterially deductive Sherlock Holmes, the

coolly analytic Mr. Spock, the genially authoritative Mr. Science (from our junior-high science films). Yet one of science's dirty secrets is that although science as a whole is as unbiased as anything human can be, scientists are just as biased as anyone else, sometimes more so. "One of the strengths of science," writes the philosopher of science David L. Hull, "is that it does not require that scientists be unbiased, only that different scientists have different biases." Another dirty secret is that, no less than the rest of us, scientists can be dogmatic and pigheaded. "Although this pigheadedness often damages the careers of individual scientists," says Hull, "it is beneficial for the manifest goal of science," which relies on people to invest years in their ideas and defend them passionately. And the dirtiest secret of all, if you believe in the antiseptic popular view of science, is that this most ostensibly rational of enterprises depends on the most irrational of motives—ambition, narcissism, animus, even revenge. "Scientists acknowledge that among their motivations are natural curiosity, the love of trust, and the desire to help humanity, but other inducements exist as well, and one of them is to 'get that son of a bitch,'" says Hull. "Time and again, scientists whom I interviewed described the powerful spur that 'showing that son of a bitch' supplied to their own research."

Many people, I think, are bewildered by this unvarnished and all too human view of science. They believe that for a system to be unprejudiced, the people in it must also be unprejudiced. In fact, the opposite is true. Far from eradicating ugly or stupid ideas and coarse or unpleasant motives, intellectual pluralism relies upon them to excite intellectual passion and redouble scientific effort. I know of no modern idea more ugly and stupid than that the Holocaust never happened, nor any idea more viciously motivated. Yet the deniers' claims that the Auschwitz gas chambers could not have worked led to closer study and in 1993, research showing, at last, how they actually did work. Thanks to prejudice and stupidity, another opening for doubt has been shut.

An enlightened and efficient intellectual regime lets a million prejudices bloom, including many that you or I may regard as hateful or grotesque. It avoids any attempt to stamp out prejudice, because stamping out prejudice really means forcing everyone to share the same prejudice, namely that of whatever is in authority. The great American philosopher Charles Sanders Peirce wrote in 1877: "When complete agreement could not otherwise be reached, a general massacre of all who have not thought in a certain way has proved a very effective means of settling opinion in a country." In speaking of "settling opinion," Peirce was writing about one of the two or three most fundamental problems that any human society must confront and solve. For most societies down through the centuries, this problem was dealt with in the manner he described: errors were identified by the authorities—priests, politburos, dictators—or by mass opinion, and then the error-makers were eliminated along with their putative mistakes. "Let all men who reject the established belief be terrified into silence," wrote Peirce, describing this system. "This method has, from the earliest times, been one of the chief means of upholding correct theological and political doctrines."

Intellectual pluralism substitutes a radically different doctrine: we kill our mistakes rather than each other. Here I draw on another great philosopher, the late Karl Popper, who pointed out that the critical method of science "consists in letting our hypotheses die in our stead." Those who are in error are not (or are not supposed to be) banished or excommunicated or forced to sign a renunciation or required to submit to "rehabilitation" or sent for psychological counseling. It is the error we punish, not the errant. By letting people make errors—even mischievous, spiteful errors (as, for instance, Galileo's insistence on Copernicanism was taken to be in 1633)—pluralism creates room to challenge orthodoxy, think imaginatively, experiment boldly. Brilliance and bigotry are empowered in the same stroke.

Pluralism is the principle that protects and makes a place in human company for that loneliest and most vulnerable of all minorities, the minority who is hounded and despised among blacks and whites, gays and straights, who is suspect or criminal among every tribe in every nation of the world, and yet on whom progress depends: the dissident. I am not saying that dissent is always or even usually enlightened. Most of the time it is foolish and self-serving. No dissident has the right to be taken seriously, and the fact that Aryan Nation racists or Nation of Islam anti-Semites are unorthodox does not entitle them to respect. But what goes around comes around. As a supporter of gay marriage, for example, I reject the majority's view of family, and as a Jew I reject its view of God. I try to be civil, but the fact is that most Americans regard my views on marriage as a reckless assault on the most fundamental of all institutions, and many people are more than a little discomfited by the statement "Jesus Christ was no more divine than anybody else" (which is why so few people ever say it). Trap the racists and anti-Semites, and you lay a trap for me too. Hunt for them with eradication in your mind, and you have brought dissent itself within your sights.

The new crusade against prejudice waves aside such warnings. Like earlier crusades against antisocial ideas, the mission is fueled by good (if cocksure) intentions and a genuine sense of urgency. Some kinds of error are held to be intolerable, like pollutants that even in small traces poison the water for a whole town. Some errors are so pernicious as to damage real people's lives, so wrongheaded that no person of right mind or goodwill could support them. Like their forebears of other stripe—the Church in its campaigns against heretics, the McCarthyites in their campaigns against Communists—the modern anti-racist and anti-sexist and anti-homophobic campaigners are totalists, demanding not that misguided ideas and ugly expressions be corrected or criticized but that they be eradicated. They make war not on errors but on error, and like other totalists they act in the name of public safety—the safety, especially, of minorities.

The sweeping implications of this challenge to pluralism are not, I think, well enough understood by the public at large. Indeed, the new brand of totalism has yet even to be properly named. "Multiculturalism," for instance, is much too broad. "Political correctness" comes closer but is too trendy and snide. For lack of anything else, I will call the new anti-pluralism "purism," since its major tenet is that society cannot be just until the last traces of invidious prejudice have been scrubbed away. Whatever you call it, the purists' way of seeing things has spread through American intellectual life with remarkable speed, so much so that many people will blink at you uncomprehendingly or even call you a racist (or sexist or homophobe, etc.) if you suggest that expressions of racism should be tolerated or that prejudice has its part to play.

The new purism sets out, to begin with, on a campaign against words, for words are the currency of prejudice, and if prejudice is hurtful then so must be prejudiced words. "We are not safe when these violent words are among us," wrote Mari Matsuda, then a UCLA law professor. Here one imagines gangs of racist words swinging chains and smashing heads in back alleys. To suppress bigoted language seems, at first blush, reasonable, but it quickly leads to a curious result. A peculiar kind of verbal shamanism takes root, as though certain expressions, like curses or magical incantations, carry in themselves the power to hurt or heal—as though words were bigoted rather than people. "Context is everything," people have always said. The use of the word "nigger" in *Huckleberry Finn* does not make the book an "act" of hate speech—or does it? In the new view, this is no longer so clear. The very utterance of the word "nigger" (at least by a non-black) is a racist act. When a *Sacramento Bee* cartoonist put the word "nigger" mockingly in the mouth of a white su-

premacist, there were howls of protest and 1,400 canceled subscriptions and an editorial apology, even though the word was plainly being invoked against racists, not against blacks.

Faced with escalating demands of verbal absolutism, newspapers issue lists of forbidden words. The expression "gyp" (derived from "Gypsy") and "Dutch treat" were among the dozens of terms stricken as "offensive" in a much-ridiculed (and later withdrawn) *Los Angeles Times* speech code. The University of Missouri journalism school issued a *Dictionary of Cautionary Words and Phrases* which included *"Buxom:* Offensive reference to a woman's chest. Do not use. See 'Woman.' *Codger:* Offensive reference to a senior citizen."

As was bound to happen, purists soon discovered that chasing around after words like "gyp" or "buxom" hardly goes to the roots of the problem. As long as they remain bigoted, bigots will simply find other words. If they can't call you a kike then they will say Jewboy, Judas, or Hebe, and when all those are banned they will press words like "oven" and "lampshade" into their service. The vocabulary of hate is potentially as rich as your dictionary, and all you do by banning language used by cretins is to let them decide what the rest of us may say. The problem, some purists have concluded, must therefore go much deeper than laws: it must go to the deeper level of ideas. Racism, sexism, homophobia, and the rest must be built into the very structure of American society and American patterns of thought, so pervasive yet so insidious that, like water to a fish, they are both omnipresent and unseen. The mere existence of prejudice constructs a society whose very nature is prejudiced.

This line of thinking was pioneered by feminists, who argued that pornography, more than just being expressive, is an act by which men construct an oppressive society. Racial activists quickly picked up the argument. Racist expressions are themselves acts of oppression, they said. "All racist speech constructs the social reality that constrains the liberty of nonwhites because of their race," wrote Charles R. Lawrence III, then a law professor at Stanford. From the purist point of view, a society with even one racist is a racist society, because the idea itself threatens and demeans its targets. They cannot feel wholly safe or wholly welcome as long as racism is present. Pluralism says: There will always be some racists. Marginalize them, ignore them, exploit them, ridicule them, take pains to make their policies illegal, but otherwise leave them alone. Purists say: That's not enough. Society cannot be just until these pervasive and oppressive ideas are searched out and eradicated.

And so what is now under way is a growing drive to eliminate prejudice from every corner of society. I doubt that many people have noticed how far-reaching this anti-pluralist movement is becoming.

In universities: Dozens of universities have adopted codes proscribing speech and other expression that (this is from Stanford's policy, which is more or less representative) "is intended to insult or stigmatize an individual or a small number of individuals on the basis of their sex, race, color, handicap, religion, sexual orientation or national and ethnic origin." Some codes punish only persistent harassment of a targeted individual, but many, following the purist doctrine that even one racist is too many, go much further. At Penn, an administrator declared: "We at the University of Pennsylvania have guaranteed students and the community that they can live in a community free of sexism, racism, and homophobia." Here is the purism that gives "political correctness" its distinctive combination of puffy high-mindedness and authoritarian zeal.

In school curricula: "More fundamental than eliminating racial segregation has to be the removal of racist thinking, assumptions, symbols, and materials in the curriculum," writes theorist Molefi Kete Asante. In practice, the effort to "remove racist thinking" goes well beyond striking egregious references from textbooks. In many cases it becomes a kind of mental engi-

neering in which students are encouraged to see prejudice everywhere; it includes teaching identity politics as an antidote to internalized racism; it rejects mainstream science as "white male" thinking; and it tampers with history, installing such dubious notions as that the ancient Greeks stole their culture from Africa or that an ancient carving of a bird is an example of "African experimental aeronautics."

In criminal law: Consider two crimes. In each, I am beaten brutally; in each, my jaw is smashed and my skull is split in just the same way. However, in the first crime my assailant calls me an "asshole"; in the second he calls me a "queer." In most states, in many localities, and, as of September 1994, in federal cases, these two crimes are treated differently: the crime motivated by bias—or deemed to be so motivated by prosecutors and juries—gets a stiffer punishment. "Longer prison terms for bigots," shrilled Brooklyn Democratic Congressman Charles Schumer, who introduced the federal hate-crimes legislation, and those are what the law now provides. Evidence that the assailant holds prejudiced beliefs, even if he doesn't actually express them while committing an offense, can serve to elevate the crime. Defendants in hate-crimes cases may be grilled on how many black friends they have and whether they have told racist jokes. To increase a prison sentence only because of the defendant's "prejudice" (as gauged by prosecutor and jury) is, of course, to try minds and punish beliefs. Purists say, Well, they are dangerous minds and poisonous beliefs.

In the workplace: Though government cannot constitutionally suppress bigotry directly, it is now busy doing so indirectly by requiring employers to eliminate prejudice. Since the early 1980s, courts and the Equal Employment Opportunity Commission have moved to bar workplace speech deemed to create a hostile or abusive working environment for minorities. The law, held a federal court in 1988, "does require that an employer take prompt action to prevent . . . bigots from expressing their opinions in a way that abuses or offends their co-workers," so as to achieve "the goal of eliminating prejudices and biases from our society." So it was, as UCLA law professor Eugene Volokh notes, that the EEOC charged that a manufacturer's ads using admittedly accurate depictions of samurai, kabuki, and sumo were "racist" and "offensive to people of Japanese origin"; that a Pennsylvania court found that an employer's printing Bible verses on paychecks was religious harassment of Jewish employees; that an employer had to desist using gender-based job titles like "foreman" and "draftsman" after a female employee sued.

On and on the campaign goes, darting from one outbreak of prejudice to another like a cat chasing flies. In the American Bar Association, activists demand that lawyers who express "bias or prejudice" be penalized. In the Education Department, the civil-rights office presses for a ban on computer bulletin board comments that "show hostility toward a person or group based on sex, race or color, including slurs, negative stereotypes, jokes or pranks." In its security checks for government jobs, the FBI takes to asking whether applicants are "free of biases against any class of citizens," whether, for instance, they have told racist jokes or indicated other "prejudices." Joke police! George Orwell, grasping the close relationship of jokes to dissent, said that every joke is a tiny revolution. The purists will have no such rebellions.

The purist campaign reaches, in the end, into the mind itself. In a lecture at the University of New Hampshire, a professor compared writing to sex ("You and the subject become one"); he was suspended and required to apologize, but what was most insidious was the order to undergo university-approved counseling to have his mind straightened out. At the University of Pennsylvania, a law lecturer said, "We have ex-slaves here who should know about the Thirteenth Amendment"; he was banished from campus for a year and required to make a public apology, and he, too, was compelled to attend a "sensitivity and racial awareness" session.

Mandatory reeducation of alleged bigots is the natural consequence of intellectual purism. Prejudice must be eliminated.

Ah, but the task of scouring minds clean is Augean. "Nobody escapes," said a Rutgers University report on campus prejudice. Bias and prejudice, it found, cross every conceivable line, from sex to race to politics: "No matter who you are, no matter what the color of your skin, no matter what your gender or sexual orientation, no matter what you believe, no matter how you behave, there is somebody out there who doesn't like people of your kind." Charles Lawrence writes: "Racism is ubiquitous. We are all racists." If he means that most of us think racist thoughts of some sort at one time or another, he is right. If we are going to "eliminate prejudices and biases from our society," then the work of the prejudice police is unending. They are doomed to hunt and hunt and hunt, scour and scour and scour.

What is especially dismaying is that the purists pursue prejudice in the name of protecting minorities. In order to protect people like me (homosexual), they must pursue people like me (dissident). In order to bolster minority self-esteem, they suppress minority opinion. There are, of course, all kinds of practical and legal problems with the purists' campaign: the incursions against the first Amendment; the inevitable abuses by prosecutors and activists who define as "hateful" or "violent" whatever speech they dislike or can score points off of; the lack of any evidence that repressing prejudice eliminates rather than inflames it. But minorities, of all people, ought to remember that by definition we cannot prevail by numbers, and we generally cannot prevail by force. Against the power of ignorant mass opinion and group prejudice and superstition, we have only our voices. If you doubt that minorities' voices are powerful weapons, think of the lengths to which Southern officials went to silence the Reverend Martin Luther King Jr. (recall that the city commissioner of Montgomery, Alabama, won a

$500,000 libel suit, later overturned in *New York Times v. Sullivan* [1964], regarding an advertisement in the *Times* placed by civil-rights leaders who denounced the Montgomery police). Think of how much gay people have improved their lot over twenty-five years simply by refusing to remain silent. Recall the Michigan student who was prosecuted for saying that homosexuality is a treatable disease, and notice that he was black. Under that Michigan speech code, more than twenty blacks were charged with racist speech, while no instance of racist speech by whites was punished. In Florida, the hate-speech law was invoked against a black man who called a policeman a "white cracker"; not so surprisingly, in the first hate-crimes case to reach the Supreme Court, the victim was white and the defendant black.

In the escalating war against "prejudice," the right is already learning to play by the rules that were pioneered by the purists activists of the left. [In 1994] leading Democrats, including the President, criticized the Republican Party for being increasingly in the thrall of the Christian right. Some of the rhetoric was harsh ("fire-breathing Christian radical right"), but it wasn't vicious or even clearly wrong. Never mind: when Democratic Representative Vic Fazio said Republicans were "being forced to the fringes by the aggressive political tactics of the religious right," the chairman of the Republican National Committee, Haley Barbour, said, "Christian-bashing" was "the left's preferred form of religious bigotry." Bigotry! Prejudice! "Christians active in politics are now on the receiving end of an extraordinary campaign of bias and prejudice," said the conservative leader William J. Bennett. One discerns, here, where the new purism leads. Eventually, any criticism of any group will be "prejudice."

Here is the ultimate irony of the new purism: words, which pluralists hope can be substituted for violence, are redefined by purists *as* violence.

"The experience of being called 'nigger,' 'spic,' 'Jap,' or 'kike' is like receiving a slap in the face," Charles Lawrence wrote in 1990. "Psychic injury is no less an injury than being struck in the face, and it often is far more severe." This kind of talk is commonplace today. Epithets, insults, often even polite expressions of what's taken to be prejudice are called by purists "assaultive speech," "words that wound," "verbal violence." To me, racial epithets are not speech," one University of Michigan law professor said. "They are bullets." In her speech accepting the 1993 Nobel Prize for Literature in Stockholm, Sweden, the author Toni Morrison said this: "Oppressive language does more than represent violence; it is violence."

It is not violence. I am thinking back to a moment on the subway in Washington, a little thing. I was riding home late one night and a squad of noisy kids, maybe seventeen or eighteen years old, noisily piled into the car. They yelled across the car and a girl said, "Where do we get off?"

A boy said, "Farragut North."
The girl: "*Faggot* North!"
The boy: "Yeah! Faggot North!"
General hilarity.

First, before the intellect resumes control, there is a moment of fear, an animal moment. Who are they? How many of them? How dangerous? Where is the way out? All of these things are noted preverbally and assessed by the gut. Then the brain begins an assessment: they are sober, this is probably too public a place for them to do it, there are more girls than boys, they were just talking, it is probably nothing.

They didn't notice me and there was no incident. The teenage babble flowed on, leaving me to think. I became interested in my own reaction: the jump of fear out of nowhere like an alert animal, the sense for a brief time that one is naked and alone and should hide or run away. For a time, one ceases to be a human being and becomes instead a faggot.

The fear engendered by these words is real. The remedy is as clear and as imperfect as ever: protect citizens against violence. This, I grant, is something that American society has never done very well and now does quite poorly. It is no solution to define words as violence or prejudice as oppression, and then by cracking down on words or thoughts pretend that we are doing something about violence and oppression. No doubt it is easier to pass a speech code or hate-crimes law and proclaim the streets safer than actually to make the streets safer, but the one must never be confused with the other. Every cop or prosecutor chasing words is one fewer chasing criminals. In the world rife with real violence and oppression, full of Rwandas and Bosnias and eleven-year-olds spraying bullets at children in Chicago and in turn being executed by gang lords, it is odious of Toni Morrison to say that words are violence.

Indeed, equating "verbal violence" with physical violence is a treacherous, mischievous business. Not long ago a writer was charged with viciously and gratuitously wounding the feelings and dignity of millions of people. He was charged, in effect, with exhibiting flagrant prejudice against Muslims and outrageously slandering their beliefs. "What is freedom of expression?" mused Salman Rushdie a year after the ayatollahs sentenced him to death and put a price on his head. "Without the freedom to offend, it ceases to exist." I can think of nothing sadder than that minority activists, in their haste to make the world better, should be the ones to forget the lesson of Rushdie's plight: for minorities, pluralism, not purism, is the answer. The campaigns to eradicate prejudice—all of them, the speech codes and workplace restrictions and mandatory therapy for accused bigots and all the rest—should stop, now. The whole objective of eradicating prejudice, as opposed to correcting and criticizing it, should be repudiated as a fool's errand. Salman Rushdie is right, Toni Morrison wrong, and minorities belong at his side, not hers.

Statement on Freedom of Expression and Campus Speech Codes
American Association of University Professors

Editor's Note: This is a policy statement issued by the American Association of University Professors (AAUP). The AAUP is a national association or union of college and university faculty.

Freedom of thought and expression is essential to any institution of higher learning. Universities and colleges exist not only to transmit existing knowledge. Equally, they interpret, explore, and expand that knowledge by testing the old and proposing the new.

This mission guides learning outside the classroom quite as much as in class, and often inspires vigorous debate on those social, economic, and political issues that arouse the strongest passions. In the process, views will be expressed that may seem to many wrong, distasteful, or offensive. Such is the nature of freedom to sift and winnow ideas.

On a campus that is free and open, no idea can be banned or forbidden. No viewpoint or message may be deemed so hateful or disturbing that it may not be expressed.

Universities and colleges are also communities, often of a residential character. Most campuses have recently sought to become more diverse, and more reflective of the larger community, by attracting students, faculty, and staff from groups that were historically excluded or underrepresented. Such gains as they have made are recent, modest, and tenuous. The campus climate can profoundly affect an institution's continued diversity. Hostility or intolerance to persons who differ from the majority (especially if seemingly condoned by the in-

American Association of University Professors, "Statement on Freedom of Expression and Campus Speech Codes," *Academe: Bulletin of the American Association of University Professors* 78 (July–August 1992): 30–31. All AAUP policy statements, including this statement on speech codes, are in the public domain.

stitution) may undermine the confidence of new members of the community. Civility is always fragile and can easily be destroyed.

In response to verbal assaults and use of hateful language some campuses have felt it necessary to forbid the expression of racist, sexist, homophobic, or ethnically demeaning speech, along with conduct or behavior that harasses. Several reasons are offered in support of banning such expression. Individuals and groups that have been victims of such expression feel an understandable outrage. They claim that the academic progress of minority and majority alike may suffer if fears, tensions, and conflicts spawned by slurs and insults create an environment inimical to learning. These arguments, grounded in the need to foster an atmosphere respectful of and welcome to all persons, strike a deeply responsive chord in the academy. But, while we can acknowledge both the weight of these concerns and the thoughtfulness of those persuaded of the need for regulation, rules that ban or punish speech based upon its content cannot be justified. An institution of higher learning fails to fulfill its mission if it asserts the power to proscribe ideas—and racial or ethnic slurs, sexist epithets, or homophobic insults almost always express ideas, however repugnant. Indeed, by proscribing any ideas, a university sets an example that profoundly disserves its academic mission. Some may seek to defend a distinction between the regulation of the content of speech and the regulation of the manner (or style) of speech. We find this distinction untenable in practice because offensive style or opprobrious phrases may in fact have been chosen precisely for their expressive power. As the United States Supreme Court has said in the course of rejecting criminal sanctions for offensive words: [W]ords are often chosen as much for their emotive as their cognitive force. We cannot sanction the view that the Constitution, while solicitous of the cognitive content of individual speech, has little or no regard for that emotive function which, practically speaking, may often be the more important element of the overall message sought to be communicated. The line between substance and style is thus too uncertain to sustain the pressure that will inevitably be brought to bear upon disciplinary rules that attempt to regulate speech. Proponents of speech codes sometimes reply that the value of emotive language of this type is of such a low order that, on balance, suppression is justified by the harm suffered by those who are directly affected, and by the general damage done to the learning environment. Yet a college or university sets a perilous course if it seeks to differentiate between high-value and low-value speech, or to choose which groups are to be protected by curbing the speech of others. A speech code unavoidably implies an institutional competence to distinguish permissible expression of hateful thought from what is proscribed as thoughtless hate. Institutions would also have to justify shielding some, but not other, targets of offensive language—not to political preference, to religious but not to philosophical creed, or perhaps even to some but not to other religious affiliations. Starting down this path creates an even greater risk that groups not originally protected may later demand similar solicitude—demands the institution that began the process of banning some speech is ill equipped to resist.

Distinctions of this type are neither practicable nor principled; their very fragility underscores why institutions devoted to freedom of thought and expression ought not adopt an institutionalized coercion of silence.

Moreover, banning speech often avoids consideration of means more compatible with the mission of an academic institution by which to deal with incivility, intolerance, offensive speech, and harassing behavior:

(1) Institutions should adopt and invoke a range of measures that penalize conduct and behavior, rather than speech, such as rules against defacing property, physical intimidation or harassment, or disruption of campus activities. All members of the campus community should be made aware of such rules, and administrators should be ready to use them in preference to speech-directed sanctions.

(2) Colleges and universities should stress the means they use best—to educate—including the development of courses and other curricular and co-curricular experiences designed to increase student understanding and to deter offensive or intolerant speech or conduct. Such institutions should, of course, be free (indeed encouraged) to condemn manifestations of intolerance and discrimination, whether physical or verbal.

(3) The governing board and the administration have a special duty not only to set an outstanding example of tolerance, but also to challenge boldly and condemn immediately serious breaches of civility.

(4) Members of the faculty, too, have a major role; their voices may be critical in condemning intolerance, and their actions may set examples for understanding, making clear to their students that civility and tolerance are hallmarks of educated men and women.

(5) Student personnel administrators have in some ways the most demanding role of all, for hate speech occurs most often in dormitories,

locker-rooms, cafeterias, and student centers. Persons who guide this part of campus life should set high standards of their own for tolerance and should make unmistakably clear the harm that uncivil or intolerant speech inflicts.

To some persons who support speech codes, measures like these—relying as they do on suasion rather than sanctions—may seem inadequate. But freedom of expression requires toleration of "ideas we hate," as Justice Holmes put it. The underlying principle does not change because the demand is to silence a hateful speaker, or because it comes from within the academy. Free speech is not simply an aspect of the educational enterprise to be weighed against other desirable ends. It is the very precondition of the academic enterprise itself.

Administrators Say Policies Serve Mainly as Deterrents

Susan Dodge

Although campus speech codes that ban slurs and epithets have set off volatile debates over students' First Amendment rights, administrators say the policies have rarely been used to penalize those who utter offensive remarks.

The so-called hate-speech codes were instituted at many public and private institutions following racial incidents on their campuses.

The codes, most of which have been adopted within the last four years, have been criticized by officials of the American Civil Liberties Union and others, who believe they violate the free-speech rights of students and, in some cases, of faculty and staff members. Hate-speech codes at the Universities of Michigan and Wisconsin were struck down by federal judges after the ACLU sued.

Most of the policies still in place ban offensive or demeaning words that are directed at someone's

gender, race, sexual orientation, religion, or handicap. The most widely known case of punishment under such a code was at Brown University, which expelled a student last year for yelling racist and anti-Semitic remarks in a dormitory courtyard. The student had been drinking, and university officials described him as unruly.

According to several college administrators, no other institution has expelled a student for offensive remarks, although a handful of students have been suspended for violating campus speech policies. Most of the time, however, administrators try to work out complaints with informal discussions between the student who used the remark and the one who was offended.

College administrators who enforce the policies say few students have used the codes to lodge complaints against others. The administrators say their policies serve primarily as a deterrent to offensive remarks rather than as an active tool to police behavior.

"I think every time you address a situation in the college with some kind of policy, it acts as an indication to everyone that it is a concern of the in-

Susan Dodge, "Campus Codes That Ban Hate Speech Are Rarely Used to Penalize Students; Administrators Say Policies Serve Mainly as Deterrents," *The Chronicle of Higher Education*, 12 February 1992: A35. Copyright (c) 1992 by The Chronicle of Higher Education, Inc. Reprinted with permission.

stitution," says Marilyn LaPlante, dean of students at Kalamazoo College. "And if it is a concern of the institution, that, I think, is the deterrent."

College officials also say that hate-speech policies can serve as a message to prospective minority students, who may feel more comfortable when institutions have written policies banning harassment.

Following are examples of how hate-speech policies are working at some institutions:

At Kalamazoo, an anti-harassment policy that has been in place since 1989 has never been used to punish a student. Kalamazoo officials developed the plan in response to reports from colleges across the country of an increase in harassment directed at members of minority groups, homosexuals, and women. "We wanted to be ready should we have any particular problems," Ms. LaPlante says.

Emory University has dealt with about two dozen allegations of violations since its anti-harassment policy was instituted in 1988. Many of the complaints have dealt with sexual harassment, although a few have involved accusations of anti-homosexual remarks. Emory suspended two graduate teaching assistants after allegations of sexual harassment, but it dealt with most of the other violations by reprimanding students who were found guilty.

Officials at the University of California at Los Angeles say that a student who violated the university's speech code and physically assaulted and sexually harassed other students has had to perform several hours of community service, establish a program to educate his fraternity about sexual harassment, and write a paper for the dean of students on the topics of "heterosexism" and the origins of programs aimed at discouraging sexual harassment. Another student who physically assaulted a student and violated the speech code has been prohibited from having any further contact with the victim of his attack and was required to write a paper on "Words of Oppression."

Eastern Michigan University has seen one violation of its anti-harassment policy. University officials would not reveal details of the case because they are still deciding on a penalty for the student involved.

Officials at the University of Arizona say they have not used the hate-speech policy they instituted in 1990. But Alexis Hernandez, associate dean of students, says that if the university were to punish students for violating the policy, "the focus would be on education." Students probably would be asked to attend workshops about harassment and participate in community-service projects.

Administrators at a variety of institutions with hate-speech policies say they prefer to resolve violations informally, rather than with official penalties.

"Generally, apologies and getting the students together help resolve a lot of the situations," says Beth Wilson, the affirmative-action officer at the University of Oklahoma.

"Most of the incidents aren't intended to be malicious," Ms. Wilson says. "They're just young, immature students who are, for the first time, getting immersed with people from different cultures. They just have to be sensitized."

Students on some campuses who use racial slurs or other types of epithets are required to go to special workshops to learn how slurs and epithets can upset others.

At Emory University, for example, administrators have held several workshops on sexual harassment for students and faculty and staff members who have been accused of using sexist remarks.

The participants are given quizzes so university officials can test their knowledge of what constitutes sexist behavior and harassment. They review legal cases involving sexual harassment, participate in "role playing" exercises to learn what the university considers to be harassment, and watch videos that feature various scenes involving sexual harassment.

"The workshop sessions are eye opening and enlightening," says Robert Ethridge, assistant vice-president for equal opportunity. "For some people, the sessions won't change their minds, but for others, being confronted with these issues has a long-term positive benefit."

Other proponents of workshops compare them to educational sessions that people convicted of drunk driving must attend in some states. "Some people might really feel remorse, and some might just be attending because they have to," says James E. Sulton, Jr., special assistant to the president for minority affairs for the University of Wisconsin system. "They can be effective in some cases in changing minds and attitudes."

Students who are punished under campus speech codes are sometimes assigned to attend courses in psychology, sociology, and ethics to increase their understanding of prejudice and stereotypes.

At the University of Wisconsin at Stevens Point, for example, a student who stole his Japanese roommate's bank card and used it to steal $60 was required to enroll in an ethics or East Asian studies course. The student who stole the card told campus officials that he resented his roommate because he was Japanese and did not speak fluent English.

Many institutions have not adopted separate codes to penalize students who say and do things that offend others. But some still punish students who say or do things that others find offensive.

Last fall, for example, Harvard University punished three medical students for an episode at a Halloween party. Two white students appeared in blackface as Clarence Thomas and Anita Hill, and a black student punched one of them.

A committee of several medical-school faculty members recommended that the white students prepare a syllabus and bibliography on medicine in a multi-ethnic society "for their own education and that of their classmates." The committee also recommended that the black student be suspended, but an appeals panel instead placed him on probation for two years. It also required him to complete 20 hours of community service working with victims of violence and to attend counseling sessions.

Officials on campuses that have not instituted hate-speech policies say that students do not have to be punished to understand the effect their remarks have had on others. Those officials say their experiences prove that speech codes aren't needed.

"I have a concern about forcing students into mandatory workshops," says Sue Wasiolek, dean for student life at Duke University, which does not have a hate-speech code. "It bothers me about our society in general that the only way people think they can change behavior is to set up a rule."

Ms. Wasiolek says she often invites students whose speech offends others to talk with her informally—talks that sometimes result in apologies.

She says: "Our mission is to facilitate the exchange of differences and different opinions—not to brainwash people."

30.

Dealing with Words That Wound

Richard Delgado and Jean Stefancic

Richard Delgado is professor of law and Jean Stefancic is research associate in law at the University of Colorado. Professor Delgado helped draft the University of Wisconsin's student conduct code dealing with hate speech and is the author of *Words That Wound: Critical Race Theory, Assaultive Speech, and the First Amendment*. In this essay, the authors argue that hateful speech aimed against women and men of color, white women, and gays and lesbians is not a *symptom* of subordination, but is itself a *source* of oppression. From our earliest years, we are exposed to a complex set of stereotypes, stories, and images that present distorted images of racial and sexual minorities; these words and images create subconscious assumptions and deep-seated expectations that cause and sustain discrimination. Delgado and Stefancic argue that unless we name and challenge this root cause of subordination, we will have a difficult time ending racial and sexual discrimination.

In recent years, some legal scholars and social activists have been seeking ways to combat the harm done to members of minority groups by hateful speech. Other scholars and activists have been focusing on the harm done to women by hard-core pornography. Today, the two groups of reformers are joining to formulate legal theories and approaches that draw on scholarly research concerning the way that the roles and identities of women, people of color, and gays and lesbians are constructed in society.

A conference held at the University of Chicago Law School in the spring was the first to bring together legal scholars, feminists, and community organizers to address hate speech and pornography in tandem.

It was just the beginning of the collaboration that will be needed, but it came at a critical time. A few years ago, when feminists in Indianapolis and Minneapolis succeeded in enacting antipornography ordinances (drafted by the writer-activist Andrea Dworkin and the University of Michigan law professor Catharine MacKinnon), courts and mayors struck them down. Later, two federal courts struck down hate-speech codes at the Universities of Wisconsin and Michigan.

When the United States Supreme Court handed down its decision in June 1992 in *R.A.V. v. St. Paul, Minn.*, prohibiting the city from banning cross burning, momentum slowed even further. Most cities and universities considering hate-speech codes put them on hold.

A possible turning point came in June, however, when the Supreme Court upheld enhanced sentences for hate-motivated crimes in a case known as *Wisconsin v. Mitchell.* That ruling, together with two Canadian Supreme Court decisions in 1990 and 1992 upholding prohibitions on pornography and hate crimes, suggest that

narrowly drawn restraints may one day be possible in the United States. (Canada has a constitutional system much like ours and shares a similar English-common-law heritage.)

A great deal of work remains to be done, however. The judiciary remains conservative, and much of the public harbors little sympathy for feminist or minority-group causes. But the emerging cooperation between two groups of reformers who previously had worked separately is notable. Those interested in restricting pornography and hate speech often have regarded each other warily, as though gains for one group could come only at the expense of the other, or as if one group's success in pricking America's conscience might cause the public to ignore the equally pressing claims of the other.

But now both groups of scholars and activists are realizing that dealing with stigmatizing expression—words that wound or degrading depictions of women—requires a fuller understanding of how subordination occurs in the first place. Unless those in the forefront of social change and legal reform understand how and why certain words acquire the power to wound, our efforts are likely to prove unsuccessful.

We are beginning to recognize that hateful speech is not the symptom of subordination (as it is often thought to be), but its very source. When a woman, black, gay, or lesbian is unfairly refused a job, that refusal hurts both the individual and society; that is why we have civil-rights laws and affirmative action. But the reason that certain people are refused jobs—as well as why the refusal hurts them and creates more than a momentary setback—stems from a background of cultural and ethnic imagery. Repetition of certain words and images recalls and reinforces that imagery.

From an early age, all of us are exposed to a host of stereotypes, stock characters, narratives, stories, and plots in which women are ornaments and people of color are stupid, happy-go-lucky, or licentious. We are beginning to

Richard Delgado and Jean Stefancic, "Dealing with Words That Wound," *The Chronicle of Higher Education*, 11 August 1993: B1. Copyright (c) 1993 by Richard Delgado and Jean Stefancic. Reprinted by the authors' permission.

understand how society uses such images to construct a social reality in which women and blacks are always at risk, one in which each new slight or injury reverberates against a history of similar ones. After years of repetition, offenses are targeted as much at groups as at individuals. Some actions, such as burning a cross or painting a swastika on a synagogue, gain a power that most insults directed at individuals lack—the power to demoralize.

Words can create categories, expectations, and subconscious assumptions so deep-seated that only troublesome mechanisms such as affirmative action can make headway against the system of subordination that they support. Unless we name and challenge this root cause of subordination, the progress of women and minorities in gaining equal access to jobs, credit, or education will be slow and limited. Indeed, gains for one group may well come at the expense of another, particularly in hard times when sympathy and money are limited.

The emerging insight into the roots and pervasiveness of subordination through symbolic depiction provides a framework that both groups of reformers can accept wholeheartedly, one that places the highest priority on exposing the harm of injurious words and images. This task will entail defining a radically new understanding of a First Amendment that protects equality as much as it has liberty; it will entail understanding the Constitution as a document that embraces not just one value, but many. Speech has never been protected absolutely— witness the dozens of "exceptions" that we have created or tolerated when free speech conflicts with other important social values, such as national security, intellectual property, the right to privacy, and the right to protect one's reputation, to name a few.

Further, it is not necessary to hold that words are actions, as some argue, to subject them to regulation. An important social interest, comparable to the interests undergirding the doctrines of libel, defamation, intentional infliction of emotional distress, or deceptive advertising, should suffice. Equality and everyone's right to be treated as a person worthy of respect represent, we believe, a comparable interest.

Earlier scholarship has already moved in this direction. Legal theorists such as Mari Matsuda of the University of California at Los Angeles and Charles Lawrence of Stanford University have urged that hate speech that takes the form of face-to-face taunts and revilement has no place in a system of protected expression. It wounds the victim while conveying no valid information; it is less akin to a political speech than to a slap in the face. In our own previous work, we have demonstrated that invective aimed at aspects of a person's core identity can seriously wound and damage, particularly young people. Some U.S. courts already afford individuals redress—through private actions for libel, assault, and intentional infliction of emotional distress—when they experience particularly vicious racial slurs, finding that the First Amendment interest of the speaker was weak or non-existent in comparison with the seriousness of the harm done.

The federal-court decisions concerning university speech codes indicate that such codes must be carefully tailored if they are to pass judicial muster, since they are broadly regulatory in impact, unlike the private tort actions mentioned above. Still, we do not believe that college administrators must sit idly by while many young minority students become embittered or leave the university because of repeated verbal abuse directed against their races or identities.

For example, although the Supreme Court ruled in last year's cross-burning case that regulations aimed at curbing insult and invective must be race-neutral—that is, apply equally to all—the Court's decision in June in *Wisconsin* v. *Mitchell* upheld statutes that impose extra penalties if conduct that is otherwise prohibited is directed at victims because of their race or on some other discriminatory basis.

As a short-term solution, then it would seem that a university's conduct code could be amended to include two separate provisions. One could penalize severe, disruptive, face-to-face insults (for example, a professor saying to a student in the professor's office, "You incompetent, illiterate fool"). A separate provision could stipulate that punishment for a campus offense would be increased for any behavior already prohibited in the code if that behavior was motivated by bias. The offenses designated in the first provision would be race-neutral (that is the lesson we should draw from the cross-burning case). Punishment could be tailored to motivation and seriousness (the lesson of the recent hate-crimes case). The combination of the two provisions might provide campus administrators with the tool that they need to deal with insults and hate speech, while remaining within Constitutional bounds.

Longer-term solutions and broader remedies will entail at least the following tasks:

- Lawyers and social scientists must be prepared to demonstrate through research the harm done by racial insults and pornography and to show how the law's conception of harm can be reasonably expanded to include notions of damaged identity.

- Lawyers and legal scholars must be ready to draw courts' attention to the experience of many other Western industrialized countries in successfully regulating pornography and hate speech. A growing literature on this topic is available.

- Scholars also need to find ways to demonstrate how "more speech"—the usual argument used by those opposed to curbing racist speech—is not a viable solution, and how talking back to the aggressor in most cases is either dangerous or futile.

- University officials must be prepared to show how institutions' interests are implicated when members of minority groups on campus must live with the fear of insult or assault, leading to demoralization and heavy dropout rates.

- We must drive home to all participants in the debate about hate speech the idea that speech without equality is a hollow illusion, and that true dialogue presupposes something like rough equality between the speakers—dialogue that cannot take place unless the most vicious forms of hate speech are curbed.

Above all, we need to explain how the old adage about "sticks and stones" may be misleading in one highly significant respect: The broken bone will heal. But the harm of being identified as a "nigger" or "fag" or "broad" will not fade—at least not without a concerted effort to challenge those pernicious categories. With the help of sympathetic scholars committed to equality and fair treatment for all, legal barriers to the regulation of hate speech and hard-core pornography will one day appear as anachronistic and inhumane as the 1896 doctrine upheld by the Supreme Court in *Plessy v. Fergusson*—that facilities could be separate but equal.

31.
Codes, Correctness, and Feminism

Marilyn Friedman

Marilyn Friedman is an associate professor of philosophy at Washington University. She has published widely on ethics, social philosophy, and feminism. She is the author of *What Are Friends For? Feminist Perspectives on Personal Relationships and Moral Theory*, and has recently coedited a collection of essays, *Feminism and Community*. In her brief essay, Friedman argues that we need to place the debate over college speech codes in a broader context. Although Friedman does not support speech codes, she is concerned that many critics of speech codes fail to show any sustained moral outrage over the prevalence of sexist, racist, and homophobic attitudes on our campuses. Perhaps in examining the details of debate over whether or not to formally regulate hateful speech acts, we have failed to attend to the deeper social problems. In the end, Friedman recommends that we not institute formal speech codes, but she cautions us against then failing to pay sufficient moral heed to the problems of offensive speech and discrimination in our academic communities.

In the fall of 1990, "political correctness" in the academy emerged as a national news media preoccupation. Political correctness comprises a host of academic reforms and attitudes that, according to their critics, are destroying higher education and threatening national survival.

The alleged culprit is the academic left, a group encompassing feminists, multiculturalists, Marxists, and deconstructionists. In their teaching and scholarship, these leftist academics are supposed to have launched a full-scale attack on Western civilization. They have replaced the classical works of Western culture with third world, anti-Western trash and have forsaken standards of truth, objectivity, and merit of any sort. They have consolidated their academic power by smuggling unqualified women and minorities into positions of educational dominance and by ruthlessly quashing dissenting voices. Their multicultural machinations will soon surely fragment the United States into an intellectual Yugoslavia.[1]

From the standpoint of the left, however, the picture is quite different. The reforms in question are intended to revamp a host of traditional academic practices and attitudes that constitute the *real* malaise of higher education. The real correctness to worry about, from a leftist perspective, is the "rectitude" of those traditionalists who resist the growing cultural diversity of academia today. The policies of the critics of political correctness would return us to the deplorably homogeneous and exclusionary educational world of yesterday.

The left has, accordingly, raised critical questions about the quality of everything academic, from esoteric scholarly research to the interpersonal dynamics of daily campus life. Most importantly, the left has challenged European, American, heterosexual, and masculine biases that continue to permeate traditional research and pedagogy. This challenge has rejuvenated age-old skeptical inquiries into such venerated notions as truth, objectivity, impartiality, and disinterested criticism. In addition, new fields of study have emerged to promote research into, and by, hitherto misrepresented or unrepresented peoples, fields such as African American studies and women's studies. Furthermore, the preeminence of Western canonical literatures in the humanities and social sciences has diminished as traditional disciplines themselves have witnessed the growth of new research paradigms emphasizing race, gender, ethnicity, and sexual orientation as analytical categories.

The left has also turned its attention to the campus environment. For some time now, the left has been contesting the persistently low numbers of women and certain minority groups in specific academic populations—students, faculty, or administration, as appropriate. The results of these challenges include the notorious affirmative action plans. The left has also worried about campus climates that are often inhospitable to students who are not white, not male, and not heterosexual. These concerns have led to student behavior codes that penalize insulting epithets used against women and minorities.

All of these developments fit under an umbrella rubric: the promotion of diversity and multiculturalism in academic life. Calls for diversity and multiculturalism have become anathema to many traditionalists and other opponents of these innovations. Most of what is

From Marilyn Friedman and Jan Narveson, *Political Correctness: For and Against* (Lanham, Maryland: Rowman & Littlefield, 1995): 1–6. Copyright (c) 1995 by Rowman & Littlefield Publishers, Inc. Reprinted with permission.

connected to the pursuit of multiculturalism is now ridiculed as being "politically correct." This label was co-opted from an earlier self-critical but friendly use by leftists themselves meant to deflate their own excesses with humor and irony. When the charge is deployed by critics of multiculturalism, however, the humor and irony vanish.

Although multiculturalism has had its share of defenders, there is still much that remains to be said on behalf of these controversial and challenging academic developments. In this spirit, my discussion [here] deals with . . . [one] topic that fit[s] under the general heading of political correctness: campus speech codes . . .

SPEECH CODES

A number of academic institutions have recently tried to implement a novel sort of student behavior code. The codes in question penalize students who use racist, sexist, or homophobic "hate speech" to insult other students. Schools that have experimented with these codes include Stanford University, the University of Michigan, and the University of Wisconsin. The codes have been drafted in an attempt to protect from verbal harassment certain groups of students who are otherwise vulnerable to taunts and insults. The intent of the codes is thus salutary. Nevertheless, they have been widely challenged as unjustified infringements on the First Amendment guarantee of freedom of speech.

Some of the challenges have taken legal form and speech codes are not faring well in the courts. In the fall of 1991, for example, the University of Wisconsin code was overturned by a U.S. district court that held that the code violated the constitutional guarantee of freedom of expression.[2] In 1992, the Supreme Court overturned a St. Paul, Minnesota, ordinance that similarly attempted to regulate racial and sexual epithets.[3]

Defenders of speech codes have tried to argue that the insults in question do not merit First Amendment protection because they are a variety of what the Supreme Court has called "fighting words." As defined by the Court in 1942, fighting words are those insults "which by their very utterance inflict injury or tend to incite an immediate breach of the peace."[4] In recent years, this court doctrine has been greatly modified but not entirely eliminated. Fighting words can still be penalized provided they pose the "clear and present danger" of a breach of the peace, for instance, a violent reaction by the insulted party.[5]

Unfortunately for the codes, court doctrine requires that an imminent danger be demonstrated in each and every case; no particular type of language can be declared punishable in advance. Nevertheless, in its 1992 decision regarding the St. Paul, Minnesota, ordinance, the Supreme Court allowed that fighting words could be banned provided the ban was not restricted to certain categories of insults, such as those focusing only on sex or race.[6] Thus, academic speech codes, if carefully drafted, may yet survive their court challenges.

The codes have, nevertheless, faced strong opposition. Regrettably, code critics too often seem far more bothered by requirements *not to express* racism, sexism, and homophobia in public than they are by the prevalence of those attitudes. In this context, however, I will not be defending academic speech codes as such. My concern focuses instead on some disturbing features in the campaign that has been waged against the codes by some of their critics.

First of all, code critics suggest that speech codes are being used to suppress criticism of policies such as affirmative action and abortion rights by treating such criticism as if it were racist or sexist language.[7] To my knowledge, this suggestion is incorrect. Speech codes have been neither designed nor implemented to suppress genuine debate over controversial issues. During the University of Wisconsin's brief period of speech code enforcement, students were penalized for calling other students such obscenities as "fucking bitch" and "fat-ass nigger."[8] If speech codes were used to punish criticism of, say, abortion or affirmative action, then that would be misuse of the codes. Misuse, however, does not show that codes against racist or sexist insults are themselves wrong. The real issue is whether or not it is legally and morally appropriate for an academic institution to penalize genuine group-based insults used by some students against other students.[9]

A second problem with the campaign being waged against speech codes is its occasional hypocrisy.[10] Code critics insistently invoke the constitutional and moral halo of a right to freedom of expression, or free speech. There have been a variety of threats to free speech in recent years, however, and someone who really wants to protect that right should have challenged all of them. Code critics have not always been so consistent.

A genuine defender of free speech would have objected to George Bush's executive order that prohibited employees in federally funded health clinics from counseling their patients about abortion services.[11] That is, a genuine defender of free speech would have been just as concerned then about the abortion "gag rule" as she was about campus speech codes. The morality of abortion was not at issue; the question was one of free speech, in this case, the freedom of a health care worker to tell a client about a legally available medical service.

Now, someone might try to justify an abortion "gag rule" by arguing that it is all right to curb the speech of anyone who is even partly supported by tax dollars if the taxpayers object to what is being said. Anti-abortion taxpayers do not want their tax dollars used to support even the merest mention of abortion. Remember, however, that opinion polls show repeatedly that only a minority of U.S. taxpayers are flatly opposed to abortion under any circumstances.[12] The relevant principle would have to be something like this: speech that is otherwise legal may be suppressed when it is partly supported by tax money and conflicts with the values of some taxpayers.

That principle, however, condones campus speech codes just as readily as it condones the abortion gag rule. Some taxpayers, I, for one, do not want our tax dollars going to support public universities in which some students may with impunity call other students "niggers," "bitches," and "faggots." Thus, using the gag rule as a model, college administrators at publicly funded universities are entitled to implement codes that penalize hate speech, as long as at least some of the taxpayers in that state oppose it. The same argument would hold by analogy for private universities whose financial supporters oppose hate speech on their campuses.

On the other hand, if it is wrong for universities to stifle racial and sexual insults, even when their financial supporters oppose such speech, then gag rules are also wrong that prevent health care workers from using polite speech to describe legally available medical services. Consistency calls for the opponents of speech codes to condemn abortion gag rules in the same breath in which they condemn the codes. In the case of those who have not done so, it is legitimate to wonder whether they are really defending all free speech or merely speech of a certain sort, in this case, racist, sexist, or homophobic insults.[13]

The third problem with the opposition to speech codes is that it sometimes blurs the issues and switches to a different target. Speech code critics sometimes try to make it seem as if leftist advocacy by itself is as much a violation of free speech rights as are the formal codes. Criticizing speech codes thereby becomes a vehicle for covertly denouncing leftist expression as such without having to respond to its content.

Nat Hentoff, for example, a journalist and veteran free speech proponent, complains that students who advocate leftist views in the classroom create a "chilling atmosphere" that leads other students to censor themselves. According to Hentoff, on one occasion at New York University Law School, a "sizable number" of leftist law students challenged the use of a case that was assigned for moot court competition. The case involved a divorced father who was trying to gain custody of his children because their mother, his ex-wife, had become a lesbian. The students who objected to using the case in moot court apparently thought that lesbian and gay students in the class might be offended by someone arguing on behalf of the father. A chilling atmosphere resulted, according to Hentoff, in which those students who wanted to discuss the case "censored themselves" from saying so.[14]

Why, we should ask, is Hentoff upset about this? Those leftist students who challenged the case were merely exercising their rights to free speech. Based on Hentoff's own principles, the fact that some students were chilled by the expression of this view is irrelevant. In a context of virtually unrestricted freedom in the expression of ideas, some people will sometimes say what others find to be chilling. Unrestricted freedom of speech is not a protection merely for those who want to insult women, minorities, lesbians, and gays.

Hentoff opposes speech codes because he does not think that black, female, lesbian, or gay students should be "insulated from barbed language." They should have to learn to respond to language they do not like "with more and better language of their own." On this subject, Hentoff quotes approvingly the words of Gwen Thomas, a "black community college administrator from Colorado." Thomas opposes speech codes on the grounds that students should have to learn "how to deal with adversarial situations."[15]

Evidently, Hentoff thinks that non-leftist students should *not* have to learn how to deal with adversarial situations. They should not have to learn to respond, with more and better language of their own, to the leftist views that chill the atmosphere for them.

The problem of free speech is that when a view is expressed by a majority of those present, or even a vocal minority, it might well suppress those who think differently. Rather than being part of the speech code framework, however, this group pressure is precisely the result of hav-

ing no prohibitions on the relevant speech. Facing virtually no restrictions, majority opinion or outspoken minority opinion will range wherever it can, and exert the pressures that it exerts. Sometimes the most vocal opinions will be leftist, and when this happens, conservatives and other nonleftists are the ones who will feel a bit of a chill.

If Hentoff really cares about freedom of *all* speech, he should gallantly accept the chilling effects exerted by vocal leftists no less than the chilling effects exerted by conservatives, racists, and bigots of all sorts as the price to be paid for whatever value we gain from freedom of speech. Why should blacks, women, and certain others have to devote extra time to responding to chilling or adversarial speech against them if students who dissent from leftist views are permitted to enjoy the luxury of not having to respond to their adversaries? After all, leftist students are entitled to exercise their own vaunted free speech rights, too.

I do not promote speech codes. I do support values of mutual respect, civility, and courtesy wherever possible—and most of the time, university life is a place where these values are eminently possible. Ideally, the members of our academic citizenries (and of our societies at large) should regard hate speech as so morally intolerable that they object to it vocally and point out the bigoted attitudes manifested by such speech. My recommendation, then, is to avoid the use of formal speech codes but to make sure that the issue of offensive speech does not die with the codes.

NOTES

1. My essay deals mainly with political correctness in U.S. postsecondary education. Many of these same issues, however, seem relevant to other Western nations.

Political correctness encompasses a variety of viewpoints, ranging from very moderate to very extreme. It is important for the critics of political correctness to engage with the most defensible versions of it; otherwise they are not giving the perspective its due and are deceiving their audiences. Thus, I do not pretend to represent the whole gamut of politically correct ideas; instead, I offer what I regard as the most reasonable versions of feminism, multiculturalism, and the rest.

2. *UWM Post v. Board of Regents of the University of Wisconsin System*, No. 90–C328, Oct. 11, 1991. See also Michele N.-K. Collison, "Hate Speech Code at U. of Wisconsin Voided by Court," *The Chronicle of Higher Education* 38, no. 9 (1991): A1, A37.

3. *R.A.V. v. City of St. Paul* (1992) 112 S.Ct. 2538.

4. *Chaplinsky v. New Hampshire*, 315 U.S. 568, 569 (1942), at 571–72.

5. Rodney A. Smolla, *Free Speech in an Open Society* (New York: Alfred A. Knopf, 1992), p. 162.

6. Christopher Shea, "Court's Decision on 'Hate Crimes' Sows Confusion," *The Chronicle of Higher Education* 38, no. 47 (1992): A26–27.

7. Nat Hentoff intermingles his criticism of formal speech codes with examples of students who wanted to criticize, say, affirmative action but did not do so because they feared the wrath of intolerant leftists (" 'Speech Codes' on the Campus and Problems of Free Speech," in *Debating P.C.*, ed. Paul Berman [New York: Dell, 1992], pp. 217–18. Reprinted from *Dissent* [Fall 1991]). Hentoff's juxtaposition erroneously makes it seem as if speech codes themselves contribute to this supposed repression.

8. Martha Albert Fineman, "Who Pays for Free Speech?," *Women's Review of Books* 9, no. 5 (1992): 17.

9. For an argument that such codes are appropriate, see Stanley Fish, "There's No Such Thing as Free Speech and It's a Good Thing, Too," in *Debating P.C.*, ed. Berman, pp. 231–45.

10. This problem does not show that the arguments against the codes are logically flawed. It pertains instead to the sincerity of code critics.

11. The gag rule was upheld by the U.S. Supreme Court in *Rust v. Sullivan* (1991) 111 S.Ct. 1759. That one particular group of U.S. Supreme Court justices decided the case in a particular way in 1991 does not mean, of course, that the issue is not further debatable.

12. Cf. Hyman Rodman, Betty Sarvis, and Joy Walker Bonar, *The Abortion Question* (New York: Columbia University Press, 1987), p. 137. According to these authors, the percentage of support among U.S. adults for the availability of legal abortion varies with the circumstances of the pregnancy. In case of danger to the pregnant female's health, pregnancy due to rape, or strong chance of fetal abnormality, a strong majority (89 percent, 81 percent, and 79 percent, respectively) approved of abortion in a 1985 survey. Other reasons received less support; for example, only 40 percent of those surveyed in 1985 approved of abortion for a married woman who simply did not want any more children. However, an astonishing 36 percent (more than one-third) of those surveyed approved of abortion "for any reason."

13. Someone might argue against my analogy that there is a significant difference between a salaried employee and a consumer of a service. Workers at federally funded health care clinics are partly salaried by the federal government and are, therefore, like employees who are paid partly out of tax dollars. Students, by contrast, are more like consumers of a service. One could argue that there is no basis for regulating the speech of those who merely consume a service, even if the service-providers do not like the speech, but that an employer has a legal right to withhold the salary of an employee who speaks in a manner that the employer does not like.

As mentioned in the text, however, it is doubtful that even a majority of the U.S. taxpaying population would have agreed to support the gag rule, had they been asked. Lack of "employer" unanimity in this case makes the employer-based argument of questionable relevance.

Rodney A. Smolla is one opponent of campus speech codes who also opposed the abortion gag rule. He argues that the government should not be permitted to attach, to the receipt of its funds, conditions that "brazenly prefer one set of ideas over another," and thus accomplish indirectly the "viewpoint discrimination" that is supposed to be precluded by the guarantee of freedom of expression (*Free Speech*, pp. 216–19).

14. Hentoff, "'Speech Codes,'" pp. 218–19.

15. Ibid., pp. 221, 224.

Top 75 Reasons Why Women . . . Should Not Have Freedom of Speech
Four Cornell University Undergraduates

Editor's Note: This list was written by four undergraduate males at Cornell University in the fall semester of 1995. It was written as a private document and sent through their campus Internet system to a few friends, who apparently did not find it offensive. However, the list was then widely circulated on the Internet and read by students and faculty at many universities throughout the country. It quickly drew angry responses and sparked heated debates on numerous Internet discussion lists. It raised questions about freedom of speech and the subtle ways in which women students might find their campuses to be hostile environments even in the mid-1990s. It also demonstrated the power of the electronic medium, and raised questions about the responsibilities of a university to regulate how its students use their campus Internet accounts. Finally, it showed the difficulties in distinguishing between private and public forms of speech.

The decision to include this document in this chapter was not an easy one, and I apologize to readers who may find it offensive. I decided that reprinting the list and the accompanying articles from *The Chronicle of Higher Education* had pedagogical value.

"Let's go back to the good old days when men were men and women were ribs."

1. She doesn't need to talk to get me a beer.
2. If she's in the kitchen like she should be, no one can hear her anyway.
3. If she can talk, all she'll do is complain.
4. Because she won't say "I will" instead of "I do."
5. No man wants to hear "first down" during a basketball game.
6. Because PMS is no excuse for whining.
7. No man needs or wants to hear the word "period" unless it has to do with hockey.
8. Women created tampon and yeast infection commercials during football.
9. Affirmative Action.
10. When men whistle at them in the street, they should just shut up and obey anyway.
11. If my . . . in her mouth, she can't talk anyway.
12. Oprah.
13. Feminists.
14. Because that stupid look on her face should not be accompanied by an equally stupid statement.
15. The 2nd and 19th amendments.
16. I don't want to be made to lie and say "I love you" after sex.
17. Highway fatalities would decrease by over 90%.
18. When I sneak out at four in the morning, I don't want to hear anybody calling me back.
19. "No, I will NOT buy you tampons while I'm at the store."
20. This is my . . . I'm gonna . . . you. No more stupid questions.
21. Don't waste your breath, I won't respect you in the morning.

22. Women sportscasters.
23. Women congressman [sic].
24. God forbid, a woman president. (Oops, my bad—see #66)
25. Marge Schott.
26. Stupid says as stupid does (and is).
27. Dikes (unless I can jump in the middle).
28. Where does speaking come into "barefoot and pregnant"?
29. Yes that toilet seat was yellow in the first place.
30. TLC and Salt-N-Pepa.
31. I could give a . . . if you're pregnant.
32. I don't care if you're in labor. For the love of god, let me sleep.
33. Women caused the 18th amendment.
34. The life expectancy of the average male goes down with every bitchy word.
35. Female drunks are annoying unless they put out (for which they don't need to talk).
36. We're tired of their "We can't pee standing up" shit.
37. That damn apple.
38. If she can't speak, she can't cry rape.
39. Of course, if she can't speak, she can't say no.
40. Rosanne. Nuff said.
41. Suzanne Powter. Too much said.
42. Honestly, do they really have anything useful to say?
43. Only one set of lips should be moving at a time.
44. If she can't talk, she can't bitch when I forget important dates.
45. There are no speaking parts in pornos anyway.

46. When she talks she's not drinking; it's hard to get her drunk when she's talking.

47. Nothing should come out a woman's mouth, SWALLOW. . . !

48. The mute button only works on the TV.

49. Whores get payed [sic] by the hour not by the word.

50. Helen Keller was the ultimate woman.

51. Equality is for math.

52. The credit card bill speaks for itself.

53. If it hurts, I don't wanna hear it.

54. Marcia Clark.

55. Chick-flicks.

56. You don't see Victoria's Secret models talking, do you?

57. Janet, Mariah, and Whitney.

58. Michael Jackson.

59. Silence and sex make a great combination.

60. N.O.W.? NO. NOW BITCH? YES.

61. Intelligent car conversation? Hell no. Her head should never be above the dashboard.

62. That annoying fat bitch from Snapple.

63. Your mouth is useful in so many other ways.

64. High phone bills really suck.

65. Women should be seen and not heard.

66. Do you think it was BILL Clinton who . . . up the country?

67. If I want romance, I'll turn on Playboy (hopefully not her).

68. Because they're not men.

69. 69, finally a use for both lips at the same time.

70. If I wanted your opinion, I'd ask for it.

71. Hell, if I wanted your opinion, I'd give it to you.

72. "Where've you been?" Who the . . . are you, my mother?

73. Women on radio? You can't see them, do you really want to hear them?

74. Unless the words are "Doctor, can you make these bigger?" shut the . . . up.

75. Big breasts should speak for themselves.

Misogynistic E-Mail Sparks Controversy on Cornell Campus

David Wilson

Four freshmen at Cornell University are facing allegations that they violated the university's code of conduct by writing what many observers considered a misogynistic message, which was widely disseminated via the Internet. Their message was called, "75 reasons why women (bitches) should not have freedom of speech."

Cornell's computer system was flooded with electronic mail from people around the country who had seen the list—which also contained the names of its four authors—and wanted the institution to do something about it. Many threatened to overload Cornell's computer systems, and a few even sent death threats to the four students.

The list contained a number of declarations that left many readers enraged. One of the least vulgar was: "If she can't speak, she can't cry rape."

The university had not taken action against the students by last week. It was awaiting the judgment of its judicial administrator, who will determine whether the conduct code was violated, and, if so, what punishment is appropriate. A decision in the case is expected by the end of the month, university administrators said.

Cornell has no speech code, but it does have rules against sexual harassment and a policy, instituted last year, that is aimed at insuring the responsible use of electronic communications. Administrators said it was unlikely that the four

David Wilson, "Misogynistic E-Mail Sparks Controversy on Cornell Campus," *The Chronicle of Higher Education*, 24 November 1995: A20. Copyright (c) 1995 The Chronicle of Higher Education, Inc. Reprinted with permission.

men would be found guilty of sexual harassment, since the message was not aimed at an individual.

The students—Evan Camps, Rikus Linschoten, Patrick Sicher, and Brian Waldman— could not be reached for comment. But in an apology printed in Cornell's student newspaper, they said they had written and distributed the list only to a small group of friends. One or more of those friends then distributed it to someone else, until eventually it was posted on an electronic mailing list or on one of the thousands of "newsgroups" that make up USENET, an electronic bulletin-board system accessible through the Internet.

Once that happened, many other people saw it and forwarded it to still other newsgroups and lists. It became a hot topic on several lists, with some of those who forwarded the message urging others to complain to Cornell officials.

Thousands did so. The four students and Cornell administrators found themselves deluged with messages. Other people used the telephone to complain, prompting the university to issue a statement that said, in part, "We very much regret that this incident has occurred and that Cornell's good name and reputation have been damaged in the process."

Colleges Criticized for Response to Offensive On-Line Speech

Thomas J. DeLoughry

Colleges and universities from New York to California continue to take heat for how their students behave on the Internet, and for the ways in which the institutions respond.

E-mail from critics across the country poured into Cornell University last week after officials there decided not to charge four freshmen with violating the campus code of conduct. The students had written a misogynistic note that was widely circulated on line. It was called "Top 75 reasons why women (bitches) should not have freedom of speech."

The message suggested that women should be silenced to keep them from crying rape or saying No to sex; made several references to forcing women to perform oral sex; and took aim at affirmative action, Oprah Winfrey, and feminists.

Its circulation triggered immediate, angry responses from Internet users across the country, thousands of whom appealed to Cornell through e-mail and telephone calls to discipline the four men. . . .

But university officials said the statements did not violate Cornell's computer-use or harassment policies, because the authors themselves had shared their note only with a small number of friends, who were not offended by it.

The Cornell decision came several weeks after Virginia Polytechnic Institute and State University penalized a student for posting a note on the World-Wide Web page of a gay organization suggesting that gay men be castrated and killed. The university, which has not revealed the student's name or the punishment levied, was accused by many observers of infringing upon the student's First Amendment rights.

The California Institute of Technology, meanwhile, has come under fire from critics who charge that the expulsion of a graduate student for harassing his former girlfriend was based on e-mail that may have been forged to appear as if it had come from him. Caltech officials said the e-mail constituted a small portion of the evidence against the student and had not been the deciding factor in the case.

Controversy is also certain to re-emerge in Michigan, where the federal government last week appealed a judge's dismissal of its case against a former University of Michigan student charged with using the Internet to transmit threats.

Thomas J. DeLoughry, "Colleges Criticized for Response to Offensive On-Line Speech," *The Chronicle of Higher Education*, 01 December 1995: A32. Copyright (c) 1995 by The Chronicle of Higher Education, Inc. Reprinted with permission.

The defendant, Jake Baker, was prosecuted on the basis of a rape-and-torture fantasy that he had posted on the Internet, and e-mail messages about abducting and raping a female classmate that he had exchanged with a correspondent in Canada. He was jailed for nearly a month before a judge decided in June that he was guilty only of creating "a rather savage and tasteless piece of fiction."

College administrators say the four cases are high-profile examples of the kind of on-line behavior that is becoming common on their campuses. Some say that offensive remarks are more common on computer networks because offenders are encouraged by the impersonal nature of the medium, and that recipients are often more upset by having the distasteful messages in their personal mailboxes than if the words were spoken on a campus quadrangle.

In the Cornell case, the university's judicial administrator was responsible for determining whether the four students—Evan Camps, Rikus Linschoten, Pat Sicher, and Brian Waldman— could be charged under the institution's conduct code. The code does not ban hate speech, but it does forbid sexual harassment and includes rules governing the use of computer systems.

Cornell's judicial administrator, Barbara L. Krause, decided that the four men could not be charged with harassment because they had not directed their message at anyone they believed would be harassed by it. She also determined that they had not violated computer policies prohibiting students from tying up machines by transmitting a note all over the world. She found that the four men had shared their message with fewer than 20 friends, and that people who were offended by it had been primarily responsible for duplicating it and sharing it with others.

The four students apologized for their message in a letter to *The Cornell Daily Sun* and agreed to apologize in person to Cornell administrators. Each also agreed to perform 50 hours of community service and to attend a rape-awareness program sponsored by the university's health center. They could not be reached for comment last week.

Criticism of Ms. Krause's decision came last week from free-speech advocates as well as from feminists concerned about Cornell's failure to punish the four freshmen for offending women and for creating what the critics believe is a hostile environment for women.

Harvey Silverglate, a Boston lawyer familiar with free-speech cases on college campuses, described Cornell's decision as "a plea bargain," in which the four students escaped punishment by agreeing to community service and "re-education."

He criticized university officials for failing to embrace the First Amendment and for basing their decision not to discipline the students on the fact that the four men had sent the message only to a small number of friends. "That's a very interesting line to draw between protected and unprotected speech," he said. "The time when it is most important to protect speech is when it is outrageous, provocative, annoying, and even hostile."

Others accepted Cornell's decision but suggested that the incident pointed up the need for further discussions on the campus.

Anjana Samant, a Cornell junior who is co-president of a student group called the Feminist Majority, said administrators were more concerned with the university's image and free-speech principles than with the content of the e-mail that the four students had written. "To me, it's disappointing that this has been the administration's focus, not the fact that what they did was wrong," she said. "I have met very few people who are satisfied with this at all. We're concerned that the students are not really apologetic."

Kathryn March, an associate professor of anthropology and women's studies, who brought the message to the attention of computer administrators, said she agreed with Cornell's decision that the four men had not violated the university's conduct code. But she said the case indicated the need for a debate over whether electronic mail should be protected in the same way that other speech is protected on the campus.

The ability to take a piece of private e-mail and transmit it in seconds to thousands of people sets the new medium apart from others and raises the question of whether users can assume the level of privacy that they intend, Ms. March said.

The university also should debate whether it should extend free-speech rights to students who are using university-owned computers and are attaching Cornell's name to everything sent from those computers, she said.

Limits on what students can do on university-owned computers are already in place on other campuses, including Virginia Tech, where they played a prominent role in the case of the student who sent a threatening note to a gay organization.

Cathryn T. Goree, the university's dean of students, said the student would not have been disciplined if he had used an e-mail account other than the one at Virginia Tech.

Administrators judged the posting to be "threatening," she said, but did not impose harsher penalties, because it had been directed at an organization rather than an individual.

A barrage of e-mail from people on both sides of the free-speech debate did not change her mind, she added. "Our policy comes down to the fact that your right to free speech stops when you associate the name of the university with it."

Ms. Goree acknowledged that differences among policies at Virginia Tech, Cornell, and other institutions would continue to confuse Internet users who want to know what is appropriate conduct on the network. The only solution, she said, is to determine the policy of the university from which the offensive note was sent.

7

Same-Sex Marriage

Introduction

32.

John Finnis, "Homosexual Conduct Is Wrong"

Barbara J. Cox, "A Personal Essay on Same-Sex Marriage"

33.

Adrian Alex Wellington, "Why Liberals Should Support Same Sex Marriage"

United States Congress, The 1996 "Defense of Marriage Act"

34.

Andrew Sullivan, "The Conservative Case"

William Bennett and Andrew Sullivan, "An Exchange on Same-Sex Marriage"

35.

James Q. Wilson, "Against Homosexual Marriage"

Melissa George, "More Retailers Are Recognizing Gay Marriages"

36.

Cheshire Calhoun, "Family's Outlaws: Rethinking the Connections Between Feminism, Lesbianism, and the Family"

Frank Browning, "Why Marry?"

BACKGROUND

Of late, we have seen a vigorous debate arise over whether or not our society ought officially sanction unions between persons of the same sex, that is, "same-sex" marriages. This recent round of debates arose in part when widespread public attention was drawn to the possibility that one state, Hawaii, might grant legal recognition to same-sex unions; and that, as states generally tend to recognize marriage licenses issued by other states, this could conceivably lead other states to recognize gay and lesbian marriages legally performed in Hawaii. In order to preclude the outcome of the Hawaiian court cases from, in effect, deciding the issue for the rest of the country, the United States Congress passed "The Defense of Marriage Act" (DOMA) in 1996, which defined a marriage as a union of a man and a woman. This federal statute permits individual states to deny recognition of same-sex marriages performed in other states, so for example, the state of Utah would not be bound to recognize same-sex marriages legally performed in Hawaii. Similar bills were introduced, debated, and approved by numerous state legislatures in the mid- to late-1990s.

THE MORAL DEBATE OVER
SAME-SEX MARRIAGE

In this chapter, our focus is again on the underlying *moral* issues, not the narrow legal or constitutional ones. Should society recognize and support same-sex unions, thus according gay and lesbian couples the same economic, social, and psychological benefits that heterosexual married couples enjoy? Or would official recognition of same-sex unions erode traditional marriages and families?

Proponents of same-sex marriage argue that the government discriminates against gay and lesbian citizens by barring them from taking part in this type of legally binding contract. They contend that it is fundamentally unfair and unjust to limit the privileges of legally recognized marriages to heterosexual adult couples, and thus bar gay and lesbian partners from receiving the economic and social benefits available to heterosexual couples who choose to marry. Many defenders of same-sex marriages remind opponents of the inflamed debate that arose a generation ago over interracial marriages: As recently as the 1960s, the U. S. Supreme Court had to act to strike down laws banning interracial marriages in a dozen or more states. Just as our society once failed to recognize the injustice of anti-miscegenation laws, we now resist acknowledging the unfairness of laws limiting marriage licenses to heterosexual couples. Activists working to secure the right to marry for gay and lesbian couples argue that recognition of same-sex marriages is simply one more step toward a more just society in which the rights of all minorities are protected against the unjust prejudices of the majority.

Other supporters of same-sex marriages, such as Andrew Sullivan, attend to the long-term psychological and health benefits of marriage. In defense of same-sex marriages, they point to the advantages of publicly sanctioning these unions: the emotional and economic security associated with committed, long-term, monogamous relationships; the presumably reduced rates of promiscuity with concomitant reductions in sexually transmitted diseases. Thus, a society that recognizes same-sex marriages will be more stable, healthy, and just than one that does not.

Opponents of same-sex marriage, including William Bennett, John Finnis, and James Q. Wilson, argue that it is morally wrong for society to recognize these unions. They assert that official recognition of same-sex unions will threaten the value and stability of heterosexual marriages in our society. John Finnis argues that homosexual conduct is fundamentally wrong in that it fails to "actualize" "a real common good." He claims that "the orgasmic union of the reproductive organs of husband and wife really unites them biologically (and their biological reality is part of, not merely an instrument of, their personal reality); that orgasmic union therefore can actualize and allow them to experience their real common good—their marriage with the two goods, children and friendship, which are the parts of its wholeness as an intelligible common good."[1] Critics contend that permitting same-sex marriages will lead to all sorts of undesirable consequences in terms of the family, an institution whose health many judge to be essential to the good of society as a whole. Some critics, such as William Bennett, fear that permitting same-sex marriages will open a nuptial Pandora's box, making it difficult for society to impose any conceptual limits on marriage, and thus opening the door for public sanction of bigamy, polygamy, and intrafamily marriages.

RETHINKING THE INSTITUTIONS OF MARRIAGE AND FAMILY

The debate over same-sex marriages has also prompted philosophers to examine more critically the purpose and moral value of marriage as it is conventionally understood in our society. Feminist theorists have often criticized the oppressive elements of heterosexual marriage in a patriarchal society. They have sought to challenge traditional divisions of labor within the private family so as to allow more opportunities for women. Some feminists and lesbian theorists who criticize the traditional practices of heterosexual marriage may very well wish to reform marriage altogether, and they are deeply skeptical that the current institution of marriage is desirable as it stands. Thus, they are less concerned about extending the opportunity to marry to lesbian and gay couples than they are about radically revisioning marriage and family. Rather than working toward the goal of securing marriage rights for same-sex couples, they urge us to direct our efforts toward fundamentally reforming marriage and the family.

Other critics are less concerned with the fact that the institution of marriage has and continues to perpetuate the oppression of women; they encourage us to rethink the family on different grounds. Particularly, they ask if the family is the appropriate social institution for organizing the distribution of certain social benefits and burdens. In short, some theorists who attend carefully to social class structures find that traditional marriage and family policies may work more to the advantage of the middle classes than to lower classes. And thus the "right to marry movement" might be viewed by some as an elitist movement that fails to recognize how traditional marital and familial practices do not confer the same benefits on the poor and working classes as on the middle classes, for example, tax exemptions and deductions, inheritance rights, and spousal employee health care benefits and retirement fund benefits. As Cheshire Calhoun states in her article in this chapter, ". . . arguments for lesbian and gay marriage rights on the grounds that lesbians and gays lack privileges that heterosexual couples enjoy—

such as access to a spouse's health insurance benefits—are insufficiently radical. Distributing basic benefits like health insurance through the middle-class family neglects the interests of poor and working-class families as well as single individuals in having access to basic social benefits. If access to such benefits is the issue, then universal health insurance, not marriage, is what we should be advocating."[2]

NOTES

1. John Finnis "Homosexual Conduct Is Wrong," page 423.

2. Chesire Calhoun, "Family's Outlaws: Rethinking the Connections Between Feminism, Lesbianism, and the Family," p. 462.

32.
Homosexual Conduct Is Wrong
John Finnis

John Finnis is professor of law and legal philosophy at Oxford University. Finnis gave this testimony in a deposition for the 1993 trial in Colorado over that state's Amendment 2, which would have barred local ordinances protecting gays and lesbians from discrimination. Amendment 2 was adopted in 1992 after a statewide referendum, and was then immediately challenged in the courts. The legal battle eventually reached the United States Supreme Court, which ruled in 1996 in *Romer* v. *Evans* that Colorado's Amendment 2 was unconstitutional since it singled out homosexuals as a class by judging them ineligible for protective legislation.

Finnis's testimony obviously was used by supporters of Amendment 2. In this excerpt, he argues that homosexual conduct is fundamentally wrong because it fails to actualize a real common good, namely, reproduction. Homosexual sexual activity and, more broadly, all forms of masturbation, involve treating one's own body as an instrument for self-gratification; such conduct thus fails to actualize and incorporate a real common good.

The underlying thought is on the following lines. In masturbating, as in being masturbated or sodomized, one's body is treated as instrumental for the securing of the experiential satisfaction of the conscious self. Thus one disintegrates oneself in two ways, (1) by treating one's body as a mere instrument of the consciously operating self, and (2) by making one's choosing self the quasi-slave of the experiencing self which is demanding gratification. The worthlessness of the gratification, and the disintegration of oneself, are both the result of the fact that, in these sorts

of behavior, one's conduct is not the actualizing and experiencing of a real common good. Marriage, with its double blessing—procreation and friendship—is a real common good. Moreover, it is a common good that can be both actualized and experienced in the orgasmic union of the reproductive organs of a man and a woman united in commitment to that good. Conjugal sexual activity, and—as Plato and Aristotle and Plutarch and Kant all argue—*only* conjugal activity is free from the shamefulness of instrumentalization that is found in masturbating and in being masturbated or sodomized.

At the very heart of the reflections of Plato, Xenophon, Aristotle, Musonius Rufus, and

---

Excerpts from legal depositions from the 1993 trial over the constitutionality of Colorado Amendment 2.

Plutarch on the homoerotic culture around them is the very deliberate and careful judgment that homosexual *conduct* (and indeed all extramarital sexual gratification) is radically incapable of participating in, or actualizing, the common good of friendship. Friends who engage in such conduct are following a natural impulse and doubtless often wish their genital conduct to be an intimate expression of their mutual affection. But they are deceiving themselves. The attempt to express affection by orgasmic nonmarital sex is the pursuit of an illusion. The orgasmic union of the reproductive organs of husband and wife really unites them biologically (and their biological reality is part of, not merely an instrument of, their *personal* reality); that orgasmic union therefore can actualize and allow them to experience their real common good—their marriage with the two goods, children and friendship, which are the parts of its wholeness as an intelligible common good. But the common good of friends who are not and cannot be married (man and man, man and boy, woman and woman) has nothing to do with their having children by each other, and their reproductive organs cannot make them a biological (and therefore a personal) unit. So their genital acts together cannot do what they may hope and imagine.

In giving their considered judgment that homosexual conduct cannot actualize the good of friendship, Plato and the many philosophers who followed him intimate an answer to the questions why it should be considered shameful to use, or allow another to use, one's body to give pleasure, and why this use of one's body differs from one's bodily participation in countless other activities (e.g., games) in which one takes and/or gets pleasure. Their response is that pleasure is indeed a good, when it is the experienced aspect of one's participation in some intelligible good, such as a task going well, or a game or a dance or a meal or a reunion. Of course, the activation of sexual organs with a view to the pleasures of orgasm is sometimes spoken of as if it were a game. But it differs from real games in that its point is not the exercise of

skill; rather, this activation of reproductive organs is focused upon the body precisely as a source of pleasure for one's consciousness. So this is a "use of the body" in a strongly different sense of "use." The body now is functioning not in the way one, as a bodily person, acts to instantiate some other intelligible good, but precisely as providing a service to one's consciousness, to satisfy one's desire for satisfaction.

This disintegrity is much more obvious when masturbation is solitary. Friends are tempted to think that pleasuring each other by some forms of mutual masturbation could be an instantiation or actualization or promotion of their friendship. But that line of thought overlooks the fact that if their friendship is not marital . . . activation of their reproductive organs cannot be, in reality, an instantiation or actualization of their friendship's common good. In reality, whatever the generous hopes and dreams with which the loving partners surround their use of their genitals, *that use* cannot express more than is expressed if two strangers engage in genital activity to give each other orgasm, or a prostitute pleasures a client, or a man pleasures himself. Hence, Plato's judgment, at the decisive moment of the *Gorgias*, that there is no important distinction in essential moral worthlessness between solitary masturbation, being sodomized as a prostitute and being sodomized for the pleasure of it. . . .

Societies such as classical Athens and contemporary England (and virtually every other) draw a distinction between behavior found merely (perhaps extremely) offensive (such as eating excrement) and behavior to be repudiated as destructive of human character and relationships. Copulation of humans with animals is repudiated because it treats human sexual activity and satisfaction as something appropriately sought in a manner that, like the coupling of animals, is divorced from the expressing of an intelligible common good—and so treats human bodily life, in one of its most intense activities, as merely animal. The deliberate genital coupling of persons of the same sex is repudiated for a very similar reason. It is not simply that it is sterile and disposes the participants to an abdication of responsibility for the future of humankind. Nor is it simply that it cannot *really* actualize the mutual devotion that some homosexual persons hope to manifest and experience by it; nor merely that it harms the personalities of its participants by its disintegrative manipulation of different parts of their one personal reality. It is also that it treats human sexual capacities in a way that is deeply hostile to the self-understanding of those members of the community who are willing to commit themselves to real marriage [even one that happens to be sterile] in the understanding that its sexual joys are not mere instruments or accompaniments to, or mere compensation for, the accomplishments of marriage's responsibilities, but rather are the *actualizing and experiencing* of the intelligent commitment to share in those responsibilities. . . .

This pattern of judgment, both widespread and sound, concludes as follows. Homosexual orientation—the deliberate willingness to promote and engage in homosexual acts—is a standing denial of the intrinsic aptness of sexual intercourse to actualize and give expression to the exclusiveness and open-ended commitment of marriage as something good in itself. All who accept that homosexual acts can be a humanly appropriate use of sexual capacities must, if consistent, regard sexual capacities, organs, and acts as instruments to be put to whatever suits the purposes of the individual "self" who has them. Such an acceptance is commonly (and in my opinion rightly) judged to be an active threat to the stability of existing and future marriages; it makes nonsense, for example, of the view that adultery is per se (and not merely because it may involve deception), and in an important way, inconsistent with conjugal love. A political community that judges that the stability and educative generosity of family life is of fundamental importance to the community's present and future can rightly judge that it has a compelling interest in denying that homosexual conduct is a valid, humanly acceptable choice and form of life, and in doing whatever it properly can, as a community with uniquely wide but still subsidiary functions, to discourage such conduct.

A Personal Essay on Same-Sex Marriage

Barbara J. Cox

Very little since Stonewall, and the break from accepting the status quo that those riots symbolize, has challenged the lesbian and gay community as much as the debate we have had over the past several years on whether seeking the right to marry should be the focus of our community's efforts, political influence, and financial resources. As is often true in most such political debates, both "sides" to the debate make important arguments about the impact that the right to marry will have on each

From Barbara J. Cox, "Same-Sex Marriage and Choice-of-Law: If We Marry in Hawaii, Are We Still Married When We Return Home?" *Wisconsin Law Review* (1994): 1033, 1035–1037. Copyright (c) 1994 by the Board of Regents of the University of Wisconsin System. Reprinted by permission of the Wisconsin Law Review, and the author.

member of our community, on the community as a whole, and on our place in society.

Arguing against same-sex marriage in her article, "Since When is Marriage a Path to Liberation?" Paula Ettelbrick believes that it will not liberate lesbians and gay men but will make us more invisible, force assimilation, and undermine the lesbian and gay civil rights movement. She also argues that it will not transform society into respecting and encouraging relationship choice and family diversity, which are primary goals of that civil rights movement. Ruth Colker in "Marriage" echoes Ettelbrick's concerns, arguing that rather than expanding the couples who can marry, we should change the institution of marriage to eliminate its marriage-dependent benefits, so that people will choose it for symbolic, rather than legal or utilitarian, reasons. She also recognizes the class-based assumptions inherent in the marriage debate, realizing that for most poor people, marriage offers few economic advantages.

Nitya Duclos examines four reasons advanced for same-sex marriage (political reform, public legitimation, socioeconomic benefits, and safeguarding children of lesbian or gay parents) in her article, "Some Complicating Thoughts on Same-Sex Marriage." She concludes that the effects of allowing same-sex marriage will not be felt uniformly throughout lesbian and gay communities and questions whether it will exacerbate differences of power and privilege in those communities.

In a companion piece to Ettelbrick's, Thomas Stoddard, in "Why Gay People Should Seek the Right to Marry," while recognizing the oppressive nature of marriage in its traditional form, believes that lesbians and gay men should be able to choose to marry and the civil rights movement should seek full recognition of same-sex marriages. His three reasons for pursuing this right are the practical advantages associated with marriage-related benefits, the political reason that marriage is the issue most likely to end discrimination against lesbians and gay men, and the philosophical explanation that lesbians and gay men should have the right to choose to marry and that providing that right will be the principal means toward eliminating marriage's sexist trappings.

Nan Hunter, in "Marriage, Law and Gender: A Feminist Inquiry," argues that legalizing lesbian and gay marriage will destabilize marriage's gendered definition by disrupting the link between gender and marriage. She analyzes both marriage and domestic partnership against the feminist inquiry of how law reinforces power imbalances within the family and views same-sex marriage as a means to subvert gender-based power differentials. Mary Dunlap finds that same-sex marriage is constructive when lesbians and gay men are encountering gay-bashing resulting from *Bowers*. [*Bowers v. Hardwick* (1986)] She examines the values underlying the push for same-sex marriage (such as equality, autonomy, fairness, privacy, and diversity) and encourages expansion of the marriage debate outside legal circles. One way to expand this debate is to read the interviews of lesbian and gay couples, some of whom have chosen to have public ceremonies celebrating their commitment and some of whom have chosen to keep their commitment private.

The debate continues to rage, as seen from the recent articles contained in the *Virginia Law Review's* symposium issue. Without resolving the debate here, it seems clear that obtaining the right to marry will drastically impact the lesbian and gay civil rights movement. My response to the debate is best expressed in the following short (and personal) essay, explaining the vital political change that can result from the simple (and personal) act of same-sex marriage.

Yes, I know that weddings can be "heterosexual rituals" of the most repressive and repugnant kind. Yes, I know that weddings historically symbolized the loss of the woman's self into that of her husband's, a denial of her existence completely. Yes, I know that weddings around the world continue to have that impact on many women and often lead to lives of virtual slavery. Yes, I know. Then how could a feminist, out, radical lesbian like myself get married a year ago last April? Have I simply joined the flock of lesbians and gay men rushing out to participate in a meaningless ceremony that symbolizes heterosexual superiority?

I think not.

When my partner and I decided to have a commitment ceremony, we did so to express the love and caring that we feel for one another, to celebrate that love with our friends and family, and to express that love openly and with pride. It angers me when others, who did not participate or do not know either of us, condemn us as part of a mindless flock accepting a dehumanizing ceremony. But more it distresses me that they believe their essentialist vision of weddings explains all— because they have been to weddings, both straight and queer, they can speak as experts on their inherent nature.

Perhaps these experts should consider the radical aspect of lesbian marriage or the transformation that it makes on the people around us. As feminists, we used to say that "the personal is political." Have we lost that vision of how we can understand and change the world?

My commitment ceremony was not the mere "aping" of the bride that I supposedly spent my childhood dreaming of becoming. (In fact, I was a very satisfied tomboy who never once considered marriage.) My ceremony was an expression of the incredible love and respect that I have found with my partner. My ceremony came from a need to speak of that love and respect openly to those who participate in my world.

Some of the most politically "out" experiences I have ever had happened during those months of preparing for and having that ceremony. My sister and I discussed for weeks whether she would bring her children to the ceremony. Although I had always openly brought the women I was involved with home with me, I had never actually sat down with my niece and nephews to discuss those relationships. My sister was concerned that her eldest son, particularly, might scorn me, especially at a time when he and his friends tended toward "faggot" jokes. After I expressed how important it was for me to have them attend, she tried to talk with her son about going to this euphemistically-entitled "ceremony." He kept asking why my partner and I were having a "ceremony" and she kept hedging. Finally he just said, "Mom, Barb's gay, right?" She said yes, they all came, and things were fine. Her youngest son sat next to me at dinner after the ceremony trying to understand how it worked. "You're married, right?" "Yes." "Who's the husband?" "There is no husband." "Are you going to have children?" "No." "So there's no husband and no children but you're married, right?" "Yes." "OK," and he happily turned back to his dinner.

My partner invited her large Catholic family to the ceremony. We all know how the Pope feels about us. Despite that, her mother and most of her siblings, some from several states away, were able to attend. Her twin brother later told us that our ceremony led him to question and resolve the discomfort that had plagued his relationship with his sister for many years.

As a law professor leaving town early for the ceremony, I told my two classes (one of 95 and one of 20 students) that I was getting "married" to my partner, who is a woman. (I actually used "married" because saying I was getting "committed" just didn't quite have the right ring to it.) The students in one of my classes joined together to buy my partner and myself a silver engraved frame that says "Barb and Peg, Our Wedding." My colleagues were all invited to the ceremony and most of them attended. One of them spoke to me of the discussion they had within their family explaining to their children that they were going to a lesbian wedding.

How can anyone view these small victories in coming out and acceptance as part of flocking to imitate, or worse join, an oppressive heterosexual institution? Is it not profoundly transformative to speak so openly about lesbian love and commitment? The impact was so wide-ranging, not just on my partner and myself, but on our families, our friends, and even the clerks in the jewelry stores when we explained we were looking for wedding rings for both of us. Or on the 200 people who received my mother's annual xeroxed Christmas letter with a paragraph describing the ceremony. Or the clerk in the store who engraved the frame for my students. Or the young children who learned that same-sex marriage exists.

Yes, we must be aware of the oppressive history that weddings symbolize. We must work to ensure that we do not simply accept wholecloth an institution that symbolizes the loss and harm felt by women. But I find it difficult to understand how two lesbians, standing together openly and proudly, can be seen as accepting that institution? What is more anti-patriarchal and rejecting of an institution that carries the patriarchal power imbalance into most households than clearly stating that women can commit to one another with no man in sight? With no claim of dominion or control, but instead of equality and respect. I understand the fears of those who condemn us for our weddings, but I believe they fail to look beyond the symbol and cannot see the radical claim we are making.

References

Colker, Ruth. "Marriage." *Yale Journal of Law & Feminism.* Vol. 321 (1991).

Duclos, Nitya. "Some Complicating Thoughts on Same-Sex Marriage." *Law and Sexuality: A Review of Lesbian and Gay Legal Issues.* Vol. 1 (1991).

Dunlap, Mary. "Symposium, The Family in the 1990s: An Exploration of Lesbian and Gay Rights." *Law and Sexuality: A Review of Lesbian and Gay Legal Issues.* Vol. 1 (1991).

Ettelbrick, Paula. "Since When Is Marriage a Path to Liberation?" *OUT/LOOK, National Gay and Lesbian Quarterly.* Issue 6 (Fall 1989).

Hunter, Nan D. "Marriage, Law, and Gender: A Feminist Inquiry." *Law and Sexuality: A Review of Lesbian and Gay Legal Issues.* Vol. 1 (1991).

Tom Stoddard, "Why Gay People Should Seek the Right to Marry," *OUT/LOOK, National Gay and Lesbian Quarterly.* Issue 6 (Fall 1989).

33.

Why Liberals Should Support Same Sex Marriage

Adrian Alex Wellington

Adrian Alex Wellington teaches philosophy at York University, Ontario. Wellington argues that a society committed to liberalism—defined in terms of the conjunctive claim that each person should have the freedom to determine what constitutes for him or her the good life, that the government shall not give privilege to any one conception of the good life over another in its policies, and that society should be organized so as to allow individuals maximal liberty to pursue their respective accounts of the good life provided they do not harm others—must recognize the validity of same-sex marriages as an option for gays, lesbians and bisexuals.

This paper is about the state sponsorship of same sex unions, or about "family values, queer-style," as one commentator has put it.[1] The simple claim of this paper is that gays, lesbians, and bisexuals should have the right to marry if they so choose.[2] This simple claim can be characterized as a claim about formal equality—the same sex marriage bar is a denial of the formal equality rights of lesbians, gays,[3] and bisexuals. However, the simple claim does not adequately capture the complexity of the issue, either for those who argue against same sex marriage or for those who argue for it.

In this paper I will present a more complex version of the above argument in the context of contemporary secular liberalism. The argument can be broken down into the following components:

A. In a liberal society, sexual relations between consenting adults is beyond the purview of the state—"the state has no business in the bedrooms of the nation."[4]

B. It is not possible to justify anything other than a functional account of marriage in contemporary secular liberal society.

C. If some relationships—namely opposite sex ones—are to be given state sponsorship, there must be rational reasons consistent with liberal principles to deny that sponsorship to analogous relationships.

D. On a functional account of marriage same sex relationships are analogous to opposite sex relationships.

E. As a matter of formal equality, same sex unions should be entitled to state sponsorship.

F. Any other arguments against the provision of state sponsorship to same sex unions could only make claim to liberal principles by reference to some formulation of the harm principle.

G. There is no valid argument against same sex marriage based on the grounds of harm consistent with the harm principle.

Adrian Alex Wellington, "Why Liberals Should Support Same Sex Marriage," *Journal of Social Philosophy* 26 (Winter 1995): 98–106. Reprinted by permission of the *Journal of Social Philosophy.*

All of these claims taken together provide a compound argument for the claim that gays, lesbians, and bisexuals should have the right to participate in state sponsored same sex unions if they so choose. The policy claim that corresponds to my argument is that legislative reform would be required in order to ensure the provision of that right.

The main claim of this paper is that as a matter of social justice liberalism requires the provision of the opportunity for state sponsorship and state recognition of same sex couples. The paper is concerned with an issue of political philosophy—whether a commitment to liberalism entails a commitment to support the rights of lesbians, gays, and bisexuals to marry persons of the same sex, should they so desire. Whether gays, lesbians, and bisexuals should choose to exercise the option, if available, of marrying persons of the same sex is a separate issue. The position that liberalism must, as a matter of political philosophy, recognize the validity of same sex marriage as an option for gays, lesbians, and bisexuals as well as for heterosexuals (should any heterosexuals choose to marry persons of the same sex) is distinct from the position that state sponsorship of same sex marriages should be pursued as a strategy for achieving gay rights or gay liberation. One can acknowledge that liberalism entails the commitment to support state sponsorship of same sex marriage without insisting that lesbians, gays, and bisexuals should participate in, or even advocate the provision of the opportunity to participate in same sex marriages.

I

This paper begins with certain crucial assumptions about the basic claims of liberalism and the fluidity of human sexuality and emotional attachment. The first basic claim of liberalism as a broadly defined concept is the claim that each person in a liberal society should be able to determine for her/himself just what constitutes the "good life." Corollary to that claim is another basic claim that the state should be neutral between conceptions of the "good life." The third basic claim is that a liberal society not only need not, but actually should not, be based on any specific picture of "human nature." A liberal society is one in which there are many diverse conceptions of "human nature," as with conceptions of the "good life," and that none should be accorded primacy or specific state endorsement. The fourth basic claim is that legal intervention in the lives of the members of a liberal society should be constrained as far as possible by the notion of liberty contained in the formulation of the harm principle.[5]

The claims concerning human sexuality and emotional attachment are simpler, but probably no less contentious. These claims are that human beings as a species have a remarkably diverse range of potential sexual practices and emotional affiliations. Even given tremendous levels of socialization aimed at producing compulsory heterosexuality, many people resist this socialization and choose to reject, partly or completely, heterosexuality. One can assume that many more people would adopt homosexuality or bisexuality in practice or identify with either by inclination if those socialization pressures were ameliorated. The picture of a traditional marriage is that of heterosexual adults taking on a pair bonding union sanctioned by religion and/or the state involving fidelity and reproduction. Yet, many, many people who enter into the state of marriage, who partake of the status of the social practice of marriage, actually do not adhere to that traditional picture. Many marriages do not rest upon fidelity, and many marriages do not result in procreation. Further, many marriages are between parties, or involve parties, who do not primarily perceive themselves as heterosexual.

It seems clear that a liberal conception of sexuality must be one that recognizes the contingency of heterosexuality. There may be many subcultures or segments of a liberal society—religious fundamentalists, certain kinds of anti-homosexual moralists—which do not accept the assertion of heterosexuality as contingent. These groups may wish to entrench heterosexuality socially, morally, and legally, yet the very fact that they seek to entrench it and to force compliance with the norm of heterosexuality itself attests to the very contingency of the norm. It is because some people are unwilling to live in compliance with the norm, and are able to resist the supposed necessity of the norm, that these groups wish to adopt harsh measures of policing and enforcement of the norm. These groups who categorically oppose the assertion of contingent heterosexuality, nevertheless, are only part of liberal society. Liberal society also includes those who wish to partake in homosexual or bisexual pair bonding unions as well as those who wish to, or at least are willing to, tolerate such unions.

A liberal society is one that rests upon the provision of choice for individuals to determine what sorts of people they want to be, as well as what sorts of lives they want to lead. Part of the choices that one undertakes during the process of self construction and life construction is whether, and to what extent, to participate in pair bonding unions. In a society which is premised upon the separation of religion and democratic governance, indicated by the institution of civil marriage, these unions must be interpreted in the context of liberal and not religious norms. Despite the holdover of religious notions in the wording of the marriage ceremony itself, it is clear that people can engage in the practice of marriage without any specific commitment to religious conceptions of marriage. Marriage thus becomes a state sanctioned pair bonding union, an affirmation of state endorsement of the pair bonding itself. There is no requirement that one engage in heterosexual practices with one's marriage partner, and no requirement that one attempt to produce children. The only conditions one need meet in order to undertake civil marriage are that the partners are of opposite sex, of sufficient age, legally sane, and not too closely related (con-

sanguinity conditions).[6] Of course, the partners must also be able to pay the required fee for the ceremony.

It is interesting to note that once the religious basis for marriage is removed or at least elided that there is no longer any rational reason—rational in the sense of related to the purpose of the practice—to insist that parties to a civil marriage be of the opposite sex. A civil marriage is a self-defining ceremony, intended to accord a certain social status. The state cannot require that marriage partners endorse and live up to the ideal of fidelity, or endorse and live by the norm of heterosexuality, or endorse and live in accordance with the intention to reproduce. The marriage union in a secular liberal society is one that is interpreted by the parties in the context of the purported absence of teleological conceptions of human nature and of state sanctioned conceptions of the good life. The parties themselves determine what marriage means to them, and shape the practice to their needs and wants. How then can the state insist upon the condition that parties must be of opposite sexes in order to participate in that kind of practice?

Marriages are intended to be unions, unions which apparently automatically create "couples" and then "families." There are of course couples outside of marriage and marriage partners who do not perceive themselves to be couples. There are of course families outside of marriage and marriages which do not actually function like families. The point is that civil marriages produce a certain kind of coupling—state sanctioned coupling. Other than the requirement that the parties be adults and be of opposite sex, the civil marriage ceremony can be tailored by the parties to incorporate their values and beliefs and preferences. The parties can undertake civil marriage in order to attain the social status of marriage but intend to be "unfaithful" to one another sexually with persons of the opposite or same sex. The parties can intend to be celibate, to avoid procreation or to engage in procreation, to have sex only with each other, or to never have sex with each other. In other words, marriage does not depend upon any particular set of sexual or emotional practices. Why then does it depend upon an arbitrary condition of membership in the opposite sex to one's intended partner?

If a homosexual person can marry another homosexual person of the opposite sex or a heterosexual person of the opposite sex, or a bisexual person marry a homosexual or heterosexual person of the opposite sex, why should lesbians, gays, and bisexuals be excluded from marrying a homosexual or bisexual or heterosexual person of the same sex? Heterosexuals are also prevented from marrying a heterosexual or homosexual person of the same sex as well. If one looks at marriage in the context of a liberal conception of the practice, divorced from the religious interpretation of the practice and the historical background of the practice, these restrictions make no sense. Apart from social prejudice and discrimination, there is no reason to insist that individuals of the same sex cannot form couples in the same way that parties to marriage form couples. Civil marriage is a self-defining, self-obligating union. The parties will determine what the union provides for them, and what need they have for the state sanction—from expression of commitment to tax breaks. Same sex couples are no less capable of determining this than opposite sex couples.

One does not have to be able to recognize the capacity in oneself to respond sexually to persons of either sex or the of the same sex in order to recognize that the capacity exists in many others. One does not have to be able to recognize the capacity in oneself to form emotional affiliations with persons of either sex or of the same sex in order to recognize that the capacity exists in many others. There is no biological, or psychological reason that human beings must have sex or emotional affiliations only with persons of the opposite sex. There are only political or social reasons that motivate people to insist that heterosexuality is natural, or normal. Liberals are predisposed to resist arguments of the form that it is only "natural" or "normal" for humans to be X or to do Y. On my reading of liberalism the central driving force behind the adoption of liberal political philosophy and policy historically was to counteract precisely those kind of arguments in favor of the divine right of monarchs or in favor of religious morality. Divorce is one of the clearest examples of the movement towards a secularization of social practices that were initially the exclusive preserve of religion.

It seems clear that secular liberal societies can no longer rely upon outdated and archaic religious notions about the purpose of coupling and specifically of marriage. The attempts of courts to deal with common law opposite sex coupling point to several interesting things about contemporary civil marriage. The courts in some cases have attempted to develop functional characterizations of "spouses" and thus functional definitions of "couples."[7] These definitions include factors like the following: Did the parties share a bank account? Did the parties own property in common? Did the parties visit each other's relatives? Did the parties purchase shared items? Did the parties entertain guests together? Did the parties divide up household chores between them? Did the parties share meals? Did the parties provide nurturance and caring for each other when ill?

It is obvious that all these factors apply equally to same sex couples as to opposite sex couples. Same sex couples share bank accounts, own property in common, visit each other's relatives, purchase shared items, entertain guests together, divide up household chores, share meals, and provide nurturance and care for each other when ill. And of course, same sex couples, like opposite sex couples, have sex with each other. Any functional characterization of a couple—which I would argue is the only kind that could be endorsed by a full-fledged liberalism—is going to apply equally to same sex couples as to opposite sex couples.

If functional definitions are appropriate to determine whether unmarried couples were or are effectively married, and thus fall under "common law" marriage provisions of family law, then would functional definitions not be appropriate to determine whether same sex couples are suitable candidates for characterizations of "spouses" and thus suitable candidates to be deemed effectively married as well? Same sex couples look indistinguishable from opposite couples on the basis of functional definitions—that is, the differences among particular opposite and same sex couples would be as great as differences between opposite and same sex couples. The only reason that same sex couples do not fall under "common law" marriage provisions of family law is that same sex couples cannot marry, and thus they cannot be "effectively married." I should point out that "common law" marriage designation has to do with both the division of property and family assets, and the custody of, and access to, children. Both of these factors can be relevant to same sex couples who may own property together, have been in a relationship of economic dependence and support, and have children together (not the children of both of them together, but the children of each of them who they parent together or the children they have adopted together or singly previously).

None of the criteria in a functional definition of "spouse"—a person with whom one may share a bank account, own property, visit relatives, purchase shared items, entertain guests, divide up household chores, share meals, and have sex, and for whom one may provide nurturance and care—are gender specific. All are functional and relational. The significant issue in the determination of "spouse" is whether the two people relate to each other, and think of each other, in the manner of a "couple." What is a couple then, on this account, is a provisional definition that is something along the lines of a "voluntary relation premised on intimacy and connection." This phrase is my choice of wording; similar ideas based on functional definitions are suggested by the wording found in domestic partnership provisions and in certain court

decisions.[8] My functional definition of marriage explicitly excludes the requirement of procreation, or even intended procreation. It is inconsistent, I argue, with a liberal account of marriage to include such a requirement. Thus, there is no basis to the attempt to privilege procreative or potentially procreative heterosexual marriage to encourage reproduction. Such an attempt could not be justified on my account.

Of course, the phrase "voluntary relation premised on intimacy and connection" could apply to affairs, and special friendships, so what needs to be added is the clause intended to produce the union of coupling. Thus, it is self-defining. What is distinctive about "couples" is that two people self-identify as a couple, and then other people identify those two people as a couple. There is no reason, once the notion of "couple" is characterized as functional and self-defining, to restrict the notion to opposite sex couples. And then if marriage is simply the legitimation by state sanction of self-defined, functional couples, there is no reason to restrict civil marriage to opposite sex couples.

The argument might be made that a significant feature of marriage is that the status of marriage represents a certain expression of social approval for the union. Thus, the state provides for couples to marry to express social approval for opposite sex coupling. It is of course arguments like this that make advocates of gay rights argue that gays, lesbians, and bisexuals need to have the opportunity to marry in order to be accorded the expression of social approval for their unions. The idea is that marriage is a legitimating social practice—that the status of marriage legitimates the coupling. Therefore, some lesbians, gays, and bisexuals wish to have their same sex coupling legitimated. The counter argument then is that "society," whatever that is, does not wish to bestow social approval on same sex coupling. Therefore, same sex couples should not be provided with the option of legitimating state sanctioned marriage.

This counter argument does not work, for several reasons. One reason is that people who marry engage in myriad forms of coupling which are not socially approved by large segments of the population—for example, childless marriages (by choice), open marriages, adulterous marriages, opportunistic marriages or marriages of convenience (for immigration purposes, for example), tabloid marriages ("grandmother- or grandfather-aged person marries teen" type of thing). It simply is not the case that whatever unions result from opposite sex marriages would be subject to social approval. It is not simply by virtue of the fact that parties are of opposite sexes that civil marriage expresses social approval. Another reason is that many, many people do support the idea of state sanctioned social approval for same sex unions. Obviously, most if not all gays, lesbians, and bisexuals support the idea of state sanctioned social approval for same sex unions.[9] Whether or not all gays, lesbians, and bisexuals would actually want to participate in the practice of same sex marriages, they would nevertheless not want to endorse a continuation of a source of discrimination against gays, lesbians, and bisexuals. There may be some homosexuals who object to the campaign for gay marriage, but the basis of their denial of support may be something other than a wish to see discrimination against gays, lesbians, and bisexuals continued.

It is also the case that some heterosexuals who would not wish to have the option to undertake same sex marriages for themselves would still support the provision of state sanctioned same sex marriages to those who do want them. Liberals are notorious for arguing for the rights of people to do things that liberals themselves may not want to do, and that other people (non liberals) do not support for anyone. Why should same sex marriage be any different? A liberal society is one in which the fullest possible range of options for human flourishing is to be encouraged, consistent with the need for respect of the civil rights and liberties of individuals. One important civil liberty is the freedom to engage in a state sanctioned union. The only possible reason that a liberal could have for rejecting same sex

marriage is that the practice would in some way violate the harm principle.

It is important to clarify why the harm principle is even relevant in this context. The harm principle purports to stipulate the conditions under which the state could legitimately interfere with the liberty of its citizens; it sets out the bounds of individual liberty which must be respected by a liberal government. The harm principle is clearly germane to the issue of whether (homosexual) sodomy should be subject to criminal prohibition.[10] It makes sense therefore to apply the harm principle to that issue, but it is less clear why the harm principle should be applied to the issue of same sex marriage. There are several reasons why the application may be problematic.

Criminal prohibitions against sexual activity between consenting adults obviously violate the liberty of those subject to them. Thus, these prohibitions could only be justified if there was sufficient reason to do so, reasons which satisfy the requirements of the harm principle. If it could be shown that some harm—harm of the sort envisaged by Mill—results from the activity, then the prohibition could be justified. It cannot be shown that any harm of the sort envisaged by Mill results from the activity, and thus the criminal prohibition of homosexual activity cannot be justified. Any justifications of such criminal prohibitions could only be based on illiberal principles and prejudices.

The question of permitting homosexual marriage does not involve any clear violation of liberty. It could be argued that marriage law is an instance of power-conferring and entitlement-allocating legislation. Marriage law determines which couples are entitled to state sanction for their unions, and which couples are not. Marriage constitutes "an affirmation by the state, a larger-than-life acknowledgment of one's relationship, a seal of approval."[11] The question of whether the state can legitimately deny same sex couples the right to marry seems thus to be a question of equality. Are same sex couples equal to opposite sex couples, such that they should be entitled to the same state sponsorship of their unions? I argue that on a functional account of marriage formal equality would dictate that same sex couples are entitled to the same state sponsorship as opposite sex couples. I also argue that a functional account of marriage is the only type of account consistent with contemporary secular liberal society.

It should be sufficient, then, to say that the same sex marriage bar violates the formal equality of gays, lesbians, and bisexuals. Yet, it is not sufficient because the literature addressing the issue of same sex marriage does not facilitate a straightforward treatment in terms of formal equality. To respond to the objections that have been raised by critics of homosexual marriage, it is necessary to depart from a neat and simple analysis of equality.

The critics of homosexual marriage (both straight and gay) are not satisfied with the characterization of the issue as one of formal equality. Those critics who object to homosexual marriage because they object to homosexuality will not accept the claim of equality between same sex couples and opposite sex couples. That claim is contentious for them, and their response to that claim is typically to point out some kind of harm that is imputed to homosexual marriage. Those critics who object to homosexual marriage, or at least raise concerns about the pursuit of state sponsorship, but who do not object to homosexuality *per se* are concerned with issues of substantive equality. To address same sex marriage in the context of substantive equality is to talk about benefit and disbenefit, it is to talk about harm to interests.

Some readers might wonder whether the kind of harm that is being discussed in this section of the paper is really the kind of harm that Mill would have had in mind when he proposed the Harm Principle. I have two responses to that potential interjection. Firstly, what Mill would have had in mind is not determinative of the articulation of harm to be covered by the Principle for contemporary society. The debates over hate literature, pornography, and the lim-

its of free speech are not really foreshadowed in Mill's formulation, yet these issues have become an integral part of how the Harm Principle is understood in contemporary liberal society. Secondly, the kinds of harms that are covered by the term stigmatization include the loss of jobs, physical assaults ("gay bashing"), and other violations of the civil rights of gays, lesbians, and bisexuals. These are certainly the kinds of things Mill's own formulation would have been intended to cover.

On the usual reading of Mill's harm principle, preventing harm to others is the only justified rationale for state interference with the liberty of individuals.[12] I propose to apply a variant of the harm principle which can accommodate the concerns about putative harm raised by both sets of critics of same sex marriage, but still does justice to liberal principles. That variant is the following: the only justification for the denial by the state of a benefit required by formal equality is that the provision of that benefit would harm others in the society. Thus, as a matter of public policy, the state must sponsor power-conferring or entitlement-allocating legislation required by formal equality unless it can be shown that significant harm (of the kind covered by the harm principle) would result from that sponsorship. It could be argued that my formulation has departed so far from Mill's principle that it could not be included under the same label. Nevertheless, I think that the term harm is irreplaceable in this context—since it is harm that justifies the denial of state benefits. My version could be called the State Benefits Version of the Harm Principle.

The objections to same sex marriage which need to be countered involve conceptions of harm. I contend that in order to make sense of the objections, and in order to make a valid case for state sponsorship, it is necessary to respond to the assertions about putative harm. I have found that the most efficacious way to do so is examine the application of my proposed formulation of the harm principle in the context of the legitimation of homosexual marriage.

II

There are effectively two distinct sets of criticisms of same-sex marriage on the grounds of imputed harm resulting from state sanction. One set of criticisms includes several variations on the idea that allowing same-sex marriages will bring about a threat to the nuclear family, marriage in general, or even to society. This set of criticisms is based on a claim that I will call the Harm to Heterosexuality claim. The other set of criticisms includes several variations on the idea that advocating and pursuing state sponsorship of same sex marriage will bring about a threat to the goals and objectives of gay liberation. This set of criticisms is based on a claim that I will call the Harm to Homosexuality claim. The objection to same sex marriage can make use of conceptions of harm that are either symbolic or empirical, or both. In other words, the kind of harm that is imputed can be harm that can be determined and measured empirically or it can be symbolic harm that is simply perceived.

The Harm to Heterosexuality is supposed to consist in the threat that same sex marriages pose to opposite sex marriages, harm in the form of decline in the sanctity of the institution of marriage, inconsistency with traditional definitions of family, or even in the most extreme articulations of the position, harm in the form of a contribution to an overall breakdown in social order. People who make these kinds of criticisms are motivated by the rejection of gay rights and liberation, and often even a "fear and loathing" of homosexuality.

Many versions of the Harm to Heterosexuality position are premised upon religious conceptions of sex, family, and society. As such, the harm that is claimed tends to be more symbolic than empirical. Insofar as the Harm to Heterosexuality position is based upon religious conceptions of sex, family, and society, it is easily dispensed with in the context of a discussion of liberalism. Given that liberalism requires the separation of church and state, it cannot be argued that the state should outlaw same sex marriages because such marriages are inconsistent with religious morality. Insofar as the Harm to Heterosexuality position is based upon some empirical sounding claim about actual harm to the institutions of marriage and family, or to "society" itself, it is obvious that this would have to be based on some kind of evidence. What kind of evidence could one possibly produce to argue that same sex marriages would erode the institutions of marriage and family?

Someone who wants to claim that same sex marriages will produce some kind of distinct social harm has to be able to show what harm is caused by the state sponsorship of marriage that is distinct from the harm that is imputed to same sex relationships themselves. Same sex coupling will continue with or without state sponsorship, and even with or without criminalization of some of the acts that are targeted as part of an attempt to outlaw homosexuality. People who object to same sex marriage may also object to homosexuality, but the point is that to make any kind of a case for why a liberal society should not provide legal sanction for relationships that are already occurring, an argument specifically against state sponsorship of marriage is needed. If liberalism is based, as I want to argue, on the notions of privacy, autonomy, and individual liberty, no argument against homosexuality based on mere moral or social disapproval is acceptable. There has to be evidence of actual harm that will be experienced by members of the society that amounts to more than mere offense at the actions or choices of others. Therefore, the critics of same sex marriage cannot argue that they object to state sponsorship because they object to homosexuality and state sponsorship legitimates homosexuality.

What quickly becomes clear once one looks at the various articulations of the Harm to Heterosexuality position is that it is difficult to separate the objection to same sex marriage from the objection to homosexuality. It is of course important to be able to separate these objections, because the only basis a liberal could accept for outlawing, or denying legitimacy to, same sex relationships, is that those relationships will actually cause harm to others. If we recognize that the harm that can be considered is not harm that consists of mere offense, then the symbolic element of the objection is disallowed. That leaves the empirical element of the objection.

One candidate for the requisite kind of harm that is proposed is the potential for gay marriage to undermine the legitimacy of straight marriage. This claim can be understood in two ways: one in which the delegitimation consists of symbolic harm to the institution and the other in which the delegitimation consists of actual harm to the institution in the form of decreased participation. The notion of symbolic harm to the sanctity of heterosexual marriage rests upon illiberal commitments and concerns, and thus does not raise issues germane to the consideration of what liberals should support.

The notion of the latter form of harm, one of decreased participation, underlies the claim that the opportunity for gay marriage will weaken the institution of heterosexual marriage. Yet, as others have pointed out, this argument rests upon (at least one) fallacy. As one commentator puts it "[g]ay marriage could only delegitimize straight marriage if it were a real alternative to it."[13] That is, it could only delegitimize it if those who would otherwise participate in straight marriage chose to participate instead in gay marriage. Obviously, heterosexuals will continue to marry other heterosexuals. The people who will no longer participate in straight marriages if offered the opportunity to participate in gay marriages will be gays, lesbians, and bisexuals. Assuming that some gays who marry straights do so in order to be married and to have families, and not simply to avoid social stigma, then they would continue to do so. Those gays who marry straights in order to stay closeted and to avoid social stigma would continue to do so as long as the social stigmatization continues. Of course, the legalization of gay marriage would contribute to the erosion of the social stigma surrounding homosexuality, which would in turn encourage lesbians, gays,

and bisexuals to participate in gay marriage. None of this suggests that there would be any real threat of significantly decreased participation in heterosexual marriage.

It thus seems as if the objection to same sex marriage characterized in terms of harm rests solely upon the objection to homosexuality itself. There is no argument against marriage of same sex persons that is not an argument against homosexuality. I want to assert that there is no valid empirical evidence that same sex relationships, in and of themselves, cause actual harm to any other persons. The claim that these relationships are harmful to the participants—even assuming there could be a factual basis to this dubious supposition—is of course an irrelevant claim, given liberalism's *prima facie* commitment to nonpaternalism. It is particularly illegitimate when the paternalism is based on contentious moral, religious, or social conceptions of the "good" of the intended beneficiaries of the paternalism.[14]

The Harm to Homosexuality is supposed to consist in the threat that state sponsorship poses to the achievement of gay liberation and to the project of reconceiving heterosexuality, homosexuality, and relations between the sexes. People who make these kinds of claims are motivated by a commitment to gay liberation, and to some articulations of gay rights—ones that do not amount to presumption of the notion of "sameness" between gays and straights but rather assume the notion of "difference" between gays and straights. The position of those in gay, lesbian, and bisexual communities[15] who reject the pursuit of state sponsorship for same sex relationships, is not of course that there is anything wrong with same sex relationships. Their position is that there is something wrong with state sponsorship, and something wrong with marriage.

It should be pointed out that those in lesbian, gay, and bisexual communities who raise objections to the prospect of gay marriage do so largely on grounds of strategy and tactics. The debate over gay marriage within gay, lesbian, and bisexual communities is mainly a debate over the priority of different venues or policies for the allocation of resources and the expenditure of efforts. The discussion in much of the literature thus addresses the advisability of pursuing gay marriage as a strategy for gay activists, and raises concerns about the diversion of efforts and resources from other significant issues. These debates—whether putting too much effort into this one option will divert efforts from other options that may be more central to sexual liberation, whether the pursuit of domestic partnership legislation should take priority over removal of the same sex marriage bar,[16] whether the potential backlash from the pursuit of this particular option will have repercussions, or whether the gay, lesbian, and bisexual community is too divided over the option to make it a priority—could all be seen to involve questions about goals and strategies for queer activism.[17] For instance, some "regard domestic partnership agreement registration as a distraction from the need to gain full rights to marry with full access to benefits and protections," while others perceive that registration is better because it "recognizes alternative family structures."[18] These questions about which is the better target begin with the assumption that gays, lesbians, and bisexuals are entitled to equality and then move to the attempt to articulate and clarify the appropriate way to characterize and pursue that equality.

The point is that gays, lesbians, and bisexuals who call into question the desirability of gay marriage generally do not dispute the position that the opposite sex requirement of marriage laws is "socially discriminatory and offensive to the basic liberal principles that underlie human rights legislation."[19] Even those who raise objections to same sex marriage do not deny that the same sex marriage bar is illiberal. Yet, it is still possible to construct an objection to state sponsorship to same sex marriage that imputes some type of potential harm that would result from the policy. This objection could take several different forms:

1. one based on an objection to perceived conformity to "straight standards;"[20]

2. one based on an objection to the oppressive patriarchal nature of the institution of marriage; and

3. one based on an objection to the involvement of the state in the regulation of lesbian, gay, and bisexual intimate relationships.

These objections tend to overlap and are difficult to disentangle.

The first form of the objection, based on rejection of the perceived conformity to "straight standards" inherent in same sex marriage, implies that the pursuit of conformity on the part of some gays, lesbians, and bisexuals—namely those who would want to get married—could indirectly harm the interests of those who would not want to get married, and thus who do not conform. The harm would consist of the further stigmatization of those lesbians, gays, and bisexuals who choose not to get married once the option becomes available.[21]

It is possible to construct the imputed argument along the following lines. Homosexual sex is stigmatized and a cause for oppression of gays, lesbians, and bisexuals. If homosexuals could marry, those who would already tend to benefit from certain social privileges (class, race, ethnicity, and so forth) will likely be the ones to exercise the option. Those homosexuals who do not marry will be further stigmatized and oppressed, relative to the otherwise more privileged homosexuals who will marry.[22]

It is difficult to determine in what sense there would be more stigmatization or oppression of the lesbians, gays, and bisexuals who choose not to marry—absolutely or in terms of perception of relative privilege. It is at least partly an empirical question. What is relevant to the issue in question is whether the provision of state sponsorship for same sex marriage would result in more harm overall, harm of the sort that is germane to liberalism.

The significant issue for the question of whether liberalism should support same sex marriage is whether the resulting "extra" stigmatization would result from the provision of same sex marriage itself, or would be an unintended byproduct of pre-existing homophobia.[23] It is unclear whether the stigmatization of non-married or single gays, lesbians, and bisexuals would be more after the option of state sponsored same sex marriage is available or whether it would be the same amount of stigmatization, but would seem more in relation to the other married gays, lesbians, and bisexuals. That is, it is unclear whether it would be extra stigmatization or simply continuing stigmatization. Either way, the "extra" stigmatization should be the focus of additional efforts to reduce and eventually overcome homophobic societal attitudes. Unless one could show that denying same sex couples the right to marry would, in and of itself, decrease the stigmatization, it is necessary to address the resulting harm by other measures than continuing the same sex marriage bar.

The first objection to same sex marriage can be presented still more abstractly, in terms of the "politics for validating difference,"[24] and a general critique of "rights discourse" and "rights claims." The presumption is that there is something one could identify as lesbian and gay identity and culture that resists assimilation. There is no denial, however, that some gays and lesbians as individuals do not resist, and even welcome, assimilation. The concern is that whenever society extends rights to some previously disenfranchised group of persons—in this case the lesbians, gays, and bisexuals who do want to get married—then other members of the group who "forswear or forego such rights risk being even more marginalized than before."[25] The objection seems to highlight the tension between individual rights which would be asserted by the group of same sex couples who want to marry, and collective interests which would be represented by the interests of the remainder of the group, the non-marrying gays and lesbians.[26]

The second form of the Harm to Homosexuality objection is the claim that marriage is an oppressive institution which lesbians and gay men should condemn, rather than lobby to join.[27] There are two different aspects of characterizing the harm of marriage in this objection. One aspect concerns the patriarchal nature of marriage as a social institution.[28] The other aspect emphasizes the balance of benefits and burdens that marriage may provide for particular same sex couples. The latter aspect is related to the former in that the reason some couples would not realize the potential benefits of marriage would have to do with the underlying oppressive features, and structural constraints of society. What Nitya Duclos calls the "hierarchy of privilege" ensures that some couples—whether opposite sex or same sex couples—will benefit more from the bundle of benefits that constitute marriage.[29] The provision of state sponsored marriage for same sex couples will also have effects on cohabiting same sex couples that may or may not be welcomed by those cohabiting couples.

Both aspects of the second objection—the particular and the general—have in common the focus on marriage. It is marriage as a social institution that is an oppressive patriarchal institution. It is marriage as a particular legislative scheme that has better or worse effects for particular couples. The important point for the purposes of this paper is that the putative harm does not result from the provision of same sex marriage, but rather from marriage itself. For the liberal, the question is whether it is justifiable for the state to continue to deny to same sex couples the option that is available to opposite sex couples—to participate in the potentially undesirable, arguably harmful institution of marriage. The liberal rejection of paternalism entails that individuals should be allowed to choose for themselves whether or not to participate in activities that may be harmful to themselves. The issue is not the desirability of marriage, but the desirability of the right.[30]

Several feminists have argued for the position that while marriage may be oppressive in its present form, it need not always be that way. Marriage, the argument goes, is a creature of law dependent upon the power of the state; as such, it is an historically and culturally contingent institution.[31] The further claim is made that same sex marriage could have the potential to "disrupt both the gendered definition of marriage and the assumption the marriage is a form of socially, if not legally, prescribed hierarchy."[32] At the very least, same sex marriages would require the rethinking of the content of the marriage vows and the exercise of linguistic creativity to replace the "husband" and "wife" terminology. These improvements would have symbolic value, and would contribute to the larger project of reforming marriage as a social institution. Same sex marriage, then, would produce no distinctive harm and might even ameliorate the current harm produced by marriage.

What makes the issue complicated is that it is possible to characterize the benefits that would accrue to lesbians, gays, and bisexuals upon provision of the right to state sponsorship of same sex marriage in two ways. One way is to emphasize the benefits that would be realized by individual members of same sex couples who could participate in marriage. The other way is to emphasize the benefits that would be realized by all queers consisting of increased tolerance of homosexuality and increased legitimacy for same sex unions. Some advocates of state sponsorship of same sex marriage argue that it is actually the "issue most likely to lead ultimately to a world free of discrimination against lesbians and gay men."[33] The characterization of benefits—the determination of which benefits will result and who specifically will benefit—is addressed in the literature in the context of the identification of attendant harms—the determination of which harms will result and who specifically will be harmed.

It is important to distinguish between the claim that same sex couples should be entitled to equal treatment with opposite sex couples—whether through domestic partnership arrangements or civil marriage—and the claim that these legal measures should be the focus of advocacy and struggle for gay rights. It is also important to distinguish between the claim that the right to choose X—for example, the right to choose to marry—will benefit those for whom X is a likely option and the claim that the right to choose X is a benefit to only those who do choose X. There is a difference between the concern that gay activists should not direct their energies to the pursuit of marriage and domestic partnership arrangements because only some gays and lesbians would want to participate in those institutions and the claim that only those who (will) participate in those institutions will be benefited by the existence of the choice.

The objection to same sex marriage based on the rejection of conformity should properly locate the harm in homophobia. The objection to same sex marriage based on the suspicion of marriage should properly locate the harm in marriage itself. The objection to same sex marriage based on the perniciousness of state regulation of sexuality should properly locate the harm in the combination of homophobia and marriage itself. It is obvious why queers would be suspicious of any manifestation of state regulation of sexuality.[34] The question, however, is whether gays, lesbians, and bisexuals would be worse off with the provision of state sponsorship for same sex coupling. It is hard to see how they would be. The problem rests with state initiatives that amount to the entrenchment of intolerance of homosexuality.

According to the third form of the Harm to Homosexuality objection, marriage simply presents yet another vehicle of state regulation of sexuality. Marriage, however, does present some potential for protection from state regulation and other benefits. Nitya Duclos lists four objectives of the advocates of gay and lesbian marriage:

1. "to revolutionize marriage and force society to rethink its collective views of sex and sexuality;"
2. to provide validation and legitimation of same sex relationships;
3. to enable lesbian and gay families to partake in the range of socioeconomic benefits of marriage;

4. to legitimate gay and lesbian relationships in the eyes of courts to help lesbians and gays keep their children.[35]

It is clear that merely removing the obstacles to same sex marriage is not going to be sufficient for the realization of these objectives.

State sponsorship of same sex coupling will entail toleration of homosexuality, but it alone will not provide for respect and full equality without other social, political, legal, and economic changes.[36] For example, changes in judicial attitudes and child custody legislation will be necessary for the achievement of the fourth objective.[37] The effect of marriage breakdown will cause same sex couples to come under the purview of courts under divorce legislation. Same sex couples who separate and divorce will be subject to provisions concerning division of property, support, and custody of children. For some people, that will be a benefit and for others that will be a burden. The point is that it is not same sex marriage that increases the points of contact but the legislative regime governing marriage and divorce. The fear of state regulation should not amount to a fear of same sex marriage, but rather a fear of homophobia and a fear of the potential effects of the legislative regime governing marriage and divorce. Thus, harm would result from homophobia and the effects of marriage and divorce, but not from same sex marriage itself.

The consideration of the Harm to Homosexuality objections points to the need to distinguish between formal and substantive equality. The conceptions of harm contained in the various forms of the objection indicate concerns of substantive equality. The question of whether same sex couples should be denied the state sponsorship available to opposite sex couples is really a question of formal equality. The position of this paper is that the same sex marriage bar is a clear denial of formal equality for gays, lesbians, and bisexuals. It is important to make clear, then, the relation between formal equality and substantive equality on this issue, if there is any relation.

The opponents to same sex marriage who are motivated by some version of the Harm to Homosexuality objection could be making one of three different claims about the effects of same sex marriage on substantive equality. These three claims are:

1. same sex marriage would increase substantive equality;

2. same sex marriage would decrease substantive equality; or

3. same sex marriage would neither decrease nor increase substantive equality.

On the basis of the above discussion it seems that the three forms of the Harm to Homosexuality objection—the rejection of conformity, the suspicion of marriage, and the fear of state regulation—all attempt to implicate same sex marriage in the charge of jeopardizing substantive equality.

I have tried to argue, however, that what actually jeopardizes substantive equality is not the possibility of same sex marriage, in and of itself, but the effects of pre-existing inequalities resulting from homophobia, the legal regime governing marriage and divorce, and other social inequalities. I would contend then, that same sex marriage at the least could be said to neither decrease nor increase substantive equality. It may even increase substantive equality if the claims concerning the potential liberatory effects of same sex marriage upon the institution of marriage are viable. The provision of state sponsored same sex marriage would certainly further the pursuit of formal equality for homosexuals, and for that reason it is incumbent upon liberals to support it.

III

Richard Posner in *Sex and Reason* presents several other arguments against same sex marriage. Posner argues that there are significant differences between punishing sodomy and prohibiting homosexual marriage such that the former is not justifiable but the latter might be. Posner claims that the laws criminalizing sodomy are unjustifiable and should be repealed, but that the bar to same sex marriage is probably justifiable and should be upheld. He gives three reasons for his claim, but only one amounts to an argument.

The first reason seems to be that homosexual unions do not deserve state approval, although they do not deserve state condemnation either.

This first reason involves multiple assertions:

1. that permitting homosexual marriage would be interpreted as "placing a stamp of approval on homosexuality, while decriminalizing sodomy would not;"

2. that permitting homosexual marriage is tantamount to declaring that "homosexual marriage is a desirable, even a noble, condition in which to live;"[38]

3. that permitting homosexual marriage would "place government in the dishonest position of propagating a false picture of the reality of homosexuals' lives."[39]

What Posner is not saying explicitly is as significant as what he is saying. He is saying that most people do not think that homosexual marriage is a noble or a desirable condition in which to live. He is implying that homosexual marriage is not entitled to a stamp of approval. Posner does not specifically say why homosexual unions do not deserve a stamp of approval. One can only assume that it has something to do with the claim that homosexual unions generate "unstable, temporary, and childless" marriages.[40] It is the pretense that they are otherwise that seems to constitute the false picture the government would be propagating if it permitted homosexual marriage.

Posner assumes that he has provided empirical evidence for his claims in the earlier part of the chapter, "Homosexuality: The Policy Questions." Yet, some homosexual unions include children, some are very stable, and some are very long lasting, as Posner himself recognizes. Posner is either making sweeping generalizations and then contradicting himself, or else he is not providing sufficient support for his argument. Posner seems to assume that the information that a certain couple is married gives the picture that the couple has

a stable, long-lasting, and child-producing union. He then seems to claim on the basis of empirical studies that homosexual couples are statistically less likely to be stable or permanent than are heterosexual couples. Thus, he argues that the government would be propagating a false picture by permitting homosexual marriage.

Of course many heterosexual unions also generate "unstable, temporary, and childless" marriages. Thus, for many opposite sex couples the information that a couple is married gives, according to Posner's reasoning, a false picture. Posner even acknowledges this fact. He allows that the suggestion that heterosexual marriages and prospective homosexual marriages differ fundamentally along these lines comes to seem ever more implausible. This then leads him to suggest that the appropriate response is one of "chucking the whole institution of marriage in favor of an explicitly contractual approach that would make the current realities of marriage transparent."[41] Gay and lesbian sexual liberationists might support the proposal to get rid of marriage altogether, but it is difficult to imagine that this prospect is imminent. In the interim, as long as opposite sex couples can choose to marry Posner needs to explain why same sex couples cannot have that choice. Posner needs to explain why same sex unions do not deserve state approval.

If it the case, as Posner assumes, that most people do not consider homosexual unions to be noble and desirable, than what would follow from that? Homosexual unions are obviously desirable to those who participate in them, and likewise same sex marriages would be desirable to those who would participate in them. Homosexual unions are not ignoble to those who participate in them and they are inherently no more or no less noble than heterosexual unions to those who are tolerant and respectful of them. Posner argues for the decriminalization of homosexuality on the grounds of toleration. For liberals, however, the issue is not merely whether the political value of liberty requires the tolerance and acceptance of homosexuals. The question is whether the political value of equality further requires the state to provide the stamp of approval for same sex unions. Posner needs to provide an argument for the violation of equality that the denial of state sponsorship represents.

The second reason seems to be inconclusive—he identifies both an information cost and an information benefit to the prospect of same sex marriage. The information cost is that the more inclusive the concept of marriage becomes the less information the world "marriage" conveys. But as Posner would recognize, this argument would apply equally to other expansions of the concept of marriage. Posner then goes on to point out that the label same sex marriage would convey more information about the particular same sex relationship. Thus, same sex marriage would also provide an information benefit. Since they cancel each other out, the information cost consideration counts neither for nor against his argument.[42]

The third reason that Posner provides for distinguishing between decriminalization of sodomy and the legalization of gay marriage concerns the entitlements of marriage. He points out that authorizing same sex marriage would confer certain benefits on some homosexual couples, and then simply asks whether society would want this. On the question of costs and benefits, I think it is important to point out that Posner does not deal with the issue of the social and moral costs of leaving state sponsored discrimination unchallenged.[43] If the question of state sponsorship of same sex unions is simply a matter of determining whether there is a violation of formal equality, then the issue of costs and benefits is incidental. It is because those who address the question do not simply view it as a matter of formal equality that these other issues—such as costs and benefits—continue to be raised.

Posner has not presented sufficient argument for the claim that homosexual marriages should not be given the stamp of approval. Posner himself admits that his arguments are inconclusive.[44] All Posner has succeeded in showing is that removing the bar on same sex marriage has some-

what different implications than decriminalizing (homosexual) sodomy. He has not succeeded in showing that there is anything actually wrong with same sex marriage that does not amount to either rejection of homosexuality or the illiberal claims about the threat to the sanctity of marriage.

IV

I am not making any claim of the sort that gays, lesbians, or bisexuals should want to get married in order to mimic opposite sex coupling.[45] I am only claiming that the benefits of state sanctioned civil marriage—from expression of commitment to employee benefits and tax breaks—should be available to any self-defined couple, whether same sex or opposite sex. Same sex marriages can facilitate the provision of "spousal" benefits and establish the basis for same sex couple adoptions. The status of marriage thus provides more opportunities for people, and liberals should endorse that, if nothing else, about same sex state sanctioned union. Opposite sex couples can choose to marry or to remain in common law relationships or to register as domestic partnerships. Why shouldn't same sex couples have those same choices? Opposite sex couples can have the "benefits" of pursuing extra-marital affairs (given that some people find a certain pleasure in transgressing the bounds of marriage). Opposite sex couples can have the "benefits" of legal provisions concerning division of property and family assets upon marriage breakdown. Why shouldn't same sex couples have these same options? As an issue of equality and fairness, liberals should insist that the same range of coupling options and their attendant benefits be available to same sex couples as are available to opposite sex couples.

There are larger questions, of course, of why people should and do identify themselves as "couples," and of why the state should provide legal, political, and social benefits upon that identification. Those questions are not relevant to the specific claim that if the state does provide these benefits and if coupling is self-defining, then same sex coupling should not be deprived the state sanction accorded to opposite sex coupling. The larger questions aside, it is a matter of social justice and equality and non-discrimination that same sex couples should have access to, and be entitled to, equivalent benefits and privileges as opposite sex couples.

NOTES

1. Chris Bull, "Till Death Do Us Part," p. 41. As Bull and others point out gays and lesbians are "openly marrying, raising children, and demanding official recognition of their partners as spouses." Bull says that same sex marriage is the "new hot issue in the nation's [the United States] gay and lesbian community." See Michelangelo Signorile's article, "Bridal Wave," for an account of how the issue is developing in Hawaii, which may end up being the first United States state to legally recognize homosexual marriages.

2. Gays and lesbians have been participating in commitment ceremonies (also called bonding or union ceremonies) for some time, but these of course do not have the "stamp of approval" nor the legal consequences of state sponsored marriage. In Canada, several challenges to the exclusion of same sex couples from legal provisions concerning "spouses" are working their way through the courts. These challenges are typically based on equality claims involving Section 15 of the Canadian Charter of Rights and Freedoms. See Bruce Ryder's, "Equality Rights and Sexual Orientation: Confronting Heterosexual Family Privilege," for more on the specifics of the Canadian context.

3. As per common usage, I will assume that gay refers to gay men and lesbian refers to gay women. Some people take the term "queer" to refer to gay men, lesbian women, bisexual women, bisexual men, transsexuals, and transvestites collectively.

4. This is the gist of what then Prime Minister Pierre Elliot Trudeau said when recommending the decriminalization of any sexual activity between consenting adults in private. This claim is a prior assumption to my version of a functional definition of marriage.

5. Clearly, I am developing my formulation of liberalism and its basic assumptions and commitments in reliance upon certain exponents of the liberal tradition—namely John Stuart Mill in *On Liberty*, Ronald Dworkin in "Liberalism," from Hampshire, ed., *Public and Private Morality*, and Joel Feinberg in *Harmless Wrongdoing*. There is a vast literature on liberalism, but interestingly very little of that literature that I am aware of actually addresses the question of a liberal position on the state sponsorship of same sex marriages.

6. These are the usual conditions for marriage—there will likely be some variation among jurisdictions. Nitya Duclos, in "Some Complicating Thoughts on Same Sex Marriage,"

says the common bars to marriage include: "minimum age limits, insanity, absence of consent (mistake, duress, and fraud), prohibited degrees of affinity and consanguinity, and a prior existing marriage." Duclos, p. 44, fn. 48.

7. Nan Hunter, in "Marriage, Law and Gender: A Feminist Inquiry," points out that the functionalist approach—which posits the identification of objective criteria to determine which relationships are the functional equivalents to marriage—underlay the recognition of common law marriage. See Hunter, p. 21 ff.

8. The San Francisco Domestic Partnership law states, "[d]omestic partners are two adults who have chosen to share one another's lives in an intimate and committed relationship of mutual caring, who live together, and who have agreed to be jointly responsible for basic living expenses incurred during the Domestic Partnership." See Appendix A: San Francisco Domestic Partnership Ordinance (1990) in David Chambers' article, "Tales of Two Cities . . . ," p. 204. The New York Court of Appeals found in *Braschi v. Stahl Associates* that a gay couple must be treated as a family in relation to New York's rent control law. The Court found that the couple satisfied the following criteria: "the exclusivity and longevity of the relationship, the level of emotional and financial commitment, the manner in which the parties have conducted their everyday lives and held themselves out to society, and the reliance placed upon one another for daily family services." Chambers provides an extended discussion of that case from p. 192 ff. See Hunter, supra, p. 23.

9. I should point out that the support is often a qualified support, for a series of complicated reasons. I will touch briefly on some of those reasons in the section concerning the Harm to Homosexuality objection to same sex marriages below, but it will not be possible for me to do justice in this paper to the fascinating complexity of the debates over same sex marriage in the lesbian, gay, and bisexual community. For some sense of what the issues are see the papers by Nitya Duclos, Mary Dunlap, and Nan Hunter in the Symposium on Lesbian and Gay Marriage in *Law and Sexuality: A Review of Lesbian and Gay Legal Issues*, Volume 1, Summer 1991 and see the papers by Thomas Stoddard and Paula Ettelbrick in *Lesbian and Gay Marriage*, edited by Suzanne Sherman. See also Chris Bull, "Till Death Do Us Part" and Michelango Signorile, "Bridal Wave."

10. Laws in several states in the United States which criminalize sodomy do not distinguish between heterosexual and homosexual sodomy. Yet, in *Bower vs. Hardwick* the Georgia law was challenged by a homosexual man and the court dealt with the issue as if the law were intended to outlaw homosexual sodomy. In Canada, the federal criminal code was amended in May 1969 to remove the criminalization of any sexual acts between consenting adults.

11. Harlon Dalton, "Reflections on the Lesbian and Gay Marriage Debate," p. 7.

12. This general conception covers both narrower and broader conceptions of the Harm Principle. See Lyons,

"Liberty and Harm to Others," for a discussion of the debate over how narrowly or broadly Mill's principle—which he calls the Principle of Liberty—should be construed. Brown argues that the principle should cover only harm producing conduct and Lyons argues that it should be expanded to include harm preventing conduct, which may not itself be harm producing—for example, good Samaritan behavior and joint cooperation behavior. My conception differs from that of both of these versions in that I focus on the justification of the denial of state benefits rather than the justification of the interference with liberty.

13. Andrew Sullivan, in "Here Comes the Groom: A (Conservative) Case for Gay Marriage," p. 20. Catharine MacKinnon points out that "persons secure in their heterosexuality would not be threatened by the availability of this option," i.e., gay marriage. MacKinnon, p. 27.

14. Michael Levin, in "Why Homosexuality is Abnormal," for example, attempts to provide a teleological account of the harm that homosexuality presents. If his argument were persuasive, then paternalism would seem to follow. Michael Ruse's discussion of the claim that homosexuality is unnatural in, "Is Homosexuality Bad Sexuality?" tends to undercut Levin's claims.

15. It would be inaccurate and inappropriate to speak of "the" gay, lesbian, and bisexual community; but it would be equally inaccurate and inappropriate to speak of "the" gay, "the" lesbian, or "the" bisexual community. There are communities, and communities within communities. It might be possible to speak of a community of communities, but even that might be misleading. One can get a sense of the remarkable range of conceptions of equality for gays, lesbians, and bisexuals and of the range of recommended strategies from reading Paul Berman's essay, "Democracy and Homosexuality," in *The New Republic*, and from the following books (two of which Berman reviews): Bruce Bawer, *A Place at the Table: The Gay Individual in American Society*; Mark Blasuis, *A Politics of Sexuality: The Emergence of a Lesbian and Gay Ethos*; Diana Fuss, *Essentially Speaking: Feminism, Nature and Difference*; Marshall Kirk and Hunter Madsen, *After the Ball: How America Will Conquer Its Fear and Hatred of Gays in the 1990s*; Shane Phelan, *Identity Politics: Lesbian Feminism and the Limits of Community*, Michelangelo Signorile's *Queer in America: Sex, the Media and the Closets of Power*. There are many more references that could be given, but this list is sufficient to cover the range from separatist liberation perspectives to conservative assimilationist perspectives. Chris Bull's article in the *Advocate*, "Till Death Do Us Part," and Michelangelo Signorile's article in *Out*, "Bridal Wave," give some indication of the range of positions on same sex marriage among gays and lesbians.

16. See David Chambers, "Tales of Two Cities: AIDS and the Legal Recognition of Domestic Partnerships in San Francisco and New York." Domestic Partnership ordinances have been enacted by municipalities in various United States cities. The domestic partnership arrangements usually contain a requirement that same sex couples register as partners—"two people who have chosen to share one another's lives in an intimate

and committed relationship of mutual caring." Chambers, p. 185. The other feature of the arrangements is the provision by public and private employers that those couples who have registered will be entitled to the benefits provided to "spouses." Domestic Partnership regimes in the United States have usually been open to both homosexual and heterosexual unmarried couples. See Dunlap, p. 94, and Posner, pp. 313–314, on the arrangements in Denmark and Sweden.

17. Many of the discussions of the issue by gay and lesbian activists focus on this aspect. For example, Michael Lowenthal, in "Wedding Bells and Whistles," says that "[w]inning domestic-partnership privileges won't lead to acceptance for all lesbians and gay men, only for those in domestic partnerships." He then goes on to say: "[r]ather than lobbying for policies that will benefit only those who choose to register domestic partnerships, we should be fighting for the fundamental civil rights that will guarantee equal treatment for us all." See Lowenthal, p. 5.

18. Suzanne Sherman points to the divided opinion on the topic among the interviewees for her book, *Lesbian and Gay Marriage: Private Commitments, Public Ceremonies*. See p. 8.

19. Nitya Duclos, "Some Complicating Thoughts on Same Sex Marriage," p. 31. Paula Ettelbrick, one of those most strongly opposed to same sex marriages admits that: "[w]hen analyzed from a standpoint of civil rights, certainly lesbians and gay men should have a right to marry." Ettelbrick, "Since When Is Marriage a Path to Liberation?," p. 21.

20. Michael Lowenthal says, in "Wedding Bells and Whistles," that he was part of efforts to obtain legal recognition of domestic partnerships but came to realize that the administration of the college where he worked "would accept us only to the degree that we conformed to straight standards." Lowenthal, p. 5.

21. The objection is framed this way by Mary Dunlap in "The Lesbian and Gay Marriage Debate: A Microcosm of Our Hopes and Troubles in the Nineties," p. 78 and Nan Hunter in "Marriage, Law and Gender...," p. 12. Dunlap asks, "If Outlaws Can Have In-Laws Then Won't Those Without In-Laws Become Outer Outlaws?" Nitya Duclos discusses the issue several times in "Some Complicating Thoughts on Same Sex Marriage." Paula Ettelbrick says, "gay marriage, instead of liberating gay sex and sexuality, would further outlaw all gay and lesbian sex that is not performed in a marital context." See Ettelbrick, "Since When Is Marriage a Path to Liberation?," p. 23.

22. This is a reconstruction of the various positions presented in the papers by Hunter, Duclos, and Ettelbrick.

23. Homophobia has become a common term for the unjust denial of civil rights to homosexuals, as well as to the irrational fear and hatred of homosexuals and homosexuality. The term was initially used in psychiatric literature to refer to the "phobia" that one might be a homosexual oneself. The term has taken on a broader meaning, one which functions in many respects analogously to sexism, racism, ableism, and classism. The term heterosexism is often used in the same contexts as homophobia.

24. Nan Hunter, supra, p. 11.

25. Harlon Dalton, "Reflections on the Lesbian and Gay Marriage Debate," p. 5. As Dalton points out, "legal rights would never be extended if the bare fact that a subset of the class might thereby be disadvantaged were deemed to constitute a sufficient ground for inaction." He goes on to say that it is still problematic to pursue policies which will have the unintended effects of favoring some class members over others.

26. While this conflict is most readily treated as a conflict between individual and collective interests, it can also be conceived as a conflict between different collective interests and thus competing versions of collective rights—the interests of assimilationists and the interests of anti-assimilationists respectively. Cf. Leslie Green, "Two Views of Collective Rights," p. 235.

27. Hunter, supra, p. 11. Hunter identifies two arguments that opponents to same sex marriage within lesbian, gay, and bisexual communities have relied on: the one about assimilation and stigmatization and the other one about the oppressiveness of marriage. Duclos and Dunlap also provide extensive discussion of the claim concerning marriage.

28. See Duclos, Dunlap, and Hunter for extensive discussions of marriage as a patriarchal institution. Duclos points out that the provision of same sex marriage may serve to legitimate marriage, which would have bad consequences for heterosexually identified women. It is of course the legitimation of marriage that would have the bad consequences.

29. Dunlap, p. 86, reproduces the following list of rights enjoyed by persons who marry: the right to obtain health insurance, bereavement leave, and make decisions when the partner is incapacitated; the right to visit the partner in hospitals, jails, mental institutions, and other places restricted to family members; the right to claim dependency deductions and statuses; the right to claim estate and gift tax benefits; the right to file joint tax returns; the right of inheritance (particularly in case of intestacy); the right to sue for infliction of emotional distress by injury to the partner, for loss of consortium, wrongful death and other personal injuries; the right to claim marital communication privilege; the right to live in housing for married persons; and more. See Duclos, pp. 52–53, for a more extensive list. Duclos also sets out a list of burdens the marriage brings, which includes the following: "spouse in the house" rules for state welfare assistance; "spouse's" credit history taken into account in credit rating; disentitlement from government student loans on the basis of "spouse's" income; anti-nepotism rules in employment, and more. See Duclos, pp.53–54 for the complete list.

30. Thomas Stoddard makes this point in "Why Gay People Should Seek the Right to Marry," p. 18.

31. Nan Hunter, p. 13. See also Dunlap and Duclos for similar arguments.

32. Hunter, supra, p. 16. As Catherine MacKinnon puts it in "Not By Law Alone," from *Feminism Unmodified: Discourses on Life and Law*: "I do think it might do something amazing to the entire institution of marriage to recognize the unity of "two" persons between whom no superiority or inferiority could be presumed on the basis of gender." MacKinnon, p. 27.

33. Thomas Stoddard, "Why Gay People Should Seek the Right to Marry," p. 17.

34. See Dunlap for an extensive discussion of the harmful effects of the *Bowers v. Hardwick* decision and other homophobic state measures.

35. Duclos, p. 42.

36. Nan Hunter suggests that more encompassing changes be based on "gender dissent," which she says does not connote identity based on sexual orientation but rather conveys an active intent to disconnect power from gender and conveys an adversary relationship to dominance. Hunter, pp. 29–30. She argues that the pursuit of domestic partnership laws should complement the pursuit of legalizing lesbian and gay marriage, and that "neither strategy is complete without the other." Hunter, p. 26. For more, on domestic partnership agreements, see David Chambers, "Tales of Two Cities. . . ."

37. It is interesting, and disconcerting, to note that the Danish government which provided the right to marry for same sex couples by an act of Parliament still restricted the right of lesbian and gay couples to adopt children. There would be no rationale for the continuing restriction on a liberal treatment of the issue such as I have been developing. See Dunlap, p. 94.

38. Posner is echoing the wording of the United States Supreme Court decision in *Griswold v. Connecticut*. The court said that marriage is "an association for as noble a purpose as any involved in our prior decisions." See *Sexual Orientation and the Law* by the Editors of the *Harvard Law Review*, pp. 95 ff. for further discussion.

39. Posner, pp. 311–312.

40. Posner, p. 312.

41. Posner, p. 312.

42. In fact it is difficult to understand why Posner even brings the point up, since it is inconclusive and the things he says, on his own admission, seem to represent a "trivial addendum." See Posner, p. 312. It seems as if he needed to find a way to bring in some economic concept, since the context of his discussion is his use of a "law and economics" approach.

43. Harlan Dalton raises this point. Dalton articulates five questions on the issue of lesbian and gay marriage as follows: (1) Can the state legitimately deny lesbian and gay couples the right to marry? (2) Were such a right to exist, would lesbians and gay men gain or lose? (3) Can anyone, gay or straight, who enters into the institution of marriage avoid its misogynist and proprietary taint? (4) What impact does the struggle to make lesbian and gay marriage an option have on the politics of lesbian and gay liberation? (5) What would be the effect of a successful struggle to legalize lesbian and gay marriage on the institution of marriage itself? Dalton, p. 3. I would argue that it is really only the first

question which raises specifically philosophical issues, and thus it is that question which has been the focus of the present paper. The other questions are important questions, but they really concern matters of political strategy and political sociology. It should be clear from the discussion in this paper that it is necessary to address issues that arise as a result of asking the other questions, but it is not necessary to be able to provide definitive answers to those other questions to be able to provide an answer to the first question.

44. Posner, p. 313.

45. Nitya Duclos says: "[g]iven that a same-sex marriage bar is a bad thing for the state to impose, lesbians and gay men still need to ask whether marriage is a good thing for them to seek." Duclos, p. 42. Her article raises many significant issues for lesbians and gay men to consider about the desirability of marriage.

The 1996 "Defense of Marriage Act"

United States Congress

In September, 1996, both the U.S. House and Senate passed "The Defense of Marriage Act" ("DOMA"). The House vote was 342–67; the Senate voted 85–14.

PUBLIC LAW 104–199
DATE: SEPT. 21, 1996

"No State, territory, or possession of the United States, or Indian tribe, shall be required to give effect to any public act, record, or judicial proceeding of any other State, territory, possession, or tribe respecting a relationship between persons of the same sex that is treated as a marriage under the laws of such other State, territory, possession, or tribe, or a right or claim arising from such relationship.

In determining the meaning of any Act of Congress, or of any ruling, regulation, or interpretation of the various administrative bureaus and agencies of the United States, the word 'marriage' means only a legal union between one man and one woman as husband and wife, and the word 'spouse' refers only to a person of the opposite sex who is a husband or a wife."

34.

The Conservative Case

Andrew Sullivan

Andrew Sullivan's essay on growing up a young gay man appears in Chapter 1 of this book. An ardent and vocal supporter of same-sex marriages, he has recently published a collection of essays, *Same-Sex Marriage: Pro and Con, A Reader*. In this essay, Sullivan identifies and critically evaluates what he calls one of the most common conservative arguments against same-sex marriage, namely, that public acceptance of same-sex unions would undermine the stability of the traditional heterosexual family. Sullivan directly challenges the assumption that public recognition of homosexuality could "potentially destabilize the whole system of incentives for stable family relationships."

The [most common] . . . conservative argument, however, is a much stronger one: that the public acceptance of homosexuality subverts the stability and self-understanding of the heterosexual family. But here too the conservative position undermines itself somewhat. Since conservatives, unlike prohibitionists, concede the presence of a number of involuntarily homosexual persons, they must also concede that these persons are already part of "heterosexual" families. They are sons and daughters, brothers and sisters, even mothers and fathers, of heterosexuals. The distinction between "families" and "homosexuals" is, to begin with, empirically false; and the stability of existing families is closely linked to how homosexuals are treated within them. Presumably, it is against the interest of heterosexual families to force homosexuals into roles they are not equipped to play and may disastrously perform. This is not an abstract matter. It is quite common that homosexual fathers and mothers who are encouraged into heterosexual marriages subsequently find the charade and dishonesty too great to bear: spouses are betrayed, children are abandoned, families are broken, and lives are ruined. It is also common that homosexual sons and daughters who are denied the love and support of their families are liable to turn against the institution of the family, to wound and destroy it, out of hurt and rejection. And that parents, inculcated in the kind of disdain of homosexuality conservatives claim is necessary to protect the family, react to the existence of gay children with unconscionable anger and pain, and actually help destroy loving families.

Still, conservatives may concede this and still say that it's worth it. The threat to the stability of the family posed by public disapproval of homosexuality is not as great as the threat posed by public approval. How does this argument work? Largely by saying that the lives saved by preventing wavering straights from becoming gay are more numerous than the lives saved by keeping gay people out of heterosexual relationships and allowing greater tolerance of gay members of families themselves; that the stability of the society is better served by the former than by the latter. Now, recall that conservatives are not attempting to assert moral truths here. They are making an argument about social goods, in this case, social and familial stability. They are saying that a homosexual life is, on the face of it, worse than a heterosexual life is, as far as society is concerned. In Pattullo's words,

Though we acknowledge some influences—social and biological—beyond their control,

we do not accept the idea that people of bad character had no choice. Further, we are concerned to maintain a social climate that will steer them in the direction of the good.

The issue here is bad character and the implied association of bad character with the life of homosexuals. Although many conservatives feel loath to articulate what they mean by this life, it's clear what lies behind it. So if they won't articulate it, allow me. They mean by "a homosexual life" one in which emotional commitments are fleeting, promiscuous sex is common, disease is rampant, social ostracism is common, and standards of public decency, propriety, and self-restraint are flaunted. They mean a way of life that deliberately subverts gender norms in order to unsettle the virtues that make family life possible, ridicules heterosexual life, and commits itself to an ethic of hedonism, loneliness, and deceit. They mean by all this "the other," against which any norm has to be defended and any cohesive society protected. So it is clear that whatever good might be served by preventing gay people from becoming parents or healing internal wounds within existing families, it is greatly outweighed by the dangers of unleashing this kind of ethic upon the society as a whole.

But the argument, of course, begs a question. Is this kind of life, according to conservatives, what a homosexual life *necessarily* is? Surely not. If homosexuality is often indeed involuntary, as conservatives believe, then homosexuals are not automatically the "other"; they are sprinkled randomly throughout society, into families that are very much like anybody else's, with characters and bodies and minds as varied as the rest of humanity. If all human beings are, as conservatives believe, subject to social inducements to lead better or worse lives, then there is nothing inevitable at all about a homosexual leading a depraved life. In some cases, he might even be a paragon of virtue. Why then is the choice of a waverer to live a homosexual rather than a heterosexual life necessarily a bad one, from the point of view of society? Why does it lead to any necessary social harm at all?

Of course, if you simply define "homosexual" as "depraved," you have an answer; but it's essentially a tautologous one. And if you argue that in our society at this time, homosexual lives simply *are* more depraved, you are also begging a question. There are very few social incentives of the kind conservatives like for homosexuals *not* to be depraved: there's little social or familial support, no institution to encourage fidelity or monogamy, precious little religious or moral outreach to guide homosexuals into more virtuous living. This is not to say that homosexuals are not responsible for their actions, merely that in a large part of homosexual subculture there is much a conservative would predict, when human beings are abandoned with extremely few social incentives for good or socially responsible behavior. But the proper conservative response to this is surely not to infer that this behavior is inevitable, or to use it as a reason to deter others from engaging in a responsible homosexual existence, if that is what they want; but rather to construct social institutions and guidelines to modify and change the behavior for the better. But that is what conservatives resolutely refuse to do.

Why? Maybe for conservatives, there is something inherent even in the most virtuous homosexual life that renders it less desirable than the virtuous heterosexual life, and therefore merits social discouragement to deter the waverers. Let's assume, from a conservative perspective, the best-case scenario for such a waverer: he can choose between a loving, stable, and responsible same-sex relationship and a loving, stable, and responsible opposite-sex relationship. Why should society preference the latter?

The most common response is along the lines of Hadley Arkes, the conservative commentator, who has written on this subject on occasion. It is that the heterosexual relationship is good for men not simply because it forces them to cooperate and share with other human beings on a daily basis but because it forces them into daily contact and partnership with *women:*

It is not marriage that domesticates men; it is women. Left to themselves, these forked creatures follow a way of life that George Gilder once recounted in its precise, chilling measures: bachelors were twenty-two times more likely than married men to be committed to hospital for mental disease (and ten times more likely to suffer chronic diseases of all kinds). Single men had nearly double the mortality rate of married men and three times the mortality rate of single women. Divorced men were three times more likely than divorced women to commit suicide or die by murder, and they were six times more likely to die of heart disease.

I will leave aside the statistical difficulties here: it's perfectly possible that many of the problems Arkes recounts were reasons why the men didn't get married, rather than consequences of their failing to do so. Let's assume, for the sake of argument, that Arkes is right: that marriage to a woman is clearly preferable to being single for an adult man; that such a man is more likely to be emotionally stable, physically healthy, psychologically in balance; and that this is good for the society as a whole. There is in this argument a belief that women are naturally more prone to be stable, nurturing, supportive of stability, fiscally prudent, and family-oriented than men, and that their connection to as many men as possible is therefore clearly a social good. Let's assume also, for the sake of argument, that Arkes is right about that too. It's obvious, according to conservatives, that society should encourage a stable opposite-sex relationship over a stable same-sex relationship.

But the waverer has another option: *he can remain single.* Should society actually encourage him to do this rather than involve himself in a stable, loving same-sex relationship? Surely, even conservatives who think women are essential to the successful socialization of men would not deny that the discipline of domesticity, of shared duties and lives, of the inevitable give-and-take of cohabitation and love with anyone, even of the same sex, tends to benefit men more than the option of constant, free-wheeling, etiolating bachelorhood. But this would mean creating a public moral and social climate which preferred stable gay relationships to gay or straight bachelorhood. And it would require generating a notion of homosexual responsibility that would destroy the delicately balanced conservative politics of private discretion and undiscriminating public disapproval. So conservatives are stuck again: their refusal to embrace responsible public support for virtuous homosexuals runs counter to their entire social agenda.

Arkes's argument also leads to another (however ironic) possibility destabilizing to conservatism's delicate contemporary compromise on the homosexual question: that for a wavering woman, a lesbian relationship might actually be socially *preferable* to a heterosexual relationship. If the issue is not mere domesticity but the presence of women, why would two women not be better than one, for the sake of children's development and social stability? Since lesbianism seems to be more amenable to choice than male homosexuality in most studies and surveys, conservatism's emphasis on social encouragement of certain behaviors over others might be seen as even more relevant here. If conservatism is about the social benefits of feminizing society, there is no reason why it should not be an integral part of the movement for women to liberate themselves completely from men. Of course, I'm being facetious; conservatives would be terrified by all the single males such a society would leave rampaging around. But it's not inconceivable at all from conservative premises that, solely from the point of view of the wavering woman, the ascending priorities would be: remaining single, having a stable, loving opposite-sex relationship, and having a stable, loving same-sex relationship. And there is something deliciously ironic about the sensibility of Hadley Arkes and E. L. Pattulo finding its full fruition in a lesbian collective.

Still, the conservative has another option. He might argue that removing the taboo on ho-

mosexuality would unravel an entire fabric of self-understanding in the society at large that could potentially destabilize the whole system of incentives for stable family relationships. He might argue that now, of all times, when families are in an unprecedented state of collapse, is not the occasion for further tinkering with this system; that the pride of heterosexual men and women is at stake; that their self-esteem and self-understanding would be undermined if society saw them as equivalent to homosexuals. In this view, the stigmatization of homosexuals is the necessary corollary to the celebration of traditional family life.

Does this ring true? To begin with, it's not at all clear why, if public disapproval of homosexuals is indeed necessary to keep families together, homosexuals of all people should bear the primary brunt of the task. But it's also not clear why the corollary really works to start with. Those homosexuals who have no choice at all to be homosexual, whom conservatives do not want to be in a heterosexual family in the first place, are clearly no threat to the heterosexual family. Why would accepting that such people exist, encouraging them to live virtuous lives, incorporating their difference into society as a whole, necessarily devalue the traditional family? It is not a zero-sum game. Because they have no choice but to be homosexual, they are not choosing that option over heterosexual marriage; and so they are not sending any social signals that heterosexual family life should be denigrated.

The more difficult case, of course, pertains to Arkes's "waverers." Would allowing them the option of a stable same-sex relationship as a preferable social option to being single really undermine the institution of the family? Is it inconceivable that a society can be subtle in its public indications of what is and what is not socially preferable? Surely, society can offer a hierarchy of choices, which, while preferencing one, does not necessarily denigrate the others, but accords them some degree of calibrated respect. It does this in many other areas. Why not in sexual arrangements?

You see this already in many families with homosexual members. While some parents are disappointed that their son or daughter will not marry someone of the opposite sex, provide grandchildren and sustain the family line for another generation, they still prefer to see that child find someone to love and live with and share his or her life with. That child's siblings, who may be heterosexual, need feel no disapproval attached to their own marriage by the simple fact of their sibling's difference. Why should society as a whole find it an impossible task to share in the same maturity? Even in the most homosexualized culture, conservatives would still expect over eighty percent of couples to be heterosexual: why is their self-esteem likely to be threatened by a paltry twenty percent—especially when, according to conservatives, the homosexual life is so self-evidently inferior?

In fact, it's perfectly possible to combine a celebration of the traditional family with the celebration of a stable homosexual relationship.

The one, after all, is modeled on the other. If constructed carefully as a conservative social ideology, the notion of stable gay relationships might even serve to buttress the ethic of heterosexual marriage, by showing how even those excluded from it can wish to model themselves on its shape and structure. This very truth, of course, is why liberationists are so hostile to the entire notion. Rather than liberating society from asphyxiating conventions, it actually harnesses one minority group—homosexuals—and enlists them in the conservative structures that liberationists find so inimical. One can indeed see the liberationists' reasons for opposing such a move. But why should conservatives oppose it?

REFERENCES

Arkes, Hadley. "The Closet Straight." *National Review*, July 5, 1993.

Pattullo, E.L. "Straight Talk About Gays. *Comentary,* December 2, 1992.

An Exchange on Same-Sex Marriage
William Bennett and Andrew Sullivan

Let Gays Marry
Andrew Sullivan

A state cannot deem a class of persons a stranger to its laws," declared the Supreme Court last week. It was a monumental statement. Gay men and lesbians, the conservative court said, are no longer strangers in America. They are citizens, entitled, like everyone else, to equal protection—no special rights, but simple equality.

For the first time in Supreme Court history, gay men and women were seen not as some powerful lobby trying to subvert America, but as the people we truly are—the sons and daughters of countless mothers and fathers, with all the weaknesses and strengths and hopes of everybody else. And what we seek is not some special place in America but merely to be a full and equal part of America, to give back to our society without being forced to lie or hide or live as second-class citizens.

That is why marriage is so central to our hopes. People ask us why we want the right to marry, but the answer is obvious. It's the same reason anyone wants the right to marry. At some point in our lives, some of us are lucky enough to meet the person we truly love. And we want to commit to that person in front of our family and country for the rest of our lives. It's the most simple, the most natural, the most human instinct in the world. How could anyone seek to oppose that?

Yes, at first blush, it seems like a radical proposal, but, when you think about it some more, it's actually the opposite. Throughout American history, to be sure, marriage has been between a man and a woman, and in many ways our society is built upon that institution. But none of that need change in the slightest. After all, no one is seeking to take away anybody's right to marry, and no one is seeking to force any church to change any doctrine in any way. Particular religious arguments against same-sex marriage are rightly debated within the churches and faiths themselves. That is not the issue here: there is a separation between church and state in this country. We are only asking that when the government gives out *civil* marriage licenses, those of us who are gay should be treated like anybody else.

Of course, some argue that marriage is *by definition* between a man and a woman. But for centuries, marriage was *by definition* a contract in which the wife was her husband's legal property. And we changed that. For centuries, marriage was *by definition* between two people of the same race. And we changed that. We changed these things because we recognized that human dignity is the same whether you are a man or a woman, black or white. And no one has any more of a choice to be gay than to be black or white or male or female.

Some say that marriage is only about raising children, but we let childless heterosexual couples be married (Bob and Elizabeth Dole, Pat and Shelley Buchanan, for instance). Why should gay couples be treated differently? Others fear that there is no logical difference between allowing same-sex marriage and sanctioning polygamy and other horrors. But the issue of whether to sanction multiple spouses (gay or straight) is completely separate from whether, in the existing institution between two unrelated adults, the government should discriminate between its citizens.

This is, in fact, if only Bill Bennett could see it, a deeply conservative cause. It seeks to change no one else's rights or marriages in any way. It seeks merely to promote monogamy, fidelity and the disciplines of family life among people who have long been cast to the margins of society. And what could be a more conservative project than that? Why indeed would any conservative seek to oppose those very family values for gay people that he or she

supports for everybody else? Except, of course, to make gay men and lesbians strangers in their own country, to forbid them ever to come home.

Leave Marriage Alone

William Bennett

There are at least two key issues that divide proponents and opponents of same-sex marriage. The first is whether legally recognizing same-sex unions would strengthen or weaken the institution. The second has to do with the basic understanding of marriage itself.

The advocates of same-sex marriage say that they seek to strengthen and celebrate marriage. That may be what some intend. But I am certain that it will not be the reality. Consider: the legal union of same-sex couples would shatter the conventional definition of marriage, change the rules which govern behavior, endorse practices which are completely antithetical to the tenets of all of the world's major religions, send conflicting signals about marriage and sexuality, particularly to the young, and obscure marriage's enormously consequential function—procreation and child-rearing.

Broadening the definition of marriage to include same-sex unions would stretch it almost beyond recognition—and new attempts to expand the definition still further would surely follow. On what *principled* ground can Andrew Sullivan exclude others who most desperately want what he wants, legal recognition and social acceptance? Why on earth would Sullivan exclude from marriage a bisexual who wants to marry two other people? After all, exclusion would be a denial of that person's sexuality. The same holds true of a father and daughter who want to marry. Or two sisters. Or men who want (consensual) polygamous arrangements. Sullivan may think some of these arrangements are unwise. But having employed sexual relativism in his own defense, he has effectively lost the capacity to draw any lines and make moral distinctions.

Forsaking all others is an essential component of marriage. Obviously it is not always honored in practice. But it is the ideal to which we rightly aspire, and in most marriages the ideal is in fact the norm. Many advocates of same-sex marriage simply do not share this ideal; promiscuity among homosexual males is well known. Sullivan himself has written that gay male relationships are served by the "openness of the contract" and that homosexuals should resist allowing their "varied and complicated lives" to be flattened into a "single, moralistic model." But that "single, moralistic model" has served society exceedingly well. The burden of proof ought to be on those who propose untested arrangements for our most important institution.

A second key difference I have with Sullivan goes to the very heart of marriage itself. I believe that marriage is not an arbitrary construct which can be redefined simply by those who lay claim to it. It is an honorable estate, instituted of God and built on moral, religious, sexual and human realities. Marriage is based on a natural teleology, on the different, complementary nature of men and women—and how they refine, support, encourage and complete one another. It is the institution through which we propagate, nurture, educate and sustain our species.

That we have to engage in this debate at all is an indication of how steep our moral slide has been. Worse, those who defend the traditional understanding of marriage are routinely referred to (though not to my knowledge by Sullivan) as "homophobes," "gay-bashers," "intolerant" and "bigoted." Can one defend an honorable, 4,000-year-old tradition and not be called these names?

This is a large, tolerant, diverse country. In America people are free to do as they wish, within broad parameters. It is also a country in sore need of shoring up some of its most crucial institutions: marriage and the family, schools, neighborhoods, communities. But marriage and family are the greatest of these. That is why they are elevated and revered. We should keep them so.

A Reply to Bennett

Andrew Sullivan

It wasn't that we hadn't prepped. Testifying on the Hill was a first for me, and those of us opposing the "Defense of Marriage Act" had been chatting for days about possible questions. But we hadn't quite expected this one. If a person had an "insa-

tiable desire" to marry more than one wife, Congressman Bob Inglis of South Carolina wanted to know, what argument did gay activists have to deny him a legal, polygamous marriage? It wasn't a stray question. Republican after Republican returned gleefully to a Democratic witness who, it turned out, was (kind of) in favor of polygamy. I hastily amended my testimony to deal with the question. Before long, we were busy debating on what terms Utah should have been allowed into the Union and whether bisexuals could have legal harems.

Riveting stuff, compared to the Subcommittee on the Constitution's usual fare. But also revealing. In succeeding days, polygamy dominated the same-sex marriage debate. . . . Bill Bennett . . . used the polygamy argument as a first line of defense against same-sex marriage. . . . Bennett in particular accused the same-sex marriage brigade of engaging in a "sexual relativism" with no obvious stopping place and no "principled ground" to oppose the recognition of multiple spouses.

Well, here's an attempt at a principled ground. The polygamy argument rests, I think, on a couple of assumptions. The first is that polygamous impulses are morally and psychologically equivalent to homosexual impulses, since both are diversions from the healthy heterosexual norm, and that the government has a role to prevent such activities. But I wonder whether Bennett really agrees with this. Almost everyone seems to accept, even if they find homosexuality morally troublesome, that it occupies a deeper level of human consciousness than a polygamous impulse. Even the Catholic Church, which believes that homosexuality is an "objective disorder," concedes that it is a profound element of human identity. It speaks of "homosexual persons," for example, in a way it would never speak of "polygamous persons." And almost all of us tacitly assume this, even in the very use of the term "homosexuals." We accept also that multiple partners can be desired by gays and straights alike; that polygamy is an *activity*, whereas both homosexuality and heterosexuality are *states*.

So where is the logical connection between accepting same-sex marriage and sanctioning polygamy? Rationally, it's a completely separate question whether the government should extend the definition of marriage (same-sex or different-sex) to include more than one spouse or whether, in the existing institution between two unrelated adults, the government should continue to discriminate between its citizens. Politically speaking, the connection is even more tenuous. To the best of my knowledge, there is no polygamists' rights organization poised to exploit same-sex marriage to return the republic to polygamous abandon. Indeed, few in the same-sex marriage camp have anything but disdain for such an idea. And, as a matter of social policy, same-sex marriage is, of course, the opposite of Bennett's relativism. Far from opening up the possibilities of multiple partners for homosexuals, it actually closes them down.

Bennett might argue, I suppose, that any change in marriage opens up the possibility of any *conceivable* change in marriage. But this is not an argument, it's a panic. If we're worried about polygamy, why not the threat of legally sanctioned necrophilia? Or bestiality? The same panic occurred when interracial marriage became constitutional—a mere thirty years ago—and when women no longer had to be the legal property of their husbands. The truth is, marriage has changed many, many times over the centuries. Each change should be judged on its own terms, not as part of some seamless process of alleged disintegration.

So Bennett must move to his next point, which is that homosexuals understand the institution of marriage so differently than heterosexuals do that to admit them into it would be to alter the institution entirely. To argue this, he has to say that gay men are so naturally promiscuous that they are constitutively unable to sustain the monogamous requirements of marriage and so fail to meet the requirements of membership. He has even repeatedly—and misleadingly—quoted my book, *Virtually Normal,* to buttress this point.

Bennett claims that I believe male-male marriage would and should be adulterous—and cites a couple of sentences from the epilogue to that effect. In context, however, it's clear that the sentences he cites refer to some cultural differences between gay and straight relationships, as they exist today *before same-sex marriage has been made legal.* He ignores the two central chapters of my book—and several articles—in which I unequivo-

cally argue for monogamy as central to all marriage, same-sex or opposite-sex.

That some contemporary gay male relationships are "open" doesn't undermine my point; it supports it. What I do concede, however, is that, in all probability, gay male marriage is not likely to be identical to lesbian marriage, which isn't likely to be identical to heterosexual marriage. The differences between the genders, the gap between gay and straight culture, the unique life experiences that divide as well as unite heterosexuals and homosexuals, will probably create an institution not easily squeezed into a completely uniform model. And a small minority of male-male marriages may perhaps fail to uphold monogamy as successfully as many opposite-sex marriages. But what implications does that assertion have for the same-sex marriage debate as a whole?

Bennett argues that non-monogamous homosexual marriages will fatally undermine an already enfeebled institution. He makes this argument for one basic reason: men are naturally more promiscuous and male-male marriages will legitimize such promiscuity. But this argument has some problems. If you believe that men are naturally more promiscuous than women, then it follows that lesbian marriages will actually be more monogamous than heterosexual ones. So the alleged damage male-male marriages might do to heterosexual marriage would be countered by the good example that lesbian marriages would provide. It's a wash. And if you take the other conservative argument—that marriage exists not to reward monogamy but to encourage it—then Bennett is also in trouble. There is surely no group in society, by this logic, more in need of marriage rights than gay men. They are the group that most needs incentives for responsible behavior, monogamy, fidelity, and the like.

I'm not trying to be facetious here. The truth is, I think, marriage acts both as an incentive for virtuous behavior—and as a social blessing for the effort. In the past, we have wisely not made nitpicking assessments as to who deserves the right to marry and who does not. We have provided it to anyone prepared to embrace it and hoped for the best.

Imagine the consequences if you did otherwise. The government would spend its time figuring out whether certain groups of people were more or less capable of living up to the responsibilities of marriage and denying their right to it on that basis. The government might try to restrict it for more sexually active men under 20; or for women who have had an abortion. The government could argue, grotesquely, that because African Americans have, in general, higher illegitimacy rates, their right to marry should be abrogated. All these options rightly horrify us—but they are exactly the kind of conditions that Bennett and those who agree with him are trying to impose on gay citizens.

Or, in an equally troubling scenario, we could put conditions on the right to marry for certain individuals. People with a history of compulsive philandery in their relationships could be denied the right to marry; or people who have already failed at marriage once or twice or more; or people who are "free-riders" and marry late in life when the social sacrifice of marriage isn't quite so heavy. If we imposed these three restrictions, of course, three leading proponents of the Defense of Marriage Act would have their own right to marry taken away: chief-sponsor Congressman Bob Barr of Georgia (married three times), Bill Bennett (married at age 39) and Bill Clinton (ahem).

So how's this for a compromise: accept that human beings have natural, cultural and psychological differences. Accept that institutions can act both as incentives and rewards for moral behavior. Grant all citizens the same basic, civil institutions and hope that the mess and tragedy and joy of human life can somehow be sorted out for the better. That, after all, is what marriage does today for over 90 percent of the population. For some, it comes easily. For others, its commitments and responsibilities are crippling. But we do not premise the right to marry upon the ability to perform its demands flawlessly. We accept that human beings are variably virtuous, but that, as citizens, they should be given the same rights and responsibilities—period. That—and not the bogeyman of polygamy and adultery—is what the same-sex marriage debate is really about.

35.
Against Homosexual Marriage

James Q. Wilson

James Q. Wilson is Collins professor of management and public policy at the University of California at Los Angeles. He is the author of *Moral Sense*, and more recently, *Moral Judgment*. Wilson reviews and criticizes many of Andrew Sullivan's arguments in favor of same-sex marriages. Rejecting Sullivan's objections, Wilson reaffirms the conservative argument that permitting same-sex unions would jeopardize the institution of marriage at a time when it is already weakened by the widespread acceptance of divorce and single-mother households.

Wilson also questions Sullivan's premise that permitting same-sex marriages would lend stability to gay relationships. He believes that we have no proof that homosexual marriages would create stability; nor have we any evidence that permitting them won't further destabilize heterosexual marriages. Given these uncertainties, Wilson argues against same-sex marriage.

Editor's Note: By the end of 1996, two important court cases mentioned in the opening pages of Wilson's essay (published in March of 1996) had been decided. In the first case to which he refers—the Hawaiian case—a lower court in Hawaii ruled on December 3, 1996 that the state of Hawaii could not prove that it had a "compelling interest" in sustaining discrimination against same-sex couples who sought marriage licenses. Thus the Hawaiian Supreme Court will be asked to affirm its 1993 decision, *Baehr v. Lewin*, in which it judged that a marriage license could not be denied to a same-sex couple unless the state could first demonstrate a compelling interest that might justify limiting marriage licenses to heterosexual couples. The second case to which Wilson refers is the legal battle over Colorado Amendment 2. As noted in the introduction to John Finnis's article in this chapter, in the *Romer v. Evans* (1996) decision, the United States Supreme Court upheld the Colorado State Supreme Court in finding this amendment to be unconstitutional.

Our courts, which have mishandled abortion, may be on the verge of mishandling homosexuality. As a consequence of two pending decisions, we may be able to accept a homosexual marriage.

In 1993 the supreme court of Hawaii ruled that, under the equal-protection clause of that state's constitution, any law based on distinctions of sex was suspect, and thus subject to strict judicial scrutiny.[1] Accordingly, it reversed the denial of a marriage permit to a same-sex couple, unless the state could first demonstrate a "compelling state interest" that would justify limiting marriages to men and women. A new trial is set for early this summer. But in the meantime, the executive branch of Hawaii appointed a commission to examine the question of same-sex marriages; its report, by a vote of five to two, supports them. The legislature, for its part, holds a different view of the matter, having responded to the court's decision by passing a law unambiguously reaffirming the limitation of marriage to male-female couples.

No one knows what will happen in the coming trial, but the odds are that the Hawaiian version of the equal-rights amendment may control the outcome. If so, since the United States Constitution has a clause requiring that "full faith and credit shall be given to the public acts, records, and judicial proceedings of every other state," a homosexual couple in a state like Texas, where the population is overwhelmingly opposed to such unions, may soon be able to fly to Hawaii, get married, and then return to live in Texas as lawfully wedded. A few scholars

believe that states may be able to impose public-policy objections to such out-of-state marriages—Utah has already voted one in, and other states may follow—but only at the price of endless litigation.

That litigation may be powerfully affected by the second case. It concerns a Colorado statute, already struck down by that state's supreme court, that would prohibit giving to homosexuals "any claim of minority status, quota preferences, protected status, or claim of discrimination." The U.S. Supreme Court is now reviewing the appeals. If its decision upholds the Colorado supreme court and thus allows homosexuals to acquire a constitutionally protected status, the chances will decline of successful objections to homosexual marriage based on considerations of public policy.

Contemporaneous with these events, an important book has appeared under the title *Virtually Normal*.[2] In it, Andrew Sullivan, the editor of the *New Republic*, makes a strong case for a new policy toward homosexuals. He argues that "all *public* (as opposed to private) discrimination against homosexuals be ended.... *And that is all.*" The two key areas where this change is necessary are the military and marriage law. Lifting bans in those areas, while also disallowing anti-sodomy laws and providing information about homosexuality in publicly supported schools, would put an end to the harm that gays have endured. Beyond these changes, Sullivan writes, American society would need no "cures [of homophobia] or reeducations, no wrenching private litigation, no political imposition of tolerance."

It is hard to imagine how Sullivan's proposals would, in fact, end efforts to change private behavior toward homosexuals, or why the next, inevitable, step would not involve attempts to

James Q. Wilson, "Against Homosexual Marriage," *Commentary* 101 (March 1996): 34–39. Copyright (c) 1996 by the American Jewish Committee. Reprinted by permission. All rights reserved.

accomplish just that purpose by using cures and reeducations, private litigation, and the political imposition of tolerance. But apart from this, Sullivan—an English Catholic, a homosexual, and someone who has on occasion referred to himself as a conservative—has given us the most sensible and coherent view of a program to put homosexuals and heterosexuals on the same public footing. His analysis is based on a careful reading of serious opinions and his book is written quietly, clearly, and thoughtfully. In her review of it in *First Things* (January 1996), Elizabeth Kristol asks us to try to answer the following question: what would life be like if we were not allowed to marry? To most of us, the thought is unimaginable; to Sullivan, it is the daily existence of declared homosexuals. His response is to let homosexual couples marry.

Sullivan recounts three main arguments concerning homosexual marriage, two against and one for. He labels them prohibitionist, conservative, and liberal. (A fourth camp, the "liberationist," which advocates abolishing all distinctions between heterosexuals and homosexuals, is also described—and scorched for its "strange confluence of political abdication and psychological violence.") I think it easier to grasp the origins of the three main arguments by referring to the principles on which they are based.

The prohibitionist argument is in fact a biblical one; the heart of it was stated by Dennis Prager in an essay in the *Public Interest* ("Homosexuality, the Bible, and Us," Summer 1993). When the first books of the Bible were written, and for a long time thereafter, heterosexual love is what seemed at risk. In many cultures—not only in Egypt or among the Canaanite tribes surrounding ancient Israel but later in Greece, Rome, and the Arab world, to say nothing of large parts of China, Japan, and elsewhere—homosexual practices were common and widely tolerated or even exalted. The Torah reversed this, making the family the central unit of life,

the obligation to marry one of the first responsibilities of man, and the linkage of sex to procreation the highest standard by which to judge sexual relations. Leviticus puts the matter sharply and apparently beyond quibble:

> Thou shalt not live with mankind as with womankind; it is an abomination. . . . If a man also lie with mankind, as he lieth with a woman, both of them have committed an abomination; they shall surely be put to death; their blood shall be upon them.

Sullivan acknowledges the power of Leviticus but deals with it by placing it in a relative context. What is the nature of this "abomination"? Is it like killing your mother or stealing a neighbor's bread, or is it more like refusing to eat shellfish or having sex during menstruation? Sullivan suggests that all of these injunctions were written on the same moral level and hence can be accepted or ignored *as a whole*. He does not fully sustain this view, and in fact a refutation of it can be found in Prager's essay. In Prager's opinion and mine, people at the time of Moses, and for centuries before him, understood that there was a fundamental difference between whom you killed and what you ate, and in all likelihood people then and for centuries earlier linked whom you could marry closer to the principles that defined life than they did to the rules that defined diets.

The New Testament contains an equally vigorous attack on homosexuality by St. Paul. Sullivan partially deflects it by noting Paul's conviction that the earth was about to end and the Second Coming was near; under these conditions, all forms of sex were suspect. But Sullivan cannot deny that Paul singled out homosexuality as deserving of special criticism. He seems to pass over this obstacle without effective retort.

Instead, he takes up a different theme, namely that on grounds of consistency many heterosexual practices—adultery, sodomy, premarital sex, and divorce, among others—

should be outlawed equally with homosexual acts of the same character. The difficulty with this is that it mistakes the distinction alive in most people's minds between marriage as an institution and marriage as a practice. As an institution, it deserves unqualified support; as a practice, we recognize that married people are as imperfect as anyone else. Sullivan's understanding of the prohibitionist argument suffers from his unwillingness to acknowledge this distinction.

The second argument against homosexual marriage—Sullivan's conservative category—is based on natural law as originally set forth by Aristotle and Thomas Aquinas and more recently restated by Hadley Arkes, John Finnis, Robert George, Harry V. Jaffa, and others. How it is phrased varies a bit, but in general its advocates support a position like the following: man cannot live without the care and support of other people; natural law is the distillation of what thoughtful people have learned about the conditions of that care. The first thing they have learned is the supreme importance of marriage, for without it the newborn infant is unlikely to survive or, if he survives, to prosper. The necessary conditions of a decent family life are the acknowledgment by its members that a man will not sleep with his daughter or a woman with her son and that neither will openly choose sex outside marriage.

Now, some of these conditions are violated, but there is a penalty in each case that is supported by the moral convictions of almost all who witness the violation. On simple utilitarian grounds it may be hard to object to incest or adultery; if both parties to such an act welcome it and if it is secret, what differences does it make? But very few people, and then only ones among the overeducated, seem to care much about mounting a utilitarian assault on the family. To this assault, natural-law theorists respond much as would the average citizen—never mind "utility," what counts is what is right. In partic-

ular, homosexual uses of the reproductive organs violate the condition that sex serve solely as the basis of heterosexual marriage.

To Sullivan, what is defective about the natural-law thesis is that it assumes different purposes in heterosexual and homosexual love: moral consummation in the first case and pure utility or pleasure alone in the second. But in fact, Sullivan suggests, homosexual love can be as consummatory as heterosexual. He notes that as the Roman Catholic Church has deepened its understanding of the involuntary—that is, in some sense genetic—basis of homosexuality, it has attempted to keep homosexuals in the church as objects of affection and nurture, while banning homosexual acts as perverse.

But this, though better than nothing, will not work, Sullivan writes. To show why, he adduces an analogy to a sterile person. Such a person is permitted to serve in the military or enter an unproductive marriage; why not homosexuals? If homosexuals marry without procreation, they are no different (he suggests) from a sterile man or woman who marries without hope of procreation. Yet people, I think, want the form observed even when the practice varies; a sterile marriage, whether from choice or necessity, remains a marriage of a man and a woman. To this Sullivan offers essentially an aesthetic response. Just as albinos remind us of the brilliance of color and genius teaches us about moderation, homosexuals are a "natural foil" to the heterosexual union, "a variation that does not eclipse the theme." Moreover, the threat posed by the foil to the theme is slight as compared to the threats posed by adultery, divorce, and prostitution. To be consistent, Sullivan once again reminds us, society would have to ban adulterers from the military as it now bans confessed homosexuals.

But again this misses the point. It would make more sense to ask why an alternative to marriage should be invented and praised when we are having enough trouble maintaining the institution at all. Suppose that gay or lesbian marriage were authorized; rather than producing a "natural foil" that would "not eclipse the theme," I suspect such a move would call even more seriously into question the role of marriage at a time when the threats to it, ranging from single-parent families to common divorces, have hit record highs. Kenneth Minogue recently wrote of Sullivan's book that support for homosexual marriage would strike most people as "mere parody," one that could further weaken an already strained institution.

To me, the chief limitation of Sullivan's view is that it presupposes that marriage would have the same, domesticating, effect on homosexual members as it has on heterosexuals, while leaving the latter largely unaffected. Those are very large assumptions that no modern society has ever tested.

Nor does it seem plausible to me that a modern society resists homosexual marriages entirely out of irrational prejudice. Marriage is a union, sacred to most, that unites a man and woman together for life. It is a sacrament of the Catholic Church and central to every other faith. Is it out of misinformation that every modern society has embraced this view and rejected the alternative? Societies differ greatly in their attitude toward the income people may have, the relations among their various races, and the distribution of political power. But they differ scarcely at all over the distinctions between heterosexual and homosexual couples. The former are overwhelmingly preferred over the latter. The reason, I believe, is that these distinctions involve the nature of marriage and thus the very meaning—even more, the very possibility—of society.

The final argument over homosexual marriage is the liberal one, based on civil rights.

As we have seen, the Hawaiian supreme court ruled that any state-imposed sexual distinction would have to meet the test of strict scrutiny, a term used by the U.S. Supreme Court only for racial and similar classifications. In doing this, the Hawaiian court distanced itself

from every other state court decision—there are several—in this area so far.[3] A variant of the suspect-class argument, though, has been suggested by some scholars who contend that denying access to a marriage license by two people of the same sex is no different from denying access to two people of different sexes but also different races. The Hawaiian supreme court embraced this argument as well, explicitly comparing its decision to that of the U.S. Supreme Court when it overturned state laws banning marriages involving miscegenation.

But the comparison with black-white marriages is itself suspect. Beginning around 1964, and no doubt powerfully affected by the passage of the Civil Rights Act of that year, public attitudes toward race began to change dramatically. Even allowing for exaggerated statements to pollsters, there is little doubt that people in fact acquired a new view of blacks. Not so with homosexuals. Though the campaign to aid them has been going on vigorously for about a quarter of a century, it has produced few, if any, gains in public acceptance, and the greatest resistance, I think, has been with respect to homosexual marriages.

Consider the difference. What has been at issue in race relations is not marriage among blacks (for over a century, that right has been universally granted) or even miscegenation (long before the civil-rights movement, many Southern states had repealed such laws). Rather, it has been the routine contact between the races in schools, jobs, and neighborhoods. Our own history, in other words, has long made it clear that marriage is a different issue from the issue of social integration.

There is another way, too, in which the comparison with race is less than helpful, as Sullivan himself points out. Thanks to the changes in public attitudes I mentioned a moment ago, gradually race was held to be not central to decisions about hiring, firing, promoting, and schooling, and blacks began to make extraordinary advances in society. But then, in an effort to enforce this new view, liberals came to embrace affirmative action, a policy that said that race *was* central to just such issues, in order to ensure that *real* mixing occurred. This move created a crisis, for liberalism had always been based on the proposition that a liberal political system should encourage, as John Stuart Mill put it, "experiments in living" free of religious or political direction. To contemporary liberals, however, being neutral about race was tantamount to being neutral about a set of human preferences that in such matters as neighborhood and schooling left groups largely (but not entirely) separate.

Sullivan, who wisely sees that hardly anybody is really prepared to ignore a political opportunity to change lives, is not disposed to have much of this either in the area of race or in that of sex. And he points out with great clarity that popular attitudes toward sexuality are anyway quite different from those about race, as is evident from the fact that wherever sexual orientation is subject to local regulations, such regulations are rarely invoked. Why? Because homosexuals can "pass" or not, as they wish; they can and do accumulate education and wealth; they exercise political power. The two things a homosexual cannot do are join the military as an avowed homosexual or marry another homosexual.

The result, Sullivan asserts, is a wrenching paradox. On the one hand, society has historically tolerated the brutalization inflicted on people because of the color of their skin, but freely allowed them to marry; on the other hand, it has given equal opportunity to homosexuals, while denying them the right to marry. This, indeed, is where Sullivan draws the line. A black or Hispanic child, if heterosexual, has many friends, he writes, but a gay child "generally has no one." And that is why the social stigma attached to homosexuality is different from that attached to race or ethnicity—"because it attacks the very heart of what makes a human being human: the ability to love and be loved." Here is the essence

of Sullivan's case. It is a powerful one, even if (as I suspect) his pro-marriage sentiments are not shared by all homosexuals.

Let us assume for the moment that a chance to live openly and legally with another homosexual is desirable. To believe that, we must set aside biblical injunctions, a difficult matter in a profoundly religious nation. But suppose we manage the diversion, perhaps on the grounds that if most Americans skip church, they can as readily avoid other errors of (possibly) equal magnitude. Then we must ask on what terms the union shall be arranged. There are two alternatives—marriage or domestic partnership.

Sullivan acknowledges the choice, but disparages the domestic-partnership laws that have evolved in some foreign countries and in some American localities. His reasons, essentially conservative ones, are that domestic partnerships are too easily formed and too easily broken. Only real marriages matter. But—aside from the fact that marriage is in serious decline, and that only slightly more than half of all marriages performed in the United States this year will be between never-before-married heterosexuals—what is distinctive about marriage is that it is an institution created to sustain child-rearing. Whatever losses it has suffered in *this* respect, its function remains what it has always been.

The role of raising children is entrusted in principle to married heterosexual couples because after much experimentation—several thousand years, more or less—we have found nothing else that works as well. Neither a gay nor a lesbian couple can of its own resources produce a child; another party must be involved. What do we call this third party? A friend? A sperm or egg bank? An anonymous donor? There is no settled language for even describing, much less approving of, such persons.

Suppose we allowed homosexual couples to raise children who were created out of a prior heterosexual union or adopted from someone else's heterosexual contact. What would we think of this? There is very little research on the matter. Charlotte Patterson's famous essay, "Children of Gay and Lesbian Parents" (*Journal of Child Development,* 1992), begins by conceding that the existing studies focus on children born into a heterosexual union that ended in divorce or that was transformed when the mother or father "came out" as a homosexual. Hardly any research has been done on children acquired at the outset by a homosexual couple. We therefore have no way of knowing how they would behave. And even if we had such studies, they might tell us rather little unless they were conducted over a very long period of time.

But it is one thing to be born into an apparently heterosexual family and then many years later to learn that one of your parents is homosexual. It is quite another to be acquired as an infant from an adoption agency or a parent-for-hire and learn from the first years of life that you are, because of your family's position, radically different from almost all other children you will meet. No one can now say how grievous this would be. We know that young children tease one another unmercifully; adding this dimension does not seem to be a step in the right direction.

Of course, homosexual "families" with or without children, might be rather few in number. Just how few, it is hard to say. Perhaps Sullivan himself would marry, but, given the great tendency of homosexual males to be promiscuous, many more like him would not, or if they did, would not marry with as much seriousness.

That is problematic in itself. At one point, Sullivan suggests that most homosexuals would enter a marriage "with as much (if not more) commitment as heterosexuals." Toward the end of his book, however, he seems to withdraw from so optimistic a view. He admits that the label "virtually" in the title of his book is deliberately ambiguous, because homosexuals as a group are *not* "normal." At another point, he writes that the "openness of the contract" between two homosexual males means that such

a union will in fact be more durable than a heterosexual marriage because the contract contains an *"understanding of the need for extramarital outlets"* (emphasis added). But no such "understanding" exists in heterosexual marriage; to suggest that it might in homosexual ones is tantamount to saying that we are now referring to two different kinds of arrangements. To justify this difference, perhaps, Sullivan adds that the very "lack of children" will give "gay couples greater freedom." Freedom for what? Freedom, I think, to do more of those things that heterosexual couples do less of because they might hurt the children.

The courts in Hawaii and in the nation's capital must struggle with all these issues under the added encumbrance of a contemporary outlook that makes law the search for rights, and responsibility the recognition of rights. Indeed, thinking of laws about marriage as documents that confer or withhold rights is itself an error of fundamental importance—one that the highest court in Hawaii has already committed. "Marriage," it wrote, "is a state-conferred legal-partnership status, the existence of which gives rise to a multiplicity of rights and benefits. . . ." A state-conferred legal partnership? To lawyers, perhaps; to mankind, I think not. The Hawaiian court has thus set itself on the same course of action as the misguided Supreme Court in 1973 when it thought that laws about abortion were merely an assertion of the rights of a living mother and an unborn fetus.

I have few favorable things to say about the political system of other modern nations, but on these fundamental matters—abortion, marriage, military service—they often do better by allowing legislatures to operate than we do by deferring to courts. Our challenge is to find a way of formulating a policy with respect to homosexual unions that is not the result of a reflexive act of judicial rights-conferring, but is instead a considered expression of the moral convictions of a people.

NOTES

1. *Baehr, et al., v. Lewin*, 852 P.2d 44.

2. Knopf, 209 pp.

3. Minnesota refused a claim for a marriage license by two gay men even though the relevant state statute does not mention sex; the federal Ninth Circuit rejected a claim that

Congress, in defining a spouse in the Immigration and Naturalization Act of 1982, meant to include same-sex spouses. In Pennsylvania a court refused to allow a same-sex couple to contract a common-law marriage. A Kentucky court did the same in the case of two lesbians applying for a marriage license, as did a Washington court in the case of two gay men. The District of Columbia Court of Appeals acted similarly (by a divided vote) in 1995.

More Retailers Are Recognizing Gay Marriages

Melissa George

Before Patricia Koch tied the knot last summer, she considered doing what many brides do when they plan a wedding—signing up for a bridal planning seminar.

Koch, 37, wanted to take a seminar with her partner of the past 10 years, Ginger, but she was put off when a Crate & Barrel sales clerk mistook the two women for friends instead of a couple and said it would cost $35 per bride to attend.

"I was surprised by the retailers that didn't have it together," said Koch, a radio host whose "union" ceremony took place last Labor Day. "People in the gay community tend to have a little more discretionary income to spend."

Koch's experience is an example of the pitfalls retailers are increasingly trying to avoid as they seek to lure more gay couples to their gift registry counters.

Despite the recent political push to ban gay marriages, the flow of same-sex couples to the altar remains strong, retailers and gay groups said.

While these union ceremonies are not legally binding and make up just a small percentage of the overall wedding business, they often are lavish affairs that add up to big sales for stores in the bridal trade.

In Koch's case, 105 guests attended the modest garden party with a buffet dinner, bar and dancing—all of which cost about $3,000. Other gay couples, however, throw much more elaborate events with tabs running to tens of thousands of dollars.

"Some gay couples are very affluent and have a lot of disposable income," said Kimberly Miller, a promotion director for Macy's West Coast division. "If retailers in certain markets are resistant to servicing them in any way, they're turning away a lot of business."

Chains such as Macy's have reviewed their wedding service operations to make them more appealing to gays.

At Macy's stores on the West Coast, the words *bride* and *groom* soon will be purged from the computerized gift registry system, replaced by the word *partner.*

Dayton Hudson Corp. of Minneapolis, parent of Marshall Field's, Dayton's and Hudson's department stores, still uses traditional wedding titles in its computer system but gives gay couples the option of signing up for a "special occasion."

Other retailers said they have advertised their wedding services in gay publications or participated in wedding fairs.

Rick Karlin, a teacher from Chicago, said he didn't know what retailers to call when he was planning his marriage two years ago.

"My partner and I wanted to have a ceremony, and I had trouble figuring out where to go," said Karlin, who also is an activist in the gay community. "If I didn't know where to go, the average person doesn't know either."

After registering for gifts at Marshall Field's, where he and his lover were waited on by "a little old grandma who didn't bat an eye," Karlin decided to organize a wedding fair in Chicago to help other gays steer through the process.

Most of the 40 vendors that participate in the annual event, which Karlin said drew about 300 people, already operate in the gay community.

Homosexuals make up an estimated 3 percent of the U.S. population, and many gay couples want to get married. A poll of readers by the gay magazine *The Advocate* showed 81 percent of same-sex couples would get married if it were legal.

While gay union ceremonies often are held in church, they are not legally binding and do not entitle couples to federal health, Social Security and tax benefits. The House recently passed legislation to bar federal recognition of same-sex unions, although a court case pending in Hawaii may make gay marriages legal in that state.

Meanwhile gay union ceremonies are big moneymakers for department stores, bridal chains and jewelry stores. Gays are good customers because they usually get married later in life when their incomes are higher, and many don't have dependents.

36.

Family's Outlaws: Rethinking the Connections Between Feminism, Lesbianism, and the Family

Cheshire Calhoun

Cheshire Calhoun is associate professor of philosophy and director of women's studies at Colby College. She writes on feminist ethics and gay and lesbian ethics. Many of the other articles in this chapter have taken for granted the notion that marriage is a desirable institution, and that the crucial issue is whether or not to extend this cherished social institution to gays and lesbians. Yet, feminists have often raised concerns over the oppressive nature and history of heterosexual marriage. One might assume that feminists and lesbian theorists would have similar reservations about seeking to re-create traditional marital practices.

Cheshire Calhoun challenges this assumption; she argues that lesbians need to critically evaluate marriage from distinctively lesbian theoretical frameworks. She claims that "lesbians' distinctive relation to the family, marriage, and mothering is better captured by attending to the social construction of lesbians as *familial outlaws* than by attending exclusively to the gender structure of family, marriage, and mothering."

How should we understand lesbians' relation to the family, marriage, and mothering? Part of what makes this a difficult question to answer from a feminist standpoint is that feminism has undertheorized lesbian and gay oppression as an axis of oppression distinct from gender oppression.[1] As a result, lesbians' *difference* from heterosexual women is often not visible—

even, oddly enough, within explicitly lesbian-feminist thought. In Parts I, II, and III of this essay, I critically review feminist analyses—particularly lesbian-feminist ones—of lesbians' relation to the family, marriage, and mothering. In Part IV, I develop a historical account of the construction of lesbians (and gays) as outlaws to the family.

My aim is to suggest that lesbians' distinctive relation to the family, marriage, and mothering is better captured by attending to the social construction of lesbians as familial outlaws than by attending exclusively to the gender structure of family, marriage, and mothering.

Cheshire Calhoun, "Family's Outlaws: Rethinking the Connections Between Feminism, Lesbianism, and the Family," *Feminism and Families*, ed. Hilde Lindemann Nelson (New York: Routledge, 1997): 131–150. Copyright (c) 1997 by Routledge. Reprinted with permission.

I. FEMINISM AND THE FAMILY

Feminist depictions and analyses of the family, marriage, and mothering have been driven by a deep awareness that the family centered around marriage, procreation, and child-rearing has historically been and continues to be a primary site of women's subordination to and dependence on men, and by an awareness that the gender ideology that rationalizes women's subordinate status is heavily shaped by assumptions about women's natural place within the family as domestic caretakers, as reproductive beings, and as naturally fit for mothering. It has been the task and success of feminism to document the dangers posed to women by family, marriage, and mothering in both their lived and ideological forms.

The ideology of the loving family often masks gender injustice within the family, including battery, rape, and child abuse. Women continue to shoulder primary responsibility for both child-rearing and domestic labor; and they continue to choose occupations compatible with child care, occupations which are often less well paid, more replaceable, and less likely to offer benefits and career-track mobility. The expectation that women within families are first and foremost wives and mothers continues to offer employers a rationale for paying women less. Women's lower wages in the public workforce in turn make it appear economically rational within marriages for women to invest in developing their husband's career assets. No-fault divorce laws, which operate on the assumption that men and women exiting marriage have equally developed career assets (or that those career assets could be developed with the aid of short-term alimony) and that fail to treat the husband's career assets as community property, result in women exiting marriage at a significant economic disadvantage.[2] Women's custody of children after divorce, their lower earning potential, the unavailability of low-cost child care, the absence of adequate social support for single mothers, and, often, fathers' failure to pay full child support combine to reduce divorced women's economic position even further, resulting in the feminization of poverty.

The ideology of the normal family as the self-sufficient, two-earner, nuclear family is then mobilized to blame single mothers for their poverty, to justify supervisory and psychological intervention into those families, and to rationalize reducing social support for them.

This picture, although generally taken as a picture of women's relation to the family, marriage, and mothering, is not, in fact, a picture of *women's* relation to the family, but is more narrowly a picture of *heterosexual* women's relation to the family, marriage, and mothering. It is a picture whose contours are shaped by an eye on the lookout for the ways that marriage, family, and mothering subordinate heterosexual women to men in the private household, in the public economy, and in the welfare state. Thus it fails to grasp lesbians' relation to the family.[3]

It has instead been the task of lesbian feminism from the 1970s through the 1990s to develop an analysis of lesbians' distinctive relation to the family. However, although lesbian feminism has developed feminist arguments for rejecting lesbian motherhood, lesbian marriages, and lesbian families, it too has failed to make lesbian difference from heterosexual women central to its analyses. It is to the promise and, I will argue, the failure of lesbian feminism to grasp lesbians' distinctive relation to the family that I now turn.

II. LESBIAN FEMINISM, THE FAMILY, MOTHERING, AND MARRIAGE

In understanding what lesbians' relation to the family, motherhood, and marriage is and ought to be, lesbian feminists took as their point of departure feminist critiques of heterosexual women's experience of family, motherhood, and marriage. Lesbian feminists were particularly alive to the fact that lesbians are uniquely positioned to evade the ills of the heterosexual, male-dominated family. In particular, they are uniquely positioned to violate the conventional gender expectation that they, as women, would be dependent on men in their personal relations, would fulfill the maternal imperative, would service a husband and children, and would accept confinement to the private sphere of domesticity. Because of their unique position, lesbians could hope to be in the vanguard of the feminist rebellion against the patriarchal family, marriage, and institution of motherhood.

Family. In the 1970s and '80s, lesbian feminists used feminist critiques of heterosexual women's subordination to men within the family as a platform for valorizing lesbian existence. Lesbian feminists like Monique Wittig and Charlotte Bunch, for instance, argued that the nuclear family based on heterosexual marriage enables men to appropriate for themselves women's productive and reproductive labor.[4] Because lesbians do not enter into this heterosexual nuclear family, they can be read as refusing to allow their labor to be appropriated by men.

Lesbian feminists similarly made use of feminist critiques of heterosexual women's confinement to the private sphere of family and exclusion from the public sphere of politics and labor to argue for a new vision of lesbians' personal life. In that vision, passionate friendships, centered around a common life of work, could and should replace the depoliticized, isolated life within the nuclear family. Janice Raymond, for instance, argued for the feminist value of historical all-women's communities, such as the pre-enclosure nunneries and the nineteenth-century Chinese marriage resisters' houses where women combined intimate friendships, community, and work.[5]

Lesbian-feminist interpretation of lesbians' relation to the family as nonparticipation in *heterosexual*, male-dominated, private families is then translated into nonparticipation in *any* form of family, including lesbian families. In a 1994 essay, for instance, Ruthann Robson argues against recent liberal legal efforts to redefine the family to include lesbian and gay families that are functionally equivalent to heterosexual ones.[6] She argues that, in advocating legal recognition of lesbian families, "we have forgotten the lesbian generated critiques of family as oppressive and often deadly."[7] In particular we

have forgotten the critiques of the family as an institution of the patriarchal state, of marriage as slavery,[8] and of wives as property within marriage.[9] In her view, the category "family" should be abolished.

Motherhood. Feminist critiques of heterosexual women's experience also supplied the point of departure for lesbian-feminist critiques of lesbian motherhood. Lesbian motherhood, on this view, represents a concession to a key element of women's subordination—compulsory motherhood. By refusing to have children, or by giving up custody of their children at divorce, lesbians can refuse to participate in compulsory motherhood. They can thus refuse to accept the myth "that only family and children provide [women] with a purpose and place, bestow upon us honor, respect, love, and comfort."[10] Purpose and place is better found in political activities in a more public community of women. Lesbian feminists thus challenge lesbians contemplating motherhood to reflect more critically on their reasons for doing so and on the political consequences of participating in the present lesbian baby boom.

Not only does resistance to motherhood signal a rejection of conventional understandings of womanhood and women's fulfillment, it also frees lesbians to devote their lives to public political work for lesbians and heterosexual women. Thus lesbian resistance to motherhood is seen as instrumental to effective political action. Nancy Polikoff, for instance, claims that "[t]o the extent that motherhood drains the available pool of lesbians engaging in ongoing political work, its long-term significance is overwhelming."[11]

Lesbian motherhood also facilitates the closeting of lesbian existence. Even when lesbian mothers are careful not to pass as heterosexual, their very motherhood works against their being publicly perceived as deviants to the category "woman." And in her study of lesbian mothers, Ellen Lewin argues that motherhood enables lesbians to claim a less stigmatized place in the gender system; in particular, it enables them to claim for themselves the conventional womanly attributes of being altruistic, nurturant, and responsible—attributes which lesbians typically are stereotyped as lacking.[12]

Marriage. Like lesbian motherhood, lesbian (and gay) marriage seems antithetical to the lesbian-feminist goal of radically challenging conventional gender, sexual, and familial arrangements. Historically, the institution of marriage has been oppressively gender-structured. And, as Polikoff points out in a recent essay, the historical and cross-cultural record of same-sex marriages does not support the claim that same-sex marriages will revolutionize the gender structure of marriage. On the contrary, same-sex marriages that have been legitimized in other cultures—for instance, African woman-marriage, Native American marriages between a berdache and a same-sex partner, and nineteenth-century Chinese marriages between women—have all been highly gender-structured. Thus there is no reason to believe that "'gender dissent' is inherent in marriage between two men or two women."[13]

Moreover, the attempt to secure legal recognition for lesbian and gay marriages is highly likely to work against efforts to critique the institution of marriage. In particular, by attempting to have specifically *marital* relationships recognized, advocates of marriage rights help to reinforce the assumption that long-term, monogamous relationships are more valuable than any other kind of relationship. As a result, the marriage rights campaign, if successful, will end up privileging those lesbian and gay relationships that most closely approximate the heterosexual norm over more deviant relationships that require a radical rethinking of the nature of families.[14]

Finally, arguments for lesbian and gay marriage rights on the grounds that lesbians and gays lack privileges that heterosexual couples enjoy—such as access to a spouse's health insurance benefits—are insufficiently radical.[15] Distributing basic benefits like health insurance through the middle-class family neglects the interests of poor and some working-class families as well as single individuals in having access to basic social benefits. If access to such benefits is the issue, then universal health insurance, not marriage, is what we should be advocating.

III. LESBIAN DISAPPEARANCE

The difficulty with the lesbian-feminist viewpoint is that it is one from which lesbian difference from heterosexual women persistently disappears from view.

First, the value of the family and marriage for *lesbians* is judged largely by evaluating the *heterosexual* nuclear family's effects on *heterosexual* women. Lesbians are to resist family and marriage because the family centered around the heterosexual married couple has been gender structured in a way that made marriage a form of slavery where heterosexual women could be treated as property and their labor appropriated by men. But to make this a principal reason for lesbians' not forming families and marriages of their own is to lose sight of the difference between lesbians and heterosexual women. Lesbian families and marriages are not reasonably construed as sites where women can be treated as property and where their productive and reproductive labor can be appropriated by men. It thus does not follow from the fact that heterosexual marriage and family has been oppressive for heterosexual women and a primary structure of patriarchy that *any* form of marriage or family, including lesbian ones, is oppressive for women and a primary structure of patriarchy.

The alternative argument—that creating lesbian families and marriages will not remedy the gender structure in heterosexual marriages and families—drops lesbians from view in a different way. Here, heterosexual women's interests are substituted for those of lesbians as the touchstone for determining what normative conclusions about the family, marriage, and mothering lesbians should come to. Lesbians are to resist forming marriages and families of their own because heterosexual women's struggle against the institution of marriage and family will not be promoted and may in fact be hindered by lesbian endorsement of the value of marriage and family. This line of reasoning ignores the possibility that lesbians may have interests of their own in forming families and marriages, interests that may conflict with heterosexual women's political aims.

Second, resistance to the forms of gender oppression and gender ideology to which lesbians, *as women*, are subject is presented as a distinctively lesbian task (that is, as a distinctively lesbian version of feminist resistance), when in fact these are broadly feminist tasks whose burden should be equally shared by heterosexual women and lesbians. Both lesbians and heterosexual women have reason to resist the construction of mothering as an unpaid, socially unsupported task. Both have reason to reject women's confinement to the domestic sphere and reason to value participation in politically oriented communities of women. Both have reason to resist their gender socialization into the myth of feminine fulfillment through mothering and to assert their deviance from the category "woman." Both can have justice interests in objecting to a social and legal system that privileges long-term, monogamous relationships over all other forms of relationship and that does not provide universal access to basic benefits like health insurance. All of these are broadly feminist concerns. As a result, the lesbian-feminist perspective does not articulate any distinctively *lesbian* political tasks in relation to the family, marriage, and mothering. Instead, lesbians are submerged in the larger category "feminist."

Finally, the political relation between heterosexuals and nonheterosexuals and the ideologies of sexuality that support the oppression of lesbians and gays simply do not inform the lesbian-feminist analysis of lesbians' relation to the family, marriage, or mothering. What governs the lesbian-feminist perspective is above all the political relations between men and women, and to a lesser extent class relations and the political relations between those in normative long-term, monogamous relations (whether heterosexual or nonheterosexual) and all other human relations. As a result, the radicalness of lesbian and gay family, marriage, and parenting is measured on a scale that looks only at their power (or impotence) to transform gender relations, the privileging of long-term, monogamous relations, and class privilege. Not surprisingly, lesbian and gay families, marriages, and parenting fail to measure up. But this ignores the historical construction of lesbians and gays as outlaws to the natural family, as constitutionally incapable of more than merely sexual relationships, and as dangerous to children.

Within gender ideology, for instance, lesbians have not been and are not constructed as beings whose natural place is within the family as domestic caretakers, as reproductive beings, and as naturally fit mothers. On the contrary, the gender ideology that rationalizes the oppression of both lesbians and gays consists in part precisely in the assumption that both are aliens to the natural family, nonprocreative, incapable of enduring intimate ties, dangerous to children, and ruled by sexual instincts to the exclusion of parenting ones. Moreover, unlike heterosexual women, it is not their subordination *within* the family that marks their oppression but rather their denial of access *to* a legitimated and socially instituted sphere of family, marriage, and parenting.

Lesbians and gays are, for instance, denied the legal privileges and protections that heterosexuals enjoy with respect to their marital and familial relations. Among the array of rights related to marriage that heterosexuals enjoy but gays and lesbians do not are the rights to legal marriage, to live with one's spouse in neighborhoods zoned "single-family only," and to secure U.S. residency through marriage to a U.S. citizen; the rights to Social Security survivor's benefits, to inherit a spouse's estate in the absence of a will, and to file a wrongful death suit; the rights to give proxy consent, to refuse to testify against one's spouse, and to file joint income taxes.

Lesbians and gays similarly lack access to the privileges and protections that heterosexuals enjoy with respect to biological, adoptive, and foster children. Sexual orientation continues to be an overriding reason for denying custody to lesbian and gay parents who exit a heterosexual marriage. Gays and lesbians fare equally poorly with respect to adoption and foster parenting. New Hampshire prohibits gay and lesbian adoption and foster parenting, while other states, like Massachusetts, have policies making a child's placement with lesbian or gay parents unlikely. Even while adoption is successful, joint adoption generally is not—nor is adoption of a partner's biological child.

What comes into view in this picture of the legal inequities that lesbians and gays confront is the fact that the family, marriage, and parenting are a primary site of heterosexual privilege. The family centered around marriage, procreation, and child-rearing has historically been and continues to be constructed and institutionalized as the natural domain of heterosexuals only, and thus as a domain from which lesbians and gays are outlawed. This distinctively lesbian and gay relation to family, marriage, and parenting is what fails to make its appearance within feminist analyses and critiques of the family. But so long as the political position of lesbians and gays in relation to heterosexual control of family, marriage, and parenting remains out of view, distinctively lesbian (and gay) interests in family, marriage, and parenting and distinctively lesbian (and gay) political goals in relation to the family cannot make their appearance. It is to the construction of lesbians and gays as outlaws to the family that I now turn.

IV. FAMILIAL OUTLAWS

A constitutive feature of lesbian and gay oppression since at least the late nineteenth century has been the reservation of the private sphere for heterosexuals only. Because lesbians and gays are ideologically constructed as beings incapable of genuine romance, marriage, or families of their own, and because those assumptions are institutionalized in the law and social practice, lesbians and gays are displaced from this private sphere.

In what follows, I want to suggest that the historical construction of gays and lesbians as familial outlaws is integrally connected to the history of social anxiety about the failure and potential collapse of the heterosexual nuclear family. In particular, I want to suggest that in periods where there was heightened anxiety about the stability of the heterosexual nuclear family because of changes in gender, sexual, and family composition norms within the family, this anxiety was resolved by targeting a group of persons who could be ideologically constructed as outsiders to the family, identifying the behaviors that most deeply threatened the family with those outsiders, and stigmatizing that group. In each of the periods of anxiety about the family that I intend to consider, lesbians and gays had achieved fairly high social visibility, making them natural candidates for the group to be constructed as outsiders to the family. The construction of gays and lesbians as highly stigmatized outsiders to the family and as displaying the most virulent forms of family-disrupting behavior allayed anxieties about the potential failure of the heterosexual nuclear family in three ways. First, it externalized the threat to the family. As a result, anxiety about the possibility that the family was disintegrating from *within* could be displaced onto the spectre of the hostile outsider to the family. Second, stigma threatening comparisons between misbehaving members of the heterosexual family and the dangerous behavior of gays and lesbians could be used to compel heterosexual family members' compliance with gender, sexual, and family composition norms. Third, by locating the genuinely deviant, abnormal, perverse behavior outside the family, members of heterosexual families were enabled to adjust to new, liberalized norms for acceptable gender roles and sexual behavior within families[16] as well as new, liberalized norms for acceptable family composition. They could, in essence, reassure themselves with the thought: "At least we aren't like them!"

The coincidence of anxiety about the failure of the heterosexual nuclear family and the ideological construction of gays and lesbians as familial outlaws is particularly striking in three periods: the 1880s to 1920s, the 1930s to 1950s, and the 1980s to 1990s. Although a variety of factors threatened the family in each of these periods, I want to suggest that the three periods differ with respect to the familial norms that were most seriously challenged. In the 1880s to 1920s it was especially norms governing (women's) gender behavior, in the 1930s to 1950s, it was most critically norms governing (male) sexuality, and in the 1980s and 1990s it has been, above all, norms governing acceptable family composition that have been most centrally challenged.

1880s to 1920s. The 1880s to 1920s witnessed significant challenges to the gender structure of marriage. By the mid-1800s, the first wave of the feminist movement was underway, pressing for changes in women's gender roles within the family. First-wave feminists pushed for legal reforms that would recognize women as separate individuals within marriage by, for example, securing women property rights within marriage, and that would give women access to divorce. (Between 1860 and 1920 the divorce rate increased over 600 percent.[17]) They also pushed for increased access to higher education and employment as well as for contraception, abortion, and (through the temperance movement) control of male sexuality, all of which would enable women to limit family size and free women from a life devoted exclusively to childbearing and child-rearing.

First-wave feminists' explicit critique of women's gender role within the family produced an anxiety about the family that focused on its gender structure. Because turn-of-the-century gender ideology tied gender tightly to biology, the violation of gender norms was interpreted as having significant biological repercussions. From the mid-1800s on, physicians argued that "unnatural" women—that is, "over" educated women, women who worked

at gender-atypical occupations, and women who practiced birth control or had abortions—were likely to suffer a variety of physically based mental ailments including weakness, nervousness, hysteria, loss of memory, insanity, and nymphomania.[18] Worse yet, their gender-inappropriate behavior might result in sterility or inability to produce physically and mentally healthy offspring. In particular, they risked producing children who were themselves inappropriately gendered—effeminate sons and masculine daughters. Not only could departure from women's traditional gender role as wife and mother have dire physical and mental consequences for both herself and her offspring, she herself might be suspected of being at a deep level not really a woman. Indeed, she might be suspected of being one of the third sex.

Beginning roughly in 1869 with the publication of Carl von Westphal's essay on the congenital invert, medical theorists began developing a new gender category variously labelled the sexual invert, the intermediate sex, the third sex, the urning, the man-woman. The image of the sexual invert crystallized anxiety about women's, and to a lesser extent, men's gender-crossing and symbolized the dangers of deviance from conventional gender norms. Although the invert is the historical precursor to the contemporary categories "lesbian" and "homosexual," the turn-of-the-century sexual invert was not constructed primarily *sexually*. What distinguished the invert was her or his *gender* inversion. The sexually inverted woman, for example, was distinguished from noninverted women by her masculine traits: short hair, independent and aggressive manner, athleticism, male attire, drinking, cigarette and sometimes cigar smoking, masculine sense of honor, dislike of needlework and domestic activities, and preference for science and masculine sports. The sexually inverted woman's attraction to conventionally gendered women and to effeminate men was simply a natural result of her generally masculine genderization. In her sexual relations, whether with women or with a husband, she would wear the pants.

Medical theorists postulated that, at a biological level, sexually inverted women were not real women. Some imagined that inverts were really hermaphrodites. Others, like Havelock Ellis, imagined that they possessed an excess of male "germs."[19] Others, like Krafft-Ebing, imagined that the invert was a throwback to an earlier evolutionary stage of bisexuality (that is, bi-*genderization*) and that in spite of her female brain and body, the psychosexual center in her brain was masculine.[20]

Because the mark of the sexual invert was her lack of conformity with women's conventional gender role, the line between the nonconforming sexual invert and the nonconforming feminist was often blurred. Feminist views and feminist-inspired deviance from gender norms might be both symptom and cause of sexual inversion. Like sexual inverts, feminists threatened to disrespect appropriate gender relations between women and men in marriage. One author of a 1900 *New York Medical Journal* essay, for instance, "warned that feminists and sexual perverts alike, both of whom he classed as 'degenerates,' married only men whom they could rule, govern and cause to follow [them] in voice and action."[21]

In short, the sexually inverted woman, sometimes indistinguishable from the feminist, symbolized the dangers of departing from women's conventional gender role. The idea that this new medical category of sexual inversion was created in direct response to first-wave feminists' challenge to gender norms is not new. Both Lillian Faderman and George Chauncey, Jr., for instance, have argued that given both the influence of feminist ideas and the burgeoning of economic opportunities for women, there was a cultural fear that women would replace marriages to men with Boston marriages or romantic friendships.[22] One response to that fear was greater attention to the ideal of companionate marriage, and thus to making marriage more attractive to women.[23] A second response,

however, was a cultural backlash—or as Chauncey describes it, a heterosexual counter-revolution—against Boston marriages, romantic friendships, schoolgirl "raves," and same-sex institutions. The pathologizing of both gender deviance and same-sex relationships brought what were formerly taken to be innocent and normal intimacies between women under suspicion of harboring degeneracy and abnormality.

The pathologizing of relations between women was not confined to medical literature. As Lisa Duggan has documented, newspapers sensationalized violent intimate relationships between women, such as the case of Alice Mitchell, a sexual invert, who intended to elope with and marry Freda Ward and to cross-dress as a man, adopting the name Alvin. When their plan was discovered and the engagement forcibly terminated, Alice Mitchell murdered Freda so that no one else could have her. Duggan argues that Alice's clear intent to forge a new way of life outside the heterosexual, gender-structured family marked her as dangerous. In sensationalizing cases like Alice's,

> [t]he late-nineteenth century newspaper narratives of lesbian love featured violence as a boundary marker; murders or suicides served to abort the forward progress of the tale, signaling that such erotic love between women was not only tragic but ultimately hopeless. . . . The stories were thus structured to emphasize, ultimately, that no real love story was possible.[24]

Not only was no real love story possible, no real family relation was possible either. And this is the point I want to underscore. Controlling challenges to the conventional gender structure within heterosexual marriages was accomplished by constructing the fully gender-deviant woman as someone who was not only pathological and doomed to tragedy, but who was constitutionally unfit for family life. Her masculinity unfitted her for the marital role of wife, unfitted her for the task of producing properly gendered children, and unfitted her for any stable, intimate relationships. The cultural construction of the lesbian was thus, from the outset, the construction of a kind of being who was, centrally, an outsider to marriage, family, and motherhood.

The image of the doomed, mannish lesbian could be used to compel heterosexual women's compliance with gender norms. In addition, by equating the worst forms of gender deviance with lesbians, heterosexual families were helped to adjust to new gender norms for women (which, by comparison to lesbians, seemed normal). Finally, attributing the worst forms of gender deviance to a third sex externalized the threat to the heterosexual family, suggesting that the heterosexual family was not in fact being challenged from within by *real* women.

1930s to 1950s. The Depression of the 1930s and World War II in the 1940s created a new set of threats to the stability of the heterosexual family.[25] During the Depression, many men lost their traditional gender position in the family as breadwinners as a result of both massive unemployment and a drop in marriage rates. The sense of a cultural crisis in masculinity was reflected in numerous sociological studies of "The Unemployed Man and His Family."[26] Men's traditional position in the family and family stability itself was additionally undermined during World War II, which brought a rise in the frequency of prolonged separations, divorce, and desertion.[27]

One response was the attempt to reposition men as primary income earners in their families by discouraging or prohibiting married women from working. A second response, however, appears to have been a shift in the cultural construction of masculinity from being gender-based to being sexuality-based. In his historical study of New York gay culture during the first third of the twentieth century, for instance, George Chauncey argues that sexual categories for men underwent a significant transformation during the '30s and '40s. The gender-behavior-based contrast between "fairies," that is, effeminate men and "men" (who might be "queer,"

"trade," that is, heterosexual men who accepted advances from homosexual men, or strictly heterosexual) gave way to the contemporary binarism between homosexual and heterosexual. Real manhood ceased to be secured by simply avoiding feminine behaviors, and instead came to rest on exclusive heterosexuality.[28] The depiction of gay men, during the sex crime panics of 1937 to 1940 and 1949 to 1955, as violent child molesters further solidified the boundary between real, heterosexual men and homosexuals, while depiction of the heterosexual sexual psychopath as hypermasculine underscored the centrality of (hetero)sexuality to manhood.[29]

Compounding the shifts in gender arrangements within the family brought on by the Depression and World War II were shifts in cultural understandings of women's and children's sexuality. The idea of female sexual satisfaction, the use of birth control, and sexuality outside of marriage all gained increased acceptance. And the publicization of Freudian ideas underscored not only the sexuality of women, but the sexuality of children as well. The sexualization of women and children meant that both might fail to be merely innocent victims of male sexual aggression; they might instead play a role in inviting it.[30] These factors contributed to a changed understanding of sexuality and sexual norms both outside and inside the family. They also contributed to cultural anxiety about the power of sexuality to destabilize and undermine the family.

Those anxieties were crystallized during the sex crime panics in the twin figures of the heterosexual psychopathic rapist and the homosexual psychopath who seduced youth and molested children. Both figures symbolized sexuality run dangerously amok. The image of the dangerously sexual homosexual received added reinforcement during the McCarthy era's purge of "sex perverts" from governmental service on the grounds that they threatened not only the nation's children but its national security and the heterosexuality of its adult population as well.[31]

The images of the sexual psychopath and the homosexual child molester helped to redefine the sexual norm, setting the outer limits of acceptable sexual behavior: violent sex, sex with men, and sex with children.[32] By constructing new understandings of sexual abnormality, the images of the sexual psychopath and the homosexual child molester also helped Americans adjust to new sexual norms, such as the acceptability of nonprocreative sex, as well as to new understandings of both women and children as "normally" sexual beings. The location of the sexual danger posed to women and children outside the family also allayed anxiety that the family risked disruption by the potentially violent sexuality of its own members.

Again, the point I want to underscore is that resolving cultural anxiety about shifting gender and sexual patterns within the family was integrally connected with the social construction of gay men as familial outlaws. The very nature of homosexuality unfitted gay men for family. Constitutionally prone to uncontrolled and insatiable sexuality, gay (and lesbians) could not be trusted to respect prohibitions on adult-child sexual interactions.[33] Nor, given the compulsive quality of their sexual desire, could gay men or lesbians be expected to maintain stable relationships with each other.

1980s to 1990s. The 1980s and 1990s have posed a different challenge to the family. Technological, social, and economic factors have combined to produce an explosion of new family and household forms that undermine the nuclear, biology-based family's claim to be *the* natural, normative social unit.

Increasingly, sophisticated birth control methods and technologically assisted reproduction using in-vitro fertilization, artificial insemination, contract pregnancy, fertility therapies, and the like undermine cultural understandings of the marital couple as a naturally reproductive unit, introduce nonrelated others into the reproductive process, and make it possible for women and men to have children without a heterosexual partner. The institutionalization of child care, as mothers work to support families, involves nonfamily members in the familial task of raising children. Soaring divorce rates have made single-parent households a common family pattern—so common that Father's Day cards now include ones addressed to mothers, and others announcing their recipient is "like a dad." The high incidence of divorce has also meant an increase in divorce-extended families that incorporate children, grandparents, and other kin from former marriages as well as former spouses who may retain shared custody or visitation rights.[34] As a result of remarriage, semen donation, and contract pregnancy, the rule of one-mother, one-father per child (both of whom are expected to be biological parents) that has dominated legal reasoning about custody and visitation rights has ceased to be adequate to the reality of many families. Multiple women and/or multiple men become involved in children's lives through their biological, gestation, or parenting contributions.[35] The extended kinship networks of the Black urban poor, including "fictive kin," which enable extensive pooling of resources, have become increasingly common in the working class as the shift from goods to service production and the decline of industrial and unionized occupations has made working class persons' economic position increasingly fragile.[36] And the impoverishment of single-parent households has increasingly involved welfare agencies in family survival.

In short, as Judith Stacey observes,

> No longer is there a single culturally dominant family pattern to which the majority of Americans conform and most of the rest aspire. Instead, Americans today have crafted a multiplicity of family and household arrangements that we inhabit uneasily and reconstitute in response to changing personal and occupational circumstances.[37]

We now live, in her view, in the age of the postmodern family. It is an age where one marriage and its biological relations have ceased to determine family composition. Choice increasingly appears to be the principle determining family composition: choice to single-parent, choice of fictive kin, choice to combine nuclear families (in extended kin networks, in remarriage, or in divorce-extended families), choice of semen donors or contract birthgivers, choice to dissolve marital bonds, choice of who will function as a parent in children's live (in spite of the law's failure to acknowledge the parental status of many functional parents.) That is, what Kath Weston describes as a distinctively gay and lesbian concept of "chosen families," contrasted to heterosexuals' biological families, in fact characterizes the reality of many heterosexual families who fail in various ways to construct a nuclear family around a procreative married couple.[38]

As family forms multiply, the traditional, heterosexual and procreative, nuclear family delimited by bonds of present marriage and blood relation and capable of sustaining itself rather than pooling resources across households has ceased to be the "natural" family form.[39] Not only has the pluralization of family forms undermined the credibility of the claim that the traditional family is the most natural family form, it has also highlighted the failure of the traditional family to satisfy individual needs better than other personal relationships or alternative family forms.[40]

Cultural anxiety about the future of the family crystallized in the 1980s and 1990s in at least two major images: those of the unwed welfare mother and of the lesbian or gay whose mere public visibility threatens to undermine family values and destroy the family. The depiction of lesbians and gays as beings whose "lifestyle" contradicts family values was preceded in the 1970s by the gay liberation movement, and with it, a rise in lesbian custody suits and in litigation contesting the denial of marriage licenses to gays.[41] Both the sheer visibility of gays and lesbians as well as their specific bid for acknowledgment of gay and lesbian marriages and families made gays and lesbians natural targets for the expression of cultural anxieties about the family.

In the late 1980s, for instance, Britain passed Clause 28 of the Local Government Act that, in addition to prohibiting the promotion of homosexuality, also forbade local authorities from promoting "the teaching in any maintained school of the acceptability of homosexuality as a pretended family relationship."[42] The pretended nature of gays' and lesbians' family relationships has, in the United States, been repeatedly underscored in court rulings affirming that marriage requires one man and one woman. The pretend nature of lesbian motherhood has also been underscored in custody rulings that have assumed that being parented by a lesbian is not in a child's best interests—because the child may be molested, or may fail to be socialized into her or his appropriate gender or into heterosexuality, or may be harmed by the stigma of having a lesbian parent.[43]

Not only are gays and lesbians constructed as beings whose "marriages" and "families" fail to be the genuine article, they are also constructed as beings who, simply by being publicly visible or mentionable, assault family values. As a result, antidiscrimination measures are equated with hostility to the family, even though ending workplace discrimination or punishing hate crimes would appear to have little to do with advocating one family form rather than another. So, for instance, the author of a 1995 law journal article argues that gays and lesbians should not be protected against discrimination because gay sexuality is "deeply hostile to the self-understanding of those members of the community who are willing to commit themselves to real marriage."[44] He makes it clear that any policy protecting a "gay lifestyle" threatens the stability of the family, and for that reason should be rejected:

> A political community which judges that the stability and protective and educative generosity of family life is of fundamental importance to that community's present and future can rightly judge that it has a compelling interest in denying that homosexual conduct—a "gay lifestyle"—is a valid, humanly acceptable choice and form of life,

and in doing whatever it *properly* can, as a community with uniquely wide but still subsidiary functions, to discourage such conduct.[45]

So threatening to the family are gays and lesbians taken to be that even protecting them against hate crimes may be interpreted as dangerously close to attacking the family. Thus the Hate Crimes Act passed by Congress in 1990 (which covers sexual orientation) includes the affirmation that "federal policy should encourage the well-being, financial security, and health of the American family," almost immediately followed with the warning that "[n]othing in this Act shall be construed, nor shall any funds appropriated to carry out the purpose of the Act be used, to promote or encourage homosexuality."[46]

As in previous periods, constructing lesbians and gays as dangerous outlaws to the family serves several functions. First, it externalizes the threat to the heterosexual, procreative, nuclear family, diverting attention from heterosexuals' own choices to create multiple, new family arrangements that undermine the hegemony of the traditional family. Second, depicting gay and lesbian relationships as "pretended" families, by comparison to which even the most deviant heterosexual families can appear normal, helps heterosexual families adjust to changing norms for family composition. Finally, the equation of heterosexuality with family values and homosexuality and lesbianism with hostility to the family serves to compel loyalty to the sexual norm prescribing heterosexuality. It also renders suspect some of the alternative family arrangements that heterosexuals might be inclined to choose, such as supportive, familylike relationships between women involved in single parenting.

V. NOT FOR HETEROSEXUALS ONLY

I have argued for the existence of a historical pattern in which anxiety about the stability of the family goes hand in hand with the ideological depiction of gays and lesbians as unfit for marriage, parenting, and family. The construction of lesbians and gays as natural outlaws to the family and the masking of heterosexuals' own family-disrupting behavior results in the reservation of the private sphere for heterosexuals only.[47]

It is because being an outlaw to the family has been so central to the social construction of lesbianism that I think lesbians' relation to the family is better captured by attention to their outlaw status than to the gender structure of marriage and motherhood (as is characteristic of lesbian feminism). Indeed, on the historical backdrop of the various images of family outlaws—the mannish lesbian, the homosexual child molester, and their pretended family relationships—lesbian-feminist resistance to lesbian and gay marriages, lesbian motherhood, and the formation of lesbian and gay families looks suspiciously like a concession to the view of lesbians and gays as family outlaws. Because being denied access to a legitimate and protected private sphere has been and continues to be central to lesbian and gay oppression, the most important scale on which to measure lesbian and gay political strategies is one that assesses their power (or impotence) to resist conceding the private sphere to heterosexuals only. On such a scale, the push for marriage rights, parental rights, and recognition as legitimate families measures up.

For similar reasons, it seems to me a mistake to make advocacy of "queer families" *the* political goal for lesbians and gays. By "queer families" I mean ones not centered around marriage or children, but composed instead of chosen, adult, supportive relationships (which would include lesbian-feminist political communities of women).

Equating gay families with queer, nonmarital, and nonparenting families concedes too much to the ideology of gays and lesbians as family outlaws, unfit for genuine marriage and dangerous to children. In addition, describing families that depart substantially from traditional family forms as distinctively gay conceals the queerness of many heterosexual families. I have tried to show that, historically, gays and lesbians have become family outlaws not because *their* relationships and families were distinctively queer, but because *heterosexuals'* relationships and families queered the gender, sexual, and family composition norms. The depiction of gays and lesbians as deviant with respect to family norms was a product of anxiety about that deviancy within heterosexual families. Thus claiming that gay and lesbian families are (or should be) distinctively queer and distinctively deviant helps conceal the deviancy in heterosexual families, and thereby helps to sustain the illusion that heterosexuals are specially entitled to access to a protected private sphere because they, unlike their gay and lesbian counterparts, are supporters of the family.

All this is not to say that there is no merit in lesbian feminists' concern that normalizing lesbian motherhood will reinforce the equation of "woman" with "mother." Overcoming the idea that lesbian motherhood is a contradiction in terms may very well result in lesbians' being expected to fulfill the maternal imperative just as heterosexual women are. But this is just to say that the oppression of lesbians and gays is structurally different from gender oppression. Thus, strategies designed to resist *lesbian* oppression (such as pushing for the legal right to coadopt) are not guaranteed to counter *gender* oppression (which might better be achieved by resisting motherhood altogether). In gaining access to a legitimate and protected private sphere of mothering, marriage, and family, lesbians will need to take care that it does not prove to be as constraining as the private sphere has been for heterosexual women.

Nor have I meant to claim that there is no merit in both lesbian feminists' and queer theorists' concern that normalizing lesbian and gay marriage will reinforce the distinction between good, assimilationist gays and bad gay and heterosexual others whose relationships violate familial norms (the permanently single, the polygamous, the sexually nonmonogamous, the

member of a commune, and so on). Overcoming the idea that lesbian and gay marriages are merely pretended family relationships may very well result in married lesbians and gays being looked upon more favorably than those who remain outside accepted familial forms. But this is just to say that countering lesbians' and gays' family outlaw status is not the same thing as struggling to have a broad array of social relationships recognized as (equally) valuable ones. It is, however, important not to exaggerate the level of conformity involved in having familial status. I have argued that families often fail to conform to gender, sexual, and family composition norms. This has not prevented heterosexuals from claiming that, their deviancy notwithstanding, they still have real marriages and real families, and are themselves naturally suited for marriage, family, and parenting. Thus, lesbians and gays who resist their construction as family outlaws are not bidding for access to one, highly conventional family form (such as the nuclear, two-parent, self-sufficient, procreative family). They are instead bidding for access to the same privilege that heterosexuals now enjoy, namely the privilege of claiming that *in spite of their multiple deviations* from norms governing the family, their families are nevertheless *real* ones and they are themselves naturally suited for marriage, family, parenting *however* these may be defined and redefined.

NOTES

1. I have argued that this claim in both "Separating Lesbian Theory from Feminist Theory," *Ethics* 104 (1994), pp. 558–581, and in "The Gender Closet: Lesbian Disappearance Under the Sign 'Women'," *Feminist Studies* 21 (Spring 1995), pp. 7–34.

2. For discussion of women's vulnerability in marriage and after divorce, see Susan Moller Okin, *Justice, Gender and the Family* (New York: Basic Books, 1989), and Lenore J. Weitzman, *The Divorce Revolution: The Unexpected Social and Economic Consequences for Women and Children in America* (New York: Free Press, 1985).

3. This is not to say that lesbians are entirely left out of the picture. Although drawn from a heterosexual viewpoint, this picture of the family, marriage, and mothering as a primary

site of women's subordination and dependence is one that lesbians do nevertheless fit into in many ways. Lesbians, too, can find themselves in heterosexual marriages, undergoing divorce, becoming single parents, disadvantaged in a sex-segregated workforce that pays women less, without adequate child care or child support, vulnerable to welfare bureaucracies, and so on.

4. Monique Wittig, *The Straight Mind and Other Essays* (Boston: Beacon Press, 1992); Charlotte Bunch, "Lesbians in Revolt," in *Passionate Politics, Essays 1968–1986* (New York: St. Martin's Press, 1987).

5. Janice G. Raymond, *A Passion for Friends* (Boston: Beacon Press, 1986).

6. Ruthann Robson, "Resisting the Family: Repositioning Lesbians in Legal Theory," *Signs* 19 (1994), pp. 975–996.

7. *Ibid,* p. 977.

8. *Ibid,* p. 976.

9. *Ibid,* pp. 986–987.

10. Irena Klepfisz, "Women Without Children/Women Without Families/Women Alone," in *Politics of the Heart: A Lesbian Parenting Anthology*, ed. Sandra Pollack and Jeanne Vaughn (New York: Firebrand Books, 1987), p. 57.

11. Nancy D. Polikoff, "Lesbians Choosing Children: The Personal Is Political," in Pollack and Vaughn, *Politics of the Heart*, p. 51.

12. Ellen Lewin, *Lesbian Mothers: Accounts of Gender in American Culture* (Ithaca, N.Y.: Cornell University Press, 1993), p. 16.

13. Nancy D. Polikoff, "We Will Get What We Ask For: Why Legalizing Gay and Lesbian Marriage Will Not 'Dismantle the Legal Structure of Gender in Every Marriage'," *Virginia Law Review* 79 (1993), 1535–1550, p. 1538.

14. Robson's objection to functionalist approaches to the family in legal thinking is precisely that functionalist approaches are inherently conservative and "guarantee exclusion of the very relationships that might transform the functions," such as sexual relationships among three lesbians (Robson, "Resisting the Family," p. 989).

15. Paula Ettelbrick, "Since When Is Marriage a Path to Liberation?" in *Lesbians, Gay Men, and the Law,* ed. William B. Rubenstein (New York: The New Press, 1993); and Polikoff, "We Will Get What We Ask For."

16. Estelle B. Freedman develops this thesis in "'Uncontrolled Desires': The Response to the Sexual Psychopath 1920–1960," in *Passion and Power: Sexuality in History*, ed. Kathy Peiss and Christina Simmons with Robert A. Padgug (Philadelphia: Temple University Press, 1989).

17. Eli Zaretsky, "The Place of the Family in the Origins of the Welfare State," in *Rethinking the Family: Some Feminist Questions*, ed. Barrie Thorne with Marilyn Yalom (New York: Longman, 1982), p. 199.

18. Carroll Smith-Rosenberg and Charles Rosenberg, "The Female Animal: Medical and Biological Views of Woman and Her Role in Nineteenth-Century America," in *Concepts of Health and Disease: Interdisciplinary Perspectives,* ed. Arthur L. Caplan, H. Tristram Engelhardt, Jr., James J. McCartney (Reading, Mass.: Addison-Wesley Publishing Co., 1981).

19. Havelock Ellis, *Studies in the Psychology of Sex*, Vol II: *Sexual Inversion* (Philadelphia: F.A. Davis Co., 1928).

20. Richard von Krafft-Ebing, *Psychopathia Sexualis: A Medico-Forensic Study* (New York: Pioneer Publications, Inc., 1947).

21. Quoted in George Chauncey, Jr., "From Sexual Inversion to Homosexuality: The Changing Medical Conceptualization of Female 'Deviance,'" in *Passion and Power*, p. 92.

22. Chauncey, Jr. "From Sexual Inversion to Homosexuality"; Lillian Faderman, *Surpassing the Love of Men: Romantic Friendship and Love between Women from the Renaissance to the Present* (New York: William Morrow, 1981); Lillian Faderman, "Nineteenth-Century Boston Marriage as a Possible Lesson for Today," in *Boston Marriages: Romantic but Asexual Relationships Among Contemporary Lesbians*, ed. Esther D. Rothblum and Kathleen A. Brehony (Amherst: University of Massachusetts Press, 1993).

23. Chauncey, Jr., "From Sexual Inversion to Homosexuality."

24. Lisa Duggan, "The Trials of Alice Mitchell: Sensationalism, Sexology, and the Lesbian Subject in Turn-of-the-Century America." *Signs* 18 (1993), 791–814, p. 808.

25. See Estelle B. Freedman, "'Uncontrolled Desires'"; John D'Emilio, "The Homosexual Menace: The Politics of Sexuality in Cold War America," in *Passion and Power*; and George Chauncey, Jr., *Gay New York: Gender, Urban Culture, and the Making of the Gay Male World, 1890–1940* (New York: Basic Books, 1994).

26. Chauncey, Jr., *Gay New York*, pp. 353–354.

27. D'Emilio, "The Homosexual Menace," p. 233.

28. Chauncey, Jr., *Gay New York*. One of his central aims in this work is to argue that the hetero-homosexual binarism is of significantly more recent invention than generally acknowledged.

29. This point is made by Freedman in "'Uncontrolled Desires'."

30. Freedman, "'Uncontrolled Desires'."

31. John D'Emilio, in "The Homosexual Menace," points out that there was virtually no evidence supporting McCarthy-era allegations that lesbians and gays were vulnerable to blackmail and hence unsuitable for government employment. He suggests that the massive efforts to counter the "homosexual menace" can only be explained as a result of the Depression and World War II's disruption of family life, gender arrangements, and patterns of sexuality.

32. Freedman, "'Uncontrolled Desires'," and D'Emilio, "The Homosexual Menace."

33. Fear that the child will be sexually molested is one reason for denying *lesbians* custody of their children.

34. Judith Stacey cites one San Francisco study of divorced couples as revealing that one-third of them sustained kinship ties with former spouses and their relatives; *Brave New Families: Stories of Domestic Upheaval in Late Twentieth Century America* (New York: Basic Books, 1990), p. 254. "Divorce-extended" is her term.

35. For an exhaustive discussion of the inadequacies of the one-mother, one-father assumption to both heterosexual and gay/lesbian families see Nancy d. Polikoff, "This Child Does Have Two Mothers," *The Georgetown Law Journal* 78 (1990), 459–575.

36. Stacey, *Brave New Families*.

37. *Ibid*, p. 17.

38. Kath Weston, *Families We Choose: Lesbians, Gays, Kinship* (New York: Columbia University Press, 1991).

39. Indeed, it has become doubly denaturalized. First, in failing to be repetitively enacted by individuals creating families, the heterosexual, procreative, nuclear family has lost its appearance of being the natural family form. That is, just as gender is "naturalized" through repeated performances (Judith Butler, *Gender Trouble: Feminism and the Subversion of Identity* [New York: Routledge, 1990]), so too one might imagine that the family itself is naturalized through being repetitively enacted. Second, family composition extends well beyond those "naturally" linked by blood and those whose marital coupling "naturally" issues in progeny.

40. Jeffrey Weeks, "Pretended Family Relationships," in *Against Nature: Essays on History, Sexuality, and Identity* (London: Rivers Oram Press, 1991), p. 143.

41. For 1970s marriage cases, see *Lesbians, Gay Men, and the Law.*

42. Quoted in Jeffrey Weeks, "Pretended Family Relationships," p. 137.

43. Although courts are moving to the assumption that the mother's lesbianism per se is not a bar to her fitness as a parent, this did not prevent the Virginia Supreme Court in the recent case of *Bottoms v. Bottoms* from ruling that, even so, *active* lesbianism on the part of the mother could be a bar to her fitness.

44. John M. Finnis, "Law, Morality, and 'Sexual Orientation'," *Notre Dame Journal of Law, Ethics, and Public Policy* 9 (1995), 11–39, p. 32.

45. *Ibid.*, pp. 32–33.

46. U.S.C. #534, quoted in Robson, "Resisting the Family," p. 981 ftn. 16.

47. Justice White, in *Bowers v. Hardwick* argued that homosexual sodomy is not protected by the right to privacy because, in his view, the right to privacy protects the private sphere of family, marriage, and procreation and he opined that there was no connection between family, marriage, and procreation on the one hand, and homosexuality on the other.

Why Marry?

Frank Browning

Thursday morning, and it's my turn to move our cars for street cleaning. Gene has already bribed the cats into silence with food.

So begins the day here in Windsor Terrace, a quiet Brooklyn neighborhood populated by many kinds of families: a lesbian couple next door—and beyond them an Italian widow who rents out rooms, an Irish-American grandmother who shares her house with her daughter's family, the multigenerational Korean family that owns the corner grocery.

We gay couples, of course, are not considered families under the law, a fact that the bishops and Buchananites insist will never change and that many gay activists have identified as America's next great civil rights struggle. Indeed, a court case in Hawaii may soon lead to that state's recognition of same-sex marriage.

I suppose it's a good thing for gay adults to be offered the basic nuptial rights afforded to others. We call that equal treatment before the law. But I'm not sure the marriage contract is such a good plan for us.

The trouble with gay marriage is not its recognition of our "unnatural unions." The problem is with the shape of marriage itself. What we might

Frank Browning, "Why Marry?" *The New York Times*, 17 April 1996: A23. Copyright (c) 1996 The New York Times Co. Reprinted by permission.

be better off seeking is civic and legal support for different kinds of families that can address the emotional, physical and financial obligations of contemporary life. By rushing to embrace the standard marriage contract, we could stifle one of the richest and most creative laboratories of family experience.

We gay folk tend to organize our lives more like extended families than nuclear ones. We may love our mates one at a time, but our "primary families" are often our ex-lovers and our ex-lovers' ex-lovers.

The writer Edmund White noticed this about gay male life 20 years ago; he called it the "banyan tree" phenomenon, after the tree whose branches send off shoots that take root to form new trunks. Nowhere has the banyan-tree family proved stronger than in AIDS care, where often a large group of people—ex-mates and their friends and lovers—tend the sick and maintain the final watch.

Modern marriage, by comparison, tends to isolate couples from their larger families and sometimes from friends—especially if they are ex-lovers. And a nuclear family with working parents has often proved less than ideal in coping with daily stresses or serious illness.

The marriage model could prove especially problematic for rearing children. In a gay family, there are often three parents—a lesbian couple, say, and the biological father. Sometimes, four or five adults are committed to nurturing the children. In such cases, a marriage between two might bring second-class status to the rest of the extended family and diminish their parental roles.

(Those who think that only a father and mother can successfully raise a child should visit Italy, Japan, Greece, Thailand or American family archives, which show that before World War II, grandparents, aunts, uncles and older siblings had vital child-rearing roles.)

Precisely because homosexuals have resided outside the law, they have invented family forms that respond to late 20th-century needs, while formulating social and moral codes that provide love, freedom and fidelity (if not always monogamy).

All I need do is look up and down Windsor Terrace to see that the family includes all sorts of relationships and obligations.

Each of us, hetero or homo, has a stake in nurturing a diverse landscape of families. Only a minority of us have marriages like Donna Reed's or Harriet Nelson's. Even Pat Buchanan knows that.

8

Sexual Violence

THE HORRORS OF SEXUAL VIOLENCE

It is difficult to speak of the magnitude of suffering of those who have been
victimized by sexual violence. It is painful to read and to listen to others'
accounts of being forcibly violated, tortured, and beaten. In the opening

reading in this chapter, Susan Brison, a young philosophy professor, tells of her experience of being raped and nearly murdered in a violent attack by a stranger in the middle of a sunny, summer day in the French countryside. She speaks poignantly of her ongoing recovery and the reactions of others to her experience.

Sexual violence takes many forms and occurs in many contexts. The primary victims of sexual violence are girls and women, though it must be noted that boys and men are also victims, particularly males in prison. Some perpetrators of violence are well known by their victims; in other cases they are strangers. Some acts of violence take place in the context of war: countless women were viciously raped during the genocidal war in Bosnia in the early and mid-1990s. Other acts take place in the familiar surroundings of one's home. The violence takes many forms; victims suffer both physical and psychological harm. Some do not survive their attacks; others find themselves haunted for years by disturbing memories, dreams, and disabling fears. Sexual violence also takes a tremendous toll on women who have never been victims and may never be victims: Studies show repeatedly that *fear* of rape shapes and constrains the lives of women every day; researchers believe the hidden social costs of women's fears of being sexually assaulted have been greatly underestimated.

CONTRIBUTIONS OF PHILOSOPHY TO AN ANALYSIS OF SEXUAL VIOLENCE

One might very well ask what moral philosophers might contribute to the debate over sexual violence. It seems patently obvious that it is morally wrong to harm others through sexual violence; that rape is morally evil seems to require little defense. In light of this, some might suggest that the only important scholarly work to be done on sexual violence is that carried out by social scientists—sociologists, psychologists, and anthropologists. These scholars certainly can help us learn more about the causes of sexual violence, the effects of such violence on victims, and, possibly, successful means of reducing violent sexual behavior in our society. The distinctive contributions of philosophers, however, seem less clear. Yet as Susan Brison points out in her article, philosophers may very well play an important role. Philosophers help to point out the biases already implicit in our concepts of 'harm' and 'rape' and 'guilt.' Legal scholar Catharine MacKinnon examines the implicit assumptions that structure and distort legal approaches to rape. Philosophers Larry May and Robert Strikwerda discuss the idea of collective responsibility as opposed to individual responsibility. Some moral philosophers find that they are able to refine and strengthen their normative theories by considering some of the seemingly paradoxical aspects of victims' misplaced sense of guilt and responsibility.

37.

Surviving Sexual Violence: A Philosophical Perspective[1]

Susan J. Brison

Susan J. Brison is an assistant professor of philosophy at Dartmouth, where she also teaches in the women's studies program. She works in the areas of philosophy of law, social philosophy, and ethics. She coedited *Contemporary Perspectives on Constitutional Interpretation* and is working on a new book on the aftermath of sexual violence. In this essay, she recounts her own traumatic experience of being sexually assaulted and nearly killed in a vicious attack by a stranger as she walked in the French countryside one summer morning. Drawing upon her experiences, she challenges the assumption that philosophers have little or nothing to say about sexual violence and trauma. She criticizes traditional philosophical definitions of rape; she examines the concepts of self-identity and trust in the aftermath of life-altering experiences of violence. Finally, she challenges the epistemic norms implicit in much of traditional moral philosophy, namely, that the best type of knowledge is dispassionate, impartial, and acquired from an allegedly neutral point of view.

Editor's Note: Susan Brison has written more recently about the experiences examined in this article in a new essay, "Outliving Oneself: Trauma, Memory, and Personal Identity," in *Feminists Rethink the Self*, ed. Diana Tietjiens Meyers (Boulder, CO: Westview Press, 1997): 12–39.

This is an unorthodox philosophy article, in both style and subject matter. Its primary aim is not to defend a thesis by means of argumentation, but rather to give the reader imaginative access to what is, for some, an unimaginable experience, that of a survivor of rape. The fact that there is so little philosophical writing about violence against women results not only from a lack of understanding of its prevalence and of the severity of its effects, but also from the mistaken view that it is not a properly philosophical subject. I hope in this essay to illuminate the nature and extent of the harm done by sexual violence and to show why philosophers should start taking this problem more seriously.

On July 4, 1990, at 10:30 in the morning, I went for a walk along a peaceful looking country road in a village outside Grenoble, France. It was a gorgeous day, and I didn't envy my husband, Tom, who had to stay inside and work on a manuscript with a French colleague of his. I sang to myself as I set out, stopping to pet a goat

and pick a few wild strawberries along the way. About an hour and a half later, I was lying face down in a muddy creek bed at the bottom of a dark ravine, struggling to stay alive. I had been grabbed from behind, pulled into the bushes, beaten, and sexually assaulted. Feeling absolutely helpless and entirely at my assailant's mercy, I talked to him, calling him 'sir.' I tried to appeal to his humanity, and, when that failed, I addressed myself to his self-interest. He called me a whore and told me to shut up. Although I had said I'd do whatever he wanted, as the sexual assault began I instinctively fought back which so enraged my attacker that he strangled me until I lost consciousness. When I awoke, I was being dragged by my feet down into the ravine. I had often, while dreaming, thought I was awake, but now I was awake and convinced I was having a nightmare. But it was no dream. After ordering me, in a gruff, Gestapo-like voice, to get on my hands and knees, my assailant strangled me again. I wish I could convey the horror of losing consciousness while my animal instincts desperately fought the effects of strangulation. This time I was sure I was dying. But I revived, just in time to see him lunging toward me with a rock. He smashed it into my forehead,

Susan J. Brison, "Surviving Sexual Violence: A Philosophical Perspective," *Journal of Social Philosophy* 24 (1993): 5–22. Reprinted by permission of the *Journal of Social Philosophy*.

knocking me out, and eventually, after another strangulation attempt, he left me for dead.

After my assailant left, I managed to climb out of the ravine, and was rescued by a farmer who called the police, a doctor, and an ambulance. I was taken to emergency at the Grenoble hospital where I underwent neurological test, x-rays, blood tests, and a gynecological exam. Leaves and twigs were taken from my hair for evidence, my fingernails were scraped, and my mouth was swabbed for samples. I had multiple head injuries, my eyes were swollen shut, and I had a fractured trachea which made breathing difficult. I was not permitted to drink or eat anything for the first thirty hours, though Tom, who never left my side, was allowed to dab my blood-encrusted lips with a wet towel. The next day, I was transferred out of emergency and into my own room. But I could not be left alone even for a few minutes. I was terrified my assailant would find me and finish the job. When someone later brought in the local paper with a story about my attack, I was greatly relieved that it referred to me as *Mlle. M.R.* and didn't even mention that I was American. Even by the time I left the hospital, eleven days later, I was so concerned about my assailant tracking me down that I put only my lawyer's address on the hospital records.

Although fears for my safety may have initially explained why I wanted to remain anonymous, by that time my assailant had been apprehended, indicted for rape and attempted murder, and incarcerated without possibility of bail. Still, I didn't want people to know that I had been sexually assaulted. I don't know whether this was because I could still hardly believe it myself, because keeping this information confidential was one of the few ways I could feel in control of my life, or because, in spite of my conviction that I had done nothing wrong, I felt ashamed.

When I started telling people about the attack, I said, simply, that I was the victim of an attempted murder. People typically asked, in horror, "What was the motivation? Were you

mugged" and when I replied, "No, it started as a sexual assault," most inquirers were satisfied with that as an explanation of why some man wanted to murder me. I would have thought that a murder attempt *plus* a sexual assault would require more, not less, of an explanation than a murder attempt by itself. (After all, there are *two* criminal acts to explain here.)

One reason sexual violence is taken for granted by many is because it is so very prevalent. The FBI, notorious for underestimating the frequency of sex crimes, notes that, in the United States, a rape occurs on an average of every 6 minutes.[2] But this figure covers only the reported cases of rape, and some researchers claim that only about 10% of all rapes get reported.[3] Every 15 seconds, a woman is beaten.[4] The every-dayness of sexual violence, as evidenced by these mind-numbing statistics, leads many to think that male violence against women is natural, a given, something not in need of explanation, and not amenable to change. And yet, through some extraordinary mental gymnastics, while most people take sexual violence for granted, they simultaneously manage to deny that it really exists—or, rather, that it could happen to them. We continue to think that we—and the women we love—are immune to it, provided, that is, that we don't do anything 'foolish.' How many of us have swallowed the potentially lethal lie that 'If you don't do anything wrong, if you're just careful enough, you'll be safe'? How many of us have believed its damaging, victim-blaming corollary: 'If you are attacked, it's because *you* did something wrong'? These are lies, and in telling my story I hope to expose them, as well as to help bridge the gap between those of us who have been victimized and those who have not.

But what, you may be thinking, does this have to do with philosophy? Why tell my story in this academic forum? Judging from the virtual lack of philosophical writing on sexual violence, one might well conclude there is nothing here of interest to philosophers. Certainly, I came across nothing in my search for philosophical help with explaining what had happened to me and putting my shattered world back together.[5] Yet sexual violence and its aftermath raise numerous philosophical issues in a variety of areas in our discipline. The disintegration of the self experienced by victims of violence challenges our notions of personal identity over time, a major preoccupation of metaphysics. A victim's seemingly justified skepticism about everyone and everything is pertinent to epistemology, especially if the goal of epistemology is, as Wilfrid Sellars put it, that of feeling at home in the world. In aesthetics—as well as in philosophy of law—the discussion of sexual violence in—or as—art could use the illumination provided by a victim's perspective. Perhaps the most important issues posed by sexual violence are in the areas of social, political, and legal philosophy, and insight into these, as well, requires an understanding of what it's like to be a victim of such violence.

One of the very few articles written by philosophers on violence against women is Ross Harrison's "Rape: A Case Study in Political Philosophy."[6] (Harrison 1986) In this article Harrison argues that not only do utilitarians need to assess the harmfulness of rape in order to decide whether the harm to the victim outweighs the benefit to the rapist, but even on a rights-based approach to criminal justice we need to be able to assess the benefits and harms involved in criminalizing and punishing violent acts such as rape. On his view, it is not always the case, contra Ronald Dworkin, that rights trump considerations of utility, so, even on a rights-based account of justice, we need to give an account of why, in the case of rape, the pleasure gained by the perpetrator (or by multiple perpetrators, in the case of gang-rape) is always outweighed by the harm done to the victim. He points out the peculiar difficulty most of us have in imagining the pleasure a rapist gets out of an assault, but, he asserts confidently, "There is no problem imagining what it is like to be a victim. . . ." (Harrison 1986, 51) To his credit, he acknowledges the importance, to political phi-

losophy, of trying to imagine others' experience, for otherwise we could not compare harms and benefits, which he argues must be done even in cases of conflicts of rights in order to decide which of competing rights should take priority. But imagining what it is like to be a rape victim is no simple matter, since much of what a victim goes through is unimaginable. Still, it's essential to try to convey it.

In my efforts to tell the victim's story—my story, our story—I've been inspired and instructed not only by feminist philosophers who have refused to accept the dichotomy between the personal and the political, but also by critical race theorists such as Patricia Williams, Mari Matsuda, and Charles Lawrence who have incorporated first person narrative accounts into their discussion of the law. In writing about hate speech, they have argued persuasively that one cannot do justice to the issues involved in debates about restrictions on speech without listening to the victims' stories.[7] In describing the effects of racial harassment on victims, they have departed from the academic convention of speaking in the impersonal, 'universal,' voice and related incidents they themselves experienced. In her groundbreaking book, *The Alchemy of Race and Rights*, Williams describes how it felt to learn about her great-great-grandmother who was purchased at age 11 by a slave owner who raped and impregnated her the following year. (Williams 1991) And in describing instances of everyday racism she herself has lived through, she gives us imaginative access to what it's like to be the victim of racial discrimination. Some may consider such first person accounts in academic writing to be self-indulgent, but I consider them a welcome antidote to the arrogance of those who write in a magisterial voice that in the guise of 'universality' silences those who most need to be heard.

Philosophers are far behind legal theorists in acknowledging the need for a diversity of voices. We are trained to write in an abstract, universal voice and to shun first-person narratives as biased and inappropriate for academic discourse.

Some topics, however, such as the impact of racial and sexual violence on victims, cannot even be broached unless those affected by such crimes can tell of their experiences in their own words. Unwittingly further illustrating the need for the victim's perspective, Harrison writes, elsewhere in his article on rape, "What principally distinguishes rape from normal sexual activity is the consent of the raped woman." (Harrison 1986, 52) There is no parallel to this in the case of other crimes, such as theft or murder. Try "What principally distinguishes theft from normal gift-giving is the consent of the person stolen from." We don't think of theft as "gift-giving minus consent." We don't think of murder as "assisted suicide minus consent." Why not? In the latter case, it could be because assisted suicide is relatively rare (even compared with murder) and so it's odd to use it as the more familiar thing to which we are analogizing. But in the former case, gift-giving is presumably more prevalent than theft (at least in academic circles) and yet it still sounds odd to explicate theft in terms of gift-giving minus consent. In the cases of both theft and murder, the notion of violation seems built into our conceptions of the physical acts constituting the crimes, so it is inconceivable that one could consent to the act in question. Why is it so easy for a philosopher such as Harrison to think of rape, however, as "normal sexual activity minus consent"? This may be because the nature of the violation in the case of rape hasn't been all that obvious. Witness the phenomenon of rape jokes, the prevalence of pornography glorifying rape, the common attitude that, in the case of women, 'no' means 'yes,' that women really want it.[8]

Since I was assaulted by a stranger, in a "safe" place, and was so visibly injured when I encountered the police and medical personnel, I was, throughout my hospitalization and my dealings with the police, spared the insult, suffered by so many rape victims, of not being believed or of being said to have asked for the attack. However, it became clear to me as I gave my deposition from my hospital bed that this

would still be an issue in my assailant's trial. During my deposition, I recalled being on the verge of giving up my struggle to live when I was galvanized by a sudden, piercing image of Tom's future pain on finding my corpse in that ravine. At this point in my deposition, I paused, glanced over at the police officer who was typing the transcript, and asked whether it was appropriate to include this image of my husband in my recounting of the facts. The *gendarme* replied that it definitely was and that it was a very good thing I mentioned my husband, since my assailant, who had confessed to the sexual assault, was claiming I had provoked it. As serious as the occasion was, and as much as it hurt to laugh, I couldn't help it—the suggestion was so ludicrous. Could it have been those baggy Gap jeans I was wearing that morning? Or was it the heavy sweatshirt? My maddeningly seductive jogging shoes? Or was it simply my walking along minding my own business that had provoked his murderous rage?

After I completed my deposition, which lasted eight hours, the police officer asked me to read and sign the transcript he'd typed to certify that it was accurate. I was surprised to see that it began with the words, *"Comme je suis sportive . . . "*—"Since I am athletic . . . "—added by the police to explain to the court just what possessed me to go for a walk by myself that fine morning. I was too exhausted by this point to protest 'no, I'm not an athlete, I'm a philosophy professor,' and I figured the officer knew what he was doing, so I let it stand. That evening, my assailant confessed to the assault. I retained a lawyer, and met him along with the investigating magistrate, when I gave my second deposition toward the end of my hospitalization. Although what occurred was officially a crime against the state, not against me, I was advised to pursue a civil suit in order to recover unreimbursed medical expenses, and, in any case, I needed an advocate to explain the French legal system to me. I was told that since this was an "easy" case, the trial would occur within a year. In fact, the trial took place two and a half years after the assault, due to the delaying tactics of my assailant's lawyer who was trying to get him off on an insanity defense. According to Article 64 of the French criminal code, if the defendant is determined to have been insane at the time, then, legally, there was *"ni crime, ni délit"*—neither crime nor offense. The jury, however, did not accept the insanity plea and found my assailant guilty of rape and attempted murder, sentencing him to ten years in prison.

As things turned out, my experience with the criminal justice system was better than that of most sexual assault victims. I did, however, occasionally get glimpses of the humiliating insensitivity victims routinely endure. Before I could be released from the hospital, for example, I had to undergo a second forensic examination at a different hospital. I was taken in a wheelchair out to a hospital van, driven to another hospital, taken to an office where there were no receptionists and where I was greeted by two male doctors I had never seen before. When they told me to take off my clothes and stand in the middle of the room, I refused. I had to ask for a hospital gown to put on. For about an hour the two of them went over me like a piece of meat, calling out measurements of bruises and other assessments of damage, as if they were performing an autopsy. This was just the first of many incidents in which I felt as if I was experiencing things posthumously. When the inconceivable happens, one starts to doubt even the most mundane, realistic perceptions. Perhaps I'm not really here, I thought, perhaps I did die in that ravine. The line between life and death, once so clear and sustaining, now seemed carelessly drawn and easily erased.

For the first several months after my attack, I led a spectral existence, not quite sure whether I had died and the world went on without me, or whether I was alive but in a totally alien world. Tom and I returned to the States, and I continued to convalesce, but I felt as though I'd somehow outlived myself. I sat in our apartment and stared outside for hours, through the blur of a detached vitreous, feeling like Robert Lowell's newly widowed mother, described in one of his poems as mooning in a window "as if she had stayed on a train/one stop past her destination." (Lowell 1977, 82)

My sense of unreality was fed by the massive denial of those around me—a reaction I learned is an almost universal response to rape. Where the facts would appear to be incontrovertible, denial takes the shape of attempts to explain the assault in ways that leave the observers' world view unscathed. Even those who are able to acknowledge the existence of violence try to protect themselves from the realization that the world in which it occurs is their world and so they find it hard to identify with the victim. They cannot allow themselves to imagine the victim's shattered life, or else their illusions about their own safety and control over their lives might begin to crumble. The most well-meaning individuals, caught up in the myth of their own immunity, can inadvertently add to the victim's suffering by suggesting that the attack was avoidable or somehow her fault. One victims' assistance coordinator, whom I had phoned for legal advice, stressed that she herself had never been a victim and said that I would benefit from the experience by learning not to be so trusting of people and to take basic safety precautions like not going out alone late at night. She didn't pause long enough during her lecture for me to point out that I was attacked suddenly, from behind, in broad daylight.

We are not taught to empathize with victims. In crime novels and detective films, it is the villain, or the one who solves the murder mystery, who attracts our attention; the victim, a merely passive pretext for our entertainment, is conveniently disposed of—and forgotten—early on. We identify with the agents' strength and skill, for good or evil, and join the victim, if at all, only in our nightmares. Though one might say, as did Clarence Thomas, looking at convicted criminals on their way to jail, "but for the grace of God, there go I,"[9] a victim's fate prompts an almost instinctive "it could never happen to me." This may explain why there is, in our criminal justice system, so little concern for justice for victims—especially rape victims. They have no constitutionally protected rights *qua* victims. They have no right to a speedy trial or to a compensation for damages (though states have been changing this in recent years), or to privacy vis-à-vis the press. As a result of their victimization, they often lose their jobs, their homes, their spouses—in addition to losing a great deal of money, time, sleep, self-esteem, and peace of mind. The rights to "life, liberty, and the pursuit of happiness," possessed, in the abstract, by all of us, are of little use to victims who can lose years of their lives, the freedom to move about in the world without debilitating fear, and any hope of returning to the pleasures of life as they once knew it.

People also fail to recognize that if a victim could not have anticipated an attack, she can have no assurance that she will be able to avoid one in the future. More to reassure themselves than to comfort the victim, some deny that such a thing could happen again. One friend, succumbing to the gambler's fallacy, pointed out that my having had such extraordinary bad luck meant that the odds of my being attacked again were now quite slim (as if fate, though not completely benign, would surely give me a break now, perhaps in the interest of fairness). Others thought it would be most comforting to pretend nothing had happened. The first card I received from my mother, while I was still in the hospital, made no mention of the attack or of my pain and featured the "bluebird of happiness," sent to keep me ever cheerful. The second had an illustration of a bright, summery scene with the greeting: "Isn't the sun nice? Isn't the wind nice? Isn't everything nice?" Weeks passed before I learned, what I should have been able to guess, that after she and my father received Tom's first call from the hospital they held each other and sobbed. They didn't want to burden me with their pain—a pain which I now realize must have been greater than my own.

Some devout relatives were quick to give God all the credit for my survival but none of the blame for what I had to endure. Others acknowledged the suffering that had been inflicted on me, but as no more than a blip on the graph of God's benevolence—a necessary, fleeting, evil, there to make possible an even greater show of good. An aunt, with whom I have been close since childhood, did not write or call at all until three months after the attack, and then sent a belated birthday card with a note saying that she was sorry to hear about my "horrible experience" but pleased to think that as a result I "will become stronger and will be able to help so many people. A real blessing from above for sure." Such attempts at a theodicy discounted the horror I had to endure. But I learned that everyone needs to try and make sense, in however inadequate a way, of such senseless violence. I watched my own see-sawing attempts to find something for which to be grateful, something to redeem the unmitigated awfulness: I was glad I didn't have to reproach myself (or endure others' reproaches) for having done something careless, but I wished I had done something I could consider reckless so that I could simply refrain from doing it in the future. I was glad I did not yet have a child, who would have to grow up with the knowledge that even the protector could not be protected, but I felt an inexpressible loss when I recalled how much Tom and I had wanted a baby and how joyful were our attempts to conceive. It is difficult, even now, to imagine getting pregnant, because it is so hard to let even my husband near me, and because it would be harder still to let a child leave my side.

It might be gathered, from the litany of complaints, that I was the recipient of constant, if misguided, attempts at consolation during the first few months of my recovery. This was not the case. It seemed to me that the half-life of most people's concern was less than that of the sleeping pills I took to ward off flashbacks and nightmares—just long enough to allow the construction of a comforting illusion that lulls the shock to sleep. During the first few months after my assault, most of the aunts, uncles, cousins, and friends of the family notified by my parents almost immediately after the attack didn't phone, write, or even send a get well card, in spite of my extended hospital stay. These are all caring, decent people who would have sent wishes for a speedy recovery if I'd had, say, an appendectomy. Their early lack of response was so striking that I wondered whether it was the result of self-protective denial, a reluctance to mention something so unspeakable, or a symptom of our society's widespread emotional illiteracy that prevents most people from conveying any feeling that can't be expressed in a Hallmark card.

In the case of rape, the intersection of multiple taboos—against talking openly about trauma, about violence, about sex—causes conversational gridlock, paralyzing the would-be supporter. We lack the vocabulary for expressing appropriate concern, and we have no social conventions to ease the awkwardness. Ronald de Sousa has written persuasively about the importance of grasping paradigm scenarios in early childhood in order to learn appropriate emotional responses to situations. (deSousa 1987) We do not learn—early or later in life—how to react to a rape. What typically results from this ignorance is bewilderment on the part of victims and silence on the part of others, often the result of misguided caution. When, on entering the angry phase of my recovery period, I railed at my parents: "Why haven't my relatives called or written? Why hasn't my own brother phoned?" They replied, "They all expressed their concern to us, but they didn't want to remind you of what happened." Didn't they realize I thought about the attack every minute of every day and that their inability to respond made me feel as though I had, in fact, died and no one had bothered to come to the funeral?

For the next several months, I felt angry, scared, and helpless, and I wished I could blame myself for what had happened so that I would feel less vulnerable, more in control of my life. Those who haven't been sexually violated may have difficulty understanding why women who survive assault often blame themselves, and may wrongly attribute it to a sex-linked trait of masochism or lack of self-esteem. They don't know that it can be less painful to believe that you did something blameworthy than it is to think that you live in a world where you can be attacked at any time, in any place, simply because you are a woman. It is hard to go on after an attack that is both random—and thus completely unpredictable—and not random, that is, a crime of hatred towards the group to which you happen to belong. If I hadn't been the one who was attacked on that road in France, it would have been the next woman to come along. But had my husband walked down that road instead, he would have been safe.

Although I didn't blame myself for the attack, neither could I blame my attacker. Tom wanted to kill him, but I, like other rape victims I came to know, found it almost impossible to get angry with my assailant. I think the terror I still felt precluded the appropriate angry response. It may be that experiencing anger towards an attacker requires imagining oneself in proximity to him, a prospect too frightening for a victim in the early stages of recovery to conjure up. As Aristotle observed in the *Rhetoric,* Book I, "no one grows angry with a person on whom there is no prospect of taking vengeance, and we feel comparatively little anger, or none at all, with those who are much our superiors in power."[10] The anger was still there, however, but it got directed towards safer targets: my family and closest friends. My anger spread, giving me painful shooting signs that I was coming back to life. I could not accept what had happened to me. What was I supposed to do now? How could everyone else carry on with their lives when women were dying? How could Tom go on teaching his classes, seeing students, chatting with colleagues . . . and why should he be able to walk down the street when I couldn't?

The incompatibility of fear of my assailant and appropriate anger towards him became most apparent after I began taking a women's self-defense class. It became clear that the way to break out of the double bind of self-blame versus powerlessness was through empowerment—physical as well as political. Learning to fight back is a crucial part of this process, not only because it enables us to experience justified, healing rage, but also because, as Iris Young has observed in her essay "Throwing Like a Girl," "women in sexist society are physically handicapped," moving about hesitantly, fearfully, in a constricted lived space, routinely underestimating what strength we actually have. (Young 1990, 153) We have to learn to feel entitled to occupy space, to defend ourselves. The hardest thing for most of the women in my self-defense class to do was simply to yell 'No!' Women have been taught not to fight back when being attacked, to rely instead on placating or pleading with one's assailant—strategies that researchers have found to be least effective in resisting rape. (Bart and O'Brien 1984)

The instructor of the class, a survivor herself, helped me through the difficult first sessions, through the flashbacks and the fear, and showed me I could be tougher than ever. As I was leaving after one session, I saw a student arrive for the next class—with a guide dog. I was furious that, in addition to everything else this woman had to struggle with, she had to worry about being raped. I thought I understood something of her fear since I felt, for the first time in my life, like I had a perceptual deficit—not the blurred vision from the detached vitreous, but, rather, the more hazardous lack of eyes in the back of my head. I tried to compensate for this on my walks by looking over my shoulder a lot and punctuating my purposeful, straight ahead stride with an occasional pirouette, which must have made me look more whimsical than terrified.

The confidence I gained from learning how to fight back effectively not only enabled me to walk down the street again, it gave me back my life. But it was a changed life. A paradoxical life. I began to feel stronger than ever before, and more vulnerable, more determined to fight to change the world, but in need of several naps a day. News that friends found distressing in a less visceral way—the trials of the defendants in the Central Park jogger case, the controversy over *American Psycho*, the Gulf War, the Kennedy rape case, the Tyson trial, the fatal stabbing of law professor Mary Jo Frug near Harvard Square, the ax murders of two women graduate students at Dartmouth College—triggered debilitating flashbacks in me. Unlike survivors of wars or earthquakes, who inhabit a common shattered world, rape victims face the cataclysmic destruction of their world alone, surrounded by people who find it hard to understand what's so distressing. I realized that I exhibited every symptom of post-traumatic stress disorder—disassociation, flashbacks, hypervigilance, exaggerated startle response, sleep disorders, inability to concentrate, diminished interest in significant activities, and a sense of a foreshortened future.[11] I could understand why children exposed to urban violence have such trouble envisioning their futures. Although I had always been career-oriented, always planning for my future, I could no longer imagine how I would get through each day, let alone what I might be doing in a year's time. I didn't think I would ever write or teach philosophy again.

The American Psychiatric Association's *Diagnostic and Statistical Manual* defines post-traumatic stress disorder, in part, as the result of "an event that is outside the range of usual human experience."[12] Because the trauma is, to most people, inconceivable, it's also unspeakable. Even when I managed to find the words—and the strength—to describe my ordeal, it was hard for others to hear about it. They would have preferred me to just "buck up," as one friend urged me to do. But it's essential to talk about it, again and again. It's a way of remastering the trauma, although it can be retraumatizing when people refuse to listen. In my case, each time someone failed to respond it felt as though I were alone again in the ravine, dying, screaming. And still no one could hear me. Or, worse, they heard me, but refused to help.

I now know they were trying to help, but that recovering from trauma takes time, patience, and, most of all, determination on the part of the survivor. After about six months, I began to be able to take more responsibility for my own recovery, and stopped expecting others to pull me through. I entered the final stage of my recovery, a period of gradual acceptance and integration of what had happened. I joined a rape survivors' support group, I got a great deal of therapy, and I became involved in political activities, such as promoting S.15: the Violence against Women Act of 1991, currently before the United States Senate.[13] Gradually, I was able to get back to work.

When I resumed teaching at Dartmouth in the fall of 1991, the first student who came to see me in my office during freshman orientation week told me that she had been raped. Last spring four Dartmouth students reported sexual assaults to the local police. In the aftermath of these recent reports, the women students on my campus have been told to use their heads, lock their doors, not go out after dark without a male escort. They have been advised: just don't do anything stupid.

Although colleges are eager to "protect" women by limiting their freedom of movement or providing them with male escorts, they continue to be reluctant to teach women to protect themselves. After months of lobbying the administration at my college, we were able to convince them to offer a women's self-defense and rape prevention course. It was offered last winter as a Physical Education course, and nearly 100 students and employees signed up for it. Shortly after the course began, I was informed that the women students were not going to be allowed to get P.E. credit for it, since the administration had determined that it discriminated against men. I was told that granting credit for the course was in violation of Title IX, which prohibits sex-discrimination in education programs receiving federal funding—even though granting credit to men for being on the football team was not, even though Title IX law makes an explicit exception for P.E. classes involving substantial bodily contact, and even though every term the college offers several martial arts courses, for credit, that are open to men, geared to men's physiques and need, and taken predominantly by men. I was told by an administrator that, even if Title IX permitted it, offering a women's self-defense course for credit violated "the College's non-discrimination clause—a clause which, I hope, all reasonable men and women support as good policy." The implication that I was not a "reasonable woman" didn't sit well with me as a philosopher, so I wrote a letter to the appropriate administrative committee criticizing my college's position that single-sex sports, male-only fraternities, female-only sororities, and pregnancy leave policies are not discriminatory, in any invidious sense, while a women's self-defense class is. The administration has finally agreed to grant P.E. credit for the course, but shortly after that battle was over, I read in the *New York Times* that "a rape prevention ride service offered to women in the city of Madison and on the University of Wisconsin campus may lose its university financing because it discriminates against men."[14] The Dean of Students at Wisconsin said that this group—the Women's Transit Authority—which has been providing free nighttime rides to women students for nineteen years—must change its policy to allow male drivers and passengers. These are, in my view, examples of the application of what Catharine MacKinnon refers to as "the stupid theory of equality."[15] To argue that rape prevention policies for women discriminate against men is like arguing that money spent making university buildings more accessible to disabled persons discriminates against those able-bodied persons who do not benefit from these improvements.[16]

Sexual violence victimizes not only those women who are directly attacked, but *all* women. The fear of rape has long functioned to keep women in their place. Whether or not one agrees with the claims of those, such as Susan Brownmiller, who argue that rape is a means by which *all* men keep *all* women subordinate (Brownmiller 1975), the fact that all women's lives are restricted by sexual violence is indisputable. The authors of *The Female Fear*, Margaret Gordon and Stephanie Riger, cite studies substantiating what every woman already knows—that the fear of rape prevents women from enjoying what men consider to be their birthright. Fifty percent of women never use public transportation after dark because of fear of rape. Women are 8 times more likely than men to avoid walking in their own neighborhoods after dark, for the same reason. (Gordon and Riger 1991) In the seminar I taught last spring on Violence against Women, the men in the class were stunned by the extent to which the women in the class took precautions against assault every day—locking doors and windows, checking the back seat of the car, not walking alone at night, looking in closets on returning home. And this is at a 'safe,' rural New England campus.

Although women still have their work and leisure opportunities unfairly restricted by their relative lack of safety, paternalistic legislation excluding women from some of the 'riskier' forms of employment (e.g. bartending[17]) has, thankfully, disappeared, except, that is, in the military. We are still debating whether women should be permitted to engage in combat, and the latest rationale for keeping women out of battle is that they are more vulnerable than men to sexual violence. Those wanting to limit women's role in the military are now using the reported indecent assaults on the two female American prisoners of war in Iraq as evidence for women's unsuitability for combat.[18] One might as well argue that the fact that women are much more likely than men to be sexually assaulted on college campuses is evidence that women are not suited to post-secondary education. No one, to my knowledge, has proposed returning Ivy League colleges to their former all-male status as a solution to the problem of campus rape. Some have, however seriously proposed enacting after-dark curfews for women, in spite

of the fact that men are the perpetrators of the assaults. This is yet another indication of how natural it still seems to many people to address the problem of sexual violence by curtailing women's lives. The absurdity of this approach becomes apparent once one realizes that a woman can be sexually assaulted anywhere, at any time—in 'safe' places, in broad daylight, even in her own home.

For months after my assault, I was afraid of people finding out about it—afraid of their reactions and of their inability to respond. I was afraid that my professional work would be discredited, that I would be viewed as 'biased,' or, even worse, not properly 'philosophical.' Now I am no longer afraid of what might happen if I speak out about sexual violence. I'm much more afraid of what *will* continue to happen if I don't. Sexual violence is a problem of catastrophic proportions—a fact obscured by its mundanity, by its relentless occurrence, by the fact that so many of us have been victims of it. Imagine the moral outrage, the emergency response we would surely mobilize, if all of these everyday assaults occurred at the same time or were restricted to one geographical region? But why should the spatio-temporal coordinates of the vast numbers of sexual assaults be considered to be morally relevant? From the victim's point of view, the fact that she is isolated in her rape and her recovery, combined with the ordinariness of the crime that leads to its trivialization, makes the assault and its aftermath even more traumatic.

As devastating as sexual violence is, however, I want to stress that it is possible to survive it, and even to flourish after it, although it doesn't seem that way at the time. Whenever I see a survivor struggling with the overwhelming anger and sadness, I'm reminded of a sweet, motherly, woman in my rape survivors' support group who sat silently throughout the group's first meeting. At the end of the hour she finally asked, softly, through tears: "Can anyone tell me if it ever stops hurting?" At the time I had the same question, and wasn't satisfied with any answer. Now I can say, yes, it does stop hurting, at least for longer periods of time. A year ago, I was pleased to discover that I could go for fifteen minutes without thinking about my attack. Now I can go for hours at a stretch without a flashback. That's on a good day. On a bad day, I may still take to my bed with lead in my veins, unable to find one good reason to go on.

Our group facilitator told us that first meeting: "You will never be the same. But you can be better." I protested that I had lost so much: my security, my self-esteem, my love and my work. I had been happy with the way things were. How could they ever be better now? As a survivor, she knew how I felt, but she also knew that, as she put it, "When your life is shattered, you're forced to pick up the pieces, and you have a chance to stop and examine them. You can say, 'I don't want this one anymore' or 'I think I'll work on that one.'" I have had to give up more than I would ever have chosen to. But I have gained important skills and insights, and I no longer feel tainted by my victimization. Granted, those of us who live through sexual assault aren't given ticker tape parades or the keys to our cities, but it's an honor to be a survivor. Although it's not exactly the sort of thing I can put on my résumé, it's the accomplishment of which I'm most proud.

Now, more than two years after the assault, I can acknowledge the good things that have come from the recovery process—the clarity, the confidence, the determination, the many supporters and survivors who have brought meaning back into my world. This is not to say that the attack and its aftermath were, on balance, a good thing or, as one aunt put it, "a real blessing from above." I would rather not have gone down that road. It's been hard for me, as a philosopher, to learn the lesson that knowledge isn't always desirable, that the truth doesn't always set you free. Sometimes, it fills you with incapacitating terror and, then, uncontrollable rage. But I suppose you should embrace it anyway, for the reason Nietzsche exhorts you to love your enemies: if it doesn't kill you, it makes you stronger.

People ask me if I'm recovered now, and I reply that it depends on what that means. If they mean "am I back to where I was before the attack"? I have to say, no, and I never will be. I am not the same person who set off, singing, on that sunny Fourth of July in the French countryside. I left her—and her trust, her innocence, her joie de vivre—in a rocky creek bed at the bottom of a ravine. I had to in order to survive. I now understand what a friend described to me as a Jewish custom of giving those who have outlived a brush with death new names. The trauma has changed me forever, and if I insist too often that my friends and family acknowledge it, that's because I'm afraid they don't know who I am.

But if recovery means being able to incorporate this awful knowledge into my life and carry on, then, yes, I'm recovered. I don't wake each day with a start, thinking: "this can't have happened to me!" It happened. I have no guarantee that it won't happen again, although my self-defense classes have given me the confidence to move about in the world and to go for longer and longer walks—with my two dogs. Sometimes I even manage to enjoy myself. And I no longer cringe when I see a woman jogging alone on the country road where I live, though I may still have a slight urge to rush out and protect her, to tell her to come inside where she'll be safe. But I catch myself, like a mother learning to let go, and cheer her on, thinking, may she always be so carefree, so at home in her world. She has every right to be.

REFERENCES

Allen, Jeffner, 1986. *Lesbian Philosophy: Explorations*. Palo Alto: Institute of Lesbian Studies.

American Psychiatric Association. 1987. *Diagnostic and Statistical Manual of Mental Disorders*. 3rd ed., rev. Washington, D.C.: American Psychiatric Association.

Bard, Morton and Dawn Sangrey. 1986. *The Crime Victim's Book*. New York: Brunner/Mazel.

Barnes, Jonathan, ed. 1984. *The Complete Works of Aristotle*, Vol. 2. Princeton: Princeton University Press.

Bart, Pauline B. and Patricia H. O'Brien. 1984. "Stopping Rape: Effective Avoidance Strategies." *Signs: Journal of Women in Culture and Society* 10 (1): 83–101.

Benedict, Helen. 1985. *Recovery: How To Survive Sexual Assault—for Women, Men, Teenagers, Their Friends and Families.* Garden City, New York: Doubleday.

Brownmiller, Susan. 1975. *Against Our Will: Men, Women, and Rape.* New York: Bantam Books.

deSousa, Ronald. 1987. *The Rationality of Emotion.* Cambridge, Mass.: MIT Press.

Estrich, Susan. 1987. *Real Rape.* Cambridge, Massachusetts: Harvard University Press.

Gordon, Margaret T. and Stephanie Riger. 1991. *The Female Fear: The Social Cost of Rape.* Chicago: University of Illinois Press.

Harrison, Ross. 1986. "Rape—a Case Study in Political Philosophy." In *Rape: An Historical and Cultural Enquiry*, ed. Sylvana Tomaselli and Roy Porter, 41–56. New York: Basil Blackwell.

Herman, Judith Lewis. 1992. *Trauma and Recovery.* New York: Basic Books.

Janoff-Bulman, Ronnie. 1992. *Shattered Assumptions: Towards a New Psychology of Trauma.* New York: The Free Press.

Lawrence, Charles R., III. 1990. "If He Hollers Let Him Go: Regulating Racist Speech on Campus." *Duke Law Journal* 1990: 431–83.

Lowell, Robert. 1977. *Selected Poems*, 82. New York: Farrar, Straus and Giroux.

Matsuda, Mari. 1989. "Public Response to Racist Speech: Considering the Victim's Story." *Michigan Law Review* 87 (8): 2320–81.

Miedzian, Myriam. 1991. *Boys Will Be Boys: Breaking the Link between Masculinity and Violence.* New York: Doubleday.

Minow, Martha. 19990. *Making All the Difference: Inclusion, Exclusion, and American Law.* Ithaca, New York: Cornell University Press.

Noddings, Nell. 1989. *Women and Evil.* Berkeley: University of California Press.

Nozick, Robert. 1989. *The Examined Life: Philosophical Meditations.* New York: Touchstone Books.

Pineau, Lois. 1989. "Date Rape: A Feminist Analysis." *Law and Philosophy* 8: 217–243.

Russell, Diana E.H. and Nancy Howell. 1983. "The Prevalence of Rape in the United States Revisited." *Signs: Journal of Women in Culture and Society* 8 (4): 688–695.

Warshaw, Robin. 1988. *I Never Called It Rape.* New York: Harper & Row.

Williams, Patricia J. 1991. *The Alchemy of Race and Rights.* Cambridge, Massachusetts: Harvard University Press.

Young, Iris Marion. 1990. *Throwing Like a Girl and Other Essays in Feminist Philosophy and Social Theory.* Indianapolis: Indiana University Press.

Ziegenmeyer, Nancy. 1992. *Taking Back My Life.* New York: Summit Books.

NOTES

1. I would like to thank the North American Society for Social Philosophy for inviting me to give this paper as a plenary address at the Eighth International Social Philosophy Conference, Davidson College, August 1, 1992. I am also grateful to the Franklin J. Matchette Foundation for sponsoring this talk.

2. Federal Bureau of Investigation, *Uniform Crime Reports for the United States*, 1989, 6.

3. Robin Warshaw notes that "[g]overnment estimates find that anywhere from three to ten rapes are committed for every one rape reported. And while rapes by strangers are still underreported, rapes by acquaintances are virtually nonreported. Yet, based on intake observations made by staff at various rape counseling centers (where victims come for treatment, but do not have to file police reports), 70–80 percent of all rape crimes are acquaintance rapes." (Warshaw 1988, 12).

4. National Coalition against Domestic Violence, fact sheet, in "Report on Proposed Legislation S.15: The Violence against Women Act," 9. On file with the Senate Judiciary Committee.

5. After I presented this paper at Davidson College, Iris Young drew my attention to Jeffner Allen's discussion of her rape (Allen 1986).

6. Another, much more perceptive, article is Lois Pineau's "Date Rape: A Feminist Analysis" (Pineau 1989). In addition, an excellent book on the causes of male violence was written by a scholar trained as a philosopher, Myriam Miedzian (Miedzian 1991). Philosophical discussions of the problem of evil, even recent ones such as that in (Nozick 1991), don't mention the massive problem of sexual violence. Even Nell Noddings' book, *Women and Evil*, which is an "attempt to describe evil from the perspective of women's experience" (Noddings 1989) mentions rape only twice, briefly, and in neither instance from the victim's point of view.

7. See especially Patricia Williams' discussion of the Ujaama House incident in *The Alchemy of Race and Rights* (Williams 1991, 110–116), Mari Matsuda, "Public Response to Racist Speech: Considering the Victim's Story" (Matsuda 1989), and Charles Lawrence, "If He Hollers, Let Him Go: Regulating Racist Speech on Campus" (Lawrence 1990).

8. As the authors of *The Female Fear* note: "The requirement of proof of the victim's nonconsent is unique to the crime of forcible rape. A robbery victim, for example, is usually not considered as having 'consented' to the crime if he or she hands money over to an assailant [especially if there was use of force or threat of force]." (Gordon and Riger 1991, 59).

9. Quoted in *The New York Times,* September 13, 1991, p. A18. Although Judge Thomas made this statement during his confirmation hearings, Justice Thomas' actions while on the Supreme Court have belied his professed empathy with criminal defendants.

10. (Barnes, 1984, 2181–2). I thank John Cooper for drawing my attention to this aspect of Aristotle's theory of the emotions.

11. For a clinical description of Post-traumatic Stress Disorder (or PTSD), see the *Diagnostic and Statistical Manual,* 3rd ed., rev., (American Psychiatric Association 1987). Excellent discussions of the recovery process undergone by rape survivors can be found in (Bard and Sangrey 1986), (Benedict 1985), (Herman 1992), and (Janoff-Bulman 1992). I have also found it very therapeutic to read first person accounts by rape survivors such as Susan Estrich (Estrich 1987) and Nancy Ziegenmeyer (Ziegenmeyer 1992).

12. (American Psychiatric Association 1987, 247).

13. S.15, sponsored by Sen. Joseph Biden, D-Del., was drafted largely by Victoria Nourse, Special Counsel for Criminal Law, Office of the Senate Judiciary Committee. I am particularly interested in Title III, which would reclassify gender motivated assaults as bias crimes. From the victim's

perspective this reconceptualization is important. What was most difficult for me to recover from was the knowledge that some man wanted to kill me simply because I am a woman. This aspect of the harm inflicted in hate crimes (or bias crimes) is similar to the harm caused by hate speech. One cannot make a sharp distinction between physical and psychological harm in the case of PTSD sufferers. Most of the symptoms are physiological. I find it odd that in Philosophy of Law, so many theorists are devoted to a kind of Cartesian dualism that most philosophers of mind rejected long ago.

14. *The New York Times,* April 19, 1992, p. 36.

15. She characterized a certain theory of equality in this way during the discussion after a Gauss seminar she gave at Princeton University, April 9, 1992.

16. For an illuminating discussion of the ways in which we need to treat people differently in order to achieve genuine equality see (Minow 1990).

17. As recently as 1948, the United States Supreme Court upheld a state law prohibiting the licensing of any woman as a bartender (unless she was the wife or daughter of the bar owner where she was applying to work). *Goesaert v. Cleary,* 335 U.S. 464 (1948).

18. *The New York Times,* June 19, 1992, p. 1, A13.

Raped: A Male Survivor Breaks His Silence

Fred Pelka

The man who raped me had a remarkable self-assurance which could only have come from practice. He picked me up just outside Cleveland, heading east in a van filled with construction equipment. That early morning in May I'd already spent a sleepless 24 hours trying to hitchhike from Oxford, Mississippi to Buffalo, New York, so it felt good when I was offered a ride through the western fringe of Pennsylvania. First, though, the driver told me he needed to stop along the way, to pick up some building supplies. We drove to a country club undergoing renovation, where I hung out with his co-workers while he signed for several boxes of equipment which we carried back to his van. Getting back onto the turnpike he told me about one more stop he had to make.

As a man, I've been socialized never to admit to being vulnerable, to discuss those moments when I wasn't in control. I know also how women and children are routinely punished when they speak out about abuse, how they are blamed for their own victimization. The examples are endless: Witness the contempt with which Anita Hill was treated. For these reasons and more I'm still reticent, years after it happened, to recount what happened to me that day in Ohio. This article marks the first time in 15 years I have publicly discussed it under my own name.

The second building seemed deserted. We went up a flight of stairs, down a corridor into a side room. I looked around for the equipment he'd mentioned, and noticed him locking the door behind us. He slugged me before I could react, forced me down with his hands around my throat. As I began to lose consciousness I heard him say, "If you scream, if you make one wrong move, I'll kill you."

Fred Pelka, "Raped: A Male Survivor Breaks His Silence," *On the Issues: The Progressive Women's Quarterly* 22 (Spring 1992): 10–11, 40. Reprinted by permission of *On the Issues.*

The police told me later that the man who raped me was a suspect in the rapes of at least six other young men. During the assault his mood swung from vicious, when he promised to strangle me or break my neck, to self-pity, when he wept because we were both among "the wounded ones." In that enormous calm that comes after the acceptance of death, I wondered who would find my body.

Most rapes don't happen like this. Most victims know their attacker(s)—he is a neighbor, friend, husband, or father, a teacher, minister or doctor. The vast majority of rapes are committed by men against women and children, and the FBI estimates that anywhere from 80 to 90 percent go unreported. Rape is an integral part of our culture, and fully one third of all women in this country will be raped at some point in their lives. But this sexist violence does occasionally spill over onto boys and men. The National Crime Survey for 1989 estimated that one in 12 rape survivors is male.

For all this, nobody really knows how many men are raped each year, or how many boys are sexually abused. One study at the University of New Hampshire found that one in 11 young men surveyed had been sexually abused before their 18th birthday. I've seen articles which speculate that anywhere from one in nine to one in seven men will be raped or sexually abused in their lifetime, most often by other males, but these are little more than guesses.

"Since rape is generally misconstrued to be a sexually motivated crime," write Dr. A. Nicholas Groth and Anne Wolbert Burgess, "it is generally assumed that males are unlikely targets of such victimization, and then when it does occur, it reflects a homosexual orientation on the part of the offender. However, the causes of male rape that we have had an opportunity to study do not lend much support to either assumption." Groth and Burgess interviewed men in the community who had been raped, and men who admitted to raping other men, and published their findings in the *American Journal of Psychiatry*. In half the cases they studied, the gender of the victim "did not appear to be of specific significance" to the rapist. "Their victims included males and females, adults and children," and "may symbolize . . . something they want to conquer or defeat. The assault is an act of retaliation, an expression of power, and an assertion of their strength or manhood."

In their article, Burgess and Groth dispute some of the prevalent myths about male rape. The first is that men simply don't get raped, at least not outside prison. Of course, if men don't get raped then what happened to me either wasn't rape (the police asking, "Did you come?"), or I'm not a man (my male friends wanting to know how I could "let something like this" happen to me). The second myth—that all men who are raped or rape other men are gay—is a product of our culture's homophobia, and our ignorance of the realities of sexual violence. Most people find it difficult to understand why a straight man would rape another straight man. But if you see rape as a way of exerting control, of confirming your own power by disempowering others, then it makes perfect sense. If it makes you feel powerful and macho to force sex on a woman or child, think of how much more powerful you feel raping another man.

"I have a special place," the man who raped me said after a long while. "It's out in the country, where we can make all the noise we want." It seemed obvious what would happen to me once we arrived at "his special place," but I knew there was no hope for my survival as long as we stayed in that room. So I agreed to go with him to "the country." I promised not to try to escape. It is perhaps an indication of his fragile hold on reality that he believed me.

We walked back to his van and drove away. I waited until I saw some people, then jumped as we slowed to make a turn, rolling as I hit the pavement. I ran into the nearest building—a restaurant—just as patrons were finishing their lunch. Conversation stopped, and I was confronted by a roomful of people, forks raised in mid-bite, staring.

"I think you'd better call the police," I told the waitress. This was all I could say, placing my hands flat on the counter between us to control their trembling. She poured me a cup of black coffee. And then the police arrived.

The two detectives assigned to my case conformed to the standard good cop/bad cop archetype. The good cop told me how upset he'd seen "girls" become after being raped. "But you're a man, this shouldn't bother you." Later on he told me that the best thing to do would be to pull up my pants "and forget it ever happened." The bad cop asked me why my hair was so long, what was I doing hitchhiking at seven o'clock in the morning? Why were my clothes so dirty? Did I do drugs? Was I a troublemaker?

I used to be puzzled at how the bad cop obviously didn't believe me, in spite of the fact that, by his own account, in the months before my assault six other men had come to him with similar stories. Then I heard of the Dahmer case in Milwaukee, how in May 1991 Dahmer's neighbors saw him chasing a naked 14-year-old boy, bleeding from the anus, through the alley behind their building. The responding officers returned the boy to Dahmer's apartment, where Dahmer explained that this was just a lover's spat, which the police believed in spite of the youth's apparent age, and the photos scattered on Dahmer's floor of murdered and mutilated boys and men. The police reassured a neighbor who called again, saying that everything was all right—this at the very moment Dahmer was murdering Konerak Sinthasomphone. Afterwards Dahmer dismembered Sinthasomphone's body.

Sinthasomphone was one of at least 17 boys and men raped and murdered by Dahmer, their body parts stored in vats and freezers in his apartment. It was reported that his first assaults were committed in Ohio, so I had to brace myself before I could look at Jeffrey Dahmer's photo in the paper. At first I was relieved to find that he was not the man who raped me. Then I thought how this meant my assailant is likely still out there, looking for more "wounded ones."

Because I gave them such detailed information—the country club, the name painted on the side of his van—the detectives were able to locate my assailant not too many hours after I was brought into their precinct. The good cop asked, after I identified the rapist, whether I wanted to press charges. He explained how I'd have to return to Ohio to appear before a grand jury, and then return again for the trial, how the newspapers would publish my name, how little chance there was of a conviction.

"He says you seduced him," the good cop said. "So it's your word against his."

The bad cop glared at me when I told them there was no way I wanted any of this to be made public. "You mean," he fumed, "I wasted my whole afternoon on this shit?" Standing in front of me with an expression of disgust, he asked, "How do you think this makes me feel?"

By then it was getting dark. I hitchhiked the remaining 200 miles home, studying every movement of every man who offered me a ride. I arrived at my apartment after midnight, walking the last 10 miles.

In the weeks that followed the assault, every stupid, insensitive thing I'd every said about rape came back to haunt me. A friend of mine had been attacked several months earlier, also while hitchhiking. She told me just a few hours after it happened how she'd missed her bus, and didn't want to be late to work. She said the man offering her a lift seemed normal enough, even "nice."

"You should've waited for the next bus," I lectured. Today I cringe at my arrogance. Hitchhiking, like walking alone after dark, or feeling safe on a date, at work, at home, is another perquisite to which only men are entitled. How dare she not understand the limits of her freedom?

While women tell me that the possibility of rape is never far from their minds, most men never give it a first, let alone a second, thought. This may explain why they react so negatively to accounts by male survivors. To see rape as "a women's issue" is a form of male privilege most men would prefer not to surrender. They would rather believe that they can move with immunity through the toxic atmosphere of violence and fear they and their compatriots create. Being a male survivor meant I'd lost some of that immunity. No wonder I felt as if I'd been poisoned, as if I were drowning.

For years I pretended, as per the good cop's recommendation, that nothing had happened, secretly feeling that I was somehow responsible, somehow less masculine. The turning point came with the media storm that swirled up around the Big Dan rape in New Bedford, Massachusetts. The moved "The Accused" is based on that incident—a woman assaulted in a bar while other men looked on and cheered. Naïve as I was, I figured this was a pretty clear-cut case. Where the police might have doubted my will to resist (no broken bones, no massive lacerations), here was a victim overpowered by half a dozen men. How could anyone doubt that she had been brutalized? Yet, during the trial, *The Boston Herald* ran the front page headline "SHE LED US ON!" I realized then that, even had I been murdered, someone would have inevitably questioned my complicity: "He probably liked rough sex."

It's just this sort of victim-blaming that discourages survivors from reporting their trauma, or seeking treatment, but there are other factors which may discourage males in particular. Homophobia for one: The sort of gender McCarthyism that labels any man a faggot who cannot or will not conform to accepted norms of masculine feeling or behavior. Men who rape other men capitalize on this, knowing that straight victims don't want to appear gay, and gay victims might fear coming out of the closet. Groth and Burgess report, for instance, that "a major strategy used by some offenders . . . is to get the victim to ejaculate." This "strategy" was attempted in roughly half the cases they studied, and in half of those the rapist succeeded in ejaculating his victim. This confuses the victim, who often misidentifies ejaculation with orgasm. It confirms for the rapist the old canard about how victims "really want it." And, as Groth and Burgess say, it leaves the survivor "discouraged from reporting the assault for fear his sexuality may be suspect."

For male survivors of child sexual abuse there is also the unfortunate theory that boys who are abused inevitably grow up to be men who rape. One survivor told me it was for this reason he had decided never to be a father. Not that he'd ever wanted to abuse children, nor was there any evidence he ever would. He eventually came to realize that because some rapists are themselves survivors doesn't mean that all male survivors of child sexual abuse turn out to be rapists.

Finally, rape crisis centers [RCCs], the only institutions in our society founded expressly to help rape survivors, are identified by some men as hotbeds of feminism, and many men take "feminist" to mean "man-hating." It's true that the vast majority of rape crisis counselors are women, that the entire stop-rape movement is an extension of the women's movement. For the record, though, I have never felt any hostility in response when calling a rape crisis center, this in spite of the fact that RCCs are often plagued by "hotline abusers"—men who call to masturbate to the sound of a female voice.

On the other hand, I've run across a good deal of hostility towards women from male survivors with whom I've talked. One man told me how certain he was that the counselors at his local RCC hated men, even though, by his own admission, he'd never called, and knew no one who had. A while back I attended a survivors' conference organized by a Boston women's group, attended by several hundred women and maybe a dozen men. One of these men stood up during a plenary session to shout at the women on the podium. As an incest survivor, he said, he felt "marginalized" and "oppressed" by the way the conference was run, despite the fact that a number of the workshops were specifically geared toward males, and that a keynote speaker received a standing ovation when he described his work with boys and men. Some male survivors even blame women for the denial and homophobia they encounter after their assault. They openly resent the (pitifully few) resources available to female survivors, as if any help women receive is at the expense of men. Even Geraldo has picked up this theme: His show on male survivors ended with an attack on rape crisis centers for their alleged refusal to acknowledge male victimization.

This hostility has been exacerbated by the so-called men's movement, the Robert Bly/mythopoetic crowd, with their "Wild Man" and "Inner Warrior" archetypes. These men say a lot of absurd things about sexual violence, not the least of which is that "just as many men get raped as women." This last statement is often repeated by Chris Harding, editor of *Wingspan*, which *The Boston Globe* calls "the bible of the new men's movement." Harding is generally quick to add that most of these rapes "occur in prison"—a statement which is an inaccurate as it is pernicious, assuming as it does that a disproportionate number of male rapes are committed by working-class and minority men. The men's movement claims that rape is a "gender-neutral issue," and thus has nothing to do with sexism.

What is ironic about all this is that what little acknowledgment there is of male victimization generally comes from the *women's* stop-rape movement. To the extent that male survivors *can* tell their stories, it is because of the foundation laid by feminists. So this woman-bashing is as ungrateful as it is gratuitous.

One source of confusion appears to be the distinction between victimization and oppression. Male survivors charge that feminists see rape as a "man vs. woman" issue, emphasizing the central role male violence plays in stunting and destroying women's lives, and they're right. The distinction is that while many women, and some men, are victimized by rape, all women are oppressed by it, and any victimization of women occurs in a context of oppression most men simply do not understand. Rape for men is usually a bizarre, outrageous tear in the fabric of reality. For women, rape is often a confirmation of relative powerlessness, of men's contempt for women, and its trauma is reinforced every day in a thousand obvious and subtle ways.

For myself, I don't need for rape to be gender neutral to feel validated as a male survivor. And I certainly don't need to denigrate women, or to attack feminists, to explain why I was abused by the (male) police, ridiculed by my (male) friends, and marginalized by the (male dominated) society around me. It is precisely because we have been "reduced" to the status of *women* that other men find us so difficult to deal with. It was obvious to me at the police station that I was held in contempt because I was a *victim*—feminine, hence perceived as less masculine. Had I been an accused criminal, even a rapist, chances are I would have been treated with more respect, because I would have been seen as more of a man. To cross that line, to become victims of the violence which works to circumscribe the lives of women, marks us somehow as traitors to our gender. Being a male rape survivor means I no longer fit our culture's neat but specious definition of masculinity, as one empowered, one always in control. Rather than continue to deny our experience, male survivors need to challenge that definition.

As Diana E.H. Russell says in *The Politics of Rape*, "Women must start talking about rape: Their experiences, their fears, their thoughts. The silence about rape must be broken."

The same must be true for men. And so I offer this article as my first contribution to that effort.

38.

Rape: On Coercion and Consent

Catharine A. MacKinnon

Catharine A. MacKinnon is professor of law at the University of Michigan Law School. In addition to many articles, she has written *Feminism Unmodified, Toward a Feminist Theory of the State* and *Only Words*. In this essay, she challenges the conventional legal definition and social understanding of rape. MacKinnon argues that rape must be understood as more than an isolated, individual, aberrant act of sexual aggression. A more comprehensive and accurate understanding of rape requires taking into account the realities of male dominance, heterosexuality, and the status of women in society.

If sexuality is central to women's definition and forced sex is central to sexuality, rape is indigenous, not exceptional, to women's social condition. In feminist analysis, a rape is not an isolated event or moral transgression or individual interchange gone wrong but an act of terrorism and torture within a systemic context of group subjection, like lynching. The fact that the state calls rape a crime opens an inquiry into the state's treatment of rape as an index to its stance on the status of the sexes.

Catharine A. MacKinnon, *Towards a Feminist Theory of the State* (Cambridge: Harvard University Press, 1989), Chapter Nine. Copyright (c) 1989 by Catharine MacKinnon. Reprinted with the author's permission.

Under law, rape is a sex crime that is not regarded as a crime when it looks like sex. The law, speaking generally, defines rape as intercourse with force or coercion and without consent.[1] Like sexuality under male supremacy, this definition assumes the sadomasochistic definition of sex: intercourse with force or coercion can be or become consensual. It assumes pornography's positive-outcome-rape scenario; dominance plus submission is force plus consent. This equals sex, not rape. Under male supremacy, this is too often the reality. In a critique of male supremacy, the elements "with force and without consent" appear redundant. Force is present because consent is absent.

Like heterosexuality, male supremacy's paradigm of sex, the crime of rape centers on penetration.[2] The law to protect women's sexuality from forcible violation and expropriation defines that protection in male genital terms. Women do resent forced penetration. But penile invasion of the vagina may be less pivotal to women's sexuality, pleasure or violation, than it is to male sexuality. This definitive element of rape centers upon a male-defined loss. It also centers upon one way men define loss of exclusive access. In this light, rape, as legally defined, appears more a crime against female monogamy (exclusive access by one man) than against women's sexual dignity or intimate integrity. Analysis of rape in terms of concepts of property, often invoked in marxian analysis to criticize this disparity, fail to encompass the realities of rape.[3] Women's sexuality is, socially, a thing to be stolen, sold, bought, bartered, or exchanged by others. But women never own or possess it, and men never treat it, in law or in life, with the solicitude with which they treat property. To be property would be an improvement. The moment women "have" it—"have sex" in the dual gender/sexuality sense—it is lost as theirs. To have it is to have it taken away. This may explain the male incomprehension that, once a woman has had sex, she loses anything when subsequently raped. To them women have nothing to lose. It is true that dignitary harms,

because nonmaterial, are ephemeral to the legal mind. But women's loss through rape is not only less tangible; it is seen as unreal. It is difficult to avoid the conclusion that penetration itself is considered a violation from the male point of view, which is both why it is the centerpiece of sex and why women's sexuality, women's gender definition, is stigmatic. The question for social explanation becomes not why some women tolerate rape but how any women manage to resent it.

Rape cases finding insufficient evidence of force reveal that acceptable sex, in the legal perspective, can entail a lot of force. This is both result of the way specific facts are perceived and interpreted within the legal system and the way the injury is defined by law. The level of acceptable force is adjudicated starting just above the level set by what is seen as normal male sexual behavior, including the normal level of force, rather than at the victim's, or women's, point of violation.[4] In this context, to seek to define rape as violent not sexual is as understandable as it is futile. Some feminists have reinterpreted rape as an act of violence, not sexuality, the threat of which intimidates all women.[5] Others see rape, including its violence, as an expression of male sexuality, the social imperatives of which define as well as threaten all women.[6] The first, epistemologically in the liberal tradition, comprehends rape as a displacement of power based on physical force onto sexuality, a preexisting natural sphere to which domination is alien. Susan Brownmiller, for example, examines rape in riots, wars, pogroms, and revolutions; rape by police, parents, prison guards; and rape motivated by racism. Rape in normal circumstances, in everyday life, in ordinary relationships, by men as men, is barely mentioned.[7] Women are raped by guns, age, white supremacy, the state—only derivatively by the penis. The view that derives most directly from victims' experiences, rather than from their denial, construes sexuality as a social sphere of male power to which forced sex is paradigmatic. Rape is not less sexual for being violent. To the extent that coercion has become integral to male sexuality, rape may even be sexual to the degree that, and because, it is violent.

The point of defining rape as "violence not sex" has been to claim an ungendered and non-sexual ground for affirming sex (heterosexuality) while rejecting violence (rape). The problem remains what it has always been: telling the difference. The convergence of sexuality with violence, long used at law to deny the reality of women's violation, is recognized by rape survivors with a difference: where the legal system has seen the intercourse in rape, victims see the rape in intercourse. The uncoerced context for sexual expression becomes as elusive as the physical acts come to feel indistinguishable. Instead of asking what is the violation of rape, their experience suggests that the more relevant question is, what is the nonviolation of intercourse? To know what is wrong with rape, know what is right about sex. If this, in turn, proves difficult, the difficulty is as instructive as the difficulty men have in telling the difference when women see one. Perhaps the wrong of rape has proved so difficult to define because the unquestionable starting point has been that rape is defined as distinct from intercourse,[8] while for women it is difficult to distinguish the two under conditions of male dominance.

In the name of the distinction between sex and violence, reform of rape statutes has sought to redefine rape as sexual assault.[9] Usually, assault is not consented to in law; either it cannot be consented to, or consensual assault remains assault.[10] Yet sexual assault consented to is intercourse, no matter how much force was used. The substantive reference point implicit in existing legal standards is the sexually normative level of force. Until this norm is confronted as such, no distinction between violence and sexuality will prohibit more instances of women's experienced violation than does the existing definition. Conviction rates have not increased under the reform statutes.[11] The question remains what is seen as force, hence as violence, in the sexual arena.[12] Most rapes, as women live

them, will not be seen to violate women until sex and violence are confronted as mutually definitive rather than as mutually exclusive. It is not only men convicted of rape who believe that the only thing they did that was different from what men do all the time is get caught.

Consent is supposed to be women's form of control over intercourse, different from but equal to the custom of male initiative. Man proposes, woman disposes. Even the ideal it is not mutual. Apart from the disparate consequences of refusal, this model does not envision a situation the woman controls being placed in, or choices she frames. Yet the consequences are attributed to her as if the sexes began at arm's length, on equal terrain, as in the contract fiction. Ambiguous cases of consent in law are archetypically referred to as "half won arguments in parked cars."[13] Why not half lost? Why isn't half enough? Why is it an argument? Why do men still want "it," feel entitled to "it," when women do not want them? The law of rape presents consent as free exercise of sexual choice under conditions of equality of power without exposing the underlying structure of constraint and disparity. Fundamentally, desirability to men is supposed a woman's form of power because she can both arouse it and deny its fulfillment. To woman is attributed both the cause of man's initiative and the denial of his satisfaction. This rationalizes force. Consent in this model becomes more a metaphysical quality of a woman's being than a choice she makes and communicates. Exercise of women's so-called power presupposes more fundamental social powerlessness.[14]

The law of rape divides women into spheres of consent according to indices of relationship to men. Which category of presumed consent a woman is in depends upon who she is relative to a man who wants her, not what she says or does. These categories tell men whom they can legally fuck, who is open season and who is off limits, not how to listen to women. The paradigm categories are the virginal daughter and other young girls, with whom all sex is proscribed, and the whorelike wives and prostitutes, with whom no sex is proscribed. Daughters may not consent; wives and prostitutes are assumed to, and cannot but.[15] Actual consent or nonconsent, far less actual desire, is comparatively irrelevant. If rape laws existed to enforce women's control over access to their sexuality, as the consent defense implies, no would mean no, marital rape would not be a widespread exception,[16] and it would not be effectively legal to rape a prostitute.

All women are divided into parallel provinces, their actual consent counting to the degree that they diverge from the paradigm case in their category. Virtuous women, like young girls, are unconsenting, virginal, rapable. Unvirtuous women, like wives and prostitutes, are consenting, whores, unrapable. The age line under which girls are presumed disabled from consenting to sex, whatever they say, rationalizes a condition of sexual coercion which women never outgrow. One day they cannot say yes, and the next day they cannot say no. The law takes the most aggravated case for female powerlessness based on gender and age combined and, by formally prohibiting all sex as rape, makes consent irrelevant on the basis of an assumption of powerlessness. This defines those above the age line as powerful, whether they actually have power to consent or not. The vulnerability girls share with boys—age—dissipates with time. The vulnerability girls share with women—gender—does not. As with protective labor laws for women only, dividing and protecting the most vulnerable becomes a device for not protecting everyone who needs it, and also may function to target those singled out for special protection for special abuse. Such protection has not prevented high rates of sexual abuse of children and may contribute to eroticizing young girls as forbidden.

As to adult women, to the extent an accused knows a woman and they have sex, her consent is inferred. The exemption for rape in marriage is consistent with the assumption underlying most adjudications of forcible rape: to the extent the

parties relate, it was not really rape, it was personal.[17] As marital exemptions erode, preclusions for cohabitants and voluntary social companions may expand. As a matter of fact, for this purpose one can be acquainted with an accused by friendship or by meeting him for the first time at a bar or a party or by hitchhiking. In this light, the partial erosion of the marital rape exemption looks less like a change in the equation between women's experience of sexual violation and men's experience of intimacy, and more like a legal adjustment to the social fact that acceptable heterosexual sex is increasingly not limited to the legal family. So although the rape law may not now always assume that the woman consented simply because the parties are legally one, indices of closeness, of relationship ranging from nodding acquaintance to living together, still contraindicate rape. In marital rape cases, courts look for even greater atrocities than usual to undermine their assumption that if sex happened, she wanted it.[18]

This approach reflects men's experience that women they know do meaningfully consent to sex with them. *That* cannot be rape; rape must be by someone else, someone unknown. They do not rape women they know. Men and women are unequally socially situated with regard to the experience of rape. Men are a good deal more likely to rape than to be raped. This forms their experience, the material conditions of their epistemological position. Almost half of all women, by contrast, are raped or victims of attempted rape at least once in their lives. Almost 40 percent are victims of sexual abuse in childhood.[19] Women are more likely to be raped than to rape and are most often raped by men whom they know.[20]

Men often say that it is less awful for a woman to be raped by someone she is close to: "The emotional trauma suffered by a person victimized by an individual with whom sexual intimacy is shared as a normal part of an ongoing marital relationship is not nearly as severe as that suffered by a person who is victimized by one with whom that intimacy is not shared."[21]

Women often feel as or more traumatized from being raped by someone known or trusted, someone with whom at least an illusion of mutuality has been shared, than by some stranger. In whose interest is it to believe that it is not so bad to be raped by someone who has fucked you before as by someone who has not? Disallowing charges of rape in marriage may, depending upon one's view of normalcy, "remove a substantial obstacle to the resumption of normal marital relationships."[22] Note that the obstacle is not the rape but the law against it. Apparently someone besides feminists finds sexual victimization and sexual intimacy not all that contradictory under current conditions. Sometimes it seems as though women and men live in different cultures.

Having defined rape in male sexual terms, the law's problem, which becomes the victim's problem, is distinguishing rape from sex in specific cases. The adjudicated line between rape and intercourse commonly centers on some assessment of the woman's "will." But how should the law or the accused know a woman's will? The answer combines aspects of force with aspects of nonconsent with elements of resistance, still effective in some states.[23] Even when nonconsent is not a legal element of the offense, juries tend to infer rape from evidence of force or resistance. In Michigan, under its reform rape law, consent was judicially held to be a defense even though it was not included in the statute.[24]

The deeper problem is that women are socialized to passive receptivity; may have or perceive no alternative to acquiescence; may prefer it to the escalated risk of injury and the humiliation of a lost fight; submit to survive. Also, force and desire are not mutually exclusive under male supremacy. So long as dominance is eroticized, they never will be. Some women eroticize dominance and submission; it beats feeling forced. Sexual intercourse may be deeply unwanted, the woman would never have initiated it, yet no force may be present. So much force may have been used that the woman never risked saying no. Force may be used, yet the woman may prefer the sex—to avoid more force or because she, too, eroticizes dominance. Women and men know this. Considering rape as violence not sex evades, at the moment it most seems to confront, the issue of who controls women's sexuality and the dominance/submission dynamic that has defined it. When sex is violent, women may have lost control over what is done to them, but absence of force does not ensure the presence of that control. Nor, under conditions of male dominance, does the presence of force make an interaction nonsexual. If sex is normally something men do to women, the issue is less whether there was force than whether consent is a meaningful concept.[25]

To explain women's gender status on a rape theory, Susan Brownmiller argues that the threat of rape benefits all men.[26] How is unspecified. Perhaps it benefits them sexually, hence as a gender: male initiatives toward women carry the fear of rape as support for persuading compliance, the resulting appearance of which has been considered seduction and termed consent. Here the victims' perspective grasps what liberalism applied to women denies: that forced sex as sexuality is not exceptional in relations between the sexes but constitutes the social meaning of gender. "Rape is a man's act, whether it is a male or a female man and whether it is a man relatively permanently or relatively temporarily; and being raped is a woman's experience, whether it is a female or a male woman and whether it is a woman relatively permanently or relatively temporarily."[27] To be rapable, a position that is social not biological, defines what a woman is.

Marital rape and battery of wives have been separated by law. A feminist analysis suggests that assault by a man's fist is not so different from assault by a penis, not because both are violent but because both are sexual. Battery is often precipitated by women's noncompliance with gender requirements.[28] Nearly all incidents occur in the home, most in the kitchen or bedroom. Most murdered women are killed by their husbands or boyfriends, usually in the bed-room. The battery cycle accords with the rhythms of heterosexual sex.[29] The rhythm of lesbian sadomasochism is the same.[30] Perhaps violent interchanges, especially between genders, make sense in sexual terms.

The larger issue raised by sexual aggression for the interpretation of the relation between sexuality and gender is: what is heterosexuality? If it is the erotization of dominance and submission, altering the participants' gender does not eliminate the sexual, or even gendered, content of aggression. If heterosexuality is males over females, gender matters independently. Arguably, heterosexuality is a fusion of the two, with gender a social outcome, such that the acted upon is feminized, is the "girl" regardless of sex, the actor correspondingly masculinized. Whenever women are victimized, regardless of the biology of the perpetrator, this system is at work. But it is equally true that whenever powerlessness and ascribed inferiority are sexually exploited or enjoyed—based on age, race, physical stature or appearance or ability, or socially reviled or stigmatized status—the system is at work.

Battery thus appears sexual on a deeper level. Stated in boldest terms, sexuality is violent, so perhaps violence is sexual. Violence against women is sexual on both counts, doubly sexy. If this is so, wives are beaten, as well as raped, as women—as the acted upon, as gender, meaning sexual, objects. It further follows that acts by anyone which treat a woman according to her object label, woman, are in a sense sexual acts. The extent to which sexual acts are acts of objectification remains a question of one's account of women's freedom to live their own meanings as other than illusions, of individuals' ability to resist or escape, even momentarily, prescribed social meanings short of political change. Clearly, centering sexuality upon genitality distinguishes battery from rape at exactly the juncture that both existing law, and seeing rape as violence not sex, do.

Most women get the message that the law against rape is virtually unenforceable as applied to them. Women's experience is more often delegitimated by this than the law is. Women, as realists, distinguish between rape and experiences of sexual violation by concluding that they have not "really" been raped if they have ever seen or dated or slept with or been married to the man, if they were fashionably dressed or not provably virgin, if they are prostitutes, if they put up with it or tried to get it over with, if they were force-fucked for years. The implicit social standard becomes: if a woman probably could not prove it in court, it was not rape.

The distance between most intimate violations of women and the legally perfect rape measures the imposition of an alien definition. From women's point of view, rape is not prohibited; it is regulated. Even women who know they have been raped do not believe that the legal system will see it as they do. Often they are not wrong. Rather than deterring or avenging rape, the state, in many victims' experiences, perpetuates it. Women who charge rape say they were raped twice, the second time in court. Under a male state, the boundary violation, humiliation, and indignity of being a public sexual spectacle makes this more than a figure of speech.[31]

Rape, like many other crimes, requires that the accused possess a criminal mind (*mens rea*) for his acts to be criminal. The man's mental state refers to what he actually understood at the time or to what a reasonable man should have understood under the circumstances. The problem is that the injury of rape lies in the meaning of the act to its victim, but the standard for its criminality lies in the meaning of the act to the assailant. Rape is only an injury from women's point of view. It is only a crime from the male point of view, explicitly including that of the accused.

The crime of rape is defined and adjudicated from the male standpoint, presuming that forced sex is sex and that consent to a man is freely given by a woman. Under male supremacist standards, of course, they are. Doctrinally, this means that the man's perceptions of the woman's desires determine whether she is deemed violated. This might be like other crimes of subjective intent if rape were like other crimes. With rape, because sexuality defines gender norms, the only difference between assault and what is socially defined as a noninjury is the meaning of the encounter to the woman. Interpreted this way, the legal problem has been to determine whose view of that meaning constitutes what really happened, as if what happened objectively exists to be objectively determined. This task has been assumed to be separable from the gender of the participants and the gendered nature of their exchange, when the objective norms and the assailant's perspective are identical.

As a result, although the rape law oscillates between subjective tests and objective standards invoking social reasonableness, it uniformly presumes a single underlying reality, rather than a reality split by the divergent meanings inequality produces. Many women are raped by men who know the meaning of their acts to their victims perfectly well and proceed anyway.[32] But women are also violated every day by men who have no idea of the meaning of their acts to the women. To them it is sex. Therefore, to the law it is sex. That becomes the single reality of what happened. When a rape prosecution is lost because a woman fails to prove that she did not consent, she is not considered to have been injured at all. It is as if a robbery victim, finding himself unable to prove he was not engaged in philanthropy, is told he still has his money. Hermeneutically unpacked, the law assumes that, because the rapist did not perceive that the woman did not want him, she was not violated. She had sex. Sex itself cannot be an injury. Women have sex every day. Sex makes a woman a woman. Sex is what women are for.

Men set sexual mores ideologically and behaviorally, define rape as they imagine women to be sexually violated through distinguishing that from their image of what they normally do, and sit in judgment in most accusations of sex crimes. So rape comes to mean a strange (read Black) man who does not know his victim but

does know she does not want sex with him, going ahead anyway. But men are systematically conditioned not even to notice what women want. Especially if they consume pornography, they may have not a glimmer of women's indifference or revulsion, including when women say no explicitly. Rapists typically believe the woman loved it. "Probably the single most used cry of rapist to victim is 'You bitch . . . slut . . . you know you want it. You all want it' and afterward, 'there now, you really enjoyed it, didn't you?'"[33] Women, as a survival strategy, must ignore or devalue or mute desires, particularly lack of them, to convey the impression that the man will get what he wants regardless of what they want. In this context, to measure the genuineness of consent from the individual assailant's point of view is to adopt as law the point of view which creates the problem. Measuring consent from the socially reasonable, meaning objective man's, point of view reproduces the same problem under a more elevated label.[34]

Men's pervasive belief that women fabricate rape charges after consenting to sex makes sense in this light. To them, the accusations are false because, to them, the facts describe sex. To interpret such events as rapes distorts their experience. Since they seldom consider that their experience of the real is anything other than reality, they can only explain the woman's version as maliciously invented. Similarly, the male anxiety that rape is easy to charge and difficult to disprove, also widely believed in the face of overwhelming evidence to the contrary, arises because rape accusations express one thing men cannot seem to control: the meaning to women of sexual encounters.

Thus do legal doctrines, incoherent or puzzling as syllogistic logic, become coherent as ideology. For example, when an accused wrongly but sincerely believes that a woman he sexually forced consented, he may have a defense of mistaken belief in consent or fail to satisfy the mental requirement of knowingly proceeding against her will.[35] Sometimes his knowing disregard is measured by what a reasonable man would disregard. This is considered an objective test. Sometimes the disregard need not be reasonable so long as it is sincere. This is considered a subjective test. A feminist inquiry into the distinction between rape and intercourse, by contrast, would inquire into the meaning of the act from women's point of view, which is neither. What is wrong with rape in this view is that it is an act of subordination of women to men. It expresses and reinforces women's inequality to men. Rape with legal impunity makes women second-class citizens.

This analysis reveals the way the social conception of rape is shaped to interpret particular encounters and the way the legal conception of rape authoritatively shapes that social conception. When perspective is bound up with situation, and situation is unequal, whether or not a contested interaction is authoritatively considered rape comes down to whose meaning wins. If sexuality is relational, specifically if it is a power relation of gender, consent is a communication under conditions of inequality. It transpires somewhere between what the woman actually wanted, what she was able to express about what she wanted, and what the man comprehended she wanted.

Discussing the conceptually similar issue of revocation of prior consent, on the issue of the conditions under which women are allowed to control access to their sexuality from one penetration to the next, one commentator notes: "Even where a woman revokes prior consent, such is the male ego that, seized of an exaggerated assessment of his sexual prowess, a man might genuinely believe her still to be consenting; resistance may be misinterpreted as enthusiastic cooperation; protestations of pain or disinclination, a spur to more sophisticated or more ardent love-making; a clear statement to stop, taken as referring to a particular intimacy rather than the entire performance."[36] This vividly captures common male readings of women's indications of disinclination under many circumstances[37] and the perceptions that determine whether a rape occurred. The specific defense of mistaken belief in consent merely carries this to its logical apex. From whose standpoint, and in whose interest, is a law that allows one person's conditioned unconsciousness to contraindicate another's violation? In conceiving a cognizable injury from the viewpoint of the reasonable rapist, the rape law affirmatively rewards men with acquittals for not comprehending women's point of view on sexual encounters.

Whether the law calls this coerced consent or defense of mistaken belief in consent, the more the sexual violation of women is routine, the more pornography exists in the world the more legitimately, the more beliefs equating sexuality with violation become reasonable, and the more honestly women can be defined in terms of their fuckability. It would be comparatively simple if the legal problem were limited to avoiding retroactive falsification of the accused's state of mind. Surely there are incentives to lie. The deeper problem is the rape law's assumption that a single, objective state of affairs existed, one that merely needs to be determined by evidence, when so many rapes involve honest men and violated women. When the reality is split, is the woman raped but not by a rapist? Under these conditions, the law is designed to conclude that a rape did not occur. To attempt to solve this problem by adopting reasonable belief as a standard without asking, on a substantive social basis, to whom the belief is reasonable and why—meaning, what conditions make it reasonable—is one-sided: male-sided.[38] What is it reasonable for a man to believe concerning a woman's desire for sex when heterosexuality is compulsory? What is it reasonable for a man (accused or juror) to believe concerning a woman's consent when he has been viewing positive-outcome-rape pornography?[39] The one whose subjectivity becomes the objectivity of "what happened" is a matter of social meaning, that is, a matter of sexual politics. One-sidedly erasing women's violation or dissolving presumptions into the subjectivity of either side are the alternatives dictated by the terms of the object/subject split, respectively. These alternatives will only retrace that split to women's detriment until its terms are confronted as gendered to the ground.

NOTES

1. W. LaFave and A. Scott, *Substantive Criminal Law* (St. Paul: West, 1986), sec. 5.11 (pp. 688–689); R. M. Perkins and R. N. Boyce, *Criminal Law* (Mineola, N.Y.: Foundation Press, 1980), p. 210.

2. One component of Sec. 213.0 of the Model Penal Code (Philadelphia: American Law Institute, 1980) defines rape as sexual intercourse with a female not the wife of the perpetrator, "with some penetration however slight." Most states follow. New York requires penetration (sec. 130.00 [I]). Michigan's gender-neutral sexual assault statute includes penetration by objects (sec. 750.520 a[h]; 720.520[b]). The 1980 Annotation to Model Penal Code (Official Draft and Revised Comments, sec. 213.1[d]) questions and discusses the penetration requirement at 346–348. For illustrative case law, see Liptroth v. State, 335 So.2d 683 (Ala. Crim. App. 1976), *cert. denied* 429 U.S. 963 (1976); State v. Kidwell, 556 P.2d 20, 27 Ariz. App. 466 (Ariz. Ct. App. 1976); People v. O'Neal, 50 Ill. App. 3d 900, 365 N.E. 2d 1333 (Ill. App. Ct. 1977); Commonwealth v. Usher, 371 A.2d 995 (Pa. Super. Ct. 1977); Commonwealth v. Grassmyer, 237 Pa. Super. 394, 352 A.2d 178 (Pa. Super. Ct. 1975) (statutory rape conviction reversed because defendant's claim that five-year-old child's vaginal wound was inflicted with a broomstick could not be disproved and commonwealth could therefore not prove requisite penetration; indecent assault conviction sustained). Impotence is sometimes a defense and can support laws that prevent charging underage boys with rape or attempted rape; Foster v. Commonwealth, 31 S.E. 503, 96 Va. 306 (1896) (boy under fourteen cannot be guilty of attempt to commit offense that he is legally assumed physically impotent to perpetrate).

3. In the manner of many socialist-feminist adaptations of marxian categories to women's situation, to analyze sexuality as property short-circuits analysis of rape as male sexuality and presumes rather than develops links between sex and class. Concepts of property need to be rethought in light of sexuality as a form of objectification. In some ways, for women legally to be considered property would be an improvement, although it is not recommended.

4. For contrast between the perspectives of the victims and the courts, see Rusk v. State, 43 Md. App. 476, 406 A.2d 624 (Md. Ct. Spec. App. 1979) (*en banc*), *rev'd*, 289 Md. 230, 424 A.2d 720 (1981); Gonzales v. State, 516 P.2d 592 (1973).

5. Susan Brownmiller, *Against Our Will: Men, Women, and Rape* (New York: Simon and Schuster, 1975), p. 15.

6. Diana E. H. Russell, *The Politics of Rape: The Victim's Perspective* (New York: Stein & Day, 1977); Andrea Medea and Kathleen Thompson, *Against Rape* (New York: Farrar, Straus and Giroux, 1974); Lorenne M. G. Clark and Debra Lewis, *Rape: The Price of Coercive Sexuality* (Toronto: Women's Press, 1977); Susan Griffin, "Rape: The All-American Crime," *Ramparts,* September 1971, pp. 26–35. Ti-Grace Atkinson connects rape with "the institution of sexual intercourse," *Amazon Odyssey: The First Collection of Writings by the Political Pioneer of the Women's Movement* (New York: Links Books, 1974), pp. 13–23. Kalamu ya Salaam, "Rape: A Radical Analysis from the African-American Perspective," in *Our Women Keep Our Skies from Falling* (New Orleans: Nkombo, 1980), pp. 25–40.

7. Racism is clearly everyday life. Racism in the United States, by singling out Black men for allegations of rape of white women, has helped obscure the fact that it is men who rape women, disproportionately women of color.

8. Pamela Foa, "What's Wrong with Rape?" in *Feminism and Philosophy*, ed. Mary Vetterling-Braggin, Frederick A. Elliston, and Jane English (Totowa, N.J.: Littlefield, Adams, 1977), pp. 347–359; Michael Davis, "What's So Bad about Rape?" (Paper presented at the annual meeting of the Academy of Criminal Justice Sciences, Louisville, Ky., March 1982). "Since we would not want to say that there is anything morally wrong with sexual intercourse per se, we conclude that the wrongness of rape rests with the matter of the woman's consent"; Carolyn M. Shafer and Marilyn Frye, "Rape and Respect," in Vetterling-Braggin, Elliston, and English, *Feminism and Philosophy*, p. 334. "Sexual contact is not inherently harmful, insulting or provoking. Indeed, ordinarily it is something of which we are quite fond. The difference is [that] ordinary sexual intercourse is more or less consented to while rape is not"; Davis, "What's So Bad?" p. 12.

9. Liegh Bienen, "Rape III—National Developments in Rape Reform Legislation," 6 *Women's Rights Law Reporter* 170 (1980). See also Camille LeGrande, "Rape and Rape Laws: Sexism in Society and Law," 61 *California Law Review* 919 (May 1973).

10. People v. Samuels, 58 Cal. Rptr. 439, 447 (1967).

11. Julia R. Schwendinger and Herman Schwendinger, *Rape and Inequality* (Berkeley: Sage Library of Social Research, 1983), p. 44; K. Polk, "Rape Reform and Criminal Justice Processing," *Crime and Delinquency* 31 (April 1985): 191–205. "What can be concluded about the achievement of the underlying goals of the rape reform movement? . . . If a major goal is to increase the probability of convictions, then the results are slight at best . . . or even negligible" (p. 199) (California data). See also P. Bart and P. O'Brien, *Stopping Rape: Successful Survival Strategies* (Elmsford, N.Y.: Pergamon, 1985), pp. 129–131.

12. See State v. Alston, 310 N.C. 399, 312 S.E.2d 470 (1984) and discussion in Susan Estrich, *Real Rape* (Cambridge: Harvard University Press, 1987), pp. 60–62.

13. Note, "Forcible and Statutory Rape: An Exploration of the Operation and Objectives of the Consent Standard," 62 *Yale Law Journal* 55 (1952).

14. A similar analysis of sexual harassment suggests that women have such "power" only so long as they behave according to male definitions of female desirability, that is, only so long as they accede to the definition of their sexuality (hence, themselves, as gender female) on male terms. Women have this power, in other words, only so long as they remain powerless.

15. See Comment, "Rape and Battery between Husband and Wife," 6 *Stanford Law Review* 719 (1954). On rape of prostitutes, see, e.g., People v. McClure, 42 Ill. App. 952, 356 N.E. 2d 899 (1st Dist. 3d Div. 1976) (on indictment for rape and armed robbery of prostitute where sex was admitted to have occurred, defendant acquitted of rape but "guilty of robbing her while armed with a knife"); Magnum v. State, 1 Tenn. Crim. App. 155, 432 S.W.2d 497 (Tenn. Crim. App. 1968) (no conviction for rape; conviction for sexual violation of age of consent overturned on ground that failure to instruct jury to determine if complainant was "a bawd, lewd or kept female" was reversible error; "A bawd female is a female who keeps a house of prostitution, and conducts illicit intercourse. A lewd female is one given to unlawful indulgence of lust, either for sexual indulgence or profit . . . A kept female is one who is supported and kept by a man for his own illicit intercourse"; complainant "frequented the Blue Moon Tavern; she had been there the night before . . . she kept company with . . . a married man separated from his wife . . . There is some proof of her bad reputation for truth and veracity"). Johnson v. State, 598 S.W. 2d 803 (Tenn. Crim. App. 1979) (unsuccessful defense to charge of rape that "even [if] technically a prostitute can be raped . . . the act of the rape itself was no trauma whatever to this type of unchaste woman"); People v. Gonzales, 96 Misc. 2d 630, 409 N.Y. S. 2d 497 (Crm. Crt. N.Y. City 1978) (prostitute can be raped if "it can be proven beyond a reasonable doubt that she revoked her consent prior to sexual intercourse because the defendant . . . used the coercive force of a pistol).

16. People v. Liberta, 64 N.Y. 2d 152, 474 N.E.2d 567, 485 N.Y.S. 2d 207 (1984) (marital rape recognized, contrary precedents discussed). For a summary of the current state of the marital exemption, see Joanne Schulman, "State-by-State Information on Marital Rape Exemption Laws," in Diana E. H. Russell, *Rape in Marriage* (New York: Macmillan, 1982), pp. 375–381; Patricia Searles and Ronald Berger, "The Current Status of Rape Reform Legislation: An Examination of State Statutes," 10 *Women's Rights Law Reporter* 25 (1987).

17. On "social interaction as an element of consent" in a voluntary social companion context, see Model Penal Code, sec. 213.1. "The prior social interaction is an indicator of consent in addition to actor's and victim's behavioral interaction during the commission of the offense"; Wallace Loh, "Q: What Has Reform of Rape Legislation Wrought? A: Truth in Criminal Labeling," *Journal of Social Issues* 37, no. 4 (1981): 47.

18. E.g., People v. Burnham, 176 Cal. App. 3d 1134, 222 Cal. Rptr. 630 (Cal. App. 1986).

19. Diana E. H. Russell and Nancy Howell, "The Prevalence of Rape in the United States Revisited," *Signs: Journal of Women in Culture and Society* 8 (Summer 1983): 668–695; and D. Russell, *The Secret Trauma: Incestuous Abuse of Women and Girls* (New York: Basic Books, 1986).

20. Pauline Bart found that women were more likely to be raped—that is, less able to stop a rape in progress—when they knew their assailant, particularly when they had a prior or current sexual relationship; "A Study of Women Who Both Were Raped and Avoided Rape," *Journal of Social Issues* 37 (1981): 132. See also Linda Belden, "Why Women Do Not Report Sexual Assault" (Portland, Ore.: City of Portland Public Service Employment Program, Portland Women's Crisis Line, March 1979); Menachem Amir, *Patterns in Forcible Rape* (Chicago: University of Chicago Press, 1971), pp. 229–252.

21. Answer Brief for Plaintiff-Appellee, People V. Brown, Sup. Ct. Colo., Case No. 81SA102 (1981): 10.

22. Note, "Forcible and Statutory Rape," p. 55.

23. La. Rev. Stat. 14.42. Delaware law requires that the victim resist, but "only to the extent that it is reasonably necessary to make the victim's refusal to consent known to the defendant"; 11 Del. Code 761(g). See also Sue Bessmer, *The Laws of Rape* (New York: Praeger, 1984).

24. See People v. Thompson, 117 Mich. App. 522, 524, 324 N.W. 2d 22, 24 (Mich. App. 1982); People v. Hearn, 100 Mich. App. 749, 300 N.W. 2d 396 (Mich. App. 1980).

25. See Carol Pateman, "Women and Consent," *Political Theory* 8 (May 1980): 149–168: "Consent as ideology cannot be distinguished from habitual acquiescence, assent, silent dissent, submission, or even enforced submission. Unless refusal of consent or withdrawal of consent are real possibilities, we can no longer speak of 'consent' in any genuine sense . . . Women exemplify the individuals whom consent theorists declared are incapable of consenting. Yet, simultaneously, women have been presented as always consenting, and their explicit non-consent has been treated as irrelevant or has been reinterpreted as 'consent'" (p. 150).

26. Brownmiller, *Against Our Will*, p. 5.

27. Shafer and Frye, "Rape and Respect," p. 334.

28. See R. Emerson Dobash and Russell Dobash, *Violence against Wives: A Case against the Patriarchy* (New York: Free Press, 1979), pp. 14–21.

29. On the cycle of battering, see Lenore Walker, *The Battered Woman* (New York: Harper & Row, 1979).

30. Samois, *Coming to Power* (Palo Alto, Calif.: Alyson Publications, 1983).

31. If accounts of sexual violation are a form of sex, as argued [by MacKinnon elsewhere], victim testimony in rape cases is a form of live oral pornography.

32. This is apparently true of undetected as well as convicted rapists. Samuel David Smithyman's sample, composed largely of the former, contained self-selected respondents to his ad, which read: "Are you a rapist? Researchers Interviewing Anonymously by Phone to Protect Your Identity. Call . . ." Presumably those who chose to call defined their acts as rapes, at least at the time of responding; "The Undetected Rapist" (Ph.D. diss., Claremont Graduate School, 1978), pp. 54–60, 63–76, 80–90, 97–107.

33. Nancy Gager and Cathleen Schurr, *Sexual Assault: Confronting Rape in America* (New York: Grosset & Dunlap, 1976), p. 244.

34. Susan Estrich proposes this; *Real Rape*, pp. 102–103. Her lack of inquiry into social determinants of perspective (such as pornography) may explain her faith in reasonableness as a legally workable standard for raped women.

35. See Director of Public Prosecutions v. Morgan, 2 All E.R.H.L. 347 (1975), [England]; Pappajohn v. The Queen, 111 D.L.R. 3d 1 (1980) [Canada]; People v. Mayberry, 542 P.2d 1337 (Cal. 1975).

36. Richard H. S. Tur, "Rape: Reasonableness and Time," 3 *Oxford Journal of Legal Studies* 432, 441 (Winter 1981). Tur, in the context of the *Morgan* and *Pappajohn* cases, says the "law ought not to be astute to equate wickedness and wishful, albeit mistaken, thinking" (p. 437). Rape victims are typically less concerned with wickedness than with injury.

37. See Silke Vogelmann-Sine, Ellen D. Ervin, Reenie Christensen, Carolyn H. Warmsun, and Leonard P. Ullmann, "Sex Differences in Feelings Attributed to a Woman in Situations Involving Coercion and Sexual Advances," *Journal of Personality* 47 (September 1979): 429–430.

38. Estrich has this problem in *Real Rape*.

39. E. Donnerstein, "Pornography: Its Effect on Violence against Women," in *Pornography and Sexual Aggression*, ed. N. Malamuth and E. Donnerstein (Orlando, Fla.: Academic Press, 1984), pp. 65–70. Readers who worry that this could become an argument for defending accused rapists should understand that the reality to which it points already provides a basis for defending accused rapists. The solution is to attack the pornography directly, not to be silent about its exonerating effects, legal or social, potential or actual.

Sex and Language

Robert Baker

Our Conception of [Heterosexual] Sexual Intercourse

There are two profound insights that underlie the slogan "men ought not conceive of women as sexual objects"; both have the generality of scope that justifies the universality with which the feminists apply the slogan; neither can be put as simply as the slogan. The first is that the conception of sexual intercourse that we have in this culture is antithetical to the conception of women as human beings—as persons rather than objects. (Recall that this is congruent with the fact . . . that "man" can be substituted for "humanity," while "woman" cannot.)

Many feminists have attempted to argue just this point. Perhaps the most famous defender of this view is Kate Millett,[1] who unfortunately faces the problem of trying to make a point about our conceptual structure without having adequate tools for analyzing conceptual structures.

The question Millett was dealing with was conceptual—Millett, in effect, asking about the nature of our conception of sexual roles. She tried to answer this question by analyzing novels; I shall attempt to answer this question by analyzing the terms we use to identify coitus, or more technically, in terms that function synonymously with "had sexual intercourse with" in a sentence of the form "**A** had sexual intercourse with **B**." The following is a list of some commonly used synonyms (numerous others that are not as widely used have been omitted, for example, "diddled," "laid pipe with"):

> screwed
> laid
> fucked
> had
> did it with (to)
> banged
> balled
> humped

Robert Baker, "The Language of Sex: Our Conception of Sexual Intercourse," abridged from "'Pricks and Chicks': A Plea for 'Persons,'" in *Philosophy and Sex,* eds. Robert Baker and Frederick Elliston (Buffalo, NY: Prometheus Books, 1975): 57–64. Reprinted with permission of author.

slept with

made love to

Now, for a select group of these verbs, names for males are the subjects of sentences with active constructions (that is, where the subjects are said to be doing the activity); and names for females require passive constructions (that is, they are the recipients of the activity—whatever is done is done to them). Thus, we would not say "Jane did it to Dick," although we would say "Dick did it to Jane." Again, Dick bangs Jane, Jane does not bang Dick; Dick humps Jane, Jane does not hump Dick. In contrast, verbs like "did it with" do not require an active role for the male; thus, "Dick did it with Jane, and Jane with Dick." Again, Jane may make love to Dick, just as Dick makes love to Jane; and Jane sleeps with Dick as easily as Dick sleeps with Jane. (My students were undecided about "laid." Most thought that it would be unusual indeed for Jane to lay Dick, unless she played the masculine role of seducer-aggressor.)

The sentences thus form the following pairs. (Those nonconjoined singular noun phrases where a female subject requires a passive construction are marked with a cross. An asterisk indicates that the sentence in question is not a sentence of English if it is taken as synonymous with the italicized sentence heading the column.[2])

Dick had sexual intercourse with Jane.

Dick screwed Jane†

Dick laid Jane†

Dick fucked Jane†

Dick had Jane†

Dick did it to Jane†

Dick banged Jane†

Dick humped Jane†

Dick balled Jane(?)

Dick did it with Jane

Dick slept with Jane

Dick made love to Jane

Jane had sexual intercourse with Dick

Jane was banged by Dick

Jane was humped by Dick

*Jane was done by Dick

Jane was screwed by Dick

Jane was laid by Dick

Jane was fucked by Dick

Jane was had by Dick

Jane balled Dick(?)

Jane did it with Dick

Jane slept with Dick

Jane made love to Dick

*Jane screwed Dick

*Jane laid Dick

*Jane fucked Dick

*Jane had Dick

*Jane did it to Dick

*Jane banged Dick

*Jane humped Dick

These lists make clear that within the standard view of [heterosexual] sexual intercourse, males, or at least names for males, seem to play a different role than females, since male subjects play an active role in the language of screwing, fucking, having, doing it, and perhaps, laying, while female subjects play a passive role.

The asymmetrical nature of the relationship indicated by the sentences marked with an asterisk is confirmed by the fact that the form "—ed with each other" is acceptable for the sentences not marked with an asterisk, but not for those that require a male subject. Thus:

Dick and Jane had sexual intercourse with each other

Dick and Jane made love to each other

Dick and Jane slept with each other

Dick and Jane did it with each other

Dick and Jane balled with each other (*?)

*Dick and Jane banged with each other

*Dick and Jane did it to each other

*Dick and Jane had each other

*Dick and Jane fucked each other

*Dick and Jane humped each other

*(?)Dick and Jane laid each other

*Dick and Jane screwed each other

It should be clear, therefore, that our language reflects a difference between the male and female sexual roles, and hence that we conceive of the male and female roles in different ways. The question that now arises is, What difference in our conception of the male and female sexual roles requires active constructions for males and passive for females?

One explanation for the use of the active construction for males and passive construction for females is that this grammatical asymmetry merely reflects the natural physiological asymmetry between men and women: the asymmetry of "to screw" and "to be screwed," "to insert into" and "to be inserted into." That is, it might be argued that the difference between masculine and feminine grammatical roles merely reflects a difference naturally required by the anatomy of males and females. This explanation is inadequate. Anatomical differences do not determine how we are to conceptualize the relation between penis and vagina during intercourse. Thus one can easily imagine a society in which the female normally played the active role during [heterosexual] intercourse, where female subjects required active constructions with verbs indicating copulation, and where the standard metaphors were terms like "engulfing"—that is, instead of saying "he screwed her," one would say "she engulfed him." It follows that the use of passive constructions for female subjects of verbs indicating copulation does not reflect differences determined by human anatomy but rather reflects those generated by human customs.

What I am going to argue next is that the passive construction of verbs indicating coitus (that is, indicating the female position) can *also* be used to indicate that a person is being harmed. I am then going to argue that the metaphor involved would only make sense if we conceive of the female role in intercourse as that of a person being harmed (or being taken advantage of).

Passive constructions of "fucked," "screwed," and "had" indicate the female role. They also can be used to indicate being harmed. Thus, in all of the following sentences, Marion plays the female role: "Bobbie fucked Marion"; "Bobbie screwed Marion"; "Bobbie had Marion"; "Marion was fucked"; "Marion was screwed"; and "Marion was had." All of the statements are equivocal. They might literally mean that someone had sexual intercourse with Marion (who played the female role); or they might mean, metaphorically, that Marion was deceived, hurt, or taken advantage of.

Thus, we say such things as "I've been screwed" ("fucked," "had," "taken," and so on) when we have been treated unfairly, been sold shoddy merchandise, or conned out of valuables. Throughout this essay. . . I have been arguing that metaphors are applied to things only if what the term *actually* applies to shares one or more properties with what the term *metaphorically* applies to. Thus, the female sexual role must have something in common with being conned or being sold shoddy merchandise. The only common property is that of being harmed, deceived, or taken advantage of. *Hence we conceive of a person who plays the female sexual role as someone who is being harmed* (that is, "screwed," "fucked," and so on).

It might be objected that this is clearly wrong, since the unsignated terms do not indicate someone's being harmed, and hence we do not conceive of having intercourse as being harmed. The point about the unsignated terms, however, is that they can take both females and males as subjects (in active constructions) and thus *do not pick out the female role*. This demonstrates that we conceive of sexual roles in such a way that only females are thought to be taken advantage of in intercourse.

The best part of solving a puzzle is when all the pieces fall into place. If the subjects of the passive construction are being harmed, presumably the subjects of the active constructions are doing harm, and, indeed, we do conceive of these subjects in precisely this way. Suppose one is angry at someone and wishes to express male violence as forcefully as possible without actually committing an act of physical violence. If one is inclined to be vulgar one can make the sign of the erect male cock by clenching one's fist while raising one's middle finger, or by clenching one's fist and raising one's arm and shouting such things as "screw you," "up yours," and "fuck you." In other words, one of the strongest possible ways of telling someone that you wish to harm him is to tell him to assume the female sexual role relative to you. Again, to say to someone "go fuck yourself" is to order him to harm himself, while to call someone a "mother fucker" is not so much a play on his Oedipal fears as to accuse him of being so low that he would inflict the greatest imaginable harm (fucking) upon that person who is most dear to him (his mother).

Clearly, we conceive of the male sexual role as that of hurting the person in the female role—but lest the reader have any doubts, let me provide two further bits of confirming evidence: one linguistic, one nonlinguistic. One of the English terms for a person who hurts (and takes advantage of) others is the term "prick." This metaphorical identification would not make sense unless the bastard in question (that is, the person outside the bonds of legitimacy) was thought to share some characteristics attributed to things that are literally pricks. As a verb, "prick" literally means "to hurt," as in "I pricked myself with a needle"; but the usage in question is as a noun. As a noun, "prick" is a colloquial term for "penis." Thus, the question before us is what characteristic is shared by a penis and a person who harms others (or, alternatively, by a penis and by being stuck by a needle). Clearly, no physical characteristic is relevant (physical characteristics might underlie the Yiddish metaphorical attribution "schmuck," but one would have to analyze Yiddish usage to determine this); hence the shared characteristic is nonphysical; the only relevant shared nonphysical characteristic is that both a literal prick and a figurative prick are agents that harm people.

Now for the nonlinguistic evidence. Imagine two doors: in front of each door is a line of people; behind each door is a room; in each room is a bed; on each bed is a person. The line in front of one room consists of beautiful women, and on the bed in that room is a man having intercourse with each of these women in turn. One may think any number of things about this scene. One may say that the man is in heaven, or enjoying himself at a bordello; or perhaps one might only wonder at the oddness of it all. One does not think that the man is being hurt or violated or degraded—or at least the possibility does not immediately suggest itself, although one could conceive of situations where this was what was happening (especially, for example, if the man was impotent). Now, consider the other line. Imagine that the figure on the bed is a woman and that the line consists of handsome, smiling men. The woman is having intercourse with each of these men in turn. It immediately strikes one that the woman is being degraded, violated, and so forth—"that poor woman."

When one man fucks many women he is a playboy and gains status; when a woman is fucked by many men she degrades herself and loses stature.

Our conceptual inventory is now complete enough for us to return to the task of analyzing the slogan that men ought not to think of women as sex objects.

I think that it is now plausible to argue that the appeal of the slogan "men ought not to think of woman as sex objects," and the thrust of much of the literature produced by contemporary feminists, turns on something much deeper than a rejection of "scoring" (that is, the utilization of sexual "conquests" to gain esteem) and yet is a call neither for homosexuality nor for puritanism.

The slogan is best understood as a call for a new conception of the male and female sexual roles. If the analysis developed above is correct, our present conception of sexuality is such that to be a man is to be a person capable of brutalizing women (witness the slogans "The marines will make a man out of you!" and "The army builds *men*!" which are widely accepted and which simply state that learning how to kill people will make a person more manly). Such a conception of manhood not only bodes ill for a society led by such men, but also is clearly inimical to the best interests of women. It is only natural for women to reject such a sexual role, and it would seem to be the duty of any moral person to support their efforts—to redefine our conceptions not only of fucking, but of the fucker (man) and the fucked (woman).

This brings me to my final point. We are a society preoccupied with sex. As I noted previously, the nature of proper nouns and pronouns in our language makes it difficult to talk about someone without indicating that person's sex. This convention would not be part of the grammar of our language if we did not believe that knowledge of a person's sex was crucial to understanding what is said about that person. Another way of putting this point is that sexual discrimination permeates our conceptual structure. Such discrimination is clearly inimical to any movement toward sexual egalitarianism and virtually defeats its purpose at the outset. (Imagine, for example, that black people were always referred to as "them" and whites as "us" and that proper names for blacks always had an "x" suffix at the end. Clearly any movement for integration as equals would require the removal of these discriminatory indicators. Thus at the height of the melting-pot era, immigrants Americanized their name: "Bellinsky" became "Bell," "Burnstein" became "Burns," and "Lubitch" became "Baker.")

I should therefore like to close this essay by proposing that contemporary feminists should advocate the utilization of neutral proper names and the elimination of gender from our language (as I have done in this essay); and they should vigorously protest any utilization of the third-person pronouns "he" and "she" as examples of sexist discrimination (perhaps "person" would be a good third-person pronoun)—for, as a parent of linguistic analysis once said, "The limits of our language are the limits of our world."

Notes

1. *Sexual Politics* (New York: Doubleday, 1971; but see also *Sisterhood Is Powerful*, ed. Robin Morgan (New York: Vintage Books, 1970).

2. For further analysis of verbs indicating copulation see "A Note on Conjoined Noun Phrases," *Journal of Philosophical Linguistics*, vol. 1, no. 2, Great Expectations, Evanston, Ill. Reprinted with "English Sentences Without Overt Grammatical Subject," in Zwicky, Salus, Binnick, and Vanek, eds., *Studies Out in Left Field: Defamatory Essays Presented to James D. McCawley* (Edmonton: Linguistic Research, Inc., 1971). The puritanism in our society is such that both of these articles are pseudoanonymously published under the name of Quang Phuc Dong; Mr. Dong, however, has a fondness for citing and criticizing the articles and theories of Professor James McCawley, Department of Linguistics, University of Chicago. Professor McCawley himself was kind enough to criticize an earlier draft of this essay. I should also like to thank G.E.M. Anscombe for some suggestions concerning this essay.

39.
Date Rape: A Feminist Analysis
Lois Pineau

Lois Pineau taught philosophy in both Canada and the United States before leaving academic work to take up a political position with the Ontario government. She has published articles in philosophy of language, political philosophy, feminist theory, and philosophy of law. Here, she argues that acquaintance-rape is made "understandable" because of a number of prevalent myths about rape and human sexuality. In her essay, she identifies and challenges the logical underpinnings of these popular myths.

. . . Date rape is nonaggravated sexual assault, nonconsensual sex that does not involve physical injury or the explicit threat of physical injury. But because it does not involve physical injury, and because physical injury is often the only criterion that is accepted as evidence that *actus reas* is nonconsensual, what is really sexual assault is often mistaken for seduction. The replacement of the old rape laws with the new laws on sexual assault have done nothing to resolve this problem.

Rape, defined as nonconsensual sex, usually involving penetration by a man of a woman who is not his wife, has been replaced in some criminal codes with the charge of sexual assault. This has the advantage both of extending the range of possible victims of sexual assault, the manner in which people can be assaulted, and replacing a crime which is exclusive of consent, with one for which consent is a defense. But while the consent of a woman is now consistent with the conviction of her assailant in cases of aggravated assault, nonaggravated sexual assault is still distinguished from normal sex solely by the fact that it is not consented to. Thus the question of whether someone has consented to a

Excerpted from Lois Pineau, "Date Rape: A Feminist Analysis," *Law and Philosophy* 8 (1989): 217–243. Reprinted with kind permission from Kluwer Academic Publishers.

sexual encounter is still important, and the criteria for consent continues to be the central concern of discourse on sexual assault.

However, if a man is to be convicted, it does not suffice to establish that the *actus reas* was nonconsensual. In order to be guilty of sexual assault a man must have the requisite *mens rea*, i.e., he must either have believed that his victim did not consent or that she was probably not consenting. In many common law jurisdictions a man who sincerely believes that a woman consented to a sexual encounter is deemed to lack the required *mens rea*, even though the woman did not consent and even though his belief is not reasonable. Recently, strong dissenting voices have been raised against the sincerity condition, and the argument made that *mens rea* be defeated only if the defendant has a reasonable belief that the plaintiff consented. The introduction of legislation which excludes "honest belief" (unreasonable sincere belief) as a defense, will certainly help to provide women with greater protection against violence. But while this will be an important step forward, the question of what constitutes a reasonable belief, the problem of evidence when rapists lie, and the problem of the entrenched attitudes of the predominantly male police, judges, lawyers, and jurists who handle sexual assault cases, remains.

The criteria for *mens rea*, for the reasonableness of belief, and for consent are closely related. For although a man's sincere belief in the consent of his victim may be sufficient to defeat *mens rea*, the court is less likely to believe his belief is sincere if his belief is unreasonable. If his belief is reasonable, they are more likely to believe in the sincerity of his belief. But evidence of the reasonableness of his belief is also evidence that consent really did take place. For the very things that make it reasonable for *him* to believe that the defendant consented are often the very things that incline the court to believe that she consented. What is often missing is the voice of the woman herself, an account of what it would be reasonable for *her* to agree to, that is to say, an account of what is reasonable from *her* standpoint.

Thus, what is presented as reasonable has repercussions for four separate but related concerns: (1) the question of whether a man's belief in a woman's consent was reasonable; (2) the problem of whether it is reasonable to attribute *mens rea* to him; (3) the question of what could count as reasonable from the woman's point of view; (4) the question of what is reasonable from the court's point of view. These repercussions are of the utmost practical concern. In a culture which contains an incidence of sexual assault verging on epidemic, a criterion of reasonableness which regards mere submission as consent fails to offer persons vulnerable to those assaults adequate protection.

The following statements by self-confessed date rapists reveal how our lack of a solution for dealing with date rape protects rapists by failing to provide their victims with legal recourse:

> All of my rapes have been involved in a dating situation where I've been out with a woman I know. . . . I wouldn't take no for an answer. I think it had something to do with my acceptance of rejection. I had low self-esteem and not much self-confidence and when I was rejected for something which I considered to be rightly mine, I became angry and I went ahead anyway. And this was the same in any situation, whether it was rape or it was something else.

> When I did date, when I was younger, I would pick up a girl and if she didn't come across I would threaten her or slap her face then tell her she was going to fuck—that was it. But that's because I didn't want to waste time with any come-ons. It took too much time. I wasn't interested because I didn't like them as people anyway, and I just went with them just to get laid. Just to say that I laid them.

There is, at this time, nothing to protect women from this kind of unscrupulous victimization. A woman on a casual date with a virtual stranger has almost no chance of bringing a complaint of sexual assault before the courts. One reason for this is the prevailing criterion for consent. According to this criterion, consent is implied unless some emphatic episodic sign of resistance occurred, and its occurrence can be established. But if no episodic act occurred, or if it did occur, and the defendant claims that it didn't, or if the defendant threatened the plaintiff but won't admit it in court, it is almost impossible to find any evidence that would support the plaintiff's word against the defendant. This difficulty is exacerbated by suspicion on the part of the courts, police, and legal educators that even where an act of resistance occurs, this act should not be interpreted as a withholding of consent, and this suspicion is especially upheld where the accused is a man who is known to the female plaintiff.

In Glanville William's classic textbook on criminal law we are warned that where a man is unknown to a woman, she does not consent if she expresses her rejection in the form of an episodic and vigorous act at the "vital moment." But if the man is known to the woman she must, according to Williams, make use of "all means available to her to repel the man." Williams warns that women often welcome a "mastery advance" and present a token resistance. He quotes Byron's couplet,

> A little still she strove, and much repented
>
> And whispering "I will ne'er consent"—consented

by way of alerting law students to the difficulty of distinguishing real protest from pretense. Thus, while in principle, a firm unambiguous stand, or a healthy show of temper ought to be sufficient, if established, to show non-consent, in practice the forceful overriding of such a stance is apt to be taken as an indication that the resistance was not seriously intended, and that the seduction had succeeded. The consequence of this is that it is almost impossible to establish the defendant's guilt beyond a reasonable doubt.

Thus, on the one hand, we have a situation in which women are vulnerable to the most ex-ploitive tactics at the hands of men who are known to them. On the other hand, almost nothing will count as evidence of their being assaulted, including their having taken an emphatic stance in withholding their consent. The new laws have done almost nothing to change this situation. Yet clearly, some solution must be sought. Moreover, the road to that solution presents itself clearly enough as a need for a re-formulation of the criterion of consent. It is patent that a criterion that collapses whenever the crime itself succeeds will not suffice. . . .

The reasoning that underlies the present criterion of consent is entangled in a number of mutually supportive mythologies which see sexual assault as masterful seduction, and silent submission as sexual enjoyment. Because the prevailing ideology has so much informed our conceptualization of sexual interaction, it is extraordinarily difficult for us to distinguish between assault and seduction, submission and enjoyment, or so we imagine. At the same time, this failure to distinguish has given rise to a network of rationalizations that support the conflation of assault with seduction, submission, with enjoyment. . . .

RAPE MYTHS

The belief that the natural aggression of men and the natural reluctance of women somehow makes date rape understandable underlies a number of prevalent myths about rape and human sexuality. These beliefs maintain their force partly on account of a logical compulsion exercised by them at an unconscious level. The only way of refuting them effectively, is to excavate the logical propositions involved, and to expose their misapplication to the situations to which they have been applied. In what follows, I propose to excavate the logical support for popular attitudes that are tolerant of date rape. These myths are not just popular, however, but often emerge in the arguments of judges who acquit date rapists, and policemen who refuse to lay charges.

The claim that the victim provoked a sexual incident, that "she asked for it," is by far the most common defense given by men who are accused of sexual assault. Feminists, rightly incensed by this response, often treat it as beneath contempt, singling out the defense as an argument against it. On other fronts, sociologists have identified the response as part of an overall tendency of people to see the world as just, a tendency which disposes them to conclude that people for the most part deserve what they get. However, an inclination to see the world as just requires us to construct an account which yields this outcome, and it is just such an account that I wish to examine with regard to date rape.

The least sophisticated of the "she asked for it" rationales—and in a sense, the easiest to deal with—appeals to an injunction against sexually provocative behavior on the part of women. If women should not be sexually provocative, then, from this standpoint, a woman who is sexually provocative deserves to suffer the consequences. Now it will not do to respond that women get raped even when they are not sexually provocative, or that it is men who get to interpret (unfairly) what counts as sexually provocative. The question should be: Why shouldn't a woman be sexually provocative? Why should this behavior warrant any kind of aggressive response whatsoever?

Attempts to explain that women have a right to behave in sexually provocative ways without suffering dire consequences still meet with surprisingly tough resistance. Even people who find nothing wrong or sinful with sex itself, in any of its forms, tend to suppose that women must not behave sexually unless they are prepared to carry through on some fuller course of sexual interaction. The logic of this response seems to be that at some point a woman's behavior commits her to following through on the full course of a sexual encounter as it is defined by her assailant. At some point she has made an agreement, or formed a contract, and once that is done, her contractor is entitled to demand that she satisfy the terms of that contract. Thus, this view about

sexual responsibility and desert is supported by other assumptions about contracts and agreement. But we do not normally suppose that casual nonverbal behavior generates agreements. Nor do we normally grant private persons the right to enforce contracts. What rationale would support our conclusion in this case?

The rationale, I believe, comes in the form of a belief in the especially insistent nature of male sexuality, an insistence which lies at the foot of natural male aggression, and which is extremely difficult, perhaps impossible to contain. At a certain point in the arousal process, it is thought, a man's rational will gives way to the prerogatives of nature. His sexual need can and does reach a point where it is uncontrollable, and his natural masculine aggression kicks in to assure that this need is met. Women, however, are naturally more contained, and so it is their responsibility not to provoke the irrational in the male. If they do go so far as that, they have both failed in their responsibilities and subjected themselves to the inevitable. One does not go into the lion's cage and expect not to be eaten. Natural feminine reluctance, it is thought, is no protection against a sexually aroused male.

This belief about the normal aggressiveness of male sexuality is complemented by common knowledge about female gender development. Once, women were taught to deny their sexuality and to aspire to ideals of chastity. Things have not changed so much. Women still tend to eschew conquest mentalities in favor of a combination of sex and affection. Insofar as this is thought to be merely a cultural requirement, however, there is an expectation that women will be coy about their sexual desire. The assumption that women both want to indulge sexually, and are inclined to sacrifice this desire for higher ends, gives rise to the myth that they want to be raped. After all, doesn't rape give them the sexual enjoyment they *really* want, at the same time that it relieves them of the responsibility for admitting to and acting upon what they want? And how then can we blame men, who have been socialized to be aggressively seductive precisely for the purpose of overriding female reserve? If we find fault at all, we are inclined to cast our suspicions on the motives of the woman. For it is on her that the contradictory roles of sexual desirer and sexual denier have been placed. Our awareness of the contradiction expected of her makes us suspect her honesty. In the past, she was expected to deny her complicity because of the shame and guilt she felt at having submitted. This expectation persists in many quarters today, and is carried over into a general suspicion about her character, and the fear that she might make a false accusation out of revenge, or some other low motive.

But if women really want sexual pleasure, what inclines us to think that they will get it through rape? This conclusion logically requires a theory about the dynamics of sexual pleasure that sees that pleasure as an emergent property of overwhelming male insistence. For the assumption that a raped female experiences sexual pleasure implies that the person who rapes her knows how to cause that pleasure independently of any information she might convey on that point. Since her ongoing protest is inconsistent with requests to be touched in particular ways in particular places, to have more of this and less of that, then we must believe that the person who touches her knows these particular ways and places instinctively, without any directives from her.

Thus, we find, underlying and reinforcing this belief in incommunicative male prowess, a conception of sexual pleasure that springs from wordless interchanges, and of sexual success that occurs in a place of meaningful silence. The language of seduction is accepted as a tacit language: eye contacts, smiles, blushes, and faintly discernible gestures. It is, accordingly, imprecise and ambiguous. It would be easy for a man to make mistakes about the message conveyed, understandable that he should mistakenly think that a sexual invitation has been made, and a bargain struck. But honest mistakes, we think, must be excused.

In sum, the belief that women should not be sexually provocative is logically linked to several other beliefs, some normative, some empirical. The normative beliefs are (1) that people should keep the agreements they make; (2) that sexually provocative behavior taken beyond a certain point, generates agreements; (3) that the peculiar nature of male and female sexuality places such agreements in a special category, one in which the possibility of retracting an agreement is ruled out, or at least made highly unlikely; (4) that women are not to be trusted, in sexual matters at least. The empirical belief, which turns out to be false, is that male sexuality is not subject to rational and moral control.

DISPELLING THE MYTHS

The "she asked for it" justification of sexual assault incorporates a conception of a contract that would be difficult to defend in any other context, and the presumptions about human sexuality which function to reinforce sympathies rooted in the contractual notion of just deserts are not supported by empirical research.

The belief that a woman generates some sort of contractual obligation whenever her behavior is interpreted as seductive is the most indefensible part of the mythology of rape. In law, contracts are not legitimate just because a promise has been made. In particular, the use of pressure tactics to extract agreement is frowned upon. Normally, an agreement is upheld only if the contractors were clear on what they were getting into, and had sufficient time to reflect on the wisdom of their doing so. Either there must be a clear tradition in which the expectations involved in the contract are fairly well known (marriage), or there must be an explicit written agreement concerning the exact terms of the contract and the expectations of the persons involved. But whatever the terms of a contract, there is no private right to enforce it. So that if I make a contract with you on which I renege, the only permissible recourse for you is through due legal process.

Now it is not clear whether sexual contracts can be made to begin with, or if so, what sort of sexual contracts would be legitimate. But assuming that they could be made, the terms of those contracts would not be enforceable. To allow public enforcement would be to grant the state the overt right to force people to have sex, and this would clearly be unacceptable. Granting that sexual contracts are legitimate, state enforcement of such contracts would have to be limited to ordering non-sexual compensation for breaches of contract. So it makes no difference whether a sexual contract is tacit or explicit. There are no grounds whatsoever that would justify enforcement of its terms.

Thus, even if we assume that a woman has initially agreed to an encounter, her agreement does not automatically make all subsequent sexual activity to which she submits legitimate. If during coitus a woman should experience pain, be suddenly overcome with guilt or fear of pregnancy, or simply lose her initial desire, those are good reasons for her to change her mind. Having changed her mind, neither her partner nor the state has any right to force her to continue. But then if she is forced to continue she is assaulted. Thus, establishing that consent occurred at a particular point during a sexual encounter should not conclusively establish the legitimacy of the encounter. What is needed is a reading of whether she agreed throughout the encounter.

If the "she asked for it" contractual view of sexual interchange has any validity, it is because there is a point at which there is no stopping a sexual encounter, a point at which that encounter becomes the inexorable outcome of the unfolding of natural events. If a sexual encounter is like a slide on which I cannot stop halfway down, it will be relevant whether I enter the slide of my own free will, or am pushed.

But there is no evidence that the entire sexual act is like a slide. While there may be a few seconds in the "plateau" period just prior to orgasm in which people are "swept" away by sexual feelings to the point where we could

justifiably understand their lack of heed for the comfort of their partner, the greater part of a sexual encounter comes well within the bounds of morally responsible control of our own actions. Indeed, the available evidence shows that most of the activity involved in sex has to do with building the requisite level of desire, a task that involves the proper use of foreplay, the possibility of which implies control over the form that foreplay will take. Modern sexual therapy assumes that such control is universally accessible, and so far there has been no reason to question that assumption. Sexologists are unanimous, moreover, in holding that mutual sexual enjoyment requires an atmosphere of comfort and communication, a minimum of pressure, and an ongoing check-up on one's partner's state. They maintain that different people have different predilections, and that what is pleasurable for one person is very often anathema to another. These findings show that the way to achieve sexual pleasure, at any time at all, let alone with a casual acquaintance, decidedly does not involve overriding the other person's express reservations and providing them with just any kind of sexual stimulus. And while we do not want to allow science and technology a voice in which the voices of particular women are drowned, in this case science seems to concur with women's perception that aggressive incommunicative sex is not what they want. But if science and the voice of women concur, if aggressive seduction does not lead to good sex, if women do not like it, or want it, then it is not rational to think that they would agree to it. Where such sex takes place, it is therefore rational to presume that the sex was not consensual.

The myth that women like to be raped, is closely connected, as we have seen, to doubt about their honesty in sexual matters, and this suspicion is exploited by defense lawyers when sexual assault cases make it to the courtroom. It is an unfortunate consequence of the presumption of innocence that rape victims who end up in court frequently find that it is they who are on trial. For if the defendant is innocent, then either he did not intend to do what he was accused of, or the plaintiff is mistaken about his identity, or she is lying. Often the last alternative is the only plausible defense, and as a result, the plaintiff's word seldom goes unquestioned. Women are frequently accused of having made a false accusation, either as a defensive mechanism for dealing with guilt and shame, or out of a desire for revenge.

Now, there is no point in denying the possibility of false accusation, though there are probably better ways of seeking revenge on a man than accusing him of rape. However, we can now establish a logical connection between the evidence that a woman was subjected to high-pressure aggressive "seduction" tactics, and her claim that she did not consent to that encounter. Where the kind of encounter is not the sort to which it would be reasonable to consent, there is a logical presumption that a woman who claims that she did not consent is telling the truth. Where the kind of sex involved is not the sort of sex we would expect a woman to like, the burden of proof should not be on the woman to show that she did not consent, but on the defendant to show that contrary to every reasonable expectation she did consent. The defendant should be required to convince the court that the plaintiff persuaded him to have sex with her even though there are no visible reasons why she should.

In conclusion, there are no grounds for the "she asked for it" defense. Sexually provocative behavior does not generate sexual contracts. Even where there are sexual agreements, they cannot be legitimately enforced either by the state or by private right or by natural prerogative. Second, all the evidence suggests that neither women nor men find sexual enjoyment in rape or in any form of noncommunicative sexuality. Third, male sexual desire is containable, and can be subjected to moral and rational control. Fourth, since there is no reason why women should not be sexually provocative, they do not "deserve" any sex they do not want. This

last is a welcome discovery. The taboo on sexual provocativeness in women is a taboo both on sensuality and on teasing. But sensuality is a source of delight, and teasing is playful and inspires wit. What a relief to learn that it is not sexual provocativeness, but its enemies, that constitutes a danger to the world. . . .

In thinking about sex we must keep in mind its sensual ends, and the facts show that aggressive high-pressure sex contradicts those ends. Consensual sex in dating situations is presumed to aim at mutual enjoyment. It may not always do this, and when it does, it might not always succeed. There is no logical incompatibility between wanting to continue a sexual encounter, and failing to derive sexual pleasure from it.

But it seems to me that there is a presumption in favor of the connection between sex and sexual enjoyment, and that if a man wants to be sure that he is not forcing himself on a woman, he has an obligation either to ensure that the encounter really is mutually enjoyable, or to know the reasons why she would want to continue the encounter in spite of her lack of enjoyment. A closer investigation of the nature of this obligation will enable us to construct a more rational and more plausible norm of sexual conduct.

Onara O'Neill has argued that in intimate situations we have an obligation to take the ends of others as our own, and to promote those ends in a non-manipulative and non-paternalistic manner. Now, it seems that in honest sexual encounters just this is required. Assuming that each person enters the encounter in order to seek sexual satisfaction, each person engaging in the encounter has an obligation to help the other seek his or her ends. To do otherwise is to risk acting in opposition to what the other desires, and hence to risk acting without the other's consent.

But the obligation to promote the sexual ends of one's partner implies that obligation to know what those ends are, and also the obligation to know how those ends are attained. Thus, the problem comes down to a problem of epistemic responsibility, the responsibility to know.

The solution, in my view, lies in the practice of a communicative sexuality, one which combines the appropriate knowledge of the other with respect for the dialectics of desire. . . .

CULTURAL PRESUMPTIONS

Now it may well be that we have no obligation to care for strangers, and I do not wish to claim that we do. Nonetheless, it seems that O'Neill's point about the special moral duties we have in certain intimate situations is supported by a conceptual relation between certain kinds of personal relationships and the expectation that it should be a communicative relation. Friendship is a case in point. It is a relation that is greatly underdetermined by what we usually include in our sets of rights and obligations. For the most part, rights and obligations disappear as terms by which friendship is guided. They are still there, to be called upon, in case the relationship breaks down, but insofar as the friendship is a friendship, it is concerned with fostering the quality of the interaction and not with standing on rights. Thus, because we are friends, we share our property, and property rights between us are not invoked. Because we are friends, privacy is not an issue. Because we are friends we may see to each other's needs as often as we see to our own. The same can be said for relations between lovers, parents and dependent children, and even between spouses, at least when interaction is functioning at an optimal level. When such relations break down to the point that people must stand on their rights, we can often say that the actors ought to make more of an effort, and in many instances fault them for their lack of charity, tolerance, or benevolence. Thus, although we have a right to end friendships, it may be a reflection on our lack of virtue that we do so, and while we cannot be criticized for violating other people's rights, we can be rightfully deprecated for lacking the virtue to sustain a friendship.

But is there a similar conceptual relation between the kind of activity that a date is, and the sort of moral practice that it requires?

My claim is that there is, and that this connection is easily established once we recognize the cultural presumption that dating is a gesture of friendship and regard. Traditionally, the decision to date indicates that two people have an initial attraction to each other, that they are disposed to like each other, and look forward to enjoying each other's company. Dating derives its implicit meaning from this tradition. It retains this meaning unless other aims are explicitly stated, and even then it may not be possible to alienate this meaning. It is a rare woman who will not spurn a man who states explicitly, right at the onset, that he wants to go out with her solely on the condition that he have sexual intercourse with her at the end of the evening, and that he has no interest in her company apart from gaining that end, and no concern for mutual satisfaction.

Explicit protest to the contrary aside, the conventions of dating confer on it its social meaning, and this social meaning implies a relationship which is more like friendship than the cutthroat competition of opposing teams. As such, it requires that we do more than stand on our rights with regard to each other. As long as we are operating under the auspices of a dating relationship, it requires that we behave in the mode of friendship and trust. But if a date is more like a friendship than a business contract, then clearly respect for the dialectics of desire is incompatible with the sort of sexual pressure that is inclined to end in date rape. And clearly, also, a conquest mentality which exploits a situation of trust and respect for purely selfish ends is morally pernicious. Failure to respect the dialectics of desire when operating under the auspices of friendship and trust is to act in flagrant disregard of the moral requirement to avoid manipulative, coercive, and exploitive behavior. Respect for the dialectics of desire is *prima facie* inconsistent with the satisfaction of one person at the expense of the other. The proper end of friendship relations is mutual satisfaction. But the requirement of mutuality means that we must take a communicative approach to discovering the ends of the other, and this entails that we respect the dialectics of desire.

But now that we know what communicative sexuality is, and that it is morally required, and that it is the only feasible means to mutual sexual enjoyment, why not take this model as the norm of what is reasonable in sexual interaction. The evidence of sexologists strongly indicates that women whose partners are aggressively uncommunicative have little chance of experiencing sexual pleasure. But it is not reasonable for women to consent to what they have little chance of enjoying. Hence it is not reasonable for women to consent to aggressive noncommunicative sex. Nor can we reasonably suppose that women have consented to sexual encounters which we know and they know they do not find enjoyable. With the communicative model as the norm, the aggressive contractual model should strike us as a model of deviant sexuality, and sexual encounters patterned on that model should strike us as encounters to which *prima facie* no one would reasonably agree. But if acquiescence to an encounter counts as consent only if the acquiescence is reasonable, something to which a reasonable person, in full possession of knowledge relevant to the encounter, would agree, then acquiescence to aggressive noncommunicative sex is not reasonable. Hence, acquiescence under such conditions should not count as consent.

Thus, where communicative sexuality does not occur, we lack the main ground for believing that the sex involved was consensual. Moreover, where a man does not engage in communicative sexuality, he acts either out of reckless disregard or out of willful ignorance, for he cannot know, except through the practice of communicative sexuality, whether his partner has any sexual reason for continuing the encounter. And where she does not, he runs the risk of imposing on her what she is not willing to have. All that is needed then, in order to provide women with legal protection from "date rape" is to make both reckless indifference and willful ignorance a sufficient condition of *mens rea* and to make communicative sexuality the accepted norm of sex to which a reasonable woman would agree. Thus, the appeal to communicative sexuality as a norm for sexual encounters accomplishes two things. It brings the aggressive sex involved in "date rape" well within the realm of sexual assault, and it locates the guilt of date rapists in the failure to approach sexual relations on a communicative basis.

Date Rape Case Studies

Robin Warshaw

Editor's Note: The following accounts of acquaintance-rape are taken from Robin Warshaw's groundbreaking book, *I Never Called It Rape*. These cases demonstrate the range of date-rape situations, and the severe pain and suffering women experience as a result of sexual assaults by "non-strangers"—acquaintances, dates, co-workers, classmates, and neighbors in college dorms.

Lori's Story

How can a date be a rape?

The pairing of the word "date," which conjures up an image of fun shared by two companions, with

Excerpts from *I Never Called It Rape* by Robin Warshaw. Copyright (c) 1988 by The Ms. Foundation for Education and Communication, Inc., and Sarah Lazin Books. Reprinted with permission of HarperCollins Publishers, Inc.

the word "rape," which evokes the total loss of control by one person to the will of another, results in the creation of a new phrase that is nearly impossible for most people to comprehend. To understand how date rape happens, let's look at a classic case.

The Setup

It was natural. Normal. Lori's friend Amy wanted to go out with Paul, but felt awkward and shy about going out with him alone. So when Paul's roommate, Eric, suggested that he and Lori join Amy and Paul for a double date, it made sense. "I didn't feel anything for Eric except as a friend," Lori says of her reaction to the plan. "I said, 'Okay, maybe it will make Amy feel better.'"

Agreeing to go out with Eric was no great act of charity on Lori's part. He *was* attractive—tall, good-looking, in his mid-20s and from a wealthy family. Lori, who was 19 at the time, knew Eric and Paul as frequent customers at the popular Tampa Bay restaurant where she worked as a waitress when she was between college semesters.

On the day of the date, Eric called several times to change their plans. Finally, he phoned to say that they would be having a barbecue with several of his friends at the house he and Paul shared. Lori agreed.

> We went to his house and I mentioned something about Paul and Amy and he kind of threw it off, like "Yeah, yeah." I didn't think anything of it. There we are, fixing steaks, and he was saying, "Well, this is obviously something to help Amy."
>
> He kept making drinks all night long. He kept saying, "Here, have a drink," "Here, drink this." I didn't because I didn't want it. He was just downing them right and left.

The Attack

Unknown to Lori, Amy had canceled her plans to see Paul the day before. Paul told Eric, but Eric never told Lori. As the barbecue party progressed and her friend failed to show up, Lori questioned Eric again. He then lied, telling her that Paul had just called to say he and Amy weren't coming.

> I was thinking to myself, "Well, okay." Not in my wildest dreams would I have thought he was plotting something. Then all of his friends started leaving. I began to think, "Something is wrong, something is going on," but I've been known to overreact to things, so I ignored it.
>
> After his friends left, we're sitting on the couch and he leans over and he kisses me and I'm thinking, "It's a date, it's no big deal." So then we started kissing a little bit more and I'm thinking, "I'm starting to enjoy this, maybe this isn't so bad." Then the phone rang and when he came back I was standing up. He grabbed me from behind and picked me up. He had his hands over my eyes and we were walking

through his house. It was really dark and I didn't know where on earth he was taking me. I had never actually walked through his house.

> He laid me down [on a bed] and kissed me. . . . He starts taking off my clothes and I said, "Wait—time out! This is not what I want, you know," and he said to me something like this is what I owed him because he made me dinner.
>
> I said, "This is wrong, don't do this. I didn't go out with you with this intent."
>
> He said, "What do you call that on the couch?"
>
> I said, "I call it a kiss, period."
>
> And he said, "Well, I don't."

The two struggled until Eric rolled off her momentarily. Lori jumped up and went into the bathroom. Her plan was to come out in a few minutes and tell him it was time to take her home.

> The whole time I'm thinking, "I don't believe this is happening to me." I didn't even have time to walk fully out of the bathroom door when he grabbed me and threw me on the bed and starting taking my clothes off. I'm yelling and hitting and pushing on him and he just liked that. He says, "I know you must like this because a lot of women like this kind of thing." Then he says, "This is the adult world. Maybe you ought to grow up some."
>
> I finally got to the point where there was nothing I could do.

Eric pushed his penis into her and, after a few minutes, ejaculated. Lori had had only one other experience with sexual intercourse, about a year before with a longtime boyfriend.

> Then Eric just rolled over and I started to get my clothes together. He said, "Don't tell me you didn't like that." I looked at him and said, "No," and by this time I'm crying because I don't know what else to do. I never heard of anybody having that happen to them.

The Aftermath

Finally, Eric took her home.

> In the car he said, "Can I call you tomorrow? Can I see you next weekend?" I just looked at him and he just looked at me and started laughing.
>
> My mom had gone out and I just laid on my bed with the covers up. Everything I could

possibly put on I think I put on that night—
leg warmers, thermal underwear—everything
imaginable in the middle of summer I put on
my body. That night I dreamed it was all happening again. I dreamed I was standing there
watching him do it.

For two weeks I couldn't talk. People
would talk to me and I felt nothing. I felt like a
zombie. I couldn't cry. I couldn't smile, I
couldn't eat. My mom said, "What's wrong
with you? Is something going on?" I said,
"Nothing's wrong."

I thought it was my fault. What did I do to
make him think he could do something like
that? Was I wrong in kissing him? Was I wrong
to go out with him, to go over to his house?

After two weeks, she told her mother what happened and they talked about what to do. Lori decided not to report it to the police for fear Eric
would blame her. Eric continued to frequent the
restaurant where she worked. Several weeks after
their date, he cornered her in a hallway near the
kitchen.

He touched me and I said, "Get your hands off
me." At first, he thought it was funny. He said,
"What's wrong?" then he started pulling me,
trying to hug me. I pushed him and said,
"Leave me alone," and I was starting to get a
little loud. As I was walking away, he said,
"Oh, I guess you didn't get enough."

I walked into the kitchen and I picked up
this tray full of food. I don't know how it happened. I just dropped the whole tray and it
went everywhere. My friend, another waitress,
went to the manager and said, "She's not going
to be much good to you tonight," so they sent
me home.

Lori decided to move to a town about 150 miles
away to avoid continued encounters with Eric. There
she found work as an office assistant and cashier and
enrolled for a few classes at a new college.

Sitting in a darkened restaurant on her lunch
break one year after the rape, Lori is still looking
for answers.

When I moved here, nobody knew about it. I
just figured, this only happened to me. Then
my roommate told me it happened to her in
Ohio. We talked about it once and that was it.
It just upset me too much to talk about it any-

more. I mean, she understood, it upset her a
lot, too, so we just don't bring it up.

How do other women handle it? I work
two jobs and I go to school because I don't
want to have to deal with the situation of having somebody ask me on a date. If I go out
with a guy, I'm wondering, is he thinking dinner means "I'll get you into bed"?

I'm not going to be stupid enough to put
myself in that situation again. I grew out of
being naive just like that. This experience grew
me up in about two weeks.

Jill's Story

Jill lives in a cottage in the fog-shrouded foothills
of Washington state near where she grew up. Now
25, she works hard all day at her secretarial job
and then comes home to help her 8-year-old son
Donny with his homework. Jill loves her son, but
she tries to block the memory of why she became
a mother at such a young age: Donny is the result
of a date rape that happened when Jill was 16, during the summer between her junior and senior
years in high school.

She was on an outing with several male and female friends to a lake when she met the man who
would later rape her.

We asked him to come over and sit with us.
Later on, I gave him my phone number and he
called me up to take me out. He was really
cute, but he was older.

His seeming maturity (he was in his early 20s)
made him attractive, as did his sandy-colored
beard and hair and the fact that he was a carpenter,
not a high schooler. But Jill worried about what
her parents would think. She still didn't date
much, although, unknown to her mother and father, she had had one experience of sexual intercourse with a steady boyfriend her own age several
months before.

The day of the date arrived and the sandy-
haired man rode up to Jill's house on a motorcycle.
She climbed aboard and they drove further into the
countryside, to a secluded spot near a river.

We were talking, it was just like a date, you
know, when he pulled a gun out of the bag on
the back of his motorcycle and started playing
with it. I don't like guns. My parents don't

have guns. I said, "Oh, gee, that's not loaded, is it?" and he said, "Oh, yeah."

I was very scared.

Jill's date laid the gun down on the blanket they were sharing. He then put his arm around her and started kissing her, but just briefly. He almost immediately proceeded to have intercourse with her.

I remember at the time I thought, "Just go along, it doesn't matter." I didn't want to take any chances. I just wanted to get home and get out of that situation.

Like date rapists then and now, the handsome carpenter never thought about birth control or the possibility of sexually transmitting disease to his victim. He drove her home and Jill was grounded for being late; she went to her room vowing to tell no one.

She made good on that vow for several months, until her pregnancy forced her to confide in a friend. Jill wanted to have an abortion until the medical procedure that would be used was explained to her. That, coupled with her parents' feelings against abortion, led her to decide to remain pregnant and keep the child. Always a good student, Jill went through her senior year pregnant and maintained an A average. She went to graduation with her son in her arms and her dreams of going to art school set aside; instead, she faced the reality of supporting a child.

Rachel's Story

Rachel blends in easily with the attractive young crowd filling a downtown Boston street on a mild spring afternoon. Her spiky short brown hair is the arty fashion of the season; her big hoop earrings mimic the large roundness of her eyes. She comes from an intelligent and loving family. Her father is a lawyer; her mother teaches.

Rachel was raped during her freshman year in college. She has never told her parents.

I was at a big university. We had coed dorms, with two hallways on each floor being girls and two hallways were guys. This guy was a football player, about six foot five and 265 pounds. I knew he lived down the hall from me, but I didn't really know him. I thought he was an attractive guy. He was a junior.

There was a party on our floor with all the guys and girls from our floor. There were kegs and stuff. The drinking age was 18, but even though I wasn't quite 18 they let me into the party. We had already been drinking a lot and we got to the party and this guy [the football player] was talking to me.

Rachel was flattered by the attention.

He wasn't drinking, but he was feeding me alcohol. He asked me to come back to his room—it was right down the hall from where all of us were. I was just so out of it, I said, "Sure." I had no idea. I didn't think he'd hurt me.

I thought there would be other people there. I thought it was just like, "Let's get out of this party." When we got to his room and I saw there was nobody there, I didn't think I could do anything about it.

We started kissing and then he started taking off my clothes. I kept telling him to stop and I was crying. I was scared of him and thought he was going to hurt me. . . . He had a hand over my face. I was five foot two and weighed 110 pounds. I didn't have any choice.

The assault lasted about half an hour. When it was over, Rachel went to her own room, just down the hall. She went to sleep praying that she wasn't pregnant.

I just wanted to block it out. I felt ashamed because it happened. I just felt dirty, violated. I thought it was my fault. It wasn't like he did something to me, it was like I let him do something to me, so I felt very bad about myself.

He came to my room the next day and wanted to go out with me. He felt that was the normal thing to do, I guess.

Rachel turned him down, but offered no explanation. She also did not report the rape.

Who would believe me? He was a really good football player. No one would have believed me if I said anything. I wouldn't have dreamed of saying anything.

Rachel's perception about not being believed would prove prescient. Later that year, her residence hall adviser (an older student) was raped by another athlete who came into her room as she lay in bed in a drunken stupor after a party. A university disciplinary board decided that since the woman was unconscious, the action could only be considered sexual misconduct, not rape. The male student received a light reprimand.

Four years later, Rachel finally began to tell people about the rape. Her friends, men and women, have been sympathetic and supportive. One friend even related her own date-rape experience. Talking about it has helped in Rachel's recovery, helped her believe in herself again. "I made some stupid choices, but him hurting me is not my fault," she says.

> You know, you're away from home for the first time and you want to go wild. You don't know what you're getting into. You just don't think people are going to hurt you.
>
> I just had no concept that anyone would do something like that to me.

Paula's Story

Paula is a social service professional who lives in the South with her young daughter. When she was 22, she worked as a hospital ward clerk at a Virginia medical facility. For several weeks, one of the young doctors, a resident specializing in the care of cancer patients, had been pressuring her to go out with him. "He had kind of a reputation (for dating a lot of women) around the hospital," she says. "I was aware of that, which is probably why I resisted seeing him for so long." But he was tall, good-looking, and successful, traits which probably had much to do with his popularity. "He had been bugging me for maybe two months, saying, 'I just want you to come over for dinner. Nothing's going to happen.' I mean, he made a really big production out of assuring me of that," she says.

Paula had recently broken up with her boyfriend. The doctor's fiancée lived out of town. After talking with him several times, she decided that he was just trying to be friendly.

> I thought how nice it would be to spend a platonic evening with a sympathetic ear. The first couple of hours were just that—good conversation, a wonderful meal, and a bottle of wine. He lived in a nice apartment with expensive furniture.
>
> After we finished eating, I felt ready to go. He pleaded with me to stay a bit longer. He had some pot he wanted to share and told me that it would relax me and lift my spirits.

Paula had smoked marijuana before, but never anything as potent. Looking back now, she believes it was medical-strength marijuana, the kind that is sometimes given by prescription to chemotherapy patients to ease their pain.

> I got real delusional. I felt like I was having hallucinations. I remember his face and it seemed disconnected from his body. It was distorted. I can remember losing muscular control.

Her date, however, was having no such problem. He took off her clothes and dragged her up some stairs to a bedroom.

> I started to cry. It was the only coping mechanism I had. I remember saying, "No, no, no," and crying profusely.
>
> I remember feeling like it was never going to stop. He was able to maintain an erection for a long time without coming. I remember thinking, "Oh, I can't stand this anymore. Either I have to die or he has to stop." It got to the point where the crying wasn't working; nothing was working. I was feeling like I was going to burst if he didn't stop doing these things to me because it was oral sex and he tried anal sex. He was forcing me to have oral sex and I said something like, "I'm going to throw up," and I think that's what spurred him to finish.
>
> He finished and that's when I was really in shock. I was in denial and disbelief up to that point, but when it was over with, I was very much in shock and really quite unable to maneuver around much. I think he must have helped me get dressed and sort of dragged me to the door. His demeanor was real sheepish.
>
> I remember somehow getting in my car, somehow driving home. I have no idea how I got home, none whatsoever. I'm lucky I didn't kill somebody on the road.

Paula went home and told her sister-in-law, who immediately wanted to go back and confront the man. Instead, Paula made her promise that she wouldn't tell anyone. Several days later, Paula saw the doctor at work; she glared ferociously at him, but said nothing.

> Acquaintance rape was an unknown thing, at least in my world it was, so the anger at him was in the form of "You lied to me. You tricked me. You conned me." I was aware of that, but I

was totally unaware that what he had done to me was a crime. I had no idea I could report it to the police. I had no idea I could charge him with anything.

A month later I moved more than a thousand miles away and lived with my folks for a while. I couldn't stand my father to touch me; I didn't even like to be real close to him. I just didn't want any bodily contact at all.

I cut off all my hair. I did not want to be attractive to men. I started wearing real androgynous clothes—nothing tight, nothing revealing—and reduced my makeup to almost nil. I just wanted to look neutered for a while because that felt safer.

It was several years before Paula started dating again, years filled with anger and distrust and sexual problems. As for the man who assaulted her, she did not speak to him before she quit her job and left town. But she has thought about him since.

At the time, it never crossed my mind that he would do this again and again. Now I am acutely aware that he probably used the same plan of action to rape a lot of women.

The Antioch College Sexual Offense Prevention Policy (1996)

Preface

Antioch College has made a strong commitment to the issue of respect, including respect for each individual's personal and sexual boundaries. Sexual offenses are dehumanizing. They are not just a violation of the individual, but of the Antioch community.

Some of the principles fundamental to this policy are:

1. All sexual behavior occurring between Antioch community members on or off the Antioch College campus must be consensual.

2. When a sexual offense, as defined herein, is committed by a community member, such action will not be tolerated.

3. While Antioch exists within a larger society governed by existing laws, it is also part of Antioch's mission to strive for the betterment of both the individual and society. Thus, our standards for behavior may be broader than currently exist under state and federal laws. Community members are expected to respect and uphold these standards. These community standards are part of Antioch's educational mission. Any educational community which does not recognize the potentially devastating effects of sexual offenses and does not work for an atmosphere of mutual respect and safety risks undermining their educational mission.

4. When state or federal laws may be violated, the College urges the complainant to take the matter to the appropriate governmental body. . . .

5. This policy is gender neutral, and applies equally to women and man of all sexual orientations, recognizing that both women and men commit sexual offenses, and both women and men may be sexually offended.

6. Community members need to be respectful and honor the confidentiality of participants as matters proceed under this policy.

7. This policy is not intended to suggest that community members should engage in sexual behavior. Rather, it is intended to encourage and support community members to make and place appropriate physical and sexual boundaries where they choose. Community members who choose to be sexually active should practice safe sex.

This policy is a crucial part of our educational and prevention efforts but represents only a part of our commitment to the safety and well-being of our community members.

"The Antioch College Sexual Offense Prevention Policy" was approved by the Board of Trustees of Antioch College on June 8, 1996. Reprinted by permission of Antioch College, Yellow Springs, Ohio.

A support network exists that consists of the Sexual Offense Prevention and Survivors' Advocacy Program, including its director who is an advocate for both the policy and survivors; the Peer Advocacy Program; a 24-hour crisis and support line; and other support services available through both the Program and the Counseling Center. The Program Director/Advocate (or other designated administrator) shall be responsible for initiation and coordination of measures required by this policy, unless otherwise specified.

Antioch College provides and maintains educational programs for all community members, some aspects of which are required. The educational aspects of this policy are intended to prevent sexual offenses and ultimately heighten community awareness. Each community member must also contribute their efforts to insure the proper implementation of this policy.

The implementation of this policy also utilizes established Antioch governance structures and adheres to contractual obligations.

Seeking to reduce the amount of sexual offenses occurring on campus, students in fall 1990 and winter 1991 drafted Antioch's first Sexual Offense Policy. The first revision was written in winter 1992 and included the definition of consent as "willing and verbal." The second revision, written in the winter and spring of 1996, strengthens the policy based on accumulated experience. This policy has come from students with the support of faculty, staff and administrators. This policy applies to every member of the Antioch Community.

Consent

1. For the purpose of this policy, "consent" shall be defined as follows:

    the act of willingly and verbally agreeing to engage in specific sexual behavior.

    See (4) below when sexual behavior is mutually and simultaneously initiated.

    Because of the importance of communication and the potential dangers when misunderstanding exists in a sexual situation, those involved in any sexual interaction need to share enough of a common understanding to be able to adequately communicate: 1) requests for consent;

and, 2) when consent is given, denied or withdrawn.

    Note: Recognized American and international sign languages are considered a form of verbal language for the purpose of this policy.

2. When sexual behavior is not mutually and simultaneously initiated, then the person who initiates sexual behavior is responsible for verbally asking for the consent of the other individual(s) involved.

3. The person with whom sexual contact/conduct is initiated shall verbally express his/her willingness or must verbally express consent, and/or express his/her lack of willingness by words, actions, gestures, or any other previously agreed upon communication.

    Silence and/or non-communication must never be interpreted as consent.

4. When sexual behavior is mutually and simultaneously initiated, then the persons involved share responsibility for getting/giving or refusing/denying consent by words, actions, gestures or by any other previously agreed upon communication.

5. Obtaining consent is an on-going process in any sexual interaction. Verbal consent should be obtained with each new level of physical and/or sexual behavior in any given interaction, regardless of who initiates it. Asking "Do you want to have sex with me?" is not enough. The request for consent must be specific to each act.

6. If someone has initially consented but then stops consenting during a sexual interaction, she/he should communicate withdrawal of consent verbally (example: saying "no" or "stop") and/or through physical resistance (example: pushing away). The other individual(s) must stop immediately.

7. In order for consent to be meaningful and valid under this policy:
    a) the person not initiating must have judgment and control unimpaired by any drug or intoxicant administered to prevent his/her resistance, and/or which has been

administered surreptitiously, by force or threat of force, or by deception;

b) the person not initiating must have judgment and control unimpaired by mental dysfunction which is known to the person initiating;

c) the person not initiating must not be asleep or unconscious;

d) the person initiating must not have forced, threatened, coerced, or intimidated the other individual(s) into engaging in sexual behavior.

8. To knowingly take advantage of someone who is under the influence of alcohol, drugs, prescribed or over-the-counter medication is not acceptable behavior in the Antioch community.

Offenses of the Sexual Offense Prevention Policy Defined

Our standards of behavior may be broader than currently exist under state and federal laws. These community standards are part of Antioch's educational mission, to be dealt with through on-campus administrative means as part of the educational process. When state or federal laws may be violated, the College urges a complainant to take the matter to the appropriate governmental body. . . .

The following actions are prohibited under Antioch College's Sexual Offense Prevention Policy and, in addition to possible criminal prosecution, may result in sanctions up to and including expulsion or termination of employment.

Non-Consensual Sexual Conduct:

Non-consensual sexual conduct. "Sexual conduct" means vaginal intercourse, anal intercourse, fellatio and cunnilingus between persons regardless of sex. Penetration, however slight, is sufficient to complete vaginal or anal intercourse. This category includes, but is not limited to, rape and sexual battery as defined in Ohio Revised Code.

Non-Consensual Sexual Comportment:

Non-consensual sexual comportment, exclusive of sexual conduct as defined above, means any sexual behavior which includes the insertion of any part of the body or any instrument, appara-

tus, or other object into the body cavity of another. This category includes, but is not limited to, felonious sexual penetration as defined in Ohio Revised Code.

Non-Consensual Sexual Contact I:

Non-consensual sexual contact I includes when a person has non-consensual contact with another; causes another to have non-consensual sexual contact with the offender; causes another without his/her consent to sexually touch her/himself; causes two or more other persons to have non-consensual sexual contact; when, for the purpose of preventing resistance, the offender substantially impairs the other person's or one of the other persons' judgment or control by administering any drug or intoxicant to the other person, surreptitiously, deceptively, or by force or threat of force. "Sexual contact" means the touching of an erogenous zone of another, including but not limited to the thigh, genitals, buttock, pubic region, or breast, for the purpose of sexually arousing or gratifying either person. This category includes, but is not limited to, gross sexual imposition as defined in Ohio Revised Code.

Non-Consensual Sexual Contact II:

Non-consensual sexual contact II includes when a person has non-consensual contact; causes another to have non-consensual contact with the offender; causes another without his/her consent to sexually touch her/himself; causes two or more other persons to have non-consensual sexual contact; when any of the following applies: 1) the offender knows that the sexual contact is likely to be offensive to the other person, or one of the other persons, or is reckless in that regard; 2) the offended knows that the other person's ability to appraise the nature of or control the offender's or touching person's conduct is substantially impaired; 3) the offender knows that the other person, or one of the other persons, is unaware of the sexual contact. "Sexual contact" means the touching of an erogenous zone of another, including but not limited to the thigh, genitals, buttock, pubic region, or breast, for the purpose of sexually arousing or gratifying either person. This category includes, but is not limited to, sexual imposition as defined in Ohio Revised Code.

*Insistent and/or Persistent
Sexual Harassment:*

Any insistent and/or persistent intimidation or abuse considered sexually threatening and/or offensive according to the standards of the Antioch community. This includes, but is not limited to, unwelcome and irrelevant comments, references, gestures or other forms of personal attention which are inappropriate and which may be perceived as persistent sexual overtones or denigration.

*Unnecessarily Endangering
the Health of Another:*

If someone knows or reasonably should know that she/he is infected with a disease or condition which can be transmitted sexually, that person must not engage in any sexual behavior with another individual in any manner which would put that individual at risk of contracting the disease or condition.

Before engaging in any behavior considered "high risk" for transmission the person who is infected has an obligation to inform the other individual so that an informed choice regarding safety can be made. This category acknowledges an individual's right to privacy regarding personal health matters, but holds that in balance with concern for individual and community safety.

Options If a Violation
May Have Occurred

1. To make our community as safe as possible for all community members, community members who are suspected of violating this policy should be made aware of the concern about their behavior. The other provisions of this policy provide channels and guidelines for such education. Sometimes people are not aware that their behavior is sexually offensive, threatening, or hurtful. Awareness of the effects of their behavior may cause them to change their behavior.

2. If someone suspects that a violation of this Sexual Offense Prevention Policy may have occurred, she/he should contact a member of the Sexual Offense Prevention and Survivors' Advocacy Program, or the Dean of Students.

A 24-hour Crisis and Support Line has been established. From on-campus, call [phone numbers deleted]. . . .

Any discussion of a suspected violation with a member of the Sexual Offense Prevention and Survivors' Advocacy Program or the Dean of Students will be treated as confidential.

3. *Options:* When a suspected violation of this policy is reported, the person who receives the report should explain to the person reporting all of the options which are appropriate in responding to the suspected offense.

   Those options include, in no particular order, and are not limited to:

   - directly confronting the alleged offender;
   - having appropriate mediation with the alleged offender;
   - having the Dean of Students or Associate Dean of Students talk with the alleged offender;
   - filing a formal complaint;
   - filing an anonymous or confidential complaint with a member of the Sexual Offense Prevention and Survivors' Advocacy Program so the alleged action is recorded;
   - getting counseling or crisis intervention;
   - getting appropriate medical treatment;
   - filing a police report if the alleged offense is against the law;
   - taking a concern to the Community Standards Board;
   - choosing to do nothing further.

   More than one of these options may be used by the person alleging she/he was violated (hereafter referred to as the "primary witness").

4. *Criminal Complaints:* It is strongly encouraged that suspected violations be reported, and that they be reported as soon as is reasonable after a suspected violation has occurred. Where criminal misconduct is involved (see Appendix B or Ohio Revised Code for definitions), reporting the mis-

conduct to the local law enforcement agency is strongly recommended.

Because of the need to collect physical evidence for criminal complaints, if the primary witness is giving any consideration to filing a criminal complaint, the primary witness should, as soon as possible, go to the hospital, ideally in the jurisdiction where the alleged crime occurred (for example, if the incident occurred on campus, the complainant should go to Greene Memorial Hospital in Xenia).

The primary witness is not charged for the administration of a rape evidence collection kit. A peer advocate, the Advocate, or a member of the Greene County Victim-Witness Program can accompany the primary witness to the hospital to provide information and support. . . .

Remedies

1. When a policy violation by a student is found by the Hearing Board, the Hearing Board shall also determine a remedy which is commensurate with the offense, except in those cases where mandatory remedies are prescribed in this policy.

   When a remedy is not prescribed, the Hearing Board shall determine the remedy in consultation with the Dean of Students and the Advocate, and shall include an educational and/or rehabilitation component as part of the remedy.

2. *For Non-Consensual Sexual Conduct:* In the event that the Hearing Board determines that a violation of non-consensual sexual conduct has occurred, as defined under this policy, the recommended remedy is immediate expulsion or removal from the campus.

3. *For Non-Consensual Sexual Comportment:* In the event that the Hearing Board determines that a violation of non-consensual sexual comportment has occurred, as defined under this policy, then the respondent should: a) be suspended immediately for a period of no less than six months; b)

successfully complete a treatment program for sexual offenders approved by the Director of Counseling Services before returning to campus; and c) upon return to campus, be subject to mandatory class and co-op scheduling so that the respondent and primary witness avoid, to the greatest extent possible, all contact, unless the primary witness agrees otherwise.

In the event that the Hearing Board determines that a second violation of non-consensual sexual comportment has occurred, with the same respondent, then the respondent must be expelled immediately.

4. *For Non-Consensual Sexual Contact I:* In the event that the Hearing Board determines that a violation of non-consensual sexual contact I has occurred, as defined under this policy, then the recommended remedy is that the respondent: a) be suspended immediately for a period of no less than six months; b) successfully complete a treatment program for sexual offenders approved by the Director of Counseling Services before returning to campus; and c) upon return to campus, be subject to mandatory class and co-op scheduling so that the respondent and primary witness avoid, to the greatest extent possible, all contact, unless the primary witness agrees otherwise.

In the event that the Hearing Board determines that a second violation of non-consensual sexual contact I has occurred, with the same respondent, then the respondent must be expelled immediately.

5. *For Non-Consensual Sexual Contact II:* In the event that the Hearing Board determines that a violation of non-consensual sexual contact II has occurred, as defined under this policy, then the recommended remedy is that the respondent: a) be suspended immediately for a period of no less than three months; b) successfully complete a treatment program for sexual offenders approved by the Director of Counseling Services before returning to campus; and c) upon return to campus, be

subject to mandatory class and co-op scheduling so that the respondent and primary witness avoid, to the greatest extent possible, all contact, unless the primary witness agrees otherwise.

In the event that the Hearing Board determines that a second violation of non-consensual sexual contact II has occurred, with the same respondent, then the respondent must be expelled immediately.

6. *For Insistent and/or Persistent Sexual Harassment:* In the event that the Hearing Board determines that a violation of insistent and/or persistent sexual harassment has occurred, as defined under this policy, then the recommended remedy is that the respondent: a) be suspended immediately for a period of no less than six months; b) successfully complete a treatment program for sexual offenders approved by the Director of Counseling Services before returning to campus; and c) upon return to campus, be subject to mandatory class and co-op scheduling so that the respondent and primary witness avoid, to the greatest extent possible, all contact, unless the primary witness agrees otherwise.

In the event that the Hearing Board determines that a second violation of insistent or persistent sexual harassment has occurred, with the same respondent, then the respondent must be expelled immediately.

7. *For Unnecessarily Endangering the Health of Another:* In the event that the Hearing Board determines that a violation of Unnecessarily Endangering the Health of Another has occurred, as defined under this policy, then the recommended remedy is left to the discretion of the Hearing Board.

8. In all cases, *a second offense* under this policy, regardless of category, must receive a more severe consequence than did the first offense if the second offense occurred after the Hearing Board's first finding of a respondent's violation of this policy.

9. The remedy for a *third offense,* regardless of category, must be expulsion, if the third offense occurred after the Hearing Board's first or second finding of a respondent's violation of this policy.

10. It is the responsibility of the Dean of Students to ensure that the Hearing Board's remedies are carried out. . . .

The 'Date-Rape Drug'

Kit Lively

Detective Troy Castillo has never actually encountered the drug called Rohypnol, or "roofie," in his work with the Palm Springs, Cal., police department.

But when a student from the University of California at Los Angeles accused three men of raping her at a fraternity party in Palm Springs this month, he decided to have her tested for Rohypnol along with other drugs and alcohol.

Mr. Castillo won't have the results of the test for a few weeks, but based on the woman's description of the ordeal, he is pretty sure that she was sedated. She admitted smoking marijuana and drinking at the party, he says, but he also suspects a so-called "date-rape drug." Several newspapers have had stories this year about women, many of them students, who reportedly had blacked out after the drug was slipped into their drinks and who woke up unsure of what had happened.

"There has been a lot of publicity on it, which causes people to experiment, unfortunately," Mr. Castillo says.

Prescribed for Insomnia

Rohypnol, a sedative, has not been approved by the U.S. Food and Drug Administration, but it is prescribed legally for insomnia in other countries, in-

Kit Lively, "The 'Date-Rape Drug': Colleges Worry About Reports of Abuse of Rohypnol, a Sedative," *The Chronicle of Higher Education* 28 June 1996, A29. Copyright (c) 1996 by *The Chronicle of Higher Education*, Inc.

cluding Mexico and Colombia. In the United States, federal officials say, the drug is most prevalent in Florida, Texas, and California, but they fear use is increasing. The Customs Service made its importation illegal in March. The U.S. Drug Enforcement Administration and the Florida Attorney General are considering whether to control it more stringently.

Officials of the D.E.A. say the small, white pills are easy to smuggle. Available for less than $5 each, they come in blister packs marked "Roche," from the name of the manufacturer, F. Hoffmann-La Roche Ltd., a Swiss company whose American affiliate is Hoffmann-La Roche Inc.

Police at large universities in states where officials say roofies are the most common say they've heard about the drug, although most say they've had no, or only a few, reports of its use.

At the University of Florida, however, officials say they've heard from students who reported using the drug to get high, and some who believed they could have been raped under its influence. People can lose memory of events that happen within several hours after taking Rohypnol, especially if they use it with alcohol.

Cpl. Mary Brock, of the police department at the University of Maryland at College Park, says she has heard about a few curious students who tried the drug. Its actual use is hard to nail down, she says, because people who take it may not remember what happened. That also can keep them from reporting incidents soon enough to be tested, officials say.

"I have seen a couple of students who wonder what happened to them," says Charlotte Hayes, a psychological counselor at San Diego State University. "They didn't know if they were drunk and passed out or what. But that happens from time to time."

"We know it is flying across the border," she adds. "Students are talking about it."

Sarah Calhoun, research director for the Haight-Ashbury Free Clinics Inc. in San Francisco, is part of a team that interviewed 66 Rohypnol users in Texas and is interviewing more in Florida for a study commissioned by Hoffmann-La Roche.

"We talked to a lot of people in Florida who hadn't heard about the drug until they heard about it on TV," she says. "Then they went out and bought it."

Reports from U. of Florida

Young people often use Rohypnol to enhance the effects of alcohol or marijuana, Ms. Calhoun says. She and drug counselors say many college students reported using it a few times and moving on to other drugs, because Rohypnol made them sleepy or because of its amnesiac effects.

Ms. Calhoun says the amnesia, which is like an alcohol blackout, increases as more Rohypnol is taken. The effect is not necessarily unconsciousness, she says. "You can be up and walking around. You just don't store long-term memory."

Maggie Gerard, coordinator of the Victim Advocate Program at the University of Florida police department, says she first heard about the drug a year ago. Since then, she says, many students have come forward to tell about using it, and 20 to 25 women have reported blackouts that made them suspect that they had been drugged. Victim advocates at other public universities in Florida have said their students are also using the drug, she adds.

"With women who suspect Rohypnol, there is a total blackout—no memory, no flashes," she says. "You get that with alcohol. But they would have been doing more alcohol than ever—and most just remember drinking one or two drinks."

Detectable for 60 Hours

None of the women were tested for Rohypnol, she says, because they waited too long to report the incidents. The drug is detectable for only about 60 hours after it is taken, Ms. Calhoun says.

Patricia Telles-Irvin, director of the student-counseling center at Florida International University, believes that the drug is probably being used, although no students have reported incidents to her yet.

"Rape victims usually do not come forward and say what happened," she says. "If they don't remember or have a spotty memory, the potential is usually higher that they will question what happened."

"What has become apparent is that people are becoming more perceptive or vigilant about it, so that when they do go to bars they are much more careful about where they put their glasses."

Hoffmann-La Roche announced last week that it will pay to test rape victims for the drug. Carolyn

R. Glynn, a vice-president of the company, says a toll-free number will be provided to police and rape-crisis centers. The company is also starting an ad campaign, "Watch your drink!"

Ms. Calhoun, of the Haight-Ashbury clinic, says an emphasis on early testing is important. Also important, she says, is hammering home the message that rape is still rape when the woman can't consent.

"The focus of date-rape prevention," she says, "needs to be on saying, 'Guys, if you know this woman is under the influence, she can't consent to anything. Take her home and put her in *her* bed.'"

40.

Violence in Intimate Relationships: A Feminist Perspective

bell hooks

bell hooks is a professor of English at City College in New York. She is the author of many books, including *Killing Rage: Ending Racism; Teaching to Transgress: Education as the Practice of Freedom; Black Looks: Race and Representation; Talking Back: Thinking Feminist, Thinking Black; Feminist Theory: From Margin to Center;* and, *Ain't I a Woman: Black Women and Feminism.* In this essay, bell hooks calls our attention to all forms of violence in all types of intimate relationships. We need to attend to the seemingly less extreme forms of violence in intimate relationships, including instances of men occasionally hitting women, and of mothers occasionally hitting their children. If feminists want to create a world in which intimate relationships are truly free of domination and abuse, then these seemingly lesser acts of violence must be stopped.

We were on the freeway, going home from San Francisco. He was driving. We were arguing. He had told me repeatedly to shut up. I kept talking. He took his hand from the steering wheel and threw it back, hitting my mouth— my open mouth, blood gushed, and I felt an intense pain. I was no longer able to say any words, only to make whimpering, sobbing sounds as the blood dripped on my hands, on the handkerchief I held too tightly. He did not stop the car. He drove home. I watched him pack his suitcase. It was a holiday. He was going away to have fun. When he left I washed my mouth. My jaw was swollen and it was difficult for me to open it.

I called the dentist the next day and made an appointment. When the female voice asked what I needed to see the doctor about, I told her I had been hit in the mouth. Conscious of race, sex, and class issues, I wondered how I would be treated in this white doctor's office. My face was no longer swollen so there was nothing to identify me as a woman who had been hit, as a black woman with a bruised and swollen jaw. When the dentist asked me what had happened to my mouth, I described it calmly and succinctly. He made little jokes about, "How we can't have someone doing this to us now, can we?" I said nothing. The damage was repaired. Through it all, he talked to me as if I were a child, someone he had to handle gingerly or otherwise I might become hysterical.

This is one way women who are hit by men and seek medical care are seen. People within patriarchal society imagine that women are hit because we are hysterical, because we are beyond reason. It is most often the person who is hitting that is beyond reason, who is hysterical, who has lost complete control over responses and actions.

Reprinted from bell hooks, *Talking Back: Thinking Feminist, Thinking Black,* with permission from the publisher, South End Press, 116 Saint Botolph Street, Boston, MA 02115.

Growing up, I had always thought that I would never allow any man to hit me and live. I would kill him. I had seen my father hit my mother once and I wanted to kill him. My mother said to me then, "You are too young to know, too young to understand." Being a mother in a culture that supports and promotes domination, a patriarchal, white-supremacist culture, she did not discuss how she felt or what she meant. Perhaps it would have been too difficult for her to speak about the confusion of being hit by someone you are intimate with, someone you love. In my case, I was hit by my companion at a time in life when a number of forces in the world outside our home had already "hit" me, so to speak, made me painfully aware of my powerlessness, my marginality. It seemed then that I was confronting being black and female and without money in the worst possible ways. My world was spinning. I had already lost a sense of grounding and security. The memory of this experience has stayed with me as I have grown as a feminist, as I have thought deeply and read much on male violence against women, on adult violence against children.

In this essay, I do not intend to concentrate attention solely on male physical abuse of females. It is crucial that feminists call attention to physical abuse in all its forms. In particular, I want to discuss being physically abused in singular incidents by someone you love. Few people who are hit once by someone they love respond in the way they might to a singular physical assault by a stranger. Many children raised in households where hitting has been a normal response by primary caretakers react ambivalently to physical assaults as adults, especially if they are being hit by someone who cares for them and whom they care for. Often female parents use physical abuse as a means of control. There is continued need for feminist research that examines such violence. Alice Miller has done insightful work on the impact of hitting even though she is at times antifeminist in her perspective. (Often in her work, mothers are blamed, as if their responsibility in parenting is greater than that of fathers.) Feminist discussions of violence against women should be expanded to include a recognition of the ways in which women use abusive physical force toward children not only to challenge the assumptions that women are likely to be nonviolent, but also to add to our understanding of why children who were hit growing up are often hit as adults or hit others.

Recently, I began a conversation with a group of black adults about hitting children. They all agreed that hitting was sometimes necessary. A professional black male in a southern family setting with two children commented on the way he punished his daughters. Sitting them down, he would first interrogate them about the situation or circumstance for which they were being punished. He said with great pride, "I want them to be able to understand fully why they are being punished." I responded by saying that "they will likely become women whom a lover will attack using the same procedure you who have loved them so well used and they will not know how to respond." He resisted the idea that his behavior would have any impact on their responses to violence as adult women. I pointed to case after case of women in intimate relationships with men (and sometimes women) who are subjected to the same form of interrogation and punishment they experienced as children, who accept their lover assuming an abusive, authoritarian role. Children who are the victims of physical abuse—whether one beating or repeated beatings, one violent push or several—whose wounds are inflicted by a loved one, experience an extreme sense of dislocation. The world one has most intimately known, in which one felt relatively safe and secure, has collapsed. Another world has come into being, one filled with terrors, where it is difficult to distinguish between a safe situation and a dangerous one, a gesture of love and a violent, uncaring gesture. There is a feeling of vulnerability, exposure, that never goes away, that lurks beneath the surface. I know. I was one of those children. Adults hit by loved ones usually experience similar sensations of dislocation, of loss, of new found terrors.

Many children who are hit have never known what it feels like to be cared for, loved without physical aggression or abusive pain. Hitting is such a widespread practice that any of us are lucky if we can go through life without having this experience. One undiscussed aspect of the reality of children who are hit finding themselves as adults in similar circumstances is that we often share with friends and lovers the framework of our childhood pains and this may determine how they respond to us in difficult situations. We share the ways we are wounded and expose vulnerable areas. Often, these revelations provide a detailed model for anyone who wishes to wound or hurt us. While the literature about physical abuse often points to the fact that children who are abused are likely to become abusers or be abused, there is no attention given to sharing woundedness in such a way that we let intimate others know exactly what can be done to hurt us, to make us feel as though we are caught in the destructive patterns we have struggled to break. When partners create scenarios of abuse similar, if not exactly the same, to those we have experienced in childhood, the wounded person is hurt not only by the physical pain but by the feeling of calculated betrayal. Betrayal. When we are physically hurt by loved ones, we feel betrayed. We can no longer trust that care can be sustained. We are wounded, damaged—hurt to our hearts.

Feminist work calling attention to male violence against women has helped create a climate where the issues of physical abuse by loved ones can be freely addressed, especially sexual abuse within families. Exploration of male violence against women by feminists and non-feminists shows a connection between childhood experience of being hit by loved ones and the later occurrence of violence in adult relationships. While there is much material available discussing physical abuse of women by men, usually extreme physical abuse, there is not much discussion of the impact that one incident of hitting may have on a person in an intimate relationship, or how the person who is hit recovers

from that experience. Increasingly, in discussion with women about physical abuse in relationships, irrespective of sexual preference, I find that most of us have had the experience of being violently hit at least once. There is little discussion of how we are damaged by such experiences (especially if we have been hit as children), of the ways we cope and recover from this wounding. This is an important area for feminist research precisely because many cases of extreme physical abuse begin with an isolated incident of hitting. Attention must be given to understanding and stopping these isolated incidents if we are to eliminate the possibility that women will be at risk in intimate relationships.

Critically thinking about issues of physical abuse has led me to question the way our culture, the way we as feminist advocates focus on the issue of violence and physical abuse by loved ones. The focus has been on male violence against women and, in particular, male sexual abuse of children. Given the nature of patriarchy, it has been necessary for feminists to focus on extreme cases to make people confront the issue, and acknowledge it to be serious and relevant. Unfortunately, an exclusive focus on extreme cases can and does lead us to ignore the more frequent, more common, yet less extreme case of occasional hitting. Women are also less likely to acknowledge occasional hitting for fear that they will then be seen as someone who is in a bad relationship or someone whose life is out of control. Currently, the literature about male violence against women identifies the physically abused woman as a "battered woman." While it has been important to have an accessible terminology to draw attention to the issue of male violence against women, the terms used reflect biases because they call attention to only one type of violence in intimate relationships. The term "battered woman" is problematical. It is not a term that emerged from feminist work on male violence against women; it was already used by psychologists and sociologists in the literature on domestic violence. This label "battered woman" places primary emphasis on physical assaults that are continuous, repeated, and unrelenting. The focus is on extreme violence, with little effort to link these cases with the everyday acceptance within intimate relationships of physical abuse that is not extreme, that may not be repeated. Yet these lesser forms of physical abuse damage individuals psychologically and, if not properly addressed and recovered from, can set the stage for more extreme incidents.

Most importantly, the term "battered woman" is used as though it constitutes a separate and unique category of womanness, as though it is an identity, a mark that sets one apart rather than being simply a descriptive term. It is as though the experience of being repeatedly violently hit is the sole defining characteristic of a woman's identity and all other aspects of who she is and what her experience has been are submerged. When I was hit, I too used the popular phrases "batterer," "battered woman," "battering" even though I did not feel that these words adequately described being hit once. However, these were the terms that people would listen to, would see as important, significant (as if it is not really significant for an individual, and more importantly for a woman, to be hit once). My partner was angry to be labelled a batterer by me. He was reluctant to talk about the experience of hitting me precisely because he did not want to be labelled a batterer. I had hit him once (not as badly as he had hit me) and I did not think of myself as a batterer. For both of us, these terms were inadequate. Rather than enabling us to cope effectively and positively with a negative situation, they were part of all the mechanisms of denial; they made us want to avoid confronting what had happened. This is the case for many people who are hit and those who hit.

Women who are hit once by men in their lives, and women who are hit repeatedly do not want to be placed in the category of "battered woman" because it is a label that appears to strip us of dignity, to deny that there has been any integrity in the relationships we are in. A person physically assaulted by a stranger or a casual friend with whom they are not intimate may be

hit once or repeatedly but they do not have to be placed into a category before doctors, lawyers, family, counselors, etc. take their problem seriously. Again, it must be stated that establishing categories and terminology has been part of the effort to draw public attention to the seriousness of male violence against women in intimate relationships. Even though the use of convenient labels and categories has made it easier to identify problems of physical abuse, it does not mean the terminology should not be critiqued from a feminist perspective and changed if necessary.

Recently, I had an experience assisting a woman who had been brutally attacked by her husband (she never commented on whether this was the first incident or not), which caused me to reflect anew on the use of the term "battered woman." This young woman was not engaged in feminist thinking or aware that "battered woman" was a category. Her husband had tried to choke her to death. She managed to escape from him with only the clothes she was wearing. After she recovered from the trauma, she considered going back to this relationship. As a church-going woman, she believed that her marriage vows were sacred and that she should try to make the relationship work. In an effort to share my feeling that this could place her at great risk, I brought her Lenore Walker's *The Battered Woman* because it seemed to me that there was much that she was not revealing, that she felt alone, and that the experiences she would read about in the book would give her a sense that other women had experienced what she was going through. I hoped reading the book would give her the courage to confront the reality of her situation. Yet I found it difficult to share because I could see that her self-esteem had already been greatly attacked, that she had lost a sense of her worth and value, and that possibly this categorizing of her identity would add to the feeling that she should just forget, be silent (and certainly returning to a situation where one is likely to be abused is one way to mask the severity of the problem). Still I had to try. When I first gave her the book, it disappeared. An unidentified family member had thrown it away. They felt that she would be making a serious mistake if she began to see herself as an absolute victim which they felt the label "battered woman" implied. I stressed that she should ignore the labels and read the content. I believed the experience shared in this book helped give her the courage to be critical of her situation, to take constructive action.

Her response to the label "battered woman," as well as the responses of other women who have been victims of violence in intimate relationships, compelled me to critically explore further the use of this term. In conversation with many women, I found that it was seen as a stigmatizing label, one which victimized women seeking help felt themselves in no condition to critique. As in, "who cares what anybody is calling it—I just want to stop this pain." Within patriarchal society, women who are victimized by male violence have had to pay a price for breaking the silence and naming the problem. They have had to be seen as fallen women, who have failed in their "feminine" role to sensitize and civilize the beast in the man. A category like "battered woman" risks reinforcing this notion that the hurt woman, not only the rape victim, becomes a social pariah, set apart, marked forever by this experience.

A distinction must be made between having a terminology that enables women, and all victims of violent acts, to name the problem and categories of labeling that may inhibit that naming. When individuals are wounded, we are indeed often scarred, often damaged in ways that do set us apart from those who have not experienced a similar wounding, but an essential aspect of the recovery process is the healing of the wound, the removal of the scar. This is an empowering process that should not be diminished by labels that imply this wounding experience is the most significant aspect of identity.

As I have already stated, overemphasis on extreme cases of violent abuse may lead us to ignore the problem of occasional hitting, and it may make it difficult for women to talk about this problem. A critical issue that is not fully ex-

amined and written about in great detail by researchers who study and work with victims is the recovery process. There is a dearth of material discussing the recovery process of individuals who have been physically abused. In those cases where an individual is hit only once in an intimate relationship, however violently, there may be no recognition at all of the negative impact of this experience. There may be no conscious attempt by the victimized person to work at restoring her or his well-being, even if the person seeks therapeutic help, because the one incident may not be seen as serious or damaging. Alone and in isolation, the person who has been hit must struggle to regain broken trust—to forge some strategy of recovery. Individuals are often able to process an experience of being hit mentally that may not be processed emotionally. Many women I talked with felt that even after the incident was long forgotten, their bodies remain troubled. Instinctively, the person who has been hit may respond fearfully to any body movement on the part of a loved one that is similar to the posture used when pain was inflicted.

Being hit once by a partner can forever diminish sexual relationships if there has been no recovery process. Again there is little written about ways folks recover physically in their sexualities as loved ones who continue to be sexual with those who have hurt them. In most cases, sexual relationships are dramatically altered when hitting has occurred. The sexual realm may be the one space where the person who has been hit experiences again the sense of vulnerability, which may also arouse fear. This can lead either to an attempt to avoid sex or to unacknowledged sexual withdrawal wherein the person participates but is passive. I talked with women who had been hit by lovers who described sex as an ordeal, the one space where they confront their inability to trust a partner who has broken trust. One woman emphasized that to her, being hit was a "violation of her body space" and that she felt from then on she had to protect that space. This response, though a survival strategy, does not lead to healthy recovery.

Often, women who are hit in intimate relationships with male or female lovers feel as though we have lost an innocence that cannot be regained. Yet this very notion of innocence is connected to passive acceptance of concepts of romantic love under patriarchy which have served to mask problematic realities in relationships. The process of recovery must include a critique of this notion of innocence which is often linked to an unrealistic and fantastic vision of love and romance. It is only in letting go of the perfect, no-work, happily-ever-after union idea, that we can rid our psyches of the sense that we have failed in some way by not having such relationships. Those of us who never focussed on the negative impact of being hit as children find it necessary to reexamine the past in a therapeutic manner as part of our recovery process. Strategies that helped us survive as children may be detrimental for us to use in adult relationships.

Talking about being hit by loved ones with other women, both as children and as adults, I found that many of us had never really thought very much about our own relationship to violence. Many of us took pride in never feeling violent, never hitting. We had not thought deeply about our relationship to inflicting physical pain.

Some of us expressed terror and awe when confronted with physical strength on the part of others. For us, the healing process included the need to learn how to use physical force constructively, to remove the terror—the dread. Despite the research that suggests children who are hit may become adults who hit—women hitting children, men hitting women and children—most of the women I talked with not only did not hit but were compulsive about not using physical force.

Overall the process by which women recover from the experience of being hit by loved ones is a complicated and multi-faceted one, an area where there must be much more feminist study and research. To many of us, feminists calling attention to the reality of violence in intimate relationships has not in and of itself compelled most people to take the issue seriously, and such violence seems to be daily on the increase. In this essay, I have raised issues that are not commonly talked about, even among folks who are particularly concerned about violence against women. I hope it will serve as a catalyst for further thought, that it will strengthen our efforts as feminist activists to create a world where domination and coercive abuse are never aspects of intimate relationships.

In Week of an Infamous Rape, 28 Other Victims Suffer

Don Terry

From poor women, whose suffering rarely makes headlines, to bankers on the fast track, to little girls in pigtails, vulnerability to rape is shared by all women and girls, experts say.

In the week in which a white investment banker was brutally beaten and raped as she jogged through Central Park, there were 28 other first-degree rapes or attempted rapes reported across New York City, the police said.

First-degree rape involves either the threat or the use of violence.

The attack on the jogger inspired angry cries for vengeance and increased police patrols, partly, some have argued, because those charged in the attack were minority-group teen-agers and the victim was an affluent white women.

Nearly all the rapes reported during that April week were of black or Hispanic women. Most went unnoticed by the public.

Ages Range from 8 to 51

The investment banker was attacked during the late evening of Wednesday, April 19. The other victims that week—April 16–22—were attacked while walking along the street, waiting for a train and visiting a friend.

The victims that week ranged in age from 8 years old to 51. But Linda Fairstein, an assistant Manhattan district attorney who heads the sex-crimes prosecution unit, said she has seen rape victims as young as a few months and as old as their 90's.

"Sexual violence happens to women of every racial and ethnic and economic background," said Brooklyn District Attorney Elizabeth Holtzman. "And the perpetrators also come from every racial and economic background."

"The Central Park attack was treated as extraordinary," said Francoise Jacobsohn, president of the New York City Chapter of the National Organization For Women. "It was not extraordinary. Sexual violence is a continuing problem. But we only talk about it when it's on the front pages. It happens all the time."

Less than two weeks after the Central Park case made headlines across the country, a 38-year-old black woman was taken at knife point from a Brooklyn street by two men who forced her up to the roof of a four-story building, raped and beat her. Then they threw her 50 feet to the ground. She suffered two broken ankles, a fractured right leg and abdominal injuries.

In New York City last year, 3,584 rapes and attempted rapes were reported. Those figures include first-, second- and third-degree rape charges. Second- and third-degree rape charges are brought when victims are either too young or not mentally competent to consent to sexual intercourse.

Last year, there were also 1,665 reported cases of sodomy and sexual abuse in the city, bringing the total number of reported sexual assaults to 5,249, a decrease of 60 from 1987.

But the rape statistics may only scratch the surface.

Detective Ellen King, who retired in May after 14 years with the New York City Police Department's sex-crimes unit, said law-enforcement officials across the nation estimate that only 1 or 2 out of every 10 rapes or sexual assaults are reported to the police.

Fear, shame and the victims' fear of being blamed for somehow encouraging the attack keep many women from reporting rapes, say experts and some victims.

"I was afraid he'd kill me," said a 53-year-old woman who was raped by an acquaintance in his 50's. "So I didn't press charges. It's not so easy to do."

Rapists are as varied as their victims—doctors and lawyers, homeless men and teen-age boys. The attackers can be strangers, carrying guns or knives, or acquaintances, armed with the victim's trust.

And every rapist carries the specter of death.

"Rape is a life-threatening situation," Detective King said. "I often talk with women who say, 'I should have kicked, I should have screamed.' I tell them, 'Look, whatever you did was the right thing, because you are alive, because you survived.'"

The 29 first-degree rapes reported from April 16 to April 22, were recorded sketchily in police records as investigations began. Authorities withheld the names of the victims and the specific locations of the crimes.

Rape crisis counselors and authorities point out that attackers and victims are most often of the same race. That was true in nearly all of the rapes that occurred during that April week. Among the victims were 17 blacks, 7 Hispanic women, 3 whites, and 2 Asians.

Sunday, April 16

7:30 P.M. A 12-year-old girl was accosted by four boys, ages, 11, 12, 13 and 15, in an apartment building in Harlem. They pulled her into a hallway, where they each raped her. The youngest boys were arrested. The 15-year-old has not yet been charged.

10 P.M. An 18-year-old woman was in her home in Port Richmond, Staten Island, when she was raped by an acquaintance at 10 P.M. A 22-year-old man was arrested and charged the next day.

Monday, April 17

4:30 A.M. A woman, 22, was visiting a male friend in Brooklyn when he forced her into a bedroom, took her money and raped her. No arrest was made. The police said the location of the crime was unknown because the victim refused to cooperate.

9:50 A.M. A woman, 51, was alone in a small store in the Bushwick section of Brooklyn when a man walked in, carrying a gun. He took $200 and pushed her into a back room, where he ordered her to disrobe, but he fled before raping her.

3:30 P.M. As she walked through the northern reaches of Central Park on the East Side, a woman, 26, was hit in the face, robbed and raped. The suspect escaped.

4 P.M. A 14-year-old girl was walking along Prospect Place in the Crown Heights section of Brooklyn when a 22-year-old man approached her and placed an object to her neck. He forced her to a nearby apartment where he raped her.

11:35 P.M. A woman, 18, walking down a street in Jamaica, Queens, was grabbed from behind by a man with a knife. He dragged her to a roof and raped her. The attacker escaped.

Tuesday, April 18

6:40 A.M. Two brothers and two other men accosted a 20-year-old woman on the street in Brooklyn Heights and forced her to a rooftop, where each man raped her. The brothers, 24 and 29 years old, were arrested and charged with first-degree rape. Their accomplices were being sought.

2:15 P.M. A 15-year-old girl in East Harlem was taken from an elevator by a man with a knife. He pushed her into an apartment, robbed and raped her. The man was later arrested and charged in several similar rapes in the area.

6 P.M. A woman, 22, was forced into a vacant office in a building in Midtown Manhattan, where she was raped. Her suspected attacker was arrested a week later.

8:30 P.M. A woman, 24, was walking along East 138th Street in the Melrose section of the Bronx when she was grabbed from behind. The attacker blindfolded her and drove her to an unknown location, where he raped her.

9:30 P.M. On a sidewalk in Far Rockaway, Queens, a woman, 28, was approached by a man who asked her if she would have sex with him. She refused. The man, 21, then dragged her to a beach, beat her about the face with his fists and raped her. He was arrested nine days later.

11 P.M. A 25-year-old woman was assaulted by an acquaintance who invited the woman to his home in the Crown Heights section of Brooklyn. The man forced the woman to undress and then raped her.

Wednesday, April 19

12:30 P.M. As she walked in the Canarsie section of Brooklyn, a 14-year-old girl was grabbed by two teen-agers. One of the boys had a gun. They forced her to an apartment, where they raped her. Before letting her go, the boy with the gun fired a shot into a wall.

2 P.M. A 15-year-old girl walked into an apartment building in the Coney Island section of Brooklyn, where she was confronted by a man who pulled a pistol and told her to follow him. He took her to an apartment, where two other men were waiting. Each man then raped her.

10:05 P.M. A 28-year-old investment banker, jogging through Central Park, was attacked by a group of teen-agers. They kicked and beat her, smashed her in the head with a pipe and raped her. The teen-agers, who were from East Harlem, were quickly arrested.

Thursday, April 20

2 A.M. A 15-year-old girl was raped by a 36-year-old acquaintance in the Bronx.

3 A.M. A woman, 20, was sitting with a male acquaintance in the Bronx. He forced her to smoke crack, then demanded sex. When she refused, he punched and choked her. Then he raped her.

4:30 A.M. A woman, 34, was going to meet a friend when she stopped to talk with two male acquaintances in the Bathgate section of the Bronx. When she asked if a mutual friend still lived in the area, the men offered to take her to the friend. Instead, they led her to a building on Southern Boulevard, where they raped her.

10 A.M. A 27-year-old woman accompanied an 18-year-old man she had just met on a walk through Central Park. Once in the park, he raped her.

4 P.M. In the Melrose section of the Bronx, an 8-year-old girl was raped by an acquaintance, a 50-year-old man.

11 P.M. An 18-year-old woman and a 25-year-old acquaintance had been socializing when the man demanded sex and raped the woman in an apartment in midtown Manhattan.

Friday, April 21

2:30 A.M. A 42-year-old woman was visiting a 20-year-old acquaintance in his home in Far

Rockaway, Queens. At some point, the visit turned ugly, and the man raped her.

6 P.M. In an apartment building in the East Flatbush section of Brooklyn, a 13-year-old girl was riding an elevator when a 15-year-old boy grabbed her and forced her to go the roof, where he raped her.

Saturday, April 22

3:05 A.M. On a Long Island Rail Road platform in Woodside, Queens, a 27-year-old woman was confronted by a man who said he had a gun. He ordered her to undress and attempted to rape her. He could not perform sexually, a common occurrence during rape, experts say, and fled after robbing her. Four days later, a man, 28, was arrested and charged with attempted rape and robbery.

5:45 A.M. A man with a gun approached a woman, 27, from behind in Woodhaven, Queens. He marched her to an abandoned truck and raped her. Two days later, a man, 35, from Brooklyn was arrested in the assault.

6 A.M. Two men, one of them armed with a stick, confronted a 23-year-old woman on a street in the Brownsville section of Brooklyn. They beat and raped her on the street.

6:30 A.M. A woman, 20, was alone on a street in the Bedford-Stuyvesant section of Brooklyn when a man grabbed her from behind, forced her into an abandoned car and raped her.

10 P.M. Two men, one holding a gun, forced a woman, 26, beneath the Williamsburg Bridge in Brooklyn and raped her.

According to F.B.I. statistics, a forcible rape is committed in this country every six minutes.

41.

Men in Groups: Collective Responsibility for Rape

Larry May and Robert Strikwerda

Larry May is professor of philosophy at Washington University and is the author of several books on moral and political philosophy, including *The Morality of Groups and Sharing Responsibility*. Robert Strikwerda teaches philosophy at Indiana University at Kokomo and is the author of numerous articles in philosophy of social science and moral philosophy. He and Larry May co-edited *Rethinking Masculinity: Philosophical Explorations in Light of Feminism*. In this essay, they defend the controversial claim that a group can be held responsible for the harms done by individual members of the group; they apply this claim to sexual violence committed by men against women: To the extent that male bonding and male group socialization contribute to the prevalence of rape in our society, then men as a group should accept responsibility for the prevalence of rape, and should seek to reduce rape and speak out against sexual violence against women. "Rape is indeed a crime against humanity, not merely a crime against a particular woman. And rape is a crime perpetrated by men as a group, not merely by the individual rapist."

We criticize the following views: only the rapist is responsible since only he committed the act; no one is responsible since rape is a biological response to stimuli; everyone is responsible since men and women contribute to the rape culture; and patriarchy is responsible but no person or group. We then argue that, in some societies, men are collectively responsible for rape since most benefit from rape and most are similar to the rapist.

Larry May and Robert Strikwerda, "Men in Groups: Collective Responsibility for Rape," *Hypatia* 9 (Spring 1994): 134–151. Copyright (c) 1994 by Larry May and Robert Strikwerda. Reprinted with the authors' permission.

As teenagers, we ran in a crowd that incessantly talked about sex. Since most of us were quite afraid of discovering our own sexual inadequacies, we were quite afraid of women's sexuality. To mask our fear, of which we were quite ashamed, we maintained a posture of bravado, which we were able to sustain through mutual reinforcement when in small groups or packs. Riding from shopping mall to fast food establishment, we would tell each other stories about our sexual exploits, stories we all secretly believed to be pure fictions. We drew strength from the camaraderie we felt during these experiences. Some members of our group would yell obscenities at women on the street as we drove by. Over time, conversation turned more and more to group sex, especially forced sex with women we passed on the road. To give it its proper name, our conversation turned increasingly to rape. At a certain stage, we tired of it all and stopped associating with this group of men, or perhaps they were in most ways still boys. The reason we left was not that we disagreed with what was going but, if this decision to leave was reasoned at all, it was that the posturing (the endless attempts to impress one another by our dating ways) simply became very tiresome. Only much later in life did we think that there was anything wrong, morally, socially, or politically, with what went on in that group of adolescents who seemed so ready to engage in rape. Only later still did we wonder whether we shared in responsibility for the rapes that are perpetrated by those men who had similar experiences to ours.[1]

Catharine MacKinnon has recently documented the link between violence and rape in the war in Bosnia. Young Serbian soldiers, some with no previous sexual experience, seemed quite willing to rape Muslim and Croatian women as their reward for "winning" the war. These young men were often encouraged in these acts by groups of fellow soldiers, and even sometimes by their commanding officers. Indeed, gang rape in concentration camps, at least at the beginning of the war, seems to have been common. (Post, et al., in *Newsweek*) The situation in Bosnia is by no means unique in the history of war (Brownmiller, 37). But rape historically has never been considered a war crime. MacKinnon suggests that this is because "Rape in war has so often been treated as extracurricular, as just something men do, as a product rather than a policy of war" (MacKinnon 1993, 30).

War crimes are collective acts taken against humanity; whereas rape has almost always been viewed as a despicable "private" act. In this paper we wish to challenge the view that rape is the responsibility only of the rapists by challenging the notion that rape is best understood as an individual, private act. This is a paper about the relationship between the shared experiences of men in groups, especially experiences that make rape more likely in western culture, and the shared responsibility of men for the prevalence of rape in that culture. The claim of the paper is that in some societies men are collectively responsible for rape in that most if not all men contribute in various ways to the prevalence of rape, and as a result these men should share in responsibility for rape.

Most men do very little at all to oppose rape in their societies; does this make them something like co-conspirators with the men who rape? In Canada, a number of men have founded the "White Ribbon Campaign." This is a program of fund-raising, consciousness raising, and symbolic wearing of white ribbons during the week ending on December 6th, the anniversary of the murder of 14 women at a Montreal engineering school by a man shouting "I hate feminists." Should men in U.S. society start a similar campaign? If they do not, do they deserve the "co-conspirator" label? If they do, is this symbolic act enough to diminish their responsibility? Should men be speaking out against the program of rape in the war in Bosnia? What should they tell their sons about such rapes, and about rapes that occur in their home towns? If men remain silent, are they not complicitous with the rapists?

We will argue that insofar as male bonding and socialization in groups contributes to the prevalence of rape in western societies, men in those societies should feel responsible for the prevalence of rape and should feel motivated to counteract such violence and rape. In addition, we will argue that rape should be seen as something that men, as a group, are collectively responsible for, in a way which parallels the collective responsibility of a society for crimes against humanity perpetrated by some members of their society. Rape is indeed a crime against humanity, not merely a crime against a particular woman. And rape is a crime perpetrated by men as a group, not merely by the individual rapist.

To support our claims we will criticize four other ways to understand responsibility for rape. First, it is sometimes said that only the rapist is responsible since he alone intentionally committed the act of rape. Second, it is sometimes said that no one is responsible since rape is merely a biologically oriented response to stimuli that men have little or no control over. Third, it is sometimes said that everyone, women and men alike, contribute to the violent environment which produces rape so both women and men are equally responsible for rape, and hence it is a mistake to single men out. Fourth, it is sometimes said that it is "patriarchy," rather than individual men or men as a group, which is responsible for rape.[2] After examining each of these views we will conclude by briefly offering our own positive reasons for thinking that men are collectively responsible for the prevalence of rape in western society.

I. THE RAPIST AS LONER OR DEMON

Joyce Carol Oates has recently described the sport of boxing, where men are encouraged to violate the social rule against harming one another, as "a highly organized ritual that violates taboo."

> The paradox of the boxer is that, in the ring, he experiences himself as a living conduit for the inchoate, demonic will of the crowd: the expression of their collective desire, which is to pound another human being into absolute submission. (Oates 1992, 60)

Oates makes the connection here between boxing and rape. The former boxing heavyweight champion of the world, Mike Tyson, epitomizes this connection both because he is a convicted rapist, and also because, according to Oates, in his fights he regularly used the pre-fight taunt, "I'll make you into my girlfriend," clearly the "boast of a rapist." (Oates 1992, 61)

Just after being convicted of rape, Mike Tyson gave a twisted declaration of his innocence:

> I didn't rape anyone. I didn't hurt anyone— no black eyes, no broken ribs. When I'm in the ring, I break their ribs, I break their jaws. To me, that's hurting someone. (*St. Louis Post Dispatch*, March 27, 1992, 20A)

In the ring, Tyson had a license to break ribs and jaws; and interestingly he understood that this was a case of hurting another person. It was just that in the ring it was acceptable. He knew that he was not supposed to hurt people outside the ring. But since he didn't break any ribs or jaws, how could anyone say that he hurt his accuser, Desiree Washington? Having sex with a woman could not be construed as having hurt her, for Tyson apparently, unless ribs or jaws were broken.

Tyson's lawyers, attempting to excuse Tyson's behavior, said that the boxer grew up in a "male-dominated world." And this is surely true. He was plucked from a home for juvenile delinquents and raised by boxing promoters. Few American males had been so richly imbued with male tradition, or more richly rewarded for living up to the male stereotype of the aggressive, indomitable fighter. Whether or not he recognized it as a genuine insight, Tyson's lawyer points us toward the heart of the matter in American culture: misbehavior, especially sexual misbehavior of males toward females is, however mixed the messages, something that many men condone.

This has given rise to the use of the term "the rape culture" to describe the climate of attitudes that exists in the contemporary American male-dominated world (see Griffin 1971).

While noting all of this, Joyce Carol Oates ends her *Newsweek* essay on Tyson's rape trial by concluding that "no one is to blame except the perpetrator himself." She absolves the "culture" at large of any blame for Tyson's behavior. Oates regards Tyson as a sadist who took pleasure in inflicting pain both in and out of the boxing ring. She comes very close to demonizing him when, at the end of her essay, she suggests that Tyson is an outlaw or even a sociopath. And while she is surely right to paint Tyson's deed in the most horrific colors, she is less convincing when she suggests that Tyson is very different from other males in our society. In one telling statement in her essay, however, Oates opens the door for a less individualistic view of rape by acknowledging that the boxing community had built up in Tyson a "grandiose sense of entitlement, fueled by the insecurities and emotions of adolescence" (Oates 1992, 61).

Rape is normally committed by individual men; but, in our view, rape is not best understood in individualistic terms. The chief reasons for this are that individual men are more likely to engage in rape when they are in groups, and men receive strong encouragement to rape from the way they are socialized as men, that is, in the way they come to see themselves as instantiations of what it means to be a man. Both the "climate" that encourages rape and the "socialization" patterns which instill negative attitudes about women are difficult to understand or assess when one focuses on the isolated individual perpetrator of a rape. There are significant social dimensions to rape that are best understood as group-oriented.

As parents, we have observed that male schoolchildren are much more likely to misbehave (and subsequently to be punished by being sent to "time out") than are female schoolchildren. This fact is not particularly remarkable, for boys are widely believed to be more active than

girls. What is remarkable is that school teachers, in our experience, are much more likely to condone the misbehavior of boys than the misbehavior of girls. "Boys will be boys" is heard as often today as it was in previous times. (See Robert Lipsyte's (1993) essay about the Glen Ridge, New Jersey rape trial where the defense attorney used just these words to defend the star high school football players who raped a retarded girl). From their earliest experience with authority figures, little boys are given mixed signals about misbehavior. Yes, they are punished, but they are also treated as if their misbehavior is expected, even welcome. It is for some boys, as it was for us, a "badge of honor" to be sent to detention or "time out." From older boys and from their peers, boys learn that they often will be ostracized for being "too goody-goody." It is as if part of the mixed message is that boys are given a license to misbehave.

And which of these boys will turn out to be rapists is often as much a matter of luck as it is a matter of choice. Recent estimates have it that in the first few months of the war "30,000 to 50,000 women, most of them Muslim" were raped by Serbian soldiers (Post et al., 1993, 32). The data on date rape suggest that young men in our society engage in much more rape than anyone previously anticipated. It is a serious mistake in psychological categorization to think that all of these rapes are committed by sadists. (Studies by Amir show that the average rapist is not psychologically "abnormal." [Cited in Griffin 1971, 178].) Given our own experiences and similar reports from others, it is also a serious mistake to think that those who rape are significantly different from the rest of the male population. (Studies by Smithyman indicate that rapists "seemed not to differ markedly from the majority of males in our culture." [Cited in Scully 1990, 75].) Our conclusion is that the typical rapist is not a demon or sadist, but, in some sense, could have been many men.

Most of those who engage in rape are at least partially responsible for these rapes, but the question we have posed is this: are those who perpetrate rape the *only* ones who are responsible for rape? Contrary to what Joyce Carol Oates contends, we believe that it is a serious mistake to think that only the perpetrators are responsible. The interactions of men, especially in all-male groups, contribute to a pattern of socialization that also plays a major role in the incidence of rape. In urging that more than the individual perpetrators be seen as responsible for rape, we do not mean to suggest that the responsibility of the perpetrator be diminished. When responsibility for harm is shared it need not be true that the perpetrators of harm find their responsibility relieved or even diminished. Rather, shared responsibility for harms merely means that the range of people who are implicated in these harms is extended. (More will be said on this point in the final section.)

II. THE RAPIST AS VICTIM OF BIOLOGY

The most recent psychological study of rape is that done by Randy Thornhill and Nancy Wilmsen Thornhill (1992), "The Evolutionary Psychology of Men's Coercive Sexuality." In this work, any contention that coercion or rape may be socially or culturally learned is derisively dismissed, as is any feminist argument for changing men's attitudes through changing especially group-based socialization. The general hypothesis they support is that

> sexual coercion by men reflects a sex-specific, species-typical psychological adaptation to rape: Men have certain psychological traits that evolved by natural selection specifically in the context of coercive sex and made rape adaptive during human evolution. (363)

They claim that rape is an adaptive response to biological differences between men and women.

Thornhill and Thornhill contend that the costs to women to engage in sex ("nine months of pregnancy") greatly exceed the costs to men ("a few minutes of time and an energetically cheap ejaculate"). As a result women and men come very early in evolutionary time to adapt quite differently sexually.

> Because women are more selective about mates and more interested in evaluating them and delaying copulation, men, to get sexual access, must often break through feminine barriers of hesitation, equivocation, and resistance. (366)

Males who adapted by developing a proclivity to rape and thus who "solved the problem" by forcing sex on a partner, were able to "out-reproduce" other more passive males and gain an evolutionary advantage.

In one paragraph, Thornhill and Thornhill dismiss feminists who support a "social learning theory of rape" by pointing out that males of several "species with an evolutionary history of polygyny" are also "more aggressive, sexually assertive and eager to copulate." Yet, in "the vast majority of these species there is no sexual training of juveniles by other members of the group." This evidence, they conclude, thoroughly discredits the social learning theory and means that such theories "are never alternatives to evolutionary hypotheses about psychological adaptation" (364). In response to their critics, Thornhill and Thornhill go so far as to say that the feminist project of changing socialization patterns is pernicious.

> The sociocultural view does seem to offer hope and a simple remedy in that it implies that we need only fix the way that boys are socialized and rape will disappear. This naive solution is widespread. . . . As Hartung points out, those who feel that the social problem of rape can be solved by changing the nature of men through naive and arbitrary social adjustments should "get real about rape" because their perspective is a danger to us all. (416)

According to the Thornhills, feminists and other social theorists need to focus instead on what are called the "cues that affect the use of rape by adult males" (416).

The evolutionary biological account of rape we have rehearsed above would seemingly suggest that no one is responsible for rape. After all, if rape is an adaptive response to different sexual development in males and females, particular individuals who engage in rape are merely doing what they are naturally adapted to do. Rape is something to be controlled by those who control the "cues" that stimulate the natural rapist instincts in all men. It is for this reason that the Thornhills urge that more attention be given to male arousal and female stimulation patterns in laboratory settings (375). Notice that even on the Thornhills' own terms, those who provide the cues may be responsible for the prevalence of rape, even if the perpetrators are not. But Thornhill and Thornhill deny that there are any normative conclusions that follow from their research and criticize those who wish to draw out such implications as committing the "naturalistic fallacy" (see 407).

In contrast to the Thornhills, a more plausible sociobiological account is given by Lionel Tiger. Tiger is often cited as someone who attempted to excuse male aggression. In his important study he defines aggression as distinct from violence, but nonetheless sees violence as one possible outcome of the natural aggressive tendencies, especially in men.

> Aggression occurs when an individual or group see their interest, their honor, or their job bound up with coercing the animal, human, or physical environment to achieve their own ends rather than (or in spite of) the goals of the object of their action. Violence may occur in the process of interaction. (Tiger 1984, 158–59)

For Tiger, aggression is intentional behavior which is goal-directed and based on procuring something which is necessary for survival. Aggression is a "'normal' feature of the human biologically based repertoire" (159). Violence, "coercion involving physical force to resolve

conflict," (159) on the other hand, is not necessarily a normal response to one's environment, although in some circumstances it may be. Thus, while human males are evolutionarily adapted to be aggressive, they are not necessarily adapted to be violent.

Tiger provided an account that linked aggression in males with their biological evolution.

> Human aggression is in part a function of the fact that hunting was vitally important to human evolution and that aggression is typically undertaken by males in the framework of a unisexual social bond of which participants are aware and with which they are concerned. It is implied, therefore, that aggression is 'instinctive' but also must occur within an explicit social context varying from culture to culture and to be learned by members of any community. . . . Men in continuous association aggress against the environment in much the same way as men and women in continuous association have sexual relations. (Tiger 1984, 159–60)

And while men are thus predisposed to engage in aggression, in ways that women are not, it is not true in Tiger's view that a predisposition to engage in violent acts is a normal part of this difference.

Thornhill and Thornhill fail to consider Tiger's contention that men are evolutionarily adapted to be aggressive, but not necessarily to be violent. With Tiger's distinction in mind it may be said that human males, especially in association with other males, are adapted to aggress against women in certain social environments. But this aggressive response need not lead to violence, or the threat of violence, of the sort epitomized by rape; rather it merely affect noncoercive mating rituals. On a related point, Tiger argues that the fact that war has historically been "virtually a male monopoly" (81) is due to both male bonding patterns and evolutionary adaptation. Evolutionary biology provides only part of the story since male aggressiveness need not result in such violent encounters as occur in war or rape. After all, many men do not rape or go to war; the cultural cues provided by socialization must be considered at least as important as evolutionary adaptation.

We side with Tiger against the Thornhills in focusing on the way that all-male groups socialize their members and provide "cues" for violence. Tiger has recently allied himself with feminists such as Catharine MacKinnon and others who have suggested that male attitudes need to be radically altered in order to have a major impact on the incidence of rape (see the preface to the second edition of *Men in Groups*). One of the implications of Tiger's research is that rape and other forms of male aggressive behavior are not best understood as isolated acts of individuals. Rather than simply seeing violent aggression as merely a biologically predetermined response, Tiger places violent aggressiveness squarely into the group dynamics of men's interactions—a result of his research not well appreciated.

In a preface to the second edition of his book, Tiger corrects an unfortunate misinterpretation of his work.

> One of the stigmas which burdened this book was an interpretation of it as an apology for male aggression and even a potential stimulus of it—after all, boys will be boys. However I clearly said the opposite: "This is not to say that . . . hurtful and destructive relations between groups of men are inevitable. . . . It may be possible, as many writers have suggested, to alter social conceptions of maleness so that gentility and equivocation rather than toughness and more or less arbitrary decisiveness are highly valued." (Tiger 1984, 191)

If Tiger is right, and the most important "cues" are those which young boys and men get while in the company of other boys and men, then the feminist project of changing male socialization patterns may be seen as consistent with, rather than opposed to, the sociobiological hypotheses. Indeed, other evidence may be cited to buttress the feminist social learning perspective against the Thornhills. Different human societies have quite different rates of rape. In her anthropological research among the Minangkabau of West Sumatra, Peggy Reeves Sanday has found that this society is relatively rape-free. Rape does occur, but at such a low rate—28 per 3 million in 1981–82 for example—as to be virtually nonexistent (Sanday 1986, 85; also see Sanday, 1990 and Lepowsky). In light of such research, men, rather than women, are the ones who would need to change their behavior. This is because it is the socialization of men by men in their bonding-groups, and the view of women that is engendered, that provides the strongest cues toward rape. Since there may indeed be something that males could and should be doing differently that would affect the prevalence of rape, it does not seem unreasonable to continue to investigate the claim that men are collectively responsible for the prevalence of rape.

III. THE RAPIST AS VICTIM OF SOCIETY

It is also possible to acknowledge that men are responsible for the prevalence of rape in our society but nonetheless to argue that women are equally responsible. Rape is often portrayed as a sex crime perpetrated largely by men against women. But importantly, rape is also a crime of violence, and many factors in our society have increased the prevalence of violence. This prevalence of violence is the cause of both rape and war in western societies. Our view, that violence of both sorts is increased in likelihood by patterns of male socialization which then creates collective male responsibility, may be countered by pointing out that socialization patterns are created by both men and women, thereby seemingly implicating both men and women in collective responsibility for rape and war.

Sam Keen has contended that it is violence that we should be focusing on rather than sex or gender, in order to understand the causes and remedies for the prevalence of rape. According to Keen,

Men are violent because of the systematic violence done to their bodies and spirits. Being hurt they become hurters. In the overall picture, male violence toward women is far less than male violence toward other males . . . these outrages are a structural part of a warfare system that victimizes both men and women. (Keen 1991, 47)

Keen sees both men and women conspiring together to perpetuate this system of violence, especially in the way they impart to their male children an acceptance of violence.

Women are singled out by Keen as those who have not come to terms with their share of responsibility for our violent culture. And men have been so guilt-tripped on the issue of rape that they have become desensitized to it. Keen thinks that it is a mistake to single out men, and not women also, as responsible for rape.

Until women are willing to weep for and accept equal responsibility for the systematic violence done to the male body and spirit by the war system, it is not likely that men will lose enough of their guilt and regain enough of their sensitivity to accept responsibility for women who are raped. (Keen 1991, 47)

Even though women are equally responsible for the rape culture, in Keen's view, women should be singled out because they have not previously accepted their share of responsibility for the creation of a violent society.

Keen is at least partially right insofar as he insists that issues of rape and war be understood as arising from the same source, namely the socialization of men to be violent in western cultures. We agree with Keen that rape is part of a larger set of violent practices that injure both men and women. He is right to point out that men are murdering other men in our society in increasing numbers, and that this incidence of violence probably has something to do with the society's general condoning, even celebrating, of violence, especially in war.

Keen fails to note though that it is men, not women, who are the vast majority of both rapists and murderers in our society. And even if some women do act in ways which trigger violent reactions in men, nevertheless, in our opinion this pales in comparison with the way that men socialize each other to be open to violence. As Tiger and others have suggested, aggressive violence results primarily from male-bonding experiences. In any event, both fathers and mothers engage in early childhood socialization. Men influence the rape culture both through early childhood socialization and through male-bonding socialization of older male children. But women only contribute to this culture, when they do, through individual acts of early childhood socialization. For this reason, Keen is surely wrong to think that women share responsibility *equally* with men for our rape culture.

In our view, some women could prevent some rapes; and some women do contribute to the patterns of socialization of both men and women that increase the incidence of rape. For these reasons, it would not be inappropriate to say that women share responsibility for rape as well as men. But we believe that it is a mistake to think that women share equally in this responsibility with men. For one thing, women are different from men in that they are, in general, made worse off by the prevalence of rape in our society. As we will next see, there is a sense in which men, but not women, benefit from the prevalence of rape, and this fact means that men have more of a stake in the rape culture, and hence have more to gain by its continued existence.

In general, our conclusion is that women share responsibility, but to a far lesser extent than men, for the prevalence of rape. We do not support those who try to "blame the victim" by holding women responsible for rape because of not taking adequate precautions, or dressing seductively, etc. Instead, the key for us is the role that women, as mothers, friends and lovers, play in the overall process of male socialization that creates the rape culture. It should come as no surprise that few members of western society can be relieved of responsibility for this rape culture given the overwhelming pervasiveness of that culture. But such considerations should not deter us from looking to men, first and foremost, as being collectively responsible for the prevalence of rape. The women who do contribute to aggressive male-socialization do so as individuals; women have no involvement parallel to the male-bonding group.

IV. THE RAPIST AS GROUP MEMBER

Popular literature tends to portray the rapist as a demonic character, as the "Other." What we find interesting about the research of Thornhill and Thornhill is that it operates unwittingly to support the feminist slogan that "all men are rapists," that the rapist is not male "Other" but male "Self." What is so unsettling about the tens of thousands of rapes in Bosnia is the suggestion that what ordinary men have been doing is not significantly different from what the "sex-fiends" did. The thesis that men are adapted to be predisposed to be rapists, regardless of what else we think of the thesis, should give us pause and make us less rather than more likely to reject the feminist slogan. From this vantage point, the work of Tiger as well as Thornhill and Thornhill sets the stage for a serious reconsideration of the view that men are collectively responsible for rape.

There are two things that might be meant by saying that men are collectively responsible for the prevalence of rape in western culture. First, seeing men as collectively responsible may mean that men as a group are responsible in that they form some sort of super-entity that causes, or at least supports, the prevalence of rape. When some feminists talk of "patriarchy," what they seem to mean is a kind of institution that operates through, but also behind the backs of, individual men to oppress women. Here it may be that men are collectively responsible for the prevalence of rape and yet no men are individually responsible. We call this nondistributive

collective responsibility. Second, seeing men as collectively responsible may mean that men form a group in which there are so many features that the members share in common, such as attitudes or dispositions to engage in harm, that what holds true for one man also holds true for all other men. Because of the common features of the members of the group men, when one man is responsible for a particular harm, other men are implicated. Each member of the group has a share in the responsibility for a harm such as rape. We call this distributive collective responsibility (see May 1992, Ch. 2). In what follows we will criticize the first way of understanding men's collective responsibility, and offer reasons to support the second.

When collective responsibility is understood in the first (nondistributive) sense, this form of responsibility is assigned to those groups that have the capacity to act. Here there are two paradigmatic examples: the corporation and the mob (see May 1992. Chs. 2 and 4). The corporation has the kind of organizational structure that allows for the group to form intentions and carry out those intentions, almost as if the corporation were itself a person. Since men, qua men, are too amorphous a group to be able to act in an organized fashion, we will not be interested in whether they are collectively responsible in this way. But it may be that men can act in the way that mobs act, that is, not through a highly organized structure but through something such as like-mindedness. If there is enough commonality of belief, disposition and interest of all men, or at least all men within a particular culture, then the group may be able to act just as a mob is able to respond to a commonly perceived enemy.

It is possible to think of patriarchy as the oppressive practices of men coordinated by the common interests of men, but not organized intentionally. It is also productive to think of rape as resulting from patriarchy. For if there is a "collective" that is supporting or creating the prevalence of rape it is not a highly organized one, since there is nothing like a corporation that intentionally plans the rape of women in western culture. If the current Serbian army has engaged in the systematic and organized rape of Muslim women as a strategy of war, then this would be an example of nondistributive responsibility for rape. But the kind of oppression characterized by the prevalence of rape in most cultures appears to be systematic but not organized. How does this affect our understanding of whether men are collectively responsible for rape?

If patriarchy is understood merely as a system of coordination that operates behind the backs of individual men, then it may be that no single man is responsible for any harms that are caused by patriarchy. But if patriarchy is understood as something which is based on common interests, as well as common benefits, extended to all or most men in a particular culture, then it may be that men are collectively responsible for the harms of patriarchy in a way which distributes out to all men, making each man in a particular culture at least partially responsible for the harms attributable to patriarchy. This latter strategy is consistent with our own view of men's responsibility for rape. In the remainder of this essay we will offer support for this conceptualization of the collective responsibility of men for the prevalence of rape.

Our positive assessment, going beyond our criticism of the faulty responses in earlier sections of our paper, is that men in western culture are collectively responsible in the distributive sense, that is, they each share responsibility, for the prevalence of rape in that culture. This claim rests on five points: (1) Insofar as most perpetrators of rape are men, then these men are responsible, in most cases, for the rapes they committed. (2) Insofar as some men, by the way they interact with other (especially younger) men, contribute to a climate in our society where rape is made more prevalent, then they are collaborators in the rape culture and for this reason share in responsibility for rapes committed in that culture. (3) Also, insofar as some men are not unlike the rapist, since they would be rapists if they had the opportunity to be

placed into a situation where their inhibitions against rape were removed, then these men share responsibility with actual rapists for the harms of rape. (4) In addition, insofar as many other men could have prevented fellow men from raping, but did not act to prevent these actual rapes, then these men also share responsibility along with the rapists. (5) Finally, insofar as some men benefit from the existence of rape in our society, these men also share responsibility along with the rapists.

It seems to us unlikely that many, if any, men in our society fail to fit into one or another of these categories. Hence, we think that it is not unreasonable to say that men in our society are collectively responsible (in the distributive sense) for rape. We expect some male readers to respond as follows:

> I am adamantly opposed to rape, and though when I was younger I might have tolerated rape-conducive comments from friends of mine, I don't now, so I'm not a collaborator in the rape culture. And I would never be a rapist whatever the situation, and I would certainly act to prevent any rape that I could. I'm pretty sure I don't benefit from rape. So how can I be responsible for the prevalence of rape?

In reply we would point out that nearly all men in a given western society meet the third and fifth conditions above (concerning similarity and benefit). But women generally fail to meet either of these conditions, or the first. So, the involvement of women in the rape culture is much less than is true for men. In what follows we will concentrate on these similarity and benefit issues.

In our discussion above, we questioned the view that rapists are "other." Diane Scully, in her study of convicted rapists, turns the view around, suggesting that it is women who are "other." She argues that rapists in America are not pathological, but instead

> that men who rape have something to tell us about the cultural roots of sexual violence. . . .

They tell us that some men use rape as a means of revenge and punishment. Implicit in revenge rape is the collective liability of women. In some cases, victims are substitutes for significant women on whom men desire to take revenge. In other cases, victims represent all women. . . . In either case, women are seen as objects, a category, but not as individuals with rights. For some men, rape is an afterthought or bonus they add to burglary or robbery. In other words, rape is "no big deal." . . . Some men rape in groups as a male bonding activity—for them it's just something to do. . . . Convicted rapists tell us that in this culture, sexual violence is rewarding . . . these men perceived rape as a rewarding, low-risk act. (Scully 190, 162–63)

It is the prevalent perception of women as "other" by men in our culture that fuels the prevalence of rape in American society.

Turning to the issue of benefit, we believe that Lionel Tiger's work illustrates the important source of strength that men derive from the all-male groups they form. There is a strong sense in which men benefit from the all-male groups that they form in our culture. What is distinctly lacking is any sense that men have responsibility for the social conditions, especially the socialization of younger men which diminishes inhibitions toward rape, that are created in those groups. Male bonding is made easier because there is an "Other" that males can bond "against." And this other is the highly sexualized stereotype of the "female." Here is a benefit for men in these groups—but there is a social cost: from the evidence we have examined there is an increased prevalence of rape. Men need to consider this in reviewing their own role in a culture that supports so much rape.

There is another sense in which benefit is related to the issue of responsibility for rape. There is a sense in which many men in our society benefit from the prevalence of rape in ways many of us are quite unaware. Consider this example:

Several years ago, at a social occasion in which male and female professors were present, I asked off-handedly whether people agreed with me that the campus was looking especially pretty at night these days. Many of the men responded positively. But all of the women responded that this was not something that they had even thought about, since they were normally too anxious about being on campus at night, especially given the increase in reported rapes recently.[3]

We men benefitted in that, relative to our female colleagues, we were in an advantageous position vis-a-vis travel around campus. And there were surely other comparative benefits that befell us as a result of this advantage concerning travel, such as our ability to gain academically by being able to use the library at any hour we chose.

In a larger sense, men benefit from the prevalence of rape in that many women are made to feel dependent on men for protection against potential rapists. It is hard to overestimate the benefit here for it potentially affects all aspects of one's life. One study found that 87% of women in a borough of London felt that they had to take precautions against potential rapists, with a large number reporting that they never went out at night alone (Radford 1987, 33). Whenever one group is made to feel dependent on another group, and this dependency is not reciprocal, then there is a strong comparative benefit to the group that is not in the dependent position. Such a benefit, along with the specific benefits mentioned above, support the view that men as a group have a stake in perpetuating the rape culture in ways that women do not. And just as the benefit to men distributes throughout the male population in a given society, so the responsibility should distribute as well.

V. CONCLUSIONS

When people respond to conflict with violence, they coerce one another and thereby fail to treat one another with respect as fellow autonomous beings. Rape and murder, especially in war, victimize members of various groups simply because they are group members. These two factors combine to create a form of dehumanization that can warrant the charge of being a crime against humanity. What makes an act of violence more than just a private individual act in wartime is that killing and rape are perpetrated not against the individual for his or her unique characteristics, but solely because the individual instantiates a group characteristic, for example, being Jewish, or Muslim, or being a woman. Such identification fails to respect what is unique about each of us.

Our point is not that all men everywhere are responsible for the prevalence of rape. Rather, we have been arguing that in western societies, rape is deeply embedded in a wider culture of male socialization. Those who have the most to do with sustaining that culture must also recognize that they are responsible for the harmful aspects of that culture (see Porter 1986, 222–23). And when rape is conjoined with war, especially as an organized strategy, then there is a sense that men are collectively responsible for the rapes that occur in that war,[4] just as groups of people are held responsible for the crimes of genocide, where the victims are persecuted simply because they fall into a certain category of low-risk people who are ripe for assault.

Rape, especially in times of war, is an act of violence perpetrated against a person merely for being an instantiation of a type. Insofar as rape in times of war is a systematically organized form of terror, it is not inappropriate to call rape a war crime, a crime against humanity. Insofar as rape in times of peace is also part of a pattern of terror against women to the collective benefit of men, then rape in times of peace is also a crime against humanity (see Card 1991). Rape, in war or in peace, is rarely a personal act of aggression by one person toward another person. It is an act of hostility and a complete failure to show basic human respect (see Shafer and Frye 1977). And more than this, rape is made more likely by the collective ac-

tions, or inactions, of men in a particular society. Insofar as men in a particular society contribute to the prevalence of rape, they participate in a crime against humanity for which they are collectively responsible.

The feminist slogan "all men are rapists" seems much stronger than the claim "all men contribute to the prevalence of rape." Is the feminist slogan merely hyperbole? It is if what is meant is that each time a rape occurs, every man did it, or that only men are ever responsible for rape. But, as we have seen, each time a rape occurs, there is a sense in which many men could have done it, or made it less likely to have occurred, or benefitted from it. By direct contribution, or by negligence or by similarity of disposition, or by benefitting, most if not all men do share in each rape in a particular society. This is the link between being responsible for the prevalence of rape and being responsible, at least to some extent, for the harms of each rape.

The purpose of these arguments has been to make men aware of the various ways that they are implicated in the rape culture in general as well as in particular rapes. And while we believe that men should feel some shame for their group's complicity in the prevalence of rape, our aim is not to shame men but rather to stimulate men to take responsibility for re-socializing themselves and their fellow men. How much should any particular man do? Answering this question would require another paper, although participating in the Canadian White Ribbon Campaign, or in anti-sexism education programs, would be a good first step.[5] Suffice it to say that the status quo, namely doing nothing, individually or as a group, is not satisfactory, and will merely further compound our collective and shared responsibility for the harms caused by our fellow male members who engage in rape.[6]

NOTES

1. This paragraph was based on Larry May's experiences growing up in an upper middle class suburban U.S. society.

While our experiences differ somewhat in this respect, these experiences are so common that we have referred to them in the first person plural.

2. There is a fifth response, namely, that women alone are somehow responsible for being raped. This response will be largely ignored in our essay since we regard it as merely another case of "blaming the victim." See Scully (1990) for a critical discussion of this response. Undoubtedly there are yet other responses. We have tried to focus our attention on the most common responses we have seen in the literature on rape.

3. In his fascinating study of the climate of rape in American culture, Timothy Beneke also reports as one of his conclusions that the fear of rape at night "inhibits the freedom of the eye, hurts women economically, undercuts women's independence, destroys solitude, and restricts expressiveness." Such curtailments of freedom, he argues, "must be acknowledged as part of the crime" (Beneke 1982, 170).

4. The European Community's preliminary investigation into the reports of widespread Bosnian rapes of Muslim women by Serbian soldiers concluded that "Rape is part of a pattern of abuse, usually perpetrated with the conscious intention of demoralizing and terrorizing communities, driving them from their homes and demonstrating the power of the invading forces. Viewed in this way, rape cannot be seen as incidental to the main purpose of the aggression but as serving a strategic purpose in itself" (*St. Louis Post-Dispatch*, January 9, 1993, 8A).

5. We would also recommend recent essays by philosophers who are trying to come to terms with their masculinity. See our essay on friendship as well as the essay by Hugh LaFollette in our anthology *Rethinking Masculinity* (1992).

6. We would like to thank Virginia Ingram, Jason Clevenger, Victoria Davion, Karen Warren, Duane Cady and Marilyn Friedman for providing us with critical comments on earlier drafts of this paper.

REFERENCES

Beneke, Timothy. 1982. *Men on rape*. New York: St. Martin's Press.

Brownmiller, Susan. 1993. Making female bodies the battlefield. *Newsweek* (January 4): 37.

Card, Claudia. 1991. Rape as a terrorist institution. In *Violence, terrorism, and justice*, ed. R.G. Frey and Christopher Morris. New York: Cambridge University Press.

Griffin, Susan. 1971. Rape: The all-american crime. Ramparts (September) 26–35. Reprinted in *Women and values: Readings in feminist philosophy*, ed. Marilyn Pearsall. Belmont, CA: Wadsworth, 1986.

Keen, Sam. 1991. *Fire in the belly*. New York: Bantam Books.

LaFollette, Hugh. 1992. Real men. In *Rethinking masculinity*, ed. Larry May and Robert Strikwerda. Lanham, MD: Rowman & Littlefield.

Lepowsky, Maria. 1990. Gender in an egalitarian society. In *Beyond the second sex*, ed. Peggy Reeves Sanday and Ruth Gallagher Goodenough. Philadelphia: University of Pennsylvania Press.

Lipsyte, Robert. 1993. An ethics trial: Must boys always be boys? *The New York Times* (March 12): B-11.

MacKinnon, Catharine A. 1993. Turning rape into pornography: Postmodern genocide. *Ms.* (July/August): 24–30.

May, Larry. 1987. *The morality of groups*. Notre Dame, IN: University of Notre Dame Press. 1991.

———. 1992. *Sharing responsibility*. Chicago: University of Chicago Press.

Oates, Joyce Carol. 1992. Rape and the boxing ring. *Newsweek* (February 24): 60–61.

Peterson, Susan Rae. 1977. Coercion and rape: The state as a male protection racket. In *Feminism and philosophy*, ed. Mary Vetterling-Braggin, Frederick Elliston, and Jane English. Totwa, NJ: Littlefield, Adams: 360–371.

Porter, Roy. 1985. Does rape have a historical meaning? In *Rape: An historical and social enquiry*, ed. Sylvana Tomaselli and Roy Porter. Oxford: Basil Blackwell.

Post, Tony et al. 1993. A pattern of rape. *Newsweek*. (January 4): 32–36.

Radford, Jill. 1987. Policing male violence, policing women. In *Women, violence and social control*, ed. Jalna Hanmer and Mary Maynard. Atlantic Highlands, NJ: Humanities Press.

Sanday, Peggy Reeves. 1986. Rape and the silencing of the feminine. In *Rape: An historical and social enquiry*, ed. Sylvana Tomaselli and Roy Porter. Oxford: Basil Blackwell.

———. 1990. Androcentric and matrifocal gender representation in minangkabau ideology. In *Beyond the second sex*, ed. Peggy Reeves Sanday and Ruth Gallagher Goodenough. Philadelphia: University of Pennsylvania Press.

Scully, Diana. 1990. *Understanding sexual violence*. Boston: Unwin Hyman.

Shafer, Carolyn M. and Marilyn Frye. 1977. Rape and respect. In *Feminism and philosophy*, ed. Mary Vetterling-Braggin, Frederick Elliston, and Jane English. Totowa, NJ: Littlefield Adams.

Strikwerda, Robert, and Larry May. 1992. Male friendship and intimacy. *Hypatia* 7(3): 110–25. Reprinted in *Rethinking masculinity*, ed. Larry May and Robert Strikwerda, Lanham, MD: Rowman & Littlefield.

Thornhill, Randy, and Nancy Wilmsen Thornhill. 1992. The evolutionary psychology of men's coercive sexuality. *Behavioral and Brain Sciences* 15: 363–75.

Tiger, Lionel. [1969] 1984. *Men in groups* 2nd ed. New York: Marion Boyars Publishers.

For Some, Youthful Courting Has Become a Game of Abuse

Melinda Henneberger and Michel Marriott

James Fauntleroy, 15, says the teen-agers in his circle either don't date or don't admit to it.

"Nobody wants a relationship except the girls," he said, sitting on a park bench in downtown Stamford, Conn., listening to music on a hot summer night. "The guys don't want to look soft to their friends."

That fear, and the desire of boys to demonstrate their manhood by abusing or showing disrespect to girls, was repeated time and again in more than 50 interviews with teen-agers across the region last week after a series of reported sexual assaults by groups of teen-agers in a Bronx swimming pool, a Montclair, N.J., school stairwell and a Yonkers playground.

Most of the boys interviewed, though not all, described how they gain "props," or popularity, by yelling explicit propositions or fondling girls who pass by, competing to see who shows the most flair and audacity in talking trash and making moves. Many girls seem to have accepted that romantic relationships are rare, and often not worth the trouble. And though the vast majority of teenagers are not sex offenders, a growing number seem to view sexual harassment as a game, and abuse as a team sport.

While it is impossible to quantify the attitudes and alienation expressed by the inner-city and suburban teen-agers—white, black, Hispanic and Asian, from both middle-class and low-income families—sociologists and psychologists are concerned about the apparent increase of abuse as a group activity.

'No Big Deal'

A nationwide survey of high school and junior high students released last month found that a high number of girls and boys said they had been grabbed, groped and subjected to sexually explicit put-downs in school hallways. The study, conducted by Louis Harris & Associates for the American Association of University Women Educational Foundation, found that more than two-thirds of girls and 42 percent of boys reported being touched, grabbed or pinched on school grounds.

And two-thirds of the boys surveyed and 52 percent of the girls said they had harassed other students. Of those, 41 percent of the boys and 31 percent of the girls said they believed that this was "just a part of school life" and that it was "no big deal." The study surveyed 1,632 students in grades 8 through 11 in 79 schools across the country in February and March.

Behind the numbers are young people like Chilly Acevedo, 19, of the Bronx, who seem to have given up on love. "Nobody loves nobody anymore," she said. "And there's no respect, no trust."

Zuka Muratovic, 17, of the Norwood section of the Bronx said the landscape of teen-age dating has become jagged and scary. "You hear a lot about it," said Ms. Muratovic, referring to verbal, and sometimes physical abuse. "You see a lot of sun glasses and black eyes."

In discussing their attitudes, many young people reveal complicated and sometimes contradictory feelings about sex and gender. For example, Kinshasha Rhodes, 17, of Stamford, said she got a strong sense of her own worth from the powerful women in her family. But she also said:

"Females are just dumb. They're stupid. They fight for a guy. Not all of them, but the majority of them are dumb."

'It's Nature'

And Afr (Derrick) James, 18, of Bogota, N.J., said proudly, "I'm the highest there is in respect for women." And then he rationalized the psychology of group assaults.

"It's nature," he said. "Look at a female dog and a male dog: it's the same thing. You see 20 male dogs on a female dog. It's the male nature in a way."

Some young people admit they can be confused about where to draw the line between flirting and harassment, advances and abuse, media images and reality, and right and wrong.

Shuichi, a 15-year-old from Tenafly, N.J., who would not give his last name, described his ambivalence about an incident he witnessed on the Fourth of July, when he watched a bunch of younger boys chasing a girl who had put a pack of cigarettes down her shirt to keep them from taking them. When six of them reached down her shirt to get the cigarettes and later tackled her again and fondled her, he said the girl didn't tell them to stop.

"Or maybe she did, but she didn't mean it seriously," he said, laughing nervously. "She was like, 'Ha-ha-ha.' They pretended it was wrestling, but it wasn't. They were touching her. But I don't think the girl cared. She was flirting with other guys and I hear rumors about her."

'It's Like Nothing Serious'

His own reaction? "I was like, 'Oh my God,' but she didn't say anything," he said. "It's kind of stupid and funny. It's like nothing serious. It didn't look serious, but I don't think it was appropriate."

Last week, the police arrested two teen-agers involved in what the authorities said was a sexual assault at the Crotona pool in the South Bronx. Last month, seven teen-agers from Montclair, N.J., were charged with sexually assaulting two 14-year-old girls in a series of group attacks that one girl said included an assault in a school stairwell.

Also last month, eight 9- to 13-year-olds in Yonkers were charged with sexual abuse after a 12-year-old told the police she had been thrown to the ground, held down and fondled.

A Bonding Ritual

Lisa Ortiz, 23, was working in the emergency room of Bronx Lebanon Hospital when the girl who reported being assaulted in the pool was brought in. "I was devastated," she said. "When I was growing up and walking down the street I was worried about an old man looking at me. Now I have to worry about these little 13-year-olds and 14-year-olds overpowering me and ganging up and disrespecting my body."

Out of their need for acceptance and friendship, James Fauntleroy said, a lot of guys see sexual harassment—and worse—as a bonding ritual. "If you dis a girl you get respect," he said. "Like,

'Yeah, you dissed her, you're the man, you're the man.' That's how people think."

He added that he does not share that view because, unlike many of his friends, he has a father who taught him better. "If you see people slapping their girl," he said, "they probably get respect from their boys."

And if they're caught treating a girl well, he and others said, they lose the approval of their friends. As a result, in some circles the types of dating relationships that characterized adolescence in earlier generations have become rare and even clandestine, with some girls accepting the fact that their boyfriends will not acknowledge them in public.

Other girls said they wouldn't trust most guys enough to go out with them, anyway.

Old Scapegoats Blamed

"It makes me think if I get in a relationship they're just going to call me a bitch," said Paola Ocampo of Englewood, N.J., a quiet 14-year-old who already faces the daily ordeal of taunts and propositions. She is not charmed. And she is not hopeful. "You don't see that a lot, a good relationship," she said, "because the guys' main object in life is to get as many girls as possible."

While teen-agers of both sexes blamed the abusive behavior on the old scapegoats—hormones and girls who wear tight clothes—young people also said their ideas about love, sex and commitment have been skewed by the failed relationships of their parents, the violence of their times and the degrading influence of their culture, which they say de-means women, cheapens sex and promotes instant gratification.

And some teen-agers said they had been affected by their parents' materialism and resentment over changing sex roles. "Everyone is in it to see what they can get out of it," said Mike Agar, 17, who lives in the largely Irish Norwood section. "It seems that girls expect more, more attention, more jewelry."

The mindset they describe is not limited to teen-agers, because younger people look to their older siblings and friends for direction and youth trends often seep into mainstream popular culture. David Sierra, 21, stood with several male friends at Orchard Beach in the Bronx, admiring both the surf and the waves of young women drawn to the scene.

Frontin' and Bugging Out

"Girls be frontin' and guys be bugging out," he said, describing what he said was a tendency among many young girls to represent themselves as sexually available by their carriage and dress, and then men's response to the messages they believe they are receiving.

As he spoke, two teen-age girls walked by a row of teen-age boys. "Hey-hey! Sweetheart!" one yelled out as the women ignored their calls and walked on toward a vacant area of the beach.

Language is one indication that some teenagers do not really see each other as people. Some boys commonly use the word "bitch" as a synonym for "girl," while girls refer to boys as "dogs" and both talk about sex as a function. But when even murder fails to shock, as some pointed out, it is little wonder that all human life is debased.

Some girls complained that boys often chant rap lyrics, popular among white and black teenagers alike, that are singularly unflattering to women.

Davin Mintz, 18, of Stamford, said he feels that girls are just as disrespectful as boys.

'It's Equal'

"O.K., say you see a girl who's blazing," he said. "You say, 'What's up?' or, 'What school do you go to?' and she'd say something like: 'Are you a virgin? Who was the last girl you were with? How was your relationship?' She'd be like, 'Did you ever hit skins'"—have sex?

Of course, many young people do have healthy relationships and real respect for the opposite sex. And those who said they do generally credited strong family ties and religious faith.

Ricky Bobb, 22, and his wife Juliet Bobb, 21, of Brooklyn, who said they were raised in strict households in Barbados and Trinidad, blamed overly permissive or absent parents for the disturbing attitudes they notice among some other people their age.

But Mrs. Bobb said their strong relationship is still no protection from the groups of leering young men she sometimes faces on the street.

"It's demeaning," she said. "If they would talk to a girl respectfully, if they would not call her like she's a cat, someone would probably talk to them."

9

New Reproductive Technologies

Introduction

AN OVERVIEW

Our society faces new and complex moral decisions due to recent developments in reproductive technology and also the rapid changes in the field of human genetics. Advances in reproductive technologies have made it possible for formerly infertile couples and individuals to have biological or gestational offspring. We now have available a wide range of "reproduction-assisting technologies," including artificial insemination (AI), in vitro fertilization (IVF), so-called "surrogate motherhood," gamete donation, gamete intrafallopian transfer (GIFT), zygote intrafallopian transfer (ZIFT), embryo transfer (ET), the cryopreservation of embryos, and so on.

To what extent ought society regulate the use of these technologies? Should society in any way restrict individual consumers' access to these new reproductive technologies? Should the government regulate or limit or prohibit some or all of these procedures? Or should individuals have almost unlimited freedom to purchase these medical services?

ARGUMENTS IN FAVOR OF "PROCREATIVE LIBERTY"

Defenders of these new technologies argue that society should not restrict individuals' access to reproductive technologies provided that these adults are capable of making rational, well-informed, and free choices: Government intervention is not morally justified when otherwise infertile adults seek out new reproductive technologies in order to attempt to have "healthy" children with whom they will have a genetic and/or gestational bond.[1] John Robertson, whose article opens this chapter, identifies what he calls a "right to procreative liberty."[2] Robertson argues that "individuals should be free to use these techniques or not as they choose" without government intervention, unless there is the potential for significant harm to others. In other words, adults should be free to use these various forms of "collaborative reproduction" and "reproduction-assisting technologies" without government intervention unless there is the risk of "substantial harm to others." The individual's right to liberty and autonomy should extend to his or her taking advantage of all of these new technologies, provided that there is no substantial harm to others.

FEMINIST PERSPECTIVES ON REPRODUCTIVE TECHNOLOGIES

Not surprisingly, there are numerous feminist perspectives on contract pregnancy, egg "donation," collaborative reproduction, cryopreserved embryo transfer, and all of the new "procedures." The article by Rosemarie Tong examines the range of feminist responses. Some feminists are in principle concerned with any attempts by the government to regulate these procedures; they believe that feminists should consistently resist government intervention in all areas of women's reproductive freedom. Other feminists analyze these procedures in a broader social context, identifying and challenging the underlying assumptions about the nature of the family and of parenthood that are implicit in this debate. They contend that the dilemmas of infertile heterosexual couples and same-sex couples need to be put into a larger framework in order to be properly understood.

CONCERNS ABOUT SOCIAL CLASS AND RACE

Public debates over contract pregnancy and egg donation have drawn attention to the role that social class plays in these transactions and procedures. As the reading by Ronald Munson makes clear, the highly publicized case of Mary Beth Whitehead, the Stern family, and "Baby M" made social and economic class salient: The Sterns were both upper-middle class professionals who had achieved high levels of education and economic success; Ms. Whitehead, on the other hand, was a homemaker from a working class family who had a high-school degree. It is not difficult to guess who was to undertake the reproductive labor and who was to pay for it. Critics have been quick to point out that contract birth giving and egg "donations" may very well exploit the young and the poor to the advantage of the older and wealthier members of society. The article by Dorothy Roberts examines how the use of new reproductive technologies reflects and reinforces the racial hierarchies in our society.

NOTES

1. John A. Robertson, *Children of Choice: Freedom and the New Reproductive Technologies* (Princeton: Princeton University Press, 1994): 22–23. See Robertson's essay, which opens this chapter.

2. Robertson (page 557).

42.
Freedom and the New Reproductive Technologies
John A. Robertson

John A. Robertson is the Vinson and Elkins Chair and Professor of Law at the University of Texas at Austin School of Law. He is also a fellow of the Hastings Center and a member of the American Fertility Society. His recent work includes *Children of Choice: Freedom and the New Reproductive Technologies* and *The Rights of the Critically Ill*. In this essay, Robertson defends and explicates "a right to procreative liberty." He defends the primacy of this right and examines the implications of its presumptive primacy with respect to the government's role in regulating new reproductive technologies. Robertson argues that unless we can clearly prove substantial harm to the tangible interests of others, we ought not interfere with infertile persons' freedom to use these new technologies.

Procreative Liberty

Procreative liberty has wide appeal but its scope has never been fully elaborated and often is contested. The concept has several meanings that must be clarified if it is to serve as a reliable guide for moral debate and public policy regarding new reproductive technologies.

WHAT IS PROCREATIVE LIBERTY?

At the most general level, procreative liberty is the freedom either to have children or to avoid having them. Although often expressed or realized in the context of a couple, it is first and foremost an individual interest. It is to be distinguished from freedom in the ancillary aspects of reproduction, such as liberty in the conduct of pregnancy or choice of place or mode of childbirth.

The concept of reproduction, however, has a certain ambiguity contained within it. In a strict sense, reproduction is always genetic. It occurs by provision of one's gametes to a new person, and thus includes having or producing offspring. While female reproduction has traditionally included gestation, in vitro fertilization (IVF) now allows female genetic and gestational reproduction to be separated. Thus a woman who has provided the egg that is carried by another has reproduced, even if she has not gestated and does not rear resulting offspring. Because of the close link between gestation and female reproduction, a woman who gestates the embryo of another may also reasonably be viewed as having a reproductive experience, even though she does not reproduce genetically.[1]

In any case, reproduction in the genetic or gestational sense is to be distinguished from child rearing. Although reproduction is highly valued in part because it usually leads to child rearing, one can produce offspring without rearing them and rear children without reproduction. One who rears an adopted child has not reproduced, while one who has genetic progeny but does not rear them has.

In this [article] the terms "procreative liberty" and "reproductive freedom" will mean the freedom to reproduce or not to reproduce in the genetic sense, which may also include rearing or not, as intended by the parties. Those terms will also include female gestation whether or not there is a genetic connection to the resulting child.

Often the reproduction at issue will be important because it is intended to lead to child rearing. In cases where rearing is not intended, the value to be assigned to reproduction *tout court* will have to be determined. Similarly, when there is rearing without genetic or gestational involvement, the value of nonreproductive child rearing will also have to be assessed. In both cases the value assigned may depend on the proximity to reproduction where rearing is intended.

[Some] . . . further qualifications on the meaning of procreative liberty should be noted. One is that "liberty" as used in procreative liberty is a negative right. It means that a person violates no moral duty in making a procreative choice, and that other persons have a duty not to interfere with that choice.[2] However, the negative right to procreate or not does not imply the duty of others to provide the resources or services necessary to exercise one's procreative liberty despite plausible moral arguments for governmental assistance.

As a matter of constitutional law, procreative liberty is a negative right against state interference with choices to procreate or to avoid procreation. It is not a right against private interference, though other laws might provide that protection. Nor is it a positive right to have

From John A. Robertson, *Children of Choice: Freedom and the New Reproductive Technologies* (Princeton: Princeton University Press, 1994). Copyright (c) 1994 by Princeton University Press. Reprinted by permission of Princeton University Press. Portions previously published as John Robertson, "Procreative Liberty and the Control of Conception, Pregnancy, and Childbirth," *Virginia Law Review* 69 (April 1983): 405–462. Reprinted with permission of the Virginia Law Review Association and Fred B. Rothman & Co.

the state or particular persons provide the means or resources necessary to have or avoid having children.[3] The exercise of procreative liberty may be severely constrained by social and economic circumstances. Access to medical care, child care, employment, housing, and other services may significantly affect whether one is able to exercise procreative liberty. However, the state presently has no constitutional obligation to provide those services. Whether the state should alleviate those conditions is a separate issue of social justice. . . . [4]

THE IMPORTANCE OF PROCREATIVE LIBERTY

Procreative liberty should enjoy presumptive primacy when conflicts about its exercise arise because control over whether one reproduces or not is central to personal identity, to dignity, and to the meaning of one's life. For example, deprivation of the ability to avoid reproduction determines one's self-definition in the most basic sense. It affects women's bodies in a direct and substantial way. It also centrally affects one's psychological and social identity and one's social and moral responsibilities. The resulting burdens are especially onerous for women, but they affect men in significant ways as well.

On the other hand, being deprived of the ability to reproduce prevents one from an experience that is central to individual identity and meaning in life. Although the desire to reproduce is in part socially constructed, at the most basic level transmission of one's genes through reproduction is an animal or species urge closely linked to the sex drive. In connecting us with nature and future generations, reproduction gives solace in the face of death. As Shakespeare noted, "nothing 'gainst Time's scythe can make defense/save breed."[5] For many people, "breed"—reproduction and the parenting that usually accompanies it—is a central part of their life plan, and the most satisfying and meaningful experience they have. It also has primary importance as an expression of a couple's love or unity. For many persons, reproduction also has religious significance and is experienced as a "gift from God." Its denial—through infertility or governmental restriction—is experienced as a great loss, even if one has already had children or will have little or no rearing role with them.

Decisions to have or to avoid having children are thus personal decisions of great import that determine the shape and meaning of one's life. The person directly involved is best situated to determine whether that meaning should or should not occur. An ethic of personal autonomy as well as ethics of community or family should then recognize a presumption in favor of most personal reproductive choices. Such a presumption does not mean that reproductive choices are without consequence to others, nor that they should never be limited. Rather, it means that those who would limit procreative choice have the burden of showing that the reproductive actions at issue would create such substantial harm that they could justifiably be limited. Of course, what counts as the "substantial harm" that justifies interference with procreative choice may often be contested, as the discussion of reproductive technologies in this [essay] will show.

A closely related reason for protecting reproductive choice is to avoid the highly intrusive measures that governmental control of reproduction usually entails. State interference with reproductive choice may extend beyond exhortation and penalties to gestapo and police state tactics. Margaret Atwood's powerful futuristic novel *The Handmaid's Tale* expresses this danger by creating a world where fertile women are forcibly impregnated by the ruling powers and their pregnancies monitored to replenish a decimated population.[6]

Equally frightening scenarios have occurred in recent years when repressive governments have interfered with reproductive choice. In Romania and China, men and women have had their most private activities scrutinized in the service of state reproductive goals. In Ceaușescu's Romania, where contraception and abortion were strictly forbidden, women's menstrual cycles were routinely monitored to see if they were pregnant.[7] Women who did not become pregnant or who had abortions were severely punished. Many women nevertheless sought illegal abortions and died, leaving their children orphaned and subject to sale to Westerners seeking children for adoption.[8]

In China, forcible abortion and sterilization have occurred in the service of a one-child-per-family population policy. Village cadres have seized pregnant women in their homes and forced them to have abortions.[9] A campaign of forcible sterilization in India in 1977 was seen as an "attack on women and children" and brought Indira Ghandi's government down.[10] In the United States, state-imposed sterilization of "mental defectives," sanctioned in 1927 by the United States Supreme Court in *Buck v. Bell*, resulted in 60,000 sterilizations over a forty-year period.[11] Many mentally normal people were sterilized by mistake, and mentally retarded persons who posed little risk of harm to others were subjected to surgery.[12] It is no surprise that current proposals for compulsory use of contraceptives such as Norplant are viewed with great suspicion.

TWO TYPES OF PROCREATIVE LIBERTY

To see how values of procreative liberty affect the ethical and public policy evaluation of new reproductive technologies, we must determine whether the interests that underlie the high value accorded procreative liberty are implicated in their use. This is not a simple task because procreative liberty is not unitary, but consists of strands of varying interests in the conception and gestation of offspring. The different strands implicate different interests, have different legal and constitutional status, and are differently affected by technology.

An essential distinction is between the freedom to avoid reproduction and the freedom to reproduce. When people talk of reproductive rights, they usually have one or the other aspect in mind. Because different interests and justifications underlie each and countervailing interests for limiting each aspect vary, recognition of one aspect does not necessarily mean that the other will also be respected; nor does limitation of one mean that the other can also be denied.

However, there is a mirroring or reciprocal relationship here. Denial of one type of reproductive liberty necessarily implicates the other. If a woman is not able to avoid reproduction through contraception or abortion, she may end up reproducing, with all the burdens that unwanted reproduction entails. Similarly, if one is denied the liberty to reproduce through forcible sterilization, one is forced to avoid reproduction, thus experiencing the loss that absence of progeny brings. By extending reproductive options, new reproductive technologies present challenges to both aspects of procreative choice. . . .

THE FREEDOM TO PROCREATE

In addition to freedom to avoid procreation, procreative liberty also includes the freedom to procreate—the freedom to beget and bear children if one chooses. As with avoiding reproduction, the right to reproduce is a negative right against public or private interference, not a positive right to the services or the resources needed to reproduce. It is an important freedom that is widely accepted as a basic, human right.[12] But its various components and dimensions have never been fully analyzed, as technologies of conception and selection now force us to do.

As with avoiding reproduction, the freedom to procreate involves the freedom to engage in a series of actions that eventuate in reproduction and usually in child rearing. One must be free to marry or find a willing partner, engage in sexual intercourse, achieve conception and pregnancy, carry a pregnancy to term, and rear offspring. Social and natural barriers to reproduction would involve the unavailability of willing or suitable partners, impotence or infertility, and lack of medical and child-care resources. State barriers to marriage, to sexual intercourse, to conception, to infertility treatment, to carrying pregnancies to term, and to certain child-rearing arrangements would also limit the freedom to procreate. The most commonly asserted reasons for limiting coital reproduction are overpopulation, unfitness of parents, harm to offspring, and costs to the state or others. Technologies that treat infertility raise additional concerns that are discussed below.

The moral right to reproduce is respected because of the centrality of reproduction to personal identity, meaning, and dignity. This importance makes the liberty to procreate an important moral right, both for an ethic of individual autonomy and for ethics of community or family that view the purpose of marriage and sexual union as the reproduction and rearing of offspring. Because of this importance, the right to reproduce is widely recognized as a prima facie moral right that cannot be limited except for very good reason.

Recognition of the primacy of procreation does not mean that all reproduction is morally blameless, much less that reproduction is always responsible and praiseworthy and can never be limited. However, the presumptive primacy of procreative liberty sets a very high standard for limiting those rights, tilting the balance in favor of reproducing but not totally determining its acceptability. A two-step process of analysis is envisaged here. The first question is whether a distinctively procreative interest is involved. If so, the question then is whether the harm threatened by reproduction satisfies the strict standard for overriding this liberty interest.

The personal importance of procreation helps answer questions about who holds procreative rights and about the circumstances under which the right to reproduce may be limited. A person's capacity to find significance in reproduction should determine whether one holds the presumptive right, though this question is often discussed in terms of whether persons with such a capacity are fit parents. To have

a liberty interest in procreating, one should at a minimum have the mental capacity to understand or appreciate the meanings associated with reproduction. This minimum would exclude severely retarded persons from having reproductive interests, though it would not remove their right to bodily integrity. However, being unmarried, homosexual, physically disabled, infected with HIV, or imprisoned would not disqualify one from having reproductive interests, though they might affect one's ability to rear offspring. Whether those characteristics justify limitations on reproduction is discussed later.[13] Nor would already having reproduced negate a person's interest in reproducing again, though at a certain point the marginal value to a person of additional offspring diminishes.[14]

What kinds of interests or harms make reproduction unduly selfish or irresponsible and thus could justifiably limit the presumptive right to procreate? To answer this question, we must distinguish coital and noncoital reproduction. Surprisingly, there is a widespread reluctance to speak of coital reproduction as irresponsible, much less to urge public action to prevent irresponsible coital reproduction from occurring. If such a conversation did occur, reasons for limiting coital reproduction would involve the heavy costs that it imposed on others—costs that outweighed whatever personal meaning or satisfaction the person(s) reproducing experienced. With coital reproduction, such costs might arise if there were severe overpopulation, if the persons reproducing were unfit parents, if reproduction would harm offspring, or if significant medical or social costs were imposed on others.

Because the United States does not face the severe overpopulation of some countries, the main grounds for claiming that reproduction is irresponsible is where the person(s) reproducing lack the financial means to raise offspring or will otherwise harm their children. As later discussions will show, both grounds are seriously inadequate as justifications for interfering with procreative choice. Imposing rearing costs on others may not rise to the level of harm that justifies depriving a person of a fundamental moral right. Moreover, protection of offspring from unfit parenting requires that unfit parents not rear, not that they not reproduce. Offspring could be protected by having others rear them without interfering with parental reproduction.

A further problem, if coital reproduction were found to be unjustified, concerns what action should then be taken. Exhortation or moral condemnation might be acceptable, but more stringent or coercive measures would act on the body of the person deemed irresponsible. Past experience with force sterilization of retarded persons and the inevitable focus on the poor and minorities as targets of coercive policies make such proposals highly unappealing. Because of these doubts, there have been surprisingly few attempts to restrict coital reproduction in the United States since the era of eugenic sterilization, even though some instances of reproduction—for example, teenage pregnancy, inability to care for offspring—appear to be socially irresponsible.

An entirely different set of concerns arises with noncoital reproductive techniques. Charges that noncoital reproduction is unethical or irresponsible arise because of its expense, its highly technological character, its decomposition of parenthood into genetic, gestational, and social components, and its potential effects on women and offspring. To assess whether these effects justify moral condemnation or public limitation, we must first determine whether noncoital reproduction implicates important aspects of procreative liberty.

The Right to Reproduce and Noncoital Technology

If the moral right to reproduce presumptively protects coital reproduction, then it should protect noncoital reproduction as well. The moral right of the coitally infertile to reproduce is based on the same desire for offspring that the coitally fertile have. They too wish to replicate themselves, transmit genes, gestate, and rear children biologically related to them. Their infertility should no more disqualify them from reproductive experiences than physical disability should disqualify persons from walking with mechanical assistance. The unique risks posed by noncoital reproduction may provide independent justifications for limiting its use, but neither the noncoital nature of the means used or the infertility of their beneficiaries mean that the presumptively protected moral interest in reproduction is not present.

A major question about this position, however, is whether the noncoital or collaborative nature of the means used truly implicates reproductive interests. For example, what if only one aspect of reproduction—genetic transfer, gestation, or rearing—occurs, as happens with gamete donors or surrogates who play no rearing role? Is a person's procreative liberty substantially implicated in such partial reproductive roles? The answer will depend on the value attributed to the particular collaborative contribution and on whether the collaborative enterprise is viewed from the donor's or recipient's perspective.

Gamete donors and surrogates are clearly reproducing even though they have no intention to rear. Because reproduction *tout court* may seem less important than reproduction with intent to rear, the donor's reproductive interest may appear less important. However, more experience with these practices is needed to determine the inherent value of "partial" reproductive experiences to donors and surrogates.[15] Experience may show that it is independently meaningful, regardless of their contact with offspring. If not, then countervailing interests would more easily override their right to enter these roles.

Viewed from the recipient's perspective, however, the donor or surrogate's reproduction *tout court* does not lessen the reproductive importance of her contribution. A woman who receives an egg or embryo donation has no genetic connection with offspring but has a gestational relation of great personal significance. In addition, gamete donors and surrogates enable one or both rearing partners to have a biological relation with offspring. If one of them has no biological connection at all, they will still have a strong interest in rearing their partner's biologic offspring. Whether viewed singly through the eyes of the partner who is reproducing, or jointly as an endeavor of a couple seeking to rear children who are biologically related to at least one of the two, a significant reproductive interest is at stake. If so, noncoital, collaborative treatments for infertility should be respected to the same extent as coital reproduction is.

Questions about the core meaning of reproduction will also arise in the temporal dislocations that cryopreservation of sperm and embryos make possible. For example, embryo freezing allows siblings to be conceived at the same time, but born years apart and to different gestational mothers. Twins could be created by splitting one embryo into two. If one half is frozen for later use, identical twins could be born at widely different times. Sperm, egg, and embryo freezing also make posthumous reproduction possible.

Such temporally dislocative practices clearly implicate core reproductive interests when the ultimate recipient has no alternative means of reproduction. However, if the procreative interests of the recipient couple are not directly implicated, we must ask whether those whose gametes are used have an independent procreative interest, as might occur if they directed that gametes or embryos be thawed after their death for purposes of posthumous reproduction. In that case the question is whether the expectancy of posthumous reproduction is so central to an individual's procreative identity or life-plan that it should receive the same respect that one's reproduction when alive receives.[16] The answer to such a question will be important in devising policy for storing and posthumously disposing of gametes and embryos. The answer will also affect inheritance questions and have implications for management of pregnant women who are irreversibly comatose or brain dead.

The problem of determining whether technology implicates a major reproductive interest also arises with technologies that select offspring characteristics.... Some degree of quality control would seem logically to fall within the realm of procreative liberty. For many couples the decision whether to procreate depends on the ability to have healthy children. Without some guarantee or protection against the risk of handicapped children, they might not reproduce at all.

Thus viewed, quality control devices become part of the liberty interest in procreating or in avoiding procreation, and arguably should receive the same degree of protection. If so, genetic screening and selective abortion, as well as the right to select a mate or a source for donated eggs, sperm, or embryos should be protected as part of procreative liberty. The same arguments would apply to positive interventions to cure disease at the fetal or embryo stage. However, futuristic practices such as nontherapeutic enhancement, cloning, or intentional diminishment of offspring characteristics may so deviate from the core interests that make reproduction meaningful as to fall outside the protective canopy of procreative liberty.[17]

Finally, technology will present questions of whether one may use one's reproductive capacity to produce gametes, embryos, and fetuses for nonreproductive uses in research or therapy. Here the purpose is not to have children to rear, but to get material for research or transplant. Are such uses of reproductive capacity tied closely enough to the values and interests that underlie procreative freedom to warrant similar respect? Even if procreative choice is not directly involved, other liberties may protect the activity.

Are Noncoital Technologies Unethical?

If this analysis is accepted, then procreative liberty would include the right to use noncoital and other technologies to form a family and shape the characteristics of offspring. Neither infertility nor the fact that one will only partially reproduce eliminates the existence of a prima facie reproductive experience for someone. However, judgments about the proximity of these partial reproductive experiences to the core meanings of reproduction will be required in balancing those claims against competing moral concerns.

Judgment about the reproductive importance of noncoital technologies is crucial because many people have serious ethical reservations about them, and are more than willing to restrict their use. The concerns here are not the fears of overpopulation, parental unfitness, and societal costs that arise with allegedly irresponsible coital reproduction. Instead, they include reduction of demand for hard-to-adopt children, the coercive or exploitive bargains that will be offered to poor women, the commodification of both children and reproductive collaborators, the objectification of women as reproductive vessels, and the undermining of the nuclear family.

However, often the harms feared are deontological in character. In some cases they stem from a religious or moral conception of the unity of sex and reproduction or the definition of family. Such a view characterizes the Vatican's strong opposition to IVF, donor sperm, and other noncoital and collaborative techniques.[18] Other deontological concerns derive from a particular conception of the proper reproductive role of women. Many persons, for example, oppose paid surrogate motherhood because of a judgment about the wrongness of a woman's willingness to sever the mother-child bond for the sake of money.[19] They also insist that the gestational mother is always morally entitled to rear, despite her preconception promise to the contrary. Closely related are dignitary objections to allowing any reproductive factors to be purchased, or to having offspring selected on the basis of their genes.

Finally, there is a broader concern that noncoital reproduction will undermine the deeper community interest in having a clear social framework to define boundaries of families, sexuality, and reproduction. The traditional family

provides a container for the narcissism and irrationality that often drives human reproduction. This container assures commitments to the identifications and taboos that protect children from various types of abuse. The technical ability to disaggregate and recombine genetic, gestational, and rearing connections and to control the genes of offspring may thus undermine essential protections for offspring, couples, families, and society.

These criticisms are powerful ones that explain much of the ambivalence that surrounds the use of certain reproductive technologies. They call into question the wisdom of individual decisions to use them, and the willingness of society to promote or facilitate their use. Unless one is operating out of a specific religious or deontological ethic, however, they do not show that all individual uses of these techniques are immoral, much less that public policy should restrict or discourage their use.

. . . [T]hese criticisms seldom meet the high standard necessary to limit procreative choice. Many of them are mere hypothetical or speculative possibilities. Others reflect moralisms concerning a "right" view of reproduction, which individuals in a pluralistic society hold or reject to varying degrees. In any event, without a clear showing of substantial harm to the tangible interests of others, speculation or mere moral objections alone should not override the moral right of infertile couples to use those techniques to form families. Given the primacy of procreative liberty, the use of these techniques should be accorded the same high protection granted to coital reproduction.

RESOLVING DISPUTES OVER PROCREATIVE LIBERTY

As this brief survey shows, new reproductive technologies will generate ethical and legal disputes about the meaning and scope of procreative liberty. Because procreative liberty has never been fully elaborated, the importance of procreative choice in many novel settings will be a question of first impression. The ultimate decision reached will reflect the value assigned to the procreative interest at stake in light of the effects causing concern. In an important sense, the meaning of procreative liberty will be created or constituted for society in the process of resolving such disputes.

If procreative liberty is taken seriously, a strong presumption in favor of using technologies that centrally implicate reproductive interests should be recognized. Although procreative rights are not absolute, those who would limit procreative choice should have the burden of establishing substantial harm. This is the standard used in ethical and legal analyses of restrictions on traditional reproductive decisions. Because the same procreative goals are involved, the same standard of scrutiny should be used for assessing moral or governmental restrictions on novel reproductive techniques.

In arbitrating these disputes, one has to come to terms with the importance of procreative interests relative to other concerns. The precise procreative interest at stake must be identified and weighed against the core values of reproduction. As noted, this will raise novel and unique questions when the technology deviates from the model of two-person coital reproduction, or otherwise disaggregates or alters ordinary reproductive practices. However, if an important reproductive interest exists, then use of the technology should be presumptively permitted. Only substantial harm to tangible interests of others should then justify restriction.

In determining whether such harm exists, it will be necessary to distinguish between harms to individuals and harms to personal conceptions of morality, right order, or offense, discounted by their probability of occurrence. As previously noted, many objections to reproductive technology rest on differing views of what "proper" or "right" reproduction is aside from tangible effects on others. For example, concerns about the decomposition of parenthood through the use of donors and surrogates, about the temporal alteration of conception, gestation

and birth, about the alienation or commercialization of gestational capacity, and about selection and control of offspring characteristics do not directly affect persons so much as they affect notions of right behavior. Disputes over early abortion and discard or manipulation of IVF-created embryos also exemplify this distinction, if we grant that the embryo/previable fetus is not a person or entity with rights in itself.

At issue in these cases is the symbolic or constitutive meaning of actions regarding prenatal life, family, maternal gestation, and respect for persons over which people in a secular, pluralistic society often differ. A majoritarian view of "right" reproduction or "right" valuation of prenatal life, family, or the role of women should not suffice to restrict actions based on differing individual views of such preeminently personal issues. At a certain point, however, a practice such as cloning, enhancement, or intentional diminishment of offspring may be so far removed from even pluralistic notions of reproductive meaning that they leave the realm of protected reproductive choice.[20] People may differ over where that point is, but it will not easily exclude most reproductive technologies of current interest.

To take procreative liberty seriously, then, is to allow it to have presumptive priority in an individual's life. This will give persons directly involved the final say about use of a particular technology, unless tangible harm to the interests of others can be shown. Of course, people may differ over whether an important procreative interest is at stake or over how serious the harm posed from use of the reproductive technology is. Such a focused debate, however, is legitimate and ultimately essential in developing ethical standards and public policy for use of new reproductive technologies. . . .

Collaborative Reproduction

Donors and Surrogates

All reproduction is collaborative, for no moral person reproduces alone.[1] The term "collaborative reproduction" is nonetheless useful for describing those situations in which someone other than one's partner provides the gametes or gestation necessary for reproduction, such as occurs with sperm, egg, or embryo donation, or surrogate motherhood. These technologies play an increasingly central role in infertility treatment and raise basic questions about the scope of procreative liberty.[2]

THE DILEMMAS OF COLLABORATIVE REPRODUCTION

Resort to donor gametes or surrogates is not an easy choice for infertile couples. The decision arises after previous efforts at pregnancy have failed, thus confronting the couple with the fact of one or both partners' infertility. A collaborative technique is chosen because it offers an opportunity to have a child who is the biologic offspring of one or, in the case of egg donation and gestational surrogacy, both partners.[3] Yet collaborative reproduction occurs in an uncertain ethical, legal, and social milieu, where social practices and legal rules are still largely unclear.

A basic commitment to procreative liberty—to the freedom to have and rear offspring—should presumptively protect most forms of collaborative reproduction. After all, collaborative reproduction occurs for the same reason as IVF—the couple is infertile and cannot produce offspring. They need donor or surrogate assistance if they are to have children. Even if both rearing partners are not reproducing in the strict genetic sense, at least one partner will have a genetic or gestational relationship with their child. The same techniques may also be sought by a single woman or a same-sex couple that wishes to have offspring. In a few cases, donor gametes are used to avoid genetic handicap in offspring.

Despite its clear link to procreative choice, collaborative reproduction often generates controversy and even calls for prohibition. Collaborative reproduction is problematic because it intrudes a third party—a donor or surrogate—into the usual situation of two-party parenthood, and separates or deconstructs the

traditional genetic, gestational, and social unity of reproduction.[4] A child could in theory end up with three different biologic parents (a genetic mother, a gestational mother, a genetic father) and two separate rearing parents, with various combinations among them.[5] Such collaboration risks confusing offspring about who their "true" parent is and creating conflict about parental rights and duties. At the same time, the isolation of the particular components of parenthood tends to depersonalize the contributions of gamete donors and surrogates.

Collaborative reproduction thus poses several challenges for a regime of procreative liberty. On the one hand, it greatly expands procreative options, both for infertile couples seeking to form a family with biologically related offspring, as well as for persons who find satisfaction or meaning in serving as donors or surrogates.

On the other hand, it involves a novel set of practices and relationships in which social and psychological meanings and legal rights and duties have not yet been clearly defined. Given the ample room presented for misunderstanding and conflict, the use of technology to alter fundamental or traditional family relationships seems risky, and should occur only under conditions that protect the welfare of offspring, couples, and collaborators.

Indeed, the decomposition of the usually unified aspects of reproduction into separate genetic, gestational, and social strands calls into question the very meaning of procreative liberty. Are couples who use these techniques "procreating" in a significant way, even though one of them may lack a genetic or biological connection to offspring? Is a collaborator meaningfully procreating if he or she is merely providing gametes or gestation without any rearing role? Do such limited procreative roles deserve the same respect and protection that traditional coital reproduction warrants? Answers to these questions will help determine the extent to which such arrangements are permitted, regulated, or prohibited.

Although it appears too late in the game to eliminate most forms of collaborative practice, many ethical, legal, and social questions remain. This chapter addresses the extent to which procreative liberty protects a couple's access to collaborative reproduction.

HARM TO OFFSPRING

Although no organized movement to ban collaborative reproduction exists, many persons—usually those who have not themselves faced infertility—find these practices to be ethically troubling and socially deviant. In their eyes the central problem is that intrusion of a gamete donor or surrogate into the marital relationship confuses family and lineage in a way that is ultimately harmful to offspring. To protect offspring from the problems of multiple parents, they would strictly limit, if not prohibit altogether, the use of donors and surrogates to treat infertility.

Are Offspring Harmed by Collaborative Reproduction?

The concern about the impact is an important one. Genetic and biological ties are so central to our notions of individual identity and family that the possibility of adverse effects from deliberate separation of these elements must be taken seriously. Indeed, participants in these endeavors are often nervously aware that they are engaged in an enterprise for which the psychological, social, and legal rules have not yet been written.

Yet the claim that these practices should be prohibited because they are so inimical to offspring welfare is not convincing. The chief danger is that children will be reared by a person who is not their genetic mother or father, and that they may not know who their "true" father or mother is. In addition to causing conflict between the rearing partners and collaborator, the nonbiologic rearing partner may subtly or explicitly reject the child, and the child may experience a sense of loss or abandonment by the absent biologic parent.

Such experiences, of course, are not unique to donor- and surrogate-assisted reproduction. More than 25 percent of children are now raised in a nonnuclear family, and 28 percent of children are now born out of wedlock.[6] Many children are being raised by adoptive, step, or foster parents, by relatives or by other persons in situations in which they will have no or limited contact with their genetic or gestational parents and have close ties with nonbiologic rearers.

If the phenomenon of split biologic and social rearing is so widespread, one may question why collaborative reproduction should be of special concern. Of course, most instances of adoption, stepparentage, and other forms of blended or mixed families are a postnatal response to death, divorce, economic travail, abuse, or abandonment. In contrast, collaborative families are intentionally created. The intention is to create a loving home for a child who has a biological connection to one or both rearing parents.

The intentional creation of families with an absent genetic or gestational parent is a problem only if being reared in a situation in which one biologic parent is missing is itself generally harmful. Even if not ideal, we must ask what the risks of serious psychosocial problems in such families are, and what steps are possible to minimize them. Even then, one must also ask whether the likely problems are so great that offspring of collaborative reproduction, who have no other way to be born, would be better off never existing.

Empirical data is only partially helpful here, because other than some limited studies of sperm donation, no data on other forms of collaborative reproduction are available. The data available on offspring of sperm donation, however, do not show that those families or children are at especially high risk for psychological or social problems.[7] They have fewer problems than adopted children and their families. Healthy adjustment usually occurs, though problems can arise if the parents have not accepted their infertility or worked through the emotional conflicts that donor sperm raises for them. Children who learn of their missing donor father are sometimes angry at their parents for having kept it secret, and may be frustrated at not being able to obtain more information about him. But they typically do not feel rejected or abandoned as adopted children often do, and many express gratitude for the "gift" that made their existence possible. There is no reason to suppose that egg and embryo donation or gestational surrogacy will pose any greater problems. Because of the closer genetic or gestational links that exist in those cases, they may indeed pose fewer problems.

The data on sperm donation suggest that the impact of collaborative reproduction on offspring will depend largely on how well the infertile couple and their family accept and adjust to the situation. If the couple has worked through their depression, anger, and guilt at their own or their partner's infertility, they will have less difficulty in dealing with donor-assisted reproduction. If they are warned about conflicted feelings, given time to adjust to the novelty of the situation, and if their own parents are accepting of their choice for collaborative assistance, they are more likely to have a successful experience.[8] This in turn will make it easier to deal with issues of secrecy, disclosure, and uncertain legal status.

Yet even if couples or offspring have difficulties adjusting to the fact of donor or surrogate assistance, it does not follow that collaborative assistance should be discouraged in order to prevent harm to offspring. But for the technique in question, the child never would have been born. Whatever psychological or social problems arise, they hardly rise to the level of severe handicap or disability that would make the child's very existence a net burden, and hence a wrongful life.[9] Measures to minimize such effects are needed, but their absence alone would not justify banning collaborative techniques.

Protecting Offspring by Disclosure

Given that collaborative reproduction serves individual procreative interests, makes possible

children who would not otherwise be born, and does not appear to generate undue psychological or social conflict, such practices should generally be permitted. Rather than try to stop such practices, public policy should focus on preventing the problems that can arise. Legal rules for allocating rearing rights and duties among the participants are discussed in the next section. Later sections also discuss the need to protect collaborators by assuring that they act freely, and knowingly. Questions of secrecy and disclosure, which directly affect offspring, are discussed here. This concern raises two questions: (1) should children be told of their donor- or surrogate-assisted birth? (2) What information about donors and surrogates should be provided to offspring?

Secrecy vs. Disclosure of Collaborative Birth

The usual practice with donor sperm has been secrecy, anonymity, and nondisclosure. Couples usually have had little information about anonymous donors, who have been recruited by physicians or commercial sperm banks.[10] The couple is usually advised to keep the fact of sperm donation a secret from their families and the child. Although psychologists now recommend against secrecy, there is still a strong reluctance to reveal the fact of sperm donation to family and the child.

Secrecy may also inform egg and embryo donation, and even surrogacy, though often surrogates and egg donors will meet the couples whom they help.[11] Even if information is known about the donor or surrogate, the rearing parents may be reluctant to discuss it with the child, though perhaps less so if a relative or friend has helped them. As with sperm donation, the couple may feel shame, embarrassment, or guilt, or simply find it more convenient to say nothing.

As a matter of public policy, the question of secrecy or disclosure to the child is best left to the couple to resolve. Although most psychologists see no good reason for secrecy and emphasize the energy that keeping the secret entails, they recognize that disclosure entails its own complications.[12] At what age to tell the child? What information about the donor is needed? What if the child wants to meet the missing biologic parent? Such questions will recur many times, restimulating the parents' own unresolved conflicts about their infertility, and may take on special urgency during adolescence or times of conflict. The problems presented will vary with the individuals and the particular collaborative assistance involved, and cannot be adequately handled by a law requiring disclosure. Couples, however, do need to be informed of these problems in advance and given the chance to resolve them before proceeding.

Anonymity and Information About Donors and Surrogates

In practice, some families will disclose the existence of a collaborating donor or surrogate to the child. When disclosure occurs, children will be intensely interested in their missing biologic parent. They will need support and understanding in dealing with the emotions that an absent biologic parent may stimulate. Some children might, as adopted children often do, desire to meet that parent and other members of their biologic family. Given these desires, an important policy issue concerns what information should be collected about donors and surrogates, who should maintain it, and when should the child be given access to it.

Since most children who are told of their collaborative birth will desire knowledge of the missing parent, at the very least nonidentifying information about the donor or surrogate should be collected so that parents can provide as much information as possible. In many instances, however, rearing parents willing to discuss the matter may have no information to share, because the transaction was handled anonymously through an intermediary. If the intermediary has kept records, he is likely to keep

them confidential out of fear of legal liability. Because *nonidentifying* information about donors will be immensely important to offspring, physicians who perform sperm, egg, or embryo donation should collect this information and provide it to the couple so that they may later inform the child. If private actors do not adequately meet this need, legislation requiring the collection and disclosure of nonidentifying information may be justified.

The more difficult issue is whether *identifying* information about donors and surrogates should also be disclosed. If donors and surrogates prefer to remain anonymous yet the child wishes to learn their identity, a conflict between their privacy and the child's need to know her parentage may arise. Resolution of this conflict requires balancing the importance of knowing one's genetic or gestational parents against the importance to donors and surrogates of avoiding disclosure of their identity to the children whom they make possible.

Individuals and legislatures may well differ on this intensely personal issue. If government chooses to privilege the donor or surrogate's interest in privacy over the offspring's interest in knowing the biologic parent's identity, it appears to have the constitutional authority to do so.[13] On the other hand, if the state chooses to privilege the child's need to know her parent's identity over the collaborator's wish for privacy, that policy too may be constitutional.[14] Some legislatures might reasonably conclude, as Sweden has, that the need of children to know their biologic parents is more compelling than the interest of donors and surrogates in privacy. Options here include a ban on anonymous donation, a registry that offspring might access at age 18, or disclosure only if good medical or other cause is shown. One California sperm bank now permits donors and recipients to agree to have the name and address of the donor disclosed to offspring at age 18, if they request it.

The question of record-keeping and disclosure of both identifying and nonidentifying collaborative information is an important policy issue that has been too long ignored. At the very least, nonidentifying information should be collected and provided to rearing parents, so they may pass it on to inquiring children. Identifying information should also be collected, so that it may be disclosed if a particular jurisdiction determines at a later time that offspring should have the right to know their biologic parents' identity.

REARING RIGHTS AND DUTIES IN COLLABORATIVE REPRODUCTION

A major policy issue in collaborative reproduction is the allocation of rearing rights and duties in offspring. Given that there may be more than two biologic parents and multiple possible social parents, who will have the legal right or duty to rear the child? This issue is of central importance to infertile couples, to donors and surrogates, and to the children born of these arrangements.

While these issues have been largely resolved for sperm donation to a married couple, legal questions remain about the status of sperm donation to an unmarried woman and situations where donor and recipient intend to share rearing. The legal status of rearing is even less clear with donor eggs, embryo donation, and surrogacy. A major issue concerns whether the preconception intentions of the parties for rearing shall be determinative, or whether lawmakers should adopt some other system for allocating rearing roles.

In my view there are compelling reasons for recognizing the preconception intentions of the parties as the presumptive arbiter of rearing rights and duties, as long as the welfare of the offspring will not be severely damaged by honoring those intentions.[15] This standard, of course, assumes that the child's best interest does not automatically depend on being reared by a particular genetic or gestational parent.

A main reason for presumptively enforcing the preconception agreement for rearing is procreative liberty. . . . The procreative liberty of in-

fertile married couples (and arguably unmarried persons as well) should include the right to use noncoital means of conception to form families. If the couple lacks the gametes or gestational capacity to produce offspring, a commitment to procreative liberty should also permit them the freedom to enlist the assistance of willing donors and surrogates.

Reliance on preconception agreements are thus necessary to give the couple—as well as the donors and surrogates—the assurance they need to go forward with the collaborative enterprise. Without some contractual assurance, the parties may be unwilling to embark on the complicated enterprise of collaborative reproduction. The infertile couple needs assurance that their efforts to become parents, if medically successful, will be legally recognized. Donors and surrogates also need assurance that they will not acquire unwanted rearing duties, or, if they have bargained for a more active rearing role, that their intentions will be honored. Without some advance certainty about legal consequences, they or the couple might be unwilling to collaborate, thus depriving the couple of the ingredients needed to have and rear offspring.[16]

In addition to giving parties advance certainty, honoring preconception intentions will minimize the frequency of disputes and the costs of resolving them if they occur. If preconception agreements concerning rearing are generally binding, there will be less chance that participants will violate them. If disputes do arise, presumptively recognizing those intentions will be the most efficient way to resolve the dispute. Holding the parties to the promises on which the other parties relied also seems to be a fair solution. If enforcement of those agreements does not hurt the child, the only question will be whether the agreement was knowingly and freely made.[17]

The idea of allowing preconception intentions or contracts to control postbirth rearing, however, is objectionable to many people. They point to the rejection of a contractual approach to adoption, the disparities in bargaining position that may exist, and the disregard of the child's best interests. However, the position asserted here is not necessarily antithetical to those points. The parties' preconception agreement about postbirth rearing is not enforced if it was not freely made or if enforcing the rearing provisions will clearly harm the child. However, if the parties who have contracted to rear are adequate child rearers, their preconception agreement should trump the claims of donors or surrogates who later insist on a different rearing role than they had agreed upon. If all parties are equally good child rearers and the collaborative agreement was freely and knowingly entered, the preconception agreement for rearing should be enforced.

In fact, the idea of enforcing preconception agreements for collaborative reproduction is already well accepted with donor sperm. Although not stated in contract terms a similar result occurs judicially or by statute in over thirty states when the husband consents in writing to artificial insemination of his wife with donor sperm. A similar result presumably would be reached with egg and embryo donation. The main problems with enforcing preconception rearing agreements have arisen with donations to unmarried persons, agreements for greater involvement by the donor, and with surrogacy.

To explore the question of rearing rights and duties in collaborating offspring, it is helpful to distinguish between (1) agreements that exclude donors and surrogates from any rearing role, and (2) agreements that include the donor and surrogate. Within each category, further distinctions based on the collaborative technique involved, the marital status of the parties, and the timing of deviations from preconception agreements may also be relevant.

Agreements to Exclude
Donors and Surrogates

The most common arrangement in collaborative situations will be to exclude the donor or surrogate from any rearing role. The infertile couple receiving the third party's gametic or gestational contribution assumes all rearing rights and duties, while the donor or surrogate takes on no visitation, custody, or other rearing rights and assumes no duties of financial support.

The validity of such agreements could be challenged in several ways. The donor or surrogate could, despite his or her agreement, attempt to visit or see the child, or in the case of surrogacy, not relinquish the child to the contracting couple. Such attempts to rear could occur at birth or at some later point. Alternatively, the state or recipient of the collaborative service could seek to impose rearing duties of support on the third party, despite their understanding that they would have no rearing obligations. To evaluate the merits of either attempt to override the agreement, it is necessary to distinguish the collaborative techniques in which these issues might arise.

Donor Sperm: Married

The validity of preconception rearing contracts excluding the donor is firmly established only in one area—donor sperm to a consenting married couple. Statutes and court decisions in more than thirty states provide that the consenting husband is the rearing father for all purposes, with the donor having no rearing rights and duties.[18] Presumably jurisdictions without statutes or court decisions would also follow this model. Although not worded in contract terms, these laws implicitly recognize the intentions of the parties to exclude the donor from all rearing rights and duties.

Donor Sperm: Unmarried

The situation is more complicated with sperm donation to an unmarried woman (who may be single or cohabiting with a male or female partner). While a few states apply the married person model in this situation and exclude the donor, they may condition legal exclusion on a physician doing the insemination or on compliance with some other condition.[19] Where no statute applies, the question of whether the donor's intention to avoid support obligations will be upheld remains undetermined.

Courts generally do not relieve men of child support obligations even if they were misled by their sexual partner about her inability to conceive.[20] A few cases involving sperm donation to unmarried women have followed this principle when other statutory provisions for excluding the donor, such as physician insemination, have not been met.[21] In most cases, however, no legal attempt to seek support from the donor has occurred, either because the recipient has been able to provide for the child or the donor is unknown.

Resolution of this issue requires balancing financial responsibility for offspring against encouraging or facilitating the use of donor sperm by unmarried women. Holding sperm donors responsible for the costs of rearing offspring would reduce the opportunities of unmarried women to obtain sperm from physicians or sperm banks, thus relegating them to turkey baster inseminations with sperm that has not been screened for infectious diseases.[22] While one can question whether the right to procreate includes the right to impose rearing costs on others, the risk that sperm donation to unmarried women will increase welfare costs is very slight. One could reasonably conclude that this risk does not justify the reduction in reproductive options for single women that imposing rearing costs on sperm donors would create. Until legislation clarifying these issues is passed, complicated questions of inheritance could also arise.

Egg Donation

Since 1988, collaborative reproduction involving the donation of eggs to women who are unable to produce healthy eggs has been available.[23] The donor goes through ovarian stimulation and has eggs retrieved, as occurs in IVF.[24] In egg donation, however, the eggs are donated to the in-

fertile couple, inseminated with the husband's sperm, and then placed in the uterus of the wife who is unable to produce eggs. The wife carries the embryo to term, and becomes the rearing mother. In this case both rearing parents have a biologic relation with the child, though only the husband has a genetic relation.

As with sperm donation, the egg donor ordinarily will provide eggs with the intention that she will have no rearing rights or duties in the offspring, and the couple will receive them with the intention that they will assume all rearing rights and duties. At present, only Oklahoma, Texas, and Florida have statutes that gives legal effect to such intentions, following the model that they have adopted for donor sperm to a married couple.[25] A similar approach is expected in other states.

There is no good reason why preconception agreements to exclude the egg donor from any rearing role should not be followed. The egg donor who changes her mind has no persuasive claim in her own right to be involved in rearing. She knowingly provided the egg with the intention that she would be excluded from any rearing role. Nor can she argue convincingly that the best interests of the child require that she have contact with her genetic offspring. Whether or not offspring will want to know their genetic mother at a later time, it is unlikely that the child's best interests require contact with the genetic mother at such an early age, especially when the father and gestational, rearing mother object.

By the same token, the genetic mother should not have rearing duties imposed on her that she did not agree to. Because a female parent is usually in the picture to provide financial support, the situation is not like sperm donation to a single woman.[26] Imposing such obligations would greatly deter or discourage egg donation, thus impairing the ability of infertile couples to use this technique to form families.

Nor should the marital status of the recipient matter in this case, as it might with sperm donation to an unmarried woman. Egg donation always involves a woman who is present to birth and care for the child. Enforcing the agreement to exclude the egg donor from rearing rights and duties should not be dependent on marital status, as it sometimes is with sperm donation.

Embryo Donation

A collaborative technique not yet in wide use but that will be sought by a subset of infertile couples is embryo donation. Couples who are unable to produce egg and sperm themselves may form a family by having a donated embryo placed in the wife's uterus and brought to term. Or couples or women who could benefit from egg donation but who wish to avoid the expense of paying a woman to produce eggs might choose embryo donation. Here the wife has a gestational but no genetic connection with the child, and the husband has no genetic connection. In effect it combines egg and sperm donation in the precombined form of an embryo. While neither rearing partner will be reproducing in the strict genetic sense, gestation undertaken with the intent of the woman and her husband to rear deserves respect as an aspect of their procreative liberty.

No statutes or cases yet exist to regulate rearing rights and duties in embryo donation. However, if agreements to exclude sperm and egg donors from all rearing rights and duties are recognized, the same result should apply with persons who receive an embryo donation. Offspring are assured a male and female rearing parent, one of whom—the mother—has a biologic connection with the child. The couple donating the embryo did so willingly, with the clear understanding that they would have no rearing rights and duties. If separate sperm and egg donations would bar donors from a rearing role, there is no apparent reason why combining the donation in the form of an embryo should lead to a different result.[27]

The only situation in which the agreements to exclude from any rearing role might be overridden would be where the donation went to a single woman. In that case, the child would have a female rearing parent but no male rearing parent. If the jurisdiction recognized the sperm donor's obligations to offspring in those situations, then presumably it might do so in similar situations involving embryo donation. However, one can question whether such a policy is desirable for either sperm or embryo donations for single women.

Surrogacy

Collaborative reproduction is also practiced with the assistance of a woman who gestates the embryo of the infertile couple. The wife may have functioning ovaries but no uterus or is otherwise medically unable to carry a fetus to term. Through IVF, she and her husband produce an embryo which is then placed in the uterus of the gestational surrogate. The resulting child is the genetic offspring of the rearing parents, but has been gestated or carried to term by another.[28]

Surrogacy may also occur with the surrogate providing the egg as well as gestation.[29] The collaborator in this case is artificially inseminated with the husband's sperm, and relinquishes the child to the father and his wife at birth. At some point after birth she terminates her parental rights, and the father's wife—the child's stepmother—adopts the child. In this case, the rearing husband will have a biologic connection with the child. The rearing mother will have none.[30]

The question of enforcing preconception surrogacy agreements for rearing is the most controversial issue in collaborative reproduction. Although most surrogates relinquish the child as agreed, widely publicized cases of surrogates seeking custody or visitation in violation of their agreement have arisen. The few courts that have dealt with the matter have usually applied the long standing adoption law principle that preconceptual or prenatal agreements to relinquish for adoption will not be enforced. They reject the notion that the child's best interests can be determined prior to birth or conception by contract, or that women can know their true wishes about rearing offspring before birth occurs. Some persons oppose enforcing surrogate contracts because women may enter into these arrangements under financial pressure, because it is their labor that has produced the child, or because contract law reflects patriarchal notions of rights that use women's bodies for the sake of male reproduction.[31]

In my view, the preconception intentions of the parties should be binding both for gestational and full surrogacy.[32] In both cases the couple will have invested considerable time, energy, and emotion in finding the surrogate and initiating pregnancy in reliance on her promise. In the case of gestational surrogacy, they will also have entrusted their embryo to her. Given these competing interests, it is not obvious that the surrogate's disappointment or loss at having to relinquish the child as promised should be privileged over the loss which the couple will feel if she now insists on rearing. Assuming that both the couple and the surrogate are fit rearers, there is no reason to think that the child is always better off with the birth mother.[33] In addition, overriding preconception intentions interferes with the couple's procreative interest in using this method of forming a family.

The procreative liberty of both infertile couples and surrogates would be advanced by upholding preconception agreements for surrogate services. If the parties have a fundamental constitutional right to use noncoital means of forming families, that right should include enforcement of preconception surrogate contracts.[34] A failure to enforce preconception agreements to rear could block the only avenue open to infertile couples to have offspring genetically related to one or both rearing partners. It may also deny women who wish only to gestate opportunities to do so. Couples who would otherwise engage their services might be reluctant to do so if the couple's legal right to rear cannot be guaranteed in advance.

While a mix of reasons contribute to the view that the gestational mother's wish to rear

should be privileged, they are not sufficient to override the procreative interests at stake. Indeed, in the final analysis, rejection of preconception intentions to fix postbirth rearing rights and duties seems to be based on paternalistic attitudes toward women or on a symbolic view of maternal gestation. Privileging the surrogate's wishes over the reliance interests of the couple assumes that women cannot make rational decisions about reproduction and child rearing prior to conception. It also treats gestational motherhood as a near sacred endeavor, which preconception contracts that separate gestational and social parentage violate.[35] However, paternalistic and symbolic attitudes over which reasonable persons differ do not justify trumping the fundamental right to use collaborative means of procreation.

No court, however, has yet held that enforcement of preconception rearing agreements is required by procreative liberty. The New Jersey Supreme Court rejected it in the Baby M case by characterizing procreation as genetic only, ignoring the rearing relationship that William Stern and most genetic reproducers intend as a result.[36] Most states that have legislated on surrogate motherhood since Baby M also protect the surrogate's right to retain rearing rights, despite her preconception promise to the contrary.[37]

Respect for the preconception agreement however, should fare better in the case of gestational surrogacy, because the surrogate is not then claiming to rear her own genetic child. In *Anna J. v. Mark C.*, for example, the California Supreme Court held that a gestational surrogate had no claim to rear because she was not the genetic parent.[38] Still, many commentators and surrogacy statues refuse to distinguish the two types of surrogacy because of the value they assign to the gestational bond and the autonomy of birthing women.[39] Questions of custody and visitation then have to be assigned on some basis other than preconception intentions. However, as long as legislators do not prohibit surrogacy altogether (either directly or by banning payments), recognition of the surrogate's legal right to rear may not discourage all uses of surrogacy. Some couples will still proceed with the hope that the surrogate will honor her promise not to seek postbirth rearing.

Agreements to Include the Donor/Surrogate in Rearing Collaborative Offspring

Although most collaborative arrangements will exclude the donor or surrogate from rearing rights and duties, there will be some instances in which the collaborators agree—as a condition of participation—to give donors and surrogates a role in rearing offspring, including joint or limited custody, visitation, or child support.[40] Such reproduction is truly collaborative, for it involves egg, embryo, and sperm donors and surrogates in rearing the "family" that the parties jointly produce.

Such novel familial arrangements raise two separate legal issues: (1) should inclusive collaborative agreements be permitted at all, and (2) should such agreements be enforced?

Laws against such novel intentionally blended families are unlikely, and would probably be unconstitutional.[41] It is no more likely that raising a child openly with several biologic and social parents would be any more or less harmful than raising a child who has no contact with a biologic parent. Either situation may be done well or badly, depending on the parties, their economic and social situation, and their adjustment to the emotional and psychological complexities of these roles. The medical gatekeepers of the reproductive technology who are needed to construct such families may refuse access, but the law is unlikely to be a direct bar.

The second question—should inclusive collaborative rearing arrangements be enforced— will arise when the donor or surrogate wishes to avoid rearing duties that they voluntarily undertook, or the married couple or individual recipient wishes to exclude the donor or surrogate from the rearing role that had been intended.

A commitment to procreative liberty argues for presumptively enforcing these agreements, both against the primary rearing parents who wish to exclude the donor, and against the donor who wishes to escape support obligations. The parties agreed to collaborate on condition that they would have the assigned roles. Denying effect to their agreement may deprive them of parenting experiences that were the reason for their collaboration. It will also deter future collaborations because of legal uncertainty that intentions will be honored. If freedom to use noncoital technologies to treat infertility and to play partial reproductive roles is to be respected, then agreements of donors and surrogates to be included in—as well as excluded from—rearing offspring should be presumptively honored.

Whether courts or legislatures will honor these agreements depends on several factors, including the time at which the rearing claim is made, the presence of male and female rearers, whether the third party is trying to be included or trying to avoid support obligations, and, finally, on whether the aggrieved party has a biologic relation with the child in question.

The timing of the dispute will be key because of the importance of maintaining rearing relationships that have been established with biologic partners. Attempts to exclude a donor or surrogate who has been permitted to visit the child over a period of time will be less successful than attempts to exclude before the child has established a beneficial relationship with that party. If the relationship has already been established, only conflicts deemed detrimental to the child would seem to warrant exclusion of the donor or surrogate from the agreed-upon role. If the relationship has not been established, failure to enforce the agreement may not harm the child, unless a child's access to a biologic parent is deemed important. In any event, donors or surrogates who do not act to assert their contractual rearing rights immediately after birth are in danger of losing them, just as unmarried fathers are who do not timely assert their interest in rearing offspring.[42]

The primary rearing parents' success in excluding the donor or surrogate may also depend on whether a two-parent rearing family is available to the child aside from the donor or surrogate. The couple's claim to exclude is more likely to be successful in those cases because the child's interests in two parents appears to be met, and the presence of a third party could be disruptive.[43] Still, the excluded biologic parent should have standing to raise her and the child's interest in the intended contact, with disposition of the dispute determined by the child's best interests and the excluded parent's constitutional right to rear offspring.

On the other hand, if the recipient of the collaborative service is single, it will be much harder to exclude the donor or surrogate from the agreed-upon role. Courts are then more likely to find that enforcing the agreement serves the child's interest by providing a second rearer, a factor important in cases that have upheld the sperm donor's right to visit the child of a donation to a single woman.[44] This factor could be important in sperm or embryo donation to single women, or in surrogacy involving single men. It is less likely to matter with egg donation or surrogacy to a single women, since a female rearer will be present.

A third factor that will determine whether inclusive agreements are enforced is the nature of the agreed-upon rearing role. Agreements for joint custody or visitation will be more easily revoked and rejected than agreements to provide support, which the donor/surrogate now refuses to pay. As the biologic parent who would ordinarily be liable for support, he or she should still be liable even if conception was noncoital and donors/surrogates are relieved of support obligations if they agreed to be excluded from any rearing role. When they agreed to support the child whom they are directly responsible for producing, it is reasonable to hold them to their preconception promise. Of course, they may then be entitled to some rearing role as well.

A final determinative factor in these cases is whether the party claiming rearing rights pursuant to a preconception collaborative agreement has played a biologic role in the arrangement. If the collaborator is not a gamete donor or gestator, they will not have reproduced and may have little chance of having their rearing role recognized, as recent litigation concerning custody disputes in lesbian families shows.

In the Matter of Alison D. v. Virginia M., a typical case of this sort, involved a lesbian couple who had a child by artificial insemination.[45] The nonbiologic partner obtained sperm from her brother, inseminated her partner, was present at birth, gave the child her last name, and was the main financial support for the family and child for several years. When the couple separated, the nonbiologic parent was allowed to visit the child for a period. After a point, however, the biologic mother barred her former partner from further contact and litigation ensued. The New York Court of Appeals rejected that partner's claim to participate in rearing on the ground that she was not a "parent" within existing law, and thus lacked standing to raise issues of visitation on behalf of herself or the child.

This decision firmly rejects an expanded version of procreative liberty that would include nonbiologic parties who play a central role in arranging the birth of a child, as the plaintiff in *Alison D.* had. No matter what the intentions of the parties or the actual rearing relationship with the child has been, the nonbiologic rearer is not a "parent" and thus has no standing to have the child's best interests in continuing her rearing relationship considered. While the legislature can change this result, legislators appear reluctant to grant nonbiologic rearers parental status in these situations. Such cases directly challenge the importance of bloodline in determining parenting relations, and require us to rethink whether a nonbiologic party should always be barred from a prearranged rearing role when the biologic parent insists.[46]

On the other hand, *Alison D.* implicitly supports the claim of excluded biologic collaborators who are seeking to partake in rearing pursuant to a preconception agreement. They will at least have standing to raise the issue, because "parent" is defined biologically. Whether courts will find the child's best interests served by contact with the excluded biologic parent will depend on the child's need for contact with all biologic parents, on whether some parental relationship has already begun, and on other factors.[47]

Decisions such as *Alison D.* might, if adoption by the nonbiologic parent is not possible, push gay, lesbian, or other nontraditional partners to establish a biologic connection with intended offspring whenever possible, in order to protect their rearing rights in case of death, divorce, or later dispute. Lesbian couples could have one partner provide the egg for the embryo, which is then gestated by the other partner. Each would then be a biologic parent and have standing as a "parent" to protect the child's best interests.[48] Gay couples who form families with the assistance of a surrogate do not have this option. Until techniques for fusing embryos created by gametes from different partners are established, only one man can be the genetic father of a child.

PROTECTING REPRODUCTIVE COLLABORATORS

Collaborative reproduction offers infertile couples, donors, and surrogates the technical means to fulfill their differing reproductive needs in a mutually satisfying way. If done with advance counseling and full understanding of the social, psychological, medical, and legal complications, it may be a fulfilling enterprise for all parties.

But collaborative reproduction may also be frustrating, upsetting, and difficult. Even with sperm donation, which has been practiced since the 1940s, the social, psychological, and legal roles have not been fully defined. The parties will be thrust into new roles and relationships for which there is little guidance and little legal or social approval. Persons embarking on this enterprise may receive little counseling or guidance in how to deal with the complicated emotional issues that may arise. What is proper conduct for a donor or a family that has received a donation? How do they relate to each other?

To the child? What do they tell their own parents, siblings, and friends? What do donors and surrogates tell their family, friends, and own children? The opportunities for greeting-card companies and family therapists are endless.

In addition, the parties face an uncertain legal environment. Aside from donor sperm to a consenting married couple where the law is clearest, there is ample room for dispute and litigation, as donors and surrogates change their minds and assert interests that they had not previously envisaged. Also, the procedures sought may be such less efficacious than expected, requiring several cycles of artificial insemination or embryo transfer. Surrogates may miscarry, or have medical complications during pregnancy or childbirth. Donor insemination may transmit cytomegalovirus or even HIV.[49] Egg donors are also at medical risk from hyperstimulation of the ovaries and egg retrieval.

Limiting Collaborative Reproduction to Protect Donors and Surrogates

Given the problems that could arise in collaborative reproduction, some persons have argued that the enterprise should be banned altogether or greatly limited to protect the participants from pain or later disappointment. However, such paternalism is unwarranted, and would . . . appear to violate the procreative liberty of reproductive collaborators. Rather than discourage collaboration, public policy should focus on making it safe, effective, and rewarding for all the parties.[50]

Indeed, while there are risks of disappointment, emotional turmoil, and perhaps even litigation, these risks are neither so likely nor so substantial that a ban on any particular form of collaborative reproduction is justified. Even surrogacy, which poses the greatest risks to collaborators, usually is successful for the parties, even though some surrogate mothers feel such intense disappointment that they will wish that surrogacy had never been invented. Sperm, egg, and embryo donors may also at times feel a poignant sadness at never knowing their progeny. But these reactions will vary in intensity and permanence with the individuals involved. Later regret does not seem so likely or devastating that collaborative contracts should be prohibited to protect reproductive collaborators. The harm prevented is not so likely or substantial to justify paternalistic interference with the parties' procreative choice.[51]

Assuring Informed Consent and Avoiding Disappointment

An essential step to protect the collaborating parties is to make sure that they are fully informed of the particular risks that they run in participating in collaborative reproduction. In most instances, this will require actions by physicians and other intermediaries. In some cases, laws or professional guidelines will be necessary.

Infertile Couples and Recipients

Couples being treated for infertility often feel that they are riding on an unpredictable roller coaster. In confronting their infertility, they must adjust to the loss of expected children and self-esteem, and the guilt, anger, and depression that these losses usually bring. They may grasp eagerly at the hope that donor gametes or surrogacy will, at last, bring them the child that they so fervently wish.

It is thus crucial that they be fully informed about success rates and about the medical, social, and psychological risks of these procedures, so that they are prepared for later disappointment and complications. The extent of counseling will vary with the program, the parties, and the collaborative technique they choose. Overshadowing the entire enterprise will be the unanswerable questions about the longer-range psychological and social impact of collaborative reproduction.

Gamete Donors

Donors of sperm, egg, or embryos also need detailed information, and in some cases counseling, about the social, psychological, and legal ramifications of their role. Sperm donors face no medical risk in masturbating to produce sperm, though they may end up learning disturbing information about their genetic or HIV status.[52] They should be accurately informed of the legal implications of their donation, including any chance that they could be liable in the future for child support or have unwanted contact with offspring. They should also be informed of possible psychological repercussions if they wish to have contact with offspring, yet do not have any recourse. Honest discussion of these issues at the start will minimize later problems.

Egg donors face more medical risks, because they will usually undergo ovarian stimulation and surgical retrieval of eggs. They need accurate information about those risks and the legal ramifications of their donation, and counseling about the unknown social and psychological effects of separating female genetic, gestational, and social parentage. They too should be prepared for the possibility of wanting to know about or make contact with their genetic offspring, yet have no way of doing so.[53] They should also be prepared for genetic offspring seeking to make contact with them. Other complications could occur if they are donating eggs to a family member or friend.

Embryo donors face similar uncertainties. The legal effects of embryo donation are still undefined, so that even reasonable predictions about future rearing rights and duties are necessarily uncertain. In addition, donated embryos will usually have been created as part of an infertile couple's own efforts to form a family. The donor couple may feel a special bond to "their" embryos, and want very much, despite initial feelings to the contrary, to meet or protect "their" child. If their own efforts at pregnancy have failed, these feelings might intensify or even parallel the feelings of abandonment and guilt that persons who relinquish children for adoption sometimes feel. Prospective embryo donors should be informed of these possibilities, and counseling should be provided to help them adjust to these contingencies.

Surrogates

Special attention must be paid to the needs of surrogates. They will be embarking on a major life event—pregnancy and childbirth—with the intention of then relinquishing the child they have gestated. Accurate information about medical difficulties in initiating and completing pregnancy is essential. Counseling is also essential to prepare surrogates for probable feelings of disappointment, depression, and guilt. Counseling should be provided both prior to conception and after birth to help them adjust to their situation.

A class bias in most surrogacy arrangements may also be inevitable. While most surrogates are high school graduates, and many will have gone to college, they are more likely to be less educated and less well off than the infertile couples who hire them. Prospective surrogates will be driven by complex motives, including altruism, money, the wish to reexperience in order to master a previous experience of loss, enjoyment of pregnancy, or wanting to reproduce without rearing.[54] Some women may have unrealistic ideas about the experience, or not fully understand their own motivation.

Given the complexity of the situation, some persons recommend that prospective surrogates be screened according to strict criteria of psychological health. They suggest that women with previous psychological problems and women who have not had children not be accepted into surrogacy programs. Others would provide couples with the results of screening tests and leave it to the couple to decide whether to accept a particular surrogate. Still others would formalize surrogacy agreements by requiring that a judge, or alternatively, a review board, examine the prospective surrogate prior to insemination to make sure that she fully understands her rights and duties, and is acting freely.[55] Preconception ratification would bar the surrogate's later claim to custody of offspring contrary to her agreement.

Until regulatory legislation is passed, surrogate brokers have special duties to make sure that the women they recruit are well informed and counseled about the risks they face.[56] Although this has not always been the practice, surrogate brokers should inform prospective surrogates at the earliest possible time in the recruitment process, such as in the material that they send out to women responding to newspaper ads, that surrogacy is disappointing and difficult for some women. Brokers should also make clear to prospective surrogates that they represent the infertile couple, not the surrogate, and advise the surrogate to seek her own legal counsel. They should also screen prospective surrogates psychologically, so that women who appear likely to have problems are excluded or so infertile couples have full information on the psychological profile of the prospective surrogate. They may also have legal duties to make sure that medical tests that protect the surrogate are performed.[57]

Whether privately or publicly imposed, measures to assure that surrogates are adequately counseled and screened will increase costs, and interfere to some extent with the wishes of individuals to engage or function as a surrogate. Such restrictions, however, do not violate procreative liberty, for they are not likely to prevent couples from use of this technique.[58] Moreover, the additional burden they create is justified as a reasonable measure to enhance autonomy and protect the parties in surrogate reproduction.

Paying Money and the Reification of Reproduction

A major concern about collaborative reproduction arises from paying donors and surrogates for their services. Commercializing reproduction is said to exploit and depersonalize women, turning them into mere cogs in the machinery of reproduction. It also risks turning children into commodities that are purchased via the payments for donor and surrogate services that make them possible.

Objections to payment, however, vary with the procedure in question. Some countries, such as France, England, and Australia, have banned payments to gamete donors and depend solely on volunteers. The prevailing practice in the United States is for commercial sperm banks or physician intermediaries to pay sperm donors for their time and effort, thus proving the inaccuracy of the term "donor." Egg donors are also paid on a graduated schedule according to the procedures they undergo.[59] A fee of $1,500 to $2,000 is now common. Some embryo donors have requested compensation to cover the costs incurred in producing the donated embryos. Federal and state laws outlaw the sale of solid organs and nonrenewable tissue, but usually do not apply to the sale of gametes.[60]

Payment to surrogate mothers, however, is much more controversial and is illegal in many states and abroad. Several states have recently passed statutes that expressly forbid commercial surrogacy, banning payments both to surrogates and to the brokers who arrange for their services.[61] Other states reach the same result by construing laws against baby selling, which prohibit payments other than medical expenses for adoption, as prohibiting payments to surrogates, Such laws do not usually distinguish between gestational and other forms of surrogacy. In most states the legal status of payment to surrogates remains uncertain.

One could argue that these laws do not apply to surrogacy because the infertile couple is paying the surrogate for her gestational services, not for giving the child up for adoption. This argument is strongest when gestational surrogacy is involved, and weakest as the contract makes payment conditional on either producing a live baby or on fulfilling the promise to relinquish the child for adoption. Opponents of paid surrogacy, on the other hand, argue that the surrogate contract, no matter how written, is a contract for the sale of a child that falls within laws prohibiting baby selling. The New Jersey Supreme Court adopted the latter view in the *Baby M* case, and it may be followed in other jurisdictions.[62]

Paying surrogates (though perhaps not gamete donors) is probably necessary if infertile couples are to obtain surrogacy services. Although surrogates usually act out of a mix of motivations, few women not related to the couple are likely to undergo pregnancy and childbirth unless they are paid for their services. Also, it seems unfair not to pay surrogates for their very substantial efforts, while egg and sperm donors and the doctors and lawyers arranging surrogate services are well paid. If a ban on payment significantly reduced access to surrogacy, it would infringe the infertile couple's procreative liberty, for it would prevent them from obtaining the collaborative services they need to rear biologically related offspring. Such an infringement could be justified only if banning payment prevented a substantial harm that clearly outweighed the burden on procreative choice.

Yet the arguments for banning payment do not appear to reach that level of justification. A main argument is that a ban on payment will prevent exploitation of surrogates, who in most cases will be poorer and of a different social class than the infertile couples hiring them.[63] Exploitation should not be confused with coercion. Women volunteering to be paid surrogates are not being coerced, even if they need the money, because they are not deprived of anything that they are otherwise entitled to if they refuse the couple's offer.[64]

Nor is it clear that they are bing exploited to any greater degree than labor markets generally exploit financial need. In this regard, markets for the sale of gestational services are no more exploitive than the sale of other kinds of physical labor. If people are free to sell their labor as petrochemical workers, cleaning persons, or construction workers in the hot Texas sun, why should the sale of gestational services be treated any differently? Much paid labor is equally or even more risky to health.

Proponents of the exploitation claim point to the very different nature of maternal gestation, and argue that women should not be asked to trade their gestational capacity for their need for money. Their argument, in effect, rests on an objection to the perceived risks and demeaning effects of commercializing motherhood. Yet reasonable people have differing moral perceptions about paid surrogacy, with many not finding the symbolic demeaning of motherhood that others see as so glaringly wrong. With such splits in perception, such symbolic concerns alone should not override the couple's interest in having and rearing biologic offspring with the help of a freely consenting, paid collaborative.

A second argument against payment—that it commodifies children and surrogates—also reduces to a perception of the symbolic effects of treating gestation as a product to be sold for money. Professor Margaret Radin has developed this argument more fully than anyone else.[65] But she has failed to show that payment will lead to monetizing or commodifying all children or women, or why certain attributes such as gestation and sexuality may not be sold, while other attributes, such as physical size, skill, attractiveness, and intellectual prowess may be.[66] Her claim that her list of nonmonetizable attributes are more essential "to our deepest understanding of what it is to be human" is not convincing, since one could just as reasonably argue that the physical and mental attributes that drive the market for models, professional athletes, and computer scientists are also essential to "our deepest understanding of what it is to be human."[67]

In short, while some feminist critics stress the harmful effects of paid surrogacy on women, objections to paying surrogates are often more deontological than consequentialist.[68] The exploitation and commodification objections usually boil down to the judgment that it is simply wrong to pay women to gestate, because of the very essence or nature of gestation, regardless of actual effects. The problem with this objection is that perceptions of the wrongfulness of payment vary widely, with surrogates, infertile couples, and many others strongly in favor of payment. Given differing views over the symbolic significance of payment, the need to protect female gestation from the taint of filthy lucre does not seem compelling enough to justify stopping infertile couples from obtaining the services they need to rear biologic offspring. However, until courts and legislatures adopt this analysis, bans on paying surrogate mothers, though arguably a clear interference with procreative liberty, may prevent many infertile couples from using this technique to have children.

THE LOOP BACK TO ADOPTION

Recognition of the right to engage in collaborative reproduction has been grounded in the importance of rearing children who are biologically related to one or both rearing partners. One might question, however, why the biologic tie to one or both of the partners is essential. For medical or other reasons some couples will be unable to establish that tie, yet still have a strong desire to rear children. If couples may resort to donors and surrogates to form a family, why should access to collaborative assistance depend on the couple's biologic participation in the enterprise?

The importance of a minimal biologic connection as a prerequisite to collaborative reproduction may not withstand scrutiny. Adopted children are wanted and loved despite the lack of biologic tie with parents, as are collaboratively produced children who have no biologic tie with a rearing mother or father. Indeed, feminists critical of surrogate motherhood have pointed out that the bias in favor of biology may reflect patriarchal notions of kinship and inheritance that need revision in light of the social realities of rearing families. In forcing us to recognize the rearing interests of both partners, including the partner who may lack a biologic connection with offspring, collaborative reproduction may lead to a reevaluation of the importance of biologic ties in other family arrangements.[69]

Such a reevaluation might show that preconception rearing intentions should count as much as or more than biologic connection. If so, then arrangements in which several persons collaborate to produce a child for person(s) to rear who have no biologic connection with the child should also be presumptively protected.[70] Although it is not reproduction in the strict sense, the rearing couple would be exercising a choice which presumptively deserves respect because of the importance of parenting to persons who cannot themselves reproduce.

If the importance of rearing leads us to privilege rearing intentions and practices over biology, then the existing legal framework for adoption will necessarily be called into question. Under this framework, preconception or prenatal contracts to relinquish children for adoption are invalid, and payments to induce adoption are illegal. Such laws directly conflict with an expanded view of collaborative reproduction that includes a couple's right to form a family with nonbiologically related children, for preconception agreements and money payments will usually be essential to form such families.

If the right to form families is broadened beyond the confines of current adoption law, couples would be entitled to pay women to be artificially or naturally impregnated to produce children for them. The couple would have a presumptive right to rear offspring exclusive of the biologic parents, in accordance with preconception agreements to that effect.[71] After all, they were the prime movers in bringing all the parties together to produce the child, and have relied on the promise of the gamete providers and gestator not to rear in mobilizing the parties to that goal. No doubt brokers adept in finding gamete donors and surrogates and coordinating conception, pregnancy, and childbirth for the sake of intended parents would enter the market. Thus broadened, procreative liberty would lead to a widespread market in paid conception, pregnancies, and adoptions, the very antithesis of the current system.

If collaborative reproduction loops back in this way to undermine the foundations of adop-

tion law, some persons may oppose any use of donors and surrogates. The logic of collaborative reproduction, even when confined to some biologic relation, does challenge the importance of biology. The intended arrangement presumptively trumps the later claims of donors and surrogates, even though they have as strong, or in the case of full surrogacy, arguably stronger, biologic ties to offspring. The theory underlying these practices would logically extend primary rearing rights to the infertile couple who independently recruit sperm, egg, or embryo donor and surrogate to produce a child for them.[72] The need for adoption brokers and payment to collaborators to implement such arrangements would naturally follow. Laws that prevented these arrangements would then need revision.

Yet logic and practice must be distinguished. In the foreseeable future most reproductive collaboration will be for gamete donation or gestational surrogacy, both of which preserve a prime biologic connection. There will be few instances of a couple organizing gamete donors and surrogacy to provide them a child in the extreme way being discussed.[73] The adoption system can be distinguished from these practices and permitted to function independently with its own rules.

In time, however, pressure to change that system might occur. If preconception contracts with donors and surrogates are validated, some persons—infertile couples or entrepreneurs—will no doubt try to extend that principle to commissioned pregnancies and paid adoption. At that point the importance of the biologic gestational connection will have to be directly confronted, and the framework of adoption law reevaluated.[74] In the end, we may come to accept paid, commissioned pregnancies in carefully defined circumstances as another avenue for infertile couples seeking to form a family. Whether or not labeled "reproductive," the interests at stake may deserve equivalent protection. However, fear of that possibility should not prevent the present use of donors and surrogates to form families who are biologically related to one or both rearing partners.

COLLABORATIVE REPRODUCTION AND THE FUTURE OF FAMILIES

Discussion of these issues inevitably brings us to a recurring concern about collaborative reproduction—that it will accelerate the decline of the nuclear family at a time when that institution is under severe pressure from divorce, teenage pregnancy, single mothers, blended families, gay and lesbian life-styles, and other forces.

Yet such fears exaggerate the effect of collaborative reproduction and do not justify limiting the joint efforts of infertile couples, donors, and surrogates. In most cases, collaborative reproduction enables a married couple to have biologically related offspring, with the gamete donor or surrogate excluded from any significant rearing role. While contracts to include the donor or surrogate in rearing offspring are theoretically possible, they are likely to be rare except where a friend or family member provides the service. Even then, one would expect there to be at most two primary rearers, even if some contact with other biologic parents and their relatives occurs.

Given the great number of families in which nonbiologic parents are primary rearers due to death, divorce, abandonment, and the like, it is difficult to see how collaborative reproduction, with its small number of intentionally blended families, poses a threat to the nuclear family. Indeed, with its emphasis on enabling a married couple to have and rear biologic offspring, it supports that institution more than it diminishes it, despite the social, psychological, and legal complications that might ensue.

Nor would the hypothetical possibility of expanding procreative liberty to include commissioned pregnancies and paid adoptions where there is no biologic connection alter this conclusion. While this practice would increase the number of persons playing partial reproductive roles, its primary aim is to provide a couple with a child to love and rear in a two-parent family. In any event, the numbers involved are likely to be minuscule, relative to the number of births occurring annually.

CONCLUSION

This chapter has shown that collaborative reproduction is an important part of the procreative liberty of infertile couples and the donors and surrogates assisting them to reproduce. Given its increasingly important role in the treatment of infertility, the main policy issues concern how to assure that collaborative reproduction occurs in a safe, effective, and mutually satisfying way. Rather than try to discourage such practices, public policy should insure that the necessary counseling, informed-consent, record-keeping, and legal rules for allocating rearing rights and duties exist.

As collaborative reproductive technologies grow in efficacy, they will be more frequently used, particularly egg and embryo donation and gestational surrogacy. However, the incidence of donor sperm—the most frequent collaborative technique—may diminish, as micromanipulation and intrauterine insemination techniques improve treatment of male factor infertility. Overall, however, collaborative reproduction will remain a subset of noncoital reproduction and a very small subset of reproduction generally. While crucially important for the parties involved, it is likely to have only a minimal effect on female social roles, the vitality of the family, or the shape of society.

In time, acceptance of collaborative reproduction will lead to better definition of the roles and responsibilities of the various participants. This will reduce the social, legal, and psychological uncertainties that now pervade the area, and improve the chances of a satisfying experience for collaborators and offspring. The sooner that collaborative reproduction is woven into the social fabric, the better it will be for all affected parties.

NOTES

Procreative Liberty

1. Whether labeled reproductive or not, gestation is a central experience for women and should enjoy the special respect or protected status accorded reproductive activities. On this view, a woman who receives an embryo donation or who serves as a gestational surrogate is having a reproductive experience, whether or not she also rears.

2. The distinction between liberty and claim right follows Joel Feinberg's account of those terms in his "Voluntary Euthanasia and the Inalienable Right to Life," *Philosophy and Public Affairs* 7(1978):93–95.

3. Constitutional rights are generally negative rather than positive. With the exception of counsel in criminal trials, there is no obligation on the government to provide the means necessary to exercise constitutional rights.

4. Dan Brock has argued that contraceptive services are so cheap and their lack has such a substantial impact on persons that the state has a moral obligation to provide contraceptives to poor persons. Dan Brock, "Reproductive Freedom: Its Nature, Bases, and Limits" (unpublished paper, 1992).

5. Sonnet 12 ("When I do count the clock that tells the time/And see the brave day sunk in hideous night"). Sonnet 2 ("When forty winters shall besiege they brow/And dig deep trenches in thy beauty's field") also sings the praises of reproduction as an answer to death and old age.

6. Margaret Atwood, *The Handmaid's Tale* (Boston: Houghton Mifflin, 1986).

7. "Where Death and Fear Went Forth and Multiplied," *New York Times,* 14 January 1990.

8. B. Meredith Burke, "Ceaucescu's Main Victims: Women and Children," *New York Times*, 2 June 1991.

9. Sheryl WuDunn, "China, with Ever More to Feed, Pushes Anew for Small Families," *New York Times*, 2 June 1991.

10. The 1977 sterilization campaign plays a key role in the denouement of Salmon Rushdie's *Midnight's Children: A Novel* (New York: Knopf, 1981). The narrator cries, just before he too is sterilized: "They are doing nashendi—sterilization is being performed. Save our women and children. And a riot is beginning" (p. 414).

11. Phillip Reilly, *The Surgical Solution* (Baltimore: Johns Hopkins University Press, 1991).

12. This right has received explicit recognition in the United Nations' 1978 Universal Declaration of Human Rights ("men and women of full age . . . [have the right] to marry and found a family"), the International Covenant of Civil and Political Rights (Art. 23, 1976), and the European Convention on Human Rights (Art. 12, 1953).

13. See chapters 4 and 7 [of John Robertson, *Children of Choice* (Princeton, 1994)] for further discussion.

14. The low marginal value of additional reproduction would ordinarily be relevant only when one has already had a large number of children, and thus may not be important for many of the issues discussed in this book.

15. In a technical sense, genetic reproduction is not partial at all but an instance of complete reproduction. However, it is partial when separated from the gestation or rearing that usually attends reproduction.

16. In resolving this question, we will have to determine the importance to people of the knowledge that a biologic descendant will come into being an live after one has died. Is the sense of possible continuity with nature from knowing that posthumous reproduction might occur so meaningful to people that it should be respected? Could not posthumous reproduction become as important to some individuals as the prospect of the posthumous use of one's ideas or philanthropic contributions? See John Robertson, "Posthumous Reproduction," *Indiana Law Journal* (forthcoming, 1994).

17. See chapter 7 [of *Children of Choice*].

18. Catholic Church, Congregation for the Doctrine of the Faith, "Instruction on Respect for Human Life in Its Origin and on the Dignity of Procreation," *Origins* 16 (1987): 698–711.

19. They are also concerned that women will be exploited or pressured by circumstances into arrangements that turn out to harm their interests. See chapter 6 [of *Children of Choice*].

20. Such extreme cases are dealt with in chapter 7 [of *Children of Choice*].

Collaborative Reproduction

1. One has to turn to mythological events such as Athena springing full-blown from the head of Zeus for examples of truly noncollaborative reproduction. Even the Immaculate Conception of the Virgin Mary was collaborative (though noncoital), for it required divine infusion by the Godhead.

2. Only egg and embryo donation and gestational surrogacy are truly high-tech procedures. The most widely used collaborative technique, donor sperm, involves only a syringe. It is estimated that 20,000 to 30,000 children are born each year through donor sperm. United States Congress, Office of Technology Assessment, *Infertility: Medical and Social Choices* (Washington, D.C.: Government Printing Office, 1988). Egg donation, a product of IVF, is now increasingly practiced, with over fifty clinics providing the service. Embryo donation and surrogacy are occurring to a lesser extent.

3. The term "biologic" is used in this chapter to refer to either a genetic or gestational relationship with the child who is reared. For the man, the biologic connection in reproduction is always genetic. The biologic connection for the woman may be either genetic or gestational or both, depending on the particular technique used.

4. Collaborative reproduction involves varying degrees of deviance from the two-person model of biologically related parentage. Egg donation is closest to the model, because each rearing partner has a biologic connection with offspring. Gestational surrogacy provides both with a genetic connection, though the gestational tie is missing. Sperm donation allows the woman the full connection and the man none, while embryo donation gives only the woman a biological (gestational) tie. Full surrogacy, on the other hand, gives the man a genetic connection and his wife none (the surrogate presumably being out of the picture). In contrast to adoption, each technique allows at least one, and sometimes both of the partners, a biologic connection with offspring.

5. The situation becomes even more complicated if the surrogate is the sister or mother of the husband or wife, or if any of the parties divorces and remarries a person with children from a previous marriage. In practice, however, most collaborative reproduction will involve sperm or egg donation and occasionally surrogacy, thus falling short of the five-parent combination often alluded to as a danger of collaborative reproductive practices.

6. National Center for Health Statistics, "Advance Report of Final Natality Statistics, 1990," *Monthly Vital Statistics Report* 41, no. 9 supp. (1993):33, table 16.

7. R. Snowden, G. Mitchell, and E. Snowden, *Artificial Reproduction: A Social Investigation* (London, Boston: G. Allen and Unwin, 1983), 50–54, 71–82, 97–104.

8. Physicians need to be very sensitive to these aspects of treatment, for the psychological and social dimensions may be as important as the medical.

9. Preventing harm to offspring would thus not constitute the compelling state interest necessary to justify a governmental ban on use of these techniques. See chapter 4 [of *Children of Choice*] for further discussion of this point.

10. Commercial sperm banks now distribute lists of donors identified by height, weight, hair and eye color, race or ethnic background, education, and even hobbies, from which couples choose.

11. Family members who know each other may also serve as egg donors or surrogates.

12. Mahlstedt and Greenfield, "Assisted Reproductive Technology with Donor Gametes: The Need for Patient Preparation," *Fertility and Sterility* 52(1989):908.

13. Since adopted children have no constitutional right to learn the identity of their birth parents, it is unlikely that a constitutional right of collaborative offspring to identify their genetic or gestational parents would be recognized. At the very least, the state should protect collaborative offspring by requiring that identifying information be confidentially maintained so that it could be provided if later deemed essential. See John A. Robertson, "Embryos, Families and Procreative Liberty: The Legal Structure of the New Reproduction," *Southern California Law Review* 59(1986):939, 1015–1018.

14. Laws that privileged disclosure of identity over the collaborator's desire for privacy would not violate their procreative liberty. If a state determines that adopted or collaborative offspring have a substantial interest in having identifying information about their biologic parents, this interest should be sufficient to justify regulations that burden the procreative or privacy rights of collaborators. For further discussion of this issue and the paradoxes it presents, see Robertson, "Embryos, Families, and Procreative Liberty."

15. The operative standard should require clear and convincing evidence that the intended parents will abuse or neglect the child—the same standard for interfering with rearing of children produced coitally.

16. It also deprives donors and surrogates of playing a more limited reproductive role, because couples might be unwilling to go forward without the assurance of a binding contract.

17. A contract model assumes, some means for assuring that the parties are aware of the legal, binding implications of their agreement, and that agreements are freely made. Public policies to assure intelligent, noncoerced contract formation, such as review by a judge or review panel, may be appropriate in some cases.

18. Office of Technology Assessment, *Infertility: Medical and Social Choices.*

19. See Cal. Civ. Code Sec. 7005 (West 1990).

20. In re Pamela P., 443 N.Y.S.2d 343, 110 Misc.2d 978 (1981).

21. Jhordan C. v. Mary K., No. AO27810 (Cal. Ct. of App. Apr. 25, 1986).

22. See Daniel Wikler and Norma J. Wikler, "Turkey-Baster Babies: The Demedicalization of Artificial Insemination," *Milbank Quarterly* 65(1991):5, for an interesting account of the issues that such practices present.

23. In 1990, sixty-seven clinics reported performing IV-ET with donated oocytes, with 498 patients undergoing 547 donor transfers. One hundred twenty-two (22 percent) live deliveries resulted, including thirty-six sets of twins, three sets of triplets, and one set of quadruplets. Medical Research International, Society for Assisted Reproductive Technology, The American Fertility Society, "In Vitro Fertilization-Embryo Transfer (IVF-ET) in the United States: 1990 Results from the IVF-ET Registry, *Fertility and Sterility* 57(1992):15, 21.

24. Egg donors may be other women going through IVF, women undergoing abdominal surgery for other reasons, or women recruited specifically to be egg donors. In some cases the recipient recruits the donor herself, who may be a friend or even a family member. Often they are paid. Egg donation may also occur by artificial insemination and uterine lavage, so that the recipient receives the embryo at the blastocyst stage. See John A. Robertson, "Ethical and Legal Issues in Human Egg Donation," *Fertility and Sterility* 52(1989):353.

25. Okla. Stat. Ann. tit. 10, Sec. 544 (1991); Tex. S.B. 512, 73rd Leg., R.S. (1993); S. 2082, 1993 Reg. Sess., 1993 Florida Laws.

26. The presence of a female rearer distinguishes this situation from sperm donation to a single woman, where no rearing male is present. Of course, the gestational mother and her husband could die, leaving the child of egg donation without financial support, but this contingency could also occur with sperm donation to a married couple.

27. Their claim for contact with the child, however, might have special poignancy if their own efforts at IVF, which led to the donated embryo, have not resulted in offspring.

28. The surrogate could be a sister, a mother, or a stranger hired directly or through a broker for this purpose.

29. Many persons object to use of the term "surrogate" to describe this relationship. In their view, the "surrogate" is the actual mother of the child and should be referred to as such. The wife of the hiring couple is thus a surrogate rearer for the biologic mother. However, because of the wide currency of the term "surrogate," I will continue to use it here.

30. Both forms of surrogacy are products of the 1980s. Full surrogacy dates from around 1980, when Noel Keane began a surrogacy brokerage operation in Michigan. It has been the most widely publicized of these procedures due to the Baby M case. Several hundred surrogate births now occur annually, and several brokers function to meet demand. For couples in which the wife's fertility cannot be achieved by other treatments, this might be the only method for that couple to have a child. Gestational surrogacy, on the other hand, is a product of more recent advances in IVF. The first births began appearing in the late 1980s. Its use is likely to grow, and may involve sisters or even mothers of the couple who need gestational services in order to reproduce.

31. Maura Ryan, "The Argument for Unlimited Procreative Liberty: A Feminist Critique," *Hastings Center Report*, July/August 1990, 6.

32. Many feminist writers also share this view. See Lori Andrews, *New Conceptions* (New York: St. Martin's Press, 1984); M. Shultz, "Reproductive Technology and Intent-Based Parenthood: An Opportunity for Gender Neutrality," *Wisconsin Law Review* 1990(1990):298.

33. The claim that the child is bonded to the gestational mother and thus will be hurt by relinquishment is highly contestable. See Hill, "What Does It Mean to Be a 'Parent'? The Claims of Biology As the Basis for Parental Rights," *New York University Law Review* 66(1991):353, 394–400. He also refutes the claim that only a gestational parent can nurture and love a child. Id. at 400–405.

34. See Robertson, "Embryos, Families, and Procreative Liberty." John A. Robertson, "Procreative Liberty and the State's Burden of Proof in Regulating Noncoital Reproduction," *Law, Medicine and Health Care* 16(1988):27.

35. Ironically, this view of gestation reflects attitudes toward childbearing and women that underlies much gender discrimination. Privileging the gestational role also undermines the notion that women are free, autonomous actors who can, like others, be bound by promises on which others have relied.

36. In the Matter of Baby M, 537 A.2d 1227, 1234 (N.J. 1988). For a critique of this holding, see Robertson, "Procreative Liberty and the State's Burden of Proof," 27.

37. State statutes making all surrogate contracts void and unenforceable: Ariz. Rev. Stat. Ann. Sec. 25-218 (West 1991); Ind. Code Ann. Sec. 31-8-2-2 (West Supp. 1991); Mich. Comp. Laws Ann. Sec. 722.855 (West Supp. 1991); 1992 N.Y. Laws Sec. 308; N.D. Cent. Code Sec. 14-18-05 (1991); Utah Code Ann. Sec. 76-7-204 (Michie Supp. 1992). Statutes making surrogate contracts unenforceable when they involve compensation: La. Rev. Stat. Ann. Sec. 9:2713 (West 1991); Neb. Rev. State. Sec. 25-21,200 (1989); Wash. Rev. Code Ann. Secs. 26.26.230-26.26.240 (West Supp. 1992). See also Ky. Rev. Stat. Ann. Sec. 199.590 (Michie 1991). However, Arkansas will enforce the agreement to have the hiring couple rear the child. AR ST sec. 9-10-201.

38. Anna J. v. Mark C., 822 P.2d 1317, 4 Cal. Rptr. 2nd 170 (1992).

39. Professor Martha Field sees no difference between the two and would allow the birth mother in either case to assert a rearing role for some period after birth. "Surrogacy Contracts—Gestational and Traditional: The Argument for Nonenforcement," *Washburn Law Journal* 31(1992):433.

40. These arrangements are most likely when relatives or friends act as donors or surrogates. It may also arise with same-sex couples who wish to have and rear children, but only one partner has a biologic tie with offspring.

41. A law against a donor or surrogate having contact with rearing parents and offspring would interfere with rights to rear one's biologic offspring and other rights of intimate association. Although the Supreme Court in Michael H. v. Gerald D., 491 U.S. 110 (1989) upheld a California law that denied the genetic father the right to visit his daughter, the situations envisaged here, where all parties agree in advance, are distinguishable. However, one cannot reliably predict what the ultimate legal outcome of such a case would be.

42. Lehr v. Robertson, 436 U.S. 248 (1983). For a fuller account of this issue, see Janet L. Dolgin, "Just a Gene: Judicial Assumptions about Parenthood," *UCLA Law Review* 40(1993):637.

43. Thus a sperm or egg donor who insists on visitation or limited custody of a child resulting from a donation to a married couple will have more difficulty in getting the agreement recognized than a donation to a single woman. But see Crouch v. McIntyre, 780 P.2d 239 (Or. App. 1989).

44. C.M. v. C.C., 152 N.J. Super. 160, 377 A.2d 821 (Cumberland County Ct. 1977).

45. In the Matter of Alison D. v. Virginia M., 572 N.E.2d 27, 77 N.Y.2d 651, 569 N.Y.Supp.2d 586 (1991).

46. Strictly speaking, the party seeking to rear in this case has not reproduced, because she has no biologic tie with the child. However, one could argue for recognition of such arrangements because of the important interest of the nonbiologic parent, his or her role in making conception and birth possible, the previous relation with the child, and the need for reliance on such agreements if parties are to go forward with these instances of collaborative reproduction. Whether the interest at stake is labeled procreative, it may independently be worth protecting. The implications of such a view for adoption law are discussed below.

47. R. Alta Charo has argued that "having several parents to love you" can never be a bad thing, and thus should count in favor of the excluded biologic parent who wishes to rear. "And Baby Makes Three . . . Or Four, Or Five: Defining the Family after the Reprotech Revolution" (*Texas Journal of Women and the Law*, Spring 1994, 3).

48. The assumption is that the courts would recognize both genetic and gestational mothers as parents within the family code—a result that has not yet occurred. In addition, this method of forming a family—a form of egg donation—is more expensive and onerous than is artificial insemination of one partner. But it will appeal to lesbian couples who wish to protect their rights to rear collaboratively produced children or who each wish to have biologic offspring. Alternatively, and less onerously, the nonbiologic rearing partner could seek to adopt the child to protect her rearing rights. Such co-parent or second-parent adoptions have occurred in Texas, Vermont, Alaska, Massachusetts, and other states, but are not available in all states.

49. In Stiver v. Parker, 975 F.2d 261 (6th Cir. 1992), a surrogate mother sued the lawyer and doctors involved in arranging her surrogacy because she allegedly contracted cytomegalovirus infection during insemination with the contracting husband's sperm. She claimed that they failed to test his sperm for the virus before the insemination.

50. However, some persons would reject any active state encouragement of collaborative reproduction, particularly of surrogacy.

51. However, limits on the number of times one could be a egg or sperm donor might be acceptable.

52. Donors are now routinely screened—or should be—for HIV.

53. Egg donors who are themselves going through IVF (and who donate extra eggs) may be especially invested in these issues, particularly if their own IVF efforts do not succeed.

54. Phillip Parker, "Surrogate Mothers' Motivations: Initial Findings," *American Journal of Psychiatry* 140(January 1983):1.

55. Va. Code. Ann. Sec. 20-162(A)(Supp. 1991); N.H. Rev. Stat. Ann. Sec. 168-B:25(V)(Supp. 1991).

56. Surrogate brokers have been sued by surrogates disappointed in the experience for failure to inform them

adequately or for other breaches of duties alleged to be owed them.

57. See *Stiver v. Parker.*

58. Would state laws requiring the exclusion of certain women as surrogates violate their procreative liberty? Arguably not, because their reproductive role is partial, and infertile couples can select other surrogates.

59. There is some controversy over whether egg donors should be paid for their eggs or for the "time, risk and associated inconvenience" of donation, as the American Fertility Society recommends.

60. See National Organ Transplantation Act, 42 U.S.C.A. No. 274(e); Note, "Regulating the Sale of Human Organs," *Virginia Law Review* 71(1985):1015. For an analysis of the application of these laws to egg donation, see John Robertson, "Legal Uncertainties in Human Egg Donation" (1993).

61. Mich. Comp. Laws Ann. Sec. 722.855 (West Supp. 1991); 1992 N.Y. Laws 308; Utah Code Ann. Sec. 76-7-204 (Michie Supp. 1992); Va. Code Ann. Sec. 20-162(A) (Supp. 1991).

62. It is unclear how the New Jersey court would consider paid gestational surrogacy, since adoption by the infertile couple, who are biologic parents, may not be necessary.

63. The best discussion of exploitation in the surrogacy context is Alan Wertheimer, "Two Questions about Surrogacy and Exploitation," *Philosophy and Public Affairs* 21(1992):211. He concludes that "Surrogacy may be exploitive and exploitation may be wrong, but it does not follow that such exploitation is a reason for prohibiting surrogacy or refusing to enforce surrogacy contracts." Id. at 239.

64. Virginia Held, "Coercion and Coercive Offers," in *Nomos XIV: Coercion*, ed. J. Roland Pennock (Boston: Aldine-Atherton, 1972). David Zimmerman argues that some offers can be coercive. See "Coercive Wage Offers," *Philosophy and Public Affairs* 10(1981):121–145.

65. Radin, "Market-Inalienability," *Harvard Law Review*, 100(1987):1849, 1921–1936.

66. Scott Altman effectively counters her arguments in "(Com)Modifying Experience," *Southern California Law Review* 65(1992):293.

67. Radin, "Market-Inalienability, 1921–1936.

68. Debra Satz, for example, has argued that the wrong of paid surrogacy is the unequal treatment of women that arises from creating markets for their reproductive labor. "Markets in Women's Reproductive Labor," *Philosophy and Public Affairs* 21(1992):107. See also Christine Overall, *Ethics and Human Reproduction: A Feminist Analysis* (Boston: Allen and Unwin, 1987), 111–137.

69. Such an implication may not, however, be what the feminist critics of surrogacy have in mind, for it could lead to contracting with women for reproductive services in situ-

ations where the hiring male or couple will have no biologic relation with children they seek to rear.

70. In such arrangements, persons who contribute egg, sperm, and gestation to produce the child to be reared by others would have to agree in advance to the arrangement, thus avoiding the problems that arose in the 1993 Baby Jessica case, where the mother but not the father had relinquished parental rights to a couple desiring to adopt her baby.

71. John Hill has presented an elegant argument for this result in "What Does It Mean to Be a Parent."

72. Ibid.

73. In addition to the infertile couple organizing donors and surrogates to produce a child for them, one could imagine scenarios involving single men who hire a surrogate, or an egg donor and gestational surrogate, to produce a child.

74. Although she is not in favor of assisted collaborative reproduction, Elizabeth Bartholet presents a powerful critique of the current adoption system's emphasis on genetic ties in *Family Bonds: Adoption and the Politics of Parenting* (Boston: Houghton Mifflin, 1993).

The Fertility Market: Conflict and Competition

Trip Gabriel

Editor's Note: The table on page 589 explains various high- and low-tech treatments available to infertile couples.

Most mornings at 7 A.M., Sundays included, the dozens of waiting-room chairs are filled with well-turned-out, anxiously hopeful patients, as if at a casting call for a smart urban drama.

They have dropped by on their way to midtown Manhattan offices, or flown in from Hong Kong, Jerusalem and Caracas, to visit the in vitro fertilization clinic at New York Hospital-Cornell Medical Center, one of the most renowned in the world.

In a field where the average I.V.F. clinic sees about 75 couples a year, Cornell treats more than 750, and claims success rates almost double the national average. Nationwide, only 1 in 5 couples trying I.V.F., or fertilization in a laboratory dish, takes home a baby.

Because of its reputation, the Cornell clinic, on Manhattan's Upper East Side, has become a financial powerhouse, generating a $2 million annual surplus for the Cornell Medical College and making possible physicians' salaries up to $1 million, more than the hospital pays its president.

Yet, the pressure to treat more and more patients contributed to the departure of a dozen scientists from the clinic laboratory last year. They left after complaining that high volume had them working seven-day weeks in an overcrowded lab

and threatened the well-being of the human embryos they were responsible for.

Jacques Cohen, the former laboratory director, said that the clinic grew beyond its capacity because of a desire by physicians and administrators to maximize income. But Dr. William J. Ledger, chairman of obstetrics and gynecology at Cornell, who oversees the clinic, said that volume had risen because so many patients were clamoring for service.

"If you are the messiah for a kind of clinical care, you'll have people beating your door down," Dr. Ledger said.

The schism at Cornell, which ultimately led Dr. Cohen and his colleagues to join two rival clinics, highlights the combustible mix of elements in the thriving field of high-tech fertility, where there are many desperate patients who have spent years longing for a baby and not enough superior clinics to meet the demand.

In only a decade, the field has grown from 30 clinics to more than 300 in the United States, which do more than 40,000 in vitro fertilizations and similar procedures a year. A virtually free-market branch of medicine, the $350 million-a-year business has been largely exempt from government regulation and from the downward pressure on costs that insurance companies exert.

At a time when money from private insurers and the government is evaporating, successful clinics can enrich the doctors who run them and serve as profit centers for hospitals. The clinics' patients, largely affluent city dwellers, can afford to pay $25,000 or more. Because relatively few insurers cover in vitro fertilization, patients usually pay out of their own pockets.

Clinics compete aggressively for these patients, soliciting everywhere from the World Wide Web to hard-sell newspaper advertisements, like one run repeatedly by the Genetics and I.V.F. Institute in Fairfax, Va., that promises "immediate availability of eggs" from "100 fully screened donors."

Some clinics also woo star physicians, those who can prove that they can produce babies, with promises of big salaries and new laboratories, turning the doctors into real-life fertility gods.

The lack of outside oversight has been illustrated by an unfolding controversy at a clinic in Irvine, Calif., where state authorities say that as many as 80 women were duped by three doctors who removed eggs from some patients and, without their permission, implanted those eggs or fertilized embryos into other women. Some of the recipients gave birth, raising doubts about who the children's biological parents are.

Although the state has closed the clinic and patients have filed lawsuits, there has been no criminal action against the doctors. Prosecutors in Orange County, Calif., are apparently hamstrung because no laws prohibit embryo theft. The incident has drawn national attention, though it is one of only a very few controversial cases to affect the fertility business.

"I don't think I.V.F. should go away or ever will go away, but the commercialization aspects of it are very disappointing," said George Annas, a professor of health law at Boston University. "Of course, the entire medical profession is becoming more commercial, more concerned with profits and the bottom line. And I.V.F. clinics lead the way."

The Need—Many
Candidates for Technology

The growth of high-tech reproduction has been driven by advances in the laboratory and by a swell of prospective patients as many members of the baby boom generation have delayed childbearing into their 30's and 40's. As women age, the quality of the eggs stored in their ovaries declines, scientists say.

Infertility, defined as an inability to conceive after a year of unprotected sexual relations, affects about 4.9 million American couples, 1 in 12, the National Center for Health Statistics says. In 40 percent of infertile couples the woman is infertile, in 40 percent the man is infertile, and in 20 percent the infertility cannot be explained.

Fewer than half the couples are successfully treated by conventional methods like fertility drugs, artificial insemination and surgery to unblock fallopian tubes.

The millions of others, as specialists like to point out, are candidates for high-tech remedies. In the in vitro fertilization process, by far the most common of what are called assisted-reproduction technologies, a woman's egg is withdrawn from her ovary and fertilized in a laboratory dish with sperm from her partner or a donor. If her own eggs are poor, she can buy one from a donor for as much as $3,000. The resulting embryo is placed in her uterus by a catheter inserted through the vagina.

In the United States, 40,000 babies conceived through I.V.F. and similar procedures have been born since 1981. Medical entrepreneurs like to dream of how the field could be even bigger if it were as widely covered by insurance plans here as elsewhere. In France, where I.V.F. is a common benefit, it is done at a per-capita rate 5 times as high as in the United States. Only 10 states, including Massachusetts, Rhode Island and Illinois, require insurance.

In the absence of widespread benefits, 85 percent of the costs are borne by patients, which means that treatment is largely, though not exclusively, the preserve of the well-to-do. Many less affluent couples save for treatments the way others put away money for a down payment on a house. Couples postpone their lives, turning down better jobs to stay near a trusted clinic or taking leaves of absence from careers to pursue high-tech conception.

The median cost of one procedure, lasting about the length of a menstrual cycle, is $7,800, according to the American Society for Reproductive Medicine. Many patients try three, four or more times before having a baby or giving up. Success can be spectacular; more than half of all I.V.F. children are twins or triplets.

The success rate drops sharply for women 40 or over; among the New York region's 12 busiest

An Infertility Glossary

Nearly 5 million American couples are infertile, unable to conceive after a year of trying. Doctors estimate that 50 percent of infertile couples can be helped by conventional, low-tech treatments. The other 50 percent need more advanced treatment, sometimes called assisted reproductive technology (A.R.T.). When available, the estimated cost and number of procedures are shown for 1993.

CONVENTIONAL TREATMENTS

Drug Therapy Fertility drugs, like Clomid and Pergonal, are given to women to regulate and stimulate ovulation.

Intrauterine Insemination (I.U.I.) Often performed in conjunction with drug therapy, this is one of the simplest fertility treatments. Sperm, either the husband's or a donor's, is shuttled with a catheter into the uterus, where fertilization may occur. 600,000 procedures.

Surgery Surgery is performed on women to clear blocked fallopian tubes or reduce endometriosis, abnormal blood-rich tissue that grows primarily in and around female reproductive organs, causing pain and interfering with normal reproductive function. Surgery is performed on men to repair a varicocele, a varicose vein in the testicle, which causes reduced sperm counts.

ASSISTED REPRODUCTIVE TECHNOLOGY

In Vitro Fertilization (I.V.F.) Eggs produced by administering fertility drugs are retrieved from the woman's body and fertilized by sperm in a laboratory dish. The resulting embryos are transferred by catheter to the uterus. 32,000 procedures. Cost: $7,800.

Gamete Intrafallopian Transfer (G.I.F.T.) A mixture of sperm and eggs is transferred, using a minor surgical procedure, to the fallopian tubes, where fertilization may occur. 4,992 procedures.

Zygote Intrafallopian Transfer (Z.I.F.T.) Eggs are fertilized by sperm in a laboratory dish, and any resulting embryos are transferred to the woman's fallopian tubes and move into the uterus. 1,792 procedures.

Micromanipulation A variety of techniques can be performed in a laboratory dish under a microscope in which an embryologist manipulates egg and sperm, to improve the chances of a pregnancy. 1,400 procedures.

Intracytoplasmic Sperm Injection (I.C.S.I.) A new micromanipulation procedure in which a single sperm is directly inserted into a single egg, to increase the likelihood of fertilization in couples where the sperm is of poor quality. The embryo is then transferred to the uterus.

Cryopreserved Embryo Transfer (C.P.E.) Embryos frozen after a previous A.R.T. cycle are thawed and then transferred to the uterus. 6,672 procedures.

Egg Donation Eggs are removed from the ovaries of a donor and transferred, after fertilization in a laboratory dish, to the uterus of an infertile woman. 2,766 procedures. Donor is paid $1,500 to $3,000. The whole procedure, counting treatment of donor and recipient, can run $14,000 to $20,000.

Surrogacy A woman is implanted with an embryo and is paid to carry the child to term. The egg may come from the surrogate mother or from the legal mother, the sperm from the legal father or a donor. The surrogate's fee is negotiated and ranges from $10,000 to $20,000. Additional costs can include the surrogate's prenatal care and fertility drugs for the legal mother.

SOURCES: Resolve; American Society for Reproductive Medicine.

clinics, the success rate for these older women varied in 1993 from zero to 15 percent, with most clinics in the single digits. "Age, overwhelmingly, is the single most important factor," said Dr. Zev Rosenwaks, the director of the Cornell infertility program. "Fertility is negligible after the age of 45. And at age 37, the slope becomes much steeper."

Considering their chances of becoming pregnant, are patients being overcharged? The industry says no, that in vitro fertilization is labor-intensive and that the $7,800 pays for a battery of ultrasound scans, an anesthesiologist during egg retrieval, and ovulation-stimulating drugs, which alone run $2,000 an attempt.

The typical clinic's bottom line is unknown, but Peter J. Neumann of the Harvard School of Public Health persuaded one hospital I.V.F. program to open its books on the condition that its name not be made public. The costs to the clinic were $8,000 for one procedure, sometimes called a cycle. The charge to patients was $11,000, for a profit of 37.5 percent, a margin that any business might envy.

About half the fertility clinics in the United States are associated with hospitals; the rest are run by groups of physicians, or even by sole practitioners. But whether they are private or nonprofit practices, all clinics are concerned about the bottom line and compete for patients, often fiercely.

Pacific Fertility Medical Centers, a chain of five private clinics in California, advertises on the radio, holds public seminars in Chicago and New York, and offers consultations by E-mail or toll-free call. Long-distance callers give their medical history, then speak for 20 minutes with a doctor.

Critics of profit-driven chains say that to satisfy investors, doctors must pull as many patients as possible into the pipeline, even if in vitro fertilization is not necessary. Harley Earl, president of Pacific Fertility's parent company, National Reproductive Medical Centers, said the group's doctors have incentive plans tied to their clinics' profitability, but the plans are set up in such a way "that no one could ever look at a patient as your next car payment." He said the privately held company, which plans to expand to the New York area in 1996, earns a profit, though he declined to say how much.

There is no guarantee of profitability in the fertility business. Because of high fixed costs—about $1 million for equipment and about $500,000 annually for salaries—clinics that perform fewer than 100 cycles a year have a hard time breaking even.

In 1992, IVF America became the first infertility chain to sell stock to the public, ambitiously asking $8 to $10 a share and predicting its clinics would one day blanket the country. Yet the company lost money through 1994, and reported a meager $18,000 profit for the first nine months of 1995. Its stock now trades around $2.50 and the company has drastically altered its focus: it manages the business affairs of seven clinics, primarily on the East Coast, but it has withdrawn from setting uniform medical protocols.

Ethics—When to Advise: Time to Give Up

Health economists say there is no doubt prices for in vitro fertilization are higher than they otherwise would be if more insurance companies covered the treatment, exerting pressure on doctors to cut fees and unneeded procedures.

A study of infertile couples treated by one health-maintenance organization, HMO Illinois, recently found that the cost of making a woman pregnant was strikingly lower than in traditional fee-for-service practices. The H.M.O. cost was $15,000, compared with $27,000 for traditional doctors. Success rates were not significantly different.

HMO Illinois performed fewer surgeries and realistically informed patients when it was time to give up, said Dr. Arnold L. Widen, chief medical director of Blue Cross-Blue Shield of Illinois, which sponsored the study. "In the fee-for-service sector, as long as a woman is willing to go on, the doctors might say, 'Let's keep on trying,'" Dr. Widen said. "Obviously, one makes more fees that way."

Doctors inside and outside the specialty said that to increase revenue, some unscrupulous clinics push patients toward costly high-tech solutions when they would be just as successful with simpler treatments, or when their odds of success are so low they should not be encouraged at all.

"Certain providers have strong financial incentives to take patients to I.V.F., which may lead patients there who don't need it," said Dr. Norbert Gleicher, head of the Center for Human Reproduction, a group of 11 Chicago-area infertility practices.

On the other hand, impatient couples sometimes demand I.V.F., and doctors find it hard to set a more conservative course.

Critics say the clinics are not always straightforward about the odds of succeeding. "I've often said that the one thing these clinics ought to do is to tell patients at the beginning, 'You will probably not have a child,'" said Professor Annas, who is also the ethical adviser to the American Society for Reproductive Medicine. "Morally, that's the only truthful thing to say."

To desperate couples, even a 1 in 5 chance of having a baby looks good. Joey and Rosa Antico, a Staten Island couple, said they struggled with infertility for 10 years before attempting I.V.F. and were willing to try anything, even if it seemed a long shot. Mrs. Antico, now 36, became pregnant on her second try at Advanced Fertility Services, a private clinic in Manhattan. Her triplet sons just turned 5.

"I never thought about it not working," she recalled. "I was a little worried the first time it didn't take. But I thought, 'If it's meant to be, it's meant to be.'"

Direct evidence of patients' being misled about treatment is scarce, largely because very few scientifically precise studies of the effectiveness of I.V.F. have been done. It is hard to say if a couple who had a baby after treatment might have achieved pregnancy by less aggressive means.

A 1993 Canadian Royal Commission that reviewed hundreds of studies worldwide concluded that I.V.F. was unproven except for women with severe tubal blockage. For other diagnoses in which the procedure is routinely done—ovulation defects, sperm defects or unexplained infertility—the existing studies were inconclusive.

"Unproven and quite possibly ineffective procedures are being offered as medical treatment," the commission reported, "and women are undertaking the risks of these procedures without knowing whether they are more likely to have a child than if they received no treatment."

Dr. Paul W. Zarutskie, president of the Society for Assisted Reproductive Technology, a subgroup of I.V.F. specialists within the American Society for Reproductive Medicine, said that simple observation proved the effectiveness of treatment.

"You see people who can't get pregnant and then move them toward assisted reproductive technology," Dr. Zarutskie said, "and 20 percent-plus of our patients are going home with babies, and you've got to think we're doing something effective."

The Odds—Success Rates Called Misleading

A 21.2 percent success rate per cycle, which is the average of the 267 clinics that reported data to

S.A.R.T., Dr. Zarutskie's group, for 1993, the last year surveyed, still means that 78.8 percent of couples fail. Because of those long odds, a clinic that can claim to beat them by even a few percentage points has a powerful lure. But it also has an incentive to manipulate the numbers.

Since 1991, the Federal Trade Commission has won five cease-and-desist agreements over deceptive advertising claims with fertility clinics in Arizona, California, Colorado, Massachusetts and New York. In the New York case, IVF America, based in Purchase, N.Y., admitted no wrongdoing but agreed to drop claims about success rates that the F.T.C. said were misleading.

"You don't open your newspaper and see, 'We have a 21 percent success rate with transplanted hearts,'" said Michael Katz, a Federal medical investigator. "This is the only branch of medicine doing success-rate advertising on this scale. It succeeds because of the desperation and emotional vulnerability of the patients."

In 1994, Mount Sinai Medical Center in New York City paid $4 million to hundreds of childless former infertility patients to settle a suit over false success-rate claims.

The suit stemmed from an investigation conducted by the New York City Department of Consumer Affairs. It charged Mount Sinai with exaggerating success rates in a promotional brochure and a flyer, which claimed that the "take-home baby rate" was 20 percent. But according to data submitted to S.A.R.T. at the time, Mount Sinai's delivery rate was really much lower, 13.7 percent or 10.9 percent, depending on how it was measured.

The affair seems to have wounded the Mount Sinai program, once among the most popular in New York. Its director resigned soon after the charges in 1992, and recently volume dropped about 12 percent, from 408 cycles in 1994 to about 350 in 1995.

Dr. Maria Bustillo, the current director, said patients had declined because of a decision by the hospital to reduce its program and because of the rise of other clinics in the region. "There's just a lot more competition all around," Dr. Bustillo said.

Success-rate figures are easily manipulated. Advocates for patients say the most meaningful rate is the most conservative: live deliveries as a percent of the number of treatment cycles that a clinic initiates. Counting pregnancies alone can be misleading, because about 18 percent of I.V.F. pregnancies end in miscarriage.

S.A.R.T. has increasingly refined the statistics it compiles, and makes reports available to the public on 267 individual clinics. Still, the data's accuracy is impossible to confirm because it is reported voluntarily. A 1992 Federal law requires the Centers for Disease Control and Prevention in Atlanta to independently collect and publish data from all clinics. But since the law went into effect in 1994, it has not been carried out for lack of financing. During the ongoing Federal budget crisis, the Clinton Administration has declined to ask for the money.

A new round of calls for regulation has surrounded the inquiry at the once-prestigious Center for Reproductive Health in Irvine, Calif., which was shut down in June after charges of improper egg and embryo handling. State and Federal authorities are investigating claims by patients and former clinic employees against three physicians, including the former director, Dr. Ricardo Asch, a pioneer of gamete intrafallopian transfer, a variation of I.V.F.

Dr. Asch, in an interview broadcast in the fall on ABC-TV, denied making improper transfers of eggs and embryos. Now facing numerous civil suits that make the same allegations as the state authorities, Dr. Asch has sold his two Orange County houses and is now practicing in Mexico City.

So far, no criminal charges have been brought in the case, in part, it appears, because embryo theft is not a criminal offense in California. A bill to criminalize it is likely to be introduced in the next session of the California Legislature.

Despite the battery of civil suits in the case, medical malpractice suits are uncommon in infertility. "People don't sue, even when they're misled," Professor Annas said. "I think that's because many people feel shame or embarrassment about seeing a fertility doctor in the first place."

Responding to patients' concerns, the American Society for Reproductive Medicine has been drafting voluntary guidelines on record keeping, informed consent by patients and the handling of embryos that are frozen for future implantation.

Many physicians oppose more regulation, saying it would increase the cost to patients, impede research and fail to prevent the misdeeds Dr. Asch and his colleagues are accused of.

"All this bad press makes the government do things that are well-meaning but misguided," said Dr. Jamie Grifo, director of the infertility clinic at New York University Medical Center. "If we're all suspect because of one bad apple, it makes it hard to provide services. There comes a point where you have to trust the person taking care of you or you just shouldn't do it."

The $2,000 Egg

Barbara Nevins

It was a windy morning before dawn. While the University of California's Irvine campus slept, the dark green waters of Upper Newport Bay were swirling wildly. The women in the nine-person crew team were strong, but in the dim light and fierce current, they rammed a pile of floating debris, leaving a gaping hole in their shell.

Once safely on the dock, the team soberly assessed the damage. The boat was borrowed from the senior men's crew team since the women's team wasn't funded by the university—so money for repairs would have to come from their own pockets. One rower, a biology major who'd worked at a hospital the previous summer, said she'd heard that doctors would pay major money to college women who'd donate their eggs.

Jeniffer Huie remembers her teammates shouting out their outrage almost in unison. The notion of dipping into the mysterious region of the body

Barbara Nevins, "The $2,000 Egg; Donation of Eggs for Infertile Couples," *Redbook Magazine* 180/1 (November 1992): 118. Copyright (c) 1992 Barbara Nevins Taylor. Reprinted with the permission of the author.

where life is created to harvest human eggs seemed bizarre. If they gave up their eggs, they joked, would they help create a future generation of robust rowers who looked just like them?

The biology major silenced her teammates' laughter when she demanded, "If men can donate sperm, why can't we donate eggs?" It was exactly the kind of challenge that appealed to Jeniffer, 20, a junior majoring in criminal justice and social ecology. She took the good looks she was born with for granted. But she prided herself on what she felt she had worked for—being well muscled, strong, and athletic. The youngest of four children, she swam and played basketball, volleyball, and baseball in her hometown of Moraga, California.

Even though the team's volunteer coach eventually lent the women the money to repair the boat, Jeniffer didn't forget about egg donation. Her credit card bill—thanks to spending on clothes, books, airfare, and socializing—had skyrocketed to $3,000. She knew her parents would send money, but she didn't want to be dependent on them.

Although the school paper had carried an article about a local fertility clinic's search for college-student egg donors, Jeniffer couldn't locate a clinic right away. Finally, someone suggested she call the Saddleback Center for Reproductive Health in nearby Laguna Hills.

After the center sent her information, she shared it with her friends. But no one else was interested. They listened as Jeniffer called the center from her dorm room. If they had moral or emotional objections to using the body like a fertility farm, they said nothing.

The clinic told Jeniffer that she would earn $1,500 if selected as a donor, but first she'd have to complete a screening process. She went there in May and filled out the 13-page questionnaire. She described her father, a Presbyterian missionary who taught high school science and math and now invests in the stock market; her mother, a teacher of English as a second language; her older brother and two older sisters, all college graduates. No genetic diseases in the family. No drug or alcohol addiction. No criminal record.

A week after Jeniffer mailed the questionnaire, she was called in for an interview. For two hours she answered questions about everything from her alcohol consumption to her sex life. A 90-minute written psychological test was next. She answered questions like: During my free time, I _____; I hate when my father _____; I'm happy when _____. By the time the clinic called back to say they wanted her, the semester was over. Jeniffer was headed home to her parents' for the summer. She told the clinic she'd have to wait until September when she returned to school because she didn't want to tell her parents what she was doing. She didn't want to worry them or hear their objections.

That summer she worked for California's Bureau of Automotive Repair in San Francisco. She still planned to donate her eggs in the fall because her summer salary only made a small dent in her bills. "And besides, I had said I would do it. I felt committed."

Did she waver at all, or wonder about the possibility that she would soon help create a baby she would never know? "I didn't worry about the emotional things," she says flatly. "I just didn't think about it much."

Jeniffer called Saddleback when she returned to school in September. She had a series of blood tests and an ultrasound scan, to make sure that her ovaries and uterus were healthy. Then she was put on birth control pills to regulate her period and synchronize it with the cycle of the woman who would receive the eggs.

By November, her period was regulated. The center gave her a supply of syringes and the drugs Lupron, Pergonal, and Metrodin. She was told to inject the Lupron every morning for the seven days before her period was due.

She had been warned before she signed up about possible complications from the drugs. The clinic doctor told her that she might experience vaginal bleeding, dizziness, stomachaches, and feel bloated. But she wasn't fazed.

Morning came early for Jeniffer at the four-bedroom house she and her roommates rented. The crew team practiced six days a week from 5:30 a.m. to 8:30 a.m. It was still dark out when she awoke at 4:30 in the morning to deftly insert the syringe into the bottle of Lupron. Then she'd jab the fleshiest part of her thigh with the needle.

On the second day of her period, she began another series of injections, this time putting the needle in her hip: Metrodin for two days and Pergonal for ten days. She had no side effects.

During the time that she was taking the drugs, she visited Saddleback several times for ultrasound tests. She was thrilled when doctors reported that she had produced more than enough eggs. She was told that because there were a great many Asian families on the center's waiting list, the clinic hoped to divide Jeniffer's eggs between two of the families. For Jeniffer it seemed like an opportunity to make more money. "I asked if they would then double my compensation. I thought that since I was providing eggs for two families, I should get paid for it," she says. She was told she'd have to be satisfied with the original $1,500.

In early December, Jeniffer went to the clinic to have her eggs harvested. In the operating room was José Balmaceda, M.D., the clinic's medical director, an anesthesiologist, and two nurses. She was given a mild local anesthetic so she remained aware of what was going on. A probe with a long needle was inserted into her vagina. The medical team scanned a monitor as the needle pierced an ovary and then suctioned tiny follicles containing eggs. The follicles were tested immediately and 26 eggs, more than enough for two families, were harvested. It was considered a huge success: A typical donor produces between 12 and 18 eggs. Being a superdonor pleased Jeniffer almost as much as the prospect of being out of debt.

After two days, though, Jeniffer developed a rash all over her face. Her legs itched and peeled. "The doctor told me he hadn't seen anything like this in the ten years since they've been doing the procedures," she says. "He thought one of the drugs might be sun-sensitive." The clinic paid a dermatologist to treat her, and the rashes eventually vanished.

Jeniffer had already signed a release giving up her parental rights and another promissory form pledging to notify the clinic of her whereabouts, in case the child ever needs her blood or organs in a medical emergency. And when asked if she'd like to hear from the people who might make babies from her eggs, she quickly agreed. Even before they received her eggs, a Canadian couple of Chinese descent wrote to thank her. They explained that they had been trying to have a baby for ten years.

"We don't know how to express in words the gratitude toward your generosity in helping make our dream come true," the letter said. "Your generous donation is the most precious gift we ever received. The child will be ensured of a good upbringing—the best we can provide." The recipients had signed their names, Simon and Cathy. Their last name had been blacked out by someone at the center.

For the first time since she contemplated using her body to make money, Jeniffer says she felt "really emotional. I was almost in tears. I didn't need these eggs, and I was just glad that someone else could put them to good use and make a child out of them."

Jeniffer wouldn't mind meeting the couple, and the baby when it's born. But she won't press it. "If it happens, that would be nice," she says. "But I'm really not all that curious. I know I have no right to see the child."

Jeniffer has graduated from college and is working as a temp while she waits to learn if she'll be hired by one of the half-dozen local police departments where she's applied. Meanwhile, she still needs money. She signed up with the clinic for a second go-round.

Her boyfriend, George, is supportive. "So what?" he says. "Big deal. They're just eggs, and besides, there will be somebody walking around just like her. "

That's also Jeniffer's thought at the moment. She'd like to get married and have a couple of kids of her own one day. But right now being an egg donor is as close to parenthood as she wants to get. "It's kind of cool," she says, "to think that you've helped someone have a baby. It's nice to know that there's a piece of me floating around somewhere . . ."

The Fertility Market: Buying Eggs

Jan Hoffman

Dana O., a 33-year-old nurse with three children of her own, may be genetically related to one, two or perhaps three other children. She will probably never know.

That is because Dana donated her eggs anonymously through IVF America-Boston, a fertility clinic here, and through another clinic nearby. Each time, she was paid $1,500 for undergoing extensive screening, three weeks of hormone injections and outpatient surgery to retrieve her eggs. They were then mixed with sperm in a petri dish and implanted in the uterus of an infertile woman.

The money was the least of it, she said. Haunted by a sister's nine-year struggle with infertility, Dana realized that her eggs, which would be lost through menstruation every month, did not have to go to waste.

"I don't feel like I'm giving someone a child, but a chance at a child," she said. Then she laughed self-consciously, her blue eyes crinkling. "I hope they told the recipient that I have really dry skin."

Receiving eggs from donors like Dana has become an increasingly sought-after and available option for thousands of women who cannot conceive on their own. In 1993, the last year for which the American Society for Reproductive Medicine has statistics, 135 fertility clinics were offering to retrieve eggs from donors and give them to other women, up from 26 clinics in 1988. About 80 percent of the donors were anonymous; the others were relatives or friends of the women who received the eggs.

Although the first egg donor babies were born in the mid-1980's, it was not until about five years ago, when the technique was simplified, that egg donation began to take off: of the 2,500 babies born from donated eggs through 1993, 1,000 were conceived just in that year. Individual clinics report that their numbers have continued to climb,

particularly as patients discover that the success rate of this procedure can be about 50 percent.

But more than any other area of reproductive technology, egg donation raises an array of ethical concerns: whether donors are victimized, whether clinics give recipients truthful information about the donors, whether the whole process has become too commercial. The fees paid donors are rising as demand soars. Some critics are troubled at what they see as the crassness of the advertisements run by clinics and by brokers who act as intermediaries between donors and recipients.

"You can see ads for donors that say, 'We Pay Top Dollar,' and that's distasteful when you're talking about medical treatment," said Dr. Mark V. Sauer, who helped pioneer egg donation at the University of Southern California.

For recipients, egg donation is usually the end of the line. By the time most consider becoming pregnant with another woman's egg, they have descended through all the circles of infertility hell, having spent many years and thousands of dollars on inseminations, surgery and in vitro fertilization.

Most recipients are women in their late 30's to mid-40's who have an irreversible, age-related condition: their ovaries can no longer produce eggs of sufficient quality to fertilize into embryos. Other recipients may have entered premature menopause, some as early as their late 20's. And still others may carry genetic diseases or have received radiation therapy for cancer that damaged their ovaries. Even so, doctors say many such patients, whose only significant problem is their eggs, can sustain a pregnancy—if they use a healthy woman's eggs.

The donors, by contrast, tend to be fertile women in their 20's and early 30's, who usually learn about donation from advertisements. Some are attracted by the fees; others, like Dana, have altruistic motives.

Critics of egg donation are legion. Some countries, including Germany and Switzerland, ban the procedure. The Roman Catholic Church condemns egg donation and other artificial aids to conception. Some ethicists warn that donors, usually younger and poorer than the recipients, can be exploited if they are not sufficiently counseled about medical risks or the psychological consequences of giving away their genetic material.

Arthur Caplan, a philosophy professor who is the director of the Center for Bioethics at the University of Pennsylvania, said that the field of egg donation lacks industry-wide standards. "Should donors be paid?" he asked. "What's a fair price? Who should the donors be? And who should be allowed to use the egg donor services?"

Egg recipients are also vulnerable, said Dr. Hilary Hanafin, a psychologist at the Center for Surrogate Parenting and Egg Donation in Beverly Hills, Calif. "I have no doubt that some clinics leave out information about donors, intentionally to 'dress them up' or unintentionally in their desire to get a match," said Dr. Hanafin.

For many infertile couples, egg donation is a gamble worth taking, because they can have a child who is half theirs genetically. The price of a donor egg cycle is comparable to adoption, ranging from $14,000 to $20,000, depending on the donor's fee, legal costs and the extent of medical preparation.

During a recent interview at the IVF America-Boston clinic here, Patty S., a 43-year-old accountant's assistant, merrily chased after her 18-month-old son, who was conceived here with a donor egg. "He's the joy of our lives," she said. "The donor made our lives complete. I can never thank her enough."

Recipients—One Last Chance to Be Pregnant

When Mary D. turned 35, she and her husband, both producers in the entertainment industry, tried to have a baby. During the next six years, they went through fertility drugs, surgery to correct endometriosis and fibroid tumors, inseminations and three attempts at in vitro fertilization. Mary said that when she was still childless at 41, "I was completely depressed and my husband was ready to give up."

Her doctor in Santa Monica, Calif., proposed egg donation, but Mary's husband initially recoiled. "He had wanted a child with me," said Mary, who, like most of the donors and recipients contacted, spoke on the understanding that only her first name and last initial would be used, to protect the privacy of her child. "He was more comfortable with adoption than having just one of us give up a genetic tie to a baby."

But Mary's interest was piqued. "Even if it wasn't my egg," she said during a telephone interview, "I really wanted to carry the baby."

Many couples agree to try a donated egg only after great anguish, hacking their way through a thicket of difficult questions: How will the mother's relationship with the child be affected by the fact that she has no genetic tie? Should the parents reveal the child's unusual heritage to grandparents? Friends? The child? And when?

"I was worried that I'd feel like an outsider," Mary said, "less connected to her than my husband and his family."

Eventually Mary and her husband decided to proceed. To them, a successful egg donation had many advantages over adoption. Mary could fulfill her dream of being pregnant and not have to worry, as she would in an adoption, about whether the birth mother had had prenatal care. They would be able to learn a lot about their donor's background and would not have to be concerned about a birth father's reclaiming the child. And a custody claim from an egg donor seemed highly unlikely; no such case has yet surfaced.

After a few months, Mary's doctor found a donor. Following the California fashion of openness, Mary and her husband met the donor for lunch. "I wanted to learn what type of person she was, her level of sincerity," recalled Mary. "We liked her immediately. She had two boys of her own and needed money for their school. She knew someone who had been infertile and she thought, if she could donate her eggs, why not?"

It took almost a month of injections and monitoring to synchronize the two women's menstrual cycles. While Mary's donor took hormone stimulants to help her produce a high number of eggs (typically between 8 and 15), Mary took hormones to thicken her uterine lining for the embryo implant. Just before the donor ovulated, the donor went to a hospital and was given anesthesia. Her eggs were removed through her vagina with a fine needle. The procedure lasted about half an hour.

That same day, the husband's sperm were mixed with the donor's eggs. Two days later, the doctor implanted five embryos in Mary's uterus. Within two weeks, Mary finally heard the news that had eluded her for six years: she was pregnant. One month shy of her 42d birthday, she delivered a 9-pound girl.

"I was thrilled to be given the opportunity to carry her," she said. "I breast-fed her for 14 months." Her fears about not being sufficiently connected to her child vanished. "My little baby needs me and I'm her Mom," she said.

Mary's and her husband's wish list for a donor was typical: someone with the wife's coloring, who was healthy, reasonably bright and "a nice person."

But many couples specify a religious or ethnic heritage. Asian-American and Jewish donors are particularly hard to find. Because of the tradition of matrilineal descent, some Jewish women believe that the donor has to be Jewish for the child to be considered Jewish. But some rabbis refute that view, saying that a child born of a Jewish womb is automatically Jewish.

Other couples, who feel stripped of control by infertility, fantasize about the perfect donor. A doctor who does egg donations recalled one couple who said, "We'd like her to look like Christie Brinkley, have graduated from an Ivy League school—but Seven Sisters is O.K.—and now be getting a Ph.D., although medicine or law is acceptable."

Dr. David Keefe, an infertility specialist at the Yale University School of Medicine, said he reminds couples: "What you're dealing with in genetics is potentialities. Besides, every egg from every woman is different. With any child you get dealt a card. With donor egg babies, you just may not know who the dealer was."

Donors—'I Feel Like a Good Soldier'

Nearly three years ago, Monica Loustalot, who is married to the property manager of a San Diego condominium complex, figured out something extra to do while staying at home caring for their two children: With her husband's wary approval, Mrs. Loustalot became a surrogate mother and then an egg donor.

"I'm comfortable with controversy," she said as she sat in the Beverly Hills offices of the Center for Surrogate Parenting and Egg Donation, an agency that helps match recipients and donors.

In 1994 she gave birth to one child for a couple, and she is now pregnant with twins for another. In between, she donated eggs to a couple who subsequently had a daughter. "No more," said Mrs. Loustalot, who is 30. "I'm maxed out." After this next birth, she thinks her body will have had enough.

"For now, this is perfect for me," said Mrs. Loustalot, a high school graduate who worked her way up through the administrative ranks of a ceramic tile company before becoming a mother. "I'm not going to just sit home and bake cookies for my kids. I can accomplish things."

The money didn't hurt—$12,000 for the first surrogate pregnancy, $15,000 for this one and $2,000 for the egg donation—but it was not her main motivation, Mrs. Loustalot said. At first, she said, she felt uncomfortable being paid to donate her eggs.

"But I was driving to the doctor's office in L.A. from San Diego every other day," she said, "taking my shots, going for tests, so I worked really hard at this. And I thought, everyone else who works gets compensated. Why shouldn't I?"

She is delighted that her donated eggs helped end one couple's 10-year battle with infertility. "They tried so hard to make it happen that the success is that much sweeter," she said. "And I feel like a good soldier, as if God said to me, 'Hey, girl, I've done a lot for you and now I want you to do something for Me.'"

Donors give many reasons for donating. Some want to compensate for phantom children they lost through abortions. Many had friends who suffered infertility. Some, like Mrs. Loustalot, love their children so profoundly that they want another woman to share that joy. Many younger women say: If I ever want children and have this problem, I hope someone will do this for me. The notion of women helping women runs through their language.

Many clinics seek these donors by advertising in parenting magazines, weekly Pennysavers and nursing journals, as well as general-interest publications.

And while some ethicists and feminists once predicted that a donor's fee would entice poor women to turn their reproductive capacities into a commodity, that dire forecast now seems overstated. Although donors are almost always less well-off than recipients, who tend to be older and more established in their careers, they come from a cross-section of backgrounds.

Recipients selecting a donor at the Genetics and I.V.F. Institute in Fairfax, Va., for example, would find a list of potential donors that includes students, a police officer, a lawyer, several nannies, a copy editor, a secretary and a podiatrist.

The Marketplace—Bidding Wars and Finder's Fees

Egg donation threatens to become a victim of its own success: as more women seek it out, more clinics have begun to offer the procedure, stoking what is becoming a bidding war for scarce donors. In California, a middle tier of entrepreneurs known as donor brokers has emerged: mostly lawyers, nurses and psychotherapists, they charge recipients a finder's fee to locate donors.

The clinics' rates for donors range from $1,500 to $3,000. But some couples and donor finders run their own ads in college newspapers, offering to pay even more. An ad that ran in *The Harvard Crimson* last October said: "Jewish ovum donor needed for infertile couple willing to pay a fee of $3,500 plus expenses."

Guidelines from the American Society for Reproductive Medicine, an association of fertility specialists, say a donor should not be paid for her eggs, but rather for her considerable time and effort. The fee should be fixed, the guidelines say, regardless of how many eggs she produces.

"If we don't believe in buying and selling babies, then why are we comfortable buying and selling sperm and eggs?" asked Professor Caplan of the University of Pennsylvania. "Does anyone really believe that donors are just being compensated for their time?"

Many practitioners are alarmed at the rising fees and the pall that economics may cast over donation. "A donor's motive used to be primarily altruistic but nowadays it's becoming for financial reward," said Dr. Sauer, who recently joined the Columbia University College of Physicians and Surgeons.

Under his stewardship, the program at Columbia follows the tradition of sperm donation, and

seeks egg donors among childless college students, whom practitioners see as fertile, bright and in need of extra cash. "I'm a little uncomfortable with it," Dr. Sauer said. "I want to do it responsibly, in a way that's not exploitative."

Critics say that college students are too young to appreciate the consequences of what they are donating. And pragmatically speaking, unless they have had abortions, their fertility has not been proven. Moreover, the critics ask, how will the donors feel if years later, they try to become pregnant, only to discover that they have become infertile?

"In a perfect world, you'd have only married women with children donating," said Susan L. Crockin, co-author of the forthcoming book, *Family Building Through Egg and Sperm Donation* (Jones & Bartlett). "But you wouldn't get a lot of donors that way and you wouldn't demand it of men."

Being accepted as an egg donor is hardly automatic. Many clinics screen potential donors extensively over a series of appointments, a factor that drives up costs. The Reproductive Medicine society's guidelines say a donor must undergo thorough medical screening; the group also recommends psychological counseling. Sperm donors, by contrast, are screened medically but rarely psychologically.

There is an inherent conflict, however: Clinics have a lot to gain by persuading both donors and recipients to go through with the procedure. George Annas, a professor of health law at Boston University, said: "I don't have much faith in counseling, unless it's done by someone completely independent of the clinic. Is someone from the clinic going to say, 'Don't do this'?"

Donors face the same medical risks as recipients: Fertility drugs can cause temporary bloating, removal of the eggs may cause cramping, and at least one disputed study has suggested a slight connection between ovarian cancer and long-term use of fertility drugs.

"My job is to talk donors out of it," said Dr. Susan Cooper, a psychologist with IVF America-Boston. "That's not because we don't need them, but we want to sleep at night. They're not likely to ever forget they donated and we want that to be an experience they never regret."

Not all egg donation programs even include a psychologist. Some therapists are preparing standardized guidelines for counselors, urging them to watch for economic stability and coping skills in a donor, and to be wary of anyone with a chaotic life or who seems to have been coerced by a partner.

As a safety precaution for donors, most clinics limit them to four cycles. The guidelines of the Reproductive Medicine society also say that donors should contribute to no more than 10 live births, which reduces the chances—already infinitesimal—that a child would ever meet and mate with half-siblings.

Privacy—Fears of Demands from Strangers

While many donors agree to be contacted after the child turns 18, most want assurance that they will have no financial or familial obligation.

Donors sign consent forms releasing them from any parental rights or responsibilities. More than 30 states have laws that guarantee sperm donors their independence from any offspring, but only a handful so far have comparable laws for egg donation. Under the legal theory of equal protection, said Ms. Crockin, the sperm donation model would extend to egg donors.

While Mary D., the California entertainment producer, met her donor for lunch, Elizabeth M., a 42-year-old mother through egg donation at the IVF America-Boston clinic here, has never seen a picture of her donor and does not know her name. The clinic, however, did give her nonidentifying information about the woman.

"It was anonymous on both sides," Elizabeth said as she breast-fed her infant daughter. "But the law could change tomorrow. I'd support my daughter if she chose to try to locate the donor so long as she respected the donor's need for privacy."

Will children conceived with a donor egg someday want to meet donors, in the way that many adopted children search for birth parents? No one knows, because most donor children are under 5 years old. Much depends on whether parents even tell their children about their origins.

In trying to gauge the future, clinics around the country vary greatly in how much information

about donors they give recipients. At many East Coast clinics, the matches are made by doctors and nurses. Following the model of anonymous sperm donation, they tell recipients about the donor's physical characteristics and a few other nonidentifying facts, but that is all. Donors like Dana learn nothing about the recipients, not even if they became pregnant.

These programs reflect the recipients' fears that a donor could somehow find them and claim the child, the same kind of fear often expressed by adoptive parents. Donors, in turn, do not want a stranger knocking on their door in 18 years, looking for financial or emotional succor.

Contrast that philosophy with the one at the Center for Surrogate Parenting and Egg Donation in Beverly Hills, a high-end donor broker agency that charges each recipient $6,000, which covers the agency's own fee for recruiting and screening donors as well as the donor's fee.

Each couple works with a psychologist to choose a donor from a list of about 150. The couple receives a dossier on the donor and her extended family, including photographs and her Social Security number, in case they ever need to contact her. The center urges donors and recipients to meet.

"It is much more work to do open rather than closed donation," said Dr. Elaine Gordon, a psychologist at the center. "Everyone is nervous. But afterwards, they're all so glad they did it that way. They feel more finished with it and there's no residual curiosity."

The intention of the California clinics is to echo open adoption, in which birth parents and adoptive parents meet and sometimes remain in contact. The extensive information made available allows recipients one day to tell a child a story as free of mystery as possible.

"We'll find a way to tell her," said Elizabeth. "I'm so comfortable with it that I'm not worried." Besides, that day of reckoning was still years off; just now, she was blissfully absorbed in burping her daughter.

"Egg donation is a tremendously private decision," she said, "and a couple has to be able to cross all those thresholds. We did it, and now we have this absolutely beautiful child."

43.

Race and the New Reproduction

Dorothy E. Roberts

Dorothy Roberts is professor of law at Rutgers University School of Law, Newark. This is a written version of a talk she presented at Rutgers University's Center for the Critical Analysis of Culture. She has published numerous articles in law reviews. Her recent work has served to extend feminist critiques of issues in medical ethics by exploring the perspectives of women of color. In this essay, she presents and affirms certain feminist criticisms of new reproductive technologies, especially in vitro fertilization (IVF). She then examines how the use of these technologies reflects and reinforces the racial hierarchy in our country.

INTRODUCTION[1]

New means of procreating are heralded by many legal scholars and social commentators as inherently progressive and liberating. In this view, in vitro fertilization (IVF), embryo donation, and contract pregnancy expand the procreative options open to individuals and therefore enhance human freedom. These innovations give new hope to infertile couples previously resigned to the painful fate of childlessness. In addition, this view holds that the new reproduction creates novel family arrangements that break the mold of the traditional nuclear family. A child may now have five parents: a genetic mother and father who contribute egg and sperm, a gestational mother who carries the implanted embryo, and a contracting mother and father who intend to raise the child.[2] A proponent of new means of reproduction, John Robertson opens his book *Children of Choice* by proclaiming that these "powerful new technologies" free us from the ancient subjugation to the "the luck of the natural lottery" and "are challenging basic notions about procreation, parenthood, family, and children."[3]

My impression of these technologies, however, is that they are more conforming than liberating: they more often reinforce the status quo than challenge it. True, these technologies often free outsiders from the constraints of social convention and legal restrictions. They have helped single heterosexual women, lesbians, and gay men, whom society regards as unqualified to raise children, to circumvent legal barriers to parenthood.[4] Informal surrogacy arrangements between women, for example, may provide a means of self-help for women who wish to have children independently of men; moreover, they have the advantage of requiring no government approval, medical intervention, or even sexual intercourse.[5]

But these technologies rarely serve to subvert conventional family norms. Most often they complete a traditional nuclear family by providing a married couple with a child.[6] Rather than disrupt the stereotypical family, they enable infertile couples to create one. Most IVF clinics only accept heterosexual married couples as clients,[7] and most physicians have been unwilling to assist in the insemination of single women.[8] The new reproduction's conservative function is often imposed by courts and legislatures, as well. Laws regulating artificial insemination contemplate use by a married woman and recognition of her husband as the child's father,[9] and recent state legislation requiring insurance coverage of IVF procedures applies only when a wife's eggs are fertilized using her husband's sperm.[10] On the other hand, as Martha Field observes, courts have been willing to grant parental rights to sperm donors "when no other man is playing the role of father for

Dorothy E. Roberts, "Race and the New Reproduction," *Hastings Law Journal* 47 (April 1996): 25–39. Copyright (c) 1996 University of California, Hastings College of Law. Reprinted from *Hastings Law Journal* Vol. 47, No. 4, pp. 25–39, by permission.

the child," such as when the mother is a lesbian or unmarried.[11]

Feminists have powerfully demonstrated that the new reproduction enforces traditional patriarchal roles that privilege men's genetic desires and objectify women's procreative capacity.[12] They make a convincing case that IVF serves more to help married men produce genetic offspring than to give women greater reproductive freedom.[13] In this essay I will explore how these technologies reflect and reinforce the racial hierarchy in America. I will focus primarily on in vitro fertilization because it is the technology least accessible to Black people and most advantageous to those concerned about genetic linkages.[14] The salient feature of in vitro fertilization that distinguishes it from other means of assisted reproduction is that it enables an infertile couple to have a child who is genetically-related to the husband.[15]

I. THE ROLE OF RACE IN THE NEW REPRODUCTION

A. Racial Disparity in the Use of Reproductive Technologies

One of the most striking features of the new reproduction is that it is used almost exclusively by white people. Of course, the busiest fertility clinics can point to some Black patients; but they stand out as rare exceptions.[16] Only about one-third of all couples experiencing infertility seek medical treatment at all; and only 10 to 15 percent of infertile couples use advanced techniques like IVF.[17] Blacks make up a disproportionate number of infertile people avoiding reproductive technologies.

When I was recently transfixed by media coverage of battles over adopted children, "surrogacy" contracts, and frozen embryos, a friend questioned my interest in the new methods of reproduction. "Why are you always so fascinated by those stories?" he asked. "They have nothing to do with Black people."[18] Think about the images connected with reproduction-assisting technologies: They are almost always of white people. And the baby in these stories often has blond hair and blue eyes—as if to emphasize her racial purity. A "Donahue" show featured the family of the first public surrogacy adoption. Their lawyer Noel Keane describes the baby, Elizabeth Anne, as "blonde-haired, blue-eyed, and as real as a baby's yell."[19] He concludes, "The show was one of Donahue's highest-rated ever and the audience came down firmly on the side of what Debbie, Sue, and George had done to bring Elizabeth Anne into the world."[20]

In January, 1996, the *New York Times* launched a prominent four-article series entitled "The Fertility Market," and the front page photograph displayed the director of a fertility clinic surrounded by seven white children conceived there while the continuing page featured a set of beaming IVF triplets, also white.[21]

When we do read news accounts involving Black children created by these technologies they are always sensational stories intended to evoke revulsion at the technologies' potential for harm. In 1990, a white woman brought a lawsuit against a fertility clinic which she claimed had mistakenly inseminated her with a Black man's sperm, rather than her husband's, resulting in the birth of a Black child.[22] Two reporters covering the story speculated that "if the suit goes to trial, a jury could be faced with the difficult task of deciding the damages involved in raising an interracial child."[23] Although receiving the wrong gametes was an injury in itself, the fact that the gametes were of the wrong race added a unique dimension of harm to the error.

In a similar, but more bizarre, incident in the Netherlands in 1995, a woman who gave birth to twin boys as a result of IVF realized when the babies were two months old that one was white and one was Black.[24] A *Newsweek* article subtitled "A Fertility Clinic's Startling Error" reported that "while one boy was as blond as his parents, the other's skin was darkening and his brown hair was fuzzy."[25]

It is easy to conclude that the stories displaying blond-haired blue-eyed babies born to white parents are designed to portray the positive potential of the new reproduction, while the stories involving the mixed-race children reveal its potential horror.

These images and the predominant use of IVF by white couples indisputably reveal that race in some way helps to shape both the use and popularity of IVF in America. What are the reasons underlying this connection between race and the new reproduction?

First, the racial disparity in new reproduction has nothing to do with rates of infertility. Married Black women have an infertility rate one and one-half times higher than that of married white women.[26] In fact, the profile of people most likely to use IVF is precisely the opposite of those most likely to be infertile. The people in the United States most likely to be infertile are older, poorer, Black and poorly educated.[27] Most couples who use IVF services are white, highly educated, and affluent.[28]

Besides, the new reproduction has far more to do with enabling people (mostly men) to have children who are genetically related to them than with helping infertile people to have children.[29] The well-known "surrogacy" cases such as Baby M and Anna J. involved fertile white men with infertile wives who hired gestational mothers in order to pass on their own genes. Moreover, at least half of women who undergo IVF are themselves fertile, although their husbands are not.[30] These women could conceive a child far more safely and inexpensively by using artificial insemination although the child would not be genetically-related to the husband. Underlying their use of IVF, then, is often their husbands' insistence on having a genetic inheritance. In short, use of reproduction-assisting technologies does not depend strictly on the physical incapacity to produce a child.

Instead, the reason for the racial disparity in fertility treatment appears to be a complex interplay of financial barriers, cultural preferences, and more deliberate professional manipulation. The high cost of the IVF procedure places it out of reach of most Black people whose average

median income falls far below that of whites. The median cost of one procedure is about $8,000; and, due to low success rates, many patients try several times before having a baby or giving up.[31] Most medical insurance plans do not cover IVF, nor is it included in Medicaid benefits.[32] IVF requires not only huge sums of money, but also a privileged lifestyle that permits devotion to the arduous process of daily drug injections, ultrasound examinations and blood tests, egg extraction, travel to an IVF clinic, and often multiple attempts—a luxury that few Black people enjoy. As Dr. O'Delle Owens, a Black fertility specialist in Cincinnati explained, "For White couples, infertility is often the first roadblock they've faced—while Blacks are distracted by such primary roadblocks as food, shelter and clothing."[33] Black people's lack of access to fertility services is also an extension of their more general marginalization from the health care system.

There is evidence that some physicians and fertility clinics may deliberately steer Black patients away from reproductive technologies. For example, doctors are more likely to diagnose white professional women with infertility problems such as endometriosis that can be treated with in vitro fertilization.[34] In 1976, one doctor found that over 20 percent of his Black patients who had been diagnosed as having pelvic inflammatory disease, often treated with sterilization, actually suffered from endometriosis.[35]

Screening criteria not based specifically on race tend to exclude Black women, as well. Most Black children in America today are born to single mothers, so a rule requiring clients to be married would work disproportionately against Black women desiring to become mothers. One IVF clinic addresses the high cost of treatment by offering a donor oocyte program that waives the IVF fee for patients willing to share half of their eggs with another woman.[36] The egg recipient in the program also pays less by forgoing the $2,000 to $3,000 cost for an oocyte donor.[37] I cannot imagine that this program would help many Black patients, since it is unlikely that the predominantly white clientele would be interested in donation of their eggs.

The racial disparity in the use of reproductive technologies may be partially self-imposed. The myth that Black people are overly fertile may make infertility especially embarrassing for Black couples.[38] One Black woman who eventually sought IVF treatment explained, "Being African-American, I felt that we're a fruitful people and it was shameful to have this problem. That made it even harder."[39] Blacks may find it more emotionally difficult to discuss their problem with a physician, especially considering the paucity of Black specialists in this field. Blacks may also harbor a well-founded distrust of technological interference with their bodies and genetic material at the hands of white physicians.

Finally, Blacks may have an aversion to the genetic marketing aspect of the new reproduction. Black folks are skeptical about any obsession with genes. They know that their genes are considered undesirable and that this alleged genetic inferiority has been used for centuries to justify their exclusion from the economic, political and social mainstream. Only last year Richard Herrnstein & Charles Murray's *The Bell Curve* was a national bestseller, and it reopened the public debate about racial differences in intelligence and the role genetics should play in social policy.[40]

Blacks have understandably resisted defining personal identity in biological terms. Blacks by and large are more interested in escaping the constraints of racist ideology by defining themselves apart from inherited traits. They tend to see group membership as a political and cultural affiliation. Their family ties have traditionally reached beyond the bounds of the nuclear family to include extended kin and non-kin relationships.

My experience has been that fertility services simply are not a subject of conversation in Black circles, even among middle-class professionals. While I have recently noticed stories about infertility appearing in magazines with a Black middle-class readership such as *Ebony* and *Essence*, these articles conclude by suggesting that childless Black couples seriously consider adoption.[41] Black professional women I know are far more concerned about the assault that recent welfare reform efforts are inflicting on our poorer sisters' right to bear children—an assault that devalues all Black women and children in America.[42]

Moreover, Black women are also more concerned about the higher rates of sterilization in our community, a disparity that cuts across economic and educational lines. One study found that 9.7 percent of college-educated Black women had been sterilized, compared to 5.6 percent of college-educated white women.[43] The frequency of sterilization increased among poor and uneducated Black women. Among women without a high school diploma, 31.6 percent of Black women and 14.5 percent of white women had been sterilized.[44]

B. The Importance of the Genetic Tie

Race also influences the importance we place on IVF's central aim—having genetically-related children.

Of course sharing a genetic tie with children is important to people of different races and in racially homogeneous cultures. Most parents I know take great satisfaction in having children who "take after them." It seems almost natural for people to want to pass down their genes to their children, as if they achieve a form of immortality by continuing their "blood line" into future generations.

Yet we also know that the desire to have genetically-related children is influenced, if not created, by our culture. A number of feminists have advocated abandoning the genetic model of parenthood because of its origins in patriarchy and its "preoccupation with male seed."[45] We should add to these concerns the tremendous impact that the inheritability of race has had on the meaning of the genetic tie in American culture.

The social and legal meaning of the genetic tie helped to maintain a racial caste system that preserved white supremacy through a rule of racial purity.[46] The contradiction of slavery existing in a republic founded on a radical commitment to liberty required a theory of racial hierarchy. Whites took the hereditary trait of race and endowed it with the concept of racial superiority and inferiority;[47] they maintained a clear demarcation between Black slaves and white masters by a violently enforced legal system of racial classification and sexual taboos.[48]

The genetic tie to a slave mother not only made the child a slave and subject to white domination; it also passed down a whole set of inferior traits. Children born to a slave, but fathered by a white master, automatically became slaves, not members of the master's family. To this day, one's social status in America is determined by the presence or absence of a genetic tie to a Black parent. Conversely, the white genetic tie—if free from any trace of blackness—is an extremely valuable attribute entitling a child to a privileged status, what Cheryl Harris calls the "property interest in whiteness."[49]

For several centuries a paramount objective of American law and social convention was keeping the white bloodline free from Black contamination. It was only in 1967 that the United States Supreme Court in *Loving v. Virginia*[50] ruled antimiscegenation laws unconstitutional. Thus, ensuring genetic relatedness is important for many reasons, but, in America, one of those reasons has been to preserve white racial purity.

C. Value of Technologically Created Children

Finally, the new reproduction graphically reflects and reinforces the disparate values placed on members of social groups.

The monumental effort, expense and technological invention that goes into the new reproduction marks the children produced as especially valuable. It proclaims the unmistakable message that white children are precious enough to devote billions of dollars towards their creation. Black children, on the other hand, are the primary object of welfare reform measures designed to discourage poor women from procreating.

II. IMPLICATIONS FOR POLICY REGARDING THE NEW REPRODUCTION

What does it mean that we live in a country in which white women disproportionately use expensive technologies to enable them to bear children, while Black women disproportionately undergo surgery that prevents them from being able to bear any? Surely this contradiction must play a critical part in our deliberations about the morality of these technologies. What exactly does race mean for our own understanding of the new reproduction?

Let us consider three possible responses. First, we might acknowledge that race influences the use of reproductive technologies, but decide this does not justify interfering with individuals' liberty to use them. Second, we could work to ensure greater access to these technologies by lowering costs or including IVF in insurance plans. Finally, we might determine that these technologies are harmful and that their use should therefore be discouraged.

A. The Liberal Response: Setting Aside Social Justice

The liberal response to this racial disparity is that it stems from the economic and social structure, not from individuals' use of reproductive technologies. Protection of individuals' procreative liberty should prohibit government intervention in the choice to use IVF, as long as that choice itself does not harm anyone.[51] Currently, there is little government supervision of reproduction-assisting technologies, and many proponents fear legal regulation of these new means of reproduction. In their view, financial and social barriers to IVF are unfortunate but inappropriate reasons to interfere with the choices of those fortunate enough to have access to this technology. Nor, according to the liberal response, does the right to use these technologies entail any government obligation to provide access to them. And if for cultural reasons Blacks choose not to use these technologies, this is no reason to deny them to people who have different cultural values.

Perhaps we should not question infertile couples' motives for wanting genetically-related children. After all, people who have children the old-fashioned way may also practice a form of genetic selection when they choose a mate. The desire to share genetic traits with our children may not reflect the eugenic notion that these particular traits are superior to others; rather, as Barbara Berg notes, "these characteristics may simply symbolize to the parents the child's connection to past generations and the ability to extend that lineage forward into the future."[52] Several people have responded to my concerns about race by explaining to me, "White couples want white children not because of any belief in racial superiority, but because they want children who are like them."

Moreover, the danger of government scrutiny of people's motives for their reproductive decisions may override my concerns about racism. This danger leads some feminists who oppose the practice of using abortion as a sex selection technique, for example, nevertheless to oppose its legal prohibition.[53] As Tabitha Powledge explained:

> To forbid women to use prenatal diagnostic techniques as a way of picking the sexes of their babies is to begin to delineate acceptable and unacceptable reasons to have an abortion. . . . I hate these technologies, but I do not want to see them legally regulated because, quite simply, I do not want to provide an opening wedge for legal regulation of reproduction in general.[54]

It would be similarly unwise to permit the government to question the individuals' reasons for deciding to use reproduction-assisting technologies.

B. The Distributive Solution

The distributive solution does not question individuals' motives in order to question the soci-

etal impact of a practice.[55] This approach to procreative liberty places more importance on reproduction's social context than does the liberal focus on the fulfillment of individual desires.[56] Policies governing reproduction not only affect an individual's personal identity; they also shape the way we value each other and interpret social problems. The social harm that stems from confining the new reproduction largely to the hands of wealthy white couples might be a reason to demand equalized access to these technologies.

Obviously the unequal distribution of wealth in our society prevents the less well off from buying countless goods and services that wealthy people can afford. But there may be a reason why we should be especially concerned about this disparity when it applies to reproduction.

Reproduction is special. Government policy concerning reproduction has tremendous power to affect the status of entire groups of people. This is why the Supreme Court in *Skinner* v. *Oklahoma* declared the right to bear children to be "one of the basic civil rights of man."[57] "In evil or reckless hands," Justice Douglas wrote, the government's power to sterilize "can cause races or types which are inimical to the dominant group to wither and disappear."[58] This explains why in the Casey opinion Justices O'Connor, Kennedy, and Souter stressed the importance the right to an abortion had for women's equal social status. It is precisely the connection between reproduction and human dignity that makes a system of procreative liberty that privileges the wealthy and powerful particularly disturbing.

Procreative liberty's importance to human dignity is a compelling reason to guarantee the equal distribution of procreative resources in society. Moreover, the power of unequal access to these resources to entrench unjust social hierarchies is just as pernicious as government interference in wealthy individuals' expensive procreative choices. We might therefore address the racial disparity in the use of reproductive technologies by ensuring through public spending that their use is not concentrated among affluent white people. Government subsidies, such as Medicaid coverage of IVF, and legislation mandating private insurance coverage of IVF would allow more diverse and widespread enjoyment of the new reproduction.

C. Should We Discourage the New Reproduction?

If these technologies are in some ways positively harmful, will expanding their distribution in society solve the problem? The racial critique of the new reproduction is more unsettling than just its exposure of the maldistribution of fertility services. It also challenges the importance that we place on genetics and genetic ties.

But can we limit individuals' access to these technologies without critically trampling our protection of individual freedom from unwarranted government intrusion? After all, governments have perpetrated as much injustice on the theory that individual interests must be sacrificed for the public good as they have on the theory that equality must be sacrificed for individual liberty. This was the rationale justifying eugenic sterilization laws enacted earlier in this century.[59]

Even for liberals, individuals' freedom to use reproductive technologies is not absolute. Most liberals would place some limit on their use, perhaps by defining the legitimate reasons for procreation.[60] If a core view of reproduction can limit individuals' personal procreative decisions, then why not consider a view that takes into account reproduction's role in social arrangements of wealth and power? If the harm to an individual child or even to a core notion of procreation can justify barring her parents from using the technique of their choice, then why not the new reproduction's potential for worsening group inequality?

Some have concluded that the harms caused by certain reproduction-assisting practices justify their prohibition. In 1985, for example, the United Kingdom passed the Surrogacy Arrangements Act banning commercial contract pregnancy arrangements and imposing fines and/or imprisonment on the brokers who negotiate these agreements.[61] Some Marxist and radical feminists agree that paid pregnancy contracts should be criminalized to prevent their exploitation and commodification of women and children.[62]

On the other hand, the government need not depart at all from the liberal noninterference model of rights in order to discourage or refuse to support practices that contribute to social injustice.[63] Even the negative view of liberty that protects procreative choice from government intrusion leaves the state free to decide not to lend assistance to the fertility business or its clients.

We may therefore question a practice that channels millions of dollars into the fertility business, rather than spending similar amounts on programs that would provide more extensive benefits to infertile people. *New York Times* writer Trip Gabriel describes IVF clinics as "[a] virtually free-market branch of medicine, the $350 million-a-year business has been largely exempt from government regulation and from downward pressure on costs that insurance companies exert."[64]

Indeed, we can no longer avoid these concerns about the social costs and benefits of IVF. Such calculations are now part of the debate surrounding the advisability of state laws requiring insurance companies to include the cost of fertility treatment in their coverage. A study recently reported in the *New England Journal of Medicine* calculated the real cost of IVF at approximately $67,000 to $114,000 per successful delivery.[65] The authors concluded that the debate about insurance coverage must take into account these economic implications of IVF, as well as ethical and social judgments about resource allocation.[66]

Black women in particular would be better served by a focus on the basic improvement of conditions that lead to infertility, such as occupational and environmental hazards, diseases, and complications following childbirth and abortion.[67]

Taking these social justice concerns more seriously, then, might justify government efforts to reallocate resources away from expensive reproductive technologies.

CONCLUSION

These are thorny questions. It is extremely difficult to untangle white couples' reasons for using reproduction-assisting technologies and Black couples' reasons for avoiding them. Evidence is hard to come by: what doctor or fertility clinic will admit (at least publicly) to steering Black women away from their services? Few people seem to want to confront the obvious complexion of this field. Moreover, the problems raised by the racial disparity in the use of these technologies will not be solved merely by attempting to expand their distribution. Indeed, the concerns I have raised in this essay may be best addressed by placing restrictions on the use and development of the technologies, restrictions imposed by the government or encouraged by moral persuasion. This possibility is met by a legitimate concern about protection of our private decisions from government scrutiny. Indeed, Black women are most vulnerable to government efforts to control their reproductive lives.

Nonetheless, we cannot ignore the negative impact that the racial disparity and imagery of the new reproduction can have on racial inequality in America. Our vision of procreative liberty must include the eradication of group oppression, and not just a concern for protecting the reproductive choices of the most privileged. It must also include alternative conceptions of the family and the significance of genetic relatedness that truly challenge the dominant meaning of family.

NOTES

1. Dorothy Roberts, Professor, Rutgers University School of Law-Newark. B.A. 1977, Yale College; J.D. 1980, Harvard Law School. This is a written version of a talk presented at Rutgers University's Center for the Critical Analysis of Culture and University of California, Hastings College of the Law; I am grateful to the participants for their comments. Portions of this article are adapted from Dorothy E. Roberts, "The Genetic Tie," 62 *University of Chicago Law Review* 62 (1995): 209.

2. See generally John L. Hill, "What Does It Mean To Be a 'Parent'?: The Claims of Biology as the Basis for Parental Rights," *New York University Law Review* 66 (1991): 353, 355; Andrea E. Stumpf, Note, "Redefining Mother: A Legal Matrix for New Reproductive Technologies," *Yale Law Journal* 96 (1986): 187, 192–94.

3. John Robertson, *Children of Choice: Freedom and the New Reproductive Technologies* (Princeton: Princeton University Press, 1995): 3. [See Robertson, pp. 556–587]

4. See Nancy D. Polikoff, "This Child Does Have Two Mothers: Redefining Parenthood to Meet the Needs of Children in Lesbian-Mother and Other Nontraditional Families," *Georgetown Law Journal* 78 (1990): 459, 466; Sharon E. Rush, "Breaking with Tradition: Surrogacy and Gay Fathers," *Kindred Matters: Rethinking the Philosophy of the Family*, eds. Diana Tietjens Meyers, et al. (Ithaca, NY: Cornell University Press, 1993): 102, 132–133.

5. Juliette Zipper and Selma Sevenhuijsen, "Surrogacy: Feminist Notions of Motherhood Reconsidered," *Reproductive Technologies: Gender, Motherhood and Medicine,* ed. Michelle Stanworth (Minneapolis: University of Minnesota Press, 1987): 118, 137–138. Under this arrangement, a fertile woman would informally promise an infertile woman who wants a child to impregnate herself with a man's sperm and to give the baby to the infertile woman for adoption.

6. Robertson, *supra* note 3, at 145 (noting that assisted reproduction furthers the "primary aim to provide a couple with a child to live and rear in a two-parent family").

7. Thomas A. Shannon, "In Vitro Fertilization: Ethical Issues," *Embryos, Ethics, and Women's Rights: Exploring the New Reproductive Technologies*, eds. Elaine Hoffman Baruch et al. (New York: Harrington Press, 1988): 155, 163.

8. Daniel Wikler and Norma J. Wikler, "Turkey-baster Babies: The Demedicalization of Artificial Insemination," *Milbank Quarterly* 69 (1991): 5, 13–16.

9. Bartha M. Knoppers and Sonia LeBris, "Recent Advances in Medically Assisted Conception: Legal, Ethical and Social Issues," *American Journal of Law and Medicine* 17 (1991): 329, 332–33, 346–47; Lisa C. Ikemoto, "Destabilizing Thoughts on Surrogacy Legislation," *University of San Francisco Law Review* 28 (1994): 633, 636–37.

10. See, e.g., *Md. Code Ann.* (West 1995): Art. 48a, 354 DD(3); *Haw. Rev. Stat.* (West 1995) 431: 10A–116.5(3).

11. Martha Field, *Surrogate Motherhood: The Legal and Human Issues* (Cambridge: Harvard University Press, 1988): 116.

12. See, e.g., Janice G. Raymond, *Women as Wombs: Reproductive Technologies and the Battle Over Women's Freedom*

(New York: Harper Collins 1993); Barbara Katz Rothman, *Recreating Motherhood: Ideology and Technology in a Patriarchal Society* (New York: Norton, 1989); *Reproduction, Ethics, and the Law: Feminist Perspectives,* ed. Joan C. Callahan (Bloomington, IN: Indiana University Press, 1995).

13. See, e.g., Susan Sherwin, *No Longer Patient: Feminist Ethics and Health Care* (Philadelphia: Temple University Press, 1992): 127.

14. I capitalize the "B" in Black Americans because I believe that Black Americans consider themselves to be an ethnic group, like Asian-Americans, whereas I believe that white Americans do not see themselves in that way.

15. As I explain below, many women who could conceive through artificial insemination prefer the more expensive and risky IVF because it can produce a baby with a genetic link to their husband. See *infra* note 29 and accompanying text.

16. See Lori B. Andrews and Lisa Douglass, "Alternative Reproduction," *Southern California Law Review* 65 (1991): 623, 646; F. P. Haseltine et al., "Psychological Interviews in Screening Couples Undergoing In Vitro Fertilization," *Annals of the New York Academy of Science* 442 (1985): 504, 507; Martha Southgate, "Coping with Infertility," *Essence* (September 1994): 28.

17. Office of Technology Assessment, *Infertility: Medical and Social Choices* (OTA-BA-358, 1988): 7, 49–60.

18. I first recounted this story in Roberts, *supra* note 1, at 209.

19. Noel P. Keane and Dennis L. Breo, *The Surrogate Mother* (New York: Everest House, 1981): 96.

20. Id.

21. Trip Gabriel, "High-Tech Pregnancies Test Hope's Limit," *The New York Times* 07 January 1996: A1, A10. [*Editor's note:* Trip Gabriel's article, which appears in this chapter, is the first of four articles in this series. The articles by Jan Hoffman and Elisabeth Rosenthal, also in this chapter, were part of this series.]

22. Robin Schatz, "'Sperm Mixup' Spurs Debate: Questioning Safeguards, Regulations," *New York Newsday,* 11 March 1990: 3; Ronald Sullivan, "Mother Accuses Sperm Bank of a Mixup," *The New York Times,* 9 March 1990: B1.

23. Barbara Kantrowitz and David A. Kaplan, "Not the Right Father," *Newsweek,* 19 March 1990: 50.

24. Dorinda Elliott and Friso Endt, "Twins—With Two Fathers; The Netherlands: A Fertility Clinic's Startling Error," *Newsweek,* 03 July 1995: 38.

25. Id.

26. Laurie Nsiah-Jefferson and Elaine J. Hall, "Reproductive Technology: Perspectives and Implications for Low-Income Women and Women of Color," *Healing Technology: Feminist Perspectives,* eds. Kathryn Strother Ratcliff et al. (Ann Arbor: University of Michigan Press, 1989): 93, 108.

27. Sevgi O. Aral and Willard Cates, Jr., "The Increasing Concern with Infertility: Why Now?," *The Journal of the American Medical Association* 250 (1983): 2327.

28. Andrews and Douglass, *supra* note 16, at 646.

29. Joan C. Callahan, "Introduction to Reproduction, Ethics and the Law: Feminist Perspectives," *supra* note 12, at 24–25.

30. Raymond, *supra* note 12, at 6; Judith Lorber, "Choice, Gift, or Patriarchal Bargain?:" Women's Consent to In Vitro Fertilization in Male Infertility," *Feminist Perspectives in Medical Ethics,* eds. Helen Bequaert Holmes and Laura M. Purdy (Bloomington: Indiana University Press, 1992): 169, 172.

31. Gabriel, *supra* note 21, at 10–11.

32. Annetta Miller et al., "Baby Makers Inc.," *Newsweek,* 29 June 1992: 38, 38; Gabriel, *supra* note 21, at 10; George J. Annas, "Fairy Tales Surrogate Mothers Tell," *L. Ed. Health Care* 16 (1988): 27, 28. Only 10 states require insurance coverage of IVF. Gabriel, *supra* note 21, at 10.

33. Monique Burns, "A Sexual Time Bomb: The Declining Fertility Rate of the Black Middle Class," *Ebony* (May 1995): 74, 76.

34. Lisa C. Ikemoto, "Destabilizing Thoughts on Surrogacy Legislation," *U.S.F.L. Rev.* 28 (19): 633, 639.

35. Donald L. Chatman, "Endometriosis in the Black Woman," *American Journal of Obstetrics and Gynecology* 125 (1976): 987 (1976).

36. Cooper Center for IVF, "Cooper Center for IVF Responds to 'The Fertility Market,'" *The New York Times,* 14 January 1996: 16 (advertisement).

37. Id.

38. Martha Southgate, "Coping with Infetility," *Essence* (September 1994): 28.

39. Id.

40. See Richard J. Herrnstein and Charles Murray, *The Bell Curve: Intelligence and Class Structure in American Life* (New York: Free Press, 1994).

41. See, e.g., Burns, *supra* note 33, at 148; Southgate, *supra* note 38, at 28.

42. See Dorothy E. Roberts, "Welfare and the Problem of Black Citizenship," *Yale Law Journal* 105 (1996): 1563, 1582 (book review).

43. Levin and Taub, "Reproductive Rights," *Women and the Law,* ed. C. Lefcourt (1989): sec. 10A.07[3] [b], 10A–28.

44. Id.

45. Joan C. Callahan, "Introduction," *Reproduction, Ethics, and the Law: Feminist Perspectives, supra* note 12, at 1, 11. See, e.g., Rothman, *supra* note 12, at 39; Christine Overall, *Ethics and Human Reproduction: A Feminist Analysis* (Boston: Allen & Unwin, 1987): 149 (noting that "the need for a genetic connection with one's offspring seems to be of particular importance to men").

46. Roberts, *supra* note 1, at 223–30.

47. See Stephen Jay Gould, *The Mismeasure of Man* (New York: Norton, 1981).

48. Barbara K. Kopytoff and A. Leon Higginbotham, Jr., "Racial Purity and Interracial Sex in the Law of Colonial and Antebellum Virginia," *Georgetown Law Journal* 77 (1989): 1967, 1967–68.

49. Cheryl I. Harris, "Whiteness as Property," *Harvard Law Review* 106 (1993): 1707, 1713.

50. *U.S. 1* (1967): 388.

51. See generally Robertson, *supra* note 3, at 22–42.

52. Barbara J. Berg, "Listening to the Voices of the Infertile," *Reproduction, Ethics, and the Law: Feminist Perspectives, supra* note 12, at 80, 82.

53. Joan C. Callahan, "Introduction, Part II: Prenatal and Postnatal Authority," *Reproduction, Ethics, and the Law: Feminist Perspectives, supra* note 12, at 133–134.

54. Tabitha M. Powledge, "Unnatural Selection: On Choosing Children's Sex," *The Custom-Made Child?: Women-Centered Perspectives*, eds. Helen B. Holmes et al. (Clifton, NJ: Humana Press, 1981): 193, 197.

55. See Overall, *supra* note 45, at 17–39.

56. For a more extended critique of the liberal approach to reproduction-assisting technologies, see Dorothy E. Roberts, "Social Justice, Procreative Liberty, and the Limits of Liberal Theory: Robertson's *Children of Choice*," *Law and Social Inquiry* 20 (1995): 601; Joan C. Callahan and Dorothy E. Roberts, "A Feminist Social Justice Approach to Reproduc-tion-Assisting Technologies: A Case Study on the Limits of Liberal Theory," *Kentucky Law Journal* 84 (1996).

57. *U.S. 316* (1942): 535, 541.

58. Id.

59. See Mark H. Haller, *Eugenics: Hereditarian Attitudes in American Thought* (New Brunswick, NJ: Rutgers University Press, 1963).

60. See, e.g., Robertson, *supra* note 3, at 167 (positing "a core view of the goals and values of reproduction" that limits an individual's right to shape offspring characteristics).

61. Rosemarie Tong, "Feminist Perspectives on Gestational Motherhood: The Search for a Unified Focus," *Reproduction, Ethics, and the Law: Feminist Perspectives, supra* note 12, at 55, 58 (citing "Surrogacy Arrangements Act," 1985, United Kingdom, Chapter 49, p. 2 (1) (a) (b) (c).

62. Id. at 64–68.

63. Callahan and Roberts, *supra* note 56.

64. Gabriel, *supra* note 21, at 10. [See Gabriel, p. 587]

65. Peter J. Neuman et al., "The Cost of a Successful Delivery with In Vitro Fertilization," *New England Journal of Medicine* 331 (1994): 239, 239. Unlike the $8,000 cost per IVF cycle mentioned above, the figures quoted in this study refer to the cost involved in the birth of at least one live baby as a result of an IVF cycle.

66. Id.

67. See Nadine Taub, "Surrogacy: A Preferred Treatment for Infertility?" *Law, Medicine & Health Care* 16 (1988): 89.

A Record and Big Questions as Woman Gives Birth at 63

Gina Kolata

In a feat that has raised questions about the uses of medical science, a woman 63 years and 9 months old recently gave birth to a healthy baby girl. Her doctors say that as far as they know, she is the oldest woman ever to give birth.

The woman was well past menopause, but she became pregnant by using a donated egg from a much younger woman.

The woman's doctors refused to identify the woman, saying she was adamant about preserving her privacy. They said only that she lived in the Los Angeles area, that her baby was delivered by Caesarean section late last year, that the woman recovered uneventfully and that she breast-fed her baby. The fertility center that assisted her bars women over 55, but her doctor said she had lied about her age.

The woman's successful pregnancy and births to other women over age 60 raise questions about whether there should be an age limit for pregnancy and, if so, who should decide that a woman is too old to bear a child.

Doctors who run infertility centers set their own age limits for pregnancies and decide for themselves who is a suitable mother. Some find it abhorrent that women past menopause can now bear children and others find it only fair that older women, like older men, can become parents.

Gina Kolata, "A Record and Big Questions as Woman Gives Birth at 63," *The New York Times* 24 April 1997: A1, A25. Copyright (c) 1997 The New York Times Company. Reprinted by permission.

"I'm on her side," said Dr. Ronald Munson, an ethicist at the University of Missouri. Arbitrary age cutoffs are "just a matter of age discrimination," he said, and it is irrational to wink and grin at an older man who has a new baby but to look with horror at an older woman. "Quite frankly, I can understand why that woman lied," Dr. Munson said.

Until recently, and despite the growing use of donor eggs, doctors would never have suspected that a woman who was 63—or even 55—could become pregnant and carry a fetus to term, even if she used a donated egg from a younger woman.

"We really believed that, as we see in other animals, that as women reached the age of 50 or so, pregnancy wastage might be high, the uterus might not be fit to carry a baby," said Dr. Mark V. Sauer, who directs the infertility program at Columbia University in New York.

Now it has become clear that any woman who has a uterus can potentially become pregnant with a donated egg, as long as it comes from a relatively young woman. Women who have gone through menopause are just as likely as younger women to become pregnant using donor eggs and their babies are just as healthy, said Dr. Richard J. Paulson, the director of the infertility center at the University of Southern California and the doctor for the 63-year-old woman. The age of the oldest mother keeps getting pushed forward. Until now, the record-holder was a woman in Italy but she was younger by months than the woman who gave birth in California.

The donated egg is genetically unrelated to the woman, but because her husband's sperm fertilized it, the baby received half her genes from him. Dr. Arthur Wisot, executive director of the Center for Advanced Reproductive Care in Redondo Beach, Calif., said that older couples have few other options if they want to have children. Adoption agencies will not give them babies and, in any event, he added, many couples prefer using an egg from a catalogue of donors, who provide information on their appearance, interests, ethnic background and education.

It is expensive to try to become pregnant with donor eggs, costing about $15,000 for each attempt, and it takes an average of four attempts before women succeed. Health insurance virtually never covers the procedure for older women. But, doctors said, if a woman stays with the program, she is very likely to have a baby. "Persistence is the name of the game," Dr. Sauer said.

"I'm sure we are going to run into a biological clock as far as pregnancies are concerned," Dr. Paulson said, "but so far we have not."

Some doctors have loose age limits at best, saying it is the woman's choice; others say it is unnatural or medically unsound to have a baby late in life and refuse to do the procedure. Some found that their limits kept changing as women lied about their ages and had successful pregnancies.

The 63-year-old had enrolled in a program that had one of the most generous age limits of all. Women who were age 55 or under could enroll and become pregnant with donated eggs. Dr. Paulson said the 63-year-old woman conceded later she knew the program rules, so she told her doctors that she was 53. She had never had any children and had been married for 13 years.

Dr. Paulson said that he accepted the woman into the program and that her 57-year-old husband's sperm fertilized the donated eggs. On her third try, she became pregnant, Dr. Paulson said, and he referred her to an obstetrician for prenatal care. "A week later, we got a call from her obstetrician," Dr. Paulson said. "He said, 'She's 63, not 53.' I called her and said, 'How do I know this is true?'" The woman produced her passport showing she was 63.

Dr. Paulson and his colleagues reported the case in the current issue of the journal *Fertility and Sterility*.

Dr. Sauer, a pioneer in establishing pregnancies in older women and a former director of the . . . [donor egg] program at the University of Southern California, said he had seen similar situations ever since he first used donor eggs and started setting an age limit for pregnancies.

It began about a decade ago, when Dr. Sauer, like virtually everyone else running infertility clinics, decided that they would only provide donor eggs for women who were under 40. Then, he said, he discovered that some women had misled him about their ages and that he had helped women in their early 40's become pregnant. He reported seven of those pregnancies, in women ages 40 to 44 whose ovaries had failed prematurely, in a paper in *The New England Journal of Medicine*, concluding that it was possible to establish successful pregnancies "even in older women."

And so Dr. Sauer decided to raise his age limit. He set the limit at 50. Soon he discovered that there were women over 50 lying to get into the program. So he raised the age limit to 55 and added medical tests, like mammograms and treadmill tests.

But even with a limit of 55, women above that age tried to enter the program and it was hard to spot them. Many had had plastic surgery, Dr. Sauer said. The first time he discovered he had established a pregnancy in a woman over 55, Dr. Sauer had thought the woman was 50. "After she delivered, in Wyoming, one of her so-called girlfriends called to let me know she was 61," he said.

That is a common way for a woman's deception to be unmasked, Dr. Sauer said. "A friend will call us and say, 'Ha, Ha. The trick's on you.'" This month, for example, he was just about to use a donor egg on a woman from London, when "we had an anonymous call from someone in London who said she's known this woman from the time she was a child and that she was in her early 60's," Dr. Sauer said. He called the woman's doctor in London who admitted that he had put a false age on the woman's medical records to allow her to have donor eggs at Dr. Sauer's clinic. Dr. Sauer subsequently refused to help the woman become pregnant.

When Dr. Sauer confronts women who lied about their age, they say, "We knew there was a cutoff at 55 but we know we're as healthy as 50-year-olds are," Dr. Sauer said. "They'll say, 'It was just a small white lie.' I look at them and say, 'Well, yes and no.'"

And yet, doctors say, there is no particular reason that 55, or any other age, should be the limit for donated eggs and different medical centers have different age cutoffs.

"There are no hard and fast rules, there is no legislation," said Dr. Wisot at the Center for Advanced Reproductive Care. "This whole area of medicine is totally unregulated. We don't answer to anyone but our peers."

His age limit is 50, Dr. Wisot said, because he does not think that it is "fair to the child" to have a very old mother and because "we feel more comfortable using women in this age group."

Dr. Zev Rosenwaks, director of the Center for Reproductive Medicine and Infertility at New York Hospital-Cornell Medical Center in New York, said age 46 or 47 is about as high as he will go. "I believe it's not that easy for someone in their 50's to bring up a baby," he explained.

Dr. Joseph Schulman, director of the Genetics and IVF Center in Fairfax, Va., says his limit is 55 but he does not treat his guidelines "as rigid rules."

Dr. Sauer is torn. He looks at the handful of women he treated who were over 55 and whose deceptions came to light after they became pregnant and sees that "despite their dishonesty, the outcomes were really good." And so, he said, "I'm glad in my heart that they did lie to me." Yet, he said, "on the other hand, I think, 'Gee, what have I done?'"

44.
Feminist Perspectives on Artificial Insemination and In-Vitro Fertilization

Rosemarie Tong

Rosemarie Tong is Thatcher Professor of Philosophy and Medical Humanities at Davidson College. She has written extensively on feminist perspectives and feminist approaches to medical ethics. In this essay, she examines the variety of feminist perspectives on artificial insemination and in-vitro fertilization.

INTRODUCTION

Many Americans probably would not recognize the name of Louise Brown, the first child conceived in a petri dish. She may not be well known, but her birth in 1978 signaled a new age in reproductive technology.[1] For the first time ever, human beings were able to procreate a child outside of its mother's womb. As we will discover, the bioethical consequences of this event have been vast and far-reaching. . . . [Here] we consider two major reproduction-*aiding* technologies: artificial insemination, or AI (increasingly referred to as donor insemination, or DI) and in-vitro fertilization (IVF).[2] Just as nonfeminist bioethicists have varying perspectives on these technologies, so too do feminists. Issues of choice, control, and connection pervade feminists' differing analyses of so-called assisted reproduction. Working toward a common feminist policy on the reproduction-aiding technologies is no less difficult than achieving some measure of feminist consensus on the reproduction-controlling technologies.

Given that the population of the world continues to grow at an alarming rate, it seems difficult to believe that anyone has much trouble procreating. Yet many people do. Approximately 13.5 percent of American couples are infertile.[3] The term 'infertility' is used in reference to couples who fail to achieve pregnancy within one year of unprotected intercourse. There are two broad categories of infertility: *Primary infertility* is diagnosed when a couple has never successfully conceived, whereas *secondary infertility* is diagnosed when a couple has successfully conceived at least once.[4] Although a couple's reproductive difficulties may rest with only one of the partners, very often they rest with both of them or between them, as in cases of reproductive incompatibility (whereby each member of the couple is able to beget children with a different partner but, for some reason, not with the ex-

isting partner). As more physicians choose to specialize in infertility services, more infertility clinics are opening their doors. Significantly, the growing supply of infertility specialists and infertility clinics shows no sign of outstripping the demand for them. On the contrary, this demand seems to be expanding rapidly, as evidenced by the fact that the "infertility business" now exceeds the billion-dollar mark. Between 1968 and 1983, the number of couples seeking infertility services rose from about 600,000 to 2 million. At present, about 1 million couples seek infertility services annually, and each year general practitioners, obstetrician-gynecologists, and urologists see anywhere from 110,000 to 160,000 new cases.[5]

Infertility rates vary with age and socioeconomic class. In general, older women have higher rates of infertility than younger women, due largely to the biological effects of aging. However, over the last quarter-century the infertility rate of women aged twenty to twenty-four has swelled from 4 to 11 percent. The increase can be explained by rising rates of gonorrhea and other sexually transmitted diseases, which, if left untreated, can cause infertility; greater use of intrauterine devices, the filaments of which can lead infectious bacteria into the fallopian tubes at an accelerated rate; and increased environmental dangers. In addition, African-American women and poor women suffer from infertility problems more than white and middle-class women do, largely because many of them do not receive adequate preventive health care.[6]

Nonfeminist bioethicists have often debated whether infertility is a disease or simply a regrettable human limitation that causes many couples to experience guilt, disappointment, depression, low self-esteem, and often marital conflict. Those who believe that infertility is a human limitation, not a disease, observe that infertile people are just as healthy and vigorous as fertile people. They also note that if infertility were a disease, artificial insemination and in-vitro fertilization would not count as cures for it: Although these technologies enable many infertile people to have children, they leave them as infertile as ever.[7] In contrast, those who do regard infertility as a disease argue that although infertility neither threatens life nor causes physical pain or discomfort, it does prevent affected persons from functioning normally—that is, from reproducing. They also point out that physicians are often content to treat diseases in lieu of being able to cure them. Thus, in the same way that insulin is a treatment but not a cure for diabetes, AI and IVF are treatments but not cures for infertility.[8]

Whether infertility is considered a limitation or a disease is a matter of some consequence. If infertility is viewed as "just one of those things," then infertile people should focus on the advantages as opposed to the disadvantages of a childless marriage, or they should consider adoption, foster parenting, or working with children as meaningful options. In contrast, if infertility is viewed as a disease or disablement, then infertile couples should take advantage of all the reproduction-aiding technologies now available. At present, the disease or disablement view of infertility is the dominant one, inasmuch as infertile people are increasingly seeing it as a medical problem that can be remedied. . . .

There are two types of artificial insemination: artificial insemination by husband (AIH), in which the sperm donor is the woman's husband or male partner; and artificial insemination by donor (AID), in which the sperm donor is a man other than the woman's husband or male partner. AIH is the preferred method of treatment when the husband's sperm cells are normal and able to fertilize the egg but the sperm count is low. And AID is indicated when the husband's sperm count is so low that pooling his sperm is not of much use, where there is an Rh incompatibility, or when the husband suffers from a serious hereditary genetic disorder. At present, artificial insemination is the most widely used mode of assisted reproduction in the United States. In fact, the Office of Technology Assessment (OTA) recently reported that, in 1987 alone, 172,000 women had artificial insemination and 65,000 babies resulted. . . .[9]

FEMINIST BIOETHICAL PERSPECTIVES ON ARTIFICIAL INSEMINATION

In general, feminists agree that artificial insemination and, for that matter, most other reproduction-aiding technologies increase women's procreative options. If they have any basic disagreement at all about the use of these technologies, it centers on the question of whether women's right to use them should be almost absolute or considerably restricted. Philosopher Christine Overall, for one, accepts the view that "reproductive rights are derived from the central importance of reproduction in an individual's life and are limited only by a capacity to participate meaningfully and an ability to accept or transfer rearing responsibilities."[10] She also accepts the standard distinction between a *weak* sense of one's reproductive rights and a *strong* one.

Supposedly, the *weak* sense of the right to procreate implies an obligation on the part of the state not to interfere with anyone's reproductive freedom through, say, forced sterilization or contraception programs, or through racist or eugenic marriage laws. In addition, it implies an obligation on the part of the state not to limit women's reproductive freedom by requiring women to have cesarean sections in the supposed best interests of their fetuses, or by insisting that women give birth in hospitals attended by obstetrical technologists rather than at home attended by nurse midwives, family members, and friends.

In contrast to the weak sense of the right to procreate, the *strong* sense of this right implies an obligation on the part of the state not only to avoid interfering with procreation but also to facilitate it. So interpreted, the strong sense of the right to procreate presumably entitles all individuals to access "all available forms of reproductive products, technologies, and labor, including the gametes of other women and men, the gestational services of women, and the full range of procreative techniques including *in vitro* fertilization, gamete intrafallopian transfer, uterine lavage, . . . embryo freezing, and sex preselection."[11]

Some feminists believe it is vital for women that the right to reproduce be affirmed in its strong as well as its weak sense. As they see it, unless the right to reproduce is total, only certain women (and men) will be given access to gamete donors, for example; and the fortunate recipients will probably be heterosexual, married, economically well-to-do, and racially privileged.[12] This state of affairs is fundamentally unfair, insist many feminists. The fact that certain people do not want to marry someone of the opposite sex or engage in heterosexual intercourse does not mean that they should be deprived of having children genetically related to them.

Other feminists, however, believe it might be a mistake to interpret the right to reproduce in the strong sense specifically. For example, feminist Maura Ryan takes exception to law professor John Robertson's exceptionally strong interpretation of the right to reproduce, according to which "[t]he right of married persons to use noncoital and collaborative means of conception to overcome infertility must extend to any purpose, including selecting the gender or genetic characteristics of the child or transferring the burden of gestation to another."[13]

In Ryan's view, if the strong sense of the right to reproduce does in fact include what Robertson says it does, then children are little more than commodities that adults can "order" or "purchase" in accordance with their specific parental desires.[14] Worse, a strong interpretation of the right to reproduce leads to the incoherent position that having a genetic connection to one's children is both very important and not important at all. For the infertile couple who wants to use AID, for example, the genetic connection to the child is supposedly all-important, whereas for the sperm donor this type of connection is supposedly unimportant. What wor-

ries Ryan most about a strong interpretation of the right to procreate, however, is that it automatically privileges the *wants* of individuals over the *needs* of their communities. Thus, she claims that feminists, at least,

> need to ask whether we should support the right of individuals to go to any length to acquire the type of child they want when there are so many children already living who are not being take care of. And, recognizing that collaborative reproduction ordinarily has as its object a white child, we need as well to examine the kind of racial attitudes being perpetrated.[15]

In short, the mere desire to procreate does not imply the strong right to do so, as if an infertile woman could simply demand that a fertile woman give her the eggs without which she cannot reproduce.[16]

Clearly, Ryan's concerns about the strong sense of the right to procreate are not idle speculations. Considerable evidence now exists for what some critics initially dismissed as "paranoia" on the part of some feminists who, like Gena Corea, sought to expose what they viewed as the unethical practice of "snatching" eggs from unsuspecting women.[17] A case in point is the scandal uncovered in 1995 at the University of California Irvine's Center of Reproductive Health. Unapproved egg "transfers" involving at least thirty women were made between 1988 and 1992,[18] and there is some suspicion that such practices were not confined to the state of California.

As might be expected, similar concerns have arisen about the retrieval and use of men's sperm. For example, in 1984 a French woman named Corinne Parplaix sued a sperm bank to release her dead husband's sperm cells to her even though he had left no specific instructions as to what he wanted done with them. The state prosecutor argued that Mrs. Parplaix had no more right to her dead husband's sperm than to his feet or ears. Mrs. Parplaix's lawyer countered that Mr. Parplaix knew he was dying of cancer when he deposited his sperm. By so doing, he implied a contract with his wife, a contract to bear his child after his death. The court agreed with Mrs. Parplaix's lawyer. When apprised of the decision, Mrs. Parplaix said: "I'll call him Thomas. . . . He'll be a pianist. That's what his father wanted."[19]

More recently, some women have requested that physicians retrieve sperm from their near-dead or dead husbands. When the Northeast Organ Procurement Organization asked more than fifty other organ procurement organizations if they had been requested to recover sperm from organ donors, more than 80 percent of these organizations reported that they had. In seven of the reported forty-six cases, sperm retrieval was attempted. Only three of these succeeded, and none of the procurement organizations knows whether any of the three widows actually became pregnant or had a child. However, the procurement organizations that gave the widows the sperm of their dead husbands have realized that they are probably on shaky legal ground. It is not clear, for example, that a widow has a right to claim her deceased husband's sperm, especially if there is reason to think he did not want any offspring, including ones born posthumously. In this connection, Maggie Gallagher of the Center for Social Thought, a conservative think tank, has commented: "It really does violate the principle of reproductive choice. A man can't tell his wife she can't have an abortion, and a woman can't tell her husband he can't have a vasectomy. I question making a man a father when he has never indicated he would want to be a father under these circumstances."[20] Yet, despite the soundness of Gallagher's reasoning, many feminists would suggest that widows are ordinarily good interpreters of their deceased husband's desires. For example, Pam Mareska, widowed shortly after her marriage, insisted that her deceased husband, Manny, very much wanted to have children. Since Manny Maresca's family agreed with his widow's judgment, his physicians removed Manny's sperm cells from his

body. Pam Maresca then stored them in a sperm bank for her future use. Although Pam Maresca has not ruled out marrying again, she insists that "it will have to be someone special enough to accept Manny's child."[21]

As risky as it is to interpret the right to procreate too strongly, some feminists caution that it is probably just as risky—if not more so—to interpret this right too weakly. There is, after all, much evidence indicating that legal and medical authorities have inappropriately restricted access to AID and other reproduction-aiding technologies. In the past, U.S. courts refused to legally recognize the alternative families that AID enabled. In fact, some courts not only classified AID as adulterous but also branded AID children as illegitimate. Traditionally, the law regarded the genetic father, not the social father, as the child's "real" father; and any child begotten through a man other than a woman's husband was considered illegitimate. It mattered not if the woman's husband, the child's social father, viewed the child as his own.

In the United States, a legal trend toward ruling that, under certain circumstances, the social father is no less a father than the genetic father began in 1948. In a New York divorce case, *Strnad v. Strnad*, a woman sued to limit her ex-husband's right to visit their child who had been conceived through AID *with his consent*. Although the court did not explicitly rule that the child was legitimate, it held that the ex-husband, though not the genetic father of the child, was "entitled to the same rights as those acquired by a foster parent who has adopted a child, if not the same rights as those to which a natural parent under the circumstances would be entitled."[22] Later, in a 1968 California case, *People v. Sorenson*, a woman sued her ex-husband for child support. He refused to support the child on the grounds that the child was not his, even though he had consented to his ex-wife's use of AID. The supreme court of California ruled against the man. It held that since he had consented to his wife's insemination by donor, the child was his in the eyes of the law.[23]

Although decades have passed since the *Sorenson* case, no comprehensive federal statute governing AID has been written. However, several states have enacted a variety of laws to regulate certain aspects of AID. Despite the variations in these laws, most states agree that both partners must consent to AID; and that if they both consent, the child born to them is legitimate. Some states go further than this, explicitly stating that the sperm donor is not the legal father of the child. Other legal or quasi-legal attempts to regulate the practice of AID include requirements for (1) documenting the consent of sperm recipients and/or their spouses or partners to AID; (2) keeping the personal identity of sperm donors confidential; (3) limiting the number of times any one man can serve as a sperm donor in a certain geographical area; (4) regulating the quality of sperm used in AID; and (5) confirming the performance of AID to an authorized or licensed person, generally a physician.[24]

In addition to legal authorities, health-care practitioners have sought to regulate AID in a variety of ways. Recently, reputable clinics have begun to screen donor sperm rigorously and to expand informed-consent procedures to include discussions of possible legal problems associated with AID (such as breaches of confidentiality or attempts by the sperm donor to enter his genetic child's life) as well as possible medical risks.[25] What feminists find troubling are not such measures themselves but the tendency of some physicians to restrict access to AID to "childworthy," married infertile couples.[26] Apparently, these physicians believe that since *they* are the ones who enable people to have children they could not have otherwise, it is their responsibility not to use their medical skills "to create children who will suffer from their poor start in life."[27] Convinced that children need to be raised by a man and a woman who are married to each other and have all that it takes emotionally, physically, and financially to rear children to adulthood, these physicians routinely turn away single persons, lesbian couples, unmarried heterosexual couples, and married couples whom they perceive as unstable.

Generally speaking, feminists view as flawed the reasoning of those who would restrict AID to "childworthy," married heterosexual couples. They doubt not only that physicians are particularly good assessors of "childworthiness" but also that children need two (and only two) parents—one male, the other female—in order to thrive. On the contrary, they note, there is growing evidence that children fare well in any kind of family structure, including those headed by single parents, provided that their primary caregiver(s) treat them responsibly and *lovingly*.[28] Observing that it is not the number or gender of a child's parents that makes the difference in a child's life but, rather, the quality of the parent-child relationship, most feminists insist that physicians should provide AID not only to married heterosexual couples but also to unmarried ones and to single women—be they heterosexual or lesbian. The fact that a woman chooses not to marry a man or to have sex with a man is no reason, in and of itself, to deny her the opportunity to have children of her own if she is physically, emotionally, and financially able to do so. If physicians want to restrict access to AID only to people who are "good parenting material," then they should subject *all* persons who wish to use AID to the same level of *objective* scrutiny. In this connection, feminist philosopher Mary Mahowald has reported that she personally knows at least one infertility specialist who declines to perform AID unless the person(s) who request it obtain an evaluation of "competence" for parenthood from a recognized expert. Mahowald has no objections to this physician's policy per se, although she worries that the officials in charge of the evaluations might be subtly biased in the direction of married, heterosexual couples.[29]

Frustrated by legal and medical impediments to obtaining AID, some feminists urge women to take control of the situation. After all, a woman can achieve pregnancy through casual intercourse—the proverbial "one-night stand."

However, casual intercourse is anything *but* casual for lesbians or for women who believe that sex outside of a meaningful, long-term relationship is wrong or at least distasteful. Moreover, it might take multiple "one-night stands" for a woman to get pregnant, during which a woman may be exposed to sexually transmitted diseases or the HIV virus. Thus, although casual intercourse can be an effective way to get pregnant, it is not a method that feminists are eager to endorse. Instead, feminists have organized themselves into groups committed to finding a more independent and fulfilling way for women to get pregnant.

Self-insemination is a reproductive possibility that many feminists laud as being quite liberating not only from the control of the medical profession but also from that of men in general. In the early 1980s a group of lesbian feminists in London established the Feminist Self Insemination Group.[30] Using homosexual men as donors, these women inseminated themselves with every manner and fashion of syringe, including turkey basters. Says one member of the Feminist Self Insemination Group: "'Doing it ourselves' [is] . . . one of the roads to getting in charge of our reproductive capacities."[31] In addition to putting reproduction entirely within the control of women, self-insemination is inexpensive since the women who use it typically rely on altruistic males to provide them with sperm. Being able to inseminate oneself is therefore a boon not only to lesbians rejected by the medical establishment but also to those women who cannot afford the cost of AID (typically from $400 to $600 per cycle).[32] It is also a boon to those women who do not wish to involve an unfamiliar physician in what they consider a private matter, as private as the act of sex itself.

Yet for all its advantages, self-insemination has enough disadvantages to arouse some feminists' concern. Even if a woman is able to find a man willing to give her his sperm cells, she cannot be sure of their quality or safety, since she has no way to screen them for genetic defects or diseases, sexually transmitted diseases, or the HIV virus. Relying on physician-controlled AID has the advantage of removing many of these concerns since most physicians use frozen sperm from a sperm bank. And most of the nation's 138 sperm banks follow the safety guidelines of the American Fertility Society and the American Association of Tissue Banks. These guidelines (1) advise that potential sperm donors complete a medical history and undergo an extensive physical exam; (2) disqualify gay men, drug users, and men with multiple sex partners as well as men over fifty and men with low-quality or sluggish sperm; and (3) recommend appropriate genetic testing as well as screening for HIV, hepatitis B, gonorrhea, syphilis, and chlamydia. So rigorous are these guidelines that some sperm banks are forced to reject about 80–85 percent of potential donors.[33]

Granted, women who choose physician-controlled AID are not always shielded from unsafe or otherwise undesirable sperm. A minority of physicians still use fresh sperm. They claim that there is no need to screen their donors since they either know the donors personally or the donors belong to a "reliable" group: medical students, for example. Moreover, although some of these physicians inform their patients that they use fresh sperm, others do not. In one notorious case, two fertility doctors at Mount Sinai Medical Center inseminated dozens of women with fresh sperm that had been illegally sold to them by two hospital employees over a two-year period but had not been frozen and quarantined as New York state law requires.[34] Luckily, the sperm was found not to be carrying any diseases; however, many women were exposed to *possible* infection from HIV and STDs. Another physician in Vienna, Virginia, who inseminated more than seventy women at his infertility clinic with his own fresh sperm, told his patients that he used carefully screened donor sperm.[35] Fortunately, such shocking stories are rare: Physician-controlled AID generally proceeds safely and ethically for all those involved.

Perhaps the greatest risk faced by women who decide to self-inseminate (or even to use physician-controlled AID) is the possibility not of using unsafe sperm but of using a donor who will later demand access to his genetically related child. Feminist Gena Corea has cautioned that, according to U.S. law, the parental rights of sperm donors disappear or appear depending on the marital status of the woman. If a man donates his sperm to a married woman, his status shrivels to that of an anonymous "semen source" who supplies a bodily fluid; but if he donates his sperm to an unmarried woman, his status quickly swells "to that of a father with rights over his issue."[36]

Several court cases support Corea's observations. In 1977, a man gave some of his sperm to a woman friend who, after she was nearly three months pregnant, broke off all relations with him. When the child was born, the sperm donor sued for visitation rights. A New Jersey court not only granted him visitation rights but also declared him the child's legal father.[37] Significantly, the U.S. Supreme Court supported New Jersey's ruling. In another case, it ruled that, under certain circumstances, a sperm donor has a constitutional right to claim fatherhood. Apparently, state laws according to which sperm donors have no legal rights to a child produced through artificial insemination do not necessarily apply to sperm donors who have been in relatively long-term relationships with the recipients of their sperm. In the case considered by the U.S. Supreme Court, a man named McIntyre claimed to have been friends with a lesbian woman for more than thirteen years. Unable to adopt a child, he donated sperm to the woman, who supposedly agreed to his playing an active role in the child's life. Then, however, McIntyre and the woman had a falling out. After the child was born, she blocked McIntyre's access to the child, claiming she had never regarded him as anything more than a sperm donor. McIntyre filed a paternity-rights suit against the woman. Although a lower Oregon court dismissed his suit, an Oregon appeals court reversed the decision, ruling that "the due-process clause can afford no

different protection to [McIntyre] as the biological father because the child was conceived by artificial insemination rather than by sexual intercourse."[38] As a result of this ruling, McIntyre was given the right to try to prove that the lesbian woman had originally agreed to let him act as the social father of the child. Although this decision probably does not affect the 20,000 *married* women who use a sperm donor in any given year, it probably does affect the 1,500 *unmarried* women who use a sperm donor in any given year. Unless an unmarried woman can prove she was not in a long-term relationship with the sperm donor, he might be in a position to establish himself as the child's legal father.

Over and beyond the legal risks incurred by single women who use AID, lesbian women who do so put their partners (when they have partners) at special legal risk. Suppose two lesbians in a relationship decide to have a child. If their relationship breaks up, the woman who is not biologically related to the child has no legal rights to the child. Under such circumstances, some judges empathize with the lesbian "co-parent," even though there is little they can do legally to ameliorate her situation. For example, after denying a lesbian co-parent the right to visit the eight-year-old girl who was conceived by her former lover and partner, California Judge Dana Henry urged his state to reform the law "in order to adequately deal with the increasing number of children of homosexual couples."[39] Other judges have gone even further, in one instance granting parental visitation rights to the lesbian co-parent of a child. In general, the lawyers who represent lesbian co-parents argue that a person becomes a "de facto" parent to the degree that she (or he) provides longtime physical and psychological nurture to a child. Should such arguments gain wide social acceptance, they will have consequences not only of the estimated 10,000 children now being reared by lesbians but also for the thousands of children now being reared by gay men and stepparents.[40]

Having realized that women's "choice" to use AID will remain limited unless legal authorities and medical practitioners make it possible for all women and/or couples to gain access to safe, affordable sperm, some feminists urge that women take complete control over the practice of AID now. Toward this goal, some enterprising feminists have already established their own sperm banks. The Sperm Bank of California (T.S.B.C.), located in Berkeley, is one such establishment. T.S.B.C. not only carefully screens the sperm cells that are deposited there but also provides sperm to any woman, regardless of her marital status, sexual preference, or physical disability. T.S.B.C. also permits sperm recipients to examine a catalogue of donor information and to select their own donor on the basis of this information. Finally, since 1983, T.S.B.C. has asked donors if they wish to list themselves as "yes donors"—that is, donors who are willing to disclose identifying information about themselves to future offspring. T.S.B.C. releases "yes-donors" information to offspring who petition the bank in writing after they are at least eighteen years old. It does not, however, release identifying information to the donor concerning the recipient of this sperm or any child born as the result of his contribution.[41]

The rather open policies of The Sperm Bank of California invite feminists (as well as nonfeminists) to reconsider not only current U.S. laws that specify the rights and responsibilities of sperm donors and recipients, respectively, but also U.S. policies regarding both anonymous and commercial sperm donation. As noted earlier, the identity of sperm donors is kept secret, and most sperm donors are paid for their gametes (in the range of $50 per ejaculation).[42] As also noted earlier, these policies have been affirmed as serving *men's* best interests. Indeed, as Glanville Williams, a British law professor, points out, the reasons for donor anonymity are twofold: "to protect the *donor's* reputation" and "to eliminate the risk of the wife transferring her affections to the *donor*."[43] In addition to these reasons, protecting the sperm donor from an unwanted financial or personal relationship with his biological child is typically cited in support of anonymity.[44]

Recently, a variety of psychologists and counselors have challenged the assumption that an anonymous policy (if not also a commercial policy) is actually in *men's* best interests. Some recent studies show that, more often than not, sperm donors want to know whether they "fathered" a child. Moreover, many sperm donors seem willing to share not only nonidentifying but even identifying information about themselves with recipients and children. For example, psychologist Patricia P. Mahlstedt discovered that nearly all of the seventy-two sperm donors in her study were inclined to pass on significant medical and personal background information about themselves to their recipients, and 60 percent were also willing to be contacted by their potential offspring when they (the offspring) reached age eighteen.[45] Mahlstedt's empirical research is bolstered in some interesting ways by the popular media. In an episode of the television show "St. Elsewhere," one of the physicians donates sperm to the hospital's infertility program. Through a complicated chain of events, he discovers the identity of his sperm recipient and follows her pregnancy obsessively. Eventually, he assigns himself to her case, at which point he begins to act like an expectant father. The pregnant woman's husband is bewildered by the physician's inappropriate behavior and asks the chief of residents to remove him from his wife's case. As a result, the physician nearly has a nervous breakdown, protesting that the woman is carrying his child and that he has a right to be involved in his child's life.

Given studies such as Mahlstedt's and media representations such as the "St. Elsewhere" episode, a more open policy of sperm donation might indeed be in the best interests of sperm donors. Whether or not this proves to be the case, however, the question remains for feminists: Would a more open policy or the current commercial and anonymous policy of sperm donation serve *women's* best interests?

Feminists who support the current policy argue, first, that *commercialism* serves women's best interests. Because it is neither desirable nor feasible for all women to secure sperm noncommercially (i.e., from altruistic male friends, acquaintances, or contacts), women need to have a way of securing sperm commercially for a fair market price. Second, the same feminists insist that, like commercialism, *anonymity* serves women's best interests because it insulates them and their children from the intrusions of uninvited "genetic fathers." Better that sperm donors know nothing about their recipients' or children's identity than that they make nuisances of themselves. Moreover, it is up to the sperm donor's genetic children to decide whether they wish to give any identifying personal information about themselves to their genetic fathers. (Interestingly, most feminists who favor an anonymous sperm donation policy regard sperm donors' right to privacy as less weighty than AID children's right to know their genetic fathers. They claim that AID children, like adopted children, should have access to non-identifying medical information about their genetic fathers at any time and to identifying personal information about them reaching the age of majority. As it stands, however, the trend is to provide only nonidentifying medical information to children conceived through AID. Unless a donor is a "yes-donor" or voluntarily chooses to disclose his identity upon his genetic child's request, the child will remain in the dark as to his identity.)[46]

The feminist case for a commercial *and* anonymous sperm donation policy is countered by equally cogent feminist cases for sperm donation policies that are (1) noncommercial and anonymous or (2) noncommercial and open. Feminists who support noncommercial and anonymous policies regard as exemplary the policy developed by a network of twenty sperm banks in France known as CECOS (Centre d'etude et de conservation du sperme.) The guiding idea behind CECOS is that of "a gift from one couple to another." Potential donors must be married and have fathered at least one child of their own. In addition, they must have their wives' consent and cannot receive compensation for donating their sperm. The recipient couples must also be married (or in a long-term monogamous relationship) and need to have been referred to the CECOS bank for a medically proven *male* infertility problem (or for a genetically determined condition that the husband does not wish to transmit to his offspring). Finally, both donors and recipients must agree to psychological counseling, the primary purpose of which is to permit all parties to explore their feelings about this form of collaborative reproduction. Although CECOS keeps accurate records on donors and recipients, anonymity is guaranteed to all parties.[47]

Some feminists think that although the CECOS policy is a good one, it does not go far enough. They favor an open as well as noncommercial policy that includes not only infertile heterosexual couples in marriage or marriage-like relationships but also lesbian couples and single women wishing to raise children on their own. These feminists believe that if genetic connection is as important as people generally claim it is, and if men as well as women should take on full childrearing responsibilities for the sake of the child, then everyone involved in collaborative reproduction should play a more or less active role in their children's lives.

Among the family structures that meet with the approval of feminists who support open as well as noncommercial policies of sperm donation are those that bring together lesbian women and gay men to co-parent children they have conceived through AID. In one case of lesbian co-parenting, a lesbian couple, Nancy and Amy, formed a family that included Nancy's genetic child Sarah and Sarah's genetic father Doug. All three adults expressed satisfaction with the arrangement, which produced a very well-adjusted child. Indeed, Sarah's only recorded worry about the future was that she might not be able to find a "Daddy" and an "Amy" for the child she herself hopes to have someday.[48] To be sure, feminist advocates of open family structures like this one are well aware that when such families break up, a particularly great toll is taken. In the event that Nancy and Doug's relationship ruptures, Doug might sue Nancy for custody of Sarah; or if Nancy and Amy split up, Nancy could keep Amy from seeing Sarah. In addition, if both Nancy and Doug were to die, their wish that Amy should have custody of Sarah could be challenged in court by grandparents or even the state. Nevertheless, feminist advocates of such open family structures claim that the solution to these problems is not to forbid lesbians to form families or to keep sperm donors out of their genetic children's lives but, rather, to delineate the respective legal rights and responsibilities of genetic, gestational, and social parents more clearly and more fairly.

Of course, there is less inclination to invite the sperm donor to join the family when AID is used by a woman in a traditional heterosexual marriage. After all, the woman's husband usually desires to be the child's one and only social father. Therefore, if the main reason to admit the sperm donor into the family is to provide the AID child not so much with a genetic reference point as with a loving social father or male figure, then such admission seems unnecessary. If the AID child already has a stable and loving social father, she or he will probably feel little, if any, need to establish a close social relationship with his or her genetic father. Under such circumstances, a brief meeting between the genetic father and his genetic child might satisfy any curiosity they have about each other.

FEMINIST PERSPECTIVES ON IN-VITRO FERTILIZATION

The term 'test-tube baby' conjures up all sorts of Faustian and Frankensteinian images, but these do not appropriately reflect the realities of in-vitro fertilization. The phrase 'in-vitro fertilization' (literally, fertilization in glass) ordinarily denotes any fertilization procedure that occurs outside the human body. The process of IVF begins when a woman's ovaries are stimulated with fertility drugs to produce multiple eggs, which the physician then retrieves through one of two means: laparoscopy or transvaginal ultrasound-directed oocyte retrieval (TUDOR). In the case of laparoscopy, the physician makes a small incision near the navel of the woman and inserts the laparoscope, a slender fiberoptic tube with a light and an optical system at the end. After pinpointing the eggs within the ovaries, the physician retrieves them with a long hollow needle fed through the laparoscope. The needle is inserted through the vaginal wall, rather than through the abdomen as in the TUDOR procedure, and ultrasonography guides the physician's retrieval of the eggs. After retrieval, each egg is placed in a separate glass dish and combined with sperm from the woman's partner or a donor. Those eggs that are successfully fertilized are inserted in the woman's uterus when they have divided to form between four and sixteen cells.[49] . . .

Although there is no uniform feminist position regarding in-vitro fertilization, it is accurate to say that, unlike nonfeminist bioethicists, feminists rarely discuss the moral status of the pre-embryo. Instead, both feminist critics and feminist advocates of IVF worry that the women who participate in IVF programs are not always as aware of IVF's risks as they are of its benefits. Thus, they urge health-care practitioners to be honest about the *true* success rates of IVF. They also insist that health-care practitioners be as candid as possible about the physical and psychological risks of IVF. If a woman wishes to use IVF to attempt to become pregnant, she should realize just how long and arduous the process is. Feminists Gena Corea and Susan Ince note that a woman typically has to submit to at least two IVF cycles, each of which lasts approximately two weeks. First, as an outpatient, the woman is monitored for her daily plasma levels and cervical mucus and undergoes ultrasound examinations to determine her ovarian progress. Then, as an inpatient, she becomes the object of hormonal assays and the collection of eggs through laparoscopy. Finally, *if* egg collection and fertilization are successful, clinicians will transfer one or more of the pre-embryos into her womb. If any stage along the way—egg collection, egg fertilization, or pre-embryo transfer—is unsuccessful (and if additional frozen pre-embryos are not available), the whole process must be performed again. Each time the woman goes through an IVF cycle, she is subjected to several risks, including the following ones: "the adverse affects of hormones such as Clomid, which are usually taken in large, concentrated doses to stimulate hyperovulation; repeated anesthesia and surgery to extract eggs; the heightened risk of ectopic pregnancy (when the fertilized egg implants outside the uterus); the development of ovarian cysts and menstrual difficulties; and the early start of menopause and an increased risk of some forms of cancer."[50] Attempts to reduce such risks have not been very successful. For example, unlike laparoscopy, which is a relatively painful egg-extracting technique, transvaginal ultrasound-directed oocyte retrieval is, in theory, so painless that it precludes the need for general anesthesia. Nevertheless, many women claim that, in their experience of it, the TUDOR process was very painful—so much so that they had to ask for general anesthesia during it.[51]

Equally as taxing as the physical risks of IVF are its psychological risks, in feminists' estimation. Philosopher Mary Anne Warren notes that these include "the emotional ups and down inherent in the cycle of hope and disappointment; the disruption of work and, often, personal relationships; and the humiliation and depersonalization that may result from the submission to painful and embarrassing invasions of their bodies."[52] Indeed, many women in IVF programs become highly preoccupied by all the things that can, and very often do, go wrong. A woman's eggs may not be retrievable; or if retrievable, her eggs may be of poor quality. Fertilization may not occur in the petri dish; and even if it does, the pre-embryo may fail to implant in her womb. In one study of IVF patients, all the women reported that the two-week waiting period after the transfer of the pre-embryo into their wombs was nearly intolerable. One woman said: "You sit . . . and pray and pray. . . . And when it doesn't work, that's when you curse everybody. You feel depressed. You're not worth anything."[53]

Feminists are also concerned about the well-being of egg donors, who assume many of the same risks that IVF enrollees do, but without receiving the same benefit: namely, a much-wanted child. Instead, egg donors receive financial compensation for their eggs.[54] Thus, feminists urge health-care practitioners to make certain that egg donors thoroughly comprehend the risks involved in egg retrieval. They have praised one clinic in particular not only for verbally communicating the risks of serving as an egg donor but also for showing prospective egg donors videos. One such video details TUDOR (the procedure by which their eggs are removed), thus underscoring that fact that egg donation is painful enough to require the administration of a general anesthetic.[55]

As serious as IVF's risks are, however, its feminist advocates nonetheless insist that it is up to the egg recipients and egg donors to decide whether they are risks worth taking. Each woman, they insist, should decide for herself just how much *she* wants a child or just how much *she* wants to help another woman have a child. Feminist critics of IVF counter that just because a woman knows cognitively what IVF's risks and benefits are, she is not necessarily emotionally able to make a fully voluntary decision to use or not to use IVF. As they see it, Western society teaches women that their "fulfillment" depends on their mothering a child, preferably a child that is flesh of their flesh.[56] To the degree that a woman is convinced that being a genetic and gestational as well as social mother is the sine qua non for her success as a human being, she will "want" to use virtually any reproduction-aiding technology to achieve her maternal goal. Thus, as Gena Corea comments, "[t]he propaganda . . . that women are nothing unless they bear children, that if they are infertile, they lose their most basic identity as women . . . has a coercive power. It conditions a woman's choices as well as her *motivations* to choose. Her most heartfelt desire, the pregnancy for which she so desperately yearns, has been—to varying degrees—conditioned."[57]

Feminist critics of IVF also worry that, simply owing to IVF's availability, society will pressure infertile women who are currently happy without children to "do something" about their childlessness. Likewise, they are concerned that society will pressure fertile women to help out their infertile "sisters"—by providing them with the eggs they so desperately need, for example. Corea points out that, in contrast to sperm donation, egg donation has historically relied on *known* as opposed to *anonymous* donors. Given that it is considerably inconvenient, uncomfortable, risky, and even painful to serve as an egg donor, clinicians initially required that their patients use female relatives or friends as egg donors. But when it became evident that some of these "donors" felt there was no way to say "no" to their loved ones, most clinicians reconsidered their open and noncommercial egg-donation policy and moved in the direction of an anonymous and commercial one.[58] They reasoned that anonymous egg donors would be able to sell their eggs without feeling obligated to do so. They also reasoned that so long as sperm donors were being paid for their gametes, egg donors should be paid for theirs.

Although some feminist critics of IVF applaud the switch to an anonymous and commercial policy of egg donation, others view it as a matter of replacing one evil with another. They contend that many egg donors "choose" to be egg donors simply because they are financially strapped and in serious need of the $750 to $3,000 they can collect for their eggs, or because they feel obligated to do a good deed.[59] Although most infertility clinics report that their anonymous egg donors are mature women able to assess what personal risks are entailed in their act of generosity, many of the same clinics also concede that some of their donors are burdened

by heavy emotional baggage.[60] And, indeed, several recent empirical studies have confirmed that a statistically significant number of anonymous volunteers, perhaps as many as one-third, are either excessive risk-takers or the survivors of a major reproductive loss (abortion, miscarriage, giving up a child for adoption).[61] Thus, feminist critics of IVF conclude that a sizable percentage of egg donors might not be acting in their own best interests, and that such women should be discouraged from serving as egg donors. They are particularly concerned about "super donors" (who sell their eggs routinely), since these women are exposed to a level of medical risk that the average IVF patient escapes.[62] As bad as it is to take advantage of vulnerable persons, it is even worse to do so when they are exposed to considerable personal risk.

Of all the debates that IVF's feminist critics and feminist advocates have waged, none are greater than those concerning the ways that IVF and other reproduction-aiding technologies affect the childbearing experience itself. According to feminist philosopher Mary O'Brien, even though women's exclusive ability to bear children has been a source of oppression for women, it has also been a source of power—one that men have not been able to share. Thus, the experience and meaning of natural reproduction is very different for women than for men. In the first place, women experience procreation as a continuous process. For them, the spatial and temporal continuity between the egg and the resulting child is unbroken in natural reproduction, since the entire process of conception and gestation takes place inside their bodies. For men, in contrast, the spatial and temporal continuity between the sperm and the resulting child is broken in natural reproduction, since the entire process of conception and gestation takes place outside their bodies. Second, women, not men, have necessarily performed the fundamental *labor* of natural reproduction—pregnancy and birth. Without women, life could not go on. It is women who have the *individual* power to determine whether a *particular* child will be born, as well as the *collective* power to determine whether the human species will continue.[63] Third, prior to the introduction of DNA testing for paternity, women could know for certain in natural reproduction whether the children born to them were genetically related to them, whereas men could not know for certain that their female partners' genetic children were also their genetic children. For men, there was always the possibility that their female partners had been raped or had committed adultery.

CONCLUSIONS ABOUT ARTIFICIAL INSEMINATION AND IN-VITRO FERTILIZATION

Clearly, women have the advantage in natural reproduction; yet, according to some feminist critics of IVF, it is precisely this advantage that has compelled men to try to control women's sexual lives and reproductive capacities. Men have done so in the "privacy" of their homes by bullying, badgering, and even beating their wives and girlfriends. They have also used the courts, executive offices, and legislatures to control women's sexual and reproductive freedom. Finally, and in particularly effective ways, men have used medical authorities to limit women's reproductive freedom. In the past, health-care practitioners—most of whom have been men—sought to subject menstruation, pregnancy, delivery, lactation, ad menopause to their control. And, in the view of feminist critics of IVF, reproduction-controlling and reproduction-aiding technologies have provided the same health-care practitioners with the means to consolidate their control over women's reproductive powers. So concerned is Gena Corea about society's drift in the direction of assisted reproduction that she urges women to ask themselves the following questions:

> Why are men focusing all this technology on woman's generative organs—the source of her reproductive power? Why are they collecting our eggs? Why do they seek to freeze them? Why do men want to control the production of human beings? Why do they talk so often about producing "perfect" babies?
>
> Why are they splitting the functions of motherhood into smaller parts? Does that reduce the power of the mother and her claim to the child? ("I only gave the egg. I am not the real mother." "I only loaned my uterus. I am not the real mother." "I only raised the child. I am not the real mother").[64]

Corea's questions have prompted feminist critics of IVF to speculate that *men* intend to make women's experience of reproduction just as "alienated" as their own is. As soon as a woman's eggs are removed from her body, or as soon as she decides to use another woman's eggs, the stage is set for her to experience the reproductive process as a discontinuous one. Absent DNA testing, a woman who uses IVF cannot be certain that the child she births is genetically related to her. After all, the lab can always make a mistake. Someone else's eggs may be labeled with her name by mistake or by design. In the future, moreover, women may be disconnected from their genetic progeny in an even more radical way, according to feminist critics of IVF. Should researchers develop an artificial placenta, for instance, women would no longer have the sole power to gestate and to give birth. Feminist Robyn Rowland is sufficiently concerned about this possible development that she asks us to imagine a world in which only a few superovulating women are allowed to exist, a world in which eggs are taken from women, frozen, and fertilized in vitro for transfer into artificial placentas. Rowland concedes that the replacement of women's childbearing capacity by male-controlled technology would remove some of women's biological burdens. But it would also leave women "without a product" with which "to bargain": "For the history of 'mankind' women have been seen in terms of their value as childbearers. We have to ask, if that last power is taken and controlled by men, what role is envisaged for women in the new world?"[65]

Corea, Rowland, and other feminist critics of IVF also suspect that removing the fetus from a woman's womb might facilitate full-scale genetic manipulation, a concern that I will only touch upon now. Gena Corea notes than an increasing number of IVF clinical and laboratory researchers are eager to develop screening techniques to eliminate genetically defective pre-embryos.[66] Although eliminating birth defects may sound like a wonderful scientific advancement, Corea cautions that even if genetic manipulation starts out benevolently, it may not end benevolently. As Corea sees it, the stage is now being set for laws and medical practices that would prohibit women not only from conceiving or birthing "defective babies" but also from exposing fetuses to their own "defective intrauterine environments."[67] Whatever the right to procreate will mean in the future, Corea warns, it will not mean the right of a couple to conceive and bring to term a severely or even moderately disabled child for whose support society as a whole will in some measure be responsible. Indeed, philosopher Joseph Fletcher has already asserted that "the right to conceive and bear children has to stop short of knowingly making crippled children."[68] Told that they are victimizing their offspring and the whole of society by using their defective eggs and/or sperm, a shamed couple will probably willingly accept donor gametes. But however "responsible" this decision may seem, feminists worry about the long-term social implications of the ideology of human perfectibility. In their view, if people are no longer willing (or even able) to accept unconditionally the imperfect children born to them—to love these children just as they are—the human species will be morally worse for this new intolerance.

Feminists who advocate IVF disagree with its feminist critics who predict dire consequences such as the replacement of women by artificial placentas. They assert that, with sufficient safeguards, women can use IVF without being exploited. In fact, they see in IVF a valuable affirmation of the genetic connection, at least when a couple uses their own gametes. When one woman needs another woman's eggs to experience pregnancy—perhaps the most intimate of all human connecting experiences—the relationship subsequently formed need not be viewed as one woman exploiting an-other woman but simply as one woman helping another.

NOTES

1. John Robertson, *Children of Choice: Freedom and the New Reproductive Technologies* (Princeton, N.J.: Princeton University Press, 1994), pp. 4–5. [See above, pp. 556–587]

2. There are two types of artificial insemination: artificial insemination by husband (AIH) and artificial insemination by donor (AID). In order to avoid confusion between the acronym AID and the acronym AIDS (auto-immune-disease syndrome), some infertility specialists prefer to refer to AID as DI, or donor insemination.

3. U.S. Congress, Office of Technology Assessment, *Infertility: Medical and Social Choices* (Washington, D.C.: Government Printing Office, 1988).

4. V. Davajan and D. R. Mishell, Jr., "Evaluation of the Infertile Couple," in D.R. Mishell, Jr., and V. Davajan, eds., *Infertility, Contraception, and Endocrinology* (Oradell, N.J.: Medical Economics, 1986), p. 381.

5. Robertson, *Children of Choice*, p. 98.

6. *Ibid.*, p. 97.

7. Leon Kass, "Babies by Means of In Vitro Fertilization: Unethical Experiments on the Unborn?" *New England Journal of Medicine* 285 (1971): 1177.

8. Peter Singer and Deanne Wells, *Making Babies: The New Science and Ethics of Conception* (New York: Charles Scribner's Sons, 1985), p. 48.

9. U.S. Congress, Office of Technology Assessment (OTA), *Artificial Insemination: Practice in the United States: Summary of a 1987 Study* (Washington, D.C.: 1988).

10. Christine Overall, *Reproduction: Principles, Practices, Policies* (Toronto: Oxford University Press, 1993), p. 27.

11. *Ibid.*, pp. 27–28.

12. Lori B. Andrews, *New Conceptions: A Consumer's Guide to the Newest Infertility Treatments* (New York: Balantyne Books, 1985), p. 138.

13. John Robertson, "Procreative Liberty and the Control of Conception, Pregnancy, and Childbirth," *Virginia Law Review* 69 (April 1983): 450.

14. Maura J. Ryan, "The Argument for Unlimited Procreative Liberty: A Feminist Critique," *Hastings Center Report* 20, no. 4 (July–August 1990): 7.

15. *Ibid.*, p. 12.

16. Overall, *Reproduction: Principles, Practices, Policies*, p. 29.

17. Gena Corea, *The Mother Machine: Reproductive Technologies from Artificial Insemination to Artificial Wombs* (New York: Harper & Row, 1985), p. 101.

18. Tract Weber and Julie Marquis, "Staffers at Top Fertility Center Tell Horror Stories," *Charlette Observer,* July 16, 1995, pp. 1A, 4A.

19. Otto Friedrich, "A Legal, Moral, Social Nightmare," *Time,* September 10, 1984, p. 55.

20. Laura Muha, "She Lost Her Husband But Saved Their Dream," *Redbook,* May 1995, p. 80.

21. Ibid., p. 83.

22. *Strnad v. Strnad,* 78 N.Y. Supplement, 2nd Ser. (1948), at 391–392.

23. *People v. Sorenson,* 68 Cal. 2nd 280, 66 Cal. Rpt. (1968), at 437.

24. B. J. Jensen, "Artificial Insemination and the Law," *Brigham Young University Law Review* (1982): 955–956.

25. Walter Wadlington, "Reproductive Technologies: Artificial Insemination," in Warren T. Reich, ed., *Encyclopedia of Bioethics* (New York: Simon & Shuster/MacMillan, 1995), p. 2219.

26. Kamran S. Moghissi, "The Technology of AID," in Linda M. Whiteford and Marilyn L. Poland, eds. *New Approaches to Human Reproduction* (Boulder, Colo.: Westview Press, 1989), p. 129.

27. Singer and Wells, *Making Babies: The New Science and Ethics of Conception,* p. 154.

428. Maureen McGuire and Nancy J. Alexander, "Artificial Insemination of Single Women," *Fertility and Sterility* 43, no. 2 (1985): 182–184.

29. Mary B. Mahowald, *Women and Children in Health Care: An Unequal Majority* (New York: Oxford University Press, 1993), p. 30.

30. Renate Duelli Klein, "Doing It Ourselves: Self Insemination," in Rita Arditti, Renata Duelli Klein, and Shelly Minden, eds., *Test-Tube Women: What Future for Motherhood?* (Boston: Pandora Press, 1985), pp. 382–385.

31. Ibid., p. 388.

32. Lawrence J. Kaplan and Carolyn M. Kaplan, "Natural Reproduction and Reproduction-Aiding Technologies," in Kenneth D. Alpern, ed., *The Ethics of Reproductive Technology* (New York: Oxford University Press, 1992), p. 24.

33. Robin Hemran, "When the 'Father' Is a Sperm Donor," *Washington Post Health,* February 11, 1992, p. 14.

34. Jan Fisher, "4 Charged in Illegal Sperm Bank," *New York Times,* April 27, 1992, p. B2.

35. B. Drummond Ayres, Jr., "Fertility Doctor Accused of Fraud," *New York Times,* November 21, 1991.

36. Corea, *The Mother Machine,* p. 49.

37. C.M. v. C.C., 170 N.J. Superior Ct. 586, 407 A. 2nd 849, 852 (Juv. & Dom. Rel. Ct. 1979).

38. Ruth Marcus, "Court Lets Sperm Donor Sue for Parental Rights," *New York Times,* April 24, 1990, p. A4.

39. Carlyle C. Douglas, "Lesbian Child-Custody Cases Redefine Family Law," *New York Times,* April 10, 1990.

40. Ibid.

41. Herman, "When the 'Father' Is a Sperm Donor," p. 10.

42. Nadine Brozan, "Babies from Donated Eggs Growing Use Stirs Questions," *New York Times,* January 18, 1988, p. 9.

43. Glanville Williams, *The Sanctity of Life and the Criminal Law* (New York: Alfred A. Knopf, 1970), p. 120, emphasis added.

44. George J. Annas, "Artificial Insemination: Beyond the Best Interests of the Donor," *Hastings Center Report* 9, no. 4 (August 1979): 14.

45. Patricia P. Mahlstedt, cited in Herman, "When the 'Father' Is a Sperm Donor," p. 10.

46. Alison Kornet, "Should Donors Be Anonymous?" *New Women,* November 1995. Some sperm banks have "openness" policies. For example, the California Cryobank in Los Angeles responds to AID offspring's requests by contacting genetic fathers and giving them a choice about whether they want to be identified. Comments Kornet: "It does not require men to decide upon donating whether contact with their offspring will be important to them in 20 years, but unlike the yes-donor policy, the openness policy cannot guarantee AID offspring the information they want" (p. 144).

47. Simone B. Novaes, "Semen Banking and Artificial Insemination by Donor in France. Social and Medical Discourse," *International Journal of Technology Assessment in Health Care* 2, no. 2 (1986): 221–222.

48. Lindsey Van Gelder, "A Lesbian Family," in Alison M. Jaggar, ed., *Living with Contradictions* (Boulder, Colo.: Westview Press, 1994), p. 450.

49. Kaplan and Tong, *Controlling Our Reproductive Destiny: A Technological and Philosophical Perspective,* pp. 258–264.

50. Overall, *Human Reproduction: Principles, Practices, Policies,* p. 151.

51. Gena Corea and Susan Ince, "Report of a Survey of IVF Clinics in the U.S.," in Patricia Spallone and P. L. Steinberg, eds., *Made to Order: The Myth of Reproductive and Genetic Progress* (Oxford: Pergamon Press, 1987), pp. 142–143.

52. Mary Anne Warren, "IVF and Women's Interests: An Analysis of Feminist Concerns," *Bioethics* 2, no. 1 (1988): 38.

53. Christine Crow, "'Women Want It': In-Vitro Fertilization and Women's Motivations for Participation," *Women's Studies International Forum* 8, no. 6 (1986): 551.

54. Robertson, *Children of Choice,* p. 226.

55. L. R. Shover, R. L. Collins, M. M. Quigley, J. Blanstein, and G. Kanoti, "Psychological Follow-up of Women Evalu-

ated as Oocyte Donors," *Human Reproduction* 6, no. 10 (1991): 1491.

56. Martha E. Giminez, "Feminism, Pronatalism, and Motherhood," in Joyce Trebilcot, ed., *Mothering* (Totowa, N.J.: Rowan and Allenheld), pp. 300–301.

57. Corea, *The Mother Machine: Reproductive Technologies from Artificial Insemination to Artificial Wombs,* p. 170.

58. Schover et al., "Psychological Follow-up of Women Evaluated as Oocyte Donors," p. 1491.

59. Mahowald, *Women and Children in Health Care: An Unequal Majority,* p. 104.

60. Shover et al., "Psychological Follow-up of Women Evaluated as Oocyte Donors," p. 1488.

61. Ibid.

62. Mahowald, *Women and Children in Health Care: An Unequal Majority,* p. 104.

63. Mary O'Brien, *The Politics of Reproduction* (Boston: Routledge and Kegan Paul, 1981), p. 58.

64. Gena Corea, "Egg Snatchers," in Arditti, Klein, and Minden, eds., *Test-Tube Women,* p. 45.

65. Robyn Rowland, "Reproductive Technologies: The Final Solution to the Woman Question," in Arditti, Klein, and Minden, eds., *Test-Tube Women,* p. 45.

66. Gena Corea, "Effects of NRAs on Women" (unpublished manuscript), p. 8.

67. As Dr. Margery Shaw has noted, once a pregnant woman decides to carry her fetus to term, she ensures a "conditional prospective liability" for negligent acts toward her fetus should it be born alive: "These acts could be considered negligent fetal abuse resulting in an injured child. A decision to carry a genetically defective fetus to term would be an example. Abuse of alcohol or drugs during pregnancy.... [w]ithholding of necessary prenatal care, improper nutrition, [and] exposure to the mother's defective intrauterine environment caused by her genotype . . . could all result in an injured infant who might claim that his right to be born physically and mentally sound had been invaded. See M.S. Henifin, R. Hubbard, and J. Norsigian, "Prenatal Screening," in Sherill Cohen and Nadine Taub, eds., *Reproductive Laws for the 1990s* (Clifton, N.J.: Humana Press, 1989), p. 167.

68. Joseph Fletcher, *Humanhood: Essays in Biomedical Ethics* (Buffalo, N.Y.: Prometheus Books, 1979), p. 90.

The Case of 'Baby M'

Ronald Munson

On March 30, 1986, Dr. Elizabeth Stern, a professor of pediatrics, and her husband, William, accepted from Mary Beth Whitehead a baby who had been born four days earlier. The child's biological mother was Mrs. Whitehead, but she had been engaged by the Sterns as a surrogate mother. Even so, it was not until almost exactly a year later that the Sterns were able to claim legal custody of the child.

The Sterns, working through the Infertility Center of New York, had first met with Mrs. Whitehead and her husband, Richard, in January of 1985. Mrs. Whitehead, who already had a son and a daughter, had indicated her willingness to become a surrogate mother by signing up at the Infertility Center. "What brought her there was empathy with childless couples who were infer-

tile," her attorney later stated. Her own sister had been unable to conceive.

According to court testimony, the Sterns considered Mrs. Whitehead a "perfect person" to bear a child for them. Mr. Stern said that it was "compelling" for him to have children, for he had no relatives "anywhere in the world." He and his wife planned to have children, but they put off attempts to conceive until his wife completed her medical residency in 1981. However, in 1979 she was diagnosed as having an eye condition indicating that she probably had multiple sclerosis. When she learned that the symptoms of the disease might be worsened by pregnancy and that she might become temporarily or even permanently paralyzed, the Sterns "decided the risk wasn't worth it." It was this decision that led them to the Infertility Center and to Mary Beth Whitehead.

The Sterns agreed to pay Mrs. Whitehead $10,000 to be artificially inseminated with Mr. Stern's sperm and to bear a child. Mrs. Whitehead would then turn the child over to the Sterns, and Dr. Stern would be allowed to adopt the child legally. The agreement was drawn up by a lawyer specializing in surrogacy arrangements. Mr. Stern later testified that Mrs. Whitehead seemed perfectly pleased with the agreement and expressed no interest in keeping the baby she was to bear. "She said she would not come to our doorstep," he said. "All she wanted from us was a photograph each year and a little letter on what transpired that year."

The baby was born on March 27, 1986. According to Dr. Stern, the first indication that Mrs. Whitehead might not keep the agreement was her statement to the Sterns in the hospital two days after the baby's birth. "She said she didn't know if 'I can go through with it,'" Dr. Stern testified. Although Mrs. Whitehead did turn the baby over to the Sterns on March 30, she called a few hours later. "She said she didn't know if she could live any more," Dr. Stern said. She called again the next morning and asked to see the baby and she and her sister arrived at the Sterns' house before noon.

According to Dr. Stern, Mrs. Whitehead told her that she "woke up screaming in the middle of the night" because the baby was gone, that her husband was threatening to leave her, and that she had "considered taking a bottle of Valium." Dr. Stern quoted Mrs. Whitehead as saying, "I just want her for a week, and I'll be out of your lives forever." The Sterns allowed Mrs. Whitehead to take the baby home with her.

Mrs. Whitehead then refused to return the baby voluntarily and took the infant with her to the home of her parents in Florida. The Sterns obtained a court order, and on July 31 the child was seized from Mrs. Whitehead. The Sterns were granted temporary custody. Then Mr. Stern, as the father of the child, and Mrs. Whitehead, as the mother, each sought permanent custody from the Superior Court of the State of New Jersey.

The seven-week trial attracted considerable attention, for the legal issues were virtually without precedent. Mrs. Whitehead was the first to challenge the legal legitimacy of a surrogate agreement in a U.S. court. She argued that the agreement was "against public policy" and violated New Jersey prohibitions against selling babies. In contrast, Mr. Stern was the first to seek a legal decision to uphold

the "specific performance" of the terms of a surrogate contract. In particular, he argued that Mrs. Whitehead should be ordered to uphold her agreement and to surrender her parental rights and permit his wife to become the baby's legal mother. In addition to the contractual issues, the judge had to deal with the "best interest" of the child as required by New Jersey child-custody law. In addition to being a vague concept, the "best interest" standard had never been applied in a surrogacy case.

On March 31, 1987, Judge Harvey R. Sorkow announced his decision. He upheld the legality of the surrogate-mother agreement between the Sterns and Mrs. Whitehead and dismissed all arguments that the contract violated public policy or prohibitions against selling babies. Immediately after he read his decision, Judge Sorkow summoned Elizabeth Stern into his chambers and allowed her to sign documents permitting her to adopt the baby she and her husband called Melissa. The court decision effectively stripped Mary Beth Whitehead of all parental rights concerning this same baby, the one she called Sara.

The Baby M story did not stop with Judge Sorkow's decision. Mrs. Whitehead's attorney appealed the ruling to the New Jersey Supreme Court, and on February 3, 1988, the seven members of the court, in a unanimous decision, reversed Judge Sorkow's ruling on the surrogacy agreement. The court held that the agreement violated the state's adoption laws, because it involved a payment for a child. "This is the sale of a child, or at the very least, the sale of a mother's right to her child," Chief Justice Wilentz wrote. The agreement "guarantees the separation of a child from its mother . . . ; it takes the child from the mother regardless of her wishes and her maternal fitness . . . ; and it accomplishes all of its goals through the use of money." The court held that surrogacy agreements might be acceptable if they involved no payment and if a surrogate mother voluntarily surrendered her parental rights. In the present case, though, the court regarded paying for surrogacy "illegal, perhaps criminal, and potentially degrading to women."

The court let stand the award of custody to the Sterns, because "Their household and their personalities promise a much more likely foundation for Melissa to grow and thrive." Mary Beth White-head, having divorced her husband three months earlier, was romantically involved with a man named Dean Gould and was pregnant at the time of the court decision.

Despite awarding custody to the Sterns, the court set aside the adoption agreement signed by Elizabeth Stern. Mary Beth Whitehead remained a legal parent of Baby M, and the court ordered a lower court hearing to consider visitation rights for the mother.

The immediate future of the child known to the court and to the public as Baby M was settled. Neither the Sterns nor Mary Beth Whitehead had won exactly what they had sought, but neither had they lost all.

From Lives Begun in a Lab, Brave New Joy
Elisabeth Rosenthal

A few years ago, when Elizabeth Carr's class was learning how an egg combines with sperm in the mother's body to create a child, she felt compelled to interrupt.

"I piped up to say that not all babies are con-ceived like that and explained about sperm and eggs and petri dishes," said Elizabeth, now 14, the first child in the United States born through in vitro fertilization.

Because her mother's landmark pregnancy was documented in great detail by a film crew, Eliza-beth has seen pictures of the egg and sperm that united to become her, the petri dish where she was conceived, the embryonic blob of cells that grew into the bubbly young woman who now plays field hockey and sings in the school chorus.

Elizabeth and her parents, Roger and Judith Carr of Westminster, Mass., are pioneers in what is all too often a forgotten afterward to the saga of infertility: the world of children and families, hol-idays and birthday celebrations that without new technologies would never have been.

On the surface, what is most notable about these families, with their extraordinary beginnings, is just how ordinary their lives become, with par-ents swept up in the rigors of raising children.

But in so many other ways they are charting new territory, even revising the definition of family. When new reproductive technologies are used, each child can, in theory, have five different people with some role in creation: the woman who pro-vides the egg, the man who provides the sperm, the woman who carries the fetus and the woman and man who raise the child. What then does it mean to be mother, father or sibling?

This world of new reproductive possibilities is filled with new childhood mementos. Some chil-dren receive the petri dish in which they were con-ceived. There are new anxieties. How do parents avoid coddling such a hard-won child? And there are new talks about the birds and the bees custom-made for a particular child's conception or gestation.

And beyond these lies what has been for most parents a charged question: What should they tell their children? Since research on such families is sparse, there is little scientific guidance. Indeed, at a recent meeting of the American Society for Re-productive Medicine, 100 mental health profes-sionals could not agree about when or how these children should be told about their origins, or if they needed to be told at all.

Elizabeth Carr, now an eighth grader at the Overlook Middle School in Westminster, said that her parents—whose egg and sperm joined in a petri dish at the Jones Institute for Reproductive Medicine in Norfolk, Va.—have always made it clear that she was created differently from other children. Although she said she had faced taunts of "test-tube baby" or "weirdo" a few times at school, she said she had never felt resentful about her conception.

I'm so grateful that they went through all this to have me—I mean, my mom almost died," she said, referring to an ectopic pregnancy that occurred before her parents resorted to I.V.F. "Now I'm just a normal eighth grader trying to keep my room clean."

Telling the Children—Not Ashamed, Almost Boastful

On the refrigerator door at the home of Charlotte Lee and Ron Turbayne of Montclair, N.J., among the postcards, family snapshots and lists of emergency phone numbers, is a picture of a women named Dee, cradling the couple's newborn twins.

Though unrelated to the family, Dee is central to its existence, for it was she who bore and gave birth to Graham and Diana Turbayne, who are now 2, for Ms. Lee and Mr. Turbayne, the twins' biological parents.

After Ms. Lee had endured at least 10 unsuccessful cycles of I.V.F. and one ectopic pregnancy, doctors in 1992 fertilized her eggs with sperm from her husband in a petri dish and gingerly placed the embryos that resulted into Dee's uterus. Ms. Lee was born with a T-shaped uterus because of exposure to diethylstilbestrol, a hormone better known as DES that was widely prescribed to prevent miscarriages in the 1950's.

Ms. Lee signed a contract with Dee through the hospital in Pennsylvania where the procedure was performed, but during the pregnancy the two forged a close bond. Ms. Lee drove two hours each way to accompany Dee on prenatal visits. Ms. Lee, Mr. Turbayne and Dee's husband, Tom, were all in the delivery room when Dee gave birth to the twins. Dee, who has three children of her own, is now their godmother.

"Having children became something we very much did with these other people, not just as a couple," said Ms. Lee, formerly an executive with a financial services company. "I came home not just with two babies but two exceptional people in our lives."

Today, pictures of Dee are scattered around the Lee-Turbayne house and, although Ms. Lee says she knows her children are too young to understand her "ridiculous chatter," she looks for chances to tell Diana and Graham that they "grew in Dee's body before they were born."

"We don't want the children stumbling upon this or having to learn it," she said. "We hope they'll assimilate it into their lives."

Ms. Lee and Mr. Turbayne are among the growing number of couples who, after achieving pregnancy using medical technology, have elected to be open with their children about their origins—a trend that mirrors the open adoption movement of 10 years ago.

But many couples struggle with what to tell children, concerned about how society, family members, priests, rabbis and the children themselves will react. It can be a painful decision, since it forces couples to confront lingering feelings about years of infertility treatment.

In a recent survey of parents who had babies via I.V.F. at the Yale University Medical Center from 1982 to 1992, 8 percent said they were not going to tell their children about their origins, 26 percent said they were unsure and 66 percent said they planned to tell. But only 15 percent of couples had actually made the disclosure, with many saying they would wait until the child was older, generally about 7.

"There are a lot of people telling and others who are not comfortable with that," said Dorothy Greenfeld, the director of Psychological Services at the Yale Center for Reproductive Medicine. "We don't know whether it's important or whether it's like discussing with kids the circumstance of their conception—who was on top—which we normally don't do."

She added that the decision was far more difficult and the consequences greater when a donor egg or sperm was involved.

John C. Aspinwall 3d and Judy Aspinwall of Virginia Beach, Va., have chosen to tell the world as well as their 7-year-old son, John Aspinwall 4th, about his conception through in vitro fertilization. "We were so blessed by the miracle of his birth there was nothing we were going to say or do to diminish it," Mr. Aspinwall said. "We are not ashamed and, in fact, we're almost boastful. We're telling him he's special because he was conceived in this special way."

He said that they had told Jack he was an I.V.F. child, and that he had seen the laboratory at the

Jones Institute for Reproductive Medicine in Nor-folk, where the egg and the sperm were mixed. Jack even owns a special box containing the petri dish in which he was conceived and has a picture of children who were conceived at the Jones Insti-tute hanging over his bed. But his father added that he was not sure how much his son under-stood, since "he doesn't yet know about the birds and the bees."

Not Telling—Church's Reaction and Child's Fears

Other couples would like to be more open but have been forced into the closet by outside pres-sures. Sue S., a mother of 7-year-old twins con-ceived through I.V.F., has been frank with her children, telling them that doctors took a piece of Mommy and a piece of Daddy to help create them. In the past, she has told strangers in the market that the children are "test-tube babies."

Nonetheless, she said she could not be identi-fied because her children were due to take their first communion. "The church doesn't approve of I.V.F.," she said, "and my husband is worried the church wouldn't let them take communion."

Maureen H. of New York also has a 7-year-old through I.V.F., but her daughter does not know how she was conceived. She feels that the infor-mation would confuse or frighten her daughter now and imagines bringing up the subject sometime in early adolescence, with the lead-in, "Oh, by the way, let us explain to you how impor-tant you are." But she is worried that some well-meaning family member who knows how her pregnancy came to be will let the secret slip be-fore then.

Psychologists say such dilemmas are more dif-ficult when a donor egg or sperm is used; the chil-dren are no longer a simple mixture of their parents' genetic material.

When there is a donor, "children have to deal with the identity issues of being raised by a non-genetic parent," said Carole LieberWilkins, a Los Angeles family therapist who has one adopted son and one conceived with a donor egg. She has told both about their origins and advises parents to tell children even before they are old enough to un-derstand, in part so the parents can become com-fortable with the disclosure.

"I do see us moving toward more openness," she said. "I envision a day when my son is sitting in school and someone says, 'I was made with donor sperm,' and half the kids will say, 'Me, too.' It's happened with adoption. Talking will normal-ize this. A quarter of his classroom was conceived with some assistance, but no one will know un-less someone talks about it."

Although most psychologists now encourage openness because "such secrets are a weight on the family," said Susan Levin, a Boston therapist who treats infertility patients, some couples find they are not comfortable with that approach, and stud-ies suggest that many couples have not made the disclosure.

In one study conducted by Dr. Susan Klock, an assistant professor of obstetrics and gynecology and psychology at Northwestern University, 86 percent of couples who used donated sperm had not told or did not plan to tell their children.

Many regretted having discussed their treatment with family and friends, in part because they felt this knowledge would force them to tell their children as well. "If a dozen people know, you run the risk of a child finding out from someone else, which would be a real family disaster," Dr. Klock said.

Child Rearing—Seeking Normalcy After a Miracle

Another big concern for couples who have run the gauntlet of infertility treatments is how to treat chil-dren normally after having endured so much to have them. Research about these families is sparse, and some studies have suggested that the parents do have early difficulties with separation, but over all these mothers and fathers receive high marks.

"You would expect that forever these families would pack the children in cotton because these are such cherished human beings, but that doesn't seem to be true," said Dr. John Stangel, medical director of IVF America-Westchester, one of the older infertility programs in the country.

One major study published in the January 1995 issue of the journal *Child Development* found that couples who conceived with the help of technology were generally "superior" parents compared with couples who had conceived naturally, and that they reported less stress associated with parenthood. The research group, led by Dr. Susan Golombok at the City University of London, looked at numerous qualities, including the mother's warmth toward her child and her emotional involvement, as well as the quality of the interaction between both parents and the child.

Many couples say that a history of infertility has made them deeply appreciative of their children and more careful in child rearing. But, fearful of spoiling their offspring, many go to great lengths to insure that their "miracle babies" evolve into normal, independent children.

"Infertility had a profound effect on my whole life, and that has probably affected my parenting," said Ms. Lee, the woman who contracted with a surrogate. "I still can't get over the wonder of these children, and that makes me more patient and helps me keep in perspective what is petty and what is significant. But if I was ever the kind of person who was going to think of a child as a possession, this changed that."

Judith Carr said that she and her husband, an engineer, had sent Elizabeth to summer camp in Maine from the time she was 7, a decision that surprised some friends. "She is an I.V.F. child and an only child," Mrs. Carr said, "and our feeling has always been that there is no room for prima donnas around our house."

But Mrs. Carr, once a fertility pioneer and now the owner of a preschool where "test-tube babies" are common, cautioned against generalizations about I.V.F. children, based on her own observations. "It's hard to compare these kids with others," she said. "Their parents are older. They mostly have two-parent households. And the majority have mothers who stay at home."

Although most couples who have had miracle babies yearn for normalcy, they say there are always the reminders of their history—from the first picture in the baby album showing a blob of cells to the birth certificate processed six months late because the application did not have enough blanks to explain how their child entered the world.

Following the advice of their lawyer, Ms. Lee and Mr. Turbayne had filled in their names as "mother" and "father" on the applications for the birth certificates, since their own egg and sperm were involved.

But the State of Pennsylvania initially rejected their application, ruling that Dee, who had given birth to the twins, should be listed as the mother and Mr. Turbayne as the father. "They insisted I was an egg donor," Ms. Lee recalled. "But if I was an egg donor, my husband was a sperm donor. It just drove home what a new path we were walking."

And when such couples look for professional advice there is often none, since psychologists are just beginning to study these families. So parents improvise—and fret.

When Rebecca Walters, 19 months old, was dancing recently, her father, Richard, exclaimed, "I bet your donor was a great dancer, 'cause your mom is not." After several years of infertility treatments, Rebecca was conceived when her mother, Judith, was inseminated with donor sperm—and her parents want her to know it. Following the lead of adoptive parents, they have set up a play group for Rebecca with other girls conceived with donor sperm, so that she will understand that there are others like her.

"I couldn't not tell her," said Mrs. Walters, a book editor. "How can you raise a truthful child while not telling the child about the core of her existence? Children are very instinctual, and when there's a secret they sense that something's wrong."

But others feel less certain. "We're on uncharted turf, and that's what makes it scary," said Maureen H. "In learning about toilet training and diapering there were other people I could talk to. But who can tell me how to do this? Where's my book? I think this is going to be great news for them, to understand how much they're wanted. But what if they freak out?"

And experts say that even with the smoothest, most perfectly timed delivery, the issue is likely to surface.

"Kids will have questions about their identity," Ms. LieberWilkins, the family therapist, said. "When they're angry they'll go for the jugular, with statements like, 'You're not my real mom.'" But she added: "Parents should try to be able to say, 'If you want to talk about the donor, or adoption, we can, but first clean your room.'"

In The Classifieds: Seeking "Egg Donors" and "Surrogates"

[*Editor's Note*: These advertisements were found in free local newspapers and in college newspapers in the Philadelphia and San Francisco Bay areas.]

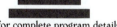

Epilogue:
Diverse Moral Perspectives
and Moral Relativism

Always there lurked the fear that one's own view...
was merely a small window in a small house.

Thornton Wilder, *The Eighth Day*

PART ONE: THE UNDERLYING FEAR
OF MORAL RELATIVISM

One popular series of undergraduate textbooks on moral problems is structured in a simple binary fashion: Each chapter introduces a problem, for example, abortion or euthanasia, and then presents two readings, one the "yes" selection, and the other the "no." Thus, it might appear to an uncritical reader that there are two, and only two, mutually exclusive positions on each moral issue and that the goal of one's study is to determine which one of the two is correct.

A student reading this anthology, on the other hand, is likely to react in a very different way. The variety and diversity of perspectives presented here with respect to each moral problem might seem to suggest that one should sample the various views on offer, selecting from among them those found to be most appealing, or perhaps least demanding. The further implication would be that others may do the same and come away with quite different conclusions about these same moral issues. Acknowledging that two people with very different experiences of race and social class might adopt very different perspectives on the morality of the death penalty, for example, might suggest that in the end there is no one "correct" position. Different individuals might draw different conclusions and adopt different moral positions depending on who they are and where they have come from. In short, the recognition of genuinely diverse moral perspectives might seem to lead *inevitably* to the view that there is no single or objective truth with respect to any particular moral problem.

Recognizing various perspectives that are in part a function of persons' gender, sexual orientation, racial identity, social class, and health status might also seem to promote the pessimistic view that our society is so fractured that the divisions are, in effect, unbridgeable.[1] If this were indeed so, an additional and very troubling implication of a book of this sort could be, effectively, a counsel of despair: In the face of such confusion, one may as well settle for a form of moral passivity. Or again, some might fear that recognition of these differences in perspective is likely to contribute to an attitude of intolerance on the part of the reader. One such critic worries that recognizing seemingly intractable moral conflicts "has made efforts to resolve moral disagreements appear futile, and it has encouraged intolerance. It has dampened efforts and hopes for moral concord."[2] In short, recognizing multiple perspectives seems, to some critics at least, to promote *moral relativism*, and in turn a certain pessimism and passivity with respect to critical public policy debates. Philosophers Lawrence Foster and Patricia Herzog point out that those who are promoting "multiculturalism" in the academic curriculum find themselves:

> . . . anxiously worrying at the underlying questions about pluralism and relativism that this multiculturalism brings to the foreground of inquiry. Their restlessness mirrors an unease in society at large, because we live in a time in which previously disempowered and silenced (or perhaps unheard) groups are finding their voices and bringing to our philosophic conversations their own social histories, cultural traditions, and prescriptions for moral behavior. The good life, it seems, has become good lives. We are discovering that the culture of the United States, which many thought was unified, was always manifold, and that what many believed was certain and settled seems now to be irrevocably contested.[3]

The underlying worry thus occasioned by a book of this type is that it might *necessarily* commit the reader to one or another seemingly undesirable position about the status and truth of moral judgments, in practice, to some form of moral relativism, with its allegedly attendant evils—moral passivity or a stubborn intolerance of moral views other than one's own.

In this essay, I argue that the diversity which is documented in this anthology need *not* commit one to moral relativism. Rather, I believe that a thoughtful consideration of more abstract ideas about the nature and structure of moral knowledge shows that studying diverse moral perspectives is logically compatible with affirming the possibility of objective moral judgments: it is logically possible to accept the importance of considering multiple perspectives *and* to assert universal moral truths.

WHAT IS MORAL RELATIVISM?

Before we can examine the relationship between acknowledging multiple perspectives and moral relativism, we need to gain some clarity with respect to the latter term. It can be used in a number of ways, and thus it is often confused with other labels. One way to get a clearer grasp of moral relativism is to sketch its relationship to other positions regarding the nature and status of moral judgments.[4] Defining *moral nihilism* and *moral objectivism* will shed light on the highly ambiguous term moral relativism.

Moral nihilism asserts that moral utterances lack truth–values, that is, they are not propositions and thus are neither true nor false, since only propositions can have truth–values. According to the moral nihilist, moral utterances amount to no more than exclamations of pleasure or displeasure, preference or distaste.[5] In short, moral expressions don't amount to much more than exclamations of a vaguely normative sort, for example, "yuck!" or "yeah!" or "boo!"

In contrast, the *moral relativist* claims that moral utterances *are* propositions, and thus do have truth–values, that is, they are either true or false. However, the moral relativist also claims that the truth–values of moral judgments must always be indexed to a particular culture or society or community at a particular time. In other words, a speaker making moral judgments must mean (even if she doesn't make it explicit) that something is good or morally correct *given* the moral principles or moral code of a particular society. Thus moral judgments are similar to legal judgments and judgments of etiquette in this respect, namely, that in order to make sense, they must always make implicit or explicit reference to a particular group's code at a particular time:

> phrases like '. . . is illegal' or '. . . is legally permissible' make sense only within such expressions as '. . . is illegal in C' or '. . . is legally permissible in C' where 'C' can be replaced by some such term as 'the legal code of Indiana' or 'the legal code of Minnesota.' When this complementary phrase is missing from a sentence uttered on a particular occasion, we must look to some factor in the context of utterance to supply it.[6]

Legal judgments always require completion by being indexed to a particular legal code at a particular time. Similarly, judgments of etiquette require completion, since these claims about what is acceptable behavior are true only with respect to a particular group or sub-culture at a particular time: "When eating food, the dinner fork should be held in the right hand with the tines facing upward." "The dinner fork should be in your left hand, tines facing down, as you begin to eat." "Never wear white shoes before Memorial Day or after Labor Day." "It is improper for a woman to chew gum in public." "A widow should not wear brightly colored clothing in public in the year immediately following her husband's death." Anyone asserting these claims must make implicit or explicit reference to a particular group's social code at some time or another.

The moral relativist claims that *moral* judgments require similar qualification in order to make sense. Thus moral relativism might be understood as a form of "code relativism."[7] The moral relativist claims that various cultures and groups adopt different moral codes that reflect their respective histories, customs, traditions, religious practices, and even economic needs. And moral judgments are deemed true (or false) only by reference to that particular code. A moral relativist might assert that while marital polygamy is morally incorrect in some societies, it is morally permissible in others. Similarly, while infanticide and cannibalism are judged morally unacceptable in our society at present, they would not necessarily be morally wrong in other cultures at certain times. Since moral judgments receive their warrant only with respect to a particular group's moral code at a particular time, one group's moral beliefs are impervious to moral criticism from those who justify their moral judgments in light of another group's moral code.

In contrast to moral relativism, we can now identify the position of *moral objectivism* or *moral universalism*. Moral objectivism is defined by two claims: that moral judgments are propositional; and that it is possible to assert and justify them *without* indexing them to the moral code of a particular culture. In other words, moral judgments are held to be true or false in light of some sort of universal moral code or a moral order which transcends particular cultures and groups—moral judgments can be determined to be true or false without being indexed to the code of a particular culture. Moral objectivists offer different accounts of what might provide the universal or objective ground of moral judgments; some, for example, appeal to certain allegedly universal and distinctive features of human nature, such as rationality. Throughout the history of moral philosophy the task of establishing the ground of an objective moral code has proved endlessly controversial. Fortunately, we need not pursue these controversies. For the purpose of this epilogue, it is sufficient if moral objectivism and moral relativism are seen to be quite distinct.

PART TWO: WILL ACKNOWLEDGING MULTIPLE PERSPECTIVES NECESSARILY LEAD TO MORAL RELATIVISM?

The central question of this epilogue is whether there is any *necessary* link between the position of moral relativism as outlined above and the implicit *epistemic* presupposition of this book, namely, that one's "social location" almost inevitably has some bearing on one's understanding of specific moral issues. We might, for convenience, label this presupposition *perspectivalism*. We need to ask, then, about the logical relationship between perspectivalism and each of the two moral positions discussed above, moral relativism and moral objectivism. If we assume that an adequate analysis of moral problems requires one to examine the social locations and complex identities of a variety of different sorts of person and group, does this implicitly commit us to adopt moral relativism and to relinquish any claim for an objective and universal basis for moral judgments?

I would argue that the answer to this question is "no." And the reason for this is quite simple. The positions outlined in the first part of this paper are *moral* positions. They are concerned with the nature of moral judgment itself: against what standard is a moral claim or judgment to be evaluated? By contrast, what I am calling perspectivalism is an *epistemic* position. It suggests that in order to acquire the knowledge to make moral judgments, one ought first draw on the widest variety of perspectives, reflecting the experiences of the variety of groups of which even the most apparently homogeneous society is composed. This is an epistemic or methodological prescription for moral philosophers generally, whether they ultimately subscribe to the objectivist or the relativist positions.

Clearly, the perspectivalist approach is compatible with moral relativism, but adopting perspectivalism does not logically compel one to accept moral relativism. How might the perspectival approach appear to the moral objectivist? It could appear threatening, obviously. And if the objectivist adopts from the start the implicit methodological approach which some philosophers have referred to as "the God's eye point of view" or "the view from nowhere," then a work like this one built on a perspectival premise, might seem misguided. However, the perspectivalist questions such a conclusion and the premise on which it is founded. Epistemologist Lorraine Code puts it this way:

> The project I am proposing, then, requires a new *geography* of the epistemic terrain: one that is no longer primarily a physical geography, but a population geography that develops qualitative analyses of subjective positions and identities and of the social-political structures that produce them. Because differing social positions generate variable constructions of reality, and afford different perspectives on the world, the revisionary stages of this project will consist in case-by-case analyses of the knowledge produced in specific social positions. These analyses derive from a recognition that knowers are always *somewhere*— and at once limited and enabled by the specificities of their locations.[8]

Her last point is critical. The situatedness of individual knowers is not just a limitation, but is also an advantage. That is, it enables such knowers to attain moral insights that might be denied to others who do not share their location, whether that location be a matter of gender, race, social class, health status or any other among the aspects of social identity that this anthology set out to document.

On the face of it, it might seem that the proponent of a perspectivalist approach in moral inquiry would inevitably end up a moral relativist. And indeed this might well happen, since the emphasis on the diversity of perspectives might well lead one to deny the possibility of going beyond some particular perspective, most likely the perspective that reflects one's own social location. Yet it might be argued that careful attention to the perspectivalist approach could lead one to question the adequacy of such a halting or stopping place. Is there not something to be learned by examining different points of view? by surveying as wide a range of contentious moral issues as possible? by modifying one's own moral starting points in the light of insights drawn from the experiences of other groups that face moral problems in an altogether unfamiliar fashion to those who have not shared their experiences?

It is this implication of perspectivalism that might encourage at least one type of moral objectivist to find this anthology congenial. For moral objectivism can take many forms and among these there are some who would view objectivism in moral judgment as an *ideal* toward which to strive and not as something already achieved or given somehow in advance (as, for example, a result of one's adopting a "God's eye point of view"). Though the perspective of each individual is inevitably partial—as on a larger scale are the perspectives of each of the many groupings to which each individual may belong—multiple and diverse partial perspectives can be brought into contact with one another, representing more and more experiences of situatedness. One may then reasonably expect (or so such an objectivist might argue) to come closer to the ideal of impartiality which the objectivist hopes to achieve.

Objectivists of this more nuanced sort would accept a premise that collaborative epistemic work is needed in order to approximate impartiality. And they might allow, further, that the absence of a particular perspective could well lessen the adequacy of the approximation reached. All of this follows quite naturally once one adopts the perspectivalist premise that sound moral judgment requires a prior awareness of a far wider variety of perspectives than any individual can possibly claim. As one proponent of perspectivalism noted: "It is a paradox. Only by admitting our partiality can we strive for impartiality."[9]

Traditionally, moral objectivism has often been linked with a set of implicit assumptions about the epistemic autonomy of moral agents. If one assumes that the project of providing a warrant for moral judgment is a more or less solitary epistemic activity to be carried out independently of any social networks, one is likely to conclude that the perspectivalist approach is irrelevant at best, inimical at worst. For perspectivalism is all about community, about the moral relevance of the various communities to which the individual belongs and the experiences these embody, as well as the larger community of communities to which the objectivist's search for universality must ultimately be addressed. The ideal knower cannot, then, be regarded as detached and solitary since the experiences of a community must be drawn on. Warrant must in the first instance be referred to that community.

The complexities consequent upon the recognition of perspectivalist principles scarcely need underlining. It is obvious that moral objectivists who adopt the perspectivalist approach face many different issues in deciding how the sort of collaborative enterprise mentioned above is to be carried out in practice: How wide an array of perspectives is to be sought out? What relative weight is to be given to each? Ought greater weight, for example, be attached to the perspectives of those who have been most marginalized in our society? How are conflicts between perspectives to be adjudicated?

Much more would need to be said in order to secure this qualified variety of moral objectivism against criticism. But this is not our purpose here. Our aim is the more limited one of showing that the perspectivalism which implicitly guides this collection of materials is compatible with a variety of positions about the nature and character of moral judgments, both relativist and objectivist. The task of sorting between these positions will, I hope, be furthered by engaging in a serious way with the diversity contained within these covers.

NOTES

1. As evidence of this, some cite the public reactions to the jury's acquittal of O. J. Simpson of the charges of murder in his criminal trial. The popular media reported markedly different reactions to the verdict which reflected strong racial polarization. This seemed to serve as evidence of the divisive power of so-called "identity politics": One's political and moral views, indeed one's very notion of the truth, are somehow a function of one's racial, ethnic background, as well as one's gender, health status, and social class.

2. Mitchell Silver, "Irreconcilable Moral Disagreement," *Contemporary Philosophical Perspectives on Pluralism and Multi-culturalism.* Ed. Lawrence Foster and Patricia Herzog. (Amherst: University of Massachusetts Press, 194): 39.

3. Lawrence Foster and Patricia Herzog, "Introduction," *Contemporary Philosophical Perspectives on Pluralism and Multi-culturalism:* 1.

4. My analysis in this section reveals a large debt to the work of J.L.A. Garcia. See his "Relativism and Moral Divergence," *Metaphilosophy* 19 (1988): 264–281.

5. Garcia, 265.

6. Garcia, 269–270.

7. Garcia.

8. Lorraine Code, *Rhetorical Spaces: Essays on Gendered Locations* (New York: Routledge, 1995): 52–53.

9. Martha Minnow, "Justice Engendered" in *Feminist Jurisprudence*, ed. Patricia Smith. (New York: Oxford University Press, 1993): 233.

REFERENCES

Code, Lorraine. *Rhetorical Spaces: Essays on Gendered Locations.* New York: Routledge, 1995.

DeCew, Judith Wagner. "Moral Conflicts and Ethical Relativism." *Ethics* 101 (1990): 27–41.

Dworkin, Ronald. "Objectivity and Truth: You'd Better Believe It." *Philosophy and Public Affairs* 25 (Spring 1996): 87–139.

Foster, Lawrence and Patricia Herzog. *Contemporary Philosophical Perspectives on Pluralism and Multiculturalism.* Amherst: University of Massachusetts Press, 1994.

Frye, Marilyn. *Willful Virgin: Essays in Feminism 1976–1992.* Freedom, California: The Crossing Press, 1992.

Garcia, J. L. A. "Relativism and Moral Divergence." *Metaphilosophy* 19 (July/October 1988): 264–281.

Garver, Eugene. "Point of View, Bias, and Insight." *Metaphilosophy* 24 (1993): 47–60.

Hampshire, Stuart. *Morality and Conflict.* Cambridge: Harvard University Press, 1983.

Nagel, Thomas. *The View From Nowhere.* Oxford: Oxford University Press, 1986.

Smith, Patricia, ed. *Feminist Jurisprudence.* New York: Oxford University Press, 1993.

Stewart, Robert and Lynn Thomas. "Recent Work on Ethical Relativism." *American Philosophical Quarterly* 28 (April 1991): 85–100.

Stocker, Michael. *Plural and Conflicting Values.* Oxford: Oxford University Press, 1990.

Wolf, Susan. "Two Levels of Pluralism." *Ethics* 102 (July 1992): 785–798.